From maps of migrations and wars to primary source documents by servants and statesmen...from the original complete texts of Thomas Paine's *Common Sense,* to video clips of modern political campaigns, MyHistoryLab brings together an amazing collection of resources for you and your students. This Web site gives students a wealth of primary sources, an electronic version of the textbook, extensive student assessment tools, twenty complete books on the *History Bookshelf*, and much more. CourseCompass, Blackboard, and WebCT course management systems give you the support you need to more efficiently manage your course.

Use MyHistoryLab with this Longman U.S. History survey text, and your students will have everything they need to succeed in your course. For the first time, icons in the margins of this text link the material presented in the text with MyHistoryLab ... connecting students of today with people, events, and ideas of the past.

Visit www.myhistorylab.com to see a live Sample Chapter, or Take a Tour!

Here's what you'll find in

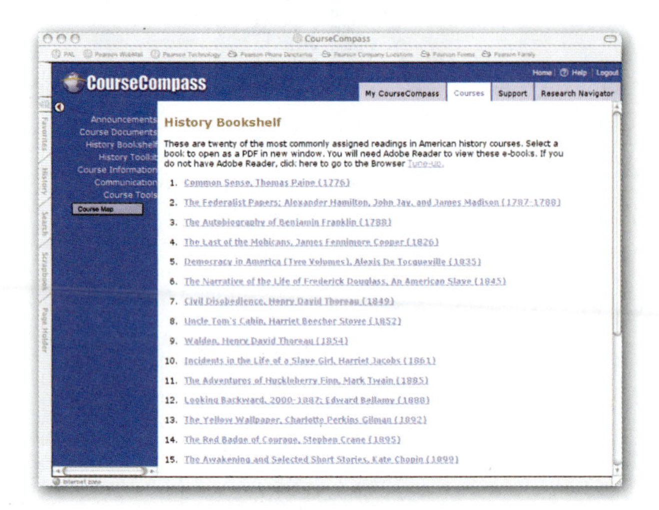

History Bookshelf.

Read, download, or print **twenty of the most commonly assigned works,** like: Thomas Paine's *Common Sense*, Upton Sinclair's *The Jungle*, or Booker T. Washington's *Up from Slavery*.

Documents, Images, Maps, and Other Sources.

Find over **1,100 primary source documents,** images, audio clips and video clips, as well as an unprecedented number of maps.

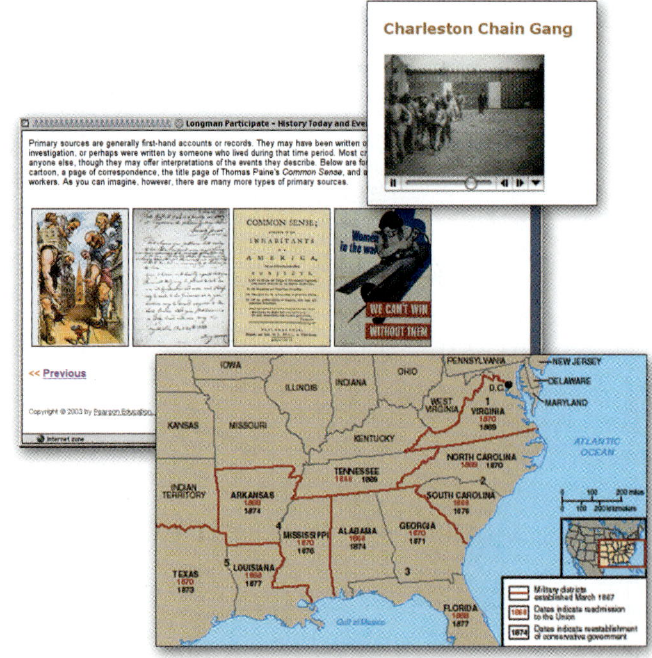

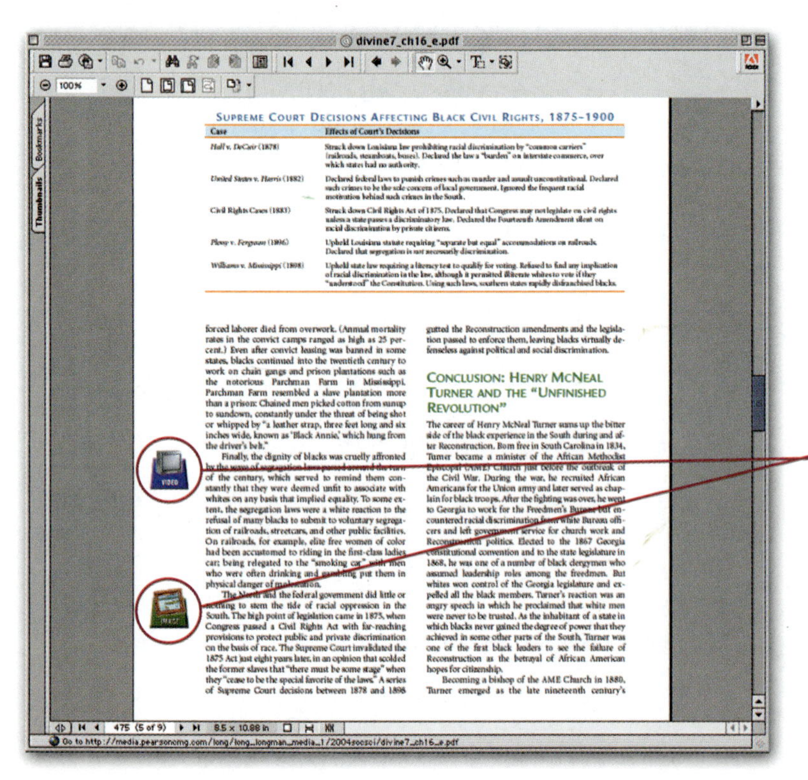

Electronic Textbook (EBook).

Matching the layout of the printed textbook, the EBook contains **multimedia icons** in the margins that launch to exciting resources, expanding upon the key topics students encounter as they read through the text.

Student Assessment.

This integrated quizzing and testing program—including **pre-tests, post-tests, and chapter exams**—helps students identify areas of strengths and weakness. Look for these icons on MyHistoryLab

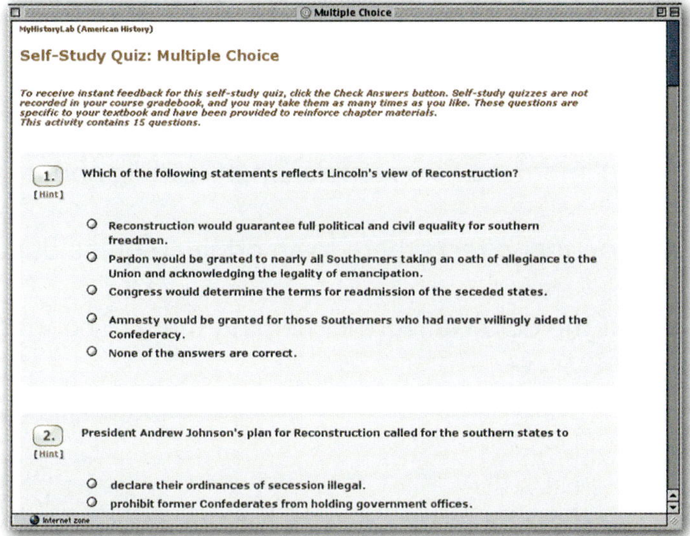

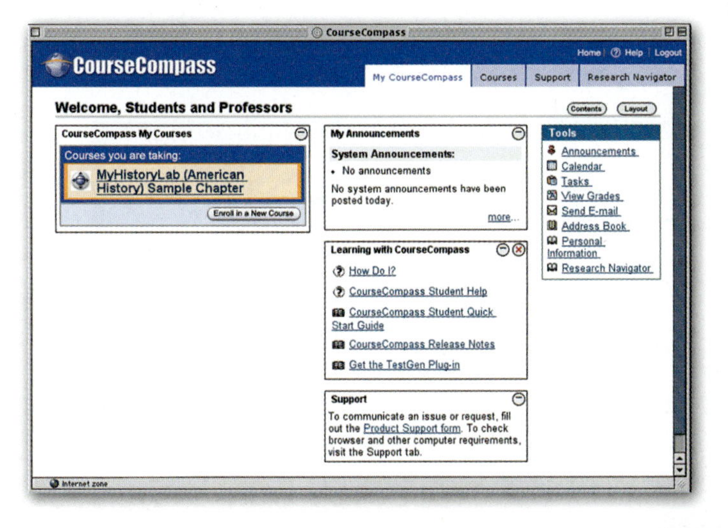

Instructor Resources.

MyHistoryLab is powered by your choice of **course management systems**—CourseCompass, BlackBoard, or WebCT®— complete with an online gradebook and a host of other features. Quickly and easily create your own tests in CourseCompass using the Test Bank material for your text, or download the Instructor's Manual or PowerPoint® presentations as you prepare for class.

Tutor Center.

Your students can now get expert, **one-on-one tutoring** help when they are most likely to be completing assignments, preparing for exams, and when you may not be available. The Tutor Center is available Sunday through Thursday from 5 pm to midnight, Eastern Standard Time.

Take a tour of MyHistoryLab at www.myhistorylab.com

Your text is now connected to myhistorylab™

Where it's a good time to connect to the past!

For the first time, this text includes icons in the margins that send students to areas in MyHistoryLab with additional material that supports what they are reading in the chapter at that moment. For example, when reading about the 1700's or the 20th century, students may find an icon that directs them to an original source document by an indentured servant or a video clip about the Cold War, further helping them to connect with the past!

430 **Chapter 16** Reconstruction and the South

THE FOURTEENTH AMENDMENT

13th, 14th, and 15th Amendments

In June 1866 Congress submitted to the states a new amendment to the Constitution. The Fourteenth Amendment was, in the context of the times, a truly radical measure. Never before had newly freed slaves been granted significant political rights. For example, in the British Caribbean sugar islands, where slavery had been abolished in the 1830s, stiff property qualifications and poll taxes kept freedmen from voting. The Fourteenth Amendment was also a milestone along the road to the centralization of political power in the United States because it reduced the power of all the states. In this sense it confirmed the great change wrought by the Civil War: the growth of a more complex, more closely integrated social and economic structure requiring closer national supervision. Few people understood this aspect of the amendment at the time.

First the amendment supplied a broad definition of American citizenship: "All persons born or naturalized in the United States, and subject to the jurisdiction thereof, are citizens of the United States and of the State wherein they reside." Obviously this included blacks. Then it struck at discriminatory legislation like the Black Codes: "No State shall make or enforce any law which shall abridge the privileges or immunities of citizens of the United States; nor shall any State deprive any person of life, liberty, or property, without due process of law." The next section attempted to force the southern states to permit blacks to vote. If a state denied the vote to any class of its adult male citizens, its representation was to be reduced proportionately. Under another clause, former federal officials who had served the Confederacy were barred from holding either state or federal office unless specifically pardoned by a two-thirds vote of Congress. Finally, the Confederate debt was repudiated.

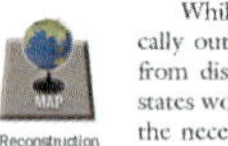

Reconstruction

While the amendment did not specifically outlaw segregation or prevent a state from disenfranchising blacks, the southern states would have none of it. Without them the necessary three-fourths majority of the states could not be obtained.

President Johnson vowed to make the choice between the Fourteenth Amendment and his own policy the main issue of the 1866 congressional elections. He embarked on "a swing around the circle" to rally the public to his cause. He failed dismally. Northern women objected to the implication in the amendment that black men were more fitted to vote than white women, but a large majority of northern voters was determined that African Americans must have at least formal legal equality. The Republicans won better than two-thirds of the seats in both houses, together with control of all the northern state governments. Johnson emerged from the campaign discredited, the Radicals stronger and determined to have their way. The southern states, Congressman James A. Garfield of Ohio said in February 1867, have "flung back into our teeth the magnanimous offer of a generous nation. It is now our turn to act."

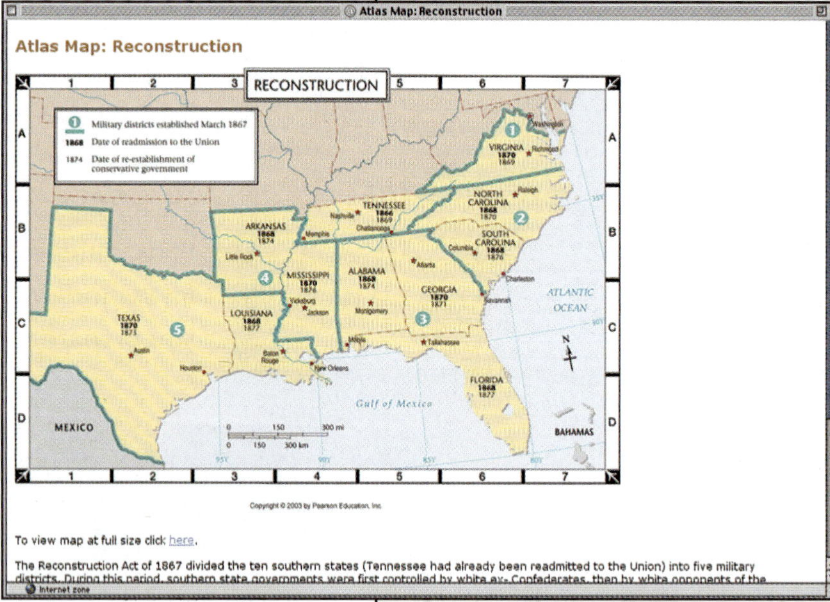

polls, whites prevented ratification in state after state. At last, in March 1868, a full year after the First Reconstruction Act, Congress changed the rules again. The constitutions were to be ratified by a majority of the voters. In June 1868 Arkansas, having fulfilled the requirements, was readmitted to the Union, and by July a

Example shown from Carnes, *The American Nation, 12/e*

Icons in this text that direct students to the resources on MyHistoryLab.com—

DOCUMENT.

This icon directs students to primary source documents that support the material that they are reading. In addition, the documents offer headnotes and analysis questions that focus students' reading.

IMAGE.

Photos, cartoons, and artwork offer students opportunities to learn the course content in a more visual way. Each image includes a headnote and analysis questions.

MAP.

Interactive maps with headnotes and questions help students visualize the material they are studying. Atlas maps and printable map activities from a Longman workbook give students hands-on experience.

AUDIO CLIP.

Historical music in original recordings, and more contemporary performances of original works, give students a sense of the impact that music had in a particular period. Audio clips are accompanied by contextual headnotes and thought questions.

VIDEO CLIP.

Historical and political video clips from the last century are included, along with headnotes and thoughtful questions.

History Bookshelf Listing.

1. *Common Sense,* Thomas Paine (1776)
2. *The Federalist Papers;* Alexander Hamilton, John Jay, and James Madison (1787-1788)
3. *The Autobiography of Benjamin Franklin* (1788)
4. *The Last of the Mohicans,* James Fennimore Cooper (1826)
5. *Democracy in America* (Two Volumes), Alexis De Tocqueville (1835)
6. *The Narrative of the Life of Frederick Douglass, An American Slave* (1845)
7. *Civil Disobedience*, Henry David Thoreau (1849)
8. *Uncle Tom's Cabin,* Harriet Beecher Stowe (1852)
9. *Walden,* Henry David Thoreau (1854)
10. *Incidents in the Life of a Slave Girl*, Harriet Jacobs (1861)
11. *The Adventures of Huckleberry Finn,* Mark Twain (1885)
12. *Looking Backward, 2000-1887,* Edward Bellamy (1888)
13. *The Yellow Wallpaper,* Charlotte Perkins Gilman (1892)
14. *The Red Badge of Courage,* Stephen Crane (1895)
15. *The Awakening and Selected Short Stories,* Kate Chopin (1899)
16. *Up From Slavery,* Booker T. Washington (1901)
17. *The Jungle,* Upton Sinclair (1906)
18. *Rise of the New West,* Frederick Jackson Turner (1906)
19. *Anarchism and Other Essays,* Emma Goldman (1917)
20. *Babbitt,* Sinclair Lewis (1922)

Looking for all the resources in MyHistoryLab but don't need an electronic textbook or course management system?

Organized to match your text's Table of Contents, LongmanAmericanHistory.com offers instructors and students all the assets of MyHistoryLab without the electronic textbook or course management.

FEATURES INCLUDE:

- **Documents, Images, Maps, and Other Sources.** Find over 1,100 primary source documents, images, and video clips, as well as an unprecedented number of maps.
- **History Bookshelf.** Read, download, or print twenty of the most commonly assigned works like Thomas Paine's *Common Sense*, and Upton Sinclair's *The Jungle*.
- **Student Assessment.** This integrated quizzing and testing program, along with pre-tests, post-tests, and chapter exams, helps students identify areas of strength and weakness.

Visit www.MyHistoryLab.com and select "Longman American History"

Dear Colleague:

We are pleased to present you with an examination copy of the second edition of *Created Equal: A Social and Political History of the United States*. If you used the first edition in your classroom, we would like to thank you and your students for embracing the book in such an enthusiastic way. Many of you have told us how excited you are by the text's new and fresh approach to American history. At the same time, you've also offered us many valuable suggestions for improving the text.

As we've taken account of those suggestions in our revision, we've also tried to keep the second edition of *Created Equal* true to the vision that inspired it. American history consists of many stories—the story of territorial expansion, the story of the rise of the middle class, the story of technological innovation and economic development, and the story of U.S. engagement with the wider world. *Created Equal* incorporates these traditional narratives into a fresh interpretation of American history, one that includes the stories of diverse groups of people and explores expanding notions of American identity. Our goal with *Created Equal* is not to overturn the familiar chronology of American history, but to integrate into that history the stories a variety of groups and individuals whose experiences allow us to provide an accurate, comprehensive, and compelling view of the past. In the second edition, as in the first, *Created Equal* tells the dramatic, evolving story of America in all its complexity—a story of a diverse people "created equal" yet struggling to achieve equality.

To users of the first edition, we again express our gratitude and we hope you will find that the second edition substantially strengthens the original text. If you are considering adopting *Created Equal* for the first time, we invite you to examine the text and discover what has made the book so popular with instructors and students alike. Whether you have already used the book in your classroom or will be using it for the first time, we are eager to learn of your reaction to and your experiences with *Created Equal*.

—The Authors

Jacqueline Jones

Peter H. Wood

Elaine Tyler May

Tim Borstelmann

Vicki L. Ruiz

CREATED EQUAL

A SOCIAL AND POLITICAL HISTORY OF THE UNITED STATES

SECOND EDITION

VOLUME II ▪ 1877 TO PRESENT

Jacqueline Jones
Brandeis University

Peter H. Wood
Duke University

Thomas Borstelmann
University of Nebraska

Elaine Tyler May
University of Minnesota

Vicki L. Ruiz
University of California, Irvine

New York San Francisco Boston
London Toronto Sydney Tokyo Singapore Madrid
Mexico City Munich Paris Cape Town Hong Kong Montreal

To our own teachers, who helped set us on the historian's path, and to our students, who help keep us there. You have touched our intellects, our hearts, and our lives.

A nuestros propios maestros, quienes nos ayudaron a seguir en el sendero de historiador, y a nuestros estudiantes que ayudan a mantenernos alli. Usted ha tocado nuestros intelectos, nuestros corazones, y nuestras vidas.

Executive Editor: Michael Boezi
Development Manager: Betty Slack
Executive Marketing Manager: Sue Westmoreland
Senior Media Editor: Patrick McCarthy
Media and Supplements Editor: Kristi Olson
Director of Market Research: Laura Coaty
Production Manager: Ellen MacElree
Project Coordination, Electronic Page Makeup, and Cartography: Electronic Publishing Services Inc., NYC
Interior Design: Pearson Education Development and Electronic Publishing Services Inc.
Cover Designer/Manager: Wendy Ann Fredericks
Photo Researcher: Photosearch, Inc.
Manufacturing Buyer: Lucy Hebard
Printer and Binder: Webcrafters
Cover Printer: Phoenix Color Corps.
Cover Photo: Japanese-American soldiers from the Jerome and Rohwer Relocation Center in Arkansas take time out from their dance at Camp Shelby to wave thir leis at the camera. © Picture History

Credits for literary selections, selected maps and figures, and timeline photos appear on pages C-1–C-2.

Library of Congress Cataloging-in-Publication Data

Created equal : a social and political history of the United States / Jacqueline Jones ... [et al.].— 2nd ed.
p. cm.
Includes bibliographical references and index.
ISBN 0-321-24188-6 (complete volume)
1. United States—History. 2. United States—Social conditions. 3. United States—Politics and government. 4. Pluralism (Social sciences)—United States—History. 5. Minorities—United States—History. 6. Pluralism (Social sciences)—United States—History—Sources. 7. Minorities—United States—History—Sources. I. Jones, Jacqueline

E178.C86 2006
973—dc22

2004030498

Please visit our website at www.ablongman.com
ISBN: 0-321-24188-6 (Complete Edition)
ISBN: 0-321-31726-2 (Volume 1)
ISBN: 0-321-31725-4 (Volume 2)
1 2 3 4 5 6 7 8 9 10—WC—06 05

Brief Contents

Detailed Contents xv
Maps xviii
Figures and Tables xviii
Features xix
Preface xx
Supplements xxvi
A Conversation with the Authors xxx
Meet the Authors xxxiv
Acknowledgments xxxvi

15 In the Wake of War: Consolidating a Triumphant Union, 1865–1877 498

PART SIX
The Emergence of Modern America, 1877–1900 534
16 Standardizing the Nation: Innovations in Technology, Business, and Culture, 1877–1890 536
17 Challenges to Government and Corporate Power: Resistance and Reform, 1877–1890 570
18 Political and Cultural Conflict in a Decade of Depression and War: The 1890s 604

PART SEVEN
Reform at Home, Revolution Abroad, 1900–1929 640
19 The Promise and Perils of Progressive Reform, 1900–1912 642
20 War and Revolution, 1912–1920 674
21 The Promise of Consumer Culture: The 1920s 706

PART EIGHT
From Depression and War to World Power, 1929–1953 736
22 Hardship and Hope in the 1930s: The Great Depression 738
23 Global Conflict: World War II, 1937–1945 772
24 Cold War and Hot War, 1945–1953 806

PART NINE
The Cold War at Full Tide, 1953–1979 838
25 Domestic Dreams and Atomic Nightmares, 1953–1963 840
26 The Nation Divides: The Vietnam War and Social Conflict, 1964–1971 874
27 Reconsidering National Priorities, 1972–1979 906

PART TEN
Global Connections, at Home and Abroad: New Threats and Possibilities, 1979–2004 938
28 The Cold War Returns—and Ends, 1979–1991 940
29 Post–Cold War America, 1991–2000 972
30 A Global Nation for the New Millennium 1002

Appendix A-1
Glossary G-1
Credits C-1
Index I-1

Detailed Contents

Maps xviii
Figures and Tables xviii
Features xix
Preface xx
Supplements xxvi
A Conversation with the Authors xxx
Meet the Authors xxxiv
Acknowledgments xxxvi

PART FIVE

Disunion and Reunion 426

CHAPTER 15

In the Wake of War: Consolidating a Triumphant Union, 1865–1877 498

The Struggle over the South 501
- Wartime Preludes to Postwar Policies 501
- Presidential Reconstruction, 1865–1867 502
- The Southern Postwar Labor Problem 505
- Building Free Communities 508
- Landscapes and Soundscapes of Freedom 510
- Congressional Reconstruction: The Radicals' Plan 510
- The Remarkable Career of Blanche K. Bruce 515

Claiming Territory for the Union 515
- Federal Military Campaigns Against Western Indians 516
- The Postwar Western Labor Problem 518
- Land Use in an Expanding Nation 521
- Buying Territory for the Union 524

The Republican Vision and Its Limits 525
- Postbellum Origins of the Woman Suffrage Movement 526
- Workers' Organizations 527
- Political Corruption and the Decline of Republican Idealism 530

Conclusion 532

Sites to Visit 532

■ INTERPRETING HISTORY
A Southern Labor Contract 509

■ CONNECTING HISTORY
Two Presidents Impeached 514

■ MAPPING HISTORY
Great Salt Lake Basin 520

PART SIX

The Emergence of Modern America, 1877–1900 534

CHAPTER 16

Standardizing the Nation: Innovations in Technology, Business, and Culture, 1877–1890 536

The New Shape of Business 539
- New Systems and Machines—and Their Price 540
- Alterations in the Natural Environment 542
- Innovations in Financing and Organizing Business 543
- New Labor Supplies for a New Economy 545
- Efficient Machines, Efficient People 548

The Birth of a National Urban Culture 549
- Economic Sources of Urban Growth 550
- Building the Cities 551
- Local Government Gets Bigger 555

Thrills, Chills, and Bathtubs: The Emergence of Consumer Culture 556
- Shows as Spectacles 556
- Entertainment Collides with Tradition 558
- "Palaces of Consumption" 559

Defending the New Industrial Order 562
- The Contradictory Politics of Laissez-Faire 563
- Social Darwinism and the "Natural" State of Society 566

Conclusion 566

Sites to Visit 568

For Further Reading 569

■ MAPPING HISTORY
Chicago, Illinois, and Gary, Indiana 554

■ CONNECTING HISTORY
Persuading People to Buy: Advertising in American History 560

■ INTERPRETING HISTORY
Andrew Carnegie and the "Gospel of Wealth" 567

CHAPTER 17

Challenges to Government and Corporate Power: Resistance and Reform, 1877–1890 570

Resistance to Legal and Military Authority 573
- Chinese Lawsuits in California 573

Blacks in the "New South" 576
"Jim Crow" in the West 579
The Ghost Dance on the High Plains 580
Revolt in the Workplace 584
Trouble on the Farm 585
Militancy in the Factories and Mines 588
The Haymarket Bombing 593
Crosscurrents of Reform 594
The Goal of Indian Assimilation 596
Transatlantic Networks of Reform 599
Women Reformers: "Beginning to Burst the Bonds" 599
Conclusion 601
Sites to Visit 602
For Further Reading 603

MAPPING HISTORY
Lower Mississippi Valley 578

CONNECTING HISTORY
Rural Protests and Rebellions 590

INTERPRETING HISTORY
"Albert Parsons's Plea for Anarchy" 595

CHAPTER 18
Political and Cultural Conflict in a Decade of Depression and War: The 1890s 604
Frontiers at Home, Lost and Found 607
Claiming and Managing the Land 608
The Tyranny of Racial Categories 610
New Roles for Schools 612
Connections Between Consciousness and Behavior 615
The Search for Alliances 616
Class Conflict 616
Rise and Demise of the Populists 620
Barriers to a U.S. Workers' Political Movement 621
Challenges to Traditional Gender Roles 623
American Imperialism 627
Cultural Encounters with the Exotic 627
Initial Imperialist Ventures 628
The Spanish-American-Cuban-Filipino War of 1898 630
Critics of Imperialism 634
Conclusion 636
Sites to Visit 638
For Further Reading 638

MAPPING HISTORY
Coeur d'Alene and Northern Idaho/Western Montana 618

CONNECTING HISTORY
The Modern Olympic Games 630

INTERPRETING HISTORY
Proceedings of the Congressional Committee on the Philippines 636

PART 7
Reform at Home, Revolution Abroad, 1900–1929 640

CHAPTER 19
The Promise and Perils of Progressive Reform, 1900–1912 642
Migration and Immigration: The Changing Face of the Nation 646
The Heartland: Land of Newcomers 647
The Southwest: Mexican Borderlands 648
Asian Immigration and the Impact of Exclusion 650
Newcomers from Southern and Eastern Europe 653
Work, Science, and Leisure 655
Reform and Science: An Uneasy Alliance 655
Scientific Management and Mass Production 657
New Amusements 658
"Sex O'Clock in America" 660
Artists Respond to the New Era 661
Reformers and Radicals 661
Muckraking, Moral Reform, and Vice Crusades 662
Women's Suffrage 664
Radical Politics and the Labor Movement 664
Resistance to Racism 665
Expanding National Power 666
The "Rough Rider" as President 666
Protecting and Preserving the Natural World 667
Expanding National Power Abroad 668
William Howard Taft: The One-Term Progressive 669
Conclusion 671
Sites to Visit 672
For Further Reading 672

CONNECTING HISTORY
Rose Freedman 645

MAPPING HISTORY
Northeast Minnesota and Northwest Wisconsin 649

INTERPRETING HISTORY
Defining Whiteness 658

CHAPTER 20
War and Revolution, 1912–1920 674
A World in Upheaval 676
The Apex of European Conquest 677

Confronting Revolutions Abroad 677
Conflicts over Hierarchies at Home 680

The Great War and American Neutrality 684
"The One Great Nation at Peace" 684
Reform Priorities at Home 685
The Great Migration 688
Limits to American Neutrality 689

The United States Goes to War 690
The Logic of Belligerency 690
Mobilizing the Home Front 692
Ensuring Unity 693
The War in Europe 694

The Struggle to Win the Peace 697
Peacemaking and the Versailles Treaty 698
Waging Counterrevolution Abroad 700
The Red and Black Scares at Home 702

Conclusion 703

Sites to Visit 704

For Further Reading 705

■ MAPPING HISTORY
The Four Corners Region 683

■ INTERPRETING HISTORY
African American Women in the Great War 696

■ CONNECTING HISTORY
The League of Nations and Internatio nal Security 701

CHAPTER 21

The Promise of Consumer Culture: The 1920s 706

The Business of Politics 708
Warren G. Harding: The Politics of Scandal 708
Calvin Coolidge: The Hands-Off President 709
Herbert Hoover: The Self-Made President 710

The Decline of Reform 711
Women's Rights After the Struggle for Suffrage 711
Prohibition: The Experiment That Failed 712
Reactionary Impulses 713
Marcus Garvey and the Persistence of Civil Rights Activism 715

Hollywood and Harlem: National Cultures in Black and White 715
Hollywood Comes of Age 716
The Harlem Renaissance 720
Radios and Autos: Transforming Leisure at Home 722

Science on Trial 723
The Great Flood of 1927 724
The Triumph of Eugenics: *Buck v. Bell* 724
Science, Religion, and the Scopes Trial 726

Consumer Dreams and Nightmares 728
Marketing the Good Life 728
Writers, Critics, and the "Lost Generation" 729
Poverty Amid Plenty 730
The Stock Market Crash 732

Conclusion 733

Sites to Visit 734

For Further Reading 735

■ CONNECTING HISTORY
The Globalization of American Popular Culture 716

■ MAPPING HISTORY
Los Angeles and Its Environs 719

■ INTERPRETING HISTORY
F. Scott Fitzgerald, The Great Gatsby *733*

PART EIGHT

From Depression and War to World Power, 1929–1953 736

CHAPTER 22

Hardship and Hope in the 1930s: The Great Depression 738

The Great Depression 740
Causes of the Crisis 741
"We Are Not Bums" 743
Surviving Hard Times 743
The Dust Bowl 745

Presidential Responses to the Depression 746
Herbert Hoover: Tackling the Crisis 747
Franklin Delano Roosevelt: The Pragmatist 750
"Nothing to Fear but Fear Itself" 752

The New Deal 752
The First Hundred Days 753
Monumental Projects Transforming the Landscape 756
Protest and Pressure from the Left and the Right 758
Eleanor Roosevelt: Activist and First Lady 761
The Second New Deal 761
FDR's Second Term 764

A New Political Culture 765
The Labor Movement 765
The New Deal Coalition 766
A New Americanism 767

Conclusion 768

Sites to Visit 769

For Further Reading 770

■ INTERPRETING HISTORY
Songs of the Great Depression 748

■ CONNECTING HISTORY
Presidents and the Media 750

■ MAPPING HISTORY
Las Vegas/Hoover Dam Area 757

CHAPTER 23
Global Conflict: World War II, 1937–1945 772

Mobilizing for War 775
The Rise of Fascism 775
Aggression in Europe and Asia 776
The Great Debate: Americans Contemplate War 776
Pearl Harbor: The United States Enters the War 778
December 7, 1941 779
Japanese American Relocation 781
Foreign Nationals in the United States 783
Wartime Migrations 783
The Home Front 784
Building Morale 784
Home Front Workers, Rosie the Riveter, and Victory Girls 787
Race and War 789
The Holocaust 789
Racial Tensions at Home 791
Fighting for the "Double V" 792
Total War 795
The War in Europe 795
The War in the Pacific 797
The End of the War 799
Conclusion 802
Sites to Visit 803
For Further Reading 804

■ MAPPING HISTORY
Hawaii 780

■ INTERPRETING HISTORY
Zelda Webb Anderson, "You Just Met One Who Does Not Know How to Cook" 794

■ CONNECTING HISTORY
The Atomic Bomb: Political and Cultural Fallout 800

CHAPTER 24
Cold War and Hot War, 1945–1953 806

The Uncertainties of Victory 808
Global Destruction 808
Vacuums of Power 809
Postwar Reconversion 811
Contesting Racial Hierarchies 812
Class Conflict 814
The Quest for Security 815
Redefining National Security 815
Conflict with the Soviet Union 816
The Policy of Containment 818
Colonialism and the Cold War 820
The Impact of Nuclear Weapons 821
A Cold War Society 822
Family Lives 823
The Growth of the South and the West 825
Harry Truman and the Limits of Liberal Reform 825
The Cold War at Home 826
Who Is a Loyal American? 827
The United States and Asia 828
The Chinese Civil War 829
The Creation of the National Security State 830
At War in Korea 833
Conclusion 836
Sites to Visit 836
For Further Reading 837

■ CONNECTING HISTORY
The Origins of the Cold War 818

■ INTERPRETING HISTORY
NSC-68 831

■ MAPPING HISTORY
Washington, D.C. 832

PART NINE
The Cold War at Full Tide, 1953–1979 838

CHAPTER 25
Domestic Dreams and Atomic Nightmares, 1953–1963 840

Cold War, Warm Hearth 842
Consumer Spending and the Suburban Ideal 845
Race, Class, and Domesticity 846
Women: Back to the Future 849
The Civil Rights Movement 851
Brown v. Board of Education 852
White Resistance, Black Persistence 853
Boycotts and Sit-Ins 854
The Eisenhower Years 856
The Middle of the Road 856
"What's Good for General Motors…" 858
Eisenhower's Foreign Policy 859
Outsiders and Opposition 862
Youth, Sex, and Rock 'n' Roll 863
Rebellious Men 864
Mobilizing for Peace and the Environment 864
The Kennedy Era 865
Domestic Policy 866
Foreign Policy 868
A Year of Turning Points 869
Conclusion 872
Sites to Visit 872

For Further Reading 873

■ MAPPING HISTORY
The Texas-Louisiana Coast 857

■ INTERPRETING HISTORY
Rachel Carson, **Silent Spring** *867*

■ CONNECTING HISTORY
Anticommunism 870

CHAPTER 26

The Nation Divides: The Vietnam War and Social Conflict, 1964–1971 874

Lyndon Johnson and the Apex of Liberalism 876
- The New President 876
- The Great Society: Fighting Poverty and Discrimination 877
- The Great Society: Improving the Quality of Life 879
- The Liberal Warren Court 881

Into War in Vietnam 882
- The Vietnamese Revolution and the United States 882
- Johnson's War 883
- Americans in Southeast Asia 885
- 1968: The Turning Point 888

The Movement 889
- From Civil Rights to Black Power 889
- The New Left and the Struggle Against the War 892
- Cultural Rebellion and the Counterculture 893
- Women's Liberation 895
- The Many Fronts of Liberation 897

The Conservative Response 899
- Backlashes 900
- The Turmoil of 1968 at Home 901
- The Nixon Administration 902
- Escalating and Deescalating in Vietnam 903

Conclusion 904

Sites to Visit 904

For Further Reading 905

■ CONNECTING HISTORY
Coming to America 880

■ INTERPRETING HISTORY
Martin Luther King Jr. and the Vietnam War 891

■ MAPPING HISTORY
The San Francisco Bay Area 894

CHAPTER 27

Reconsidering National Priorities, 1972–1979 906

Twin Shocks: Détente and Watergate 909
- Triangular Diplomacy 909
- Scandal in the White House 912
- The Nation After Watergate 913

Discovering the Limits of the U.S. Economy 916
- The End of the Long Boom 916
- The Oil Embargo 918
- The Environmental Movement 919

Reshuffling Politics 922
- Congressional Power Reasserted 922
- "I Will Never Lie to You" 925
- Rise of a Peacemaker 926
- The War on Waste 928

Diffusing the Women's Movement 931
- The Meanings of Women's Liberation 931
- New Opportunities in Education, the Workplace, and Family Life 932
- Equality Under the Law 933
- Backlash 934

Conclusion 935

Sites to Visit 936

For Further Reading 937

■ CONNECTING HISTORY
Energy Use in the United States 920

■ INTERPRETING HISTORY
The Church Committee and CIA Covert Operations 924

■ MAPPING HISTORY
Alaska 929

PART TEN

Global Connections, at Home and Abroad: New Threats and Possibilities, 1979–2004 938

CHAPTER 28

The Cold War Returns—and Ends, 1979–1991 940

Anticommunism Revived 942
- Iran and Afghanistan 942
- The Conservative Victory of 1980 944
- Renewing the Cold War 945

Republican Rule at Home 947
- "Reaganomics" and the Assault on Welfare 947
- An Embattled Environment 948
- A Society Divided 950

Cultural Conflict 954
- The Rise of the Religious Right 955
- Dissenters Push Back 958
- The New Immigration 959

The End of the Cold War 961
- From Cold War to Détente 962

The Iran-Contra Scandal 963
A Global Police? 965
Conclusion 970
Sites to Visit 970
For Further Reading 971

CONNECTING HISTORY
Is Material Success Corrupting? 952

INTERPRETING HISTORY
Religion and Politics in the 1980s 956

MAPPING HISTORY
Southern Florida 960

CHAPTER 29
Post–Cold War America, 1991–2000 972

The Economy: Global and Domestic 975
The Post–Cold War Economy 975
The Widening Gap Between Rich and Poor 977
Labor Unions 979
Tolerance and Its Limits 980
"We Can All Get Along" 980
Values in Conflict 981
Courtroom Dramas 983
The Changing Face of Diversity 984
Violence and Danger 985
Domestic Terrorism 985
Kids Who Kill 986
A Healthy Nation? 987
The Clinton Presidency 988
Clinton: The New Democrat 988
Clinton's Domestic Agenda and the "Republican Revolution" 989
The Impeachment Crisis 990
The Nation and the World 991
Trade Agreements 991
Efforts at Peacemaking 993
Military Interventions and International Terrorism 994
The Contested Election of 2000 995
The Campaign, the Vote, and the Courts 995
The Aftermath 998
Legacies of Election 2000 999
Conclusion 999
Sites to Visit 1000
For Further Reading 1001

MAPPING HISTORY
Front Range, Rocky Mountains 976

INTERPRETING HISTORY
Vermont Civil Union Law 982

CONNECTING HISTORY
Voting 996

CHAPTER 30
A Global Nation for the New Millennium 1002

The George W. Bush Administration 1004
The President and the War on Terrorism 1004
Security and Politics at Home 1005
The War in Iraq 1007
The Election of 2004 1010
America's Place in a Global Economy 1011
The Logic and Technology of Globalization 1012
Free Trade and the Global Assembly Line 1014
Who Benefits from Globalization? 1016
The Stewardship of Natural Resources 1018
Ecological Transformations 1018
Pollution 1021
Environmentalism and Its Limitations 1022
The Expansion of American Popular Culture Abroad 1023
A Culture of Diversity and Entertainment 1024
U.S. Influence Abroad Since the Cold War 1025
Resistance to American Popular Culture 1025
Identity in Contemporary America 1028
Negotiating Multiple Identities 1029
Social Change and Abiding Discrimination 1030
Still an Immigrant Society 1031
Conclusion 1032
Sites to Visit 1033
For Further Reading 1034

CONNECTING HISTORY
The Internet and the World Wide Web 1012

MAPPING HISTORY
Puget Sound and Western Washington 1019

INTERPRETING HISTORY
The Slow Food Movement 1026

Appendix A-1
The Declaration of Independence A-3
The Article of Confederation A-5
The Constitution of the United States of America A-8
Amendments to the Constitution A-13
Presidential Elections A-17
Mapping History in the United States A-20
Present Day World A-22

Glossary G-1
Credits C-1
Index I-1

Maps

15.1 Radical Reconstruction 512
15.2 Plains Indian Wars, 1865–1900 517
15.3 The Compromise of 1877 531
16.1 Agricultural Regions of the Midwest and Northeast 541
16.2 Some Places Where Chinese Located, 1865–1880 547
16.3 Population of Foreign-Born, by Region, 1880 551
17.1 Southern Tenancy and Sharecropping, 1880 576
17.2 Buffalo Soldiers 581
17.3 Indian Lands Lost, 1850–1890 583
17.4 Estimated Membership, by State, of the National Farmer's Alliance, 1890 587
18.1 Population Density, 1890 607
18.2 Indian Territory and the State of Oklahoma, 1885–1907 609
18.3 Indian Reservations, 1900 613
18.4 Compulsory School Attendance Laws, by State 614
18.5 Manufacturing in the United States, 1900 622
18.6 The Spanish-American-Cuban-Filipino War of 1898 634
19.1 Foreign-Born Population, 1900 647
19.2 Areas Excluded from Immigration to the United States, 1882–1952 651
19.3 Russian and Italian Immigrants in the United States, 1910 654
20.1 U.S. Interests and Interventions in the Caribbean Region, 1898–1939 679
20.2 Prominent National Parks of the American West 687
20.3 World War I in Europe and the Western Front, 1918 695
20.4 Europe After World War I 699
21.1 The Mississippi River Flood of 1927 725
21.2 Americans on the Move, 1870s–1930s 731
22.1 Dust and Drought, 1931–1939 747
22.2 Areas Served by the Tennessee Valley Authority 754
23.1 The Internment of Japanese Americans During World War II 781
23.2 Nazi Concentration and Extermination Camps 790
23.3 World War II in Europe 795
23.4 World War II in the Pacific 798
24.1 Occupation of Germany and Austria, 1946–1949 810
24.2 Europe Divided by the Cold War 817
24.3 Asia After World War II 820
24.4 The Korean War, 1950–1953 834
25.1 Major Events of the African American Civil Rights Movements, 1953–1963 855
25.2 Cold War Spheres of Influence, 1953–1963 860
25.3 The Nuclear Landscape 866
26.1 Percentage of Population Living Below the Poverty Line, 1969 (by State) 878
26.2 The American War in Vietnam 884
26.3 Major Social and Political Protests, 1962–1971 890
27.1 Nuclear Weapons Before Détente 910
27.2 The Gradual Liberation of Southern African from White Minority Rule 927
27.3 Building Nuclear Power Plants 930
28.1 Trouble Spots in the Middle East, 1979–1993 943
28.2 Federally Owned Lands in the West 949
28.3 The Soviet Bloc Dissolves 966
28.4 The Persian Gulf War 968
29.1 States With Large Numbers of Undocumented Immigrants, 1995 978
29.2 The Breakup of Former Yugoslavia 994
29.3 The Contested Election of 2000 997
30.1 Iraq and the Middle East 1008
30.2 Top Ten U.S. Trading Partners 1014
30.3 Water Sources in the American West 1020
30.4 State Population Growth, 1990–2000 1028

Figures and Tables

Figures

16.1 Amount of Forest Clearing Each Decade, by Major Region, 1850–1909 542
16.2 How Indians Used the Buffalo 544
16.3 Menu from Drake Hotel, Chicago, Illinois, for Thanksgiving, 1886 552
19.1 Number of Immigrants Entering the United States, 1821–1990 646
20.1 Casualties of the Great War, 1914–1918 685
21.1 Number of Immigrants and Countries of Origin, 1891–1920 and 1921–1940 714
21.2 Transformation of the Upper Midwest, 1880–1980 723
24.1 Opportunities for Veterans 813
25.1 Marital Status of the U.S. Adult Population, 1900–1995 844
25.2 The Baby Boom in Historical Context 846
26.1 U.S. Troops and Deaths in Vietnam (as of December 31 of Each Year) 886
27.1 Imported Petroleum as Share of U.S. Consumption 918
27.2 The Death Penalty: Practices and Opinions 923
28.1 Distribution of Wealth and Income 954
29.1 Childhood Obesity Rates for Boys and Girls, Aged 6–17, 1960s and 1990s 988
30.1 World Crude Oil Reserves, 2000 1006
30.2 U.S. Petroleum Imports by Leading Countries of Origin, April 2004 1007
30.3 Self-Described Religious Affiliation in the United States, 2000 1029

Tables

15.1 Comparison of Black and White Household Structure in 27 Cotton-Belt Counties 511
15.2 Estimates of Railroad Crossties Used and Acres of Forest Cleared, 1870–1910 524
15.3 National and International Union Members of the National Labor Union 529
16.1 Number of Firms by Number of Employees per Firm, 1850 and 1880 548
17.1 Percentage of Farms Operated by Tenants or Sharecroppers 585
18.1 Work Hours Needed to Produce Specified Amounts of Wheat, Corn, and Cotton, 1880 and 1900 619
18.2 Categories of Employment, 1880–1910 623
22.1 Key New Deal Legislation, 1933–1938 763

Features

Interpreting History

A Southern Labor Contract 509
Andrew Carnegie and the "Gospel of Wealth" 567
"Albert Parson's Plea for Anarchy" 595
Proceedings of the Congressional Committee on the Philippines 636
Defining Whiteness 658
African American Women in the Great War 696
F. Scott Fitzgerald, *The Great Gatsby* 733
Songs of the Great Depression 748
Zelda Webb Anderson, "You Just Met One Who Does Not Know How to Cook" 794
NSC-68 831
Rachel Carson, *Silent Spring* 867
Martin Luther King, Jr. and the Vietnam War 891
The Church Committee and CIA Covert Operations 924
Religion and Politics in the 1980s 956
Vermont Civil Union Law 982
The Slow Food Movement 1026

Connecting History

Two Presidents Impeached 514
Persuading People to Buy: Advertising in American History 560
Rural Protests and Rebellions 590
The Modern Olympic Games 630
Rose Freedman 645
The League of Nations and International Security 701
The Globalization of American Popular Culture 716
Presidents and the Media 750
The Atomic Bomb: Political and Cultural Fallout 800
The Origins of the Cold War 818
Anticommunism 870
Coming to America 880
Energy Use in the United States 920
Is Material Success Corrupting? 952
Voting 996
The Internet and the World Wide Web 1012

Mapping History

Great Lake Salt Basin 520
Chicago, Illinois, and Gary, Indiana 554
Lower Mississippi Valley 578
Coeur d'Alene and Northern Idaho/Western Montana 618
Northeast Minnesota and Northwest Wisconsin 649
The Four Corners Region 683
Los Angeles and Its Environs 719
Las Vegas/Hoover Dam Area 757
Hawaii 780
Washington, D.C. 832
The Texas-Louisiana Coast 857
The San Francisco Bay Area 894
Alaska 929
Southern Florida 960
Front Range, Rocky Mountains 976
Puget Sound and Western Washington 1019

Preface

> *"We hold these truths to be self-evident: That all men are created equal; that they are endowed by their Creator with certain unalienable rights; that among these are life, liberty, and the pursuit of happiness. . . ."*

In April 2005, at the annual meeting of the Organization of American Historians (OAH) in San Francisco, the authors and editors of *Created Equal* will gather to celebrate both the launching of the text's second edition and the inauguration of Professor Vicki L. Ruiz, a key member of our team, as the new president of the OAH. Vicki is the organization's first Latino American leader, and the event will have great symbolic significance for all of us. Celebrating in California rather than on the East Coast affirms that our history touches the Pacific as well as the Atlantic. The event will remind us why we wrote this book, and why we chose to highlight the rich regional and social diversity of the American people.

Ever since the Continental Congress approved the Declaration of Independence on July 4, 1776, that document has inspired people in the United States and around the world. Now, more than ever, "We hold these truths to be self-evident: That all men are created equal; that they are endowed by their Creator with certain unalienable rights; that among these are life, liberty, and the pursuit of happiness." Granted, the Founding Fathers conceived of the new nation in narrow terms—as a political community for white men of property. But for generations, diverse racial and ethnic groups, as well as people of different ages, genders, or sexual preference, have cited the Declaration in their struggle to achieve a more inclusive definition of American citizenship. American history is the story of various groups of men and women, rich and poor, all "created equal" in their common humanity, claiming an American identity for themselves. *Created Equal* serves to inform and inspire a new generation with an inclusive and optimistic view of what it means to be an American.

The Second Edition

We are pleased to introduce the second edition of *Created Equal.* In it we retain and strengthen the basic structure of the original text—its organization, themes, and style. This edition covers events through the presidential election of 2004, adding new material on the first administration of President George W. Bush in sections titled "The President and the War on Terrorism," "Security and Politics at Home," and "The War in Iraq." The second edition also includes new graphics and features, as well as substantial revisions that reflect the suggestions of the many instructors who used the first edition in their classrooms.

First-time users of the book told us that they appreciated the elements that make *Created Equal* unique. These elements include a strong chronological narrative emphasizing significant political developments throughout American history, the stories of individuals that enliven the narrative, and the intertwining of four themes: social diversity and inclusivity, the environment, class and power relations, and the intersection of foreign and domestic affairs. We added new material related to all of these themes. In addition, we significantly strengthened the environmental theme by introducing a major new full-page feature—in each chapter, a map of a particular region of the country, highlighting transformations within that region over time.

Several new features enhance the book's accessibility for students. A glossary at the back of the book defines terms that are highlighted in the body of the text. Study questions at the end of each "Interpreting History" primary document encourage students to hone their critical thinking skills. Website icons in the margins of the text point students toward additional Web-produced resources on a particular topic.

The second edition of *Created Equal* remains true to the vision that inspired it. The book's basic framework focuses on the political events and economic structures discussed in most American history textbooks. *Created Equal* aims not to overturn the familiar chronology of American history, but to integrate into it a variety of groups and individuals whose stories help us to provide an accurate, comprehensive, and compelling view of the past. We realize that American history consists of many stories—the story of territorial expansion, the story of the rise of the middle class, the story of technological innovation and economic development, and the story of U.S. engagement with the wider world. *Created Equal* incorporates these traditional narratives into a fresh interpretation of American history, one that includes the stories of diverse groups of people and explores expanding notions of American identity. The second edition encourages students to make connections and comparisons in new and creative ways. For example, new sections include "The Contrasting Worlds of Pennsylvania and Carolina" (Chapter 3), comparing two of colonial America's most important seaports, Philadelphia and Charleston; and "Landscapes and Soundscapes of Freedom" (Chapter 15) describing the audible evidence of emancipation—black children reciting their ABC's, congregants of newly formed black churches singing and clapping their hands.

Four Themes

The second edition highlights the four significant themes developed in the first edition and includes new material related to each of these themes.

- **Diversity.** In considering the theme of diversity, we acknowledge the formation of social identity as a central element of the American story. We examine how individual Americans have understood and identified themselves by gender, religion, region, income, race, and ethnicity, among other factors. American Indians, African Americans, Latinos, Chinese immigrants, members of the laboring classes, women of all groups—all of these people have played a major role in defining what it means to be an American. At the same time, diverse forms of identity are by no means fixed or static. For example, Chapter 9 now includes the story of Ona Judge, an enslaved woman owned by George Washington's wife, Martha. In 1796, Ona Judge took to heart the rhetoric of the American Revolution in a way that her master and mistress did not anticipate or fully understand; the young woman escaped from the Washington household in Philadelphia and fled to New Hampshire, where she made a new life for herself. In response to the Washingtons' efforts to retrieve her, Judge echoed the words of the revolutionary Patrick Henry, declaring "that she should rather suffer death than return to Slavery & [be] liable to be sold or given to any other persons."
- **Class and systems of power.** These systems have shaped American society in profound ways, and an understanding of them is fundamental to understanding events in American history. The nation was founded on the idea that, unlike European countries, the United States would not have an inherited aristocracy. However, in the early years of the republic, the privileges of citizenship were limited to a minority of residents—namely, white men who owned property. The institution of slavery denied people of African descent basic human freedoms. From the beginning, African Americans struggled against the institution of bondage and its legacy. Some groups used the law to deny other groups the right to participate in the political system. Popular ideas related to alleged social differences and innate inferiority served to justify the treatment of certain groups as second-class citizens. U.S. military leaders launched military campaigns against vulnerable peoples within and outside the nation's borders. By the end of the nineteenth century, the United States boasted the largest and most comfortable middle class in the world—and yet the most substantial political and economic power was distributed

among a relatively small contingent of white men. During the twentieth century, Americans dismantled the legal system of inequality that reduced blacks, women, and other groups to second-class citizenship. Nevertheless, a growing gap between the rich and poor continued to complicate the notion of true equality.

- **Environment.** The theme of the environment is key to understanding cultural, political, and economic developments. American Indians and European Americans differed in the ways they inhabited and used the land. Indians were more likely to use the land communally, and to incorporate natural phenomena, such as periodic burning, in their agricultural practices. European Americans based their land use on the concept of private ownership, dividing up parcels among settlers and clearing the land for profit. The vast richness of the American landscape has provoked violent conflict over the years, even as it has formed a key component in American wealth and power. We examine regional differences in all geographical areas—not just the eastern seaboard. This edition includes a new section in Chapter 22 that focuses on the monumental construction projects during the Great Depression. New bridges, dams, and other structures indicated efforts to demonstrate human mastery and grandeur during a time of national crisis.

  In the second edition, the new environmental map in the "Mapping History" feature in each chapter enhances our understanding of the ways the physical landscape has profoundly shaped American society, and the ways people have used and altered the land. For its symbolic and historical significance, a map of the heart of the continent is included in the very first chapter. This map shows the confluence of the Missouri, Illinois, and Mississippi Rivers, an ancient meeting place that saw the rise of the Cahokia moundbuilders ten centuries ago and the launching of the Lewis and Clark expedition 800 years later. Among the other regions covered by these maps (30 in all) are northeastern Alaska, the Delaware Valley, the Upper Midwest, the Lower Mississippi Valley, Chicago and its environs, the great Salt Lake basin, the Las Vegas-Hoover Dam area, and Hawaii.

- **Globalization.** Finally, the increasing globalization of the U.S. economy and society in recent decades reminds us of how deeply the country has always been engaged with the rest of the world. Since the earliest days of colonial settlement, Americans have traded goods, cultural practices, and ideas with peoples outside their borders. As an immigrant nation and the modern world's superpower, America's foreign and domestic relations have always been interconnected. After World War II, Americans' fears of communism and the Soviet Union exerted a profound effect upon the country's politics and society. In the wake of the attacks of September 11, 2001, Americans were forced to confront the role of the United States in the larger world, with all the opportunities and dangers that role entailed. This edition includes a number of new sections, graphics, and other features highlighting America's relation to the rest of the world, including a new chart in Chapter 2 clarifying the array of early European colonies that appeared in North America between 1560 and 1660; these colonizing efforts were sponsored not only by the Spanish and English, but by the French, Dutch, and Swedes as well. Chapter 25 includes a new opener detailing the life story of Tom Dooley. The renowned "jungle doctor" known for his work among the poor people of Southeast Asia, Dooley was a fervent anticommunist and a devout Catholic. The last chapter brings students up to date on the causes and aftermath of the war in Iraq.

These four themes serve as the lenses through which we view the traditional narrative framework of American history. Readers of *Created Equal* will understand the major political developments that shaped the country's past, as well as the roles of diverse groups in initiating and reacting to those developments. Chapter 13, for example, which focuses on the 1850s, includes a detailed account of the effects of the slavery crisis on Congress and the political party system, as well as a discussion of shifting group identities affecting Indians, Latinos, northern women, and enslaved and free blacks. Chapter 18, on the 1890s, covers the rise of the Populist party and stirrings of American imperialism, as well as a discussion of barriers to a U.S. workers' political party and challenges to traditional gender roles. Thus, *Created Equal* builds on the basic history that forms the foundation of most major textbooks and offers a lively and comprehensive look at the past by including the stories of many different kinds of Americans.

Chronological Organization

One of the challenges in writing *Created Equal* has been to emphasize the way the four major themes come together and influence each other, affecting specific generations of Americans. Thus, the text is organized into ten parts, most of these covering a generation. Many textbooks organize discussions of immigrants, cities, the West, and foreign diplomacy (to name a few topics) into separate chapters that cover large time periods. In contrast, *Created Equal* integrates material related to a variety of topics within individual chapters. Although the text adheres to a chronological organization, it stresses coherent discussions of specific topics within that framework. This provides students with a richer understanding of events. Chapter 15, for example, which covers the dozen or so years after the end of the Civil War, deals with Reconstruction in the South, Indian wars on the High Plains, and the rise of the women's and labor movements, stressing the relationships among all these developments. To cite another example, many texts devote a chapter exclusively to America's post–World War II rise to global power; *Created Equal* integrates material related to that development in a series of six chapters that cover the period 1945 to 2004. Each of these chapters illustrates the effects of dramatic world developments on American social relations and domestic policy on a decade-by-decade basis. This approach allows readers to appreciate the rich complexity of any particular time period and to understand that major events occur not in a vacuum but in a larger social context.

Special Features

The book includes a number of features designed to make American history clear and engaging to the reader, and to encourage students to engage with history on their own. These features include:

- **Parts and timelines.** *Created Equal* consists of ten parts covering three chapters each. An opening section that lays out the basic themes of the period introduces each part. Each part opener also includes an illustrated timeline highlighting major events covered in the three chapters that follow.
- **Chapter introductory vignettes and conclusions.** Each chapter begins with a story that introduces the reader to groups and individuals representative of the themes developed in the chapter. Among the new chapter introductory vignettes in the second edition are the story of Andrew Carnegie and an account of the Three Mile Island nuclear accident. Others introduce students to a Norwegian immigrant woman in Wisconsin (Chapter 12), a group of runaway slaves accused of treason by Confederate authorities in wartime (Chapter 14), Spanish-speaking inhabitants of northern New Mexico struggling to retain their culture in the face of an onslaught of European American settlers (Chapter 17), and a Sioux Indian boy at a government boarding school (Chapter 18). At the end of each chapter, a concluding section sums up the chapter's themes and points the reader toward the next chapter. For the second edition, these conclusions have been lengthened and expanded.
- **"Connecting History."** *Created Equal* encourages students to think outside the boundaries of specific time periods by including in each chapter a boxed feature called

"Connecting History." A topic is examined at two different periods, or as it evolved over time. Several of these mini-essays span the entire sweep of American history. New topics in this edition include a discussion of "Wind Power: Traditional and Novel," charting the harnessing of this type of energy from Dutch windmills to more recent innovations; the history of the Olympic games; the globalization of American culture; and shifts in immigration and naturalization policy throughout American history. Other topics include the history of naval navigation, civil liberties, advertising, and the Internet.

- **"Interpreting History."** This feature consists of a primary document on a topic relevant to the chapter's themes. Through this feature we hear the voices of a variety of Americans—a seventeenth-century slave, a sailmaker in post-Revolutionary New York City, a Mexican lawyer visiting New Mexico in the early nineteenth century, a group of Cherokee women in early nineteenth-century Georgia, a professor in the antebellum South, industrial titan Andrew Carnegie, anarchist Albert Parsons, writer F. Scott Fitzgerald, and environmental activist Rachel Carson. The "Interpreting History" feature takes many different forms—letters, sermons, court decisions, labor contracts, congressional hearings, and songs. Students thus have an opportunity to analyze primary documents and to better appreciate the historian's task—to read materials critically and to place them in their larger socio-historical context. Questions at the end of each document point students toward major issues and encourage them to think critically about the document.
- **"Mapping History."** This feature, new to the second edition, is intended to enhance the environmental theme that informs the book as well as acquaint students with the wide variety of geographic and environmental regions of the United States. Each "Mapping History" feature consists of a topographical map of a particular area of the country on which significant natural features are identified. Callouts on the map highlight events that occurred in the region during the time period covered in the particular chapter and other significant events that took place in time periods before and after. Accompanying each map is a brief comment noting key social and economic developments within the region over a large span of American history. For example, the environmental map for Chapter 28 zooms in on South Florida, focusing on the natural landscape of the Everglades, recounting the devastating effects of Hurricane Andrew, and stressing the importance of air conditioning as a factor in the region's development. One "Mapping History" feature appears in each chapter, focusing on such areas as Comanchería: the Lower Great Plains (Chapter 5); the Great Salt Lake basin (Chapter 15); northeast Minnesota and northwest Wisconsin (Chapter 19); and northern and eastern Alaska (Chapter 27). The areas discussed in each of the "Mapping History" features are highlighted on the U.S. map that appears on the inside front cover of the book (or, in volumes 1 and 2, in the Appendix).
- **Glossary.** The second edition includes a glossary of terms culled from the text and defined at the back of the book. Sample terms (out of several hundred) include pocket veto, aqueduct, canal locks, sit-down strike, antebellum, carpetbaggers, scalawags, vigilantes, and fatigue work. Glossary terms are highlighted in **boldface type** in the chapter text.
- **Web Assets.** Icons in the margin throughout the pages of the book identify assets on the U.S. history premium Web site—MyHistoryLab or LongmanAmericanHistory.com—that relate to the chapter content and themes. The icons indicate the kind of asset—document, map, video, or audio—and the title of each asset. These Web assets provide hundreds of additional resources including source documents, interactive maps, videos, and audio clips designed to enrich students' study of U.S. history.
- **Maps, charts, pullout quotes, and artifacts.** Illustrations—photographs, tables, pictures of objects from the time period, and figures—enhance the narrative. Large maps offer

greater geographical detail and invite students to see the relationship between geography and history. Highlighted quotes help the reader grasp the chapter's major themes.

- **"Sites to Visit" and "For Further Reading."** At the end of each chapter is a list of "Sites to Visit," identifying sites on the World Wide Web relevant to the chapter and occasionally listing the location of important historical sites and landmarks as well. There is also a list of suggested works related to each section of the chapter. We have updated these features to encourage students to follow up on major topics on their own—either on the computer or in the library.

Created Equal not only introduces students to recent scholarship in social history but provides a firm grounding in the traditional political narrative as well. In recent decades, social identity has emerged as a central theme of American history. However, exclusive attention to cultural and social diversity can overshadow the political and economic structures of American society. Students should gain an understanding of our nation's social diversity but also learn about the power relations that have shaped that past—which groups have had influence and how they have maintained and wielded that influence. Placing these issues at the forefront, *Created Equal* tells the dramatic, evolving story of America in all its complexity—a story of a diverse people "created equal" yet struggling to achieve equality.

—The Authors

Supplements

Instructor Supplements for Qualified College Adopters

- ***MyHistoryLab*** provides students with an online package complete with the entire textbook, numerous study aids, and course management. With over 1,000 primary sources, images, audio clips and video clips, as well as over 150 map activities with gradable quizzes, geographic case studies, map workbook activities, and atlas maps, the site offers students a unique, interactive experience that brings history to life. The comprehensive site also includes a history bookshelf with 20 of the most commonly assigned books in history classes and a history toolkit with tutorials and helpful links.
- ***LongmanAmericanHistory.com*** provides students with the same resources as MyHistoryLab, but without the e-book or course management.
- ***History Digital Media Archive CD-ROM.*** The Digital Media Archive CD-ROM contains electronic images and interactive and static maps, along with media elements such as video. These media assets are fully customizable and ready for classroom presentation or easy downloading into your PowerPoint™ presentations or any other presentation software. ISBN:0-321-14976-9.
- ***NEW! Visual Archives of American History, Updated Edition 0-321-18694-X.*** Available on two CD-ROMs and with added content, this encyclopedic collection of instructor resources contains dozens of narrated vignettes and videos as well a hundreds of photos and illustrations ready for use in PowerPoint™ presentations, course Web sites, or online courses.
- **Created Equal *Companion Web site*** (www.ablongman.com/jones). Instructors can take advantage of the Companion Web site that supports this text. The instructor section of the Web site includes teaching links, downloadable maps and images from the text, and PowerPoint presentations. A link to Supplements Central is also provided.
- ***Supplements Central*** (www.ablongman.com/suppscentral). At this helpful Web site, instructors can download supplements for this text, including the Instructor's Manual, Test Bank, and TestGen-EQ. Instructors will need to request a password from their sales representative to gain access.
- ***Instructor's Manual.*** Written by Yvonne Johnson of Central Missouri University and Nancy Zens of Central Oregon Community College, this tool is designed to aid both the novice and experienced instructor in teaching American history. Each chapter contains a chapter outline, significant themes, learning objectives, lesson enrichment ideas, discussion suggestions, and questions for discussing the primary source documents in the text.
- ***Test Bank.*** Written by D. Niler Pyeatt of Wayland Baptist University, the test bank contains over 1,200 test items, including multiple choice, true/false, and essay. The questions are keyed to topic and relevant text page.
- ***TestGen-EQ Computerized Testing System.*** This flexible, easy-to-use computer test bank includes all the test items in the printed test bank. Available on a dual platform CD-ROM, the software allows you to edit existing questions and add your own items. Tests can be printed in several different formats and can include graphs and tables.
- ***Text-specific Transparencies.*** A set of map transparencies from the text is available.
- ***Comprehensive American History Transparency Set.*** This vast collection of American history transparencies is a necessary teaching aid. It includes over 200 maps covering social trends, wars, elections, immigration, and demographics. Included is a set of reproducible map exercises.

• ***Discovering American History Through Maps and Views Transparency Set.*** Created by Gerald Danzer of the University of Illinois at Chicago, the recipient of the AHA's 1990 James Harvey Robinson Prize for his work in the development of map transparencies, this set of 140 four-color acetates is a unique instructional tool. It contains an introduction on teaching history through maps and a detailed commentary on each transparency. The collection includes cartographic and pictorial maps, views, and photos, urban plans, building diagrams, and works of art.

Student Supplements

• ***MyHistoryLab*** provides students with an online package complete with the entire textbook, numerous study aids, and course management. With over 1,000 primary sources, images, audio clips, and video clips, as well as over 150 map activities with gradable quizzes, geographic case studies, map workbook activities, and atlas maps, the site offers students a unique, interactive experience that brings history to life. The comprehensive site also includes a history bookshelf with 20 of the most commonly assigned books in history classes and a history toolkit with tutorials and helpful links.

• ***LongmanAmericanHistory.com*** provides students with the same resources as MyHistoryLab, but without the e-book or course management.

• ***SafariX Textbooks Online*** is an exciting new choice for students looking to save money. As an alternative to purchasing the print textbook, students can subscribe to the same content online and save up to 50 percent off the suggested list price of the print text. With a SafariX WebBook, students can search the text, make notes online, print out reading assignments that incorporate lecture notes, and bookmark important passages for later review. For more information, or to subscribe to the SafariX WebBook, visit www.SafariX.com.

• ***Study Card for American History.*** Colorful, affordable, and packed with useful information, Allyn & Bacon/Longman's Study Cards make studying easier, more efficient, and more enjoyable. Course information is distilled down to the basics, helping you quickly master the fundamentals, review a subject for understanding, or prepare for an exam. Because they're laminated for durability, you can keep these Study Cards for years to come and pull them out whenever you need a quick review.

• **Created Equal *Companion Web site*** (www.ablongman.com/jones). The Companion Web site provides a wealth of resources for students using the text. Students can access chapter summaries, interactive practice test questions, flash cards, and Web links for every chapter. The site also includes a comprehensive glossary and an online appendix.

• ***Study Guides.*** Written by William Pelz of Elgin Community College, this two-volume supplement for students contains activities and study aids for every chapter in the text. Each chapter includes a thorough summary, learning objectives, and a timeline, as well as identification, multiple-choice, map, and thought questions.

• ***Research Navigator Guide.*** This guidebook includes exercises and tips on how to use the Internet. It also includes an access code for Research Navigator™—the easiest way for students to start a research assignment or research paper. Research Navigator™ is composed of three exclusive databases of credible and reliable source material, including EBSCO's ContentSelect™ Academic Journal Database, *New York Times* Search by Subject Archive, and "Best of the Web" Link Library. This comprehensive site also includes a detailed help section.

• ***Longman American History Atlas.*** A four-color reference tool and visual guide to American history that includes almost 100 maps and covers the full scope of history. Atlas overhead transparencies available to adopters. *$3.00 when bundled with a new book.*

- ***Mapping American History: Student Activities.*** Written by Gerald Danzer of the University of Illinois at Chicago, this free map workbook for students features exercises designed to teach how to interpret and analyze cartographic materials as historical documents. Available free to qualified college adopters when bundled in advance with the textbook.

- ***Mapping America: A Guide to Historical Geography, Second Edition.*** Written by Ken Weatherbie of Del Mar College, this two-volume workbook contains 35 exercises correlated to the text that review basic American historical geography and ask students to interpret the role geography has played in American history. *Mapping America* is available free to qualified college adopters when bundled with the text.

- ***American History in a Box.*** Created by editors Julie Roy Jeffrey and Peter Frederick, this unique "reader in a box" is designed to give students an up-close and personal view of history. The collection includes loose facsimiles of written documents, visual materials and artifacts, songs and sheet music, portraits, cartoons, film posters, and more, so that students can learn firsthand what history is and what historians do. "Placing the Sources in Context" and "Questions to Consider" accompanying each set of materials in the collection help guide students through the practice of historical analysis.

- ***America Through the Eyes of Its People, Second Edition.*** This single-volume collection of primary documents reflects the rich and varied tapestry of American life. The revised edition includes more social history and enhanced pedagogy. It is available to qualified college adopters at no charge when requested by the instructor in advance.

- ***Sources of the African American Past, Second Edition.*** Edited by Roy Finkenbine of the University of Detroit at Mercy, this collection of primary sources covers key themes in the African American experience from the West African background to the present. Balanced between political and social history, it offers a vivid snapshot of the lives of African Americans in different historical periods and includes documents representing women and different regions of the United States. Available at a minimum cost to qualified college adopters when bundled with the text.

- ***Women and the National Experience, Second Edition.*** Edited by Ellen Skinner of Pace University, this primary source reader contains both classic and unusual documents describing the history of women in the United States. The documents provide dramatic evidence that outspoken women attained a public voice and participated in the development of national events and policies long before they could vote. Chronologically organized and balanced between social and political history, this reader offers a striking picture of the lives of women across American history. Available at a minimum cost to qualified college adopters when bundled in advance with the text.

- ***Reading the American West.*** Edited by Mitchel Roth of Sam Houston State University, this primary source reader uses letters, diary excerpts, speeches, interviews, and newspaper articles to let students experience how historians do research and how history is written. Every document is accompanied by a contextual headnote and study questions. The book is divided into chapters with extensive introductions. Available at a minimum cost to qualified college adopters when bundled with the text.

- ***A Short Guide to Writing About History, Fourth Edition.*** Written by Richard Marius and Melvin E. Page, this practical text teaches students how to incorporate their own ideas into their papers and to tell a story about history that interests them and their peers. Focusing on more than just the conventions of good writing, this text shows students how first to think about history, and then how to organize their thoughts into coherent essays. The *Short Guide* covers both brief essays and the document resource paper as it explores the writing and researching processes, examines different modes of historical writing, including argument, and concludes with guidelines for improving style.

- ***Library of American Biography Series.*** Each of these interpretive biographies focuses on a figure whose actions and ideas significantly influenced the course of American history and national life. At the same time, each biography relates the life of its subjects to the broader theme and developments of the times. Brief and inexpensive, they are ideal for any U.S. history course. Editions include Edmund S. Morgan, *The Puritan Dilemma: The Story of John Winthrop;* Charles W. Akers, *Abigail Adams: An American Woman;* Harold C. Livesay, *Andrew Carnegie and the Rise of Big Business;* Randolph B. Campbell, *Sam Houston and the American Southwest;* Walter L. Hixson, *Charles Lindbergh: Lone Eagle;* Jack N. Rakove, *James Madison and the Creation of the American Republic;* Sam W. Haynes, *James K. Polk and the Expansionist Impulse;* and J. William T. Youngs, *Eleanor Roosevelt: A Personal and Public Life.*
- ***Penguin Books.*** The partnership between Penguin-Putnam USA and Longman Publishers offers your students a discount on many titles when bundled with any Longman survey. Available titles include *Narrative of the Life of Frederick Douglass* by Frederick Douglass, *Why We Can't Wait* by Martin Luther King Jr., *Beloved* by Toni Morrison, and *Uncle Tom's Cabin* by Harriet Beecher Stowe.

A Conversation with the Authors

> **Created Equal** *tells stories across generations, regions, and cultures, integrating the lives of individuals within the economic, political, cultural, global, and environmental vectors shaping their lives. These tales of simple courage breathe life into history, bringing an immediacy and vibrancy to the past. We cherish the telling of stories for it is within these tales that we remember the ánimo y sueños (spirit and dreams)' of the American people.*
>
> —*Vicki Ruiz*

How Did This Project Begin?

PETER: It started with a videocassette. The Longman history editor taped a lively conversation with a dozen exceptional history teachers from very different backgrounds. They were all energized about teaching U.S. history in new ways, but they felt frustrated by their current texts. Then Longman sent the video to me. The video was not great cinematography, just talking heads, but their voices were so articulate, and I shared so many of their concerns. I remember watching the cassette on a Sunday night, and it set my mind spinning. I couldn't get much sleep. Here were real teachers like me who wanted a dramatically different text. And here was a major publisher, Longman, saying, "What do you think?"

At the time, I was teaching one of those special classes, a group of history majors that really clicked. Four of the best students had parents from other countries—South Africa, Mexico, Haiti, Vietnam—and all four were fascinated by American history. I remember thinking, "I'd love to be part of a team of historians who developed a text that would excite Darlene Aquino from Texas and Minh-Thu Pham from North Carolina." I called Longman and said, "Let's find a way to do it."

How Did You Come to the Decision to Write This Book?

JACKIE: I thought that writing a new kind of text would be a real intellectual challenge. We have the opportunity to rethink and reconfigure the traditional American history narrative, and that's exciting.

PETER: I was not eager to write a "feel good" text. American history has not been a big happy rainbow. I was convinced that we could be much more open and inclusive than most current texts. We could also be more direct and matter-of-fact in many areas. It is important to be frank about differences and contradictions in the American story in a way that actually helps explain things.

THOMAS: Writing a textbook was attractive because it's so complementary to what I do in the classroom, particularly teaching the introductory American history survey. Having the chance to try to tell the entire story of the American past was exciting as a balance to the other work we do.

How Did the Author Team Come Together, Work Together?

PETER: The Longman videotape circulated. Eventually, we had a team of people who felt that they could answer, collectively, the challenge presented by those articulate teachers. Obviously, no one could do it alone, but the right combination might be able to pull it off. Having watched the Duke basketball team for two decades, I know what five very different people can do if they pay attention to each other and if they all have the same goal in mind. An author team is like a basketball team: the players have to complement one another. (Sometimes we *compliment* each other, too!) And each person gets better and contributes more through practice and hard work. This team works hard.

VICKI: I joined the *Created Equal* team out of the profound respect I have for the scholarship of my colleagues. I had met Elaine and Jackie previously at conferences and knew Peter and Thomas only from their scholarship. The first brainstorming meeting I attended in New York City was intellectual magic, pure and simple. From the first hour onward, we exchanged our separate visions and expectations, debated periodization and conceptual frames, and began the process of intellectual coalescence that marks this truly collaborative enterprise. I left New York exhilarated and exhausted.

ELAINE: I joined this project because I was excited about the challenge of writing a textbook that would convey the drama and excitement of the nation's history. It offered an opportunity to work with a team of scholars whom I have long admired, and it has been a joy and a privilege to collaborate with them. We have become a close group of friends and colleagues, and our text reflects the lively exchanges, debates, and brainstorming sessions we've had over e-mail, phone calls, and gatherings when we have come together to work on the project.

Tell Us About the Title—Created Equal.

JACKIE: The title reflects our commitment to be inclusive in our coverage of different groups and the part they played in shaping American history. Of course, we are invoking the Declaration of Independence: "We hold these truths to be self-evident, that all men are created equal." That document, and those words, have inspired countless individuals, groups, and nations around the world.

PETER: We all recognize the phrase "created equal" from the Declaration of Independence, but we rarely ponder it. For me, it represents an affirmation of humanity, the family of mankind. But it also raises the deepest American theme: the endless struggles over defining whose equality will be recognized. I suppose you could say that there is equality in birth and death, but a great deal of inequality in between. Many of those inequities—and their partial removal—drive the story of American History. Tom Paine understood this in 1776 when he published *Common Sense.* Months before the Declaration of Independence appeared, Paine put it this way: "Mankind being originally equal in the order of creation, the equality could only be destroyed by some subsequent circumstance."

How and Why Did You Choose the Themes That Structure the Text?

THOMAS: The themes that we chose to highlight in *Created Equal* reflect what we see as the current and future state of the field of U.S. history, as well as the needs of future generations of students. The prominence of multiculturalism in recent decades made clear that identity remains a central piece of the American story: how individual Americans understand and identify themselves (by religion, class, region, sex, race, ethnicity, etc.). But too much attention to cultural issues has often led to a discounting of the political and economic structure of American society. Who has material wealth and power, and how they use it, is fundamental for determining the course of the past and present. The increasing globalization of the U.S. economy and American society (for example, through rising immigration) in recent decades has reminded us of how deeply the United States has always been engaged with the rest of the world. Because America is an immigrant nation and the modern world's superpower, America's foreign and domestic affairs have always been intertwined. And the deepening awareness in recent decades of the fragility of the earth's environment has stimulated a whole subfield of American environmental history, which we try to tap into. In a sense, the environment represents the clearest example of the interconnectedness of American and international history.

JACKIE: It was time to integrate recent scholarship related to the many different groups that have been part of the American story, and to open up that story to include all geographical areas (and not just the eastern seaboard). The theme of the environment is key to understanding American history; we explore the ways American cultural, political, and economic developments influence and are shaped by the nation's natural resources and landscape. The theme of power relations helps students to understand that differences of class, and differences in political and material resources, are significant aspects of the country's history. We balance this perspective by showing how America emerged as a uniquely open and middle-class nation—one that has attracted immigrants from all over the world throughout its history.

ELAINE: *Created Equal* brings together aspects of the nation's story that are usually examined separately. It demonstrates that the people who make change are not only those in major positions of power; they are also ordinary Americans from all backgrounds. We illuminate ways that ordinary Americans have seized opportunities to improve their lives and their nation. In *Created Equal,* the land itself is a major player in the story—the environment, the different regions, and the ways in which people, businesses, public policies, and the forces of nature have shaped it. We also address the ongoing interaction between the United States and the rest of the world, examining the nation in a truly global context.

How Is the Book Organized?

PETER: History is the study of change over time, so chronology becomes extremely important. We wanted to emphasize central themes, but we wanted to explore and explain how they related to one another at any given moment. So we made a conscious decision to be more chronological than many recent texts in our presentation. It makes for less confusion, less jumping back and forth in time, than when broad themes are played out separately. After all, this is the way we lead our own lives—sequentially.

JACKIE: Most of the 10 separate parts in the book cover about a generation each. The parts give students a sense of the big picture over a longer period—the way our themes fit together and the impact of major developments on a particular generation of Americans. The chronological organization of the book forces us to understand the "wholeness" of any particular period—to consider links among political, social, economic, and cultural developments. By maintaining a strictly chronological focus, we hope to show students how the events and developments of any one period are intertwined with each other. For example, for coverage of the period after the end of the Civil War, it is important to show links between the Indian wars in the West and the process of Reconstruction in the South. In most texts, those regional perspectives are separated into different chapters, but in *Created Equal*, these connections are presented together in Chapter 15.

What Did You Enjoy Most About Writing This Text?

JACKIE: The intellectual stimulation and the opportunity to work with a wonderful group of people.

PETER: Three things. My teammates and their different energies, for sure. Also, the staff at Longman. I had never worked on a big collective effort like this, and I still marvel at the intricacies and coordination of the whole operation. But most of all, writing this text has reinforced my sense of the intense relevance of history. We were hard at work when the World Trade Center attack occurred, and our editor lived only a few blocks from the destruction. I saw the hole in the Pentagon firsthand. Suddenly, our entire society was on a new footing. A culture oriented to the present and the future had to reexamine the past, both locally and globally, recent and distant. In reconnecting to our history in new ways—examining it openly and fearlessly and critically—we find a story that is more relevant than most of us imagined. It is complex, dramatic, sobering, and uplifting all at once, like life itself.

THOMAS: It's been a pleasure to work as a team. When I first joined the project in its early phases, I was lured by the prospect of working with Peter, and then I got that much more excited as the rest of the team was filled in. I've been deeply impressed by how well we communicate, especially the combination of serious intellectual challenges to each other and our great personal support for each other. I simply learn a lot every time we communicate, and I'm grateful for the friendships that have emerged out of our joint endeavor.

What Did You Find Most Challenging About Revising the First Edition?

JACKIE: The second edition offered us a great opportunity to get together and discuss issues related to both substance and style. In June 2004, we met in Truro, on Cape Cod, and, between walks on the beach, planned the new "Mapping History" feature. I liked working on the map for Chapter 9, on the Delaware Valley, and adding material on the area around Christiana, where I grew up.

PETER: How many times have I said to students, "I think you could make this sentence clearer"? For once, I had a chance to practice what I had been preaching, taking time to shorten and sharpen occasional paragraphs to make the meaning more clear. Historians do not often get a second chance at their own prose; I liked that part. The process of planning and creating the "Mapping History" feature also proved especially enjoyable.

THOMAS: Rewriting Chapter 30 is inherently interesting, bringing the past and present together in a very explicit way. This process matches up with the intent of the "Connecting History" features. It's also fun to test out new sections on my students in draft form, giving them a chance to help shape the history that other students will learn. And I enjoyed bringing new scholarship on environmental history to bear in Chapters 27, 28, and 30.

VICKI: The second edition provides a chance to respond to our readers' comments as we revisit and revise the features, vignettes, maps, visuals, and even certain phrases. More than fine-tuning the original text or simply adding new materials, the second edition represents a calibration and contemplation of interpretation and tone—balancing conceptual themes within regional and national narratives. We remain committed to "the telling of stories for it is within these tales that we remember the *ánimo y sueños* (spirit and dreams) of the American people."

ELAINE: I enjoyed the opportunity to include new stories and images that I had been collecting since the first edition and to reflect a bit on the original interpretations in light of new scholarship. The process of revising reminded me that our understanding and interpretation of the past continues to change and evolve in the present.

What Do You Hope Students Will Get Out of the Book?

PETER: I want readers to connect. As a child, you connect to your family, your neighbors, your schoolmates. As you get older, that circle expands; you begin to relate to people in other places and other times. In a good history class, or a strong history book, that relationship becomes close. You start to care about, argue with, and connect to the persons you are studying. Pretty soon, their tough choices and surprising experiences in life start to resemble our own in ways we never expected, even though their worlds are dramatically different from ours.

JACKIE: By presenting an inclusive view of the past, we give students a more accurate account of American history. Many texts only pay lip service to diversity. Non-elite groups are tacked on, marginalized, or segregated from the "real" story of America. In contrast, we believe that the history of all groups constitutes the real story of America.

Meet the Authors

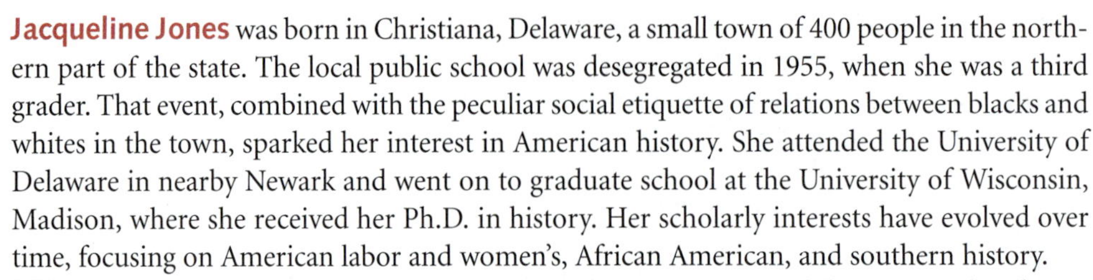

Jacqueline Jones was born in Christiana, Delaware, a small town of 400 people in the northern part of the state. The local public school was desegregated in 1955, when she was a third grader. That event, combined with the peculiar social etiquette of relations between blacks and whites in the town, sparked her interest in American history. She attended the University of Delaware in nearby Newark and went on to graduate school at the University of Wisconsin, Madison, where she received her Ph.D. in history. Her scholarly interests have evolved over time, focusing on American labor and women's, African American, and southern history.

One of her biggest challenges has been to balance her responsibilities as teacher, historian, wife, and mother (of two daughters). One of her proudest achievements is the fact that she has been able to teach full-time and still pick up her daughters at school every day at 2:30 in the afternoon (thanks to a flexible professor's schedule). She is the author of several books, including *Soldiers of Light and Love: Northern Teachers and Georgia Blacks* (1980); *Labor of Love, Labor of Sorrow: Black Women, Work, and Family Since Slavery* (1985), which won the Bancroft Prize and was a finalist for a Pulitzer Prize; *The Dispossessed: America's Underclasses Since the Civil War* (1992); and *American Work: Four Centuries of Black and White Labor* (1998). In 2001, she completed a memoir that recounts her childhood in Christiana: *Creek Walking: Growing Up in Delaware in the 1950s.*

She teaches American history at Brandeis University, where she is Harry S. Truman Professor. In 1999, she received a MacArthur Fellowship.

Peter H. Wood was born in St. Louis (before the famous arch was built). He recalls seeing Jackie Robinson play against the Cardinals, visiting the courthouse where the *Dred Scott* case originated, and traveling up the Mississippi to Hannibal, birthplace of Mark Twain. Summer work on the northern Great Lakes aroused his interest in Native American cultures, past and present. He studied at Harvard (B.A., 1964; Ph.D., 1972) and at Oxford, where he was a Rhodes Scholar (1964–1966). His pioneering book *Black Majority* (1974), concerning slavery in colonial South Carolina, won the Beveridge Prize of the American Historical Association. Since 1975, he has taught early American history at Duke University, where he also coached the women's lacrosse club for three years. The topics of his articles range from the French explorer LaSalle to Gerald Ford's pardon of Richard Nixon. He coauthored *Winslow Homer's Images of Blacks,* and he has written *Strange New Land,* a book about early African Americans. In 1989 he coedited *Powhatan's Mantle: Indians in the Colonial Southeast.* His demographic essay in that volume provided the first clear picture of population change in the eighteenth-century South. Dr. Wood has served on the boards of the Highlander Center, Harvard University, Houston's Rothko Chapel, the Menil Foundation, and the Institute of Early American History and Culture in Williamsburg. He is married to colonial historian Elizabeth Fenn; his varied interests include archaeology, documentary film, and growing gourds. He keeps a baseball bat used by Ted Williams beside his desk.

Thomas Borstelmann, the son of a university psychologist, has taught at the elementary, high school, and college levels. He taught second-grade physical education, taught and coached high school lacrosse, soccer, and basketball, and since 1991 has taught American history at Cornell University. In addition to his teaching experience, he also served as "Head Maid" of a conference center near Lake Tahoe. He lives with his wife and two sons in Syracuse, New York, where his greatest challenge—and delight—is doing the bulk of childcare while commuting 60 miles to Cornell. An avid bicyclist, runner, and cross-country skier, he earned his B.A. from Stanford University in 1980 and Ph.D. from Duke University in 1990.

He became a historian to figure out the Cold War and American race relations, in part because he had grown up in the South. His first book, concerning American relations with southern Africa in the mid-twentieth century, won the Stuart L. Bernath Book Prize of the Society for Historians of Foreign Relations. His second book, *The Cold War and the Color Line,* appeared in 2002. His commitment to the classroom remains clear at Cornell University, where he has won a major teaching award: the Robert and Helen Appel Fellowship. He found writing *Created Equal* a natural complement to what he does in the classroom, trying to provide both telling details of the American past and the broad picture of how the United States has developed as it has. A specialist in U.S. foreign relations, he is equally fascinated with domestic politics and social change. He is currently working on a book about the 1970s.

Elaine Tyler May grew up in the shadow of Hollywood, performing in neighborhood circuses with her friends. She went to high school before girls could play on sports teams, so she spent her after-school hours as a cheerleader and her summer days as a bodysurfing beach bum. Her passion for American history developed in college when she spent her junior year in Japan. The year was 1968. The Vietnam War was raging, along with turmoil at home. As an American in Asia, often called on to explain her nation's actions, she yearned for a deeper understanding of America's past and its place in the world. She returned home to study history at UCLA, where she earned her B.A., M.A., and Ph.D. She has taught at Princeton and Harvard Universities and since 1978 at the University of Minnesota. She has written four books examining the relationship between politics, public policy, and private life. Her widely acclaimed *Homeward Bound: American Families in the Cold War Era* was the first study to link the baby boom and suburbia to the politics of the Cold War. The *Chronicle of Higher Education* featured *Barren in the Promised Land: Childless Americans and the Pursuit of Happiness* as a pioneering study of the history of reproduction. *Lingua Franca* named her coedited volume *Here, There, and Everywhere: The Foreign Politics of American Popular Culture* a "Breakthrough Book." She served as president of the American Studies Association in 1996 and as Distinguished Fulbright Professor of American History in Dublin, Ireland, in 1997. She is married to historian Lary May and has three children who have inherited their parents' passion for history.

Vicki L. Ruiz is a professor of history and Chicano/Latino studies at the University of California, Irvine. For her, history remains a grand adventure, one that she began at the kitchen table, listening to the stories of her mother and grandmother, and continued with the help of the local bookmobile. She read constantly as she sat on the dock, catching small fish ("grunts") to be used as bait on her father's fishing boat. As she grew older, she was promoted to working with her mother, selling tickets for the *Blue Sea II.* The first in her family to receive an advanced degree, she graduated from Gulf Coast Community College and Florida State University, then went on to earn a Ph.D. in history at Stanford in 1982, the fourth Mexican American woman to receive a doctorate in history. Her first book, *Cannery Women, Cannery Lives,* received an award from the National Women's Political Caucus, and her second, *From Out of the Shadows: Mexican Women in 20th-Century America,* was named a *Choice* Outstanding Academic Book of 1998 by the American Library Association. She is coeditor with Ellen Carol Dubois of *Unequal Sisters: A Multicultural Reader in U.S. Women's History.* She and Virginia Sánchez Korrol coedit *Latinas in the United States: A Historical Encyclopedia,* and both were recognized by *Latina Magazine* as Latinas of the Year in Education for 2000. Active in student mentorship projects, summer institutes for teachers, and public humanities programs, Dr. Ruiz served as an appointee to the National Council of the Humanities. She has also served on the national governing bodies of the American Historical Association, the Organization of American Histories, and the American Studies Association. The mother of two grown sons, she is married to Victor Becerra, urban planner and gourmet cook extraordinaire.

Acknowledgments

As authors, we could not have completed this project without the loving support of our families. We wish to thank Jeffrey Abramson, Lil Fenn, Lynn Borstelmann, Lary May, and Victor Becerra for their interest, forbearance, and encouragement over the course of many drafts. Our children, now ranging in age from 6 to 32, have been a source of inspiration, as have our many students, past and present. We are grateful to scores of colleagues and friends who have helped shape this book, both directly and indirectly, in more ways than they know.

Special thanks are due to Steve Fraser for his insightful midcourse corrections, which came at a crucial time in the process. Along the way, Rob Heinrich, Matthew Becker, Scott Laderman, Matt Basso, Chad Cover, Eben Miller, Andrea Sachs, Mary Strunk, and Melissa Williams provided useful research and administrative assistance; their help was invaluable. Louis Balizet provided careful reading of several chapter drafts. Thanks to Deborah Anderson for a stellar job in locating images, and to Jim Hill for all his terrific work in overseeing the layout.

Our friends at Longman have shown their belief in this project from the beginning. We thank all the creative people at Longman (and there are many) who have had a hand in bringing this book to life. We are especially grateful to Priscilla McGeehon, Betty Slack, and Sue Westmoreland for their enthusiastic devotion to this project and their expertise and friendship from start to finish. Michael Boezi, joining the Longman team recently, has embraced *Created Equal* and given it his full and timely support.

Finally, we wish to express our deep gratitude to our consultants and reviewers whose thoughtful and constructive comments contributed greatly to this edition. Collectively, they pushed us hard with their high standards, tough questions, and shrewd advice. The thoughtful criticisms and generous suggestions from these colleagues have helped improve the book:

Yvonne Baldwin, *Morehead State University*; Marjorie Berman, *Red Rocks Community College*; Susan Burch, *Gallaudet University*; JoAnn D. Carpenter, *Florida Community College, Jacksonville*; Jacqueline M. Cavalier, *Community College of Allegheny County*; Ann Denkler, *Shenandoah University*; Paul E. Doutrich, *York College of Pennsylvania*; Susan Edwards, *Cy-Fair College*; Ronald B. Frankum, *Millersville University*; Mike Haridopolos, *Brevard Community College*; Andrew M. Honker, *Arizona State University*; Adam Howard, *University of Florida*; Jeremy Johnston, *Northwest College*; Dennis Kortheuer, *California State University, Long Beach*; Rebecca A. Kosary, *Texas Lutheran University*; Michael L. Krenn, *Appalachian State University*; Kurt E. Leichtle, *University of Wisconsin, River Falls*; Xiaobing Li, *University of Central Oklahoma*; Mike Light, *Grand Rapids Community College*; Michelle Espinosa Martinez, *St. Philip's College*; Gaye T. M. Okoh, *University of Texas, San Antonio*; Dolores Davis Peterson, *Foothill College*; Thomas J. Rowland, *University of Wisconsin, Oshkosh*; Mike Sistrom, *Greensboro College*; Melissa Soto-Schwartz, *Cuyahoga Community College*; and Stephen Tallackson, *Purdue University, Calumet.*

This second edition also owes much to the many conscientious historians who reviewed the manuscript of the first edition throughout its many drafts and offered valuable suggestions that led to many improvements in this revision. We acknowledge with gratitude the contributions of the following:

Ken Adderley, *Upper Iowa University*; Leslie Alexander, *Ohio State University*; John Andrew, *Franklin and Marshall College*; Abel Bartley, *University of Akron*; Donald Scott Barton, *Central Carolina Technical College*; Mia Bay, *Rutgers University*; Chris Bierwith, *Treasure Valley Community College*; Charles Bolton, *University of Arkansas, Little Rock*; Susan Burch,

Gallaudet University; Tommy Bynum, *Georgia Perimeter College*; Robert B. Carey, *Empire State College, SUNY*; Todd Carney, *Southern Oregon University*; Kathleen Carter, *Highpoint University*; Jonathan Chu, *University of Massachusetts*; Amy E. Davis, *University of California, Los Angeles*; Judy DeMark, *Northern Michigan University*; James A. Denton, *University of Colorado*; Joseph A. Devine, *Stephen F. Austin University*; Margaret Dwight, *North Carolina Agricultural and Technical University*; Nancy Gabin, *Purdue University*; Lori Ginzberg, *Pennsylvania State University*; Gregory Goodwin, *Bakersfield College*; Amy S. Greenberg, *Pennsylvania State University*; Nadine Isitani Hata, *El Camino College*; James Hedtke, *Cabrini College*; Fred Hoxie, *University of Illinois*; Tera Hunter, *Carnegie Mellon University*; David Jaffe, *City College of New York*; Jeremy Johnson, *Northwest College*; Yvonne Johnson, *Central Missouri State University*; Kurt Keichtle, *University of Wisconsin*; Anne Klejment, *University of St. Thomas*; Dennis Kortheuer, *California State University, Long Beach*; Joel Kunze, *Upper Iowa University*; Joseph Laythe, *Edinboro College of Pennsylvania*; Chana Kai Lee, *Indiana University*; Dan Letwin, *Pennsylvania State University*; Gaylen Lewis, *Bakersfield College*; Kenneth Lipartito, *Florida International University*; Kyle Longley, *Arizona State University*; Edith L. Macdonald, *University of Central Florida*; Lorie Maltby, *Henderson Community College*; Sandra Mathews-Lamb, *Nebraska Wesleyan University*; Constance M. McGovern, *Frostburg State University*; Henry McKiven, *University of South Alabama*; James H. Merrell, *Vassar College*; Earl Mulderink, *Southern Utah State University*; Steven Noll, *University of Florida*; Jim Norris, *North Dakota State University*; Elsa Nystrom, *Kennesaw State University*; Keith Pacholl, *California State University, Fullerton*; William Pelz, *Elgin Community College*; Melanie Perrault, *University of Central Arkansas*; Delores D. Petersen, *Foothill College*; Robert Pierce, *Foothill College*; Louis Potts, *University of Missouri, Kansas City*; Sarah Purcell, *Central Michigan University*; Niler Pyeatt, *Wayland Baptist University*; Steven Reschly, *Truman State University*; Arthur Robinson, *Santa Rosa Junior College*; Robert E. Rook, *Fort Hays State University*; Steven Ruggles, *University of Minnesota*; Christine Sears, *University of Delaware*; Rebecca Shoemaker, *Indiana State University*; Howard Shore, *Columbia River High School*; James Sidbury, *University of Texas*; Arwin D. Smallwood, *Bradley University*; Margaret Spratt, *California University of Pennsylvania*; Rachel Standish, *Foothill College*Jon Stauff, *St. Ambrose University*; David Steigerwald, *Ohio State University, Marion*; Kay Stockbridge, *Central Carolina Technical College*; Daniel Thorp, *Virginia Tech University*; Michael M. Topp, *University of Texas, El Paso*Clifford Trafzer, *University of California, Riverside*; Deborah Gray White, *Rutgers University*; Scott Wong, *Williams College*; Bill Woodward, *Seattle Pacific University*; Nancy Zens, *Central Oregon Community College*; David Zonderman, *North Carolina State University.*

CHAPTER 15

In the Wake of War: Consolidating a Triumphant Union, 1865–1877

CHAPTER OUTLINE

The Struggle over the South

Claiming Territory for the Union

The Republican Vision and Its Limits

Conclusion

Sites to Visit

For Further Reading

Edward Lamson Henry, *Kept In*, 1889. Fenimore Art Museum, Cooperstown, New York (N-309.61). Photo by Richard Walker

▲ The artist Edward L. Henry titled this 1888 painting *Kept In*. A pupil endures her punishment while her classmates frolic outside during recess. Former slaves of all ages eagerly embraced the opportunity to learn to read and write, and many African American communities established their own schools after the war. Some Northerners, mostly young white women, traveled south to teach freedpeople.

In Savannah, Georgia, in mid-December 1864, African American men, women, and children rejoiced when the troops of Union General William Tecumseh Sherman liberated the city: the day of jubilee had come at last! The city's black community immediately formed its own school system under the sponsorship of a new group, the Savannah Education Association (SEA). The association owed its creation to the desire of freedpeople of all ages to learn to read and write. A committee of nine black clergy began by hiring 15 black teachers and acquiring buildings (including the Old Bryan Slave Mart) for use as schools. By January 1, 1865, Savannah blacks had raised $800 to pay teachers' salaries, enabling several hundred black children to attend classes free of charge.

Following hard on the heels of the Union army, a group of northern white missionaries arrived in Savannah to seek black converts for two Protestant denominations, the Presbyterians and the Congregationalists. On the first day of school, in January 1865, these northern newcomers watched a grand procession of children wend its way through the streets of Savannah. The missionaries expressed amazement that the SEA was an entirely black-run organization; these whites had believed the former slaves incapable of creating such an impressive educational system.

In March 1865, the federal government, under the auspices of the newly formed Bureau of Refugees, Freedmen, and Abandoned Lands (Freedmen's Bureau), agreed to work with missionaries in opening schools for black children throughout the former Confederate states. In Georgia, missionaries and government officials soon became alarmed that black leaders were willing to accept financial aid from them but not willing to relinquish control of SEA schools to the whites in return. The Northerners were also distressed by the militancy of certain local black leaders. One of these leaders was Aaron Bradley, who, armed with a pistol and bowie knife, was urging other black men to vote as a bloc in all elections.

Courtesy of the Georgia Historical Society, William Wilson Collection

In Savannah, African American Sunday School pupils pose for photographer William Wilson in 1890. After the Civil War, many Southern black communities created, or enlarged and solidified, their own institutions, including schools and churches.

In an effort to wrest control of the SEA from Savannah blacks, northern missionaries and agents of the Freedmen's Bureau decided to withhold funds from the association. By March 1866, the city's black community, swollen by a refugee population, was no longer able to support its own schools. Northern whites took over SEA operations, and the association ceased to exist.

On April 11, 1865, President Abraham Lincoln appeared on the balcony of the White House and announced that the Union forces were victorious, the Confederate States of America defeated. Four years before, southern slaveholders had organized a rebellion against the federal government; their aim was to preserve slavery in the wake of the election of a Republican president, the antislavery Lincoln. The Civil War claimed more American lives (nearly 700,000) than all other conflicts in American history combined. Yet the military defeat of the rebels did not resolve fundamental problems related to black people's status in the South or in the nation at large. Contemplating the difficult task ahead of the United States, Lincoln declared in that speech on April 11, just a few days before he was assassinated, "We must simply begin with, and mould from, disorganized and discordant elements."

THIRD READER. 249

LESSON CXXXVIII.

church	as-sign	com-mun-ion	ar-range-ment
stretch	oys-ter	pro-ces-sion	op-por-tu-ni-ty
through	shoul-der	ex-am-ine	or-gan-i-za-tion

SCHOOLS IN SAVANNAH.

Rev. Mr. Alvord, whose picture is on this page, was in Savannah when the first colored schools were formed, and assisted in organizing the "Educational Association." We give his description of the scene when the members were admitted to the Association. The admission-fee was three dollars.

THE large church was full; and, as soon as opportunity was offered, the crowd came forward. About the communion-table they pressed, stretching

Courtesy, American Antiquarian Society

▲ **The Boston wing of the American Tract Society, an abolitionist group, published a series of reading primers for newly freed slaves. The primers provided moral lessons as well as reading lessons for the pupils. This page from *The Freedman's Third Reader* focuses on the work of John W. Alvord, the Freedmen's Bureau general superintendent of education. The authors suggest (wrongly) that Alvord played a major role in organizing the Savannah Education Association in Savannah, Georgia, in early 1865.**

The months and years immediately after the war unleashed a major conflict between supporters of African American rights and supporters of southern privilege. Republican congressmen hoped to *reconstruct* the South by enabling African Americans to own their own land and to become full citizens. Southern freedpeople sought to free themselves from white employers, landlords, and clergy and to establish control over their own workplaces, families, and churches. In contrast, President Andrew Johnson appeared bent on *restoring* the antebellum power relations that made southern black field laborers dependent on white landowners. For their part, many southern whites were determined to prevent blacks from becoming truly free. Most former rebels remained embittered about the outcome of the war and vengeful toward the freedpeople.

The Civil War hardened the positions of the two major political parties. The Republicans remained in favor of a strong national government, one that promoted economic growth. The Democrats tended to support states' efforts to manage their own affairs, which included regulating relations between employers and employees, whites and blacks.

After the war, western economic development presented new challenges. In order to open the West to European American miners and homesteaders, the U.S. army clashed repeatedly with Native Americans. On the Plains and in the Northwest, Indians resisted white efforts to force them to abandon their nomadic way of life and take up sedentary farming. William Tecumseh Sherman, Philip H. Sheridan, and George Custer were among the U.S. military officers who had commanded troops in the Civil War and now attempted to subdue the Plains Indians and further white settlement. Sherman declared, "We must act with vindictive earnestness against the Sioux, even to their extermination, men, women and children." The former head of the Freedmen's Bureau, General Oliver O. Howard, oversaw the expulsion of Chief Joseph and his people, the Nez Perce, from their homeland in Washington's Walla Walla Valley in 1877.

U.S. soldiers also contributed to the building of the transcontinental railroad. A former Union military officer, Grenville Dodge, served as chief civil engineer for the Union Pacific Railroad, supervising huge workforces of immigrant laborers. The railroad industry was a potent symbol of postwar U.S. nationalism. It also represented a robust, Republican-sponsored partnership between private enterprise and the federal government. Between 1862 and 1872, the government gave the industry subsidies that included millions of dollars in cash and more than 100 million acres of land. On the Plains, U.S. soldiers protected Union Pacific Railroad land surveyors against the retaliatory raids conducted by Indians who were enraged by this incursion into their territory and by the government's failure to abide by its treaties.

The Civil War, and the economic growth unleashed after the conflict, transformed the physical landscape of the nation. In the South the scars of war were everywhere, in the form of ruined crop fields, pillaged forests, and charred cities. Pursuing a strategy of "hard war" in the final months of the war, Sherman's troops had destroyed many of the towns and farms that lay in their path on their famous march from Atlanta to Savannah and then north into South Carolina. New train trestles, wharfs, and warehouses stood as monuments to the recent efforts of both rebel and Union forces to move and supply their troops. In the West, construction of new towns and railroad tracks demanded tremendous amounts of lumber. Some observers warned of an impending timber famine, spurring interest in the conservation of natural resources of all kinds.

The Republicans' triumph prompted dissent from diverse people who feared that the victorious Union would serve the interests of specific groups such as men, employers, and white property owners. Some women's rights activists, for example, felt betrayed by the suggestion that this was "the hour of the Negro [man]." These women were not willing to wait indefinitely for their own voting rights. At the same time, in the bustling workshops of the nation's cities, many workers realized that they remained at the mercy of employers bent on using cheap labor. The founding of the National Labor Union in 1866 revealed that members of the laboring classes had a national vision of their own, one that valued the efforts of working people to earn a decent living for their families.

At great cost to human life, the Civil War decisively settled several political conflicts.

At great cost of human life, the Civil War decisively settled several immediate and long-standing political conflicts. The southern secessionists were defeated, and slavery as a legal institution was destroyed. Nevertheless, the relationship between federal power and group rights remained unresolved, leading to continued bloodshed between whites and Indians on the High Plains, as well as in the former Confederate states between Union supporters and diehard rebels. During the postwar period, federal government officials attempted to complete the political process that the military defeat of the South had only begun: the consolidation of the Union, North and South, East and West. This process encompassed the nation as a whole.

The Struggle over the South

The Civil War had a devastating impact on the South in physical, social, and economic terms. The region had lost an estimated $2 billion in investments in slaves; modest homesteads and grand plantations alike lay in ruins; and gardens, orchards, and cotton fields were barren. More than 3 million former slaves eagerly embraced freedom, but the vast majority lacked the land, cash, and credit necessary to build family homesteads for themselves. Hoping to achieve social and economic self-determination, African American men and women traveled great distances, usually on foot, in efforts to locate loved ones and reunite families that had been separated during slavery. At the same time, landowning whites considered black people primarily as a source of agricultural labor; these whites resisted the idea that the freedpeople should be granted citizenship rights.

In the North, Republican lawmakers disagreed among themselves how best to punish the defeated but defiant rebels. President Abraham Lincoln had indicated early that after the war the government should bring the South back into the Union quickly and painlessly. His successor wanted to see members of the southern planter elite humiliated but resisted the notion that freedpeople should become independent of white landowners. In Congress, moderate and radical Republicans argued about how far the government should go in ensuring the former slaves' freedom.

Wartime Preludes to Postwar Policies

Wartime experiments with African American free labor in Union-occupied areas foreshadowed bitter postwar debates. As early as November 1861, Union forces had occupied the Sea Islands off Port Royal Sound in South Carolina. In response, wealthy cotton planters fled to the mainland. Over the next few months, three groups of northern civilians landed on the Sea Islands with the intention of guiding blacks in the transition from slave to free labor. Teachers arrived intent on creating schools, and missionaries hoped to start churches. A third group, representing Boston investors, also settled on the Sea Islands to assess economic opportunities; by early 1862, they decided to institute a system of wage labor that would reestablish a staple crop economy and funnel cotton directly into northern textile mills. The freed slaves, however, preferred to grow crops for their families to eat rather than cotton to sell, relying on a system of barter and trade among networks of extended families. Their goal was to break free of white landlords, suppliers, and cotton merchants.

H. P. Moore/Collection of the New-York Historical Society, Neg. #37497

Meanwhile, in southern Louisiana, the Union capture of New Orleans in the spring of 1862 enabled northern military officials to implement their own free (that is, nonslave) labor system. General Nathaniel Banks proclaimed that U.S. troops should forcibly relocate blacks to plantations "where they belong"; there they would continue to work for their former owners in the sugar and cotton fields, but now for wages supposedly negotiated annually. The Union army would compel blacks to work if they resisted doing so. In defiance of these orders, however, some blacks went on strike for higher wages, and others refused to work at all. Moreover, not all members of the Union military relished the prospect of forcing blacks to work on the plantations where they had been enslaved. Thus, federal policies returning blacks to plantations remained contested even within the ranks of the army itself.

The Lincoln administration had no hard-and-fast reconstruction policy to guide congressional lawmakers looking toward the postwar period. In December 1863 the president outlined his Ten Percent Plan. This plan would allow former Confederate states to form new state governments once 10 percent of the men who had voted in the 1860 presidential election had pledged allegiance to the Union and renounced slavery. Congress instead passed the Wade-Davis Bill, which would have required a majority of southern voters in any state to take a loyalty oath affirming their allegiance to the United States. By refusing to sign the bill before Congress adjourned, Lincoln vetoed the measure (through a **pocket veto**). However, the president approved the creation of the Bureau of Refugees, Freedmen, and Abandoned Lands, or Freedmen's Bureau, in March 1865. The bureau was responsible for coordinating relief efforts on behalf of blacks and poor whites loyal to the Union, for sponsoring schools, and for implementing a labor contract system on southern plantations. At the time of his assassination, Lincoln seemed to be leaning toward giving the right to vote to southern black men.

Presidential Reconstruction, 1865–1867

When Andrew Johnson, the seventeenth president of the United States, assumed office in April 1865, he brought his own agenda for the defeated South. Throughout his political career, Johnson had seen himself as a champion of poor white farmers in opposition to the wealthy planter class. A man of modest background, he had been elected U.S. senator from Tennessee in 1857. He alone among southern senators remained in Congress and loyal to the Union after 1861. Lincoln first appointed Johnson military governor of Tennessee when that state was captured by the Union in 1862 and then tapped him as his running mate for the election of 1864.

Soon after he assumed the presidency, Johnson disappointed congressional Republicans who hoped that he would serve as a champion of the freedpeople. He welcomed back into the Union those states reorganized under Lincoln's Ten Percent Plan. He advocated denying the vote to wealthy Confederates, though he would allow individuals to come to the White House to beg the president for special pardons. Johnson also outlined a fairly lenient plan for

▲ **Residents of Edisto Island, off the coast of South Carolina, pose with a U.S. government mule cart immediately after the Civil War. U.S. troops captured the island in November 1861. The following March, the government began to distribute to blacks the lands abandoned by their former masters. In October 1865 President Andrew Johnson halted the program. A group of angry and disappointed blacks appealed to the president, claiming, "This is our home, we have made these lands what they are." After meeting with the group, General Oliver O. Howard noted, "I am convinced that something must be done to give these people and others the prospect of homesteads."**

readmitting the other rebel states into the Union. Poor whites would have the right to vote, but they must convene special state conventions that would renounce secession and accept the Thirteenth Amendment abolishing slavery. Further, they must repudiate all Confederate debts. The president opposed granting the vote to the former slaves; he believed that they should continue to toil as field workers for white landowners.

Initiated by presidential proclamation at the end of May 1865, the pardoning process revealed a great deal about Andrew Johnson as both a Southerner and a Republican politician. He personally considered appeals from 15,000 men, all of whom were required to apply directly to the president for a pardon; these men included those who had served as high-ranking Confederate officials and who owned $20,000 or more in taxable property. Of humble origins himself, Johnson relished the sight of the wealthiest Southerners nervously crowding his office and seeking his pardon—at times hundreds of men in a single day. With these pardons, Johnson aimed to humble a group of southern leaders he considered arrogant—he wanted to "punish and impoverish them," he said. He also hoped to win support for his own reelection from southern poor whites, men who approved of his effort to humiliate the planter elite.

While he was in office, Johnson sought to reassure Southerners that he believed blacks needed "the care and civilizing influence of dependence upon the white race." In fact, many former rebels gradually came to see Johnson as their postwar political ally; they hoped that he would counter the power of what they called vengeful Yankee "fanatics." The former Confederate secretary of the treasury, Christopher Memminger, noted that Johnson "held up before us the hope of a 'white man's government' and it was natural that we should yield to our old prejudices."

Johnson also argued that individual states should make their own laws on black suffrage. Many Northerners agreed. Indeed, northern states seemed eager to impose upon the defeated South provisions that they themselves would not accept. In 1865, only five New England states (of all northern states) allowed blacks to vote. That year, three state referenda on the issue—in Minnesota, Wisconsin, and Connecticut—failed to win voter approval. Almost all northern Democrats opposed black suffrage, but many of their Republican neighbors shared the same views. During the summer of 1865, Pennsylvania Republicans proclaimed that any discussion of black voting rights was "heavy and premature."

Johnson argued that individual states should make their own laws on black suffrage.

Johnson failed to anticipate the speed and vigor with which former Confederate leaders would move to reassert their political authority. In addition, he did not gauge accurately the resentment of congressional Republicans, who thought his policies toward the defeated South were too forgiving. The southern states that took advantage of Johnson's reunification policies passed laws that instituted a system of near slavery. Referred to as Black Codes, they aimed to penalize "vagrant" blacks, defined as those who did not work in the fields for whites, and to deny blacks the right to vote, serve on juries, or in some cases even own land. The Black Code of Mississippi restricted the rights of a freedperson to "keep or carry fire-arms," ammunition, and knives and to "quit the service of his or her employer before the expiration of his or her term of service without good cause." The vagueness of this last provision threatened any blacks who happened not to be working under the supervision of whites at any given moment. People arrested under the Black Codes faced imprisonment or forced labor.

The Mississippi Black Code

At the end of the war, congressional Republicans were divided into two camps. Radicals wanted to use strong federal measures to advance black people's civil rights and economic independence. In contrast, moderates were more concerned with the free market and private property rights; they took a hands-off approach regarding former slaves. But members of both groups reacted with outrage to the Black Codes. Moreover, when the legislators returned to the Capitol in December 1865, they were in for a shock: among their new colleagues were four former Confederate generals, five colonels, and other high-ranking members of the Confederate elite, including former Vice President Alexander Stephens, now under indictment for treason. All of these rebels were duly elected senators and representatives from southern states. In a special session called for December 4, a joint committee of 15 lawmakers (6 senators and 9 members of the House) voted to bar these men from Congress.

By January 1865, both houses of Congress had approved the Thirteenth Amendment to the Constitution, abolishing slavery. The necessary three-fourths of the states ratified the measure by the end of the year. However, President Johnson was becoming more openly defiant of his congressional foes who favored aggressive federal protection of black civil rights. He vetoed two crucial pieces of legislation: an extension and expansion of the Freedmen's Bureau and the Civil Rights Bill of 1866. This latter measure was an unprecedented piece of legislation. It called on the federal government—for the first time in history—to protect individual rights against the willful indifference of the states (as manifested, for example, in the Black Codes). Congress managed to override both vetoes by the summer of 1866.

In June of that year, Congress passed the Fourteenth Amendment. This amendment guaranteed the former slaves citizenship rights, punished states that denied citizens the right to vote, declared the former rebels ineligible for federal and state office, and voided Confederate debts. This amendment was the first to use gender-specific language, guarding against denying the vote "to any of the male inhabitants" of any state.

Even before the war ended, Northerners had moved south, and the flow increased in 1865. Black and white teachers volunteered to teach former slaves to read and write. Some white Northerners journeyed south to invest in land and become planters in the staple crop economy. White southern critics called all these migrants **carpetbaggers.** This derisive term suggested that the Northerners hastily packed their belongings in rough bags made of carpet scraps—a popular form of luggage at the time—and then rushed south to take advantage of the region's devastation and confusion. To many freedpeople, whether they worked for a white Northerner or Southerner, laboring in the cotton fields was but a continuation of slavery.

Some former southern (white) Whigs, who had been reluctant secessionists, now found common ground with northern Republicans who supported government subsidies for railroads, banking institutions, and public improvements. This group consisted of some members of the humbled planter class as well as people of more modest means. Southern Democrats, who sneered at any alliances with the North, scornfully labeled these whites **scalawags** (the term referred to a scrawny, useless type of horse on the Scottish island of Scalloway).

Even before the war ended, Northerners had moved south, and the flow increased in 1865.

Soon after the war's end, southern white **vigilantes** launched a campaign of violence and intimidation against freedpeople who dared to resist the demands of white planters and other employers. Calling itself the Ku Klux Klan, a group of Tennessee war veterans soon became a white supremacist terrorist organization, and the Klan spread to other states. In May 1866, violence initiated by white terrorists against blacks in Memphis, Tennessee, left 46 freedpeople and 2 whites dead; in July, a riot in New Orleans claimed the lives of 34 blacks and 3 of their white allies. These bloody encounters demonstrated the lengths to which ex-Confederates would go to reassert their authority and defy the federal government.

Back in Washington, Johnson condemned the Fourteenth Amendment and traveled around the country, urging the states not to ratify it. He argued that policies related to black suffrage should be decided by the states. The time had come for reconciliation between the North and South, maintained the president. (The amendment would not be adopted until 1868.)

Congressional Republicans fought back. In the election of November 1866, they won a two-thirds majority in both houses of Congress. These numbers allowed them to claim a mandate from their constituents and to override any future vetoes by the president. Moderates and radicals together prepared to bypass Johnson to shape their own reconstruction policies.

The Southern Postwar Labor Problem

Throughout the South, black people aspired to labor for themselves and gain independence from white overseers and landowners. Yet white landowners persisted in regarding blacks as field hands who must be coerced into working. With the creation of the Freedmen's Bureau in 1865, Congress intended to form an agency that would mediate between these two groups. Bureau agents encouraged workers and employers to sign annual labor contracts designed to eliminate the last **vestiges** of the slave system. All over the South, freed men, women, and children would contract with an employer on January 1 of each year. They would agree to work for either a monthly wage, an annual share of the crop, or some combination of the two.

The Freedmen's Bureau established elementary schools and distributed rations to southerners who had remained loyal to the Union, blacks and whites alike. Agents also conducted wedding ceremonies for the former slaves, who had been denied the right to legalize their unions as marriages. The agency's most formidable challenge was its effort to usher in a new economic order in the South—one that relied on nonslave labor but also returned the region to prewar productivity levels in terms of planting and harvesting cotton. The Freedmen's Bureau's functions in the areas of education and labor represented a new and significant federal

Bettmann/CORBIS

▲ **Freedmen's Bureau agents distributed rations to former slaves and southern whites who had remained loyal to the Union. Agents also sponsored schools, legalized marriages formed under slavery, arbitrated domestic disputes, and oversaw labor contracts between workers and landowners. This photo shows the bureau office in Petersburg, Virginia.**

role in the realm of social welfare. Yet the agency did not have the staff or money necessary to effect meaningful change.

In April 1866, a white planter in Thomson, Georgia, wrote to a local Freedmen's Bureau official and complained that the black wives and mothers living on his land had refused to sign labor contracts. The planter explained, "Their husbands are at work, while they are nearly idle as it is possible for them to be, pretending to spin—knit or something that really amounts to nothing." These "idle" women posed a threat to plantation order, the white man asserted.

Women who stayed home to care for their families were hardly idle. Yet Freedmen's Bureau agents and white planters alike tended to define productive labor (among blacks) as work carried out under the supervision of a white man in the fields or a white woman in the kitchen. During the postwar period, a struggle ensued. Who should toil in the fields of the South? And under what conditions should they labor?

The physical devastation wrought by the war gave these questions heightened urgency. Most freedpeople understood they must find a way to provide for themselves first and foremost. They thought of freedom in terms of welfare for their family rather than just for themselves as individuals. Men and women embraced the opportunity to live and work together as a unit. For many couples, their first act as free people was to legalize their marriage vows. Black women shunned the advice of Freedmen's Bureau agents and planters that they continue to pick cotton. These women withdrew from field labor whenever they could afford to do so.

Enslaved women had been deprived of the opportunity to attend to family life. Now freedwomen sought to devote themselves to caring for their families.

According to the Northerners, the benefits of the annual labor contract system were clear. Employers would have an incentive to treat their workers fairly—to offer a decent wage and refrain from physical punishment. Disgruntled workers could leave at the end of the year to work for a more reasonable landowner. In the **postbellum** South, however, labor relations were shaped not by federal decree but by a process of negotiation that pitted white landowners against blacks who possessed little but their own labor.

For instance, blacks along the Georgia and South Carolina coast were determined to cultivate the land on which their forebears had lived and died. They urged General Sherman to confiscate the land owned by rebels in the area. In response, in early 1865, Sherman issued Field Order Number 15, mandating that the Sea Islands and the coastal region south of Charleston be divided into parcels of 40 acres for individual freed families. He also decreed that the army might lend mules to these families to help them begin planting. Given the provisions of this order, many freed families came to expect that the federal government would grant them "40 acres and a mule."

As a result of Sherman's order, 20,000 former slaves proceeded to cultivate the property once owned by Confederates. Within a few months of the war's end, however, the War Department bowed to pressure from the white landowners and revoked the order. The War Department also provided military protection for whites to return and occupy their former lands. In response, a group of black men calling themselves Commissioners from Edisto Island (one of the Sea Islands) met in committee to protest to the Freedmen's Bureau what they considered a betrayal. Writing from the area in January 1866, one Freedmen's Bureau official noted that the new policy must be upheld but regretted that it had brought the freedpeople in "collision" with "U.S. forces."

During its brief life (1865–1868), the Freedmen's Bureau compiled a mixed record.

During its brief life (1865 to 1868), the Freedmen's Bureau compiled a mixed record. The individual agents represented a broad range of backgrounds, temperaments, and political ideas. Some were former abolitionists who considered northern-style free labor "the noblest principle on earth." These men tried to ensure safe and fair working arrangements for black men, women, and children. In contrast, some agents had little patience with the freedpeople's drive for self-sufficiency. Some bureau offices became havens for blacks seeking redress against abusive or fraudulent labor practices, but other offices had little impact on the postwar political and economic landscape. For agents without means of transportation (a reliable horse), plantations scattered throughout the vast rural South remained outside their control. Because white landowners crafted the wording and specific provisions of labor contracts, the bureau agents who enforced such agreements often served the interests of employers rather than laborers.

Southern Skepticism of the Freedmen's Bureau (1866)

In fact, for the most part, postwar freedpeople pressed for their labor rights independently of the federal government. Their efforts took a dramatic form along the coastline of Georgia and South Carolina, where thousands of slaves had toiled in the steamy, muck-filled rice fields before the war. With the revocation of Sherman's Field Order Number 15, black laborers sought to negotiate with white landowners who wished to maintain rice cultivation in the region. Rice culture necessitated an intricate network of ditches, dams, and sluice gates; together these improvements amounted to a complicated hydraulic system. This system allowed for the periodic flooding of rice fields with fresh water from local canals and rivers. Resisting the heavy, hot, muddy work of conventional rice culture, and wishing to spend more time on their own crops, blacks forced landowners to institute labor-saving measures. These measures included the use of mules to pull rakes in order to clean out weed-choked ditches, and the use of wagons to carry rice from the fields to the barn. Some planters turned to other groups of workers—for example, Irish men who came out to the coast from the city of Savannah—whom they hired on a seasonal basis.

However, rice farming required year-round work to keep ditches, fences, and canals in good working order, jobs that seasonal workers could not or would not do. For their part, the freedpeople preferred to engage in subsistence farming and to fish and hunt to support their families. Gradually lowcountry planters realized they lacked the large, subordinate labor force that would make their rice competitive with the rice grown in other parts of the country and the world. In the lowcountry rice regions, then, black people's desire for economic autonomy, combined with the unhealthful and disagreeable nature of rice culture, transformed the local economy.

In the cotton regions of the South, freedpeople resisted the near-slavery system of gang labor that planters tried to enforce right after the war. Instead, extended families came together in groups called squads to negotiate collectively with landowners. Gradually, squads gave way to sharecropping families. The outlines of sharecropping, a system that defined southern cotton production until well into the twentieth century, were visible just a few years after the Civil War. Poor families, black and white, contracted annually with landlords, who advanced them supplies, such as crop seed, mules, plows, food, and clothing. Fathers directed the labor of their children in the fields. At the end of the year, many families remained indebted to their employer and, thus, entitled to nothing and obliged to work another year in the hope of repaying the debt. If a sharecropper's demeanor or work habits displeased the landlord, the family faced eviction.

A Sharecrop Contract

Single women with small children were especially vulnerable to the whims of landlords in the postbellum period. Near Greensboro, North Carolina, for example, when planter Presley George Sr. settled the year's accounts with his field worker Polly at the end of 1865, Polly was charged $69 for corn, cloth, thread, and board for a child who did not work. By George's calculations, Polly had earned exactly $69 for the labor she and her three children (two sons and a daughter) performed in the course of the year, leaving her no cash of her own. Under these harsh conditions, freedpeople looked to each other for support and strength.

Building Free Communities

Soon after the war's end, southern blacks set about organizing themselves as an effective political force and as free communities devoted to the social and educational welfare of their own people. Differences among blacks based on income, jobs, culture, and skin color at times inhibited institution building. Some black communities found themselves divided by class, with blacks who had been free before the war (including many literate and skilled light-skinned men) assuming leadership over illiterate field hands. In New Orleans, a combination of factors contributed to class divisions among people of African heritage. During the antebellum period, light-skinned freedpeople of color, many of whom spoke French, were much more likely to possess property and a formal education than were enslaved people, who were dark-skinned English speakers. After the Civil War, the more privileged group pressed for public accommodations laws, which would open the city's theaters, opera, and expensive restaurants to all blacks for the first time. However, black churches and social organizations remained segregated according to class.

For the most part, postbellum black communities united around the principle that freedom from slavery should also mean full citizenship rights: the ability to vote, own land, and educate their children. These rights must be enforced by federal firepower: "a military occupation will be absolutely necessary," declared the blacks of Norfolk, "to protect the white Union men of the South, as well as ourselves." Freedpeople in some states allied themselves with white yeomen who had long resented the political power of the great planters and now saw an opportunity to use state governments as agents of democratization and economic reform.

"Free At Last"

Networks of freedpeople formed self-help organizations. Like the sponsors of the Savannah Education Association, blacks throughout the South formed committees to raise funds and hire teachers for neighborhood schools. Small Georgia towns, such as Cuthbert, Albany, Cave Spring, and Thomasville, with populations no greater than a few hundred, raised up to $70 per month and contributed as much as $350 each for the construction of school buildings. Funds came from the proceeds of fairs, bazaars, and bake sales; subscriptions raised by local school boards; and tuition fees. In the cash-starved postbellum South, these amounts represented a great personal and group sacrifice for the cause of education.

A Southern Labor Contract

After the Civil War, many southern agricultural workers signed labor contracts. These contracts sought to control not only the output of laborers but also their lives outside the workplace.

On January 1, 1868, the planter John D. Williams assembled his workers for the coming year and presented them with a contract to sign. Williams owned a plantation in the lower Piedmont county of Laurens, South Carolina. He agreed to furnish "the said negroes" (that is, the three black men and two black women whose names were listed on the document) with mules and horses to be used for cultivating the land. The workers could receive their food, clothing, and medical care on credit. They were allowed to keep one-third of all the corn, sweet potatoes, wheat, cotton, oats, and molasses they produced. Presumably, they would pay their debts to Williams using proceeds from their share of the crop.

According to the contract, Williams's workers promised to

bind them Selves to be steady & attentive to there work at all times and to work at keeping in repair all the fences on Said plantation and assist in cuting & taking care of—all the grain crops on Said plantation and work by the direction of me [Williams] or my Agent....

And should any of them depart from the farm or from any services at any time with out our approval they shall forfeit one dollar per day, for the first time and for the second time without good cause they shall forfeit all of their interest in the crop their to me the enjured person—they shall not be allowed to keep firearms or deadly wapons or ardent Spirits and they shall obey all lawful orders from me or my Agent and shall be honest—truthful—sober—civel—diligent in their business & for all wilful Disobedience of any lawful orders from me or my Agent drunkenness moral or legal misconduct want of respects or civility to me or my Agent or to my Family or any elce, I am permitted to discharge them forfeiting any claims upon me for any part of the crop....

Moses Nathan	1 full hand
Jake Chappal	" "
Milly Williams	½ " "
Easter Williams	" "
Mack Williams	" "

At the end of the contract is this addition:

We the white labores now employed by John D. Williams on his white plains plantation have lisened and heard read the foregoing Contract on this sheet of paper assign equal for the black laborers employed by him on said place and we are perfectly Satisfied with it and heare by bind our selves to abide & be Governed & Controwed by it

Wm Wyatte	1 full hand
John Wyatte	1 full hand
Packingham Wyatte	½ " "
Franklin Wyatte	½ " "
R M Hughes	1 full hand
B G Pollard	1 full hand
George Washington Pollard	1 full hand

To sign the contract, all of the blacks and two of the whites "made their marks"; that is, they signed with an "X" because they were illiterate.

After the Civil War, many rural southern blacks, such as those shown here, continued to toil in cotton fields owned by whites.

Library of Congress

Questions

1. *In what ways did sharecropping differ from wage labor?*
2. *Do you see evidence that family or kin members worked together on Williams's plantation?*
3. *What is the significance of the contract addendum signed by white laborers?* ■

Source: Rosser H. Taylor, "Postbellum Southern Rental Contracts" [from Furman University library, Greenville, South Carolina], *Agricultural History* 17 (1943): 122–123.

All over the South, black families charted their own course. They elected to take in orphans and elderly kin, to pool resources with neighbors, and to arrange for mothers to stay home with their children. These choices challenged the power of former slaveholders and the influence of Freedmen's Bureau agents and northern missionaries and teachers. At the same time, in seeking to attend to their families and to provide for themselves, southern blacks resembled members of other mid-nineteenth-century laboring classes who valued family ties over the demands of employers and landlords.

Landscapes and Soundscapes of Freedom

Tangible signs of emerging black communities infuriated southern whites. A schoolhouse run by blacks proved threatening in a society where most white children had little opportunity to receive an education. Black communities were also quick to form their own churches, rather than continue to occupy an inferior place in white churches. Other sights proved equally unsettling: on a main street in Charleston, an armed black soldier marching proudly or a black woman wearing a fashionable hat and veil, the kind favored by white women of the planter class.

Old sounds were silenced, replaced by new ones that signaled a new order. Cannon ceased to echo through the southern countryside, as did the thunderous roar of immense armies on the march. In their place emerged the sounds of freedpeople celebrating their liberation, the "Day of Jubilee." A Florida observer complained that black people's festivities and political realities produced "noise enough to really distract every body in the vicinity." Joyful family reunions, black children reciting their ABC's, congregants of a newly formed independent black church dancing and singing, speeches presented during long-suppressed Fourth of July celebrations—these sounds proclaimed a new day of freedom.

Some southern whites sought to impose a new, ominous silence on the South. In 1868 in Virginia, a white man named John Schofield objected to the singing of four black women; he attacked them when they ignored his order to stop. When freedpeople sought to socialize in a park in Savannah, Georgia, city officials closed the park altogether. These developments help to account for the speed with which whites organized themselves in vigilante groups, aiming to preserve "the supremacy of the white race in this Republic." The emerging Ku Klux Klan made its members promise "never [to] reveal any one not a member of the Order of the KKK, by any intimation, sign, symbol, word or act, or in any manner whatsoever, any of the secrets, signs, grips, pass-words, or mysteries of the order." New sounds and silences alike marked the end of the war and the crosscurrents of African American freedom.

Tangible signs of emerging black communities infuriated southern whites.

Congressional Reconstruction: The Radicals' Plan

Reconstruction

The rise of armed white supremacist groups in the South helped spur congressional Republicans to action. On March 2, 1867, Congress seized the initiative. A coalition led by two radicals, Senator Charles Sumner of Massachusetts and Congressman Thaddeus Stevens of Pennsylvania, prodded Congress to pass the Reconstruction Act of 1867. The purpose of this measure was to purge the South of disloyalty once and for all. The act stripped thousands of former Confederates of voting rights. The former Confederate states would not be readmitted to the Union until they had ratified the Fourteenth Amendment and written new constitutions that guaranteed black men the right to vote. The South (with the exception of Tennessee, which had ratified the Fourteenth Amendment in 1866) was divided into five military districts. Federal troops were stationed throughout the region. These troops were charged with protecting Union personnel and supporters in the South and with restoring order in the midst of regional political and economic upheaval.

Congress passed two additional acts specifically intended to secure congressional power over the president. The intent of the Tenure of Office Act was to prevent the president from dismissing Secretary of War Edwin Stanton, a supporter of the radicals. The other measure, the Command of the Army Act, required the president to seek approval for all military orders from General Ulysses S. Grant, the army's senior officer. Grant also was a supporter of the Repub-

TABLE 15.1

Comparison of Black and White Household Structure in 27 Cotton-Belt Counties, 1870, 1880, 1900

1870 (*N* = 534)

Single Person %	Nuclear %	Ext. %	Aug. %	Ext./Aug. %	(Unrelated Adults %)	Total	
3.1	80.7	14.4	1.4	.3	.3	290	**Black**
2.1	71.3	7.4	17.6	1.2	.4	244	**White**
2.6	76.4	11.0	8.8	.7	.4	534	

1880 (*N* = 672)

Single Person %	Nuclear %	Ext. %	Aug. %	Ext./Aug. %	(Unrelated Adults %)	Total	
3.7	74.2	13.6	5.9	1.7	.8	353	**Black**
3.1	62.7	13.5	15.7	5.0	.0	319	**White**
3.4	68.8	13.5	10.6	3.3	.4	672	

1900 (*N* = 643)

Single Person %	Nuclear %	Ext. %	Aug. %	Ext./Aug. %	(Unrelated Adults %)	Total	
5.7	64.9	22.9	4.0	1.7	.8	353	**Black**
3.4	65.2	19.0	10.7	1.7	.0	290	**White**
4.7	65.0	21.2	7.0	1.7	.5	643	

Single person: one person living alone.
Nuclear: father, mother, and children.
Ext.: extended family consisting of parents, children, and kin.
Aug.: augmented household consisting of family and nonfamily members (boarders, servants, hired hands).
Ext./aug.: combination of extended and augmented.
Unrelated adults: more than one unrelated adult living together.

Source: Based on information from a sample of households (located in selected cotton staple counties in Alabama, Florida, Georgia, Louisiana, Mississippi, North Carolina, South Carolina, and Texas) listed in the 1870, 1880, and 1900 federal population manuscript censuses.

licans. Both of these acts probably violated the **separation of powers** doctrine as put forth in the Constitution. Together, they would soon precipitate a national crisis.

During the Reconstruction period, approximately 2,000 black men of the emerging southern Republican party served as local elected officials, sheriffs, justices of the peace, tax collectors, and city councilors. Many of these leaders were of mixed ancestry, and many had been free before the war. They came in disproportionate numbers from the ranks of literate men, such as clergy, teachers, and skilled artisans. In Alabama, Florida, Louisiana, Mississippi, and South Carolina, black men constituted a majority of the voting public.

Some states made substantial gains in terms of integrating blacks into local systems of law enforcement and justice. By 1872, Florida, Arkansas, Louisiana, and South Carolina had elected black officials. Black men served as city chiefs of police in Tallahassee, Florida, and Little Rock, Arkansas, and black men made up half the ranks of the police force in Montgomery,

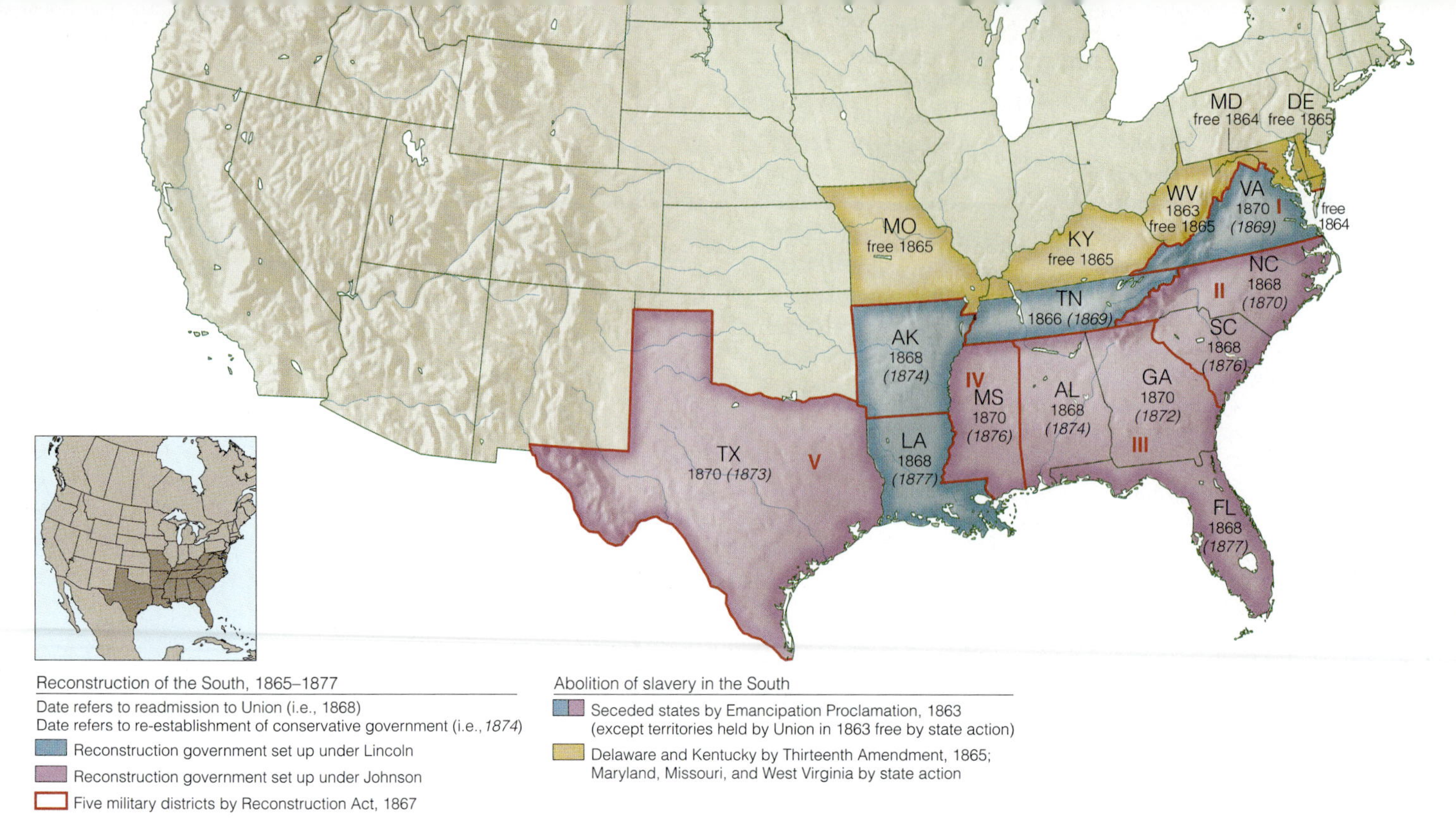

▲ MAP 15.1 RADICAL RECONSTRUCTION
Four of the former Confederate states—Louisiana, Arkansas, Tennessee, and Virginia—were reorganized under President Lincoln's Ten Percent Plan in 1864. Neither this plan nor the proposals of Lincoln's successor, Andrew Johnson, provided for the enfranchisement of the former slaves. In 1867 Congress established five military districts in the South and demanded that newly reconstituted state governments implement universal manhood suffrage. By 1870 all of the former Confederate states had rejoined the Union, and by 1877 all of those states had installed conservative (i.e., Democratic) governments.

Alabama, and Vicksburg, Mississippi. Whites found these developments profoundly unsettling. One white attorney observed that calling black jurors "gentlemen of the jury" was "the severest blow I have felt."

Throughout the South, 600 black men won election to state legislatures. Still, nowhere did blacks control a state government, although they did predominate in South Carolina's lower House. Sixteen black Southerners were elected to Congress during Reconstruction. Most of those elected to Congress in the years immediately after the war were freeborn. However, among the nine men elected for the first time after 1872, six were former slaves. All of these politicians exemplified the desire among southern blacks to become active, engaged citizens.

Newly reconstructed southern state legislatures provided for public school systems, fairer taxation methods, bargaining rights of plantation laborers, racially integrated public transportation and accommodations, and public works projects, especially railroads. All new state constitutions guaranteed black civil rights and most recognized the right of married women to hold property in their own names. With the exception of Louisiana, every new southern state constitution included a household exemption—from $1,500 to $5,000 worth of property that could not be seized by creditors.

Many of these Republican-dominated legislatures were shaped by the drive to further economic development in the largely rural, agricultural South. Black and white Republicans agreed that tax breaks and subsidies to railroads would provide jobs and update the South's transportation system. Mississippi black leader Merriman Howard noted in 1868: "The day we commence to work on a Rail Road...it would make this whole South flourish." Every southern state promoted railroads through direct cash payments and endorsement of company bonds.

Nevertheless, the legislative coalitions forged between Northerners and Southerners, blacks and whites, were uneasy and, in many cases, less than productive. Southern Democrats (and later, historians sympathetic to them) claimed that Reconstruction governments were uniquely corrupt, with some carpetbaggers, scalawags, and freedpeople vying for **kickbacks** from railroad and construction magnates. In fact, whenever state legislatures sought to promote business interests, they opened the door to the bribery of public officials. In this respect, northern as well as southern politicians were vulnerable to charges of corruption. In the long run, southern Democrats cared less about charges of legislative corruption than about the growing political power of local black Republican party organizations.

In Washington in early 1868, President Johnson forced a final showdown with Congress. He replaced several high military officials with more conservative men. He also fired Secretary of War Stanton, in apparent violation of the Tenure of Office Act. Shortly thereafter, in February, a newly composed House Reconstruction Committee impeached Johnson for ignoring the act, and the Senate began his trial on March 30. The president and Congress were locked in an extraordinary battle for political power.

The final vote was 35 senators against Johnson, one vote short of the necessary two-thirds of all senators' votes needed for conviction. Nineteen senators voted to acquit Johnson of the charges. Nevertheless, to win acquittal, he had had to promise moderates that he would not stand in the way of congressional plans for Reconstruction. Johnson essentially withdrew from policymaking in the spring of 1868. That November, with Republicans urging Northerners to "vote as you shot" (that is, to cast ballots against the former Confederates), Ulysses S. Grant was elected president.

Political reunion was an uneven process, but one that gradually eroded the newly won rights of former slaves in many southern states. By the end of 1868, Arkansas, North Carolina, South Carolina, Louisiana, Tennessee, Alabama, and Florida had met congressional conditions for readmission to the Union, and two years later, Mississippi, Virginia, Georgia, and Texas followed. The Fifteenth Amendment, passed by Congress in 1869 and ratified by the necessary number of states a year later, granted all black men the right to vote. However, in some states, such as Louisiana, reunification gave Democrats license to engage in wholesale election fraud and violence toward freed men and women. In 1870–1871, a congressional inquiry into the Klan exposed pervasive and grisly assaults on Republican schoolteachers, preachers, and prospective voters, black and white. The Klan also targeted men and women who refused

◀ This drawing by famous political cartoonist Thomas Nast depicts the first black members of Congress. Left to right, front row: Senator Hiram Revels of Mississippi (the first African American to serve in the U.S. Senate), Representatives Benjamin S. Turner of Alabama, Josiah T. Walls of Florida, Joseph H. Rainey of South Carolina, Robert B. Elliott of South Carolina. Back row: Representatives Robert G. DeLarge of South Carolina, Jefferson Long of Georgia.

Schomburg Center for Research in Black Culture, Art and Artifacts Division, New York Public Library, Astor, Lenox and Tilden Foundations

CONNECTING HISTORY

Two Presidents Impeached

Library of Congress

President Andrew Johnson.

White House Historical Association

President Bill Clinton.

The president, a Democrat, had humble roots in the South. He was raised by a hard-working single mother. His tenure as a state governor ill prepared him for the hostility he encountered as chief executive in Washington, where people persisted in gossiping about his personal life. The Republicans, firmly in control of Congress, despised him and managed to impeach him. At the same time, many observers questioned whether his misdeeds rose to the level of "high crimes and misdemeanors." With the aid of skillful lawyers, members of his own party, and a core of Republican moderates, he avoided conviction in the Senate. Nevertheless, the political battle diminished his capacity to lead forcefully for the rest of his term in office.

Andrew Johnson in 1868 or Bill Clinton 130 years later? The answer, of course, is both. Yet these superficial similarities in the careers of the two men mask dramatic differences between them. Andrew Johnson was charged with violating the Tenure of Office Act, a law that probably was unconstitutional. His impeachment took place against the backdrop of a national debate over the course of Reconstruction, a debate that was intensely ideological.

In contrast, Bill Clinton was charged with lying and obstructing justice, charges that stemmed from an extramarital affair the president had conducted with a young White House intern, Monica Lewinsky. His impeachment reflected the bitter partisanship and personal animosity between Democrats and Republicans in the 1990s. (See Chapter 29.)

Andrew Johnson was born in Raleigh, North Carolina, in 1808. At age 13, he was apprenticed to a tailor. As a young man, he moved to Tennessee. There he came to identify with the state's yeoman farmers and artisans in opposition to the great planters. Although he served as governor of Tennessee and later U.S. senator, he had little formal education; his wife, the daughter of a Scottish shoemaker, taught him how to write and do arithmetic.

In contrast, Bill Clinton attended Georgetown University and went on to graduate from Yale Law School. Clinton also appreciated the help and support of his wife, but Hillary Rodham Clinton was a unique First Lady. She possessed impressive skills as a political campaigner and maintained a keen interest in policy issues. In 2000, just as her husband was leaving office, she was elected U.S. senator from the state of New York.

Generations of historians have disagreed about Johnson's case. In the early twentieth century, pro-South scholars sympathized with Lincoln's successor. Yet many scholars later in the century looked more favorably on the radical Republicans; influenced by the civil rights movement, these historians focused on Johnson's anti-civil-rights stance. Therefore, it is difficult to predict how history will judge Bill Clinton and his battle with congressional Republicans. ■

to work like slaves in the fields. In April 1871, Congress passed the Ku Klux Klan Act, which punished conspiracies intended to deny rights to citizens. But Klan violence and intimidation had already taken their toll on Republican voting strength.

Resenting the political power of Republicans, blacks and whites, Louisiana Democrats unleashed a wave of violence during the 1875 elections. When the state's governor appealed to President Grant for military troops to quell the bloodshed, Grant replied: "The whole public are tired out with these autumnal outbreaks in the South, and the great majority now are ready to condemn any interference on the part of the Government." In the absence of law enforcement, the Democrats swept to victory in 1875.

The Remarkable Career of Blanche K. Bruce

Library of Congress

▲ This formal portrait of Blanche K. Bruce conveys his status as a wealthy and powerful politician.

The career of Blanche K. Bruce reveals the opportunities and limitations faced by an emerging black leadership during Reconstruction. Born a slave in 1841, this light-skinned mulatto spent much of his childhood working on a tobacco farm in central Missouri. He learned to read at an early age and acquired an interest in plantation management. After the war began, Bruce managed to escape from slavery. He eventually settled in Hannibal, Missouri, where he established the first school for blacks and worked as a printer's helper. In 1866 he enrolled in Oberlin College in Ohio. Though he worked hard, sawing wood to pay tuition, he could not afford to continue his formal education.

In 1867 Bruce attended a political rally in Mississippi. He became convinced that the state, especially the Delta region, afforded both economic and political opportunity. He quickly rose up the local political ranks, starting as voter registrar in Tallahatchie County, serving as sergeant at arms of the state legislature, and then tax assessor, sheriff, and member of the board of levee commissioners for Bolivar County. Bruce soon earned a reputation for fairness and honesty in public service. In 1872, he served simultaneously as education superintendent, sheriff, and tax collector in Bolivar County. He had established himself as the most powerful black politician in the Delta. Meanwhile, Bruce began to buy houses and parcels of land in the county; by the 1880s he was a wealthy man.

Blanche K. Bruce won support from the Republican-dominated state legislature in his bid to run for the U.S. Senate in 1874; a year later he was elected to that seat. As a U.S. senator, Bruce demonstrated an interest in navigation improvements and flood control of the Mississippi River. He was one of a few legislators to condemn discrimination against Chinese immigrants in California, expressing "a large confidence in the strength and assimilative power of [our] American institutions." When he lost his Senate seat in 1881, Bruce and his wife moved to Washington, D.C. There he held a series of federal patronage jobs and became a member of the city's African American elite. Ultimately, his rise to wealth and political power distanced him from poorer blacks. His four-decade odyssey from slavery to the fashionable salons of the nation's capital revealed the promise, as well as the limitations, of Radical Reconstruction.

Claiming Territory for the Union

In 1871 poet Walt Whitman celebrated the "manly and courageous instincts" that propelled a brave, adventurous people west. Whitman hailed the march across the prairies and over the mountains as a cavalcade of progress. He and other Americans believed that the postbellum migration fulfilled a mission of national regeneration begun by the Civil War. Kansas's population grew by 240 percent in the 1860s, Nebraska's by 355 percent.

To unite the entire country together as a single economic and political unit was the Republican ideal. The railroads in particular served as vehicles of national integration. When the

Central Pacific and Union Pacific Railroads met at Promontory Point, Utah, in 1869, the hammering of the spike that joined the two roads produced a telegraphic signal received simultaneously on both coasts, setting off a national celebration.

Meanwhile, regular units of United States cavalry, including two regiments of blacks, were launching attacks on Indians on the Plains, in the Northwest, and in the Southwest. Between 1865 and 1890, U.S. military forces conducted a dozen separate campaigns against western Indian peoples and met Indian warriors in battle or attacked Indian settlements in more than 1,000 engagements. In contrast to African Americans, who adamantly demanded their rights as American citizens, defiant western Indians battled a government to which, they steadfastly maintained, they owed no allegiance.

Federal Military Campaigns Against Western Indians

In 1871 the U.S. government renounced the practice of seeking treaties with various Indian groups. This change in policy opened the way for a more aggressive effort to subdue native populations. In 1848, the United States had acquired a vast amount of western territory as a result of the Mexican-American War. As a result, the U.S. government abandoned its policy of pushing Indians ever farther westward. Instead, officials expanded the reservation system, an effort begun in the antebellum period to confine specific Indian groups to specific territories.

In the Southwest, clashes between Indians and U.S. soldiers persisted after the Civil War. In 1867 at Medicine Lodge Creek in southern Kansas, the United States signed a treaty with an alliance of Comanche, Kiowa, Cheyenne, Arapaho, and Plains Apache. This treaty could not long withstand the provocation posed by the railroad. The year before, the Seventh U.S. Cavalry, under the command of Lieutenant Colonel George Custer, had been formed to ward off native attacks on the Union Pacific, snaking its way across the central Plains westward from Kansas. In November 1868 Custer destroyed a Cheyenne settlement on the Washita River, in present-day Oklahoma. The settlement's leader was Black Kettle, who had brought his people to reservation territory after the Sand Creek Massacre in Colorado in 1864. Custer's men murdered women and children, burned tipis, and destroyed 800 horses. Sickened by the scene,

▶ At Promontory Point near Ogden, Utah, workers joined the tracks linking the Central Pacific (its wood-burning locomotive, *Jupiter,* is on the left) with the Union Pacific (whose coal-burning engine No. 119 is on the right). This photo was taken during the May 10, 1869, celebration marking the completion of the transcontinental railroad. According to one eyewitness, the crowd included Indians, Chinese and Irish immigrants, European Americans, and Mexicans "grouped in picturesque confusion." Yet this official photo shows little evidence of the Chinese workers who helped engineer and build the Central Pacific line.

National Archives

▲ **MAP 15.2 PLAINS INDIAN WARS, 1865–1900**
Between 1865 and 1890, many of the conflicts between Indians and U.S. troops occurred along either railroad lines or trails used by European American settlers. For example, the Sioux, Cheyenne, and Arapaho fiercely resisted travelers along the Bozeman Trail running from Colorado to Montana.

one army officer later wrote sarcastically of the "daring dash" on the part of "heroes of a bloody day." The soldiers left piles of corpses scattered among the smoldering ruins of the village.

Geronimo and Natiche Surrender (1886)

A series of peace delegations to Washington, several led by Red Cloud of the Sioux, produced much curiosity among whites but no end to the slaughter of people or animals in the West. Indians continued to attack the surveyors, supply caravans, and military escorts that preceded the railroad work crews. Lamenting the loss of his people's hunting grounds to the railroad, Red Cloud said, "The white children have surrounded me and have left me nothing but an island."

The Apache managed to elude General George Crook until 1875. Crook employed some of these Apache to track down the war chief Geronimo of the Chiricahua. Like many other Indian leaders, Geronimo offered both religious and military guidance to his people. He believed that a spirit would protect him from the white man's bullets and from the arrows of Indians in league with government troops. Yet Geronimo was tricked into a momentary surrender in 1877. Sorrowfully, he agreed to bring his followers into the San Carlos reservation in eastern Arizona. There he was held in irons for several months before gaining release and challenging authorities for another nine years.

In 1874 Custer took his cavalry into the Black Hills of the Dakotas. Supposedly, the 1868 Treaty of Fort Laramie had rendered this land off-limits to whites. Custer's mission was to offer protection for the surveyors of the Northern Pacific Railroad and to force Indians onto reservations as stipulated in the 1868 treaty. However, the officer lost no time trumpeting the fact

▲ This European American version of the Battle of Little Big Horn illustrated a book celebrating the life of Custer. The book was published soon after the battle, which took place in June 1876. At the time, the country was in the midst of a celebration marking the centennial of the nation's birth. The engraving portrays Custer and his cavalry making a courageous "last stand."

Bettmann/CORBIS

that Indian lands were filled with gold. This report prompted a rush to the Black Hills, lands sacred to the Sioux. Within two years, 15,000 gold miners had illegally descended on Indian lands to seek their fortunes. The federal government proposed to buy the land, but leaders of the Sioux, including Red Cloud, Spotted Tail, and Sitting Bull, spurned the offer. "The Black Hills belong to me," declared Sitting Bull. "If the whites try to take them, I will fight."

During the morning of June 25, 1876, Custer and his force of 264 soldiers attacked a Sun Dance gathering of 2,500 Sioux and Cheyenne on the banks of the Little Big Horn River in Montana. Custer foolishly launched his attack without adequate backup, and he and his men were easily overwhelmed and killed by Indian warriors, led by the Oglala Sioux Crazy Horse and others. Reacting to this defeat, U.S. military officials reduced the Lakota and Cheyenne to wardship status, ending their autonomy.

Indians throughout the West maintained their distinctive ways of life during these turbulent times. Horse holdings, so crucial for hunting, trading, and fighting, varied from group to group, with the Crow wealthy in relation to their Central Plains neighbors the Oglala and the Arikara. Plains and Plateau peoples engaged in a lively trading system. They exchanged horses and their trappings (bridles and blankets) for eastern goods such as kettles, guns, and ammunition. Despite their differences in economy, these groups held similar religious beliefs about an all-powerful life force that governed the natural world. People, plants, and animals were all part of the same order.

Even in the midst of brutal repression, Indian cultural traditions survived and in some cases flourished. On the West Central Plains and the Plateau, among the Crow, Shoshone, Nez Perce, and other tribes, women developed a new, distinctive style of seed beadwork characterized by variations of triangular patterns. These designs, made of beads selected for their quality and consistency, adorned leggings, gauntlets, and belt pouches. In these ways, the decorative arts were endowed with great symbolic meaning. When a wife embellished moccasins with patterns signifying her husband's military achievements, handicrafts assumed political as well as artistic significance.

The Postwar Western Labor Problem

In 1865 the owners of the Central Pacific Railroad seemed poised for one of the great engineering feats of the nineteenth century. In the race eastward from California, they would construct trestles spanning vast chasms, and roadbeds traversing mountains and deserts. Government officials in Washington were eager to subsidize the railroad. What the owners lacked was a dependable labor force. The Irish workers who began the line in California struck for higher wages in compensation for brutal, dangerous work. These immigrants dropped their shovels and hammers at the first word of a gold strike nearby—or far away. As a result, in 1866 the Central Pacific decided to tap into a vast labor source by importing thousands of Chinese men from their native Guandong province.

The Chinese toiled to extend the railroad tracks eastward from Sacramento, California, up to ten miles a day in the desert, only a few feet a day in the rugged Sierra Nevada Mountains.

Kicking Bear, *Battle of Little Big Horn*, c.1890. Southwest Museum, Los Angeles

▲ Sioux artist Kicking Bear commemorated the Battle of Little Big Horn with this painting, completed in the 1890s. The figure in yellow buckskin at the left is Custer and the ghostlike figures behind the line of dead soldiers in the upper left are the spirits of the dead. At the center of the painting, Kicking Bear placed the figures of Sitting Bull, Rain-in-the-Face, Crazy Horse, and himself.

In nerve-wracking feats of skill, they lowered themselves in woven baskets to implant nitroglycerine explosives in canyon walls. Chinese laborers toiled through snowstorms and blistering heat to blast tunnels and cut passes through granite mountains. With the final linking of the railroad in Utah in 1869, many Chinese returned to California.

Signed in 1868, the Burlingame Treaty, named for Anson Burlingame, an American envoy to China, had supposedly guaranteed government protection for Chinese immigrants (most of whom were men) as visitors, traders, or permanent residents within the United States. Yet the treaty did not inhibit U.S. employers, landlords, and government officials from discriminating against the Chinese.

By 1870, 40,000 Chinese lived in California and represented fully one-quarter of the state's wage-earners. They found work in the cigar, woolen-goods, and boot and shoe factories of San Francisco; in the gold mining towns, now as laundry operators rather than as miners as they had before the Civil War; and in the fields as agricultural laborers. White workers complained of unfair competition from this Asian group that was becoming increasingly integrated into the region's economy.

Another labor group, California Indians, remained trapped in the traditional agricultural economy of unskilled labor. Whites appropriated Indian land and forced many men, women, and children to work as wage-earners for large landowners. Deprived of their familiar hunting and gathering lands, and wracked by disease and starvation, California Indians suffered a drastic decline in their numbers by 1870, from 100,000 to 30,000 in 20 years.

By the early 1870s, western manufacturers were faltering under the pressure of cheaper goods imported from the East by rail. At the same time, the growth of fledgling gigantic agricultural businesses opened new avenues of trade and commerce. Located in an arc surrounding the San Francisco Bay, large ("bonanza") wheat farmers grew huge crops and exported the grain to

Great Salt Lake Basin

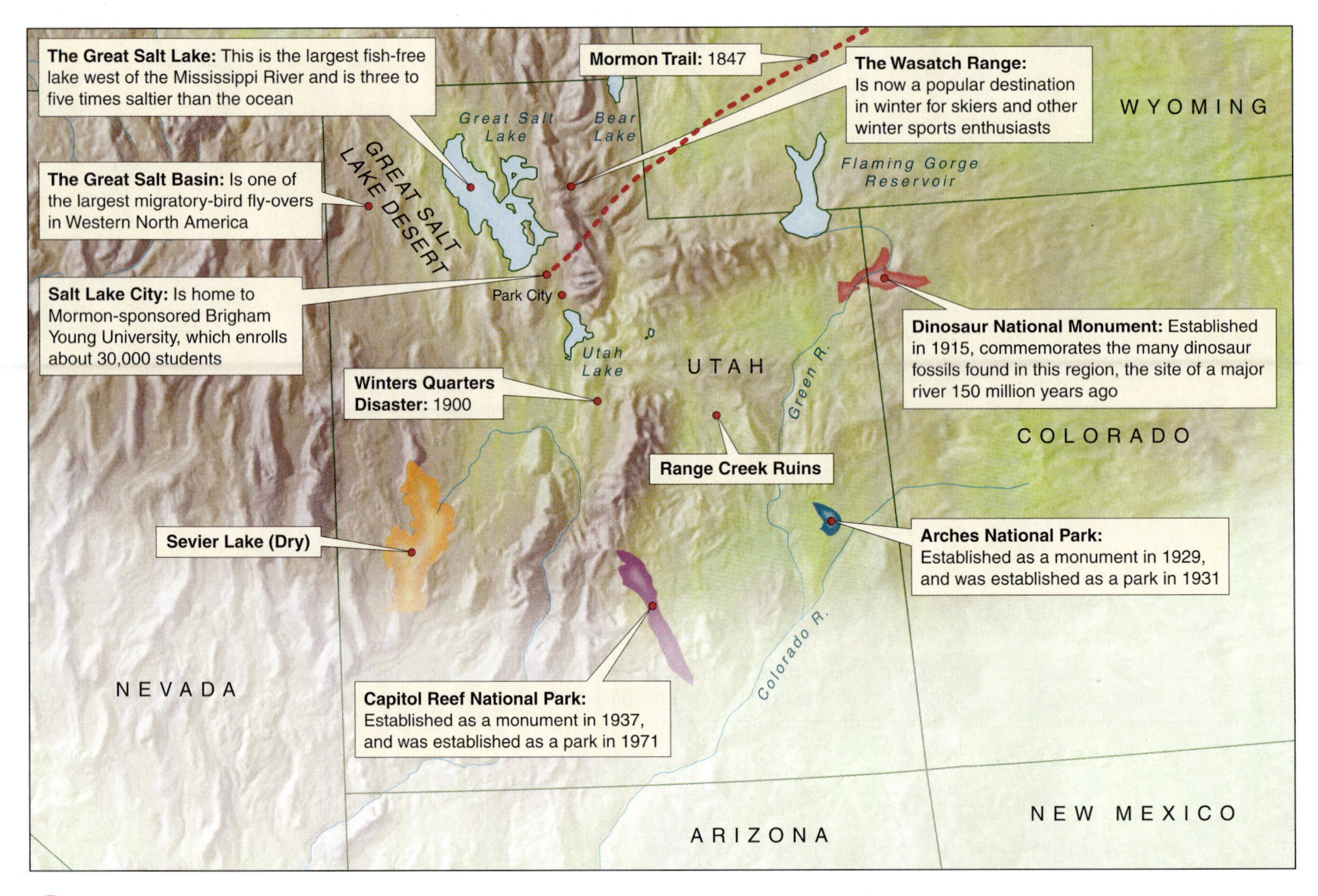

One thousand years ago, the Fremont Indians established a string of thriving villages nestled along Range Creek in the high-desert Book Cliff region of Utah. There they constructed homes made of round stones and covered with roofs of pine boughs. They also built stone walls, granaries, and silos for corn and beans. They made baskets woven of grass and willow, as well as pottery, tools, and beads. In the early 1940s, a young cowboy named Waldo Wilcox came across the ruins of this community; the dry climate had preserved many structures and artifacts to a remarkable degree. Wilcox kept the site secret until the summer of 2004. His announcement set off a debate among archaeologists and federal and local officials over the best way to keep the site intact and at the same time open it to the public.

Since the Fremont Indians made their home in central Utah, humans have used the land for a variety of purposes. Coal mining, a major enterprise in the state, was particularly dangerous. In the 1900 Winter Quarters disaster, 200 people lost their lives when coal dust caused an explosion underground.

Utah's mountainous terrain has made it a popular cultural and tourist destination. In 2000, Salt Lake City welcomed the Winter Olympics. Park City hosts the annual Sundance Film Festival, the largest independent-film festival in the United States. ■

Carleton Watkins/Union Pacific Historical Collection

◀ Chinese construction workers labor on the Central Pacific Railroad, c. 1868. Many Chinese immigrants toiled as indentured laborers, indebted to Chinese merchant creditors who paid for their passage to California. Isolated in all-male work camps, crews of railroad workers retained their traditional dress, language, and diet. After the completion of the transcontinental railroad in 1869, some immigrants returned to China, and others dispersed to small towns and cities throughout the West.

the East Coast and to England. These enterprises stimulated the building of wharves and railroad trunk lines and encouraged technological innovation in threshing and harvesting. Western enterprises showed a growing demand for labor, whatever its skin color or nationality.

Land Use in an Expanding Nation

The end of the Civil War prompted new conflicts and deepened long-standing ones over the use of the land in a rich, sprawling country. In the South, staple crop planters began to share political power with an emerging elite, men who owned railroads and textile mills. Despairing of ever achieving antebellum levels of labor efficiency, some landowners turned to mining the earth and the forests for saleable commodities. These products, obtained through extraction, included phosphate (used in producing fertilizer), timber, coal, and turpentine. Labor in extractive industries complemented labor in the plantation economy. Sharecroppers alternated between tilling cotton fields in the spring and harvesting the crop in the fall, while seeking employment in sawmills and coal mines in the winter and summer.

As European Americans settled in the West and Southwest, they displaced natives who had been living there for generations. For example, the U.S. court system determined who could legally claim property. Western courts also decided whether natural resources such as water, land, timber, and fish and game constituted property that could be owned by private interests. In the Southwest, European American settlers, including army soldiers who had come to fight Indians and then stayed, continued to place Mexican land titles at risk. Citing prewar precedents, American courts favored the claims of recent squatters over those of long-standing residents. In 1869 with the death of her husband (who had served as a general in the Union army), Maria Amparo Ruiz de Burton saw the large ranch they had worked together near San Diego slip out of her control. The first Spanish-speaking woman to be published in English in the United States, de Burton was a member of the Hispanic elite. Nevertheless, she had little political power. California judges backed the squatters who occupied the ranch.

Security Pacific Historical Photograph Collection, Los Angeles Public Library

▲ **These Cahuilla Indians were employees of Henry Dalton, a British immigrant who established a profitable trading and shipping business in California. Taken in the 1860s, this photo shows men and boys who have traveled from the area around Temecula and San Bernardino to work at Dalton's 20,000-acre Rancho Azusa.**

As they controlled more land and assumed public office, some European Americans in the Southwest exploited their political connections and economic power. In the process they managed to wield great influence over people and vast amounts of natural resources. In the 1870s the so-called Santa Fe Ring wrested more than 80 percent of the original Spanish grants of land from Spanish-speaking landholders in New Mexico. An alliance of European American lawyers, businesspeople, and politicians, the Santa Fe Ring defrauded families and kin groups of their land titles and speculated in property to make a profit. Whereas many ordinary Hispanic settlers saw land in terms of its crops, pasture, fuel, building materials, and game, the Santa Fe Ring saw land primarily as a commodity to be bought and sold.

Seemingly overnight, boom towns sprang up wherever minerals or timber beckoned: southern Arizona and the Rocky Mountains west of Denver, Virginia City in western Nevada, the Idaho-Montana region, and the Black Hills of South Dakota. In all these places, increasing numbers of workers operated sophisticated kinds of machinery, such as rock crushers, and labored for wages. When the vein was exhausted or the forests depleted, the towns went bust.

DeGolyer Library, Southern Methodist University

◀ With this 1870 photograph, the Kansas Pacific Railroad advertised the opportunity for western travelers to shoot buffalo from the comfort and safety of their railroad car. The company's official taxidermist shows off his handiwork. Railroad expansion facilitated the exploitation of natural resources while promoting tourism.

Railroads facilitated not only the mining of minerals but also the growth of the cattle-ranching industry. By 1869 a quarter of a million cattle were grazing in Colorado Territory. Rail connections between the Midwest and East made it profitable for Texas ranchers to pay cowboys to drive their herds of long-horned steers to Abilene, Ellsworth, Wichita, or Dodge City, Kansas, for shipment to stockyards in Chicago or St. Louis. Large meatpackers, such as Swift and Armour, prepared the carcasses for the eastern market.

Cattle drives were huge; an estimated 10 million animals were herded north from Texas alone between 1865 and 1890. They offered employment to all kinds of men with sufficient skills and endurance. Among the cowhands were African American horsebreakers and gunmen and Mexicans skilled in the use of the *reata* (lasso). Blacks made up about 25 percent and Hispanos about 15 percent of all cowboy outfits. Tracing the evolution of the Chisholm Trail, which linked southern Texas to Abilene, from Indian path to commercial route, one observer wrote in 1874, "So many cattle have been driven over the trail in the last few years that a broad highway is tread out, looking much like a national highway." Yet this new "national highway" traversed Indian Territory (present-day Oklahoma), lands supposedly promised to Indians forever.

Cowboys and Cattle

In knitting regional economies together, federal land policies were crucial to the Republican vision of a developing nation. Yet a series of land use acts had a mixed legacy. The Mineral Act of 1866 granted title to millions of acres of mineral-rich land to mining companies, a gift from the federal government to private interests. In 1866 Congress passed the Southern Homestead Act to help blacks acquire land, but the measure accomplished little and was repealed in 1876. The Timber Culture Act of 1873 allotted 160 acres to individuals in selected western states if they agreed to plant one-fourth of the acreage with trees. Four years later, the Desert Land Act provided cheap land if buyers irrigated at least part of their parcels.

The exploitation of western resources raised many legal questions: Must ranchers pay for the prairies their cattle grazed on and the trails they followed to market? How could one "own" a stampeding buffalo herd or a flowing river? What was the point of holding title to a piece of property if only the timber, oil, water, or minerals (but not the soil) were of value?

TABLE 15.2

Estimates of Railroad Crossties Used and Acres of Forest Cleared, 1870–1910

Year	Miles of Track	Ties Renewed Annually (millions)	Ties Used on New Construction (millions)	Total Ties Annually (millions)	Acres of Forest Cleared (thousands)
1870	60,000	21	18	39	195
1880	107,000	37	21	58	290
1890	200,000	70	19	89	445
1900	259,000			91	455
1910	357,000			124	620

Source: Michael Williams, *Americans and Their Forests* (New York: Cambridge University Press, 1989), 352.

The Apex Mining Act of 1872 sought to address at least some of these issues. This law legalized traditional mining practices in the West by validating titles approved by local courts. According to the law, a person who could locate the apex of a vein (its point closest to the surface) could lay claim to the entire vein beneath the surface. The measure contributed to the wholesale destruction of certain parts of the western landscape as mining companies blasted their way through mountains and left piles of rocks in their wake. It also spurred thousands of lawsuits as claimants argued over what constituted an apex or a vein.

It was during this period that a young Scottish-born naturalist named John Muir began to explore the magnificent canyons and mountains of California. Viewing nature as a means for regenerating the human spirit, Muir emphasized a deep appreciation of the natural world. He contrasted nature's majesty with the artificial landscape created by and for humans. In the wilderness, there is nothing "truly dead or dull, or any trace of what in manufactories is called rubbish or waste," he wrote; "everything is perfectly clean and pure and full of divine lessons." Muir believed that the need to protect breathtaking vistas and magnificent stands of giant redwoods compelled the federal government to act as land-policy regulator.

Muir was gratified by the creation of the National Park system during the postwar period. By this time, pressure had been building on the federal government to protect vast tracts of undeveloped lands. Painters and geologists were among the first Easterners to appreciate the spectacular vistas of the western landscape. In 1864 Congress set aside a small area within California's Yosemite Valley for public recreation and enjoyment. Soon after the war, railroad promoters forged an alliance with government officials in an effort to block commercial development of particularly beautiful pockets of land. In the late 1860s the invention of the Pullman sleeping car—a luxurious hotel room on wheels—helped spur tourism, and thus the drive to protect areas of natural beauty from farming, lumbering, stock raising, and mining. Northern Pacific railroad financier Jay Cooke lobbied hard for the government to create a 2-million-acre park in what is today the northwest corner of Wyoming. As a result, in March 1872, Congress created Yellowstone National Park. Tourism would continue to serve as a key component of the western economy.

Muir and others portrayed the Yosemite and Yellowstone Valleys as wildernesses, empty of human activity. In fact, both areas had long provided hunting and foraging grounds for native peoples. Since the fifteenth century, Yellowstone had been occupied by the people now called the Shoshone. This group, together with the Bannock, Crow, and Blackfoot, tried to retain access to Yellowstone's meadows, rivers, and forests after it became a national park. However, U.S. policymakers and military officials persisted in their efforts to mark off territory for specific commercial purposes, while Indians were confined to reservations.

Buying Territory for the Union

Before the Civil War, Republicans had opposed any federal expansionist schemes that they feared might benefit slaveholders. However, after 1865 and the outlawing of slavery, some Republican lawmakers and administration officials advocated the acquisition of additional territory. Secretary of State William Seward led the way in 1867 by purchasing Alaska from Russia. For $7.2 million (about 2 cents an acre), the United States gained 591,004 square miles of land. Within the territory were diverse indigenous groups—Eskimo, Aleut, Tlingit, Tsimshian, Athabaskan, and Haida—and a small number of native Russians. Though derided at the time as "Seward's icebox," Alaska yielded enough fish, timber, minerals, and water power in the years to come to prove that the original purchase price was a tremendous bargain.

The impulse that prompted administration support for the Alaska purchase also spawned other plans for territorial acquisitions. In 1870 some Republicans joined with Democrats in calling for the annexation of the Dominican Republic. These members of Congress argued that the tiny Caribbean country would make a fine naval base, provide investment opportunities for American businesspeople, and offer a refuge for southern freedpeople.

However, influential Senator Charles Sumner warned against a takeover without considering the will of the Dominican people, who were currently involved in their own civil war. Some members of Congress, in a prelude to foreign policy debates of the 1890s, suggested that the dark-skinned Dominican people were incapable of appreciating the blessings of American citizenship. In 1871 the treaty failed to win Senate approval.

Colorado Historical Society (CHS.J 2067)

▲ Chicago photographer Thomas J. Hine titled this stereograph "Old Faithful in Action, Fire Hole Basin." It is the first photograph of the eruption of the famous Yellowstone geyser. Costing 15–25 cents each, stereographs were a popular form of entertainment in middle-class households beginning in the 1860s. The stereoscope merged two identical photos to form a single three-dimensional image. Widely distributed stereographs of scenic natural wonders boosted western tourism.

The Republican Vision and Its Limits

After the Civil War, victorious Republicans envisioned a nation united in the pursuit of prosperity. All citizens would be free to follow their individual economic self-interest and enjoy the fruits of honest toil. In contrast, some increasingly vocal and well-organized groups saw the expansion of legal rights, and giving black men the right to vote in particular, as only initial, tentative steps on the path to an all-inclusive citizenship. Women, industrial workers, farmers, and African Americans made up overlapping constituencies pressing for equal political rights and economic opportunity. Together they challenged the mainstream Republican view that defeat of the rebels and destruction of slavery were sufficient to guarantee all people prosperity.

Partnerships between government and business also produced unanticipated consequences for Republicans committed to what they believed was the collective good. Some politicians and business leaders saw these partnerships as opportunities for private gain. Consequently, private greed and public corruption accompanied postwar economic growth. Thus, Republican leaders faced challenges from two very different sources: people agitating for civil rights and people hoping to reap personal gain from political activities.

Postbellum Origins of the Woman Suffrage Movement

After the Civil War, the nation's middle class, which had its origins in the antebellum period, continued to grow. Dedicated to self-improvement and filled with a sense of moral authority, many middle-class Americans (especially Protestants) felt a deep cultural connection to their counterparts in England. Indeed, the United States produced its own "Victorians," the term for the self-conscious middle class that emerged in the England of Queen Victoria during her reign from 1837 to 1901.

At the heart of the Victorian sensibility was the ideal of domesticity: a harmonious family living in a well-appointed home, guided by a pious mother and supported by a father successful in business. Famous Protestant clergyman Henry Ward Beecher and his wife were outspoken proponents of this domestic ideal. According to Eunice Beecher, women had no "higher, nobler, more divine mission than in the conscientious endeavor to create a *true home.*"

Yet the traumatic events of the Civil War only intensified the desire among a growing group of American women to participate fully in the nation's political life. They wanted to extend their moral influence outside the narrow and exclusive sphere of the home. Many women believed they deserved the vote and that the time was right to demand it.

Library of Congress

▲ The *Daily Graphic,* a New York City newspaper, carried this caricature of Susan B. Anthony on its June 5, 1873, cover. The artist suggests that the drive for women's suffrage has resulted in a reversal of gender roles. Titled "The Woman Who Dared," the cartoon portrays Anthony as a masculine figure. One of her male supporters, on the right, holds a baby, while women activists march and give speeches. On the left, a female police officer keeps watch over the scene.

In 1866 veteran reformers Elizabeth Cady Stanton, Susan B. Anthony, and Lucy Stone founded the Equal Rights Association to link the rights of white women and African Americans. Nevertheless, in 1867, Kansas voters defeated a referendum proposing suffrage for both blacks and white women. This disappointment convinced some former abolitionists that the two causes should be separated—that women should wait patiently until the rights of African American men were firmly secured. Frederick Douglass declined an invitation to a women's suffrage convention in Washington, D.C., in 1868. He explained, "I am now devoting myself to a cause [if] not more sacred, certainly more urgent, because it is one of life and death to the long enslaved people of this country, and that is: negro suffrage." But African American activist and former slave Sojourner Truth warned: "There is a great stir about colored men getting their rights, but not a word about the colored women; and if colored men get their rights, and not colored women get theirs, there will be a bad time about it."

In 1869 two factions of women parted ways and formed separate organizations devoted to women's rights. The more radical wing, including Cady Stanton and Anthony, bitterly denounced the Fifteenth Amendment because it gave the vote to black men only. They helped to found the National Woman Suffrage Association (NWSA), which argued for a renewed commitment to the original Declaration of Sentiments passed in Seneca Falls, New York, two decades earlier.

They favored married women's property rights, liberalization of divorce laws, opening colleges and trade schools to women, and a new federal amendment to allow women to vote. Lucy Stone and her husband, Henry Blackwell, founded the rival American Woman Suffrage Association (AWSA). This group downplayed the larger struggle for women's rights and focused on the suffrage question exclusively. Its members supported the Fifteenth Amendment and retained ties to the Republican party. The AWSA focused on state-by-state campaigns for women's suffrage.

In 1871 the NWSA welcomed the daring, flamboyant Victoria Woodhull as a vocal supporter, only to renounce her a few years later. Woodhull's political agenda ranged from free love and dietary reform to legalized prostitution, working men's rights, and women's suffrage. (In the nineteenth century, free love advocates denounced what they called a sexual double standard, one that glorified female chastity while tolerating male promiscuity.)

In 1872 Woodhull spent a month in jail as a result of zealous prosecution by vice reformer Anthony Comstock, a clergyman who objected to her public discussions and writings on sexuality. Comstock assumed the role of an outspoken crusader against vice. A federal law passed in 1873, and named after him, equated information related to birth control with pornography, banning this and other "obscene material" from the mails.

Susan B. Anthony used the 1872 presidential election as a test case for women's suffrage. She attempted to vote and was arrested, tried, and convicted. By this time, most women suffragists, and most members of the NWSA for that matter, had become convinced that they should focus on the vote exclusively; they therefore accepted the AWSA's policy on this issue. In the coming years, they would avoid other causes with which they might have allied themselves, including black civil rights and labor reform.

Workers' Organizations

Many Americans benefited from economic changes of the postwar era. Railroading, mining, and heavy industry helped fuel the national economy and in the process boosted the growth of the urban managerial class. In the Midwest, many landowning farmers prospered when they responded to an expanding demand for grain and other staple crops. In Wisconsin, wheat farmers cleared forests, drained swamps, diverted rivers, and profited from the booming world market in grain. Yet the economic developments that allowed factory managers and owners of large wheat farms to make a comfortable living for themselves did not necessarily benefit agricultural and manufacturing wage-workers.

Many Americans benefitted from the econmic changes of the postwar era.

Indeed, during this period, growing numbers of working people, in the countryside and in the cities, became caught up in a cycle of indebtedness. In the upcountry South (above the fall line, or Piedmont), formerly self-sufficient family farmers sought loans from banks to repair their war-damaged homesteads. To qualify for these loans, a farmer had to plant cotton as a staple crop, to the neglect of corn and other foodstuffs. Many sharecroppers, black and white, received payment in the form of credit only; for these families, the end-of-the-year reckoning yielded little more than rapidly accumulating debts. Midwestern farmers increasingly relied on expensive threshing and harvesting machinery and on bank loans to purchase the machinery.

Several organizations founded within five years of the war's end offered laborers an alternative vision to the Republicans' brand of individualism and nationalism. In 1867 Oliver H. Kelly, a former Minnesota farmer now working in a Washington office, organized the National Grange of the Patrons of Husbandry, popularly known as the Grange. This movement sought to address a new, complex marketplace increasingly dominated by railroads, banks, and grain elevator operators. The Grange encouraged farmers to form **cooperatives** that would market their crops and to challenge discriminatory railroad rates that favored big business.

Founded in Baltimore in 1866, the National Labor Union (NLU) consisted of a collection of craft unions and claimed as many as 600,000 members at its peak in the early 1870s. The group welcomed farmers as well as factory workers and promoted legislation for an eight-

State Historical Society of Wisconsin, WHi (D32) 821

▲ **A Norwegian immigrant extended family in the town of Norway Grove, Wisconsin, poses in front of their imposing home and up-to-date carriage in this photograph taken in the mid-1870s. Linking their fortunes to the world wheat market, these newcomers to the United States prospered. Wrote one woman to her brother back home in Norway, "We all have cattle, driving oxen, and wagons. We also have children in abundance."**

hour workday and the arbitration of industrial disputes.William Sylvis, a leader of the Iron Molders' International Union in Philadelphia and the second president of the NLU, sounded twin themes that would mark national labor union organizing efforts for generations to come. He called for an alliance of black and white workers. Yet at the same time, Sylvis defended the practice of excluding blacks from positions of leadership on the job and in the union. Impatient with such pronouncements, Isaac Myers, a black ship caulker from Baltimore, helped found the short-lived Colored National Labor Union in Washington, D.C., in 1868. (This association remained small, and disbanded within three years.) Myers offered a view of citizenship that differed from white Republicans' exclusive emphasis on the franchise: "If citizenship means anything at all," the black labor leader declared, "it means the freedom of labor, as broad and universal as freedom of the ballot."

In 1873 a nationwide economic depression threw thousands out of work and worsened the plight of debtors. Businesspeople in agriculture, mining, the railroad industry, and manufacturing had overexpanded their operations. The freewheeling loan practices of major banks had

TABLE 15.3

National and International Union Members of the National Labor Union (with dates of each union's founding)

National Typographical Union (printers and typesetters) (1850)	Carpenters' and Joiners' I.U. (1865)
Iron Molders' I.U. (1859)	Bricklayers' I.U. (1865)
Machinists' and Blacksmiths' I.U. (1859)	Journeyman Painters' I.U. (1865, again 1871)
American Miners' Association (1861)	Stationary Engineers' N.U. (1866?)
Miners' National Association (1873)	Mule Spinners' I.U. (textile workers) (1866)
Sons of Vulcan (steel workers) (1862)	Knights of St. Crispin (shoemakers) (1867)
National Telegraphic Union (1863)	Conductors' Brotherhood (1868)
Telegraphers' Protective League (1868)	Workingmen's Benevolent Association (1868)
Brotherhood of Locomotive Engineers (1863)	Wool Hat Finishers' N.U. (1869)
Ship Carpenters' and Caulkers' I.U. (1864)	Daughters of St. Crispin (shoemakers) (1869)
Cigar Makers' I.U. (1864)	Coopers' I.U. (barrel makers) (1870)
N.U. of Journeyman Curriers (tanners) (1864)	Morocco Dressers' N.U. (hide processors) (1870)
Plasterers' N.U. (1864, again 1871)	American Bricklayers' N.U. (1871)
Iron and Steel Heaters' I.U. (1865, again 1872)	N.U. of Woodworking Mechanics (1872)
Coachmakers' I.U. (1865)	Sons of Adam (cloth cutters) (1872)
Dry Goods Clerks' Early Closing Ass'n. (1865)	Brotherhood of Locomotive Firemen (1873)
Tailors I.U. (1865)	Boilers,' Roughers,' Catchers,' and Hookers,' N.U. (1873)

I.U.= International Union; N.U. = National Union.

contributed to this situation. The inability of these businesspeople to repay their loans led to the failure of major banks. With the contraction of credit, thousands of small businesses went bankrupt. The NLU did not survive the crisis.

However, by this time, a new organization had appeared to champion the cause of the laboring classes in opposition to lords of finance. Founded in 1869 by Uriah Stephens and other Philadelphia tailors, the Knights of Labor eventually aimed to unite industrial and rural workers, the self-employed and the wage earner, blacks and whites, and men and women. The Knights were committed to private property and to the independence of the farmer, the entrepreneur, and the industrial worker. The group banned from its ranks "nonproducers," such as liquor sellers, bankers, professional gamblers, stockbrokers, and lawyers.

This period of depression also laid the foundation for the Greenback Labor party, organized in 1878. Within three years after the end of the Civil War, the Treasury had withdrawn from circulation $100 million in wartime paper currency ("greenbacks"). With less money in circulation, debtors found it more difficult to repay their loans. The government also ceased coining silver dollars in 1873, despite the discovery of rich silver lodes in the West. To add insult to injury, the Resumption Act (1875) called for the government to continue to withdraw paper "greenbacks." Thus, hard money became dearer, and debtors became more desperate. In 1878 the new Greenback Labor party managed to win one million votes and elect 14 candidates to Congress. The party laid the foundation for the Populist party that emerged in the 1890s.

Several factors made coalition building among American workers difficult. One was the nation's increasingly multicultural workforce. Unions, such as the typographers, were notorious for excluding women and African Americans, a fact publicized by both Frederick Douglass and Susan B. Anthony, to no avail. In 1869 shoe factory workers (members of the Knights of St. Crispin) went on strike in North Adams, Massachusetts. They were soon shocked to see 75 Chinese strikebreakers arrive by train from California. Their employer praised the new arrivals for their "rare industry." The shoemakers' strike collapsed quickly after the appearance of what the Massachusetts workers called this "Mongolian battery." Employers would continue to manipulate and divide the laboring classes through the use of ethnic, religious, and racial prejudices.

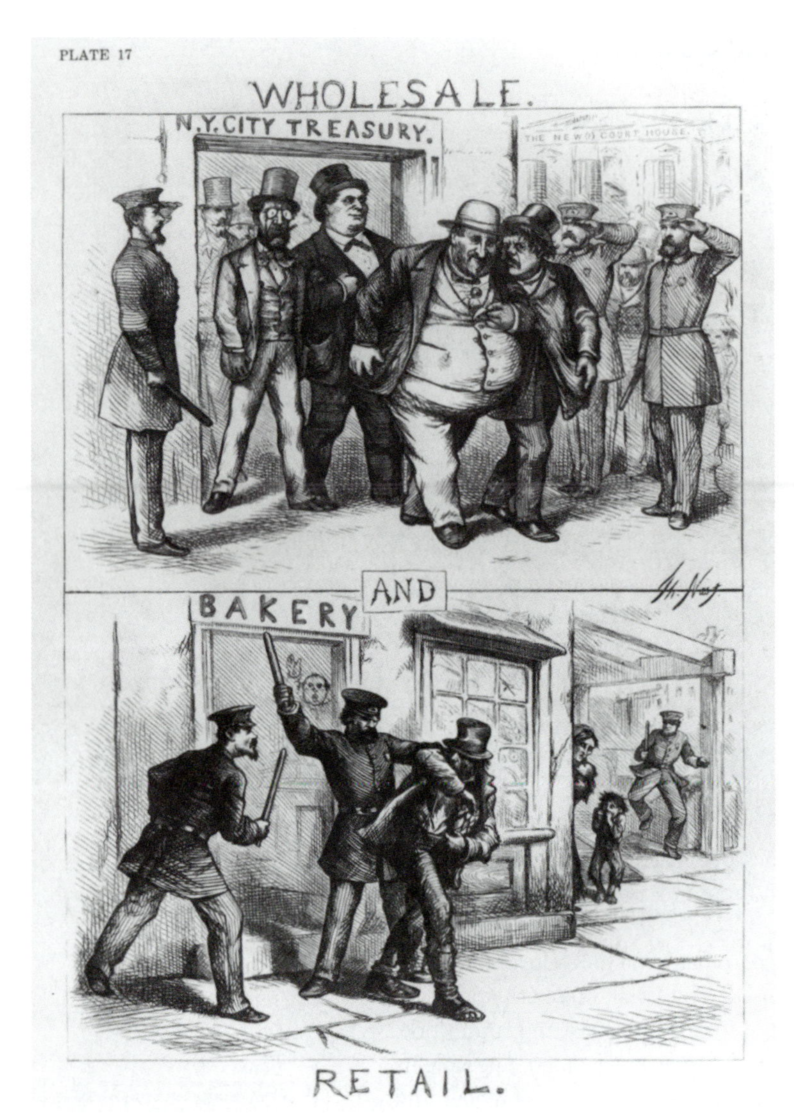

Harper's Weekly, September 16, 1871

▲ **In 1871 Thomas Nast drew a series of cartoons exposing the corruption of New York City Democratic boss William M. Tweed and his political organization, Tammany Hall. In this drawing, published in *Harper's Weekly,* Nast depicts Tweed and his cronies engaging in a "wholesale" looting of the New York City treasury with the assistance of compliant police officers. Those same officers stand ready to crack down on the impoverished father who robs a bakery to feed his family. By portraying Tweed as an enemy of the poor, Nast ignored the fact that the political boss gained a large following among immigrant voters.**

Political Corruption and the Decline of Republican Idealism

Out of the new partnership between politics and business emerged an extensive system of bribes and kickbacks. Greedy politicians of both parties challenged the Republicans' high-minded idealism.

In the early 1870s, the *New York Times* exposed the schemes of William M. "Boss" Tweed. Tweed headed Tammany Hall, a New York City political organization that courted labor unions and contributed liberally to Catholic schools and charities. Tammany Hall politicians routinely used bribery and extortion to fix elections and bilk taxpayers of millions of dollars. One plasterer employed on a city project received $138,000 in "payment" for two days' work. After the *Times* **exposé,** Tweed was prosecuted and convicted. His downfall attested to the growing influence of newspaper reporters.

Another piece of investigative journalism rocked the political world in 1872. In 1867 major stockholders of the Union Pacific Railroad had formed a new corporation, called the Crédit Mobilier, to build railroads. Heads of powerful congressional committees received shares of stock in the new company. These gifts of stock were bribes to secure the legislators' support for public land grants favorable to the new corporation. The *New York Sun* exposed a number of the chief beneficiaries in the fall of 1872, findings confirmed by congressional investigation. Among the disgraced politicians was Grant's vice president, Schuyler Colfax.

The 1872 presidential election pitted incumbent Grant against the Democratic challenger, *New York Tribune* editor Horace Greeley. Many Republicans, disillusioned with congressional corruption and eager to press forward with civil service reform, endorsed the Democratic candidate. Greeley and his Republican allies decried the patronage (or "spoils") system by which politicians rewarded their supporters with government jobs. Nevertheless, Grant won the election.

By 1872, after four bloody years of war and seven squandered years of postwar opportunity, the federal government seemed prepared to hand the South back to unrepentant rebels. The North showed what one House Republican called "a general apathy among the people concerning the war and the negro." The Civil Rights Act of 1875 guaranteed blacks equal access to public accommodations and transportation. Yet this act represented the final, half-hearted gesture of radical Republicanism. The Supreme Court declared the measure unconstitutional in 1883 on the grounds that the government could protect only political and not social rights. White Southerners reasserted their control over the region's political economy.

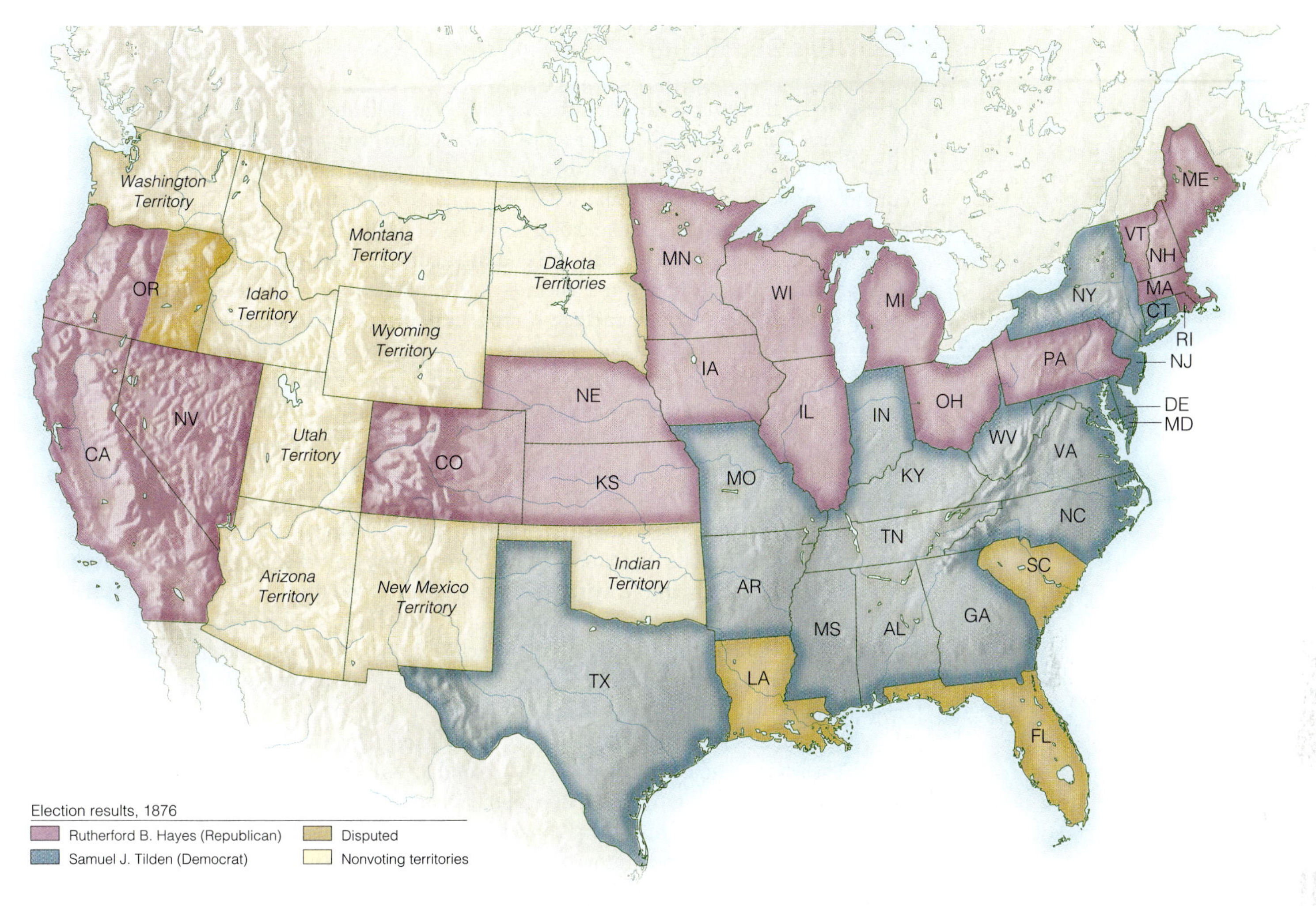

▲ **MAP 15.3 THE COMPROMISE OF 1877**
During the presidential election of 1876, returns from South Carolina, Florida, and Louisiana (the only states that remained under Republican control) were disputed. Under a compromise reached by Republicans and Democrats in Congress, Republican Rutherford B. Hayes became president and Congress removed all federal troops from the South.

The presidential election of 1876 intensified public cynicism about deal making in high places. A dispute over election returns led to what came to be known as the Compromise of 1877. In the popular vote, Democrat Samuel J. Tilden outpolled Republican Rutherford B. Hayes, a former Ohio governor. However, when the electoral votes were counted, the Democrat had only 184, one short of the necessary number. Nineteen of the 20 votes in dispute came from Louisiana, South Carolina, and Florida, and these three states submitted two new sets of returns, one from each of the two main parties. A specially appointed congressional electoral commission, the Committee of Fifteen, was charged with resolving the dispute. It divided along partisan lines. The eight Republicans outvoted the seven Democrats to accept the Republican set of returns from Florida.

To break the logjam, the Democrats agreed that Hayes could assume office in return for the withdrawal of all remaining federal troops from the South. The Republicans tacitly agreed that their work there was finished and that blacks in the region should fend for themselves. Hayes declined to enforce the Civil Rights Act of 1875. White Southerners were free to uphold the principle of states' rights that had been traditionally invoked to deny blacks their rights in the region.

Conclusion

During the dozen or so years after the Civil War, both northern Republicans and southern Democrats registered a series of spectacular wins and crushing losses. Though humiliated by the Union victory, southern white supremacists eventually won the freedom to control their own local and state governments. As landlords, sheriffs, and merchants, they defied the postwar federal amendments to the Constitution and deprived African Americans of basic citizenship rights. By the end of Reconstruction, northern Republicans had conceded local power to their former enemies. Apparently, even an aggressive nationalism could accept traditional southern hierarchies: white over nonwhite, rich over poor.

Yet the Civil War was not only a fight between whites. During the conflict, black people had served as combatants in the struggle for freedom. They saw the war in different terms than did northern white Republicans and southern white Democrats. After the war, blacks pursued full citizenship rights while attempting to maintain institutional and cultural autonomy from white people regardless of political affiliation. In their quest, freed men and women met with mixed success. They gained the status of citizens under federal amendments to the Constitution, and black men gained the right to vote. Yet white Republicans, both in Congress and in southern state legislatures, proved to be disappointing allies to blacks who found themselves, increasingly, at the mercy of white vigilante and other terrorist groups. During the Reconstruction period, blacks consolidated their families, established their own churches, and sought to work on their own terms in the fields. Yet lacking money and credit, they found it difficult to buy land and in the process achieve true independence from white landowners, bankers, and politicians.

At the end of Reconstruction, Republicans remained in firm control of national economic policy. The white South had secured its right to conduct its own political affairs, but the Republican vision of economic growth and development had become the law of the land. This vision was a guiding principle of historic national and, increasingly, international significance. Economic innovation in particular proved to be a force of great unifying power, stronger even than all the federal military forces deployed during and after the Civil War.

Sites to Visit

The Impeachment of Andrew Johnson

www.impeach-andrewjohnson.com/

This site about the impeachment includes images and text from the Reconstruction period.

Diary and Letters of Rutherford B. Hayes

www.rbhayes.org

The Rutherford B. Hayes Presidential Center in Fremont, Ohio, maintains a searchable database of his writings.

Freedmen and Southern Society Project

www.inform.umd.edu/ARHU/Depts/History/Freedman/home.html

This University of Maryland, College Park, site contains a chronology and sample documents from several collections or primary sources about emancipation and freedom in the 1860s.

History of the Suffrage Movement

www.rochester.edu/SBA

This site includes a chronology, important texts relating to women's suffrage, and bibliographical information about Susan B. Anthony and Elizabeth Cady Stanton.

Indian Memorial at Little Big Horn Battlefield National Monument

www.nps.gov/libi/indmem.htm

The National Park Service maintains this site featuring the National Monument near Crow Agency, Montana.

National Museum of the American Indian

www.si.edu/nmai

The Smithsonian Institution maintains this site, providing information about the museum.

The Northern Great Plains, 1880–1920: Photographs from the Fred Hulstrand and F. A. Pazandak Photograph Collections

www.memory.loc.gov.ammem/award97/ndfahtml/ngphome.html

This American Memory site from the Library of Congress contains two collections from the Institute for Regional Studies at North Dakota State University with 900 photographs of rural and small-town life at the turn of the twentieth century. Included are images of sod homes and the people who built them, farms and the machinery that made them prosper, and one-room schools and the children who were educated in them.

Chinese American Contribution to Transcontinental Railroad

cprr.org/museum/Chinese.html

This site contains photographs and text related to the Chinese workers who built the Transcontinental Railroad.

For Further Reading

General Works

Michael W. Fitzgerald, *Urban Emancipation: Popular Politics in Reconstruction Mobile, 1860–1890* (2002).

Eric Foner, *Reconstruction: America's Unfinished Revolution, 1863–1877* (1988).

David Montgomery, *Beyond Equality: Labor and the Radical Republicans, 1862–1872* (1967).

Amy Dru Stanley, *From Bondage to Contract: Wage Labor, Marriage, and the Market in the Age of Slave Emancipation* (1998).

Ronald Takaki, *A Different Mirror: A History of Multicultural America* (1993).

Richard White, *"It's Your Misfortune and None of My Own": A History of the American West* (1991).

The Struggle over the South

Peter Bardaglio, *Reconstructing the Household: Families, Sex and the Law in the Nineteenth-Century South* (1995).

Ira Berlin and Leslie S. Rowland, eds., *Families and Freedom: A Documentary History of African-American Kinship in the Civil War Era* (1997).

Dwight B. Billings, *Planters and the Making of a "New South": Class, Politics, and Development in North Carolina, 1865–1900* (1979).

Jane Turner Censer, *The Reconstruction of White Southern Womanhood, 1865–1895* (2003).

Frederick Cooper, Thomas C. Holt, and Rebecca J. Scott, eds., *Beyond Slavery: Explorations of Race, Labor, and Citizenship in Post-Emancipation Societies* (2000).

Wilma A. Dunaway, *The African-American Family in Slavery and Emancipation* (2003).

Michael Golay, *A Ruined Land: The End of the Civil War* (1999).

Thomas C. Holt, *Black over White: Negro Political Leadership in South Carolina During Reconstruction* (1977).

Jacqueline Jones, *Soldiers of Light and Love: Northern Teachers and Georgia Blacks, 1865–1873* (1980).

Claiming Territory for the Union

Stephen E. Ambrose, *Nothing Like It in the World: The Men Who Built the Transcontinental Railroad, 1863–1869* (2000).

Orin G. Libby, ed., *The Arikara Narrative of the Campaign Against the Hostile Dakotas, June, 1876* (1998).

Ruth B. Moynihan, Susan Armitage, and Christiane Fischer Dichamp, eds., *So Much to Be Done: Women Settlers on the Mining and Ranching Frontier* (1990).

Larry Sklenar, *To Hell with Honor: Custer and the Little Bighorn* (2000).

Robert Wooster, *The Military and United States Indian Policy, 1865–1903* (1988).

Judy Yung, *Unbound Feet: A Social History of Chinese Women in San Francisco* (1995).

The Republican Vision and Its Limits

Leon Fink, *Workingmen's Democracy: The Knights of Labor and American Politics* (1983).

Barbara Goldsmith, *Other Powers: The Age of Suffrage, Spiritualism, and the Scandalous Victoria Woodhull* (1998).

Heather Cox Richardson, *The Death of Reconstruction: Race, Labor and Politics in the Post–Civil War North* (2001).

Lyde Cullen Sizer, *The Political Work of Northern Women Writers and the Civil War* (2000).

Irwin Unger, *The Greenback Era: A Social and Political History of American Finance, 1865–1879* (1964).

C. Vann Woodward, *Reunion and Reaction: The Compromise of 1877 and the End of Reconstruction* (1956).

PART SIX

The Emergence of Modern America, 1877–1900

1877	All federal troops withdrawn from the South, ending Reconstruction. "Great Uprising" of railroad employees and other workers.
1878	Thomas Edison patents the phonograph. San Francisco Workingmen's party stages anti-Chinese protests.
1879	First telephone line connects two American cities (Boston and Lowell, Massachusetts).
1880	New York City streets lit by electricity.
1881	Charles Guiteau assassinates President Garfield.
1882	Standard Oil Trust is created. Chinese Exclusion Act.
1883	Pendleton Act (civil service reform).
1884	Mark Twain, *The Adventures of Huckleberry Finn.*
1885	Geronimo leads Apache to Sierra Madres in Mexico.
1886	Accused Haymarket bombers tried and convicted. Geronimo and his followers are sent to Fort Marion, Florida; the children are sent to the government Indian school in Carlisle, Pennsylvania.
1887	Interstate Commerce Act creates Interstate Commerce Commission. Dawes Severalty Act. United States claims right to Pearl Harbor, leases it as a coaling and repair station.
1888	Edward Bellamy, *Looking Backward.*
1889	First All-American football team, consisting of players from Yale, Harvard, and Princeton. National Farmers' Alliance is founded.

The United States became a modern nation during the last quarter of the nineteenth century. Vast reserves of coal, timber, and water helped fuel a growing industrial economy. Railroad lines criss-crossed the nation and knit together regional economies. Large numbers of immigrants, many from eastern Europe, arrived in the United States, drawn by America's rising standard of living, high demand for labor, and religious and political freedom.

To raise the money needed to purchase expensive equipment and machinery, coal and oil producers and railroad owners formed modern corporations, businesses that were owned by stockholders rather than individuals. The largest businesses sought to dominate the marketplace by eliminating their competitors. Managers could cut production and operating costs by slashing the wages of workers or by installing labor-saving machinery. Either way, workers paid the price.

The generation that came of age after the Civil War witnessed a series of violent confrontations between workers and employers. Standards of industrial work discipline required workers to labor for long hours at dangerous, disagreeable jobs. Some workers formed new kinds of labor unions to combat the power of big business. Some organizations, such as the Knights of Labor, were national in scope and inclusive in their membership; others represented the interests of specific groups of workers. Employers, local and state law enforcement officials, and judges used a variety of means to suppress strikes and other forms of collective action among workers. Nevertheless, local communities often supported the strikers, who were their friends and neighbors.

During the late nineteenth century, the national economy began to shift to the production of consumer goods. New products gave Americans new ways to spend their money. Manufacturers of everything from toothpaste to bathtubs advertised their goods to a mass market. In cities, department stores offered a dazzling array of goods.

Even as the country was becoming more ethnically diverse, advertisers promoted a single standard of physical beauty and material well-being. At the same time, some scholars and politicians seized on a revolutionary new theory of natural history to argue for the superiority of white, middle-class Americans. Social Darwinism served as the intellectual justification for unfettered economic growth and for the subjugation of darker-skinned peoples, at home and abroad.

Many Americans rejected the trends toward economic standardization and cultural homogeneity. Native Americans in the West continued to resist the railroad and its profound threat to their way of life. By 1890 the U.S. military had forcefully subdued most of these Indians, relegating many to reservations. Together with industrial workers throughout the nation, Hispanic villagers in the Southwest and African American sharecroppers in the South disputed the notion that progress could be defined exclusively in terms of economic growth and development.

Middle-class reformers sought to mediate between what they perceived to be two dangerous groups: arrogant industrialists and discontented workers. These reformers feared that rapid urban and industrial growth would cause rifts in the social fabric. Middle-class women pioneered in the founding of social settlements and other urban institutions to ease the transition of immigrants into modern American society.

The lines between national standards and local cultural interests often blurred. For example, for a short time Sioux chief Sitting Bull (Tatanka Iyotake) appeared with William ("Buffalo Bill") Cody's "Wild West" show, which played to enthusiastic audiences in the United States and Europe. Yet this Indian leader also led the Plains Indians as they attempted to resist U.S. military authorities. Some groups of Americans who sought to preserve their own cultural traditions nonetheless aspired to a middle-class way of life and its material comforts. Elite Hispanic families in the Southwest remained devoted to their Roman Catholic faith and at the same time followed up-to-date clothing fashions marketed by East Coast department stores.

The promise and the conflicts inherent in the emerging modern social order met head on in the 1890s. A new political party called the Populists mounted a brief but potent challenge to entrenched economic and political power. The Populists failed in their attempt to capture the presidency in 1896, but they offered a vision of a new kind of political party, one that would bring black and white farmers and industrial workers together in opposition to landlords, employers, and bankers.

In 1898, in an effort to protect its interests in the Western Hemisphere and to extend those interests into the Pacific, the United States went to war with Spain. This imperialist venture suggested the links among several impulses, including missionary outreach, commercial expansion, and white supremacist racial ideologies. By 1900 the United States was fast becoming a world leader in terms of manufacturing, technological innovation, and the rapid growth of its prosperous middle class.

1890 Sherman Anti-Trust Act.
Wyoming admitted to the Union, first state to enfranchise women.
National American Woman Suffrage Association is formed.
Wounded Knee Massacre.

1891 Populist Party formed.
Eleven Italian immigrants are lynched in New Orleans.

1892 Ellis Island opens as screening site for immigrants.
Miners strike in Coeur d'Alene, Idaho.
Steelworkers strike at Carnegie's Homestead plant near Pittsburgh.

1893 Columbian Exposition opens in Chicago.
Pro-American interests stage a successful coup against Queen Liliuokalani of Hawaii.
Worst nationwide economic depression to date.

1894 Coxey's Army marches on Washington, D.C.
Pullman workers strike.

1896 Supreme Court decides *Plessy v. Ferguson*, upholds segregation.
W. E. B. DuBois is first black person to receive a Ph.D. from Harvard.

1898 United States annexes Hawaii.
Maine blows up in Havana Harbor.
United States defeats Spain in Spanish-American-Cuban-Filipino War.
Spain cedes Guam and Puerto Rico to United States, turns over Philippines in return for $20 million.

1899 Gen. Emilio Aguinaldo leads Filipino revolt against 70,000 U.S. occupying forces.

1900 U.S. troops sent to China to crush Boxer Rebellion.

CHAPTER 16

Standardizing the Nation: Innovations in Technology, Business, and Culture, 1877–1890

CHAPTER OUTLINE

The New Shape of Business

The Birth of a National Urban Culture

Thrills, Chills, and Bathtubs: The Emergence of Consumer Culture

Defending the New Industrial Order

Conclusion

Sites to Visit

For Further Reading

Courtesy, Transcendental Graphics

▲ A late-nineteenth-century crowd enjoys a baseball game on a summer day. These fans show some of the same characteristics of their twenty-first-century counterparts—men and women cheer lustily for the home team, and at least one spectator is enjoying a mug of beer. During this period, the number of professional baseball teams multiplied. Games such as this one turned athletic competitions into forms of mass entertainment.

ANDREW CARNEGIE LIVED A LIFE FULL OF CONTRASTS AND CONTRADICTIONS. BORN into an immigrant family of modest means, he made a fortune in the steel industry; eventually he became the richest man in the world. At one point a strong supporter of labor unions, he nevertheless yielded day-to-day control of his steel mills to his business partner, who oversaw the brutal suppression of striking workers in 1892. A savvy manager and innovator, he remained dependent on his mother and waited until she died (when he was 43 years old) before he felt free to marry. Possessed of an immense fortune, he tried mightily to give almost all of it away.

In 1835 Will and Margaret Carnegie were living in the village of Dunfermline, Scotland, where Will was a skilled weaver. The couple had two sons—Andrew, born in 1835, and Tom, born eight years later. When steam-powered textile looms threw Will Carnegie and other handweavers out of work, the family emigrated to the United States and settled in Pittsburgh, Pennsylvania. Eager to work hard, Andrew took a series of jobs to help support the family: bobbin boy in a textile mill, tender of a steam boiler in a factory, clerk and then messenger in a telegraph office. By the time he was 18 years old, he was personal assistant to Thomas Scott, superintendent of the Western Division of the Pennsylvania Railroad. Three years later, after the death of his father, Andrew assumed the role of family breadwinner; he also took over the job of Thomas Scott, who became president of the railroad.

HultonIArchive/Getty Images

When Andrew Carnegie retired in 1901, he sold the Carnegie Steel Company to American banker and financier J. P. Morgan for $480 million. Carnegie's personal fortune was about $500 million.

Working for the railroad, Andrew Carnegie learned a great deal about running a gigantic business efficiently and profitably. He also invested in oil and railroads. In 1872 he visited England and gained firsthand information about the production of steel, a lighter, stronger material than iron. Three years later he opened his own steel plant, the Edgar Thomson works in Pittsburgh. Carnegie named the plant for the current president of the Pennsylvania Railroad. He then proceeded to buy rival steel mills. In 1892 Carnegie's business partner, Henry Clay Frick, took extraordinary steps to end a strike among 10,000 workers at Homestead, another of Carnegie's plants in Pittsburgh; Frick relied on a private security force, the Pinkertons, and 8,000 state militia to put down the strike. Nine strikers and seven Pinkertons died in the ensuing violence, and the steelworkers' union, the Amalgamated Association of Steel and Iron Workers, was virtually crushed.

In his business life, Andrew Carnegie was a man of strong principles. In 1868 he promised himself that he would not hoard the money he made; instead he would promote the "education and improvement of the poorer classes." Earning $25 million a year by the early 1890s, he nonetheless believed that "The amassing of wealth is one of the worst species of idolatry." During the course of his career, Carnegie gave away

90 percent of his fortune, founding the Carnegie Endowment for International Peace, as well as many public libraries around the country.

At the same time, Carnegie remained devoted to his mother. They shared an apartment in a fashionable New York hotel. She occasionally accompanied him when he went to meetings and otherwise attended to his business. Margaret Carnegie believed that "There is no woman good enough to marry my Andra," prompting her son to postpone marrying Louise Whitfield, his longtime romantic interest. Margaret Carnegie died in 1886, and Andrew and Louise married the following year. Their wedding was a small, intimate affair, with only 30 guests in attendance. By the end of his life, Carnegie had earned a total of $350 million—the equivalent of $3 billion in today's dollars.

By 1877 the emergence of a national rail system signaled the rise of big business.

It was significant that Carnegie spent his formative years in business learning about railroads. These lessons paved the way for his own success in the steel industry. By 1877 the emergence of a national rail system signaled the rise of big business. The railroad industry produced America's first business bureaucracies, employing gigantic workforces to maintain, schedule, operate, and staff trains that traversed 93,000 miles of track. By 1890 the Pennsylvania Railroad had become the nation's largest employer, with 110,000 workers on its payroll. About one out of seven people worked in the rail industry. The personnel in charge of coordinating these vast operations were among the country's first professional, salaried managers.

The railroad industry was both a great centralizer and a great standardizer. Trains ran on schedules that were set by a central office, and those schedules relied on definitions of actual time that were standard throughout the nation. Moreover, trains broke down regional boundaries by transporting goods to all areas of the country. For the first time, trains carried brand-name goods and commodities to a national market. A California wheat farmer could purchase replacement parts for his McCormick reaper manufactured in Chicago. An Iowa farm family ordered a new cookstove through a mail-order catalogue. Levi-Strauss, a small clothier in San Francisco, shipped its famous denim pants to cowboys in Texas. Pillsbury Flour of Minnesota distributed its products to bakeries throughout the Midwest. Armour Meatpacking of Chicago sent its sausages to the East Coast. With the introduction of the new refrigerated railroad car, trains also began carrying larger loads of fruits and vegetables over longer distances. The new traffic in produce stimulated commercial agriculture in the South and on the West Coast.

Few Americans amassed the fabulous fortunes of rich industrialists like Carnegie, yet most people aspired to a better life, even in modest terms. Proprietors, managers, and office workers filled the ranks of the comfortable middle class, men and women freed of the danger and drudgery of manual labor. Between 1880 and 1900, clerical workers tripled in number, and business managers increased from 68,000 to more than 318,000. Enjoying steady work and cash salaries, middle-class employees began to move their families out of the city. Urban areas were becoming increasingly befouled by smokestacks and congested with new factories and workshops.

Providers of goods and services celebrated a "standard" American viewed as white, native-born, middle-class, heterosexual, and Protestant. This image assumed special significance in the marketing of consumer products and in the appeal of new forms of leisure activities. Mass advertising techniques heightened distinctions that European Americans drew between themselves and people they considered inferior, exotic, or foreign.

Yet the energy and vitality associated with American popular culture served as a magnet for people all over the world. Beginning in the 1880s, eastern European immigrants streamed to the United States. They were also eager to partake of the country's plentiful jobs, material prosperity, and democratic openness. Well into the twentieth century, the nation still showed the ethnic and cultural diversity that was shaped by patterns of immigration during the late nineteenth century.

Population growth spurred the growth of industries that exploited nature. Between 1880 and 1890, the U.S. population grew from 50 million people to almost 63 million, and six new states entered the Union: North Dakota, South Dakota, Montana, and Washington in 1889; Idaho and Wyoming in 1890. Increased demand in turn hastened large-scale commercial mining, logging, and fishing.

Economic growth produced contradictory effects. Blessed with abundant and diverse natural resources, American industries became competitive in the world marketplace. However, miners and loggers tended to "cut and run," despoiling streams and forests in the process. Economic growth and development transformed natural landscapes throughout the United States. Citizens in general benefited from the proliferation of new technological marvels, but consumers bore the brunt when big business raised prices and eliminated competition within an industry. Certain workers suffered when new machines displaced them from their jobs.

During the last third of the nineteenth century, the rise of big business, the mass production of consumer goods, and innovations in transportation produced national standards that shaped the economic and social life of the nation. Placing advertisements in newspapers and popular magazines, large companies sought to market their products to all parts of the country. These products, from bathtubs to new fashions in dress, helped to set the standard for middle-class life. In addition, advertising conveyed to the buying public an image of "American" beauty; this standard was narrow by definition but supposedly universal in its appeal. New kinds of commercialized leisure activities, such as shows, athletic competitions, and amusement parks, promoted the idea that all Americans, regardless where they lived or what they did for a living, valued spectacles and thrilling forms of entertainment. At the same time, not all people embraced these standards or the assumption that underlay them—the notion that new kinds of goods and entertainment represented progress in American life.

The New Shape of Business

In 1882 prospectors discovered gold in the creeks of Idaho's Coeur d'Alene region (in Indian territory, about 90 miles east of Spokane, Washington). Multiethnic boomtowns mushroomed in the region. The Northern Pacific Railway promoted settlement, and the primitive techniques that had been used in surface mining soon yielded to far more efficient hydraulic methods of extraction (a process in which powerful water hoses wash the soil away to expose gold deposits).

The mining industry in the region soon emerged as a big business. In 1885 an unemployed carpenter named Noah S. Kellogg set in motion a dramatic chain of events. Kellogg discovered a lode containing not only gold but also zinc and lead. In short order, he sold his mines to a Portland businessman, who paid a whopping $650,000 for them. A group of eastern and California investors, and finally several large corporations, soon controlled major interests in the mines. By the mid-twentieth century, mining companies had dug more than a billion dollars' worth of metal out of Noah Kellogg's original stake.

Crucial to the process of innovation were engineers.

Crucial to the process of innovation were engineers, who mastered the technical aspects of construction and design. Many American engineers were trained in Germany, but others attended such schools as the Massachusetts Institute of Technology (MIT) or Cornell University in New York State, both of which introduced electrical engineering into their curricula in 1882. American engineers, such as those who worked in Mexico under the auspices of mining companies and the railroads, served as the vanguard of American capitalism throughout the world.

Advocates of standardized industrial processes and mass marketing hoped to break down regional barriers and create an integrated national economy. Whether they specialized in railroads or shoes, wheat or steel, business owners and managers who possessed the necessary resources and resourcefulness pursued similar goals: to mine, grow, manufacture, or process large quantities of goods and then market them as widely, cheaply, and quickly as possible. Business put a premium on technological innovation, on the efficient use of workers, and on the reduction of uncertainties that accompanied a competitive marketplace. These guiding principles, formulated during the late 1870s and 1880s, laid the foundations of economic progress in late-nineteenth-century America.

New Systems and Machines—and Their Price

The free enterprise system thrived on innovation. Indeed, during the 1880s, new machines, new technical processes, new engineering feats, and new forms of factory organization fueled the growth and efficiency of U.S. businesses. Many devices that became staples of American life appeared during this period. Alexander Graham Bell invented the telephone in 1876. Thomas A. Edison developed the phonograph in 1877 and the electric light in 1879. Cash registers, stock tickers, and typewriters soon became indispensable tools for American businesses. Beginning in the 1880s, railroad cars installed steam heat and electric lights, boosting the comfort of passengers.

DOCUMENT
Edison, "The Success of the Electric Light"

During this period, more and more businesses perfected the so-called American system of manufacturing, which dated back half a century and relied on the mass production of interchangeable parts. Factory workers made large numbers of a particular part, each part exactly the same size and shape. This system enabled manufacturers to assemble products more cheaply and efficiently, to repair products easily with new parts, and to redesign products quickly. The engineers who designed the modern bicycle (which has wheels of equal size) used the American system to make their product affordable to almost anyone who wanted one. The bicy-

Oregon Historical Society, OrHi 92918

▶ **Bonanza farms were huge agricultural enterprises, ranging in size from 15,000 to 50,000 acres. This photo shows a bonanza wheat farm in Oregon, c. 1890. Many of these farms relied not only on sophisticated machinery but also on transient labor forces (up to 1,000 workers at a time) to help plow, plant, harvest, and thresh the crop. Some of the largest landowners abandoned farming when they had an opportunity to sell their vast holdings for a profit.**

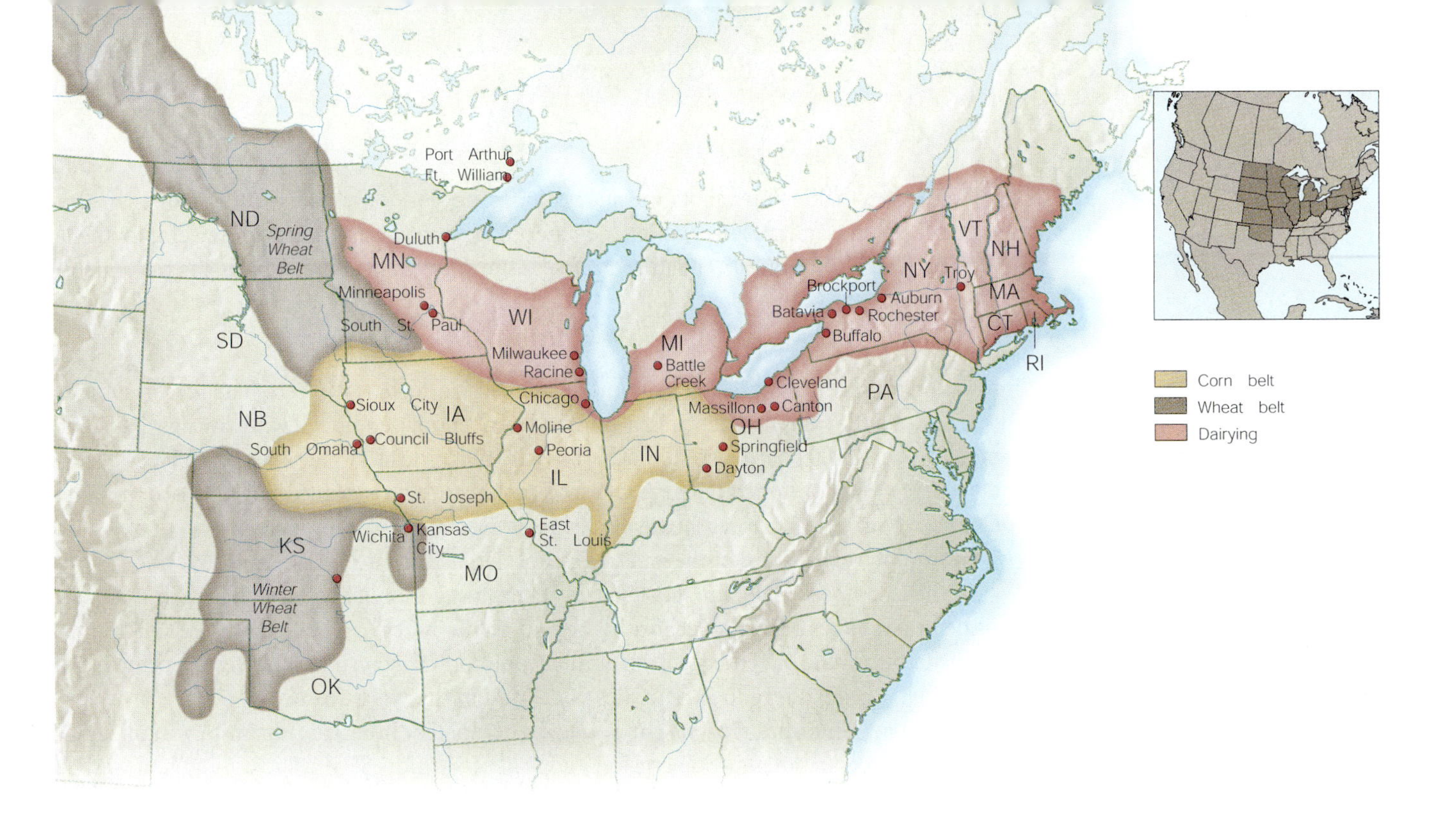

▲ **MAP 16.1 AGRICULTURAL REGIONS OF THE MIDWEST AND NORTHEAST**
By 1890 several Midwestern cities served as shipping centers, getting wheat and corn to the growing metropolitan areas of the Northeast and Mid-Atlantic. Farmers complained that the railroads gave discounts to large shippers, such as Standard Oil, and discriminated against small producers.

cle craze of the late nineteenth century resulted from the novelty and cheapness of this new form of transportation and recreation, one enjoyed by males and females of all ages. Production techniques used to make bicycles were later adapted to the manufacture of automobiles.

New technical processes also facilitated the manufacture and marketing of foods and other consumer goods. Distributors developed pressure-sealed cans, which enabled them to market agricultural products in far-flung parts of the country. Innovative techniques for sheet metal stamping and electric resistance welding transformed a variety of industries. By 1880, 90 percent of American steel was made by the Bessemer process, which injected air into molten iron to yield steel.

The agriculture business benefited from engineering innovations as well, which often reached across national boundaries. As just one example, the first modern irrigation systems in the Southwest were constructed by Native Americans and *mestizos* (people of both indigenous and Spanish ancestry). And in the 1870s, Japan began importing American farm implements and inviting U.S. engineers to construct dams and canals for new steam- and water-powered gristmills and sawmills. Technology was a universal language, one that many peoples around the globe sought to master.

Long active in territorial exploration and land surveying, the federal government continued to assume a leading role in applied science. In 1879 the U.S. Geological Survey (USGS) was formed, charged with compiling and centralizing data describing the natural landscape, an effort that had originated in 1804 with the Lewis and Clark expedition. In the 1880s, the federal government also began to systematize and disseminate information useful to farmers through the United States Department of Agriculture. In 1881, for example, the department's Entomology Bureau began to combine current research on insects with practical techniques for pest control.

Like factory machines, new agricultural machinery benefited consumers, but the need for hired hands evaporated. Early in the nineteenth century, harvesting an acre of wheat took 56 hours of labor; in 1880, that number dropped to 20 hours. One agricultural worker in Ohio observed, "Of one thing we are convinced, that while improved machinery is gathering our large crops, making our boots and shoes, doing the work of our carpenters, stone sawyers, and builders, thousands of able, willing men are going from place to place seeking employment, and finding none. The question naturally arises, is improved machinery a blessing or a curse?"

Resources and Conflict in the West

Alterations in the Natural Environment

Innovation altered the natural landscape and hastened the depletion of certain natural resources. By the mid-1870s, Texas had new steam-powered lumber mills equipped with saw rigs that could produce up to 30,000 board feet a day. This capacity made Texas lumbering a big business, especially when it was combined with infusions of capital and the expansion of railroad lines into the piney woods region, along the eastern edge of the state. Texas lumber mills were poised to benefit from the exhaustion of the great forests of the eastern and Great Lakes states.

In the Chesapeake Bay, dredge boats were becoming more efficient in harvesting oysters, and shellfish reserves began to decline. In the mid-1880s oyster harvesters took a record 15 million bushels from the bay; the shellfish simply could not replenish themselves. New means of commercial fishing also reduced supplies of salmon in the Northwest.

In 1884 in California, a federal court issued a permanent injunction against hydraulic mining, because it contributed to soil erosion and water pollution. Hydraulic mining had washed

▶ **FIGURE 16.1**
AMOUNT OF FOREST CLEARING EACH DECADE, BY MAJOR REGION, 1850–1909 (IN THOUSANDS OF ACRES)

an estimated 12 billion tons of earth into San Francisco Bay, raising the floor of the bay several feet. At the same time, mercury flowing into nearby streams from gold mines in the San Jose hills was poisoning fish in the bay, creating pollution that would be felt well into the twentieth century. Similar cases of industrial pollution despoiled other parts of the country. In the absence of any laws to restrain them, Chicago meatpackers befouled the Chicago River with the byproducts of sausage, glue, and fertilizer.

By stimulating manufacturing and **extractive enterprises** alike, the railroads powered these great environmental transformations, for better or worse. Trains enabled entrepreneurs to develop large-scale copper mines in Arizona, gigantic herds of longhorn cattle in Kansas, and vast steel mills in western Pennsylvania. Every western town clamored for a railroad station; they knew that places bypassed by the rails withered and died. The railroads enabled tourists to enjoy the beauty of western wilderness areas. Yet the railroads had an insatiable demand for lumber. Between the late 1870s and 1890, U.S. railroads accounted for 20 to 25 percent of all lumber consumed in the nation. They used wood for fuel, fences, trestles, and stations, along with countless railroad ties. In 1890 scientists estimated that the railroads would need 73 million board feet each year to make new ties to lay beneath expanding lines and to replace ties eaten by pests and decayed with age.

Since buffalo herds impeded rail travel, railroads promoted the shooting of buffalo from trains, a "sport" that almost eradicated the species. By the mid-1880s, the great herds had disappeared, victims of ecological change (the incursion of horses into grazing areas), disease (brucellosis spread by domestic livestock), and commercial enterprise. Eastern consumers prized buffalo-hide coats, and eastern factories used the hides to make steam-engine drive belts. Sioux leader Black Elk decried the slaughter and the "heaps of bones" left to rot in the sun.

Innovations in Financing and Organizing Business

As agents of economic development and cultural change, the railroads knew no peer. As private enterprises, however, they faced the same challenges that all big businesses ultimately must address. The proliferation of independent lines and the high fixed costs associated with the

Courtesy, Burton Historical Collection, Detroit Public Library

◀ **Following the wholesale slaughter of buffalo on the Great Plains, settlers earned money by gathering the skeletons. "The bones are shipped East by the carloads," reported the Dodge City *Times*, "where they are ground and used for fertilizing and manufactured into numerous useful articles." This mound of buffalo bones at the Michigan Carlson Works in Detroit, c. 1880, suggests the extent of the devastation.**

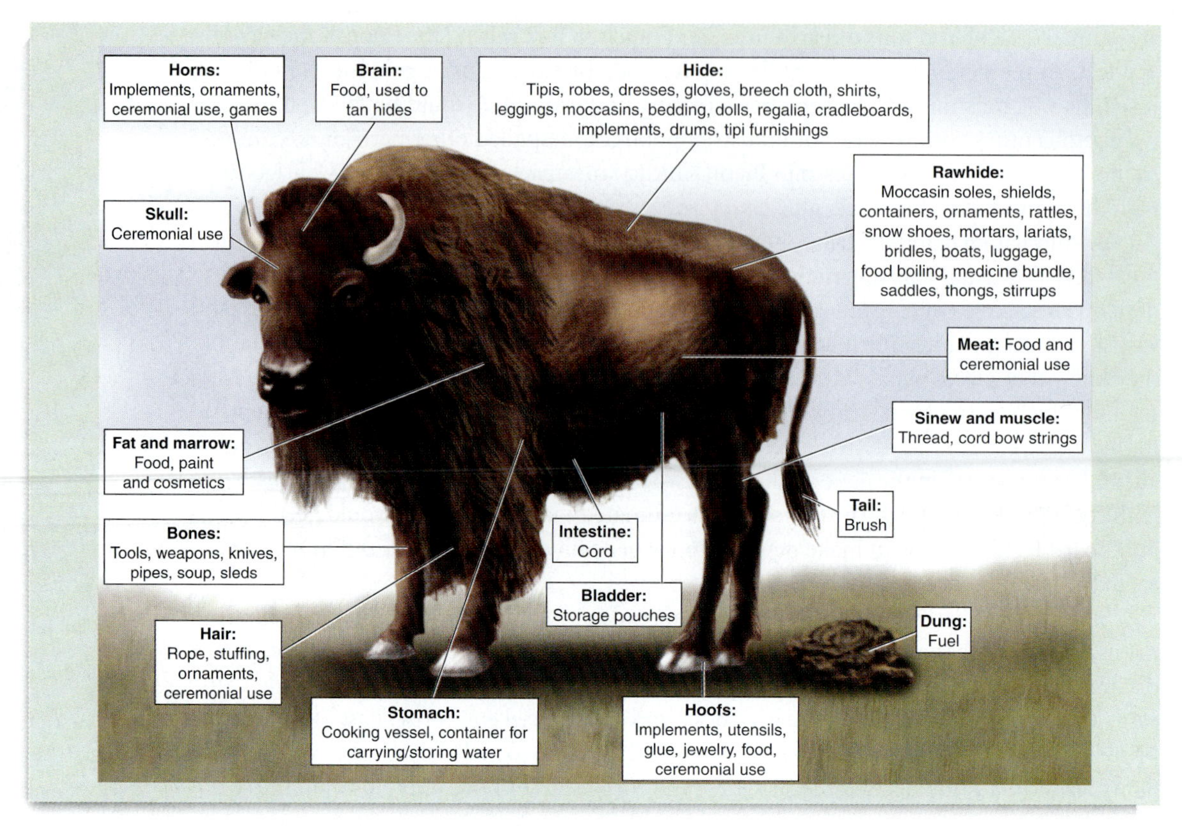

▲ **FIGURE 16.2** HOW INDIANS USED THE BUFFALO

industry made profits slim and competition intense. As a result, railroad companies began to come together in informal pools to share equipment and set prices industrywide. In the 1880s these pools gave way to consolidation, a process by which several companies merged into one large company.

In these years U.S. businesses grew larger and more quickly compared with their western European counterparts. This difference stemmed in large part from America's astonishing population growth and its rich natural resources. Equally significant, the United States possessed a social and legal culture favorable to big business. The absence of an entrenched, conservative elite, along with the spread of state and national laws that protected private property, stimulated the entrepreneurial spirit. The U.S. government refrained from owning industries, although it heavily subsidized the railroad industry. It taxed business lightly and did not tax individual incomes at all until 1913. Finally, American bankers such as J. P. Morgan aggressively promoted growth through their lending practices and bond sales.

Several large enterprises began to conquer not just local but also national markets. Examples include Bell Telephone (founded in Boston), the Kroger grocery business (Cincinnati), Marshall Field department store (Chicago), and Boston Fruit Company. In the South, Midwest, and West, investors rushed to finance gigantic mining operations and agribusinesses, such as the 1.5 million acres devoted to rice cultivation in southeastern Louisiana and bonanza wheat farms (as large as 38,000 acres) in the Red River Valley of North Dakota.

Owners of these enterprises devised new forms of business organization that helped them grow and survive in a dynamic economy. By combining, or integrating, their operations, manufacturers cut costs and monopolized an entire industry in the process. Unable to withstand the ruthless competition that favored larger enterprises, smaller companies folded. The two icons of American big business in the 1880s—Andrew Carnegie in steel and John D. Rockefeller in petroleum—proved master innovators in both the managerial and technical aspects of business.

In 1875 Carnegie opened the Edgar Thomson Steelworks in Pittsburgh. Within a year, he was producing steel at half the prevailing market price. Carnegie excelled at vertical integration, in which a single firm controls all aspects of production and distribution. Carnegie employed laborers in the Lake Superior region to mine the raw material, and he owned the ships and railroads that brought the ore to the mills in Pittsburgh.

Another form of business consolidation was horizontal integration, in which a number of companies producing the same product merge to reduce competition and control prices. In 1882 John D. Rockefeller, a former bookkeeper, horizontally integrated the petroleum industry by forming Standard Oil Trust. Stockholders in small companies turned over their shares to Standard Oil, which then coordinated operations and eliminated competition from other smaller firms. Standard Oil also practiced vertical integration. Like Carnegie, Rockefeller controlled not only a raw material (in this case, crude oil) but also processing plants, or refineries. He managed to keep transportation costs low by negotiating discount rates from rail shippers. Soon he had positioned himself to buy out his rivals—or ruin them. **Trusts** placed a premium on efficient production, but they also worked to the disadvantage of consumers, who were hostage to high prices within industries that lacked competition.

Trusts helped to eliminate some of the uncertainty associated with an unstable marketplace.

For the growing managerial class, trusts helped to eliminate some of the uncertainty associated with an unstable marketplace. They ensured industries' access to raw materials, cheap transportation, expansive markets, and reliable credit institutions. This new form of business cropped up in other industries besides steel and oil. In 1887 the so-called Sugar Trust comprised 17 of the 21 U.S. sugar refiners and monopolized sugar refining east of the Mississippi River.

New Labor Supplies for a New Economy

To operate efficiently, expanding industries needed expanding supplies of workers to grow crops, extract raw materials, and produce manufactured goods. Many of these workers came from abroad. The year 1880 marked the leading edge of a new wave of immigration to the United States. Over the next ten years, 5.2 million newcomers entered the country, almost twice the previous decade's level of 2.8 million.

In the mid-nineteenth century, most immigrants hailed from western Europe and the British Isles—from Germany, Scandinavia, England, and Ireland. Between 1880 and 1890 they were joined by numerous Italians, Russians, and Poles. In fact, these last three groups predominated among newcomers for the next 35 years, their arrival rates peaking between 1890 and 1910. At the same time, immigrants from Asia, especially from China, were making their way to the Kingdom of Hawaii, which was annexed by the United States in 1898. Between 1852 and 1887, 26,000 Chinese arrived on the islands. Almost 40 percent of all immigrants to the United States during this period were known as "birds of passage," men who were recruited by American employers and who, after earning some money, migrated back to their native land.

Many of the new European immigrants sought to escape oppressive economic and political conditions in Europe, even as they hoped to make a new life for themselves and their families in the United States. Russian Jews fled discrimination and violent **anti-Semitism** in the form of pogroms, organized massacres conducted by their Christian neighbors and Russian authorities. Southern Italians, most of whom were landless farmers, suffered from a combination of declining agricultural prices and high birthrates. Impoverished Poles chafed under cultural restrictions imposed by Germany and Russia. Hungarians, Greeks, Portuguese, and Armenians, among other groups, also participated in this great migration; members of these groups too were seeking political freedom and economic opportunity.

Immigrants replenished America's sense of itself as a haven for the downtrodden, a place where opportunity beckoned to hard-working and ambitious people. "The New Colossus," written by American poet Emma Lazarus in 1883, pays tribute to the "huddled masses yearning to breathe free"—people from all over the world who sought refuge in the United States. The words of her poem are inscribed on the Statue of Liberty at the entrance to New York Harbor. (The people of France presented the statue, called "Liberty Enlightening the World," to America in 1884.)

Most of the newcomers found work in the factories, mills, and sweatshops of New York, Philadelphia, and Chicago. At the same time, large numbers of these fresh arrivals dispersed to other areas of the country to work in a wide variety of enterprises. Scandinavians populated the prairies of Iowa and Minnesota and the High Plains of the Dakotas. Immigrants from Mexico found work in the mines and beet fields of Colorado.

William E. Wilson Photographic Collection/Historic Mobile Preservation Society

▲ A burst of technological innovation characterized many American businesses during the last quarter of the nineteenth century. Nevertheless, some, like southern cotton plantations, remained largely unmechanized. Commanding large numbers of (sometimes resistant) black and white workers, southern planters refrained from investing in labor-saving technology. This woman, working at the Savannah Cotton Exchange in 1880, carries a basket of cotton on her head, just as her enslaved foremothers did.

In the South, some planters began to recruit immigrants—especially western Europeans of "hardy peasant stock"—to take the place of blacks who resisted working for whites. Nevertheless, planters' experiments with recruiting immigrants amounted to little. Given the opportunity, many immigrants sought to flee from the back-breaking labor and meager wages of the cotton staple crop economy. A group of Germans brought over to toil in the Louisiana swamps soon after the Civil War quickly slipped away from their employers; they had agreed to the arrangement only to gain free passage to America. Thirty Swedes who arrived in Alabama also deserted at an opportune moment, declaring that they were not slaves. South Carolina planters who sponsored colonies of Germans and Italians gave up in exasperation. The few Chinese who began work in the Louisiana sugar fields soon abandoned the plodding work of the plantations in favor of employment in the trades and shops of New Orleans. Still, in 1890, immigrant worker enclaves were scattered throughout the South. Irish, Polish, and Italian men were swinging pickaxes in Florida railroad camps. Italian men, women, and children were picking cotton on Louisiana plantations. Hungarian men were digging coal out of mines in West Virginia.

The story of Rosa Cassettari, a young woman who emigrated from northern Italy to the United States in 1884, suggests the challenges that faced many newcomers during this period. Rosa's husband, Santino, had preceded her to America. He had settled in an iron mining camp in Missouri. Leaving her son with relatives, Rosa received the assurances of friends and relatives: "You will get smart in America. And in America you will not be so poor."

In the steerage section of a steamship bound for the United States, Rosa found herself surrounded not only by *paesani* (fellow Italians) but also by Germans, Swedes, Poles, and French—"every kind," she remembered later. After arriving at Castle Garden (an immigration processing center at the tip of Manhattan and a predecessor of Ellis Island), Rosa and her *paesani* were approached by a smooth-talking, well-dressed, Italian-speaking man. Overcharging them for the train trip to Missouri, he left them with no money for food.

Life in the iron camp proved harsh—nothing like what Rosa had expected. Her husband, who was much older than she, neglected her; he preferred the company of prostitutes in the town. The iron was almost depleted, and some workers and their wives had moved on to a new mine in Michigan. Rosa's days centered on caring for her new baby and cooking for 13 of the miners.

Despite these realities, within a couple of years, Rosa grew used to America and considered herself an American. She returned briefly to her hometown in Italy but expressed impatience with the rigid social etiquette that separated the rich from the poor. She also yearned for the hearty meals that

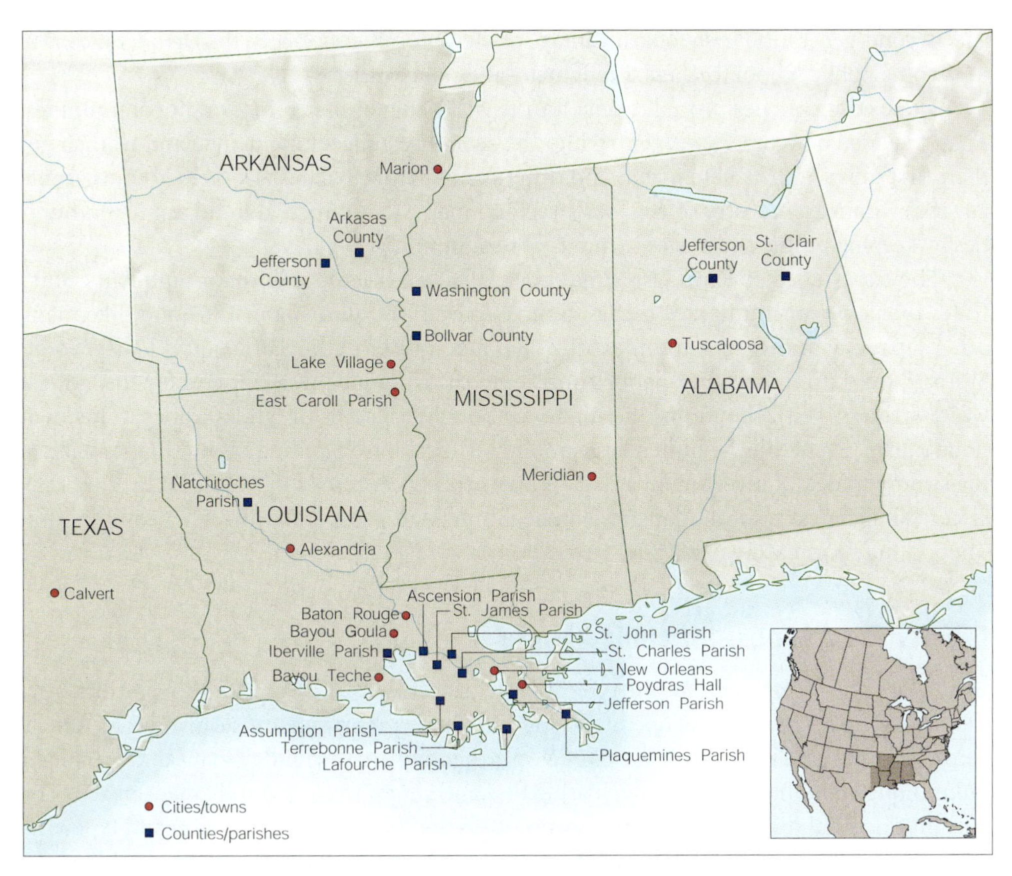

▲ MAP 16.2 SOME PLACES WHERE CHINESE LOCATED, 1865–1880
Immediately after the Civil War, some southern whites believed that immigrants would be more reliable and efficient workers than the freedpeople. Planters in Mississippi and Louisiana imported a small number of Chinese from California and others directly from Hong Kong. However, by the early 1870s most of these workers had deserted the fields and moved to nearby towns and cities to work as artisans, grocers, and laundry operators.

had become her staple in the iron camp. Back in Missouri, she mustered enough courage to leave Santino, traveling to Chicago and making a new life for herself in the Italian *colonia* (community) there. She eventually married another Italian man (the two had fallen in love in Missouri) and found work as a cleaning woman at Chicago Commons, a social settlement house. Her new husband alternated between working in construction and peddling bananas and cranberries. Rosa herself gained a reputation as a storyteller; later she said, "Me, I was always crazy for a good story."

The influx of so many foreign-born workers transformed the American labor market. Native-born Protestant men moved up the employment ladder to become members of the white-collar (that is, professional) middle class, while recent immigrants filled the ranks in construction and manufacturing. By 1890 Italian immigrants accounted for 90 percent of New York's public works employees and 99 percent of Chicago's street construction and maintenance crews. Women and children, both native and foreign born, predominated in the textile, garment-making, and food-processing industries.

Specific groups of immigrants often gravitated toward particular kinds of jobs. For example, many Poles found work in the vast steel plants of Pittsburgh, and Russian Jews went into the garment industry and street-peddling trade in New York City. California fruit orchards and vegetable farms employed numerous Japanese immigrants. Cuban immigrants rolled cigars in Florida. In Hawaii, the Chinese and Japanese labored in the sugar fields; after they had accumulated a little money, they became rice farmers and shopkeepers. In Boston and New York

City, second-generation Irish took advantage of their prominent place in the Democratic party to become public school teachers, firefighters, and police officers.

These **ethnic niches** proved crucial for the well-being of many immigrant communities. They provided newcomers with entry into the economy; indeed, many men and women got their first jobs with the help of kin and other compatriots. Niches also helped immigrants advance within an industry or economic sector. Finally, they enriched immigrant communities by keeping profits and wages within those communities.

The experience of Kinji Ushijima, later known as George Shima, graphically illustrates the power of immigrant niches. Shima arrived in California in 1887 and, like many other Japanese immigrants, found work as a potato picker in the San Joaquin Valley. Soon, Shima moved up to become a labor contractor, securing Japanese laborers for the valley's white farmers. With the money he made, he bought 15 acres of land and began his own potato farm. Eventually he built a large potato business by expanding his holdings, reclaiming swampland, and investing in a fleet of boats to ship his crops up the coast to San Francisco. Taking advantage of a Japanese niche, Shima had prospered through a combination of good luck and hard work.

Efficient Machines, Efficient People

By the late nineteenth century, the typical industrial employee labored within an immense, multistory brick structure and operated a machine powered by water or steam. Smoky, smelly kerosene lamps gave way to early forms of electric lighting, first arc and then incandescent light bulbs. Long-standing industries, such as textiles and shoes, were now fully mechanized. The new products flooding the economy—locomotives and bicycles, cash registers and typewriters—streamed from factories designed to ensure maximum efficiency from both machines *and* the people who tended them.

TABLE 16.1

Number of Firms by Number of Employees per Firm, 1850 and 1880

	Number of Firms							
	1850				1880			
	No. of Employees				No. of Employees			
Industry	0–5	6–50	50+	Total	0–5	6–50	50+	Total
Iron and steel	6	13	3	22	6	20	17	43
Hardware	76	42	7	125	114	122	27	263
Machines and tools	42	44	6	92	96	113	19	228
Printing	36	60	10	106	105	148	36	289
Building construction	83	59	3	145	588	227	18	833
Clothing	165	294	43	502	301	255	93	649
Furniture	84	66	3	153	185	105	20	310
Metal	83	11	1	95	166	47	5	218
Meat	81	3	0	84	458	23	2	483
Harness	32	15	3	50	96	21	2	119
Baking	384	29	0	413	910	73	8	991
Shoes	339	224	20	583	441	139	34	614
Blacksmith	141	18	1	160	187	12	0	199

Note: Because the census recorded only firms producing more than $500 per year, there may be serious undercounting of firms with one or no employees.

Source: Census of the United States, 1850 and 1880.

In the 1880s a few factory managers hired efficiency experts. The experts' goal was to cut labor costs in the same way that industry barons had shaved the costs of extracting raw materials or distributing final products. With huge quantities of goods flowing from factories, even modest savings in wages could mean significant profits in the long run. Frederick Winslow Taylor, chief engineer for the Midvale Steel Plant outside Philadelphia, pioneered in the techniques of efficient "scientific management."

Southern textile mill owners in the Piedmont region of South Carolina and Georgia devised their own strategies for shaping a compliant workforce. They employed only white men, women, and children as machine operators, but threatened to hire blacks if the whites protested low wages and poor working conditions. Poor whites lived in company housing, their children attended company schools, and they received cash wages. In contrast, blacks remained in the countryside, impoverished and without the right to vote. In the cities of the North as well as the textile villages of the South, factory workers remained exclusively white until well into the twentieth century.

The Birth of a National Urban Culture

In the 1880s visitors to the territory of Utah marveled at the capital, Salt Lake City, where Mormon pioneers had made the desert bloom. Situated at the foot of the magnificent snow-covered Wasach Range, this oasis in the Great Salt Basin boasted a built landscape almost as impressive as the natural beauty that surrounded it. In the heart of Salt Lake City lay Temple Square. This broad plaza contained the Mormon Tabernacle, a huge domed structure. Next to it stood the Mormon Temple, a soaring six-spired granite cathedral still under construction. The city had the advantage of rail service (Promontory Point, where the transcontinental railroad was joined, was not far away). Mines in nearby Bingham Canyon yielded rich lodes of silver, and large local smelters refined copper ores. Irrigation systems made the city self-sufficient in the production of foodstuffs. A settlement inspired by religious faith, Salt Lake City was at the same time thoroughly modern.

Cities around the country began to assume monumental proportions.

Not just Salt Lake City, but other cities around the country began to assume monumental proportions. In New York, the 1880s marked the completion of Central Park and the Brooklyn Bridge and the arrival of the Statue of Liberty from France. Chicago, rebuilding after a disastrous fire in 1871, became a sprawling rail hub dotted with yards for western cattle, northern timber, and the trains that hauled them. In 1885 Chicago also became the location for a major architectural breakthrough by engineer William LeBaron Jenney. He designed the ten-story Home Insurance Building, the world's first metal frame skyscraper. The steel skeleton weighed only one-third as much as the thick stone walls needed to support a similar masonry building, and the design left room for numerous windows. Urban architecture would never be the same again.

Cities in general represented American notions of progress and prosperity; they were places where innovation, consumer culture, and new forms of entertainment grew and flourished. From 1875 to 1900, American cities developed increasingly sophisticated systems of communications and transportation. Streetlights, transportation networks, and sewer lines provided basic services to swelling populations of immigrants and rural in-migrants. Experts in the fields of urban design and architecture and ambitious entrepreneurs in the fields of entertainment and professional sports all left their mark on cities. In a country fascinated with new and bigger and better things, cities set the standard by defining a desirable way of life for a "typical" middle-class American.

In their social and physical configurations, cities also represented a new cultural diversity in American life. At times uneasily, they accommodated immigrants from around the world. San Francisco's Chinatown formed a "city within a city" as hostile European Americans sought to circumscribe its residents. Politics, prejudice, and technology came together to shape the urban landscape.

Economic Sources of Urban Growth

Northeastern and mid-Atlantic cities emerged as centers of concentrated manufacturing activity. Yet, with the aid of eastern capital, western cities also flourished. New York's Wall Street and Boston's State Street, home to the nation's largest investment bankers, financed the Main Streets of the Midwest and West. Some urban areas prospered through milling, mining, or other enterprises, such as lumber and flour milling in Minneapolis and ore smelting in Denver. Others focused on manufacturing to serve a growing western population. Chicago was rivaled only by New York in terms of its industrial economy and the vast territory that it supplied with raw materials, processed food, and manufactured goods. Salt Lake City produced goods for the so-called Mormon Corridor of settlements that stretched west from the city to southern California. By the 1880s San Francisco had a commercial reach that encompassed much of the West as well as Hawaii and Alaska. Writer Henry George noted, "Not a settler in all the Pacific States and Territories but must pay San Francisco tribute. Not an ounce of gold dug, a pound of ore melted, a field gleaned, or a tree felled in all their thousands of square miles, but must add to her wealth."

No trend supported urban growth more than the arrival of newcomers from abroad. To stoke its furnaces, mill its lumber, and slaughter its cattle, Chicago relied on immigrants from

Museum of the City of New York/CORBIS

▲ Admirers hailed New York City's Brooklyn Bridge as the eighth wonder of the world when it was completed in 1883. With a central span of 1,595 feet, it became the largest suspension bridge in the world. Built over 14 years, the bridge linked Brooklyn to Manhattan across the East River, using steel suspension cables nearly 16 inches thick. Its total cost was about $18 million.

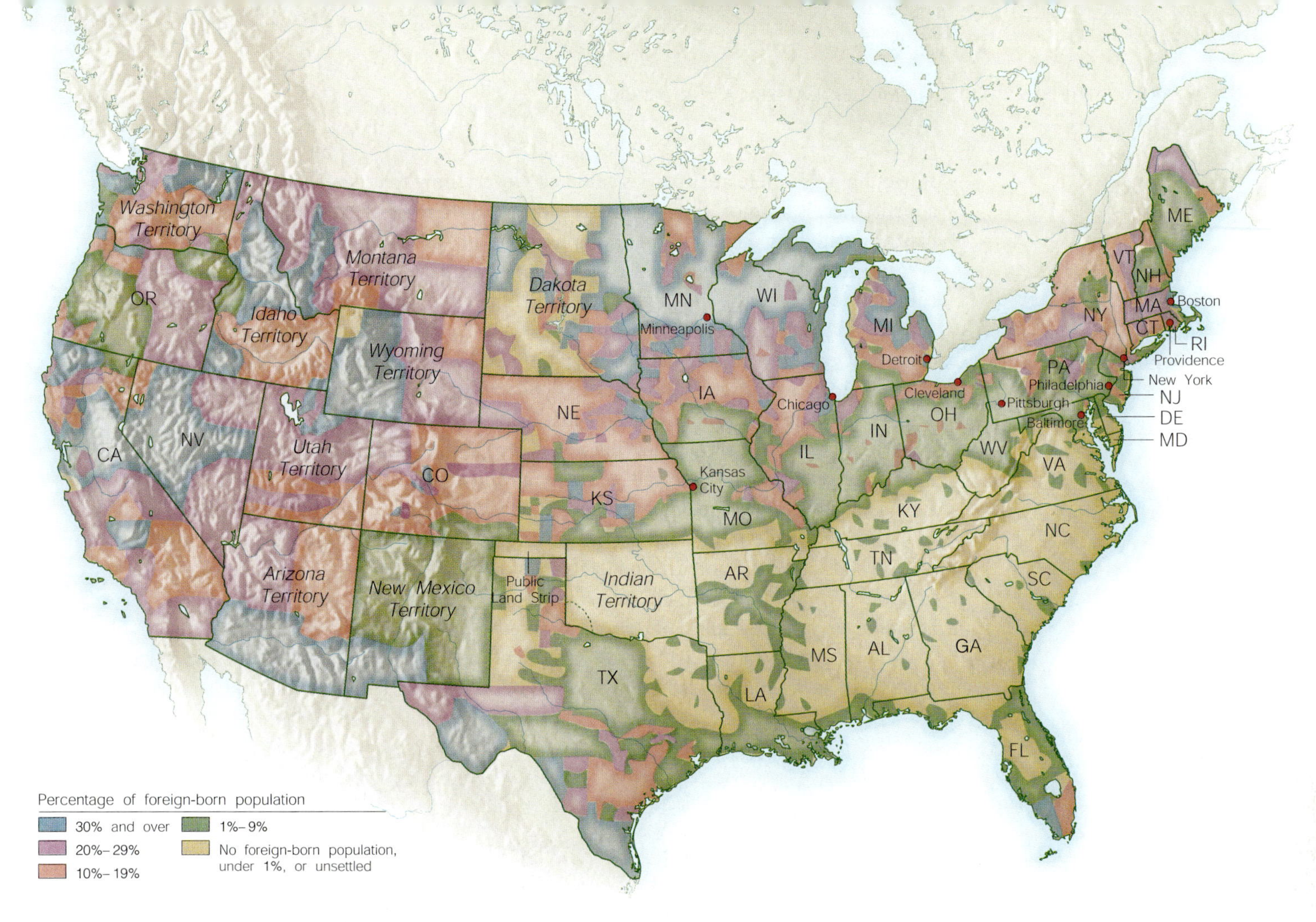

▲ MAP 16.3 POPULATION OF FOREIGN-BORN, BY REGION, 1880
After the Civil War, large numbers of immigrants settled in northeastern cities. In addition, the upper Midwest and parts of the western mining frontier drew many newcomers from western Europe. The area along the country's southwestern border was home to immigrants from Mexico. Cuban cigar makers established thriving communities in Florida.

Ireland, Slovakia, Germany, Poland, and Bohemia. Of the three cities with the highest percentage of foreign-born residents in 1880, San Francisco (45 percent) ranked higher than both Chicago (42 percent) and New York (40 percent). Yet all large cities also attracted migrants from America's own countryside, as native-born men and women fled the hardship of life on the farm. The use of increasingly efficient agricultural machines meant that rural workers had fewer job opportunities. Most of the immigrants from rural areas to the cities were young women; they included Yankee girls from the hardscrabble homesteads of New England, daughters of Swedish immigrants in Minnesota, and native-born farm tenants in Indiana.

Rural folk sought the steady work and wages afforded by jobs in the city, but they were also drawn to the excitement that had become the hallmark of the urban scene. In the early nineteenth century, Thomas Jefferson had located the heart of America in its sturdy yeoman farmers; by the late nineteenth century, that heart had shifted to the city.

Building the Cities

In 1886 the Reverend Josiah Strong, a proponent of Protestant missionary efforts abroad, condemned the American city as a "menace" to civilization. However, in decrying what he considered the evils of urban life, Strong described its appeal to people of all ages and both sexes: "It is the city where wealth is massed; and here are the tangible evidences of it piled many stories high. . . . Here are luxuries gathered—everything that dazzles the eye or tempts the appetite; here is the most extravagant expenditure." Strong was right that this conspicuous display of wealth would have profound implications for American politics and culture.

In these years the American city was emerging as a technological marvel. Through a combination of money and engineering skill, cities managed to provide an adequate water supply for private and commercial purposes, move large numbers of people and goods efficiently, get rid of waste materials, and illuminate thoroughfares at night. Professionals, such as landscape contractors, construction architects, and civil engineers, designed the parks, bridges, public libraries, and museums that made cities so attractive.

Throughout the country, new towns emerged as industrialists and factory owners sought to lure and retain workers. George M. Pullman, who manufactured railroad sleeping cars, built a town outside Chicago and named it after himself. In the South, company towns dotted the Piedmont region (textiles), the steep slopes of the Appalachian Mountains (coal and lumber), the piney woods of Texas (lumber), and the coast of Florida (phosphates). In the West, towns grew up around copper, coal, iron ore, and silver mines. These communities shared a unique characteristic: they directly linked housing, education, and commerce to a particular company.

Cities grew upward and outward as a result of developments in mass production and technology. The availability of factory-assembled building materials accelerated the construction

PROCESSION OF GAME

Soup
Venison (Hunter Style) Game Broth

Fish
Broiled Trout, Shrimp Sauce
Baked Black Bass, Claret Sauce

Boiled
Leg of Mountain Sheep, Ham of Bear
Venison Tongue, Buffalo Tongue

Roast
Loin of Buffalo, Mountain Sheep, Wild Goose, Quail, Redhead Duck, Jack Rabbit, Blacktail Deer, Coon, Canvasback Duck, English Hare, Bluewing Teal, Partridge, Widgeon, Brant, Saddle of Venison, Pheasants, Mallard Duck, Prairie Chicken, Wild Turkey, Spotted Grouse, Black Bear, Opossum, Leg of Elk, Wood Duck, Sandhill Crane, Ruffed Grouse, Cinnamon Bear

Broiled
Bluewing Teal, Jacksnipe, Blackbirds, Reed Birds, Partridges, Pheasants, Quails, Butterballs, Ducks, English Snipe, Rice Birds, Red-Wing Starling, Marsh Birds, Plover, Gray Squirrel, Buffalo Steak, Rabbits, Venison Steak

Entrees
Antelope Steak, Mushroom Sauce; Rabbit Braise, Cream Sauce; Fillet of Grouse with Truffles; Venison Cutlet, Jelly Sauce; Ragout of Bear, Hunter Style; Oyster Pie

Salads
Shrimp, Prairie Chicken, Celery

Ornamental Dishes
Pyramid of Game en Bellevue, Boned Duck au Naturel, Pyramid of Wild-Goose Liver in Jelly, The Coon out at Night, Boned Quail in Plumage, Red-Wing Starling on Tree, Partridge in Nest, Prairie Chicken en Socle

▶ FIGURE 16.3 MENU FROM THE DRAKE HOTEL IN CHICAGO, ILLINOIS, FOR THANKSGIVING, 1886

Center for Southwest Research, University of New Mexico

▲ **Many southwestern cities, such as Albuquerque, New Mexico, were laid out on an Old Town–New Town plan. The original center of settlement, Old Town was characterized by flat-roofed adobe buildings clustered on narrow streets. This photo shows Albuquerque's New Town in the 1880s. Located a mile and a half from Old Town plaza, it consists of Victorian-style buildings. The plan of New Town followed straight lines and right angles, "adapted to the railroad, the regenerator," in the words of one observer.**

of private dwellings and office buildings. Elevators extended living and office spaces upward (in the Reverend Strong's words, "wealth is massed...piled many stories high"). The invention of the electric streetcar in 1888 permitted cities to spread out.

One of the greatest challenges for modern cities was to devise means to transport numbers of people over long distances and rough terrain in an efficient and inexpensive way. For most of the nineteenth century, cities relied on carriages pulled by horses. In 1885, approximately 100,000 horses pulled urban passengers through the United States. For many reasons, horsecars were not a satisfactory method of conveyance. In order to scale a hill, drivers had to add extra teams, causing passengers to wait at the bottom of the hill while fresh animals were harnessed to the car. The cost of maintaining a full complement of horses—the feed to sustain them and the stables to shelter them—taxed the budgets of many cities.

Horsecars also threatened the health of urban residents. Each animal deposited on city streets an estimated ten pounds of waste per day, forcing pedestrians to hold their noses while they picked their way through piles of manure. In 1900 health officials in Rochester, New York, reported that the city's 15,000 horses produced an expanse of waste that would fill an acre of land 175 feet deep—a smelly pile, home to 16 billion flies.

The first successful electric trolley was developed by Julian Sprague, an engineer who founded the Sprague Electric Railway and Motor Company in 1884. The earliest electric streetcar consisted of a small four-wheel carriage connected to an overhead electric cable. Charging passengers a nickel or a dime, and averaging 10–15 miles an hour, these electric trolleys were cheaper, faster, and more versatile than horsecars. Unlike horses, trolleys did not become ill, or die, or balk at ascending a steep grade.

Chicago, Illinois and Gary, Indiana

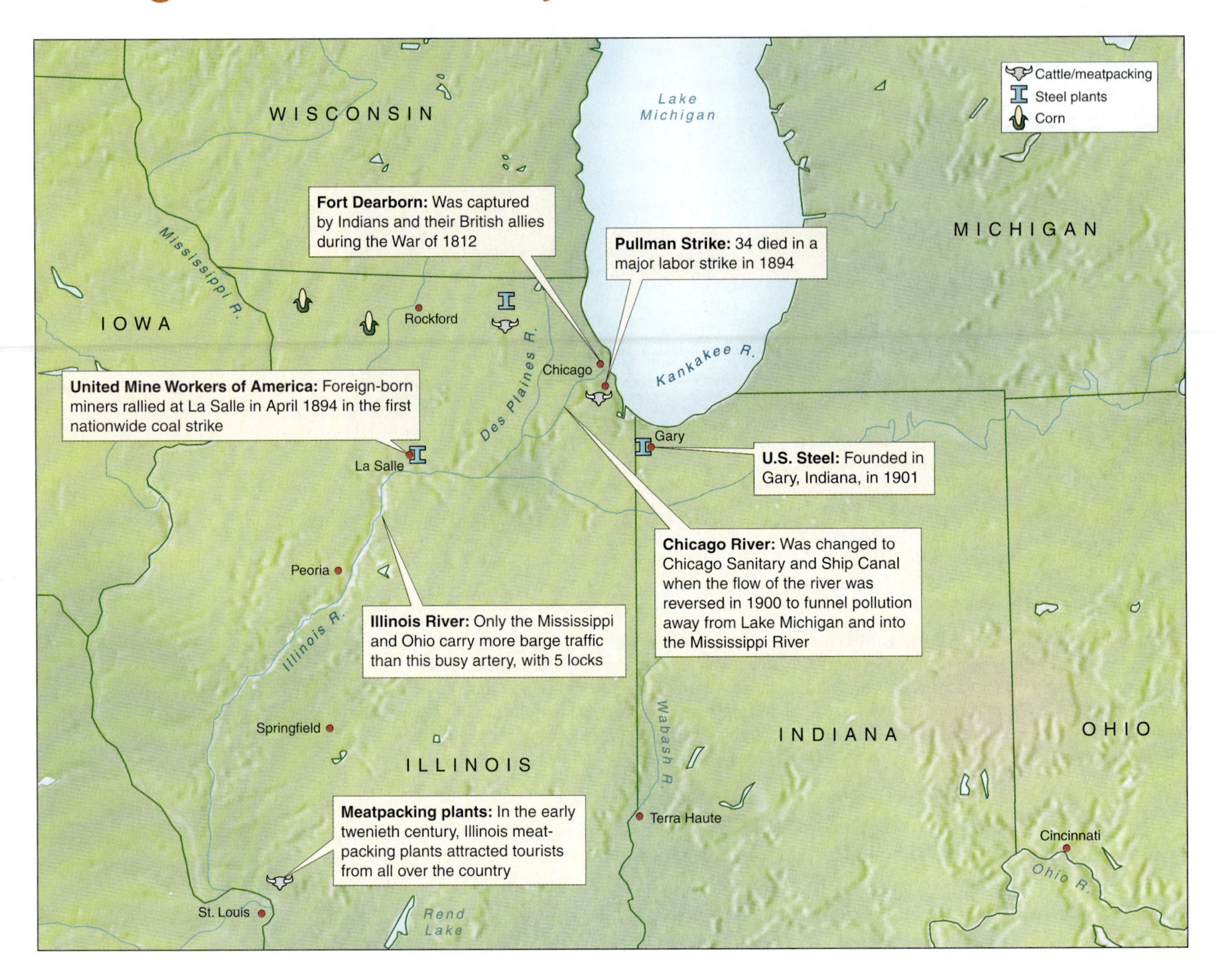

In the late nineteenth century, railroads made Chicago the Midwestern rail hub and also the nation's leading interior port city, capturing the title from Cincinnati. Marshall Field's "Grand Emporium," one of the nation's first large department stores, signified the emergence of a national consumer culture. Customers flocked to the store to ride its multifloor escalators, enjoy its central heating, and choose from a wide array of fashionable clothing and household wares.

The meatpacking industry offered plentiful jobs to people with little in the way of skills or formal education—initially Irish and German immigrants, and later Poles, Lithuanians, and Hungarians, as well as African American migrants from the South. The Chicago-Gary area also became a leading producer of steel. The region offered a superior location for steel mills by virtue of its easy access to rail and water transportation and its proximity to natural resources, including iron ore from Lake Superior, coke from Pennsylvania, limestone from Michigan, and coal from Illinois.

Today, the massive steel mills have been abandoned, replaced by smaller, high-tech "mini-mills" scattered throughout the United States. ■

In the 1880s, residential suburbs cropped up many miles from urban commercial cores. Wealthy and middle-class urban residents followed the streetcar lines out of the city, hoping to find a green refuge from the grime and noise of downtown while maintaining a manageable commute to work.

As cities expanded, the challenges associated with providing services also grew more complex and expensive. A polluted water supply, for example, meant epidemics of diphtheria and cholera, so city taxpayers demanded waterworks that delivered drinkable water through intricate systems of dams, pumps, reservoirs, and pipes. Chicago had long pumped its sewage into Lake Michigan, the source of its drinking water. In the 1880s the city financed the building of a canal and the reversal of the flow of the Chicago River. These changes sent the city's sewage away from Lake Michigan and into the Mississippi River instead. Begun in 1889, the 28-mile Chicago Sanitary and Ship Canal was completed seven years later. One awed observer marveled at the "powerful machinery for digging and hoisting, steam shovels, excavators, inclines, conveyors, derricks, cantilevers, cableways, channelers, steam drills, pumps, etc." The cost: $54 million.

Local Government Gets Bigger

These new systems of services, combined with the mushrooming immigrant neighborhoods, changed both the quality and quantity of urban problems. Zoning issues—who could build what, where, and when—became flashpoints for conflict as the interests of homeowners, developers, and municipal engineers collided. These controversies called for new forms of local government. Specifically, urban political leaders struggled to improve the city's public works while meeting the needs of multiple ethnic groups. Governing a big city was becoming a big business.

Rising tax rates and ballooning municipal debts told an even larger story. In 1845, the city of Boston spent $8.29 per resident and owed its creditors $748,000. Thirty years later, per capita annual expenditures had risen fivefold, and the city's debt had multiplied to more than $27 million. Clearly, running a city was an expensive, full-time enterprise and one that had the potential to be very lucrative to businesspeople and politicians alike.

Although New York's "Boss" Tweed had been convicted on charges of corruption in the early 1870s, the infamous Tammany Hall gang carried on his legacy. The Democratic officials associated with this social and political organization perfected a system of kickbacks linked to municipal construction projects. Under this system, contractors paid politicians for city construction contracts. For example, a New York City courthouse that was supposed to cost a quarter of a million dollars ended up costing taxpayers 52 times that amount, or twice as much as the United States paid Russia for Alaska! In the 1880s secretive networks of corruption that linked law enforcement personnel, city officials, and construction contractors flourished in many cities. These webs, or "machines," characterized urban life for decades to come.

Local officials went out of their way to support the provison of illegal services.

Urban machines existed to secure jobs for their loyal supporters and line the pockets of those at the highest levels of power. Deal-making blurred the lines between private enterprise and public service as everyone from mayors to local ward organizers benefited from the modernization of the American city. In the process, urban bosses ensured that the streets were paved, tenement buildings erected, sewer lines laid, and trolley tracks extended. But taxpayers footed the bill, which included outrageous amounts of money used for bribes and kickbacks.

Local officials went out of their way to support the provision of illegal services, such as prostitution and gambling, demanded by their constituents. Money-grubbing politicians and police extorted "hush money" from brothels, gambling parlors, and unlicensed taverns. In turn, these places became absorbed into the bosses' local empire. Extorted fees greased the palms of the cop on the beat and the judge on the take.

Urban bosses had a vested interest in sponsoring new money-making venues for professional sports and supporting other forms of commercialized leisure activity. Baseball parks, boxing rings, and racetracks yielded huge sums in the form of kickbacks from contractors. Once built, stadiums and boxing rings generated profits indefinitely. Sporting events themselves also gave a city's political, legal, and judicial leaders a chance to meet each other and seal business deals.

Thrills, Chills, and Bathtubs: The Emergence of Consumer Culture

On a hot summer day in 1890, a young mother named Emily Scanlon, with her three-year-old daughter in tow, paid the five-cent admission fee to a popular ride called the Toboggan Slide at the Brandywine Springs Amusement Park near Wilmington, Delaware. The two of them ascended a stairwell to the top of the three-story-high structure and then stepped into a car that ran on a wooden trough. When the attendant released the brakes, the car descended, pulled by gravity. It moved slowly at first, then picked up speed around a curve. Suddenly, Emily Scanlon stood up in the car (perhaps to retrieve her hat, which had blown off), and she and her daughter were thrown from the car. Mrs. Scanlon died instantly of a broken neck, but the youngster survived. Significantly, the tragedy did not provoke a shutdown of the ride or the installation of safety measures. Instead, park managers simply posted a sign that read, "Passengers must keep their seats." Patrons continued to enjoy the thrills of the toboggan.

Brandywine Springs boasted an ornate gateway that proclaimed "Let All Who Enter Here Leave Care Behind." In cities around the country, amusement parks brought men and women, girls and boys together to enjoy merry-go-rounds, prizefights, and circus sideshows. By 1880, railroads and steamships were transporting crowds out of Manhattan to Coney Island, where working-class people mingled with the self-proclaimed "respectable" middle classes.

Late in the century, Americans of all kinds began to sample a new realm of sensual experience—one of physical daring, material luxury, and visual fantasy—either as participants or as observers. The ride at Brandywine Springs was an early prototype of the modern roller coaster. The park afforded patrons not only the thrill of riding the Toboggan Slide but also the sights and sounds of a carnival. The calliope (pipe organ) music and the brightly colored signs beckoned visitors to an exciting world apart from the humdrum routine of everyday life.

Colorful spectacles became an integral part of American life.

Ticket holders at Brandywine Springs were participating in an emerging consumer culture. With economic growth and high rates of productivity came the two ingredients necessary to a culture of consumption: industries that catered to the demand for novel experiences or ready-made goods, and people with enough money to buy them. Central to this culture was mass advertising, a form of appeal that sought to instill in consumers the desire for things that were new and visually attractive. Colorful spectacles of all kinds—whether in the form of a department store window or a well-publicized athletic event—became an integral part of American life.

Shows as Spectacles

Public officials, college administrators, and ambitious entrepreneurs alike discovered that Americans craved new and stimulating forms of entertainment and were willing to pay for them. Athletic events began to draw large crowds, revealing their potential as big business. Traveling road shows promoted new products and services by charming their audiences with exotic performances. Though modest by today's standards, such spectacles found a ready market in the United States and other countries.

In the quarter-century after Reconstruction, three major sports began to attract large national audiences. Organized baseball had existed since 1846, when the Knickerbocker Base Ball Club of New York met the New York Nine in Hoboken, New Jersey. (The score was 23 to 1, in favor of the Nine.) The National Baseball League, consisting of eight professional teams, was founded

Courtesy, Transcendental Graphics

CHAMPIONS

Base Ball,
Andrews, (C.F. Philadelphia).
Anson, (1st Base, Chicago).
Brouthers, (1st Base, Detroit).
Caruthers, (P. Brooklyn).
Dunlap, (Capt, Pittsburgh).
Glasscock, (S.S. Indianapolis).
Keefe, (P. New York).
Kelly, (C. Boston).
Prince, ... Bicyclist.
Rowe, ... do.
Stevens, ... do.
Wood, ... do.
Daly, ... Billiards.
Schaefer, ... do.
Sexton, ... do.
Slosson, ... do.
Vignaux, ... do.
Broadswordsman,
Duncan C. Ross.
Capt. Mackenzie, Chess.
Steinitz, ... do.
Zukertort, ... do.
Foot Ball,
Beecher, (Capt. of Yale Team).
W. Byrd Page, High Jumper.
"Snapper" Garrison, Jockey.
Mc Laughlin, ... do.

Isaac Murphy, ... Jockey.
Charles Wood, ... do.
Beeckman, ... Lawn Tennis
Dwight, ... do.
Sears, ... do.
Taylor, ... do.
Marksman,
Captain Bogardus.
Beach, ... Oarsman.
Jake Gaudaur, do.
Hanlan, ... do.
Teemer, ... do.
James Albert, Pedestrian.
Pat Fitzgerald, do
Rowell, ... do
D'oro, ... Pool.
Jack Dempsey, Pugilist
Jake Kilrain, ... do
Mitchell, ... do
Jem Smith, do
Sullivan, ... do.
Myers, ... Runner.
Strongest Man in the World,
Emil Voss.
Wild West Hunter,
"Buffalo Bill."
Joe Acton, Wrestler
Muldoon, ... do.

GOODWIN & CO.
NEW YORK.

CARD COLLECTOR'S CO.
REPRINT

Courtesy, Transcendental Graphics

◀ Baseball cards, like this one featuring New York Giants player Tim Keefe, were sold at department stores. On the back of the card are listed other national athletes featured in the series. One "Wild West Hunter" is included: "Buffalo Bill" Cody. This card was also a cigarette advertisement.

in 1876, the American League in 1900. In the 1880s, several new regulations—those governing the overhand pitch, foul balls, and swingless strikes—helped to standardize the game.

Also in the 1880s, Walter Camp, a former Yale University football player, introduced rules—for instance, the system of downs and the center snap to the quarterback—that made that sport quicker and more competitive. Camp was also behind the selection of the first "All America" team (1889) to stimulate fan interest. By this time towns, high schools, and colleges were fielding football teams.

Likewise, boxing emerged as a national, regulated sport. John L. Sullivan, an American, won renown as the world's bare-knuckled champion in 1882, even as more and more fighters had started wearing gloves. Sullivan then joined a traveling theatrical group and demonstrated gloved boxing to enthusiastic crowds all over the country. These exhibitions revealed the fine line between displays of physical prowess and theatrical performances. In 1889, Sullivan defeated an opponent in a 75-round match, the last heavyweight, bare-knuckled championship.

Performances based on skills of all kinds gained national audiences, as the career of William "Buffalo Bill" Cody reveals. Born in Iowa in 1846, Cody parlayed his early years as a Pony Express postal rider, cavalry scout, Indian fighter, and buffalo hunter into a form of mass entertainment. In his "Buffalo Bill Combination" show, cowboy and Indian actors performed skits depicting dramatic events in western history (from a European American point of view, at least). In 1876 Cody briefly left the stage to join a U.S. cavalry skirmish against the Sioux and Cheyenne. Soon he returned to the show to exhibit the dried scalp of the Cheyenne warrior Yellow Hand, whom he claimed he had killed in battle. Cody thus presented the subjugation of the Indians as a form of high drama, a scripted performance that audiences applauded from the comfort of their seats.

In 1882 Cody produced "Buffalo Bill's Wild West," a traveling road show that featured sharpshooter Annie Oakley, cowboy musicians, and Sioux warriors performing authentic Native American dances. Sioux leader Sitting Bull (Tatanka Iyotake), long an admirer of Annie Oakley (he called her "Little Sure Shot"), joined the show in 1885. Like other Indians who worked for Cody, Sitting

Denver Public Library/Western History/Genealogy Department (Neg. #B-133)

▲ "Buffalo Bill" Cody and Sitting Bull pose for a promotional photo for the 1885 season of the "Wild West." Cody refrained from calling the production a "show," maintaining that it demonstrated frontier skills and recreated historical encounters (such as Custer's Last Stand and stagecoach robberies). The "Wild West" toured Canada and Europe and inspired many imitators.

Bull took advantage of the opportunity to escape the confines of the reservation (in his case, Standing Rock in North Dakota). As a member of the "Wild West" troupe, he also enjoyed decent food and accommodations. At a time when whites were denigrating Indian culture, Sitting Bull affirmed that culture by demonstrating his shooting and riding skills. However, white audiences jeered him—they saw him as less an entertainer and more an enemy warrior—and he left after just a year. By the 1890s, Cody was playing to audiences in Europe as well as the United States, dramatizing a West that was fast disappearing. Still, the sight of Annie Oakley shooting glass balls and clay pigeons out of the air, as well as mounted cowboys leading "Custer's last charge," gave customers their money's worth.

Entertainment Collides with Tradition

After the Civil War, various forms of mass entertainment gained huge, enthusiastic followings all over the country. The traveling circus provides a case in point. By the 1870s, such shows were erecting their tents in small towns and big cities alike. The largest shows employed hundreds of people as performers, cooks, carpenters, and wagon drivers. Circus owners provided their customers with exciting sights and sounds—death-defying lion-tamers, gravity-defying gymnasts and tightrope walkers, exhibits of wild animals such as elephants and tigers, rollicking brass bands, and the hilarious antics of clowns. Even people who could not afford to attend the main show enjoyed the elaborate parade that marked the circus's arrival in town. Sideshows featured people with unusual physical characteristics related to height, body weight, facial hair, and limb flexibility. On the circus grounds, people sold a variety of exotic foods, and performers provided previews of the afternoon or evening show. These early circuses foreshadowed several forms of popular twentieth-century entertainment, including movie spectacles, magic shows, and daredevil stunts.

Not everyone cheered when the circus wagons rolled into town. Men and women with conservative religious views often disapproved of circuses. They found much that offended them in the three rings under the "Big Top"—the bawdy humor of clowns; the displays of young female acrobats and other performers clad only in tights or, even worse, appearing in various states of undress; the rowdy audiences that cheered wildly for each act. Outside, on the circus grounds, gamblers and other tricksters were intent on cheating children and other naive persons out of their money. Frequently, fistfights and gunfights broke out among circus employees and local youths, fights often fueled by an excess of alcohol all around. Moreover, the arrival of the circus caused schoolchildren to drop their books, field workers their hoes, and domestic servants their dish towels in their rush to the ticket office. Some people also charged that the circus encouraged the poor to squander what little money they had on frivolous pursuits.

These concerns were especially prominent in the rural South. In 1876, a newspaper editor in southern Georgia warned his readers, "Of all the demoralizing things ever permitted to run at large through any town, a circus takes the lead. It completely unjoints every particle of social, moral, and religious machinery in any small town." Circus owners reacted to these warnings in creative ways. Many of them stressed the wild-animal exhibits as proof of God's power, worthy of the patronage of the most devout church member. Promoters of the John Robinson Circus claimed that its show possessed "the Largest and most Complete Menagerie, Aviary, and Aquarium in the World, Containing Living Specimens of our CREATOR'S GREAT HANDIWORK, of which 'They went in two and two, and Noah into the Ark, the male and female as God had commanded Noah.'" The Great Eastern Circus beckoned customers to view its wild animals "just as God made them, in his infinite wisdom." However, many people, circus-goers of all ages, needed no encouragement to spend an afternoon or an evening in a world apart from their everyday routines.

"Palaces of Consumption"

During the late nineteenth century, the act of shopping in cities for goods, especially luxury goods, became an adventure in itself. A new piece of the cityscape, the department store, welcomed customers into a world of luxury and abundance, a place of color, light, and glamour. These "palaces of consumption" showcased a variety of technological innovations. In Marshall Field's "Grand Emporium" (Chicago), Wanamaker's (Philadelphia), and Lord & Taylor (New York), shoppers glided from story to story on escalators and in elevators. Warmed by central heating, they browsed display cases, racks, and tables laden with enticing goods and illuminated by arc lighting. Their money streamed into cash registers or to a central clerk through cash conveyors.

Thus, department stores not only offered a dazzling array of goods but also made shopping an exciting experience. This type of adventure appealed particularly to middle-class women, who had the leisure time and the cash to indulge in daylong shopping excursions. In 1880 a New Yorker could arrive at Macy's by taking the Sixth Avenue elevated train and spend the morning exploring any number of specialized departments: ribbons, women's and children's muslin underwear, toys, candy, books, men's furnishings, china and glassware, and so on. Fatigued at noon, she might visit the lunchroom to partake of a modest meal and then devote the rest of her day to examining the colored dress silks, a new department established the year before.

Harper's Weekly, 1881

▲ In the Bowery, at the southern tip of Manhattan, a "barker" stands in the doorway of a dime museum and urges the curious—in this case, mainly children—to pay the admission fee and come inside to view unusual specimens of humanity. This drawing appeared in *Harper's Weekly* in 1881.

During the 1880s, Macy's expanded its line of goods, introducing items as varied as dog collars and telescopes, mirrors, seeds and garden tools, and Goodyear's rubber boots. The store sold brand names and products manufactured by the company itself, including Red Star silk and Red Star velveteen (a soft, plush fabric). One New York newspaper marveled at the selection and pronounced the store "a bazaar, a museum, a hotel and a great fancy store all combined."

The department store was an exclusively urban phenomenon, but mass merchandising reached far beyond cities. The material riches of American society became accessible to rural people through the mail-order catalogue. This marketing device was pioneered in 1872 by the Chicago company Montgomery Ward, the official supply house for the Farmers' Grange. On homesteads throughout the Midwest, family members gathered to pore over the thousands of items displayed in "The Great Wish Book." The company's motto? "Satisfaction guaranteed or your money back." Farm wives delighted in the latest Parisian fashions, their husbands pondered the intricacies of McCormick threshing machinery, and the children studied the newest line of toys and fishing rods.

"Rural Free Delivery Mail"

Late in the decade, a competitor appeared on the scene in the form of the Sears, Roebuck Catalogue. A former mail-order watch salesman, Richard Sears soon gained a reputation as a man who could "sell a breath of fresh air." Sears helped pioneer the field of modern advertising **hyperbole,** claiming, for example, that the sewing machine he offered was the "Best on Earth." Selling was fast becoming a circus sideshow.

The mass production needed to satisfy eager customers depended on mass advertising, an enterprise still in its infancy in the 1880s. Yet some of the principles that would shape the future of this business were in place even at this early date. For instance, soon after the Civil War, the makers of Sozodont dentifrice (toothpaste) plastered the name of their product

Refugio Amador and her five daughters, Emilia, Maria, Clotilde, Julieta, and Corina, were members of an elite Hispanic family in Las Cruces, New Mexico. Her husband, Martin Amador, was a prominent politician, merchant, hotel owner, and freighter. A subcontractor for the U.S. government, he supplied military troops in the area. The family shopped by mail-order catalogue from Bloomingdale's Department Store in New York City.

all over weekly religious magazines and more mainstream publications, such as *Harper's* and *Scribner's*. They labeled the natural landscape as well. Indeed, the word *Sozodont* on Maiden's Rock in Red Wing, Minnesota, was so large that steamboat passengers on the Mississippi River three miles away could plainly read it.

The career of L. Frank Baum illustrates the convergence of modern ideas about theatrical performances and sales spectacles. Born to a wealthy German American family in 1856, Baum grew up in upstate New York. His father had made a great deal of money from the oil industry, particularly Pennsylvania gushers that yielded a distinctive emerald green oil. The younger Baum was drawn to what he called the "dream life," with its guilt-free indulgence in pleasure. Together with his wife, he founded a theater troupe that toured the Midwest in the 1880s. He then made a brief foray into merchandising. He marketed Baum's Castorine (axle grease) and opened his own department store, Baum's Bazaar, in Aberdeen, South Dakota, in the northeast corner of the state. There, he also became editor of the town newspaper, the *Aberdeen Saturday Pioneer*.

Baum eventually moved his family to Chicago, where he embarked on a career as a department store window designer. He founded the National Association of Window Trimmers in 1898 and started a trade magazine, *The Show Window*. The magazine encouraged designers to strive for a "sumptuous display" of goods and to highlight their rich textures and colors. Baum went on to become a popular writer of children's fiction. His famous book *The Wizard of Oz* (1900), an allegory of late-nineteenth-century life, covered themes as diverse as feminism and rural poverty. An accomplished and successful showman, Baum understood that Americans were eager to buy fantasy wherever they could find it: in a theater, department store, or children's book.

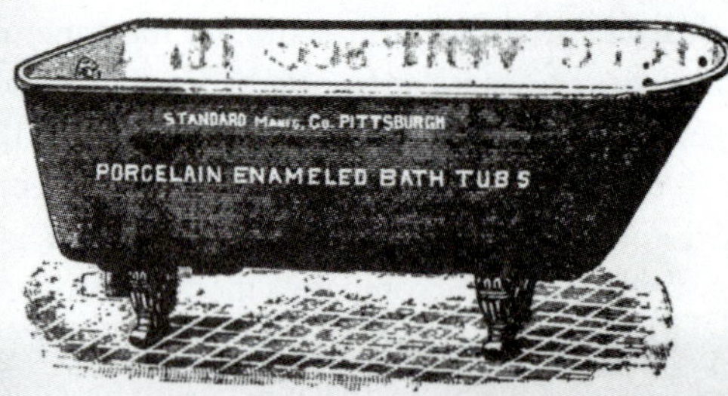

▶ This advertisement for a Standard bathtub appeared in the May 1890 issue of *Century Magazine*. Early on, advertisers used sophisticated psychological techniques to convince consumers that a wide array of products, formerly considered luxuries, were necessities. This ad suggests that a husband can show his affection for his wife by buying her a new bathtub.

Persuading People to Buy: Advertising in American History

Over the last four centuries, American advertisers have become increasingly creative in using new media to reach potential customers. During the colonial period, inns and taverns identified themselves by hanging sideboards easily recognizable to pedestrians. Peddlers called to passersby. Chimney sweeps hawked their services with their distinctive "Sweep O!" refrain. Dry goods merchants distributed cards (handbills) that listed their wares, from corduroy cloth to colorful ostrich feathers.

Early newspapers, such as Benjamin Franklin's *Philadelphia Gazette* (founded in 1728), pioneered in print advertising. Among the items in Franklin's paper were descriptions of runaway slaves wanted by their owners as well as ads for slaves offered for sale. When the Stamp Act of 1765 imposed a two-shilling tax on every print advertisement, colonial merchants rightly feared that this tax would hinder commercial development.

In the antebellum period, mass circulation newspapers featured advertisements as prominently as news stories. In 1833 the *New York Sun* announced that it would provide "ALL THE NEWS OF THE DAY, and at the same time afford an advantageous medium for advertising."

After the Civil War, advertising served as the engine of an emerging consumer economy that depended on the marketing of large quantities of packaged goods. In the 1880s the Proctor & Gamble company initiated an

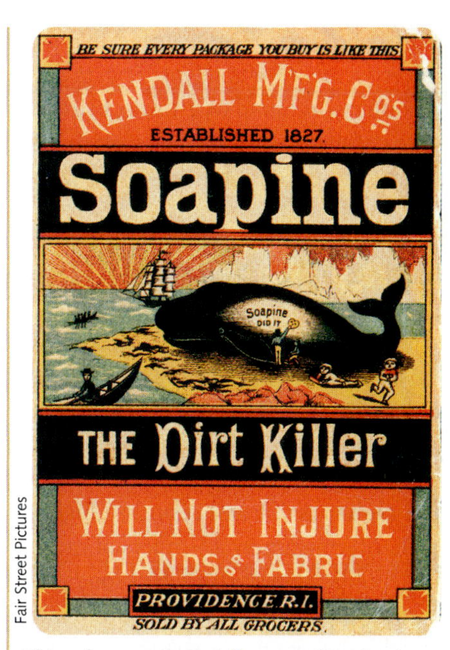

Fair Street Pictures

This ad suggests that the soap Soapine is powerful enough to bleach the black shine out of a whale's hide. Soapine's "scrubbed whale" logo became a familiar sight to late-nineteenth-century consumers.

aggressive marketing campaign, touting its brand of Ivory Soap ("99 and 44/100 percent pure") with full-page ads in monthly magazines. (In 1890 the company sold 30 million cakes of the soap.) Traveling road shows advertised patent medicines and at the same time entertained young and old.

The retail sales concerns Montgomery Ward and Sears, Roebuck took advantage of Rural Free Delivery offered by the U.S. Postal Service and sent lavishly illustrated catalogues to households all over the country. In the fall of 1908, Sears distributed 3.7 million copies of its catalogue.

An African American businesswoman, Madame C. J. Walker, built a successful cosmetics company through a variety of modern means. She used print advertising, attractive packaging, endorsements by such celebrities as dancer Josephine Baker, and door-to-door saleswomen called "Walker agents" to enhance her own fame and sell more products.

By the 1920s large advertising agencies were drawing on research in the field of psychology in an effort to create ads that appealed to people's deepest desires and deepest insecurities. In 1957, in *The Hidden Persuaders,* author Vance Packard argued that advertisers used subtle psychological techniques to persuade people to buy goods and services they did not need.

In its 1976 *Virginia State Board of Pharmacy v. Virginia Citizens Council, Inc.* decision, the Supreme Court ruled that advertising was a form of free speech, protected under the Constitution. As a result, professionals such as physicians and lawyers began to advertise their services.

Innovations in communication and transportation opened new channels of advertising. As early as the 1920s, billboards and the sides of barns were used to advertise products to automobile passengers. Radio advertisers specialized in catchy slogans and jingles. In the 1950s television ads became increasingly sophisticated in their use of music and striking visuals. By the late twentieth century, movies and orbiting space capsules provided opportunities for product placement. Airplanes flew advertising banners over crowded summertime beaches and packed football stadiums. Telemarketers pitched their wares over the telephone. Channel One, a closed-circuit television outlet, offered corporate-sponsored educational programming for public school students.

In 1999, U.S. companies, entrepreneurs, and individuals spent more than $200 billion to advertise. By this time, advertising represented a blend of traditional and high-technology methods. The World Wide Web was full of ads, but passersby on city streets were still receiving a barrage of handbills advertising a variety of goods and services. ■

Whether the products were featured in a department store display case, show window, magazine advertisement, or mail-order catalogue, the face of modern merchandising was bound to be young, white, and well-to-do, brimming with health and material well-being. The new consumer culture was marked by a glaring double standard: Although advertisers marketed to the millions, they established a very narrow standard of the "normal" American.

Defending the New Industrial Order

By the late 1870s, intense conflict over fundamental issues had all but evaporated from national politics. Although ethnic and cultural loyalties continued to inflame local and state elections, Republicans and Democrats at the national level disagreed about little except the tariff. Adhering to tradition, Republicans favored a higher tariff that would benefit domestic businesses by making imported goods more expensive. In contrast, Democrats argued that a higher tariff, and resulting higher prices for goods produced in the United States, would harm consumers. Members of the Republican Party called themselves the Grand Army of the Republic; they "waved the **bloody shirt**"—that is, reminded voters that many of their Democratic opponents, especially those in the South, had supported secession a generation before. Still, the two major parties openly shared a similar goal: to win as many jobs as possible for their respective supporters. Politics served as a vehicle for patronage and favors rather than as a conduit for ideas and alternative visions of the nation's future.

Many politicians also shared a belief in the idea of *laissez-faire* (a French phrase meaning to leave alone, referring to the absence of government interference in the economy). Laissez-faire was actually a flexible concept, invoked to justify government indifference in some areas but government intervention in others. Indeed, politicians tended to favor laissez-faire in social matters more than in the economy. Thus, support for manufacturers and railroads in the form of tariff protection and land grants, for example, was justified. At the same time, however, Congress, the president, and the Supreme Court were reluctant to enact bold measures to redress the growing gap between rich and poor. In fact, certain clergy, businesspeople, and university professors sought to explain and defend the inequality between the captains of industry and the masses of ill-paid laborers. They argued that the system of industrial capitalism was desirable because it was "natural."

Nevertheless, many advocates of laissez-faire in social welfare policy supported government intervention in the economy. These observers argued that the government was justified in providing tariff protection to manufacturers and in using federal power to quell strikes of railroad workers.

In the summer of 1877, the president of the Pennsylvania Railroad, Thomas Scott, and other railroad officials were forced to contend with a workers' strike that spread throughout the country. Trying to cut costs in what had become a bitterly competitive business, many of the railroads had demanded that workers labor for longer hours for 10 percent less pay. Managers instituted the practice of "double-heading"—adding more cars to a train but not hiring more workers to tend them, placing added burdens on engineers and other workers. In response, beleaguered rail workers walked off the job. Men and women in other struggling industries—from laundresses and longshoremen in Galveston, Texas, to coal miners in Scranton, Pennsylvania, to packinghouse laborers in Chicago—also went on strike during what came to be known as the Great Labor Uprising of 1877. That July the federal government deployed army troops as a strike-breaking force in Chicago, East St. Louis, Illinois, and Terre Haute, Indiana, among other cities.

Many advocates of laissez-faire in social welfare policy supported government intervention in the economy.

In a letter to the *North American Review* magazine in August 1877, Thomas Scott justified his railroad's wage cuts and charged that the strikers were under the sway of vicious criminals. Scott hailed the railroads as truly national enterprises, "closely interwoven with the interests not only of our own but other countries." During the Civil War, Union forces had commandeered private rail lines, Scott pointed out. Now it was appropriate that the federal government protect the railroads in this time of crisis. Indeed, according to Scott, "this insurrection," the strike, presented a national emergency "almost as serious as that which prevailed at the outset of the Civil War."

In 1873 writer Mark Twain (Samuel Clemens) published his first novel, which he co-wrote with friend and fellow writer Charles Dudley Warner. Titled *The Gilded Age,* the book satirized the trend toward corruption in public affairs and the wild financial speculation that produced both poverty and great wealth. The growth of large businesses that received economic and political support from government officials served to enrich employers, investors, and politicians at the expense of workers and farmers. The term *Gilded Age* became synonymous with the excess and extravagance on the part of politicians and businesspeople alike during the last quarter of the nineteenth century.

The Contradictory Politics of Laissez-Faire

In 1880 the undistinguished President Rutherford B. Hayes chose not to run for office again. That summer the Republicans nominated James A. Garfield of Ohio, a former mule driver who had become a Civil War general. To counter the "bloody-shirt" effect, Democrats put forth their own former Union general: Winfield S. Hancock, who had been wounded at Gettysburg. Garfield won the popular vote by a narrow margin and overwhelmed Hancock in the electoral college.

Garfield's arrival in the White House set off a race for patronage jobs among loyal Republicans. Indeed, overwhelmed by office-seekers, the new president remarked, "My God! What is there in this place that a man should ever want to get into it?" Then on July 2, 1881, Charles J. Guiteau, who had unsuccessfully sought the position of U.S. consul in Paris, shot Garfield in a Washington, D.C., train station. Garfield languished for a few months, finally dying on September 19.

Vice President Chester A. Arthur, a former New York politician, assumed the reins of government. Arthur's administration supported certain forms of government intervention in society, or "social engineering." Arthur and others believed that laissez-faire policies had their limits; strong measures were needed to counter what they and other conservatives considered immoral personal behavior. In 1882 Congress passed the Edmunds Act. Targeting Mormons, the act outlawed polygamy (the practice of having more than one wife at a time), took the right to vote away from the law's offenders, and sent a five-member commission to Utah to oversee local elections.

That same year, Congress responded to pressure from West Coast European American politicians, the San Francisco's Workingmen's Party in particular, and approved the Chinese

Carnegie Library of Pittsburgh (#P-1987)

◀ **The Great Labor Uprising of July 1877 was the first national strike in U.S. history. As railroad lines proliferated, owners slashed wages in a bid to remain competitive. Railroad workers in some cities destroyed trains, tracks, and other equipment. Spreading eventually to 14 states, the conflict claimed the lives of more than 100 people and resulted in the loss of millions of dollars worth of private property.**

Exclusion Act. The act became the first piece of legislation to bar a particular group from entering the United States. Most Chinese immigrants took jobs that native-born whites shunned. Moreover, unemployment among California's white manufacturing workers in the 1870s was caused not by Chinese competitors but by the flood of cheap eastern-made goods carried into the state by the transcontinental railroad. As eastern goods entered California, manufacturers in the West laid off workers and closed factories. The Chinese thus became scapegoats for groups hit hard by larger economic changes.

In 1883 the Supreme Court hurt the cause of blacks' civil rights by declaring the Civil Rights Act of 1875 unconstitutional. The five cases involved in the Court's decision focused on exclusions of blacks from hotels, railroad cars, and theaters. The Court held that state governments could not discriminate on the basis of race but that private individuals could do so. This decision put an official stamp of approval on racist practices of employers, hotels, restaurants, and other providers of jobs and services.

Arthur surprised his critics by embracing the cause of civil service reform. This movement sought to inject professional standards into public service and rid the country of the worst excesses of the corrupt "spoils system," where political victors put loyal supporters into public jobs regardless of their qualifications. In response to Garfield's assassination by Guiteau, the disappointed patronage-seeker, Congress passed the Pendleton Act (1883). This measure established a merit system for federal job applicants and created the Civil Service Commission, which administered competitive examinations to candidates in certain classifications.

In 1884 Arthur fell ill (he would die shortly), and the Republicans nominated James G. Blaine of Maine as their candidate for the presidency. Blaine, who had benefited from corrupt deals in the past, offended the sensibilities of a group of reform-minded Republicans, who called themselves Mugwumps. (The term reportedly had its roots in an Indian word that meant "holier than thou.") As a result, Blaine was bested in the national election by the former mayor of Buffalo, Grover Cleveland, who became the first Democratic president in 28 years.

Eastman Johnson, *Finding His Way*, 1866. Chrysler Museum of Art, Norfolk, VA. Bequest of Walter P. Chrysler, Jr. 89.60

▲ **This painting by Eastman Johnson, *Fiddling His Way* (1866), depicts a traveling African American fiddler who makes his living by entertaining people in their homes. Here, family members of all ages take time out from their daily routine to listen to him play.**

Smithsonian National Anthropological Archives

▲ Dakota Indians gather at the Standing Rock Reservation to receive government rations, c. 1880. To counter the Indians' increased dependence on the government for food, Congress passed the Dawes Severalty Act of 1887. U.S. agents cited the act in their efforts to ban crucial aspects of Indian culture, including native practices related to religion, education, language, and even dress and hairstyles.

Throughout the 1880s, Congress and the chief executive applied the laissez-faire principle selectively—for example, to the status of Indians. Like other critics of federal Indian policy, writer Helen Hunt Jackson in her 1881 book *A Century of Dishonor* called for applying the "protection of the law to the Indian's rights of property." Moved to act, Congress passed the Dawes General Allotment (Severalty) Act. The new act was intended to improve the economic condition of Indians by eliminating common ownership of tribal lands in favor of a system of private property. The law distributed plots of land to individual Indians who renounced traditional customs. The law also encouraged these landowners to become sedentary farmers and to adopt "other habits of civilized life." In the end, however, the act amounted to little more than a land-grab on the part of whites; between 1887 and 1900, Indian-held lands decreased from 138 million acres to 78 million acres.

DOCUMENT

The Dawes Act

By the 1880s, local citizens, through the Grange and their elected public officials, were calling for the states to restrict the monopolistic practices of the railroads. Nevertheless, in *Wabash v. Illinois* (1886), the Supreme Court invalidated a state law regulating railroads, ruling that only Congress, and not the states, could control interstate transportation. The next year Congress took the initiative and passed the Interstate Commerce Act of 1887. This legislation mandated that the railroads charge all shippers the same rates and refrain from giving rebates to their largest customers. The act also established the Interstate Commerce Commission to oversee and stabilize the railroad industry. Congress thus acknowledged that the public interest demanded some form of business regulation, although enforcement of the act was less than vigorous.

DOCUMENT

Interstate Commerce Act

Cleveland invoked laissez-faire principles in 1887 when he vetoed legislation that would have provided seeds for hard-pressed farmers in Texas. As the president put it, "Though the people support the government, the government should not support the people." Cleveland also favored lower tariff rates, but most Americans favored government protection of domestic manufacturing in the form of higher tariffs. The Republicans exploited Cleveland's unpopular views on this issue, nominating Benjamin Harrison, grandson of President William Henry ("Tippecanoe") Harrison. The younger Harrison defeated his rival in the electoral college but not in the popular vote.

The principle of government laissez-faire was of little use in addressing a central paradox of the late nineteenth century: the free enterprise system was being undermined by the very forms of business organization it had spawned and nourished. Trusts and combinations were inherently hostile to competition. In 1890 Congress passed a piece of landmark legislation, the Sherman Anti-Trust Act, designed to outlaw trusts and large business combinations of all kinds.

Social Darwinism and the "Natural" State of Society

In the late nineteenth century, manufactured devices and engineering feats helped create a new social order, one marked by a few very wealthy industrialists, a growing middle class, and an increasingly diverse workforce of ill-paid field and factory hands. Brazenly borrowing from the theories of Charles Darwin, a British naturalist who had pioneered the study of evolution, some prominent clergy, businesspeople, journalists, and university professors sought to defend this new order as God-ordained, or "natural." These observers drew parallels between Darwin's theory of "survival of the fittest" and the workings of modern society. (In his book *Origin of the Species,* Darwin had discussed the study of animals, not people or societies.) In the United States, Social Darwinists warned that "unnatural" forms of intervention—specifically, labor unions or social welfare legislation—were misguided, dangerous, and ultimately doomed to failure. In essence, Social Darwinists distorted a sound scientific theory, misusing it to justify exploitation of the poor and laboring classes.

The ideology of **Social Darwinism** evolved in response to class conflict and other forms of social turbulence in the 1870s and 1880s. Famed Brooklyn minister Henry Ward Beecher cited what he called "the great laws of political economy" to preach the virtues of poverty ("it was fit that man should eat the bread of affliction") and the evils of labor unions. Beecher and like-minded thinkers agreed that the government had the right and the obligation to come to the rescue of private companies threatened by angry workers or consumers. These observers also made a distinction between public subsidies to railroads and tariff protection for domestic manufacturers on one hand, and public intervention on behalf of workers on the other.

Yale sociologist William Graham Sumner declared that society was like a living organism. For the species to remain healthy, individuals must prosper or decline according to their inherent characteristics. "Society, therefore, does not need any care or supervision," Sumner wrote in his 1883 treatise *What the Social Classes Owe to Each Other.* These views rationalized not only the hierarchies of the workplace but also the triumph of "Anglo Saxons" on the North American continent and beyond. Editors of the *New York Times* interpreted Darwin's ideas as suggesting that "the red man will be driven out, and the white man will take possession. This is not justice, but it is destiny." In his book *Our Country* (1885), the Reverend Josiah Strong also drew on the ideas of Social Darwinism to claim that just as the fittest plants and animals endure in the natural kingdom, so "civilized" whites would eventually displace "barbarous," dark-skinned peoples, whether on the High Plains of South Dakota or on the savannas of Africa.

The ideology of Social Darwinism evolved in response to class conflict.

Not all Americans studied or debated the theories of Charles Darwin, of course. Nevertheless, middle-class opinion-makers, many of them Victorian Protestants, believed that their own religious and cultural values remained culturally superior to those of other groups of people, at home and abroad. The United States was becoming increasingly diverse in both economic and ethnic terms. At the same time, white, prosperous, native-born Protestants contended that they set the standards for the rest of the nation. These standards revolved around the middle-class domestic ideal, with its rigidly proscribed gender roles, devotion to personal achievement (for men at least), and commitment to moral suasion (that is, regulating a person's behavior by appealing to his or her conscience). Agents of the Victorian middle class included schoolteachers, clergy, magazine editors, business leaders, and other well-educated people able and willing to influence the beliefs and behavior of others.

Conclusion

Some historians suggest that the great captains of industry were the chief representatives of widely held values in late-nineteenth-century America. Men such as Carnegie and Rockefeller had the vision and personal ambition necessary to build large corporate enterprises. They became fabulously wealthy by providing the United States with the ingredients neces-

Andrew Carnegie and the "Gospel of Wealth"

In an article titled "Wealth," published in the North American Review *in 1889, steel manufacturer Andrew Carnegie defended the amassing of large fortunes on the part of a few. He hailed this trend as a sign of progress.*

The conditions of human life have not only been changed, but revolutionized, within the past few hundred years. In the former days there was little difference between the dwelling, dress, food, and environment of the chief and those of his retainers. The Indians are to-day where civilized man then was. When visiting the Sioux, I was led to the wigwam of the chief. It was just like the others in external appearance, and even within the difference was trifling between it and those of the poorest of his braves. The contrast between the palace of the millionaire and the cottage of the laborer with us to-day measures the change which has come with civilization.

This change, however, is not to be deplored, but welcomed as highly beneficial. It is well, nay, essential for the progress of the race, that the houses of some should be homes for all that is highest and best in literature and the arts, and for all the refinements of civilization, rather than that none should be so. Much better this great irregularity than universal squalor. . . . Whether the change be for good or ill, it is upon us, beyond our power to alter, and therefore to be accepted and made the best of. It is a waste of time to criticise the inevitable.

Judge, July 25, 1903

This *Judge* cartoon depicts Andrew Carnegie dispersing his fortune. Many of his donations were used for the establishment of public libraries, a worthy cause according to Carnegie's "gospel of wealth."

Carnegie believed that wealthy people had the responsibility to give away their money before they died, although he had distinct ideas about to whom—or to what—such money should be given. He elaborated on what came to be called the "gospel of wealth":

There remains, then, only one mode of using great fortunes; but in this we have the true antidote for the temporary unequal distribution of wealth, the reconciliation of the rich and the poor—a reign of harmony—another ideal, differing indeed, from that of the Communist in requiring only the further evolution of existing conditions, not the total overthrow of our civilization. . . . Under its sway we shall have an ideal state, in which the surplus wealth of the few will become, in the best sense, the property of the many, because it is administered for the common good, and this wealth, passing through the hands of the few, can be made a much more potent force for the elevation of our race than if it had been distributed in small sums to the people themselves. Even the poorest can be made to see this, and to agree that the great sums gathered by some of their fellow-citizens and spent for public purposes, from which the masses reap the principal benefit, are more valuable to them than if scattered through the course of many years in trifling amounts.

In 1901, Carnegie sold his steel company to banker J. P. Morgan for $480 million. By the time of his death, Carnegie had given away an estimated $350 million to a variety of causes and institutions.

Questions

1. *How does Carnegie link extremes of wealth and poverty with progress?*
2. *Why did Carnegie focus his philanthropic energies on building public libraries?*
3. *Why would Carnegie have rejected as impractical and unreasonable the argument that he should have paid his workers higher wages rather than distributing his profits to charity?* ■

Source: Andrew Carnegie, "Wealth," *North American Review* (1889).

sary to an economic revolution: steel, oil, and other materials. Their ideology of unbridled individualism encouraged many people to aspire to entrepreneurial independence: the tailor hoped to someday own a store, the cook dreamed of opening a restaurant. The explosion of economic activity during this period—a second American industrial revolution—widened the middle class and lent credence to the notion of widespread upward mobility, modest though it was in most cases.

Nevertheless, a case can be made that engineers were the true representatives of the age. As designers of railroad routes, gravity-defying skyscrapers, and new systems of factory management, they oversaw the technical aspects of economic growth and development.

Engineers melded science with mass production to yield a form of capitalism that thrived on consumers' deepest desires and anxieties. In the process, a new, complex national culture emerged. On the one hand, this culture valued innovation, newness, fashion, change, and sensory stimulation. Advertisers sought to convince consumers that they should buy products that were up to date. Customers all over the country desired to experience theatrical spectacles and athletic contests that were thrilling and novel. "Desires" replaced more traditional "needs" when Americans of all ages contemplated buying clothes and household furnishings. On the other hand, this culture also embraced impulses that were conservative, promoting the idea that white, Protestant, native-born Americans set the standard against which other Americans were judged, and often found wanting. Still, many native-born Americans and immigrants to the United States found this vital, new consumer culture enormously appealing.

At the same time, the effort to homogenize and standardize American cultural impulses was not without complications. Throughout the nation, various groups rejected standardization in favor of local tradition or new forms of collective action. Thus, politicians and the Social Darwinists were forced to defend their outlook on life. Some of their critics advanced the idea that society was not a living organism at all. Rather, it was like a machine, a creation of people who had the ability—and the duty—to repair or adjust it. Around the country, in fact, the standardizers met with stiff resistance.

Sites to Visit

Alexander Graham Bell Family Papers at the Library of Congress

www.memory.loc.gov/ammem/bellhtml/bellhome.html

This site contains papers from 1862 to 1839 as well as a chronology, images, selected documents, and interpretive essays about Bell.

John D. Rockefeller and the Standard Oil Company

www.micheloud.com/FXM/SO/

This study, with accompanying images by François Micheloud, tells of the rise of Rockefeller and his mammoth company.

The Transcontinental Railroad

www.sfmuseum.org/hist1/rail.html

This Museum of the City of San Francisco site has excellent information on the railroad.

Touring Turn-of-the-Century America: Photographs from the Detroit Publishing Company, 1880–1920

www.memory.loc.gov/ammem/detroit/dethome.html

This Library of Congress collection has thousands of photographs from turn-of-the-century America.

Negro Baseball Leagues

http://www.blackbaseball.com/

This site includes information about the history of the Negro Baseball Leagues, including teams and players.

African American Perspectives: Pamphlets from the Daniel A. P. Murry Collections, 1818–1907

www.memory.loc.gov/ammem/aap/aaphome.html

This collection includes writings of famous African Americans, including Frederick Douglass, Booker T. Washington, Ida B. Wells-Barnett, Benjamin W. Arnett, Alexander Crummel, and Emanuel Love.

The Evolution of the Conservation Movement, 1850–1920

www.memory.loc.gov/ammem/amrvhtml/conshome.html

This American Memory site brings together scores of primary sources and photographs about the historical formations and cultural foundations of the movement to conserve and protect America's natural heritage.

Inside an American Factory: The Westinghouse Works, 1904

http://memory.loc.gov/ammem/papr/west/westhome.html

Part of the American Memory Project at the Library of Congress, this site provides a glimpse inside a turn-of-the-century factory.

For Further Reading

General Works

Thomas Augst, *The Clerk's Tale: Young Men and Moral Life in the Nineteenth-Century America* (2003).

Alfred D. Chandler, *The Visible Hand: The Managerial Revolution in American Business* (1977).

Edwin S. Gaustad, *Proclaim Liberty Throughout All the Land: A History of Church and State in America* (2003).

Jon Gjerde, *The Minds of the West: Ethnocultural Evolution in the Rural Middle West, 1830–1917* (1997).

Andrew C. Isenberg, *The Destruction of the Bison: An Environmental History, 1750–1920* (2000).

T. Jackson Lears, *Fables of Abundance: A Cultural History of Advertising in America* (1994).

Walter Licht, *Industrializing America: The Nineteenth Century* (1995).

Carroll Pursell, *The Machine in America: A Social History of Technology* (1995).

Alan Trachtenberg, *The Incorporation of America: Culture and Society in the Gilded Age* (1982).

C. Vann Woodward, *Origins of the New South, 1877–1913* (1951).

The New Shape of Business

James R. Barrett, *Work and Community in the Jungle: Chicago's Packinghouse Workers, 1894–1922* (1987).

Ron Chernow, *Titan: The Life of John D. Rockefeller, Sr.* (1998).

Thomas C. Cochran, *Two Hundred Years of American Business* (1977).

Wendy Gamber, *The Female Economy: The Millinery and Dressmaking Trades, 1860–1930* (1997).

Thomas Parke Hughes, *American Genesis: A Century of Invention and Technological Enthusiasm, 1870–1970* (1989).

A. J. Millard, *Edison and the Business of Innovation* (1990).

Daniel Nelson, *Managers and Workers: Origins of the New Factory System in the United States, 1880–1920* (1975).

David E. Nye, *Electrifying America: Social Meanings of a New Technology, 1880–1940* (1990).

Dominic A. Pacyga, *Polish Immigrants and Industrial Chicago: Workers on the South Side, 1880–1922* (2003).

Donald J. Pisani, *Water, Land, and Law in the West: The Limits of Public Policy, 1850–1920* (1996).

C. J. Schmitz, *The Growth of Big Business in the United States and Western Europe, 1850–1939* (1993).

George Rogers Taylor and Irene D. Neu, *The American Railroad Network, 1861–1890* (1956).

David O. Whitten, *The Emergence of Giant Enterprise, 1860–1914* (1983).

The Birth of a National Urban Culture

Gunther Paul Barth, *City People: The Rise of Modern City Culture in Nineteenth-Century America* (1980).

Edwin G. Burrows and Mike Wallace, *Gotham: A History of New York City to 1898* (1999).

Howard P. Chudacoff and Judith E. Smith, *The Evolution of American Urban Society,* 5th ed. (2000).

William Cronon, *Nature's Metropolis: Chicago and the Great West* (1991).

Robert V. Hine and John Mack Faragher, *The American West: A New Interpretive History* (2000).

Eric Monkkonen, *America Becomes Urban: The Development of U.S. Cities and Towns, 1780–1980* (1988).

David Nasaw, *Going Out: The Rise and Fall of Public Amusements* (1993).

Steven A. Riess, *City Games: The Evolution of American Urban Society and the Rise of Sports* (1989).

Stanley K. Schultz, *Constructing Urban Culture: American Cities and City Planning, 1800–1920* (1989).

Robert Twombly, *Louis Sullivan: His Life and Work* (1986).

Thrills, Chills, and Bathtubs

Boris Emmet and John E. Jeuck, *Catalogues and Counters: A History of Sears, Roebuck and Company* (1950).

Allen Guttmann, *A Whole New Ball Game: An Interpretation of American Sports* (1988).

Harold Kaese, ed., *The Boston Braves, 1871–1953* (2004).

John F. Kasson, *Amusing the Millions: Coney Island at the Turn of the Century* (1978).

Joy S. Kasson, *Buffalo Bill's Wild West: Celebrity, Memory and Popular History* (2000).

William Leach, *Land of Desire: Merchants, Power, and the Rise of a New American Culture* (1993).

Kathy Lee Peiss, *Cheap Amusements: Working Women and Leisure in New York City, 1880 to 1920* (1986).

Bessie Louise Pierce, *As Others See Chicago: Impressions of Visitors, 1673–1933* (2004).

Greg Renoff, "'Wait for the Big Show!': The Circus in Georgia, 1865–1930," *Atlanta History* 46 (2004): 4–23.

Robert C. Toll, *On with the Show! The First Century of Show Business in America* (1976).

Defending the New Industrial Order

Thomas L. Haskell, *The Emergence of Professional Social Science: The American Social Science Association and the Nineteenth-Century Crisis of Authority* (1977).

Richard Hofstadter, *Social Darwinism in American Thought, 1860–1914,* rev. ed. (1955).

Morton Keller, *Affairs of State: Public Life in Late Nineteenth-Century America* (1977).

Valerie S. Mathes, *Helen Hunt Jackson and Her Indian Reform Legacy* (1990).

Louis Menand, *The Metaphysical Club: A Story of Ideas in America* (2001).

CHAPTER 17

Challenges to Government and Corporate Power: Resistance and Reform, 1877–1890

▲ The Ute chief Sevara poses with his family. In the mid-nineteenth century, European American miners began to push the Ute out of their territory in eastern Utah and western Colorado. Although many Ute resisted government pressure to give up hunting and become farmers, even engaging in gun battles with U.S. troops in 1879, they were gradually forced to yield their remaining lands to whites.

CHAPTER OUTLINE

Resistance to Legal and Military Authority

Revolt in the Workplace

Crosscurrents of Reform

Conclusion

Sites to Visit

For Further Reading

IN THE SPRING OF 1889, MEN IN SAN MIGUEL COUNTY, NORTHERN NEW MEXICO territory, armed themselves and donned masks. Mounting their horses, they rode out to attack their enemies. As members of a secret organization called *las Gorras Blancas* (the Whitecaps), they banded together in the dead of night and destroyed the fences of local cattle ranchers, chopping the wooden posts to pieces and scattering the barbed wire. In some of their raids, the rebels shot and wounded ranchers. Over the next year and a half, *las Gorras Blancas* broadened their targets. They burned bridges, haystacks, and piles of lumber; they cut telegraph wires and took axes to electric light poles and railroad ties belonging to the Atcheson, Topeka, and Santa Fe Railroad. The membership of the group overlapped with that of the Knights of Labor, a national labor union that boasted 20 local assemblies in San Miguel County, east of Santa Fe. On the night of March 11, 1890, *las Gorras Blancas* nailed pieces of paper to the buildings of East Las Vegas, the largest town in the county. These pages, copies of the insurgents' "platform," declared: "Our purpose is to protect the rights and interests of the people in general; especially those of the helpless classes."

By 1889, Santa Fe, New Mexico, had seen several centuries of cultural conflict.

Who were these determined nightriders? They consisted of Hispanos—Spanish-speaking natives of the area. Their movement began when Juan José Herrera, together with his two brothers, Pablo and Nicanor, organized their neighbors in an effort to block European American ranchers from fencing their land. Labeled *las masas de los hombres pobres* (the masses of the poor people) by a local newspaper, *las Gorras Blancas* were desperately struggling to preserve a traditional way of life that was rapidly disappearing. Fenced lands prevented the area's Hispanic settlers from grazing their stock herds in the customary, open-range manner.

The fence-cutters believed they were upholding American principles of justice and fair play. Released from jail in the town of Las Vegas, New Mexico, a group of them marched down the main street. At the head of their procession, women waved the American flag and sang "John Brown's Body," a song beloved by Union supporters during the Civil War.

Many Hispanos lived in adobe (baked-clay) dwellings in small river-valley villages surrounded by breathtaking mesas, ponderosa pine forests, and high dry plains. In addition to raising chickens and grazing sheep, families grew chiles, pinto beans, squash, and wheat. Together, villagers relied on the common lands that had come down to them from their ancestors—land originally bestowed through grants from Spain and then Mexico. After the Civil War, European American interlopers—sheep and cattle ranchers, lawyers, speculators, commercial lumberers, and the railroads—began to encroach on these common lands. Through local courts, the newcomers installed a system of private property that granted exclusive ownership to single individuals. It was these groups, with their fences and their laws governing land title registration, that *las Gorras Blancas* targeted.

Northern New Mexico had long witnessed battles between successive waves of settlers; for example, *Mexicanos* had fought Comanche and Jicarilla Apache for the land in earlier generations. Yet the upheaval in San Miguel County in 1889 and 1890 did not simply pit Hispanic subsistence farmers against European American "land grabbers." The Spanish-speaking population itself was divided between poor villagers and elite *ricos* (merchants and landowners). Members of *las Gorras Blancas* quarreled among themselves over whose fences to cut and whose barns to burn. They also broke with European American members of the Knights of Labor, insisting that, as Hispanos, they had the right and the obligation to protect their common lands, by force if necessary. The insurgents even renounced some of their own Hispanic political leaders. These men, they charged, had become corrupted by greed and were willing to do the bidding of European American interlopers.

Las Gorras Blancas had only mixed success. They managed to discourage new European Americans from settling in the area, and they prevented the railroads from buying more rail ties in northern New Mexico. Yet the nightriders could not stem the tide of land loss throughout the Southwest. The Court of Private Land Claims, established in 1891 by the U.S. government, resolved land disputes between Hispanic and European American claimants. Of the more than 35 million acres of land in dispute in the early 1890s, Hispanic claimants received title to little more than 2 million acres—barely one-twentieth of the land they had held in common.

Las Gorras Blancas represented a unique response to local conditions. But the group was also part of a growing, nationwide movement against the standards imposed by industrialization and capitalism. Around the country, a wide variety of individuals and organizations emerged in the late 1870s and the 1880s to challenge employers, landlords, and military and government officials. Members of these latter groups responded with a challenge of their own. Business, they proclaimed, must be allowed to develop fully and freely without "unnatural" intervention in the form of regulatory legislation or grassroots rebellions such as that of *las Gorras Blancas*.

The motto of the Knights of Labor was "An injury to one is an injury to all."

It is difficult to generalize about those who contested the emerging order. Even their own names could be misleading. In the early 1890s, another group called "white caps," this one in Mississippi, consisted of whites who terrorized black landowners. And although the Knights of Labor was a national union, it shaped its program in accordance with local issues. In San Miguel County, for instance, the issue was land—who controlled it and under what conditions. In Washington, D.C., the Knights' concern was the welfare of workers in the building trades. The Richmond, Virginia, Knights pioneered interracial organizing, living up to the group's motto, "An injury to one is an injury to all." In contrast, the San Francisco Knights spearheaded the move to bar Chinese laborers from the United States and to limit job opportunities for those who remained. Indeed, groups that challenged the authority of government and large business interests often disagreed among themselves about goals and strategies for change.

Rejecting new business principles that favored aggressive profit-seeking above all else, nightriders, union organizers, machine breakers, visionary prophets, investigative journalists, and settlement house workers all offered alternative visions for America. Members of these groups debated among themselves the changes overtaking American society and the means to control them. Some wielded pens or typewriters to effect change; others took photographs, collected data, or conducted interviews. Still others shouldered arms or torched haystacks. In some cases they sought to preserve local religious and social customs; in others they promoted the health and welfare of factory workers.

Some proponents of change advocated radical action that challenged the very foundations of American society. Others stressed the need to reform, but not change radically, certain elements of society and politics. Radicals and reformers alike derived ideas and inspiration from their European counterparts, for the issues confronting a rapidly industrializing society were not unique to the United States during this period. Nevertheless, Americans remained divided in their vision of the good and just society—a vision that would require the commitment of more than any one political party, labor union, reform association, or band of rebels to become reality.

Resistance to Legal and Military Authority

America's march toward national economic centralization and integration was not steady. On the battlefield and in the courts, European Americans pressed their advantage, but these efforts met with stiff resistance from a variety of aggrieved groups. Members of these groups rightly believed they had much to lose from so-called progress. Often the term was used to protect the interests of white men of property and did not result in any real progress for others.

Violent prejudice characterized the tactics of elites in expanding and preserving their privileges; vulnerable groups used various strategies to protect themselves and assert their own interests. European Americans repeatedly used the notion of "racial" difference as a justification for depriving darker-skinned peoples of their claims to land, jobs, and even life itself. For example, California lawmakers at both the state and local levels approved legislation that discriminated against the Chinese as workers and as parents of school-age children. In an effort to seek redress, some Chinese took their claims to court.

A variety of aggrieved groups rightly believed they had much to lose from so-called progress.

In a similar vein, prejudice against African Americans assumed the form of discriminatory legislation and random violence. Blacks chafed under restrictions intended to bar them from good jobs and from associating with white people on an equal basis. Varieties of black resistance to white authority included migration out of the South, creation of community institutions, and violent retaliation.

For their part, during the late 1880s the Plains Indians responded to encroaching railroads, settlers, and military regiments by embracing a movement of spiritual regeneration. On the Plains, whites, and especially U.S. military officers, perceived this movement as more dangerous than an armed uprising, and they reacted accordingly.

Chinese Lawsuits in California

In San Francisco in 1878, Irish-born Denis Kearney founded the Workingmen's Party of California, composed primarily of unemployed whites. Kearney and others agitated for the violent expulsion of Chinese from jobs. They blamed Chinese shoemakers, tailors, and cigarmakers for the distress that native-born factory workers and tradespeople were suffering. One critic remarked that the temperance Kearney "practiced and preached as to liquor and tobacco did not extend to opinions or their expression."

Farwell, The Chinese at Home and Abroad

In rural California, job-hungry whites formed anti-Chinese groups such as the American and European Labor Association, founded in Colusa County in 1882. The association also included employers who resented Chinese demands for equal pay (most received two-thirds the wages of their white counterparts for the same work). Yet despite all the personal and legal discrimination, the Chinese resisted.

Opposition to the Chinese hardened in the 1880s. In San Francisco, the Knights of Labor and the Workingmen's Party of California helped to engineer the passage of the

Chinese Exclusion Act, approved by Congress in 1882. This measure denied any additional Chinese laborers entry into the country while allowing some Chinese merchants and students to immigrate. (Put to the voters of California in 1879, the possibility of *total* exclusion of Chinese had garnered 150,000 votes for and only 900 against.) In railroad towns and mining camps, vigilantes looted and burned Chinese communities, in some cases murdering or expelling their inhabitants. In 1885 in Rock Springs, Wyoming, white workers massacred 28 Chinese and drove hundreds out of town in the wake of an announcement by Union Pacific officials that the railroad would begin hiring the lower-paid immigrants. Cheered on by others, a mob burned the Chinese section of town to the ground. Such attacks erupted more and more frequently throughout the West in the late 1880s and into the 1890s. Whites contended that they must present a united front against all Chinese, who, they claimed, threatened the economic well-being of white working-class communities.

Whites held that the Chinese, with their distinctive customs, would never fit into American life. Nevertheless, early on the Chinese demonstrated an understanding and appreciation of American political and legal processes. Beginning in Gold Rush days, Chinese immigrants had taken their grievances to court. Chan Young sued for citizenship in San Francisco's federal district court in 1855. In 1862 in the same city, Ling Sing protested the $2.50 personal tax levied on Chinese exclusively. The California Supreme Court agreed (in *Ling Sing v. Washburn*) that the group could not be singled out for special taxes. In the 1870s Chinese merchants used the provisions of the Civil Rights Act to challenge state and local laws that forbade them from holding certain jobs, living in white neighborhoods, and testifying in court. In the fall of 1885, Chinese residents of Rock Springs, Wyoming, wrote a lengthy appeal to the Chinese consul in San Francisco, relating their story of the massacre and appealing for justice; 559 people signed the document.

In San Francisco in 1885, laundry operator Yick Wo was convicted under an 1880 municipal law prohibiting the construction of wooden laundries without a license. A native of China, Yick Wo had arrived in the United States in 1861. By the time of his arrest, he had operated a legal laundry for 22 years. When he applied for a license, the board of supervisors turned

▶ In the West, Chinese mining companies used water management techniques based on traditional Chinese machinery such as the waterwheel. This photo shows a Chinese river-mining operation in Siskiyou, California, c. 1890. Chinese workers also constructed flumes, dams, canals, tunnels, and pumps to drain areas efficiently.

Courtesy, California History Room, California State Library, Sacramento (Neg. #23,239)

San Diego Historical Society Photograph Collection

◀ Some Chinese made a prosperous life for themselves in the United States. This photo shows Ah Sue, her husband, Ah Quin, and their 12 children. Ah Sue found refuge in the San Francisco Chinese Mission Home in 1879. Two years later she and Ah Quin celebrated their Christian wedding in the Mission Home. Ah Quin rose from the position of cook to become a successful railroad contractor and merchant in San Diego.

him down. His prominent European American lawyers soon learned that the board had denied licenses to all Chinese laundry operators who applied. However, it had granted licenses to almost all of their white counterparts. In 1885 the lawyers petitioned the California Supreme Court, which upheld Yick Wo's arrest. The lawyers continued their appeal to the U.S. Supreme Court, maintaining that the board of supervisors intended to bar Chinese from independent laundry work altogether.

In *Yick Wo v. Hopkins* (1886), the Supreme Court reversed the state court's decision. The higher court held that the San Francisco laundry-licensing board had engaged in the discriminatory *application* of a law that on the surface was nondiscriminatory. (The local board had admitted favoritism toward white license applicants but offered no justification for its actions.) The majority opinion noted, "The very idea that one may be compelled to hold his life, or the means of living, or any material right essential to the enjoyment of life, at the mere will of another" has been considered "intolerable in any country where freedom prevails, as being the essence of slavery itself." (In 1954, the Supreme Court cited this case in *Hernandez v. Texas* when it overturned the criminal conviction of a Mexican American defendant who showed that the county judicial system systematically excluded people of his background from jury service.)

Still, many cases challenging discriminatory laws never made it to the nation's highest court. And state and local courts in general often refused to acknowledge that Chinese immigrants had any civil rights at all. (Chinese immigrants were not granted citizenship until World War II, although their children born in this country qualified as citizens.) In 1885 the California Supreme Court heard the case *Tape v. Hurley,* brought by Joseph and Mary Tape on behalf of their daughter Mamie. Joseph Tape was a Chinese immigrant with some standing in the San Francisco

▲ **MAP 17.1 SOUTHERN TENANCY AND SHARECROPPING, 1880**
Tenants and sharecroppers were landless families who worked for a landowner. Tenant families usually owned a mule (to pull a plow); sharecropping families depended on their employers for food and farm supplies. This map shows that rates of tenancy and sharecropping were highest in the areas dominated by the cotton staple crop economy, the same areas where slavery prevailed in the antebellum period.

Chinese community. Mary Tape had been raised in a Shanghai orphanage and had come to the United States with missionaries when she was 11 years old. She grew up to speak English fluently and dressed as a European American. Their daughter Mamie was quite westernized as well.

Even so, Mamie Tape was barred from the city's public school system. The school board claimed that Mamie's presence in the classroom would be "very mentally and morally detrimental" to her classmates. The Tapes sued the city and won *(Tape v. Hurley)*, but the school board retaliated by creating a separate school for children of Asian descent within Chinatown. Mary Tape wrote an angry letter to the board: "Dear Sirs, Will you please to tell me! Is it a disgrace to be Born a Chinese? Didn't God make us all!!! What right! have you to bar my children out of the school?" In the end, the Tapes decided to enroll their two children in the segregated school. Yet their legal protest kept alive the ideal of equality under the law.

In other instances, local white prejudice overwhelmed even Chinese who sought legal redress from violence and discrimination. In 1886 the Chinese living in the Wood River mining district in southern Idaho faced down a group of whites who had met and announced that all Chinese had three months to leave town. Members of the Chinese community promptly hired lawyers and took out an advertisement in the local paper stating their intention to hold their ground. As a community they managed to survive. Still, their numbers dropped precipitously throughout Idaho as whites hounded many of them out of the state.

Blacks in the "New South"

In 1886 Henry Grady, the young editor of the Atlanta *Constitution,* traveled north to deliver a speech to the New England Society of New York. A graduate of the University of Georgia, the 36-year-old Grady had achieved prominence in Georgia politics. In his speech that day, Grady hailed what he called the "New South." The former Confederate states, he claimed, were now forward looking, prepared to embrace industrialization and promote the reconciliation of blacks and whites. According to the journalist, it was time for the South to march forward and join with a larger, modernizing America.

Grady's speech about the "New South" provided a label that stuck. Yet he doubtless spoke too soon and in terms too grandiose. True, he could point with pride to some dramatic industrial developments in the South. The eastern Piedmont (foothills region), for example, was undergoing a fledgling industrial revolution in the 1880s. Soon after James Bonsack invented a cigarette-rolling machine in 1880, James Buchanan Duke pioneered the production of machine-made cigarettes. In 1884 Duke's Durham, North Carolina, company was selling 400,000 of them each day. The southern textile labor force more than doubled between 1880 and 1890, from 17,000 men, women, and children to 36,000, many of them concentrated in the Carolinas and Georgia.

In the mid-1880s, with the backing of the Tennessee Coal, Iron, and Railway Company, the city of Birmingham, Alabama, specialized in pig iron production. Local manufacturers remained at the mercy of high shipping rates imposed by northern-owned railroads, which provided discounts only to raw materials going north and manufactured goods coming south. However, in 1889 even Andrew Carnegie acknowledged the formidable challenge posed by Birmingham blast furnaces to iron and steel producers in the North and abroad.

Factory and professional work in towns and cities offered new opportunities in the South as industry developed. However, these jobs were dominated by white men. Low-paid heavy labor, primarily in rural areas, continued to be the primary source of work for black men. After they finished harvesting cotton in the fall, many black men worked at sawmills or in railroad construction camps during the winter.

The hardest and lowest-paid jobs, such as digging ore out of a hill in northern Alabama or constructing a railroad through the swamps of Florida, often went to convicts whom private employers had leased from the state. Most of these "convict lease" workers were black men who had been arrested on minor charges and then bound out when they could not pay their fines or court costs. In Mississippi a black man could be picked up for "some trifling misdemeanor," in the words of one observer, fined $500, and compelled to work off the fine (at a rate of 5 cents a day) for a local planter. With an almost unlimited supply of such workers, employers had little incentive to ease the brutal living and working conditions endured by these convicts.

Patterns of migration within and outside the South reveal blacks' efforts to resist discrimination. Some blacks fled the countryside and settled in southern cities where good jobs were limited but personal freedom was greater. In 1890, 15 percent of the southern black population lived in towns and cities; they represented a third of the South's total urban population.

George François Mugnier, The John N. Teunisson Photograph Collection, Louisiana Division, New Orleans Public Library

◀ This bustling New Orleans waterfront scene, c. 1885, suggests the commercial vitality often associated with the "New South." However, a closer look reveals that all of the activity revolves around loading and unloading bales of cotton. In fact, the New South remained locked in a low-wage, staple crop economy based on the production of cotton.

Lower Mississippi Valley

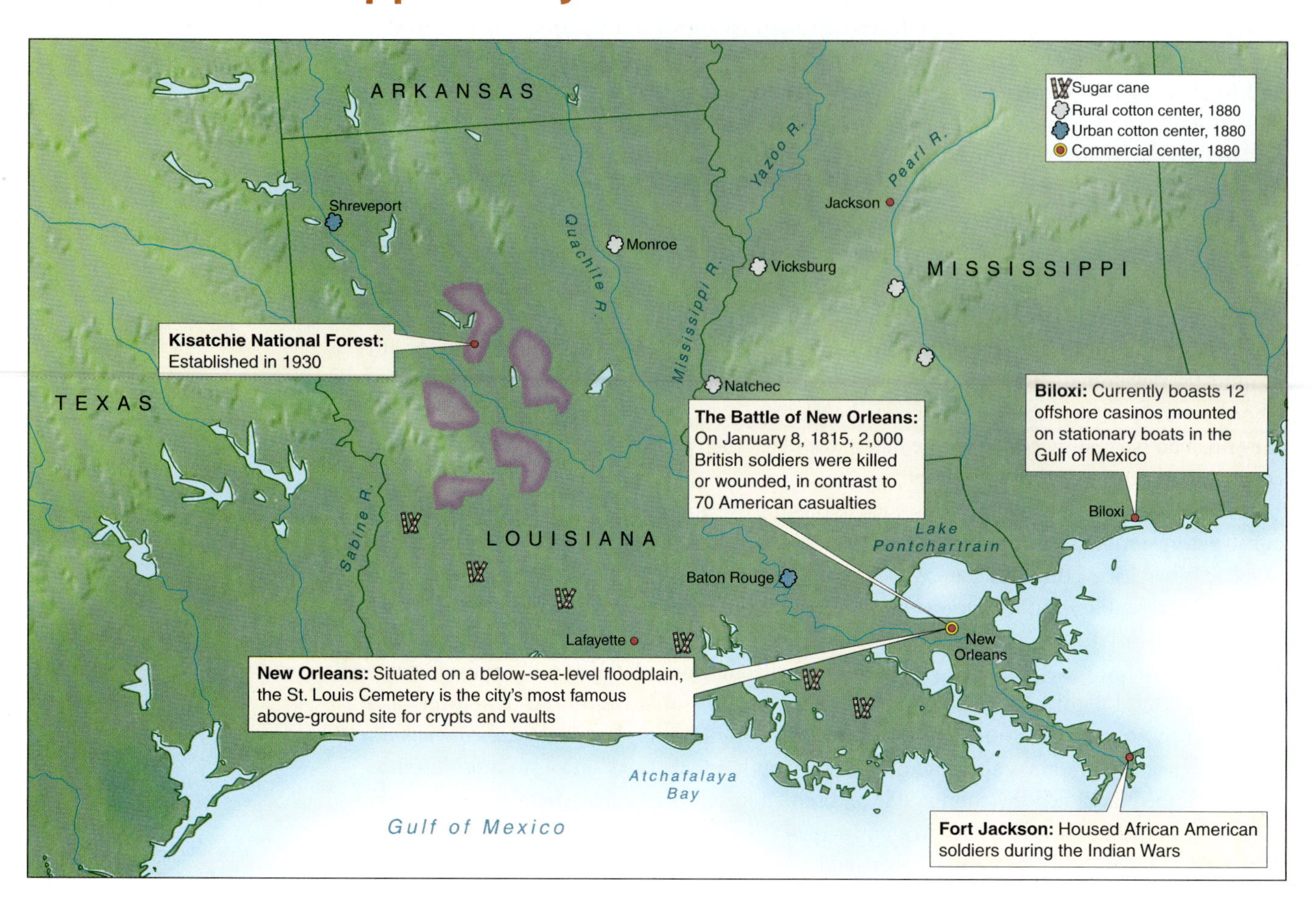

The political economy of the Lower Mississippi Valley has changed dramatically over the centuries. In the seventeenth century, a frontier exchange economy facilitated trade among Indians, enslaved Africans and their descendants, and French colonists. In the early 1800s, migrants from the southern seaboard, with the labor of many slaves, created expansive sugar and cotton plantations in the rich, fertile Delta soil. After the Civil War, the Delta region was the site of large agribusinesses, huge cotton farms employing many black workers under the exploitative sharecropping system. In the mid-1950s, the introduction of the mechanical cotton picker reduced the demand for field labor, and many blacks left the region for a better life in the upper Midwest.

In the early twentieth century, forests covered two-thirds of Louisiana. In 1910 the state was the country's top lumber producer. By the late 1920s, when the forests had been cut over, the sawmills closed down.

Today, the rural Delta is known for its chicken and catfish processing plants, which rely on low-wage labor. Casinos in Biloxi and along the Mississippi River draw fortune-seekers from a wide area. In 2003 alone, the state of Mississippi took in $330 million in taxes from gambling establishments. ■

The Image Bank/Getty Images

Gradually, a new black elite arose. These physicians, lawyers, insurance agents, and undertakers reached out to an exclusively black clientele. They also nourished a sense of community. Black men and women continued to sustain their own institutions, such as schools, lodges, benevolent societies, burial organizations, and churches. Black men formed fraternal organizations such as the Colored Masons and the Colored Odd Fellows. Black women created social and service organizations, such as the United Daughters of Ham and the Order of the Eastern Star.

Despite Henry Grady's pronouncements, clearly the South had not abandoned its historical legacy of white supremacist ideologies. In fact, in the late 1880s white Democrats feared the assertiveness of the new black elite. According to whites, this generation of men and women born as free persons and not as slaves must be "put in their place," quite literally. As a result, new state and local laws mandated separate water fountains for blacks and whites, restricted blacks to separate railroad cars and other forms of public transportation, and excluded them altogether from city parks and other public spaces. Long-standing customs barring black people from white-owned theaters, restaurants, and hotels now carried the weight of law. Taxpayers' money went into state school funds, which were then sent back to local districts. There the money was used to support two separate school systems, one white and well funded, one black and starved of cash. Legal discrimination against blacks came to be called the "Jim Crow" system. (The term, a reference to a minstrel show character named Jim Crow, had originated during the antebellum period.)

Black leaders throughout the country tried to keep a national spotlight on the Jim Crow system, its legal and violent manifestations. A rising tide of lynching (it would crest in the 1890s) engulfed the South, but white officials did little or nothing to halt it. Black men, women, and children were all vulnerable to the fury of the white lynch mob—on the most flimsy pretext. Perpetrators of these atrocities were rarely if ever apprehended and punished. Other blacks throughout the segregated South rightly feared that they too would be targeted if they spoke out against lynching. Yet northern blacks did not hesitate to highlight the hypocrisy of the federal government, which turned a blind eye toward this practice. Frances Ellen Watkins Harper, an educator and writer living in Philadelphia, issued the following challenge to an audience of white club women: "A government which has the power to tax a man in peace, draft him in war, should have the power to defend his life in the hour of peril." Harper condemned "the government which can protect and defend its citizens from wrong and outrage and does not."

"Jim Crow" in the West

Racial segregation was not limited to the South. The U.S. military enforced its own set of Jim Crow regulations. In 1869 Congress created the 24th and 25th Infantries (Colored) composed of African American soldiers. White officers were appointed to lead these segregated units; consequently, black men who aspired to positions of military leadership found their way blocked. (Before 1900, only three black men received commissions from West Point, and they faced systematic harassment at the academy and after graduation.) Some white officers, such as George Custer, refused to command black troops at all.

Military officials assigned black soldiers to the West, where they became known as buffalo soldiers. (The origins of the term are unclear. It may refer to the buffalo robes worn by many of the soldiers or to Plains Indians' respect for the black men's skills on horseback.) Many of these men were proud to wear a U.S. soldier's uniform, an emblem of their newly won citizenship rights. Organized in two cavalry and two infantry regiments, the soldiers stationed in western outposts found that military duty entailed a combination of new opportunities and old forms of humiliation.

Within their garrisons, they performed a variety of tasks related to everyday military drills and maintenance. Black soldiers helped to construct new roads and forts, protect wagon trains of settlers, and patrol the border between the United States and Mexico. They were an

William Katz Collection

▶ **Among the "buffalo soldiers" who served with the U.S. military were these Seminole scouts. The Seminole traced their history to the eighteenth century, when Creek Indians and runaway slaves of African descent established communities together in Florida. After the Seminole Wars (1818–1858), many Seminole were relocated to Indian Territory (present-day Oklahoma). Some fled to Mexico before the Civil War. In 1870 they were recruited by the U.S. Army as scouts. Their unit was disbanded 11 years later. Racist policies of the military caused some to return to Mexico.**

integral part of campaigns to subdue the Cheyenne, Comanche, Sioux, Ute, Kiowa, and Apache Indians. They were among the soldiers deployed to quash strikes among workers (silver miners in Idaho, for example) and to fight forest fires in the Northwest. As members of a novel, all-black regimental musical band, one group played for white audiences from Montana to Texas.

Often the buffalo soldiers encountered hostility from local townspeople, who resented their patronage of local establishments. In 1881 Tenth Cavalry troops stationed at Fort Concho near San Angelo, Texas, reacted angrily when a local white man killed a black soldier in a saloon. Another soldier had died at the hands of a local white within the previous two weeks. In the absence of justice for the murderers, the soldiers blanketed San Angelo with handbills. Signed "U.S. soldiers," the message read, "If we do not receive justice and fair play...someone will suffer, if not the guilty, the innocent. It has gone far enough." When some of the black soldiers attacked one of the men they believed guilty, the Texas Rangers entered the town to restore order. The army transferred the black companies out of the area and disciplined the leaders of the protest.

Once they were mustered out of the army, some black soldiers decided to settle permanently in the West. There they joined thousands of black migrants who were fleeing the Jim Crow South. In the late 1870s, 20,000 blacks from Tennessee, Mississippi, and Louisiana, called "Exodusters," migrated into western Kansas. The migrants cited the South's convict lease system, poor schools, and pervasive violence and intimidation as reasons for their flight. Henry Adams, a native of Shreveport, Louisiana, and a U.S. army veteran, expanded on the migrants' grievances when he pointed to the failed promise of Reconstruction as the root cause of migration: "The whole South—every State in the South—had got into the hands of the very men that held us as slaves...and we thought that the men that held us slaves was holding the reins of government over our heads in every respect almost, even the constable up to the governor."

Some of these migrants established all-black towns in Kansas, Colorado, Nebraska, and New Mexico. Though generally small and poor, such towns were necessarily free of the trappings of Jim Crow. They provided places for blacks to live on their own terms.

The Ghost Dance on the High Plains

Their lands and way of life threatened by whites, western Indians sought desperately to revitalize their culture and protect themselves. In 1889 an Indian named Wovoka offered the Plains

▲ **MAP 17.2 BUFFALO SOLDIERS**
In 1866 Congress authorized the creation of four permanent military units consisting of African American Civil War veterans. These soldiers played a prominent role in the Indian wars of the West from 1866 to 1890. They were stationed in federal forts scattered throughout the western states.

Indians a mystical vision of the future, a vision that promised a return to the beloved past. A leader of the Paiute in Nevada, Wovoka preached what came to be called the Ghost Dance, part religion and part resistance movement. In 1889 a solar eclipse occurred while Wovoka was wracked by fever, and he claimed that the conjunction of the two events enabled him to glimpse the afterworld. The Indians could usher in a new day of peace, Wovoka proclaimed, and this new day would be a time free of disease and armed conflict. The buffalo would return, he promised, and the Indian men and women who had died would come back to replenish depleted villages.

Sioux Ghost Dance

Wovoka's call found its warmest reception among the Plains Indians. In 1890 an anthropologist recorded an exhortation that Wovoka (called Jack Wilson by whites) delivered to the Cheyenne and Arapaho: "When you get home you must make a dance to continue five days. Dance four successive nights, and the last night keep up the dance until the morning of the fifth day, when all must bathe in the river and then disperse to their homes. You must all do in the same way." Some Indians donned "ghost shirts" made of white muslin and adorned with images of the sun, moon, stars, and various animals. They believed these garments would provide them with magical powers and protect them from the white men's bullets.

Many of the Indians who performed the Ghost Dance fell into a trance-like state, bringing inspiration to impoverished and disheartened reservation communities. However, as the ritual spread across the Plains, U.S. military officials panicked. In November 1890, E. B.

Reynolds, a Special U.S. Indian Agent, described to his superiors in Washington the strange, seemingly dangerous behavior that had gripped the Indians on Pine Ridge Reservation in South Dakota: "The religious excitement aggravated by almost starvation is bearing fruits in this state of insubordination; Indians say they had better die fighting than to die a slow death of starvation, and as the new religion promises their return to earth, at the coming of the millennium, they have no fear of death."

As tensions between whites and Indians mounted, the Sioux leader Sitting Bull came to the fore. Born in the early 1830s, he had gained respect among his people as a Wichasa Wakan ("holy man"). At the Battle of the Little Big Horn, he helped protect Indian women and children from Custer's soldiers. Wooden Leg, a Northern Cheyenne, later described Sitting Bull as "altogether brave, but peaceable. He was strong in religion—the Indian religion." After leading his followers into Canada, Sitting Bull returned to the United States in 1881. He surrendered at Fort Buford, Dakota Territory, where he was held prisoner for two years. His brief stint as a performer in Buffalo Bill Cody's "Wild West" show left him disgusted with the ways of white people.

Sitting Bull offered a pointed critique of the sedentary, materialistic way of life promoted by whites:

> White men like to dig in the ground for their food. My people prefer to hunt buffalo as their fathers did. White men like to stay in one place. My people want to move their tepees here and there to different hunting grounds. The life of white men is slavery. They are prisoners in towns or farms. The life my people want is a life of freedom. I have seen nothing that a white man has, houses or railways or clothing or food, that is as good as the right to move in open country, and live in our own fashion.

Frederic S. Remington, *The Ghost Dance by the Ogallala Sioux at Pine Ridge Agency, Dakota,* 1890. Amon Carter Museum, Fort Worth, Texas

▲ A popular artist whose work was featured in leading magazines of his time, Frederic Remington drew a scene from the Oglala Sioux Ghost Dance of 1890. Throughout the Great Plains and the Rocky Mountain region, men, women, and children participated in the ritual dance, moving in a circle and singing. The strange sight frightened many whites. In December 1890, U.S. troops attacked and killed several hundred Indians on the Pine Ridge Reservation in South Dakota. The Wounded Knee massacre marked the end of the Indian wars of the nineteenth century.

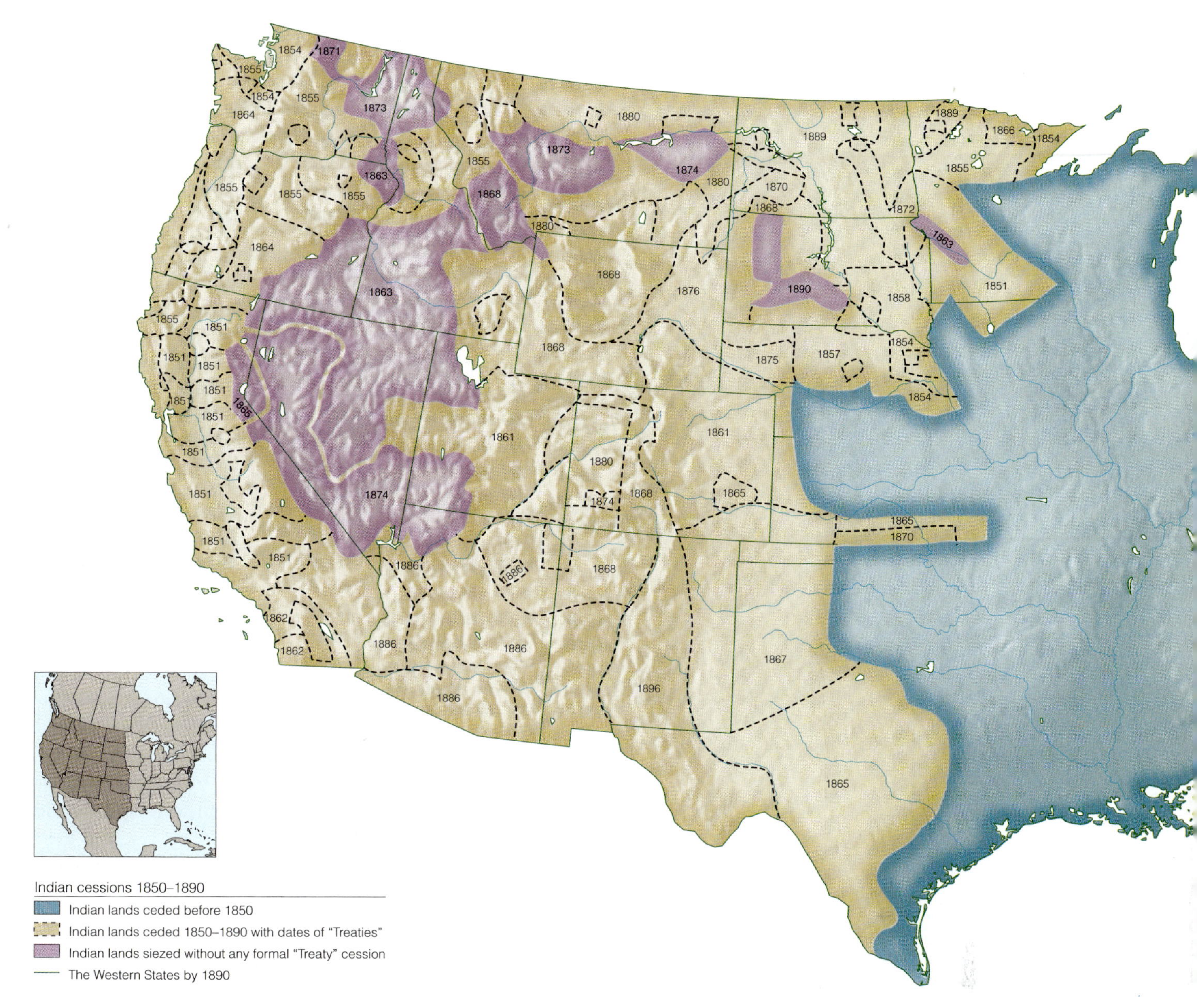

▲ **MAP 17.3 INDIAN LANDS LOST, 1850–1890**

Between 1850 and 1890, many "treaties" signed by Indian groups and the U.S. government provided that Indians turn over land in exchange for cash payments. Yet U.S. military forces seized a large portion of western Indian lands by force, without signing any treaty agreements at all. By 1890 many Indians lived on reservations, apart from European American society.

Sitting Bull rejected white notions of "progress" in favor of his people's traditions.

In mid-December 1890, military officials ordered Indian police to arrest Sitting Bull at his cabin on the Standing Rock Reservation in South Dakota. Alarmed by what they perceived as rising Indian militancy, white settlers in Nebraska and South Dakota pressured the government to rid the area of the "savages…armed to the teeth," men who were "traitors, anarchists, and assassins." While arresting Sitting Bull, his Indian captors killed him. The great man's followers, who had revered him as a prophet, decried the murder.

A week later, on December 28 and 29, soldiers of the Seventh Cavalry under Colonel James Forsyth, agitated by the tensions over Sitting Bull's death, attacked Indians at Wounded Knee Creek, South Dakota. Estimates of the number of Indians killed range from 150 to 250. More than 60 women and children were among those slain as they fled the oncoming troops. Of the 25 U.S. soldiers who perished, most apparently died from shots fired by their own comrades; according to a government eyewitness, the Indian men were unarmed when the cavalry attacked.

Accounts of the Wounded Knee Massacre

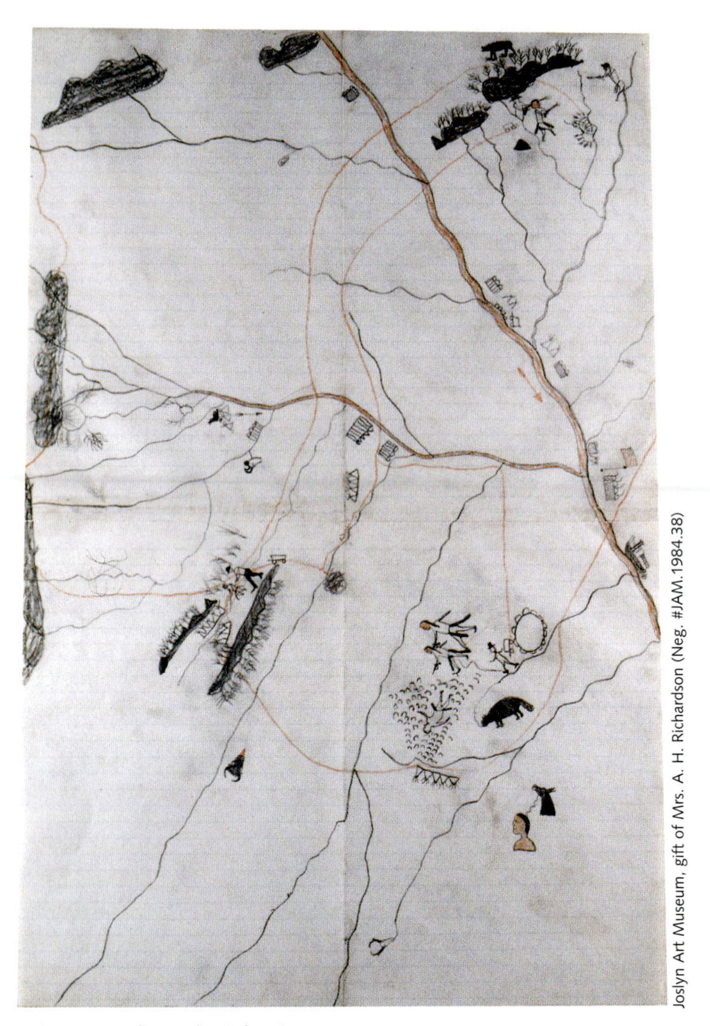

Joslyn Art Museum, gift of Mrs. A. H. Richardson (Neg. #JAM.1984.38)

▲ A map drawn by John Crazy Mule, a Cheyenne warrior and U.S. Army scout, illustrates several historic encounters between Indians and soldiers. Places and events are designated with pictographs. For example, the Missouri River is marked with a steamboat (center right). Among the events depicted is the capture of Chief Joseph of the Nez Perce in the Bear Paw Mountains in 1877.

The massacre at Wounded Knee proved the last major violent encounter between Plains Indians and U.S. cavalry forces. By this time, many Indians throughout the Midwest lived on reservations and engaged in farming. In Oklahoma, for example, the Cheyenne learned how to grow cotton and watermelons. Government agents, eager to create independent farmers, instructed Indian men in the use of the plow. But John Stands-in-Timber, a Cheyenne, later recalled how plowing became a collective effort. It engaged the energies of Indian men from Oklahoma to Montana, he noted, as bands would work together until their task was done. Thus some Indian groups attempted to maintain customs of collective endeavor in opposition to the European Americans' glorification of ambition and individualism.

Revolt in the Workplace

During the late nineteenth century, workers challenged employers and the new industrial order for many reasons. Factory operatives objected to long hours and to low pay in return for tending dangerous machines. Miners labored daily under hazardous conditions, often without necessary safety equipment or precautions. Field hands worried that they would soon be displaced by machines such as the giant threshers that were far more efficient—quicker and cheaper—than human labor. Small farmers resented their dependence on bankers and owners of **grain elevators** and railroads. Throughout the country, many different kinds of workers feared that the large influx of immigrants would provide a vast reserve of cheap labor that would depress the wages, and threaten the job security, of everyone.

Workers launched different kinds of challenges against the system of industrial capitalism, which, many charged, enriched a few industrialists and bankers at the expense of the vast majority of laboring people. Workers joined together in unions, and in many cases they fought the violence of security forces with violence of their own. Some men and women destroyed the machinery that threatened to replace them in the workplace. Southern tenants and sharecroppers challenged the exploitative labor system that left their families perpetually in debt.

By the early 1890s, critics of the new industrial and agribusiness order had come together in the form of a new political group, the People's party. This organization aimed to bring together urban and rural, male and female, agricultural and industrial workers to protest the hardships suffered by laborers of all kinds and to demand that the federal government take strong action in rectifying social ills.

Nevertheless, in workplace conflicts, the lines were not always strictly drawn between employees and employers. For example, the late-nineteenth-century laboring classes never achieved the level of unity called for by the Populists. White workers often expressed intense hostility toward their African American and Chinese counterparts. Within small towns, shopkeepers and landlords at times showed solidarity with striking workers; in these cases community ties were stronger than class differences. Also, despite their critique of big business, workers often embraced the emerging consumer culture. In fact, many of them fought for shorter workdays and higher wages so that they could enjoy their share of the material blessings of American life—in department stores, movie theaters, and amusement parks. In the end, Populism was primarily a rural movement composed of small farmers, sharecroppers, and wage hands.

Trouble on the Farm

In the late summer of 1878, the combined effects of the recent national economic depression and the loss of jobs to labor-saving technology catalyzed a rash of machine breaking throughout rural Ohio. The tactics of the machine-breakers bore some resemblance to those of *las Gorras Blancas* in northern New Mexico. In the Midwest, displaced farm hands burned the reapers, mowers, and threshers of their former employers. By autumn the violence had spread to Michigan and Indiana. Scattered reports of torched reapers, mowers, barns, and crops emanated from Illinois, Iowa, Wisconsin, and Minnesota. Some wealthy farmers responded by abandoning their machinery and rehiring their farm hands. Technology, one noted, "ought to be dispensed with in times like these." Critics charged the machine-breakers with "short-sighted madness." True, seasonal farm hands were fast losing their usefulness in the new machine age. However, the protests revealed that even family farming had become a business. Now farmers needed to secure bank loans, invest in new machinery, and worry about the price of crops in the world market. These changes had profoundly altered labor relations between farm workers and farmers and between farmers and their creditors.

On the Northern Plains, farmers endured extremes of weather and the anxiety of uncertain harvests. This area was home to immigrants from Scandinavia and Russia, drawn to the region by abundant rainfall and cheap land prices in the late 1870s and early 1880s. These men and women concentrated on ranching and farming. They built sod houses out of rectangular bricks cut from the hard prairie soil. Warm in winter and cool in summer, the houses nevertheless had roofs that needed shoring up after every rainfall. In Madison County, Nebraska, a family of five lived in a dirt-floor sod house built into the side of a ravine. Their furnishings consisted of a cookstove, a bed, a milk cooler, "and a few other articles."

In the mid-1880s the plight of these Plains farmers worsened when a series of natural disasters highlighted their vulnerability to the elements. No form of modern technology could prevent the drought of 1886, which dragged on for a decade. Combined with declining wheat prices, the prolonged dry weather drove fully half the population of western Kansas and

TABLE 17.1

Percentage of Farms Operated by Tenants or Sharecroppers

	1880	1890	1900	1910	1920
North	19.2	22.1	26.2	26.5	28.2
New England	8.5	9.3	9.4	8.0	7.4
Middle Atlantic	19.2	22.1	25.3	22.3	20.7
East North Central	20.5	22.8	26.3	27.0	28.1
West North Central	20.5	24.0	29.6	30.9	34.2
South	36.2	38.5	47.0	49.6	46.9
South Atlantic	36.1	38.5	44.2	45.9	46.8
East South Central	36.8	38.3	48.1	50.7	49.7
West South Central	35.2	38.6	49.1	52.8	52.9
West	14.0	12.1	16.6	14.0	17.7
Mountain	7.4	7.1	12.2	10.7	15.4
Pacific	16.8	14.7	19.7	17.2	20.1
U.S.	25.6	28.4	35.3	37.0	38.1

Source: U.S. Special Committee on Farm Tenancy, *Farm Tenancy* (1937), pp. 39, 36.

▶ **A Nebraska farm family poses proudly with their new windmill, c. 1890. Such devices powered water pumps that reached deep into the earth. Though expensive, windmills were necessities for drought-stricken farmers on the Plains, especially during the harsh years of the mid-1880s to the mid-1890s.**

Nebraska State Historical Society, Solomon D. Butcher Collection

Nebraska back east to Iowa and Illinois during 1888 to 1892. Meanwhile, the bitterly cold winter of 1886–1887 decimated cattle herds throughout the region. The resulting "great die up" ended the days of the huge herds that ranged the Plains. Thereafter, ranchers would concentrate on smaller stock holdings and selective breeding.

Some American writers captured the bleakness of prairie life, highlighting the condition of farmers dependent on predatory institutions and machines, such as banks and railroads. Writing from firsthand experience of his native Wisconsin, Hamlin Garland portrayed the harsh life endured by men and women who toiled "under the lion's paw" of scheming creditors and landlords. Other chroniclers of life on the Plains portrayed nature as a pitiless adversary that promised bountiful harvests one day but rained plagues of locusts the next.

Things took a radical turn in the 1880s, when a national movement of farmers emerged and tapped into a wellspring of anger and discontent in farming regions throughout the nation. Men and women from the Plains states organized in the National Farmers' Alliance, or Northern Alliance, joined with their Louisiana, Texas, and Arkansas counterparts in the National Farmers' Alliance and Industrial Union, or Southern Alliance. The Colored Farmers' Alliance was formed in 1886.

The Southern Alliance pressed for an expanded currency, taxation reform, and government ownership of transportation and communication lines. Its members tended to ally with the Democratic party. The Northern Alliance also focused on the expansion of the currency supply—specifically, the coinage of silver—but advocated the formation of a third political party to advance its interests. Both of these large regional groups found adherents in the mountain West. There, miners and farmers joined together to protest the monopolistic powers of the railroads, privately owned water companies, and silver mining interests. These monopolies drove up consumer prices and depressed workers' wages.

Most Alliance men and women farmed modest parcels of land. As small producers, they felt powerless to influence the businesspeople and politicians who affected their livelihoods and their life possibilities. Members of the alliance also presented themselves as the last line of defense for the noble yeoman in the face of the corrupting influences of modern capitalism. In rural Alabama, where the Farmers' Alliance had links with local schools and churches, the group's newspapers railed against the "filthy city," a "wicked place" of vice, crime, and dissipation. Farm folk thus distanced themselves from the "New South Creed," which promoted materialism and industrialization.

In many local groups, or suballiances, women stepped forward to claim their due as wives, mothers, and workers. In Tennessee, farm wives who raised chickens and produced milk and butter for market encountered middlemen who set unfair prices for both producers and consumers. Women argued that they were more than their husbands' helpmeets; they were partners in a family enterprise. As such, they demanded respect and a political voice. Wrote one woman to the *Weekly Toiler,* the paper of the state's Farmers' Alliance, "It would be better, methinks, if the men would say, 'come join us in the fight against your enemy' with as bold a front as he says, 'come Betsy, help me hang the meat, and drop the corn and potatoes.'"

Suffering from a recession in the late 1880s, farmers in the Dakotas, Nebraska, Kansas, and Texas began to mobilize into a new political party. Organizing work among Alliance members at the local level laid the foundation for the creation of the People's, or Populist, party. In Johnson County, Wyoming, in 1890, small farmers joined the Populist party in response to attacks on their property by gunmen hired by the Wyoming Stock Growers Association, a monopoly of large cattle ranchers.

Although the Farmers' Alliance identified itself primarily with agricultural interests, it made some notable forays into coalition-building. In 1889 the northern and southern groups attempted to combine with the Colored Farmers' Alliance. Together, these groups claimed more than 4 million members. They also sought to join with the Knights of Labor and thus bring all members of the "producing classes" together. By representing the financial interests of all farmers and highlighting the vulnerabilities of debtors, the organization foreshadowed the wider national appeal of the Populist party in the 1890s.

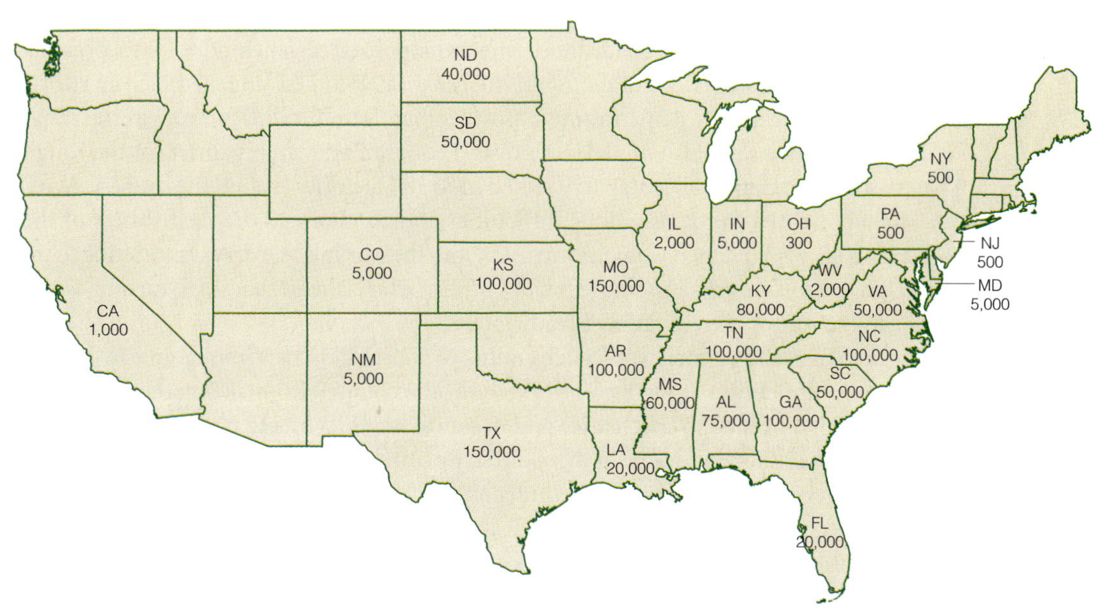

▲ **MAP 17.4 ESTIMATED MEMBERSHIP, BY STATE, OF THE NATIONAL FARMER'S ALLIANCE, 1890**

Clay County Historical Society, Moorhead, Minnesota (Neg. #F/W 12971)

▲ **In the Midwest, farmers had to contend with monopolies that charged high prices for goods and services. Farmers depended on grain elevators (such as this one in Minnesota in 1879) to store their harvests for shipment by rail. In the early 1890s the Populist party exploited the image of the small family farmer at the mercy of powerful industrialists, merchants, banks, and railroads.**

Militancy in the Factories and Mines

The new economy wrought profound hardship on members of the urban laboring classes as well as on small farmers. Many industrial workers faced layoffs and wage cuts during the economic depressions of the 1870s and 1880s. The great railroad strikes of 1877 (see Chapter 16) foreshadowed an era of bitter industrial conflict. Because no laws regulated private industry, employers could impose 10- to 15-hour workdays, six days a week. (By the 1890s, bakers were working as long as 65 hours a week.) Industrial accidents were all too common, and some industries lacked safety precautions. Steelworkers labored in excessive heat; miners and textile mill employees contracted respiratory diseases. With windows closed and machines speeded up, new forms of technology created new risks for workers. The Chicago meatpackers, who wielded gigantic cleavers in subfreezing lockers, and the California wheat harvesters, who operated complex mechanical binders and threshers, were among those confronting danger on the job.

In 1884 the Massachusetts Bureau of Statistics of Labor issued a report outlining the occupational hazards for working women in the city of Boston. In button-making establishments, female workers often got their fingers caught under punch and die machines. Employers provided a surgeon to dress an employee's wounds the first three times she was injured; thereafter, she had to pay for her own medical care. Women operated heavy power machinery in the garment industry and exposed themselves to dangerous chemicals and other substances in paper-box making, fish packing, and confectionery manufacturing.

Some women workers, especially those who monopolized certain kinds of jobs, organized and struck for higher wages. Three thousand Atlanta washerwomen launched such an effort in 1881 but failed to get their demands met. Most women found it difficult to win the respect not only of employers but also of male unionists. Leonora Barry, an organizer for the Knights of Labor, sought to change all that. Barry visited mills and factories around the country. At each stop, she highlighted women's unique difficulties and condemned the "selfishness of their brothers in toil" who resented women's intrusion into the workplace. Barry was reacting to men such as Edward O'Donnell, a prominent labor official who claimed that wage-earning women threatened the role of men as family breadwinners.

For both men and women workers, the influx of 5.25 million new immigrants in the 1880s stiffened job competition at worksites throughout the country. To make matters worse, vast outlays of capital needed to mechanize and organize manufacturing plants placed pressure on employers to economize. Many of them did so by cutting wages. Like the family farmer who could no longer claim the status of the independent yeoman, industrial workers depended on employers and consumers for their physical well-being and very survival.

Organizing American Labor in the Late 19th Century

Not until 1935 would American workers have the right to organize and bargain collectively with their employers. Until then, laborers who saw strength in numbers and expressed an interest in a union could be summarily fired, **blacklisted** (their names circulated to other employers), and harassed by private security forces. The Pinkerton National Detective Agency, founded in 1850 by a Scottish immigrant named Allan Pinkerton, initially found eager clients among the railroads. The Pinkertons, as they were called, served as industrial spies and police during some of the most bitter and violent strikes of the late nineteenth century.

For example, in 1876 a Pinkerton detective, James McParlan, was hired by railroad operators to infiltrate a local union of Irish immigrant miners in Schuylkill County, Pennsylvania. The miners, members of a secret society called the Molly Maguires, were determined to do battle against the mine owners, who not only suppressed union activity but also controlled local courts and law enforcement agencies. In 1875 the Mollies had called a strike, but their leaders were arrested and charged with waging a guerrilla war against the mines (and their Welsh and English superintendents). In court McParlan offered testimony against the men, evidence that led to the conviction and execution (by hanging) of 20 of them. In the coming years, employers in a number of industries justified their repressive tactics by claiming that all unions represented a threat to law and order.

In small towns where one or two large industries predominated, workers often could count on their middle-class neighbors as allies. In many cases, shopkeepers, tradespeople, clergy, and landlords objected to the arrival of out-of-town strikebreakers, Pinkerton detectives, or federal troops during labor disputes. Local politicians solicited the support of their working-class constituents. As members of churches and voluntary associations, middle-class and working-class people together upheld community values of family welfare in opposition to large industrialists concerned only with profits and worker productivity. During a boycott of anti-union hat factories in Orange, New Jersey, in 1885, the community rallied around the workers. Brewers and bakers refused to supply establishments that opposed the boycott. Service providers of all kinds, from owners of roller-skating rinks to "knights of the razor" (barbers), closed their doors to patrons who expressed sympathy with what was generally called "the foul." In Orange and other towns, then, coalitions of middle-class and working-class residents severely curtailed the industrialists' power.

◀ **Mining was one of the most hazardous occupations in the United States. Below-surface miners worked with explosives and sophisticated kinds of machinery. As a result, the chances of explosions, cave-ins, rockslides, and fires increased. These conditions help to account for the labor militancy of miners throughout the country. This photo shows a mining operation at Marysville, near Helena, Montana, c. 1885.**

Rural Protests and Rebellions

In New Mexico in the 1880s, *las Gorras Blancas* expressed the grievances of Hispanic farmers against commercial interests. Throughout American history, groups of farmers have protested government policies they considered unfair and harmful to their own interests. Specific farmers' grievances, and the strategies used to express those grievances, have varied through the generations.

In the seventeenth and eighteenth centuries, impoverished backcountry settlers charged that colonial authorities were indifferent to their plight. Some settlers turned their wrath on the Indians in their midst and on government officials located in eastern towns. Sometimes protest turned into organized uprising, as in Bacon's Rebellion in Virginia in 1676 and Culpeper's Rebellion in North Carolina the following year.

Minnesota Historical Society/CORBIS

In Midwestern states during the economic depression of the 1930s, some farmers formed "holiday associations" to withhold crops from the market and to prevent creditors from seizing farm homesteads.

In 1763 farmers of backcountry Pennsylvania staged a revolt, claiming that the government promoted trade with Indians over the safety of settlers. The so-called Paxton Boys attacked the nearby Conestoga Indians, although their real grievances lay with the colonial legislature. In 1770 the Green Mountain Boys in Vermont disrupted local courts to protest the proprietary

The Knights of Labor, a secret fraternal order founded in 1869, came under the leadership of Terence V. Powderly a decade later. With this Irish American at the helm (he was called Grand Master Workman), the labor union made impressive gains in the 1880s. Under Powderly, the Knights launched a concerted effort to organize European American, African American, and Hispanic men and women workers.

In the late 1880s the Knights attempted to organize the laboring classes of San Miguel County, New Mexico, and the other parts of the Southwest. The Knights welcomed cowboys into their organization at the same time they were urging railroad workers to join their ranks. One cowhand said, "No class is harder worked, none so poor paid for their services." A cattle drive north from Texas could last for three months and cover more than a thousand miles. On such drives, a single cowboy would be responsible for keeping 250 to 300 head of cattle in line. Wages remained miserable, and unrest spread.

In the spring of 1883, an extensive strike among cowboys enraged the owners of large ranches in the Texas panhandle. To quell the uprising, ranchers paid gunmen to intimidate the strikers and enlisted the support of the state's law enforcement agency, the Texas Rangers. It was a year before the strikers gave up.

In appealing to many different kinds of workers around the country, the Knights blended a critique of the late-nineteenth-century wage system with a belief in the dignity of labor rights of large landowners. In all of these cases, a lack of available land, plus official policies that appeared to favor entrenched political and economic interests, fueled resentment among farmers.

Many farmers believed that the American Revolution failed to go far enough in securing their rights. During the postwar monetary crisis, they faced foreclosures on their property and long sentences in debtors' prison. Shays's Rebellion in the Connecticut River Valley and western Massachusetts in 1786–1787 and the Whiskey Rebellion in western Pennsylvania in 1793–1794 pitted local farmers against militia mobilized by the new national government.

The Civil War represents the country's most dramatic agrarian revolt against the central government. With the election of Abraham Lincoln, wealthy southern planters claimed that Washington was in the hands of Republicans who favored free, as opposed to slave, labor. The Confederates' uprising cost the country nearly 700,000 lives and culminated in the abolition of the institution that they were seeking to defend.

Postwar national economic development put family farmers at risk. In the 1890s the Populist party appealed to farmers in the South, the Midwest, and the Rocky Mountain region. Faced with rising costs and the monopolistic power of railroads and banks, these farmers called for government policies that would be more responsive to the needs of the small landowner. The party achieved some success at the local and state levels.

Rural interest groups continued their activism throughout the twentieth century. In the 1930s a number of different farmers' groups protested government policies that drove down crop prices. In the Midwest the Farmers' Holiday Association sought to intimidate local bankers and judges. The Sharecroppers' Union in Alabama and the Southern Tenant Farmers Union in Missouri, like the Populist party of the 1890s, represented biracial coalitions of farmers.

In 1979 the Nevada state legislature seized 49 million acres of federal land within the state. This measure ushered in the "Sagebrush Rebellion" by a political coalition of western ranchers who opposed government regulation of the land.

In 1999 the U.S. Department of Agriculture settled a class action suit brought by southern African American farmers, the largest class action civil rights settlement in U.S. history, worth $2 billion. The claimants, most of whom came from Mississippi, Arkansas, Georgia, and Tennessee, successfully charged that for decades the government had engaged in racial discrimination in its farm lending program. Although the judge in the case vowed that the claims process would be quick and "virtually automatic," by 2004 only 13,445 farmers had been awarded a total of $814 million, while 80,000 other claimants had been denied restitution, many because of the complicated, cumbersome application process with its strict deadlines. ■

and a call for collective action. According to the Knights, business monopolies and corrupt politicians everywhere shared a common interest in exploiting the labor of ordinary men and women. The Knights advocated a return to the time when workers controlled their own labor and received a just price for the products they made. "We declare an inevitable and irresistible conflict between the wage system of labor and republican system of government," the Knights proclaimed.

In condemning the concentration of wealth in the hands of a few, the Knights drew on the ideas of popular social critics of the day. In New York City, Henry George, an economist and land reformer, gained the Knights' support when he ran for mayor on the United Labor party ticket in 1886. (He came in second, with 31 percent of the vote, ahead of a young, up-and-coming Republican named Theodore Roosevelt.) George had achieved national prominence with his book *Progress and Poverty* (1879), in which he advocated a single tax on property as a means of distributing wealth more equally.

Journalist-turned-novelist Edward Bellamy echoed these themes. In his popular novel *Looking Backward* (1888), Bellamy envisioned a "cooperative commonwealth" in the year 2000, a socialist paradise in which poverty and greed had disappeared and men and women of all classes enjoyed material comfort and harmonious relations with their neighbors. This utopia was within reach, the author argued, if Americans could simply share in the nation's abundance.

Bellamy, from *Looking Backward*

▲ A card extols the Knights of Labor by suggesting that all people, regardless of age or gender, can labor in harmony together without the intrusion of bosses or supervisors. Terence V. Powderly became the group's leader, called Grand Master Workman, in 1879.

The Nationalist movement, a network of clubs inspired by Bellamy's book, included Terence Powderly as a member. Powderly declared, "We work not selfishly for ourselves alone, but extend the hand of fellowship to all mankind." Between 1885 and 1886, the Knights undertook the difficult task of organizing black workers. Many blacks remained suspicious of white-led unions, and for good reason. Historically, the white labor movement had conceived itself as a way to exclude black men and women from stable, well-paying jobs.

In the city of Richmond, Virginia, where workplaces were strictly segregated by race, the Knights made great gains. African American women there found their job opportunities limited to domestic service, laundry work, and unskilled jobs in tobacco factories. Black men were almost entirely excluded from the artisan crafts. By the mid-1880s, the Richmond Knights boasted a total membership of 7,000, with a ratio of four blacks to three whites. Yet members were organized into two district assemblies, one for blacks, the other for whites.

In early 1886 a wave of strikes hit Richmond as painters, coopers (barrel makers), typographers, **cotton press** workers, and foundry workers, among others, all decried their low wages. A coalition between the Knights and black Republicans posed a formidable threat to the entrenched Democratic leadership. That spring, labor Republican candidates won a majority of seats on the Richmond city council and gained half the board of aldermen slots. Yet the issue of racial equality proved the undoing of the Knights' fragile biracial coalition. Throughout the South, a generation of blacks and whites had allied themselves with different political parties (the Republicans and Democrats, respectively). Moreover, white workers widely perceived blacks as potential strikebreakers. In Richmond, mutual distrust, combined with pressure from white groups such as the local Law and Order League, fragmented the Knights.

Throughout the South, segregation was the norm within biracial unionism. Whites, whether New Orleans dockworkers, Birmingham district coal miners, or lumber workers in East Texas and Louisiana, insisted on separate locals for blacks. Yet African Americans did not necessarily acquiesce to this arrangement. In 1886 Jere A. Brown, a member of the Carpenter and Joiners' Union of Cleveland, wrote to the *New York Freeman,* declaring to readers of the black newspaper, "For years I have been importuned to enter into the formation of an assembly to be composed exclusively of colored men, but have persistently refused, believing as I do in mixing and not in isolating and ostracizing ourselves, thereby fostering and perpetuating the prejudice as existing today."

In 1886 workers around the country began to mobilize on behalf of the eight-hour day. "Eight hours to constitute a day's work" was their slogan. The issue had broad appeal, but the growing diversity of the labor force made unity difficult. For example, among the white workers of the Richmond Knights were leaders with names such as Kaufman, Kaufeldt, Kelly, and Molloy, suggesting the ethnic variety of late-nineteenth-century union leadership. This diversity paralleled the composition of the general population. In 1880, between 78 and 87 percent of all workers in San Francisco, St. Louis, Cleveland, New York, Detroit, Milwaukee, and Chicago were either immigrants or the children of immigrants. Most hailed from England, Germany, or Ireland, although the Chinese made up a significant part of the laboring classes on the West Coast. By 1890 Poles and Slavs were organizing in steel mills, and New York Jews were providing leadership in the garment industry. Italians were prominent in construction and the building trades. In many places, the laboring classes remained vulnerable to divisive social and cultural animosities. The diversity of ethnic groups, coupled with the fact that many newcomers adopted racist ideas to become "Americans," drove wedges between workers.

The Haymarket Bombing

The year 1886 marked the end of an era dominated by the Knights of Labor, as the organization experienced firsthand the difficulties of overcoming its members' diverse crafts, racial loyalties, and political allegiances. In 1886 the Knights suffered serious setbacks in their efforts to organize railroad workers. Industrialists dug in their heels and, with the aid of hired detectives, took union leaders to court on charges of sabotage, assault, conspiracy, and murder.

▲ Though their lives were later romanticized in novels, movies, and television programs, nineteenth-century cowboys engaged in hard, dangerous labor on the range. Against a backdrop of a large herd of cattle, these men pose for the photographer.

On May 1, 1886, 350,000 workers in 11,562 business establishments went out on a one-day strike as part of the eight-hour-workday movement. In Chicago, home to militant labor anarchists (men and women who opposed government authority of any kind), 40,000 workers participated in the strike. Among the Chicago leaders was Albert Parsons. A descendant of New England Puritans and a printer by trade, Parsons had lived in Waco, Texas, where he met his future wife, Lucia Gonzalez, an Afro-Latina (probably born a slave). In 1873 the Parsonses had moved to Chicago to avoid Texas laws against "race mixing," which prohibited interracial marriage. There Albert joined the International Typographical Union, and Lucia took up dressmaking. They were counted among the most famous and feared radicals in the city.

On May 4, things took a bloody turn. Strikers called a rally in Chicago's Haymarket Square to protest the murder of two McCormick Reaper strikers the day before. During the rally, a bomb went off, killing a police officer and wounding seven others, who later died. Although the identity of the culprit was never discovered, eight **anarchists,** including Albert Parsons, were arrested. All eight (several of whom were German immigrants) were tried and sentenced to death for conspiring to provoke violence. Parsons and several of the others had not been present when the bomb exploded. Nevertheless, in November 1887, he and three other detainees were hanged. Another committed suicide in his cell. The rest received pardons years later. After her husband's death, Lucia ("Lucy") Parsons remained active in Chicago anarchist circles. In 1905 she became a founding member of a new, radical labor union called the Industrial Workers of the World.

Engel, Address by a Haymarket Anarchist

The Haymarket hangings demoralized the labor movement nationwide. Now associated in the minds of the middle class with wild-eyed bomb throwers, the Knights suffered repercussions from employers and local police forces alike. After reaching a membership high of 700,000 in 1886, the Knights saw their ranks plummet to 100,000 by the end of the decade. Still, the execution of the Haymarket anarchists inspired young radicals—among them a recent Russian immigrant named Emma Goldman—to devote their lives to the cause of working people.

With the demise of the Knights of Labor, the American Federation of Labor (AFL) emerged to become the most powerful national labor movement. Samuel Gompers, an English immigrant cigarmaker, had founded the new group in 1886 partly in response to the Knights' attempts to usurp the Cigar Makers' International Union with a socialist-dominated local. The AFL garnered the allegiance of skilled trade workers (most of them white men) and promoted basic goals such as better wages and working conditions. The AFL emphasized the

Stock Montage, Inc/Historical Pictures Collection

▲ **Contemporary drawings such as this one convinced many Americans that labor activists, and anarchists in particular, were committed to violence, murder, and mayhem. The trials of the eight men arrested for the Haymarket bombing in Chicago were carried out in an atmosphere of public fear and hysteria. In 1893, Illinois Governor John P. Altgeld pardoned the three surviving defendants, declaring that they had not received fair trials.**

walkout and boycott as strategies of labor protest. By the mid-1890s, the AFL had embraced a narrow base: skilled trades dominated by white men.

Yet the radical labor tradition persisted. Meeting in Paris in 1889, a congress of world socialist parties voted to commemorate the American workers who had marched in support of the eight-hour day during the turbulent year of 1886. The congress voted to set aside May 1, 1890, as a day of worldwide celebrations in support of labor and demonstrations in favor of the eight-hour workday. (May 1 became an international labor day, celebrated annually.) In the United States, the United Mine Workers (founded in 1890) and the American Railway Union (1893) followed the radical labor-organizing principles of the Knights of Labor long after the AFL attained its ascendancy.

Crosscurrents of Reform

In the 1880s a young Danish-born journalist named Jacob Riis prowled New York's East Side slum district in search of stories for the New York *Tribune* and the Associated Press bureau. In this part of the city, more than 37,000 tenement buildings housed more than 1 million people—newcomers from the far reaches of Europe and Asia. As a result of Riis's stories documenting the inhuman living conditions endured by so many men, women, and children, the city formed the Tenement House Commission in 1884. Riis persisted in his exposés. In 1890 he published a collection of his own photographs, along with explanatory notes, under the title *How the Other Half Lives.*

"Albert Parsons's Plea for Anarchy"

On August 10, 1886, the New York Herald published an essay by convicted Haymarket defendant Albert R. Parsons. In it, Parsons defends his views on anarchism. His theories on the inevitable clash between workers and capitalists echo the arguments of Karl Marx, the German political theorist. Marx predicted that the capitalist system would inevitably self-destruct and that the working classes would rise to rule the world.

Albert Parsons

Library of Congress

So much is written and said nowadays about socialism or anarchism, that a few words on the subject from one who holds to these doctrines may be of interest to the readers of your great newspaper.

Anarchy is the perfection of personal liberty or self-government. It is the free play of nature's law. . . . It is the negation of force or the domination of man by man. In the place of the law maker it puts the law discoverer and for the driver, or dictator, or ruler, it gives free play to the natural leader. It leaves man free to be happy or miserable, to be rich or poor, to be mean or good. The natural law is self-operating, self-enacting, and cannot be repealed, amended or evaded without incurring a self-imposed penalty....

The capitalist system originated in the forcible seizure of natural opportunities and rights by a few, and converting these things into special privileges, which have since become vested rights formally entrenched behind the bulwarks of statute law and government....

And what of the laborer who for twelve or more hours weaves, spins, bores, turns, builds, shovels, breaks stones, carries loads, and so on? Does his twelve hours weaving, spinning, boring, turning, building, shoveling, etc. represent the active expression or energy of his life? On the contrary, life begins for him exactly where this activity, this labor of his ceases—viz: at his meals, in his tenement house, in his bed. His twelve hours work represents for him as a weaver, builder, spinner, etc., only so much earnings as will furnish him his meals, clothes, and rent. . . . The wage slaves are "free" to compete with each other for the opportunity to serve capital and capitalists to compete with each other in monopolizing the laborer's products.

Parsons argues that it is only a matter of time before the capitalist system "will collapse, will fall of its own weight, and fall because of its own weakness." He asserts that the fall of capitalism will usher in a new era of socialism, a system in which all property is held in common and workers can govern themselves. He concludes:

To quarrel with socialism is silly and vain. To do so is to quarrel with history; to denounce the logic of events; to smother the aspirations of liberty. Mental freedom, political freedom, industrial freedom—do not these follow in the line of progress? Are they not the association of the inevitable?

Ten days after this essay was published, Albert Parsons and the other Haymarket defendants were found guilty and sentenced to be hanged. Four of them, including Parsons, were executed on November 11, 1887. The true identity of the bomb-thrower remains a mystery to this day.

Questions

1. *What is the significance of Parsons's claim that the triumph of socialism is "inevitable" and "natural"?*
2. *Why did many Americans identify anarchists with violence?* ■

Reformers later called Riis "the most useful citizen of New York." His book galvanized the public in support of slum clearance and housing codes. *How the Other Half Lives* is a powerful indictment of greedy landlords, indifferent city officials, and rapacious sweatshop owners. The photos of sleeping street urchins huddled around sidewalk heating grates, of impoverished English coal heavers and Indian needleworkers, are powerful even today.

During the last decades of the nineteenth century, reformers adopted a range of causes. Some, like Riis, focused on the plight of the urban poor. Others challenged the Indian reservation system, which, they charged, left Indians poor and dependent on the federal government. Settlement house workers aimed to improve the lives of immigrant families. Middle-class women sought to protect and empower women by aiding abused or vulnerable wives and mothers, promoting temperance in alcohol use, and supporting women's suffrage. Many reformers participated in a transatlantic community of ideas, learning about reform strategies and institutions from their European counterparts. They stressed legislation, education, and moral rewards over coercion in their efforts to change society.

▲ **Jacob Riis titled this photograph *Street Arabs in Sleeping Quarters (Areaway, Mulberry St.)*. Riis's photos, collected in his book *How the Other Half Lives*, exposed the poverty and wretched living conditions endured by many immigrants in New York's Lower East Side. In certain cases, Riis carefully positioned his subjects before photographing them. It is doubtful that these little boys were sleeping while the photographer noisily set up his equipment a few feet away.**

One factor leading to reform was middle-class Americans' fear that the poor would lash out in angry frustration in order to call attention to social injustice. The reformers reasoned that even modest improvements in the lives of the poor would stave off violent conflict between the classes. Dramatic labor disputes, from the railroad workers' "great uprising" of 1877 to the Haymarket bombing of 1886, frightened many well-to-do people, especially in the nation's largest cities. Yet many reformers were also motivated by a genuine sense of concern for less privileged groups—including American Indians, the country's earliest inhabitants.

Although reformers professed to favor the full integration of various ethnic groups into American life, at times they could hardly help but look down on the people they aimed to help. (*How the Other Half Lives,* for all its sympathetic portrayals of the poor, reinforces negative stereotypes of many immigrants.) Some of the people reformers hoped to help rejected part of their benefactors' package of values—Protestantism, for example—while accepting forms of concrete aid, such as shelter from abusive husbands. Thus the history of late-nineteenth-century reform reveals the values and goals of not just middle-class Americans but of a wide variety of other social groups as well.

The Goal of Indian Assimilation

In the mid-nineteenth century many European Americans, including government officials, believed that the reservation system was a much-needed reform to protect western Indians. Reservations were tracts of land set aside for the exclusive use of Indians. Whites reasoned that reservation Indians would remain separate from the rest of American society, to the benefit of everyone. Indians could preserve their own culture, and they would remain safe from the attacks of both homesteaders and U.S. troops. By segregating this group, European Americans were free to settle on rich farmlands, mine for gold and silver, and take advantage of timber resources in the West.

By the 1870s the harsh reality of the reservation system had prompted a group composed of both Native Americans and European Americans to call for reform. The reformers pointed out that most western Indians had previously roamed the Plains in search of buffalo and other sources of food, clothing, and shelter; confining whole tribes to reservations meant that they lost not only their traditional means of feeding and housing themselves but their entire way of life. Reservation lands were often unsuitable for farming, leaving the residents on them without jobs or any other means to make a living. They depended on supplies of food, blankets, and clothing provided by the federal government. Kept apart from the rest of American society, denied the rights of citizenship such as education and the vote, many Indians fell victim to self-destructive behavior, including alcoholism and suicide.

Convinced that the reservation system was a failure, in 1879 reformers began to call for the assimilation of Native Americans into mainstream American life. This cause was promoted by some Indians as well as Protestant missionaries. In 1879, Ponca chief Standing Bear toured the East Coast, speaking before large, receptive audiences in Chicago, Boston, New York, Philadelphia, and Washington.

The chief had already received national attention for his role in the case *Standing Bear v. Crook* (1879). Attempting to leave Indian Territory and return to his homeland in Dakota Territory, to bury his son and daughter who had recently died, the chief and 30 warriors were captured by a U.S. cavalry force commanded by General George Crook. The Indians were imprisoned in Omaha, Nebraska. Two European American lawyers offered to represent the aging Indian. They argued, "In time of peace, no authority, civil or military, exists for transporting Indians from one section of the country to another…nor to confine them in any particular reservation against their will." In his decision, the judge ruled that Indians were indeed persons under the law, with inalienable rights. The decision called into question the government's attempts to force Indians onto reservations and to keep them there.

Omaha Funeral Song

On tour, addressing well-to-do listeners, Standing Bear criticized the federal Indian Office and demanded that Indians be granted full citizenship rights. When he spoke, he was accompanied by two young Omaha Indians who seemed to represent the promise of assimilation. Susette LaFlesche, of French and Indian heritage, assumed the name Bright Eyes for the purpose of the tour. She announced that her people "ask you for their liberty." Her brother Joseph, attired in European American clothing, served as translator for Standing Bear, who appealed to crowds saying, "We are bound; we ask you to set us free."

Standing Bear's appeal helped to galvanize eastern reformers. The Boston Indian Citizenship Committee, the Women's National Indian Association, and the Indian Rights Association, all founded between 1879 and 1882, proclaimed the need to abolish the reservation system, much as their antebellum predecessors had called for the abolition of slavery. Indeed, the campaign for Indian assimilation bore a marked resemblance to the antislavery crusade before the Civil War. Both movements focused on the wrongs perpetrated by the U.S. government (slavery and the Indian reservation system). Both argued that the group in question deserved full citizenship rights. And both promoted the ideal of group self-sufficiency: blacks and Indians tilling the soil, embracing mainstream Christianity, and learning trades.

In 1879 reformers began to call for the assimilation of Native Americans into mainstream American life.

Beginning in 1883, advocates of Indian assimilation sponsored annual conferences at Lake Mohonk, New York, to plot strategy for the coming year. These conferences brought together scholars, clergy, reformers, and politicians, all of whom considered their cause as part of the tradition of Protestant missionary outreach work.

The reformers believed that the values of white middle-class Protestants provided the best guide for Indians seeking to rid themselves of the hated reservation system. The Women's National Indian Association promoted "civilized home-life" on Indian reservations throughout the West. The Connecticut Branch organized a medical mission to the Omaha tribe in the 1880s. Branch

Courtesy, Hampton University Archives

▲ **Susan LaFlesche was the first Indian woman to become a physician in the United States. Together with her sisters Marguerite and Lucy, Susan attended Hampton Institute in Virginia, a vocational school for African Americans and Indians. This photo, c. 1885, shows Hampton students performing in a pageant at the school. Susan, center, and the woman to her left represented "Indians of the Past." The other students represented "Indians of the Present." Hampton's mission was to prepare its students for farming and the skilled trades.**

members also paid for the education of another LaFlesche sibling, Susan (a graduate of Hampton Institute) at the Woman's Medical College of Philadelphia. Although LaFlesche's sponsors believed that Indian women could serve as effective agents of civilization, they had less faith in the capacity of Indian men to abandon their traditions and embrace the ways of whites.

Advocates of assimilation received support from people who simply wanted the Plains Indians removed from their land to make way for European American settlers. The *New Orleans Times-Picayune* agreed that the reservation system was flawed, but not because Indians had suffered hardships under the system. The editorialist charged that Indians should not "any longer be permitted to usurp for the purpose of barbarism, the fertile lands, the products of mines, the broad valleys and wooded mountain slopes," which the dominant white society needed.

Out of these conflicting impulses—one on behalf of the Indians' welfare, the other in support of the destruction of Indians' claims to large tracts of land—came two major initiatives that would shape federal Indian policy in the years to come. The first was the Indian boarding school movement, begun in 1879 with the founding of a school in Carlisle, Pennsylvania. The purpose of the movement was to convert Indian children to Christianity, and to force them to abandon their native culture and learn literacy skills. The second was the Dawes Severalty Act, passed by Congress in 1887 with the intention of encouraging Indians to farm and apply for citizenship. By allowing reservation land to be divided into separate farms for individual Native American families, the federal act attacked the Indian tribal way of life directly. Moreover, ambitious land speculators and corrupt government officials sought to enrich themselves from the provisions of the act which allowed the sell-off of Indian lands to white buyers.

Transatlantic Networks of Reform

American reformers derived ideas and inspiration from their European counterparts. This transatlantic exchange of ideas was greatly facilitated by improvements in sea transportation. During the 1870s and 1880s, ocean travel became cheaper and safer as well as more efficient and comfortable. The great shipping lines, such as Cunard, began to offer intermediate fares for middle-class passengers who did not want to travel in **steerage** but could not afford first-class compartments. In 1890 a tourist embarking from New York could cross the Atlantic in just ten days for about $30 (the price of a bicycle) on a well-appointed steamship. Writer Henry James (1843–1916) traveled extensively in Europe before making his home in London in the mid-1870s. In his 1881 novel *Portrait of a Lady,* the main character, Isabel Archer, replies to an English gentleman who says he finds her motives for touring Europe "mysterious": "Is there anything mysterious in a purpose entertained and executed every year, in the most public manner, by fifty thousand of my fellow countrymen—the purpose of improving one's mind by foreign travel?"

Contacts between European and American scholars, students, artists, clergy, writers, and reformers enriched the intellectual life of the United States and bolstered the reform impulse. American women's rights supporters conferred with their counterparts in London. American college students attended classes at German universities. There American scholars absorbed ideas related to "reform Darwinism," the notion that state and private charitable intervention could improve modern social relations. Out of these ideas came the Social Gospel, a moral reform movement that stressed the responsibility of Americans to address the ills of modern urban life. Furthering this exchange of ideas, municipal and federal commissions studied labor unions and prisons on both sides of the Atlantic. Popular journals such as the *Nation* and the *New Republic* reported on social policy initiatives of European governments.

An idealistic graduate of Rockford (Illinois) Female Seminary, Jane Addams journeyed to Europe for the first time in 1883. The sight of large numbers of poor people in London's East End made a lasting impression on her. She returned home, searching for a way to be useful and for "an outward symbol of fellowship...some blessed spot where unity of spirit might claim right of way over all differences." In 1888 she went again to England and visited Toynbee Hall, a social settlement founded to alleviate the problems of the laboring classes. Back in Chicago, she and her friend and fellow classmate Ellen Gates Starr decided to open a settlement house of their own. Called Hull House, it was located in the Nineteenth Ward, home to 5,000 Greek, Russian, Italian, and German immigrants.

Hull House was located in Chicago's Nineteenth Ward, home to 5,000 immigrants.

Social settlement houses—so called because their goal was to help immigrants with the transition of settling in the United States—provided a variety of services for immigrants, including English language classes, neighborhood health clinics, after-school programs for children, and instruction in personal hygiene and infant care. In 1891, six settlements were in operation, including the Neighborhood Guild of New York City (1886) as well as Addams's Hull House in Chicago (1889). By 1900, the number stood at 200.

Later, Addams recalled that, with the opening of Hull House, she hoped to counter the anarchists and strikers. Like other reformers, Addams believed that social welfare activities would improve the lot of the poor and thus diffuse their radical, violent impulses. Moreover, she hoped to offer a sphere of useful work for young, well-educated women. Within the settlement house, she believed, these women reformers "might restore a balance of activity along traditional lines and learn of life from life itself." This was a place "where they might try out some of the things they had been taught."

Women Reformers: "Beginning to Burst the Bonds"

Like the Indian assimilation movement, women's reform work in general during this period had a strong missionary strain. In San Francisco, the Occidental Branch of the Women's Foreign Missionary Society enlisted the aid of well-to-do women in sponsoring a rescue home for Chinese prostitutes. Without the protection of traditional kin ties, these immigrants remained vulnerable to sexual and physical abuse. The rescue home enabled the young women to escape the men who exploited them and, in some cases, to reenter society as married women, factory wage-earners, or small merchants.

In Salt Lake City, a group of women challenged the Mormon practice of plural marriage. In 1886 their Industrial Christian Home Association received a subsidy from Congress to provide shelter for "women who renounce polygamy and their children of a tender age." That same year some Denver women founded the Colorado Cottage Home, a rescue home for pregnant girls and women. Many women sought out by these reformers welcomed services such as job training and shelter from abusive men. However, some women declined to embrace other aspects of these charitable organizations, such as religious lessons.

The Women's Christian Temperance Union (WCTU) is an apt example of the missionary impulse behind late-nineteenth-century reform. Though best known for its antialcohol crusade, the WCTU also sponsored homes for unwed mothers and day and night nurseries for the children of working women. It also stressed the need for women's "purity," claiming that women and children were the chief victims of men's alcohol consumption. But the group went further to denounce women's victimization at the hands of men in general.

Like national labor unions at the time, the WCTU organized African American women into local chapters separate from those of whites. Frances Ellen Watkins Harper served as head of the black division of the organization between 1883 and 1890. Harper, much in demand as a lecturer, also organized Sunday schools for black children and enlisted the aid of black clergy in her campaign against juvenile delinquency in Philadelphia. In 1887 middle-class black women in Atlanta formed the West Atlanta chapter of the WCTU. The group reached out to the students of Atlanta University with talks on topics with titles such as "Character Building," "Mother's Influence," and "Unfermented Wine."

Frances Willard proved a popular national speaker from the time she founded the WCTU in 1879 until her death in 1898. She served as the organization's first president during those years and in 1883 formed a world temperance union. Willard believed in the power of direct action. She exhorted groups of women to descend on taverns and rum shops and to shame customers into taking the "cold water pledge." The pledge required its adherents to quench their thirst with cold water, not alcohol.

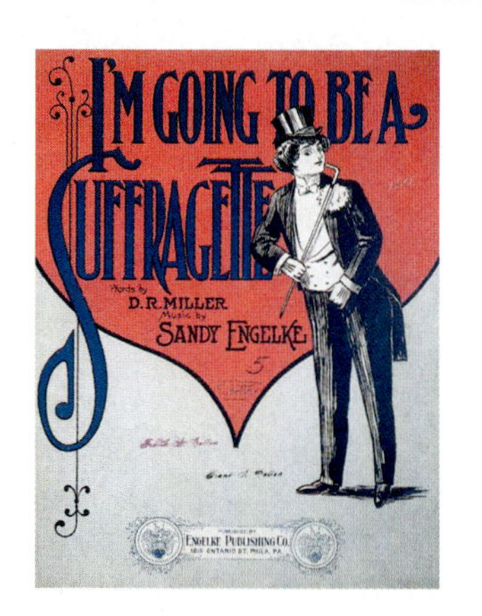

An enthusiastic advocate of women's suffrage, Willard was instrumental in bringing women's issues into the political realm. In her speeches, she quoted women such as "a Presbyterian lady" who declared, "For my part, I never wanted to vote until our gentlemen passed a prohibition ordinance...and a month later...chose a saloon keeper for mayor."

By the 1870s the issue of women's suffrage had captured the attention of men and women throughout the country. In fact, the issue had special resonance in the West for several reasons. When European American women overcame the hardships associated with the challenge of settling the trans-Mississippi West, they considered themselves worthy of having an equal voice in the polling booth. Reflecting on her hard life as a settler in Circle Valley, Utah, Mrs. L. L. Dalton wrote in 1876 that she was "proud and thankful" to see women "beginning to burst the bonds of iron handed custom" and asserting their "co-heirship" with fathers, brothers, and husbands. Abigail Scott Duniway, who sympathized with the plight of overworked and lonely farm wives, published a women's rights journal, *New Northwest,* in Portland, Oregon, from 1871 to 1887. In 1873 she had helped found the Oregon Equal Suffrage Association and served as its president.

Western politics pitted cattle ranchers against farmers, and religious and cultural groups against each other. These conflicts prompted the men of various groups to seek allies wherever they could find them—within their own households if necessary. The territorial legislature of Wyoming granted women the right to vote in 1869. Utah Territory followed suit in 1870, and Washington Territory in 1883. Territorial governments facilitated the enactment of women's suffrage, for they required only that the measure win the approval of a majority of the legislature and the approval of the governor. In contrast, states had to approve a constitutional amendment, which required support of two-thirds of the legislators and a majority of the voters. The states of Wyoming (in 1890), Colorado (in 1893), and Utah and Idaho (both in 1896) approved suffrage for women. Colorado's victory was the only one resulting from a successful statewide referendum.

In 1884 a group of women calling themselves the National Equal Rights Party convened in California. Delegates to the convention nominated Belva Lockwood for president of the United States. Born in Royalton, New York, in 1830, Lockwood was the first woman admitted to practice law before the Supreme Court (in 1879). She was a staunch proponent of women's suffrage and equal pay for equal work. Lockwood believed that her presidential candidacy would bring much-needed publicity to the cause of women's rights. In her acceptance speech, she called for "a fair distribution of the public offices to women as well as to men." She promised that, if elected, she would recommend in her inaugural speech "a uniform system of laws" that would reform marriage and divorce statutes in order to "make the wife equal with the husband in authority and right, and an equal partner in the common business." She also advocated breaking up the Indian reservation system and granting all Indians full citizenship rights. In the 1884 election, Lockwood received 4,149 votes cast in six states. In the late 1880s and 1890s she devoted her energies to the cause of world peace. Belva Lockwood died in Washington, D.C., in 1917.

May Wright Sewall Collection/Library of Congress

▲ Frances Willard (1839–1898) grew up on a farm in Wisconsin Territory. She served as the first dean of women at Northwestern University in Illinois. In the mid-1870s, she decided to devote her life to the cause of temperance. From 1879 until her death, she was president of the Woman's Christian Temperance Union. Willard developed what she called a "Do-Everything policy." Under her leadership, the WCTU addressed a range of issues, including women's suffrage and workers' rights.

The nature of the western suffrage movement points to the need to view women's rights, and women's activism in general, in their historical and regional contexts. For example, African American women also pressed for the right to vote, and their demands assumed special urgency amid violence and terrorism. Ida B. Wells would later lead an African American women's suffrage club in Chicago and play a pivotal role in the national suffrage movement. She began her public career as a crusading journalist in Memphis in the 1880s. In the early 1890s she clashed with Frances Willard over the issue of lynching, charging that the WCTU president refused to condemn the barbaric practice. Although Willard had been an active abolitionist and a steadfast campaigner for women's suffrage, according to Wells she was "no better or worse than the great bulk of white Americans on the Negro question." Thus women's political issues reflected tensions between blacks and whites as well as between women and men.

Conclusion

In the 1870s and 1880s, the Americans who challenged the power of government and big business represented a wide spectrum of ideologies, tactics, and goals. Some resisted violently, smashing the machines, trains, and telegraph poles that were transforming American society. The Ohio machine-breakers and southwestern *Gorras Blancas* destroyed property in an effort to assert their claims to a traditional way of life. Others formed new institutions such as settlement houses, reform associations, or political parties to advance their agenda on the national scene. Some people hoping to effect social change used the language of evangelical Protestantism, echoing the abolitionists who had called for the eradication of slavery before the Civil War. Others collected data and interviewed specific groups of workers, women, or immigrants in an effort, first, to expose the conditions under which these groups lived and labored, and second, to propose specific legislation to remedy those conditions. Plains Indians embraced religious mysticism in a failed attempt to halt the incursion of European Americans into their ancient hunting grounds. Thus, powerful groups encountered much resistance from people opposed to their narrow idea of progress—the idea that bigger factories, more efficient farm machinery, and a nationwide network of railroad lines would bring prosperity to all Americans.

At the same time, some groups agitated for full inclusion into American society, as citizens and as consumers. Some blacks resisted Jim Crow by voting with their feet and fleeing the oppressive system of southern sharecropping. They claimed citizenship rights in defiance of the white lawmakers and employers who aimed to keep all blacks in a state of near slavery. Too, mainstream women suffragists aspired to the rights and privileges of male voters; they hoped to achieve full integration into the American political system, rather than overhauling that system. In contrast to their radical counterparts in the Knights of Labor, members of the emerging American Federation of Labor refrained from criticizing the capitalist system; instead, AFL members argued that they deserved their fair share of American prosperity in the form of better wages and working conditions. None of these groups—black activists, women suffragists, or union members—found a welcoming home in either of the two main political parties. For evidence of lively critiques of American society and economy during this period, we must look beyond the Republicans and Democrats to those groups that offered innovative ideas and novel tactics to affect political discussions throughout the nation.

As Americans began to think more broadly about their own society, they began to think more broadly about their place in the world. Some men and women hoped to apply the principles of moral and civic reform to other countries west of the United States. The 1880s thus laid the foundations not only for a transatlantic republic of cultural exchange, but also for a transpacific empire of missionary work and trade. In the process, a new ideology of expansionism emerged, one that blended elements of economic gain, national security, and Christian missionary outreach to peoples in far-off lands.

Sites to Visit

Anarchy Archives at Pitzer University

http://dwardmac.pitzer.edu/Anarchist_Archives/haymarket/Haymarket.html

This archive includes classic anarchist texts, especially information about and graphics of the Haymarket Riot.

Labor-Management Conflict in American History

http://www.publichistory.org/reviews/view_review.asp?DBID=93

This Ohio State University site includes primary accounts of some of the major events in the history of the labor-management conflict in the late nineteenth and early twentieth centuries.

Samuel Gompers Papers at the University of Maryland

www.history.umd.edu/Gompers/

This site includes information about the papers project. It also has a photo gallery, selected documents, and a brief history of the first president of the American Federation of Labor.

African American Perspectives: Pamphlets from the Daniel A. P. Murry Collections, 1818–1907

http://memory.loc.gov/ammem/aap/aaphome.html

This collection includes writings of famous African Americans, including Frederick Douglass, Booker T.

Washington, Ida B. Wells-Barnett, Benjamin W. Arnett, Alexander Crummel, and Emanuel Love.

The Haymarket Affair Digital Collection

http://www.chicagohistory.org/hadc/index.html

The Chicago Historical Society maintains this site about a pivotal moment in American labor history.

African American Women Writers of the Nineteenth Century

www.digital.nypl.org/schomburg/writers_aa19/

The New York Public Library's Schomburg Center for Research in Black Culture maintains this site, which contains a large number of digital texts by African American women of the nineteenth century.

For Further Reading

General Works

Edward L. Ayers, *The Promise of the New South: Life After Reconstruction* (1992).

Sarah Deutsch, *No Separate Refuge: Culture, Class, and Gender on an Anglo-Hispanic Frontier, 1880–1940* (1987).

Lawrence Goodwyn, *Democratic Promise: The Populist Moment in America* (1976).

Patricia N. Limerick, *The Legacy of Conquest: The Unbroken Past of the American West* (1987).

David Montgomery, *The Fall of the House of Labor: The Workplace, the State, and American Labor Activism, 1865–1925* (1987).

Elizabeth Sanders, *Roots of Reform: Farmers, Workers, and the American State, 1877–1917* (1999).

Resistance to Legal and Military Authority

Tomás Almaguer, *Racial Fault Lines: The Historical Origins of White Supremacy in California* (1994).

Dee Brown, *Bury My Heart at Wounded Knee: An Indian History of the American West* (1970).

Arlen L. Fowler, *The Black Infantry in the West, 1869–1891* (1971).

Steve Hahn, *A Nation Under Our Feet: Black Political Struggles in the Rural South from Slavery to the Great Migration* (2003).

Alex Lichtenstein, *Twice the Work of Free Labor: The Political Economy of Convict Labor in the New South* (1996).

Leon Litwack, *Trouble in Mind: Black Southerners in the Age of Jim Crow* (1998).

Robert J. Rosenbaum, *Mexicano Resistance in the Southwest: The Sacred Right of Self-Preservation* (1981).

Alexander Saxton, *The Indispensable Enemy: Labor and the Anti-Chinese Movement in California* (1971).

Robert M. Utley, *The Lance and the Shield: The Life and Times of Sitting Bull* (1993).

Revolt in the Workplace

Paul Avrich, *The Haymarket Tragedy* (1984).

Leon Fink, *Workingmen's Democracy: The Knights of Labor and American Politics* (1983).

Philip S. Foner, *The Great Labor Uprising of 1877* (1977).

Jacquelyn Dowd Hall, James Leloudis, Robert Korstad, Mary Murphy, LuAnn Jones, and Christopher B. Daly, *Like a Family: The Making of a Southern Cotton Mill World* (1987).

Stuart B. Kaufman, *Samuel Gompers and the Origins of the American Federation of Labor, 1848–1896* (1973).

Theodore R. Mitchell, *Political Education in the Southern Farmers' Alliance, 1887–1900* (1987).

Bruce Nelson, *Beyond the Martyrs: A Social History of Chicago's Anarchists, 1870–1900* (1988).

Richard Steven Street, *Beasts of the Field: A Narrative History of California Farmworkers, 1769–1913* (2004).

Crosscurrents of Reform

Sarah Deutsch, *Women and the City: Gender, Space, and Power in Boston, 1870–1940* (2000).

Jean Bethke Elshtain, *Jane Addams and the Dream of American Democracy* (2001).

Barbara L. Epstein, *The Politics of Domesticity: Women, Evangelism, and Temperance* (1980).

Paula Giddings, *When and Where I Enter: The Impact of Black Women on Race and Sex and America* (1984).

Frederick E. Hoxie, *A Final Promise: The Campaign to Assimilate the Indians, 1880–1920* (1984).

Jane Taylor Nelsen, ed., *A Prairie Populist: The Memoirs of Luna Kellie* (1992).

Peggy Pascoe, *Relations of Rescue: The Search for Female Moral Authority in the American West, 1874–1939* (1990).

Jacob Riis, *How the Other Half Lives: Studies Among the Tenements of New York* (1971).

Daniel T. Rodgers, *Atlantic Crossings: Social Politics in a Progressive Age* (1998).

Stephen J. Stein, *Communities of Dissent: A History of Alternative Religions in America* (2003).

CHAPTER 18

Political and Cultural Conflict in a Decade of Depression and War: The 1890s

Julius L. Stewart, *On the Yacht "Namouna,"* Venice, 1890. Wadsworth Atheneum Museum of Art, Hartford, Connecticut. Ella Gallup Sumner and Mary Catlin Sumner Collection Fund, 1965.32

▲ Several Americans relax on the yacht *Namouna* as it sails in the waters off the coast of Venice, Italy. By the late nineteenth century, innovations in ocean transportation had made travel cheaper and faster. Wealthy Americans flocked to Europe, contributing to a transatlantic culture of ideas, literature, and fashion.

CHAPTER OUTLINE

Frontiers at Home, Lost and Found

The Search for Alliances

American Imperialism

Conclusion

Sites to Visit

For Further Reading

IN THE EARLY 1890S, LUTHER STANDING BEAR, A YOUNG MAN OF LAKOTA SIOUX ORIGIN, found himself suspended between two worlds. Born in 1868 in South Dakota, he had learned to hunt buffalo in the traditional manner of the Western Sioux. In 1879 he bowed to the wishes of his father, Standing Bear (not to be confused with the Ponca leader of the same name), who insisted that he learn the ways of "Long Knives," or whites. The youth was among the first pupils to attend the new federal Indian boarding school in Carlisle, Pennsylvania. En route to Carlisle, the 11-year-old regarded his journey—by boat and train—as an ordeal that he must endure with honor. Once at the school, he discovered that he was to become an "imitation of a white man"—and quickly.

This group of Chiricahua Apache students arrived at the Carlisle Indian boarding school in 1890. Government-sponsored Indian education included dressing them in European American clothing and cutting their hair.

Called Ota Kte (Plenty Kill) at home, he was now required to pick a new first name from among those listed on a classroom blackboard. He chose Luther. His teachers took away his blanket and moccasins and gave him a coat, pants, and vest to wear. They forbade him to speak his native language, and they cut his long hair. One of his classmates protested, "If I am to learn the ways of the white people, I can do it just as well with my hair on." Like most other youths at Carlisle, Luther Standing Bear learned to read and write English and to practice a craft (in his case, tinsmithing). His teachers encouraged him to embrace Christianity.

In 1884, as part of his government-sponsored training, Luther Standing Bear traveled to Philadelphia to work at the Wanamaker department store. The head of the Carlisle school, Captain Richard Henry Pratt, had sent the youth on his way with the words, "You are to be an example of what this school can turn out. Go, my boy, and do your best. Die there if necessary, but do not fail." After spending a year stocking shelves and performing other tasks at the famous store, the young man returned to South Dakota. There he taught Sioux children in a school near the place of his birth, now the Rosebud Indian Reservation. He married the daughter of an Indian mother and a white father.

In December 1890, U.S. military officials attacked and killed from 150 to 250 Indians at Wounded Knee, South Dakota. This massacre, which took place near Luther Standing Bear's home, left the young man fearful for the safety of his family. He subsequently moved with them to the nearby Pine Ridge Reservation, where he began work as a shopkeeper and postal clerk. In the late 1890s, Luther Standing Bear served as an interpreter for Buffalo Bill's "Wild West" show during its tour in London. By 1912 he had become an

American citizen and settled in southern California, where he began his acting career in the new motion picture industry. He appeared in some of the first movie westerns with famous actors Douglas Fairbanks and William S. Hart. At the same time, Luther Standing Bear also became an Indian activist, serving as president of the Los Angeles American Indian Progressive Association and speaking out against the "government prison" known as the reservation. Standing Bear died in 1939 while working on a film called *Union Pacific.*

In the 1890s, Luther Standing Bear's journey took place amid economic depression, civil strife, and war. Throughout the decade, workers challenged the idea that the United States was immune to the bloody class conflict that had long plagued Europe. Some scholars lamented the closing of the western frontier, prompting fears that America's unique dynamic of growth and social improvement had come to an end.

Domestic developments had a profound effect on American foreign policy.

Domestic developments had a profound effect on American foreign policy. Native-born whites began to seize upon new categories of racial difference to draw distinctions between various groups in the United States and around the world. Faced with declining consumer demand at home, politicians and businesspeople joined forces to expand American markets and American influence abroad. Economic and humanitarian interests often went hand in hand. Reformers claimed that the blessings of American consumer society would "civilize" darker peoples everywhere. In 1896 Merrill Gates, a philanthropist and advocate of Indian boarding-school education, described the goal of such education: "We need to *awaken in him* [the Indian] *wants.* . . . Discontent with the tepee and the starving rations of the Indian camp in winter is needed to get the Indian out of the blanket and into trousers—and trousers with a pocket in them, and with a *pocket that aches to be filled with dollars!*" America's imperialistic ventures would reveal a similar blend of economic interests and missionary outreach.

Thus, the 1890s was a time of stark contrasts. The same year the depression hit, the Chicago World's Fair, called the Columbian Exposition, celebrated American architectural and technological progress. Among the exhibits was an early motion picture camera. This was a decade when bicycling became a craze, and the syncopated rhythms of a new form of music called ragtime were all the rage. But during the same decade, southern lynch mobs burned alive black men and women, and American military forces pursued a brutal war in Cuba and the Philippines.

Whereas some Americans tried to define rigid racial and nationalistic boundaries, others sought avenues of connection. A new political party, the Populist, or People's, party, aimed to bring together men and women of all backgrounds and regions. By advocating **grassroots democracy** as well as government action to regulate the economy, the party paved the way for the Progressive reforms of the early twentieth century.

Relying on a variety of means, from new legal and educational systems to commercial expansion and the deployment of military might, American elites attempted to consolidate their political power and cultural influence. In the process, the United States confronted not only the domestic challenges of sustaining a modern industrial society but also the worldwide challenges that pitted the enduring ideal of democracy against the emerging reality of colonialism.

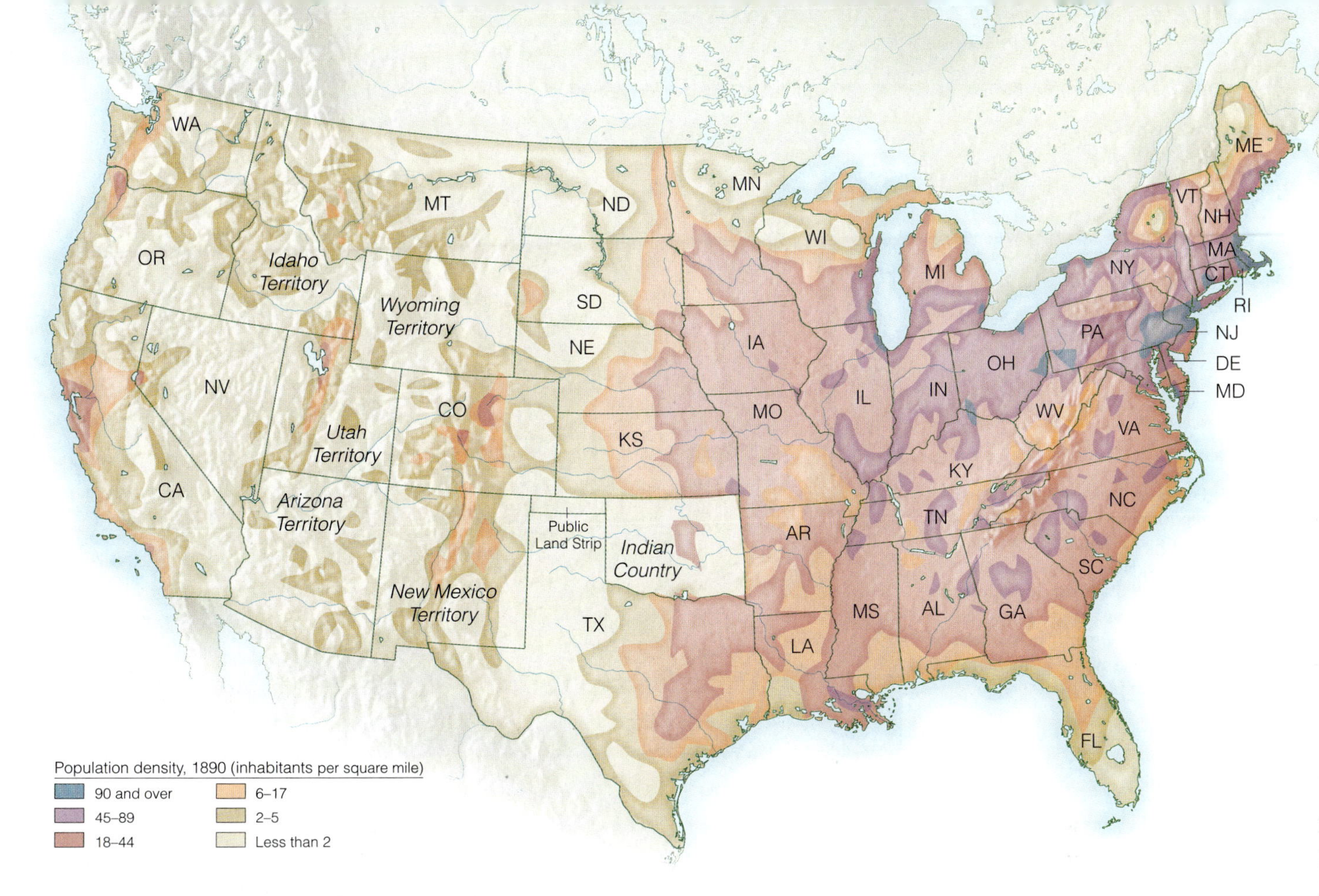

▲ **MAP 18.1 POPULATION DENSITY, 1890**
In 1890 the United States contained vast tracts of wilderness. Some Americans worried that the Northeast was overpopulated and that, as a result, the country would face the same problems as Europe—class conflict, poverty, and urban ills.

Frontiers at Home, Lost and Found

In 1893 historian Frederick Jackson Turner wrote an essay titled "The Significance of the Frontier in American History." Delivered as an address to a group of historians at the Columbian Exposition in Chicago, the essay presented a new way of thinking about American history. According to Turner, the process of settling the West had shaped all of American history. He argued that during the colonial period, the rigors of taming the land had transformed English colonists into more resourceful, more democratic people—in other words, into Americans. With each successive wave of western settlement, American society renewed itself. In his view, the West served as a **safety valve,** a place of opportunity that beckoned people out of crowded eastern cities. However, Turner noted, an 1890 Census Report had concluded that the frontier—the unsettled area of the western part of the country—had recently disappeared. The historian sounded an ominous note at the end of his address: "And now, four centuries from the discovery of America, at the end of a hundred years of life under the Constitution, the frontier has gone, and with its going has closed the first period in American history."

Turner's thesis promoted the idea of American "exceptionalism": the idea that its individualism and democratic values made the United States unique among the nations of the world. Yet his association of geography with an "American character" was simplistic at best.

National Archives

▶ Frederick Jackson Turner's 1893 announcement that the western frontier had disappeared was premature. Here, homesteaders in Washington State cut down trees to carve a farm out of the forest, c. 1900. Felling gigantic hardwoods in the Northwest was a formidable challenge to family farmers.

In his celebration of the sturdy settlers of the frontier, Turner ignored the bloody legacy of western settlement and its devastating effects on native and Spanish-speaking peoples.

Nevertheless, at the end of the nineteenth century, Turner and others were asking whether America needed to conquer new lands and "tame" certain peoples to preserve its distinctive character. Now that the frontier had disappeared, what was to prevent the United States from becoming more like Europe? These concerns led to efforts to assimilate and Americanize certain groups of people and to tighten systems of legal discrimination against others. These concerns also inspired some Americans to advocate extending the nation's military might and political authority beyond U.S. territorial boundaries. If the American frontier at home was closing, the American frontier abroad should expand, in the view of imperialists.

Claiming and Managing the Land

As less and less land was available for cultivation, grazing, and mining, the politics of rural development entered a new phase. In the early 1890s, the last great parcel of Indian land was opened to European American farmers. Congress established the Territory of Oklahoma in 1890, and three years later, the Cherokee Outlet in the north central part of the territory, combined with Tonkawa and Pawnee reservations, was thrown open to settlers and oil developers. On September 16, 1893, 100,000 people claimed 6.5 million newly opened acres in a single day. The "sooners," people who rushed to claim the land, gave the state of Oklahoma its nickname. The "Sooner State" was admitted to the Union in 1907.

Congress took other steps to manage western lands during the 1890s. The Court of Private Land Claims (1891) oversaw land disputes in New Mexico, Colorado, and Arizona. This court favored recent European American claimants over the Hispanic settlers who had received title to the lands from either Spain or Mexico generations earlier.

Land courts were only one example of an expanded federal role in the settlement of the West and management of the land. During the 1890s, the federal government continued to provide information and services for farmers through the U.S. Department of Agriculture. Policymakers argued over the proper balance between conserving natural resources for use by farmers, loggers, and oilmen and preserving the beauty of unspoiled panoramas for the enjoyment of all. In 1890 Congress established a national park in California's spectacular Yosemite Valley, where the Yosemite Indians had lived for hundreds of years. The 1891 Forest Reserve Act set aside forest reserves in the **public domain** (the vast tracts of land owned by the federal government). Logging companies were allowed to exploit these areas for their timber.

With his appointment as chief of the Division of Forestry in 1898, Gifford Pinchot sought to bring the issue of natural resource conservation to national attention. He believed that a managed forest could provide lumber and then renew itself. By contrast, John Muir and others argued that uninhabited regions should be preserved in their natural state, unmarred by dams, mines, or logging operations. In 1892 Muir founded the Sierra Club, a group devoted to preserving wilderness. In 1899 both Muir and the Northern Pacific Railroad lobbied successfully for two new national parks, Mount Rainier in Washington and Glacier in Montana, highlighting the ongoing significance of railroad tourism. The philosophical disagreements between Pinchot and the **conservationists** on one hand and Muir and the **preservationists** on the other shaped a wider debate between conservationists and preservationists in the early twentieth century.

"Rusticating," or hiking and enjoying the beauty of nature, became a popular pastime for many Americans in the 1890s. By 1890, tourists from Boston could board a train and, eight hours later, reach the rocky coast of Maine's Frenchman's Bay, where large hotels provided comfortable accommodations and breathtaking views. Throughout northern New England, religious groups and extended families established summer colonies on the coast and in the mountains so that they could live close to "the great outdoors," renewing social ties and refreshing the spirit. Although the frontier of the cattle rancher and farmer was receding, the frontier of recreational tourism was growing by leaps and bounds, as excursion trains provided greater access to beach resorts and mountain retreats.

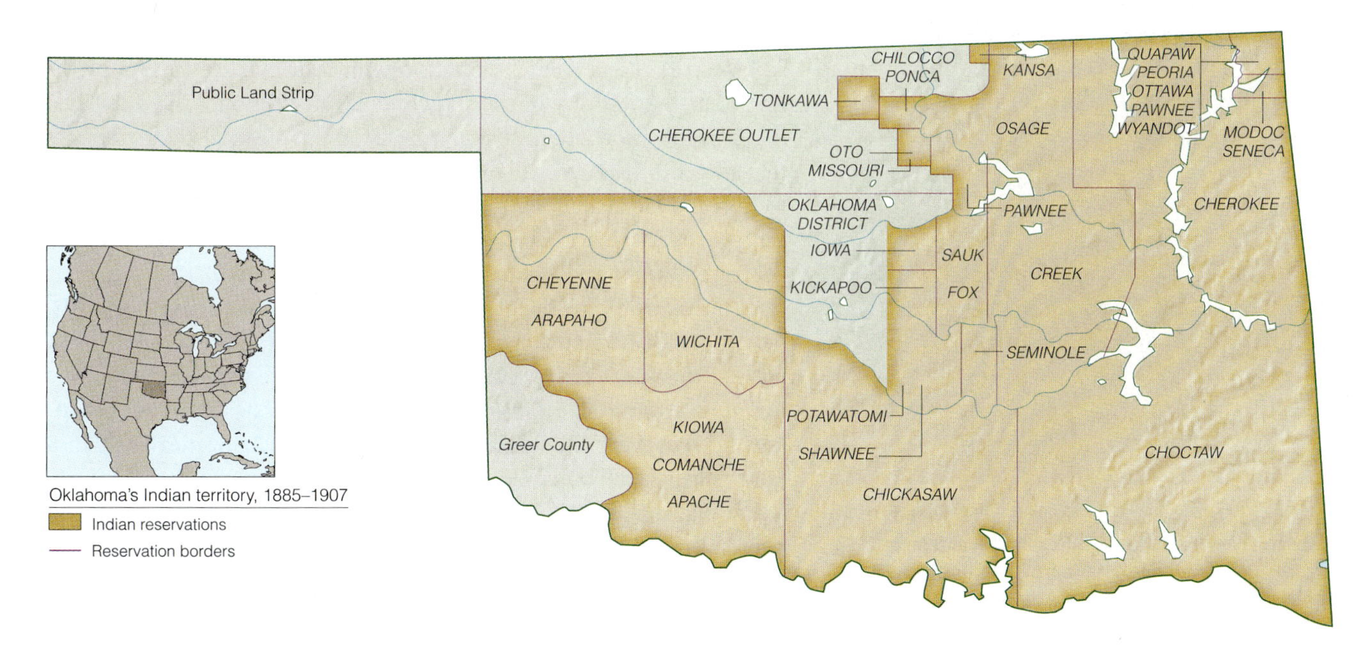

▲ **MAP 18.2 INDIAN TERRITORY AND THE STATE OF OKLAHOMA, 1885–1907**
In the early 1890s, the federal government began to purchase land from the Five Civilized Tribes and other Indian groups to open Indian Territory to European American settlement. The lands of the Potawatomi, Shawnee, Iowa, Sauk, and Fox were opened in 1891; Cheyenne and Arapaho in 1892; the Cherokee Outlet in 1893; Kickapoo in 1895; and Kiowa, Comanche, Apache, and Wichita between 1901 and 1906. In 1907, Indian Territory and Oklahoma Territory merged to become the state of Oklahoma.

The Tyranny of Racial Categories

The supposed closing of the western frontier, and with it the disappearance of the "safety valve" for restless Easterners, highlighted urban America's increasing class and cultural diversity. In an effort to categorize social groups, many national opinionmakers—scholars, journalists, and politicians—claimed that people should be distinguished from one another by their inborn, "natural" characteristics, ranging from skin color to facial bone structure and intelligence. Supposedly, these differences defined specific racial categories, such as Caucasoid, Mongoloid, and Negroid. In fact, so-called racial differences between groups were cultural differences. Prewar nativists had opposed foreign immigration because they considered native-born Protestants superior to people born in other countries. In contrast, late-nineteenth-century scientific racists ranked "superior" and "inferior" races on an elaborate hierarchy encompassing all groups, native and foreign born.

Several factors account for this renewed obsession with race in the 1890s. European and American efforts to colonize and explore the far reaches of the globe brought whites face-to-face with darker-skinned peoples, whom scholars in the new discipline of **anthropology** studied and classified. The "New Immigration" from eastern Europe raised concerns about conferring citizenship on non-Anglos, such as Russian Jews, Poles, and Italians. Persistent violence along the U.S.-Mexican border, combined with the resistance of Indians and African Americans to the authority of white people, alarmed local and federal officials. Theories of "racial difference" were used to justify attempts to subordinate these groups, by violence if necessary.

National Anthropological Archives, Smithsonian Institution (#858)

▲ A middle-class Powhatan Indian family in Virginia poses for the camera, c. 1900. Since the seventeenth century, the Powhatan had intermarried with the Nanticoke of Delaware as well as African Americans of the Mid-Atlantic region. Communities such as these defied the efforts of scientists and others to rigidly categorize people according to race.

Identification of racial categories pervaded the nation's popular, political, and legal cultures. Scientists filled scholarly journals and books with "evidence" of the superiority of the "white race," citing the size and weight of bones of various groups and comparing blacks and Jews in the United States with each other and with Eskimos in Greenland and Tapuyan Indians in Brazil. Based on poor science, this scholarship revealed the researchers' fascination with factors irrelevant to intelligence, such as the size of the skull and jaw projection. First published in 1895, the *Encyclopedia Britannica* listed the physical characteristics that allegedly distinguished the races from each other, including jaw projection and facial angles. Most people did not read these highly technical reports, but images in advertising and other forms of popular culture portrayed blacks and Asians as inferior, servile people.

In the South, the doctrine of white supremacy had disastrous consequences for African Americans. Beginning with Mississippi in 1890, over the next 20 years, white Democrats in all the southern states met in state constitutional conventions and imposed restrictions on the voting rights of African American men, using a variety of means: literacy requirements, poll taxes (fees that people had to pay to vote), and "grandfather clauses." These last measures stipulated that only men whose grandfathers had been eligible to vote before ratification of the Fifteenth Amendment could vote themselves. In some instances, the literacy requirements and poll taxes disenfranchised poor white men as well.

In 1896 the Supreme Court put its stamp of approval on segregated schools, trains, and streetcars in its *Plessy v. Ferguson* opinion. Four years earlier in New Orleans, a black man named Homer Plessy had refused to sit in a segregated railroad car. By a 7–1 majority, the Supreme Court ruled that states could exercise "reasonable" authority by segregating public accommodations. Such Jim Crow laws, according to the Court, did "not necessarily imply the inferiority of either race." Justice John Marshall Harlan dissented from the majority view, pointing out the obvious: "The white race deems itself to be the dominant race," a view that conflicted with the "colorblind" U.S. Constitution.

Between 1882 and 1901, more than 100 people, most of them black men, were lynched every year in the United States; the year 1892 set a record of 230 deaths. In the South, lynch mobs targeted black men and women who refused to subordinate themselves to whites. In 1892 a black woman born in slavery, newspaper editor Ida B. Wells, incurred the wrath of whites in her native Memphis when she condemned the killings of three black men. They had operated a Memphis store, the People's Cooperative Grocery Store, which competed for black customers with a nearby white-owned establishment. While defending their store from a mob of whites, the three men were lynched, their bodies mutilated. In the words of a friend, "They were succeeding too well. They were guilty of no crime but that."

Many black men victimized by lynch mobs were falsely accused of raping white women. In her newspaper *Free Speech,* Wells charged that accusations of rape were merely a pretext for the murder of black men. The southern white man, wrote Wells, "had never gotten over his resentment that the Negro was no longer his plaything, his servant, and his source of income." Death threats forced the editor to move north.

Whites targeted assertive black men and women, those "out of their place," especially professionals and property owners. In Wilmington, North Carolina, in November 1898, whites attacked Alex Manly, an African American newspaper editor who had labeled white men "a lot of carping hypocrites." He charged that white men who exploited black women sexually felt free to call for the murder of alleged black rapists. In retaliation, a mob destroyed Manly's offices and then turned on the city's black residents, driving them into the swamps and chasing them out of town at gunpoint. At least ten blacks were killed in the violence.

Courtesy, Atlanta History Center

▲ As a region, the South lacked the ethnic diversity characteristic of the rest of the country. However, small numbers of Jewish immigrants did settle in the South, and some managed to turn modest dry goods establishments into major urban department stores. Atlanta's Rich & Brothers Dry Goods store, shown here in the 1880s, was founded and owned by Jews.

Yet even in the South, racial definitions were never as clear-cut or self-evident as racists, scientific or otherwise, claimed. For example, Italians and Jews occupied a middle ground between black and white, as class issues intermingled with racial categories. In 1891 in New Orleans, the lynching of a group of 11 Italian prisoners accused of conspiring to murder the city's chief of police met with no public outcry. Instead, a local newspaper condemned the "lawless passions" and "cutthroat practices" that it claimed were characteristic of all Italian immigrants. However, the Italian government protested loudly against the incident. Armed conflict between the two nations was averted only when the United States agreed to compensate the victims' families.

At the same time, Jewish shopkeepers and merchants in the South gained a conditional entry into the ranks of "whites." In Natchez, Mississippi, the small but prosperous Jewish community owned 45 businesses, about a third of all in the town. Merchant Simon Moses and others like him built grand, Victorian-style houses and worshipped in an imposing synagogue, Temple B'Nai Israel. However, anti-Jewish feeling manifested itself in subtle ways. Living in an overwhelmingly Protestant region of the country, many southern Jews found themselves barred from local social organizations.

A variety of organizations sought to enforce the notion of Anglo superiority in the workplace and in the courts. In 1890 the San Francisco Boot and Shoemakers' White Labor League convinced a shoe manufacturer to fire 15 Japanese workers. The 1891 lynching of the New Orleans Italian workers (deemed nonwhites) was organized by the White League, a terrorist group similar to the Ku Klux Klan. In 1893 the newly formed Immigration Restriction League launched a campaign to impose a literacy test on incoming **aliens.** Thus definitions of race served as political strategies to limit the power of blacks and other minorities as workers and as voters.

New Roles for Schools

Between 1890 and 1899, nearly 3.7 million immigrants entered the United States; fewer than 1.4 million were English speakers from the United Kingdom and Ireland, while nearly 2.3 million were non-English speakers from Germany, Italy, Austria-Hungary, and Russia. During this period, public displays of patriotism became increasingly characteristic of American life. The recitation of the Pledge of Allegiance was introduced into public classrooms and courtrooms in the 1890s.

Victorians (in England and the United States) saw formal education as a great equalizer of social groups. Moreover, many younger immigrants and the children of immigrants eagerly embraced American schooling as a means of upward mobility. However, schools did not always fulfill their promise as agents of equal opportunity for all. Increasingly, schools separated and grouped children according to their culture, religion, and class as well as race.

Reformers, missionaries, philanthropists, and government officials alike extolled the virtues of schooling tailor-made for particular groups. Presbyterian missionary women founded the Presbyterian College of the Southwest to instruct Spanish-speaking girls in both English and Protestantism. European American teachers taught young Indian women at the Cherokee Female Seminary near the Cherokee Nation capital at Tahlequah, Oklahoma.

Whether designed for Indians, Hispanos, or African Americans, boarding schools enabled teachers to exercise authority over pupils day and night. The head of the Indian boarding school in Carlisle, Captain Richard Henry Pratt, expressed the school's principles this way: "I am a Baptist, because I believe in immersing the Indians in our civilization and when we get them under holding them there until they are thoroughly soaked." At the school, boys learned to make harnesses, tin pots and pans, wagons, and carriages, among other products, many of which were sold to local residents to raise money for the school. Girls took in laundry and ironed, also part of the school's money-making effort. The goal of such activities was to enable the pupils to become self-supporting upon graduation.

Indians who taught in Indian schools tried to counter the message that whites had nothing to learn from Indian culture. Born on the Yankton Sioux Reservation in Dakota Territory, Gertrude Bonnin chose the pen name Zitkala-Sa to write about her experiences as a teacher at the Carlisle school. She recounted the shame she felt when one of the white teachers taunted a young man by reminding him "that he was nothing but a 'government pauper.'" She lamented, "I wished my heart's burdens would turn me to unfeeling stone. But alive, in my tomb, I was destitute!"

Autobiographical Narrative by Zitkala-Sa

The school as a vehicle for **vocational instruction** also found support among northern philanthropists concerned about education for southern black children and young people. A generation after the Civil War, the persistent poverty of many rural southern blacks convinced northern reformers that this group of Americans should be educated for a distinct form of second-class citizenship. Philanthropists, such as Julius Rosenwald of Chicago, upheld the notion of segregated public education. They created new institutions, or modified existing ones, to stress the trades and "domestic arts" at the expense of such subjects as philosophy, mathematics, and foreign languages. Embracing the "industrial education movement," the white trustees of the state-sponsored North Carolina Agricultural and Mechanical College (a segregated black college) voted to exclude women from the school altogether. They reasoned that "neither the girls or boys wanted to engage in the harder kinds of manual labor in the presence of the other sex, but would strive to dress up in fine clothes to impress the other."

This emphasis on vocational training provoked varied reactions from African American leaders. Born a slave in 1858, Booker T. Washington had labored in a West Virginia coal mine

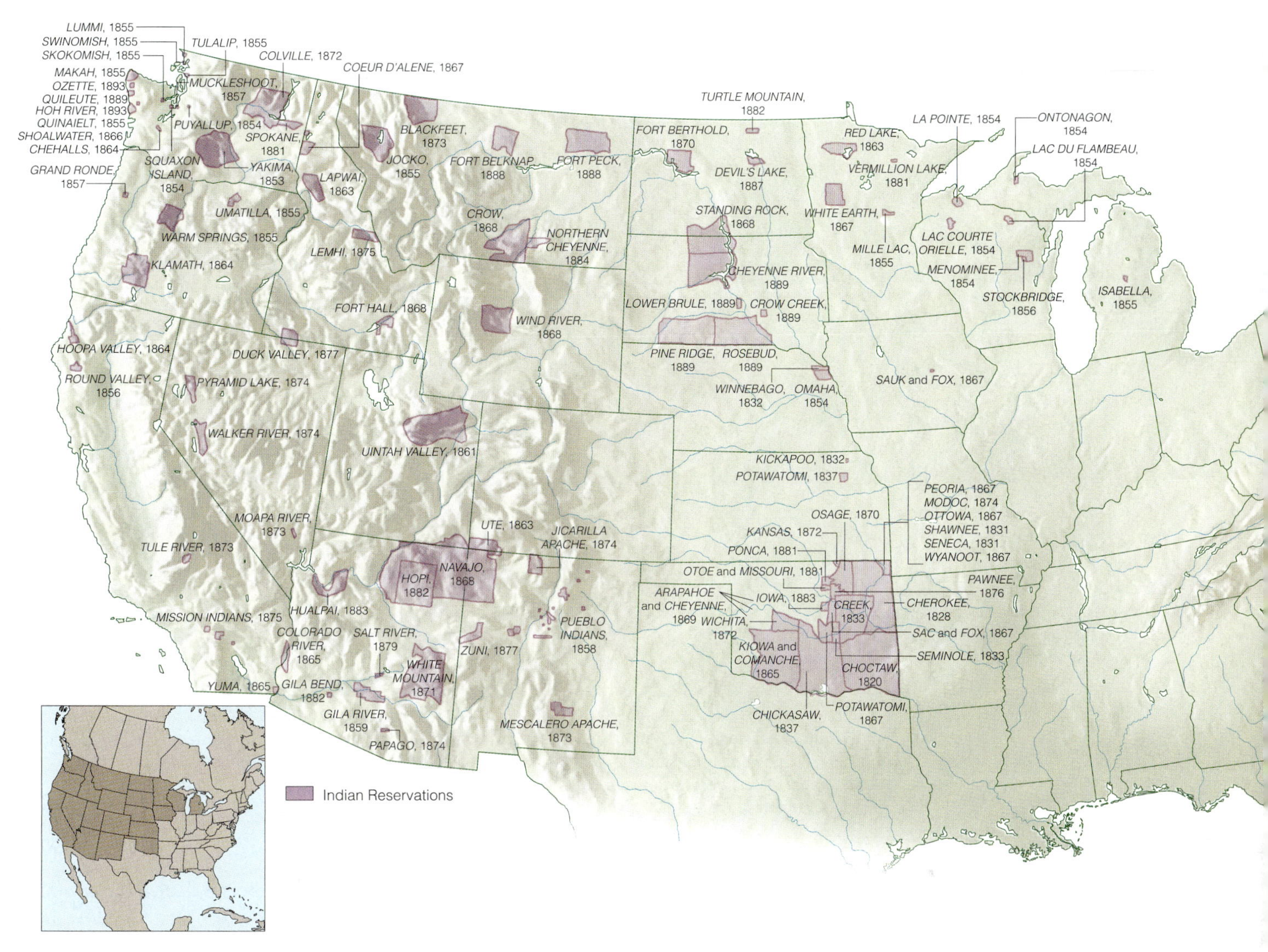

▲ **MAP 18.3 INDIAN RESERVATIONS, 1900**

The Dawes Severalty Act, passed by Congress in 1887, intended to abandon the reservation system and integrate Indians into mainstream American society. Nevertheless, many reservations remained intact. As a group, Indians remained apart from European Americans. By the early twentieth century, the Indian as a "vanishing American" had become a stock character in novels and films. Yet Indian activists continued to press the cause of their people: to preserve native cultures and, at the same time, protest persistent poverty.

before attending Hampton Normal (teacher-training) and Agricultural Institute in Virginia. In 1881 he assumed the leadership of Tuskegee Institute, an Alabama school for blacks founded on the Hampton model. Speaking at the Cotton States Exposition, a fair held in Atlanta in 1895, Washington urged southern blacks to "Cast down your buckets where you are"—in other words, to concentrate on acquiring manual skills that would bring a measure of self-sufficiency to black families and communities. In the same address, Washington proposed that blacks refrain from agitating for civil rights, such as the vote. In return, whites should refrain from attacking innocent men, women, and children. Ignoring this last part of the speech, whites hailed Washington's "Atlanta Compromise" proposal as one that endorsed racial segregation and second-class citizenship for blacks. Nevertheless, in the coming years, Washington worked secretly to undermine the legal foundations of some of the white South's most cherished institutions, including segregated railroad cars and rural forced labor.

Booker T. Washington, Atlanta Exposition Address

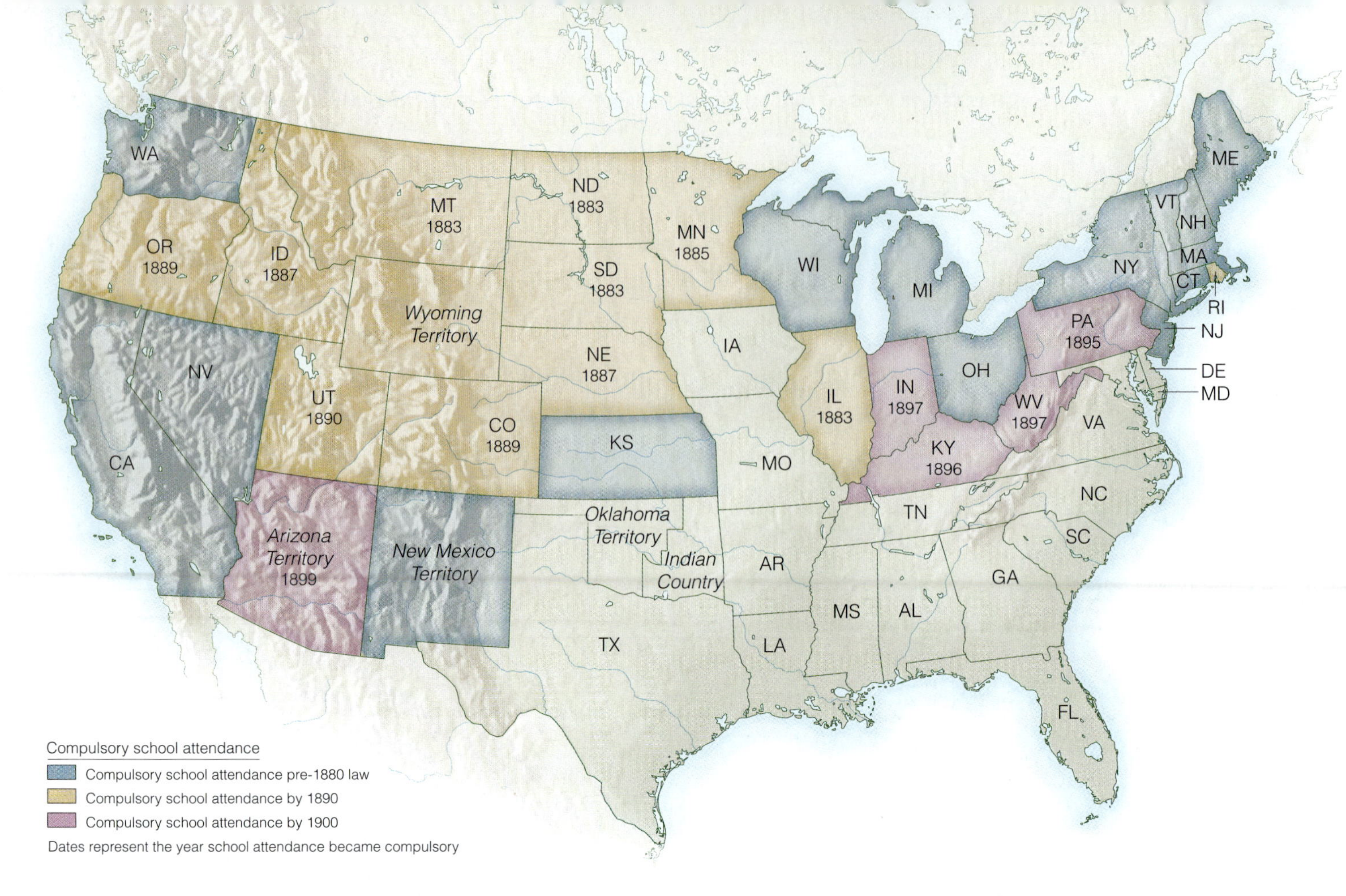

▲ MAP 18.4 COMPULSORY SCHOOL ATTENDANCE LAWS, BY STATE
Several northeastern, midwestern, and West Coast states enacted compulsory school attendance laws before 1880. A large number of states joined this trend in the 1880s and 1890s. By 1900 the former Confederate and border states, plus Iowa, were the only states not to have laws requiring young children to attend school for part of the year.

Challenging Washington's message, scholar-activist W. E. B. Du Bois ridiculed the notion that blacks should be content to become maids, carpenters, and sharecroppers. Similarly, in 1896, John Hope, a young professor at Roger Williams University in Nashville, Tennessee, and future president of Morehouse College and later Atlanta University, renounced Washington's apparent **accommodationist** stance: "If we are not striving for equality, in heaven's name for what are we living?" he demanded. "Rise, Brothers! Come let us possess this land. Never say, 'Leave well enough alone.'"

Some immigrant groups, responding specifically to the Protestant agenda of most public school systems, preferred to sponsor their own schools. In many urban areas, Roman Catholic nuns founded and staffed **parochial** (parish) schools that appealed to certain immigrant communities. By 1900 Catholics constituted the largest single denomination in the country, with 9 million members from diverse backgrounds. Catholic newcomers from southern and eastern Europe opposed what they claimed was the attempt by the Irish-dominated church hierarchy to "Americanize" Catholicism. One Chicago Catholic communicant, writing in the Polish-language paper *Zgodat,* charged that the effort to force Polish churchgoers to listen to and speak English was "an insult to all Polish parishes in Chicago as well as in the United States." Catholic churches and schools "built with the hard-earned money of us Polish people" should be kept under community control, he argued.

New forms of schooling reinforced class and cultural distinctions. No longer dependent on the income their children might earn in the workplace, late-nineteenth-century urban middle-class families could allow their sons and daughters to prolong their schooling. High school came to be considered a logical extension of public schooling. Between 1890 and 1900, the number of students graduating from high school doubled, from 43,731 to 94,883.

The spread of private institutions of higher education reflected the wealth of a new industrial owner class and new forms of socialization for young people of privilege. In 1891 Central Pacific Railroad builder Leland Stanford founded Stanford University in California in honor of his recently deceased son. The previous year, Standard Oil's John D. Rockefeller established the University of Chicago.

College life was becoming associated with a particular stage of personal development, a stage marked not only by academic endeavors, but also by uniquely American group activities, such as playing on or cheering for the school football team. In 1893 an editorial in the *Nation* decried "the inordinate attention given to athletics in college" and suggested that "debt, drink, and debauchery" were the natural consequence. The writer singled out athletic scholarships and the recruitment of college baseball players by professional scouts as especially unfortunate developments. College football games had become spectacles, drawing thousands of paying spectators but also costing a great deal of money to produce and staff. The 1892 Yale University athletic budget included funds to pay for transporting the football team and its retinue of doctors, trainers, cooks, and coaches from one game to the next. The game of basketball was invented in 1891, and soon many colleges formed teams that played the new sport.

Connections Between Consciousness and Behavior

In the 1890s some scholars and writers proposed that, although America's geographic frontier was closed, the "interior" frontier (of the human will and imagination) still attracted the curious. In Vienna, professor-physician Sigmund Freud pioneered the study of the human unconscious, the mysterious realm of thought and feeling that lies hidden beneath the mundane activities of everyday life. Freud's *The Interpretation of Dreams* (1900) suggested that dreams reveal the dreamer's unconscious desires and that these desires shape routine behavior.

In the United States, the new discipline of psychology owed much to the work of Harvard University professor William James. In his *Principles of Psychology* (1890), James described the human brain as an organism constantly adjusting itself to its environment; people's surroundings profoundly influence their behavior, he argued. In *The Will to Believe* (1897), he explored the psychology of religious faith. According to James, religion, science, and philosophy all have immediate relevance to the way people live their lives, and these ways of thinking and believing can cast light on social problems and their possible solutions.

Rex Geissler, http://greatcommission.com, The University of Chicago

▲ Like Andrew Carnegie, John D. Rockefeller gave away a great deal of his fortune—about $520 million—in his lifetime. Among Rockefeller's philanthropic endeavors was the University of Chicago. Shown here are buildings that today house several museums, including the university's Oriental Institute.

Henry James, William's brother, explored the psychological dimensions of class, gender, and national identities in his works of fiction and literary criticism. In much of his fiction, Henry James probed the consciousness of his subjects and experimented with methods of controlling points of view. Such works as *Daisy Miller* (1878), *The Wings of the Dove* (1902), *The Ambassadors* (1903), and *The Golden Bowl* (1904) reveal his intense interest in encounters between European and American elites and the clash of cultures between the two groups.

Novelist Stephen Crane combined an unflinching look at reality—a blood-soaked Civil War battlefield or the slums of New York City—with a sensitive probing of human psychology. In *The Red Badge of Courage* (1894), Crane explores the fears and self-delusions of a Union soldier, basing his account on firsthand descriptions of the fighting a generation before. By stripping the story of all ideology—northern soldiers are hardly distinguishable from southern soldiers, and political issues are never mentioned—Crane suggests that the real war was that of the combatants battling their own private demons.

Psychologists, novelists, and religious leaders explored the uncharted territory of the mind.

Kate Chopin wrote about gender roles in New Orleans Creole, or French-influenced, society. Her novel *The Awakening* (1899) prompted outrage among critics. They objected to the sympathetic portrayal of the wealthy married heroine, Edna Pontellier, who anguishes over her inability to reconcile her artistic, free-spirited temperament with her roles of wife and mother. At the end of the story, she chooses to commit suicide rather than submit to a life of convention. The novel focuses on Edna's reaction to the expectations other people have of her and on her gradual awakening to the idea that she must live life—or die—on her own terms.

Psychologists and novelists were not the only people to explore the uncharted territory of the mind. Some religious leaders saw human consciousness as the key to understanding spiritual growth and development. In the late nineteenth century, the Church of Christ, Scientist, founded by Mary Baker Eddy in 1879, prospered and grew. Eddy held that physical illness was a sign of sin and that such illness could be healed by Christian faith and prayer. By linking religious life to physical health, Eddy affirmed a crucial link between belief and personal well-being. She also suggested that reality was spiritual in nature and not bounded by the material, or physical, realm. In 1892 she reorganized her Christian Science faith around a mother church in Boston. Through branch churches, the American-born sect spread to more than 60 countries throughout the world.

The Search for Alliances

In the 1890s, groups of Americans seemed to be estranged from each other as they rarely had been before. A few were enjoying the fruits of astonishing wealth, building for themselves magnificent, multimillion-dollar "summer cottages" reminiscent of glittering European palaces. In 1899 University of Chicago sociologist Thorstein Veblen coined the term **conspicuous consumption** to describe the expensive tastes of the ostentatious rich. Meanwhile, working men and women toiled long hours under dangerous conditions—when they had jobs. In 1895 the average worker was unemployed for three months of the year. Categories of race pitted various groups, native-born and immigrant, against one another. Self-styled sophisticated city folk derided the **hayseeds** on the farm.

Still, the prosperous middle class hoped that certain unifying forces would connect different classes and ethnic groups. Businessmen, lawyers, and other professionals placed their faith in public schools, such cultural institutions as public museums and libraries, and the consumer impulse to instill "American" values in newcomers and the poor. The 1890s also witnessed some remarkable alliances between groups of people who had never before found common ground. The Populist party had a profound impact on the nation's political landscape in the 1890s. And women, through their local and national organizations, helped to blend domestic concerns with politics, offering a new model of civic involvement.

Class Conflict

Congress passed the Pension Act of 1890 to provide pensions for all disabled men who had served in the Union army during the Civil War. To pay for the pensions, Congress imposed a high tariff (named the McKinley Tariff after Representative William McKinley of Ohio) on a wide variety of imported goods. The northeastern states, dependent on domestic manufacturing, traditionally supported a high tariff. Western states supported the McKinley Tariff in return for the Sherman Silver Purchase Act of 1890, under which the federal government promised to buy a total of 4.5 million ounces of silver each month and to issue banknotes for that amount redeemable in gold or silver. As a result, Westerners benefited from the infusion of federal cash used to purchase silver mined in the West.

But the pairing of a high tariff with the purchase of silver produced explosive political and economic results. The tax on imported manufactured goods hurt consumers, and when wages did not keep pace with prices, workers revolted. In 1892 steel magnate Andrew Carnegie and his company chairman Henry Clay Frick initiated a drastic wage cut at the Carnegie Steel Company's Homestead plant, near Pittsburgh. Workers struck in June. They armed themselves with rifles and dynamite and engaged in a pitched battle with some 300 detectives from the Pinkerton agency, men hired by Frick to break the strike. (Homestead town officials had refused Frick's request to subdue the strikers.) Ten people died, and 60 were wounded. In response to the violence, the governor of Pennsylvania mobilized the state's National Guard. The troops escorted strikebreakers to work. The company cut its workforce by 25 percent and reduced the wages of the strikebreakers. The steelworkers' union lay in ruins. Gloated Frick, "Our victory is now complete and most gratifying."

The pairing of a high tariff with the purchase of silver produced explosive political and economic results.

In the West, gold, copper, and silver miners faced daunting barriers to labor organization from within and outside their ranks. Protestants harbored suspicions of Roman Catholics. Ancient hatreds prevented the Irish from cooperating with the English. European Americans disdained Mexicans and the Chinese. However, the workers in Idaho's Coeur d'Alene mines managed to overcome these animosities and strike for union recognition. In March 1892 mine owners in the region formed a "protective association" and slashed wages. When workers walked off the job, the owners imported strikebreakers from other areas of the West. The strikers retaliated by blowing up a mine with dynamite. Fifteen hundred state and federal troops arrived on the scene, and the resulting clash left seven miners dead. The troops confined 300 striking miners in bullpens, where they remained for several weeks before their trials. In this case, too, the strikers met with defeat. However, out of this conflict came a new organization, founded in Butte, Montana, in 1893: the Western Federation of Miners.

Widespread discontent over the tariff and simmering resentment on the part of debtors clamoring for unlimited coinage of silver helped unseat President Harrison in the election of 1892. The victorious Democratic candidate, Grover Cleveland, who had held the presidency before Harrison, took office once more in 1893 (the only defeated president to be reelected). A new and noteworthy player in the election of 1892 was the People's (Populist) party, which had nominated an old Greenback Labor party man, James B. Weaver. Weaver polled more than 1 million votes, putting both the Republicans and Democrats on notice that the Populists had the potential to swing future national elections.

The first national convention of the Populist party took place in Omaha, Nebraska, in the summer of 1892. The party had emerged from the Farmers' Alliances that had so effectively organized black and white midwestern and southern farmers in the 1880s. In the 1890s the plight of western farmers reflected the state of American agriculture in general. On the Plains, farmers incurred ever deeper debts as they bought more land and invested in expensive machinery to raise pigs, cattle, wheat, and fruit for market. But to put food on their own tables, they had to pay cash for bacon, beef, bread, and canned peaches at the store. The price of wheat had been a dollar a bushel in 1870, but it was only 35 cents 20 years later. Dakota farmers lost 15 cents on every bushel of wheat they sent to market.

As early as 1890 the Populist party was making gains in state legislatures, and a number of Populist orators were making their mark on the political scene. In Nebraska, party activist Luna Kellie explained the fine points of international finance to her listeners, denouncing foreign investors in the state economy and at the same time extolling the opening of foreign markets for the state's crops. "Stand up for Nebraska, so fertile and fair," she urged farmers.

The Populist party platform endorsed at the Omaha convention supported "free and unlimited coinage of silver and gold at the present legal ratio of sixteen to one"; a graduated income tax; government ownership of railroad, telegraph, and telephone companies; and an end to land speculation. The delegates also condemned government subsidies to private corporations (for example, land grants to railroads) and called for the direct election of U.S. senators. Populists supported other measures designed to make the political process more open

Coeur d'Alene and Northern Idaho/Western Montana

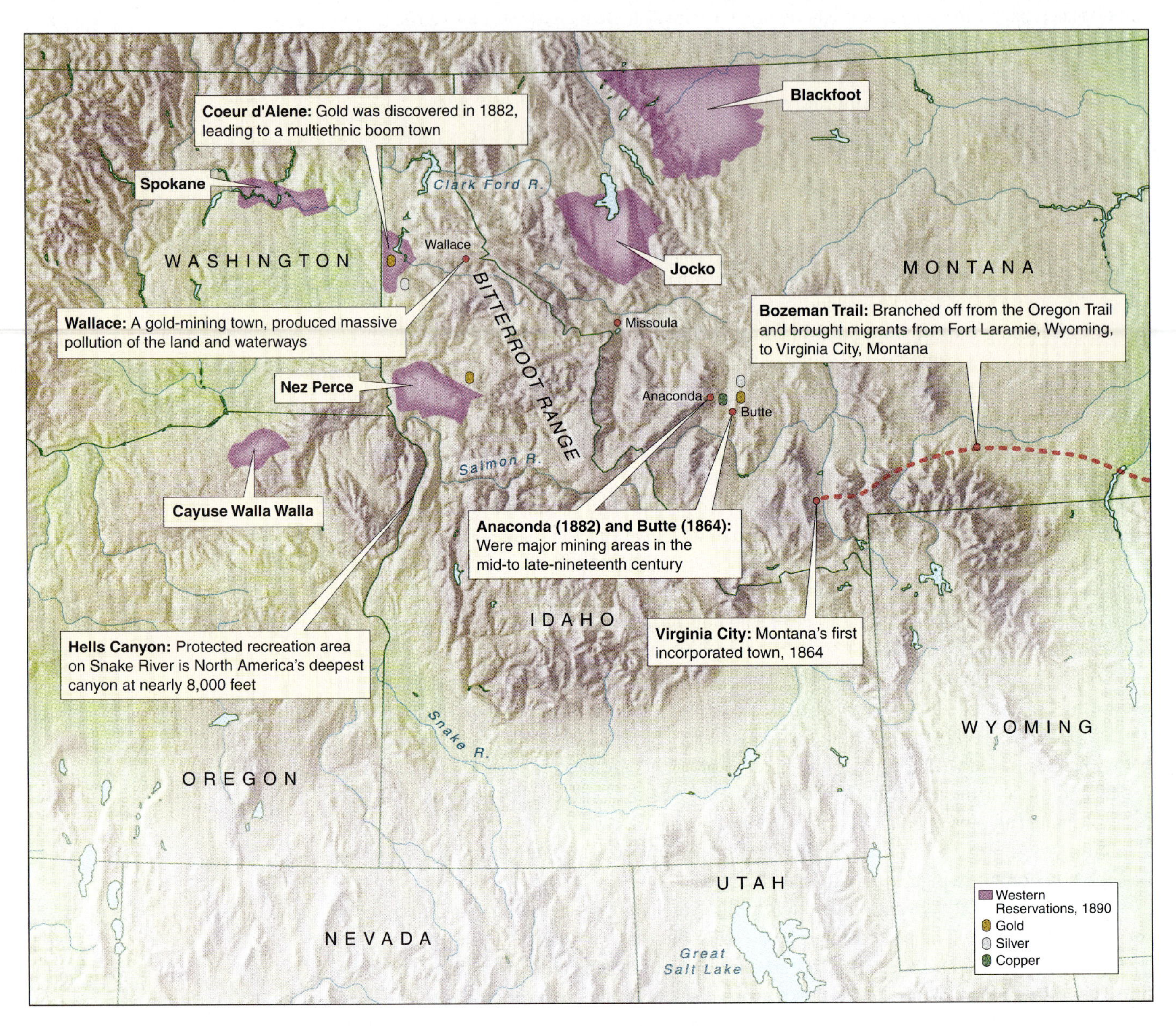

Since the late nineteenth century, much of the history of the northern Idaho and western Montana region has been shaped by gold, silver, and copper mining. Boomtowns attracted European American workers and displaced large numbers of Indian groups in the process. When gold was discovered on the reservation of the Nez Perce, the government confiscated 90 percent of the land and forced many of the group's members into Oregon.

Today the region combines natural beauty with the toxic aftermath of large-scale mining. Forests cover more than 40 percent of Idaho. Two-fifths of the state's territory consists of national forests, which serve as a sanctuary for moose, elk, and black bear. Idaho is among the nation's most sparsely populated states, with 17 persons per square mile. Montana has only two persons per square mile.

Idaho has six hazardous-waste sites listed on a national cleanup priority list; these sites consist of the remnants of large-scale mining operations. Montana has 14 sites. In some cases, long-abandoned mines continue to release toxic chemicals into the air and water. ■

and democratic, such as provisions for voters to recall corrupt elected officials and public referenda on pressing policy issues of the day.

The Populists sought to extend their reach beyond the cotton fields of the South and the plains of the Midwest to working men and women in the nation's cities. Though separated by geography and history, farmers and wage earners could lay claim to certain common interests. The Populists' 1892 platform included resolutions sympathizing "with the efforts of organized workmen to shorten the hours of labor" to an eight-hour workday (many workers were forced to toil 12–14 hours daily) and expressing solidarity with the Knights of Labor in their struggles against "tyrannical" employers. Although the Populist platform sounded radical in comparison to its Democratic and Republican counterparts, it foreshadowed both the substance and spirit of the early twentieth-century Progressives and the New Deal of the 1930s.

TABLE 18.1

Work Hours Needed to Produce Specified Amounts of Wheat, Corn, and Cotton, 1880 and 1900

	1880	1900
Wheat		
Work hours per acre	20	15
Yield per acre (bu)	13.2	13.9
Work hours per 100 bushels	152	108
Corn		
Work hours per acre	46	38
Yield per acre (bu)	25.6	25.9
Work hours per 100 bushels	180	147
Cotton		
Work hours per acre	119	112
Yield of lint per acre (bl)	179	191
Work hours per bale[a]	318	280

[a] Yields are five-year averages, centered on year shown. For statistical purposes, a bale of cotton is 500 pounds gross weight or 480 pounds net weight of lint. Actual bale weights vary widely.

Source: Historical Statistics of the United States, Colonial Times to 1957 (Washington, D.C.: U.S. Government Printing Office, 1960), p. 281.

The Populists gained strength when a national economic depression hit in 1893. This dramatic downturn stemmed from several causes. As debtors clamored for "free silver," foreign investors in the United States became nervous, and European bankers began to call in their loans. A bubble of overbuilding and land speculation burst.

The effects of the depression were widespread. Within six months, 8,000 businesses failed, throwing thousands of men and women out of work. As many as 20 percent of all workers lost their jobs. Some took to the road as tramps or hoboes to seek employment; others begged for handouts. In 1894, Jacob S. Coxey, an Ohio quarry owner, dubbed himself a "general" and mobilized his own "army" of 5,000 men to march to Washington, D.C. There, the marchers protested the failure of the federal government to provide relief, now that the country was in the midst of the worst depression ever. "Coxey's Army" petitioned Congress to create extensive public works projects at the federal and local levels. However, the "army" met with an abrupt end when Coxey and his men were arrested for trampling the grass on Capitol Hill.

Also in 1894, Eugene V. Debs, head of the American Railway Union (ARU), inspired the union's 150,000 members to protest conditions at the Pullman Palace Car Company. Employees in the company town of Pullman near Chicago felt squeezed when the Pullman company cut their wages by one-third but left intact the rents on their company-owned houses. The resulting strike crippled railroads from Chicago to California. The U.S. attorney general, Richard Olney, a former attorney for the railroads, urged President Cleveland to intervene in the strike. Cleveland heeded Olney's advice, declaring that he could not stand by while the strikers interfered with the delivery of the U.S. mail. The president sent troops to quell the uprising, crushing the strike. For the first time, a federal court issued an **injunction** to force workers to go back to their jobs. Debs and other ARU leaders defied the order and went to jail.

To workers all over the country, the response to the Pullman strike signaled a troublesome alliance between government and big business, two powerful forces that the poor and the unemployed could not hope to counter. That alliance seemed to be solidified in 1895 when federal gold reserves fell to a dangerous low of $41 million (it was widely believed that a minimum of $100 million in gold was necessary to sustain the paper currency in circulation). Cleveland authorized the sale of government bonds for gold, but he also turned to J. P. Morgan, a Wall Street banker, for a loan. Morgan and a group of bankers agreed to

Picturehistory

▲ Police and soldiers rout Jacob S. Coxey's "Army" in 1894. Coxey led a group of unemployed men in a march on Washington, D.C. They were seeking government relief—in the form of a public works program—to alleviate economic distress caused by the Depression of 1893. As they marched, they sang a song that exaggerated their numbers one-hundred fold: "We're coming, Grover Cleveland, 500,000 strong."

lend the government $65 million, earning a $7 million commission for themselves in the process.

Judicial decisions confirmed the belief of many farmers and workers that all branches of the federal government were conspiring to favor the rich at the expense of the poor. In 1895 the Supreme Court rendered two opinions that favored big business and the wealthiest Americans. In *United States v. E. C. Knight*, the court ruled that the Sherman Anti-Trust Act of 1890 applied only to interstate commerce and not to manufacturers. The court had decided in favor of the subject of the suit, the sugar trust that controlled 98 percent of the industry. In *Pollock v. Farmers' Loan and Trust Company*, the court struck down a modest federal income tax (2 percent on incomes over $4,000 per year). These decisions helped set the stage for the showdown between the Populists and the two major parties in 1896.

Rise and Demise of the Populists

In 1896 the Republicans nominated Congressman William McKinley of Ohio, whose name had graced the widely unpopular tariff bill of 1890. The Democrats turned their back on Cleveland, regarded as a pariah by members of his own party for his deal with Morgan and his high-handed tactics against the Pullman strikers. Without an obvious presidential candidate at their convention in Chicago in July, the Democrats seemed at loose ends. Then, out of the audience, a man rose to address the 15,000 delegates. William Jennings Bryan, a 36-year-old Populist from Nebraska, electrified the assembly with his passionate denunciation of arrogant industrialists and indifferent politicians. The country must abandon the gold standard once and for all, he thundered: "You shall not press down upon the brow of labor this crown of thorns, you shall not crucify mankind upon a cross of gold." One awestruck listener, an alternate member of the Nebraska delegation, later said of Bryan's "Cross of Gold" speech, "There are no words in our language to picture the effect it produced upon the vast multitude which heard it." The next day, the Democrats chose Bryan as their candidate for president.

As a political movement encompassing disparate elements, the Populists left a mixed legacy.

By nominating this eloquent upstart, the Democrats took on the Populist cause of free silver. Conservative Democrats bolted the party or sat out the election. Meanwhile, some Populists were appalled that the Democrats had picked conservative Maine banker Arthur Sewall as Bryan's vice-presidential running mate. Meeting in their own convention later in the summer, the Populists chose Bryan as their candidate for president and Thomas E. Watson of Georgia for vice president. Thus, during his presidential campaign in the fall, Bryan had to contend with two different running mates from two different parties.

In the general election, McKinley received much support from his friend and political supporter Marcus (Mark) Hanna. A wealthy iron magnate and chair of the Republican National Committee, Hanna coordinated an effort to raise large sums of money for the Republicans ($16 million in total, far more than the Democrats' $1 million). He also fueled a nationwide hysteria over the possibility that Bryan would become president, blanketing the country with leaflets declaring "In God we trust, in Bryan we bust." Hanna charged that Bryan as president would mean disaster for businesspeople, bankers, and other creditors, who would now be at the mercy of working people, small farmers, and other debtors. Benefiting from Hanna's strategy and from divisions between the Populists and Democrats, McKinley triumphed in November. As a national force, the People's party rapidly disintegrated after the election of 1896.

Yet as a political movement encompassing disparate elements, the Populists left a mixed legacy. In some areas of the country, the party yielded some remarkable, if short-lived, interracial coalitions. In Grimes County, Texas, in the cotton-growing eastern part of the state, the Populist spirit survived for a few years beyond 1896. Some whites had split from the Democratic party, and some blacks had renounced their traditional allegiance to the Republican party. The alliance brought together blacks, such as school principal Morris Carrington, and whites, such as Garrett Scott, a Populist sheriff.

In the fall of 1899, the White Man's Union (WMU) emerged to oppose this biracial coalition. A member of the WMU tried to express its aims in poetry:

> 'Twas nature's laws that drew the lines
> Between the Anglo-Saxon and African races,
> And we, the Anglo-Saxons of Grand Old Grimes,
> Must force the African to keep his place.

The WMU made good on its vow to rid the county of "Negro rule." A November 1900 shootout at Anderson, the county seat, left Garrett Scott wounded and his brother Emmett and two other men dead. The gun battle effectively ended the Populist presence in Grimes County.

The Populists were unable to sustain a regionwide biracial coalition in the South. This failure suggests the power of white supremacist beliefs. The threat of cooperation between Republican and Populist voters was powerful, especially in such states as North Carolina. In that state, Republican-Populist **fusion** had captured the state legislature in 1894 and the governorship in 1896. Throughout the South, the black population was growing—a total of 10 million people in 1890, more than double the 4.5 million on the eve of the Civil War. Frightened by this development, white southern Democrats campaigned to disfranchise black men, beginning in the 1890s. Landless blacks and whites would find no common political ground again until the 1930s.

California Views Historical Photo Collection, Monterey, California

▲ **The diversity of the American workforce and the American economy inhibited the development of a national workers' political party. By the 1890s, some industries were fully mechanized. Others relied on traditional forms of manual labor. In California, Asian workers faced persistent discrimination from labor unions. These immigrants are picking oranges near Santa Ana, c. 1895.**

Barriers to a U.S. Workers' Political Movement

In the 1890s, workers in Europe were forging new political parties to represent their interests, and in some cases to press a bold socialist agenda, in the forum of national politics. Although late-nineteenth-century America showed dramatic evidence of bitter class conflict, it produced no viable workers' party or socialist movement. Why? The answer is not simple. Together, farmers and members of the industrial laboring classes aspired to self-sufficiency, a life free of debt that released their wives and children from unremitting toil and provided some measure of material comfort. Nevertheless, both groups found it difficult to ally with each other.

The large influx of immigrants meant that competition for even low-paying jobs remained fierce among wage-earning men and women. Employers manipulated racial, ethnic, and religious prejudices among workers to keep them estranged. Between 1890 and 1900, at least 29

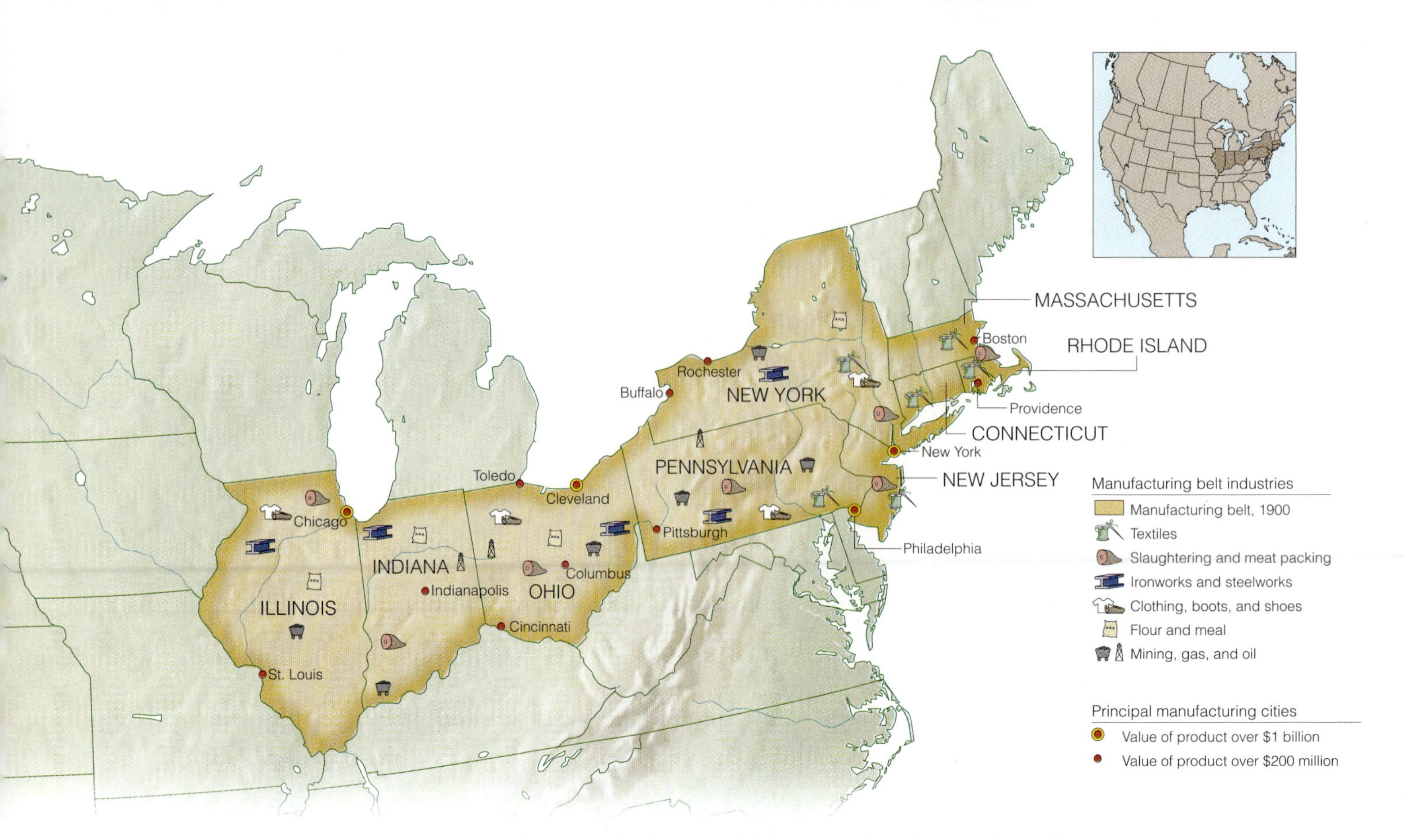

▲ **MAP 18.5 MANUFACTURING IN THE UNITED STATES, 1900**
During the late nineteenth century, most manufacturing took place in the northeastern United States. Exceptions included flour milling in Minneapolis, meatpacking in Chicago, the growing textile industry in the southern Piedmont, and the emergence of steel production in Birmingham, Alabama, due to rich local deposits of iron and coal ore.

major strikes—primarily in the iron, steel, coal-mining, meatpacking, railroad, and longshore industries—prompted management to employ African American strikebreakers.

White Protestant workers seized on ethnic and religious distinctions to win for themselves advantages in the workplace. Their unions excluded certain racial and ethnic groups altogether. Even somewhat egalitarian unions fell prey to racial prejudice. For example, the United Mine Workers (UMW) professed to welcome both black and white workers into its ranks. However, an 1892 report from an African American organizer in Jellico, Tennessee, stated that "the whites declare that they won't work" under an African American boss. At best, whites relegated their black and female coworkers to segregated unions and enforced a discriminatory division of labor within the workplace.

Moreover, the pace and processes of mechanization and technological development varied from job to job, making it difficult for workers in one industry to form alliances with workers in another. By 1900 the steel, shoe, and textile industries were fully mechanized. In contrast, skilled craft workers dominated the cigar, garment, and glass-blowing industries, although women machine operatives were beginning to challenge male cigarmakers. Taking pride in their craft and its traditions, skilled workers distanced themselves from those who tended machines.

Many American workers, regardless of ethnicity, religion, or industry, continued to believe that they could eventually own their own businesses; thus, they resisted casting their lot permanently with unions or other working-class organizations. High rates of **geographic mobility** also prevented workers from committing themselves to a particular union in a particular place. The power of antistrike forces proved daunting. Private security agencies, such as the Pinkertons, as well as state-deployed National Guard troops, backed up the authority of employers, judges, mayors, and governors. Finally, unlike European parliamentary systems, U.S. politics was based on a "winner take all" principle. In America, the two major parties tried to capture the political center, discouraging coalition-building among smaller parties. Such alliances might have pushed the country farther to the left or right.

These factors help to account for the success of the American Federation of Labor (AFL) in attracting and retaining members. By the end of the nineteenth century, the AFL had rejected the rhetoric of radical labor leaders in favor of organizing a select group of workers, mostly skilled white men. Leaders of AFL union affiliates denounced "cheap labor" competitors, whether women workers or Japanese or Chinese immigrants. In the coming years, the AFL would prove that it had staying power, although it represented primarily the interests of white male craftsmen.

Challenges to Traditional Gender Roles

In the 1890s the women's suffrage, club, missionary, and social settlement movements emerged as significant political forces. Nevertheless, for the most part, white women in these movements remained steadfast in their refusal to embrace their nonwhite counterparts.

In 1890 the two major national women's suffrage associations, the National Woman Suffrage Association and the American Woman Suffrage Association, merged to form the National-American Woman Suffrage Association (NAWSA). Elizabeth Cady Stanton served as the new group's first president for two years. The suffrage movement exhibited contradictory impulses. On one hand, it brought together supporters from around the country and yielded striking examples of international cooperation. Beginning in 1890 and every year thereafter until 1920, members of NAWSA branches scattered throughout the United States met in convention to debate strategy. American women consulted with their counterparts in England and western Europe to advance their cause.

Women's Suffrage before the 19th Century

On the other hand, in an effort to become "respectable," white native-born Protestant American suffragists sought to distance themselves from the poor, immigrants, African Americans, and the laboring classes within their own country. When NAWSA leaders called for an **educated franchise,** they implicitly left out immigrant and poor women. They also refused to admit black women's suffrage clubs into their umbrella organization. In the process, the white women turned their backs on some of the most committed supporters of their own cause.

TABLE 18.2

Categories of Employment, 1880–1910

Occupation	1880	Percentage	1890	Percentage	1900	Percentage	1910	Percentage
Agriculture, forestry, and fishing	8,705	50.1	10,170	42.8	10,920	37.6	11,590	31.6
Extractive industries	310	1.8	480	2.0	760	2.6	1,050	2.9
Manufacturing	3,170	18.2	4,750	20.0	6,340	21.8	8,230	22.4
Construction	830	4.8	1,440	6.1	1,660	5.7	2,300	6.3
Commerce and finance	1,220	7.0	1,990	8.4	2,760	9.5	3,890	10.6
Transportation and communications	860	4.9	1,530	6.4	2,100	7.2	3,190	8.7
Services	2,100	12.1	3,210	13.5	4,160	14.3	5,880	16.0
Other	195	1.1	170	0.7	370	1.3	600	1.6
Total	17,390	100	23,740	100	29,070	100	36,730	100

Numbers given in thousands.

Source: International Historical Statistics (New York: Palgrave McMillan, 2003), p. 154.

Virginia Historical Society

▲ In 1896 Charles H. Epps, the city sergeant of Richmond, Virginia, ran for reelection. He distributed these cards to prospective voters. The cards suggest the masculine nature of politics at this time. This one doubled as a scorecard for the city's professional baseball team and carried advertisements for a local whiskey manufacturer and liquor and tobacco store.

Identifying themselves primarily as wives and mothers, some women entered the political realm through local women's clubs. They believed that personal intellectual development and group political activity would benefit both their own families and society in general. In the 1880s, the typical club focused on self-improvement through reading history and literature. By the 1890s, many clubs had embraced political activism. They lobbied local politicians for improvements in education and social welfare and raised money for hospitals and playgrounds. The General Federation of Women's Clubs (GFWC), founded in 1892, united 100,000 women in 500 affiliate clubs throughout the nation.

Yet the GFWC specifically excluded African American clubs. Black women formed their own national federation, the National Association of Colored Women (NACW), in 1896. Through club work, they spoke out against lynch mobs and segregationists and worked to improve their local communities. In 1899 the first president of NACW, Mary Church Terrell, appeared before a mostly white organization, the National Congress of Mothers. She minced no words in contrasting the resources available to white mothers and children with the inferior medical care afforded their African American counterparts. Declared Terrell, "So rough does the way of her infant appear to many a poor black mother that instead of thrilling with the joy which you feel, as you clasp your little ones to your breast, she trembles with apprehension and despair."

In some areas of the country, black and white women did make common cause—to further the goals of temperance, for example—although white women embraced these alliances uneasily. At the end of the century, black women in North Carolina sought to circumvent the sometimes violent political realm dominated by white men. They worked with middle-class white women through voluntary organizations, such as the Young Women's Christian Association and the Women's Christian Temperance Union.

In the West, Protestant-sponsored "mission homes" ministered to women in need. The San Francisco Presbyterian Chinese Mission Home offered a safe haven for Chinese women fleeing abuse and exploitation. In 1898 a young Chinese woman, Lee Yow Chun, appeared before a government official and testified to the poverty of her family in Hong Kong and to the web of deception that had led to her arrival in the United States as a prostitute. Encountering an immigration official in San Francisco, Lee "fell in a lump on the floor and cried loudly, saying I did not want to be landed by those people [who had tricked her]; that I would jump into the sea rather than be taken by them." As a result, she was allowed to go to the mission home. In response to stories such as Lee's, eastern women opened their pocketbooks to support not only the San Francisco mission but also shelters for unwed mothers and abused girls in other cities, in the name of virtuous womanhood.

Religious beliefs inspired some women to go beyond national boundaries in their efforts to reach out to like-minded people. In the 1880s and 1890s, a group of American women participated in an interdenominational, international campaign to support the work of Pandita Ramabai, a native of India who had converted to Christianity and worked to challenge the subordinate role of women in her own country. In 1890 almost 60 "Ramabai Circles" claimed more than 4,000 members in the United States and Canada. Ramabai chose not to ally herself with the growing Indian nationalist movement (in opposition to Great Britain, the colonial power that ruled India); in her view, Christianity, not nation-state loyalties, should shape the identities of both men and women.

Social settlements were unique institutions, founded and staffed by well-educated women, many of whom had attended elite women's colleges. The daily operations of the settlement house reflected the priorities of its founders, who often brought activists, public health officials, journalists, and laboring men and women together around the dinner table to discuss problems of the poor. Settlement house workers hoped to instill in poor women the values of domesticity and pride in American citizenship. By 1900 more than 200 social settlement houses were helping to acculturate immigrants by offering classes in a variety of subjects, including English, health, and personal hygiene. In 1893 the women social workers of Hull House successfully lobbied Illinois state legislators for the passage of anti-**sweatshop** legislation that would protect female employees and prohibit child labor. Florence Kelley, who served for three decades as the general secretary of the National Consumer League, was a resident of Hull House in the early 1890s. In 1899 she moved to New York's Henry Street Settlement (founded by a nurse named Lillian Wald in 1893). The settlement's neighbors included the 500,000 people packed into the Lower East Side, many of them from Italy, Russia, Germany, Greece, and Hungary.

Although often associated with immigrants in the largest cities, settlement houses reached diverse populations. In the late 1890s, a coalition of the Kentucky Federation of Women's Clubs and other organizations sponsored several teachers who organized a summer settlement called Camp Cedar Grove in the eastern part of the state. This venture provided the foundation for the Hindman Settlement School. The school, still in existence, initially aimed to **acculturate** mountain people to middle-class ways in dress, eating habits, and manners and to preserve traditional mountain music and crafts.

Sensitive to the racial prejudices of their clients and their neighbors, most early settlements failed to reach out to African Americans. This policy stimulated the development of black-led settlements, such as the Phyllis Wheatley Settlement in Minneapolis and the Neighborhood

Culver Pictures

▲ To the modern eye, the Victorian parlor looks cluttered. Yet to late-nineteenth-century middle-class people, the parlor was a place to display possessions that testified to their comfortable way of life. Books, family photographs, and musical instruments had great social and symbolic value. Families gathered to read aloud, pore over photo albums, and sing old favorites. Some men, worried that their opportunities for "manly" activity were vanishing with the western frontier, thought of parlors as female spaces.

Union in Atlanta. Founded by Lugenia Burns Hope in 1908, the Neighborhood Union aimed "to bring about a better understanding between the races."

In the tradition of Frances Wright (an antebellum abolitionist who favored cooperative living arrangements over private households) and Victoria Woodhull, some women challenged traditional gender relations that relegated women to dependence on men. Emma Goldman, a Russian immigrant and self-proclaimed anarchist, paired the sexual liberation of women with the rights of workers to live a decent life. A radical by any measure, Goldman was, nevertheless, not alone in rejecting the idea that marriage should always be permanent. Between 1890 and 1900, the divorce rate increased from 1 out of every 17 new marriages to 1 out of 12. More and more couples, middle class and working class, native born and immigrant, were seeking means to dissolve marriages that had failed.

Charlotte Perkins Gilman was among the most prolific and well-known critics of the conventional division of labor in the home. Through fiction, nonfiction, and poetry, she claimed that humankind had progressed beyond the point where brute strength was the determinant of social status. Gilman proclaimed that women, no longer content to remain dependent on men, must take their rightful place within the economy, working as equals with their brothers and husbands. In *Women and Economics: A Study of the Economic Relations Between Men and Woman as a Factor in Social Evolution* (1898), she proposed that housework be divided into its specialized tasks to be performed by professionals. This system would free women from the unpaid, mind-numbing task of combined "cook-nurse-laundress-chambermaid-housekeeper-waitress-governor." In her critique of gender conventions, Gilman anticipated the feminist movement of the 1960s.

Yale collection of Western Americana, Beinecke Rare Book and Manuscript Library

▲ **This interior of a Tlingit Indian chief's house in Chilkat, Alaska, c. 1900, suggests that the Victorians were not the only group of people to arrange crowded displays of art and other cultural artifacts in central living spaces. Indians of the Northwest Coast enjoyed an abundance of marine foods. They had time to devote to making intricate wood carvings in the form of masks and totem poles. Social status was based on inheritable wealth, as revealed by works of art and other material goods.**

Men also pondered the effects of industrializing society on their own roles. Some elite men revolted against the trappings of Victorian culture. These men worked every day in business offices, not out of doors. Some yearned for "manly" activities such as courageous exploits against nature or other men. They believed that overstuffed parlors represented "feminine" interiors. Life indoors—singing religious hymns around the piano or reading aloud to family members—stifled men's "natural" instincts for bravery and adventure, they claimed. They yearned to embrace the outdoors and prove their masculinity in the process. As assistant secretary of the U.S. Navy in the late 1890s, Theodore Roosevelt worried that, in this age of machines, young men lacked the opportunities for "the strenuous life" their grandfathers had enjoyed. He argued that unapologetic masculine bravado provided the key to American strength and **rejuvenation** on both a national and personal level. In his multivolume history *The Winning of the West* (1889–1896), Roosevelt extolled America's relentless march to the Pacific: "The rude, fierce settler who drives the savage from the land lays all civilized mankind under a debt to him." Imperialism at home and abroad, he declared, was a "race-important work," one that should claim the energies of men as politicians and soldiers.

American Imperialism

In the 1890s the United States began to extend its political reach and its economic dominance to other parts of the world. Americans looked beyond their borders and saw exotic peoples who represented a variety of opportunities—as consumers of American goods, producers of goods Americans wanted to buy, and objects of American benevolence. This view represented an extension of the reform impulse at home. Indeed, broader thinking about the United States' place in the world reflected a new desire among those who benefited from prosperity to spread American standards—in behavior, productivity, and quality of life—to other peoples.

The country's mighty industrial manufacturing sector demanded new markets and a wider consumer base. The economic depression of 1893, in particular, raised fears that manufacturers would have to contend with surpluses of goods that Americans could not afford to buy. American businesspeople and State Department officials established a partnership that combined private economic self-interest with national military considerations. Some molders of public opinion used the new languages of race and masculine virility to justify an "Anglo-Saxon" mission of conquest of "childlike" peoples. Meanwhile, European countries were carving up Africa and making economic inroads into China. Many Americans believed their own country should join the "race" for riches and "march" to glory as part of the international competition to exploit the natural resources and trade potential of weaker countries.

American Museum of Natural History Library, Image No. 220545

▲ The Greenland Eskimo Minik is shown here soon after his arrival in New York City in 1897. Minik was devastated by the death of his widowed father, Qisuk; the two were among six Eskimos brought to New York by Arctic explorer Robert E. Peary. Later in his life, Minik spoke of his father to a newspaper reporter, saying, "He was dearer to me than anything else in the world, especially when we were brought to New York, strangers in a strange land."

Cultural Encounters with the Exotic

In early October 1897, 30,000 spectators paid their 25-cent fee to enter New York's Excursion Wharf and observe the strange cargo of the recently arrived steamship *Hope*. Arctic explorer Robert Peary had returned from Greenland, bringing with him six Greenland Eskimos and a 37.5-ton meteorite dislodged from the Cape York region. Among the native Greenlanders were Qisuk and his seven-year old son, Minik. The American public hailed the intrepid explorer Peary as a hero. The American Museum of Natural History put the Eskimos on display, and New Yorkers regarded their odd clothing, language, and eating habits with intense curiosity. But their curiosity was only superficial and did not extend to protection for the young Minik.

Over the next year, four of the Eskimos (including Qisuk) died, and one other returned to his native land. The orphaned Minik survived and remained in the United States. Within a few years, he was abandoned by Peary and museum officials who had initially touted him as a significant scientific discovery. Minik returned to Greenland when he was a young man, but he was restless and unhappy there. He returned to the United States in 1916, eventually finding some peace with a New Hampshire farm family. He died in 1918, a victim of a worldwide flu epidemic.

Minik's short, tragic life reveals certain aspects of Americans' encounter with "exotic" peoples in the late nineteenth century. The Museum of Natural History subjected him and the other members of his group to close study. When Qisuk died, the museum conducted a mock burial for the benefit of his son but then created a public exhibit of Qisuk's bones. (Nearly 100 years later, the passage of the Native American Grave and Burial Protection Act provided an incentive for museum authorities to send the remains of the four Eskimos back to Greenland for burial.)

During the late nineteenth century, Americans were fascinated by artifacts and images dealing with faraway places, especially Africa, the Middle East, and Asia. This impulse, revealed in high art as well as popular culture, stereotyped darker-skinned, non-Christian peoples as primitive, sensual, and inscrutable. Chicago's Columbian Exposition of 1893 featured exhibits depicting harems, spice merchants, and turbaned warriors and performances of "hootchy kootchy dancers," scantily clothed young women writhing to the music of exotic instruments.

Throughout the late nineteenth century, photographers took pictures of Middle Eastern nomads and African villagers. American artists, such as Frederic Edwin Church and John Singer Sargent, traveled abroad to render romantic scenes of deserts, ancient ruins, and mysterious peoples in oils and in watercolors. Painter Eric Pape arranged to have himself tied to a pyramid so that he could partake of an "Egyptian experience"; he produced a painting called *Site of Ancient Memphis* in 1891.

Cultural tendencies could be used to sell products and entertainment.

These cultural tendencies could be used to sell products and entertainment. The glassmaker-jeweler Tiffany and Co. evoked Islamic art in its tea services and silver patterns. Tobacco companies marketed mass-produced cigarettes with "Oriental" brand names: Fatima, Omar, and Camel. Thus, a fascination with the exotic encompassed a wide range of impulses in American life and letters, bringing together explorers, scientists, artists, and advertising agents.

Initial Imperialist Ventures

The opening of Asia to American trade, combined with the military challenges posed by the major European imperial powers, stimulated the growth of the U.S. Navy in the 1880s. In 1883, Congress appropriated funds to build 90 small ships, one-third made of wood, the rest out of steel. Seven years later, Captain Alfred Thayer Mahan argued for a modern force of large seagoing battleships. In his book *The Influence of Sea-Power in History, 1660–1763* (1890), Mahan contended that if the United States aspired to be a world power, it must control the seas.

Seeking way stations for its ships, the United States negotiated control over both Pearl Harbor in Hawaii and the harbor at Pago Pago in Samoa in 1887. The State Department even achieved a voice in Samoan foreign relations to stave off rivals Great Britain and Germany, which also coveted Pago Pago. In 1889 warships of these three powers gathered in the Samoan harbor. Fortunately, a hurricane thwarted a showdown. The powers, unnerved by their near brush with war, agreed to establish joint control over the islands for the next ten years.

In October 1890, Secretary of State James G. Blaine hosted the first Pan-American Conference in Washington, D.C., a gathering of representatives from 19 independent Latin American republics. Topics included the adaptation of standardized weights and measures for all participants in the conference and a possible intercontinental railroad. These developments suggested the blurring of military, diplomatic, strategic, and economic interests—a mix that characterized American foreign policy for decades to come.

In 1895 the United States signaled to Great Britain that it was prepared to go to war to bar Europeans from colonizing or intervening in the Americas, a policy outlined in the Monroe Doctrine more than 70 years before. Britain had persisted in its long-standing claims to the jungle boundary between its colony of British Guiana and the country of Venezuela on the north central coast of South America. President Cleveland made clear his intention to enforce the Monroe Doctrine. Britain, sensitive to other threats posed by European imperial powers on the far-flung British empire, backed down. Thereafter, Britain began to concentrate on strengthening its diplomatic ties with the United States.

Meanwhile, in the South Pacific, the Hawaiian Islands seemed to pose both a threat and an opportunity for American interests. Located 2,000 miles from the California coast, Hawaii had a population of 150,000 in 1890. When English explorer James Cook landed there in 1778, the islands were inhabited exclusively by the descendants of ancient seafaring Polynesians. Protestant missionaries began to arrive in 1820, and the first sugar plantation appeared 15 years later. In 1875 sugar planters and merchants, many of whom were related to missionaries, negotiated a treaty with the United States that let them ship the crop to the United States duty free. Production of Hawaiian sugar increased from less than 10,000 tons in 1870 to 300,000 tons 30 years later.

By this time, the Chinese, Koreans, Filipinos, Puerto Ricans, Japanese, and Portuguese had made their way to the Hawaiian Islands. These groups formed the bulk of the plantation labor force, for disease had decimated the native population. In the fields and in their barracks, immigrant contract workers followed a disciplined regimen under the supervision of mounted, whip-wielding overseers called *lunas.* Indeed, these laborers' workday bore a marked resemblance to that of sharecroppers on the largest cotton plantations of the U.S. South.

Not surprisingly, both clergy and growers were alarmed by the laborers' resistance to regimentation in the fields and in the quarters. Some men and women workers drank on Saturday night, smoked opium, and gambled. Worse, in the eyes of their employers, many grabbed any opportunity to flee the plantation in search of jobs as wage-earners or shopkeepers in the city of Honolulu. Some even became rice farmers on their own. Planters were forced to suspend operations to accommodate traditional festivals, such as the Chinese New Year, when workers decorated their barracks and cottages with colorful flags and lanterns. Missionaries and sugar planters alike hoped to transform the workers into more stable, predictable employees.

The McKinley Tariff of 1890 raised duties on imports of the islands' sugar. This served to overturn the 1875 pro-planter treaty, causing planters (mostly Americans) to panic about their livelihood. They received no support from the islands' native leader, Queen Liliuokalani, who believed foreigners should be barred from running the country. In 1893 the planters, backed by American Marines, launched a successful revolt that deposed the queen. They then called for the United States to annex the islands as a territory. Upon investigation, President Cleveland

The Granger Collection, NY

▲ Born in 1838, Lydia Kamekeha became Queen Liliuokalani of Hawaii in 1891, after the death of her brother, King David Kalakaua. She reigned just two years before planters, backed by American Marines, deposed her. She died in 1917.

CONNECTING HISTORY

The Modern Olympic Games

In 1896, Athens, Greece, hosted the first modern Olympic Games.The founding members of the International Olympic Committee hoped to recapture the spirit of the ancient games and further the ideal of international peace. However, for more than a century, the modern games have more often mirrored rather than lessened existing rivalries between countries.

The first Olympic games took place in Greece sometime before 1400 BC. Held every four years, the original games were primarily religious festivals honoring the Greek god Zeus. Only men were allowed to compete, and only men were allowed to watch as spectators. Women competed for the first time in 1900. The winter games as a separate competition began in 1924; after 1994 the winter and summer games were held two years apart, on four-year cycles.

At various points in history, divisive racial ideologies—ideas that were developed in the late nineteenth century—intruded into the games. German dictator Adolf Hitler wanted the 1936 Berlin games to highlight what he called the superiority of whites over darker-skinned peoples. Yet the athletic prowess of Jesse Owens, an African American, helped expose Hitler's racist myths. The son of Alabama sharecroppers, the 23-year-old track and field star won four gold medals and set Olympic records in the 200-meter race and the broad jump, as Hitler watched, distressed, from the grandstand.

During the 1970s and 1980s, Middle Eastern conflicts and Cold War tensions disrupted the Olympics. In 1972 in Munich, Germany, eight Arab terrorists stormed the quarters of the Israeli athletes, killing two Israelis and taking nine others hostage. Soon after, in a shootout with West German police, all the hostages, five of the terrorists, and a police officer were killed. In 1980, the United States, Canada, and 52 other nations boycotted the Moscow summer games as a protest against the Soviet Union's invasion of Afghanistan in 1979–1980. Four years later, the Soviet Union and other Eastern bloc countries kept their athletes out of the Los Angeles games, charging that U.S. authorities were lax in security arrangements.

In recent years, a number of scandals and logistical problems have plagued the games. Since 1960, when a cyclist died of a drug overdose, Olympic officials have tried, with only partial success, to monitor athletes' use of banned performance-enhancing drugs. Members of the powerful International Olympic Committee, responsible for choosing sites for the games, periodically find themselves accused of taking bribes as cities around the world vie for the lucrative prize of hosting the games.

discovered that native Hawaiians opposed annexation and so refused to agree to the move. His refusal incurred the wrath of American imperialists, who claimed that the "Hawaiian pear" had been "ripe for the plucking."

The Spanish-American-Cuban-Filipino War of 1898

In the Caribbean, Cuban nationalists staged an uprising against the Spanish in 1895. The leader of the insurrection was José Julian Martí. He had lived in exile in the United States from 1881 to 1895. Rebelling against the repressive Spanish colonialists who had ruled the island for more than 400 years, native *insurrectos* under the leadership of Martí burned crops of sugar cane and attacked passenger trains. American companies with large investments in the Cuban sugar industry (a total of about $50 million) were outraged at the destruction of their property; they had no sympathy for the *insurrectos.* Yet the arrival of Spanish military officials, who herded the rebels into barbed-wire concentration camps, inflamed public opinion in the United States. Both businesspeople and humanitarians urged McKinley to intervene in Cuba.

Two American newspaper publishers, William R. Hearst and Joseph Pulitzer, seized the chance to boost their respective circulations by highlighting Spanish atrocities against Cubans. Pulitzer owned the St. Louis *Post Dispatch* and the *New York World,* and Hearst challenged him with the *San Francisco Examiner* and the *New York Journal.* On February 9, 1898, Hearst

By the time the games returned to Athens in 2004, it was clear that the Olympics showcased commercialism and modern science as much as idealism. Though hopeful of profiting from television-broadcast rights and tourist dollars, the city had to spend millions of dollars building new venues and improving local roads and other forms of infrastructure. In preparation for the contests, athletes from wealthy countries enlisted the aid of sports psychologists and personal trainers, studied the latest findings related to nutrition, and learned about Athens weather patterns and pollution trends. Technicians perfected timing devices that measured speeds within a fraction of a second.

In August 2004, 10,500 athletes from 202 countries converged in Athens. Concerns about a possible terrorist attack prompted the International Olympic Committee and the city of Athens to institute extraordinary security measures. Several thousand closed circuit TVs monitored the activities of the athletes, judges, spectators, and support staff. Seventy thousand security personnel patrolled the Olympic Village as well as the various venues where contests related to 28 different sports were held. An airship full of high-tech surveillance equipment hovered over the city.

A police officer armed with a semi-automatic weapon stands guard over the summer Olympic games in Athens in 2004.

Despite a number of controversies over judging (especially in gymnastics and fencing) and over drug use among some athletes, the games proceeded smoothly. The cost to the country of Greece, with a total population of 11 million? At least $7 billion, more than 30 times the amount that Atlanta had spent to host the games eight years earlier. ■

published a letter written by the Spanish minister in Washington, D.C., Dupuy de Lôme, in which de Lôme denounced President McKinley as a spineless politician. Six days later, the American battleship *Maine,* which had been sent to Havana harbor to evacuate Americans should the need arise, exploded and sank. Two hundred sixty officers and men were killed. Subsequent investigations concluded that the heat from one of the coal bins had ignited an adjacent powder magazine. But the Hearst papers implied that the Spanish were responsible for the blast.

Attempting to expand their readership, the Hearst and Pulitzer newspapers engaged in **yellow journalism:** sensational news reporting that blurred the line between fact and fiction, spontaneous reality and staged theater. War sold papers. During the crisis in Cuba, the *Journal* was selling at a rate of a million copies a day.

McKinley responded to American businesspeople who feared for their interests in Cuba and to other Americans who decried Spain's brutality toward the *insurrectos.* On April 11, 1898, McKinley called on Congress to declare a U.S. war against Spain. His own assistant secretary of the navy, Theodore Roosevelt, had reportedly called the president a "white-livered" poor excuse for a man. To Roosevelt and other supporters of war, much was at stake: the large American sugar investment, trade with the island, and American power and influence in the Western Hemisphere. Congress responded to McKinley's message by adopting the Teller Amendment, which declared that the United States would guarantee Cuba its independence once the Spanish were driven from the island. America went to war on April 29.

Granger Collection, New York

▲ The battleship *Maine* exploded and sank in Havana harbor on February 15, 1898.

McKinley hoped to hobble the Spanish navy by making a **preemptive attack** on the fleet in the Philippines. Commodore George Dewey, stationed with the American Asiatic Squadron in Hong Kong, was dispatched with his ships to Manila Bay, where on May 1, 1898, his force of four battleships sank all ten rickety Spanish vessels, killing 400, with only a few minor American casualties. Dewey waited in the harbor until American reinforcements arrived in August. Then, with the help of Filipino nationalists led by Emilio Aguinaldo, U.S. forces overran Manila on August 13.

Meanwhile, congressional Republicans had found the necessary votes to annex Hawaii. They claimed that the United States needed the Pacific islands to secure a refueling way station for Dewey's troops. McKinley signed the congressional resolution on July 7, 1898. Hawaiian residents were granted citizenship rights, and the islands became an official U.S. territory in 1900.

Roosevelt's Rough Rider's

Earlier in the summer of 1898, halfway around the globe, 17,000 American troops traveled to Tampa, Florida, in preparation for their incursion into Cuba. Among them were the Rough Riders, a crew of volunteers organized by Lieutenant Colonel Theodore Roosevelt, who had resigned his post as assistant secretary of the navy to serve as an officer. The troops, woefully unprepared for combat in the tropical heat, landed near Santiago, Cuba, in late June.

On July 1, the Rough Riders engaged an unprepared Spanish force of about 2,000 at El Caney and San Juan Hill. The Rough Riders charged up nearby Kettle Hill (they were on foot, not on horses) and into American legend. Later in speeches, Roosevelt boasted of shooting a Spanish soldier at point-blank range. But Roosevelt neglected to mention that he and his men had received crucial backup support from two African American regiments that day. Blacks had formed a skirmish line at the bottom of the hill, and, according to an eyewitness, "with an unearthly yell, charged up it" in company with the white soldiers. Federal military authorities had assigned African American men prominent combat roles in Cuba and the Philippines, believing that blacks were better able than whites to withstand the withering heat of the tropics.

By late July, American warships had destroyed the Spanish fleet in Santiago Bay. Again, Spanish losses were high (500 men killed) and American losses slight (1 man killed). According to Secretary of State John Hay, it had been "a splendid little war," just 113 days long. Battles claimed 385 American lives (although many times that number died from disease—malaria, typhoid, dysentery, and yellow fever—and from the rotten meat the soldiers ate). On August 12, 1898, Spain signed an **armistice** and later in the year ceded its claim to remnants of its empire, including Cuba and Puerto Rico in the Caribbean and the island of Guam in the Pacific. The United States forced Cuba to incorporate into its constitution (written in 1901) the Platt Amendment, which guaranteed continuing U.S. influence over the country, including the stationing of American troops at a naval station on Guantanamo Bay.

Meeting with Spanish negotiators in Paris, the United States agreed to pay $20 million for the Philippines. McKinley's motives in acquiring the islands stemmed from both commercial interests (the Philippines as a gateway to China) and religious concerns (the opportunity for Protestants to convert Spanish-speaking Roman Catholics).

World Colonial Empires, 1900

But Filipino rebels were not about to bow to a new colonial power. Over the next two years, the United States committed 100,000 troops to subdue the rebels, using tactics that foreshadowed the U.S. war in Vietnam 70 years later. Hunting down guerrillas hiding in the jungle, American soldiers torched villages and crops. Using a form of torture known as the "water cure," they forced water down the throats of suspected rebel leaders in an effort to extract information. Four thousand Americans and 20,000 Filipinos died in combat. As many as 600,000 Filipino civilians succumbed to disease and starvation. Not until 1901 could the Americans claim victory over their "little brown brothers," as future president William Howard Taft referred to the Filipino people.

Ownership of the Philippine Islands gave the United States a foothold in Asia. In 1894–1895, Japan had waged a successful war against China, and European traders rushed into China to monopolize local markets and establish their own spheres of influence. Secretary of State John Hay issued a communication called the Open Door note in the summer of 1899; in it, he urged the imperial powers to respect the trading interests of all nations. The Europeans were reluctant to cede anything to their international competitors, and only Italy agreed to the terms of Hay's policy. But in 1900, the Boxer uprising in China prompted cooperation between the western powers. The Boxers, Chinese ultranationalists, killed 200 foreign missionaries and other whites in an effort to purge China of outsiders. Together, the Germans, Japanese, British, French, and Americans sent 18,000 troops to quell the revolt. The United States and European nations continued to compete for the China market well into the twentieth century.

San Diego University

▲ This contemporary Chinese drawing shows two of the country's mythic creatures—a dragon and a large serpent—vanquishing interlopers from Western Europe and the United States during the Boxer Rebellion of 1900.

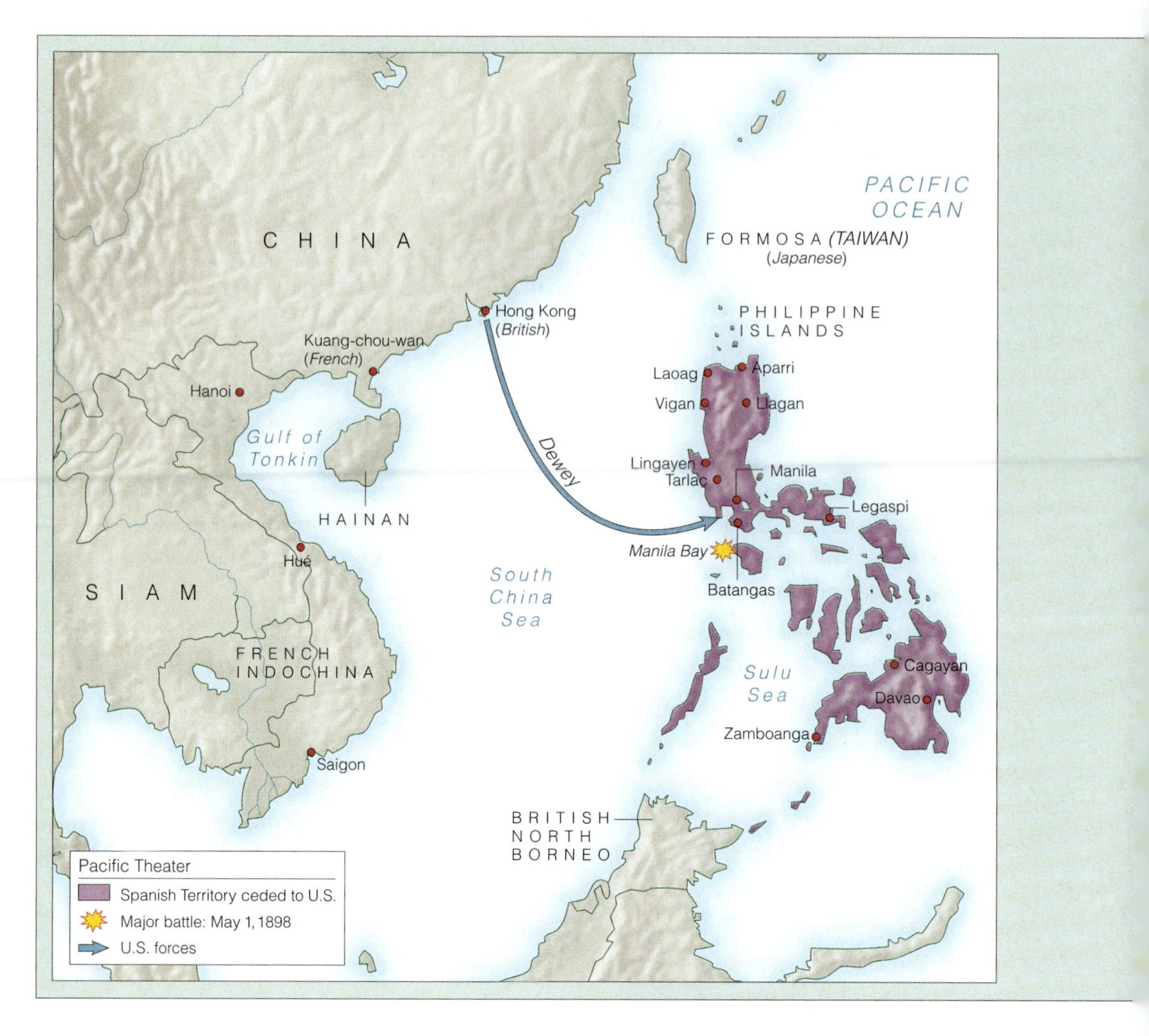

▲ **MAP 18.6 THE SPANISH-AMERICAN-CUBAN-FILIPINO WAR OF 1898**
In Cuba, the United States combined a blockade of the island with an army invasion to defeat Spanish forces. In the Philippines, the U.S. triumph over the Spanish opened a wider war between American occupying forces and native Filipinos.

Critics of Imperialism

Theodore Roosevelt seemed to personify the late-nineteenth-century idea of American manifest destiny: the notion that the core of the nation's history was a militant mission to expand its territorial reach. However, not all Americans agreed with Roosevelt. New York financier Mark Hanna called him a "madman" and "that damned cowboy." Writer Mark Twain believed him "clearly insane" and "insanest upon war and its supreme glories." Twain and other prominent people founded the Anti-Imperialist League in 1898 in an attempt to stem the rising tide of militarism.

It is difficult to generalize about the politics of anti-imperialists during this period. AFL president Samuel Gompers and industrialist Andrew Carnegie both considered themselves members of the anti-imperialist camp, but clearly that stance did not mean they agreed on much, or even on anti-imperialism. Some critics of imperialism advocated a hands-off policy toward other nations in the belief that all peoples were entitled to self-determination.

The scholar-activist W. E. B. Du Bois predicted that the "color line" would constitute a fundamental division between the earth's peoples in the twentieth century. Du Bois warned that the aggressive political and military leaders of industrialized nations would continue to colonize and exploit people of color, whether in Africa, Asia, or Latin America. He argued that this divide, between white and black, rich and poor, industrialized and agricultural societies would be a decisive factor in shaping foreign relations in the century to come.

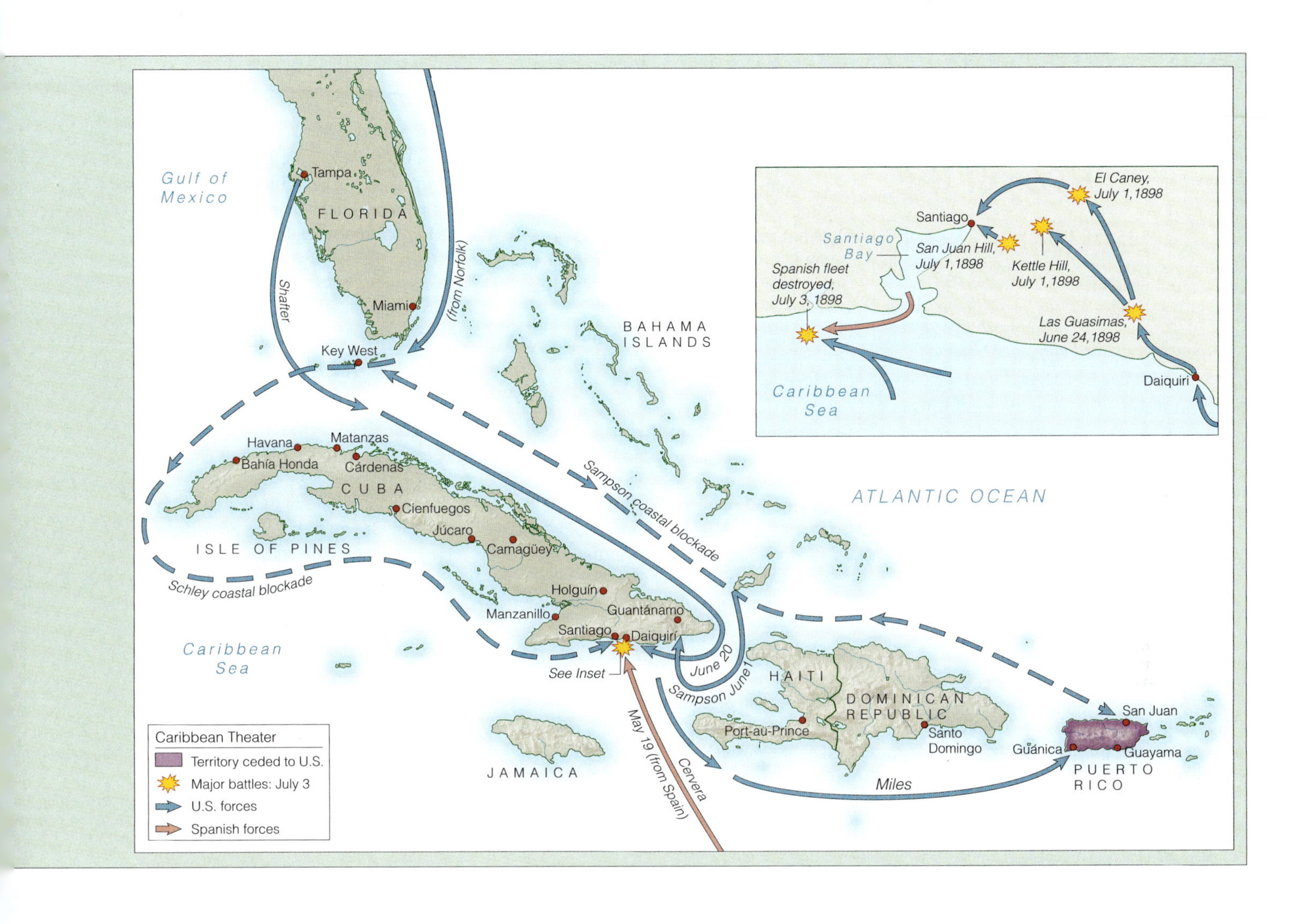

In contrast, other anti-imperialists used arguments about racial hierarchies to justify their opposition to expansion. Yale sociology professor William Graham Sumner, a proponent of Social Darwinism, argued that "uncivilized and half-civilized peoples" were hostile to democratic self-government and unprepared for its rigors. Thus, Sumner believed that American efforts to "civilize" and colonize foreign peoples would inevitably fail because those peoples were incapable of embracing American values.

Sumner, "On Empire and the Philippines"

Recent newcomers to the United States resented the idea that the "march of the flag" was an enterprise to be led by Anglo-Saxons (that is, people of English descent), as some imperialists claimed. German immigrants invoked their heritage of conquest, and the Irish juxtaposed their native culture with what they called the historic "brutal savagery" of the English. Nevertheless, supporting imperialism was one way for immigrants to proclaim their own Americanness and distance themselves from allegedly inferior peoples.

In the summer of 1900, the Democrats and Republicans prepared for the upcoming presidential election. Receiving the Democratic nomination once again, William Jennings Bryan was eager to press the outdated cause of free silver. He also condemned the American presence in the Philippines, although this issue, too, was rapidly losing the attention of the electorate. At the Republican convention, Roosevelt's supporters managed to win for him the slot as McKinley's running mate. That fall, the former Rough Rider waged an exuberant campaign. Accompanied by a retinue of gun-toting cowboys, he wrapped the Republicans in the American

Proceedings of the Congressional Committee on the Philippines

In January 1900, Congress established the Committee on the Philippines. Senator Henry Cabot Lodge of Massachusetts was appointed chair. The committee's task was to review the American conduct of the war. The testimony of two U.S. officers, which follows, foreshadows the difficulties faced by the United States in fighting a guerrilla war in Vietnam six decades later.

Brigadier General Robert P. Hughes testified in response to questions posed by committee members:

Q: In burning towns, what would you do? Would the entire town be destroyed by fire or would only offending portions of the town be burned?

GEN. HUGHES: I do not know that we ever had a case of burning what you would call a town in this country; but probably a *barrio* or a *sitio;* probably a half dozen houses, native shacks, where the *insurrectos* [rebels] would go in and be concealed, and if they caught a detachment passing they would kill some of them.

Q: What did I understand you to say would be the consequence of that?

GEN. HUGHES: They usually burned the village.

Q: All of the houses in the village?

GEN. HUGHES: Yes, every one of them.

Q: What would become of the inhabitants?

GEN. HUGHES: That was their lookout....The destruction was as a punishment.

Q: The punishment in that case would fall, not upon the men, who would go elsewhere, but mainly upon the women and little children.

GEN. HUGHES: The women and children are part of the family, and where you wish to inflict a punishment you can punish the man probably worse in that way than in any other.

Q: But is that within the ordinary rules of civilized warfare? Of course you could exterminate the family, which would be still worse punishment.

Gen. Hughes: These people are not civilized.

Sergeant Charles S. Riley also testified in response to the committee's questions:

Q: During your service there [in the Philippine Islands] did you witness what is generally known as the water cure?

A: I did.

Q: When and where?

A: On November 27, 1900, in the town of Igbaras, Iloilo Province, Panay Island.

Riley described to the committee a Filipino man, 40–45 years of age, stripped to the waist, with his hands tied behind him.

Q: Do you remember who had charge of him?

A: Captain Glenn stood there beside him and one or two men were tying him. . . . He was then taken and placed under the tank, and the faucet was opened and a stream of water was forced down or allowed to run down his throat; his throat was held so he could not prevent swallowing the water, so that he had to allow the water to run into his stomach. . . . When he was filled with water it was forced out of him by pressing a foot on his stomach or else with their hands. . . .

flag. When McKinley swept back into office in the fall, few Americans could have anticipated how central Roosevelt's vision would become to the country over the next two decades.

Conclusion

As Americans greeted the twentieth century, they might have marveled at the dramatic changes that had occurred in their country over the last 100 years. In 1800 the United States was home to 5.3 million people who lived in 16 states. One hundred years later, the country included 45 states and boasted a population of 76 million people. Many workplaces, fields as well as factories, were dominated by machines and the people who tended them. The economy was shifting toward the mass production of consumer goods.

In the United States, the 1890s was a decade of great contrasts, a time of coalition-building among some political and social groups, but also a time of often violent conflict based on ethnic, religious, and racial ideologies of social difference. Some Americans embraced common ground through the public education system; they suggested that universal schooling was the best way to prepare children, regardless of their cultural or class backgrounds, to live together in a growing, diverse nation. The People's party attempted to overcome historic divisions between Republicans and Democrats, farmers and factory workers, especially in the South; the Populists aimed to forge new alliances that would be responsive to a rapidly changing soci-

This photograph of a United States soldier during the War of 1898 is titled *The Church Saint sat on by a Washington "Johnnie" [soldier]*. During the war, photographers produced vivid images that conveyed the dramatic effects of the U.S. invasion on the society and culture of the Philippines. Led by Emilio Aguinaldo, insurrectionists fought for Philippine independence, beginning in January 1899. Two years later, American forces captured Aguinaldo and established a colonial government in the country.

Q: What had been his crime?

A: Information had been obtained from a native source as to his being an insurgent officer. After the treatment he admitted that he held the rank of captain in the insurgent army—an active captain. . . .

Q: His offense was treachery to the American cause?

A: Yes, sir.

Questions

1. *In what ways did the Filipino insurrection challenge the conventions of what congressional committee members called "civilized warfare"?*
2. *How did General Hughes justify the destruction of whole villages as part of the U.S. effort to suppress the insurrectionists?*
3. *What are the arguments for and against the practice of torture as a means of extracting information from enemy combatants?* ■

Source: Proceedings of the Congressional Committee on the Philippines, in Harvey Graff, ed., *American Imperialism and the Philippine Insurrection* (Boston, 1969),pp. 64–79.

ety. On the other hand, deep and bitter divisions emerged among Americans. Some whites invoked what they called scientific research to classify and categorize various groups and thus "prove" that all whites were superior to all people of color. Other Americans pointed to changing gender relations as proof that women and men would, and should, follow different destinies in terms of their contributions to society. These divisions and debates had a profound effect not only on domestic policy at the end of the nineteenth century but on foreign relations as well.

In 1900 the United States exerted control over the land and peoples of Alaska, the Hawaiian and Samoan Islands, the Philippines, Guam, Puerto Rico, and (through the Platt Amendment) Cuba. These holdings, notable for their strategic significance, illustrated the growing willingness of the United States to extend its influence and economic reach—by armed force if necessary—to the far corners of the earth.

The 1890s foreshadowed many of the major themes of the twentieth century. The Populists looked to the federal government to address social ills, paving the way for Progressives in the early twentieth century and New Dealers in the 1930s. Conservationists provided the foundation for the environmentalist movement of the 1970s. And suffragists were the foremothers of the modern women's movement. Yet for Americans, a generations-old contradiction lingered between prosperity and political equality for some groups, and poverty and political subordination for others. On the international stage, the United States was quick to take advantage of weaker nations if such action was deemed crucial to the "national interest." The new drive for worldwide economic and political power was fast eclipsing America's revolutionary heritage, with its values of democracy and self-determination.

Sites to Visit

The Spanish-American War

www.loc.gov/rr/hispanic/1898

This site provides resources and documents about the Spanish-American War, the period before the war, and the people who participated in the fighting or commented on it.

Imperialism Web Page

www.smplanet.com/imperialism/toc.html

Focusing on the late nineteenth and early twentieth centuries, this site includes much information about American expansionism.

Hispanic Voices/Voces Hispanas

bancroft.berkeley.edu/collections/latinamericana.html

This interactive site on Latinos in California is maintained by the Bancroft Library in Berkeley. The autobiographical narratives include late-nineteenth-century oral histories with Latinos.

Late Nineteenth-Century Authors

http://xroads.virginia.edu/~hyper/hypertex.html

This University of Virginia site includes material on prominent nineteenth-century writers, including William Dean Howells, Mark Twain, and Joel Chandler Harris.

Mary Baker Eddy

http://www.tfccs.com/index.jhtml;jsessionid

Sponsored by the Christian Science Church, this site looks at the founding of Christian Science.

National Arts and Crafts Archives

www.arts-crafts.com/index.html

This site serves as a guide to materials related to the Arts and Crafts movement, which lasted from about 1890 to 1929.

Era of William McKinley

http://history.osu.edu/projects/McKinley/Default.htm

This Ohio State University site contains a bibliography and numerous images from various periods of McKinley's career. It also includes a section with an excellent collection of McKinley-era cartoons.

"Votes for Women" Suffrage Pictures

http://lcweb2.loc.gov/ammem/vfwhtml/vfwhome.html

This site, part of the Library of Congress American Memory Series, includes images of parades and picket lines, as well as antisuffragist activity.

Hawaii's Last Queen

http://www.pbs.org/wgbh/pages/amex/hawaii/index.html

This site complements the PBS program on the overthrow of Hawaii's hereditary monarchy in 1893.

American Environmental Photographs, 1891–1936

http://www.memory.loc.gov/ammem/award97/icuhtml/aephome.html

This site includes approximately 4,500 photographs from the University of Chicago Library.

For Further Reading

General

Glenda Elizabeth Gilmore, *Gender and Jim Crow: Women and the Politics of White Supremacy in North Carolina, 1896–1920* (1996).

Matthew Frye Jacobson, *Barbarian Virtues: The United States Encounters Foreign Peoples at Home and Abroad, 1876–1917* (2000).

Walter LaFeber, *The New Empire: An Interpretation of American Expansion, 1860–1898* (1963).

Emily S. Rosenberg, *Spreading the American Dream: American Economic and Cultural Expansion, 1890–1945* (1982).

Robert W. Rydell, *All the World's a Fair: Visions of Empire at American International Expositions, 1876–1916* (1984).

Frontiers at Home, Lost and Found

David Wallace Adams, *Education for Extinction: American Indians and the Boarding School Experience, 1875–1928* (1995).

Karen L. Cox, *Dixie's Daughters: The United Daughters of the Confederacy and the Preservation of Confederate Culture* (2003).

Willard B. Gatewood Jr., *Black Americans and the White Man's Burden, 1898–1903* (1975).

Matthew Frye Jacobson, *Whiteness of a Different Color: European Immigrants and the Alchemy of Race* (1998).

Neil R. McMillen, *Dark Journey: Black Mississippians in the Age of Jim Crow* (1989).

Michael J. Pfeifer, *Rough Justice: Lynching and American Society, 1874–1947* (2004).

Donald J. Pisani, *From the Family Farm to Agribusiness: The Irrigation Crusade in California, 1850–1931* (1984).

Jonathan Sarna, *American Judaism: A New History* (2004).

Barbara M. Solomon, *In the Company of Educated Women: A History of Women and Higher Education in America* (1985).

Mark David Spence, *Dispossessing the Wilderness: Indian Removal and the Making of the National Parks* (1999).

David B. Tyack, *Managers of Virtue: Public School Leadership in America, 1820–1980* (1982).

The Search for Alliances

Paul Buhle, *From the Knights of Labor to the New World Order: Essays on Labor and Culture* (1997).

Sarah Deutsch, *Women and the City: Gender, Space, and Power in Boston, 1870–1940* (2000).

Patricia R. Hill, *The World Their Household: The American Woman's Foreign Mission Movement and Cultural Transformation, 1870–1920* (1985).

Elisabeth Lasch-Quinn, *Black Neighbors: Race and the Limits of Reform in the American Settlement House Movement, 1890–1945* (1993).

Seymour Martin Lipset and Gary Marks. *It Didn't Happen Here: Why Socialism Failed in the United States* (2000).

Vicki L. Ruiz and Ellen Carol Du Bois, eds., *Unequal Sisters: A Multicultural Reader in U.S. Women's History* (2000).

David E. Whisnant, *All That Is Native and Fine: The Politics of Culture in an American Region* (1983).

American Imperialism

Robert L. Beisner, *Twelve Against Empire: The Anti-Imperialists, 1898–1900* (1968).

H. W. Brands, *Bound to Empire: The United States and the Philippines* (1992).

Paul A. Cohen, *History in Three Keys: The Boxers as Event, Experience, and Myth* (1997).

Kenn Harper, *Give Me My Father's Body: The Life of Minik, the New York Eskimo* (2000).

Thomas J. McCormick, *China Market: America's Quest for Informal Empire, 1893–1901* (1967).

William Appleman Williams, *The Tragedy of American Diplomacy* (1972).

1901 McKinley is assassinated; Vice President Theodore Roosevelt becomes president.

1902 New Lands Act spurs dam building and irrigation in the Southwest.

1903 First motorized flight by Orville and Wilbur Wright.
Henry Ford founds Ford Motor Company.

1904 Roosevelt Corollary to Monroe Doctrine.

1905 Industrial Workers of the World founded.
Japan defeats Russia.

1906 San Francisco earthquake.
Upton Sinclair, *The Jungle*.
Pure Food and Drug Act.

1907 "Gentlemen's Agreement" with Japan.
Oklahoma (former Indian Territory) becomes state.
Indiana becomes first state to pass compulsory sterilization law.

1908 *Muller v. Oregon* limits maximum hours for working women.

1909 New York City garment workers' "Uprising of the 20,000."
Peary-Henson expedition reaches North Pole with four Greenland Inuit.

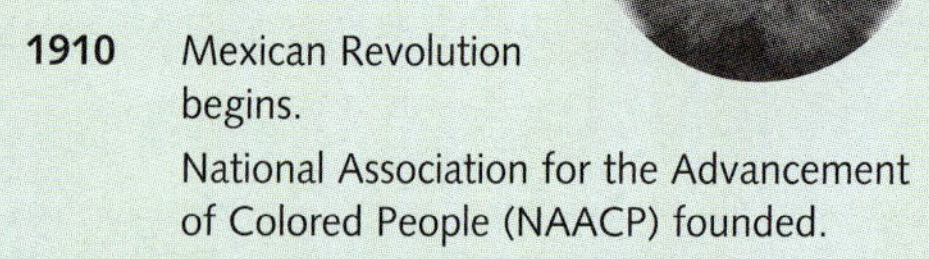

1910 Mexican Revolution begins.
National Association for the Advancement of Colored People (NAACP) founded.

1911 Triangle Shirtwaist Company fire, New York City.
Society of American Indians founded.

1912 Theodore Roosevelt helps form Progressive party.
Woodrow Wilson elected president.

1913 Federal Reserve Act.
Sixteenth Amendment (federal personal income tax) ratified.

1914 U.S. troops block German arms shipment to Mexico.
World War I breaks out in Europe.

1915 U.S. marines occupy Haiti.

PART SEVEN

Reform at Home, Revolution Abroad, 1900–1929

Many Americans greeted the first years of the twentieth century with optimism. Developments at home and abroad seemed to promise a new era of prosperity and progress. The mass manufacturing of automobiles proved a boon to the economy and transformed patterns of travel, leisure, and consumption. The beginning of commercial air flights heralded a revolution in communication and transportation. Moving pictures and new musical forms such as jazz delighted millions.

Focused on the new challenges of urbanization and industrialization, Progressive reformers sought to use science to solve a wide range of problems related to public health and welfare. Some advocated overhauling the system of public education; others pressed for legislation banning the sale and distribution of alcohol. Some lobbied for worker health and safety legislation, and still others sought to exercise social control through eugenics and state-mandated sterilization.

A variety of groups challenged white men's exclusive claim to civil rights. African Americans took the national stage to argue for equality under the law and for freedom from state-sanctioned violence in the form of lynching and debt peonage. Beginning with the Great Migration of World War I, southern blacks abandoned the cotton fields to seek jobs in northern cities.

The changing roles of women bolstered the women's suffrage movement. Growing numbers of women were becoming labor organizers, reformers, and college professors. Rising divorce rates and the emergence of birth control as a political as well as a medical issue signaled challenges to the traditional patriarchal family. At the same time, conflicts among reformers emerged. For example, white middle-class suffragists hoped to maintain their "respectability" in an effort to win the support of reluctant male leaders; in the process, these women distanced themselves from members of the working class and African American women active in the suffrage movement. Suffragists' efforts paid off in 1920, with the ratification of the Nineteenth Amendment to the Constitution.

With its lively consumer culture and rising standard of living, the United States continued to attract newcomers from abroad. Immigrants from Mexico and eastern Europe sought refuge from poverty, oppression, and civil strife at home. In 1914, 1.2 million immigrants came to America, the largest number in a single year before or since that date. Between 1900 and 1930, more than 1 million Mexicans migrated north, most settling into existing Mexican American communities in the Southwest or creating new communities there or in the Midwest.

World War I shattered the belief among many Progressives that conflicts could be solved in a rational, peaceful way. The end of the war had permanently entangled U.S. interests in European affairs. Moreover, revolutions in Mexico (1910) and Russia (1917) affected the United States directly, the former by spurring immigration across the country's southwest border, the latter by challenging the nation's system of industrial capitalism. Nevertheless, many Americans remained convinced that the country could and should isolate itself from world affairs.

Natural forces also remained beyond the control of reformers and government officials. The San Francisco earthquake of 1906, the great Mississippi flood of 1927, and the Florida hurricane of 1928 exacted devastating tolls in terms of human life and property damage. The local communities that were directly affected struggled for years to recover from these disasters.

But for many Americans, the 1920s was a period of peace and prosperity. New household appliances and conveniences lightened the burdens of housework. Radios and movies proved to be popular forms of entertainment. Traditional social mores gave way to expressions of sexual freedom. Progressive impulses waned as business values rose to take their place.

The decade after the end of World War I revealed both the persistence of old conflicts and the emergence of new conflicts within American society. Conservatives branded labor union organizers and socialists as unpatriotic and subversive. Asian immigrants on the West Coast and blacks in the rural South and urban North faced continued legal discrimination in the workplace and in the courts. Protestant fundamentalists challenged the move toward secularism and rationalism, claiming that religious faith, not science, set the standard for morality in modern life. Responding to those who feared that foreign immigration represented a threat to American society, Congress imposed immigration restrictions in 1924. Put into effect in 1920, the Eighteenth Amendment to the Constitution prohibited the sale and distribution of alcoholic beverages. The three Republican presidents who served during the 1920s—Harding, Coolidge, and Hoover—retreated from the activist stance favored by their predecessors, including Theodore Roosevelt and Woodrow Wilson.

The stock market crash of 1929 revealed fundamental weaknesses in the American economy. A tide of bank failures engulfed individual American families even as it threatened businesses abroad. As the depression deepened, Americans looked to the federal government to address the crisis.

Germans sink *Lusitania*.
Film *Birth of a Nation* released.

1916 Jeannette Rankin elected first female member of Congress.
U.S. marines occupy Dominican Republic.

1917 United States enters World War I.
U.S. marines occupy Cuba.
Russian Revolution.
Residents of Puerto Rico granted U.S. citizenship.

1918 Spanish influenza epidemic kills 20 million worldwide.
Sedition Act.
Wilson's "Fourteen Points" speech to Congress.

1919 Versailles Treaty ends World War I.
U.S. Senate rejects League of Nations.
Eighteenth Amendment (prohibition) ratified.

1920 Nineteenth Amendment (women's suffrage) ratified.

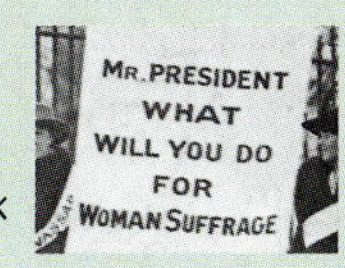

1921 Tulsa whites attack black community.
Sheppard-Towner Act.

1922 Five-Power Naval Treaty.

1923 Equal Rights Amendment proposed.

1924 Johnson-Reid Act.
Portable radio introduced.

1925 Scopes Trial, Dayton, Tennessee.
F. Scott Fitzgerald, *The Great Gatsby*.

1926 Gertrude Ederle is first woman to swim across English Channel.

1927 Charles Lindbergh flies nonstop from New York to Paris.
Al Jolson stars in *The Jazz Singer*, first talking movie.
Sacco and Vanzetti executed.
Buck v. Bell upholds compulsory sterilization laws.

1928 Tamiami Trail across Florida Everglades completed.

1929 Stock market crash.

CHAPTER 19

The Promise and Perils of Progressive Reform, 1900–1912

Abraham Walkowitz, *In the Street*, 1909. Hirshhorn Museum and Sculpture Garden, Smithsonian Institution, Washington, D.C. (66.5446) Gift of Joseph H. Hirshhorn, 1966. Photograph by Lee Stalsworth

▲ Abraham Walkowitz's 1909 painting *In the Street* depicts a Jewish immigrant couple on a crowded urban street.

CHAPTER OUTLINE

Migration and Immigration: The Changing Face of the Nation

Work, Science, and Leisure

Reformers and Radicals

Expanding National Power

Conclusion

Sites to Visit

For Further Reading

"I am a working girl," declared Clara Lemlich in her native **Yiddish,** "one of those striking against intolerable conditions." Still in her teens, the petite young woman took the podium on the night of November 22, 1909, in front of thousands of striking workers in New York, and roused them with her passionate, direct call for action: "I am tired of listening to speakers who talk in generalities. What we are here for is to decide whether or not to strike. I offer a resolution that a general strike be declared—now." The next morning, 15,000 garment workers went on strike, demanding that the workweek be reduced to 52 hours, with overtime pay and union recognition. Soon, the strikers swelled in number to more than 20,000. Observers at the time were astonished to see lively, fashionably dressed young women filling the picket lines. Ninety percent of the striking workers were women, and they were overwhelmingly young Jewish immigrants along with some Italians. The strikers drew on a wide coalition of support that included labor unions, middle-class reformers, and activists for women's suffrage.

The strike was a demand for union recognition, reasonable wages and hours, and safe and decent working conditions, including an end to sexual harassment on the job. At the same time, the young women strikers insisted that they should be treated as "ladies" and have access to the consumer goods and leisure culture taking shape in American cities. Although the young women were bullied and arrested by police, their high spirits prompted some observers to make light of their struggle. Sarah Comstock, a reporter for *Collier's* magazine, wrote of the strike, "This was a scene of gaiety and flirtation. My preconceived idea of a strike was a somber meeting where somber resolutions were made. . . . But they don't look as if they had any grievances." In response to those who tried to trivialize their massive mobilization, and in defense of their desire to be part of the new consumer culture, Lemlich stated, "We like new hats as well as other young women. Why shouldn't we?"

Victims of the Triangle Shirtwaist Company fire.

Ultimately, the strike ended when the striking workers overwhelmingly rejected an offer of better wages and working conditions that did not include recognition of their union. Calling the strikers "socialists," their more moderate allies broke from the union and left the young female workers vulnerable to the power of the company owners. The coalition of support fell apart, and most of the strikers eventually went back to work.

Less than two years later, a fire broke out in the top floors of the Triangle Shirtwaist Company, one of the centers of the 1909 strike. Eight hundred workers, most of them young Jewish and Italian women, were trapped in the inferno because company officials had locked interior doors to prevent the women from taking unauthorized breaks or leaving work early. The flames tore through the building in less than half an hour, leaving 146 young women dead. Those who did not succumb to flames and smoke jumped to their deaths. "One girl after another fell, like shot birds, from above, from the burning floors," remembered one witness. "They hit the pavement just like hail," reported a firefighter.

Parents rushed to the scene to find their young daughters dead, dying, or maimed. "My little girl lies dead, shrouds instead of a wedding gown," cried one of the bereaved.

One reporter wrote, "I looked upon the dead bodies and I remembered these girls were the shirtwaist makers. I remembered their great strike of last year in which the same girls had demanded more sanitary conditions and more safety precautions in the shops. Their dead bodies were the answer." In the investigation that followed, the owner of the factory was never charged with a crime or held responsible for the tragedy. He claimed that his building was in full compliance with safety laws, but compliance with the laws did not ensure safety for the workers. No laws required sprinklers, adequate fire escapes, or fire drills. Just a few months before the fire, the building had been inspected and declared "fireproof."

The "uprising of the 20,000," as the 1909 strike came to be called, and the tragic factory fire that ignited in its aftermath are two among many dramatic episodes in the early twentieth century that expose the fractures and tensions within the nation at the time. Immigrants and racial minorities demanded the full promise of American life. Workers struggled against the exploitation, poor pay, and dangerous conditions that characterized industrial jobs. Young women insisted on respect at work and access to the playful environment of urban fashion and popular culture; female voices called for full citizenship, the vote, and their right to be heard by male bosses and union leaders. Activists across the political spectrum tried to control and manage the changes taking place around them in accord with their widely differing values.

Library of Congress

▲ An earthquake devastated San Francisco on April 18, 1906. Here a Chinese immigrant watches as the city goes up in flames. Chinatown was destroyed, along with much of the downtown.

During the first years of the twentieth century, the nation began to emerge as something profoundly different than it had been in the past. Even the landscape changed as cities continued to grow not only outward but also upward, with the construction of towering skyscrapers, and downward, with the creation of subway systems. Brothers Orville and Wilbur Wright seemed to defy nature itself when they designed and flew the first airplane at Kitty Hawk, North Carolina, in 1903. But human enterprise continued to be vulnerable to the forces of nature. On April 18, 1906, an earthquake virtually leveled San Francisco. The nation saw in one deadly instant that human technological genius paled in the face of nature's fury. After the quake, fire devoured the city. In the words of the writer Jack London, "All the cunning adjustments of a twentieth century city had been smashed by the earthquake. The streets were humped into ridges and depressions, and piled with the debris of fallen walls. The steel rails were twisted into perpendicular and horizontal angles. The telephone and telegraph systems were disrupted. And the great water mains had burst. All the shrewd contrivances and safeguards of man had been thrown out of gear by thirty seconds' twitching of the earth-crust."

If New York's Triangle Shirtwaist Company building—almost unscathed, although the young women inside had perished in flames—was a monument to corporate arrogance, the crumbled buildings of San Francisco offered a lesson in humility. "Never, in all San Francisco's history, were her people so kind and courteous as on this night of terror," noted Jack London. Railroads carried thousands of refugees out of the city, free of charge. And the national government stepped in immediately, as it would countless times throughout the twentieth century in the face of disaster.

Rose Freedman

Major historical events sometimes take on a life of their own, locked in a single frame of historical memory. The 1911 Triangle Shirtwaist Company fire is one such event. Rose Rosenfeld Freedman, one of the young women working at the factory on that fateful day, provides a reminder that events are not simply frozen in time. The tragic fire that she survived fueled in her a lifelong commitment to the rights of workers.

Rose Rosenfeld was not born into a working-class community that might have nurtured her commitment to workers' rights. The daughter of a prosperous business owner, she was 15 years old when she emigrated from Vienna to the United States in 1909. She did not need a job, but as a young Jewish immigrant, she recalled, "I wanted to show that I'm [a] real American and I want to work like everybody else. And I went on my own, found a job. . . . And then, I almost paid with my life." She was 16 when she went to work at Triangle, sewing buttons at a wage of $3 for a six-day week.

Rose was working on the ninth floor when the fire alarm sounded at 4:43 p.m. on March 25, 1911. Finding the exit doors locked, she ran up to the tenth floor, where the executives worked, but the bosses were gone. "They saved themselves already." She pulled her dress over her head and followed the bosses to the roof, where firefighters hoisted her to safety on the top of the adjacent building.

The fire inspired her to action. Nearly a century later, her memory of the fire remained vivid: "The executives with a couple steps could have opened the door. But they thought they were better than the working people. . . . What good is a rich man [if] he hasn't got a heart? I feel it. Still. I feel very bad about it." Outrage over the fire led to the passage of 36 labor and safety laws in the next three years. Rose Rosenfeld left the garment business and went on to college, but she remained a passionate advocate for workers' rights.

(Both photos) Courtesy, Bud Freedman

Rose Rosenfeld Freedman as a young immigrant, and decades later as a labor activist.

In another dramatic brush with history, Rosenfeld demonstrated her willingness to stand up for others whose rights and safety were threatened. She was visiting Austria just as World War I erupted. A Russian Jew who had been spying for Austria arrived at the house where she was staying, begging for protection from Russian soldiers. She hid him in a coal bin in the basement; when the soldiers arrived, she told them to leave. Weeks later, the wife of the man she hid came to the house to thank her for saving the father of their five children.

In 1927, Rose married Harry Freedman, who ran a typewriter business. During World War II, in the midst of a terrifying polio epidemic, she escaped another tragedy. Two of her children were stricken with the disease but recovered. For Freedman, it was another miracle, like her escape from the Triangle fire. Widowed in 1952, Freedman entered business school at age 59 and got a job with a pen company in New York. At 64, she lied about her age and got a job in customer relations at the Metropolitan Life Insurance Company. She stayed there for 15 years, retiring at age 79.

Still an active crusader, Freedman moved to Los Angeles when she was in her 90s. At age 100, she went to Mexico to study Spanish. Like the shirtwaist workers who wore hats and stylish clothes on the picket line in 1909, Rose Freedman still wore high heels, had her hair done every week, and did her own shopping. Cherishing her independence, she refused to move in with her children, explaining that "young people belong together and I have a life of my own."

In 2000, at age 106, Rose Freedman lectured on sweatshops to enthralled students at Occidental College in Los Angeles. "She loved her career. . . . She believed quite fully in doing things that make you happy," said her granddaughter Dana Walden, head of 20th Century Fox Television. Rose Freedman died in 2001 at age 107, the last survivor of the Triangle Shirtwaist Company fire. ■

Migration and Immigration: The Changing Face of the Nation

Charismatic young labor leader Clara Lemlich was one of millions of immigrants at the time who were changing the face of the nation. This migration, which began in the latter decades of the nineteenth century, resulted largely from international economic and political upheavals. Facing severe hardships in their home countries, many people took the desperate action of departing for foreign lands. Between 1900 and 1910, nearly 9 million immigrants entered the United States, by far the largest number for any single decade in the nation's history before or since. The United States was one of several potential destinations for these courageous and hopeful sojourners. America was particularly appealing because of its often exaggerated, but nonetheless real, opportunities for jobs and economic advancement, its official commitment to freedom of religion and political thought, and its reputation as a nation that welcomed newcomers from abroad.

Ellis Island Immigrants, 1903

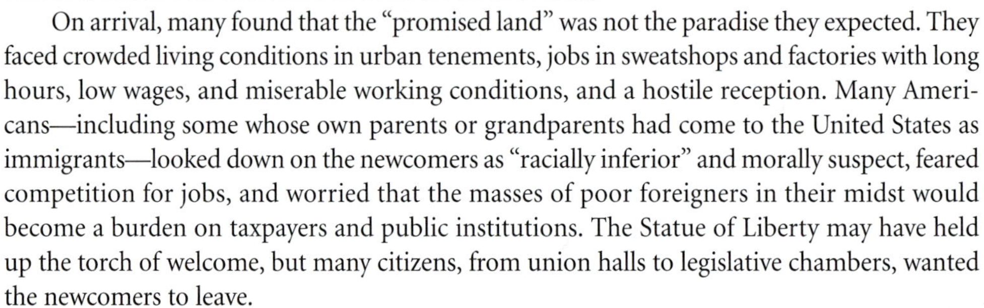

On arrival, many found that the "promised land" was not the paradise they expected. They faced crowded living conditions in urban tenements, jobs in sweatshops and factories with long hours, low wages, and miserable working conditions, and a hostile reception. Many Americans—including some whose own parents or grandparents had come to the United States as immigrants—looked down on the newcomers as "racially inferior" and morally suspect, feared competition for jobs, and worried that the masses of poor foreigners in their midst would become a burden on taxpayers and public institutions. The Statue of Liberty may have held up the torch of welcome, but many citizens, from union halls to legislative chambers, wanted the newcomers to leave.

Many did leave. One-third of immigrants to the United States returned to their home countries. Some came for only a few years and returned to their native lands, including nearly 90 percent of those from the Balkans. Other groups, especially those who faced severe hardships in the lands of their birth, were more likely to make the United States their permanent home, settling with their families and building communities. Only 11 percent of the Irish and 5 percent of the Jews returned between 1908 and 1923.

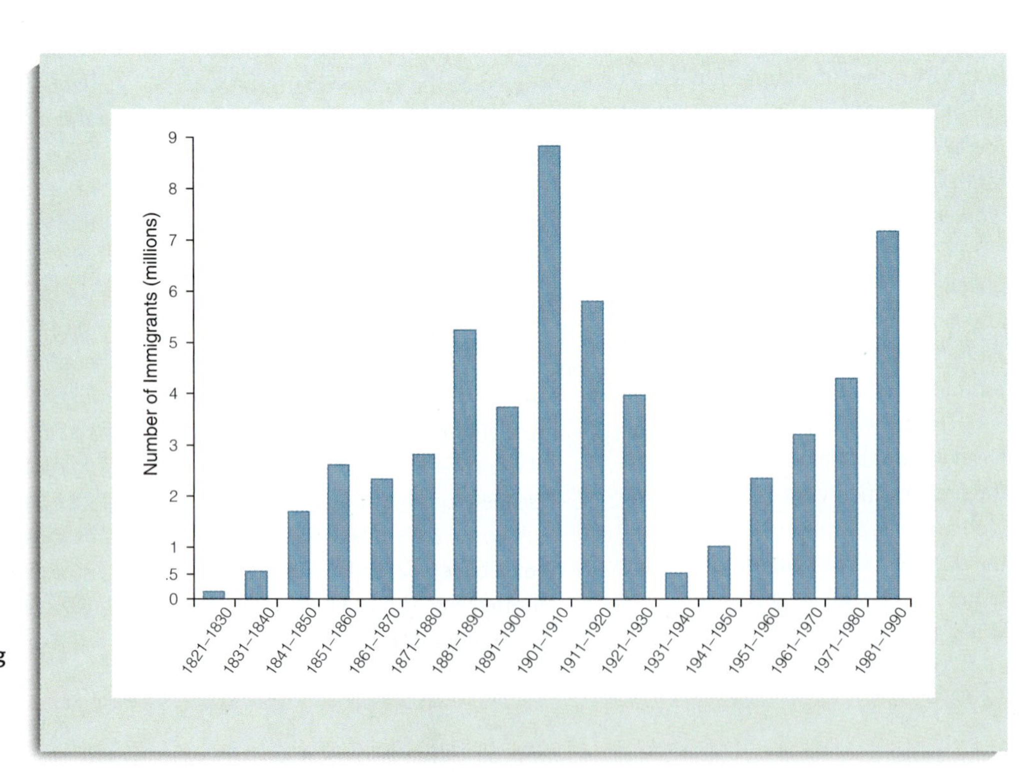

▶ FIGURE 19.1 NUMBER OF IMMIGRANTS ENTERING THE UNITED STATES, 1821–1990 The number of immigrants entering the United States peaked in the first decade of the twentieth century and dropped drastically as a result of the immigration restriction laws passed by Congress in the 1920s. Immigration increased again as laws changed after World War II, allowing new immigrant groups to enter.

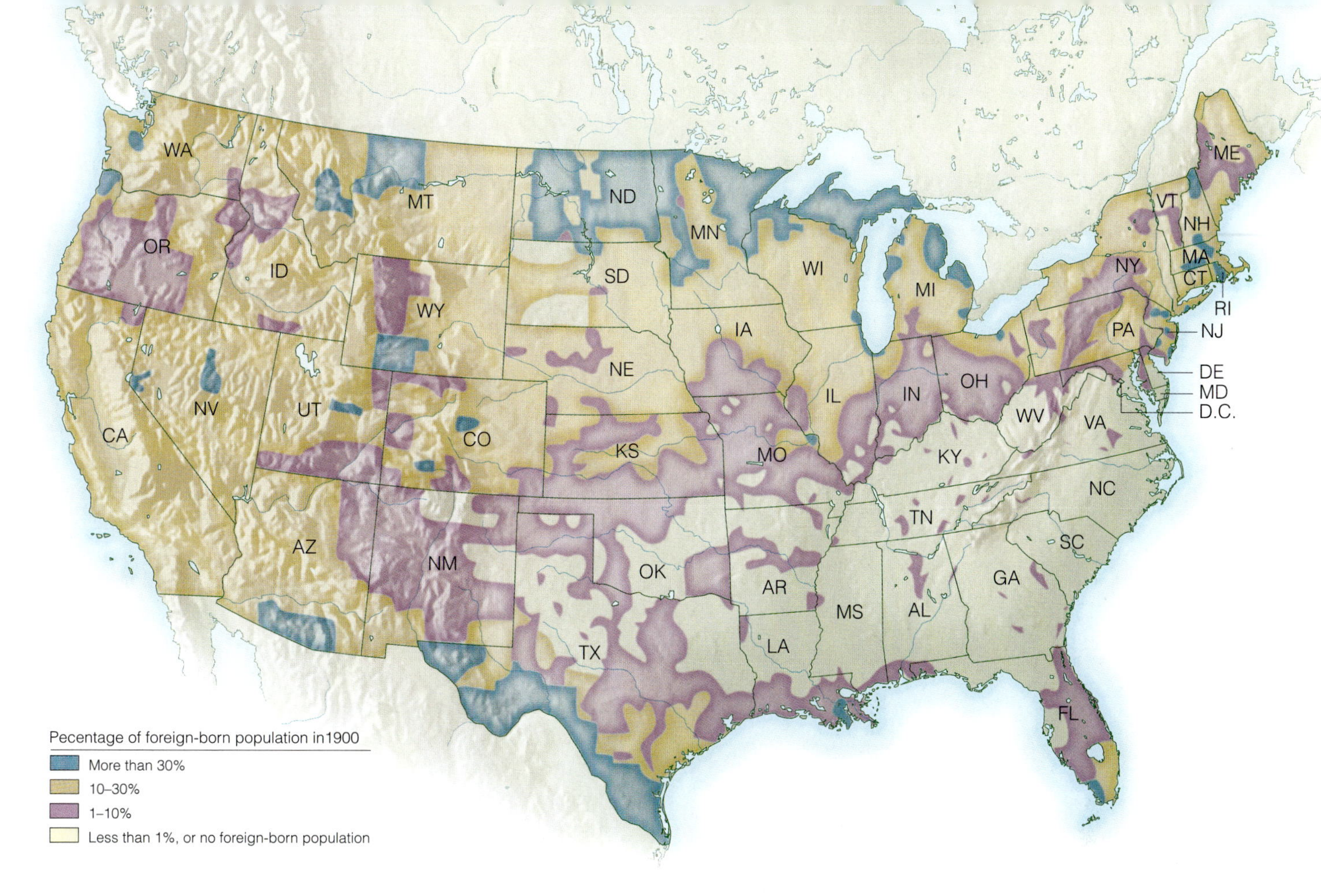

▲ **MAP 19.1 FOREIGN-BORN POPULATION, 1900** **The most famous points of entry for immigrants during the turn-of-the-century decades were New York's Ellis Island for people from Europe, and Angel Island off San Francisco for people from Asia. Most immigrants actually settled in the upper Midwest and the southwestern region bordering Mexico.**

Although some of the newcomers moved to rural areas and worked in agriculture, most settled in the cities, where they were joined by rural Americans leaving farms for new opportunities in the rapidly growing urban centers. In the first decade of the twentieth century, more than 4.5 million Americans moved from east to west, and nearly 80,000 migrated from south to north. All those on the move—from abroad and within the country—brought hopes and anxieties to their adopted homes. But over time, these newcomers would transform virtually every aspect of American life: political, economic, cultural, and social.

The Heartland: Land of Newcomers

At the dawn of the twentieth century, the greatest concentration of foreign-born residents lived not in the coastal cities, with their visible immigrant ghettos, but in the settlements of the upper Midwest and lower Southwest. In the growing towns and cities of the Midwest, newcomers from central Europe and Italy joined the earlier settlers from Germany and Scandinavia to form farming and mining communities on the rich soil and abundant iron deposits of the region.

In the 1890s, the upper Midwest was sparsely settled. As a result of the Dawes Act of 1887, which allocated tribal lands into individual parcels, much of the land originally held by Indians had been divided and sold. Most of the Indians who were native to that region were removed to reservations. The iron-rich areas near Lake Superior, previously the hunting, fishing, and gathering areas of the Native Americans, were now inhabited by lumberjacks who cut the forests. Mining companies discovered the iron deposits and began recruiting workers, first from northern Europe and then, after 1900, from southern and eastern Europe. By 1910, the iron range was home to 35 European immigrant groups. Gradually, these cohesive

Jessie Tarbox Beals, "Women and Children in the Kitchen," 1915. Community Service Society, New York. © Jewish Museum

▲ An immigrant family manages the daily routines of life in a tenement flat in 1910. Crowded conditions, poor ventilation, and inadequate plumbing made it impossible for impoverished residents such as these to maintain a clean and healthy environment.

working-class communities, like others elsewhere, developed their own brand of ethnic Americanism, complete with elaborate Fourth of July celebrations and other festivities that expressed both their distinctive ethnic identities and their allegiance to their adopted country.

The Southwest: Mexican Borderlands

In 1904 a train carrying Irish orphans from a New York Catholic **foundling home** chugged westward to deliver its small passengers to waiting Catholic families in Clifton and Morenci in the Arizona territory. Church officials at the New York orphanage had screened the families carefully to be certain that the couples hoping to adopt these children were devout churchgoing Catholics, industrious workers, and respectable members of the community. The local parish priest approved these couples, and on the appointed day, they waited eagerly as the orphans, dressed in their best clothes with their pink cheeks scrubbed clean, departed from the train. But when the Anglo-Protestant residents of the town discovered that Mexican Catholic foster parents claimed these fair-skinned children, they were outraged.

That night, the Anglo women gathered to mobilize their husbands into a vigilante posse. In the middle of the night, during a driving rainstorm, the men went to the homes of the Mexican couples and kidnapped the children at gunpoint. The next day, the children were distributed among the vigilantes' families and other Anglo foster parents. Although the Catholic foundling home that had placed the children with the Mexican couples fought a lengthy legal battle to regain custody of the children, the Anglos managed to keep the orphans. The Arizona Supreme Court validated the kidnapping in the name of the "best interests of the children," and the U.S. Supreme Court let the ruling stand.

Longtime residents of this borderland region of Arizona included many Mexicans, mainly farmers, ranchers, and miners. They were among nearly half a million Mexicans who lived in the Southwest at the turn of the twentieth century. The upheavals of the Mexican Revolution increased migration after 1911. Most of the migrants to the Southwest found work in mining, railroads, and agriculture, usually as unskilled workers earning meager wages. Men, women, and children migrated in families or alone. Some estimates suggest that half were under the age of 18. Mexican migrant women as well as Hispanas born in the Southwest had to be particularly resourceful. According to one New Mexico native, "They were their own doctors, dressmakers, tailors and advisers."

The struggle over the orphans reflected tensions and divisions in the region along lines of class as well as race. The year before the arrival of the orphans, Mexican mine workers had struck for better wages and working conditions against the Anglo owners of the Arizona Copper Company. The owners put down the strike, and the conflict left bitter feelings on both sides. The vigilante kidnapping of the orphans was, in part, retaliation against the Mexican workers who had organized the strike the previous year. Excluded from most labor unions until the 1920s, Mexican workers across the Southwest nevertheless organized strikes from time to time to improve wages and working conditions. During the first decade of the century, and especially after the Mexican Revolution, nativist hostility to the Mexicans intensified. Although the orphan abduction was unique, the conditions and tensions that gave rise to it existed across the region.

Northeast Minnesota and Northwest Wisconsin

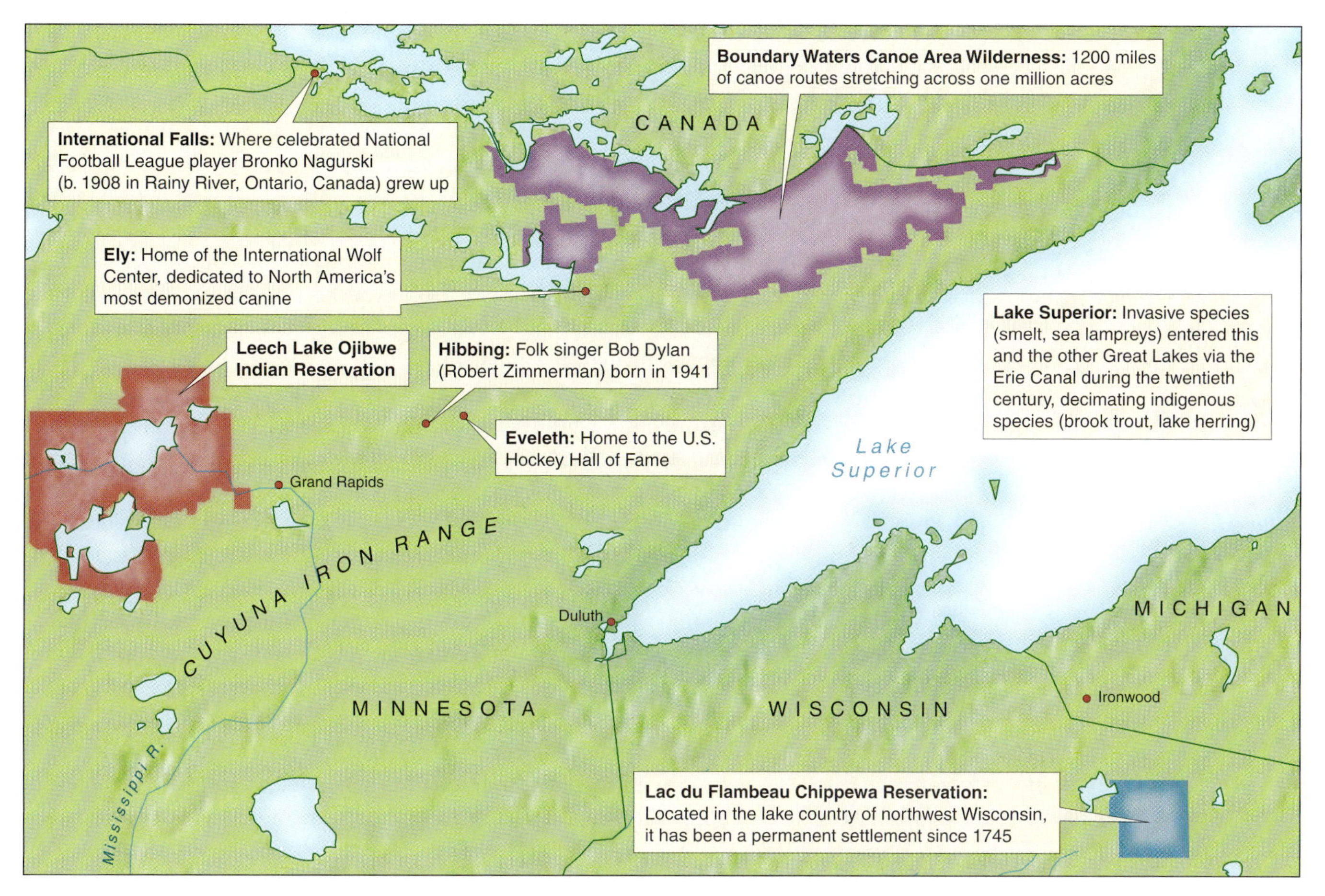

Mid-nineteenth-century prospectors seeking gold in northeastern Minnesota, an area historically occupied by Ojibwa and Dakota Indians, instead found iron ore. By the early twentieth century, iron mining in the region attracted migrants seeking work, and towns such as Hibbing were built to accommodate the newcomers. The largest of the region's iron ranges, Mesabi, has yielded more than 3 billion tons of ore and supplied most of the iron for the armaments of World War II. By mid-century, much of the high-grade ore had been depleted, leaving only lower-grade taconite. Despite recession and repeated layoffs, iron mining still remains the area's chief industry.

In the 1890s Duluth, located on the western tip of Lake Superior, began shipping iron ore, and its population swelled with new immigrants. The city rivaled Chicago in the late 1800s as a grain-shipping port. Duluth remains an international port, shipping iron-ore pellets, grain, and wood products.

Further north, the Boundary Waters Canoe Area (BWCA)—1.1 million acres of unbroken forest and some 2,500 lakes—stretches more than 100 miles along the Canadian border. Throughout the twentieth century, controversy erupted over land use in the BWCA, and in 1978 Congress enacted the BWCA Wilderness Act, eliminating logging and snowmobiling, restricting mining, and allowing motor boats on only a fourth of the water area. ■

Fenske Lake, Boundary Waters Canoe Area

Asian Immigration and the Impact of Exclusion

Asians continued to face the most severe restrictions on immigration. The Chinese Exclusion Act of 1882, which prohibited most Chinese from immigrating to the United States, was renewed and extended in 1902. As a result, the mostly bachelor Chinese community in the United States declined by nearly half between 1890 and 1920. Many died or returned to China, reducing the numbers from more than 107,000 to about 61,000. The sex ratio remained severely unbalanced, with about 14 men for every woman.

During the exclusion era, certain categories of Chinese immigrants were allowed entry. Wives of Chinese men already in the United States could enter, as could teachers, students, and merchants. More than 20,000 Chinese arrived during the first decade of the new century. One such emigrant was Sieh King King, an 18-year-old student. In 1902, at a meeting of the Protect the Emperor Society, a reform party that advocated restoring the deposed emperor and establishing a constitutional monarchy in China, she addressed a packed hall in San Francisco's Chinatown. The *San Francisco Chronicle* reported that she "boldly condemned the slave girl system, raged at the horrors of foot-binding [a traditional Chinese practice in which girls' feet were tightly bound to keep them small] and, with all the vehemence of aroused youth, declared that men and women were equal and should enjoy the privileges of equals." Like Clara Lemlich, her eastern European Jewish peer in New York, Sieh King King expressed ideas that were emerging among urban radicals in the United States but also reflected political movements in their home countries.

Individual Chinese could also immigrate if they had family members in the United States. But sometimes it was extremely difficult to prove that the relationship existed. Immigration officials were particularly suspicious of women entering the country as wives. They had to prove that they were truly married and not prostitutes or concubines. If they were married in China, that proof was often difficult to establish. For example, Lau Dai Moy applied for admission as the wife of a U.S. citizen. She and her husband, Fong Dai Sing, were separately brought before authorities for questioning. They were interrogated for hours about the details of their wed-

Courtesy, Arizona Historical Society/Tucson (#58785)

▶ Mexican miners in Arizona struck against their Anglo employers in 1903. The mining company paid Mexican workers less than their Anglo counterparts. In addition to the human toll of death and disease caused by the dangerous conditions in the mines, copper mining also caused permanent damage to the environment.

▲ MAP 19.2 AREAS EXCLUDED FROM IMMIGRATION TO THE UNITED STATES, 1882–1952 In 1882 the United States barred Chinese immigrants from entering the country; Japanese and Koreans were barred in 1924. In 1917 the exclusion was extended to people from India, Indonesia, and the Arabian Peninsula. Those laws remained in effect until 1943 and 1952, respectively.

ding, and their answers were expected to match exactly, even though the wedding had taken place more than a year earlier. The young wife was asked about gifts or ornaments given to her by her husband, when certain hair ornaments had been given to her, where the ornaments were purchased, how long she wore a beaded headdress at her wedding, and the names of guests for whom she poured tea. If her description of details of the ceremony did not exactly match her husband's account, she would not be able to enter the country, regardless of the documentation she carried. Often the process could take several weeks or even months. Hopeful immigrants were detained as virtual prisoners in wretched conditions on Angel Island, the immigrant gateway in San Francisco Bay.

Many immigrants slipped into the country illegally, through Ellis Island or over the borders from Canada or Mexico. But entry for the Chinese at Angel Island was particularly difficult during the period of exclusion. To make it possible for others to emigrate, American-born Chinese frequently traveled back and forth, claiming on their return that they left a child in China and requesting permission for their offspring to emigrate. In this way they created space holders for imaginary kin, allowing other Chinese to enter the country. U.S. authorities knew of this system of "paper sons" and "paper fathers" and tried to stop the practice with elaborate and lengthy investigations that could last a year or more. But the hopeful new arrivals were not easily thwarted. Chinese Americans on the mainland smuggled information to their fictional relatives, cleverly providing details of their families and communities back home so that their stories would match. Since it was illegal to transmit such information and letters were read and confiscated, these messages often arrived concealed in walnut shells or other camouflages.

Lee Chi Yet was one such "paper son." As a poor farmer in China, he was not among those who could enter the country legally, so he purchased papers and posed as the son of

Erika Lee

▲ **Wong Lan Fong and Lee Chi Yet, on their wedding day in China. When she came to the United States to join her husband, Wong Lan Fong submitted this photograph as proof that she was married to Lee Chi Yet. The Immigration and Naturalization Service confiscated the photo to use it as evidence in her case for admission to the country. The photo was later discovered by the couple's granddaughter, Erika Lee, while working on her Ph.D. in history and doing research on Chinese immigration during the exclusion era.**

another immigrant. After a humiliating physical examination, he faced intensive questioning. Fortunately, he had memorized all the details that went with his new name, identity, and family history, and he was allowed to enter. Eight years later he returned to China and married Wong Lan Fong. When his wife followed him to the United States the next year, she had a photo of their wedding as proof of her eligibility to enter. Like thousands of others, Lee Chi Yet and Wong Lan Fong overcame enormous odds to enter the country during the era of exclusion.

Although most Chinese were prohibited, Japanese immigrants could still enter the country, and nearly 300,000 did so between 1890 and 1920, when opportunities for relatively well-paying jobs in Hawaii and California offered an alternative to the economic crisis they faced in Japan. As one Japanese immigrant wrote in traditional *haiku* form,

> Huge dreams of fortune
> Go with me to foreign lands
> Across the ocean.

As in China, marriages in Japan generally were arranged by families, and some men returned to Japan to meet and marry their brides. But cost and distance often prevented those meetings. Some women came to the United States as "picture brides" after an exchange of photographs. Although some women were disappointed with their often much older husbands, most accepted their fate as they would have accepted an arranged marriage in Japan. Others were delighted with the opportunity for adventure and life in the new land. As one picture bride explained, many of the people from her village had already gone to the United States, and she wanted to go, too: "I didn't care what the man looked like."

Although the Japanese formed less than 1 percent of California's population, they faced intense nativist hostility. The Japanese in California protested against the discrimination they faced, and in one case they successfully turned a local case of school segregation into an international incident. In response to the segregation of Japanese children in San Francisco, the Japanese government expressed its extreme displeasure. Hoping to avoid a confrontation with Japan—a significant military power that had just won a war with Russia—President Theodore Roosevelt interceded and convinced the San Francisco school board to rescind its segregation order. This incident led to the "Gentlemen's Agreement" of 1907, in which the Japanese government agreed to limit the number of immigrants to the United States. The numbers of new arrivals from Japan dwindled, and Japanese migrants instead began to settle in Brazil.

Newcomers from Southern and Eastern Europe

Eastern European Jews were among the most numerous of the "new" immigrants in the early twentieth century. In 1880, there were about 250,000 Jews in America; by 1920, there were 4 million, the vast majority from eastern Europe. During those 40 years, a number of factors motivated Jews to leave their small towns, or *shtetls*. Economic turmoil and restrictions on Jewish land ownership, trade, and business left many Jews impoverished. Anti-Semitic policies

International Museum of Photography at George Eastman House, Rochester, New York

▲ **At Ellis Island this immigrant family received identification tags indicating that they had been examined and declared healthy. Those who were ill, or youngsters without relatives to meet them, were sent to quarantine houses. Some were refused entry and sent back to their home countries.**

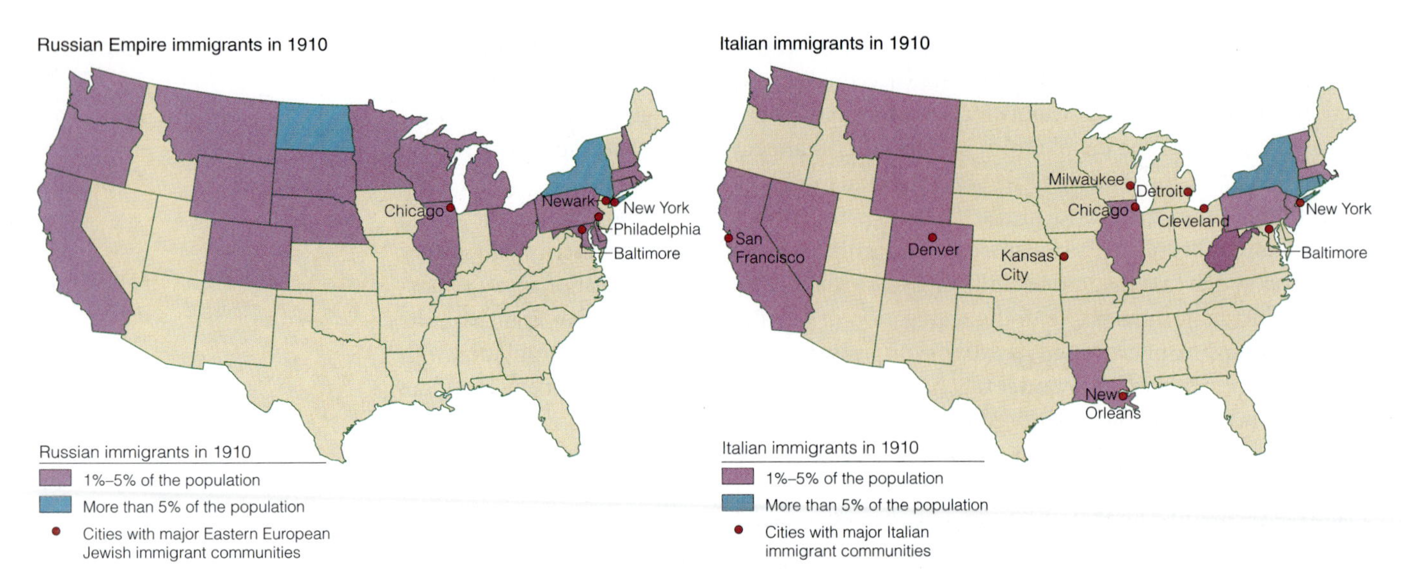

▲ **MAP 19.3 RUSSIAN AND ITALIAN IMMIGRANTS IN THE UNITED STATES, 1910**
Immigrants from Russia and Italy settled across the Northeast, Midwest, and West, with concentrations in large cities. Louisiana was the only southern state with a large concentration of immigrants from eastern or southern Europe.

in Russia and eastern Europe confined many Jews to live in restricted areas. Even more devastating was the increase in anti-Semitic violence in the form of riots, or *pogroms,* in which Jewish towns were attacked and many Jews were beaten and killed. Although Jews faced intense persecution, they were nevertheless subject to the draft. Many young Russian Jews emigrated to avoid being conscripted into the czar's army.

One such emigrant was young Morris Bass. At the age of 12, he left his family and ventured alone across the Atlantic. The uncle who was to meet him forgot about his arrival, leaving Morris stranded in the quarantine building on Ellis Island. Although he was among the lucky ones who passed the medical exam and was declared healthy enough to enter the country, he could not be released until a relative came to claim him and guarantee that the boy would be provided with support. After two weeks, just as immigration officials were preparing to send the boy back to Russia, his uncle appeared. He brought Morris home and showed him where to sleep. But as soon as the boy heard his uncle snoring, Morris ran away, furious at this relative who had left him to suffer two miserable weeks in captivity. He did not wander long in the crowded Jewish neighborhood of New York's Lower East Side before a butcher offered him a job, along with a place to sleep on a straw mat behind the shop.

Like many others, Morris prospered modestly. After a few years, he was able to strike out on his own as a pushcart peddler. Eventually, he sent home enough money to bring his parents and siblings to America. Some Jewish immigrants struggled to retain the faith and practices of Jewish orthodoxy that had defined their lives in the *shtetl.* But Morris was among those who wanted to assimilate into American life. He retained Jewish cultural practices but abandoned many religious rituals, such as refraining from work on Saturdays (the Jewish Sabbath) and wearing distinctive clothes. Nevertheless, he lived his life as a Jew among Jews, speaking Yiddish, celebrating the religious holidays, and maintaining a kosher home according to Jewish dietary laws, even though he rarely set foot in a synagogue.

Foreign-Born Population, 1890

Italian immigration also reached its peak between 1900 and 1914. While 90 percent of the Jews who migrated from Russia came to the United States, Italians ventured to many countries around the world. Turmoil in their home country resulting from the political and economic consequences of unification of the Italian peninsula prompted 27 million Italians—a third of Italy's population—to emigrate between 1870 and 1920. The majority of Italians who came to the United States arrived with their families and settled permanently, establishing strong communities and mutual aid societies. Most Italians were committed Catholics, and they preserved their rituals, festivals, and faith in the new country.

Work, Science, and Leisure

As the nineteenth century gave way to the twentieth, working women and men could increasingly expect to be employed in industry rather than farms, in large organizations rather than small shops, and in enterprises that relied more on efficiency than skilled craftswork. Towering skyscrapers began to dot the urban landscape, symbolic of the triumph of commerce and corporate power. Science and technology reigned, changing the nature of work as well as the fruits of production. Professional organizations of educators, social workers, physicians, and scientists emerged, while experts with academic credentials became leaders of many public institutions. It seemed as though science could solve virtually any problem. Advances in medical science contributed to improved public health. But in some cases, experts relied on scientific principles to address social problems rather than confronting the underlying structural causes, such as widespread poverty.

Reform and Science: An Uneasy Alliance

As standards for medications improved, reformers exposed the dangers of potions and remedies sold by street vendors. But crowding and lack of sanitation still fostered the spread of disease, especially among the poor. Lack of access to clean water was one of the major causes of disease, along with crowding, lack of medical care, and other chronic problems of poverty. Public sanitation alleviated the problem considerably in the early years of the twentieth century, reducing the incidence of typhoid fever by 70 percent. Among those who contributed to better conditions were community nurses. In 1900 the New York Charity Organization Society hired Jessie Sleet Scales, the first African American public health nurse, to address problems related to tuberculosis. Scales and other public health professionals implemented sanitation standards and provided care for poor communities, helping to control the spread of disease.

Public sanitation remained a problem, however, especially in crowded cities. An outbreak of typhoid among well-to-do New Yorkers led to Mary Mallon, an Irish immigrant, who had worked as a cook for a number of prominent families. When six members of a household where she worked developed typhoid, she was identified as a carrier of the disease. Authorities later discovered that typhoid outbreaks occurred in seven of eight households that had employed her. Although Mallon had no symptoms, she was forced to remain in a hospital for people with contagious diseases until she sued for her release in 1909; she was released in 1910. Mallon was instructed not to cook for a living, but as she had no other means to support herself, she went back to work as a cook. In 1915 she was arrested again after more typhoid cases were traced to her, and this time she was placed in isolation on an island, virtually as a prisoner, for 26 years, until her death in 1939.

The local press vilified Mallon, whom they dubbed "Typhoid Mary," and blamed her for the spread of the illness. As a carrier of the disease, she did indeed infect several people. But she was not the only source of contagion in the city. Typhoid, like many other diseases, was a public health problem. Although Mallon was an otherwise healthy

New York American, June 20, 1909, p. 6.

▲ "Typhoid Mary" unwittingly mixes death into an omelet in this 1909 poster warning against bad hygiene.

person and had never been accused of a crime, she was imprisoned for what amounted to a life sentence. City officials might have pursued other alternatives, such as helping Mallon find a job in which she would not endanger others and developing a broad-based public health approach to the disease that would have improved sanitation in the city.

Reflecting an impulse to blame social problems on allegedly flawed individuals or groups was the eugenics movement, which advocated scientific breeding to improve the nation's racial stock. Drawing on theories of white racial superiority and unscientific notions of genetic inheritance, eugenicists believed that character traits were inherited, including tendencies toward criminality, sexual immorality, and lack of discipline leading to poverty. Eugenicists claimed that social problems resulted from the high birthrate of immigrants and others they considered racially inferior to Anglo-Saxon Americans and from the low birthrate of educated middle-class whites.

President Theodore Roosevelt was an outspoken advocate of eugenics reform. One of his major concerns was that Americans were shirking their duty to create a robust citizenry for the future. Alarmed by the dramatic decline in the birthrate of native-born Americans and the tendency of college-educated women to remain single and childless, he feared that the immigrants, with their much higher birthrate, would overrun the nation. Roosevelt called upon Anglo-Saxon women to prevent what he called **race suicide,** much as male citizens had an obligation to defend the country if called to military duty. In his sixth annual Message to Congress in 1903, Roosevelt warned:

> When home ties are loosened, when men and women cease to regard a worthy family life...as the life best worth living, then evil days of the commonwealth are at hand. There are regions in our own land, and classes of our population, where the birth rate has sunk below the death rate. Surely it should need no demonstration to show that willful sterility is, from the standpoint of the nation...the one sin for which the penalty is national death, race death. . . . No man, no woman, can shirk the primary duties of life, whether for love of ease and pleasure, or for any other reason, and retain his or her self-respect.

Some eugenics crusaders proposed compulsory sterilization of those they deemed unfit for parenthood. Indiana enacted a eugenic sterilization law in 1907, and other states soon followed. These laws gave legal sanction to the surgical sterilization of thousands of men and even greater numbers of women whom government and medical officials deemed "feebleminded." Approximately one-third of these sterilizations occurred in California. The criteria for determining "feeblemindedness" were vague at best; often sexual impropriety or out-of-wedlock pregnancy landed young women—generally poor and often foreign born—in institutions for the feebleminded, where the operations took place. The Supreme Court upheld compulsory sterilization laws in the 1920s. Not everyone with reformist impulses supported eugenic sterilization. Organized opposition came from the Catholic Church, which saw sterilization not only as a violation of bodily integrity and human dignity, but also as unfairly targeting poor people and immigrants. As the field of genetics developed, scientists became increasingly uncomfortable with eugenics and eventually distanced themselves from the movement. Nevertheless, eugenic sterilization continued. Increasingly, women of color were targeted, and the practice continued well into the 1980s.

> ***Roosevelt called upon Anglo-Saxon women to prevent what he called "race suicide," much as male citizens had an obligation to defend the country.***

Eugenic sterilization was not the only issue that divided reformers over matters of science and medicine. Vaccination was another controversial issue in the early decades of the twentieth century. Although vaccination against the dreaded disease smallpox minimized the risk of infection, it was by no means without its own potential dangers. Complications from the vaccination could cause infection in the vaccinated individual, leading to severe illness or even death. In many localities, the medical profession promoted compulsory vaccination for children in the public schools. Opposition by parents and other activists who wanted to be able to make their own decisions regarding whether to vaccinate their children reached the level of a mass movement in some locations. In Portland, Oregon, for example, parents kept their

Lora C. Little became an antivaccination crusader after her son, Kenneth Marion Little, died of complications from a smallpox vaccination.

children home and virtually closed the public schools in protest against compulsory vaccination. Leading the charge was Lora C. Little, whose seven-year-old son died as a result of the smallpox vaccination. Little believed that the people, not the experts, should decide what is in their best interests. She was an avid health reformer, supporter of women's suffrage, vigorous opponent of eugenic sterilization, and critic of what she and other health reformers considered the tyranny of the medical establishment.

Scientific Management and Mass Production

In 1911 Frederick Winslow Taylor wrote *The Principles of Scientific Management,* his guide to increased efficiency in the nation's industries. He began his career as a laborer in the Midvale Steel Works near Philadelphia in 1878 and rose through the ranks to become the plant's chief engineer. Taylor developed a system to improve mass production in factories in order to make more goods more quickly. His principles included analysis of each job to determine the precise motions and tools needed to maximize each worker's productivity, detailed instructions for workers and guidelines for their supervisors, and wage scales with incentives to motivate workers to achieve high production goals. Over the next decades, industrial managers all over the country drew on Taylor's studies. Business leaders rushed to embrace Taylor's principles, and Taylor became a pioneering management consultant.

Taylor, Scientific Management

Henry Ford was among the most successful industrialists to employ Taylor's techniques. Born in 1863 on a farm near Dearborn, Michigan, the mechanically inclined Ford became an apprentice in a Detroit machine shop in 1879. Although he did not invent the automobile—the first motorcars were manufactured in Germany—he developed design and production methods that brought the cost of an automobile within the reach of the average worker. Ford experimented with the new internal combustion engine in the 1890s and built his first automobile in 1896. In 1903 he established the Ford Motor Company and began a profitable business. He introduced the popular and relatively inexpensive, mass-produced Model T automobile in 1908, which sold for $850. In 1913 Ford introduced **assembly line** production,

INTERPRETING HISTORY

Defining Whiteness

Naturalization laws pertaining to immigrants in the early twentieth century were based on racial categories. Asian immigrants, classified racially as "Mongolians," were not allowed to apply for U.S. citizenship. Naturalization was available only "to aliens being free white persons and to aliens of African nativity and to persons of African descent." Because racial theories were imprecise and fluid, and racial identities were not linked to nationality, immigrants occasionally challenged their racial classification to claim that they were "white." John Svan, who was Finnish, petitioned in federal court to contest the labeling of Finns as Mongolians, claiming that he was white and, therefore, allowed to apply for U.S. citizenship. The petition demonstrates the acceptance of racial definitions based on phenotype—particularly skin color—as well as the imprecise nature of those definitions. The court granted Svan's petition, legally changing his racial identity from Mongolian to white and reclassifying Finns as white people. Here is the court's memorandum, which allowed Svan to become a citizen:

John Svan was born in Finland and calls himself a Finn. . . . According to ethnologists, the Finns in very remote times were of Mongol origin; but the various groupings of the human race into families is arbitrary and, as respects any particular people, is not permanent but is subject to change and modification through the influences of climate, employment, intermarriage and other causes. There are indications that central and western Europe was at one time overrun by the Finns; some of their stock remained, but their racial characteristics were entirely lost in their remote descendants, who now are in no danger of being classed as Mongols. The Osmanlis, said to be of Mongol extraction, are now among the purest and best types of the Caucasian race. Changes are constantly going on and those occurring in the lapse of a few hundred years with any people may be very great.

The chief physical characteristics of the Mongolians are as follows: They are short of stature, with little hair on their body or face; they have yellow-brown skins, black eyes, black hair, short, flat noses, and oblique eyes. In actual experience we sometimes, though rarely, see natives of Finland whose eyes are slightly oblique. We sometimes see them with sparse beards and sometimes with flat noses; but Finns with a yellow or brown or yellow-brown skin or with black eyes or black hair would be an unusual sight. They are almost universally of light skin, blue or gray eyes, and light hair. No people of foreign births applying in this section of the country for the full rights of citizenship are lighter-skinned than those born in Finland. In stature they are quite up to the average. Confessedly, Finland has often been overrun with Teutons and by other branches of the human family, who, with their descendants, have remained within her borders and are now called Finns. They are in the main

a system in which each worker performed one task repeatedly as each automobile in the process of construction moved along a conveyor. Assembly line manufacturing increased production while cutting costs. In 1914 Ford increased his workers' wages to $5 per day at a time when industrial laborers averaged only $11 per week. By 1916 the price of the Model T dropped to $360. In this sense Ford was a pioneer not only in production but also in consumption.

Although an industrial genius, Ford was narrow-minded and bigoted. A ferocious anti-Semite, he later became an active supporter of Adolf Hitler. He fought unionization fiercely with a private police force. But his production methods, as well as the Ford motorcar, became fixtures of twentieth-century business and consumer culture. Ford embodied many contradictions: he helped create modern life, but he was also repulsed by it. He built a nostalgic theme park in Deerfield Village, Michigan, where he brought together old houses and artifacts to replicate a small town of the nineteenth century, where there were no cars or factories. Yet Ford's own life's work had contributed to the disappearance of the way of life idealized in Deerfield Village.

New Amusements

As Americans increasingly moved from rural to urban areas, and from farms to factories, new institutions of leisure emerged in the growing cities. Consumer culture was the flipside of business culture. One of the great ironies of American history in the twentieth century is that its popular culture—which more than anything else identifies the United States to the rest of the world—was largely a creation of immigrants and people of color. During the very years when these groups faced intense discrimination, they developed the cultural products that came to define America itself.

Minnesota Historical Society, Negative #93125. Photo by Maki of Virginia, Minnesota

These Finnish men living in Minnesota were among those whose racial classification was changed from "Mongolian" to "white" as the result of one Finnish immigrant's petition. Along with the Jews, Italians, Irish, and other immigrant groups now considered "white," Finns were classified as nonwhite until the laws and customs changed. Racial categories were fluid and imprecise, but whiteness conferred status and privileges.

indistinguishable in their physical characteristics from those of purer Finnish blood. Intermarriages have been frequent over a very long period of time. If the Finns were originally Mongols, modifying influences have continued until they are now among the whitest people in Europe. It would, therefore, require a most exhaustive tracing of family history to determine whether any particular individual born in Finland had or had not a remote Mongol ancestry. This, of course, cannot be done and was not intended. The question is not whether a person had or had not such ancestry, but whether he is now a "white person" within the meaning of that term as usually understood. This is the practical construction which has uniformly been placed upon the law. . . . Under such law Finns have always been admitted to citizenship, and there is no occasion now to change the construction.

The applicant is without doubt a white person within the true intent and meaning of such law.

The objections, therefore, in my opinion should be overruled and it will be so ordered.

Questions

1. *According to the court, what might cause changes in the "groupings of the human race into families" over time? How does the court's opinion reflect prevailing attitudes toward race during the Progressive Era?*
2. *How did the court explain the transformation of Finns from the classification as "Mongols" to becoming "among the whitest people in Europe"?* ■

The motion picture industry is a case in point. In 1888 Thomas Edison invented the kinetoscope, the early motion picture camera. The pragmatic Edison thought that his new device might be used in education and industry. But he did not see much commercial potential for the gadget. Not until the early twentieth century did the moving picture begin to reach a wide audience. Moviemakers left the East Coast and moved to the West, taking advantage of the even climate, cheap land, and nonunion labor. Within a few years, the moviemakers, mostly Jewish immigrants from Europe, established the film industry. By the late 1910s and 1920s, Paramount, Metro Goldwyn Mayer, and Fox Studios—all founded by Jews—had become leaders in movie making. Hollywood emerged as a major center of American popular culture, sending its products across the nation and abroad.

The first audiences for the motion pictures were in the working-class neighborhoods of the growing cities. In New York alone, by 1910, there were 1,000 small storefront theaters and fun houses known as penny arcades where there had been none 20 years earlier. The numbers of saloons also increased, from 7,000 to 9,000, while the Coney Island amusement park drew thousands to its shimmering lights and thrilling rides. During these same years, the sounds of African American music began to attract audiences among immigrants as well as native-born whites. Youths from all ethnic groups flocked to dance halls, where they danced to the lively tunes often played by black musicians who "ragged" the beat with new jazz rhythms.

Coney Island, 1904

Working-class youth were not the only ones drawn to the new urban amusements. Glamorous nightclubs, known as cabarets, also began to appear, offering dining, dancing, music, and entertainment to the wealthy. Jesse Lasky opened the Follies Bergeres in New York in 1911. Lasky filled his cabaret with lavish furnishings, hired black musicians to play ragtime music, and charged high prices. "Everything about the Follies," Lasky wrote, "was unheard of in New York, including the prices." In an effort to render these upper-class cabarets respectable and

George Luks, *The Café Francis*, c. 1909. Butler Institute of American Art, Youngstown, Ohio

▶ ***The Café Francis*, by George Luks, c. 1909. Luks was one of the "Ashcan school" artists who celebrated urban street life and popular culture. Their raw and sensual depictions of city entertainments stirred controversy among art critics at the time.**

distinguish them from the rowdy working-class dance halls, owners tamed the erotic dances to express a more moderate sensuality.

"Sex O'Clock in America"

The sexual mores and behavior of Americans seemed to be changing so dramatically that one observer announced "sex o'clock" had struck. Indeed, the codes of the past were challenged at every turn. Among the middle class, unchaperoned dating began to replace the previous system of a man "coming to call" at the home of a woman he hoped to court. Automobiles gave young couples more freedom and privacy. Physical intimacy became more acceptable, and even unacceptable sexual behavior became more common.

Immigrants often brought traditional courtship patterns to the new world and extended them into the next generation. One Italian man described his thwarted efforts to woo his fiancée. When he visited her home, "She sat on one side of the table, and I at the other. They afraid I touch." Finally, less than a month before their wedding, he got permission to take her to the theater. But the family was unwilling to let them go alone. "We came to the aisles of the theater. My mother-in-law go first, my fiancée next, my little sister, my father-in-law. I was the last one. I had two in between. . . . I was next to the old man." He tried to steal a kiss a few days before the wedding, but his fiancée rebuffed him: "No, not yet."

In spite of efforts by their elders, native-born as well as immigrant youth challenged the sexual codes of the past. Young working women looked forward to fun in their leisure hours and sometimes exchanged physical intimacies for "treats" from men who took them out to a meal or a dance. These women were known as "charity girls," to distinguish them from prostitutes. Increasing sexual intimacy among unmarried men and women reflected heightened expectations for sexual satisfaction—for women as well as men. These years also witnessed a rise in the proportion of brides who were pregnant at marriage, from a low of 10 percent in the mid-nineteenth century to 23 percent by 1910.

Marriage increasingly held the promise not only of love, intimacy, and mutual obligation, as it had in the nineteenth century, but also of sexual fulfillment and shared leisure pursuits. As expectations for marital happiness rose, so did the divorce rate. Liberal divorce laws, combined with expanding opportunities for women to support themselves, prompted increasing numbers of men and women to end unhappy marriages and try again. The rising divorce rate did not signal a decline in the popularity of marriage, however; a greater proportion of Americans married, and at increasingly younger ages. Those who divorced were likely to remarry, a pattern that continued through the twentieth century.

Some women did not marry but instead formed lifelong attachments to other women. Rarely identified as lesbian but often described as **Boston marriages,** these unions signified long-term emotional bonds between women who lived together. The widely admired reformer Jane Addams shared her life with Mary Rozet Smith for more than 30 years. Meanwhile, lesbians as well as gay men gained greater visibility in the cities. They frequented bars and clubs in such places as Greenwich Village and Harlem, hoping to avoid the attention of police, who were likely to arrest them for indecent conduct.

As expectations for marital happiness rose, so did the divorce rate.

Artists Respond to the New Era

Artists of all kinds contributed to enriching, expressing, interpreting, and transforming the urban industrial landscape. Among the most controversial was a group of painters who focused their attention on portrayals of life in the cities—including urban amusements and diverse working-class subjects. Although these artists did not pioneer new styles of painting, their content was revolutionary. Robert Henri painted scenes of the city including ethnic minorities, William Glackens depicted cabarets and nightlife, Everett Shinn portrayed prostitutes and other "low life" characters, John Sloan evoked New York's Lower East Side, immigrants, and theaters. Treating their subjects with dignity and humanity, these artists created works that exuded the vitality of urban life and conveyed a gritty reality free of moral condemnation. Contemptuous critics referred to the artists as the "Ashcan school," a label they embraced.

The artistic movement known as realism also infused the writing of fiction. Theodore Dreiser's 1900 novel *Sister Carrie* narrates the story of an independent young woman who moves to Chicago and uses her sexuality to advance her ambition. Contrary to the morality tales popular at the time, Carrie does not suffer for her sins. Rather, she prospers, while her male lovers are destroyed by their infatuation with her. Because of the novel's scandalous content, Dreiser's publisher did not promote the book, although it was revived and republished in later years.

Photography also began to exhibit a new realism in the work of such documentary photographers as Lewis Hine, who photographed immigrants, industrial work, and urban street life, and such avant-garde artists as Alfred Stieglitz and Edward Steichen, who drew inspiration from artistic innovations in Europe, such as Cubism. Popular music flourished in the first decade of the century, especially jazz. From its roots in slave songs, spirituals, and ragtime, jazz brought together the various strains of African American music and developed new forms, centered in New Orleans. Artists such as pianist Ferdinand "Jelly Roll" Morton and cornet player Charles "Buddy" Bolden were among the musicians who played the new syncopated rhythms.

Reformers and Radicals

The broad movement for social reform known as **Progressivism** included two distinct impulses. On the one hand, many Anglo-Saxon Protestants tried to impose order on a rapidly changing nation. They hoped to stem the tide of immigration, bolster the rapidly eroding sexual codes, and quell the movements for social change. On the other hand, women's rights activists, workers, and African Americans struggled to achieve the rights and privileges available to white men of property and standing. The tensions between these two very different approaches to reform shaped the politics of the era.

A century later, in 2003, California voters recalled a governor for the first time and elected film star Arnold Schwarzenegger to replace him.

Reform movements reshaped the relationship between citizens and their government at all levels. Reformers at the national level, including President Theodore Roosevelt, sought to increase the power of the federal government in order to regulate big business, manage the environment, and strengthen the position of the United States abroad. At the local level, radicals and reformers sought to retain power in the hands of the citizens. Particularly in the western states, Progressive reformers adopted reforms that would foster direct democracy. Oregon was the first state to adopt three reform procedures designed to allow voters more direct control over the political process. In 1902, Oregon approved the *initiative,* which allowed voters to bypass the state legislature and petition the state directly to submit specific measures to popular vote. The *referendum,* approved in the same year, permitted state legislatures to refer bills directly to the voters for approval or rejection. In 1908, Oregon adopted the *recall,* which gave citizens the right to call a special election to remove elected officials from office before the end of their term. These procedures have enabled voters to initiate measures at the grass roots. A century later, in 2003, California voters used the recall to unseat a governor for the first time. They voted to unseat unpopular governor Gray Davis and elected Hollywood film star Arnold Schwarzenegger to replace him.

Muckraking, Moral Reform, and Vice Crusades

In the early twentieth century, a group of investigative journalists began to expose the ills of industrial life. President Theodore Roosevelt dubbed them **muckrakers** in 1906, to signal their tendency to unearth the dirtiest aspects of the nation's political and economic institutions. Although Roosevelt intended the term as an insult, the muckrakers embraced their label. Their best-known works illuminated corruption in business and politics. Ida Tarbell wrote a powerful exposé of the ruthless business practices of John D. Rockefeller, who transformed the Standard Oil Company into a monopoly. Lincoln Steffens unearthed scandals in city and state politics. By 1912, more than 1,000 muckraking articles appeared in widely read and popular magazines such as *McClure's, Everybody's,* and *Colliers.*

Steffens, from *The Shame of the Cities*

One of the best-known muckraking novels was Upton Sinclair's *The Jungle,* published in 1906. A dedicated socialist, Sinclair hoped that his novel would reveal the exploitation of immigrant workers. *The Jungle* tells the story of Jurgis Rudkus, a Lithuanian immigrant, and his family and friends and provides a grim exposé of the squalid working conditions in the meatpacking plant where Rudkus worked. The book includes descriptions of the filth, rats, and even the body parts of workers that end up ground into the packages of meat. *The Jungle* had a powerful impact, but the effect was not what Sinclair had hoped. Rather than spark interest in socialism, or even improved wages and working conditions, the novel aroused consumer indignation and led to the passage of the Pure Food and Drug Act and a Meat Inspection Act, which prohibited adulterated or fraudulently labeled food and drugs from interstate commerce. Sinclair later wrote with regret, "I aimed at the public's heart and by accident hit it in the stomach." The Pure Food and Drug Act was the first of a series of consumer protection laws passed in the twentieth century.

Child labor was another concern of reformers. Children worked in fields and factories across the country, picking cotton in Texas, mining coal in West Virginia, working in the textile mills of North Carolina, and sewing buttons in urban sweatshops. Children of immigrants and rural migrants often assisted parents on farms or in shops, their labor an accepted part of the household economy. Many parents believed that work also offered children opportunities to learn discipline as well as a trade, and to gain a sense of pride and satisfaction as contributors to the family's needs. But the sorts of jobs available to children in the urban industrial world often were dangerous and unhealthy, characterized by long hours, low pay, and miserable working conditions. Reformers attempted to improve the conditions under which children worked and to establish age limits so that children could attend school and spend time in healthful recreation rather than in grim sweatshops and factories. Ultimately, child labor activists succeeded in passing legislation at the state level that restricted child labor, although these efforts were more successful in northern states than in the South.

Mother Jones, "The March of the Mill Children"

Protective legislation for women was also controversial. Reformers campaigned for laws that would establish minimum wages, maximum hours, regulations against night work, and restrictions on heavy lifting. When they were unable to secure such safety measures for all workers, they argued that women needed special protections because of their physical frailty and their role as future mothers. Women's rights activists disagreed over these measures. Some argued that they were necessary to protect women from exploitation and dangerous working conditions. Others claimed that women should be treated the same as men, arguing that protective legislation implied that women needed special care and were not suited for particular kinds of work. These debates continued throughout the century.

Women were prominent among Progressive reformers. Jane Addams, founder of Hull House, the immigrant neighborhood center in Chicago, became the most admired woman of her day. Many other influential women also left their stamp on the culture and public policies of the era. Florence Kelley, daughter of a prominent Philadelphia Quaker family, joined Addams's Hull House community and later headed the National Consumers' League (NCL) from 1898 until her death in 1932. Under her leadership, the NCL became the most effective lobbying agency for protective labor legislation for women and children. Kelley was instrumental in the successful defense of the ten-hour working day for women, which was affirmed by the Supreme Court in its 1908 decision *Muller v. Oregon.*

Another noted reformer was Helen Keller, whose work on behalf of the blind called attention to the needs of the disabled. Keller lost her sight and hearing from an illness at the age of 19 months and learned to communicate through Braille and sign language, which she mastered through touch, with the help of her extraordinary teacher, Anne Sullivan. Keller went on to study at schools for the deaf and graduated with honors from Radcliffe College in 1904. A passionate socialist and advocate of women's rights along with other radical causes, Keller wrote several books, and she lectured worldwide with the assistance of interpreters.

Most Progressive reformers were prosperous American-born Anglo-Saxon Protestants. Along with their efforts to improve living and working conditions and alleviate the suffering of the poor, they also hoped to eradicate vice from their society. At the level of local government, many reformers promoted zoning laws that would keep commercial entertainments out of residential neighborhoods. Vice crusaders in most of the nation's large cities tried to eliminate prostitution and to patrol dance halls, movie theaters, and saloons. Gay men and lesbians risked arrest. At the national level, vice crusading culminated in the passage of the Mann Act in 1910, which made it illegal to transport women across state lines for "immoral purposes." The Mann Act resulted in 1,537 convictions by 1916. Over the years, authorities used the Mann Act not only to police prostitution but also to regulate interracial sex.

International Museum of Photography at George Eastman House, Rochester, New York

▲ **In the early twentieth century, many children such as this young boy worked long hours doing hard labor. Photographer Lewis Hine, who took this picture, worked for the National Child Labor Committee. His photographs documented the exploitation of child workers and helped generate support for child labor laws.**

One such case garnered national attention. African American boxer Jack Johnson had defeated white fighters in the ring to become the world heavyweight champion in 1910. He was a hero to black Americans but a villain to many whites, who resented not only his athletic success but also his relationships with white women. In 1912 Lucille Cameron, a young white woman from Minnesota, visited Johnson's Chicago nightclub and the two began an affair. Cameron's mother brought charges of abduction against Johnson, but the young woman refused to testify so the case was dismissed. The couple later married. Authorities continued their efforts to punish Johnson for his racial and sexual transgressions. When federal agents persuaded one of Johnson's former lovers, a white prostitute, to testify that Johnson had paid for her travel from Pittsburgh to Chicago, he was convicted under the Mann Act and sentenced to one year in prison.

Women's Suffrage

The crusade for women's rights, including the effort to gain the vote, was already more than half a century old by 1900. But the movement gained momentum at the dawn of the twentieth century. A new generation of women's rights leaders came together in the suffrage movement. They included working-class women and young college-educated women, some of them with experience in the settlement houses, and others who had participated in socialist and labor circles. They initiated new grassroots strategies such as door-to-door campaigns to gather support for women's suffrage. The militancy of the suffrage movement in England inspired American activists to develop new tactics and international alliances. These activists achieved legislative success when several western states granted women the right to vote: Washington in 1910, California in 1911, and three more states in 1912. Eventually the movement united around the goal of enacting a federal amendment. In the nation's capital, women demonstrating peacefully for the right to vote faced violence and brutal treatment from hostile crowds and officials. Finally, the required three-quarters majority of the states ratified the Nineteenth Amendment in 1920, granting women the vote.

In the nation's capital, women demonstrating peacefully for the right to vote faced violence and brutal treatment from hostile crowds and officials.

Women's suffrage was achieved with a sometimes uneasy coalition. Some white suffrage leaders feared that any alliance with women of color would alienate southern voters whose support they needed to ensure ratification of the Nineteenth Amendment. They also hoped to win over to their cause racist and nativist critics in the North who feared that granting the vote to women would enfranchise "undesirable" voters, specifically immigrant and minority women. Some women's rights leaders, such as Belle Kearney, a southern suffragist, saw the ballot for women as a means of keeping African Americans in their place: "The enfranchisement of women would insure immediate and durable white supremacy, honestly attained." The suffrage movement also gained the support of conservatives who believed that women would vote for conservative causes such as prohibition and immigration restriction.

Many minority women, such as Hispanic activist Adelina Otero Warren, participated fully in the suffrage movement and became powerful allies of leading white suffragists. As Otero Warren wrote to Alice Paul, who became leader of the National Women's Party, "I will take a stand and a firm one whenever necessary for I am with you now and always." Otero Warren's efforts helped secure New Mexico's ratification of the Nineteenth Amendment. These sorts of alliances built a strong multiracial reform movement, but the leaders did not always agree on priorities. The African American antilynching activist Ida B. Wells (also known by her married name as Ida B. Wells-Barnett) supported women's suffrage but was unable to convince the white women's rights leaders to denounce lynching. Ultimately, passage of the Nineteenth Amendment resulted from a combination of factors, including radical politics, civil rights and labor activism, strong support from a wide range of reformers, and an alliance with some conservative, racist, and anti-immigrant forces.

Radical Politics and the Labor Movement

Progressive reformers believed that American capitalist democracy was a fundamentally sound system that simply needed to be fixed to achieve its full promise. Radicals of the era, however, believed that the system was flawed and needed to be fundamentally transformed. Emma Goldman, a Russian Jewish immigrant, was one of many radical activists who gained both fame and notoriety for her outspoken support of radical causes. Like Sieh King King and Clara Lemlich, Goldman was among the growing numbers of women who were leaders in the labor struggles of the day, although women were excluded from most unions. Only 3.3 percent of the 4 million women engaged in nonagricultural jobs in 1900 were members of trade unions. In 1903 the Women's Trade Union League (WTUL) brought together elite reformers and female laborers to help working women in their efforts to unionize. The number of women in unions doubled in the wake of the successful wave of strikes by young immigrant garment workers in 1909–1910, including the 1909 shirtwaist-makers' strike.

Socialism also attracted followers during these years. Although it was never as strong in the United States as it was in Europe, socialism gained strength in America at the turn of the century. Socialists promoted labor unions and the rights of women and formed their own political party. Socialist leader Eugene V. Debs, who had gained national fame for his role in the 1894 railroad strike, became the spokesperson and leader of the Socialist party. Between 1900 and 1920, he was the party's candidate for president, gaining nearly a million votes, or 6 percent of the electorate, in the 1912 election. Although the socialists never gathered a large enough following to win national elections, they elected hundreds of candidates to local office.

The Industrial Workers of the World (IWW), also known as the **Wobblies,** offered another possibility for labor radicalism. Organized in 1905 by socialists and labor militants, the IWW included women, blacks, immigrants, and unskilled and migratory laborers, workers generally shunned by the American Federation of Labor (AFL). The Wobblies organized workers in the mines of the Rocky Mountain states, in the lumber camps of the Pacific Northwest and the South, and in the eastern textile and steel mills. Its membership reached about 3 million people, although no more than 150,000 were members at any one time. Although the Socialist party and the IWW were open to black members, they had no particular interest in combating racism or addressing the unique needs of African American workers. They assumed that labor activism would improve the lives of all workers. To address their unique concerns, black Americans organized on their own behalf.

Brown Brothers

▲ Elizabeth Gurley Flynn of the Industrial Workers of the World (IWW) addresses a crowd of women in 1913. Flynn was one of the organizers of the IWW, known as the Wobblies, an organization of workers from diverse backgrounds that enrolled nearly 3 million members.

Logo for the Industrial Workers of the World

Resistance to Racism

The Progressive Era was anything but progressive for nonwhite Americans. Although there were notable exceptions, such as antiracist reformer Jane Addams, many white Protestant reformers were either indifferent to racial minorities or actively hostile to them. Moreover, most blacks lived in the rural South, not in northern cities where Progressives were most active. Lynching continued into the twentieth century, with nearly 100 lynchings per year between 1900 and 1910. African Americans were the primary targets of lynch mobs, although other minorities were also vulnerable. Between 1850 and 1930, 597 Mexicans died at the hands of vigilante mobs, half of them in Texas. Civil rights leaders spoke out against lynching and other forms of racial injustice. Ida B. Wells-Barnett, who had launched an international crusade against lynching in the 1890s, worked to establish local and national networks of black women's clubs. Although she was unable to persuade white suffrage leaders to support the cause of racial justice, she worked closely with Jane Addams to prevent the establishment of segregated schools in Chicago.

A number of other black leaders came to prominence in the first decade of the twentieth century. In 1905 scholar and civil rights leader W. E. B. Du Bois joined with other black leaders to form the Niagara Movement, which called for an end to segregation and discrimination in unions, the courts, and public accommodations, as well as for equal economic and educational opportunity. In 1908 black leaders joined with white Progressive allies to establish the National Association for the Advancement of Colored People (NAACP). The new organization adopted the platform of the Niagara Movement, and Du Bois became the editor of its journal, *The Crisis.* Ida B. Wells-Barnett insisted that the organization go on record as opposed to lynching. The NAACP has remained a major voice for African American civil rights and racial justice to this day.

Expanding National Power

Along with flourishing radical and reform movements at the grassroots, the Progressive Era gave rise to a reformist impulse at the national level. The person who most fully embodied the national Progressive movement was Theodore Roosevelt, president from 1901 to 1908. Roosevelt used his power to regulate big business, intervene in labor disputes, extend the reach of the nation across the world, and control the uses of the natural environment.

The "Rough Rider" as President

Theodore Roosevelt rose to prominence in the Republican party in the 1880s and held a number of important political posts, including assistant secretary of the navy (1897–1898) and governor of New York (1899–1900). In 1900 Roosevelt became vice president. But in September 1901, President McKinley was assassinated, and at age 42 Roosevelt became the youngest person ever to occupy the Oval Office.

Roosevelt was a strong proponent of American military and commercial presence in the world. He expanded the power of the federal government both at home and abroad and used the "bully pulpit" of the presidency to exert moral leadership. Using the Sherman Anti-Trust Act of 1890, which gave the federal government the power to break up monopolies, Roosevelt in 1902 ordered the Justice Department to prosecute the Northern Securities Company, a $400 million monopoly that controlled all railroad lines and traffic in the Northwest. Within a year, the company was dissolved. Although this bold act earned Roosevelt the title of "trust-buster," it was not his intention to weaken big business. In fact, he believed that a strong country needed large, powerful industries, and he hoped to regulate them to keep big business strong.

Roosevelt was proud of appointing a cabinet in which "Catholic and Protestant and Jew sat side by side."

The same year that Roosevelt took on the Northern Securities Company, he also used the powers of the federal government to intervene in a labor dispute. Striking coal miners in eastern Pennsylvania wanted recognition of their union, a 10 to 20 percent increase in wages, and an eight-hour day. But the mine owners refused to negotiate. Roosevelt summoned the mine owners and John Mitchell, president of the United Mine Workers union, to the White House for a meeting. He threatened to send in troops if the mine owners did not agree to the union's request for arbitration. The mine owners backed down, and the arbitrators negotiated a compromise that awarded the miners a 10 percent wage increase and a nine-hour day.

Roosevelt's efforts to strengthen the state and foster American nationalism extended to his attitudes toward immigrants. He believed that discrimination against loyal newcomers harmed democracy: "It is a base outrage to oppose a man because of his religion or birthplace. . . . A Scandinavian, a German, or an Irishman who has really become an American has the right to stand on exactly the same footing as any native-born citizen in the land, and is just as much entitled to the friendship and support, social and political, of his neighbor." He was proud of appointing a cabinet in which "Catholic and Protestant and Jew sat side by side." But to Roosevelt, becoming an American meant renouncing any loyalties to one's original homeland or culture:

> We must Americanize them in every way...[the immigrant] must not bring in his Old-World religious[,] race[,] and national antipathies, but must merge them into love for our common country, and must take pride in the things which we can all take pride in. He must revere our flag; not only must it come first, but no other flag should ever come second. He must learn to celebrate Washington's birthday rather than that of the Queen or Kaiser, and the Fourth of July instead of St. Patrick's Day. . . . Above all, the immigrant must learn to talk and think and be United States.

Roosevelt did not believe in cultural pluralism, the idea that the United States could include citizens who retained their ethnic heritage. Rather, Roosevelt promoted the idea of a melting pot that would blend all diverse cultures into a unique American "race."

Although Roosevelt was a firm believer in Anglo-Saxon superiority, he was the first president to invite an African American leader, Booker T. Washington, to the White House. Roosevelt's meeting with Washington demonstrated his willingness to stand up to southern politicians, but he did not follow that gesture with meaningful policy initiatives such as anti-lynching or civil rights laws. In the 1904 presidential election, the popular and energetic Roosevelt won 57 percent of the popular vote against his Democratic rival, Alton B. Parker.

Protecting and Preserving the Natural World

Industrial smoke had long been a problem in both European and American cities, and Progressive Era reformers established organizations in major cities to fight air pollution. At the same time, mining and other industries were depleting natural resources while destroying the natural beauty of the land. More than any previous president, Theodore Roosevelt used the federal government to manage the natural world. Although his actions did not please everyone on all sides of the debate, Roosevelt's environmental efforts were among his most enduring legacies.

Roosevelt advocated both preservation and conservation. His preservation policies doubled the number of national parks, created 16 national monuments, and established 51 wildlife refuges. At the same time, he shared the view of conservationists that timberlands, areas for livestock grazing, water, and minerals needed federal government management. Roosevelt transferred 125 million acres of public land into the forest reserves to prevent the depletion of timber, and he set aside land for dam sites, oil and coal reserves, and grazing lands. Some of these efforts faced strong opposition from preservationists, because of their negative impact on the natural environment.

Conservationists and preservationists battled frequently, and no issue was more divisive than water.

Conservationists and preservationists battled frequently, and no issue was more divisive than water. Dams, reservoirs, and aqueducts brought water and electricity to arid regions, allowing such cities as Las Vegas and Los Angeles to flourish in areas that would otherwise be unable to support large populations. Conservationists favored such projects, but environmentalists opposed the flooding of river valleys. One of the most heated of these debates surrounded the damming of the secluded and pristine Hetch Hetchy Valley in Yosemite National Park. The controversy involved the protection of the environment, the need for water and power in San Francisco, and the question of public ownership of utilities to provide affordable energy to urban residents.

In the early twentieth century, San Francisco relied on two private corporations to provide its water and power, Spring Valley Water Company and Pacific Gas & Electric Company (PG&E). But Spring Valley's water supply was inadequate to meet the needs of the growing city, and PG&E's electricity was too expensive. City planners looking for alternatives proposed damming the Tuolumne River flowing through Hetch Hetchy Valley. The resulting reservoir was to supply the city with fresh water, and the dam was to provide San Francisco residents with cheap hydroelectric power.

The idea of damming and flooding Hetch Hetchy Valley met with considerable resistance, especially from the recently formed Sierra Club. Its founder, John Muir, railed against the city

Sierra Club

▲ **The Hetch Hetchy Valley in Yosemite National Park as it looked before the damming of the Tuolumne River (above), and after (right). The dam provided San Francisco with electricity, and the reservoir provided the city with water. Environmental activists at the time opposed the damming of the river, and controversy over the project continues to this day.**

officials: "These temple destroyers, devotees of ravaging commercialism, seem to have a perfect contempt for Nature and, instead of lifting their eyes to the God of the mountains, lift them to the Almighty Dollar. . . . Dam Hetch Hetchy! As well dam for water-tanks the people's cathedrals and churches, for no holier temple has ever been consecrated by the heart of man."

The bitter dispute ultimately came to Congress. Because Hetch Hetchy is located within a national park, its development required federal approval. After several weeks of hearings, in 1913 Congress passed the Raker Act, authorizing the construction of the reservoir. Progressive reformers suspicious of private utility monopolies made certain that the Raker Act required that the hydroelectric power generated by the dam be sold to San Francisco residents through a public power agency.

But the controversy did not end there. For years San Francisco officials failed to abide by this federal mandate and continued to allow PG&E to control the distribution and sale of the energy. By 1940 the matter reached the Supreme Court, which ruled eight to one against San Francisco. The Supreme Court decision did not settle the matter, however. As late as the early twenty-first century, when power shortages in California reached a crisis level, public power remained a major issue. Meanwhile, the Sierra Club and other environmental groups continued to call for a removal of the dam and the restoration of the Hetch Hetchy Valley to its natural state, along with the development of alternative energy sources.

Expanding National Power Abroad

The decades surrounding the turn of the twentieth century marked the high point of European and American imperial expansion, bringing 80 percent of the world's land under the control of Europeans or their descendants. Roosevelt hoped to strengthen the federal government at home, develop the nation's military and commercial might, and extend American power abroad. To further these ends, he sent troops to China as part of the international expedition to crush the Boxer uprising in 1900. He also proposed the construction of a canal across the Isthmus of Panama, and Congress approved the Panama Canal project in 1902.

Sierra Club

In 1904 Roosevelt increased the authority of the United States to intervene in the affairs of nations in the Western Hemisphere through what came to be known as the Roosevelt Corollary to the Monroe Doctrine. Fearing political uprisings that might threaten American commercial interests, Roosevelt asserted that "chronic wrongdoing" might require the intervention by "some civilized nation" in the affairs of another. "In the Western Hemisphere," he concluded, this "may force the United States…to the exercise of an international police power." The Roosevelt Corollary justified later interventions into the Dominican Republic, Cuba, Nicaragua, Mexico, and Haiti.

In the Pacific, the bloody U.S. war against Filipino nationalists that began in 1899 lasted four years before the Americans crushed the revolt and established firm colonial rule in the Philippines. William Howard Taft became the colony's first governor-general in 1901. Taft developed a program of public works that included an infrastructure of roads, bridges, and schools. He also transferred government functions to those Filipinos who cooperated with American colonial powers. Although the United States promised to grant Philippine independence, that promise was deferred until 1946.

William Howard Taft: The One-Term Progressive

A financial panic in 1907 prompted Theodore Roosevelt to increase his efforts to overhaul the banking system and the stock market. But the president's critics among Republican conservatives and the business elite blamed Roosevelt's reform policies for the economic downturn. In the face of increasing rifts within his own party and his earlier pledge to step down, Roosevelt declined to run for reelection in 1908. The Republicans chose as their candidate William Howard Taft. Prior to his service in the Philippines, Taft had been a federal circuit judge. In 1904 Roosevelt appointed him secretary of war. Taft was a loyal ally who worked closely with Roosevelt on foreign and domestic policies. Roosevelt assumed that Taft, after his victory in the general election, would fulfill Roosevelt's reform agenda.

Taft's respect for the separation of powers spelled out in the U.S. Constitution made him dubious about some of Roosevelt's extensions of the powers of the presidency. Nevertheless, Taft initiated far more antitrust suits than Roosevelt had during his presidency. Despite similar political inclinations, Roosevelt's support for his protégé cooled. Although Roosevelt counted major business leaders among his own advisers, he was displeased when Taft appointed corporate lawyers rather than activist reformers to his cabinet. His displeasure increased when Taft abandoned the fight for an inheritance tax and a reduction in tariffs.

Taft departed from Roosevelt's foreign policy as well. In contrast to Roosevelt, who emphasized military might, Taft claimed that "Dollar Diplomacy" was the best way for the United States to exert influence in the world:

> This policy has been characterized as substituting dollars for bullets. It is one that appeals alike to idealistic humanitarian sentiments, to the dictates of sound policy and strategy, and to legitimate commercial aims. It is an effort frankly directed to the increase of American trade upon the axiomatic principle that the government of the United States shall extend all proper support to every legitimate and beneficial American enterprise abroad.

Yale Collection of Western Americana, Beinecke Rare Book and Manuscript Library

▲ Lumberjacks topple a giant spruce tree in a forest in Washington State around 1900. President Theodore Roosevelt believed that the federal government should manage timberlands and other natural resources to prevent depletion while allowing their use. Roosevelt preserved some Pacific Northwest forests in national parks and refuges but allowed others to be cultivated for timber.

Taft's relationship with the Philippines illustrates both his policy of Dollar Diplomacy and his reinforcement of American imperialism abroad. Taft took Roosevelt's military rule of the islands a step further by establishing U.S. business interests there. As *El Renacimiento,* a Filipino newspaper, put it at the beginning of Taft's administration:

> For [Taft] the present generation is a generation of children, incapable of assuming the responsibilities of self-government; and this point of view we can never accept. Yet we recognize the power that lies in his hands. . . . President Taft, with the avowed purpose of helping the Filipinos, will encourage the introduction into this country of large capital which will buy up and exploit everything here worth having; and the inevitable result will be the complete domination of American commercial interests. When that day comes, of what benefit will be all this policy of education, this long preparation for self-government, except to make servitude more intolerable?

When Taft signed the higher Payne-Aldrich Tariff in 1909, he disappointed Republican Progressives and aligned himself with the conservative old guard of the party, those who had been most critical of Roosevelt. The breach between Taft and the Progressives widened when Taft's secretary of the interior, Richard A. Ballinger, opened up for commercial development 1 million acres of land that Roosevelt had placed under federal protection. In a further affront to conservationists, Gifford Pinchot, still head of the National Forest Service, discovered that Ballinger had sold Alaskan coal deposits to corporate moguls J. P. Morgan and David Guggenheim. When Taft defended Ballinger, Pinchot leaked the news to the press and called for a congressional investigation. Taft subsequently fired Pinchot, but Roosevelt publicly supported Pinchot and signaled his break from Taft.

Roosevelt returned from big-game hunting in Africa to enter the political spotlight once again. He toured the country in 1910, describing his plan for a "New Nationalism," a far-reaching expansion of the federal government to stabilize the economy and institute social reforms.

The election of reformers of both parties to Congress in 1910 encouraged Roosevelt to challenge Taft for leadership of the Republican party. Although Roosevelt had wide public support and easily defeated Taft and the other challenger, Robert La Follette, in the 13 states that held preferential primaries, the old guard still dominated the national party, and they nominated Taft at the Republican National Convention.

The day after Taft's nomination, Roosevelt and his supporters withdrew from the Republican party and formed the Progressive party. They nominated Roosevelt for president and California governor Hiram W. Johnson for vice president. Roosevelt boasted, "I am as strong as a bull moose," inspiring his followers to call themselves the **Bull Moosers.** Their reformist platform called for extensive controls on corporations, minimum wage laws, child labor laws, a graduated income tax, and women's suffrage. The Democrats nominated Woodrow Wilson, former president of Princeton University and governor of New Jersey. Wilson also ran on a strong reform platform. Eugene V. Debs, the Socialist party candidate, vowed reform as well.

The three reform candidates, Wilson, Debs, and Roosevelt, all agreed that the large corporations had too much power. But they disagreed as to what to do about it. Debs argued that the national government should take over the trusts. Roosevelt argued for a "New Nationalism," in which a strong federal government would regulate the trusts and, if necessary, curb their power. Wilson, reluctant to vest so much power in the government, called his approach the "New Freedom," believing that the government should dismantle the trusts and then revert to limited powers. The Republican vote split between Taft and Roosevelt, and the victory went to the Democratic candidate, Woodrow Wilson. Wilson took office amid an overwhelming popular mandate for reform.

Conclusion

When Woodrow Wilson entered the White House in 1913, the nation looked and behaved differently than it had at the turn of the century. Millions of immigrants from Europe, Asia, and Mexico had arrived in the United States and settled in towns and cities across the nation. Growing urban areas with new amusements and increasingly diverse populations emerged as centers of a national mass culture. New developments in science and technology brought the automobile and the motion picture to American consumers. At the same time, industrial production contributed to environmental damage, pollution, and dangerous working conditions.

Progressive reformers and labor activists mounted efforts to curb the ill effects of urban industrial society. Faith in science and expertise gave rise to pervasive optimism that social problems could be solved. Technological changes converged with the widespread belief that society is the sum of interdependent parts that can work together to mitigate the harmful effects of industrial life. At the local level as well as through state and national institutions, reformers sought to solve society's ills. Muckrakers exposed corruption, women's rights activists pushed for the vote, and African American leaders organized for civil rights and against lynching. In the West and Southwest, Mexicans and Asians challenged discriminatory laws and labor practices. At the same time, moralists and vice crusaders sought to tame what they considered dangerous challenges to the social order.

These years also witnessed a major expansion of national power. Presidents Roosevelt and Taft strengthened the role of the federal government through new efforts to regulate big business and by extending American military and economic presence abroad. By 1912 most Americans supported a strong reform agenda. But within a few years, the nation became embroiled in a major world war that would challenge the inherent optimism of Progressivism, signaling the end of an era.

Sites to Visit

Touring Turn-of-the-Century America: Photographs from the Detroit Publishing Company, 1880–1920.

www.memory.loc.gov/ammem/detroit/dethome.html

This Library of Congress site includes thousands of photographs from turn-of-the-century America.

Coal Mining During the Gilded Age and Progressive Era

www.history.ohio-state.edu/projects/Lessons_US/Gilded_Age/Coal_Mining/default.htm

This Ohio State University site examines the development of the coal industry, including experiences of miners and sometimes violent labor-management conflict.

W. E. B. Du Bois Resources

www-unix.oit.umass.edu/%7Ecscpo/db.html

Included here are writings by and about the great African American intellectual and civil rights leader W. E. B. Du Bois.

Triangle Shirtwaist Factory Fire, March 25, 1911

www.ilr.cornell.edu/trianglefire/

Oral histories, cartoons, images, and essays about the fire are included here.

Inside an American Factory: The Westinghouse Works, 1904

lcweb2.loc.gov/ammem/papr/west/westhome.html

This site provides a glimpse inside a turn-of-the-twentieth-century factory.

Theodore Roosevelt

www.ipl.org/ref/POTUS/troosevelt.html

This Internet Public Library site contains biographical information about Theodore Roosevelt and his election to the presidency and links to Internet biographies and resources about him.

William Howard Taft

www.ipl.org/ref/POTUS/whtaft.html

This Internet Public Library site contains biographical information about William Howard Taft and his election to the presidency and links to Internet biographies and resources about him.

Emma Goldman Papers

sunsite.berkeley.edu/Goldman/

This site includes information about the famous immigrant radical and selections of writings by and about her.

For Further Reading

General Works

Gail Bederman, *Manliness and Civilization: A Cultural History of Gender and Race in the United States, 1800–1917* (1995).

John R. Borchert, *America's Northern Heartland: An Economic and Historical Geography of the Upper Midwest* (1987).

Herbert Croly, *The Promise of American Life* (1909).

Steven J. Diner, *A Very Different Age: Americans of the Progressive Era* (1998).

Sara Evans, *Born for Liberty: A History of Women in America* (1989).

Gary Gerstle, *American Crucible: Race and Nation in the Twentieth Century* (2001).

Migration and Immigration: The Changing Face of the Nation

Albert Camarillo, *Chicanos in a Changing Society* (1977).

Catherine Ceniza Choy, *Empire of Care: Nursing and Migration in Filipino American History* (2003).
Gilbert G. Gonzalez and Raul A. Fernandez, *A Century of Chicano History: Empire, Nations, and Migration* (2003).
Linda Gordon, *The Great Arizona Orphan Abduction* (1999).
Matthew Frye Jacobson, *Barbarian Virtues: The United States Encounters Foreign Peoples at Home and Abroad* (2000).
Erika Lee, *At America's Gates: Chinese Immigration During the Exclusion Era, 1882–1943* (2003).
Riv-Ellen Prell, *Fighting to Become Americans: Jews, Gender, and the Anxiety of Assimilation* (1999).
Vicki L. Ruiz, *From Out of the Shadows: Mexican Women in Twentieth-Century America* (1998).
George J. Sanchez, *Becoming Mexican American: Ethnicity, Culture, and Identity in Chicano Los Angeles, 1900–1945* (1993).
Judith Smith, *Family Connections: A History of Italian and Jewish Immigrant Lives in Providence, Rhode Island, 1900–1940* (1985).
Ronald Takaki, *Strangers from a Different Shore: A History of Asian Americans* (1989).
Mark Wyman, *Round Trip to America: The Immigrants Return to Europe, 1880–1930* (1996).

Work, Science, and Leisure

George Chauncey, *Gay New York* (1994).
John D'Emilio and Estelle Freedman, *Intimate Matters: A History of Sexuality in America* (1988).
Elaine Tyler May, *Great Expectations: Marriage and Divorce in Post-Victorian America* (1980).
Lary May, *Screening Out the Past: The Birth of Mass Culture and the Motion Picture Industry* (1980).
Stephen Meyer III, *The Five Dollar Day: Labor Management and Social Control in the Ford Motor Company, 1908–1921* (1981).
David Von Drehle, *Triangle: The Fire That Changed America* (2003).

Reformers and Radicals

Jane Addams, *Twenty Years at Hull House* (1910).
W. E. B. Du Bois, *The Souls of Black Folk* (1903).
Nan Enstad, *Ladies of Labor, Girls of Adventure: Working Women, Popular Culture, and Labor Politics and the Turn of the Twentieth Century* (1999).
Dorothy Herrmann, *Helen Keller: A Life* (1999).
Robert D. Johnston, *The Radical Middle Class: Populist Democracy and the Question of Capitalism in Progressive Era Portland, Oregon* (2003).
Louise Michelle Newman, *White Women's Rights: The Racial Origins of Feminism in the United States* (1999).
Viviana A. Zelizer, *Pricing the Priceless Child: The Changing Social Value of Children* (1985).

Expanding National Power

Kathleen Dalton, *Theodore Roosevelt: A Strenuous Life* (2002).
Richard Drinnon, *Facing West: The Metaphysics of Indian-Hating and Empire-Building* (1980).
Richard Hofstadter, *The Age of Reform* (1960).
Walter LaFeber, *The Cambridge History of American Foreign Relations: Volume 2, The American Search for Opportunity, 1865–1913* (1993).
Edmund Morris, *The Rise of Theodore Roosevelt* (2001).
Edmund Morris, *Theodore Rex* (2002).
Robert Weibe, *The Search for Order* (1966).

CHAPTER 20

War and Revolution, 1912–1920

Jacob Lawrence, *The Migration of the Negro Panel no. 57*, 1940–1941. Acquired 1942, Phillips Collection, Washington, D.C. Courtesy, Francine Seders Gallery

▲ Two million Americans experienced World War I as soldiers serving in France, while all citizens at home felt the impact of that global conflict. *Migration of the Negro* by painter Jacob Lawrence suggests the burdensome toil of southern African Americans, and why so many moved to northern cities after 1914 in search of better jobs.

CHAPTER OUTLINE

A World in Upheaval

The Great War and American Neutrality

The United States Goes to War

The Struggle to Win the Peace

Conclusion

Sites to Visit

For Further Reading

On the morning of April 6, 1909, six people arrived at the top of the world. They had fulfilled at last the dream of two generations of Arctic explorers to reach the North Pole. Exhausted from a month of walking across the treacherous ice of the Arctic Sea, they rested for 30 hours at their polar camp. Then they turned south—the only direction available—and raced for their lives against the brutal cold that threatened to kill them.

Who were these men? Four were Greenland Inuit ("Eskimos"), for whom the Arctic region was home, even if they rarely ventured out on the frozen sea that covered the last 400 miles to the Pole. Two were American. The leader of the party, Bowdoin College graduate and renowned Arctic adventurer Robert Peary, had already built a reputation as a leading figure in the explorations of the planet's last remote places. The other American to reach the North Pole that day received no such fame. Yet by the accounts of his fellow travelers, Matthew Henson was the indispensable man on the trip. A skilled dogsled driver, a master carpenter who built the expedition's shelters and fixed its sleds, and the only American on the voyage to learn the Inuit language, Henson was the one person Peary said he could not get along without. Henson was also African American. He had grown up during Reconstruction in rural Maryland and Washington, D.C. As a young man he developed a taste for exotic travel by working as a sailor on ships that took him to East Asia, North Africa, and the Black Sea.

American Robert Peary led the first expedition to reach the North Pole.

Back in Washington, Henson worked as a clerk at an exclusive fur company to which Peary brought furs from his early trips to Greenland. Despite living on opposite sides of the increasingly stark color line of Jim Crow, the two men made strongly positive impressions on each other. Peary, ten years older, hired Henson as his assistant in 1888. Over the next 21 years, as white Americans unleashed a growing torrent of violence against their black fellow citizens, these two men built a relationship of great mutual respect as they pressed northward on several journeys into the icy wilderness of the Arctic. In his intimate working relationship with Henson, Peary acted so much as an equal that he sometimes offended other white Americans on the expeditions.

American Matthew Henson accompanied Peary on the epic 1909 expedition.

Twelve years after Henson and Peary stood together to plant the American flag in the Inuit world of the far North, the relations between white and black Americans appeared in a sharply different light in Oklahoma. The former Indian Territory had become a state in 1907 and had more than 50,000 Cherokee and other Native American residents, more than any other state. The discovery at the turn of the century of vast oil reserves along the Arkansas River made Tulsa a boom town, with all the social tensions that accompany rapid growth. The vibrant African American section of the segregated city along Greenwood Avenue offered a strong example of black economic independence.

That entire community was destroyed on the night of May 31, 1921, in the largest American race riot of the twentieth century. In previous years, similar riots had erupted in St. Louis, Chicago, and elsewhere, when white resentment over black mobility and declining deference exploded around a petty pretext. In Tulsa, a false charge against a young black man of attempted rape of a white elevator operator sparked thousands of angry white Tulsans to descend on the county courthouse to seize the suspect from jail. The city's white newspaper spurred them on with an editorial titled "To Lynch Negro Tonight." But many black Tulsans were determined not to let that happen. Veterans just back from World War I insisted that their sacrifices to make the world "safe for democracy" not be marred by terrorism. A group of 75 African Americans drove down to the courthouse to defend it from the mob. Their leader was a former serviceman who, others remembered, "came back from France with exaggerated ideas of equality."

The two groups exchanged words and then gunfire. Several people fell dead. Enraged, the much larger and better-armed white crowd poured across the railroad tracks into Greenwood, shooting and burning. Rather than restraining them, the Tulsa police force deputized hundreds of the marauders with instructions to kill. In the next few hours, the invaders executed as many as 300 African Americans and burned the entire Greenwood district to the ground. Mary E. Jones Parrish, a Greenwood resident, felt as though World War I had come to her town: "The enemy had organized in the night and was invading our district, the same as the Germans invaded France and Belgium." No white Tulsans were ever punished by the law for their actions that night.

The invaders executed as many as 300 African Americans and burned the entire Greenwood district to the ground.

The decade that stretched from the discovery of the North Pole to the Tulsa race riot was marked by unusual turbulence in American life. From 1910 to 1914, optimism about solving the nation's social problems rose as reformers attempted to ameliorate some of the worst aspects of modern industrial life. International developments then turned American attentions abroad. Traumatic social revolutions swept through Mexico, China, and Russia, and the conflagration of the Great War—World War I—consumed all of Europe and eventually drew in the United States. What President Woodrow Wilson called the war "to make the world safe for democracy" encouraged people of color, both in the vast European-ruled colonies of Asia and Africa and in the segregated United States, to claim a place of greater equality. But at home the war also created pressures for conformity and intolerance for dissent. The events in Tulsa were part of a broad pattern of violence against political radicals and people of color that was rampant by 1920. The United States emerged from the war with great prestige and power, but most Americans were not yet convinced of the nation's obligations abroad, and the Versailles Treaty ending World War I failed to create a lasting structure for world peace.

A World in Upheaval

American politics between 1910 and 1920 and the U.S. involvement in World War I must be understood within the context of change and uncertainty in the international system. While world affairs were still dominated by the wealthy nations of western Europe and North America, the first wave of the great revolutions of the twentieth century was beginning to wash away much of the old order. Tensions also sharpened within the United States over traditional hierarchies of color, gender, and class. The struggle between reform and reaction pervaded public life in the United States and much of the rest of the world.

The Apex of European Conquest

On the eve of World War I, all but a quarter of the world's population lived under the rule of Europeans or their descendants. Explorations of the most remote parts of the globe filled in the last blank spaces on world maps, including the North (1909) and South (1911) Poles. A 1913 expedition led by Episcopalian missionary Hudson Stuck reached the top of Alaska's Mt. McKinley, at 20,320 feet the highest peak in North America. The granting of statehood to Arizona and New Mexico in 1912 filled out the 48 mainland states, and the country's native inhabitants began to seem to white Americans less a current threat than a piece of the past to be preserved. The U.S. Treasury issued the first Indian head nickel the following year.

Technological innovations in transportation and communication tied the world more closely together. Just as the Suez Canal (1870) and the trans-Siberian railroad (1904) linked Europe more directly to Asia, the Panama Canal (1914) cut in half the travel time by water between the East and West Coasts of the United States. Cables laid on the floor of the Atlantic Ocean in 1914 inaugurated telephone service between Europe and the United States. The first motorized flight by Orville and Wilbur Wright along the Outer Banks of North Carolina in 1903 led to transcontinental airmail service by 1920.

The competition that arose from the expansion of European power sowed the seeds of World War I. Germany, France, Britain, Italy, and Russia raced each other for new colonies and greater influence across Africa and Asia. Conflicts within Europe over disputed borders (Alsace-Lorraine) and nationalist movements (the Balkans) further heightened tensions. The central rivalry emerged between a newly unified Germany (1871) and traditionally dominant Britain. Anticipating trouble, each of the major European powers sought allies to bolster its position. Britain, France, and Russia formed the Triple **Entente** against the Triple Alliance of Germany, Austria-Hungary, and Italy. These unprecedented peacetime alliances between global empires meant that a single spark could ignite a worldwide war.

The United States emerged as a global power in this same period around the turn of the century. Fifteen years after it seized an overseas empire in 1898, the country's economic growth was stunning. U.S. consumption of energy from modern fuels (coal and oil) in 1913 equaled that of Britain, Germany, France, Russia, and Austria-Hungary combined. The United States brought a different history to the world stage. It had been born in 1776 in the first successful revolution by colonies against a European empire. Americans had long understood themselves as a people who opposed empires and supported self-government. The events of 1898 contradicted this legacy, and Americans remained ambivalent about their country's imperial venture. The U.S. Congress promised eventual independence to the Philippines in 1916 and granted U.S. citizenship to residents of Puerto Rico in 1917.

Confronting Revolutions Abroad

More than most people, President Wilson feared social upheaval. Born in 1856, he had grown up in Augusta, Georgia, amid the destruction of the Civil War, and he made his career as a political scientist and as governor of New Jersey (1910–1912) during a period of labor strife. Whatever Wilson's hopes for a stable social order at home and abroad, the global process of western capitalist expansion into decentralized, preindustrial societies was producing a widespread backlash by 1910. The first signs had already appeared of a broad rejection of the world order dominated by the white nations of Europe and North America. Ethiopia crushed an invading Italian army in 1896 in the first victory of an African state over a modern European one. In 1905 Japan destroyed the Russian army and naval fleet, putting Europeans on notice that their days of having their way in Asia were over. Harassed across eastern Europe in brutal pogroms, Jews under the leadership of Theodor Herzl founded the Zionist movement in 1897 for a national homeland in Palestine. Blacks organized the African National Congress in 1912 to struggle against racial oppression in South Africa, just as African Americans formed the National Association for the Advancement of Colored People (**NAACP**) in 1910.

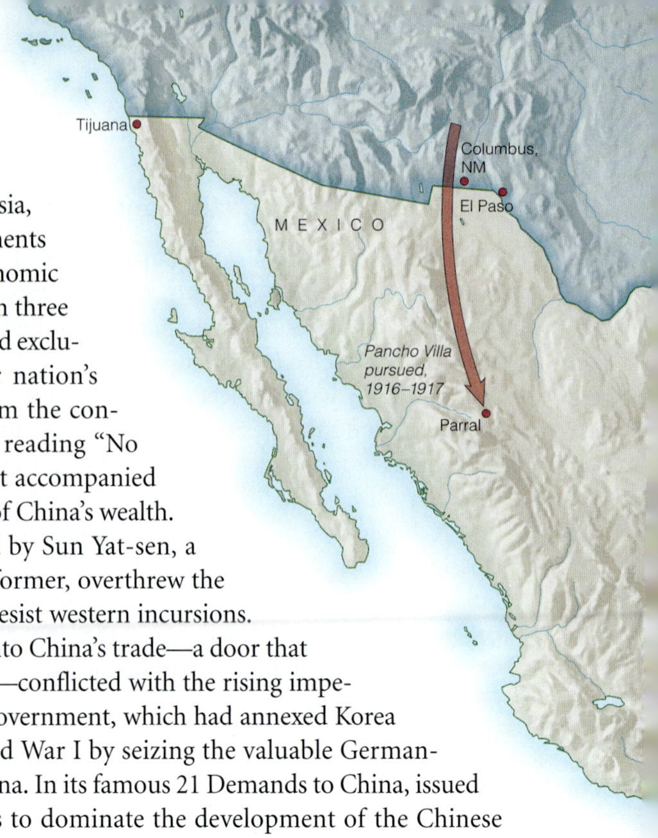

As nationalist movements in China, Russia, and Mexico overturned weak central governments controlled by foreign investors, American economic and security interests seemed to be at stake on three continents. In Asia, the Chinese deeply resented exclusive foreign enclaves that dominated their nation's coastal region and exempted foreigners from the constraints of Chinese laws. Signs in Shanghai reading "No dogs or Chinese" suggested the attitudes that accompanied European and American control of the bulk of China's wealth. In 1911 nationalist revolutionaries inspired by Sun Yat-sen, a Hawaiian-educated Christian democratic reformer, overthrew the Manchu dynasty that had proven unable to resist western incursions.

The American desire for an open door into China's trade—a door that no other powerful nation could close at will—conflicted with the rising imperial power of the region: Japan. The Tokyo government, which had annexed Korea in 1910, responded to the outbreak of World War I by seizing the valuable German-held Shantung Peninsula in northeastern China. In its famous 21 Demands to China, issued in January 1915, Japan made clear its plans to dominate the development of the Chinese economy. The American relationship with both China and Japan was undercut at home by continued discrimination and violence against immigrants from Asia, who remained ineligible for naturalization as U.S. citizens. In 1913 the California legislature passed the Alien Land Act to prevent ownership of land in the state by people "ineligible to citizenship"—people born in Asia, particularly those from Japan.

People of Asian descent on the West Coast of the United States did their best under conditions of enforced inequality. Unable to own land, Chinese immigrants eked out a daily living as migrant farm laborers or worked in laundries or restaurants. Cooks adapted their food to local tastes, creating dishes that looked Chinese but appealed to American tastes. One cook apparently created chow mein ("fried noodles") by accidentally dropping some Chinese pasta into a pot of simmering oil. The crisp, golden-brown result was a hit with his customers. David Jung opened a noodle company in Los Angeles in 1916 and is credited with inventing the fortune cookie—not a traditional Chinese dessert. Other Chinese immigrants worked as herbalists, tapping traditional Chinese medicines for a growing white clientele. Tom Leung developed a booming herbal business in Los Angeles. He also built a national mail-order business for his herbal products. Eventually he became wealthy enough to own a mansion, filled with elegant Chinese art and cared for by cooks and maids.

Revolutionary struggles with implications for America also threatened the monarchs who ruled eastern Europe. For Russians, defeat at the hands of Japan in 1905 helped precipitate a thwarted revolution in 1905 followed by two years of political turmoil. The **czar** survived to rule another decade, and thousands of political activists—unionists, anarchists, and socialists—joined a growing wave of immigration from Russia to the United States. The wave crested in 1914 at 1.2 million people, most of them from east or south of the Alps. That same year, the assassination of the heir to the Austro-Hungarian throne by a Serbian nationalist in Sarajevo in June provided the spark that ignited the Great War. Russia's defense of the Serbs put the alliance system into action as the Entente went to war with the Central Powers.

The most important region of the world for the United States before World War I was Latin America, especially Central America and the Caribbean islands. This area guarded the nation's strategic southern flank, and American citizens and corporations invested more money in Latin America than in any other region of the world. President Wilson spoke of the ability of Latin Americans to govern themselves "when properly directed" and proceeded to provide that direction. U.S. marines occupied Haiti (1915), the Dominican Republic (1916), and Cuba (1917) and maintained their earlier presence in Nicaragua to defend American-owned property and ensure that local debts

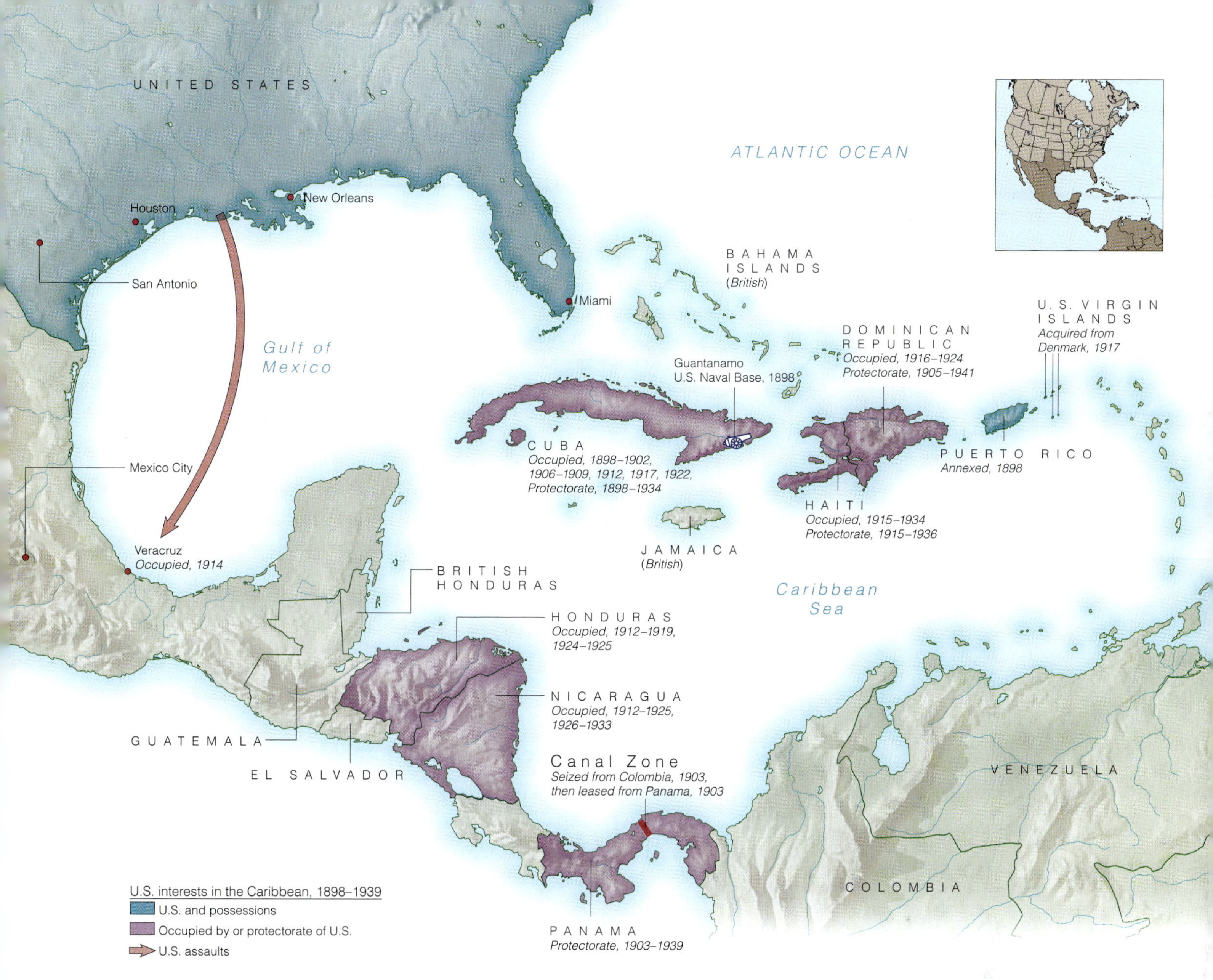

▲ **MAP 20.1 U.S. INTERESTS AND INTERVENTIONS IN THE CARIBBEAN REGION, 1898–1939**

By its size, wealth, and military power, the United States dominated the Caribbean region to its south. American capitalists invested heavily in Mexico, Central America, and the Caribbean islands, and U.S. troops often intervened to protect those investments. Puerto Rico (by acquisition from Spain) and the Panama Canal Zone (by lease from Panama) became particularly important territories ruled by the United States.

were paid to American creditors. The Bryan-Chamorro Treaty of 1916 guaranteed that no other nation would build a competitor to the Panama Canal through Nicaragua. The United States purchased the Danish Virgin Islands in 1917 to keep them out of German hands.

American anxieties about stability to the south centered on Mexico. "Land for the landless and Mexico for the Mexicans" became the slogan of revolutionaries there between 1910 and 1920. U.S. stakes in the Mexican revolution were high. American investors owned 43 percent of all Mexico's wealth (other foreigners owned another 25 percent), and more than half of the country's trade flowed north to the United States. Moreover, by 1921 Mexico became the world's second largest exporter of oil. Washington feared the spread of radical political ideas northward as almost a million Mexicans crossed their northern border during the revolutionary decade, tripling the number of Americans with recent roots south of the Rio Grande.

Many came through El Paso, the "Ellis Island" for immigrants from the south. Fleeing poverty and violence, they found both discrimination and employment. Since the Newlands Act of 1902, dam building and irrigation in the Southwest had created a boom in commercial

▲ Louis Brandeis was an extraordinary figure in early twentieth-century American life. Born in a Jewish family in Louisville, Kentucky, in 1856—when race slavery still prevailed—he excelled at Harvard Law School and became a prominent attorney in Boston, known for his sympathy for working people. He was one of the nation's leading Progressive reformers when Woodrow Wilson named him to the U.S. Supreme Court in 1916, where he served until 1939 and developed a reputation as a principled defender of free speech. Brandeis was also a strong supporter of **Zionism,** the international movement to create a Jewish state in the British-controlled territory of Palestine. Brandeis University in Waltham, Massachusetts, founded in 1948, was named in his honor.

agriculture across California and Arizona and a desperate need for farm workers. Employers often recruited south of the border. "I believe that the Mexican laborers are the solution to our common labor problem in this country," one cotton company executive told President Wilson. It was not an easy life, especially for women who had to balance paid employment with taking care of families. Grace Luna remembered picking cotton in Madera, California, where women scaled ladders with 100 pounds of cotton on their backs and "some carried their kids on top of their picking sacks." Most immigrants sought unskilled positions, but members of Mexico's professional classes—teachers, architects, and lawyers—also came north, for political asylum. The new arrivals joined Mexican Americans who had lived in the region since it was part of Mexico. They had not crossed the border; in 1848, the border had crossed them.

Wilson sought unsuccessfully to reestablish in Mexico a political order respectful of the rights of foreign property owners. Wilson twice sent U.S. troops into Mexico, at Veracruz in April 1914 to block a German arms shipment and then in pursuit of Francisco ("Pancho") Villa and his army after their 1916 assault on Columbus, New Mexico. The American forces under General John J. Pershing withdrew in early 1917 as the president prepared to enter the much larger war in Europe. Land redistribution and national control of the country's abundant mineral wealth, particularly oil, were written into Mexico's new constitution passed a few days later, and the revolutionary upheaval ended by 1920.

Conflicts over Hierarchies at Home

Just as social upheaval threatened monarchies and international investors abroad, less privileged Americans contested traditional lines of hierarchy and control in the United States. For example, racial lines were not always clear. Native-born whites continued to disagree about whether the millions of new immigrants from eastern and southern Europe were also "white." Anthropologists led by Franz Boas at Columbia University began to question the supposed significance of racial differences. Americans of all colors applauded the spectacular successes of Native American athlete Jim Thorpe at the 1912 Olympic Games in Sweden. In 1916 Wilson appointed Louis Brandeis as the first Jewish justice of the Supreme Court, but that same year anxieties about the future of white supremacy found a voice in the popular new book of a conservative New York intellectual named Madison Grant. *The Passing of the Great Race,* a bigoted sociology tract, identified Jesus as "Nordic" to distance the central figure of the Christian faith from the many new Jewish immigrants in America.

The Wilson administration's "New Freedom" slogan did not apply to African Americans, who faced continuing discrimination in employment and housing. The president filled his cabinet with white Southerners who segregated the few federal agencies that had employed blacks. When Wilson took office, African Americans continued to be murdered publicly by vigilante mobs across the South at a rate of more than one person per week. But the president ignored requests from the recently formed NAACP for an antilynching law, and the United States remained one of the few societies in which human beings were burned at the stake. The historian-president endorsed D. W. Griffith's 1915 film *Birth of a Nation* as "history written with lightning." Griffith, a Kentucky-born champion of the "Lost Cause" of slavery in the South, had created a racist blockbuster that celebrated the Ku Klux Klan of the 1860s and helped inspire the Klan's rebirth that fall at Stone Mountain, Georgia.

Women of all colors lived under particular burdens of discrimination. Their uniquely intimate relationships—as daughters, wives, mothers—with those who did not treat them as equals

Library of Congress

▲ **In February 1917, as the United States broke relations with Germany and began to prepare to enter World War I, supporters of women's suffrage continued to picket on the sidewalk outside the White House. College women joined the effort to ensure that winning liberty at home would go hand in hand with fighting for democracy abroad.**

complicated their efforts at reform. So did their dilemma about women's roles in society: some sought full legal equality with men, and others wanted special protections for women on the grounds that they were fundamentally different. At issue was the nature of women's political identity. Was their primary identification in their attachment to individual men or to the nation? American women lost their U.S. citizenship by marrying a foreigner, whereas American men did not. A growing chorus of female activists rejected this kind of double standard and focused on the key issue of **suffrage.**

American women's long struggle to vote came to a head in this decade. By 1912, a growing number of European nations and nine American states, all in the West, granted the franchise to citizens of both sexes. Jeannette Rankin, a Republican feminist and pacifist from Montana, won election in 1916 as the nation's first female member of Congress. But suffragists varied in the tactics they believed most effective for winning the vote. The moderate National American Women Suffrage Association under the leadership of Carrie Chapman Catt worked within the political system, building an alliance with President Wilson after he endorsed women's suffrage in 1916 and supporting the U.S. entry into World War I the next year. Alice Paul and other militants formed the National Women's Party and opposed the war effort as inherently undemocratic because half the adult population could not vote. In 1917 five picketers were imprisoned for seven months for obstructing traffic in front of the White House; despite brutal force-feedings, Paul and Rose Winslow persisted in a hunger strike so "that women fighting for liberty may be considered political prisoners." In 1918 suffragist organizers helped elect a more sympathetic Congress that passed the Nineteenth Amendment, ending sex discrimination in voting two years later.

Contention over women's social roles also divided Americans. Traditionalists promoted the declaration of the first Mother's Day in 1913. The desire to provide special protections for women resulted in the Sheppard-Towner Act of 1921, which expanded the role of the new federal Children's Bureau in providing infant and maternal health services. The struggle over contraception foreshadowed the conflict over abortion that dominated women's politics in the last quarter of the twentieth century. Socialist Margaret Sanger campaigned for women's access to contraception, opening the nation's first birth control clinic in Brooklyn in 1916. Sanger's experiences as a public health nurse with working-class New Yorkers convinced her that controlling pregnancy was the central issue for helping women gain greater autonomy. Unable to separate sexual experience from reproduction and facing poverty and unsanitary living conditions, married women in the lower classes suffered frequent pregnancies and the often debilitating and sometimes fatal consequences of abortion, an illegal but common operation. Sanger reached a turning point after hearing the joking response of a physician to the desperate plea of one frail 28-year-old mother of three for help in preventing another pregnancy: "Tell Jake to sleep on the roof!" Sanger was appalled, and the young woman's subsequent death as a result of a botched abortion pushed Sanger to begin her crusade for contraception.

Most adult Americans—workers—continued to find themselves in frequent conflict with the owners who employed them. Industrial capitalism's efficiency produced great material wealth, but 60 percent of it belonged to 2 percent of the population, whereas two-thirds of Americans owned only 2 percent of the wealth. The anticapitalist aspirations of the Socialist party and the Industrial Workers of the World (IWW) frightened both industrialists and the more conservative labor leaders of the American Federation of Labor (AFL), especially when the western-based IWW led two major strikes in the East, one a success in Lawrence, Massachusetts, in 1912 and the other a failure in Paterson, New Jersey, in 1913. The campaign against a wage cut at the vast Lawrence textile factory was especially impressive in uniting 20,000 workers of 40 different national backgrounds.

Some owners sought to undercut union campaigns by providing better working conditions and even company-run "unions." These carrots of concession were accompanied by the stick of force. Bolstered by sympathetic federal courts and state governors, companies usually refused to negotiate with workers who went on strike. This pattern reached a shocking climax on Easter night in 1914 outside Ludlow, Colorado, in a mining camp owned by John D. Rockefeller Jr.'s Colorado Fuel and Iron Company. State militia and company guards broke a strike there with torches and machine guns, burning the miners' tent colony and killing 2 women and 11 children. A

Denver Public Library, Western History Collection

▲ **Children of the striking coal miners gather in their tent colony outside Ludlow on the high plains of south central Colorado, at the base of the mountains of the Front Range. Winter snows and cold temperatures made for a difficult life, as did the grueling and dangerous work of mining coal that was common across the state. Miners' children died with their mothers and fathers in the Ludlow massacre on April 20, 1914.**

Southern Colorado and Northern New Mexico

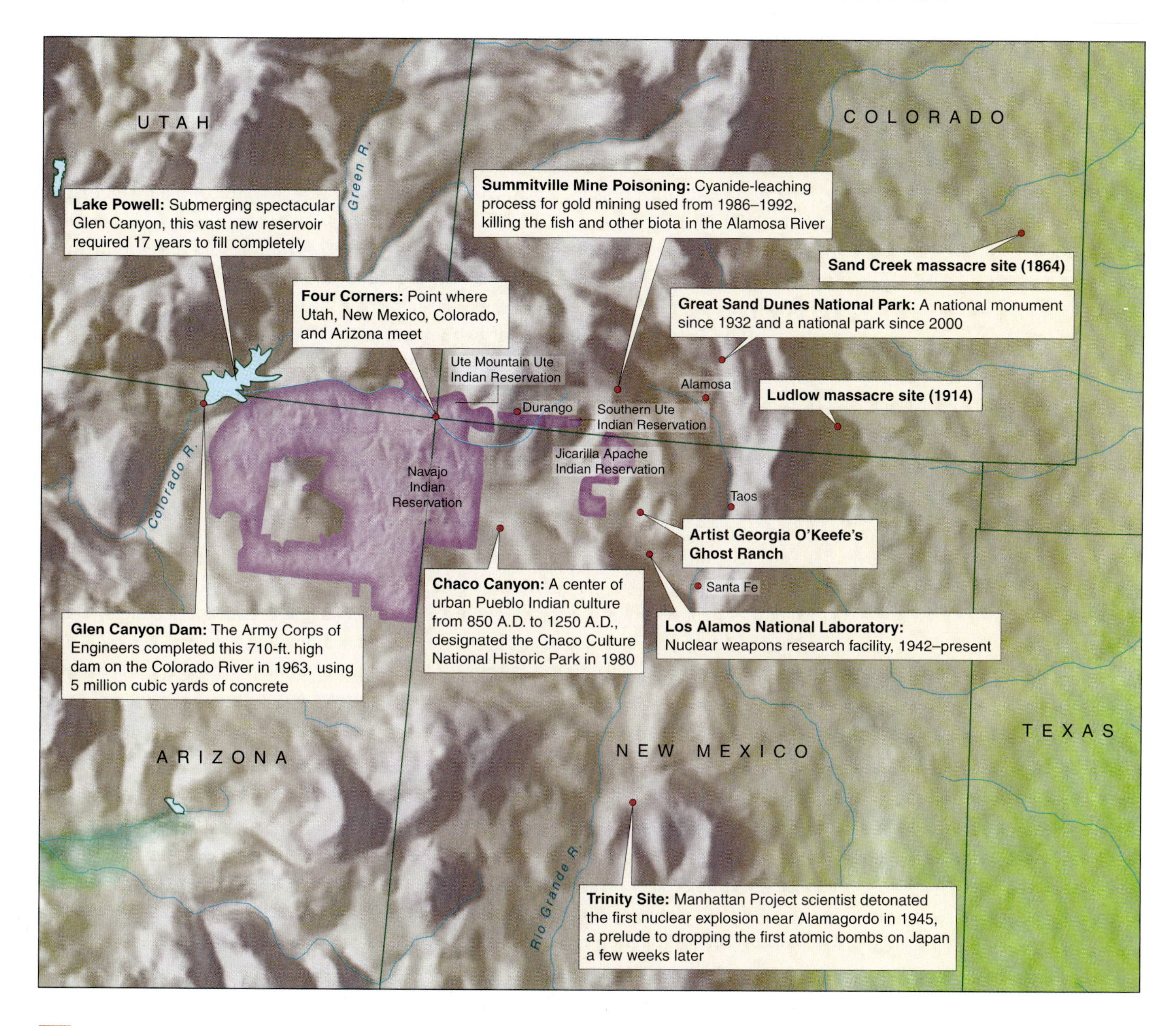

The mountainous region of southern Colorado and northern New Mexico in the 1910s had an economy based on ranching, mining, and lumbering—like much of the rural West. A large Indian population included Navajo, Apache, Pueblo, and Ute. Since the 1920s, Santa Fe and Taos supported important communities of artists enchanted by the area's natural beauty. That same beauty attracted growing numbers of visitors later in the twentieth century, including a wave of counterculture youth in the late 1960s and early 1970s. By the beginning of the new millennium, the tourist trade surpassed older extractive industries as the chief source of employment in much of the mountainous West. This change began to alter the region's traditional political stance of supporting exploitation of natural resources regardless of the environmental impact, whether soil erosion from clear-cutting and overgrazing or water pollution from hard-rock mining. Tourists and new residents, many of them affluent retirees and second-home owners, valued scenery and recreation above all. The image of rural Westerners as primarily cowboys and miners faded more slowly. ■

total of 66 strikers and strike supporters died before federal troops eventually restored order. Ludlow recalled the actions of the Colorado militia exactly 50 years earlier, when it had destroyed the Cheyenne Indian camp at Sand Creek. Immigrant coal miners and their families had replaced Native Americans as the apparent threat to Colorado's social order.

Such brutality by owners against workers appalled most Americans. The Wilson administration slowly began supporting the right of laborers to organize for collective bargaining with their employers. Wilson's strong backing from Samuel Gompers and the AFL in the 1912 election initiated the modern alliance between labor and the Democratic party. The president named William B. Wilson, a U.S. congressman from Pennsylvania and a former labor activist with the Knights of Labor and the United Mine Workers, to head the new U.S. Department of Labor, the permanent agency established "to foster, promote and develop the welfare of working people" by improving their working conditions and mediating labor disputes. The president appointed labor lawyer Frank Walsh to chair the separate short-term U.S. Committee on Industrial Relations, which for two years explored the causes of industrial violence in public hearings. Walsh even grilled Rockefeller about the events at Ludlow, embarrassing the corporate titan by revealing his close involvement and clear responsibility for what happened.

The Great War and American Neutrality

Most Americans had roots of some kind in Europe and had long defined themselves in relation to life on "the continent." But they also considered themselves part of the New World that was separate from the Old World of kings, castles, and rigid social classes. When Europe stepped off the precipice in August 1914 into a war larger than any previously fought or imagined, few Americans wanted any part of it. Make "no entangling alliances," George Washington had urged his fellow citizens. Europeans must stay out of our hemisphere, the Monroe Doctrine had declared. But international ties ultimately proved too important to the well-being of Americans for the country to remain indefinitely on the sidelines of World War I.

"The One Great Nation at Peace"

When war came in 1914, Italy switched sides, joining Britain, France, and Russia to form the Allied Powers, or Allies. The Ottoman Empire—modern Turkey—joined Germany and Austria-Hungary, forming the Central Powers. Americans were stunned as "civilized" Europe slid into savage conflict. "The lamps are going out all over Europe," British Foreign Secretary Edward Grey observed. "We shall not see them lit again in our lifetime." Following traditional U.S. policy, Wilson urged Americans to remain neutral "in fact as well as in name" to promote an eventual "peace without victory."

"The lamps are going out all over Europe," British Foreign Secretary Edward Grey observed. "We shall not see them lit again in our lifetime."

Neutrality was profitable. Wilson stoutly defended the rights of neutrals to trade with belligerents, the same principle that had led the United States into the War of 1812 against England. American industries depended on overseas trade, he believed, and "they will burst their jackets if they cannot find a free outlet to the markets of the world." After the recession of 1913–1914, war-related demands from abroad for American farm and factory products jump-started the economy. In the course of World War I, American bankers extended $10 billion in loans to the Allies (primarily Britain and France), and the United States changed from a debtor nation to the world's largest creditor.

The nature of the fighting in Europe bolstered the American determination to avoid being drawn into the conflict. Industrialized warfare brought fiendish new ways to kill human beings, including machine guns and poison gas. Gone were the days of bold maneuvers and dashing cavalry charges; now was the time of trench warfare, with its unrelenting misery, terror, and helplessness. Eight and a half million young men lost their lives and another 21 million were wounded, devastating an entire generation of European society.

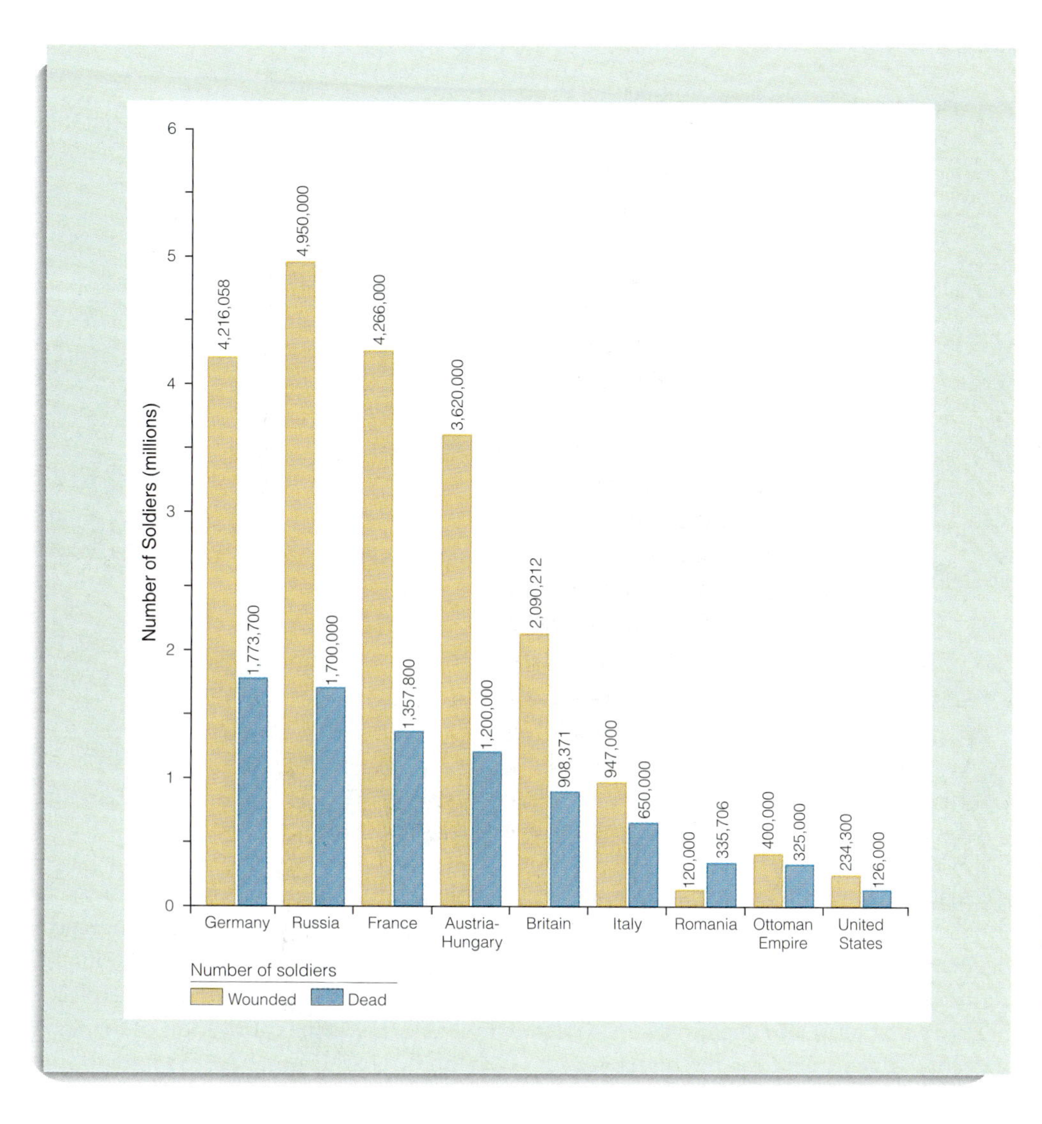

◀ **FIGURE 20.1**
CASUALTIES OF THE GREAT WAR, 1914–1918 Compared to the European combatants who fought for several years, the United States suffered far fewer casualties in its 18 months in World War I.

Eight million civilians also died as a result of the fighting, and an international outbreak of influenza in 1918 killed another 20 million around the world. Continuous shelling rendered whole sections of the landscape of northern France a wasteland. Prewar optimism about human progress swiftly disappeared.

In the United States, neutrality also made political sense. Immigrants from every part of Europe lived and voted in the United States, so Americans had blood ties to all the belligerents. Commercial and political elites tended to identify with Britain and France, as did many other Americans. But among two of the largest groups of Americans, those with roots in Germany and Ireland, many took a different view. Few Irish Americans equated England with the cause of democracy after centuries of British rule in Ireland, and London's severe repression of the 1916 Easter Rising in Dublin underscored their case. The sheer scale of the immigrant stream to the United States between 1900 and 1914 reinforced the need to avoid Europe's conflicts. Native-born white Americans were already concerned with preserving unity in their increasingly varied and urban society. Allowing in the hatreds from Europe's battlefields would only exacerbate the ethnic and class tensions that worried social reformers and many politicians, including President Wilson.

Reform Priorities at Home

Americans traditionally considered powerful government a primary threat to individual liberty, but the rise of mammoth corporations at the start of the twentieth century altered that

▶ A former professor and university president, Woodrow Wilson was the only holder of a Ph.D. to become president of the United States. He was also the first native Southerner elected to the Oval Office since before the Civil War. Wilson's self-confidence and tendency toward self-righteousness alienated some citizens, but a majority found him to be a compelling public speaker.

Hulton|Archive/Getty Images

calculation. Competition was disappearing, particularly in critical sectors of the economy such as oil production and railroads. Laissez-faire policies, by which federal agencies encouraged economic expansion, were no longer adequate; only government could balance the new might of the largest companies. This meant modest regulation of some aspects of the marketplace. Wilson's first term also encouraged such democratic reforms as the ratification of the Seventeenth Amendment for the direct popular election of U.S. senators (1913), previously chosen by state legislatures. Until American entry into the Great War in 1917 turned the nation to a very different task, this period marked the climax of the first chapter of twentieth-century liberalism.

Three areas topped the Wilson administration's reform agenda: taxes, the money system, and monopolies. The Underwood-Simmons Tariff of 1913 cut duties—taxes—on imported goods by almost one-half, helping American consumers and promoting freer trade. The Sixteenth Amendment (1913) allowed a federal income tax, which the 1916 Revenue Act put into effect. This was a progressive tax, one that took a larger percentage of the income of the rich than it took from the poor. The legislation also levied higher taxes on corporate profits and created the first federal estate tax on inheritances. Though small, a tax on inheritances supported the principle of equality of opportunity. It implied that children of the wealthy should not receive an enormous head start in life and that Americans growing up without an inheritance should not be handicapped by the large inequalities among past generations.

Congress moved to regulate money in another new way as well. The absence of a centrally managed money system had long contributed to the exaggerated boom-and-bust cycles in the American economy. The Federal Reserve Act of 1913 created a system of 12 Federal Reserve Banks to control the amount of currency in circulation, increasing it in deflationary times and decreasing it when inflation threatened. The system aimed to abolish economic depressions and prevent bank closures. It did not fully succeed, as the years after 1929 showed, but the Federal Reserve System stabilized the American banking industry and helped position the dollar to become the central global currency.

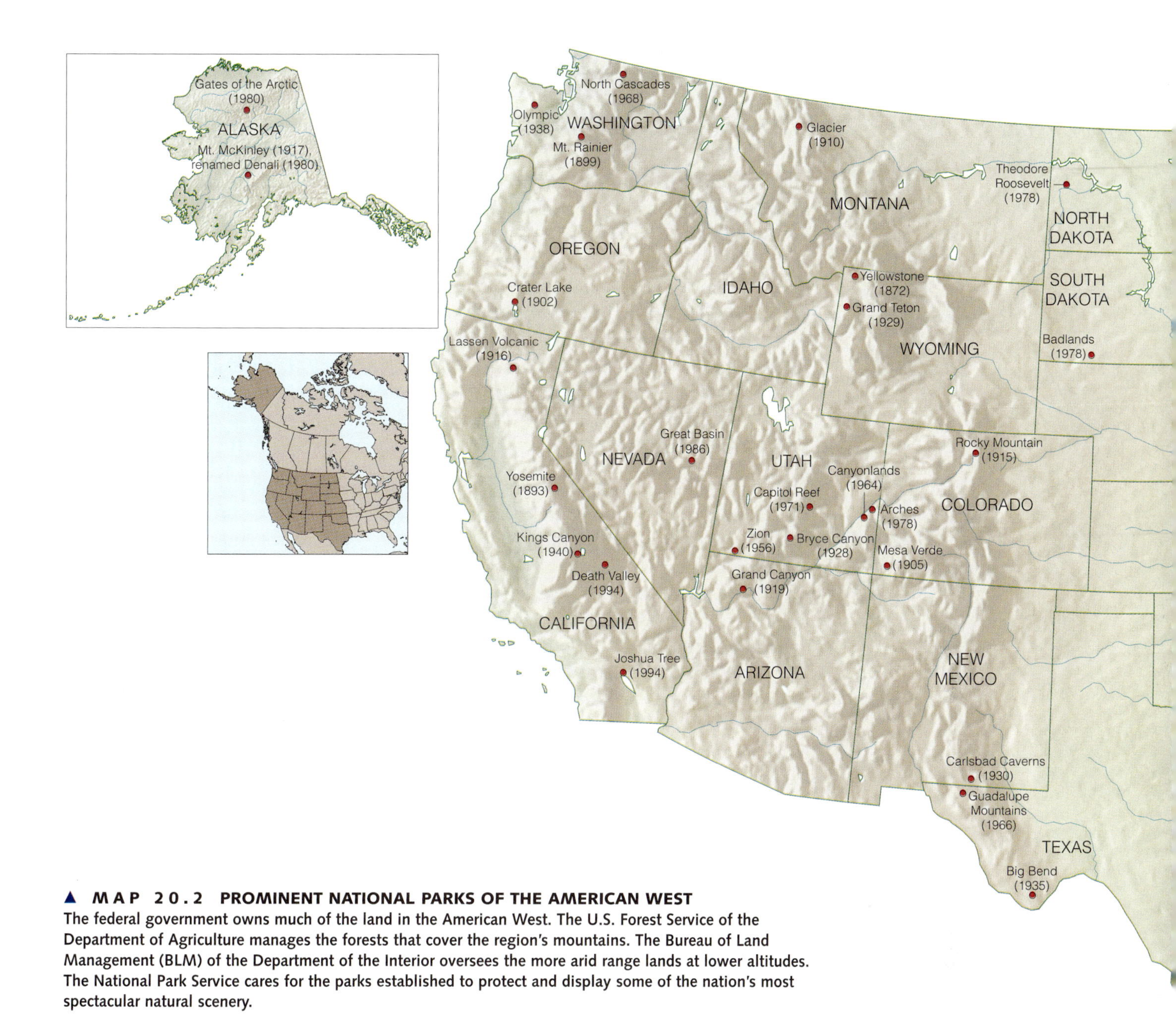

▲ **MAP 20.2 PROMINENT NATIONAL PARKS OF THE AMERICAN WEST**
The federal government owns much of the land in the American West. The U.S. Forest Service of the Department of Agriculture manages the forests that cover the region's mountains. The Bureau of Land Management (BLM) of the Department of the Interior oversees the more arid range lands at lower altitudes. The National Park Service cares for the parks established to protect and display some of the nation's most spectacular natural scenery.

No issue so dominated American politics between 1913 and 1915 as the tension between huge new corporations and the nation's antimonopoly tradition. The size and market share of companies such as U.S. Steel, American Tobacco, and Du Pont (chemicals) inhibited competition, just as Microsoft dominated computer software at the end of the twentieth century. Investigations by a congressional committee chaired by Arsene Pujo in 1913 revealed the concentration of financial power in the hands of J. P. Morgan and a few other New York bankers, dubbed the Money Trust. Congress created the Federal Trade Commission (1914) to investigate business practices that unfairly prevented competition. The Clayton Anti-Trust Act of 1914 supplemented the 1890 Sherman Anti-Trust Act by outlawing specific unfair business practices such as local price cutting and granting rebates to undermine competitors. The Clayton Act also delighted the AFL by declaring that unions should not be "construed to be illegal combinations in restraint of trade." Most federal judges remained unsympathetic to unions, but they could no longer wield the Sherman Act against striking workers rather than against the corporate trusts it had originally intended to target.

The early years after 1910 witnessed the rise of legislation to protect particular groups of citizens, especially women, children, and certain workers. States led the way, with half by

1913 passing workers' compensation laws to provide assistance to workers injured on the job and their families. Many states passed laws banning child labor. The Adamson Act (1916), providing for an eight-hour day for railroad workers, was the first case of the federal government regulating the hours of workers in the private sector.

Another kind of protective legislation focused on conservation through the preservation of natural landscapes. An increasingly urban, industrial society looked to its most beautiful rural places for solace. Local and state governments set aside parklands throughout the Progressive Era. Wilson followed in Theodore Roosevelt's conservationist footsteps by creating the National Park Service in 1916 to provide unified management of such new national treasures as Glacier National Park in Montana (1910), Rocky Mountain National Park in Colorado (1915), Lassen Volcanic National Park in California (1916), and Acadia National Park in Maine (1919).

The Great Migration

The Progressive Era of 1900–1920 was anything but progressive from the viewpoint of many African Americans. White mob violence reached its apex in these years, with hundreds of lynchings and dozens of race riots. Most African Americans lived in the South, where segregation and discrimination trapped the majority in poverty. Many therefore seized the unprecedented opportunity offered by the outbreak of the Great War. War-related orders created huge needs for workers in northern factories, and the war also closed the spigot of European immigration, drying up the standard source of new labor. Along with other cities, Chicago and Detroit became centers of the **Great Migration** of more than half a million African Americans out of Dixie during the war years.

Encouraged by black newspapers such as the *Chicago Defender* and sometimes assisted by northern labor recruiters, black Southerners wanted to go "where a man is a man" regardless of his color. They still found plenty of discrimination in the urban North. But the large black communities of Philadelphia, Cleveland, and New York offered far greater independence

Historical Pictures/Stock Montage, Inc.

▶ **A migrant family from the South arriving in Chicago, c. 1916. Southerners of all colors, like Europeans, were drawn by the lure of better jobs to the industrial cities of the American Northeast and Midwest. With immigration from Europe slowed to a trickle by the onset of World War I, industry's demand for southern immigrants increased sharply.**

than the rural South they left behind. Here "I don't have to humble to no one," one former Southerner wrote home. African Americans could vote, earn higher wages, send their children to better schools, and even sit where they wanted on streetcars. One woman newly arrived in Chicago was stunned the first time she boarded a trolley and saw black people sitting next to whites. "I just held my breath, for I thought any minute they would start something. Then I saw nobody notices it, and I just thought this is a real place for Negroes."

African American Population, 1910 and 1950

The Great Migration fit in a broader pattern of oppressed peoples seeking greater freedom and opportunity in the industrial workplaces of the American North. African Americans could not change their color and escape from discrimination, as could ethnic Europeans such as Irish, Italians, and Jews who struggled successfully against widespread prejudice to be identified as "white" (while still enduring elements of discrimination). But black Southerners moving to northern cities in pursuit of work and liberty acted much as European immigrants had, and they joined other newcomers seeking urban work. The 1920 U.S. Census showed for the first time a majority of Americans living in towns and cities of at least 2,500 people.

When war in Europe shut off most Atlantic immigration after 1914, it opened the door to newcomers who did not have to cross the submarine-infested ocean. Blacks who boarded trains for the North were joined by a similar number of white Southerners leaving rural poverty to look for jobs. A small stream of French Canadians found work in New England factories. A much larger stream of Mexicans and Mexican Americans flowed to jobs across the American Southwest and Midwest. Like African Americans, who had been leaving the South since the Civil War, people of Mexican descent had been moving across the American West for economic reasons since the mid-nineteenth century. World War I and the Mexican Revolution increased their numbers sharply, with the growing cities of Los Angeles, San Antonio, and El Paso remaining particular magnets for new immigrants. The number of Mexican Americans in Los Angeles soared from 6,000 in 1910 to nearly 100,000 in 1930.

Limits to American Neutrality

A steady undertow of interests and inclinations pulled against American neutrality after 1914. Most Americans who paid attention to events abroad favored the Allies over the Central Powers. The diversity of Americans' ethnic roots across Europe, Africa, Asia, and Latin America could not mask fundamental cultural and linguistic connections to England, the one-time "mother country." President Wilson deeply admired British political values and institutions, and most influential newspaper editors supported the British cause. Even Americans critical of the British Empire did not want to see the European continent under the autocratic rule of German Kaiser Wilhelm II.

Bishop Museum

▲ Workers of Japanese descent pause from their labor on a sugar cane plantation in Koloa, Kauai, in the Hawaiian Islands, c. 1916. Women and men labored side by side in the cane fields, as in the *ho hana* (hoe cultivation) team. Like African Americans moving from the South to northern cities for better work opportunities during World War I, migrants from Japan and other parts of Asia moved east to the U.S. territory of Hawaii in search of better farming options.

Concrete economic interests also tied the United States to the Allied side. During three years of neutrality, American bankers lent 85 times as much to the Allied nations as to the

Central Powers ($2.3 billion versus $27 million). Opponents of American entry into the war later pointed out that bankers and weapon makers had lobbied for joining the British cause, which fattened their wallets. But millions of other Americans also benefited from the nation's trade with Britain and France. Large corporations reaped the bulk of the profits, and agricultural and industrial workers earned decent wages in filling Allied war orders.

Certain powerful Americans, concentrated on the East Coast, tried from the start to prepare the country for entering the war. They emphasized that the U.S. military was much smaller than the forces of European states because of Americans' traditional aversion to large standing armies. Republicans such as Theodore Roosevelt and former Secretary of State Elihu Root led the war preparedness movement, which sought to pressure new immigrants into "100 percent Americanism" and to establish universal military training as "the only way to yank the hyphen out of America."

Progressives split over the war. More radical reformers opposed joining it as a matter of principle. "Let the capitalists do their own fighting and furnish their own corpses," socialist Eugene Debs wrote in 1914, "and there will never be another war on the face of the earth." Settlement house leader Jane Addams and black labor organizer A. Philip Randolph likewise opposed the war throughout, as did writer Randolph Bourne. They feared, presciently, that going to war would take the wind out of the sails of domestic reform.

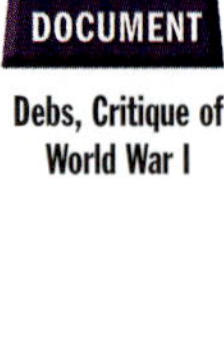

Debs, Critique of World War I

Most Progressives followed President Wilson's leadership, opposing U.S. involvement in Europe at first but gradually shifting to support it. Roosevelt's return to mainstream Republicanism and his enthusiasm for war left Wilson the standard-bearer of Progressivism in the 1916 election. This allowed the president to squeak by conservative Republican nominee Charles Evans Hughes, winning a second term in the White House. "He kept us out of war," his supporters declared, but Wilson himself was less optimistic. He knew where German submarine warfare might lead: "Any little German lieutenant can put us into the war at any time by some calculated outrage."

The United States Goes to War

Like Lyndon Johnson in 1964 regarding Vietnam, Wilson won reelection as a liberal reformer and a man of peace, only to go to war within six months. On April 2, 1917, Wilson asked Congress for a declaration of war against Germany "to make the world safe for democracy." Congress agreed by a large majority, and four days later the United States entered the Great War. Mobilization went slowly; it took almost a year before American soldiers in large numbers saw combat in the trenches of northern France. But troops of the Allied nations took heart from the knowledge that the Yanks were finally coming. American foodstuffs and munitions arrived more quickly, as did American naval ships protecting cargo vessels bound for England. The U.S. entry into the war ultimately provided the narrow margin of victory against the Central Powers.

The Logic of Belligerency

Wilson's War Message to Congress

Wilson's insistence on the traditional rights of neutral nations to trade with belligerents clashed with German and British efforts to prevent trade destined for their enemy. The German use of the new submarines, or U-boats (from the German *Unterseeboote*), against superior British surface forces pulled Americans into the war. Submarines were extremely vulnerable when not submerged. Before firing on a merchant or passenger ship that might be armed or carrying contraband (war materials), they refused to surface and warn civilian passengers—as required under international law—to evacuate on lifeboats. With Britain arming merchant ships and stowing munitions in the holds of passenger ships, U-boats were the key element in the German campaign to weaken the enemy. The British navy, in turn, seized American goods bound

HultonlArchive/Getty Images

▲ **The body of a soldier lies caught in barbed wire in the "no man's land" between opposing trenches on the western front. Technological advances in weaponry helped make the fighting vastly more destructive in World War I than in previous wars. The sheer scale of the slaughter stunned combatants and observers, both in Europe and America, and helped turn many in the postwar generation to deep skepticism regarding the use of military force.**

for Germany. But Britain's blockade of the German coastline and neutral ports nearby did not endanger civilians in the same way. "One deals with life; the other with property," Secretary of State Robert Lansing explained.

The deaths of civilians without warning on the high seas shocked and angered the American public, especially the sinking of the magnificent British ocean liner *Lusitania* in May 1915, which killed 128 U.S. citizens and a thousand others. However, some Americans believed Wilson to be less than neutral in negotiating with the British over their offenses while giving ultimatums to Germany. Lansing's predecessor as secretary of state, William Jennings Bryan, resigned in June 1915 to protest the president's manner of defending American trading rights. Bryan found both sides—stalemated and unable to gain victory in the trenches—reprehensible for trying to win by killing "noncombatant men, women, and children." Only their methods differed: Germany drowned innocent civilians; England starved them with its blockade. Hoping not to draw the United States into the war, the German government twice put its unrestricted submarine warfare on hold (the *Arabic* pledge of September 1915 and the *Sussex* pledge of May 1916). By January 1917 the British blockade had reduced German food rations per person to less than half the prewar level. Facing imminent starvation, Berlin decided to take one last chance with unrestricted submarine warfare. The German government calculated that it could force a British and French surrender before enough American assistance arrived.

Preparing for war with the Americans, German Ambassador Arthur Zimmermann secretly offered German aid to the revolutionary Mexican government "to reconquer the lost territory in Texas, New Mexico, and Arizona" if it joined the Central Powers. Mexico declined, but the Zimmermann telegram leaked to the press on March 1 and outraged Americans. The German threat seemed finally to have reached American soil. One last hindrance to joining the Allies disappeared with the revolution that same month in Russia, which replaced the monarchy with a social democratic government, which Wilson called "a fit partner for a league of honor." The president could now more genuinely call for a war to make the world "safe for democracy," with France a republic and Britain ruled by Parliament.

▶ European demand for war-related goods brought the U.S. economy out of the deep recession of 1913–1914 and created hundreds of thousands of new jobs. U.S. entry into the war in April 1917 took several million men into the armed forces, opening better-paying opportunities in manufacturing to many women. Four workers at the Westinghouse Electric Company pause from their labors in 1918.

Courtesy, Hagley Museum and Library (Neg. #69.170.13,622)

Still jealous of American autonomy and wary of close identification with the French, British, and Russian empires, however, Wilson took the nation into war as an "Associated" power rather than a full-blown member of the Entente. The president believed that the United States, unique among the belligerents, sought only to defend principles rather than to acquire territory, assuring it of distinctive moral leadership at an eventual postwar peace conference. "We have no quarrel with the German people" but only with the "Prussian autocracy" whose U-boats were engaged in "a warfare against mankind," Wilson declared in calling Americans to a great crusade in Europe. "We desire no conquest, no dominion," but merely to be "one of the champions of the rights of mankind."

Mobilizing the Home Front

Going to war entailed a complete reorientation of the American economy. For the U.S. Army and Navy to succeed abroad, mass production of war materials had to be centrally planned, and only the federal government could fulfill this role. Such an expansion of government regulation fit with the broader agenda of Progressive reform. Federal agencies could mediate some of the tensions between capital and labor as they focused on ensuring adequate food, clothing, and weapons for the troops at the front.

The Wilson administration created several new agencies to manage the war effort at home. The Selective Service Act established local boards to draft young men into the military. The U.S. Railroad Administration took control of the nation's primary transportation system to solve railroad tie-ups caused by heavy demands for war materials. The War Industries Board supervised all war-related production, allowing large manufacturers to coordinate their schedules without fear of antitrust action. The War Labor Board resolved disputes between workers and employers, providing the most advanced solution to industrial conflict before the New Deal of the 1930s. The Committee on Public Information (CPI), run by Progressive journalist George Creel, provided the government's version of information about the war. The CPI had the crucial task of inspiring and maintaining public support for Wilson's war policies.

The close cooperation between industry and government, combined with strong demand for American goods from the Allied governments, caused corporate earnings to soar. Cost-plus contracts guaranteed profits by eliminating competition and risk. "We are all making more money out of this war than the average human being ought to," one steel company official admitted privately. And some of the war gains were spread, for a collaborative effort entailed keeping workers productive and content. Taking a position unprecedented in the U.S. government, the War Labor Board promoted an 8-hour workday and the right of workers to form unions. But even as the economy bustled, social unity proved elusive, especially when word of American casualties arrived from Europe.

Ensuring Unity

The deaths of U.S. soldiers and sailors made support for the war an emotional issue, and a pattern of repressing dissent took hold that outlasted the war itself. Everything German was particularly suspect. Several states banned teaching the German language (Nebraska briefly banned teaching any foreign language, even Latin). Sauerkraut became "liberty cabbage," frankfurters became hot dogs, and many German Americans anglicized their names. Temperance reformers cited German beer drinking in their successful campaign for a constitutional prohibition of alcohol production. Congress approved the controversial Eighteenth Amendment in December 1917 as a way to save grain for the war effort, and the states ratified it in 1919. Anti-German sentiment led to sometimes deadly violence against Americans of German descent by the summer of 1918. Congress passed sharply restrictive immigration legislation in 1917 as anti-German feelings fed broader prewar fears of new immigrants.

Buffington, "Friendly Words to the Foreign Born"

A wave of discontent among working Americans redoubled anxieties about national unity. The draft and reduced immigration thinned the ranks of labor as the war created a greater need for workers. For the first time in memory, laborers could choose between jobs, and corporations were dismayed by rising employee turnover rates. Workers worried about inflation, which doubled between 1914 and 1920. Seeking better wages and more control over the workplace, they joined unions and went out on 6,000 strikes during the year and a half in which the United States was in the war. Working-class women and men identified their cause with the war for democracy abroad by calling for the "de-Kaisering of industry" at home.

The Speech That Sent Debs to Jail

Industrialists saw the strikers differently. "All they seem to think of is money," one complained, mirroring what workers often said of employers. Anti-unionists tried to tar all of organized labor with the brush of disloyalty. The government passed the Espionage Act (1917) and Sedition Act (1918) to ban written and verbal organizing against the war. Socialists who encouraged draft resistance, such as Eugene Debs and Wisconsin Congressman Victor Berger, went to prison. The Supreme Court in *Schenck v. United States* (1919) upheld restrictions on free speech in the case of a "clear and present danger" to the nation's security. The Justice Department worked closely with private "patriotic" organizations such as the National Security League, which helped spy on potential dissidents.

Hostility to unions mixed with fervent prowar sentiment to produce a devastating campaign against labor activists in the West. Along the Rocky Mountains from Montana to the Mexican border, striking copper miners under IWW leadership found federal, state, and local police forces as well as vigilantes lined up against them. Sheriff Harry Wheeler of Bisbee, Arizona, arrested more than a thousand strikers, many of them Mexican Americans suspected of sympathies with Pancho Villa. Wheeler, a former Rough Rider with Theodore Roosevelt in Cuba, locked the strikers into boxcars in the July heat of 1917 and towed them into the southern New Mexico desert before releasing them. Federal agents eviscerated the antiwar IWW by raiding its offices two months later and putting 166 of its leaders on trial. A visiting British coal-mining executive found "hostility to a quite unbelievable extent against organized labor."

Most African Americans agreed with W. E. B. Du Bois's call to "close our ranks shoulder to shoulder" with white fellow citizens in support of the war effort, despite escalating antiblack violence. The arrival of 300,000 to 500,000 black Southerners in northern cities increased competition for jobs and housing, causing resentment among many whites. Employers contributed to tensions by recruiting African Americans as strikebreakers and pitting them against white workers. Whites rioted in East St. Louis on July 1, 1917, causing at least 47 fatalities, most of them black. Black soldiers from the North rebelled against the Jim Crow restrictions they found on southern military bases. On August 23, 1917, African American troops from Camp Logan near Houston intervened to protect a black woman being beaten by police on a downtown street. The resulting gunfire killed 16 whites and 4 African Americans. Swift Army court-martials resulted in executions of 19 of the black soldiers and life imprisonment of 63 others.

Library of Congress

▲ **Once the United States joined the Allies in World War I, dissent against the war became associated for many Americans, including this cartoonist, with aiding the enemy: Germany. Here the antiwar Industrial Workers of the World (IWW) are depicted as allies of the German kaiser. The IWW's radical politics and fervent opposition to colonialism, capitalism, and monarchy—all features of the German state—made this a particularly ironic portrayal.**

The War in Europe

When the United States entered the war in Europe in 1917, crisis gripped the Allies. In the east, much of the war effort collapsed in the confusion of Russia's revolution against the czar. In the west, 49 divisions of the French army mutinied, refusing orders to make further suicidal advances. In the south, at Caporetto, Austro-Hungarian forces inflicted a disastrous defeat on the Italian army. It was not clear whether the Americans had joined soon enough to stave off Allied defeat.

No battle-ready American army waited at ports for immediate shipment to the trenches of northern France. U.S. commanders instead had to conscript and train nearly 5 million young men for an American Expeditionary Force (AEF) under General Pershing, and 16,000 young women volunteered for service overseas as nurses and Red Cross workers. U.S. troops participated in their first offensive operations in February 1918, although the veteran French and British lines had to stand largely on their own against the final German spring offensive. American soldiers later engaged in fierce combat at Belleau Wood, Château-Thierry, and St. Mihiel, ultimately losing 114,000 men. German General Erich Ludendorff attributed the sense of "looming defeat" among his troops to "the sheer number of Americans arriving daily at the front." As the only army growing stronger in 1918, the AEF contributed crucially to the fall offensive that convinced Germany to surrender on November 11.

Fighting with French and British allies gave many American GIs an appreciation for Europeans that balanced the anti-immigrant sentiments common back home. White U.S. soldiers also bonded with each other across ethnic and religious lines while engaged in the supremely dangerous task of deadly combat. One young captain from Missouri, Harry Truman, returned from the war with a stronger appreciation for Europe that would help alter America's role in the world when he became president in 1945. Truman wrote home to his fiancée, Bess Wallace, from Nice on the south coast of France, "There is no blue like the Mediterranean blue." Almost 400,000 African American soldiers served with particular determination to prove their loyalty and courage, despite being segregated and given the hardest and least inspiring work. The French, delighted to have all who would help defend them, treated black GIs with a respect they had rarely known from whites in America. When acceptance led to growing pride among black troops abroad, U.S. commanders reacted with consternation. "It has gone to their heads," President Wilson worried.

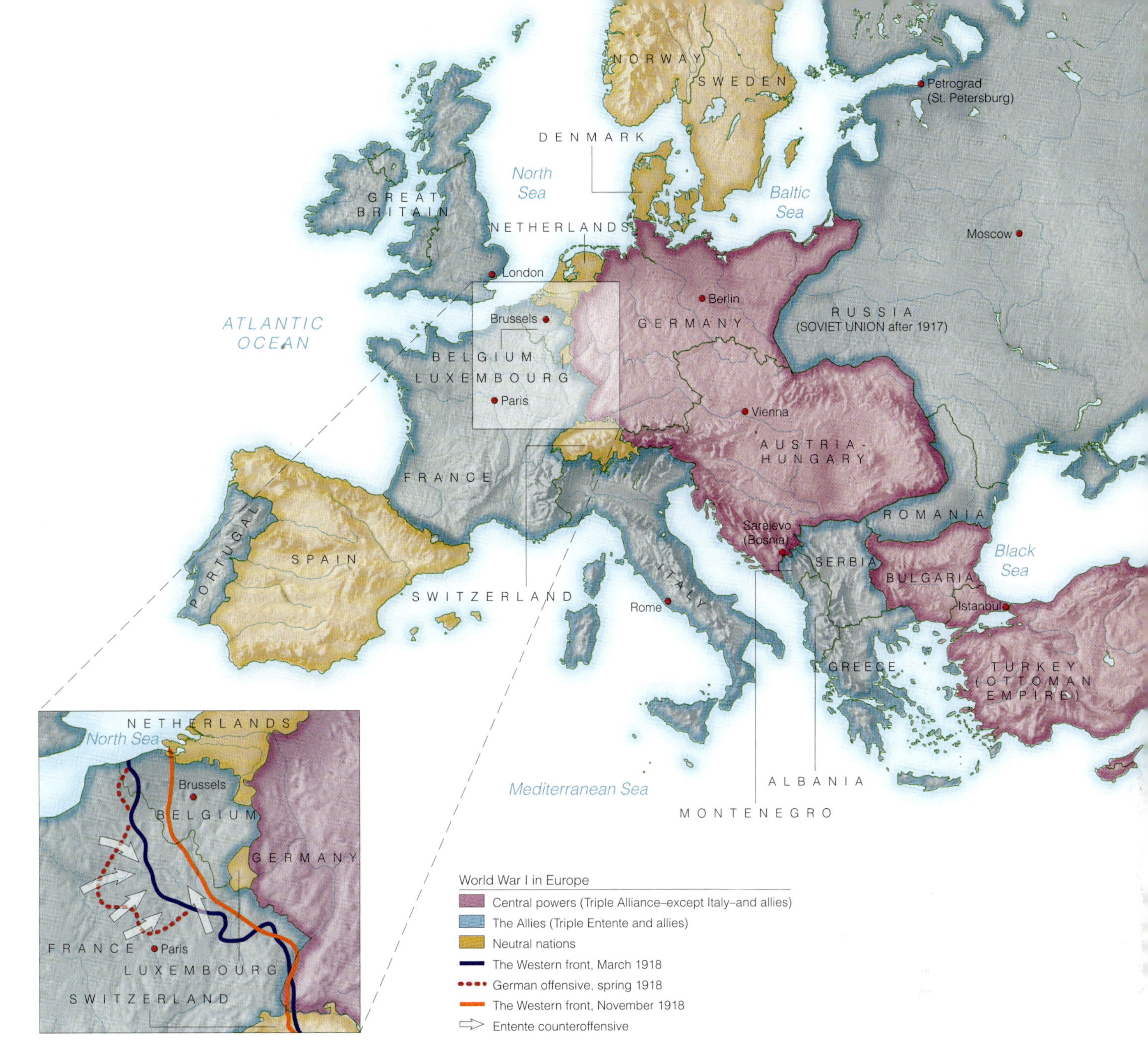

▲ **MAP 20.3 WORLD WAR I IN EUROPE AND THE WESTERN FRONT, 1918**
By the time U.S. troops arrived in force in northern France, the new Bolshevik (Communist) government of Russia had made peace with the Germans and withdrawn from the war. Germany now faced enemies only on one front—the western front—and moved all its troops there. In this dire situation for the French and British, American soldiers helped fill the gap in 1918.

Events in Russia provoked the greatest long-term concerns. On April 8, 1917, just two days after the United States entered the war, Vladimir Lenin and 32 fellow **Bolshevik** refugees from czarism left their asylum in Zurich, Switzerland, on a train ride into history. They arrived in the Russian capital of St. Petersburg and in October seized control of the government, building a dictatorship of the Communist party in the name of the working class. The Bolsheviks opposed the Great War, condemning the battle for greater wealth and power as a demonstration of pure greed among rival capitalists. In the czar's archives, they found and published the secret treaties of the Entente for dividing up their prospective conquests after the war, both in Europe and in the colonies overseas. While Wilson spoke of a war for democracy, the Bolsheviks asked Russians, "Are you willing to fight for this, that the English capitalists should rob Mesopotamia and Palestine?"

African American Women in the Great War

Just as black American men served in the American Expeditionary Forces in France in 1917–1918, black American women served in auxiliary organizations such as the Red Cross and the Young Men's and Women's Christian Associations (YMCA and YWCA), which worked to boost the soldiers' morale. They staffed canteens set up to provide social and educational support for American troops as an alternative to entertainments such as prostitution and gambling. Addie W. Hunton and Kathryn M. Johnson felt a particular calling to encourage African American soldiers, who suffered from discrimination and segregation even as they fought for democracy. As devout Christians, the two women believed they must model a life of service and compassion, even in the face of persecution. An account of their time in Europe published soon after they returned to the United States suggests some of the complications of a segregated society sending people abroad.

National Archives

American women supported the war effort in many ways, including working in munitions factories, buying war bonds, single-parenting while husbands were away in the military, and volunteering as nurses for the armed forces in France. Here, African American women entertain black soldiers with music in a service club in Newark, New Jersey, 1918.

Two Colored Women with the American Expeditionary Forces

The relationship between the colored soldiers, the colored welfare workers, and the French people was most cordial and friendly and grew in sympathy and understanding, as their associations brought about a closer acquaintance. It was rather an unusual as well as a most welcome experience to be able to go into places of public accommodation without having any hesitations or misgivings; to be at liberty to take a seat in a common carrier, without fear of inviting some humiliating experience; to go into a home and receive a greeting that carried with it a hospitality and kindliness of spirit that could not be questioned.

These things were at once noticeable upon the arrival of a stranger within the gates of this sister democracy, and the first ten days in France, though filled with duties and harassed with visits from German bombing planes, were nevertheless a delight, in that they furnished to some of us the first full breath of freedom that had ever come into our limited experience.

The first post of duty assigned to us was Brest. Upon arriving there we received our first experience with American prejudices, which had not only been carried across the seas, but had become a part of such an intricate propaganda, that the relationship between the colored soldier and the French people is more or less a story colored by a continued and subtle effort to inject this same prejudice into the heart of the hitherto unprejudiced Frenchman.

[An order posted by a white officer of a black battalion read:] "Enlisted men of this organization will not talk to or be in company with any white women, regardless of whether the women solicit their company or not."

[Another order read:]"There are two Y.M.C.A.'s, one near the camp, for white troops, and one in town, for the colored troops. All men will be instructed to patronize their own Y."

The account also describes segregation imposed during the return voyage to the United States:

Quite a bit of unpleasantness was experienced on the boats coming home. . . . On [one] boat there were nineteen colored welfare workers; all the women were placed on a floor below the white women, and the entire colored party was placed in an obscure, poorly ventilated section of the dining-room, entirely separated from the other workers by a long table of Dutch civilians. The writer immediately protested; the reply was made that the southern white workers on board the ship would be insulted if the colored workers ate in the same section of the dining-room with them, and, at any rate, the colored people did not expect any such treatment as had been given them by the French.

Questions

1. *How did serving in France affect the ways African American men and women viewed their own country?*
2. *What might the impact of blacks' service in France have been on American society when they returned home after the war?*

Source: Addie W. Hunton and Kathryn M. Johnson, *Two Colored Women with American Expeditionary Forces* (New York: Brooklyn Eagle Press, 1920), pp. 28–30, 182–183, 186.

National Archives

◀ Members of the 369th Infantry Regiment wear the Croix de Guerre (Cross of War) awarded to them for bravery by the French government. Like their white fellow soldiers, African American troops often fought bravely and with distinction on the fields of northern France. But they were segregated and given the hardest, most demeaning work by U.S. commanders, following the same pattern at home in the United States.

The answer, as Wilson feared, was no. In January 1918 the president gave the famous "Fourteen Points" speech to the U.S. Congress, outlining his aims of a postwar world built not on expansion and revenge but on national self-determination, open diplomacy, and freedom of commerce and travel, to be guaranteed by a new League of Nations. He hoped to dissuade the Bolsheviks from making a separate peace with Germany that would allow Germany to move all its troops to the western front. But Lenin, facing civil war at home, conceded huge swaths of the old czarist empire in eastern Europe to the Germans to gain peace with the Brest-Litovsk Treaty of March 3, 1918.

The competing visions of Wilson and Lenin for world order contained the roots of the Cold War that would dominate American life after 1945. Both leaders agreed that the old diplomacy of imperialist states competing for pieces of property around the globe would no longer work and that only the creation of democratic states would prevent further wars. But they understood democracy very differently. For Wilson, it meant self-governing nations with capitalist economies and republican political practices (at least in Europe and North America, and eventually elsewhere). For Lenin, it meant workers in every land overthrowing the owners of capital and setting up Soviet governments. Whereas Wilson viewed the world as a collection of nations, Lenin saw it as a battleground between two classes.

The Struggle to Win the Peace

World War I killed more than 16 million people and wrought immeasurable physical, social, and psychological damage. Was it worth it? Citizens of the belligerent nations emerged from 1918 convinced that only a guarantee of a future free of war could legitimate such suffering. Some put their hopes in the radical solution unfolding in Russia. Some in the Entente states believed that severe measures against Germany would ensure peace. Most looked to Woodrow Wilson in the winter and spring of 1919 as the world leader whose vision for a more peaceful, democratic postwar order was "all that had made the war tolerable to many of us," as one admirer put it. The president sailed for Europe in January to lead the conference that would shape the peace. Vast crowds greeted him enthusiastically as he toured England, Italy, and France.

Peacemaking and the Versailles Treaty

War and revolution destroyed the four great empires of Russia, Germany, Austria-Hungary, and the Ottomans (based in modern Turkey). Meeting in Paris from January to June 1919, the "Big Three" of Wilson, French President Georges Clemenceau, and British Prime Minister David Lloyd George took on two major tasks to shape the postwar order. First, the three leaders redrew the map of eastern and central Europe to create nation-states out of the vanished empires. Second, they had to decide what to do about a defeated Germany. The possible spread of revolution gave the negotiations a particular urgency. Anticolonial revolts broke out in India and China, and pro-Soviet workers' councils seized power briefly in Hungary and southern Germany. "We are running a race with Bolshevism," Wilson warned, "and the world is on fire."

To put out the fire, the Big Three created a string of new nations running from Finland in the north to Yugoslavia in the south. Eastern Europeans were to be self-governing within the new political boundaries. Ultimately, some of the new states—Czechoslovakia and especially Yugoslavia—lacked the sense of nationhood necessary for success and broke apart into smaller ethnic components in the 1990s. But a major purpose of these new nations for the negotiators in Paris was to establish an anticommunist belt keeping Russian communism out of Europe while satisfying their residents' desire for greater self-determination.

How far would "self-determination" go? Secretary of State Lansing worried that the president's language of democracy was "loaded with dynamite." The world's nonwhite majority wondered whether it applied to them. "Security of Life for Poles and Serbs—Why Not for Colored Nations?" asked one black newspaper in New York. A young nationalist from Vietnam named Ho Chi Minh tried but failed to get an audience with Wilson to ask for the Fourteen Points to apply to his French-ruled country; a generation later, Ho led the Vietnamese people's armed struggle against France and then the United States. The Big Three instead created the mandate system to provide for eventual self-determination for colonies after a period of tutelage under an established power, and they rejected Japan's proposal to include racial equality as a principle of the new League of Nations.

"We are running a race with Bolshevism," President Wilson warned, "and the world is on fire."

The German question predominated at the Paris conference. To create a long-term peaceful order in Europe, Wilson wanted lenient terms for Germany. But the French and British had lost much more in the war than the Americans, and they believed Germany must pay for that. French security seemed to depend on keeping its powerful and aggressive neighbor down. The Versailles Treaty (named for the famous estate of King Louis XIV outside Paris, where it was signed) reflected compromises that gave each of the allies what it most wanted. To satisfy France and England, Germany had to admit guilt for causing the war and pay $33 billion in reparations, while losing much of its eastern territory to the new Polish and Czechoslovakian states. For Wilson the League of Nations was the key: this new and unprecedented global organization would keep the peace by ensuring collective security for all nations. Disputes between nations would be mediated before they escalated to armed conflict, and potential aggressors would be deterred by the promise of collective action in defense of any threatened league member.

The absence of certain crucial players from the Paris negotiations undermined the resulting international order. The Soviets and the Germans did not participate. Wilson took in his entourage no representatives of the Republican party. This proved important, for Republicans had won the congressional elections two months earlier, giving them control of the process for ratifying any treaties. Most Republicans objected on principle to one key aspect of the

▲ **MAP 20.4 EUROPE AFTER WORLD WAR I**
The outcome of World War I led to significant changes in the boundaries of Europe, particularly its eastern parts. Four great empires in the region—Russia, Germany, Austria-Hungary, and the Ottomans—collapsed. Negotiations at Versailles created a band of new nations, providing both self-determination and a bulwark against Russian communism.

Versailles Treaty: Article 10 of the League of Nations charter, guaranteeing ahead of time a collective response to defend any member's territory from attack. Treaty opponents were determined to preserve complete American autonomy, including freedom of action in Latin America. Henry Cabot Lodge Jr. of Massachusetts, the powerful Republican chair of the Senate Foreign Relations Committee, organized the two Senate votes rejecting American membership in the League. Hoping to stave off defeat for his idealistic plan, Wilson undertook an ill-advised national speaking tour to promote the international organization. His strenuous effort failed to win American participation in the League, and it ultimately broke his fragile health. Wilson suffered a stroke on October 2, 1919, that left him incapacitated for the rest of his presidency.

Henry Cabot Lodge's Objections to Treaty of Versailles

Waging Counterrevolution Abroad

Soon after Russia withdrew from the war, western powers intervened in the civil war there between the Bolsheviks (the "Reds") and the various counterrevolutionary forces (the "Whites"). The initial military rationale in the summer of 1918 was to reopen the eastern front against Germany. The United States landed 7,000 troops in Vladivostock, on Russia's far Pacific coast, to help rescue a large group of former Czech prisoners of war from the Austro-Hungarian army who now wanted to join the Allied side and to deter Japanese expansion into Siberia. In conjunction with the British, 5,000 U.S. soldiers went ashore at Archangel in northern Russia to prevent Allied supplies from falling into German hands. They quickly became involved in fighting the Red Army. The Wilson administration meanwhile funneled money and military intelligence to leaders of the White forces.

From *Art of the October Revolution*, Leningrad, Aurora Art Publishers, 1979

▲ "Comrade Lenin Sweeps the Globe Clean." This Bolshevik (Communist) drawing shows Vladimir I. Lenin (1870–1924), the leader of the Russian revolution and founder of the world's first communist government, ridding the world of capitalists and monarchs. But Lenin also sought western trade and investment, especially from the United States, as a stimulus to reconstructing the devastated postwar economy of the new Union of Soviet Socialist Republics (USSR).

The Bolsheviks rejected certain values cherished by most Americans: the sanctity of private property and contracts, political liberty, and religious freedom. They liberalized divorce laws and legalized abortion, challenging conservative American attitudes about the relationships between women and men. And they established the Comintern in 1919 to promote similar revolutions around the world. Allied intervention in the Russian civil war failed to overthrow Lenin's government, and American troops pulled out in 1920. They left behind a powerful legacy of anti-American sentiment in Russia, exacerbated by Washington's refusal for the next 13 years to recognize the Soviet government.

Anticommunists used the metaphor of infection to describe Bolshevism. The kaiser, they said, had allowed Lenin to pass through Germany on a "sealed train," lest the bacillus of revolution leak out and spread through the German population. This image had unusual power in 1918–1919 because of the spread of one of the twentieth century's worst killers. The "Spanish influenza" (named for one of its early victims, the king of Spain) hit the United States much harder than the Great War had, killing six times as many people (675,000). In an era before effective vaccines and antibiotic drugs, little could be done for the 20 million stricken Americans besides comforting them, so nurses were in much greater demand than doctors. Not until the longer-lasting AIDS crisis after 1980 did Americans again live in such fear of a disease.

The wave of revolutionary upheaval that had begun in Mexico in 1910 and washed over Russia in 1917 continued to challenge imperial authorities around the globe. During World War I and the postwar negotiations at Versailles, Indians protested British rule of their land, Arab states rebelled against their Ottoman rulers, and Chinese students demonstrated against Japanese control of the Shantung peninsula. Western Europe was not immune to the forces of revolution. Americans of Irish descent cheered for the Irish Republican forces whose guerrilla warfare from 1919 to 1921 helped persuade Great Britain finally to grant independence to the Catholic majority of the island. Irish Americans also contributed money to the Irish Republican effort. Eamon de Valera, the leading political figure in the Irish struggle for independence, had been born in the United States. De Valera was imprisoned for his part in the unsuccessful Easter Rising of 1916, but after he escaped (with a key smuggled in to him inside a cake), he spent most of 1919–1920 in America raising political support and $5 million for the Irish cause. Enthusiastic crowds greeted him from Boston to San Francisco. In 1922, the Irish Free State (later the Republic of Ireland) became Europe's newest independent nation, although the northern six counties remained under British rule.

Warning of Influenza Epidemic, 1918

The League of Nations and International Security

The experience of World War I stunned Europeans and Americans. Never before had an armed conflict killed and wounded so many people in so brief a time. Observers from outside the Central Powers, like most historians since, placed primary responsibility for the onset of the war on the aggressive actions of German Kaiser Wilhelm II. Other critics noted the expansive empires of every member of the Entente and wondered whether more than just German imperialism was troubling the international system. The sheer scale of the carnage, especially the continuing slaughter of soldiers in indecisive battles on the almost immovable western front for four long years, suggested that something deeper might be wrong with the way nations waged both diplomacy and war.

The intensifying rivalry of the European nations after 1910 created the conditions for the Great War. In the international arena, few rules guided how powerful nations behaved, in contrast to the domestic sphere of any particular nation, which had clear guidelines for how its citizens could act. A handful of international conventions created some general expectations for "civilized" actions in peace and war, but no form of effective enforcement backed these up. When a rising power such as Germany (unified in 1871) chose to upset the existing balance of power between nations, the only recourse available was on the battlefield. The new tools of warfare on display in World War I—machine guns, poison gas, submarines, airplanes—made this a grim prospect.

Courtesy, Janice L. and David Frent

Some supporters of the League of Nations wrote popular sheet music in its honor.

Woodrow Wilson's original vision for the League of Nations was a bold effort to come to terms with this challenge. Rejecting the amoral old diplomacy of nations strengthening themselves at the cost of weakening others, Wilson called for a new diplomacy of collective security. All nations would agree to protect each other and the status quo, deterring potential aggressors by promising to come to the defense of any nation under attack. Without arms races to destabilize the international order, militarism would subside. The U.S. failure to join the League of Nations undermined the organization's effectiveness, however, as did the competing desire of national leaders to preserve maximum autonomy for pursuing their nations' own interests.

World War II seemed to prove Wilson correct. His vision of substituting collective internationalism for competitive nationalism helped shape the United Nations (UN) in 1945, especially its General Assembly of all nations. However, the UN's powerful Security Council with its five permanent members (Britain, France, Russia, China, and the United States), who each retained the right to veto any action by the organization, limited the degree of collective security that members could depend on. The Cold War (1946–1989) also reduced the UN's effectiveness by dividing the world into two competing collective security systems, one headed by the Soviet Union and one by the United States.

In the 1990s the UN gained renewed prominence, first in the international coalition fighting against Iraq in the 1991 Gulf War and subsequently as the source of mediation efforts and peacekeeping forces for civil conflicts around the globe. The growing seriousness of problems that were unarguably international in nature, such as global warming and the proliferation of nuclear weapons, provided a potent argument in favor of collective action. Americans nonetheless remained ambivalent about the UN at the start of the new millennium. As the world's most powerful nation in military and economic terms, the United States expected to lead the UN. But U.S. leaders did not like to be hemmed in by its collective decision-making process. Unilateral freedom of action in the international sphere, like that suggested two centuries earlier by George Washington's warning to avoid "entangling alliances," continued to appeal to many citizens. ■

Museum of History & Industry, Seattle, Washington/Pemco, Webster & Stevens Collection

▲ **The Seattle General Strike Committee took on the responsibility of keeping essential services running in the city. Here its members issue groceries to union families, January 1919. The cooperation necessary among organized workers to keep a strike going offered a different model of community interaction than did the individualism often touted by wealthier Americans.**

The Red and Black Scares at Home

Four million American workers, one out of every five, went out on strike in 1919—the highest proportion of the workforce ever. They sought improved wages and working conditions as well as recognition of the right to collective bargaining. The scale of industrial unrest provoked fears of a Soviet-style revolution. In Seattle a walkout by shipyard workers mushroomed into a general strike that shut down most of the city for a week. In Pittsburgh, the AFL led a bitter strike against U.S. Steel in pursuit of union recognition. The United Mine Workers led walkouts by hundreds of thousands of coal miners, which evolved into open warfare between miners and coal companies in West Virginia over the next two years. In Boston three-quarters of the police force went on strike to protest wages lower than those of common laborers. Between April and June, anarchists mailed or delivered bombs to 36 prominent public figures, including Attorney General A. Mitchell Palmer. All were defused except two, one wounding the wife and maid of a U.S. senator from Georgia, the other destroying the front of Palmer's house and dismembering its anarchist deliverer.

Whereas many Americans sympathized with struggles for unionization, others viewed them as dangerous to private property and social order. They associated strikes with radical immigrants and anarchists and considered them "un-American." The **"Red Scare"** of 1919 associated reform and social justice of any kind with subversion. To break strikes, employers hired private armies from "detective" agencies such as the Pinkertons and the Baldwin-Felts, often staffed by World War I veterans. Private organizations promoting "100 percent Americanism," such as the Ku Klux Klan and the new American Legion, monitored and harassed potential subversives and the foreign born. Attorney General Palmer directed the deportation to Russia of 249 foreign-born radicals aboard the *Buford* in December 1919, including anarchist and feminist Emma Goldman. "Palmer raids" led to the arrest of thousands more within a month. U.S. Army troops and state militias brought the ultimate force to bear against union organizers, as at the Battle of Blair Mountain on August 31, 1921, against several thousand striking West Virginia miners.

Violence against workers extended to African Americans after World War I. An upsurge in lynching included at least ten black veterans still in uniform and was not limited to the South. In Nebraska white residents of Omaha butchered William Brown with such frenzy that thousands of federal troops had to be called in to restore calm. White mobs burned entire black communities to the ground, including Tulsa's Greenwood neighborhood (1921) and the all-black town of Rosewood, Florida (1923). The Red Scare and the "Black Scare" merged in Phillips County, Arkansas, where black sharecroppers, many of them veterans, formed a union in 1919 to pursue equitable crop settlements from landlords. Fearing insurrection, local white leaders used 2,500 federal troops and white vigilantes to massacre more than 200 sharecroppers. But any inclination toward deference in the face of brutality was gone, and African Americans fought back fiercely against white marauders in deadly riots in Washington and Chicago in the summer of 1919. One black woman recalled that when she heard "our men had stood like men" in Washington, she cried for joy: "Oh, I thank God, thank God!"

Where was the president during this turmoil? Incapacitated by his stroke, Wilson lay resting in his bed in Washington, the administration managed largely by his wife, Edith, and his secretary, Joseph Tumulty. In any case, Wilson's segregationist policies suggested that he

Bettmann/CORBIS

▲ **Death by hanging or burning, often preceded by torture, at the hands of a white mob constituted one end of a range of tactics of intimidation and coercion used against black Southerners in the early twentieth century. Outnumbered and outgunned, African Americans fought back fiercely when they could. Lynchings sometimes had a festive air for the white participants, with children often present.**

would have been unlikely to provide effective leadership in bridging the nation's racial divides. The only Republican of similar stature, Theodore Roosevelt, had died a few months earlier. "There is no leadership worthy of the name," a veteran reporter lamented. Wilson's breakdown came in the middle of the 1919 baseball World Series, which the heavily favored but poorly paid Chicago White Sox intentionally lost to the Cincinnati Reds, in an arrangement with gamblers. Eight "Black Sox" were banned from the sport. With its president out of action and its national pastime corrupted, the nation seemed adrift as the lights dimmed on the Progressive Era.

Conclusion

No American citizen better exemplified the international connections of his society in the revolutionary era of the 1910s than John Reed. Born in 1887, the Portland, Oregon, native graduated from Harvard University in 1910 and moved to New York City to work as a journalist. A socialist and a supporter of Progressive reforms, he became associated with the Greenwich Village radical artists and their patrons, such as Mabel Dodge, who supported left-wing politics and opposed Victorian social mores. He shared the quest for love and revolution with feminist Louise Bryant, another journalist and Oregon native, whom he married in 1917. Reed traveled south of the border in 1914 to report on the Mexican Revolution, where he met and traveled with revolutionary commander Pancho Villa. On the way home, Reed toured Ludlow, Colorado, to report on the coal miners' strike there. Then he went to Europe to cover the First World War, sending home stories from the less well-known eastern front. In 1917 he and Bryant were in Russia for the Bolshevik Revolution, the *Ten Days That Shook the World,* as he entitled his widely read 1919 book. A founding member of the American Communist party, Reed died of typhus on a return visit to Russia in 1920. He was given a state funeral and was buried in the Kremlin. Reed's journey had taken him from an affluent family in provincial Portland, to the mainstream of Progressive reform, and on into full-blown radicalism and revolution.

How much success could a varied generation of Progressive reformers claim? Women had won the vote with the Nineteenth Amendment, in an expansion of democracy second only to the combination of the Emancipation Proclamation of 1863 and the Thirteenth Amendment, outlawing slavery. African Americans who moved to the North usually could vote as well, unlike those who stayed in Dixie. On either side of the Mason-Dixon line, however, daily life for Americans of darker hue entailed picking one's way through a maze of discrimination. Most union campaigns stalled by 1920, beaten back by the physical force and cleverness of corporate employers and their government sympathizers. When the Red Scare dissipated, Americans did not return to the reform spirit of Progressivism. Many turned away from politics. Voter turnout in 1920 dipped below 50 percent for the first time in a century. Those who did vote that year gave the Republican party a sweeping victory. Promising "not revolution, but restoration," Ohio Senator Warren G. Harding took the White House. His speeches may have been, as one rival said, "an army of pompous phrases moving over the landscape in search of an idea," but most of the nation sought calm after the upheavals of the previous decade.

American contributions to democracy abroad were similarly ambivalent. Whereas eastern Europeans named streets in their newly independent nations for President Wilson, few Latin Americans believed that U.S. invasions of Caribbean and Central American countries promoted self-government. Russians admired much about American society and the U.S. economy while resenting American troops in their land. Above all hung the problem of Germany, still the most powerful single nation in Europe. The Versailles Treaty imposed harsh terms and embittered a generation of German people. "If I were a German, I think I should not sign it," Wilson admitted privately. The Weimar Republic that replaced the abdicated German kaiser lasted through the 1920s. But the storms of the Great Depression swamped Germany's republican experiment and gave rise to Adolf Hitler.

Sites to Visit

World War I Document Archive

www.lib.byu.edu/~rdh/wwi

This site offers an array of reminiscences, photos, and documents, plus links to other useful World War I sites.

Women and Social Movements in the United States, 1775–1940

womhist.binghamton.edu

Maintained by two Binghamton University historians, this site has a rich trove of documents on the history of American women as well as excellent links to others.

Avalon Project at the Yale Law School: Documents in Law, History, and Diplomacy

www.yale.edu/lawweb/avalon

Researchers can find here the texts of a large number of the most important primary documents illuminating U.S. relations with other countries, including materials on American responses to the Bolshevik Revolution in Russia.

Temperance and Prohibition

prohibition.history.ohio-state.edu/Contents.htm

Cartoons, newspaper articles, and other primary documents available here illuminate in fascinating ways the struggle over whether to prohibit the sale of alcoholic beverages.

Emma Goldman Papers

sunsite.berkeley.edu/Goldman/

This site has photos and excerpts from the writings and speeches of one of America's most influential radicals and feminists from this era.

Divining America: Religion and the National Culture

www.nhe.ntp.nc.us/tserve/divam.htm

This site has essays by prominent historians on diverse aspects of the religious history of the United States.

Up South: African American Migration in the Era of the Great War

www.ashp.cuny.edu/video/south.html

Maintained by the American Social History Project at the Graduate Center of the City University of New York, this site offers details of the mass migration of rural black Southerners to the urban North during World War I.

Influenza Pandemic of 1918

www.stanford.edu/group/virus/uda/

A variety of information, documents, and photos of the deadly global outbreak of the "Spanish flu" can be found here.

For Further Reading

General

Kendrick A. Clements, *Woodrow Wilson: World Statesman* (1987).

John M. Cooper, *Pivotal Decades: The United States, 1900–1920* (1990).

Alan Dawley, *Struggles for Justice: Social Responsibility and the Liberal State* (1991).

Alan Dawley, *Changing the World: American Progressives in War and Peace* (2003).

Nell Irvin Painter, *Standing at Armageddon: The United States, 1877–1919* (1987).

Daniel T. Rodgers, *Atlantic Crossings: Social Politics in a Progressive Age* (1998).

A World in Upheaval

Iris Chang, *The Chinese in America* (2003).

John Mason Hart, *Empire and Revolution: The Americans in Mexico Since the Civil War* (2002).

Paul Kennedy, *The Rise and Fall of the Great Powers: Economic Change and Military Conflict from 1500 to 2000* (1987).

Arthur Link, ed., *Woodrow Wilson and a Revolutionary World* (1982).

Joseph A. McCartin, *Labor's Great War: The Struggle for Industrial Democracy and the Origins of Modern American Labor Relations, 1912–1921* (1997).

George J. Sánchez, *Becoming Mexican American: Ethnicity, Culture, and Identity in Chicano Los Angeles, 1900–1945* (1993).

The Great War and American Neutrality

John W. Coogan, *The End of Neutrality: The United States, Britain, and Maritime Rights, 1899–1915* (1981).

Steven J. Diner, *A Very Different Age: Americans of the Progressive Era* (1998).

James Grossman, *Land of Hope: Chicago, Black Southerners, and the Great Migration* (1989).

Vicki I. Ruiz, *From Out of the Shadows: Mexican Women in Twentieth-Century America* (1998).

Martin Sklar, *The Corporate Reconstruction of American Capitalism, 1890–1916: The Market, the Law, and Politics* (1988).

The United States Goes to War

Edward M. Coffman, *The War to End All Wars: The American Military Experience in World War I* (1987).

Martin Gilbert, *The First World War: A Complete History* (1994).

David M. Kennedy, *Over Here: The First World War and American Society* (1980).

Kathleen Kennedy, *Disloyal Mothers and Scurrilous Citizens: Women and Subversion During World War I* (1999).

Richard Polenberg, *Fighting Faiths: The Abrams Case, the Supreme Court, and Free Speech* (1987).

Nick Salvatore, *Eugene V. Debs: Citizen and Socialist* (1982).

The Struggle to Win the Peace

Alfred W. Crosby, *America's Forgotten Pandemic: The Influenza of 1918*, 2nd ed. (2003).

Scott Ellsworth, *Death in a Promised Land: The Tulsa Race Riot of 1921* (1982).

David S. Foglesong, *America's Secret War Against Bolshevism: U.S. Intervention in the Russian Civil War, 1917–1920* (1995).

Thomas J. Knock, *To End All Wars: Woodrow Wilson and the Quest for a New World Order* (1992).

Gordon N. Levin Jr., *Woodrow Wilson and World Politics: America's Response to War and Revolution* (1968).

William M. Tuttle Jr., *Race Riot: Chicago in the Red Summer of 1919* (1970).

Betty M. Unterberger, *The United States, Revolutionary Russia, and the Rise of Czechoslovakia* (1989).

CHAPTER 21

The Promise of Consumer Culture: The 1920s

Florine Stettheimer, "Portrait of My Sister Ettie," 1923. Columbia University in the City of New York, Gift of the Estate of Ettie Stettheimer, 1967 (Neg. #57675)

▲ Florine Stettheimer's *Portrait of Ettie* (1923) conveys the glamour and sensuality of the 1920s "flapper."

CHAPTER OUTLINE

The Business of Politics

The Decline of Reform

Hollywood and Harlem: National Cultures in Black and White

Science on Trial

Consumer Dreams and Nightmares

Conclusion

Sites to Visit

For Further Reading

IN THE SUPERIOR COURT OF LOS ANGELES IN 1920, LORIMER LINGANFIELD, A RESPECTABLE barber, filed for divorce. Although his wife, Marsha, held him in "high regard and esteem as her husband," there were "evidences of indiscretion" in her conduct. She wore a new bathing suit, "designed especially for the purpose of exhibiting to the public the shape and form of her body." To his further humiliation, she was "beset with a desire to sing and dance at cafes and restaurants for the entertainment of the public." When Lorimer complained about her "appetite for beer and whisky" and extravagant tastes for luxury, she replied that he was "not the only pebble on the beach, she had a millionaire 'guy' who would buy her all the clothes, automobiles, diamonds and booze that she wanted." The ultimate insult was her refusal to have any sexual intercourse, claiming that she did not want any "dirty little brats around her." The judge was sympathetic, and Lorimer Linganfield won his suit.

The Linganfields' difficulties represent a larger struggle as Americans shifted their sensibilities from the **producer economy** of the nineteenth century, complete with clearly defined gender roles and sexual mores, to the consumer ethic of the twentieth century, with its new amusements, changing sexual behavior, and flamboyant "new women." Marsha Linganfield was a **"flapper,"** one of the young women of the 1910s and 1920s who broke from time-honored conventions. With short, "bobbed" hair, knee-length dresses, and boyish styles unencumbered by layers of petticoats, flappers flirted, petted, and danced "wild" dances like the Charleston, an African American dance brought north from South Carolina **juke joints.** Flappers blurred the line between "good girls" and "bad girls" that had previously defined proper female behavior.

Gertrude Ederle swims the English Channel.

Marsha was fond of fancy clothes and nightlife. Lorimer undoubtedly was attracted to the lively young flapper whom he wooed and wed. He was surely anticipating conjugal bliss, as experts at the time promoted the healthy enjoyment of sex within marriage for women as well as men. New patterns of courtship allowed couples some intimacy now that chaperones were no longer required when a man "came calling." The widespread availability of automobiles offered increased mobility and privacy. So Marsha's sexual refusal, as well as her scandalous rejection of motherhood, must have been intolerable for Lorimer. The "new woman" of the age was allowed more leeway in her dress, demeanor and behavior, but she was still expected to be virginal at marriage and eager for marital sex and motherhood.

New forms of popular entertainment that developed in the 1920s, especially Hollywood movies and jazz music, became defining features of America. At a time when white, Anglo-Saxon, Protestant men had control of nearly all government and business institutions, Jewish moviemakers and African American musicians were creating the culture that would soon represent the nation. During the years when Congress largely closed off immigration, Jewish immigrants built Hollywood into the most American of all industries. In the midst of the Jim Crow era, African Americans created the music that gave the 1920s its identity as "the Jazz Age."

The great heroes of the 1920s were celebrities admired for their individual achievements in sports and adventure. In 1927, the same year that Babe Ruth hit a record 60 home runs, Charles Lindbergh flew his small monoplane, *The Spirit of St. Louis,* nonstop from New York to Paris in 33½ hours, a feat that electrified the world and made him an instant hero. Professional sports came of age in the 1920s, giving rise to star athletes such as baseball's Babe Ruth, football's Red Grange, and boxing's Jack Dempsey. It was also a decade of tremendous visibility in women's sports, with such stars as tennis sensation Helen Wills and swimmer Sybil Bauer. In 1926, 19-year-old Olympic gold medalist Gertrude Ederle became the first woman to swim the English Channel. She broke the world's record with her time of 14 hours and 31 minutes, 2 hours faster than the times of the six men who had preceded her. On her return to the United States, 2 million cheering fans lined the streets of New York City to welcome her home. The nation idolized this new generation of heroes, who dominated headlines and drew cheering crowds wherever they went.

The glamorous life, however, was out of reach for many. Often characterized as the "roaring twenties" of giddy prosperity and reckless good times, these were also years of widespread poverty, especially in rural areas and urban ghettos. Many Americans were unable to afford the new consumer goods that were being mass-produced. At the end of the decade, fewer than half of all households owned a car or radio; fewer than one in three owned a washing machine or a vacuum cleaner.

Conservative politics at the national level prevailed throughout the decade. Disenchantment after World War I prompted national leaders to promote a foreign policy based on economic ties and trade and to shrink from military entanglements. The politics of the era favored big business, but the disparity between rich and poor left the country vulnerable to the downturn of the economy. The expansion of consumer credit weakened the traditions of saving and frugality. For those with money to invest, Wall Street beckoned. The stock market rose to perilous heights, only to collapse at the end of the decade.

The Business of Politics

In 1924, President Calvin Coolidge declared, "The business of America is business." Despite its many critics, with the support of national political leaders, business reigned. After an initial recession following World War I, the economy grew steadily. The Gross National Product (GNP) increased 5.5 percent per year, from $149 billion in 1922 to $227 billion in 1929. Official unemployment remained below 5 percent throughout the decade, and real wages rose 15 percent. These trends fueled the popularity of the conservative, business-friendly presidents of the 1920s. Economic interests also drove foreign policy during the decade. After World War I, with much of Europe in shambles, the United States made loans to foreign countries, becoming the world's leading creditor nation. International markets opened up for American-made products, leading to a tremendous expansion in foreign trade.

Warren G. Harding: The Politics of Scandal

Warren G. Harding, a former newspaper editor and U.S. senator from Ohio, won the 1920 presidential election by the biggest landslide since 1820. Harding established the conservative agenda that would last throughout the decade. He supported immigration restriction, opposed labor unions, and favored tariff protection, which placed a tax on goods entering the United States from abroad. In the wake of World War I, Harding distanced himself from Woodrow Wilson's peace settlement but promoted international **treaties.** In 1921 and 1922 Secretary of State Charles Evans Hughes achieved the first major disarmament accord, the Five-Power Treaty, signed by Japan, Britain, France, Italy, and the United States. The five nations agreed to scrap more than 2 million tons of warships in the first such pact of its kind. Hughes extended the power of the United States abroad through economic ties and encouraging banks to provide loans to war-ravaged Europe.

Harding's presidency was marred by scandal. He had built his political base by handing out favors and deals to his friends, and he continued to do so as president. His buddies used their offices and influence for personal gain, while Harding caroused with them, drinking, despite Prohibition, and engaging in notorious extramarital affairs. At first, the press ignored these obvious abuses, but by 1923, the many scandals finally broke. Harding's cronies were exposed for selling government appointments and providing judicial pardons and police protection for bootleggers.

The most serious scandal of Harding's presidency involved the large government oil reserves at Teapot Dome, Wyoming, and Elk Hills, California. At the urging of Secretary of the Interior Albert Fall, Harding transferred control over the reserves from the U.S. Navy to the Department of the Interior. After accepting a bribe of nearly $400,000 from two oil tycoons, Harry F. Sinclair and Edward L. Doheny, Fall secretly issued leases to them without opening up the competition to other oil companies, thereby allowing Sinclair and Doheny to pump oil from the wells in exchange for providing fuel tank reserves to the navy. Fall went to jail for a year as a result. In another scandal, Charles R. Forbes, head of the Veteran's Bureau, went to prison for swindling the government out of $200 million worth of hospital supplies. When Harding learned of the scandals that occurred in his close circle, he grew deeply worried. The stress probably contributed to the illness that killed him in 1923.

Warren G. Harding

Calvin Coolidge: The Hands-Off President

Harding's vice president, Calvin Coolidge, took over the presidency when Harding died in 1923. Sober and serious, this aloof New Englander was not vulnerable to scandal as his predecessor had been. Coolidge believed that the government should meddle as little as possible in the affairs of the nation. He took long naps every day and exerted very little presidential leadership. Known mostly for his hostility to labor unions and his laissez-faire attitude toward business, he was a popular president during the complacent mid-1920s.

Not everyone was pleased with Coolidge's probusiness politics, and opposition mobilized for the 1924 election. Progressive Republicans formed a new Progressive party and nominated Robert M. La Follette for president. The Progressive platform promoted conservation measures, higher taxes on the wealthy, doing away with the Electoral College in favor of direct election of the president, and the abolition of child labor. The Democrats deadlocked between Catholic candidate Alfred E. Smith, an urban politician from New York, and Protestant William G. McAdoo, who had a base of support in the South and West. On the 103rd ballot, the delegates finally chose a compromise candidate, John W. Davis, a corporation lawyer. Coolidge claimed responsibility for the nation's prosperity and won easily, receiving more votes than the other two candidates combined.

Coolidge believed that the government should meddle as little as possible in the affairs of the nation.

Coolidge took pride in measures that prevented the government from interfering in the economy, such as his vetoes of the 1926 and 1928 McNary-Haugen bills, which would have provided government subsidies to farmers if farm prices dropped. The passage of the Revenue Act of 1926, a form of **trickle-down economics** intended to boost the economy, reduced the high income and estate taxes that Progressive reformers had put into place during World War I. Coolidge also continued Harding's efforts to sustain world

Bettman/CORBIS

▲ **A cartoonist's view of the Teapot Dome scandal that plagued the Harding administration depicts the scandal blowing the lid off the Capitol building.**

peace. In 1928, under the leadership of Secretary of State Frank Kellogg and French Foreign Minister Aristide Briand, delegates from the United States, France, and 13 other nations gathered in Paris to sign the Kellogg-Briand Pact, in which they agreed to resolve conflicts through peaceful solutions rather than war. Unfortunately, with no means to enforce the agreement, the pact did nothing to alleviate the international hostilities that later erupted into World War II.

Herbert Hoover: The Self-Made President

The 1928 election was a major turning point for the presence of ethnic minorities in politics, for the Democrats broke tradition by selecting an Irish Catholic, Governor Alfred E. Smith of New York, as their candidate. It was the first time a major party had nominated a Catholic for president. Coolidge decided not to run for reelection in 1928, and the Republican party selected Secretary of Commerce Herbert Hoover as its nominee. Prohibition figured prominently in the 1928 presidential campaign. Although the Democratic platform gave lukewarm support to the continuation of Prohibition, Smith made no secret of his support for the repeal of the Eighteenth Amendment. By contrast, Republican Herbert Hoover praised Prohibition as "a great social and economic experiment." The other major issue of the campaign was religion. Anti-Catholic sentiment was strong throughout the country, especially in the South, where Democrats either sat out the election or voted Republican. Smith's opponents attacked his Catholicism, charging that he was more loyal to the international headquarters of the Catholic Church at the Vatican in Rome than he was to the United States. Although Hoover won by a substantial majority, Smith carried the nation's 12 largest cities. Smith's candidacy also laid the groundwork for another Irish Catholic, John F. Kennedy, who ran successfully on the Democratic ticket 32 years later.

Herbert Hoover epitomized the values of the self-made man. He was orphaned as a child and raised by relatives of modest means. After graduating from Stanford University, he went into mining and rose through the ranks to become a wealthy corporate leader. By age 40 he was already a millionaire. Hoover began his career in government during World War I, when he earned widespread admiration for handling the distribution of food relief to European war refugees. He then served ably as secretary of commerce in the Harding and Coolidge administrations. Shortly after winning the 1928 election, he predicted, "We in America today are nearer to the final triumph over poverty than ever before in the history of any land." But less than a year into his presidency, his optimism, along with the nation's economy, came crashing down.

The Decline of Reform

The voices of workers, sharecroppers, and other poor people were muffled in the 1920s. Reformers who had championed the causes of the marginalized and disadvantaged lost influence in the 1920s. After achieving the vote, the women's rights movement splintered as younger women sought new freedoms not through politics but through a social and sexual revolution. Widespread hostility toward immigrants and various ethnic groups was at the root of the outlawing of liquor, new laws restricting immigration, and the rise of the Ku Klux Klan. But progressive political impulses did not entirely disappear, especially among African Americans, who continued to mobilize and organize for civil rights.

Reformers who had championed the causes of the marginalized and disadvantaged lost influence in the 1920s.

Women's Rights After the Struggle for Suffrage

One indication of the waning of progressive reform was the fragmentation of women's rights activism in the 1920s. The more radical wing of the suffrage movement, the National Women's Party (NWP) in 1923 launched a campaign for the Equal Rights Amendment (ERA) to add these words to the Constitution: "Equality of rights under the law shall not be denied or abridged by the United States or by any state on account of sex."

The debate over the ERA in the 1920s reflected the fundamental question that would permeate women's rights activism throughout the rest of the twentieth century. On one side were those who believed that women were fundamentally the same as men and deserved equal rights; on the other side were those who argued that women were different and deserved special privileges and protections. Many women's rights activists opposed the ERA because it would undercut efforts to gain special legislative protections for women based on their presumed physical weakness and their potential for childbearing, such as maximum hours, regulations against night work, and limitations on the weights they could lift. These women disapproved of the goals and tactics of the NWP and formed their own nonpartisan organization, the League of Women Voters, which promoted social and political reform.

Legislative gains for women did not entirely disappear in the 1920s. In 1921 Congress passed the Sheppard-Towner bill, which provided for public health nurses to educate mothers in prenatal and infant health care to reduce infant mortality. Physicians opposed the legislation because they did not want nurses providing medical care even though the nurses offered only preventive health care and advice. Doctors also worried that government-sponsored programs would compete with their private practices. Nevertheless, Sheppard-Towner remained in force until the end of the decade, when its budget was cut—a casualty of the conservative temperament in Congress that saw such forms of government support as socialistic.

Along with voting, women continued their political influence by seeking elective office. But they often faced intense public scrutiny for entering the political arena. In 1922, for example, Adelina Otero Warren ran as a Republican candidate for the U.S. House of Representatives, the first New Mexican woman and the first Hispanic woman to run for national office. During the campaign, a cousin publicly revealed that Warren had lied about her marital status, claiming to be widowed when she was really divorced. That revelation dashed her political ambitions. But neither her divorce nor her effort to pass as a widow was unusual at a time when marital breakdown still carried a heavy negative stigma, especially for women. The divorce rate doubled between 1900 and 1920 and continued to rise throughout the 1920s, in part the result of women's increasing independence. As job opportunities for women increased, more women felt able to abandon unhappy marriages.

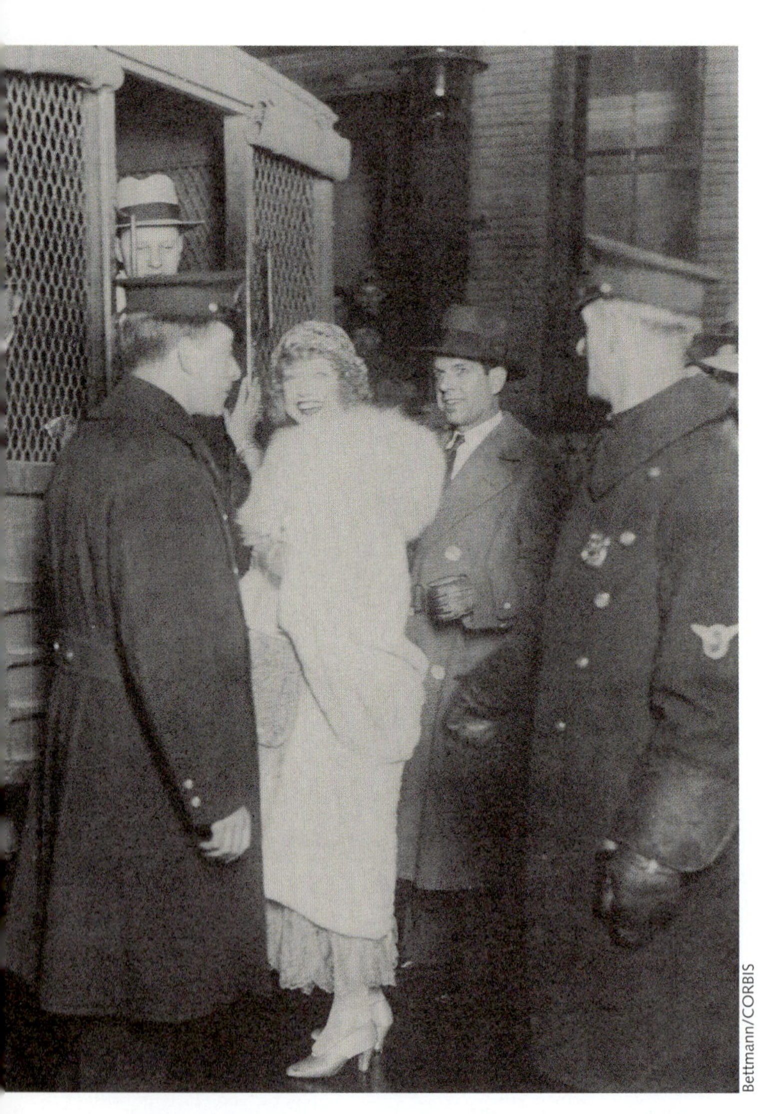

Bettmann/CORBIS

▲ Speakeasy hostess Mary Louise Guinan appears unrepentant as she is arrested for selling alcohol during the Prohibition era. Law enforcement was futile because speakeasies that were raided and closed simply reopened in new locations.

Prohibition: The Experiment That Failed

The Eighteenth Amendment, prohibiting the manufacture and sale of alcohol, went into effect in January 1920. Several diverse interests came together to promote the ban on liquor. Temperance crusaders in the Anti-Saloon League and the Women's Christian Temperance Union had argued since the late nineteenth century that women and children suffered when men spent their paychecks at the saloon and returned home drunk and violent. World War I prompted others to support a ban on the manufacture of liquor to save grain for the war effort. Anti-immigrant "drys" had political motives for promoting Prohibition. They hoped to undercut the power bases of immigrant and ethnic politicians who used local saloons to forge their constituencies and **political machines.** The "wets" included alienated intellectuals, Jazz Age rebels, and many city dwellers whose social lives revolved around neighborhood pubs, especially in Irish and German communities.

The 1919 Volstead Act established a Prohibition Bureau within the Treasury Department. Federal agents had responsibility for enforcing the law, but their numbers were inadequate. In order to be effective, federal agents had to work closely with local law enforcement officials. In some urban areas, local officials refused to cooperate with federal agents. New York repealed its Prohibition enforcement law in 1923, leaving small numbers of federal agents with the daunting task of shutting down the illegal clubs where liquor was sold, known as **"speakeasies."** In sporadic raids, the beleaguered agents closed down some of the speakeasies, only to have them pop up again in new locations. Americans who wanted to drink liquor found many ways to acquire it. Illegal speakeasies abounded where customers could buy drinks delivered by rumrunners who smuggled in liquor from Canada, Mexico, and the West Indies. Many people concocted their own "bathtub gin" or "moonshine whiskey," homemade brews using readily available ingredients and household equipment.

Prohibition was intended to cure society's ills. Instead, it provided vast opportunities for crime and profit, both among criminals and law enforcement agents. Without the profits from liquor, many nightclubs and restaurants went out of business, opening the way for gangsters and petty criminals to cater to the nightlife crowd. Organized crime received a major boost in the scramble to profit from illegal liquor. By 1929 Chicago mob king Al Capone controlled a massive network of speakeasies that raked in $60 million annually. Violence also increased. Chicago witnessed 550 gangland killings in the 1920s, with few arrests or convictions.

Prohibition also led to corruption. Authorities in St. Paul, Minnesota, for example, struck a bargain with gangsters who smuggled in liquor from Canada through the wilderness in northern Minnesota. After paying a bribe to the local police, the smugglers hid their stash in St. Paul's chalk caves along the banks of the Mississippi River until they were able to transport it down the river.

"Prohibition is a Failure"

Prohibition failed to live up to its promise. Within a year of the passage of the amendment, alcohol consumption declined by two-thirds. But by 1929 the consumption of alcohol had climbed back up to 70 percent of its pre-Prohibition level. Expenditures for alcoholic beverages actually increased by 50 percent during the Prohibition era, no doubt due in part to higher black-market prices. In 1933 Congress repealed Prohibition.

Reactionary Impulses

The Red Scare after World War I (see Chapter 20) inaugurated a decade of hostility to political radicals and foreigners. Shoemaker Nicola Sacco and fish peddler Bartolomeo Vanzetti were both: Italian immigrants and self-proclaimed anarchists. In May 1920 the paymaster and guard of a South Braintree, Massachusetts, shoe company was robbed and murdered, and Sacco and Vanzetti were arrested and charged with the crime. Sacco testified that he was in Boston at the time, applying for a passport, and his alibi was corroborated. Both men proclaimed their innocence and insisted that they were on trial for their political beliefs rather than the crime itself. Their Italian accents and advocacy of anarchism in the courtroom did not help their case with many Americans suspicious of foreign radicals, including the judge presiding at their trial. Despite a weak case against them, Sacco and Vanzetti were convicted of first-degree murder and sentenced to death.

Lawyers for the two anarchists appealed the case several times to no avail. The convictions sparked outrage among Italian Americans, political radicals, labor activists, and liberal intellectuals who believed the two men were falsely convicted. The case soon generated mass demonstrations, appeals for clemency, and petitions from around the world. In response the governor of Massachusetts appointed a commission to review the case, but the commission concluded that there were no grounds for a new trial. Finally, on August 23, 1927, Sacco and Vanzetti were executed by electric chair at Charlestown State Prison.

The case of Sacco and Vanzetti underscored the anti-immigrant sentiment that prevailed in the 1920s. Although efforts to curtail immigration since the late nineteenth century had resulted in numerous federal laws, none were as harsh as those passed in the 1920s, which cut the flow of immigrants down to a tiny trickle. The 1921 immigration restriction act set a limit on the number of European immigrants allowed into the United States. The number permitted to enter was limited to a percentage of immigrants from each country who lived in the United States in 1910. In that year large numbers of immigrants from southern and eastern European countries lived in the United States, so the quota from each country, while limited, still allowed newcomers from those countries to enter. Then, in 1924, Congress passed the Johnson-Reid Act, imposing a limit of 165,000 immigrants from countries outside the Western Hemisphere and pushing back the quota basis to 1890, a time when British, German, and Scandinavian

▶ Nicola Sacco and Bartolomeo Vanzetti, Italian self-proclaimed anarchists, were accused of murder in May 1920. The men and their supporters claimed they were on trial not for the crime but for their political beliefs and their immigrant status. After all appeals failed, the two were executed in 1927.

Bettmann/CORBIS

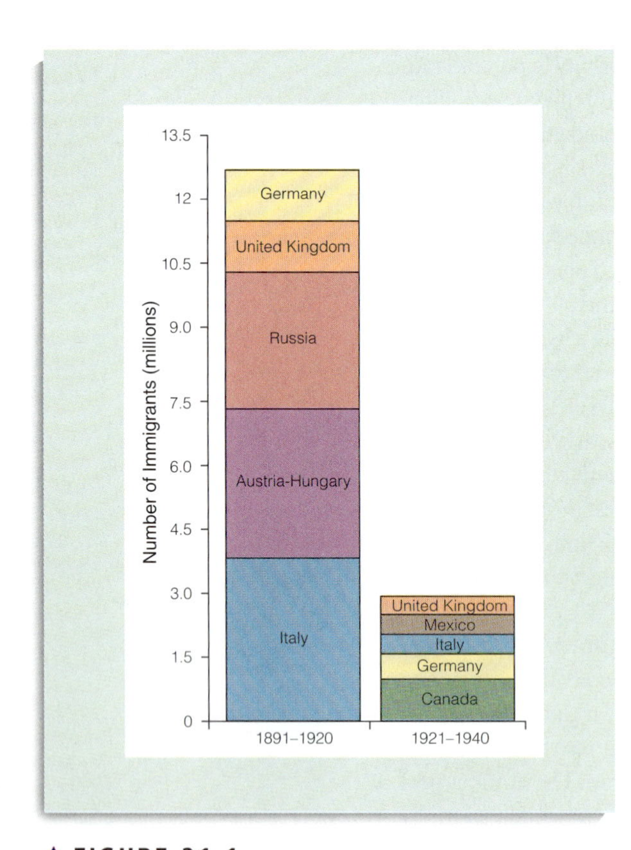

▲ **FIGURE 21.1**
NUMBER OF IMMIGRANTS AND COUNTRIES OF ORIGIN, 1891–1920 AND 1921–1940 Before the immigration restriction laws passed in the 1920s, most immigrants came from Russia and southern and eastern Europe. After immigration restriction, most came from western Europe and Canada.

immigrants dominated the foreign-born population. The Johnson-Reid Act limited entry every year to 2 percent of the total number of immigrants from each country who were present in 1890. This measure effectively barred Jews, Slavs, Greeks, Italians, and Poles because their numbers were so small in 1890. In addition, the 1924 law reaffirmed the exclusion of Chinese immigrants and added Japanese and other Asians to the list, effectively closing the door to all migrants from Asia.

Agricultural interests in California and Texas lobbied hard to keep the door open to Mexicans because of the low-wage labor they provided. In the aftermath of the Mexican Revolution, many Mexicans hoped to find stability and jobs in the United States. Between 1910 and 1930, more than 1 million Mexicans, nearly one-tenth of Mexico's population, migrated to the United States, where they found work in the farms, railroads, and mines. Recruiters often stood along the border, waiting to sign up laborers. In 1930 Mexican agricultural workers picked more than 80 percent of the perishable goods produced in the Southwest.

One of the most reactionary developments of the 1920s was the revival of the Ku Klux Klan (KKK), which became the most powerful white supremacy group in the nation, remaining active throughout the twentieth century. The Klan revival remained relatively small in the North until 1920, when its leaders mounted a national membership drive. Klan membership included laborers, businesspeople, physicians, judges, social workers, and women who felt that their homogeneous small-town Protestant culture was threatened by the evils of modern life, brought on by the presence and influence of morally suspect outsiders.

The Klan used vigilante violence as well as political mobilizations to attack African Americans, Jews, Catholics, communists, feminists, and other radicals, as well as divorced or allegedly promiscuous women. Growing to 3 million members by the early 1920s, the Klan wielded considerable power, especially in Texas, Oklahoma, Oregon, and Indiana. Some Klan members continued to engage in vigilante violence, while others held elaborate rallies and parades, burned crosses to intimidate and threaten their foes, and endorsed political candidates. Klan efforts in Oregon persuaded the state's lawmakers to pass a compulsory public schooling bill in 1922 that would have closed private and parochial schools, but the U.S. Supreme Court overturned the law. The Klan-controlled legislature in Oklahoma impeached and removed an anti-Klan governor. The power of the Klan persisted through the twentieth century. As late as the 1990s, the Klan still held considerable influence in some localities, running candidates for office, holding rallies and parades, and seeking legitimacy through civic volunteer projects.

Hulton|Archive/Getty Images

▲ Marcus Garvey, founder of the Universal Negro Improvement Association (UNIA), c. 1920. Born in Jamaica, the African American nationalist leader encouraged black people to move to Africa and establish their own nation.

Marcus Garvey and the Persistence of Civil Rights Activism

In the midst of a decade of reactionary policies toward outsiders and political activists, African Americans continued their struggle for civil rights. Jamaican-born black nationalist Marcus Garvey moved to New York City's Harlem in 1916 and opened a branch of his Universal Negro Improvement Association (UNIA). Garvey urged black people to establish their own nation-state in Africa: "Africa was peopled with a race of cultured black men, who were masters in art, science, and literature. . . . Africa shall be for the black peoples of the world." The UNIA staged colorful parades, which Garvey led in military uniform. His followers proudly wore the UNIA uniform to express their support for the movement and joined the parades in large numbers. Garvey published a journal, *The Negro World,* and encouraged the establishment of black-owned businesses. By the 1920s the UNIA had nearly 1 million followers and called for political justice and labor rights for black Americans.

In keeping with his belief in black-owned businesses, Garvey established the Black Star Line and encouraged his followers to invest in the shipping company. Nearly 40,000 African Americans invested three-quarters of a million dollars to purchase shares of Black Star stock. But the business ran into problems. Managers purchased ships that needed extensive and costly repairs, and the company ran up huge debts. Garvey claimed that he had paid for a ship that was never delivered. In 1922 Garvey was arrested and charged with mail fraud for advertising and selling stock for a ship that did not exist. Although the government lacked any concrete evidence to prove the case against him, Garvey was convicted and sentenced to five years in prison.

Garvey kept up his political activities from prison, sending a message to his followers: "My work is just begun. Be assured that I planted well the seed of Negro or black nationalism which cannot be destroyed even by the foul play that has been meted out to me." Garvey was released after two years and deported to Jamaica as an undesirable alien. Nevertheless, the momentum he sparked continued. The black publication *The Spokesman* declared, "Garvey made thousands think, who had never thought before. Thousands who merely dreamed dreams, now see visions."

Hollywood and Harlem: National Cultures in Black and White

In 1920, for the first time, the majority of Americans lived in towns and cities with populations greater than 2,500. Although this shift often is considered a watershed in the transformation from rural to urban America, it is worth noting that because the census defined

CONNECTING HISTORY

The Globalization of American Popular Culture

American movies, music, and other cultural products have long been popular in countries around the world. But American popular culture is also a product of international artistic exchanges that date back to the early twentieth century. In the silent movie era of the 1910s and 1920s, filmmakers in Hollywood drew on the artistic innovations of European directors, and some of the greatest American films stars, such as Italian Rudolph Valentino, Swedish Greta Garbo, and British Charlie Chaplin, were immigrants. By the 1920s, films set in foreign lands often played in lavish movie palaces designed by immigrants and stylized to evoke exotic locales, such as the monumental Egyptian Theater or Grauman's Chinese in Los Angeles. Producers in European countries successfully barred American films from entering their markets in the 1920s, but other forms of popular art, especially jazz music, found large audiences abroad.

The rise of fascism in Europe during the 1930s, and the war years that followed, closed down much artistic exchange. But after World War II American popular culture spread around the world, with the help of the U.S. government, as part of the nation's cultural diplomacy during the early years of the Cold War. American movies, rock 'n' roll, and clothing styles became major U.S. exports. At the same time, cultural products from around the world entered the United States and helped shape American popular arts. Films from Europe and Asia gained fans throughout the United States, and foreign artists such as Japanese director Akiro Kurosawa, Italian director Frederico Fellini, and Swedish director Ingmar Bergman had a profound influence on American filmmaking. Rock 'n' roll became an international phenomenon, emanating largely from the United States. But some of the most popular rock bands—notably the Beatles and the Rolling Stones—came not from America but from England. These groups drew on the artistic innovations of African American rhythm and blues, and their creativity in turn influenced American popular music that followed.

In the last third of the twentieth century, popular culture became a truly global phenomenon. While some observers bemoaned what they saw as pervasive Americanization, others celebrated the mixing and sharing of popular artistic forms. Turkish youth in Berlin created their own forms of rap music; filmmakers from China and the United States collaborated on productions; media stars performed for millions of viewers on the Indian version of MTV. Large corporations from outside the United States, such as the Japanese media giant Sony, began to purchase major American production companies such as Metro-Goldwyn-Mayer (MGM), one of the studios that had dominated the film industry since the 1920s.

any town with more than 2,500 inhabitants as urban, the majority of Americans still lived in small and ethnically homogeneous towns. Many small-town Americans still viewed big-city life with suspicion. They feared the decline of traditional Protestant American values of hard work, thrift, and discipline. Yet they were drawn to the new urban life. Jewish filmmakers, African American jazz artists, Irish and Italian club owners, and other "outsiders" created new leisure institutions where mainstream Americans shed their daytime routines for nightlife pleasures.

Hollywood on the West Coast and Harlem on the East Coast became centers of cultural innovation that spanned the nation. Eventually, the artistic productions of both centers attracted audiences of all racial, class, and regional backgrounds. Increasingly, as Americans moved from place to place, they encountered similar entertainments, music, arts, and consumer products. Movies, automobiles, radios, and advertising all fostered this emerging national culture.

Hollywood Comes of Age

As movie theaters spread into towns and cities across the country, the messages of Hollywood began to reach a mass audience and forge a nationwide popular culture. Movie stars and their films provided models for how to adopt new patterns of consumerism, leisure, city life, manhood and womanhood. Douglas Fairbanks showed middle-class men how to break free from the humdrum of white-collar work into the world of leisure. His attire of sports

One example of this transnational flow of artistic influence is the career of Hong Kong director John Woo, whose movies have become extremely popular in the United States. Drawing on a history of artistic exchange dating back to the early twentieth century, Woo's cinematic inspirations include American as well as Chinese filmmaking and cultural traditions. His productions involve the flow of capital, movie stars, and genres between Hollywood and Hong Kong. Describing his highly stylized scenes of action and violence, Woo explained, "When I shoot action sequences I think of great [American] dancers, Gene Kelly, [Fred] Astaire.... In action I feel like I'm creating a ballet, a dance. That's what I like. Even though there's violence, it's a dance. I make it a dance." This type of cross-cultural adaptation characterized Woo's 2002 film *Windtalkers,* the story of the Navajo code talkers during World War II. The Chinese director described his Hollywood film about Native Americans in the United States military as a "story about friendship and humanity rather than war and hatred...all about two different kinds of people. They come from different backgrounds but they both learn how to work and live together and influence each other. At the end of the film they become friends."

© Dean Conger/CORBIS

The Mongolian band Bayan Mongol, performing at a concert in Ulan Bator, Mongolia, in February 1984, shows the influence of American rock 'n'roll artists such as Elvis Presley and James Brown. The band trained in Poland and its repertoire ranges from Glenn Miller to Presley and Chuck Berry.

Although many fans as well as critics still identify most forms of popular culture as American phenomena, as Hong Kong/Hollywood director John Woo demonstrates, they are the result of a century of international artistic exchange in all directions. ■

clothes changed the way men dressed in their off-work hours. Female stars, such as Clara Bow, epitomized the flapper and taught female viewers how to be "naughty but nice."

Clara Bow, the "It" Girl

The most successful film director of the era, Cecil B. DeMille, made several films in which modern couples seek the right balance between fun and virtue in marriage. The popular DeMille formula offered a blueprint for couples like the Linganfields, whose divorce is described at the beginning of this chapter. In the typical DeMille plot, either the husband or the wife becomes bored with a spouse who, unable to shed drab old-fashioned virtue, refuses to take part in the leisure-oriented, sexually charged life of the 1920s.

In *Why Change Your Wife* (1920), for example, the heroine loses her husband by refusing to go dancing with him or to wear the sexy lingerie he buys for her. He abandons his wife for a fun-loving flapper, but he leaves the new flame when he finds that she wants only his money and has no interest in settling down to family life. By this time his ex-wife has discovered the error of her ways and transformed herself into an alluring "new woman." The former husband finds her at a beach resort, wearing a revealing swimsuit and surrounded by admiring men. The two renew their love and settle again into marriage, now combining the virtues of domestic life with the excitement of modern consumer culture and sexuality. The final caption of the film warns, "Ladies, if you want to be your husband's sweetheart, you must simply forget when you are his wife."

Ironically, as the nation closed its doors to immigrants, foreigners on screen captivated the imagination of a native-born population drawn to the allure of the outsider. Movie stars like

State Historical Association of North Dakota, A2938

State Historical Society of North Dakota, C0223

▲ **Views of Broadway in Fargo, North Dakota, the first taken in 1881, the second in the 1920s. By 1920, Fargo had developed into a bustling town with retail shops, paved roads, automobiles, and a streetcar line.**

Greta Garbo from Sweden, Dolores del Rio, Lupe Velez, and Ramon Navarro from Mexico, and Rudolph Valentino from Italy drew audiences with their foreignness. And yet, because movies were silent, their accented voices were not heard. Sound arrived in the late 1920s, bringing the voices and dialects of ethnic performers into the movies. For native-born Americans watching films in small towns and cities, sound movies brought the diverse voices of the cities into their communities. For immigrants, sound movies carried their own familiar accents and allowed for a greater sense of identification with the stars on the screen.

Photofest

▲ **Rudolph Valentino dances the tango in this famous scene from the 1920 film *The Four Horsemen of the Apocalypse.* Films in the 1920s featured exotic locales with foreign stars such as the Italian-born Valentino. In keeping with the public's taste for grandeur, lavish movie palaces emerged in cities across the country.**

Los Angeles and Its Environs

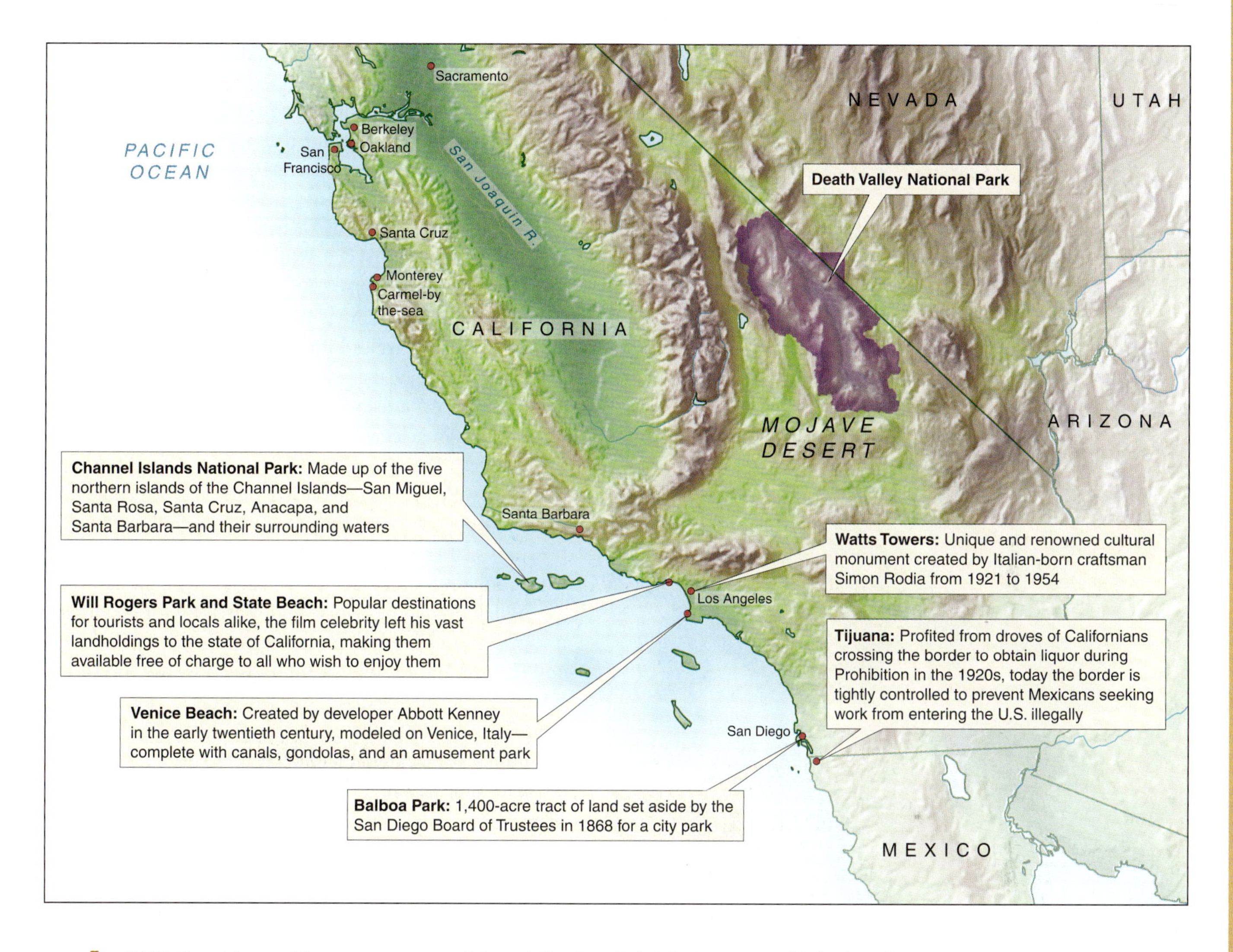

In 1780, Spanish-speaking newcomers arriving at the San Gabriel Mission established a village named Our Lady of the Angels that in time became the city of Los Angeles. Prior to statehood in 1850, California was part of Mexico. When the transcontinental railroad connected Los Angeles to the East Coast in 1876, this city grew rapidly, jumping from a population of 2,300 in 1860 to 100,000 in 1900. To meet its needs, the city constructed a harbor at San Pedro in 1914 and built aqueducts to carry melted snow from the Sierra Mountains for drinking water, a controversial system that is still in use. The discovery of oil, the development of the film industry (centered in Hollywood), and the establishment of defense industries ensured that Los Angeles would become a financial and cultural leader in the twentieth century. Located on the San Andreas Fault, however, the Los Angeles metropolitan area (population 15.8 million) is constantly threatened with earthquakes, as well as mudslides, fires, and other hazards from the unstable geography of the region.

Further south, San Diego grew quickly during World War II when the headquarters of the U.S. Pacific Fleet moved there from Hawaii after the bombing of Pearl Harbor.

The boundary between California and Mexico has been a continuous site of border crossings in both directions. ■

The Harlem Renaissance

While Hollywood in the 1920s developed on the West Coast, a flourishing center of African American culture emerged on the East Coast. The black arts movement known as the Harlem Renaissance drew on European as well as African and African American artistic traditions and gathered white as well as black intellectuals and artists. The young black poet Arna Bontemps was among the many artists drawn to Harlem. In 1924 he described Harlem as "a foretaste of paradise. A blue haze descended at night and with it strings of fairy lights on the broad avenues. From the window of a small room in an apartment on Fifth and 129th Street, I looked over the rooftops of Negrodom and tried to believe my eyes. What a city! What a world!"

©Donna VanDerZee

▲ Women out for a night on the town on a street in Harlem, New York City. During the years of the Harlem Renaissance, Harlem became the center of a flourishing music, literary, and artistic scene as well as home to lively jazz clubs that appealed to blacks and whites alike.

Like many other Americans in the 1920s, Bontemps had moved around the country. Born in Louisiana, at age four he moved to Los Angeles with his parents, who left the South in the hope of raising their children in an atmosphere less hostile to African Americans. The family settled in Watts, in the center of Los Angeles, and at the time a white neighborhood. He recalled, "We moved into a house in a neighborhood where we were the only colored family. . . . The people next door and up and down the block were friendly and talkative, the weather was perfect, there wasn't a mud puddle anywhere, and my mother seemed to float about on the clean air."

When Bontemps's Uncle Buddy arrived from Louisiana bringing stories of black life in the South, filled with "signs and charms and mumbo-jumbo," the boy was entranced. His father thoroughly disapproved of these stories, but Bontemps was drawn to the earthy sensuality of Uncle Buddy. He did not realize then that life in Jim Crow Louisiana had crushed Buddy's Creole pride and left him ruined and penniless.

When Bontemps finished school, the 21-year-old moved to Harlem. There he looked for the "Negro-ness" he felt his upbringing in California had lacked. In Harlem he found a thriving black community unlike anything he had known before. He landed a teaching job, married, and settled with his family, becoming one of the most prolific writers of the Harlem Renaissance.

Renaissance writers laid claim to their identity as Americans while articulating the culture, aesthetics, and experiences of African Americans. The poet Langston Hughes challenged white America to accept African Americans in his 1925 poem, "I, too, sing America":

> I, too, sing America.
> I am the darker brother.
> They send me to eat in the kitchen
> When company comes,
> But I laugh,
> And eat well,
> And grow strong
> Tomorrow,
> I'll be at the table
> When company comes.

Nobody'll dare
Say to me,
"Eat in the kitchen,"
Then.
Besides,
They'll see how beautiful I am
And be ashamed—
I, too, am America.

Schomburg Center for Research in Black Culture, Portrait Collection

▲ Poet Langston Hughes as a student at Lincoln University, Pennsylvania, in 1927. One of the major literary figures of the Harlem Renaissance, Hughes expressed the hopes, dreams, and sorrows of black Americans.

Although portraying the "exotic" and sensual in black culture was controversial among Renaissance critics, some of its greatest artists attracted huge followings among black as well as white audiences with unabashed and uninhibited celebrations of sexuality. Josephine Baker attracted large audiences dancing to jazz rhythms in her trademark banana skirt. She also used her visibility to criticize American racism and to crusade against lynching. Moving to Paris in 1925, Baker opened her own Paris nightclub, Chez Josephine, where she danced every night. Later, during the Cold War era, she defied anticommunist censors by traveling and performing all over the world and speaking out against American racial discrimination.

The music of black America was such an important marker of the era that it provided the decade with its most lasting moniker, *the Jazz Age.* Emanating not from Harlem but from New Orleans, Chicago, and St. Louis, jazz was, nevertheless, central to the black arts movement and the emerging national culture. With the help of the recording industry and radio, jazz and the blues began to reach a wide audience, primarily among blacks but increasingly among whites as well. Blues lyrics expressed themes of working-class protest and resistance to racism. Women who sang the blues, including Bessie Smith, Ma Rainey, and Ethel Waters, asserted their sexuality, their passion for men or for women, their resistance to male domination, their sorrows, and their strength. In "I'm No Man's Mamma Now," Waters sang about divorce not in lament but in celebration:

You may wonder what's the reason for this crazy smile,
Say I haven't been so happy in a long while
Got a big load off my mind, here's the paper sealed and signed,
And the judge was nice and kind all through the trial.
This ends a five-year war, I'm sweet Miss Was once more.

I can come when I please, I can go when I please.
I can flit, fly and flutter like the birds in the trees.
Because I'm no man's mamma now. Hey, hey.

I can smile, I can wink, I can go take a drink,
And I don't have to worry what my hubby will think.
Because I'm no man's mamma now.

Carter, "'These Wild Young People' by One of Them"

Black filmmaking also flourished during the Harlem Renaissance. Pioneer filmmaker Oscar Micheaux made dozens of films spanning three decades, including *Within Our Gates* (1919) and *Body and Soul* (1924). His films addressed complex themes of class and racial conflict. Known for his style as well as his talent, the six-foot-tall Micheaux wore long Russian coats and wide-brimmed hats and used his charm to raise the necessary funding for his films. As one of his leading actors recalled, he entered meeting halls as if "he were God about to deliver a sermon. . . . Why, he was so impressive and so charming that he could talk the shirt off your back." Micheaux managed to persuade white theater owners in the South to show his films because of the revenues they promised. Southern theater owners showed Micheaux's films during all-black matinees and at special midnight screenings to white audiences drawn to the allegedly sensual and exotic black experience.

Few people outside the black community took the Harlem Renaissance seriously as a major artistic movement until the civil rights era decades later. Nevertheless, the cultural vitality of the black community in the 1920s contributed to the forging of a national mass culture. White patrons who went "slumming" in Harlem or danced to jazz music in clubs across the country incorporated the creativity and vitality of black America into their understanding and experience of modern American life. Still, African Americans continued to face segregation and lynching as well as limited political and economic opportunities.

Radios and Autos: Transforming Leisure at Home

Radio played a major role in linking people across regions through shared information, advertising, and entertainment. By the end of the decade, more than 6 million radios were in use nationwide. Radios brought jazz and other forms of popular music to the airwaves, transforming the way music was enjoyed in American homes. Americans became more inclined to listen to music on their Victrolas and radios than to make music themselves. By the mid-1920s, sales of records surpassed those of sheet music; production and sales of pianos also dropped precipitously.

The number of radio stations soared from 30 in 1922 to 556 the following year, and national broadcasts began to supersede local ones. Airwaves became so cluttered that by the mid-1920s, the federal government, through the leadership of Secretary of Commerce Herbert Hoover, created the Federal Radio Commission to regulate and organize access. Meanwhile, American Telephone and Telegraph (AT&T) and the National Broadcasting Company (NBC) combined to form the first national network system, which gave programs and advertisers access to audiences across the country.

As radios entered millions of American homes, automobiles began to extend the mobility of Americans. The automobile offered the possibility of commuting to work without relying on public transportation, encouraging the expansion of suburban communities. The number of passenger cars in the nation more than tripled during the 1920s. The Federal Highways Act of 1916 had produced a network of roads all over the country, providing construction jobs and a slew of new roadside businesses, from restaurants to garages. Automobiles also stimulated the tourist industry; Florida, California, and Arizona became vacation destinations in this period. At the same time, tourism disrupted Native American communities in the Southwest as curious motorists intruded into previously isolated reservations.

Automobile production also revolutionized the consumer industry. The pragmatic Henry Ford built inexpensive, functional automobiles that he expected his workers to be able to purchase and keep. But Ford faced serious competition from General Motors' Alfred P. Sloan Jr., who developed the concept of **planned obsolescence** and put a new emphasis on auto styling to encourage customers to trade in their old cars for newer and more expensive models.

Wembridge, "Petting and the Campus"

More than style, however, automobiles offered Americans mobility. Many people mortgaged their homes or did without indoor plumbing in order to purchase a car. In the late 1920s, writer Ernesto Galarza noted that the Mexican migrant laborer knew "the Ford is not a perennial flower...far too much of his meager income is left in the tills of gasoline stations and tire shops in his long treks along the Pacific Coast." Cherokee humorist Will Rogers quipped that "America is the only nation in the world that is going to the poor house in an automobile."

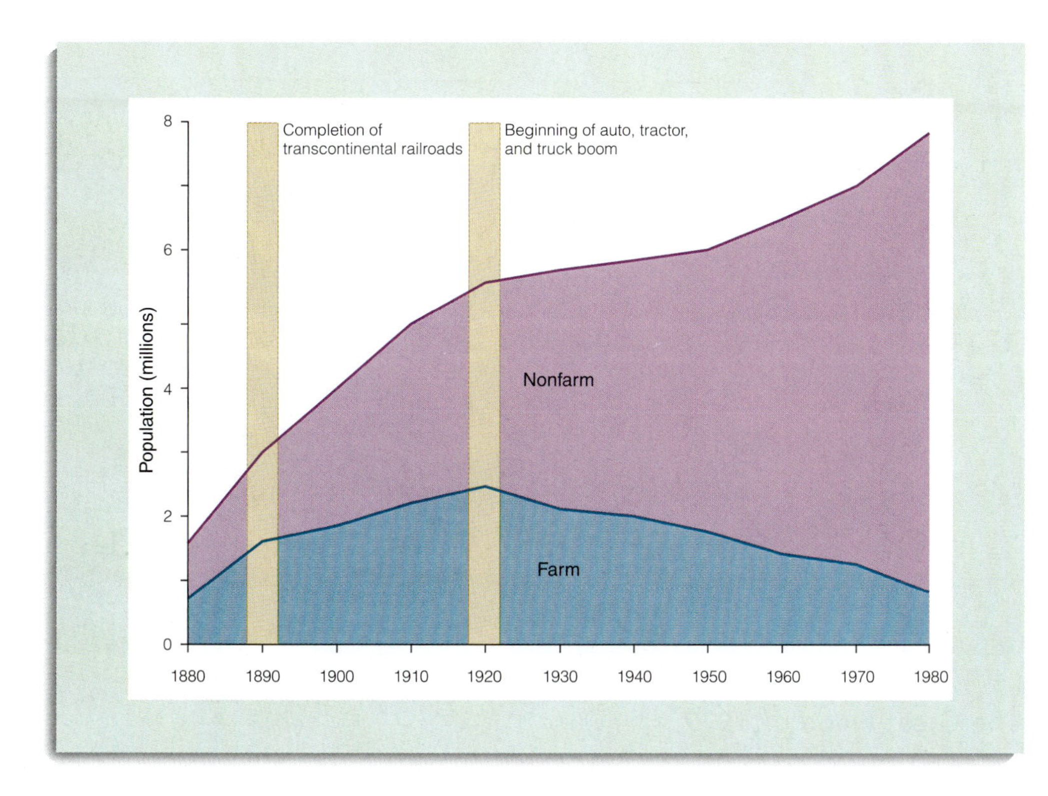

FIGURE 21.2
TRANSFORMATION OF THE UPPER MIDWEST, 1880–1980
With the completion of the transcontinental railroad, the population of the upper Midwest increased in both farm and nonfarm areas. When automobiles, tractors, and trucks became available, the farm population of the nation's "heartland" began to decline as the population of towns and cities increased.

The automobile was part of a consumer society increasingly focused on leisure, pleasure, and intimacy. Courtship patterns changed, and sexual activity increased as young couples abandoned the front porch for the back seat. Women gained new freedom and autonomy when they, too, took the wheel. Moralists worried that the automobile would provide youth with too much independence and privacy. One juvenile court judge announced that "the automobile has become a house of prostitution on wheels."

Science on Trial

Although advances in technology and medicine improved the quality of life for many Americans in the early twentieth century, scientific efforts to alter the natural world did not always lead to expected social benefits. One case in point was the engineering project to build levees along the Mississippi River to prevent flooding. These structures were expected to protect the settlements and agricultural developments in the fertile floodplains where the river would normally expand. As it turned out, the engineers were no match for the river. Scientific ideas were tested not only along the banks of the Mississippi River but also in the nation's courtrooms. Two major cases, the Scopes trial and the Supreme Court's decision in *Buck v. Bell*, subjected scientific ideas to judicial and cultural scrutiny. Although decisions in both cases resolved the immediate legal issues, the questions they raised continued to generate controversy and debate throughout the rest of the century.

"Oh, I beg your pardon! I thought you were extinct."

▲ This cartoon from the *New Yorker* reflects the intrusive aspects of tourism that developed in the Southwest, as well as the widespread erroneous assumption that Native American communities had died out by the twentieth century.

Bettmann/CORBIS

▶ The Mississippi River flood of 1927 devastated 26,000 square miles of prime farmland and homes across seven states. Levees built along the river's banks proved inadequate, despite engineers' assurances that the structures would prevent flooding. More than 900,000 people lost their homes, and crops and livestock worth more than $120 million were destroyed.

The Great Flood of 1927

For half a century the engineers of the Mississippi River Commission had adhered to a policy of building levees, assuming that strong barricades against the river's banks would prevent flooding. Presumably, the levees would allow the rich soil of the floodplains along the river to be settled and farmed rather than leaving the basins empty to provide places for the river to expand and contract. But the levee policy proved to be a disastrous example of human efforts to master the natural contours of the land. In March 1927, the rains came, and the river rose. Public authorities and river experts assured those who watched and worried that the levees would hold. They were wrong. Torrential rains caused the river to rage across the levees and the land beyond. The flood caused more than $100 million in crop losses and $23 million in livestock deaths. Journalists at the time called it "America's greatest peacetime disaster."

With the help of the Department of Commerce and the National Guard, the Red Cross set up 154 relief camps for flood victims. The camps were racially segregated. Refugees in the white camps were free to come and go and had more comfortable and generous accommodations and rations than those in the black camps. Armed guards patrolled the camps for black refugees and restricted people attempting to enter or leave. Black laborers had to register and give the names of their employers to receive any shelter or assistance. Only those planters were allowed to enter the camps and reclaim their workers. Relations between plantation owners and sharecroppers had been strained across the South before the flood, and many black laborers hoped to leave the plantations and find work elsewhere. But when labor agents came to the camps looking for workers to fill northern jobs, those patrolling the camps denied them entry. Federal authorities, including Secretary of Commerce Herbert Hoover, refused to intervene in local camp management. As a result, southern whites were able to force black sharecroppers back to work on their plantations. Despite the prisonlike conditions, many African American refugees managed to escape and made their way north.

The Triumph of Eugenics: *Buck v. Bell*

In 1924 racial theorist Lothrop Stoddard wrote a best-selling book, *The Rising Tide of Color Against White World Supremacy.* In this polemic, Stoddard predicted a war among the "primary" races of the world and warned of the "weakening" of the white race through immigration and "mongrelization." Stoddard wrote, "The melting pot may mix, but does not melt. Each race type, formed ages ago...is a stubbornly persistent entity. Each type possesses a spe-

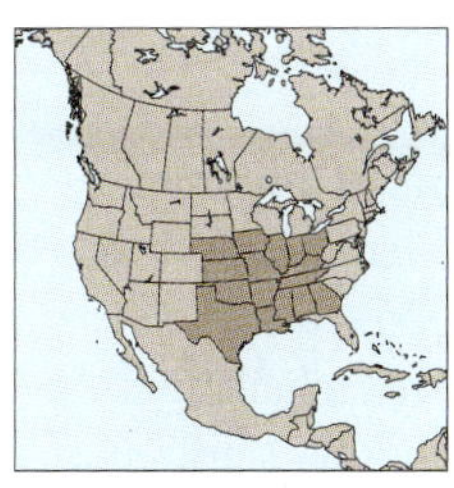

▲ **MAP 21.1 THE MISSISSIPPI RIVER FLOOD OF 1927**
The Mississippi River flood in 1927 sent water across a huge area of the South, extending as far west as Texas, covering most of Louisiana, Arkansas, and Mississippi, and reaching north into Kansas, Illinois, and Indiana.

cial set of characters: not merely the physical characters visible to the naked eye, but moral, intellectual, and spiritual characters as well." Stoddard's views were so familiar that F. Scott Fitzgerald placed them in the dialogue of his 1925 novel *The Great Gatsby.* Fitzgerald's intention was to discredit the theory by showing it to be as ludicrous as other fantasies of his hapless protagonist, Tom Buchanan, who mused, "The idea is if we don't look out the white race will be—will be utterly submerged. It's all scientific stuff; it's been proved."

Fitzgerald may have hoped to discredit Stoddard's ideas, but many Americans, including large numbers of policymakers, believed in white racial superiority. Supposedly scientific theories of race bolstered claims that distinct, biologically based characteristics divided humans into superior and inferior races. These theories had no scientific merit and were later thoroughly discredited. But in the 1920s, these dubious theories of racial superiority supported measures such as immigration restriction and eugenic sterilization laws. Eugenics was a pseudo-science based on notions of racial superiority. Eugenicists claimed that the Anglo-Saxon Protestant "race" was superior to all others, including Jews, Southern Europeans, Catholics, as well as nonwhites. Racial superiority, according to eugenic reformers, might be compromised not only by mixing with inferior groups but also by the propagation of individuals whose mental or moral condition rendered them inferior, and whose offspring would diminish the quality of the Anglo-Saxon "stock."

These ideas were consistent with the theories of Social Darwinists, who misused the ideas of Charles Darwin. Darwin's work on evolution focused on the origins of species in the animal world. Darwin found that weaker species died out, while stronger species evolved. Darwin did not study humans. But Social Darwinists claimed that Darwin's evolutionary theories were relevant to human society, arguing that only the fittest ought to survive. Social Darwinists argued against government aid to the poor and infirm, claiming that such assistance interfered with "natural selection" of the "fittest." Social Darwinism also supported eugenic theories that provided the rationale for sterilization of the "unfit."

Beginning in 1907, several states enacted eugenic laws that allowed the state to sterilize "inferior" individuals without their knowledge or consent. These laws authorized government and medical officials to determine whether or not an individual was inferior, or "feebleminded," and to order that the person be sterilized. Opponents of eugenic sterilization, mostly Catholic activists, challenged these laws in several states. In an effort to put an end to such challenges, eugenic advocates decided to test the constitutionality of the Virginia compulsory sterilization law. Their plan was to bring the case all the way to the U.S. Supreme Court, which they expected to uphold the law.

The proponents of the law selected the case of Carrie Buck, in part because she was white. Eugenic advocates did not want race to be at the center of the case, especially because eugenic sterilization laws did not target particular races; they simply targeted the "feebleminded." Feeblemindedness was a loosely defined criterion often used to label poor, immigrant, or minority women who were sexually active. At the age of 17 Carrie Buck, the daughter of an unmarried woman, was raped and became pregnant; as a result she was sent to a state institution for the feebleminded. Buck was labeled as feebleminded because she had borne a child out of wedlock and was therefore deemed morally unfit for parenthood. The noted eugenicist Harry Laughlin pointed out that Buck herself was born out of wedlock, as was her daughter, and described them as part of the "shiftless, ignorant and worthless class of anti-social whites of the South."

In the 1930s the Nazis in Germany modeled their sterilization policies on the California law.

Carrie Buck was sterilized in 1927. The following year, Buck's sister Doris was taken to the Virginia Colony for Epileptics and the Feebleminded and sterilized at age 16. She was told that she had had an appendectomy. Later, Doris Buck married and tried to get pregnant. None of the physicians she consulted told her why she could not conceive. She finally learned the truth in 1979. "I broke down and cried. My husband and I wanted children desperately. We were crazy about them. I never knew what they'd done to me."

No evidence established that Carrie Buck, her mother, or her daughter was below normal intelligence. Buck's daughter died as a child, but her teachers described the girl as bright. In writing the majority opinion for the Supreme Court that upheld the law, Justice Oliver Wendell Holmes wrote, "Three generations of imbeciles are enough." Within the next few years, 30 states had compulsory sterilization laws, and the number of operations rose dramatically. In the 1930s the Nazis in Germany modeled their sterilization policies on the California law. Finally, in the 1980s, a rare alliance of traditional Catholics and feminist activists succeeded in repealing compulsory sterilization laws.

Science, Religion, and the Scopes Trial

Many Americans were troubled by eugenics and its corollary, Social Darwinism. The populist leader William Jennings Bryan was among them. Bryan, three times the Democratic candidate for president and Woodrow Wilson's secretary of state, for 30 years had been a powerful voice for reform and social justice. Bryan believed that Social Darwinism was an ill-founded misapplication of scientific theory used to support the subjugation of women, the second-class status of ethnic and racial minorities, the neglect of the poor, and the practice of eugenic sterilization.

In Bryan's last public crusade, he defended his principles in a courtroom in Dayton, Tennessee, in July 1925. Tennessee had recently enacted the Butler Act, which made it illegal to teach the theory of evolution in the schools. The American Civil Liberties Union (ACLU) announced that it would defend any teacher charged with violating the Butler Act. A 24-year-old science teacher from the local high school, John Thomas Scopes, agreed to test the law. Using a state-approved textbook, Scopes taught a lesson on evolutionary theory on April 24 to his Rhea County High School science class. He was arrested on May 7 and quickly indicted by a grand jury. Bryan agreed to represent the prosecution; famed Chicago criminal lawyer Clarence Darrow headed the ACLU's team of defense lawyers.

The Rise and Fall of Man

▲ **This satiric political cartoon, published during the Scopes trial, depicts the theory of evolution as the development of humans from their origins as apes to the "survival of the fittest," portrayed as William Jennings Bryan. Bryan argued the case against evolution in the famous courtroom drama.**

Bryan did not oppose science, but he objected to its misapplication. Darrow did not oppose religion, but he argued that religious fundamentalists—"creationists" who believed in the literal interpretation of the Bible—should not determine the way science was taught in the schools. Reporters at the time, and since, cast the trial as a struggle between religion and science, with rural and small-town Americans on the side of creationism and secular urbanites supporting evolution. But the divide was not so clear-cut. Almost all advocates on both sides of the Scopes trial were Christians who disagreed over how to interpret the Bible. They were also believers in science; those opposed to the teaching of evolution considered it an unscientific theory.

The Scopes trial also contained elements of popular entertainment. Dubbed "the Monkey trial" because Darwin's theory of evolution demonstrated that humans evolved from an earlier primate form that included monkeys and chimpanzees, the trial was one of the first national media events. The judge invited reporters from around the country, including broadcast journalists. The Scopes trial was the first jury trial broadcast on live radio. More than 900 spectators packed the courtroom, and hundreds more gathered in the streets, where a carnival atmosphere prevailed, complete with souvenir stands, food vendors, itinerant preachers, and hucksters, including numerous chimpanzees accompanied by their trainers.

The trial did not deal with the question of the First Amendment, which guaranteed freedom of speech, nor the matter of who should decide the content of classroom education. Rather, religious fundamentalism was on trial. Although rules of evidence cannot apply to matters of faith, Darrow forced Bryan to defend his religious beliefs in a court of law. Darrow fully expected to lose the case so he could appeal it to the U.S. Supreme Court, and the jury obliged, reaching a guilty verdict in just nine minutes. Exhausted by the trial and ill with diabetes, Bryan died a week later.

Bryan technically won the case, but most reporters deemed the spectacle a victory for Darrow and the teaching of evolution. That assessment was premature. The Tennessee Supreme Court overturned the verdict on a technicality, robbing Darrow of his chance to take the case to the U.S. Supreme Court. Before the trial, most science textbooks included discussion of evolution; after the trial, material on evolution began to disappear. Laws against the teaching of evolution remained on the books until the U.S. Supreme Court overturned an Arkansas law in 1968.

The Scopes trial did not resolve the debate between creationists and evolutionists, and the controversy continued throughout the century. As late as 2000, the Board of Education in Kansas ruled that creationism and evolution were both unproven theories and that both could be taught in the schools. The Scopes trial may not have resolved anything, but it did have one significant unintended consequence. The trial generated tremendous interest in nonhuman primates. After the trial, attendance at the nation's zoos skyrocketed, boosting their funding and their prestige and improving the environment for animals in zoos. So in the end, the real winners in the "Monkey trial" were the monkeys.

Consumer Dreams and Nightmares

During the 1920s, spending on leisure and recreation nearly doubled. Faith in continuing prosperity promoted the extension of consumer credit to unprecedented heights. Previously, the only major item routinely purchased on credit was a house. But in the 1920s, installment buying became the rage for a wide range of consumer goods, from autos and radios to household appliances. Consumer debt rose from $2.6 billion in 1919 to $7.1 billion in 1929. As one official in a midwestern loan company remarked, "People don't think anything nowadays of borrowing sums they'd never have thought of borrowing in the old days. They will assume an obligation for $2,000 today as calmly as they would have borrowed $300 or $400 in 1890." This habit of buying on credit boosted the standard of living for many but also left families in a precarious situation and vulnerable to the vagaries of the broader economy.

Advertising Archive Ltd.

▲ In the 1920s advertisers used sexualized images to sell all sorts of products. This advertisement for automobile tires provides very little information about the product but evokes images of fun and romance to capture consumers' attention.

Marketing the Good Life

Advertising fueled much of the new spending. As one contemporary reporter noted, "Advertising is to business what fertilizer is to a farm." According to advertisers, consumer goods promised health, beauty, success, and the means to eliminate personal and embarrassing flaws, such as bad breath or dandruff. Cigarette companies used advertising to promote smoking as a symbol of independence for women and as a means to achieve beauty. Clever advertising campaigns promised women that if they would "reach for a Lucky Strike" instead of a sweet they would remain slim, healthy, and sexually appealing.

Advertising also fostered a vision of big business as a benevolent force, promoting individual happiness. In his 1925 best-seller *The Man That Nobody Knows,* advertising executive Bruce Barton portrayed Jesus as a businessman who gathered a group of 12 followers who believed in his enterprise and, through effective public relations and advertising, sold his product to the world. The consumer culture had its temples: movie palaces, department stores, and the 1920s innovation, the shopping center. Kansas City's Country Club Plaza, the first shopping center in the nation, was the brainchild of Jesse Clyde (J. C.) Nichols, who purchased 55 acres of swampland for the project. Like the architects of the movie palaces, Nichols looked to European aristocratic styles for inspiration. He chose a Spanish-Moorish theme for the plaza that included courtyards and stucco buildings with red tile roofs and ornate towers. He adorned the plaza's streets and sidewalks with works of art, columns, wrought iron, and fountains. Most significantly, he designed his shopping center with the car in mind. The shopping center originally boasted eight filling stations and numerous garages and parking lots. Skeptical city leaders called it "Nichols' Folly," but the Country Club Plaza was a commercial success.

DOCUMENT
Advertisements from 1925 and 1927

A much less successful venture was the Florida land boom, based on fantasies of a consumer paradise. When World War I closed off routes to the European playgrounds of the American elites, shrewd developers began to lure people to buy property in Florida with visions of "the graceful palm, latticed against the fading gold of the sun kissed sky." These promotional efforts sparked a frenzy of investment in Florida real estate. To create "earthly paradises" and resorts, developers rushed to construct roads and find new land on which to build. Forging the Tamiami Trail across 90 miles of Everglades swamp entailed dredging a canal, blowing up the submerged limestone layer with dynamite, piling the broken limestone beside the canal, and then crushing it into a road surface. The dangerous work claimed the lives of many laborers and severely damaged the sensitive ecology of the vast Everglades wetland. When the road was finally completed in 1928, the land boom had collapsed, claiming the fortunes of many hopeful but misguided investors.

Human folly and nature's fury contributed to the Florida land boom and bust. The boom peaked in 1925 and quickly collapsed. In 1926 a Danish ship, being renovated to become a floating cabaret, sank and blocked the entrance to the Miami harbor, stranding dozens of ships filled with building materials necessary for ongoing construction. Devastating hurricanes hit Florida in 1926 and again in 1928, killing thousands of people and destroying several towns. The destruction wrought by the hurricanes, and the exposure of exaggerated promotional advertisements and inflated prices, quickly put an end to land speculation in Florida.

Writers, Critics, and the "Lost Generation"

Some social critics claimed that the infatuation with consumerism fostered not only economic disasters such as the Florida land boom but also a stifling conformity. Sinclair Lewis was one of several novelists of the 1920s whose books expressed biting criticism of the frantic pursuit of material gain and status. George Babbitt, the protagonist of Lewis's novel *Babbitt* (1922), struggles to become accepted and successful in his small town by conforming to the empty materialism and standardized opinions accepted and prized by his neighbors.

F. Scott Fitzgerald wrote not about small-town conformity, as Lewis did, but about the modern urban life that was its antithesis. Fitzgerald glamorized, criticized, and in many ways embodied the giddy nightlife and status seeking of the Jazz Age. Born in St. Paul, Minnesota, into a family of modest means, he grew up admiring and emulating the wealthy. He married flamboyant flapper Zelda Sayre, daughter of a prominent Alabama judge, and together they embodied the dizzy, indulgent, free-spirited life of the decade. But Fitzgerald's novels, including *This Side of Paradise* (1920), *The Beautiful and the Damned* (1922), and *The Great Gatsby* (1925), criticized the era's obsessions with success, glamour, consumerism, advertising, and status. The Fitzgeralds, along with other writers who were critical of American superficiality and conformity, moved to Paris. Eventually, the life Fitzgerald both lived and criticized caught up with him. By the end of the decade, he—like the nation—was broken by his excesses. In 1931 he came home to Baltimore an alcoholic; Zelda was diagnosed with schizophrenia and spent the rest of her life in and out of mental institutions.

Hulton Archive/Getty Images

▲ **Gertrude Stein at age 70 and Alice B. Toklas with their white poodle, Basket II, posing on the doorstep of their villa in France.**

During their years in Paris, the Fitzgeralds often joined other expatriate writers at the salon of Gertrude Stein, a prolific author of novels, plays, operas, poems, and biographies.

Born in 1874 to German Jewish parents in Pennsylvania, she grew up in California and attended Radcliffe College in Massachusetts. In 1903 she moved to France, where she remained for the rest of her life, looking back to America for her subject matter. In Paris she met another American, Alice B. Toklas, who became her lifetime partner. Their openly lesbian relationship gave Stein material for her writing, including *The Autobiography of Alice B. Toklas* (1933). In the 1920s, she dubbed the writers who gathered at her salon the **"Lost Generation."**

Poverty Amid Plenty

Most Americans in the 1920s were neither investing in Florida real estate nor frequenting expatriate American writer Gertrude Stein's Paris salon. Even so, they were not immune to the desires and dreams that the consumer society sparked. The middle class and the more prosperous members of the working class enjoyed many of the comforts, amusements, and appliances that the booming economy made available; the poor struggled just to make ends meet. Throughout the 1920s, the nation's poorest people continued to be the most mobile, moving in search of jobs, security, and a place they could settle and call home. Henry Crews, son of a white Georgia sharecropper, longed for "that single house where you were born, where you lived out your childhood…your anchor in the world." But he never had such a home. Like that of many other hardworking sharecroppers and factory workers, his family moved frequently in search of a better life, a dream that often proved elusive.

If Zelda Sayre Fitzgerald embodied the Jazz Age, Myrtle Terry Lawrence embodied the experience of the sharecropper. Born in Alabama in 1893, she began chopping and hoeing cotton at age six. She spent two weeks in school in the first grade, which was the full extent of her formal education. She married Ben Lawrence when they were both 13 years old and had her first child at 14. With her husband she worked in the cotton fields for nearly three decades, eventually becoming a major organizer of black and white sharecroppers in the Southern Tenant Farmers' Union (STFU), which fought for the rights of landless farmers.

Myrtle Lawrence was poor, but she did not consider herself a victim. Her children described her as a "lady," although the tough-talking, tobacco-chewing Lawrence was hardly a southern belle. She took pride in vigorous outdoor work, which she preferred to indoor housework. As her daughter-in-law recalled, "She wasn't no housekeeper. Bless her heart." One of her sons boasted that his mother was paid extra to set the pace for the other workers, including the men, because "she was the best man." In the words of one daughter, "Mama wasn't slow at nothing." Myrtle Lawrence's energy and wits, as well as her refusal to be bullied, won her the admiration of her family and the respect of coworkers and propelled her in the 1930s to leadership in the STFU.

Sharecropping required hard work and careful planning to carve out a meager life, but many did so with pride.

Sharecropping required hard work and careful planning to carve out a meager life, but many did so with pride. Ed Brown, a young black sharecropper, had no formal education but considered himself "pretty schemy." He worked on six different plantations, moving about in search of better circumstances or to escape from debt or threats of violence. Although he and his wife, Willie Mae, were never able to buy a place of their own, they did improve their circumstances over time. When they finally got out of debt and secured a bit of cash, they used it to adorn their meager cabin. In 1929 they bought an old Model T Ford. But finding it too costly to maintain, they swapped it for a cow and a butter churn and dasher, which provided more practical benefits. Meanwhile, Ed took odd jobs to earn extra money, while Willie Mae took care of the children, picked cotton, took in laundry, and as Ed noted with appreciation, kept "things…lookin very pretty."

Life was a struggle for southern sharecroppers, black and white. African Americans faced the most difficult jobs and the added insults of racism. Blacks continued to move north in large numbers in search of improved opportunities. Immigrants had a better chance of moving into semiskilled jobs, while blacks were relegated to unskilled jobs. Many ended up in domestic service, where they worked long hours for low pay. They tried to avoid live-in work, where

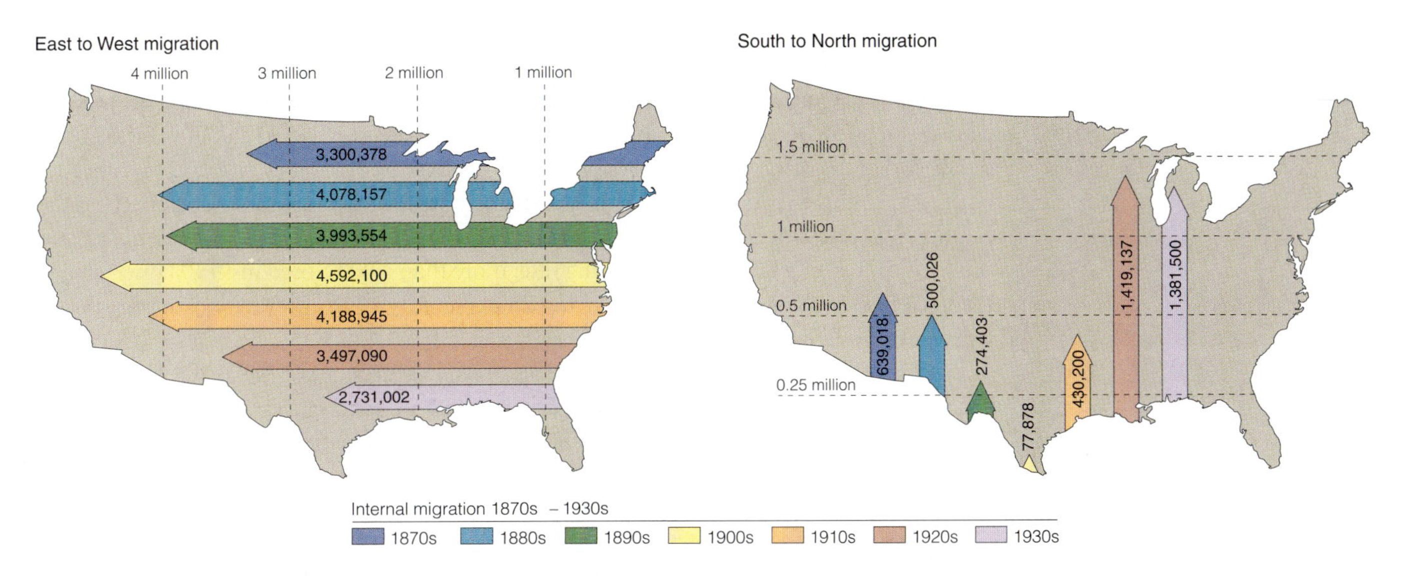

▲ **MAP 21.2 AMERICANS ON THE MOVE, 1870s–1930s**
Between the 1870s and the 1930s, millions of Americans moved around the country, mostly from east to west, but also from south to north.

they had little freedom from the watchful gaze of employers and barely any time with their own families. If they returned to the South, they faced work in the fields or factories for long hours under miserable conditions or in the extracting industries of coal mining, logging, and saw milling, where dangerous working conditions killed thousands of laborers.

Latinos joined African Americans at the bottom of the socioeconomic ladder in the Southwest and Midwest, working in jobs that offered almost no opportunity to save money or acquire property. Immigrants from Asia also faced difficulty finding stable jobs with decent pay and working conditions. Many ended up in domestic service. A young Japanese woman went to work for a family in Oakland, California. "I had to bring the coal up, all the time I went up and down," she later recalled. "Then I had to wash diapers. Me, I grew up on a farm, so I never had to do that. When I came to America, I didn't know anything. So I just had to cry." For many domestic workers, loss of a job also meant loss of housing, creating constant mobility. Nevertheless, the poor maintained strong ties of kinship and community and helped each other survive under difficult conditions.

Industrial workers struggled throughout the decade, especially in a political climate hostile to unions. With the crushing of labor radicalism in the Red Scare after World War I, union organizing and strikes declined. But workers continued to protest low wages and poor working conditions. In March 1929 young women textile workers in Elizabethton, a small town nestled in the Blue Ridge Mountains of eastern Tennessee, closed down the American Glanzstoff plant in protest against low wages, petty rules, and arrogant employers. Soon, the protest spread to textile mills across the region. At Glanzstoff, the strikers returned to work when the company promised better pay and agreed not to discriminate against union members. But the employers broke their promises, so the women struck again. The governor sent in the National Guard, armed with machine guns. More than 1,000 people were arrested in confrontations with the troops.

The strikers were young women mostly in their teens and early 20s. They combined labor militance with an air of playfulness. On the picket lines, they expressed their autonomy and independence, but they also found opportunities to flirt and carouse beyond the watchful eyes of parents. Although the strike was ultimately crushed and many of the participants were blacklisted, few expressed regrets. Bessie Edens knew she would not get her job back, but she "didn't care whether they took me back or not. I didn't! If I'd starved I wouldn't of cared, because I knew what I was a'doing when I helped to pull it. And I've never regretted it in any way. . . . And it did help the people, and it's helped the town and the country."

The Stock Market Crash

The symbolic end of the 1920s arrived on "Black Tuesday," October 29, 1929, when the inflated and overextended stock market came crashing down. In one day, stocks fell in value $14 billion. By end of the year, stock prices were down 50 percent; by 1932, they had dropped another 30 percent. In three years, $74 billion of the nation's wealth had vanished. The effect on the economy was catastrophic. Industrial production fell by half. More than 100,000 businesses went bankrupt. Banks failed at an alarming rate: more than 2,000 closed in 1931 alone. Unemployment rose to staggering levels, reaching 25 percent by 1932 and rarely dropping below 17 percent throughout the 1930s.

In keeping with the social policies that had prevailed throughout the 1920s, relief efforts were slim. No federal relief or welfare, no unemployment insurance, no Social Security, no job programs existed to help those who had lost their jobs, their savings, and their homes. Although many wealthy people lost their fortunes, which had been built on speculative investments, the poor suffered the most. People who lost their homes and farms moved into makeshift shelters in shantytowns, which they nicknamed **"Hoovervilles"** to mock the ineffectual efforts of President Herbert Hoover to respond to their plight.

The causes of the stock market crash and the decade-long economic depression that followed were complex and varied. Stock prices had risen dramatically, especially at the end of the 1920s. Speculators had been purchasing stocks on 10 percent margins, meaning they put down only 10 percent of the cost and borrowed the rest from brokers and banks. The popularity of installment buying in the consumer goods market had devastating effects when applied in this manner to the stock market. Investors expected to get rich quickly by selling their stocks at a higher price and paying back the loans from their huge profits. This system worked for a few years, encouraging investors with limited funds to make risky investments in the hope of gaining large fortunes. When the price of stocks spiraled out of control, far beyond their actual value, creditors demanded repayment of their loans, and investors were unable to pay their debts.

The collapse of the stock market alone would not necessarily have caused such a severe and prolonged depression. Poor decision making by financial and political leaders exacerbated underlying weaknesses in the economy. The Federal Reserve curtailed the amount of money in circulation and raised interest rates, making it more difficult for people to get loans and pay off their debts. These policies had profound worldwide implications and contributed to an international crisis. Banks in Germany and Austria, for example, depended on loans from the United States, and many went bankrupt, causing a ripple effect across Europe. The Hawley-Smoot Tariff of 1930 also contributed to the downward spiral. Although industrialists had convinced the Republican-controlled Congress that the tariff would protect American commodities from competition from cheaper foreign goods, they were wrong. Foreign governments retaliated by raising their own tariffs to keep out American goods. These monetary and trade policies backfired, and the economic crisis spread throughout the western industrial world.

No federal relief or welfare, no unemployment insurance, no Social Security, no job programs existed to help those who had lost their jobs, their savings, and their homes.

Within the United States, the unequal distribution of wealth exacerbated the effects of the economic downturn. Throughout the decade, the nation may have looked prosperous, but most of the wealth was concentrated in the hands of a small number of people. The gap between the rich and the poor widened during the 1920s, in part because of Coolidge administration policies that lowered taxes on the wealthy. The majority of the population lost purchasing power, resulting in the decline of consumer-oriented industries as the market for their products shrank. Although the wealthy spent money extravagantly, they spent a smaller percentage of their money on consumer goods than wage earners. If average Americans had been able to buy more cars, household appliances, and other products, those industries might have survived, and the economy might have recovered more quickly. Political leaders, and the business-oriented public policies they had promoted throughout the decade, left the country ill prepared to address the crisis and meet the needs of families deprived of their means of livelihood.

"Prosperity of the 1920s and the Great Depression"

F. Scott Fitzgerald, *The Great Gatsby*

F. Scott Fitzgerald's 1925 novel, The Great Gatsby, *expressed the longings of many Americans of the 1920s to partake of the glamorous life of the wealthy and live out their vision of the American dream. The story revolves around the desires of the newly wealthy Jay Gatsby to be accepted into the ranks of New York's elite. He is infatuated with Daisy Buchanan, who lives across the Sound from him in Long Island, a green light from her dock beckoning to him. In this passage from final paragraphs of the book, the narrator, Nick Carraway, comments on the elusiveness of Gatsby's dream—the American dream. The poignant ending of the novel foreshadows the collapse of the overextended leisure and consumer culture of the 1920s that led to the Great Depression of the 1930s.*

I spent my Saturday nights in New York because those gleaming, dazzling parties of his were with me so vividly that I could still hear the music and the laughter, faint and incessant, from his garden, and the cars going up and down his drive. One night I did hear a material car there, and saw its lights stop at his front steps. But I didn't investigate. Probably it was some final guest who had been away at the ends of the earth and didn't know that the party was over.

On the last night, with my trunk packed and my car sold to the grocer, I went over and looked at that huge incoherent failure of a house once more. On

Writer F. Scott Fitzgerald and his flapper wife, Zelda, personified the glamorous literati of the Jazz Age. In his writing, Fitzgerald both romanticized and criticized the decadent consumerism of the aspiring and upwardly mobile middle class. In this page from a scrapbook, their photos are adorned with autographs of other famous literary figures.

F. Scott Fitzgerald Papers, Manuscript Division, Department of Rare Books and Special Collections/Princeton University Library

the white steps an obscene word, scrawled by some boy with a piece of brick, stood out clearly in the moonlight, and I erased it, drawing my shoe raspingly along the stone. Then I wandered down to the beach and sprawled out on the sand.

Most of the big shore places were closed now and there were hardly any lights except the shadowy, moving glow of a ferryboat across the Sound. And as the moon rose higher the inessential houses began to melt away until gradually I became aware of the old island here that flowered once for Dutch sailors' eyes—a fresh, green breast of the new world. Its vanished trees, the trees that had made way for Gatsby's house, had once pandered in whispers to the last and greatest of all human dreams; for a transitory enchanted moment man must have held his breath in the presence of this continent, compelled into an aesthetic contemplation he neither understood nor desired, face to face for the last time in history with something commensurate to his capacity for wonder.

And as I sat there brooding on the old, unknown world, I thought of Gatsby's wonder when he first picked out the green light at the end of Daisy's dock. He had come a long way to this blue lawn, and his dream must have seemed so close that he could hardly fail to grasp it. He did not know that it was already behind him, somewhere back in that vast obscurity beyond the city, where the dark fields of the republic rolled on under the night.

Gatsby believed in the green light, the orgiastic future that year by year recedes before us. It eluded us then, but that's no matter—tomorrow we will run faster, stretch out our arms farther. . . . And one fine morning—

So we beat on, boats against the current, borne back ceaselessly into the past. ■

Questions

1. *Why would Fitzgerald use the Dutch sailors of the colonial period as a point of reference in this passage?*
2. *Critics have often pointed to Fitzgerald's ambivalence about modern urban life as expressed in* The Great Gatsby. *Do you see any ambivalence in this passage?*
3. *According to this passage, is Fitzgerald optimistic or pessimistic about the American dream?*

Source: F. Scott Fitzgerald, *The Great Gatsby*, 1925.

Conclusion

The 1920s witnessed the decline of the reform spirit that had prevailed in the Progressive era, the rise of conservative political leadership, and an economy spinning out of control. On the surface the country looked prosperous. Cities grew, an urban culture flourished, automobiles and other trappings of consumer culture proliferated. But beneath the visible affluence was the hidden poverty that prevailed throughout the decade. National leaders promoted business interests and paid little attention to social welfare, the environment, or the need to regulate the economy.

After achieving the right to vote, the women's movement fragmented. Radicals of all sorts faced a repressive political environment that curtailed union activism and political dissent. The movement for black economic empowerment persisted, especially under the leadership of black nationalist Marcus Garvey. But hostility to minorities and outsiders persisted.

Reactionary impulses led to Prohibition, immigration restriction, the Supreme Court's validation of compulsory sterilization laws, persecution of radicals and outsiders, and a revival of the Ku Klux Klan. The Scopes trial illustrated tensions between new scientific theories and traditional religious beliefs. By the end of the 1920s, it was clear that Prohibition was a dismal failure and that the federal government was ill equipped to enforce it.

Although political reform withered, cultural vitality flowered. Hollywood emerged as a major industry, and the Jazz Age reflected the widespread appeal of African American music. A black arts movement flourished, centered in Harlem, and writers of the "Lost Generation"—disenchanted with the status quo—gathered in Greenwich Village or moved to France. Across the country, a youth culture challenged the gender and sexual mores of the past. Consumer culture expanded as increasing numbers of families purchased cars, radios, and new fashions.

Few who were involved in the private preoccupations of the decade could have foreseen the disaster ahead. When the stock market crashed and the Great Depression set in, President Hoover tried to address the crisis by extending the political philosophy that had prevailed throughout the decade: Private enterprise would bring the economy back to health. But Hoover soon discovered that the old formulas would not work.

Sites to Visit

Harlem: The Mecca of the New Negro

etext.lib.virginia.edu/harlem/

This site is the online text of the March 1925 *Survey Graphic Harlem Number,* which includes writings of many Harlem Renaissance writers.

Calvin Coolidge

www.ipl.org/ref/POTUS/ccoolidge.html

This site contains basic information about Coolidge's election and presidency and an online biography.

Warren G. Harding

www.ipl.org/ref/POTUS/wgharding.html

This site contains basic information about Harding's election and presidency and an online biography.

Herbert Hoover

www.ipl.org/ref/POTUS/hchoover.html

This site contains basic information about Hoover's election and presidency and an online biography.

Harlem 1900–1940: An African American Community

www.si.umich.edu/CHICO/Harlem/

This site of the New York Public Library's Schomburg Center for Research in Black Culture includes information and articles about the history of Harlem as a center of African American cultural life.

The Scopes Trial

xroads.virginia.edu/~UG97/inherit/1925home.html

This site from the University of Virginia's American Studies program includes images, documents, and articles relating to the Scopes trial.

Temperance and Prohibition

prohibition.history.ohio-state.edu/

This site from Ohio State University covers the history of temperance and prohibition in the United States.

The Flappers

www.geocities.com/flapper_culture/

This site includes images, descriptions, and information on famous "flappers" of the 1920s.

For Further Reading

General

Ann Douglas, *Terrible Honesty: Mongrel Manhattan in the 1920s* (1995).

Lynn Dumenil, *The Modern Temper: American Culture and Society in the 1920s* (1995).

David J. Goldberg, *Discontented America: The United States in the 1920s* (1999).

Robert S. Lynd and Helen Merrell Lynd, *Middletown* (1929).

George Mowry, *The Twenties: Fords, Flappers, and Fanatics* (1963).

The Business of Politics

Kendrick A. Clements, *Hoover, Conservation, and Consumerism: Engineering the Good Life* (2000).

John Kenneth Galbraith, *The Great Crash, 1929* (1955).

William E. Leuchtenberg, *The Perils of Prosperity, 1914–1932* (1958, 1993).

Robert K. Murray, *The Politics of Normalcy: Governmental Theory and Practice in the Harding-Coolidge Era* (1973).

Burl Noggle, *Teapot Dome: Oil and Politics in the 1920s* (1962).

The Decline of Reform

Kathleen Blee, *Women of the Klan: Racism and Gender in the 1920s* (1991).

Nancy Cott, *The Grounding of Modern Feminism* (1987).

Kenneth Jackson, *The Ku Klux Klan in the City* (1967).

Matthew Frye Jacobson, *Whiteness of a Different Color: European Immigrants and the Alchemy of Race* (1998).

Desmond S. King, *Making Americans: Immigration, Race, and the Origins of the Diverse Democracy* (2000).

Nancy MacLean, *Behind the Mask of Chivalry: The Making of the Second Ku Klux Klan* (1994).

Andrew Sinclair, *Prohibition: The Era of Excess* (1962).

Hollywood and Harlem

Beth Bailey, *From Front Porch to Back Seat: Courtship in 20th Century America* (1988).

Ray Batchelor, *Henry Ford, Mass Production, Modernism and Design* (1994).

Nathan Irvin Huggins, *The Harlem Renaissance* (1971).

Angela J. Latham, *Posing a Threat: Flappers, Chorus Girls, and Other Brazen Performers of the American 1920s* (2000).

Virginia Scharff, *Taking the Wheel: Women and the Coming of the Motor Age* (1991).

Science on Trial

John M. Barry, *Rising Tide: The Great Mississippi Flood of 1927 and How It Changed America* (1997).

Richard Hofstadter, *Social Darwinism in American Thought, 1860–1915* (1944).

Daniel Kevles, *In the Name of Eugenics: Genetics and the Uses of Human Heredity* (1985).

Edward J. Larson, *Summer for the Gods: The Scopes Trial and America's Continuing Debate over Science and Religion* (1997).

Lawrence Levine, *Defender of the Faith: William Jennings Bryan, The Last Decade, 1915–1925* (1987).

Garry Wills, *Under God: Religion and American Politics* (1990).

Consumer Dreams and Nightmares

William Frazer and John J. Guthrie Jr., *The Florida Land Boom: Speculation, Money, and the Banks* (1995).

Jacqueline Jones, *The Dispossessed: America's Underclass from the Civil War to the Present* (1992).

Jackson Lears, *Fables of Abundance: A Cultural History of Advertising in America* (1994).

Roland Marchand, *Advertising the American Dream* (1985).

Nancy Milford, *Zelda: A Biography* (1970).

1930	Beginning of construction of Hoover Dam. Hawley-Smoot Tariff. 1,352 U.S. banks fail.
1931	Nine young African Americans (the "Scottsboro Boys") arrested on charges of rape.
1932	Black unemployment rates reach 50 percent. "Bonus Army" marches on Washington, D.C.
1933	Initial New Deal ("Hundred Days") legislation: AAA, FERA, CCC, TVA, NIRA. Adolf Hitler becomes chancellor of Germany. Twenty-First Amendment ratified.
1934	Indian Reorganization Act. Securities and Exchange Commission (SEC) created. Federal Housing Authority created.
1935	National Labor Relations (Wagner) Act. Social Security Act. Committee of Industrial Organizations (CIO) organized.
1936	Civil war in Spain. Hoover Dam on Colorado River completed, creating Lake Mead.
1937	Japan invades China. 170,000 workers participate in sit-down strikes. FDR's court-packing plan fails.
1938	Boxer Joe Louis defeats Max Schmeling. Fair Labor Standards Act. Congress creates Special Committee on Un-American Activities.
1939	First meeting of El Congreso de Pueblos de Habla Española.
1940	Smith Act. Nazis invade Denmark, Norway, Holland, Belgium, Luxembourg, and France.
1941	A. Philip Randolph's March on Washington Movement. FDR's "Four Freedoms" speech. Japan bombs Pearl Harbor.
1942	Executive Order 9066 (internment of Japanese and Japanese Americans). Congress of Racial Equality (CORE) founded. Japan conquers the Philippines.

PART EIGHT

From Depression and War to World Power, 1929–1953

THE GREAT DEPRESSION AND WORLD WAR II TESTED AMERICANS' faith in their federal government to a degree unmatched in the nation's history. Economic collapse in the 1930s and the threat of Nazi and Japanese aggression from 1941 to 1945 presented challenges beyond the reach of ordinary citizens, local communities, and businesses acting alone. The federal government began to take more responsibility for economic and social well-being at home and for the spread of American values around the world.

The Great Depression resulted in a fundamental reordering of American politics. President Franklin Delano Roosevelt (FDR), who took office in 1933, believed that the federal government must assume an active role in banking, agriculture, and social welfare. He sponsored a large number of federal initiatives, known collectively as the New Deal. The New Deal aimed to put people back to work, restore faith in American businesses, boost purchasing power among consumers, and cushion the effects of economic downturns on industrial workers.

The effects of the New Deal were uneven. Many workers, including domestic servants, agricultural laborers, and part-time and seasonal employees, did not qualify for Social Security and other benefits. In the South, government policies that discouraged landowners from planting crops led to the displacement of many black and white sharecropping families. On the other hand, employees of many large companies won higher wages and improved job security as a result of militant labor protests. African American civil rights activists, such local communist organizations as urban Unemployed Councils, and southern sharecroppers' and tenants' unions gave voice to the groups hit hardest by the Depression.

The New Deal did not end the Depression. On the morning of December 7, 1941, the Japanese conducted a surprise air attack on the U.S. Pacific naval fleet stationed in Pearl Harbor, Hawaii. Americans reacted with shock and outrage to what the president called this "day of infamy." The U.S. entry into World War II put large numbers of Americans back to work, many of them in the expanding defense industries.

The conflict brought Americans together in shared hardship, sacrifice, and national purpose. At the same time, the war placed strains on the social fabric. All over the country, family members separated from one another to search for work. In the Midwest, blacks and whites competed for scarce wartime resources, such as housing. On the West Coast, more than 100,000 Japanese immigrants and U.S. citizens of Japanese descent were forced into internment camps.

Elected to an unprecedented fourth term in 1944, Roosevelt proved to be a commanding leader during wartime as well as economic depression. In the last stages of the war, the president met several times with his British and Soviet counterparts, Winston Churchill and Josef Stalin, to plan for the postwar reconstruction of Europe and Asia. Roosevelt's death in April 1945 catapulted Vice President Harry S. Truman into the presidency. Germany surrendered to the Allies the next month. In August 1945, the new president authorized the dropping of atomic bombs on the Japanese cities of Hiroshima and Nagasaki, effectively ending the war in the Pacific. Together, the two bombs killed 120,000 Japanese civilians and wounded at least 130,000 more. The Atomic Age ushered in a new chapter in the history of human warfare.

Together with its allies, the United States emerged victorious from the war, but unlike its allies, America had escaped extensive physical destruction. The Soviet Union, an ally in the war against Germany and Japan, emerged as America's greatest enemy. The development of weapons of mass destruction introduced a new and profound threat to the natural environment, as well as to humans. To secure its supremacy in world affairs, the United States helped form the North Atlantic Treaty Organization (NATO). For the first time, Americans were part of a multination peacetime alliance, one that required them to defend a member of the alliance even if they themselves were not attacked.

World War II also profoundly altered life in the United States. The perceived communist threat led some Americans to suspect domestic groups of internal subversion: African Americans agitating for their civil rights, labor leaders attempting to organize southern factories, and leftists who expressed support for communism in general and the Soviet Union in particular. Supported by government contracts, the defense industry became an integral part of the nation's economy.

Recovering quickly from the disruptions of war, returning soldiers and their wives hoped to settle down to a normal family life. These couples produced the baby boom, a generation that shaped American culture and society in significant ways. In the new and growing suburbs, many (predominantly white) Americans achieved their dream of home ownership, and businesses found plenty of room to expand in new industrial parks. Yet, not all Americans shared in this newfound prosperity and security, and not all were willing to forgo their rights to free speech and free assembly in the struggle against communism.

1943 Smith-Connally Act.
Zoot-suit riots in Los Angeles. Attacks on blacks in Detroit.

1944 Normandy invasion on D-Day (June 6).
Servicemen's Readjustment Act (GI Bill).

1945 Harry S. Truman becomes president upon death of Roosevelt.
First test of atomic bomb, Alamogordo, New Mexico.
Atomic bombs dropped on Hiroshima and Nagasaki.
V-E Day (May 7); V-J Day (September 2).
United Nations created.

1946 *Morgan v. West Virginia* outlaws segregation in interstate transportation.
Winston Churchill gives "Iron Curtain" speech, Fulton, Missouri.

1947 Jackie Robinson joins Brooklyn Dodgers.
Taft-Hartley Act.
Truman Doctrine of containing communism announced.

1948 New Mexico and Arizona grant Indians right to vote.
Modern state of Israel founded.
Armed Services desegregated.
Organization of American States (OAS) founded.

1949 Billy Graham launches his first evangelical crusade in Los Angeles.
Establishment of People's Republic of China.
USSR acquires nuclear weapons.

1950 North Korean troops invade South Korea.
Internal Security Act of 1950.
Sen. Joseph McCarthy accuses State Department of harboring communists.

1951 Ethel and Julius Rosenberg convicted of treason.

1952 McCarran-Walter Act.
Puerto Rico becomes self-governing commonwealth.

1953 Korean War ends.
Soviet leader Josef Stalin dies.

CHAPTER 22

Hardship and Hope in the 1930s: The Great Depression

Joe Jones, *We Demand*, 1934. Gift of Sidney Freedman, 1948. Butler Institute of American Art, Youngstown, Ohio (948-0-110)

▲ This 1934 painting by Joe Jones, *We Demand*, expresses the increasing strength and militance of labor unions in the 1930s.

CHAPTER OUTLINE

The Great Depression

Presidential Responses to the Depression

The New Deal

A New Political Culture

Conclusion

Sites to Visit

For Further Reading

In 1934, Will Rogers commented on the causes of the Great Depression during his weekly radio broadcast. He noted that it was "not the working classes that brought on the economic crisis, it was the big boys that thought the financial drunk was going to last forever, and overbought, overmerged and overcapitalized." As a result, the "difference between our rich and poor grows greater every year. . . . Our rich are getting richer all the time. . . . There was not a millionaire in the country whose fortune did not come from the labor of others. We need to arrange it so that a man that wants work can get work, and give him a more equal division of the wealth the country produces."

Presidential candidate Franklin Roosevelt (left) delighted in the support of comic Will Rogers (right) in 1932.

Rogers was a Cherokee, a comedian, a plainspoken critic of the nation's rich and powerful, a movie star, a journalist, and an adviser to President Franklin Delano Roosevelt (FDR). Rogers articulated a new vision of American national identity that took shape in the 1930s. In contrast to an earlier notion of the United States as an Anglo-Saxon country into which newcomers might assimilate, this new Americanism included ethnic minorities, particularly those of European immigrant background. The Great Depression tarnished the status of the nation's business elite and opened up the political process to party realignments and new leaders. The popular culture expressed and reflected this new Americanism; Will Rogers was its most prominent voice. When the *Wall Street Journal* and the *New York Times* condemned him for his criticism of corporate elites, Rogers responded with a humorous assault on the nation's Anglo-Saxon leaders and their myths:

> I have a different slant on things, for my ancestors did not come over on the Mayflower. They met the boat. . . . I hope my Cherokee blood is not making me prejudiced, I want to be broad minded, but I am sure it was only the extreme generosity of the Indians that allowed the Pilgrims to land anywhere. Suppose we reverse the case. Do you reckon the Pilgrims would have ever let the Indians land? Yeah, what a chance, what a chance. The Pilgrims wouldn't even allow the Indians to live after the Indians went to the trouble of letting them land, of course, but they'd always pray. . . . You've never in your life. . .seen a picture of one of the old Pilgrims praying when he didn't have a gun right by the side of him. That was to see that he got what he was praying for.

Born in Oolagah in the Indian Territory of Oklahoma in 1879, Rogers got his start as a rope-twirling Indian cowboy on the vaudeville circuit. Like earlier Indian adventurers, including Sitting Bull, he worked his way through Wild West shows, which offered him an opportunity to demonstrate his impressive riding and roping skills, even though he found the spectacles demeaning to Native Americans, who were always defeated in the shows' mock battles. He worked as an entertainer in Hollywood in the 1920s, where his Cherokee identity shaped both his humor and his social criticism.

In the 1930s the Great Depression gave rise to a cultural and political upheaval that helped propel Rogers to stardom and political influence. President Franklin Roosevelt coveted his support, and Rogers obliged by promoting the New Deal, the president's program for economic recovery. However, Rogers also pushed the president to the left by advocating such measures as taxing the rich and redistributing wealth. In 1932 Oklahoma nominated Rogers for president as the state's favorite son; three years later, California Democratic leaders urged him to run for the Senate. But in 1935, before any of these possibilities could come to fruition, Rogers died in a plane crash.

The response to Rogers's death illustrates his stature as a national leader and spokesperson for a new multicultural America. Congress adjourned in his memory, President Roosevelt sent a well-publicized letter to Rogers's family, the governor of California proclaimed a day of mourning, flags flew at half mast, bells rang in Rogers's honor in more than 100 cities, and nearly 100,000 people filed by his coffin at Forest Lawn Cemetery. Radio stations across the country broadcast his memorial service from the Hollywood Bowl, presided over by a Protestant minister and a Catholic priest, while a Jewish performer sang a Hebrew mourning chant. Across town, Mexican American citizen groups placed a wreath on Olvera Street that read "Nosotros Lamentamos la Muerte de Will Rogers" ("We Mourn the Death of Will Rogers"). In the predominantly black Los Angeles community of Watts, an African American fraternal group joined black performers from Rogers's films in a parade to honor the Cherokee movie star. Back in his hometown of Claremore, Oklahoma, the Cherokee Indians performed a death dance in memory of their fallen kinsman.

The economic crisis unleashed changes in society that opened the door for a politically radical Cherokee Indian to become one of the most popular figures of the decade.

This massive national grieving reveals not only Rogers's popularity, but also the culture of 1930s America. The economic crisis unleashed changes in society that opened the door for a politically radical Cherokee Indian to become one of the most popular figures of the decade. Millions of Americans experienced poverty—many for the first time. The shared experience of loss and suffering permeated the country.

Franklin Roosevelt drew a new political coalition into the Democratic party that elected him to the presidency four times. It included native born and foreign born, working class and middle class, Anglo-Saxons and ethnic minorities, and people of color. The Depression gave Roosevelt the opportunity to forge a strong national government and to promote a more representative democracy. His inclusiveness efforts brought citizens of recent immigrant background into the political mainstream but stopped short of the color line. Nevertheless, African American voters abandoned the Republican party to vote for FDR.

The New Deal, a package of remedies put together by Franklin Roosevelt to address the problems of the Depression, provided relief to many Americans in need but did not eradicate poverty or end the Depression. Yet, as American families from every region of the country drew around their radios to hear the president's **fireside chats,** as they made heroes of Will Rogers and other outsider celebrities, and as they held onto their faith in the nation's promise in spite of its worst economic crisis, they helped forge a more inclusive nation.

The Great Depression

The Great Depression defined the 1930s in the United States. It shaped American culture, the political life of the nation, the public policies that resulted, and the cultural expressions that reflected the spirit of the people during a time of national crisis. Its effects permeated the lives of Americans from the mansions of the wealthy to the shanties of the poor and from the boardrooms to the bedrooms. But the story is not simply one of despair and hardship. It is also one of strong communities, resourcefulness, and hope.

Causes of the Crisis

The Great Depression of the 1930s was the worst economic depression in the nation's history. But it was neither the first nor the last. Capitalism, the economic system that forms the basis of the American economy, has cycles of ups and downs. Under capitalism, the free market operates with minimal interference from the government. In the United States, prior to the 1930s, the government stepped in to regulate the economy primarily to protect economic competition. Progressive Era reforms prevented corporations from establishing monopolies, so that competition could flourish. In the free market economy, consumers would determine which companies would succeed, based on the quality of their products and services. Because the government did not determine the levels of industrial or agricultural productivity, and did not set the prices, the economy was subject to changing circumstances that led to times of prosperity and times of recession or, in the case of severe economic downturns, depression. The circumstances that affected the up-and-down cycles of the economy included international economic trends as well as the workings of capitalism itself.

Communism and socialism provide different economic systems, with greater levels of government regulation. Communist countries have state-directed economies in which the government owns and operates the means of production, sets prices, and pays all workers' wages.

Margaret Bourke-White/TimePix/Getty Images

▲ **Margaret Bourke-White in her 1937 photograph "At the time of the Louisville Flood" depicts the painful irony of poverty in the midst of affluence. Here, hungry Americans line up at a breadline in front of a billboard proclaiming American prosperity.**

There is no free market and no competition among businesses. In socialist states, governments own and operate certain industries and services, such as electricity and other utilities, or health care systems. Socialist countries also provide citizens with certain welfare benefits such as medical care, relief from poverty, income for the unemployed, and old-age insurance. A number of capitalist countries offer these kinds of benefits to their citizens. These countries operate under a system known as welfare capitalism, or a **welfare state.**

Before the 1930s the United States provided none of these welfare state benefits. Without any policies that would serve as a safety net for workers who lost their jobs, many wage-earners and their families fell into poverty during times of economic downturn. In the Great Depression of the 1930s, the economic crisis was so severe that one quarter of the nation's workers, nearly 14 million people, lost their jobs, leaving them and their families—40 million people in all—without any income or security. Many of these people had never known poverty before. Among the newly poor were thousands of middle-class Americans who now faced the loss of their homes and savings. For working-class and poor Americans, the impact of the Depression was devastating because they had little economic security to begin with.

The Great Depression was a global economic catastrophe. Of the major world powers, only the Soviet Union—as a communist society, with state-directed labor, agriculture, and industry—was immune to the collapse of the capitalist system after 1929. In fact, the Soviet economy grew throughout the 1930s, and its relative health led many people in troubled capitalist systems to look to communism as an alternative. Socialism also gained many converts across Europe. The powerful nations of the world all moved toward greater government intervention in their economies. England, France, and the United States moved toward deficit spending to help stimulate the economy and instituted relief programs. Italy, Germany, and Japan also increased government intervention into the economy, but they used different strategies to address the crisis, particularly military spending. These varied responses to the Depression contributed to the conflicts and alliances that would eventually culminate in World War II.

Within the United States, the business values that had prevailed throughout the 1920s were now suspect. Business practices in every area of the economy, from finance to factories to agriculture, contributed to the disaster. For many Americans the Depression really began in the 1920s. Food production and distribution stumbled along weakly throughout the 1920s, leaving widespread rural poverty in its wake. Large corporations bought up smaller companies, putting many independent shops and manufacturers out of business. During the 1920s, 1,200 big corporations absorbed more than 6,000 independent businesses. By 1929, 200 corporations controlled nearly half of all industry, which limited competition and made it difficult for new, smaller businesses to flourish.

The concentration of wealth among the richest Americans during the 1920s contributed to the persistence of the crisis in the 1930s.

Although the economy in the 1920s looked healthy on the surface, prosperity rested on an unsound foundation. Many people obtained consumer goods on credit, so when people lost their jobs, they could not pay their debts. Throughout the decade, the gap between the rich and poor increased. By 1929 the top 1 percent of Americans earned 14.7 percent of the nation's income, while the poorest 40 percent shared 12.5 percent. Nearly 80 percent of the nation's families had no savings at all. Americans with high annual incomes of $10,000 or more—2.3 percent of the people—held two-thirds of all savings. As Will Rogers and many other social critics would later point out, the concentration of wealth among the richest Americans during the 1920s contributed to the persistence of the crisis in the 1930s.

International factors also played a role in the economic collapse. American overseas loans soared in the 1920s, reaching $900 million by 1924 and $1.25 billion by 1928. Germany was a large borrower, for example. Following its defeat in World War I, Germany had been required to make large reparation payments to France and other countries. The United States provided loans to Germany to help the country make its payments. When the stock market crashed, foreign economies like that of Germany also weakened and could not repay their debts. To make matters worse, American exports fell $1.5 billion between 1929 and 1933. The United States had established high tariffs to keep foreign goods out of the country so that Americans would buy only American-made goods. This, in turn, encouraged other countries to establish their own tariff barriers. Between 1929 and 1933, the Gross National Product (GNP) fell by $12 billion.

"We Are Not Bums"

In human terms the Depression of the 1930s dealt a devastating blow to large numbers of Americans: crushing poverty, hunger, humiliation, and loss of dignity and self-worth. Many felt a profound shame that they could no longer earn a living and support their families. The few jobs available often went to the young, strong, well fed, and well groomed. Thousands of citizens poured out their hearts in letters to the president, hoping that the government could provide some assistance. In 1934 an Oklahoma woman lamented, "The unemployed have been so long without food-clothes-shoes-medical care-dental care etc—we look prety bad—so when we ask for a job we dont' get it. And we look and feel a little worse each day—when we ask for food they call us bums—it isent our fault...no we are not bums." Yet the shabby appearance of the jobless helped neither their self-respect nor their work prospects. An unemployed worker from Oregon explained the difficult choices: "We do not dare to use even a little soap when it will pay for an extra egg [or] a few more carrots for our children."

Families provided the first line of defense against disaster, especially in the early days of the crisis. Many families adapted to hard times by abandoning time-honored gender roles. As men lost jobs, women went to work. More than 6 million single women held jobs during the Depression. Married women also took jobs to support their families, often providing the only source of income if husbands were out of work. These women faced hostility from those who assumed that employed wives with husbands who should be able to support them took jobs from unemployed men. But, in fact, working women did not take jobs from men; rather, they held jobs defined as "traditional women's work" as secretaries, nurses, and waitresses. These jobs offered lower wages than most jobs held by men. A white woman working for wages earned, on average, 61 percent of a white man's wages; a black woman earned a mere 23 percent. Still, they provided at least a modicum of much-needed income.

Sons and daughters also went to work, taking on the responsibilities of adulthood. Marriage rates plummeted as young people helped support their families in the face of economic hardship. Many parents struggled to provide for their families under difficult conditions, sometimes risking their health and safety to do so. Erminia Pablita Ruiz Mercer remembered when her father was injured while working in the beet fields in 1933. "He didn't want to live if he couldn't support his family," so he risked experimental back surgery and died on the operating table. Young Erminia then dropped out of school to work as "a doughnut girl" to support her mother and sisters.

Surviving Hard Times

For many poor families, hard times were nothing new. As one black man noted, "The Negro was born in depression. It only became official when it hit the white man." Throughout the 1930s black Americans suffered the impact of economic hard times disproportionately. By 1932 black unemployment reached 50 percent. Unemployed white workers began seeking the jobs that were usually held by black workers, even though they would have shunned such work during prosperous times. With local white authorities in charge of relief, impoverished Southern blacks had few places to turn for assistance. African Americans also faced increasing violence; the number of lynchings increased from 8 in 1932 to 20 in 1935.

Many poor people joined the growing ranks of **hobos,** riding the rails from town to town looking for work. But poverty did not erase racial hierarchies or sexual codes, especially for nine young African Americans who came to be known as the "Scottsboro Boys." On March 25, 1931, the youths, ranging in age from 13 to 21, were taken from a train in Paint Rock, Alabama, after a

▶ The Scottsboro Boys, pictured here surrounded by the National Guard, were sentenced to death on unsubstantiated accusations that they raped two white women on a railroad car in 1931. Although none were executed, they spent years in prison and became the focus of an international effort to gain their release.

Bettman/CORBIS

fight with a group of white men. Two white women, also on the train, accused the nine of rape. Narrowly avoiding a lynching, the youths were taken to jail in Scottsboro, where they began a long ordeal. Within two weeks an all-white jury convicted them of rape, and they were sentenced to death. The communist-backed International Labor Defense (ILD) took up the case and appealed it to the Alabama Supreme Court. The ILD also organized protests and rallies across the country, calling for justice for the Scottsboro Boys. The case gained international attention. The National Association for the Advancement of Colored People (NAACP) tried to get control of the case but withdrew when the defendants committed themselves to the ILD. In spite of the ILD efforts, the Alabama Supreme Court upheld the convictions, but in November 1932 the U.S. Supreme Court ordered a new trial on the grounds that the defendants did not get a fair trial.

The first defendant to be retried was quickly convicted again and sentenced to death. At this point, the ILD and the NAACP organized new protests and gained support from across the political spectrum. The case became a major rallying point for civil rights activists, liberals, and radicals throughout the 1930s. Support for the young men came from all over the world, including the British Parliament and the Communist party. In 1935 the U.S. Supreme Court reversed the second set of convictions on the grounds that excluding blacks from the jury denied the defendants due process. Yet in the next two years, five of the defendants were again tried and found guilty. Although none of the Scottsboro Boys was executed, they all spent long years in prison. The charges against the youngest four were eventually dropped. Although all appeals failed and the five remaining prisoners were never cleared of the crime, several were paroled, and the last of the nine was released from prison in 1950. In 1976 the repentant former segregationist governor of Alabama, George Wallace, pardoned one of the nine, Clarence Norris.

Racial discrimination intensified the suffering of African Americans during the Depression. By 1935, 90 percent of employed black women worked as either domestics or agricultural laborers. As these jobs became scarce, black women's labor-force participation fell from 42 percent to 38 percent over the decade.

Mexican American families could barely survive on the low wages paid to Mexican laborers. According to a 1933 study, working children's earnings constituted more than one-third of their families' total income. The work was often grueling. Julia Luna Mount recalled her first day at a Los Angeles cannery: "I didn't have money for gloves so I peeled chilies all day long by hand. After work, my hands were red, swollen, and I was on fire! On the streetcar going home, I could hardly hold on my hands hurt so much." Young Julia was lucky—her father saw her suffering and did not make her return to the cannery. But Carmen Bernal Escobar's father could not afford to be soft-hearted about work: "My father was a busboy and to keep the family going...in order to bring in a little more money...my mother, my grandmother, my mother's brother, my sister and I all worked together" at the cannery.

Those with cannery work, hard as it was, were among the fortunate. Many more Mexicans were deported. Most were children born in the United States. Throughout the century, the United States opened or closed its doors to Mexican immigrants depending on the need for their labor. They were deported during the Depression when unemployment was high, then recruited again during the labor shortage of World War II. In the 1930s, Mexicans who applied for relief were offered assistance only if they agreed to return to Mexico. But deportation brought more sorrows. In Ciudad Juarez, 2,000 repatriates lived in a large open corral without resources or shelter; dozens died from disease.

The Dust Bowl

Severe drought exacerbated the difficulties of farmers across Oklahoma, Texas, Kansas, Colorado, and New Mexico, an area that came to be known as the **Dust Bowl.** Farmers had

Arthur Rothstein, 1936. Library of Congress

◀ An Oklahoma farmer and his sons try to find shelter from the storm of dust that blew across the plains in 1935. Severe drought after years of excessive plowing created dry loose topsoil that was picked up by high winds. More than half of the residents of the Dust Bowl moved out of the area as a result of the devastation.

Interview about Life in a Government Camp

used the land mainly for grazing until high grain prices during World War I enticed them to plow under millions of acres of natural grasslands to plant wheat. Plowing removed root systems from the soil, and years of little rainfall caused the land to dry up. By the middle of the decade, high winds picked up the loose topsoil, creating dust storms across the open plains. The worst storm occurred on April 14, 1935, when winds up to 70 miles per hour carried clouds of dust that turned the sky black, suffocated livestock, and lodged in people's homes, clothes, hair, and lungs. The ecological disaster drove 60 percent of the population out of the region.

Migrant farm families fleeing the Dust Bowl came to symbolize the suffering wrought by the Depression. The photographs of Dorothea Lange, the songs of Woody Guthrie, and the writings of John Steinbeck all immortalized their plight. Steinbeck's Pulitzer prize–winning novel *The Grapes of Wrath* and its film version have remained classics of American popular art. Writing in *The Nation* three years before the publication of *The Grapes of Wrath* (1939), Steinbeck described the Dust Bowl migrants streaming into California:

> Poverty-stricken after the destruction of their farms, their last reserves used up in making the trip, they have arrived so beaten and destitute that they have been willing at first to work under any conditions and for any wages offered. . . . They are not drawn from a peon class, but have either owned small farms or been farm hands in the early American sense, in which the "hand" is a member of the employing family. They have one fixed idea, and that is to acquire land and settle on it. . . . They are not easily intimidated. They are courageous, intelligent, and resourceful. Having gone through the horrors of the drought and with immense effort having escaped from it, they cannot be herded, attacked, starved, or frightened.

Thousands of **Okies** piled belongings on their cars and made their way to California in hopes of starting over. There they joined Mexican migrant farm workers, African American laborers, and others down on their luck hoping for work.

Library of Congress

▲ Dorothea Lange took photographs for the Farm Security Administration (FSA) documenting the lives of Depression Era migrants. This 1939 photo, "Mother and Children on the Road, Tulelake, Siskiyou County, California," is one of Lange's many portraits of impoverished families.

Presidential Responses to the Depression

Until the collapse of the economy, President Herbert Hoover's political achievements had earned wide admiration. He seemed the perfect embodiment of the spirit of the prosperous 1920s. But his ideas about politics and economics were ill suited to the crisis of the 1930s. Dissatisfaction with Hoover's response to the Depression gave Franklin Delano Roosevelt a landslide victory in the 1932 presidential election. Promising to take action to ease the nation's suffering, the optimistic Roosevelt seemed to embody hope for an end to the crisis.

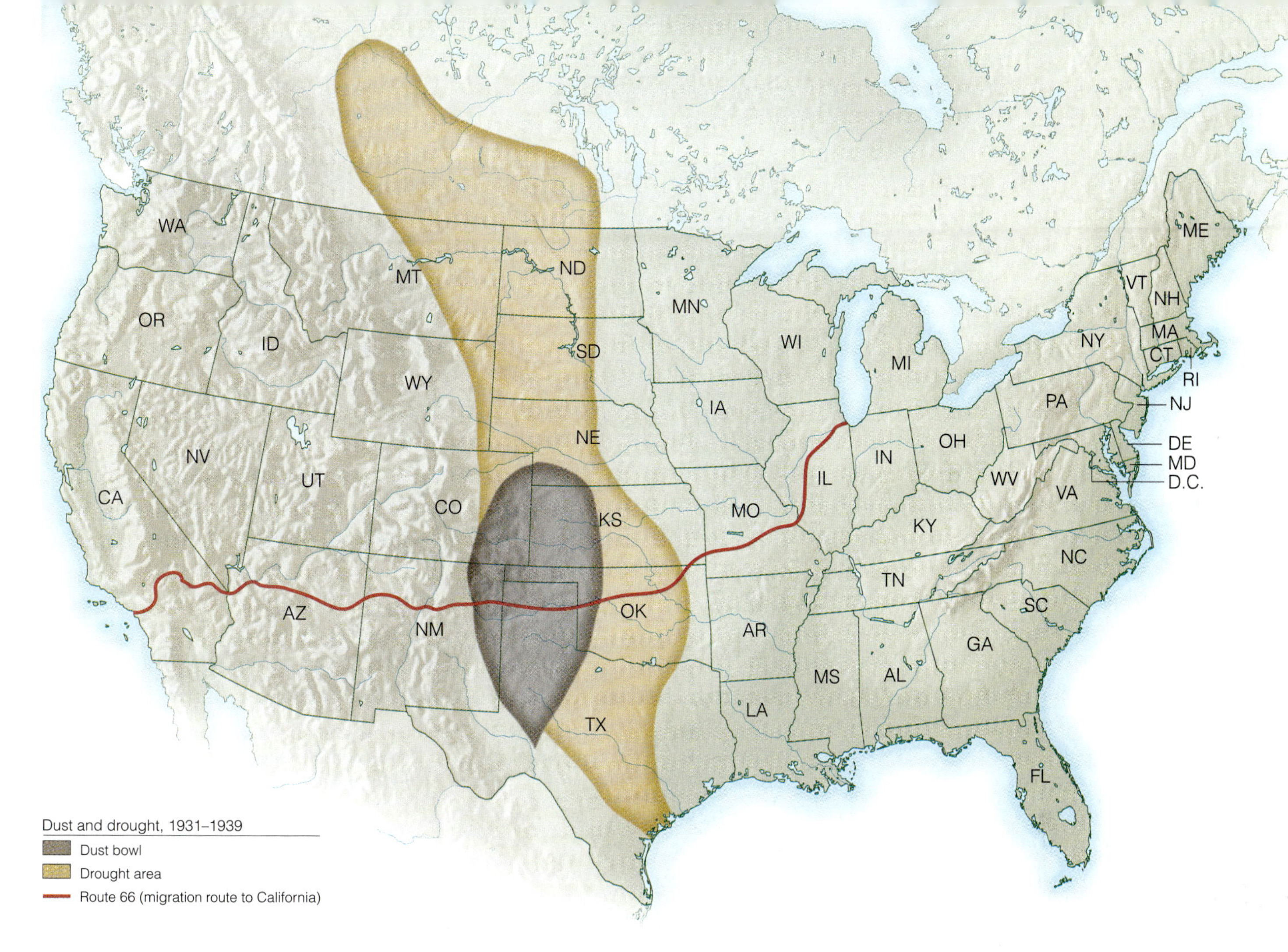

▲ **MAP 22.1 DUST AND DROUGHT, 1931–1939**
Drought cut a giant swath across the middle of America during the years of the Great Depression. The hardest hit region was the Dust Bowl area of Oklahoma, Texas, New Mexico, Colorado, and Kansas. Many people fled the afflicted areas, abandoning farms, piling their belongings on their cars, and driving along Route 66 to California.

Herbert Hoover: Tackling the Crisis

Hoover's first major political achievement came in Europe during World War I, when he headed the Commission for Relief in Belgium. There he organized a massive effort funded by private and government contributions that fed more than 9 million people for nearly five years. Later, he became the U.S. food administrator and headed the American Relief Administration. He earned praise as a visionary Progressive for his ability to mobilize volunteer efforts and to find efficient ways to meet people's needs. President Warren Harding then appointed him secretary of commerce.

It is no surprise that the popular Republican won the presidency in 1928. But even Hoover worried about "the exaggerated idea the people have conceived of me. They have a conviction that I am a sort of superman, that no problem is beyond my capacity. . . . If some unprecedented calamity should come upon the nation. . . I would be sacrificed to the unreasoning disappointment of a people who expected too much." The unprecedented calamity arrived, and Hoover's predictions were correct.

Had prosperity continued, Hoover might have left a legacy of presidential leadership to match his earlier achievements as a Progressive administrator of food relief in Europe. Declaring that "excessive fortunes are a menace to true liberty," he favored steeply graduated inheritance and income taxes on the wealthy, with no tax burden on the poor. He believed that society

Songs of the Great Depression

Popular songs expressed the spirit, sorrows, and longings of Depression Era Americans. According to folk-music historian Alan Lomax, the 12-year-old daughter of a striking Harlan County, Kentucky, mineworker wrote "Which Side Are You On?" in 1937. The song became a popular anthem for labor militancy.

Woody Guthrie (1912–1967) wrote more than a thousand songs about the struggles of common people and the dispossessed. As a teenager, Guthrie left home to hitchhike, ride the rails, live in hobo camps, and follow migrant workers around the country. His song "Union Maid" expresses the hopes and spirit of union workers, and "So Long, It's Been Good to Know Yuh" captures the sorrows of Dust Bowl migrants.

Bettmann/CORBIS

Woody Guthrie, singer and songwriter, immortalized the spirit of ordinary Americans during the struggles of the Great Depression. His songs became anthems of the era and remain classics of American folk music.

Which Side Are You On? By Florence Reece (sung to the tune of an old English song, "Jack Munro")

Come all of you good workers
Good news to you I'll tell
Of how the good old union
Has come in here to dwell.

Chorus
Which side are you on,
Tell me, which side are you on?

My daddy was a miner,
He's now in the air an' sun,
Stick with him, brother miners,
Until this battle's won.

They say in Harlan County
There are no neutrals there
You'll either be a union man,
Or a thug for J. H. Blair.

O gentlemen, can you
stand it,
O tell me if you can,

had a responsibility to care for those in need and that the prosperous should bear much of the burden. After the stock market crash, Hoover increased spending for public works—programs in which the government created jobs for people who needed employment—to the unprecedented sum of $700 million. He established the Reconstruction Finance Corporation to make government credit available to banks and other financial institutions. Seeking to restore confidence in the economy, he strove for a balanced budget by raising taxes and cutting spending—a strategy that underestimated the depth of the Depression and made the situation worse.

As the Depression set in and brought widespread misery, Hoover fully expected that charitable organizations would step in and provide assistance to the poor. He believed that government relief to the needy had demoralizing effects on people. In 1931 he pledged that if voluntary and local efforts were unable "to prevent hunger and suffering in my country, I will ask the aid of every resource of the Federal Government." But he had "faith in the American people that such a day [would] never come." Even when it was clear that the crisis was beyond the help of charitable groups, Hoover remained strongly opposed to direct relief for the poor. Private giving did increase to record levels; unfortunately, it was not sufficient.

Hoover felt that giving people the means to make a living was better than offering them direct relief. Thus, for example, he approved a grant of $45 million to feed livestock during the 1930 drought but rejected a proposed grant of $25 million to feed farmers and their fam-

Will you be a lousy scab,
Or will you be a man?

Don't scab for the bosses,
Don't listen to their lies,
Us poor folks haven't got a chance,
Unless we organize.

Source: "Which Side Are You On?" by Florence Reece © 1947 by Stormking Music, Inc. All rights reserved. Used by permission.

Union Maid By Woody Guthrie (first verse and chorus)

There once was a union maid
Who never was afraid
Of goons and ginks and company finks
And the deputy sheriffs who made the raids;
She went to the union hall
When a meeting it was called
And when the company boys came 'round
She always stood her ground.

Chorus
Oh, you can't scare me.
I'm sticking to the union, (3 times)
Oh, you can't scare me.
I'm sticking to the union, (2 times)
Till the day I die.

Source: "Union Maid." Words and music by Woody Guthrie. TRO-© Copyright 1961 (Renewed) 1963 (Renewed) Ludlow Music, Inc., New York, NY. Used by permission.

"So Long, It's Been Good to Know Yuh (Dusty Old Dust)" By Woody Guthrie (selected verses and chorus)

I've sung this song, but I'll sing it again,
Of the place that I lived on the wild, windy plains,
In the month called April, the county called Gray
And here's what all of the people there say:

Chorus
So long, it's been good to know you; (3 times)
This dusty old dust is a-getting my home,
And I've got to be driftin' along.

A dust storm hit, and it hit like thunder;
It dusted us over, and it covered us under;
Blocked out the traffic and blocked out the sun.
Straight for home all the people did run.

The sweethearts sat in the dark and they sparked,
They hugged and they kissed in that dusty old dark,
They sighed and cried, hugged and kissed
Instead of marriage, they talked like this:
Honey, so long, it's been good to know you...

Now, the telephone rang, and it jumped off the wall;
That was the preacher a-making his call.
He said, "Kind friend, this may be the end;
You've got your last chance of salvation of sin."

The churches was jammed, and the churches was packed,
And that dusty old dust storm blowed so black;
The preacher could not read a word of his text,
And he folded his specs and he took up collection, said:
So long, it's been good to know you. . . .

Source: "So Long It's Been Good To Know Yuh (Dusty Old Dust)." Words and music by Woody Guthrie. TRO-© Copyright 1940 (Renewed) 1950 (Renewed) 1963 (Renewed) Folkways Music Publishers, Inc., New York, NY. Used by permission.

Questions

1. *What makes the songs emblematic of the era in which they were written?*
2. *How are issues of class addressed in these folk tunes?*

ilies. His logic was consistent: Livestock provided farmers with the means to make a living so they could feed their families. But this philosophy offered little comfort to farmers who watched their families starve as their hogs lapped up food provided by the government.

Hoover's popularity reached its lowest ebb in 1932. A group of World War I veterans in Portland, Oregon, organized a march on Washington, D.C., called the Bonus March. The veterans were due to receive a bonus of $1,000 each in 1945. The group had asked to have their bonuses early, in 1932, to help ease their suffering during the Depression. But Hoover refused. More than 20,000 veterans traveled to Washington to petition Congress. The House passed a bill to pay the bonus immediately, but the Senate refused to follow suit. The determined veterans set up a tent city and settled in with their families. On the last day of the congressional session, when Hoover again refused to meet with the protesters, the veterans began to leave. But some did not depart quickly enough, and a police officer began shooting at the unarmed demonstrators, killing one person.

Bonus Expeditionary Force March on Washington

Army Chief of Staff Douglas MacArthur stepped in and escalated the violence. His troops used tear gas and bayonets to prod the veterans and their families to vacate the area, then set fire to the tent city. The attack injured more than 100 people and killed one baby. The image of federal troops assaulting a group of peaceful veterans horrified the public. Although MacArthur had ordered the brutality, the public directed its outrage against Hoover. As most

Presidents and the Media

Franklin Delano Roosevelt was one of several American presidents who used the media and the realm of popular culture to communicate effectively with the public and achieve political goals. Roosevelt broke new media ground with his use of the radio, particularly in his "fireside chats," in which he reassured the people during the Great Depression and explained his New Deal programs in order to gain public support. Before the radio, presidents used their oratorical skills in stump speeches and public declarations. Abraham Lincoln was a gifted orator at a time when political rallies were not only important civic events but also major arenas of popular entertainment. Some of Lincoln's major speeches, including his Gettysburg Address and Second Inaugural, have become part of the national democratic canon.

Theodore Roosevelt used the expanding popular press as a "bully pulpit" to gain public support for his domestic agenda of progressive reform and "trust busting" of large corporations, as well as for his military exploits abroad. John F. Kennedy took the media presidency to new heights with his effective mastery of television. Kennedy was the first president to inject an element of celebrity stardom into his media image, projecting an air of charm, grace, and wit. Although some found his media presence arrogant and aggressive, especially in televised debates during the 1960 campaign with his Republican opponent, Richard M. Nixon, he used television effectively throughout his

Franklin D. Roosevelt Library

Franklin Delano Roosevelt during a radio broadcast, October 14, 1938. Roosevelt mastered the medium of radio and used it effectively to communicate directly to the people. In what came to be known as "fireside chats," Roosevelt addressed his millions of listeners as "my friends."

people saw it, Hoover had heartlessly spurned the veterans' legitimate request. By the time of the 1932 election, Hoover had lost most of his public support.

Franklin Delano Roosevelt: The Pragmatist

In contrast to Hoover, Franklin Delano Roosevelt was born into a family of wealth and privilege whose ancestors included European aristocrats and passengers on the *Mayflower.* Pampered as a child, at age 14 he went to Groton, the nation's most exclusive boarding school; from there he attended Harvard College and Columbia Law School. In 1905, during his first year at Columbia, he married a distant cousin, Eleanor Roosevelt, the niece of president Theodore Roosevelt.

Franklin Roosevelt was elected to the New York State Senate in 1911, and in 1913 he became assistant secretary of the navy. He ran unsuccessfully as the Democratic vice presidential nominee in 1920. His political plans derailed suddenly in 1921 when he was stricken with polio. The painful and incapacitating illness threw the normally ebullient young man into despair. He had always assumed that he would control his own destiny. Now he could no longer use his legs. The formerly athletic Roosevelt depended on braces, crutches, and a wheelchair to move around. But his upbringing had given him extraordinary reserves of self-confidence and optimism, and these qualities helped to sustain him in the face of his paralysis.

presidency to cast himself as a tough Cold War warrior, a vigorous athlete (despite serious chronic disabilities), and a devoted family man (despite his adulterous behavior). During tense moments of the Cold War, particularly in the midst of confrontations with the Soviet Union over control of Berlin and missiles in Cuba, he appeared on television to warn the Soviet leadership of his resolve and to rally the nation behind him.

Ronald W. Reagan, known as the "great communicator," was the first professional actor elected to the presidency. His ease in front of the camera and his talent as a communicator allowed him to achieve a personal connection with his audience. Reagan's mastery of the media enabled him to convey his conservative political ideology to the nation and maintain broad-based popular support throughout his presidency. In the 1990s, Bill Clinton went one step further, appearing on talk shows, comedy hours, and MTV, where he played his saxophone, talked about his marital troubles, and answered personal questions about such things as the style of underwear he wore. By the time Clinton became president, the private lives and sexual behavior of politicians had become fair game for reporters. FDR and JFK had used the media to cultivate their images as strong leaders, while keeping their physical disabilities and their adulterous affairs far from public view. In those years journalistic ethics and etiquette placed the sexual behavior of presidents out of bounds. But all that had changed by the 1990s. The media exposed Clinton's affair with a White House intern, flooding the nation and the world with massive and detailed coverage.

Lynn Goldsmith/CORBIS

Taking his cues from media celebrities and attempting to appeal to the nation's youth, President Bill Clinton rouses the crowd at the 1993 MTV Rock 'n' Roll Inaugural Ball. Political leaders increasingly used the nation's mass media to promote their campaigns and develop a public persona.

FDR's bout with polio and subsequent paralysis did nothing to dampen his political ambitions. He became governor of New York in 1928, following the same career path as Theodore Roosevelt. But, unlike his Republican cousin, Franklin was a Democrat. In the 1932 presidential campaign, FDR made few specific proposals, but he promised the American people a "New Deal." Although Hoover was intensely unpopular, he had supporters within the Republican party who defended his record and supported his efforts to balance the budget. There were others on the ballot, notably socialist Norman Thomas and communist William Z. Foster. Polls showed that 5 percent of the electorate favored Thomas, but in the end only half of those, fewer than 1 million voters, actually marked their ballots for Thomas, and a much smaller number for Foster. Many voters on the left cast their ballots for Roosevelt, fearing that a vote for Thomas might throw the election to Hoover. FDR won a landslide victory, the largest electoral margin since 1864.

Like Theodore Roosevelt before him, FDR was committed to strengthening the federal government. But Franklin was less interested in protecting and preserving old-stock Anglo-Saxon Americans from the cultural and demographic impact of immigration than his Republican cousin had been. Lawmakers in the 1920s had closed off immigration, silenced dissenters, deported foreign radicals, and suppressed labor insurgency. In contrast, FDR identified the Depression as the nation's enemy rather than particular groups of Americans. His strategy was one of inclusion rather than exclusion; he welcomed the newcomers into his vision of America and cultivated their allegiance. Immigrants from southern and eastern Europe were among FDR's most ardent supporters. Millions of them became naturalized citizens and voted for the first time in the 1930s, overwhelmingly as Democrats.

"Nothing to Fear but Fear Itself"

Franklin D. Roosevelt, First Inaugural Address (1933)

In his inaugural address, Roosevelt endeavored to ease the nation's anxieties with reassuring words: "Let me assert my firm belief that the only thing we have to fear is fear itself—nameless, unreasoning, unjustified terror which paralyzes needed efforts to convert retreat into advance." Roosevelt launched his advance immediately. Panic had prompted many Americans to pull out their bank savings, causing many banks to fail. To stop the run on banks, FDR called Congress into a special session and announced a "bank holiday," temporarily closing all the nation's banks. He could have nationalized the banking system, a move toward socialism that would likely have received widespread support. But Roosevelt favored government regulation, not government ownership. He proposed the Emergency Banking Bill, providing government support for private banks. Congress passed the bill instantly, to the applause of the bankers who helped draft it.

Franklin Roosevelt, fireside chat (September 6, 1936)

In the first of his "fireside chats" to millions of radio listeners, whom he addressed as "my friends," Roosevelt assured citizens that the banks that reopened were sound. He used the medium of radio skillfully to explain his policies and to communicate comforting and reassuring messages that reached people in the intimate setting of their homes. FDR urged Americans to join with him in an effort to rebuild trust:

> There is an element in the readjustment of our financial system more important than currency, more important than gold, and that is the confidence of the people themselves. Confidence and courage are the essentials of success in carrying out our plan. . . . We have provided the machinery to restore our financial system; and it is up to you to support and make it work. It is your problem, my friends, your problem no less than it is mine. Together we cannot fail.

The next day, bank deposits exceeded withdrawals as a result of the confidence he inspired. Will Rogers spoke for many when he said, "My bank opened today. Instead of being there to draw my little dab out, I didn't even go to town. Shows you I heard Roosevelt on the radio." Mildred Goldstein from Joliet, Illinois, was among thousands who wrote to FDR in response to his "fireside chats." She explained what prompted her letter:

> You are the first President to come into our homes; to make us feel you are working for us; to let us know what you are doing. Until last night, to me, the President of the United States was merely a legend. A picture to look at. A newspaper item. But you are real. I know your voice; what you are trying to do. Give radio credit. But to you goes the greater credit for your courage to use it as you have.

The New Deal

The New Deal drew on Progressive Era reform impulses to extend the reach of the federal government to solve social problems. It provided assistance to many Americans suffering the effects of the Great Depression and established the welfare state that would last half a century. Based on pragmatism, experimentation, and shrewd political calculation, FDR's plan began with a flurry of activity in the first 100 days of his administration and developed into a more progressive agenda by 1935, often called the **second New Deal.** New Deal programs countered the cyclical nature of capitalism and offered a safety net for industrial workers.

They legitimized labor unions and established a system of regulation and cooperation between industry and labor. Many New Deal programs failed, but those that succeeded created the foundation of the modern American state. The broad-based reform effort, however, did not end the Depression or eradicate poverty.

The First Hundred Days

FDR understood that the people wanted "action, and action now." Roosevelt acted quickly and pragmatically. As one of his first acts, he encouraged Congress to repeal Prohibition. In 1933 the states quickly ratified the Twenty-First Amendment, repealing the Eighteenth. Repeal of Prohibition helped the economy by providing additional tax revenues from liquor sales, since they were now legal, and a market for farmers' corn and wheat, which were used in the production of liquor. Congress created the Securities and Exchange Commission (SEC) to oversee the stock market and the Federal Deposit Insurance Corporation (FDIC) to reform the banking system and provide insurance for deposits.

Roosevelt appointed a cabinet composed of a number of liberals, including Henry A. Wallace of Iowa as secretary of agriculture, Harold L. Ickes of Illinois as secretary of the interior, and Frances Perkins of New York as secretary of labor—the first woman ever appointed to the cabinet. In addition to his cabinet, FDR appointed several academics to serve as advisers known as the Brain Trust.

One of FDR's most pressing challenges was to prop up prices for producers while keeping them low enough for consumers. Poverty in the midst of plenty was one of the Depression's cruelest ironies. Because farmers could no longer afford to transport their goods to market, food rotted while millions of people went hungry. FDR took action by developing the Farm Relief Act, which included the Farm Mortgage Act that lowered mortgage rates for farmers to help them keep their farms. Also included was the Agricultural Adjustment Act (AAA). In a highly controversial provision of the AAA, the government sought to prop up farm prices by limiting supply. That is, it paid farmers to destroy livestock and take acreage out of production.

Many Americans recoiled at the systematic slaughter of 6 million piglets and the plowing under of 10 million acres of cotton. This policy boosted profits for larger farms but did little to alleviate the problems of smaller, poorer farmers. Sharecroppers and tenant farmers fared even worse.

Most Americans in need desperately wanted to work. They considered government relief a signal of failure and a source of deep shame and humiliation. Many citizens searched for ways to preserve their pride. One woman wrote to Eleanor Roosevelt asking to borrow money in order to avoid charity:

> *Please* Mrs. Roosevelt, I do not want charity, only a chance from someone who will trust me. . . . I am sending you two of my dearest possessions to keep as security, a ring my husband gave me before we were married, and a ring my mother used to wear. . . . If you will consider buying the baby clothes, please keep [the rings] until I send you the money you spent. It is very hard to face bearing a baby we cannot afford to have, and the fact that it is due to arrive soon, and still there is no money for the hospital or clothing, does not make it any easier. I have decided to stay home, keeping my 7 year old daughter from school to help with the smaller children when my husband has work. . . . The 7 year old one is a good willing little worker and somehow we must manage—but without charity.

In May 1933 Congress passed legislation creating the Federal Emergency Relief Administration (FERA), which provided $500 million in grants to the states for aid to the needy. Roosevelt placed Harry Hopkins in charge. Hopkins, an energetic and brash young reformer, disbursed $2 million during his first two hours on the job. He then persuaded Roosevelt to launch a temporary job program, the Civil Works Administration (CWA). The CWA provided

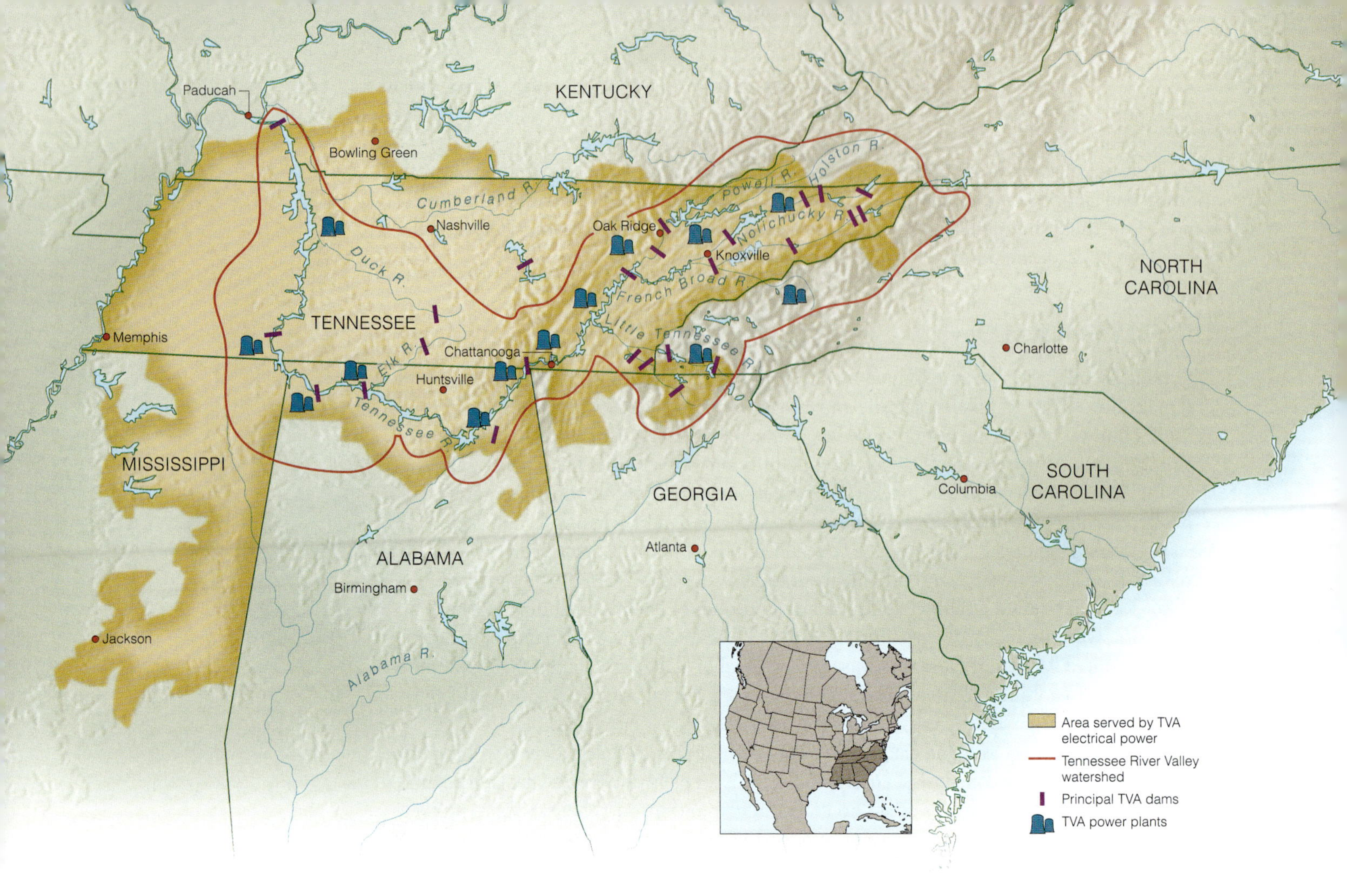

▲ MAP 22.2 AREAS SERVED BY THE TENNESSEE VALLEY AUTHORITY
The Tennessee Valley Authority (TVA) brought electricity to a large area in western Appalachia, one of the poorest regions in the country. The government-owned project strengthened the economy and improved living conditions in the area.

government-sponsored jobs for more than 4 million workers. But the program came under fire from conservatives, and FDR ended it a few months later.

The New Deal included two major programs that addressed conservation and environmental issues. In 1933, Roosevelt combined his interest in conservation with his goal of providing work for unemployed young men. The Civilian Conservation Corps (CCC) operated under the control of the U.S. Army. CCC workers lived in camps, wore uniforms, and conformed to military discipline. They planted millions of trees, dug canals and ditches, built more than 30,000 wilderness shelters, stocked rivers and lakes with nearly 1 billion fish, and preserved historic sites. Their work revived depleted forests and provided flood control. By 1935 the CCC had employed more than 500,000 young men and kept them, in FDR's words, "off the city street corners."

Another measure that linked natural resources to the recovery effort was the Tennessee Valley Authority (TVA), an experiment in government-owned utilities that brought power to rural areas along the Tennessee River in seven states in western Appalachia—among the poorest areas in the nation. This far-reaching government-owned project offered a radical alternative to American private-enterprise capitalism. Under the TVA, the government built 5 dams, improved 20 others, and constructed power plants; it produced and sold electricity to the valley's farmers and facilitated the development of industry in the region. The TVA also boosted local economies by selling fertilizer and electricity, and by providing flood control, and improving river navigation. Business conservatives and Southern Democrats in Congress opposed the plan because it used government money to provide jobs and electricity to rural African Amer-

The Tennessee Valley Authority

icans in the Tennessee Valley. Nevertheless, the TVA became one of the largest and cheapest suppliers of power in the nation. Years later, President Dwight D. Eisenhower condemned the TVA as a New Deal example of "creeping socialism," but it was one of Roosevelt's most successful and enduring projects.

The National Industrial Recovery Act (NIRA), passed by Congress in 1933, became the centerpiece of the first New Deal. The NIRA established the National Recovery Administration (NRA) to oversee the regulation of the economy. In his second "fireside chat," Roosevelt called the NRA "a partnership in planning" between business and government. The NRA enabled businesses in each sector of the economy to form trade associations and set their own standards for production, prices, and wages. But in return, businesses had to agree to recognize labor unions. Section 7(a) of the NIRA guaranteed collective bargaining rights to workers, sparking new hope for union organizers.

FDR's first hundred days also included the creation of the Home Owners' Loan Corporation, providing refinancing of home mortgages at low rates. Because the plan helped stem the tide of foreclosures and also guaranteed the repayment of loans, it pleased homeowners, banks, and real-estate interests. It helped gain for FDR the support of a large segment of the middle class.

One of the boldest New Dealers was John Collier, whom Roosevelt appointed as commissioner of Indian affairs. Collier opposed the policy of land allotment that resulted from the 1887 Dawes Severalty Act. Under allotment, Native American land holdings had dwindled from 130 million acres to 49 million acres—much of it desert. Collier rejected the assumption that Indians' survival depended on their assimilation into white culture. He altered the government boarding schools' curriculum to include bicultural and bilingual education and eliminated military dress and discipline.

Collier's ideas came to fruition in the 1934 Indian Reorganization Act, which recognized the autonomy of Indian tribes, did away with the allotment program, and appropriated funds to help Indians add to their land holdings. It also provided for job and professional training programs as well as a system of agricultural and industrial credit. In keeping with Collier's goal of Indian self-government, each tribe decided whether to accept the terms of the Indian Reorganization Act. In the end, 181 tribes voted to accept the law, while 77 opted out of it.

AP/Wide World

◀ On October 28, 1935, Commissioner of Indian Affairs John Collier stands with a group of Flathead Indian chiefs as Secretary of the Interior Harold L. Ickes signs the first constitution providing for Indian self-rule. Franklin Roosevelt appointed Collier to bring the New Deal to Native Americans.

TimePix/Getty Images

▲ The gigantic concrete walls of the Fort Peck Dam adorned the cover of the first issue of *Life* magazine in a 1936 photograph by Margaret Bourke-White. The dam was one of the monumental construction projects erected during the Great Depression.

The Navajo were among the tribes that rejected the Indian Reorganization Act. Many Navajo perceived Collier as yet another heavy-handed government agent. This tension heightened during an environmental conflict over Navajo herding rights. Convinced that the Navajo were herding far more sheep and goats than the fragile desert ecosystem could support, Collier proposed a plan by which the federal government would purchase 400,000 head of Navajo livestock. Although Collier had been more receptive to Indian concerns than almost any other federal authority who had preceded him, he could not reconcile the conflicting interests of tribal autonomy, environmentalism, and development.

Monumental Projects Transforming the Landscape

The New Deal years gave rise to monumental construction projects that altered the landscape and affected the natural environment. Skyscrapers, bridges, dams, and monuments built during the 1930s symbolized human and technological triumph in the midst of hardship. They provided jobs, sources of energy, and inspiration for many—but they also cost the lives of many workers, the natural contours of the land, and in some cases the homes and livelihoods of people living in their path.

In addition to the dams built as part of the TVA, gigantic new dams provided electricity and irrigation in the arid West. Construction on Hoover Dam on the Colorado River 30 miles from Las Vegas began in 1931. Working in the desert heat that sometimes reached 143 degrees, laborers built the colossal dam in four years. Heat prostration and accidents claimed several lives.

The huge Grand Coulee Dam piled 12 million cubic yards of concrete across the Columbia River in Washington State. Higher than Niagara Falls, standing 46 stories high and 12 city blocks long, it provided jobs to thousands of workers—77 of them died during its construction. The dam provided electricity to much of the Northwest and irrigation for over half a million acres of land in the Columbia basin. Some called it the Eighth Wonder of the World. In 1941 the Bonneville Power Administration hired folk singer Woody Guthrie to compose music to celebrate the dam's completion. Among the 26 songs Guthrie wrote was "Roll On Columbia," later designated the official state song.

While some rejoiced, others saw the dam as a tragedy. Members of the Arrow Lake Tribe (now part of the Colville Confederated Tribes) whose village, homes, and livelihood were destroyed when the river basin flooded, held a "ceremony of tears" commemorating the loss of the salmon and their habitat which had been the source of the tribe's economy.

Las Vegas/Hoover Dam Area

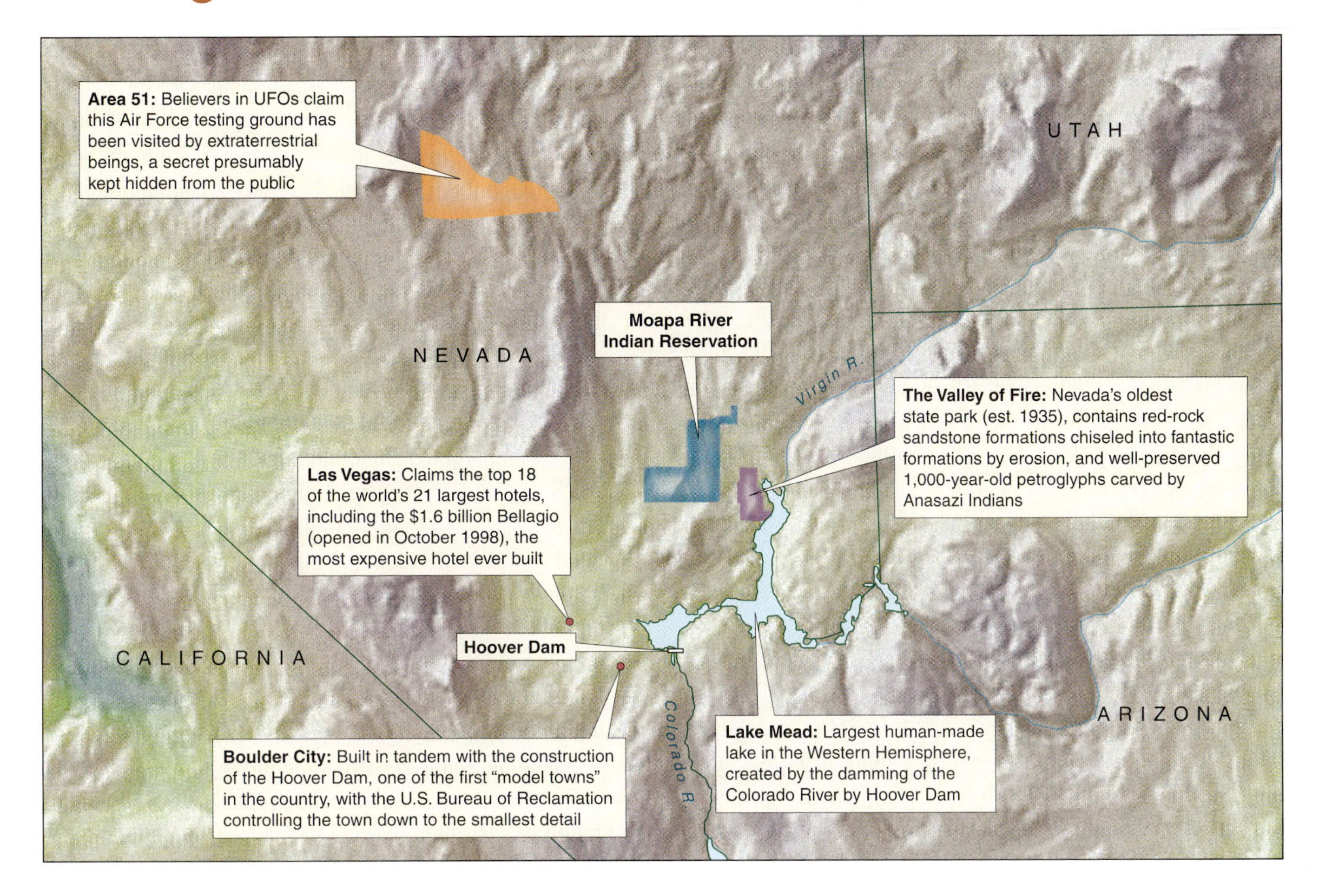

Four thousand years ago, the last remnants of the cold and wet ice-age climate that had covered southern Nevada began to retreat and the land began its transformation into the arid environment that it is today. Around 700 years ago, Paiute Indians settled the desert, followed in the 1700s and 1800s by Spanish missionaries and Anglo trappers. In 1830 a Mexican trader named Antonio Armijo explored an area in the region that he called Las Vegas, Spanish for "the Meadows."

In 1931, the U.S. Bureau of Reclamations began construction of the Hoover Dam, which lies 30 miles to the east of Las Vegas on the Colorado River. The cost of construction exceeded $175 million and involved more than 5,000 laborers who worked day and night for 46 months to complete the project in 1935. The energy and water provided by the enormous dam (725 feet high and 1,244 feet across) enabled the rapid growth of Las Vegas. The gambling industry also spurred the city's population, which increased from 8,400 in 1935 to 600,000 in 1990. Among the first grand casinos were the El Cortez, Desert Inn, and The Flaming Flamingo—opened by mobster Ben "Bugsy" Siegel in 1946. Today, Las Vegas is the fastest-growing metropolitan area in the United States, with much of its expansion centering on entertainment and tourism. An estimated 33 million tourists visit Las Vegas each year. ■

Taxi/Getty Images

Elephant rock in Valley of Fire State Park

The Golden Gate Bridge, another Depression-era project, spanned the entrance to San Francisco Bay. In spite of hard times, voters in the six counties surrounding the bridge approved a $35 million bonding bill to pay for it. The project was the first to employ a dramatic safety device: a huge net slung under the bridge. It saved the lives of 19 workers who fell during construction, but it gave way when a platform broke off, plunging 11 men to their deaths. When the bridge opened in 1937, 32,000 vehicles and 19,000 pedestrians passed over the picturesque engineering marvel on the first day.

Monumental architecture also soared skyward in the nation's cities. In 1930, construction began on the Empire State Building in New York City, the tallest building in the world up to that time. Other grandiose buildings altered the Manhattan skyline, including the dazzling and ornate Rockefeller Center, which opened its doors in 1937.

Farther west in South Dakota's Black Hills, a determined sculptor named Gutzon Borglum blasted tons of granite from 5,725-foot Mount Rushmore to carve out the portraits of four U.S. presidents—Washington, Jefferson, Lincoln, and Theodore Roosevelt. The project gained funding from Congress during the New Deal and reached completion in 1941. The site remains a major tourist destination to this day.

Protest and Pressure from the Left and the Right

Challenges to Roosevelt's New Deal took many forms. In spite of FDR's efforts to help businesses survive and remain profitable during the Great Depression, many business leaders continued to oppose the New Deal, charging that FDR was a dictator and that his program amounted to socialism. At the same time, FDR faced criticism from the left. Many people believed that Roosevelt's policies did not go far enough to ease the suffering caused by the economic crisis. Some thought that New Deal policies aimed at bolstering capitalism were ill-advised, and that capitalism itself was the problem. Disenchantment with capitalism drew many Americans to the cause of socialism and swelled the ranks of the small Communist party.

The Communist party drew its inspiration from the Soviet Union and, during the 1930s, developed a strategy known as the Popular Front to build alliances with sympathetic American liberals. Not all liberals belonged to the Popular Front, but many people with progressive political leanings shared with the socialists and the Communist party a commitment to economic justice, unemployment relief, civil rights, and union organizing. The actual membership of the Communist party remained small—it peaked at 100,000 during World War II, when the United States and the Soviet Union were allies—but its influence increased during the Depression.

> *"We were obliged to work very quietly, like Abolitionists in the South during the Civil War. . . ."*

By 1934 and 1935, much of the pressure on Roosevelt came from workers, whose hopes that the NIRA would guarantee collective bargaining rights were dashed by the intransigence of employers. The 1920s had taken a toll on labor unions. Membership had declined from a high of 5 million in 1920 to 2 million by 1933. But workers continued to strike for improved wages and working conditions. In 1934 nearly 1.5 million workers participated in 1,800 strikes. Often, unemployed laborers joined picket lines, refusing to work as strikebreakers.

Workers all over the country organized for better working conditions. Birmingham, Alabama, provides an apt example. The Depression hit Birmingham early and hard. By 1928, unemployment had reached 18 percent. Many impoverished black steelworkers, along with farm laborers in the surrounding countryside, joined the "invisible army" of the Communist party. Together, they fought for better working conditions and racial justice. One young black coal miner, Angelo Herndon, recalled the dangers of organizing and the need for secrecy: "With our few pennies that we collected we ground out leaflets on an old rickety mimeograph machine, which we kept concealed in the home of one of our workers. We were obliged to work very quietly, like the Abolitionists in the South during the Civil War, behind drawn shades and locked doors." Although most African Americans supported FDR and the Democratic party during the Depression, between 3,000 and 4,000 members of the black community of Birmingham, Alabama, joined the Communist party and related organizations.

Mexican laborers in California faced not only persistent exploitation in fields and factories but also the constant threat of deportation. During the Depression, approximately one-third of the Mexican population in the United States—more than half a million people—was deported to Mexico, even though the majority were native-born American citizens. Some of those who remained organized unions and struck for better pay and working conditions. During 1933, agricultural workers mounted 37 major strikes in California alone. They scored a number of successes; more than half of the conflicts led to wage increases.

Library of Congress

▲ By 1930 Mexicans were the predominant labor force in California agriculture. During the 1933 San Joaquin Valley Cotton Strike, between 12,000 to 20,000 workers walked out of the fields in protest over living conditions and poor wages. In particular, the strikers wanted their pay increased from 60 cents to $1 for every 100 pounds of cotton they picked. The photo here is of Mexican families on strike in Corcoran, California.

Dorothy Ray was only 16 years old when she began organizing Mexican workers at the grassroots level in California. She found it particularly rewarding to witness "the diminishing of bigotry...watching all those Okies and Arkies...all their lives they'd been on a little farm in Oklahoma; probably they had never seen a Black or a Mexicano. And you'd watch in the process of a strike how those white workers soon saw that those white cops were their enemies and that the Black and Chicano workers were their brothers." Another successful effort at multiracial organizing occurred in the Arkansas delta in 1934. The Southern Tenant Farmers' Union (STFU) brought together black and white tenants and sharecroppers to fight for better working conditions.

In addition to the communists, socialists, labor unions, and grassroots organizations that sprang up all over the country, a number of individuals proposed alternatives to Roosevelt's program and gained large followings. The most influential of these were Dr. Francis Townsend, Father Charles E. Coughlin, and Senator Huey P. Long. In 1934 Townsend, a retired physician and health commissioner from Long Beach, California, introduced an idea for a pension plan that sparked a nationwide grassroots movement. Townsend proposed a 2 percent national sales tax that would fund a pension of $200 a month for Americans over age 60. The **Townsend Plan** became hugely popular, especially among elderly Americans. In 1936, a national survey indicated that half of all Americans favored the plan. Though the plan was never implemented, the groundswell of support that it generated probably hastened the development and passage of the old-age insurance system contained in the 1935 Social Security Act.

Coughlin also inspired a huge following. A Catholic priest from Canada, he served as pastor of a small church outside Detroit, Michigan. He began to broadcast his sermons on the radio, using his magnetic personality to address political as well as religious issues. Soon he became a media phenomenon, broadcasting through 26 radio stations to an audience estimated at 40 million. The "Radio Priest" called for a redistribution of wealth and attacked Wall Street, international bankers, and the evils of capitalism. When a Minnesota radio station polled listeners to see whether they wanted to hear Coughlin's program, 137,000 said yes. Only 400 said no.

Initially, Coughlin strongly supported Franklin Roosevelt and the New Deal. But he soon grew impatient with what he considered the slow pace of New Deal reforms. In 1934 Coughlin launched his own political party, the National Union for Social Justice, which he used to challenge Roosevelt's leadership. The activist priest promoted a populist message that was hostile to both capitalism and communism. He told his radio listeners, "I call upon every one of you who is weary of drinking the bitter vinegar of sordid capitalism and upon everyone who is fearsome of being nailed to the cross of communism to join this Union which, if it is to

Coughlin, "A Third Party"

succeed, must rise above the concept of an audience and become a living, vibrant, united, active organization, superior to politics and politicians in principle, and independent of them in power." Soon, his message turned from social justice populism to right-wing bigotry. His virulent anti-Semitism and admiration for the fascist regimes of Adolf Hitler in Germany and Benito Mussolini in Italy drove away many of his followers. By 1940 Coughlin had ceased broadcasting and abandoned all political activities, under orders of the Catholic Church.

Huey P. Long was among the most powerful, and colorful, politicians of the era. He rose from modest origins to become a lawyer and a public service commissioner. In 1928, Long won the governorship of Louisiana. His progressive leadership inspired tremendous loyalty, especially among poor workers and farmers. He did more for the underprivileged people of Louisiana than any other governor. He expanded the state's infrastructure; developed social services; built roads, hospitals, and schools; and changed the tax code to place a greater burden on corporations and the wealthy. He proved unique among Southern politicians in that his public statements were free of racial slurs. But he also trampled the democratic process. His ambition had no bounds, and he used any means to accumulate power. Through his tremendous popular appeal, Long developed a huge power base and eventually gained control of Louisiana's legislature, courts, state bureaucracies, and even local governments.

In 1932 Long resigned the governorship and won election to the U.S. Senate. Soon, he gained a national following. Initially he supported FDR, but by 1933 he had broken with the president and forged his own political movement based on his Share-Our-Wealth Plan. Giving voice to the resentments many Americans felt toward "wealthy plutocrats," Long advocated a radical redistribution of the nation's wealth. He called for new taxes on the wealthy and proposed to use the funds to guarantee a minimum annual income of $2,500 for all those in need. As he put it, "How many men ever went to a barbecue and would let one man take off the table what was intended for nine-tenths of the people to eat? The only way you'll ever be able to feed the balance of the people is to make that man come back and bring back some of the grub he ain't got no business with." Long's plainspoken radicalism won the hearts of his followers, including Will Rogers, who publicly urged FDR to back Long's proposals. However, many of his congressional colleagues considered him an agitator. Such skepticism did little to limit Long's ambition, and by 1935 he was planning to challenge FDR in the next presidential election. But he never had the chance. In September 1935 the son-in-law of one of his vanquished political opponents assassinated him.

"How many men ever went to a barbecue and would let one man take off the table what was intended for nine-tenths of the people to eat?"

Other challenges took the form of viable third parties. In Wisconsin, the legacy of Progressive senator Robert M. La Follette was alive and well, particularly in the political popularity of his two sons, Senator Bob and Governor Phil. In 1934, the brothers formed the Wisconsin Progressive party, which supported the New Deal but pulled it strongly to the left.

Meanwhile in neighboring Minnesota, a coalition of workers and farmers formed the Minnesota Farmer-Labor party. In 1930 populist Floyd Olson became the nation's first Farmer-Labor governor. At the party's 1934 convention, Olson made his position clear: "I am not a liberal. I enjoy working on a common basis with liberals for their platforms, etc., but I am not a liberal. I am what I want to be—I am a radical. I am a radical in the sense that I want a definite change in the system, I am not satisfied with tinkering, I am not satisfied with patching, I am not satisfied with hanging a laurel wreath upon burglars and thieves and pirates and calling them code authorities or something else." Olson considered the possibility of a third-party bid for the presidency in 1936, but his plans never reached fruition. He contracted cancer and died in August 1936 at the age of 44.

On the West Coast, discontented voters mounted a similar challenge to party-politics-as-usual. Some Democrats persuaded Upton Sinclair, a veteran socialist and author of the 1906 muckraking novel *The Jungle,* to run for governor on their ticket in 1934. Sinclair ran on his End Poverty in California (EPIC) plan, which would have let the state take over idle land and factories and permit unemployed laborers to use them for their own needs. Sinclair won the 1934 California Democratic primary with an overwhelming majority. But Democratic party regulars, including FDR, refused to support his candidacy. Without the support of his own party, and facing opposition from wealthy Republicans who spared no expense to defeat him, Sinclair lost the election. Nevertheless, Sinclair's tremendous popularity signaled to Roosevelt that if he hoped to retain the support of his constituents, he would need to move significantly to the left.

Eleanor Roosevelt: Activist and First Lady

One of the most influential of FDR's advisers was First Lady Eleanor Roosevelt. An activist in her own right, Eleanor Roosevelt was widely considered the most powerful woman in American politics until her death in 1962. Like Franklin, Eleanor came from a sheltered, upper-class background. But her early life, unlike his, was filled with sadness. Both her parents died when she was a young child, and at age 10 she went to live with her grandmother, who left her in the care of a harsh governess. The young woman began to flourish when she went abroad to study. The rigorous education developed her strengths and confidence, which would serve her well throughout her life.

Eleanor bore six children in ten years. But she and Franklin had a partnership that was more political than sexual. Upon her discovery in 1918 that Franklin was having an affair with her secretary, Lucy Mercer, Eleanor moved into a separate house on the Roosevelt estate. The two remained married, developing a strong bond of friendship and a deep political alliance.

A powerful advocate for civil rights, social justice, women's equality, and international cooperation, Eleanor Roosevelt was largely responsible for many of the most humane programs of the New Deal. She spoke out publicly on a wide range of issues and prodded FDR to adopt her positions. Although FDR was reluctant to support an antilynching bill in Congress for fear of alienating Southern white voters, the First Lady campaigned vigorously against lynching. When the Daughters of the American Revolution (DAR) denied the African American opera star Marian Anderson the right to perform at Constitution Hall in Washington, D.C., Eleanor promptly resigned from the DAR in protest and arranged for Anderson to perform at the Lincoln Memorial on Easter Sunday 1939, where a huge audience stood in the cold to hear her sing.

After FDR died in 1945, Eleanor Roosevelt remained politically active until her own death at age 78. She was a major force in the adoption of the United Nations' Declaration of Human Rights in 1948, and she remained involved in Democratic politics throughout the 1950s. In 1962 President John F. Kennedy appointed her chair of the President's Commission on the Status of Women, which issued a report that identified widespread discrimination and helped to launch the feminist movement of the 1960s and 1970s.

UPI/Bettmann/CORBIS

▲ African American contralto Marian Anderson sings on the steps of the Lincoln Memorial on April 9, 1939. Eleanor Roosevelt arranged the concert after the DAR refused to allow Anderson to sing in Constitution Hall. The event attracted a live audience of 75,000, while millions more listened on the radio.

The Second New Deal

Although Eleanor Roosevelt exhorted FDR to promote civil rights, the president depended on southern white voters to be reelected and to get his New Deal measures through Congress. So he was careful not to alienate Southern Democrats by cultivating African American voters in the North. However, he did reach out to industrial workers. In the spring of 1935, Congress passed the National Labor Relations Act, also known as the Wagner Act, which strengthened and guaranteed collective bargaining and gave a huge boost to labor unions.

Also in 1935, Congress passed the Social Security Act, perhaps the most important and far-reaching of all New Deal programs. The act established a system of old-age pensions, unemployment insurance, and welfare benefits for dependent children and the disabled. The framework of the Social Security Administration shaped the welfare system for the remainder of the century. The welfare state established by the Social Security Act, extensive as it was, did not reach all Americans and left out many of the most needy. It also established a two-track system of welfare. One track provided workers with unemployment insurance and support in their old age. Programs like Social Security, designed primarily for male wage-earners, paid retired workers based on a percentage of the wages they earned while in the workforce. Social Security provided an important safety net for large numbers of workers and the elderly, but it did not cover domestic employees, seasonal or part-time workers, agricultural laborers, or housewives. The other track made matching funds available to states to provide relief for the needy, mostly dependent women and children with no means of support. Unlike Social Security, which was provided to many retired workers regardless of their circumstances, relief programs, which came to be known as "welfare," were administered according to need.

The architects of this welfare system included top New Deal advisers, many of them women who had been active reformers, such as Eleanor Roosevelt. These advocates hoped to protect women and children from the destitution that almost certainly resulted if a male breadwinner lost his job, deserted his family, or died. The system presumed that a man ordinarily earned a **family wage** that let him support his wife and children and that women were necessarily eco-

▲ In this mural on San Francisco's Coit Tower, "Industries of California," Works Projects Administration (WPA) artist Ralph Stackpole depicts the city's diverse workforce. Across the country, government-funded artists created works of public art that portrayed life in local communities.

TABLE 22.1

Key New Deal Legislation, 1933–1938

Year	Act or Agency	Key Provisions
1933	Emergency Banking Act	Reopened banks under government supervision
	Civilian Conservation Corps (CCC)	Employed young men in reforestation, flood control, road construction, and soil erosion control projects
	Federal Emergency Relief Act (FERA)	Provided federal funds for state and local relief efforts
	Agricultural Adjustment Act (AAA)	Granted farmers direct payments for reducing crop production; funds for payment provided by a processing tax, later declared unconstitutional
	Farm Mortgage Act	Provided funds to refinance farm mortgages
	Tennessee Valley Authority (TVA)	Constructed dams and power projects and developed the economy of a seven-state area in the Tennessee River Valley
	Home Owners' Loan Corporation	Provided funds for refinancing home mortgages of nonfarm homeowners
	National Industrial Recovery Act (NIRA)	Established a series of fair competition codes; created National Recovery Administration (NRA) to write, coordinate, and implement these codes; NIRA's Section 7(a) guaranteed labor's right to organize (act later declared unconstitutional)
	Public Works Administration (PWA)	Sought to increase employment and business activity by funding road construction, building construction, and other projects
	Federal Deposit Insurance Corporation (FDIC)	Insured individual bank deposits
	Civil Works Administration (CWA)	Provided federal jobs for the unemployed
1934	Securities and Exchange Act	Created Securities and Exchange Commission (SEC) to regulate trading practices in stocks and bonds according to federal laws
	Indian Reorganization Act	Restored ownership of tribal lands to Native Americans; provided funds for job training and a system of agricultural and industrial credit
	Federal Housing Administration (FHA)	Insured loans provided by banks for the building and repair of houses
1935	Works Progress Administration (WPA)	Employed more than 8 million people to repair roads, build bridges, and work on other projects
	National Youth Administration (NYA)	WPA program that provided job training for unemployed youths and part-time jobs for students in need
	Federal One	WPA program that provided financial assistance for writers, artists, musicians, and actors
	National Labor Relations Act (Wagner Act)	Recognized the right of employees to join labor unions and to bargain collectively, reinstating the provisions of NIRA's Section 7(a); created the National Labor Relations Board (NLRB) to enforce laws against unfair labor practices
	Social Security Act	Created a system of social insurance that included unemployment compensation and old-age survivors' insurance; paid for by a joint tax on employers and employees
1938	Fair Labor Standards Act	Established a minimum wage of 25 cents an hour and a standard work week of 44 hours for businesses engaged in interstate commerce

nomically dependent on men. Thus, a deeply entrenched gender system prevailed through the 1930s. As a result, some—though not all—male breadwinners received benefits like Social Security. Impoverished women and children, on the other hand, received public charity. These payments were usually meager, not enough to lift a woman and her children out of poverty.

Because there were no nationally established guidelines on how to distribute welfare funds, states could determine who received assistance. The Social Security Act did little to assist African Americans, especially in the South, where black women were deliberately excluded by local authorities who preferred to maintain a pool of cheap African American labor rather than provide relief for black families.

In 1935 Congress allocated the huge sum of nearly $5 billion for the Emergency Relief Appropriation. Roosevelt used a significant portion of the money to expand his public works program. By executive order he established the Works Progress Administration (WPA), which provided millions of jobs for the unemployed. The project mandated that WPA jobs would make a contribution to public life and would not compete with private business. The jobs included building streets, highways, bridges, and public buildings; restoring forests; clearing slums; and extending electricity to rural areas. The WPA National Youth Administration gave work to nearly 1 million students.

WPA Project at Tonawanda Reservation

The wages paid to WPA workers proved pitifully low. And like most other New Deal programs, the WPA left out the most needy. It provided work only to those already on the relief roles, and just one person per family could hold a WPA job. This policy ruled out most women as well as older children. It also neglected the vast majority of the unemployed who were not on relief. A 1937 letter to Harry Hopkins from the Workers' Council of Colored People in Raleigh, North Carolina, pointed to the failure of the WPA to provide jobs for black women. The writer explained that the wages paid to domestic and farm laborers were so low that, even if they worked 14-hour days, they could not pay their rent.

The most effective WPA program was Federal One, which provided financial support for writers, musicians, artists, and actors. The Federal Theater Project, under the direction of Hallie Flanagan, former head of Vassar College's Experimental Theater, became an arena for experimental community-based theater. The Federal Theater Project included 16 black theater units. Their most notable production was an all-black version of *Macbeth* set in Haiti and staged in Harlem. Federal One supported thousands of artists and brought the arts to a wide public audience through government-funded murals on public buildings, community-theater productions, local orchestras, and the like. By the late 1930s the program came under political attack for supporting artists who expressed leftist sensibilities, and Congress cut off its funding. In 1943 the WPA was dissolved.

The New Deal did not reach everyone. Programs were geared toward full-time industrial workers, most of whom were white men. Domestic workers, Mexican migrant laborers, black and white sharecroppers, Chinese and Japanese truck farmers—all were among those ineligible for Social Security, minimum wages and maximum hours, unemployment insurance, and other New Deal benefits. But the New Deal established the national welfare state and provided assistance and security to millions of working people along with disabled, dependent, and elderly Americans. Such sweeping programs also solidified Roosevelt's popularity among the poor, workers, and much of the middle class.

FDR's Second Term

In the 1936 campaign, FDR claimed that the election was a battle between "the millions who never had a chance" and "organized money." He boasted that the "forces of selfishness and of lust for power" had united against him: "They are unanimous in their *hate* for *me—and I welcome their hatred.*" His strategy paid off. Roosevelt won the election by a landslide of more than 60 percent of the popular vote. Six million more voters cast ballots than had done so in 1932, and 5 million of those new votes went to Roosevelt. His strongest support came from the lower ends of the socioeconomic scale. The election also swept Democrats into Congress, giving them a decisive majority in both the House and the Senate.

In the 1936 campaign, FDR claimed that the election was a battle between "the millions who never had a chance" and "organized money."

With such a powerful mandate, Roosevelt was well positioned to promote a new legislative program. As his first major effort, he took on the Supreme Court. Dominated by conservative justices, the court had invalidated some major legislation of Roosevelt's first term, including the AAA and the NIRA. Roosevelt feared that the justices would unravel the New Deal by striking down its progressive elements. To shift the balance of power on the court, he proposed a measure that would let the president appoint one new justice for every one on the court who had at least ten years of service and who did not retire within six months after turning 70.

Emboldened by his landslide victory, FDR believed that he could persuade Congress and the nation to go along with any plan he put forward, but he was mistaken. Many viewed his "court packing" plan as a threat to the fundamental separation of powers and feared that it would set a dangerous precedent. Some considered it an affront to the more aged justices, such as the respected liberal Louis Brandeis, a man in his 80s. Powerful Republicans in Congress forged an alliance with conservative Democrats, mostly from the South, to defeat the plan. This informal alliance dominated Congress for the following two decades. The court blunder cost Roosevelt considerable political capital and empowered his opponents. In the end, his plan proved unnecessary anyway. The court did not undercut the New Deal. Within the next few years, retirements allowed Roosevelt to appoint several new justices who tipped the balance in his favor.

A New Political Culture

FDR continued to face strong opposition from conservatives on the right and radicals, communists, and socialists on the left. But his political fortunes benefited from the emergence of a new and more inclusive national culture. This new Americanism emanated from the working class and found expression in the labor movement, the popular culture, and the political coalition that came together in the Democratic party. These nationalizing forces cut across lines of class and region and occasionally challenged hierarchies of gender and race.

The Labor Movement

The labor insurgency that erupted during the early years of the New Deal demonstrated the need for a new national labor movement. The American Federation of Labor (AFL), restricted to skilled workers, left out most of the nation's less skilled industrial laborers. John L. Lewis of the United Mine Workers (UMW) and Sidney Hillman of the Amalgamated Clothing Workers of America were among several union leaders from a number of industries—including mining, steel, rubber, and automobile—who left the AFL to form a new and more broad-based labor organization, the Congress of Industrial Organizations (CIO). Hillman and others argued that higher wages were good for the economy because workers would then be able to purchase consumer products, benefiting industry as well as workers. Lewis and Hillman played key roles in the CIO's growth into a national force, but the impetus came from the workers themselves.

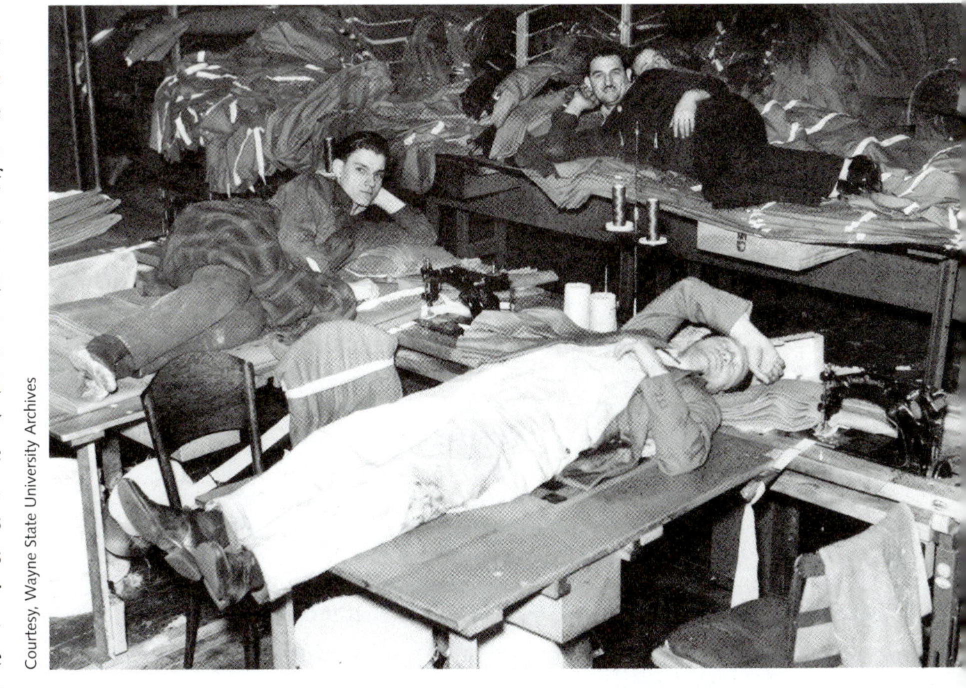

Courtesy, Wayne State University Archives

▲ These sit-down strikers at the Dodge Main plant in Hamtramck, Michigan, slept on their sewing tables while occupying the factory, shutting down production. The sit-down strike became an effective form of labor protest during the 1930s.

The CIO's first major action came in 1936 in Akron, Ohio, where workers in the rubber industry organized a **sit-down strike,** a new strategy whereby laborers stopped work and simply sat down, shutting down production and occupying plants so that strikebreakers could not enter and take their jobs. Sit-down strikes became a prominent labor tactic during 1936 when 48 strikes broke out across the nation. The numbers shot up the following year to about 500 strikes that lasted more than one day. March 1937 alone witnessed 170 sit-down strikes that affected about 170,000 workers. Striking workers expressed their enthusiasm for the tactic in song:

> When they tie the can to a union man, sit down! Sit down!
> When they give him the sack, they'll take him back, sit down! Sit down!
> When the speed up comes, just twiddle your thumbs, sit down! Sit down!
> When the boss won't talk, don't take a walk, sit down! Sit down!

The most powerful demonstration of workers' discontent came in the automobile industry, where speed-ups of the assembly line drove workers to rebellion. Charlie Chaplin's poignant film *Modern Times* (1936) expressed workers' frustration at being treated as little more than cogs in machines. "Where you used to be a man," lamented one auto worker, "now you are less than their cheapest tool." In 1936 a spontaneous strike erupted against General Motors in Atlanta; it soon spread to Kansas City, Missouri; Cleveland, Ohio; and the main plants at Flint, Michigan. Two weeks into the strike, workers clashed with police. Frank Murphy, Michigan's prolabor governor, refused to use National Guard troops against the strikers, and Roosevelt declined to send in federal troops. John L. Lewis negotiated on behalf of the workers, who demanded recognition of their union.

Women as well as men participated actively in the Flint strike. Twenty-three-year-old Genora Johnson Dollinger, wife of a striker and mother of two young sons, organized 500 women into the Women's Emergency Brigade, made up primarily of strikers' wives, sisters, and girlfriends. Wearing red berets and armbands, they ran soup kitchens and first-aid stations. They also entered the fray when necessary, as when they broke plant windows so that the company could not use tear gas effectively against the strikers inside. Dollinger arranged a children's picket line as well, in which her two-year-old carried a sign that read, "My daddy strikes for us little tykes." Reflecting on the Women's Emergency Brigade after the strike, Dollinger wrote, "It's a measure of the strength of those women of the Red Berets that they could perform so courageously in an atmosphere that was often hostile to them. We organized on our own without the benefit of professional leadership, and yet, we played a role, second to none, in the birth of a union and in changing working families' lives forever."

The sit-down strike at Flint lasted 44 days and forced General Motors to recognize the United Auto Workers (UAW), which was a CIO union. The strike scored a clear victory for the workers and boosted the CIO's stature as a national union of industrial workers. Membership in the UAW quadrupled in the next year. Bowing to the formidable power of the national union in the wake of the UAW success, U.S. Steel surrendered to the CIO even without a strike, ending its policy of hiring nonunion workers and signing an agreement with the Steel Workers' Organizing Committee. The CIO brought together workers from all over the country. Most of its member unions were open to racial and ethnic minorities and women.

The New Deal Coalition

FDR's support of labor unions brought workers solidly into the Democratic fold. They joined a coalition that included voters who had never before belonged to the same party, particularly northern blacks and southern whites. Although African Americans in the South were disenfranchised, blacks in the North had voted Republican for 60 years, loyal to the party of Lincoln. In a dramatic shift, black voters in northern cities overwhelmingly backed FDR in 1936 and remained in the Democratic party for the rest of the century.

FDR continued to cater to powerful southern congressmen and southern white voters. Nevertheless, he made some gestures on behalf of African Americans and put civil rights measures on the liberal agenda for the first time since Reconstruction. In May 1935 FDR issued Executive

Order 7046, banning discrimination in WPA projects. By the late 1930s, 15 to 20 percent of those with WPA jobs were black. Although the pay was meager—$12 a week—it was double what many blacks had been able to earn previously. In spite of FDR's lukewarm support for civil rights, African Americans in the North benefited from New Deal programs. As one black preacher exhorted his congregation prior to the 1936 election, "Let Jesus lead you and Roosevelt feed you."

Other racial and ethnic minorities also joined the New Deal coalition. In 1939, Latinos organized their first national civil rights assembly, El Congreso de Pueblos de Habla Española—the Spanish-Speaking People's Congress, which opened with a congratulatory telegram from Eleanor Roosevelt. Immigrants from Europe and their children also became loyal Democratic voters.

In spite of this diverse coalition, many Americans remained bitterly opposed to FDR. Socialists and communists criticized the New Deal for patching up capitalism rather than transforming the economic system. Conservative business leaders despised Roosevelt for the constraints he placed on business and the intrusion of the government into the economy. Critics from the political right considered the New Deal akin to communism. In 1938, Congress created the House Un-American Activities Committee (HUAC), chaired by Martin Dies of Texas. Formed ostensibly to investigate American fascists and Nazis in the United States, the committee instead pursued liberal and leftist groups throughout World War II and the Cold War.

A New Americanism

The New Deal coalition reflected not only Roosevelt's popularity but also a new and more inclusive American identity. An expanding mass culture fostered this sensibility, spread largely through the national media. It is no accident that Franklin Roosevelt found his way into the homes and hearts of Americans through his "fireside chats" over the radio; his mastery of that technology made him the first media-savvy president. During the 1930s, 70 percent of all households owned a radio—more than owned a telephone. The motion-picture industry also expanded into small towns across the country.

Movie plots portrayed the triumph of common people over the rich and powerful and celebrated love across class and ethnic lines. Even gangsters appeared as sympathetic characters whose illegal activities seemed somehow justified by the corrupt system they tried to thwart. Although racial stereotypes persisted in motion pictures throughout the decade, notable exceptions, such as Will Rogers's films, featured strong minority characters.

Popular movies also challenged traditional gender and class hierarchies. Female stars, such as Katharine Hepburn, Rosalind Russell, Bette Davis, and Mae West, portrayed feisty, independent women. For example, the 1931 film *Front Page* was remade at the end of the decade. In the original version the hero, Hildy Johnson, was a man—but in the remake, entitled *His Girl Friday,* Hildy became a woman. The feisty reporter, played by Rosalind Russell, divorces her work-obsessed boss, played by Cary Grant, and then competes with him on the job. Kicking off her high heels to race barefoot down a street, she rescues a man thought to be a communist from a threatening lynch mob.

New sports celebrities also embodied the nation's diversity. Baseball star Joe DiMaggio, son of an Italian immigrant fisherman, became a national hero. African American boxer Joe Louis, the "Brown Bomber" who was born into a sharecropper family in Alabama, became heavyweight champion of the world at age 23.

Photofest

▲ **This poster for the movie *His Girl Friday* shows the strong heroine (Rosalind Russell) and her ex-husband and boss (Cary Grant). Although the two reconcile and remarry in the end, there is no indication that the feisty reporter will become a full-time homemaker.**

National Air & Space Museum, Smithsonian Institution (SI A-A45874)

▲ **Amelia Earhart was the first woman to fly solo across the Atlantic. The legendary aviator gave preliminary flying lessons to her friend Eleanor Roosevelt. FDR convinced his wife not to take up flying, but the First Lady always regretted her decision.**

In 1938, when Louis fought German boxer Max Schmeling at Yankee Stadium, the fight attracted 70,000 fans and grossed more than $1 million. When the black fighter knocked out Schmeling in the first round, he seemed to strike a blow for America against Hitler's Nazi Germany.

A number of women also became heroes in the 1930s for their daring exploits, personal courage, and physical prowess. Athletes like tennis champion Helen Wills and Olympic track star and brilliant golfer "Babe" (Mildred) Didrikson (later Zaharias) greatly expanded the popularity of women's sports. Renowned aviator Amelia Earhart, the first woman to fly solo across the Atlantic, devoted her life to advancing both feminism and commercial aviation. When her plane disappeared during an attempted around-the-world flight in 1937, many of her admirers were so convinced of her invincibility that they refused to believe she had died. Even today, people still speculate about her fate.

One of the most beloved celebrities of the decade was a horse: the unlikely champion Seabiscuit. The little Thoroughbred overcame a crippling injury and beat the odds to win major national races, becoming a symbol of hope for Depression-weary Americans.

Conclusion

The Great Depression of the 1930s was the nation's worst economic crisis. When Franklin Delano Roosevelt became president, he put into place a wide range of programs aimed at solving the crisis and providing relief to suffering Americans. His New Deal set in place a welfare state that established the principle of government responsibility for the well-being of vulnerable citizens. Before the New Deal, people suffered the fluctuations of the market economy with no recourse beyond the assistance of kin, communities, and charities. Older Americans who could no longer work had no government-guaranteed pensions and often faced poverty in old age. Bank failures could wipe away life savings. Unemployment could mean starvation for a worker's family. The New Deal provided Social Security for the elderly, unemployment compensation for workers who had lost their jobs, minimum hours and wages, and economic aid to women and children who had no means of support. It also established national economic regulations, such as the Federal Deposit Insurance Corporation (FDIC) and the Security and Exchange Commission (SEC), as well as the right of workers to unionize and engage in collective bargaining. Labor unions grew and flourished under the New Deal. Government protections offered many Americans an unprecedented level of economic security.

The Roosevelt administration addressed many of the nation's problems and used the federal government in innovative ways to intervene in the economy and to mitigate some of the misfortunes caused by the Depression. Most New Deal policies protected factory workers in large companies. The safety net did not extend to many of the neediest Americans, including Mexican American migrant workers, African American and white sharecroppers, seasonal agricultural laborers, or domestic workers. Although the national government extended its reach considerably, at the local level many persistent problems remained entrenched. FDR

AP/Wide World

▲ **The famous equine-human team of Seabiscuit and Red Pollard won the hearts of Americans during the 1930s. Both came from humble and unpromising beginnings—the horse too small and the jockey too big—and both overcame devastating injuries not only to recover and race again, but to triumph. Here the champions pose with Seabiscuit's proud owners.**

was reluctant to press for antilynching legislation for fear of alienating southern congressmen who still retained enormous power. FDR faced critics from the left as well as the right. Although FDR's conservative opponents accused him of socialist leanings, the New Deal actually rescued and shored up capitalism.

The Depression caused widespread suffering, but it also gave rise to a new national culture. Farm families uprooted from the Dust Bowl found themselves in similar circumstances with Mexican agricultural workers and unemployed African Americans. A spirit of cooperation born of crisis strengthened communities. The popular culture reflected a new multicultural Americanism that elevated former outsiders like the radical Cherokee Will Rogers to national stardom. Immigrants and their children became part of mainstream America.

In spite of the new multicultural spirit, the cruel fate of the Scottsboro Boys and the failure to enact antilynching legislation illustrate the persistence of institutionalized racism. But civil rights activists continued to work for social justice, with support from communists, radicals, and First Lady Eleanor Roosevelt. Although the New Deal reinforced women's economic dependence on men, the popular culture featured strong women who challenged traditional gender roles.

The New Deal was the Roosevelt administration's response to a global economic crisis. With the exception of the communist Soviet Union, which had already abandoned capitalism, almost every industrialized nation responded to the Depression by increasing the role of the state in the economy. Italy, Germany, and Japan moved to fascism and the nearly total state direction of the economy, while Britain and France established welfare states that would become more fully developed after World War II. The United States' system of social welfare was not as extensive and inclusive as those that emerged in some western European democracies. But it was part of a larger trend toward government intervention in the economy and greater protections for citizens. Within the United States, the New Deal neither reached nor satisfied everyone. Some groups thought that it went too far; others believed it did not go far enough. But it eased some of the harshest effects of the Depression and established a national safety net that included several programs which have endured to this day.

Sites to Visit

African American Odyssey: The Depression, New Deal, and World War II

lcweb2.loc.gov/ammem/aaohtml/exhibit/aopart8.html

This Library of Congress site covers the history of African Americans during the years of the Great Depression and World War II.

Southern Mosaic: The John and Ruby Lomax 1939 Southern States Recording Trip

memory.loc.gov/ammem/lohtml/lohome.html

This site from the American Folklife Center, Library of Congress, provides audio, text, and photos of the Lomax collection of American folk songs collected and recorded across the South.

The 1930s Project

xroads.virginia.edu/~1930s/front.html

This site from the University of Virginia's American Studies program contains materials about the culture and history of the 1930s.

Voices from the Dust Bowl: The Charles L. Todd and Robert Sonkin Migrant Worker Collection, 1940–1941

memory.loc.gov/ammem/afctshtml/tshome.html

This Library of Congress site includes Farm Security Administration studies of migrant work camps in California in 1940 and 1941, with audio, images, manuscripts, and publications.

New Deal Network

newdeal.feri.org

This site includes images, documents, texts, artifacts, and other materials from the New Deal era.

Franklin Delano Roosevelt

www.ipl.org/ref/POTUS/fdroosevelt.html

This Internet Public Library site contains biographical information about Franklin Delano Roosevelt and his election to the presidency and links to Internet biographies and resources about him.

The Crash of 1929

www.btinternet.com/~dreklind/thecrash.htm

This site includes a discussion of the causes of the 1929 stock market crash, along with audio clips of songs related to the crash.

Franklin D. Roosevelt Library and Digital Archives

www.fdrlibrary.marist.edu/

This site includes documents, images, audio, and other primary source material from the Franklin D. Roosevelt Library.

A New Deal for the Arts

www.archives.gov/exhibit_hall/new_deal_for_the_arts/

This site of the National Archives includes artwork, documents, photographs, and information from the New Deal programs that funded artists in the 1930s.

American Life Histories: Manuscripts from the Federal Writers Project, 1936-1940

memory.loc.gov/ammem/wpaintro/wpahome.html

This site from the Library of Congress includes manuscripts written by Federal Writers Project authors who interviewed Americans all over the country and wrote about them.

For Further Reading

General

Steve Fraser and Gary Gerstle, eds., *The Rise and Fall of the New Deal Order, 1930–1980* (1989).

Robert S. McElvaine, *The Great Depression: America, 1929–1941* (1984, 1993).

James R. McGovern, *And a Time for Hope: Americans in the Great Depression* (2000).

Studs Terkel, *Hard Times: An Oral History of the Great Depression* (1986).

The Great Depression

Glen Elder Jr., *Children of the Great Depression: Social Change in Life Experience* (1974).

Robert S. McElvaine, ed., *Down and Out in the Great Depression: Letters from the Forgotten Man* (1983).

Vicki L. Ruiz, *From Out of the Shadows: Mexican Women in Twentieth-Century America* (1998).

Judith Smith, *Family Connections: A History of Italian and Jewish Immigrant Lives in Providence, Rhode Island, 1900–1940* (1985).

Presidential Responses to the Depression

Edward D. Berkowitz, *America's Welfare State: From Roosevelt to Reagan* (1991).

Blanche Wiesen Cook, *Eleanor Roosevelt* (1999).

Frank Friedel, *Franklin D. Roosevelt: A Rendezvous with Destiny* (1990).

Lawrence W. Levine and Cornelia R. Levine, *The People and the President: America's Conversation with FDR* (2002).

The New Deal

Anthony Badger, *The New Deal* (1988).

Alan Brinkley, *Voices of Protest: Huey Long, Father Coughlin and the Great Depression* (1982).

Steven Fraser, *Labor Will Rule: Sidney Hillman and the Rise of American Labor* (1991).

Linda Gordon, *Pitied but Not Entitled: Single Mothers and the History of Welfare* (1994).

A New Political Culture

Lizabeth Cohen, *Making a New Deal: Industrial Workers in Chicago, 1919–1939* (1992).

Michael Denning, *Cultural Front: The Laboring of American Culture in the Twentieth Century* (1998).

Laura Hillenbrand, *Seabiscuit: An American Legend* (2001).

Lary May, *The Big Tomorrow: Hollywood and the Politics of the American Way* (2000).

CHAPTER 23

Global Conflict: World War II, 1937–1945

Tom Lea, *Marines Call It That Two Thousand Yard Stare*, September 16, 1944. U.S. Army Center of Military History, Army Art Collection

▲ Tom Lea's haunting painting of a soldier, *Marines Call It That Two Thousand Yard Stare* (1944), evokes the horrors of World War II.

CHAPTER OUTLINE

Mobilizing for War

Pearl Harbor: The United States Enters the War

The Home Front

Race and War

Total War

Conclusion

Sites to Visit

For Further Reading

On December 7, 1941, Keith Little was out hunting rabbits with friends at their boarding school on the Navajo reservation of Ganado, Arizona. When they heard the news that the Japanese had attacked the U.S. naval base in Hawaii at Pearl Harbor, the teenage boys pledged to fight for their country. The next morning, Little and his friends showed up with their hunting rifles at the office of the reservation superintendent, ready to enlist. The previous year, the Tribal Council had voted unanimously to defend the United States against invasion. "There exists no purer concentration of Americanism than among the First Americans," the council declared.

The council vote was no idle gesture, especially given the complex status of Indian tribes within the United States. In some respects the tribes were semiautonomous nations within a nation. Several states, including Arizona, denied Indians the basic rights and obligations of citizenship, such as voting. Moreover, the Navajo were still embroiled in disputes with Commissioner of Indian Affairs John Collier and the Roosevelt administration over Collier's request that they destroy their sheep to reduce soil erosion and overgrazing. So it was by no means obvious that the Navajo would, or even should, fight for a nation they had bitterly fought against only 80 years earlier. Although large numbers of Indian soldiers had fought in earlier wars, especially World War I, the boarding-school boys could not have known that they would soon become part of a Navajo unit of "code talkers" that helped win the war.

Little and about 400 other Navajo became part of a special unit that developed an intricate code, based on the Navajo language, to transmit top-secret information without risk of detection. Ironically, many of these men were educated in government boarding schools that forbade them to speak their native language. Now that same government called upon them to use their language to help win the war. The Navajo language was particularly well suited to code because very few people besides Navajo knew it. In a process code named "Magic," the all-Navajo 382nd Platoon of the U.S. Marine Corps encoded and decoded sensitive military information almost instantly and flawlessly. In two days on the Pacific island of Iwo Jima, six code talkers transmitted more than 800 messages, working around the clock, without a single error. Signal Officer Major Howard Conner recalled, "Without the Navajos the Marines would never have taken Iwo Jima."

Navajo "code talkers" operate a portable radio in the Pacific combat zone in 1943.

The experiences of the Navajo code talkers echo many larger themes of America's involvement in World War II. Along with other ethnic and racial minorities, the Navajo willingly fought—and many died—for a nation that had treated them as second-class citizens. African Americans also joined the war effort, though in segregated units, to fight for the **Double V**—victory against fascism abroad and racial discrimination at home. Young Japanese Americans left internment camps where their families had been forcibly detained to join a war against the country from which their parents came.

World War II was a global war, affecting countries and peoples all over the world. The conflict demanded human and technological resources on an unprecedented scale and left massive destruction in its wake. The huge scale of destruction was unlike that of any previous war. At least 55 million people died, including 25 million in the Soviet Union, 10 million in China, and 6 million in Poland. In the Holocaust, Nazi Germany's campaign of genocide, 6 million European Jews perished along with thousands of Romani (Gypsies), Poles, mentally and physically disabled people, homosexuals, and others deemed "racially inferior." The war also had a tremendous impact on countries under colonial rule. Germany's bombardment of England and occupation of France, Holland, and Belgium weakened these countries' hold over their vast colonies. Japan's defeat of the American, British, Dutch, and French forces in Southeast Asia from 1940 to 1942 shocked the Western powers and ended white rule in the region, setting in motion a wave of decolonization in Asia and Africa after the war.

The United States was the only major combatant that did not suffer massive destruction on its home territory. It had two powerful advantages: an ocean barrier on its east and west coasts, plus tremendous natural resources that could provide the materials needed for modern warfare, such as steel and oil. In order to minimize American casualties, President Franklin Delano Roosevelt (FDR) pursued a strategy to make the United States the "arsenal of democracy," providing armaments and supplies to the other Allied powers so that their armies would do most of the fighting. Although the Soviet Union carried the largest burden of fighting the war and suffered the highest losses, millions of Americans also fought, and many died in the conflict. Military service had a leveling effect on social relations, as soldiers came together from all classes and ethnic groups. The vast majority of the troops—more than 85 percent—were white men from a wide variety of backgrounds. Soldiers of color generally fought in segregated units, but their battlefield successes and sacrifices gave them a sense of belonging to the nation and fueled postwar movements for equality and civil rights.

Soldiers of color fought not simply to preserve the American way of life, but also to gain access to it.

No bombs dropped on the American mainland, yet the war reached into every aspect of national and personal life. Although wartime brought prosperity, the rationing of essential goods and the scarcity of consumer products brought nearly all Americans into the war effort. As soldiers and war industry workers moved around the country, local and regional sensibilities gave way to a stronger national identity. Factories stopped making consumer items and instead turned out war machines. Scientists developed new weapons of mass destruction. Cities burgeoned as workers flooded into the lucrative war industries. The U.S. military and defense establishment expanded to the formidable scale it would maintain during and after the war, making the United States the most powerful nation in the world.

Initially, there was widespread opposition to entering the conflict. But after the attack on Pearl Harbor, most Americans supported the war effort and did their part to stop German and Japanese aggression. Early in 1941, well before the United States entered the war, Roosevelt stressed the need to protect the "Four Freedoms": freedom of speech, freedom of religion, freedom from want, and freedom from fear of armed aggression. For many American GIs, the Four Freedoms translated into intensely personal terms. They fought to stay alive and to return to their sweethearts and families. They fought in hopes of reaping the "good life" that had become the symbol of America. Others, especially soldiers of color, fought not simply to preserve the American way of life, but also to gain access to it.

Mobilizing for War

During the 1930s, the rise of fascism and militarism in Italy, Germany, and Japan created a terrible dilemma for Americans. Disillusioned by World War I and preoccupied with the hardships of the Great Depression, they disagreed strongly with one another about how to respond to overt aggression in Africa, Europe, and Asia. The ensuing "Great Debate" became a turning point in the nation's relationship with the outside world. Mobilizing for the enormous crusade of World War II gave rise to a unity of purpose that lasted throughout the war and into the postwar era.

The Rise of Fascism

In the 1930s, Depression-era Americans grappled with their problems at home and avoided entanglements abroad. But they found it difficult to ignore events in Europe and Asia. In Italy, Spain, and Germany, where a weak economy and high unemployment created political unrest, fascist leaders rose to power with strong popular support. These new leaders promised economic recovery through strengthening military and national expansion. They also encouraged intense nationalist sentiments, urging people to identify strongly with the state. Fascist party leader Benito Mussolini had held power in Italy since 1921, suppressing dissident voices and imposing one-party rule. According to Mussolini, "The fascist conception of the state is all-embracing, and outside of the state no human or spiritual values can exist, let alone be desirable." By the early 1930s fascism had gained strength in Germany and Spain. The term *fascist* has since been applied to the various right-wing dictatorships that arose during the period between the two world wars. Fascist governments were antidemocratic, antiparliamentary, and frequently anti-Semitic. Appealing to nationalistic and often racist sentiments, these governments generally ruled by coercion, brutality, and police surveillance.

Germany emerged as the most powerful fascist state in Europe. After Germany's defeat in World War I and the severe economic depression that Germany experienced in the 1920s, Adolf Hitler's National Socialist (Nazi) party won broad support in the weakened country. On January 30, 1933, Hitler became chancellor of Germany. Extolling fanatical nationalism and the racial superiority of "Aryan" Germans, Hitler blamed Jews for Germany's problems. He began a campaign of terror against Jews, homosexuals, suspected communists, and anyone else he saw as promoting "un-German" ideas. Hitler vowed to unite all German-speaking peoples into a new empire, the "Third Reich."

The fascist governments forged alliances to increase their power and launched campaigns of aggression and expansion. As conflict increased in Europe, hostilities spread into Africa as well. In 1935 Italy invaded Ethiopia, the sole independent African nation. The following year, Nazi troops seized the Rhineland, in the western region of Germany, in violation of the Versailles agreement. Hitler and Mussolini signed the **Axis** Pact, and Japan forged an alliance with Germany. Soon after that, civil war erupted in Spain. Hitler and Mussolini extended aid to the fascist General Francisco Franco, who was trying to overthrow Spain's republican government.

Although Spanish republicans appealed to antifascist governments for help in the fight against Franco, only the Soviet Union came to their assistance. The United States maintained an official policy of neutrality. American Catholics and State Department conservatives believed that the anticommunist Franco would promote social stability. But many on the left, including large numbers of writers and intellectuals, championed the beleaguered Spanish government and denounced the fascists. Cadres of Americans sympathetic to the republican cause, including the "Abraham Lincoln Brigade," joined Soviet-organized international forces to fight against Franco.

In Germany anti-Semitic fervor reached a frenzy on the evening of November 7, 1938. In a spasm of violence known as *Kristallnacht* ("Night of the Broken Glass"), Hitler launched a massive assault against Jews throughout Germany. For three days German mobs attacked synagogues, smashed windows, and vandalized Jewish homes and businesses. Thirty-five Jews were killed, and thousands arrested. The rioters destroyed 7,500 shops and 119 synagogues. The Nazi reign of terror against the Jews continued throughout the war, culminating in death camps and genocide.

Aggression in Europe and Asia

In the spring and summer of 1938, Hitler annexed Austria to the Third Reich and then demanded that the Sudetenland be turned over to Germany. In the breakup of the Austro-Hungarian Empire after World War I, this German-speaking area became part of the newly formed Czechoslovakia. The Sudetenland was key to Hitler's goal of uniting all German-speaking Europe into the Third Reich. Soviet leader Josef Stalin offered to join France and Britain to keep Hitler out of the Sudetenland and halt his aggression. But the leaders of France and Britain rebuffed Stalin's suggestion. In September they met with Hitler in Munich and agreed to let him have the Sudetenland in return for his promise that he would seek no more territory. Stalin feared that the anticommunist leaders of France and Britain would try to turn Hitler's aggression toward the Soviet Union. To prevent that possibility, Stalin signed a nonaggression pact with Hitler. Eventually, Hitler broke all his promises. Throughout the war and after, the Munich meeting became the symbol of "appeasement," a warning that compromise with the enemy leads only to disaster.

In the next few years, the fascist states expanded their power and territory. In 1939, with the help of the Soviet Union and in violation of the Munich agreement, Germany invaded Poland, which fell quickly. At that point Britain and France declared war on Germany. That same year Madrid finally fell to Franco's forces. Britain, France, and the United States recognized Franco as victor of the Spanish Civil War. The Soviet Union sent troops into Finland, gaining Finnish territory in 1940.

Hitler and Mussolini in Munich, 1940

By 1940 Hitler was sweeping through Europe, invading Denmark, Norway, Holland, Belgium, Luxembourg, and then France. In just six weeks the Nazis had seized most of western Europe. Hitler then turned his forces on Great Britain. In the summer and fall of 1940, German raids on British air bases nearly destroyed the British Royal Air Force (RAF). Hitler then ordered the bombing of London and other English cities, attacking civilians day and night in what came to be called the Battle of Britain.

In the Far East in the 1930s, events had taken an equally alarming turn. Nationalistic militarists gained control of the Japanese government in Tokyo and began a course of expansion. In 1931–1932, Japanese troops occupied the large Chinese province of Manchuria, installed a puppet government, and gave the province a Japanese name: Manchukuo. Five years later, the Japanese launched a full-scale war against China. The United States extended aid to China and discontinued trade with Japan. In 1940 Japan joined Germany and Italy in the Axis alliance and invaded the French colony of Indochina. Kazuko Kuramoto remembered the nationalist propaganda she learned as a Japanese child raised in Manchuria:

> I was born into a society of Japanese supremacy and grew up believing in Japan's "divine" mission to save Asia from the "evil" hands of Western imperialism. . . . "You are Japan's only future, a glorious future," adults around us used to say. We believed it with passion. . . . I joined the Red Cross Nurse Corps to help my country win the war. . . . "Asia for the Asians!"

Japan's efforts to rid Asia of white Western imperialism inspired some other Asians who saw Japan as a model of strength. But it was also a cynical ploy of the Japanese leaders, who sought to conquer all of Asia and considered other Asian peoples racially inferior to the Japanese. The Japanese treated the people in the countries they occupied with extreme brutality.

The Great Debate: Americans Contemplate War

In the mid-1930s the overwhelming majority of Americans still opposed intervention in foreign conflicts. Congress passed the Neutrality Acts of 1935, 1936, and 1937, outlawing arms sales or loans to nations at war and forbidding Americans from traveling on the ships of belligerent powers. In 1937 a Gallup poll indicated that 70 percent of Americans believed that the United States should have stayed out of World War I. A peace movement spread across college campuses. Students marched with banners bearing such slogans as "Scholarships, not Battleships." In a "peace strike" in the spring of 1936, half a million students boycotted classes and attended antiwar events. Nevertheless, President Roosevelt and others believed that the United States would be unable to remain aloof from the mounting international crises.

When Japan invaded China in 1937, FDR refused to comply with the provisions of the latest Neutrality Act, on the technicality that neither combatant had officially declared war. By creatively interpreting the law, he was able to offer loans to the embattled Chinese. Roosevelt felt strongly that the United States should actively help resist the Axis powers. In 1940 he told the nation, "Frankly and definitely there is danger ahead—danger against which we must prepare. But we well know that we cannot escape danger, or the fear of danger, by crawling into bed and pulling the covers over our heads."

U.S. citizens still remained bitterly divided over the question of whether to get involved in the conflict. Those who agreed with Roosevelt believed that the nation should take any action "short of war" to help defeat the aggressors in Europe. By sending supplies, for example, the United States could become the "arsenal of democracy" to fight fascism without sending troops and risking American lives. But opponents to this idea spanned the political spectrum. They included moral or religious pacifists, peace activists of the Communist and Labor parties, and anti-Semites who supported Hitler. The pro-Nazi German American Bund, an organization that supported Germany, complained about Roosevelt's "Jew Deal"—a reference to Jews among FDR's advisers.

Lindbergh, Radio Address

The largest organization to resist Roosevelt's effort was the America First Committee. With 450 chapters, the group claimed several hundred thousand members. Centered largely in the Midwest, the America Firsters included some active Nazi supporters. But conservative businesspeople also took part. Others, long opposed to Roosevelt and the New Deal, feared that war would give additional power to the already strong federal government. The group's most visible spokesperson was famed aviator Charles Lindbergh, whose anti-Semitism fueled his staunch opposition to any involvement in the conflict. Although Lindbergh's position antagonized many who once admired him, he also attracted followers.

Despite intense nonintervention sentiments, public opinion began to shift. Many Americans were shocked when Hitler swiftly conquered much of Europe. News reports of the German occupation of France and the intense bombardment of England in the Battle of Britain bolstered FDR's efforts to take action. When he gave his "Four Freedoms" speech to Congress in January 1941, the United States was not yet officially at war. But the president pledged his support for England against the Nazis. A few months later, Congress approved the Lend-Lease agreement to lend rather than sell military equipment to the Allied countries.

When Hitler broke his promise to Stalin and attacked the Soviet Union in June 1941, FDR extended Lend-Lease to the Soviets. During the summer, FDR and British Prime Minister Winston Churchill met on a ship off the coast of Newfoundland to develop a joint declaration known as the Atlantic Charter. The two leaders announced that the United States and Britain sought no new territories. Furthermore, they recognized the right of all peoples to choose their own form of government and to approve any territorial changes that might affect them. The charter called for international free trade and navigation as well.

▲ **Norman Rockwell's depiction of the "Four Freedoms" adorned the cover of the *Saturday Evening Post*, inspired the purchase of war bonds, and came to symbolize the democratic values for which the nation was fighting. These four scenes by the popular artist evoked an American ideal of close families and harmonious communities.**

The charter articulated the **Allies'** war aims, but it also had profound implications for colonial rule around the world. Realizing the possible cost of losing colonies, Churchill retreated from the global implications of the charter. The declaration, he claimed, applied primarily to European nations under Nazi rule. Roosevelt walked a fine line between contradicting Churchill and supporting the idea of empire. However, the words of the charter—along with the Allies' condemnation of racism and territorial expansion by Germany and Japan—emboldened anticolonial activists around the world. Within 15 years after the end of World War II, 800 million previously colonized people won their independence, and 40 new nations formed.

As the United States inched closer to entry into the conflict, FDR still faced political and economic troubles at home. Although Allied munitions orders had already stimulated the economy, as late as 1939, 9.4 million Americans—17.2 percent of the labor force—remained jobless. In the 1940 presidential election, Roosevelt defeated Republican challenger Wendell Wilkie. FDR began his third term as war loomed and economic hardship at home persisted. But Japan's surprise attack on Pearl Harbor in 1941 would end both the neutrality debate and the economic depression.

Pearl Harbor: The United States Enters the War

The Japanese attack on Pearl Harbor shocked the nation and catapulted the United States immediately into World War II. President Roosevelt somberly told millions of Americans gathered around their radios that the day of the attack would "live in infamy." Most former doubters now joined the war effort. The entire nation shifted into high gear to defeat brutal, aggressive regimes intent on conquering much of the world. For some, wartime mobilization offered new opportunities; for others, it brought sacrifice.

AP/Wide World Photos

▶ **On December 7, 1941, the Japanese launched a surprise attack on the U.S. naval base at Pearl Harbor, Hawaii. The attack brought the United States immediately into World War II and was the only time that the war came to American soil.**

December 7, 1941

For nearly a decade, tensions had been mounting between the United States and Japan as American leaders tried to contain Japan's expansion in Asia. Roosevelt assumed that a strong U.S. military presence in the Pacific would persuade Japan's premier, General Hideki Tojo, to avoid a confrontation with the United States. When Japan continued its aggression in Asia, FDR froze Japanese assets in the United States, putting trade with Japan under presidential control. This move, he hoped, would bring Japan to the bargaining table. Instead, on November 25, the Japanese dispatched aircraft carriers toward Hawaii and sent troops to the border of Malaya in the South Pacific.

Although U.S. intelligence sources had broken the codes with which the Japanese encrypted messages about their war plans, they did not realize that the Japanese intended to strike Hawaii. One memo indicating that the Japanese were heading toward Pearl Harbor lay buried under a pile of intelligence reports. As a result, American military officials failed to warn the U.S. forces stationed in Pearl Harbor. At 7:55 a.m. on December 7, Japanese planes swooped over Pearl Harbor and bombed the naval base. The assault caught the American forces completely off guard and destroyed most of the U.S. Pacific fleet. Only a few aircraft carriers that were out at sea survived. Two hours after the attack on Pearl Harbor, the Japanese also struck the main U.S. base at Clark Field in the Philippines, destroying half of the U.S. Air Force in the Far East.

At roughly the same time that Keith Little heard the news about Pearl Harbor at his Navajo reservation boarding school, another 16-year-old, John Garcia, watched flames rising at Pearl Harbor from his house 4 miles away. The young Hawaiian reached the scene in time to witness the second round of bombings. "I spent the rest of the day swimming inside the harbor, along with some other Hawaiians. I brought out I don't know how many bodies, and how many were alive and how many dead. . . . We worked around the clock for three days."

In less than two hours the Japanese had wrecked 188 planes—most of the American aircraft on the island—and sunk 19 ships, including 8 battleships, 3 destroyers, and 3 cruisers. When the smoke cleared, 2,323 American service personnel were dead. Congress immediately

National Archives

◀ The attack on Pearl Harbor prompted an immediate mobilization of vast proportions. Within months, thousands of young recruits, such as these sailors boarding ship in San Diego, shouldered their gear and headed overseas. More than 400,000 did not return alive. The government calculated that over four grim years of U.S. involvement, 292,131 Americans died in combat, and there were 115,185 additional service deaths from other causes. Though huge, American losses still proved small in comparison to the destruction suffered in other countries.

Hawaii

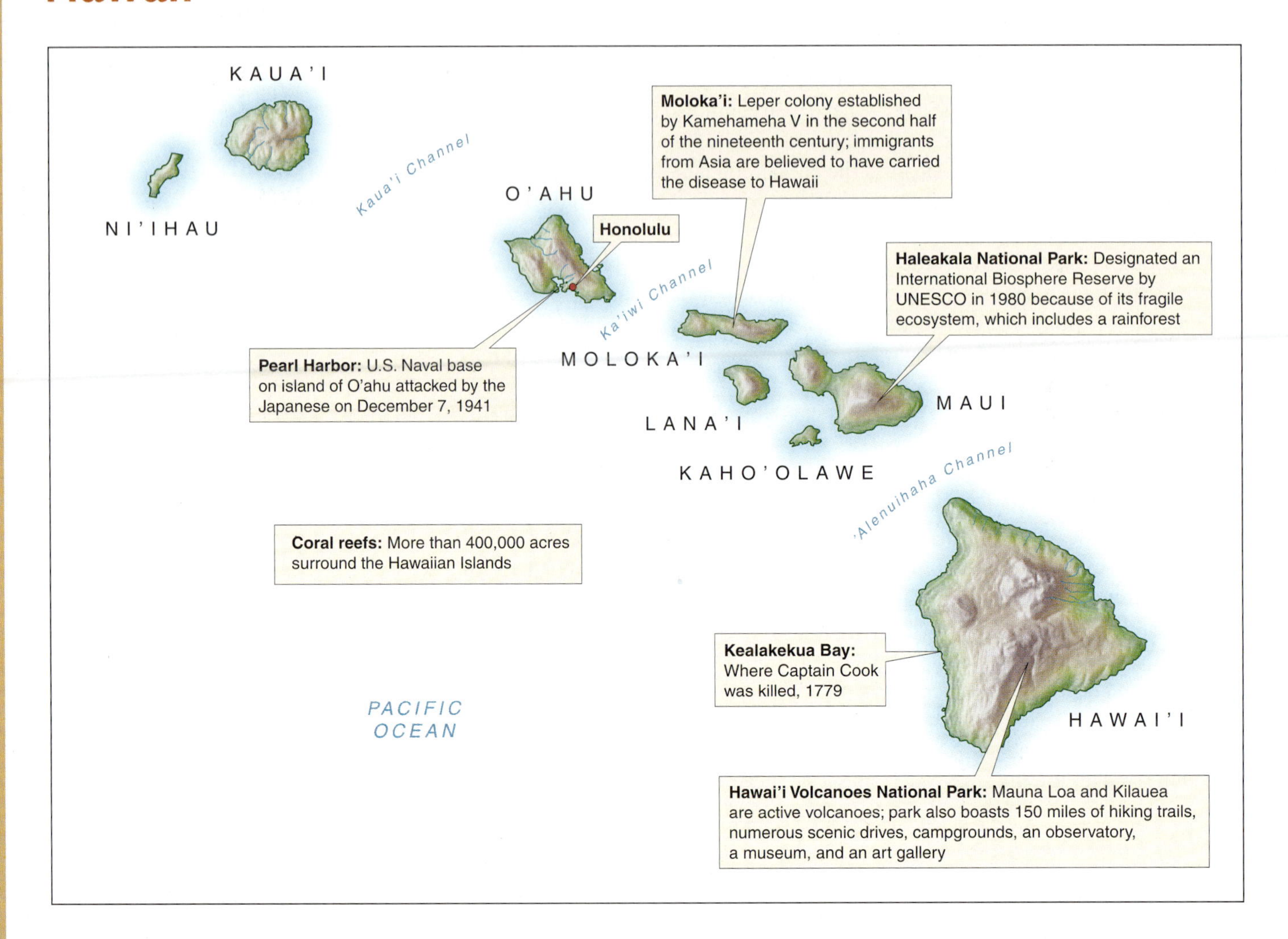

The Hawaiian Islands are massive volcano peaks that arose as molten rock from the Pacific Ocean 25 to 40 million years ago. Polynesian explorers first colonized the islands over 1,500 years ago, developing complex social patterns based on the concept of *aloha,* meaning "love." In 1778, the English explorer Captain James Cook encountered the islands, and his journals provide an important glimpse into early Hawaiian life. Hawaii's greatest king, Kamehameha, united the islands in 1795, and a generation later, American Protestant missionaries arrived to convert the Hawaiians to Christianity.

With its tropical climate, strategic Pacific location, and natural beauty, Hawaii proved increasingly attractive to American interests. The United States officially annexed Hawaii in 1898, although American sugar-cane barons already controlled much of the land and government. In 1908, the U.S. Navy began constructing facilities at Pearl Harbor, the finest sheltered harbor in the Pacific. When Congress granted the islands statehood in 1959, Hawaii entered a boom of tourism and building that shows little signs of abating.

Today, tourism continues to dominate the Hawaiian economy, accounting for $9.2 billion spent by more than 8 million out-of-state visitors annually. The people of Hawaii provide a microcosm of a diverse America, with the population about one-third Hawaiian, one-third Caucasian, and one-third Asian. ■

▲ **MAP 23.1 THE INTERNMENT OF JAPANESE AMERICANS DURING WORLD WAR II**
After the Japanese attack on Pearl Harbor, President Franklin Delano Roosevelt signed an order authorizing the removal of people of Japanese descent from the West Coast. These Japanese Americans were relocated to internment camps built in arid and isolated areas in the West, as well as in two locations in Arkansas.

declared war against Japan. Representative Jeannette Rankin from Montana cast the only dissenting vote. (The first woman elected to Congress and a lifelong pacifist, Rankin had also voted against the United States' entry into World War I.) Three days later Germany and Italy declared war against the United States.

Japanese American Relocation

The assault on Pearl Harbor sparked widespread rumors along the U.S. West Coast that Japanese and Japanese Americans living there planned to sabotage the war effort. Although no charges of criminal activity or treason were ever brought against any Japanese Americans, powerful farming interests eager to eradicate Japanese competition pushed for an evacuation. General John L. DeWitt, chief of the Western Defense Command, argued that people of Japanese ancestry posed a particular threat: "The Japanese race is an **enemy race** and while many second and third generation Japanese born on United States soil, possessed of United States citizenship, have become 'Americanized,' the racial strains are undiluted. . . . It therefore follows that along the vital Pacific Coast over 112,000 potential enemies, of Japanese extraction, are at large today."

Not everyone agreed that Japanese Americans should be removed from the West Coast. U.S. Attorney General Francis Biddle protested that there was "no reason" for a mass relocation. J. Edgar Hoover, director of the FBI, also opposed the plan, arguing that DeWitt's suggestion reflected "hysteria and lack of judgment." Nevertheless, the Roosevelt administration gave in to the pressure, with the support of California Attorney General Earl Warren. In February 1942, Roosevelt signed Executive Order 9066, which suspended the civil rights of American citizens of Japanese descent. The order authorized the removal of 110,000 Japanese and Japanese Americans from the West Coast. Of those, 70,000 were ***Nisei,*** native-born American citizens. Families received at most a week's notice to evacuate their homes and move to prison-like camps surrounded by barbed wire and guarded by armed soldiers. There were ten such camps in seven states, most of them located

▲ **The family pictured here was among thousands of loyal citizens of Japanese ancestry removed from their homes on the West Coast and relocated to internment camps. Here, the Hirano family, George, Hisa, and Yasbei (left to right), pose at the Colorado River Relocation Center in Poston, Arizona. Hisa holds a photo of her son, an American soldier, who is off fighting the war.**

in arid, desolate spots in the West. At the camps internees lived in makeshift wooden barracks, where entire families crowded into one room.

Not all Japanese Americans were evacuated. General Delos Emmons, the military governor of Hawaii, insisted that removing the Japanese from those islands would cripple the economy, as well as the defense of Oahu. In Hawaii, Japanese and Japanese Americans made up more than 90 percent of the skilled workers and agricultural laborers needed to rebuild and sustain the island. In their defense, Emmons proclaimed, "There have been no known acts of sabotage committed in Hawaii." Business leaders concurred, hoping to retain their labor force. But the Japanese living on the West Coast lacked the broad support that those in Hawaii enjoyed.

The experience of internment proved so devastating that, after the war, 5,766 *Nisei* renounced their American citizenship. One of those was World War I veteran Joseph Y. Kurihara, who recalled, "It was really cruel and harsh. To pack and evacuate in 48 hours was an impossibility. Seeing mothers completely bewildered with children crying from want and peddlers taking advantage and offering prices next to robbery made me feel like murdering those responsible." Kurihara emigrated to Japan—a country he had never seen.

While the internment experience alienated some Japanese Americans, fully 33,000 joined the armed services—including 1,200 who enlisted from the internment camps—and proved their patriotism on the battlefield. In the Pacific, their knowledge of the Japanese language proved critical in translating intercepted Japanese military documents. General Charles Willoughby, chief of intelligence in the Pacific, estimated that Japanese American military contributions shortened the war by two years. They also served ably in Europe, suffering huge casualties. The Japanese Americans of the 442nd Regiment lost one-fourth of their soldiers in battles in North Africa and Italy. They suffered another 800 casualties rescuing the Texan "Lost Battalion," 211 men surrounded by German troops in the Vosges Mountains of France. As one Texan recalled, "We were never so glad to see anyone as those fighting Japanese Americans."

The 442nd Regiment won 18,143 individual decorations for distinguished service. Welcoming them home in 1946, President Harry Truman declared, "You fought not only the enemy, you fought prejudice—and you won."

Nevertheless, the U.S. government would take its time acknowledging that the internment had been a grave injustice. The Supreme Court upheld the constitutionality of the policy, and Roosevelt would not rescind the evacuation order until after his reelection in 1944. The camps finally closed in 1945. All told, Japanese Americans lost property valued at $500 million. Not until 1968 would the government reimburse former internees for some of their losses. And not until 1983 would a Special Commission on Wartime Relocation and Internment of Civilians concede that because of "race prejudice, war hysteria and a failure of political leadership," the U.S. government had committed "a grave injustice" to more than 110,000 people of Japanese ancestry. In 1988 Congress would enact legislation awarding restitution payments of $20,000 each to 60,000 surviving internees—a small gesture for Americans whose only "crime" was their Japanese ancestry.

Foreign Nationals in the United States

Although Japanese Americans were the only U.S. citizens interned solely on the basis of their ancestry, German and Italian nationals living in the United States were also subject to new regulations, and in some cases relocation and incarceration. The Smith Act of 1940 required all foreign-born residents to be registered and fingerprinted, and broadened the grounds for deportation. In 1942, all enemy aliens (citizens of countries at war with the United States) were required to be fingerprinted and photographed, and to carry registration cards at all times. On the West Coast they were subject to travel restrictions, curfews, and in certain designated areas, relocation.

Six hundred thousand Italians and 314,000 Germans living in the United States were subject to these requirements. Several thousand who belonged to organizations that were considered sympathetic to the German or Italian government were arrested and given hearings to determine if they posed a security risk. Several hundred were deemed potentially dangerous and interned for the duration of the war. Approximately 10,000 Italian nationals were forced to relocate from their homes on the West Coast. A few hundred German and Italian immigrants who were naturalized U.S. citizens were also relocated from designated coastal areas.

German and Italian nationals living in the United States were also subject to new regulations, and in some cases relocation and incarceration.

Wartime conditions also prompted large numbers of émigrés to become American citizens. Between 1941 and 1945, more immigrants became naturalized citizens than in any previous five-year period. More than 112,000 were naturalized during their service in the armed forces. But the vast majority of those naturalized—1,539,000—were civilians. For the first time, the majority were women. The largest numbers came from countries that were embroiled in the war: the British Empire, Italy, Germany, Poland, and the Soviet Union. Naturalization was a concrete way for newcomers to clarify their status and their loyalty.

Wartime Migrations

Even before the United States officially entered World War II, the conflict had begun to change the face of the nation. The sleepy town of Richmond, California, perched near the north end of San Francisco Bay, underwent a profound transformation when the nation stepped up war production. The town's mostly white population of 23,000 ballooned to 120,000 after industrialist Henry Kaiser constructed four shipyards there. The yards employed over 150,000 workers, more than one-fourth of them African American. Most were young, married migrants from the South, and there were slightly more women than men. They came to Richmond attracted by the better pay and benefits, along with the opportunity for greater freedom than they had known in the Jim Crow South.

Margaret Starks, daughter of Southern tenant farmers, moved to Richmond. She established a blues club, edited a black newspaper, and played an active role in the National Association for the Advancement of Colored People (NAACP). Her club became a center for African American cultural and political life. Thus, black migrants not only established their own community institutions but also transformed the life of the city. This same process unfolded all over the country, bringing black culture into cities and creating a diverse urban landscape.

Many cities, however, were ill equipped to handle the influx of migrants. An estimated 60,000 African Americans moved into Chicago, for example, causing an enormous housing crisis. Many newcomers lacked even a modicum of privacy as they crowded into basements and rooms rented from total strangers. Huge numbers of whites also moved north, many leaving hardscrabble farms, hoping to prosper in booming war industries.

Wartime also saw new migration from abroad and a reversal of earlier immigration policies. Because of the alliance with China in the war against Japan, in 1943 Congress repealed the Chinese Exclusion Act, and migrants from China became eligible for citizenship for the first time. Few Chinese actually arrived, however, and most immigration restrictions remained in force. The most significant wartime migration came from Mexico. In 1942, Mexico joined the Allies and provided an air force squadron trained in the United States that fought in the Pacific. An executive agreement between the United States and Mexico created the *bracero* program, which stipulated that the migrants were to be hired on short-term contracts and treated fairly. Under the *bracero* program, 300,000 Mexicans, mostly agricultural workers, came to the United States to labor in rural areas such as California's San Joaquin Valley, taking the place of "Okies" who migrated to cities for defense work. By the mid-1960s, nearly 5 million Mexicans had migrated north under the program.

The Home Front

Wartime mobilization brought Americans from all regions and backgrounds together in shared service and sacrifice. Industries as well as citizens dedicated themselves to the war effort. Automobile manufacturers stopped making cars and instead turned out tanks, jeeps, and other military vehicles. Citizens made do with government-rationed basic staples, from food to gasoline. As able-bodied men left their jobs to fight the war, new work opportunities opened up for women as well as for disabled Americans. Cities and centers of war production brought together young women and men who found new opportunities for sexual experimentation, while gay men and lesbians discovered newly visible communities in both military and civilian life. Although class, gender, and racial injustices persisted, the war offered new sources of pride and patriotism for women and minorities and raised expectations that they would achieve full inclusion in the American promise.

Many Americans hoped that the liberal spirit of the New Deal would endure during the war; others were eager for an end to what they perceived as Depression-era class conflict and hostility to business interests. To some extent, both sides got their wish. Full employment, the increasing strength of unions, and high taxes on the wealthy pleased New Deal liberals. Profit guarantees, freedom from antitrust actions, no-strike pledges, and low-cost imported labor gratified pro-business conservatives. Congress dismantled some of the New Deal's most successful agencies, including the Civilian Conservation Corps (CCC), the Works Projects Administration (WPA), and the National Youth Administration. Full employment during wartime made these job programs unnecessary.

Building Morale

The United States, like all other major powers involved in the conflict, mounted a propaganda drive to promote support for the war effort. FDR created the Office of War Information (OWI) in 1942 to coordinate morale-boosting and censorship initiatives. Working in partnership with the motion picture industry and other media outlets, the OWI sponsored movies, radio programs, publications, and posters. These productions portrayed the war as a crusade to preserve the "American way of life" and encouraged American women and men to work in war industries, enlist in the armed forces, and purchase war bonds. Eric Johnston, head of the Motion Picture Producers' Association and FDR's business adviser, insisted that Hollywood remove class conflict from its films: "We'll have no more *Grapes of Wrath,* we'll have no more *Tobacco Roads,* we'll have no more films that deal with the seamy side of American life. We'll have no more films that treat the banker as a villain."

John Ford and Greg Toland heard the message. In the 1930s, these noted filmmakers had made movies that carried themes of political dissent. Now they helped build consensus. In one of their first wartime films, *December 7,* produced for the U.S. Navy in 1942, the protagonist is Uncle Sam himself. Visiting Hawaii before the attack on Pearl Harbor, Uncle Sam tolerates labor strikes and lets Japanese Americans speak their own language and practice their Shinto religion. But he learns his lesson when fictional Japanese Americans pass military secrets to the Japanese Imperial Navy, which attacks Pearl Harbor. Uncle Sam then insists that the Japanese Americans shed their distinct traditions, forbids class conflict, and brings all groups together to win the war. Although there was never any evidence of Japanese American sabotage, the film suggested otherwise and warned that ethnic minorities must assimilate into the American mainstream to demonstrate their patriotism.

Dwight D. Eisenhower Library

John F. Kennedy Library

Lyndon Baines Johnson Library and Museum

Richard Nixon Library and Birthplace Foundation, Album 43.6

Gerald R. Ford Library

Jimmy Carter Library

Ronald Reagan Presidential Library

George Bush Presidential Library

▲ Eight American presidents elected consecutively following World War II were veterans of that war. Pictured in wartime service, from top left, are: Dwight D. Eisenhower, John F. Kennedy, Lyndon Johnson, Richard Nixon, Gerald Ford, Jimmy Carter, Ronald Reagan, and George H. W. Bush.

Maintaining the morale of the fighting men was critical to sustaining the war effort. Officials tried to ease the hardships of combat by providing cigarettes and beer, entertainment by and for the troops, and live performances by Hollywood celebrities such as Bob Hope and Ginger Rogers. Promises of the good life waiting at home—especially images of cozy houses, warm hearths, and sexual fulfillment—reminded the men overseas why they were fighting. "Pinups"—photos of sexy but wholesome-looking women—adorned the walls of barracks, suggesting the joys that would follow victory.

Under government sponsorship, all the major radio networks aired a series of programs in 1942 to mobilize support for the war. One highly acclaimed segment, "To the Young," included this conversation:

> YOUNG MALE VOICE: "That's one of the things this war's about."
> YOUNG FEMALE VOICE: "About us?"
> YOUNG MALE VOICE: "About *all* young people like us. About love and gettin' hitched, and havin' a home and some kids, and breathin' fresh air out in the suburbs...about livin' an' workin' *decent,* like free people."

The enemy drew on the same images in their efforts to persuade American fighting service personnel to surrender. One lurid piece of propaganda that the Japanese scattered among the American troops in the Pacific pictured a young Caucasian man and woman locked in a passionate kiss under the moonlight. The leaflet read:

> That unforgettable embrace under the beautiful moon with the warmth of HER shapely body nestled against yours; that blood-tingling kiss; that over-powering sense of passion that sweeps over you—these and many other pleasant memories you'll be able to relive again if you'll throw down your arms, surrender and prepare to get out of this hell-hole.

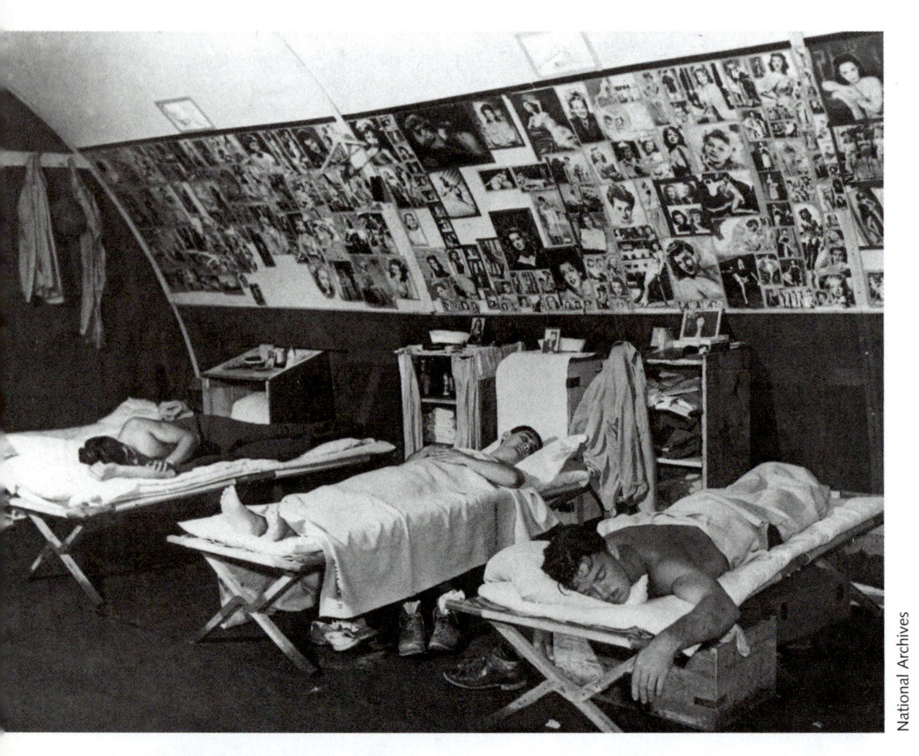

National Archives

▲ **Sailors relax in the Aircraft Repair Unit (ARU-145) during their free time at Guadalcanal. The walls above their cots are decorated with "pinups" of young women in alluring poses, reminding the men of the pleasures that await them after the war.**

Inside the card was the grim alternative: the same young man's bloody body with the warning: "BUT if you continue to resist—Then, under the beautiful tropical moon, only DEATH awaits you. Bullet-holes in your guts—agonizing death! You have the two alternatives. Take your choice."

Within the United States, government censors made sure that no photographs showing badly wounded soldiers or mutilated bodies reached the public. The censors also removed any images that might elicit sympathy for the enemy, such as pictures of injured or frightened enemy soldiers suffering at the hands of American soldiers. Photographs that appeared in the American media generally sanitized the horror of war, depicting noble American soldiers and a shadowy, faceless enemy. Rarely, if ever, did those on the home front see the true extent of the war's destructiveness and brutality. When men returned home severely traumatized by what they had seen, even their trauma was censored. As just one example, for more than three decades, the army suppressed John Huston's *Let There Be Light,* a film documentary of World War II veterans in a psychiatric hospital suffering from post-traumatic stress disorder.

Home Front Workers, Rosie the Riveter, and Victory Girls

Wartime opened up new possibilities for jobs, income, and labor organizing, for women as well as for men, and for new groups of workers. Disabled workers entered jobs previously considered beyond their abilities, fulfilling their tasks with skill and competence. Norma Krajczar, a visually impaired teenager, served as a volunteer aircraft warden; her sensitive hearing gave her an advantage over sighted wardens in listening for approaching aircraft. Deaf people streamed into Akron, Ohio, to work in the tire factories that became defense plants, making more money than they ever made before.

Along with new employment opportunities, workers' earnings rose nearly 70 percent. Income doubled for farmers and then doubled again. Labor union membership grew 50 percent, reaching an all-time high by the end of the war. In spite of no-strike pledges, strikes pressured the aircraft industry in Detroit and elsewhere. A major strike of the United Mine Workers Union erupted in 1943. Congress responded with the Smith-Connally Act of 1943, which gave the president power to seize plants or mines wherever strikes interrupted war production.

Women and minorities joined unions in unprecedented numbers. Some organized unions of their own. Energetic labor organizers like Luisa Moreno and Dorothy Ray Healy organized Mexican and Russian Jewish workers at the California Sanitary Canning Company into a powerful CIO cannery union that achieved wage increases and union recognition. Unions with white male leadership, however, admitted women and minorities reluctantly and tolerated them only during the war emergency. Some unions required women to quit their jobs after the war.

Nevertheless, World War II ushered in dramatic changes for American women. Wartime scarcities led to increased domestic labor as homemakers made do with rationed goods, mended clothing, collected and saved scraps and metals, and planted "victory gardens" to help feed their families. Employment opportunities for women also increased. As a result of the combined incentives of patriotism and good wages, women streamed into the paid labor force. Many women took "men's jobs" while the men went off to fight.

Rosie the Riveter became the heroic symbol of the woman war worker. Pictures of attractive "Rosies" building planes or constructing ships graced magazine covers and posters. Future Hollywood star Marilyn Monroe first gained attention when her photograph appeared in *Yank*, a magazine for soldiers. The magazine pictured her not as the sex goddess she later became, but as a typical Rosie the Riveter, clad in overalls, working at her job in a defense plant.

Until 1943, black women were barred from work in defense industries. Poet Maya Angelou recalled that African Americans had to fight for the jobs they wanted. She became the first black streetcar conductor in San Francisco during the war, but not without a struggle. She made herself a promise that "made my veins stand out, and my mouth tighten into a prune: I WOULD HAVE THE JOB. I WOULD BE A CONDUCTORETTE AND SLING A FULL MONEY CHANGER FROM MY BELT. I WOULD." And she did.

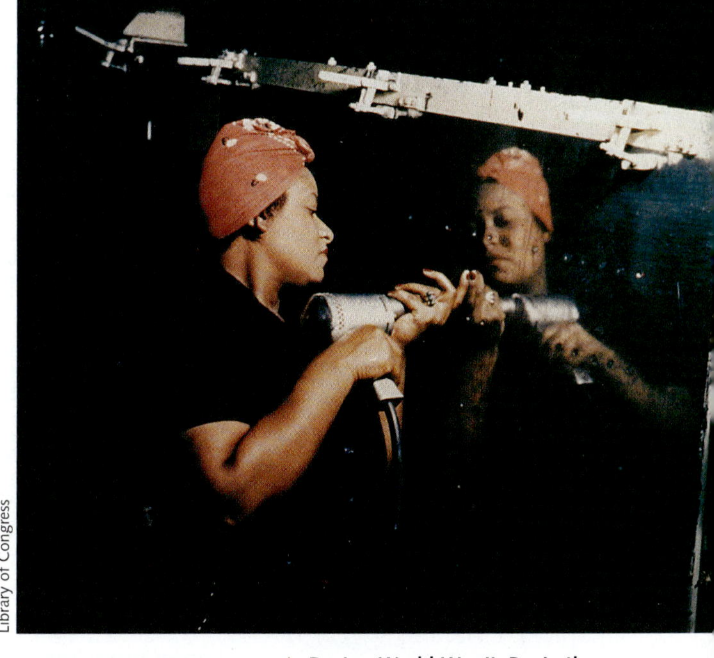

Library of Congress

▲ During World War II, Rosie the Riveter became an icon of the working woman doing a "man's job" in the war production industries. The Rosie pictured here riveting was one of thousands who enjoyed the excitement and high wages of wartime work.

For the first time, married women joined the paid labor force in droves and public opinion supported them. During the Great Depression, 80 percent of Americans had objected to the idea of wives working outside the home; by 1942, only 13 percent still objected. However, mothers of young children found very little help. In 1943 the federal government finally responded to the needs of working mothers by funding daycare centers. More than 3,000 centers enrolled 130,000 children. Still, the program served only a small proportion of working mothers. Most women relied on family members to care for their children. A Women's Bureau survey in 1944 found that 16 percent of mothers working in war industries had no child care arrangements. Meager to begin with and conceived as an emergency measure, government funding for child care would end after the war.

Before the war, most jobs for women were low-paying, nonunion positions that paid an average of $24.50 a week. Wartime manufacturing jobs paid almost twice that—$40.35 a week. During the conflict, 300,000 women worked in the aircraft industry alone. Almira Bondelid recalled that when her husband went overseas, "I decided to stay in San Diego and went to work in a dime store. That was a terrible place to work, and as soon as I could I got a job at Convair [an aircraft manufacturer]. . . . I worked in the tool department as a draftsman, and by the time I left there two years later I was designing long drill jigs for parts of the wing and hull of B-24s."

New opportunities for women also opened up in the armed services. All sectors of the armed forces had dwindled in the years between the two wars and needed to gain size and strength. Along with the 10 million men age 21 to 35 drafted into the armed services and the 6 million who enlisted, 100,000 women volunteered for the Navy WAVES (Women Accepted for Voluntary Emergency Service) and 140,00 for the Women's Army Auxiliary Corps (WAAC). In 1943, the WAAC became the Women's Army Corps (WAC), dropping "Auxiliary" from the name.

Most female enlistees and war workers enjoyed their work and wanted to continue after the war. The extra pay, independence, camaraderie, and satisfaction that their jobs provided had opened their eyes to new possibilities. Although most of the well-paying positions for women disappeared after the war as the returning veterans reclaimed their jobs, women did not disappear from the paid labor force. The numbers of employed women continued to rise in the postwar years. Edith Speert, like many others, was never again content as a full-time housewife and mother. Edith's husband, Victor, was sent overseas in 1944. During the 18 months of their separation, they penned 1,300 letters to each other, sometimes two or three times a day. The letters revealed the love and affection they felt for one another, but Edith did not hesitate to tell Victor how she had changed. In a letter from Cleveland, dated November 9, 1945, she wrote:

> Sweetie, I want to make sure I make myself clear about how I've changed. I want you to know *now* that you are not married to a girl that's interested solely in a home—I shall definitely have to work all my life—I get emotional satisfaction out of working; and I don't doubt that many a night you will cook the supper while I'm at a meeting. Also, dearest—I shall never wash and iron—there are laundries for that! Do you think you'll be able to bear living with me? . . .
> I love you, Edith

Despite the shifting priorities of women, the war reversed the declining marriage and fertility rates of the 1930s. Between 1941 and 1945 the birthrate climbed from 19.4 to 24.5 per 1,000 population. The reversal stemmed, in part, from economic prosperity, as well as the possibility of draft deferments for married men in the early war years. However, the desire to solidify relationships and establish connections to the future during a time of great uncertainty perhaps served as the more powerful motivation. Thus, a curious paradox marked the war years: a widespread disruption of domestic life accompanied by a rush into marriage and parenthood.

At the same time that the war prompted family formation, wartime upheaval sent the sexual order topsy-turvy. For many young women, moving to a new city or taking a wartime job opened up new possibilities for independence, excitement, and sexual adventure. One young worker recalled:

> Chicago was just humming, no matter where I went. The bars were jammed . . . you could pick up anyone you wanted to. . . . There were servicemen of all varieties roaming the streets all the time. There was never, never a shortage of young, healthy bucks. . . . We never thought of getting tired. Two, three hours of sleep was normal. . . . I'd go down to the office every morning half dead, but with a smile on my face, and report for work.

Some young women, known as "victory girls," believed that it was an act of patriotism to have a fling with a man in uniform before he went overseas. The independence of these women raised fears of female sexuality as a dangerous, ungoverned force. The worry extended beyond the traditional concern about prostitutes and "loose women" to include "good girls" whose sexual standards might relax during wartime. Public health campaigns warned enlisted men that victory girls would have their fun with a soldier and then leave him with a venereal disease, incapable of fighting for his country.

Wartime also intensified concerns about homosexuality. Urban centers and the military provided new opportunities for gay men and lesbians to form relationships and build communities. Although the military officially banned homosexuals from the forces, many served by keeping their orientation secret. If discovered, gay men faced severe punishment, including confinement in cages called "queer stockades" or in psychiatric wards. Lesbians faced similar sanctions, although the women's corps, in an effort to assure the civilian world of their recruits' femininity, often looked the other way.

Antigay crusades and policies sometimes backfired. Nowhere is this more evident than in the 1943 wartime propaganda film *This Is the Army,* starring future U.S. president Ronald Reagan. Sponsored by the Office of War Information and produced by Warner Brothers, the film centers on the romance between a soldier and an army nurse. The two wed just before the hero leaves to fight on foreign shores. The film uses humor to diffuse uneasiness and discomfort with the disrupted gender roles and sexual identities brought about by war. Soldier-comedians joke about their female superior officers. A group of he-men in drag do a clumsy chorus-line routine showing their hairy legs and bulging muscles beneath their skirts. In an ironic twist, *This Is the Army* became a popular wartime cult film among gays and lesbians.

Race and War

The Holocaust, Nazi Germany's campaign to exterminate European Jews, demonstrated the horrors of racial hatred taken to its ultimate extreme. The U.S. government did little to help Jewish refugees or to stem the slaughter of Jews in Europe. Official indifference and widespread anti-Semitism prevailed throughout the war. Nevertheless, Nazi policies against the Jews discredited racial and ethnic prejudice, forcing Americans to confront the reality of racism in their own country. Anthropologist Ruth Benedict, in her 1943 book *The Races of Mankind,* urged the United States to "clean its own house" and "stand unashamed before Nazis and condemn, without confusion, their doctrines of a Master Race." Swedish sociologist Gunnar Myrdal's *American Dilemma: The Negro Problem and Modern Democracy* called on the nation to live up to its democratic promise: "The great reason for hope is that this country has a national experience of uniting racial and cultural diversities and a national theory, if not a consistent practice, of freedom and equality for all." Americans of color responded to the call for unity and demonstrated their patriotism; in return, they expected full inclusion in the democracy. There would be no return to the old racial order. As black leader W. E. B. Du Bois noted, World War II was a "War for Racial Equality" and a struggle for "democracy not only for white folks but for yellow, brown, and black."

The Holocaust

Nazi Murder Mills

Hitler's war aims included conquering all of Europe and destroying European Jewry. Throughout the war, Nazi anti-Jewish policies escalated from persecution and officially sanctioned violence to imprisonment in concentration camps, slave labor, and ultimately Hitler's "final solution," genocide. Nazis developed increasingly efficient means of killing Jews. Some Jewish men, women, and children perished by firing squads in mass executions. Others died of

▲ **MAP 23.2 NAZI CONCENTRATION AND EXTERMINATION CAMPS**
Under Hitler, the Nazis established dozens of concentration camps where Jews and others whom the Nazis deemed "undesirable" were imprisoned. In addition to these sites, there were hundreds of slave labor camps attached to factories across Germany where Jews were forced to work for Nazi enterprises. After Hitler began his genocidal "final solution," six camps became sites of systematic mass murder, with efficient killing operations, including gas chambers disguised as shower rooms.

disease and malnutrition in concentration camps or at the hands of Nazi doctors in gruesome medical experiments. In the infamous Nazi death camps, guards herded prisoners into "shower rooms" that were actually gas chambers. Out of a prewar European Jewish population of 10 million, the Holocaust claimed the lives of 6 million Jews, along with homosexuals, the disabled, and Romani (also known as Gypsies).

American officials knew of the Nazi persecution of the Jews but did little about it. Throughout the 1930s, American Jewish groups pressured the Roosevelt administration to ease immigration laws to allow Jewish refugees to enter the country. But the United States raised the legal quota of Jewish immigrants only slightly. In 1938, Roosevelt organized an international conference on the refugee crisis in Evian, Switzerland, with 32 nations attending. But no nation agreed to accept large numbers of refugees, so the conference had little practical impact. In 1939, a pro-Nazi rally in New York City drew 20,000. That same year, congressional leaders defeated the Wagner-Rogers bill, which would have amended immigration quotas to allow the entry of 20,000 Jewish children.

When the Nazis began their policy of extermination in 1941, they tried to keep it a secret. But Dr. Gerhard Riegner, the World Jewish Congress representative in Geneva, Switzerland, learned about the Holocaust from a German source and informed American diplomats. U.S. State Department officials heard reports of the Holocaust but decided to keep the information quiet. Despite official silence, Rabbi Stephen S. Wise, a prominent American Jewish leader, heard the news and held a press conference in November 1942. But the American press, preoccupied with military events and reluctant to publish stories of atrocities without official verification, gave the Holocaust little coverage. Meanwhile, despite news of Nazi genocide, the U.S. government turned away boatloads of Jewish refugees, sending them back to Germany to their deaths.

Nazi persecution of the Jews raised American sensitivity to the issue of racism but did little to diminish anti-Semitism within the United States. In fact, American hostility toward Jews reached new heights during World War II and exceeded the level of prejudice against any other group. In a 1942 survey of American voters, 51 percent agreed that Jews "have too much power in the United States." At the height of Nazi genocide against the Jews in 1944, when asked to identify the greatest "menace" to the nation, 24 percent of Americans polled listed Jews—more than those who listed Germans, Japanese, radicals, Negroes, and foreigners.

In Europe, American military strategists knew of the existence and location of Nazi death camps, but they refused to destroy them or to bomb the railroad lines leading to the camps. Some Europeans under Nazi domination, however, risked their lives to rescue and shelter Jews. While the United States stood by, smaller nations took action. For example, Denmark defied the Nazis even though occupied by them—taking a far greater risk than anything the United States might have done—and managed to save nearly all Danish Jews. And the tiny Dominican Republic took in more Jewish refugees than any other country in the Western Hemisphere.

Racial Tensions at Home

Throughout the war years, racial tensions within the United States persisted. Black workers, who were excluded from the best-paying jobs in the defense industries, mobilized against discrimination on the job. Their most powerful advocate was African American civil rights leader A. Philip Randolph, who had organized the overwhelmingly black Brotherhood of Sleeping Car Porters and won the union a contract with the railroads in 1937. At the beginning of American involvement in the war in 1941, Randolph pressured FDR to ban discrimination

Dr. Seuss Collection, Mandeville Special Collections Library, University of California, San Diego (June 11, 1942)

Dr. Seuss Collection, Mandeville Special Collections Library, University of California, San Diego (June 11, 1942)

▲ These two political cartoons by Dr. Seuss, known for his whimsical children's books and progressive political ideas, demonstrate that even among liberal activists, racial tolerance during World War II did not include Japanese Americans. Dr. Seuss created dozens of cartoons that criticized anti-Semitic and anti-black prejudices, but he also promoted the idea that Japanese American citizens were disloyal and dangerous. Stereotyped images such as these contributed to anti-Japanese sentiment that ultimately resulted in the relocation of Japanese Americans from the West Coast into internment camps.

Randolph, "Why Should We March"

in defense industries. He threatened to organize a massive march on Washington if Roosevelt did not respond. Roosevelt issued Executive Order 8802, which created the Fair Employment Practices Commission (FEPC) to ensure that blacks and women received the same pay as white men for doing the same job. The FEPC narrowed pay gaps somewhat, but it did not solve the problem. The American Federation of Labor, which included the highest-paid workers, still refused to accept blacks as members and fought with the FEPC over the equal-pay policy.

Sometimes the presence of racial minorities in previously all-white work settings led to hostilities. White men who labored on the home front resented the women and minorities who were filling "men's jobs," as well as the soldiers who earned praise for their heroic military manhood. Many worried about losing their jobs to returning veterans, as well as their privileged status as white men.

For example, Montana's copper workers asked the federal government to issue them special certificates equating their wartime contribution with that of soldiers. The government denied their request and in 1942 sent a regiment of black miners from the South to help fill the labor shortage in Montana's copper mines. White miners—many of whom had immigrant parents and had only just begun to enjoy full inclusion in white America—were now being told that black men were their equals. The white miners refused to work next to black men and walked out of the mines en masse.

In 1943, white workers at the Packard auto plant in Detroit walked off the job when three black employees were promoted. With increasing numbers of black Southerners arriving to work in the city's war industries, overcrowding strained the boundaries of traditionally segregated neighborhoods. White residents at a new housing complex attacked black newcomers attempting to move in. The violence escalated into several days of rioting, resulting in 34 deaths and 1,800 arrests.

Pachucos wore the zoot suit as an expression of ethnic pride and rebelliousness, as well as incipient political consciousness.

In Los Angeles, the death of a Mexican American youth, José Diaz, at a gravel pit called Sleepy Lagoon sparked sensational news coverage and whipped up anti-Mexican fervor. Although police never determined the cause of Diaz's injuries, they filed first-degree murder charges against 22 Mexican American boys from the neighborhood. The jury found the young men guilty, but an appeals court overturned the convictions. Nevertheless, hostility continued to mount against Mexican American youths, particularly ***pachucos*** who sported **zoot suits**, distinctive attire with flared pants, long coats, and wide-brimmed hats. Pachucos wore the zoot suit as an expression of ethnic pride and rebelliousness, as well as incipient political consciousness. Both young men and young women flaunted their distinctive clothing and enjoyed the sense of unity it inspired. Some zoot-suiters would later become active in the Chicano Movement of the 1960s—including the future leader of the United Farm Workers, Cesar Chavez. Chavez remembered that it took "a lot of guts to wear those pants, and we had to be rebellious to do it, because the police and a few of the older people would harass us."

For eight days in June 1943, scores of soldiers hunted zoot-suiters in Los Angeles bars, theaters, dance halls, and even in their homes, pulling off their clothes and beating them. Soon the attacks expanded to all Mexican Americans, and then to African Americans as well, some of whom also wore the zoot-suit style. The Los Angeles police sided with the rioters. They stood by during the beatings and then arrested the naked and bleeding youths and charged them with disturbing the peace. The rioting raged until the War Department made the entire city of Los Angeles off limits to military personnel. Only a handful of soldiers, but more than 600 Mexican Americans, were arrested. President Roosevelt worried that the zoot-suit violence might strain relations with Mexico. He therefore allocated federal funds for job training, educational improvements, and greater access to higher education for Spanish-speaking Americans.

Fighting for the "Double V"

In spite of discrimination at home, members of minority groups responded enthusiastically to the war effort. The numbers of blacks in the U.S. Army soared from 5,000 in 1940 to 700,000

HultonArchive/Getty Images

▲ **African American pilots, known as the Tuskegee Airmen, served in the U.S. Army air force. Here members of the Mustang fighter group listen to a mission briefing in Italy in September 1944.**

by 1944, with an additional 187,000 in the U.S. Navy, Coast Guard, and Marine Corps. Four thousand black women joined the WACs. Almost all soldiers fought in segregated units, despite protests by the NAACP that "a Jim Crow army cannot fight for a free world." Nearly 1 million blacks also joined the industrial labor force during the war. African Americans fought for the "Double V"—victory over fascism abroad and racial discrimination at home. Wartime experiences and sacrifices would inspire African Americans, along with Mexican Americans and other minority citizens, to mobilize for civil rights after the war.

Like Keith Little and his boarding-school buddies who became Navajo code talkers, American Indians all over the country declared their willingness to fight for the cause. The Iroquois League announced: "It is the unanimous sentiment among the Indian people that the atrocities of the Axis nations are violently repulsive to all sense of righteousness of our people. This merciless slaughter of mankind upon the part of those enemies of free peoples can no longer be tolerated."

The Cheyenne agreed, vowing to defeat an "unholy triangle" determined to "conquer and enslave the bodies, minds and souls of all free people." Fully 25,000 Indians, including 800 women, served in the military during the war. By 1945, nearly one-third of all able-bodied Indian men between 18 and 50 had served. Five percent of them were killed or wounded in action. Native Americans enlisted at a higher rate than the general population, prompting the *Saturday Evening Post* to editorialize, "We would not need the Selective Service if all volunteered like the Indians."

In addition to those who enlisted, half of all able-bodied Native American men not in the service and one-fifth of women left reservations for war industry jobs. At the beginning of the war, men on reservations earned a median annual income of $500, less than one-fourth the national average. One-third of all Indian men living off reservations were unemployed. Worse, the average life expectancy for Native Americans in 1940 was just 35 years, but 64 years for the population at large. Like others who found new opportunities during the conflict, Indians hoped that the economic progress they made would be permanent. But the boom would end for them when the war ended. Fewer than 10 percent of Native Americans who relocated to cities found long-term employment after the war.

Zelda Webb Anderson, "You Just Met One Who Does Not Know How to Cook"

Zelda Webb Anderson became one of the first black women to enter military service during World War II. She served as an officer in the Women's Army Auxiliary Corps (WAACS), renamed the Women's Army Corps (WAC) in 1943. After the war she earned a doctorate in education at the University of California, Berkeley. Her 42-year career in education included a stint teaching at the University of East Africa in Dar-es-Salaam, Tanzania. She related her wartime experiences to the University of Nevada Oral History Program in 1995.

I reported for duty in January 1942. . . . This was so exciting to me. We had black officers, and our basic training was the same as for men. They would simply tell us, "You wanted to be in a man's army, so now you got to do what the men do." We learned military courtesy, history, how to shoot an M-1, go on bivouac, bathe in a teacup of water, eat hardtack rations....

Every evening troops of male soldiers would march by our barracks en route to the mess hall. I told the commanding officer that we would like to have some shades at the windows. "Oh, no. You wanted to be in the man's army. Fine—you have to do what the men do." I told all the girls, "Listen, they won't give us any shades. So I want you to get right in front of the windows buck naked." The next day we had shades at all the windows. . . .

They pulled me out of basic training the third week and sent me to officer training in Des Moines. All of the instructors were white, but white and black officers were being trained in the same facility, in the same classes, and we slept in the same barracks. After OCS I was assigned to a laundry unit.

Courtesy, Zelda Webb Anderson and University of Nevada Oral History Project

Zelda Webb Anderson

A black enlisted WAAC could either be in the laundry unit or she could be in the hospital unit. In the laundry unit, if she had a college degree, she could work at the front counter. . . . If she had less than that, then she did the laundry—very demeaning. And in the hospital unit they let her wash walls, empty basins, wash windows—all that menial work. . . .

I was assigned to duty at Fort Breckenridge, Kentucky. The post commander's name was Colonel Throckmorton. In a pronounced southern accent he told me, "You're going over to that colored WAC company, and you're going to be the mess officer."

I said, "Sir, I have not had any mess training."

"All you nigras know how to cook."

I said, "You just met one who does not know how to cook; but if you send me to Fort Eustis, Virginia, for training I will come back and be the best mess officer you have on this post."

"I ain't sending you to no school, and you're going over there to be a mess officer." When I about-faced, I kept on going. I didn't even salute him. . . .

[Much later, after developing a more cordial relationship with Colonel Throckmorton,] I told him that segregation has not allowed white people to know black people: "We know you very intimately, but you don't know how we think, how we react, and so you just try to push your stuff on us, not giving a damn about how we feel about this. And then when we rebel, or you meet somebody like me, who decides that you can't do this to me, then you think I'm cantankerous; you think I'm an agitator. I'm just trying to give you an education. . . ."

I lived out the rest of my days very happy in the Army. If I had succumbed to the treatment that they had given other blacks before, and not spoken up for myself, my morale would have been down. . . . In this life, you've got to speak up for yourself. You can't go around shuffling your feet with your head hung down acting apologetic. If you see something you want, you must go after it. One day somebody will recognize it, and it's a victory for you, especially when it's somebody who has denigrated you because of your race. . . .

Our country has not solved all of its problems. You have to live democracy before you can preach democracy. I've got four granddaughters, and I don't want them put in a position where they don't have equal opportunities, equal chances, and then they have to fight the same old battles that I fought again.

Questions

1. *Why do you think Anderson, as a woman and an African American, would choose to enlist in the U.S. Army during World War II?*
2. *According to Anderson, in what ways did the segregation of the armed forces distort white officers' views of blacks?*

Total War

World War II consisted of two wars, one centered in Europe and the other in the Pacific. Combatants in both conflicts engaged in **total war**—the bombing of civilian as well as military targets. The advantageous geographic position of the United States enabled it to wage total war without attacks on its own cities.

The war transformed much of the world. By the time it ended, Hitler had killed 6 million Jews and destroyed the Jewish communities in Europe. Large parts of the Soviet Union, Europe, and Asia lay in ruins. The United States had deployed the most powerful weapon ever used in warfare. Of all the combatants, only the United States escaped physical destruction on its own national soil, with the exception of Pearl Harbor. Coming out of the war physically whole, economically sound, and politically strong, the United States became the most prosperous and powerful nation in the world.

MAP

World War II in Europe

The War in Europe

The attack on Pearl Harbor brought the United States immediately into the war in both Europe and the Pacific. The leaders of the Allied Powers, including the United States, Britain, and the Soviet Union, had to develop a strategy to defeat the Nazis. But the Allies did not always agree on how to conduct the war, and relations between

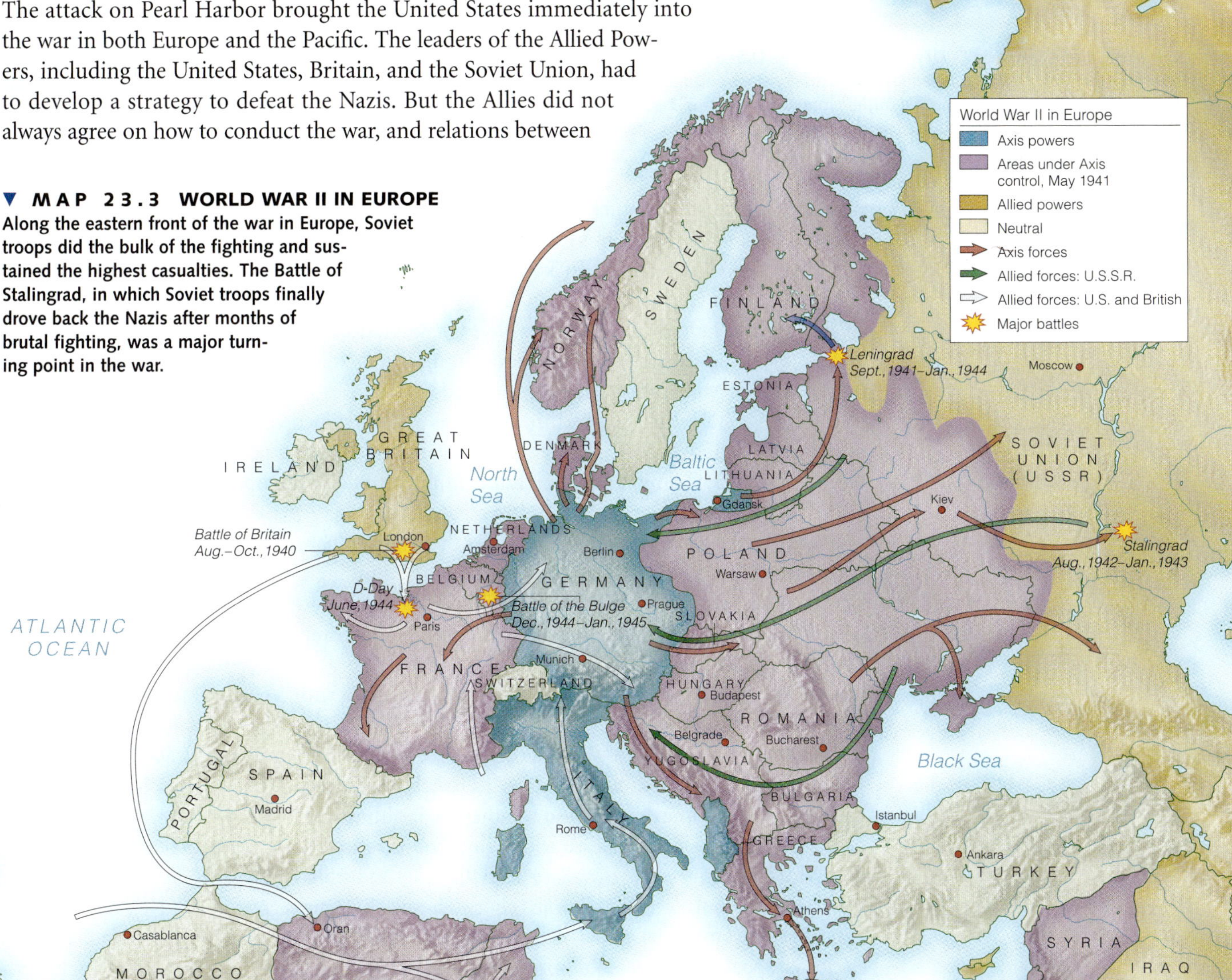

▼ **MAP 23.3 WORLD WAR II IN EUROPE**
Along the eastern front of the war in Europe, Soviet troops did the bulk of the fighting and sustained the highest casualties. The Battle of Stalingrad, in which Soviet troops finally drove back the Nazis after months of brutal fighting, was a major turning point in the war.

National Archives

▲ A photograph taken on D-Day, June 6, 1944, as U.S. troops waded to shore from their landing craft and faced German artillery fire on Omaha Beach. This is a rare surviving photograph from the initial Normandy invasion because so many of the photographers, along with thousands of soldiers, died at the scene.

the United States and the Soviet Union remained strained. Unable to fully overcome the hostility and suspicion that had marked their earlier encounters, leaders of both countries fought the war with postwar power considerations in mind.

Like the United States at Pearl Harbor, the Soviet Union suffered a shocking blow when the Nazis launched a surprise invasion in June 1941 in violation of the nonaggression pact Hitler had signed with Stalin in 1938. The Soviets suffered huge losses as 200 German divisions advanced across Eastern Europe and into the Soviet Union toward Moscow. With the full might of the Nazi forces concentrated on the front lines against the Russians in Eastern Europe, Soviet premier Joseph Stalin wanted the United States to open a second front in Western Europe to divert the Nazis toward the west and relieve pressure on the Soviet Union. In May 1942 Roosevelt assured Stalin that the United States would support an Allied invasion across the English Channel into France. But British Prime Minister Winston Churchill persuaded FDR to delay that dangerous maneuver and instead launch an invasion of French North Africa, which was controlled by the Nazi occupation forces in Vichy, France.

While the Allies turned their attention to North Africa, the Soviets managed single-handedly to force the German army into retreat at Stalingrad, where fierce fighting lasted from August 1942 to January 1943. The Battle of Stalingrad was a major turning point in the war and stopped Nazi aggression on the eastern front. Axis soldiers in North Africa surrendered in May 1943. The following summer the Allied forces overran the island of Sicily and moved into southern Italy. Italians overthrew Mussolini and opened communication with General Dwight D. Eisenhower, commander of the Allied forces in Europe. By 1944 the Allied forces reached Rome. Roosevelt and Churchill continued to delay the opening of the second front as the Soviets waited for relief.

The long-awaited Allied invasion across the English Channel finally began on June 6, 1944, code named D-Day. On D-Day, the force assembled in England crossed the English Channel to France. At dawn, in the largest amphibious landing in history, more than 4,000 Allied ships descended on the French beaches at Normandy. As the troops splashed onto shore, they met a barrage of German fire. Many thousands died on the beach that day. Over the next ten days, more than 1 million soldiers landed at Normandy, along with 50,000 vehicles and more than 100,000 tons of supplies, opening the way for an advance into Nazi-occupied France.

As the war continued to rage, Roosevelt prepared for the November election. Much of the 1944 campaign swirled around Roosevelt's suitability for reelection: whether he should serve an unprecedented fourth term, and whether his health would hold up—the 62-year-old president suffered from heart disease and high blood pressure. Party regulars persuaded FDR to drop Vice President Henry A. Wallace from the ticket and replace him with Senator Harry S. Truman from Missouri. The Republicans chose Thomas E. Dewey, governor of New York, to run against FDR. Democrats campaigned on the slogan "Don't change horses in midstream," and the electorate apparently agreed. Roosevelt won the election and continued his wartime leadership.

In the months after D-Day, the Allies liberated Paris and went on to defeat the Germans in Belgium at the Battle of the Bulge, sending the Nazis into full retreat. The Allied armies then crossed the Rhine River and headed for Berlin. Eisenhower stopped his troops at the Elbe River to let Soviet troops take Berlin. Eisenhower hoped that giving the Soviets the final triumph would ease postwar relations with the Soviet Union—but he also wanted to save American lives. Huge numbers of Soviet troops died in the siege of Berlin, but the war in Europe was nearly over. With the Soviets approaching his bunker in April 1945, Hitler committed suicide. Germany surrendered at Reims, France, on May 7, 1945—V-E (Victory in Europe) Day.

FDR did not live to see the Nazis defeated. On April 12, 1945, he died suddenly of a cerebral hemorrhage. As a stunned nation mourned, Vice President Harry S. Truman took the oath of office as the nation's thirty-third president.

The War in the Pacific

World War II in the Pacific

As the conflict in Europe came to an end, the war in the Pacific continued to rage. Following the attack on Pearl Harbor, Japan continued its conquests in the Pacific. In April 1942 General Douglas MacArthur, driven from the Philippines to Australia, left 12,000 American and 64,000 Filipino soldiers to surrender on the Bataan peninsula and the island of Corregidor. On the infamous "Bataan Death March" to the prison at Camp O'Donnell, the Japanese beat, tortured, and shot the sick and starving troops. As many as 10,000 died on the march.

Now in control of Indochina, Thailand, the Philippines, and the chain of islands from Sumatra to Guadalcanal, Japan's military leaders planned to destroy what remained of the U.S. fleet. But MacArthur marshaled his forces and achieved a major victory in the Battle of the Coral Sea in May 1942. U.S. intelligence sources discovered that the Japanese were planning a massive assault on Midway Island, a naval base key to Hawaii's defense. Under the command of Admiral Chester Nimitz, the United States launched a surprise air strike on June 4, 1942, sinking four Japanese carriers, destroying 322 planes, and virtually destroying Japanese offensive capabilities. Two months later, Nimitz's forces landed at Guadalcanal in the Solomon Islands, subduing the Japanese in five months of brutal fighting. Having seized the offensive, U.S. troops continued toward Japan. MacArthur's forces took New Guinea, and by February 1944, Nimitz secured the Marshall Islands and the Marianas.

At about the same time that Allied forces in Europe were landing in Normandy, the U.S. invaded Saipan, the main island bastion that protected Japan's mainland. In a savage air battle on June 19, the Americans shot down 346 Japanese planes and lost 50 of their own. The attack killed 22,000 Japanese civilians—two-thirds of the island's population. The United States suffered 14,000 casualties. The grueling battle secured for the United States a strategic base for launching bombing raids on Tokyo. The bloody war in the Pacific continued, with critical Allied victories on the islands of Iwo Jima and Okinawa in the spring of 1945. Crucial to these victories were the sensitive radio communications achieved by the special Marine unit of Navajo code talkers.

In China the struggle against Japanese aggression grew complicated because China was also engaged in a civil war. Initially, the Chinese Nationalists appeared to have the largest military forces to resist the Japanese, so Roosevelt declared support for Jiang Jieshi (Chiang Kai-shek), the corrupt and unpopular Nationalist leader. Jiang continued to demand Allied support as a growing communist movement, led by Mao Zedong (Mao

Joe Rosenthal/National Archives

▲ Associated Press photographer Joe Rosenthal took this photo, "Old Glory Goes Up on Mt. Suribachi, Iwo Jima," and won a Pulitzer Prize for it in 1945. Although controversy surrounded the photo (some witnesses claimed it was staged with a larger flag after the original flag had been planted), it became an icon of American determination and unity in World War II.

▲ **MAP 23.4 WORLD WAR II IN THE PACIFIC**
During World War II, the Japanese occupied vast territories in Asia and the Pacific. The Battle of Midway in 1942 was the first major victory for the United States in the Pacific and helped turn the tide of the war in favor of the Allies.

Tse-tung), challenged the Japanese and gained support among Chinese peasants. Although the Nationalists failed to stop the Japanese, Roosevelt continued to back Jiang's ineffective leadership, setting the stage for political tensions that persisted after the war.

The war in the Pacific was particularly vicious. Racism on both sides fueled acts of extreme brutality. Japan's leaders believed that their racial superiority gave them a divine mission to conquer Asia. The Japanese tortured prisoners of war and civilians in their conquered lands. They tested biological weapons and conducted medical experiments on live subjects. Japanese troops forced Chinese and Korean women into sexual slavery, euphemistically calling them **"comfort women."**

Racial hostility also promoted American battlefield savagery. U.S. troops in the Pacific often killed Japanese combatants instead of taking prisoners and desecrated the enemy dead with disrespect equal to that meted out by the Japanese on the bodies of their foes. On the home front, American cultural images and popular sentiments vilified the Japanese not only as a hated enemy but also as a monstrous race. War correspondent Ernie Pyle explained that "in Europe we felt that our enemies, horrible and deadly as they were, were still people. But…the Japanese were looked upon as something subhuman and repulsive, the way some people feel about cockroaches or mice." Respectable magazines such as *Science Digest* ran articles titled "Why Americans Hate Japs More Than Nazis."

As American troops closed in on Japan, Roosevelt approved a plan to firebomb Japanese cities. The Allies had already bombed German cities, destroying much of Hamburg and Dresden and killing thousands of civilians. To persuade Americans to accept the bombing strategy with its inevitable civilian casualties, government censors lifted the ban on stories of Japanese treatment of American war prisoners. Reports of atrocities, as well as virulently racist images of the Japanese, flooded the media. On March 9 and 10, 1945, bombing raids led by General Curtis LeMay leveled 16 square miles of Tokyo—one-fourth of the city—and left 185,000 dead or wounded. LeMay's bombers then turned to other cities. Firebombs reportedly killed more civilians than Japanese soldiers who died in battle.

The End of the War

Allied leaders met several times to plan for the postwar era. Roosevelt hoped to ensure American dominance and to limit Soviet power. At a conference in Teheran, Iran, in 1943 Roosevelt insisted that the Eastern European states of Poland, Latvia, Lithuania, and Estonia should be independent after the war. As the war wound down, Churchill, Stalin, and Roosevelt met again at Yalta, in Ukraine, in February 1945. They agreed to demand Germany's unconditional surrender and to divide the conquered nation into four zones to be occupied by Britain, the Soviet Union, the United States, and France. It became obvious at Yalta that separate spheres of influence would prevail after the war. Poland was a source of contention. Although Stalin nominally agreed to allow free elections in Eastern Europe, he intended to make sure that the countries bordering the Soviet Union would be under his control. He also pledged to enter the war against Japan and received assurances that the Soviet Union would regain the lands lost to Japan in the 1904–1905 Russo-Japanese War.

In July 1945 the newly sworn-in American president, Harry Truman, joined Stalin and Churchill (replaced by Clement Attlee after Churchill's election loss) at Potsdam, near Berlin. The three leaders issued a statement demanding "unconditional surrender" from Japan while privately agreeing to let Japan retain its emperor. The rest of the conference focused on postwar Europe. At Potsdam Truman learned of the successful test of the atomic bomb. With the new weapon in his hands, he now knew that Soviet assistance would not be needed to end the war in the Pacific.

As the war ended in Europe, Allied troops liberated the Nazi concentration camps. At that moment, the world finally learned the extent of Hitler's "final solution." Among the soldiers who first entered the camps were a number of Japanese Americans. Ichiro Imamura described the sight at Dachau: "When the gates swung open, we got our first good look at the prisoners. . . . They were like skeletons—all skin and bones. . . . They were sick, starving and dying." Some of the survivors saw the Japanese American soldiers and feared that they were Japanese allies of the Germans. A *Nisei* soldier reassured them, "I am an American soldier, and you are free."

National Archives

▲ **Slave laborers rest in the Buchenwald concentration camp near Jena, Germany. These inmates were among those who were still alive when troops of the 80th Division entered the camp on April 16, 1945. At labor camps such as this one, and death camps such as Auschwitz, 6 million Jews, along with thousands of Romani (Gypsies), Poles, mentally and physically handicapped people, and homosexuals, died in the Holocaust.**

The Atomic Bomb: Political and Cultural Fallout

Since the dawn of the Atomic Age, the United States has been the only nation that has actually waged nuclear war. The dropping of the atomic bombs on the Japanese cities of Hiroshima and Nagasaki unleashed not only massive death and destruction but also ongoing controversies over the development and use of nuclear weapons and the nature of modern warfare. The level of destruction inflicted on the Japanese civilian population shocked the nation and the world. But well before the nuclear attacks on Japan, hundreds of thousands of civilians had already perished in the war.

During World War II, bombing of civilian targets became commonplace. The Japanese bombed civilians in Nanjing, China; the Germans did the same in Guernica, Spain. Allied bombing raids nearly demolished the German cities of Berlin and Dresden and the Japanese capital of Tokyo. One night of conventional bombing in Tokyo in March 1945 killed as many civilians as the atomic bomb dropped on Hiroshima. With its huge air force, the United States became the greatest bombing power during the war. But the atomic bombs took civilian casualties to a new level, not only because of the enormous death toll wrought by a single bomb but also because of the deadly radioactive fallout that lingered. Conventional bombing raids did not create fallout to harm survivors, their descendants, or the environment.

With the successful 1952 test of the hydrogen (fusion) bomb—1,000 times more powerful than the bombs dropped on Japan—scientists warned that the use of such weapons in warfare could create a "nuclear winter" that would destroy life on Earth. Horror at the impact of the bombs discouraged their use throughout the remainder of the twentieth century.

Civilian casualties, however, remained a fact of warfare. Guerrilla warfare increased the likelihood of civilian casualties in Vietnam, where American troops found it nearly impossible to distinguish combatants from noncombatants. American forces made widespread use of napalm, the antipersonnel weapon that set fire to anyone in its path, civilian or military. Massacres of villagers, such as the infamous killings at My Lai, turned many Americans against the Vietnam War.

Although the United States and the Soviet Union refrained from using atomic weapons during the many hot wars that erupted during the Cold War, the two superpowers developed tens of thousands of nuclear weapons with sophisticated delivery systems to launch attacks from land, sea, and air. Proponents argued that the nuclear deterrent prevented the outbreak of

As the victors carved up Hitler's Third Reich, the war in the Pacific continued. The United States persisted in demanding "unconditional surrender" and vowed to continue to blockade Japan's ports, firebomb its cities, and possibly launch an invasion if the Japanese refused to surrender. A land invasion would have resulted in thousands of American casualties. Truman also worried about the impact on the postwar balance of power in Asia if the Soviet Union were to join the invasion.

The atomic bomb offered Truman an alternative means to end the war. The secret project to develop the bomb had been under way for several years, initially for possible use against Germany. In 1939 scientists in Berlin had achieved atomic fission by splitting the uranium atom, making it possible to release the tremendous energy stored in the atom. Albert Einstein, the German Jewish physicist who came to the United States after Hitler came to power in 1933, had warned Roosevelt that the Germans might be developing an atomic weapon. Einstein urged the United States to establish a small research program to keep pace. In 1942, Roosevelt authorized the Manhattan Project, the research program to develop nuclear weapons at a top-secret laboratory in Los Alamos, New Mexico. The building of the bomb was the work of 125,000 people and cost nearly $2 billion. The first test of the device took place on July 16, 1945, at Alamogordo, New Mexico.

Einstein, Letter to President Roosevelt

When Truman learned of the successful test, he hoped to avoid an invasion of Japan that would have cost the lives of many American soldiers, and he wanted to send a message to the Soviet Union that the United States would be the dominant power in the postwar world. But

World War III. But detractors claimed that the arms race increased international tensions and strained the economies of both nations. In 1962 the Cuban Missile Crisis nearly led to nuclear war.

Fifty years after the end of World War II, the controversy over the use of the weapons remained heated. The Smithsonian Institution planned an exhibit to display the *Enola Gay,* the plane that dropped the atomic bomb over Hiroshima, with an explanation of the arguments for and against the weapon. Because the proposed exhibit included viewpoints of those who opposed the dropping of the bombs on Japan, which questioned the judgment of top U.S. military and political officials, fierce opposition forced the Smithsonian to abandon the plan, prompting the institute's director to resign in protest.

At the dawn of the twenty-first century, the arms race continued to generate policy debates. President George W. Bush revived the "Star Wars" plan of President Ronald Reagan to build a satellite shield against incoming missiles. Advocates of the plan claimed that it would protect the United States from nuclear attack. Critics charged that the system would not work and that it would probably generate a new arms race. As the debate continued, around the world—in missile silos, submarines, and bomber planes—nuclear warheads remained poised to strike. ■

Harry S. Truman Library

This atomic bomb was dropped on Nagasaki, Japan, on August 8, 1945, two days after the first bomb destroyed the city of Hiroshima. The Japanese surrendered soon afterward, bringing World War II to an end. Controversy still surrounds the dropping of these weapons, which killed hundreds of thousands of civilians.

Truman's advisers did not all agree about whether or how the new weapon should be deployed. Some argued against using the bomb and favored responding to Japanese peace overtures. They believed that the Japanese would be willing to surrender if they knew that the emperor would not be executed.

Even the scientists who had developed the bomb disagreed about the wisdom of using it. Some urged a demonstration in a remote, unpopulated area that would impress the Japanese but would not cause loss of life. General George C. Marshall and other military leaders argued in favor of dropping the bomb on military or industrial targets, with ample warning ahead of time to enable civilians to leave target areas. But others agreed with Truman that dropping the bomb on a major city, without warning, would be the only way to persuade the Japanese to surrender unconditionally. Given the death and destruction already inflicted on Japanese cities by firebombing, the atomic bomb seemed to some an escalation of current strategy.

But when the first bomb exploded over Hiroshima on August 6, 1945, and the second on Nagasaki two days later, the horrifying destructiveness of nuclear weapons became apparent. Even though the American public saw few images of the carnage on the ground, the huge mushroom cloud and the descriptions of cities leveled and people instantly incinerated shocked the nation and the world. In addition to the immediate devastation wreaked by the bomb, deadly radioactive fallout remained in the atmosphere, causing illness and death for months and even years after the attack. On August 14, 1945—V-J (Victory in Japan) Day—the Japanese agreed to surrender; the official ceremony of surrender took place on September 2. Many people breathed a sigh of relief that the war was finally over. But doubts and controversies over the use of the weapon, and the nuclear arms race that it sparked, have continued to this day.

National Archives

▲ On V-J Day, August 14, 1945, New Yorkers of Italian descent celebrate Japan's surrender. Although the United States fought against the country of their ancestors, these Americans showed their spirited support for the Allied cause.

Conclusion

The Japanese attack on Pearl Harbor on December 7, 1941, put an end to the debate over whether the United States should enter the conflict. FDR immediately declared war, and within days Americans were fighting against fascist regimes in Europe and the Pacific. Millions of American men and women joined the military and served overseas. Although fighting did not take place on the American mainland, there were major disruptions on the home front. The government evacuated 110,000 Japanese Americans from their homes on the West Coast and interned them in detention camps. Americans coped with rationing of food and consumer goods.

The booming wartime economy put an end to the economic depression and brought full employment. African Americans from the rural South, Mexican American agricultural laborers, and American Indians from impoverished reservations joined thousands of other men and women who migrated to industrial centers to work in war-related industries, or entered the armed forces. Many who faced discrimination at home served heroically overseas, including the African American Tuskegee Airmen, the Navajo code-talkers, and the highly decorated Japanese American troops who fought in Europe. The war sparked a campaign for the Double V: victory over fascism abroad and racism at home.

World War II left massive devastation in its wake all across the globe. The Holocaust destroyed most of European Jewry. The waging of "total war" killed millions of civilians as well as soldiers, and caused devastation across the world. The United States dropped two atomic bombs on Japanese cities, ending the war in the Pacific and ushering in the Atomic Age.

The United States was the only country involved in the war that emerged from it stronger than before the conflict began. Although thousands of Americans died in the conflict, American casualties were far below those suffered by other countries. At the end of the war, the United States was the most powerful nation in the world.

The war changed life for Americans in profound ways. Although wartime forged a sense of unity as the nation came together to fight against fascism, it also highlighted fissures within American society. Members of minority groups fought in segregated units, while racial tensions and conflicts erupted at home, even as the country fought against a racist foe. Women joined the paid labor force and the armed services in unprecedented numbers, while at the same time official and cultural messages reminded them that their primary service to the nation was as wives and mothers.

At the end of the war, veterans of color returned to fight for the still unfulfilled side of the Double V: victory against racism at home. Women joined returning veterans to form families and have babies in the most dramatic rush into parenthood in the nation's history, but they did not retreat from the paid labor force. World War II marked the beginning of a steady increase in employment for women that continued for the rest of the century.

AP/Wide World

▲ **Two days after the atomic bombing of Hiroshima, Americans dropped another atom bomb on the ancient city of Nagasaki, pictured here after the attack. Critics argued that Japan was about to surrender and that the destruction of a second city was unnecessary. But military strategists insisted that the second attack was necessary to end the war.**

While life at home changed dramatically, so did the place of the United States in the world. The war's conclusion did not usher in the era of peace Americans expected. European empires staggered on the brink of collapse. Only the United States and the Soviet Union remained as major military powers, shifting the international balance of power from a multipolar to a bipolar system. The victors carved up countries in Europe and Asia according to geopolitical considerations, with little regard for national affinities. Soon American troops would fight again in the artificially divided lands of Korea and Vietnam. For the next half century, the fallout from World War II, as well as the power struggle between the United States and the Soviet Union, would shape political relationships across the globe.

Sites to Visit

Powers of Persuasion—Poster Art of World War II

www.archives.gov/exhibit_hall/powers_of_persuasion/powers_of_persuasion_home.html

This Library of Congress site includes posters created during World War II to encourage support for the war and to build morale.

A-Bomb WWW Museum

www.csi.ad.jp/ABOMB/

This site includes information about the impact of the atomic bombs dropped on Japan during World War II as well as materials and images about the development of nuclear weapons.

A People at War

www.archives.gov/exhibit_hall/a_people_at_war/a_people_at_war.html

This National Archives site includes materials and images about the contributions millions of Americans made to the war effort.

The United States Holocaust Memorial Museum

www.ushmm.org/index.html

This official Web site of the U.S. Holocaust Memorial Museum in Washington, D.C., covers the history and documents of the Holocaust.

Tuskegee Airmen

www.wpafb.af.mil/museum/history/prewwii/ta.htm

This site of the Air Force Museum at Wright-Patterson Air Force Base includes information and photographs of the African American pilots of World War II.

Abraham Lincoln Brigade Archives

www.alba-valb.org/aboutalb.htm

This site has information and articles about the Spanish Civil War and the unit of American volunteers who fought in it.

The Zoot Suit Riots

www.pbs.org/wgbh/amex/zoot/

This Web site from the Public Broadcasting Service (PBS) documentary series *The American Experience* covers the World War II Zoot Suit Riots in Los Angeles.

William P. Gottlieb Photographs of the Golden Age of Jazz

memory.loc.gov/ammem/wghtml/wghome.html

This Library of Congress site includes images, audio, and articles from *Down Beat* magazine in the 1940s.

America from the Great Depression to World War II: Photographs from the FSA and OWI, c. 1935–1945

memory.loc.gov/ammem/fsahtml/fahome.html

This site from the Library of Congress includes photographs in the Farm Security Administration–Office of War Information Collection taken during the Depression and World War II years.

For Further Reading

General

Paul Fussell, *Wartime: Understanding and Behavior in the Second World War* (1989).

John Keegan, *The Second World War* (1990).

Richard Polenburg, *War and Society: The United States, 1941–1945* (1972).

Studs Terkel, *"The Good War": An Oral History of World War II* (1984).

Mobilizing for War

Michael E. Birdwell, *Celluloid Soldiers: The Warner Brothers Campaign Against Nazism* (1999).

Justus D. Doenecke, *Storm on the Horizon: The Challenge to American Intervention, 1939–1941* (2000).

Thomas J. Fleming, *The New Dealers' War: Franklin D. Roosevelt and the War Within World War II* (2001).

Cecelia Lynch, *Beyond Appeasement: Interpreting Interwar Peace Movements in World Politics* (1999).

Leila J. Rupp, *Mobilizing Women for War: German and American Propaganda, 1939–1945* (1978).

Pearl Harbor: The United States Enters the War

Allan Berube, *Coming Out Under Fire: The History of Gay Men and Women in World War Two* (1990).

Allan M. Brandt, *No Magic Bullet: A Social History of Venereal Disease in the United States* (1987).

Akira Iriye, *Pearl Harbor and the Coming of the Pacific War: A Brief History with Documents and Essays* (1999).

Michael S. Sherry, *The Rise of American Air Power: The Creation of Armageddon* (1987).

The Home Front

John Morton Blum, *V Was for Victory: Politics and American Culture During World War II* (1976).

Lewis A. Erenberg and Susan E. Hirsch, *The War in American Culture* (1996).

Susan Hartmann, *The Home Front and Beyond: American Women in the 1940s* (1982).

Elaine Tyler May, *Pushing the Limits: American Women, 1940–1961* (1994).

Emily Yellin, *Our Mothers' War: American Women at Home and at the Front During World War II* (2004).

Race and War

Beth Bailey and David Farber, *The First Strange Place: The Alchemy of Race and Sex in World War II Hawaii* (1992).

Aaron Berman, *Nazism, the Jews and American Zionism, 1933–1948* (1990).

John W. Dower, *War Without Mercy: Race and Power in the Pacific War* (1987).

Barbara Dianne Savage, *Broadcasting Freedom: Radio, War, and the Politics of Race, 1938–1948* (1999).

Davis S. Wyman, *The Abandonment of the Jews: America and the Holocaust, 1941–1945* (1984).

Total War

Ronald Powaski, *March to Armageddon: The United States and the Nuclear Arms Race, 1939 to the Present* (1987).

George H. Roeder Jr., *The Censored War: American Visual Experience During World War Two* (1993).

Michael S. Sherry, *In the Shadow of War: The United States Since the 1930s* (1995).

Martin J. Sherwin, *A World Destroyed: Hiroshima and the Origins of the Arms Race* (1987).

CHAPTER 24

Cold War and Hot War, 1945–1953

David Parks, "Boys on Bikes," 1950. Curtis Galleries, Minneapolis, MN

▲ David Park's 1950 painting *Kids on Bikes* reminds viewers that in the midst of the high drama of Cold War international conflicts, most Americans tried to carry on with their normal daily lives. Park himself opted out of the comfortable life of his prominent Boston family, quitting high school and moving to Berkeley, California, to work as an artist.

CHAPTER OUTLINE

The Uncertainties of Victory

The Quest for Security

A Cold War Society

The United States and Asia

Conclusion

Sites to Visit

For Further Reading

AT 11:30 A.M. ON APRIL 25, 1945, U.S. ARMY PRIVATE JOSEPH POLOWSKY GLIMPSED what looked like the future. The young Chicago native was riding in the lead jeep of an American force along the Elbe River in central Germany when he spotted Russian soldiers on the far side, their medals glistening in the morning sun. Elated, he and five of his comrades found a small boat and paddled across to the eastern bank. Using Polowsky's knowledge of German to communicate, the American soldiers embraced their Soviet allies with laughs and tears. The Russians produced bottles of vodka, and toasts, pledges, singing, and dancing followed. After years of pressing Germany from east and west, the Allies had finally linked up in the heart of Hitler's empire. A reporter wrote of the scene, "You get the feeling of exuberance, a great new world opening up."

Despite his conservative Republican background, Polowsky spent much of his life advocating American-Russian friendship. He could not forget the transforming experience of that April day along the Elbe and the hopes it engendered for a peaceful future. However, what followed the Allied victory turned out not to be a "great new world" of international peace and brotherhood but the **Cold War** of U.S.-Soviet hostility that lasted for more than four decades. The opposing ideologies—**communism** and capitalist democracy—joined with conflicting national interests to produce this armed standoff. The American effort to contain the expansion of communist influence entailed a radical reorientation of American involvement abroad in peacetime, including the nation's first peacetime military alliance, the North Atlantic Treaty Organization (NATO). At times the Cold War turned into a hot war of actual shooting, most importantly in the Korean War of 1950–1953 and the Vietnam War in the following decade.

Soviet and American troops meet in central Germany in May 1945.

Soon after the end of World War II, Jim Forman enlisted in the U.S. Air Force. In 1948, he shipped out with his battalion to the huge U.S. base on the island of Okinawa in Japan. There some of the social changes unleashed by World War II caught up with him. President Harry Truman ordered the racial desegregation of the armed forces, and officers chose Forman to be the first African American to join the 625th Aircraft and Warning Company. He reported to his new assignment across the island, expecting trouble from white soldiers: harassment, assaults, and worse. Fearful, he slept only a few hours his first night. When Forman went to the mess hall for breakfast the next morning, he was stunned. "Fresh eggs. I saw them crack fresh eggs. I did not believe what I saw: fresh eggs. I had been on the Rock [Okinawa] some six months and I had never tasted a fresh egg unless I bought it at the restaurant in town." The white cook asked him how he wanted his eggs cooked and how many. "How many?" Forman asked in amazement. "Do you mean I can have more than two?" It was the same with milk: he could have a whole quart of fresh milk and then come back for more. In his former all-black battalion, he had been served only powdered eggs and powdered milk and only in carefully limited quantities. "I cursed the Air Force for its segregation, but I ate my fresh milk and eggs."

Jim Forman was trying to make sense of the changes and uncertainties that pervaded American society in the late 1940s. Popular support at home was needed for expansive new military commitments abroad, yet Americans had just fought in the largest war in their history, and most were eager to get back to something close to normal peacetime life. For some citizens the war years had provided new opportunities for better work and more independence. Women, workers, and African Americans, for example, did not want to retreat from the advances they had made. Struggles over the place of these groups of citizens helped shape the contours of the immediate postwar years, both in family lives and in the public sphere.

In some ways, the Cold War encouraged efforts at social reform. America's new leading role in world affairs brought its domestic life into the spotlight of world attention. Racial discrimination and violence at home embarrassed American leaders as they spoke of leading the anticommunist "free world" abroad. But in other ways, the Cold War constrained efforts to bring American life more fully into line with its democratic and egalitarian promise. Rising tensions with communist movements and governments overseas stimulated great anxieties about possible subversion within the nation's own borders. Anticommunist fervor put unions on the defensive and encouraged women to shun the workplace in favor of family life and parenting, particularly in the nation's growing suburbs. This second Red Scare—the first had followed World War I in 1919—reached flood tide by 1950 with the rise to prominence of Senator Joseph McCarthy. The young Republican from Wisconsin made a career of blaming supposedly disloyal Americans at home for setbacks to U.S. goals abroad in places such as China and Korea. He left a bitter legacy that long outlasted his political demise in 1954.

In some ways, the Cold War encouraged efforts at social reform.

The Uncertainties of Victory

It was five o'clock in the afternoon when the Senate recessed on April 12, 1945. The vice president walked through the Capitol building to the private office of his old friend and mentor, Sam Rayburn of Texas, the House majority leader. He had just mixed himself a cocktail when an aide told him that he was to call the White House immediately. Picking up the phone, he was instructed to come to the White House right away. "Jesus Christ and General Jackson," he said as he put down the receiver, his face suddenly pale. Within 15 minutes, Harry Truman was being ushered into the private quarters at 1600 Pennsylvania Avenue. Eleanor Roosevelt greeted him with the somber news: "Harry, the president is dead." Stunned, he finally said, "Is there anything I can do for you?" She replied, "Is there anything *we* can do for *you?* For you are the one in trouble now."

Franklin Roosevelt was dead; it was almost unimaginable. Elected four times to the presidency, he had dominated American politics like no figure before or since. Just as the unprecedented destruction of World War II was finally ending, the leadership of the nation passed into new and less tested hands. Peace brought an array of uncertainties and immediate needs. The victors had to reconstruct a world that had been damaged, physically and psychologically, almost beyond recognition. Spared the destruction visited elsewhere, the United States faced the different challenge of demobilizing its military forces and reconverting to a peacetime economy. Intense conflicts along the color line and in the workplace revealed real differences between Americans about the shape of the democracy they had fought to defend.

Global Destruction

World War II wrought death on a scale that defies comprehension: 60 million human beings lost their lives. From England in the west to the islands of New Guinea in the east, from Scandinavia in the north to the Sahara Desert in the south, much of Europe and Asia was left in ruins. Soviet and American power had finally crushed the Axis, with Berlin now a "city of

Ed Clark/TimePix/Getty Images

◀ **Franklin D. Roosevelt's death at his vacation home in Warm Springs, Georgia, stunned a nation and a world that had not known another U.S. president since 1932. Navy bandsman Graham Jackson was one of Roosevelt's favorite musicians. As the procession began to transport the president's body north for burial in Hyde Park, New York, Jackson captured the grief of millions of Americans as he played the sweet, slow strains of "Going Home."**

the dead" and Japan's urban landscape devastated by firebombing and nuclear attacks. Most of the victors were only marginally better off.

Only one of the major combatants emerged from the war in better shape than at the beginning. With no fighting on their soil after the initial Japanese attack on Pearl Harbor, American civilians spent the war years in safety. Orders for war materials ended the Great Depression in the United States and created full employment as factories worked overtime to supply the Allied armies. The American people, one official remarked in 1945, "are in the pleasant predicament of having to learn to live 50 percent better than they have ever lived before." Many Americans suffered terribly in the war, of course; 400,000 died, leaving behind desolate families, and millions of veterans returned with traumas that colored the remainder of their lives. But such casualties paled in comparison to those of other belligerent nations. With just 6 percent of the world's population and 50 percent of its wealth, the United States enjoyed a position of staggering economic advantage.

Americans' overriding fear was that the end of the fighting might return the country to the state it had faced when the war began: economic depression. The nation's awesome industrial productivity depended on government spending, which was now to be cut back sharply. International trade might pick up much of the slack, but the war had destroyed most of the purchasing power of U.S. trading partners in Europe and Asia. Rising tensions between the two primary victors—the United States and the Soviet Union—hampered the process of postwar reconstruction. President Truman showed his frustration with the Soviet military occupation of Eastern Europe by lecturing Soviet diplomats and abruptly cutting off Lend-Lease aid to the USSR. Soviet dictator Joseph Stalin feared America's new global military might, manifest in its monopoly of the atomic bomb, and was determined to secure his European border against future invasion from the West.

Vacuums of Power

World War II altered the world's ideological and physical landscape. Japan and Germany, the centers of prewar power in Asia and continental Europe, were vacuums waiting to be filled and reshaped by their conquerors. In addition to defeating two nations, the Allies had also discredited the ideas on which those governments had been built: fascism and militarism. These were the ideas of the extreme political right: the glorification of the racially defined state and its aggressive military expansion. Fascism's murderous character tarred those who had collaborated with the Axis during the war, primarily conservatives in countries such as France who preferred fascism to socialism.

Into many of the postwar vacuums of power flowed a newly prominent worldwide political left. Socialists, communists, and other radicals espoused communal rather than individualistic values. The Red Army's primary role in defeating the German troops who had overrun Europe evoked admiration for the Soviet Union among antifascists everywhere. The occupying Soviet forces installed communist governments in Eastern Europe by force (sometimes called "Red Army socialism"), and Socialist and Communist parties rose sharply in popularity in France, Italy, Belgium, and Scandinavia. The nominally socialist Labor party took power in Great Britain, defeating war leader Winston

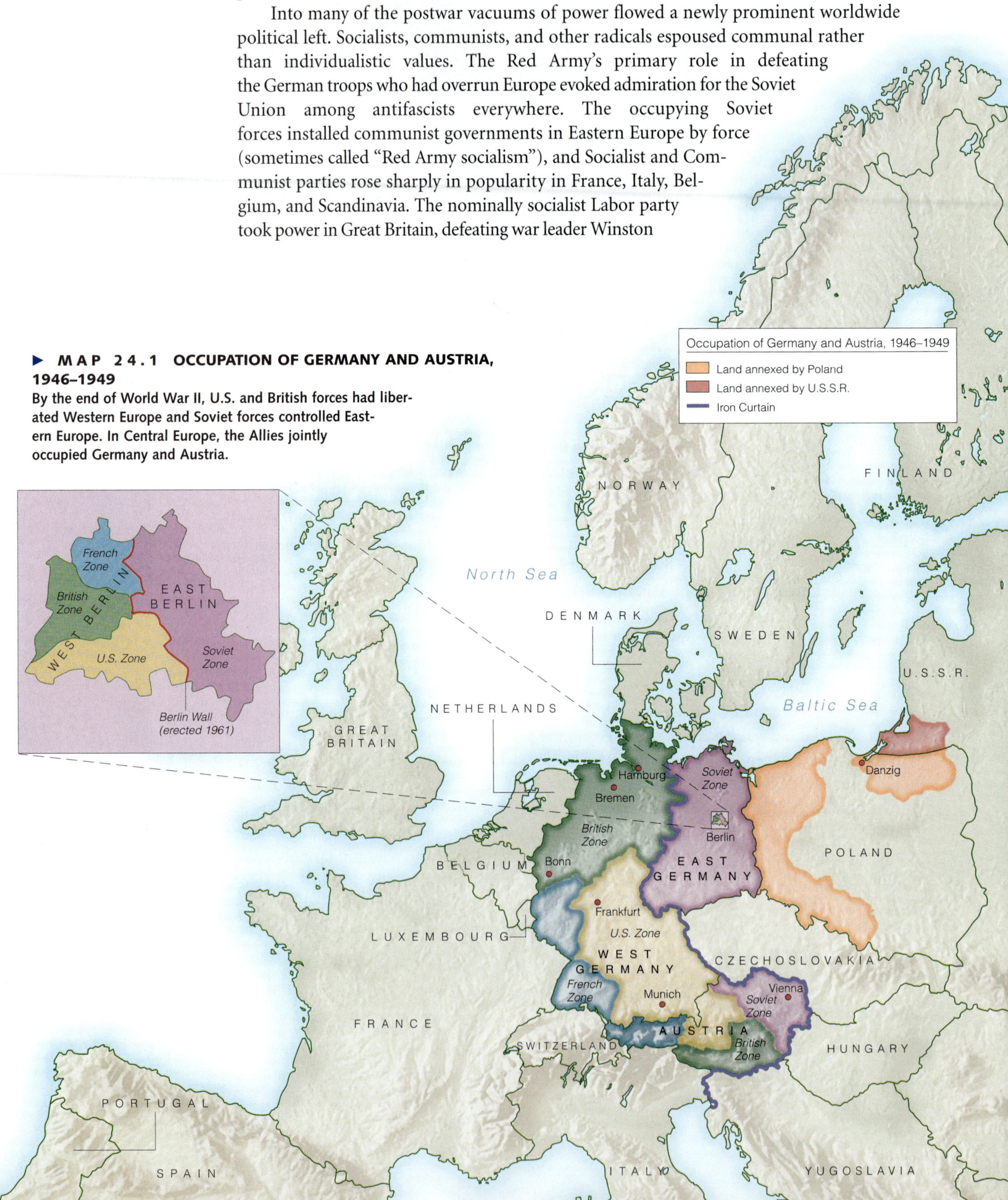

▶ MAP 24.1 OCCUPATION OF GERMANY AND AUSTRIA, 1946–1949
By the end of World War II, U.S. and British forces had liberated Western Europe and Soviet forces controlled Eastern Europe. In Central Europe, the Allies jointly occupied Germany and Austria.

Churchill and his Conservative party at the polls. Europeans across the continent established welfare states to provide a minimum standard of living for all their citizens.

This turn to the left encompassed most of the globe. Africans began organizing for eventual independence from European rule, and Asians launched the final phase of their anticolonial struggle for liberation. Indonesia fought its way free from the Dutch, and India gained its freedom from Britain. In French Indochina, Ho Chi Minh quoted from Thomas Jefferson's Declaration of Independence as he announced the creation of an independent Vietnam. (Truman ignored Vietnam's appeal for American recognition, just as Wilson had done 26 years earlier at the Versailles peace conference after World War I; see Chapter 20). Masters of much of the world a few years earlier, the European colonial powers fought desperately to hold onto the last pieces of their escaping empires. The Allies created the new United Nations (UN) in San Francisco in April 1945, just days after Truman succeeded FDR. Eventually housed in New York, it embodied hopes for a more peaceful and democratic world. Its General Assembly gave all nations an equal voice and vote in deliberations, and its small Security Council—responsible for guiding any UN military actions—gave a permanent seat and veto power to five nations: the United States, the USSR, Britain, France, and China. The 1948 UN Human Rights Charter helped put practitioners of colonialism and racial discrimination on the defensive by declaring worldwide support for the principles of national self-determination and equal treatment for all peoples.

National Archives

▲ **American sailors at Pearl Harbor in Hawaii gather around a radio to celebrate the news of Japan's surrender on August 14, 1945. Their lives were suddenly free from the perils of the brutal warfare in the Pacific, where Japanese pilots known as kamikazes had crashed suicide planes into U.S. warships.**

Postwar Reconversion

The fundamental task for Americans at home was to reconvert from a wartime society back to a peacetime one. They were especially eager to bring home the 12 million men in uniform serving abroad. Eager to resume their civilian life, the returning servicemen walked off ships' gangplanks into a country in transition. Factories were trying to convert from producing war materials to making consumer products. Wartime rationing was lifted on goods such as sugar and gasoline, and the 35 mph speed limit was withdrawn, but unemployment and inflation threatened. Orders for war materials dried up, taking jobs with them, but wartime inflation ("too many dollars chasing too few goods") persisted. Housing remained especially scarce. In the richest country in the world, one-third of the citizens still lived in poverty, with neither running water nor flush toilets.

To ease the transition home, Congress had passed the Servicemen's Readjustment Act of 1944 (the GI Bill) to extend crucial financial aid to veterans. It provided low-cost mortgages that helped create an explosion in home ownership. It created Veterans Administration hospitals to provide lifetime medical care. And it paid tuition and stipends for colleges and vocational training, making higher education broadly available for the first time. The 2 percent of veterans who were women also made use of these benefits. In the postwar era, when

John Vachon

▲ Japanese American women pack lima beans into boxes for freezing at Seabrook Farms, near Bridgeton, New Jersey, in 1947. Unlike the northern part of the state, which was closely tied to New York City, rural southern New Jersey was a rich fruit- and vegetable-growing region. After their release from the internment camps of World War II, Americans of Japanese descent joined their fellow citizens in finding work where they could in a peacetime economy no longer shrouded by the Great Depression.

American politics generally became more conservative—shifting away from the New Deal reform spirit and toward an anticommunist emphasis—the GI Bill was the one area in which the United States expanded its own welfare state. The $14.5 billion spent on veterans over the next decade marked a public investment that helped propel millions of families into an expanding middle class.

The postwar transition presented particular challenges to American women. Millions of them had gone to work outside the home during the war and found economic independence in doing so. Now they faced powerful pressures to leave the workforce and return to a domestic life of old and new families. Many women accepted this return to the domestic sphere, content to focus on marriage and family life. But millions felt varying degrees of resentment over their loss of hard-earned compensation and self-esteem. "War jobs have uncovered unsuspected abilities in American women," one argued. "Why lose all these abilities?"

Contesting Racial Hierarchies

African Americans faced a similar problem. After finding new opportunities in industrial employment during the war, they were laid off afterward in favor of returning white veterans. Like women, blacks were expected by others to retreat into deference. Black veterans spearheaded the resistance to this notion. They had fought in disproportionate numbers for their country and for the cause of defeating the world's most murderous racists, the Nazis. They then returned to a nation still deeply segregated, by law in the South and by practice elsewhere. Like Native American, Latino American, and Asian American veterans, they were determined to be full citizens in the country for which they had spilled their blood. "I went into the Army a nigger," one black soldier said about typical white views of him, but "I'm coming out a man."

African American efforts to overcome discrimination met fierce white resistance in 1946 and 1947. In the South, where most black Americans still lived, a wave of beatings and lynchings greeted black veterans in uniform and their attempts to register to vote. White Northerners also used violence to preserve the segregated character of neighborhoods in Chicago, Detroit, and other cities. They destroyed the property and threatened the lives of blacks who dared to move to previously all-white blocks, effectively confining African Americans to impoverished areas. Sometimes local authorities encouraged such extralegal use of force. The police chief of Cicero, Illinois, was indicted for conspiracy to incite a riot in 1951 after several thousand white residents destroyed an all-white apartment building to prevent African American veteran Harvey E. Clark and his family from moving in.

The retreat of European colonialism and American competition with the Soviet Union nonetheless encouraged many white Americans to acknowledge the contradiction between leading the "free world" and limiting the freedoms of Americans of color. A series of Supreme Court decisions validated the long-term strategy of the National Association for the Advancement of Colored People (NAACP) for contesting segregation in the courts. Court rulings outlawed segregation in voting primaries (*Smith v. Allwright,* 1944), interstate transportation (*Morgan v. Virginia,* 1946), contracts for house sales (*Shelley v. Kraemer,* 1948), and graduate schools (*Sweatt v. Painter* and *McLaurin v. Oklahoma,* 1950). The California Supreme Court in 1948 overturned a state law banning interracial marriage, pointing the way toward the elimination two decades later of similar laws in other states in the U.S. Supreme Court's *Loving v. Virginia* decision (1967).

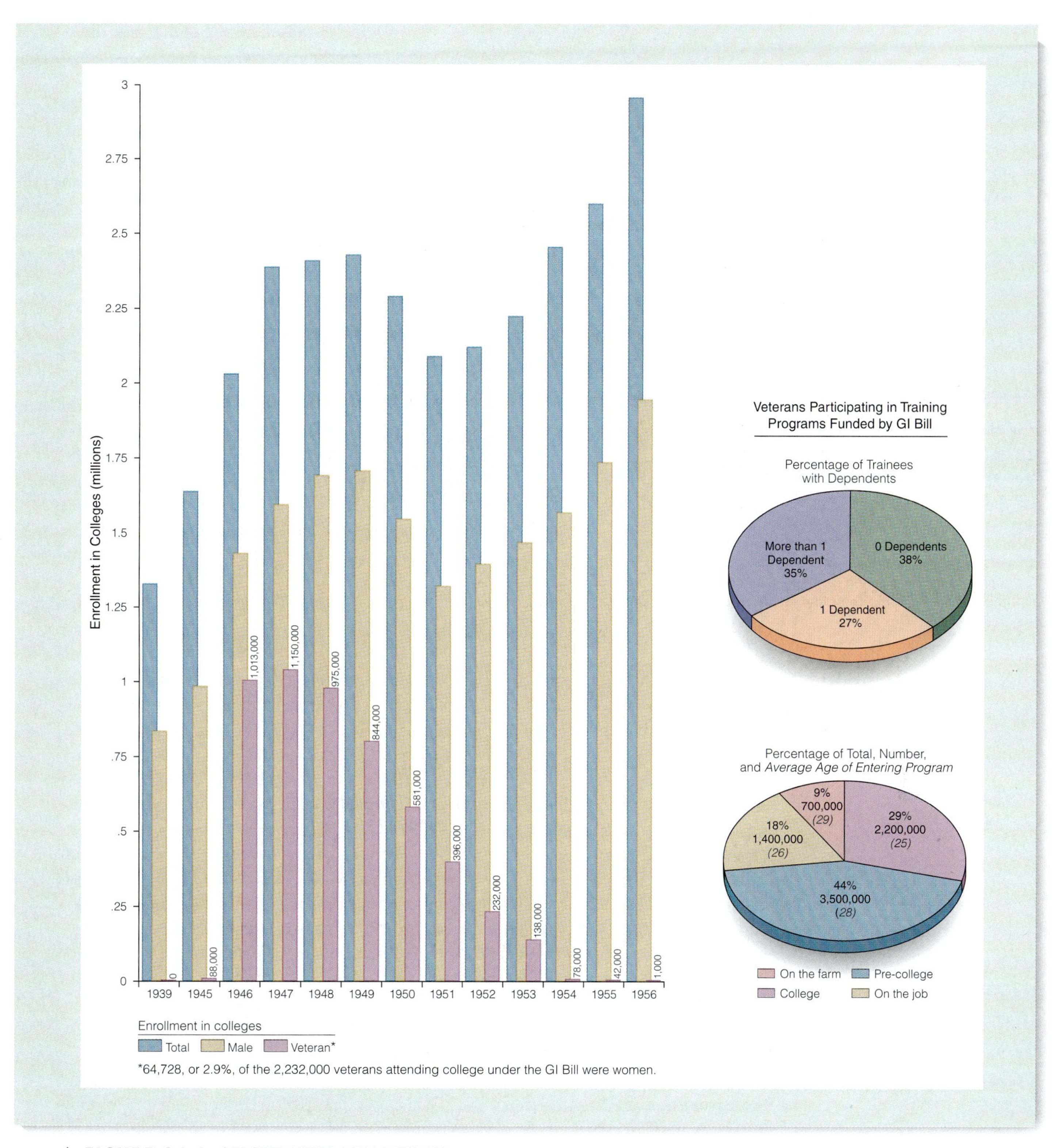

▲ **FIGURE 24.1** OPPORTUNITIES FOR VETERANS

The number of Americans attending college increased sharply after World War II. In the early postwar years, federal government spending through the 1944 GI Bill gave veterans unprecedented opportunities for access to education and other job training programs.

AP/Wide World Photos

▲ **The first person of color to play major league baseball, Jackie Robinson starred for the Brooklyn Dodgers from 1947 to 1956, helping them win six National League pennants and one world championship. His success opened the way for other black players to follow, eventually bringing the demise of the old professional Negro Leagues. Robinson credited Dodgers general manager Branch Rickey for his willingness to break the color line in what was still the nation's favorite game.**

Popular culture moved in the same direction of breaking down racial barriers. *Billboard* magazine in 1949 changed the category of "race music" to "rhythm and blues" as white record producers and radio disc jockeys such as Alan Freed began to bring the early rock 'n' roll of African American musicians to mainstream white audiences. By 1955 young white musicians such as Bill Haley and Elvis Presley joined black stars such as Chuck Berry and Little Richard in creating a wildly popular sound that transcended racial categories. Professional baseball erased its color line when Jackie Robinson, a former four-sport star at the University of California, Los Angeles, and lieutenant in the U.S. Army, joined the Brooklyn Dodgers in 1947. Despite vicious verbal taunting and threats of bodily harm by some fans and players, Robinson refused to lose his temper and remained a model of dignity and excellence as he won the National League's Rookie of the Year honors. Two years later he won the Most Valuable Player award.

Native Americans and Mexican Americans faced similar discrimination in the Southwest and elsewhere. With war veterans in the fore, they also organized to contest unfair education and election practices. "If we are good enough to fight, why aren't we good enough to vote?" asked returning Navajo soldiers in New Mexico and Arizona, where the state constitutions prohibited Indian residents from voting until successfully challenged in 1948. When the family of Private Felix Longoria, who died in combat in the Philippines, was denied the right to bury him in the all-white cemetery in Three Rivers, Texas, a new Latino veterans' organization called American GI Forum publicized the injustice. A young Texas senator named Lyndon Johnson, destined for the White House, stepped in and arranged a burial with full military honors in prestigious Arlington National Cemetery instead. The League of United Latin American Citizens (LULAC) followed a strategy similar to that of the NAACP regarding educational discrimination, leading to the Supreme Court's decision in *Mendez v. Westminster* (1946) outlawing segregated schools for Mexican Americans in California. In parallel fashion, indigenous Alaskans organized in the Alaska Native Brotherhood successfully lobbied the territorial legislature in Juneau to pass an antidiscrimination law in 1945.

Class Conflict

In many ways 1946 seemed like 1919. A world war had just ended, in which corporations had made handsome profits. American workers had enjoyed nearly full employment and improving wages and had joined unions in large numbers. In 1946 one-third of the workforce held a union card, the largest portion ever. But the end of war-related orders led to job cuts and the loss of overtime wages, and by the spring of 1946, 1.8 million workers were out on strike.

Mirroring World War I, the conclusion of hostilities in 1945 revealed rising tensions between the United States and the Soviet Union. The spread of leftist revolutions abroad amplified fears of communist influence in American unions, especially because a few of the most effective Congress of Industrial Organizations (CIO) organizers were Communist party members or at least sympathetic to an emphasis on class conflict between owners and workers. As in 1919, a Red Scare began to develop, egged on by a business community that used the supposed threat of the tiny U.S. Communist party to weaken the much larger and less radical union movement. In contrast to the end of World War I, however, federal law guaranteed the right of workers to bargain collectively, and the strikes of 1946 resulted in some negotiated wage increases.

The tide turned against unions as anticommunism intensified. President Truman, long considered a friend to organized labor, helped crush major strikes by railroad workers and coal miners in 1946 when he saw them as threatening the nation's economy. The CIO's Operation Dixie to organize southern workers of all colors failed, defeated by the skillful appeals of local businesses to white supremacist sentiment among the working class. The Republican party claimed a sweeping victory in the 1946 congressional elections, taking control of both the House and the Senate in a stark rejection of Truman's leadership. Republicans and conservative Democrats then passed the Taft-Hartley Act in 1947 over the president's veto, weakening unions by prohibiting secondary boycotts (against the products of a company whose workers were on strike) and requiring union officials to swear anticommunist oaths. Two years later the increasingly conservative CIO expelled 11 unions that still had leftist and communist leadership. At the same time, the expanding U.S. economy after 1947 pulled many skilled workers up into the middle class and gave them a larger stake in the status quo.

The Quest for Security

On February 21, 1947, a British official in Washington informed the U.S. government that Britain could no longer provide financial assistance to the anticommunist governments of Greece and Turkey. This information marked a watershed in modern world history. Long the greatest imperial power and the dominant outside force in the Middle East, Britain was beginning a long, slow retreat. Left in its wake were vacuums of power, particularly in the Middle East, South Asia, and Africa. President Truman and his advisers believed that either Soviet or American influence would flow into those regions. The Truman administration formulated a policy to contain communism in the eastern Mediterranean that it quickly expanded to encompass the entire noncommunist world.

Redefining National Security

U.S. policymakers had ended World War II with one primary goal. They were determined to revive the global capitalist economy that had nearly dissolved in the Great Depression of the 1930s and had then been battered by the war. American prosperity and freedom, they believed, depended on a world system of free trade because Americans simply could not consume all the products of their efficient farms and factories. If they could not sell the surplus abroad, the United States would slide back into a depression. The 1930s had shown that closed economic doors led to despair, poverty, and aggression, as in Germany and Japan. "We can't go through the thirties again," President Truman emphasized to his aides. He and other

TimePix/Getty Images

▲ The cover of *Time* magazine on May 15, 1950, suggested the growing worldwide popularity of Coca-Cola, a quintessential American product. Not only did the United States have vast military and political influence in the early Cold War, but its powerful economy also exported American goods and values around the world. The international diffusion of American popular culture—movies, clothes, food, and music—helped shape world history in the twentieth century, particularly after 1945.

political leaders hoped for a world with greater liberty and more democracy. But Dean Acheson, the powerful undersecretary (1945–1947) and then secretary of state (1949–1953), emphasized that U.S. foreign policy was not primarily concerned with "a lot of abstract notions." Instead, the emphasis with each country was on "what you do—these business transactions."

"National security" was expanding to mean something very different from simply defending the nation's territory against invasion. For the disproportionately powerful United States, national security after 1945 came to be identified with the creation and preservation of a free-trading capitalist world order. American national security was seen to be at stake almost everywhere around the globe—a recipe for riches but also for trouble.

The primary threat to that security came from the Soviet Union. The Red Army's occupation of Eastern Europe was part of the problem, as it symbolized the Soviets' military prowess. Even more troubling to the Truman administration was the political influence of the USSR in a world turning leftward. The real danger lay in Soviet encouragement, by example and assistance, of revolutions that rejected market economies and individualist ethics. Demoralized by the war's destruction and by grim postwar economic conditions, Western Europeans and others seemed to be considering the paths of socialism and communism. "Hopeless and hungry people," Acheson warned, "often resort to desperate measures."

Conflict with the Soviet Union

The antifascist alliance of the Soviet Union and the United States dissolved rapidly as their conflicting interests reemerged after the war. Long skeptical of the capitalist world it wanted to replace, the Soviet government viewed expansive U.S. interests as evidence of "striving for world supremacy." Yet Moscow was just as clearly expanding its own sphere of national security, with Soviet troops remaining in areas they had occupied during the war: Manchuria, northern Korea, Iran, and especially Eastern and Central Europe. These forward military positions, combined with Moscow's rhetoric of encouraging revolution abroad, increased American anxieties about rising communist movements in Asia and Europe. Each side spoke of the other's goal as "world domination."

"Hopeless and hungry people," Acheson warned, "often resort to desperate measures."

Contrasting experiences in World War II amplified historical and ideological differences. Whereas the war brought the United States out of the global capitalist depression (which the Soviets had avoided), it brought the USSR into a depression caused by the invading Germans' destruction of the western portion of the country. With a decimated population, a battered economy, and minimal air and naval forces, the postwar Soviet Union remained a regional power based on its army. The United States was the only truly global power, with a vast naval armada and air force projecting military might to every continent, undergirded by the most productive economy in world history.

The two nations' visions of the postwar world order reflected these relative positions. Americans sought an open world for the free flow of goods and most ideas and proved willing to tolerate and even embrace dictatorial governments as long as they were anticommunist and open to foreign trade and investment. Meanwhile, the Soviets called for a more traditional division into separate spheres of influence for the great powers. The horrific experience of near national extinction at the hands of the Nazis ensured that Stalin would not budge on issues of fundamental Soviet security.

Conflicts over specific areas liberated from the Nazis hastened the onset of the Cold War in the first 18 months after the end of World War II. Whereas the Soviets wanted reparations and a deindustrialized Germany that could never threaten it again, the United States considered a rebuilt industrial German state crucial for a healthy, integrated Western European economy. Britain and France had gone to war in defense of an independent Poland, but for Stalin control of Poland was not negotiable because it had been "the corridor for attack on Russia."

▲ **MAP 24.2 EUROPE DIVIDED BY THE COLD WAR**
For centuries Europe had controlled much of the rest of the world. After 1945, the Soviet Union occupied the eastern half of the continent and Americans wielded dominant influence in the western half. This division of Europe into communist and noncommunist blocs lasted until the end of the Cold War in 1989.

Moscow and Washington also clashed over Iran, on Russia's southern border, where the Soviets briefly encouraged a leftist uprising in the northern part of the oil-rich country to counteract British and American influence in the capital city of Tehran. U.S. policymakers worried about Soviet requests to Turkey for greater control of the Bosporus and Dardanelles, the straits leading out of the Black Sea into the Mediterranean. When the British announced in February 1947 their imminent withdrawal from Greece, where leftists and monarchists were fighting a fierce civil war, the Truman administration believed it was time to respond decisively.

The Origins of the Cold War

Joseph Sohm; ChromoSohm Inc./CORBIS

Cathy Crawford/CORBIS

American and Soviet patriotic symbols predominated in the Cold War era. The Stars and Stripes and the eagle faced off against the hammer and sickle in a global competition for influence.

The earliest American accounts of how the Cold War began were written by officials who had participated in the decisions that cemented U.S.-Russian hostility for two generations (1946–1989). Officials such as the State Department's Herbert Feis and academic historians through the 1950s and early 1960s accepted the U.S. government view that Soviet aggression and subversion made the Cold War unavoidable. They pointed to the absence of political and religious freedom and the severe restrictions on the ownership of private property in communist nations, combined with the expansion of communist control into Eastern Europe and China. Stalin and his successors in the Kremlin, they believed, were at fault for trying to take over the world. Arthur Schlesinger Jr. summarized this view in 1967 when he called early U.S. Cold War policies "the brave and essential response of free men" to totalitarian provocations.

America's deepening involvement in the Vietnam War destroyed the Cold War consensus among historians. Schlesinger's "orthodox" interpretation of the events of the late 1940s seemed increasingly suspect to a group of mostly younger historians who saw their own government as the aggressor in Southeast Asia in the mid-1960s. They took their lead in part from the iconoclastic William Appleman Williams of the University of Wisconsin, who in 1959 declared U.S. expansionism "the tragedy of American diplomacy." Casting a skeptical eye back a generation, these "revisionists" found evidence indicating a greater American than Soviet responsibility in bringing on the Cold War. Gar Alperovitz identified the use of atomic bombs on Japan as unnecessary for the military defeat of Tokyo but useful as "atomic diplomacy" to intimidate Moscow in regard to the postwar world order. Gabriel Kolko emphasized the structural need of U.S. capitalism to expand abroad in search of new markets and new sources of raw materials. As U.S. actions in Vietnam alienated more and more Americans, and as the Watergate scandal (1972–1974) starkly revealed the readiness of top U.S. leaders to deceive the public, the early histories blaming the Soviet Union exclusively for the onset of the Cold War lost much of their credibility.

By the 1980s historians had largely exhausted the debate over responsibility for Soviet-American hostilities. Then the fall of the Berlin Wall in 1989 and the dissolution of the USSR in 1991 (turning back into Russia and independent neighboring nations such as Ukraine) encouraged rethinking of the early Cold War. Even Washington's staunchest defenders could admit that the U.S. government had acted in an often imperial fashion. But was it perhaps a matter primarily of the expansion of American popular culture abroad—a kind of "cultural imperialism" that other peoples often welcomed, from Paris to Beijing? Jazz and later rock 'n' roll music, along with Hollywood movies, American consumer goods, and the English language, proved more powerful agents for spreading the American way of life than U.S. armed forces or even democratic political institutions. Though still concerned with the role of national governments, armies, and diplomats, some historians of the Cold War are exploring issues such as race relations and gender relations, which were also frontiers of freedom after 1945. Improved U.S.-Russian relations and the release of once-secret documents added interest to Cold War studies. ■

The Policy of Containment

Diplomat George Kennan best articulated the policy of **containment** in an influential telegram sent from his post at the U.S. embassy in Moscow in February 1946. Kennan explained Soviet hostility as a function of traditional Russian insecurity overlaid with newer Marxist justifications. He called for "the adroit and vigilant application of counterforce" against all Soviet efforts at expanding their influence. One month later, on March 5, 1946, former British prime minister Winston Churchill warned that a Russian "iron curtain" had descended across Europe from the Baltic Sea in the north to the Adriatic Sea in the south, imprisoning all those to the east of it. "The reins of world leadership are fast slipping from Britain's competent but now very weak hands," the U.S. State Department argued. "These reins will be picked up either by the United States or by Russia."

Churchill's "Iron Curtain" Speech

Picking up those reins meant a fundamental reorientation for the United States. No longer just the dominant force in the Western Hemisphere, it would have to maintain its wartime projection of military forces around the globe—permanently. To do so would take huge expenditures that Congress had to approve and public support for an unprecedented international role. In an address to Congress on March 12, 1947, asking for $400 million in aid for Greece and Turkey, the president simplified the world system into two "ways of life," those of "free peoples" and those of "terror and oppression" under communist rule. All nations must choose between them, he declared, and the United States must support "free peoples who are resisting attempted subjugation by armed minorities or outside pressures."

The **Truman Doctrine,** as it became known, exaggerated a real problem in order to win public support for a new international role for the United States. It funded the governments of Turkey and Greece but it framed the new policy broadly, opening the path to supporting anticommunist regimes and opposing revolutions around the world for decades to come. The most important immediate step was the reconstruction of a vibrant, reintegrated Western European economy. The United States provided $13 billion between 1948 and 1952 to fund the European Recovery Program, commonly known as the Marshall Plan for its chief architect, Secretary of State George Marshall (1947–1949). His assistant, Dean Acheson, reminded Americans doubtful about such expenditures that Western Europe's recovery was "chiefly a matter of national self-interest" for the United States, for European markets were crucial for American economic health.

The Marshall Plan

Ensuring Western European security against the Red Army also entailed the first U.S. military alliance in peacetime. The victors of World War II divided a defeated Germany into separate zones of occupation, based on wartime agreements that reflected their respective military positions. The Allies also shared occupation of the capital city of Berlin, although it was deep in the Soviet-controlled eastern sector of the country, in the expectation that a reunified, de-Nazified Germany would be governed from there someday. The British, French, and American decision in March 1948 to create a unified state out of the western sectors of Germany led a few months later to a year-long Soviet blockade of western access to Berlin and fears of a general war. The joint U.S.-British "Operation Vittles" airlifted tons of food to the isolated residents of West Berlin, preserving that city as a capitalist island in a communist country. The creation of NATO in 1949 made the American military commitment to Europe permanent. Headquartered first in Paris and later in Brussels, Belgium, NATO was the first U.S. military alliance in peacetime. The point of NATO for Western Europe, its British first secretary general said, was to "keep the Americans in, the Russians out, and the Germans down."

The onset of the Cold War determined the fate of the defeated powers of World War II. The Truman administration was determined to "push ahead with the reconstruction of those two great workshops of Europe and Asia—Germany and Japan." This agenda replaced initial concerns about rooting out Nazism and punishing war criminals, as at the Nuremberg trials of surviving Nazi leaders in 1945–1946. A similar story unfolded in Japan. The American occupation under General Douglas MacArthur initially (1945–1947) emphasized democratization of Japanese society, including building labor unions, weakening corporate monopolies, ensuring women's political rights, and punishing war criminals. But rising U.S. tensions with the Soviets and the imminent victory of the Communist forces in China's civil war prompted American officials to shift course by 1948. Henceforth, they focused on rebuilding as quickly as possible Japan's industrial economy as the hub of capitalist Asia and reduced efforts at social reforms that might slow that process.

"The reins of world leadership are fast slipping from Britain's . . . hands. These reins will be picked up either by the United States or Russia."

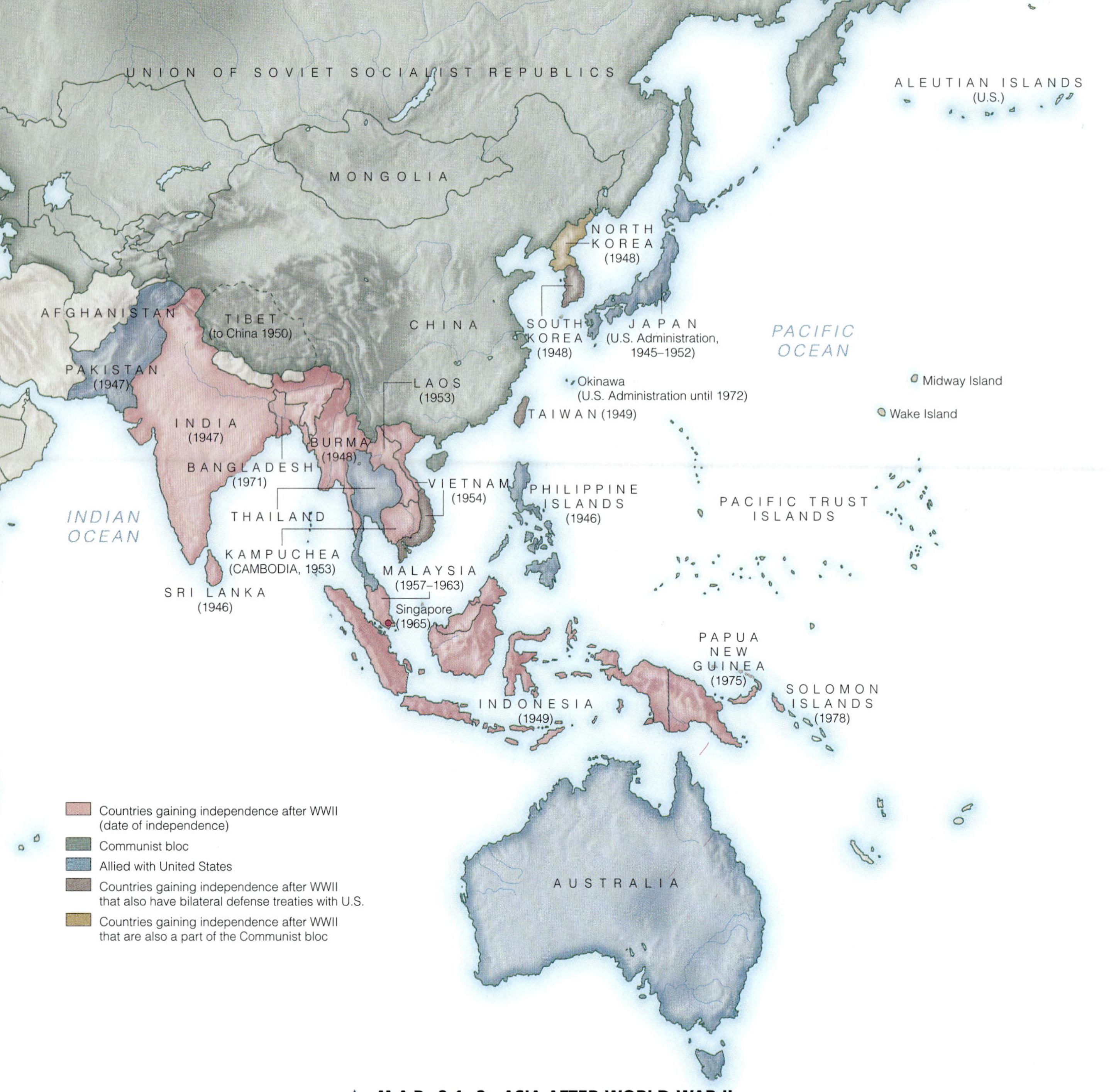

▲ **MAP 24.3 ASIA AFTER WORLD WAR II**
The weakening of Western colonial powers in the war with Japan paved the way for national independence across Asia after 1945. Some of these newly independent nations chose a capitalist form of society and others a communist form. The new East-West tensions of the Cold War complicated the longer North-South struggle for freedom from colonial control.

Colonialism and the Cold War

The world's nonwhite majority still lived under European colonial control, and for them the struggle for national independence and racial equality was the great issue of the late 1940s and 1950s. In this North-South conflict of **colonialism,** as opposed to the East-West conflict of the Cold War, the United States held an awkward position. Its primary NATO partners included the greatest colonial powers: Britain, France, Belgium, Holland, and Portugal. Racial segregation in the United States further undercut American leadership of the "free world."

With European rule in Asia and Africa on the way out, the Truman administration sought a gradual transfer of colonial rule into the hands of local pro-West elites. Violent revolutions—in the spirit of 1776—were to be avoided. The U.S. grant of official independence to the Philippines in 1946, though masking significant continued American influence, was offered as a model, as was the British departure from India a year later. However, America's European priorities included support even for imperialists who did not leave peacefully, such as the French digging in against Communist-led revolutionaries in Vietnam.

The British withdrawal from Palestine in 1948 created a peculiar dilemma for the United States. Jewish settlers—primarily from Europe and often survivors of the Holocaust—proclaimed the new state of Israel against the wishes of the Arab majority. Secretary of State Marshall and others urged Truman not to recognize Israel to avoid imperiling U.S. relations with the Arab oil-producing states. The president sympathized with the Jewish desire for a homeland, however, and understood the importance of American Jews as constituents of the Democratic party in the 1940s. His decision to recognize Israel, which most Middle Easterners viewed as a new colonial state, set the United States on a course of enduring friendship with that nation and enduring conflict with Israel's Arab neighbors and the Palestinians.

For the world's nonwhite majority, the struggle for national independence and racial equality was the great issue of the late 1940s and 1950s.

Events in the Middle East struck closer to home for some Americans. Not all Jewish Americans were Zionists, but many fervently supported the new nation of Israel. Some joined the thousands of World War II veterans from around the world who volunteered in the Israeli military forces. West Point-trained Colonel David Marcus, former commandant of the U.S. Army Ranger school, lost his life in the fighting around Jerusalem in 1948, where he commanded four Israeli brigades and planned strategy crucial for Israel's military success. Americans of Arab descent experienced the events of that year very differently. For the hundreds of thousands of Palestinians who lost their lands, houses, and livelihoods as a result of the Israeli-Arab fighting, the Israeli War of Independence was a disaster. Most wound up in refugee camps in the region, but some found their way to the United States. Edward Said grew up in a Christian Palestinian family in Jerusalem, but his family fled to Cairo during the UN partition of the territory in 1947. Said's father held American citizenship, however, and Said eventually came to the United States, where he attended the Mt. Hermon School in Massachusetts, Princeton University, and Harvard University. He became a prominent scholar of comparative literature at Columbia University and served as one of the most articulate defenders of the rights of the Palestinian people.

The Impact of Nuclear Weapons

Scientists in the 1940s dramatically increased Americans' sense of personal safety by introducing the use of antibiotics. "Miracle drugs" such as penicillin cured common bacterial infections that had previously been debilitating or fatal. Antibiotics suggested a future of personal health and longevity unimaginable to previous generations. What science gave with one hand, it threatened to take away with the other, however. The use of atomic weapons on Japan foreshadowed a future of utter insecurity in which instantaneous destruction of entire nations could occur without warning.

Even without being used again in war after 1945, nuclear weapons altered the American environment. Weapon tests with such code names as "Dirty Harry" released vast quantities of radiation into the atmosphere. The Atomic Energy Commission assured those near the mushroom clouds, "Fallout does not constitute a serious hazard." But local cancer rates spiked upward for Bikini Islanders in the Pacific, where the first tests occurred, and then for farmers and ranchers in Utah and Nevada, when tests began 65 miles northwest of Las Vegas in 1953.

Duck and Cover

Related dangers stalked other parts of the "nuclear West." Navajo Indians mining uranium in the Four Corners region (where Utah, Colorado, Arizona, and New Mexico meet) paid dearly for their intensive exposure to the poisonous material, as did thousands of workers involved in nuclear weapon production. Weapon assembly plants in Hanford, Washington, and Rocky Flats, Colorado, leaked radioactivity into the groundwater. In combination with the nuclear power industry, atomic weapon development resulted in an enormous supply of radioactive

Bettmann/CORBIS

▶ Soldiers watch as "Dog," a 21-kiloton nuclear device, is dropped from a bomber at the Nevada Test Site at Yucca Flat, northwest of Las Vegas, in November 1951. U.S. atomic specialists tested nuclear weapons first in the Marshall Islands of the western Pacific Ocean, especially the Bikini atoll, beginning in 1946, and then in Nevada beginning in January 1951. Residents downwind from the test sites suffered various deleterious health effects from radiation exposure, including high cancer rates.

waste—deadly for 10,000 more years—that the U.S. government still does not know how to dispose of safely.

The government offered reassurances about the safety of the atom, and the Atomic Energy Commission covered up evidence of radioactivity's ill effects. But many Americans were deeply anxious about this destructive new power that loomed over their lives, especially as the Soviet-American arms race intensified. Science fiction stories painted frightening pictures of a future devastated by nuclear war. Movies such as *The Blob* and *The Attack of the Crab Monsters* portrayed a world haunted by exposure to radiation. *Them!* featured mutant ants the size of buses crawling out of a New Mexico atomic test site. Concerns about a nuclear world escalated with the successful 1952 test of an American hydrogen bomb, a thousand times more powerful than the device that destroyed Hiroshima. Always suspicious of centralized power, Americans worried that one person in the Oval Office or the Kremlin could almost instantaneously obliterate entire continents.

A Cold War Society

Expanding economic opportunities and narrowing political freedoms characterized American society in the first decade of the Cold War. A withering fire of anticommunist repression pushed dissident views to the margins of the nation's political life. Americans largely accepted this new conformity for two reasons: their desire to support their government during international crises, especially the Korean War (1950–1953), and a consumer cornucopia that surrounded them with attractive material goods. A generation that had survived the Great Depression embraced the culture of consumption and convenience that emerged after World War II. Factories that had produced jeeps, tanks, and weaponry turned to manufacturing cars

Michael Melford/Getty Images

▲ **American farms were fabulously more productive in 2000 than they had been in 1900. At the end of the nineteenth century, for example, 35–40 hours of planting and harvesting labor were required to produce 100 bushels of corn; a century later the same amount of corn required only 2 hours and 25 minutes of labor. A crucial innovation was the center pivot irrigation system, devised in the 1940s by eastern Colorado tenant farmer Frank Zybach. With the sprinkler pipe rotating around the hub, this system irrigated a field in a grand circular sweep. Cross-country airplane passengers can admire the green circles that dot the arid Great Plains below them.**

and appliances; men who had learned to build roads and barracks for the military now began to erect suburban housing with equal speed.

By 1947 the United States was launching into an era of extraordinary economic expansion that continued for 25 years. Since Ben Franklin's time, Americans had been known for thrift in their pursuit of wealth, but after 1945 the long-cherished principle of delaying gratification declined steeply. "Buy now, pay later," General Motors urged, as it offered an installment plan to customers. Diner's Club introduced the first credit card in 1950. In a formulation breathtaking for its distance from Puritan and immigrant traditions of saving for the future, writer William Whyte observed that "thrift is now un-American."

Family Lives

Many white Americans embraced the opportunity to move to the suburbs after World War II. Seeking larger homes and yards and quieter neighborhoods, they flocked to new developments such as Levittown outside New York City on Long Island. In their first three hours of business in 1949, Levittown's developers sold 1,400 houses. In 1944 construction had begun on just 114,000 new houses; in 1950, the number jumped to 1.7 million. Suburbs were not for everyone, however. Even as federal courts struck down segregation laws in some spheres of American life, the Veterans Administration and the Federal Housing Administration agencies were encouraging residential separation by race. Private banks did the same, and the contracts that developers such as Alfred and William Levitt signed with homebuyers prohibited resale to nonwhites. Other government policies, including highway construction and tax benefits for homeowners, promoted the growth of suburbs at the cost of cities. A third epoch in

Levittown

Bettmann/CORBIS

▲ **A new cloverleaf intersection on a freeway arches across the northern New Jersey suburbs in 1949. Multilane, limited-access highways became common after World War II. A new word, "smog" (neither smoke nor fog), emerged to describe the urban pollution caused by trucks and commuter vehicles.**

American residential history began by 1970 when more Americans resided in suburbs than cities, parallel to the 1920 shift from a rural majority to an urban one.

Suburban life encouraged a sharpening of gender roles among the growing middle class. Men commuted to work while women were expected to find fulfillment in marriage and motherhood, including a nearly full-time job of unpaid housework. Most women did so while either feeling isolated in their homes or finding community with other women in their neighborhoods and churches. "We married what we wanted to be," one female college graduate said. "If we wanted to be a lawyer or a doctor we married one." An enormous amount depended on a woman's choice of a husband, including class status and lifelong material well-being. Despite this partial retreat from wartime employment, however, fully one-third of American women continued to work for pay outside the home. The economic circumstances of most black women offered them little choice, and most wound up doing double housework: their own and that of families employing them as domestics. Middle-class women tended to view their paid work as a job rather than a career, a way to increase the family income if they did not have small children at home. Quotas in graduate schools and sex-segregated employment limited the number of female professionals.

After a lengthy decline during the 1930s, marriage and birth rates picked up during the war and then accelerated sharply after 1945. From 1946 to 1964, women giving birth at a younger age to more children created the demographic bulge known as the baby boom. Large families reinforced the domestic focus of most women, putting the work of child-rearing at the center of their lives. Fatherhood became increasingly a badge of masculinity, with Father's Day emerging as a significant holiday for the first time. Family physician Benjamin Spock published *Baby and Child Care* (1946), a runaway best-seller that helped shift the emphasis in American parenting from strictness to greater nurturance.

Strong feelings about pregnancy hinged on the marital status of the expectant mother. Married mothers were celebrated, but unmarried ones were rebuked. Despite the greater freedom of the war years, the sexual double standard remained in place, with women's virtue linked directly to virginity in a way that men's was not. Birth control devices such as the diaphragm were legal only for married women and only in certain states. Women seeking to terminate unwanted pregnancies had to consider illegal abortions, the only kind available before 1970; millions did so, including one-fifth of all married women and a majority of single women who became pregnant. Two studies of American sexual behavior by Dr. Alfred Kinsey of Indiana University revealed that Americans often did not practice what they preached. The Kinsey reports of 1948 and 1953 shocked the public with their revelation of widespread premarital and extramarital sexual intercourse as well as homosexual liaisons.

> *"We married what we wanted to be," one female college graduate said. "If we wanted to be a lawyer or a doctor we married one."*

The Growth of the South and the West

Before World War II, American cultural, industrial, and financial power had always been centered in the urban North, but federal expenditures during the war began to change this pattern. The U.S. Army built most of its training bases in the South, where land close to the coasts was thinly populated and inexpensive. Military bases and defense industries sprang up along the West Coast to project power into the Pacific against Japan. The San Francisco Bay area sprawled with shipyards and sailors, and southern California became the center of the nation's aircraft industry. U.S. troops built the Alcan (Alaska-Canada) Highway, and millions of GIs passed through Hawaii en route to the Pacific battlefront. Fighting against the Japanese to defend Pearl Harbor and the Aleutian Islands brought the once distant territories of Hawaii and Alaska more into Americans' consciousness, setting them on the path to statehood in 1959.

The **Sunbelt** of the South, the Southwest, and California grew rapidly after the war, whereas older Rustbelt cities of the Northeast and Midwest such as Buffalo and Detroit began to lose manufacturing jobs and population. Like the 440,000 people who moved to Los Angeles during the war, postwar migrants to California and Arizona appreciated the weather and the economic opportunities. Military spending underwrote half the jobs in California during the first decade of the Cold War. Migrants from south of the border, meanwhile, found work primarily in California's booming agricultural sector. The U.S. government continued to use the *bracero* program as an exception to immigration laws for Mexicans willing to do arduous labor in the hot fields of the Golden State, thus encouraging the large influx of Mexicans into the U.S. Southwest.

Population Shifts, 1940–1950

Two industries particularly stimulated the growth of the Sunbelt: cars and air conditioning. Automobiles helped shape the economies of western states, where new cities were built out of sprawling suburbs, and governments erected highways rather than railroads, subways, or other forms of public transportation. New car sales shot up from 70,000 in 1945 to 7.9 million in 1955. Inexpensive gasoline, refined from the abundant crude oil of Texas and Oklahoma, powered this fleet. Automobile exhaust pipes replaced industrial smokestacks as the primary source of air pollution, which by the 1960s shrouded Los Angeles—the "city of angels"—in smog. Air conditioning also became widely available after World War II and contributed to the breakdown of the South's regional distinctiveness. From Miami and Atlanta to Houston and Washington, D.C., the new Sunbelt depended on the indoor comfort brought by controlling summertime heat and humidity.

Harry Truman and the Limits of Liberal Reform

The onset of the Cold War narrowed the range of American political discourse. In seeking to consolidate the New Deal legacy, President Truman found himself boxed in by conservative

Republican opponents. Allied governments in Western Europe had embraced the idea that access to health care was a right of every citizen in a modern democratic state. But when Truman proposed a system of national health care, conservatives quashed his proposal in Congress, pushed by an American Medical Association lobbying campaign that denounced the idea as a "monstrosity of Bolshevik bureaucracy."

Perhaps the most blatant omission of the New Deal was protection against racial discrimination. Now, as the Cold War intensified, the fact that millions of Americans still lacked basic guarantees for their civil rights was a glaring and embarrassing contradiction amid rhetoric about ensuring rights and liberties throughout the "free world." The President's Committee on Civil Rights called in 1947 for a strong federal commitment to racial equality. Truman campaigned for reelection in 1948 on a platform of support for civil rights that was unprecedented in the White House, including the first presidential address to the NAACP. That summer he ordered the desegregation of the armed forces and the federal civil service.

African American voters in Chicago, Cleveland, and other northern cities played a key role in swing states; their solid support lifted Truman to a narrow and surprising victory over the heavily favored Republican candidate, New York governor Thomas Dewey. Truman's reelection was all the more impressive because of the fracturing of the Democratic party. Alienated by the civil rights plank, white Southerners walked out of the Democratic convention and ran South Carolina governor Strom Thurmond as an independent candidate. The "Dixiecrats" won four states in the Deep South, foreshadowing the abandonment by white Southerners of the party of their parents in the 1960s. From the opposite side of the party, many liberals jumped ship for Henry Wallace, Roosevelt's former vice president, running as the Progressive party candidate. Truman won as a man of the moderately liberal center, fierce against communism, usually supportive of the rights of organized labor, and opposed to discrimination.

McCarthy talked about communists, but his show was about Democrats. As the war in Korea raged, he mercilessly red-baited the Truman administration.

The Cold War at Home

Anticommunism turned out to be an inadequate shield for liberals and moderates in the partisan warfare pervading American politics in the late 1940s and early 1950s. In a pattern that became known as **McCarthyism,** mostly Republican conservatives blamed liberal Democrats in the administration for communist successes abroad—especially in China and Korea. Using a tactic called "red-baiting," conservatives accused liberals of sympathizing with and even spying for the Soviet Union. The hunt for domestic subversives to explain international setbacks was grounded in the reality of a handful of actual Soviet spies, most notably Julius Rosenberg (who was executed for treason in 1953 along with his wife, Ethel) and nuclear scientist Klaus Fuchs. But this second Red Scare expressed primarily the frustration of being unable to translate vast U.S. power into greater control of world events. And it served, above all, to cast suspicion on the patriotism of liberals at home.

Despite his general support for civil liberties, Truman helped set the tone for pursuing suspected traitors. In an unsuccessful effort to fortify his right flank against Republican attacks, he established a federal employee loyalty program in March 1947 as the domestic equivalent of the Truman Doctrine. Attorney General Tom Clark drew up a list of supposedly subversive organizations that the FBI and state committees on "un-American activities" then hounded. In a case with sobering implications for free speech, federal courts in 1949 convicted the leaders of the U.S. Communist party of promoting the overthrow of the U.S. government. Words alone, the courts ruled, could be treasonable—the same logic as the wartime Sedition Act of 1918 (see Chapter 20). Conservative congressional Democrats pushed through the Internal Security Act of 1950 to require Communist party members to register with the government and allow emergency incarceration of suspected subversives. Calling it "a long step toward totalitarianism," Truman vetoed the measure, but Congress overrode the veto by a huge margin.

Republicans reaped the benefits of the Red Scare. Most Americans who had sympathized in any way with the Soviet Union in the Depression years were by the late 1940s merely liberal Democrats, but the House Un-American Activities Committee (HUAC) zeroed in on their earlier records. Investigating Hollywood, the television industry, and universities as well as the executive branch of the U.S. government, HUAC destroyed the careers of prominent figures and average Americans.

The era found its name in the previously obscure junior senator from Wisconsin, Republican Joseph McCarthy. With a single speech in Wheeling, West Virginia, on February 9, 1950, this genial but ambitious politician soared to prominence. "I have here in my hand a list of 205" Communist party members working in the State Department, he declared. Over the next four years, the numbers and names changed as McCarthy stayed one step ahead of the evidence while intimidating witnesses before his Senate subcommittee. In reality, one reporter joked, McCarthy "couldn't find a Communist in Red Square" in Moscow. He talked about communists, but his show was about Democrats. As the war in Korea raged, he mercilessly red-baited the Truman administration. But after the Republican electoral victory in 1952, his excesses lost their partisan utility. With the end of the war in Korea and his ill-advised attacks on the U.S. Army itself as supposedly infiltrated by communists (the Army-McCarthy hearings), he was at last censured by his Senate colleagues in 1954 and died an early, alcohol-related death in 1957.

Bettmann/CORBIS

▲ **Americans later knew Richard M. Nixon as the president who traveled to China in 1972 and brought his administration down in disgrace two years later with the Watergate scandal. Nixon first gained prominence as a young California congressman on the House Un-American Activities Committee (HUAC) who led the investigation into accusations that prominent U.S. diplomat Alger Hiss had spied for the USSR in the 1930s.**

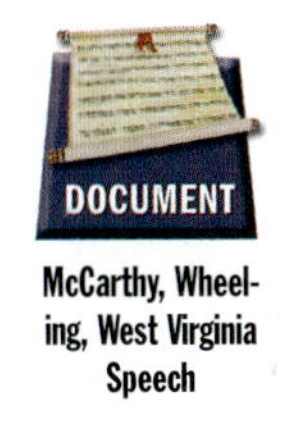

McCarthy, Wheeling, West Virginia Speech

Who Is a Loyal American?

The Cold War politics of inclusion and exclusion established a new profile for loyal Americans. Private familial and material concerns were expected to replace public interest in social reform. "No man who owns his own house and lot can be a Communist," real estate developer William Levitt declared. "He has too much to do." He also had a wife, presumably, in an era when anticommunists launched a withering assault on homosexuals as "perverts" and threats to the nation's security. Church membership climbed in tandem with condemnations of "godless Communism," and Congress added the words "under God" to the Pledge of Allegiance. Warning that "God is giving us a desperate choice, a choice of either revival or judgment," revivalist preacher Billy Graham launched his first evangelical crusade in Los Angeles in 1949, en route to becoming the nation's foremost religious figure. Discrimination against Roman Catholics and Jews, though still evident, declined as Catholics such as McCarthy proved intensely anticommunist and as pictures and stories emerged to reveal the horrors of the Nazi Holocaust against the Jews. More inclusive references to the "Judeo-Christian tradition" became common.

American leadership of the global anticommunist cause strengthened the struggle for racial equality at home, within certain limits. The NAACP and most African Americans took an anticommunist position in accord with Truman, in return for his support of civil rights. They downplayed their concern for colonial independence in Africa and Asia to support NATO. The American GI Forum (Latino veterans) and the Japanese American Citizen League also worked within the confines of Cold War politics to end discrimination. More radical black leaders such as scholar W. E. B. Du Bois and actor and singer Paul Robeson refused to make any such accommodation to anticommunism. Offended by the hypocrisy of segregation in the land of liberty,

▶ **From 1951 to 1953 Mexican American miners went on strike against the Empire Zinc Mining Company in Silver City, New Mexico. Women took on major roles in this labor action, which inspired a famous movie, *Salt of the Earth*. Defiant in the face of police and company shotguns and billy clubs, Elvira Molano (center) served as co-chair of the union negotiating committee and became known as "the most arrested woman" during the strike.**

Courtesy, Los Mineros Collection, Chicano Research Collection, Arizona State University Libraries

they insisted on full freedom everywhere in the "free world." The government responded by restricting their travel and diminishing their livelihoods. In a move right out of the Soviet playbook, Robeson's name was erased from the list of football All-Americans for 1917 and 1918 (he had starred for Rutgers University), leaving only ten men on those teams.

For impoverished Native Americans, the government seemed to give with one hand and take away with the other. In 1946 Truman established the Indian Claims Commission to consider payment for lands taken and treaties broken. But gestures toward compensation led to policies of termination. Developers seeking access to Indian lands joined reformers troubled by reservation poverty in urging Congress—with limited success—to terminate the special status Indian tribes had held with the federal government since its founding. Dillon S. Myer, who had overseen internment camps for Japanese Americans during World War II, became director of the Bureau of Indian Affairs in 1950. He closed reservation schools, withdrew support for traditional cultural activities, and launched an urban relocation program, all intended to move Native Americans into the mainstream and get the government "out of the Indian business."

Immigrants also received mixed messages. The McCarran-Walter Act (1952) ended the long-standing ban on allowing people of Asian descent not born in the United States to become U.S. citizens. But it preserved the discriminatory 1924 system of "national origins" for allocating numbers of immigrants from different countries. The bill also strengthened the attorney general's authority to deport aliens who were suspected of subversive intentions. Like Guatemalan-born leftist Luisa Moreno, a successful labor organizer in California who was deported in 1950, immigrants learned that their welcome depended on their politics.

The United States and Asia

Japan did not conquer independent nations in its sweep southward at the start of World War II. Tokyo's army defeated imperial powers: the French in Indochina, the Dutch in Indonesia, the British in Singapore and Malaya, and the Americans in the Philippines. In a single swoop, Japanese soldiers demonstrated the absurdity of white supremacy and cleared the way for the end of colonialism in Asia. Then Japan's retreat in 1945 left vacuums of power throughout the region. Into them flowed two contenders: the returning but gravely weakened European imperialists and Asian nationalists such as Ho Chi Minh in Vietnam (part of French Indochina). Americans were not passive observers of this struggle as they sought to establish a new free-trading order in the region. Less than five years after millions of American citizens had served in the war in the Pacific, hundreds of thousands returned to Asia to fight for an anticommunist regime in South Korea. In Asia, as in much of the Third World, the Cold War quickly turned hot.

The Chinese Civil War

Despite frequent discrimination against Chinese immigrants in the United States, Americans had long felt a special connection to China. Half of the thousands of Christian missionaries sent out by American churches in the early twentieth century had been posted there. Entrepreneurs eyed the Chinese market, home to one-fifth of the world's potential consumers. Selling cigarettes to the Chinese brought tobacco baron James B. Duke much of his wealth, which he then used to endow the university in North Carolina that bears his name. During World War II, Chinese resistance to Japan's invasion occupied millions of Tokyo's soldiers who would otherwise have been shooting at American GIs. The close U.S. alliance with the government of Jiang Jieshi seemed to confirm American hopes that Asia's largest nation would follow a pro-American path. Republican senator Kenneth Wherry of Nebraska declared that the United States would "lift Shanghai up and up, ever up, until it looks just like Kansas City."

However, many Chinese wanted Shanghai to look just like itself—or perhaps like Moscow. The partisans of the Chinese Communist party (CCP) under Mao Zedong's leadership fought more effectively against the Japanese than Jiang's soldiers did. Japan's withdrawal in 1945 initiated four years of warfare between the Communists and Jiang's anticommunist Nationalists. Younger American diplomats and journalists in China, many of them missionaries' children who had grown up there, argued that the CCP was more popular than the corrupt Nationalist regime and was independent of the USSR. Rejecting the advice of these "China hands," the Truman administration provided $3 billion in aid to Jiang. The logic of the Truman Doctrine required containment of communism everywhere. Nevertheless, it failed in China. Americans watched in frustration as the CCP defeated the Nationalists, who retreated to the island of Taiwan. On October 1, 1949, Mao announced the establishment of the People's Republic of China (PRC).

Xu Xiaobing/China Stock, Beijing

▲ **Mao Zedong led the Communist party that took power in China during the civil war of 1945–1949. Although Americans called this "the fall of China," Mao officially introduced the new government in Beijing by declaring that "China has stood up." Mao (left) talks here with his favorite son, Mao Anying, who was killed in Korea on November 25, 1950, apparently in a U.S. bombing raid.**

This was the first communist government created without the presence of Soviet troops. Might the rest of Asia also choose communism? Profound suspicions on both sides prevented any Sino-American accommodation. The U.S. government refused to recognize the People's Republic, just as it had done with the USSR in 1917. Faced with U.S. hostility and sharing a common ideology with the Soviet Union, Mao papered over historic Chinese-Russian tensions and signed a mutual defense pact with Moscow in February 1950. The so-called loss of China

▶ **Were all Communists conspiring together against the United States and its interests? New Chinese leader Mao Zedong (left) helps Soviet ruler Josef Stalin celebrate his birthday on December 21, 1949. Two months later, the two men signed a mutual defense treaty. But, as their expressions suggest, they shared little personal warmth. Conflicting Chinese and Russian national interests soon strained—and eventually broke—their alliance.**

increased the importance for American policymakers of building capitalist societies in the rest of Asia, particularly Japan and—fatefully—South Korea and Vietnam. China's revolution also became a major issue in American politics. "Who lost China?" Republicans demanded rhetorically and effectively, presuming that it had once been America's to lose.

No one in the United States cared more about events in China than citizens and residents of Chinese descent. The FBI suspected of espionage any Chinese Americans who had sympathies toward the new Communist government, and many lost their jobs. Most Chinese students and professors visiting in the United States when the Communists took power did not want to go home. Meanwhile, Chinese immigrants who had already worked for years or decades to improve their status in America shared the broad post-1945 desire to build comfortable material lives. Upwardly mobile young families moved to the suburbs, aided by the 1948 Supreme Court decision banning racial restrictions on real estate sales. William Chew's grandfather had worked on the transcontinental railroad; his father served in World War I and then became a cannery superintendent; and Chew himself became an engineer, with children who also succeeded him in the professions. Chew and his family made the difficult choice to leave the urban Chinese community in which he had grown up: "I longed to mow a green lawn and wax my car on weekends; to take my children to Sunday school and have backyard bar-b-ques with our neighbors and friends." In 1940, 28 cities had had Chinatowns. By 1955, that number had fallen to 16.

The Creation of the National Security State

A week before Mao's announcement that China had become a communist country, President Truman shared some equally grim news with the American public: the Soviet Union had detonated its first nuclear device. The United States had lost the atomic monopoly that for four years had assured Americans of their unique position of military strength. Truman asked his advisers for a full reevaluation of the nation's foreign policy.

The result was the top-secret National Security Council document 68, or **NSC-68,** which articulated the logic of what became the **national security state:** a government focused on the

NSC-68

Concerned about the trend of international events in the wake of the Communist revolution in China and the Soviet Union's acquisition of nuclear weapons, President Truman ordered his National Security Council on January 31, 1950, to conduct "a reexamination of our objectives in peace and war and of the effect of these objectives on our strategic plans." The resulting study, known as NSC-68, called for a military buildup to counter Soviet expansionism. Some specialists on the USSR, such as George Kennan, questioned NSC-68's accuracy regarding Soviet intentions and successes. But the subsequent North Korean invasion of South Korea seemed to confirm the idea of "international communism" on the march.

Bettmann/CORBIS

Workers at the Douglas Aircraft Company's Santa Monica factory assemble Nike guided missiles for the U.S. Army in 1955. Large military contracts proliferated during the Cold War and stimulated the growth of Sunbelt states like California.

From NSC-68: U.S. Objectives and Programs for National Security (April 14, 1950)

The Soviet Union, unlike previous aspirants to hegemony, is animated by a new fanatic faith, antithetical to our own, and seeks to impose its absolute authority over the rest of the world. . . .

Any substantial further extension of the area under the domination of the Kremlin would raise the possibility that no coalition adequate to confront the Kremlin with greater strength could be assembled. It is in this context that this Republic and its citizens in the ascendancy of their strength stand in their deepest peril.

The issues that face us are momentous, involving the fulfillment or destruction not only of this Republic but of civilization itself. . . . The assault on free institutions is world-wide now, and in the context of the present polarization of power a defeat of free institutions anywhere is a defeat everywhere. . . .

Our policy and actions must be such as to foster a fundamental change in the nature of the Soviet system. . . . In a shrinking world, which now faces the threat of atomic warfare, it is not an adequate objective merely to seek to check the Kremlin design, for the absence of order among nations is becoming less and less tolerable. . . .

The integrity of our system will not be jeopardized by any measures, covert or overt, violent or non-violent, which serve the purposes of frustrating the Kremlin design, nor does the necessity for conducting ourselves so as to affirm our values in actions as well as words forbid such measures. . . .

The total economic strength of the U.S.S.R. compares with that of the U.S. as roughly one to four. . . . The military budget of the United States represents 6 to 7 percent of its gross national product (as against 13.8 percent for the Soviet Union). . . . This difference in emphasis between the two economies means that the readiness of the free world to support a war effort is tending to decline relative to that of the Soviet Union.

It is true that the United States armed forces are now stronger than ever before in other times of apparent peace; it is also true that there exists a sharp disparity between our actual military strength and our commitments. . . . It is clear that our military strength is becoming dangerously inadequate. . . .

In summary, we must. . . [engage in] a rapid and sustained build-up of the political, economic, and military strength of the free world.

Questions

1. *What is the precise problem that the United States faces, according to NSC-68?*
2. *How does NSC-68's analysis of the Soviet threat in 1950 compare with American understandings today of the threat from Islamic terrorist organizations such as Al Qaeda?*

Washington, D.C.

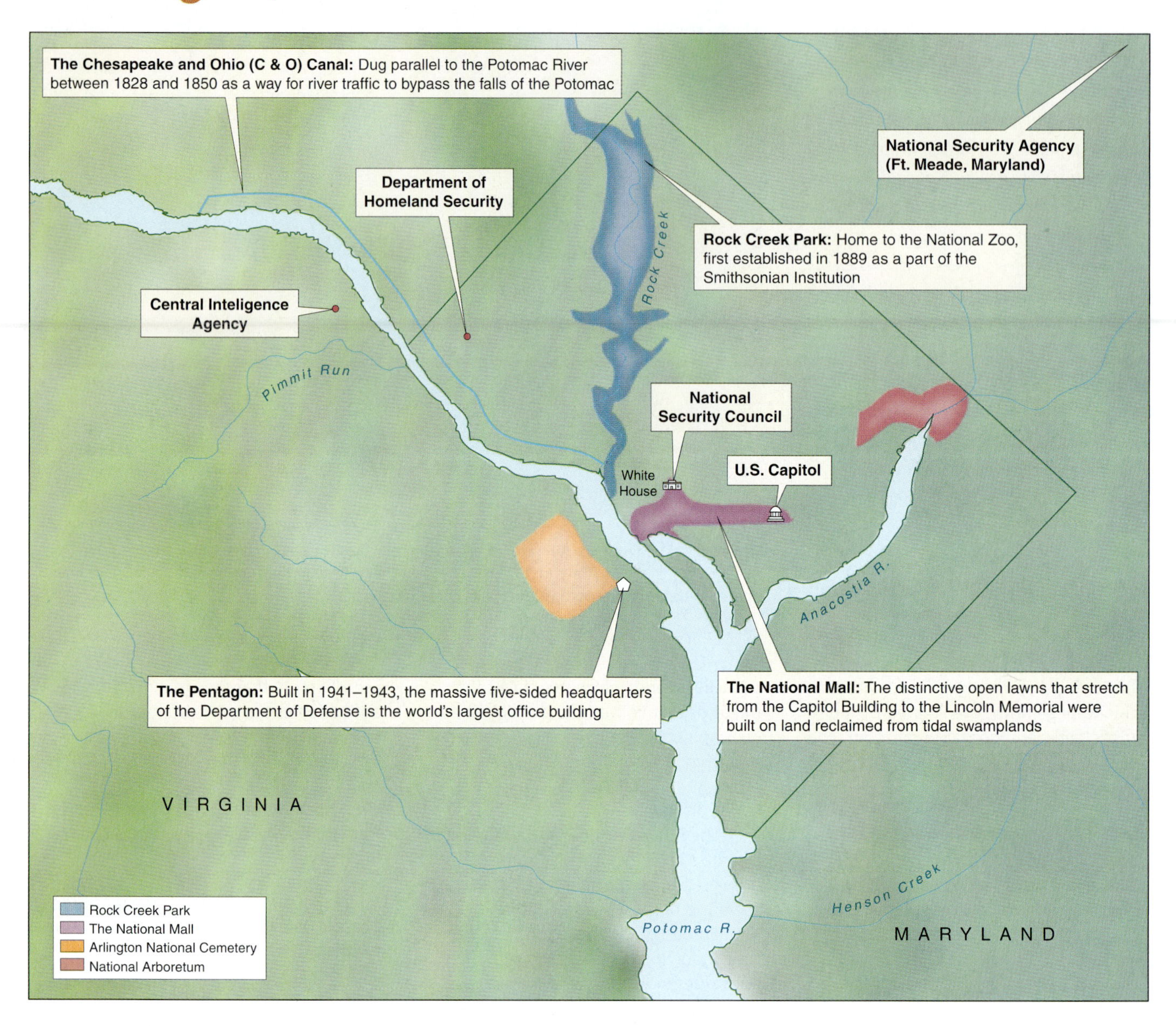

Congress created the District of Columbia in 1790–1791 with land from Maryland and Virginia, including the existing towns of Georgetown and Alexandria, as a compromise between southern and northern interests. In 1846 Congress decided to return the land in Virginia to that state. By the end of the nineteenth century, the city of Washington and the District of Columbia had become identical. After World War II, the U.S. government created several new agencies in order to wage the Cold War against the Soviet Union. The Defense Department (housed in the Pentagon), the National Security Council, the Central Intelligence Agency, and the National Security Agency (for electronic intelligence gathering) became some of the most powerful and well-funded institutions of the U.S. government. After the attacks of September 11, 2001, Congress created the Department of Homeland Security to further centralize security planning. ■

imperatives of military power, global involvement, and radically increased defense spending. NSC-68 argued that there was no longer any such thing as peacetime. The United States had entered an era of permanent crisis because of the expansion of communism and the hostile intentions of the Soviet Union. America's worldwide interests meant that it must oppose revolutions or radical change anywhere on the globe. NSC-68 went beyond the containment policy of the Truman Doctrine to call for fostering "a fundamental change in the nature of the Soviet system." This armed struggle necessitated secrecy and centralization of power in the hands of the federal government.

The National Security Act of 1947 and its 1949 amendments created the institutions of the new national security state. The Central Intelligence Agency (CIA) organized spying and covert operations, the Department of Defense unified the separate branches of the military, and the National Security Council (NSC) coordinated foreign policy information for the president. NSC-68 called for permanent military expenditures at a level of war readiness; it argued that this policy would stimulate rather than bankrupt the U.S. economy. Scores of communities became dependent on military spending—a kind of military welfare state. NSC-68's call for secrecy encouraged government deception of the public in the interest of "national security," with a consequent decline in democratic input into the nation's foreign relations.

America's new global military power included large U.S. military installations around the world, even in peacetime. American soldiers occupied Japan and Western Germany, and U.S. military bases remain in those nations even today. Locals were often amazed by GIs' physical health, abundant provisions, and casual style. One young Japanese woman recalled the shock of seeing men chewing gum in public, something "unthinkable for a well-brought-up person to do." Yet "the Japanese people liked the American soldiers. Instantly. They were young boys, healthy, smiling all the time, very friendly." She also recalled American efforts to democratize Japanese society. "Almost all the old rules disappeared" as schools changed overnight. "We could talk back to teachers. We could discuss things." And "they made no distinction between boys and girls," as women gained political equality with men under the American occupation. Many German and Austrian women married American soldiers. One woman from Vienna recalled how she and her friends were "fascinated by these young men; they seemed so carefree, happy, and well-fed." The GIs' casual manner—such as walking with their hands in their pockets—intrigued young Germans. American soldiers also brought with them American products that proved very popular abroad, especially jazz music (and soon rock 'n' roll) and Hollywood movies.

Sfc. Al Chang/Defense Visual Information Center (Department of Defense), HD-SN-99-03118

▲ Near Haktong-ni, Korea, on August 28, 1950, an Army corpsman fills out casualty tags, while one American soldier comforts another who has just seen his buddy killed in action. Men who fought together on the front lines in Korea, as in other wars, experienced physical and psychological traumas unparalleled in civilian life. They often developed strong friendships with each other but sometimes had difficulty making the transition back to peacetime routines at home.

At War in Korea

Two months after NSC-68 arrived on the president's desk and four months after Senator McCarthy began his attacks on the Democratic administration, troops from communist North Korea poured across the 38th parallel into South Korea on June 25, 1950. The alarmist recommendations of NSC-68 now seemed fully justified to U.S. policymakers. The origins of the conflict on the Korean peninsula were more complicated than they appeared at first glance, however, and the United States was deeply involved.

Korea had been colonized by Japan since 1910. After Japan's defeat in 1945, Soviet and U.S. forces each occupied half of the

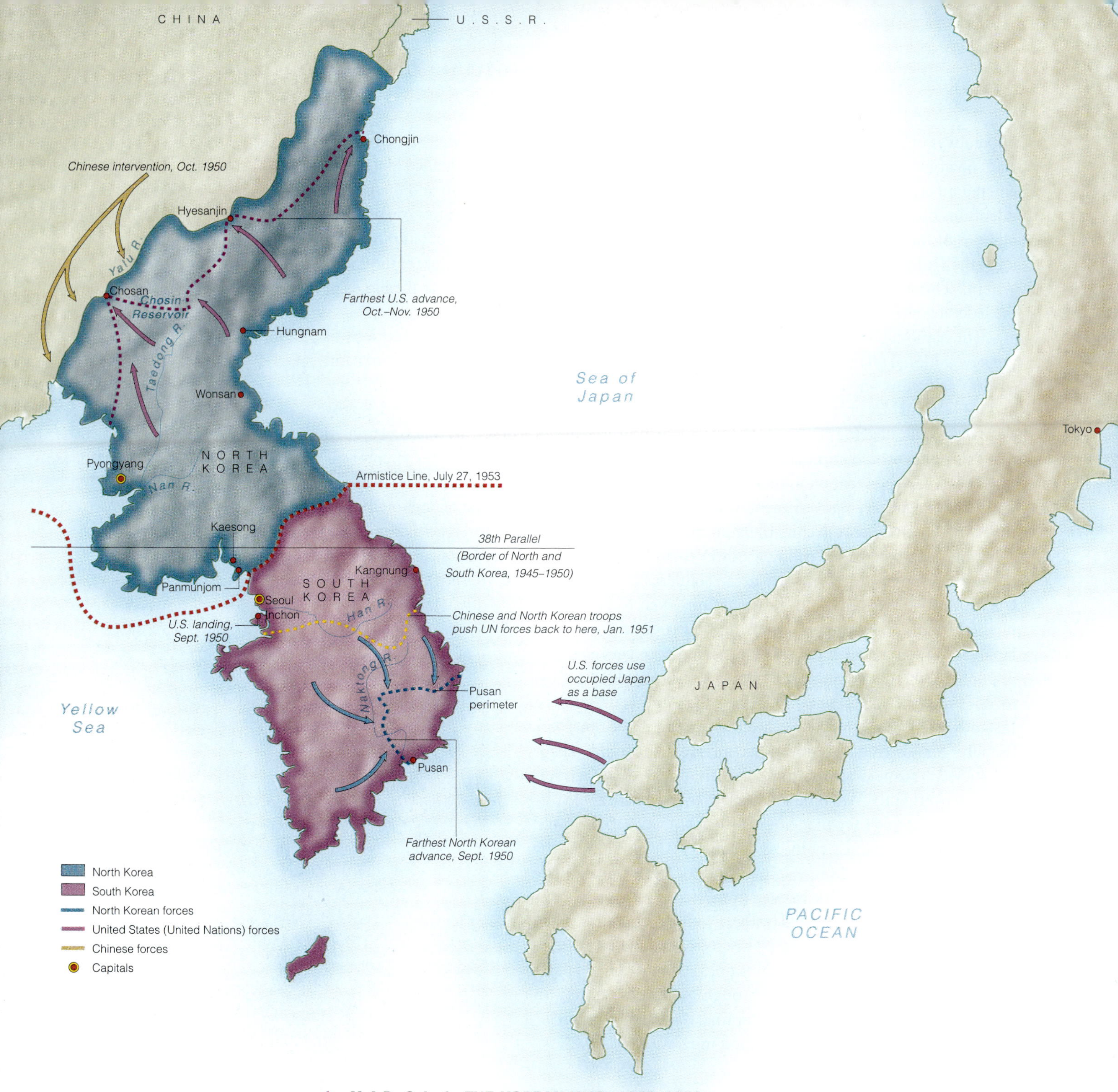

▲ **MAP 24.4 THE KOREAN WAR, 1950–1953**
The strategic location of the Korean peninsula enhanced the importance of what had originally been a civil conflict among Koreans. Korea's close proximity to China, the Soviet Union, and U.S.-occupied Japan made the outcome of that conflict very important to all of the great powers. The Americans and Chinese carried on the bulk of the fighting against each other in the full-scale war that unfolded in 1950.

The Korean War, 1950–1953

peninsula. In the north, the Soviets installed a dictatorial Communist regime under Kim Il Sung, who had fought with the Chinese Communists in their common struggle against Japan. In the south, the Americans established an authoritarian capitalist regime led by Syngman Rhee, who had taken classes at Princeton University with Woodrow Wilson and had lived in the United States most of the previous four decades. The 38th parallel was an arbitrary dividing line for a nation that had been unified for 1,300 years, and both governments sought to reunite

Korea under their control. Border skirmishes intensified after the Soviets and Americans withdrew in 1948, and leftist rebellions continued across much of the south. The CIA acknowledged that Rhee was "unpopular among many—if not a majority—of non-Communist Koreans." Some 100,000 Koreans lost their lives in the fighting between 1945 and 1950.

U.S. forces arrived in late June 1950, just in time to prevent the South Korean army from being driven off the peninsula, and then slowly pushed the North Koreans backward toward the 38th parallel in hard fighting. Truman received UN approval for this "police action," along with a small number of troops from several other nations.

Americans assumed the North Korean invasion had been orchestrated by Moscow as part of a plan of worldwide communist aggression. The Truman administration considered defense of South Korea crucial to demonstrate the credibility of U.S. power. The U.S. government took preemptive actions against possible aggression elsewhere. It sent the 7th Fleet to defend Taiwan, which it had previously assumed China would eventually conquer and reabsorb; it increased assistance to anticommunist forces in the Philippines and Vietnam; and it rearmed West Germany as part of NATO. The U.S. annual military budget increased from $13 billion in 1950 before the war to $50 billion in 1953, setting a pattern for vast military expenditures ever since.

National Archives

▲ Korean refugees carry what they can of their worldly goods through heavy snow near Kangnung, on the east coast just south of the 38th parallel, on January 8, 1951. Wild swings in fortune in the Korean War contributed to the devastation wreaked on the peninsula's civilians who were caught in the fighting, sometimes more than once. First North Korean troops conquered almost all of South Korea, except the Pusan perimeter; then U.S. and UN troops pushed all the way to the Chinese border in the north. At that point, Chinese forces entered the war and hurled the Americans back far south of the 38th parallel. Finally, U.S. and UN troops fought their way back to just north of the 38th, where the cease-fire in 1953 drew the new border between the two Koreas.

General Douglas MacArthur's brilliantly executed landing of fresh U.S. troops at the port of Inchon behind North Korean lines on September 15, 1950, created a turning point in the war. North Korean forces abandoned the South's capital city of Seoul, fleeing northward to avoid being caught between two American armies advancing from different directions. South Korea was retaken; containment had succeeded. Should American commanders now shift to rolling back communism by proceeding north of the 38th parallel? The opportunity was irresistible, despite Truman's determination to keep this a limited war. MacArthur ignored signals that the Chinese would not allow U.S. soldiers to come all the way to their border at the Yalu River—the equivalent for Americans of having the Soviet Army arrive at the Rio Grande. On November 27, 200,000 Chinese soldiers struck hard, driving American soldiers south of the 38th parallel again in the longest retreat in U.S. history, some 300 miles.

MacArthur wanted to take this "entirely new war" directly to the Chinese, using conventional or even nuclear bombing campaigns against the People's Republic. However, Joint Chiefs of Staff chair General Omar Bradley called this idea "the wrong war, at the wrong place, at the wrong time, and with the wrong enemy." MacArthur's growing insubordination forced Truman to fire the popular general in April 1951 because the president had no desire to start a larger war that would draw in the USSR. The bloody fighting in Korea stalemated that spring close to the original dividing line, where the front remained as the two sides negotiated for two years before signing a cease-fire in July 1953. All the while, the U.S. Air Force used its supremacy in the skies to rain down extraordinary destruction on the North. "We burned down *every* town in North Korea," boasted General Curtis LeMay. American deaths totaled 37,000, and China lost nearly a million soldiers. Three million Koreans on both sides died—10 percent of the population of the peninsula—and another 5 million were made refugees. Containment succeeded at enormous cost, and the Korean peninsula remains divided and heavily armed.

Conclusion

The Korean War shaped subsequent American politics and society in critical ways. The stalemate frustrated those who agreed with MacArthur that there was "no substitute for victory." But the ominous threat of nuclear weapons meant that wars had to be limited. The fighting in Korea enabled McCarthy and the Red Scare to dominate political life in the United States. The results were sometimes absurd, with the Democratic authors of the containment policy and the national security state being red-baited as "soft on communism." The Republican party rode such charges to electoral victory in November 1952. (They also benefited from evidence of petty corruption among some Truman administration officials, such as the president's appointment secretary accepting bribes). Republican presidential nominee General Dwight Eisenhower was perhaps the most popular American alive because of his leadership of the Allied victory in Europe in World War II, and he swept into the White House over Democrat Adlai Stevenson, the governor of Illinois.

The war in Korea ensured a generation of hostility between the United States and China. It tied the People's Republic more closely to the USSR, strengthening the common belief that international communism was a unified movement. The United States committed itself to defending Taiwan from recapture by the Beijing government. The firing of the "China hands" deprived the State Department of the bulk of its Asian expertise, smoothing the path to an ill-informed war in Vietnam. The Korean War also jump-started the moribund Japanese economy as American dollars poured into Japan, where the U.S. war effort was based. Japanese conservatives called it "a gift from the gods."

Frustrations with the course of war in Korea affirmed the inward focus of American society in the 1950s. Despite the organizing efforts of political activists such as civil rights workers, most citizens seemed to look increasingly to their personal and familial lives for satisfaction and meaning. From the powerful U.S. economy flowed an unprecedented river of consumer goods, including the new artificial materials—plastic, vinyl, nylon, polyester, Styrofoam—that have pervaded and polluted American life ever since. As peace came to Korea and U.S. soldiers returned from across the Pacific, Americans sought the good life at home.

Sites to Visit

National Security Archive at George Washington University

www.gwu.edu/~nsarchiv/

This extraordinary site includes the most recent declassified documents on the making of U.S. foreign policy.

Cold War International History Project

http://wwics.si.edu/index.cfm?topic_id=1409&fuseaction=topics.home

The Woodrow Wilson International Center for Scholars maintains this excellent site, which offers newly released documents and up-to-date interpretive essays on the American-Soviet struggle.

The Ad*Access Project of Duke University Library

http://scriptorium.lib.duke.edu/adaccess/

This site presents fascinating images from over 7,000 advertisements in U.S. and Canadian newspapers and magazines between 1911 and 1955, offering insights into popular culture and consumer life.

Truman Presidential Museum and Library

www.trumanlibrary.org/index.html

The Harry Truman Presidential Library maintains this site, which contains an especially useful collection of documents regarding crucial foreign policy decisions in the early Cold War.

The Avalon Project at the Yale Law School: Documents in Law, History, and Diplomacy

www.yale.edu/lawweb/avalon/avalon.htm

Researchers can find here the texts of a large number of the most important primary documents illuminating U.S. relations with other countries.

Korea + 50: No Longer Forgotten

www.trumanlibrary.org/korea/

The Truman Library's site on the Korean War has documents, photos, and interpretative essays by prominent historians.

Bancroft Library Collections

http://bancroft.berkeley.edu/collections/

The Bancroft Library of the University of California at Berkeley has extensive collections, exhibits, and links revealing the history of California, the nation's most populous state.

For Further Reading

General

William H. Chafe, *The Unfinished Journey: America Since World War II*, 5th ed. (2003).

Alonzo Hamby, *Man of the People: A Life of Harry S. Truman* (1995).

Godfrey Hodgson, *America in Our Time* (1976).

Walter LaFeber, *America, Russia, and the Cold War, 1945–1996*, 9th ed. (2002).

James T. Patterson, *Grand Expectations: The United States, 1945–1974* (1996).

The Uncertainties of Victory

Thomas Borstelmann, *The Cold War and the Color Line: American Race Relations in the Global Arena* (2001).

Robert R. Korstad, *Civil Rights Unionism: Tobacco Workers and the Struggle for Democracy in the Mid-Twentieth-Century South* (2003).

Melvyn P. Leffler, *The Specter of Communism: The United States and the Origins of the Cold War, 1917–1953* (1994).

Richard Polenberg, *One Nation Divisible: Class, Race, and Ethnicity in the United States Since 1938* (1980).

Thomas Sugrue, *The Origins of the Urban Crisis: Race and Inequality in Postwar Detroit* (1996).

The Quest for Security

Carolyn Woods Eisenberg, *Drawing the Line: The American Decision to Divide Germany, 1944–1949* (1996).

Michael J. Hogan, *The Marshall Plan: America, Britain, and the Reconstruction of Western Europe, 1947–1952* (1987).

Walter Isaacson and Evan Thomas, *The Wise Men: Six Friends and the World They Made: Acheson, Bohlen, Harriman, Kennan, Lovett, McCloy* (1986).

Melvyn P. Leffler, *A Preponderance of Power: National Security, the Truman Administration, and the Cold War* (1992).

Thomas G. Paterson, *On Every Front: The Making and Unmaking of the Cold War* (1992).

Martin J. Sherwin, *A World Destroyed: The Atomic Bomb and the Grand Alliance* (1975).

A Cold War Society

Paul S. Boyer, *By the Bomb's Early Light: American Thought and Culture at the Dawn of the Atomic Age* (1985).

Richard M. Fried, *Nightmare in Red: The McCarthy Era in Perspective* (1990).

Kenneth T. Jackson, *Crabgrass Frontier: The Suburbanization of the United States* (1985).

Elaine Tyler May, *Homeward Bound: American Families in the Cold War Era* (1988).

Ellen Schrecker, *Many Are the Crimes: McCarthyism in America* (1998).

Stephen J. Whitfield, *The Culture of the Cold War* (1991).

The United States and Asia

Warren I. Cohen, *America's Response to China: A History of Sino-American Relations*, 4th ed. (2000).

Bruce Cumings, *The Origins of the Korean War*, 2 vols. (1981, 1990).

Jon Halliday and Bruce Cumings, *Korea: The Unknown War* (1988).

Michael J. Hogan, *A Cross of Iron: Harry S. Truman and the Origins of the National Security State, 1945–1954* (1998).

Christina Klein, *Cold War Orientalism: Asia in the Middlebrow Imagination, 1945–1961* (2003).

Walter LaFeber, *The Clash: A History of U.S.-Japan Relations* (1997).

1953 CIA engineers coup in Iran, restores Shah to power.

1954 *Brown v. Board of Education.*
Founding of Southeast Asia Treaty Organization (SEATO).
French leave Vietnam, which is divided into South Vietnam and North Vietnam.

1955 Polio vaccine approved for use.
Disneyland opens in Anaheim, California.
Montgomery, Alabama, bus boycott begins.

1956 Interstate Highway Act.

1957 Central High School in Little Rock, Arkansas, integrated.
USSR launches satellite *Sputnik.*
Eisenhower Doctrine.

1958 National Defense Education Act.

1959 Nixon-Khrushchev Kitchen Debate.
Cuban Revolution.

1960 Oral contraceptive pill comes on the market.
Beginning of lunch counter sit-ins (Greensboro, North Carolina).
American U-2 spy plane shot down over USSR.

1961 First American launched into space.
Bay of Pigs invasion of Cuba.
Berlin Wall constructed.
Freedom Rides begin.

1962 Rachel Carson, *Silent Spring.*
Cuban missile crisis.
Students for a Democratic Society (SDS) founded.

1963 Lyndon B. Johnson becomes president after assassination of John F. Kennedy.
Equal Pay Act of 1963.
Betty Friedan, *The Feminine Mystique.*

1964 Gulf of Tonkin Resolution.
Civil Rights Act of 1964 (employment).
Wilderness Act.

1965 Civil Rights Act of 1965 (voting rights).
Griswold v. Connecticut legalizes birth control for married couples.
Watts (Los Angeles) riot.

1966 Clean Water Act.
National Organization for Women (NOW) founded.

PART NINE

The Cold War at Full Tide, 1953–1979

DURING THE THIRD QUARTER OF THE TWENTIETH CENTURY, THE Cold War cast a long shadow over the United States and the rest of the world. Tensions mounted at home and abroad as the United States and the Soviet Union vied for power among the world's nations. In poor Third World countries, insurgents attempted to throw off the yoke of colonialism and play the two superpowers against each other. The United States used a variety of strategies to counter Soviet influence in Latin America, Africa, the Middle East, and Southeast Asia, including military force in Korea and Vietnam, white-knuckle diplomacy in Cuba, extensive aid to non-aligned countries, and covert operations worldwide.

Soviet advances in science and technology spurred the U.S. government to sponsor bold new domestic initiatives in the areas of public education and space exploration. The Cold War even helped shape a post–World War II domestic ideal: a nuclear family living in a house in the suburbs, with a breadwinner father and a full-time homemaker mother. Many Americans believed that their prosperous, consumer-oriented economy, with its emphasis on individualism and personal choice, was a key weapon in the fight against communism.

In a feverish arms race, both the United States and the USSR rushed to stockpile weapons of mass destruction. Constant innovations in the technology of nuclear weaponry (such as intercontinental ballistic missiles) made the bombers used in World War II obsolete. The hydrogen bomb, tested successfully for the first time in 1953, dwarfed the power of the atomic bomb that had leveled Hiroshima. Nevertheless, citizens who criticized the arms buildup risked being branded unpatriotic. More than ever before, domestic policy was intertwined with foreign policy.

The rise of multinational corporations meant that large, impersonal institutions, whether government or private, were shaping American life. Middle-level managers—men in "grey flannel suits"—represented the corporate ethos of loyalty to the company above all else. At the same time, many Americans sought to work within their local communities for social and political change. In the South, African American men and women launched a dramatic assault on the system of legal segregation known as "Jim Crow." Working at the grassroots level, these activists boycotted buses, marched, sat in at lunch counters, and went to jail. Their efforts provoked the courts and Congress to act, culminating in the Civil Rights Acts of 1964 and 1965. For the first time in American history, the federal government assumed responsibility for eliminating discrimination in the workplace and guaranteeing all its citizens the right to vote.

Other groups also organized and entered the political arena. Indians, disabled Americans, California farm workers, and gay men and lesbians all formed organizations to counter discrimination and advance their civil rights. The women's movement affected all aspects of American society, enabling women to play a greater role in the political and economic life of the country. A new environmentalist movement secured legislation protecting wilderness areas and endangered species and ensuring that Americans had clean air to breathe and clean water to drink.

Lyndon B. Johnson assumed the presidency after the assassination of John F. Kennedy in 1963. Johnson hoped to revitalize the New Deal legacy by expanding social welfare programs. His program, called the Great Society, sought to address seemingly intractable problems such as poverty, lack of health care for the elderly, and the deterioration of inner-city neighborhoods. But Johnson also expanded the U.S. military presence in Vietnam, an effort that cost an increasing number of American lives. Even constant bombing proved futile to stem the civil war that pitted Americans and anticommunist Vietnamese against the National Liberation Front of South Vietnam and their comrades in the north. Johnson's successor, Richard M. Nixon, also found himself mired in a war that was becoming increasingly unpopular among Americans.

Protests against the war in the late 1960s and early 1970s highlighted an emerging youth culture. The baby boom generation, born in the two decades after World War II, embraced sexual freedom and new forms of music (such as rock 'n' roll) in an apparent attempt to defy their parents and "the Establishment" in general. Many Americans felt betrayed by both Johnson and Nixon, believing that tens of thousands of American soldiers had died in vain in Vietnam. The Watergate break-in at Democratic headquarters, leading eventually to Nixon's resignation, contributed to a growing, widespread disenchantment with government authority.

By the late 1970s, developments abroad had greatly complicated Cold War politics. Middle Eastern oil-producing nations imposed an oil embargo on the United States, highlighting U.S. dependence on fossil fuels. Islamic fundamentalists were beginning to retaliate violently against the spread of American influence and culture in Muslim countries. And at home, a conservative backlash emerged to counter the expansion of the welfare state, the heightened visibility of the feminist movement, and widening civil rights protests.

1967 Thurgood Marshall appointed first African American to U.S. Supreme Court.
Riots in Detroit, Michigan, and Newark, New Jersey.

1968 Martin Luther King Jr. assassinated.
Robert Kennedy assassinated.
My Lai massacre.
Wild and Scenic Rivers Act.
Tet offensive.

1969 Huge antiwar protests in Washington, D.C.
Indians occupy Alcatraz Island in San Francisco Bay.
Stonewall raid, New York City.
Astronauts Neil Armstrong and Buzz Aldrin walk on the moon.

1970 United States invades Cambodia.
National Guard troops kill four students, Kent State University in Ohio.

1971 Pentagon Papers published.
Nixon administration creates "plumbers" for illegal activities.

1972 Watergate break-in.
Nixon visits China.
Founding of *Ms.* magazine.

1973 *Roe v. Wade* legalizes abortion.
American Indian Movement members occupy Wounded Knee.
Endangered Species Act.
OPEC oil embargo.
American troops withdrawn from Vietnam.

1974 Nixon resigns presidency; Gerald R. Ford becomes president.

1975 *Mayaguez* incident.
Vietnam reunified under communist rule.
Congressional investigations of CIA covert operations.

1976 Hyde Amendment prohibits use of Medicaid funds for abortions.
Nation celebrates bicentennial.

1977 Carter issues general amnesty for draft evaders.
Trans-Alaska Pipeline system completed.
ABC airs miniseries *Roots*, based on book by Alex Haley.

1978 Bakke Supreme Court decision.
California Proposition 13.

1979 Camp David peace accords.
Partial meltdown of nuclear core at Three Mile Island nuclear plant.
Iranian Revolution.

CHAPTER 25

Domestic Dreams and Atomic Nightmares, 1953–1963

Ernest Crichlow, *By the Gate*, 1953. Harmon and Harriet Kelley Foundation for the Arts

▲ Ernest Chrichlow's 1953 painting *By the Gate* evokes the longings of a young African American.

CHAPTER OUTLINE

Cold War, Warm Hearth

The Civil Rights Movement

The Eisenhower Years

Outsiders and Opposition

The Kennedy Era

Conclusion

Sites to Visit

For Further Reading

Dr. Tom Dooley was known as the "jungle doctor." A native of St. Louis and a devout Catholic, Dooley joined the Navy medical corps during World War II and remained in the Navy reserves until 1950. After earning his medical degree, he moved to Southeast Asia, where he set up clinics to provide medical care for impoverished villagers. He quickly became a major celebrity. In a 1960 Gallup poll, Dooley was among the ten most admired Americans. President Dwight D. Eisenhower said of Dooley, "Few, if any, men have equaled [Dooley's] exhibition of courage, self-sacrifice, faith in his God and his readiness to serve his fellow man." When Dooley died of cancer in 1961 at the age of 34, he was honored by Congress and posthumously awarded the U.S. Navy's Legion of Merit. His legacy helped inspire John F. Kennedy's creation of the Peace Corps.

Dooley's life personifies the complex legacy of U.S. cultural diplomacy during the early years of the Cold War. Although he was a practicing Catholic, he rejected the role of the religious missionary—a role largely discredited in the anticolonial post–World War II years as tied to racist and imperialist designs. Rather, Dooley promoted modernization and development, embracing an internationalist vision that was grounded in respect and appreciation for the local culture and customs of the people with whom he lived. Dooley was the model for the protagonist of the best-selling novel *The Ugly American,* written by Far East correspondent William Lederer and political theorist Eugene Burdick, both navy veterans. *The Ugly American* was a scathing attack on American diplomats working in Asia who had disdain for Asian people and who never bothered to learn the language, history, or cultures of the countries where they were stationed. In contrast to the arrogant diplomats, the character modeled on Dooley was sensitive to the people and well loved. As a result, he was the most effective ambassador for the nation, in contrast to the official diplomats who fostered hatred for Americans.

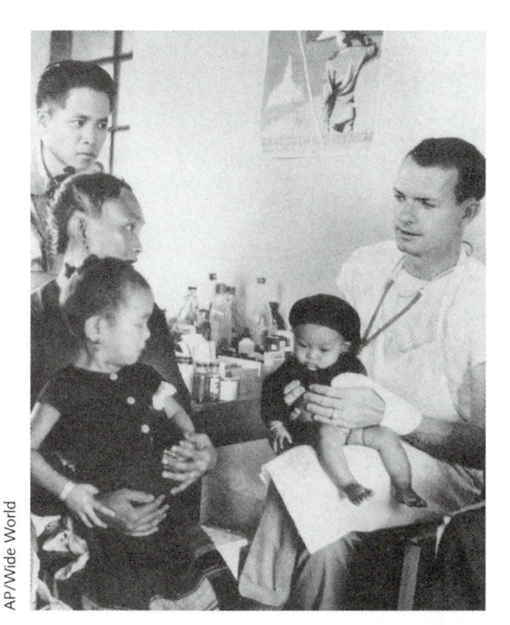
AP/Wide World

Dr. Tom Dooley is pictured here providing medical care to Laotian children. Known as the "jungle doctor," he represented American expertise and benevolence, as well as fervent anticommunism, during the early years of the Cold War.

Dooley's zeal to help the people of Southeast Asia went far beyond medical care. A passionate anticommunist, in 1956 he assisted the Central Intelligence Agency (CIA) and the U.S. Navy in leading the exodus of 900,000 Catholic refugees from newly created communist North Vietnam to South Vietnam, where the United States backed a noncommunist dictatorship under Ngo Dinh Diem. He recounted that experience in a best-selling book, *Deliver Us from Evil,* and wrote two other books that chronicled his activities at the clinics he founded in the villages and jungles of Laos. His books praised Diem's regime in South Vietnam and promoted the cause of anticommunism in Southeast Asia. He portrayed himself as a peaceful crusader against communism who spread American values in Southeast Asia and opposed imperialism. The CIA supported Dooley's efforts and helped publicize his cultural diplomacy.

Dooley's work in Southeast Asia provided essential medical care to people in need and also served American interests in the early years of the Cold War. But his decision to live and work in the remote villages of Laos was not based simply on self-sacrifice. As a homosexual, Dooley would have had a difficult life within the United States in the 1950s. Anticommunist crusaders purged homosexuals from government employment, and gay men and lesbians faced harassment, ostracism, and often the loss of their jobs. Dooley escaped the intense homophobia of his home country by creating communal living situations with other men in remote areas of Laos, far from public view. There he could keep his sexual

orientation private. If he had remained in the United States, the anticommunists whose political passions he shared would have purged him from their ranks.

It is fitting that a doctor spreading the benefits of American medicine to Asia would become a Cold War hero. Science and expertise reigned supreme during the Cold War years. Parents turned to another famous physician, Dr. Benjamin Spock, whose 1946 guide to raising children, *Baby and Child Care,* became an instant best-seller. Unlike prewar child-rearing experts who encouraged discipline and discouraged coddling, Dr. Spock emphasized nurture and affection. He urged parents to hold and comfort their infants, feed them on demand, and abandon rigid toilet-training routines. Dr. Jonas Salk became a hero for developing a vaccine against polio. Approved for use in 1955 and distributed widely to children in schools and clinics, the Salk vaccine virtually eliminated the dreaded illness within a few years. The oral contraceptive pill, which came on the market in 1960, provided relatively safe and effective birth control. Hailed initially as a boon to family planning, the pill also helped to usher in the sexual revolution of the 1960s.

Scientific discoveries in the 1950s also inaugurated the modern era of exploration beyond the Earth's atmosphere, fueled by the space race between the United States and the Soviet Union. The National Aeronautics and Space Administration (NASA), established in 1958, sent the first American into space in 1961. But science also brought pesticides, smog, and other pollutants. Americans, at the time, rarely considered the environmental effects of consumer goods, cars, petrochemicals, or nuclear power.

The oral contraceptive pill, which came on the market in 1960, provided relatively safe and effective birth control. Hailed initially as a boon to family planning, the pill also helped to usher in the sexual revolution of the 1960s.

The decade from 1953 to 1963 was a time of expansive optimism about the future. The **baby boom** demonstrated widespread faith in the future for American children. It was also a decade of growth for U.S. influence abroad, the domestic economy, consumer culture, and television. Suburbs, highways, and shopping malls expanded to meet the needs of increasing numbers of families with young children. The nation expanded with the addition of Hawaii and Alaska as states.

It was also a decade of anxiety. Americans worried about the perils of the atomic age as the nuclear arsenals of both superpowers continued to grow. The brainwashing of prisoners of war in Korea raised fears about communist propaganda and psychological warfare. Science fiction films about alien invaders reflected concerns about foreign dangers. The Soviet Union's 1957 launching of *Sputnik,* the first artificial satellite to orbit the Earth, alarmed Americans and forced the nation to confront the possibility of Soviet technological superiority. The United States appeared to be at the height of its strength and power, yet at the same time, more vulnerable than ever before.

Cold War, Warm Hearth

In 1959 Vice President Richard M. Nixon traveled to the Soviet Union, where he engaged in one of the most noted verbal sparring matches of the century. In a lengthy and often heated debate with Soviet Premier Nikita Khrushchev at the opening of the American National Exhibition in Moscow, Nixon extolled the virtues of the American way of life; his opponent promoted the communist system. The two leaders did not discuss missiles, bombs, or even modes of government. Rather, they argued over the relative merits of American and Soviet washing machines, televisions, and electric ranges in what came to be known as the "Kitchen Debate."

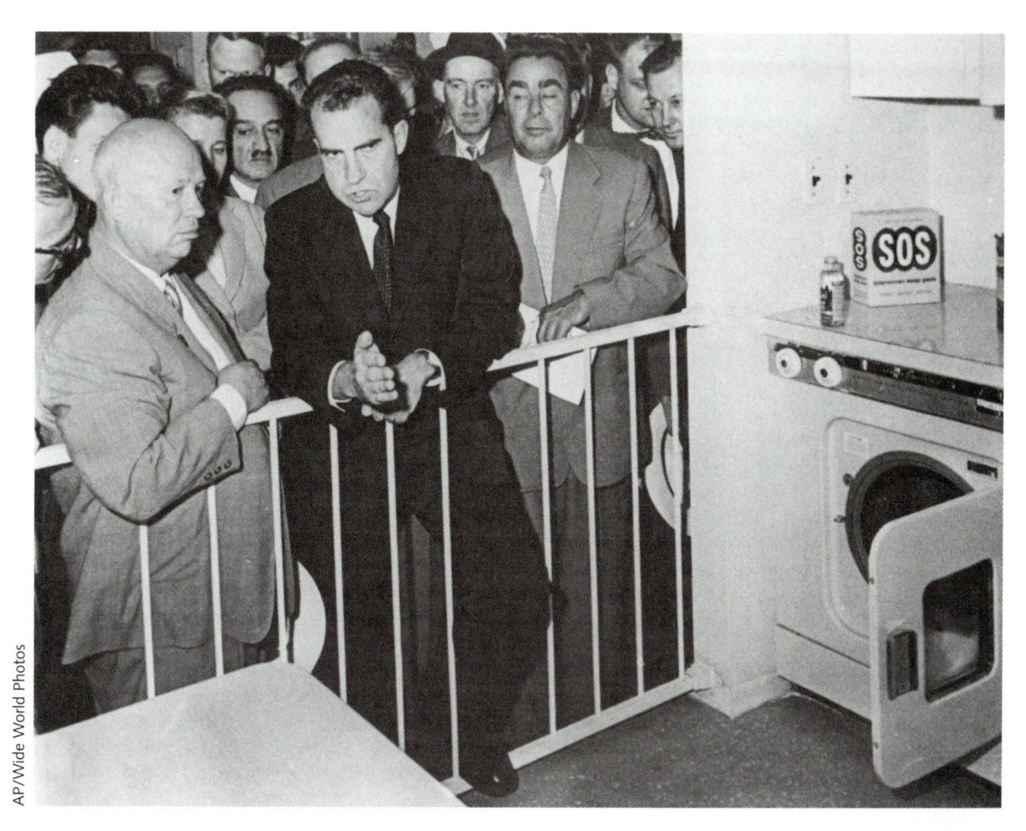

AP/Wide World Photos

▲ **Vice President Richard M. Nixon and Soviet Premier Nikita Khrushchev touring the 1959 American National Exhibition in Moscow.**

The Kitchen Debate was a major skirmish on the Cold War's cultural battleground, where the two superpowers struggled for ideological supremacy. For Nixon, American superiority rested on the ability of average Americans to purchase a suburban home, complete with modern appliances. He proclaimed that the home adorned with a wide array of consumer goods represented the essence of American freedom:

> To us, diversity, the right to choose, . . .is the most important thing. We don't have one decision made at the top by one government official. . . . We have many different manufacturers and many different kinds of washing machines so that the housewives have a choice. . . . Would it not be better to compete in the relative merits of washing machines than in the strength of rockets?

Nixon's focus on household appliances was not accidental. After all, arguments over the strength of rockets would only point out the vulnerability of the United States in the event of a nuclear war between the superpowers. Debates over consumer goods provided a reassuring vision of the good life available in the atomic age. So Nixon insisted that American superiority in the Cold War rested not on weapons but on prosperous families living in comfortable suburban homes. Freed by modern appliances from the drudgery of household chores, mothers could spend their time nurturing happy, well-adjusted children. Consumerism provided the means for achieving individuality, leisure, domestic bliss, and upward mobility.

The American National Exhibition in Moscow was a showcase of American consumer goods and leisure equipment. But the main attraction, which the two leaders toured under international media spotlight, was a full-scale, six-room, ranch-style model house. This model home, filled with labor-saving devices and presumably available to Americans of all classes, offered tangible proof, Nixon claimed, of the superiority of free enterprise over communism.

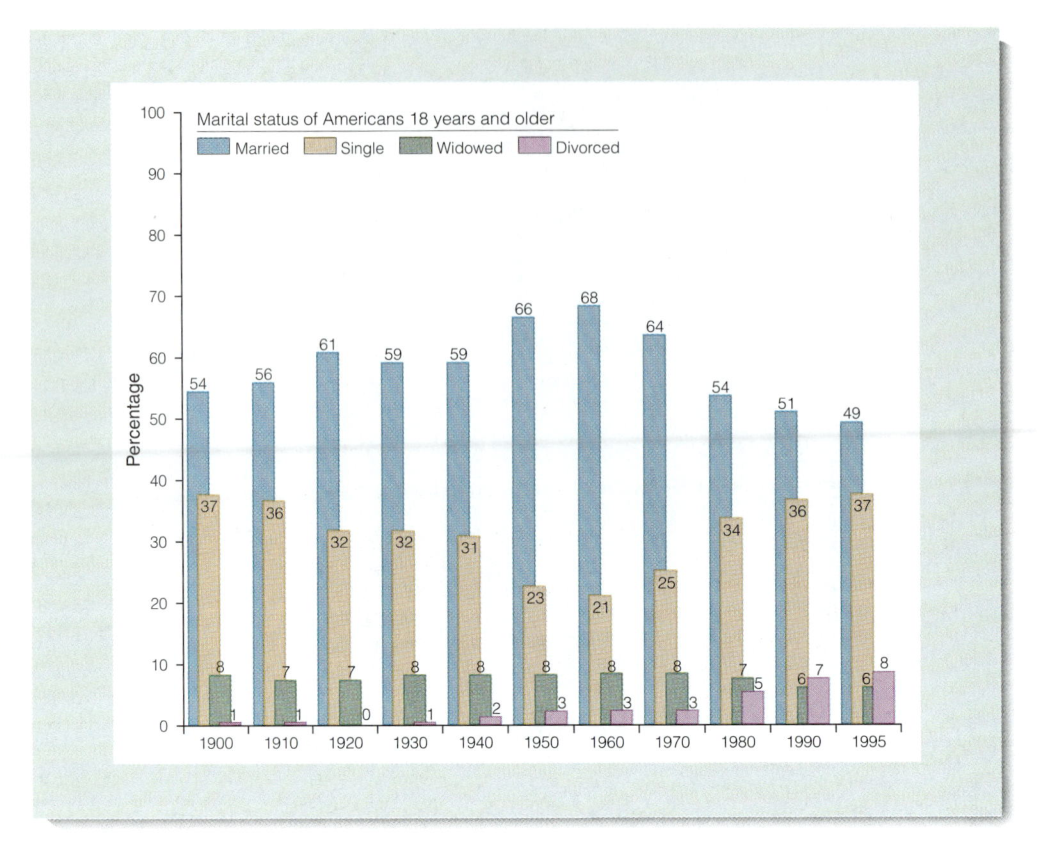

▶ **FIGURE 25.1** MARITAL STATUS OF THE U.S. ADULT POPULATION, 1900–1995
Following World War II, Americans married in record numbers. The high rate of marriage corresponded with a relatively low divorce rate. Beginning in the 1970s, the marriage rate plummeted and the divorce rate rose dramatically.

Nixon called attention to a built-in panel-controlled washing machine. "In America," he said, "these [washing machines] are designed to make things easier for our women." Khrushchev countered Nixon's boast of comfortable American housewives by expressing pride in productive Soviet female workers. The Soviets, he claimed, did not share that "capitalist attitude toward women."

According to American journalists, Nixon's knock-out punch in his verbal bout with the Soviet premier was his articulation of the American postwar domestic dream: successful breadwinners supporting attractive homemakers in well-appointed, comfortable homes. Sharing Nixon's sentiments about politics, consumerism, and gender, most reporters hailed the vice president's trip as a major triumph. The American National Exhibition in Moscow seemed to demonstrate the superiority of the American way of life.

Nixon's emphasis on the home and family during the Kitchen Debate reflected the central concerns of postwar Americans. In spite of deep divisions in American society, in certain ways Americans behaved with remarkable conformity. This is nowhere more evident than in the overwhelming embrace of the nuclear family. The GI Bill, with its provisions for home mortgage loans, enabled veterans of modest means to purchase homes. Although residential segregation prevailed throughout the postwar era, limiting most suburban developments to prosperous white middle- and working-class families, many veterans of color were able to buy their first homes.

Family fever swept the nation and affected all Americans. The trends that began during and immediately after World War II, including the rising rates of marriage and childbirth and the declining age at marriage, continued during the 1950s. Americans of all racial, ethnic, and religious groups, of all socioeconomic classes and educational levels, brought the marriage rate up and the divorce rate down. Popular television shows such as *The Honeymooners*, featuring working-class couples, and *Leave It to Beaver*, depicting middle-class families, placed the consumer-oriented home at the center of attention. So did mainstream *Life* magazine and the African American glossy *Ebony*. The "American way of life" embodied in the suburban nuclear family, as a cultural ideal if not a universal reality, motivated countless postwar Americans to strive for it, to live by its codes, and—for Americans of color—to demand it.

Courtesy, Herb and Dorothy McLaughlin Collection, Arizona State University Libraries

▲ Following World War II, hospital nurseries barely had room for all the babies. After a century and a half of steady decline, the birthrate rose dramatically in the 1940s and 1950s. Americans from all backgrounds and socioeconomic levels contributed to the surge in births.

Consumer Spending and the Suburban Ideal

The postwar years witnessed a huge increase in spending power. Between 1947 and 1961, the number of families rose 28 percent, national income increased more than 60 percent, and the number of Americans with money to spend beyond basic necessities doubled. Rather than putting this money aside for a rainy day, Americans were inclined to spend it. Investing in one's home, along with the trappings that would enhance family life, seemed the best way to plan for a secure future.

Between 1950 and 1970, the suburban population more than doubled, from 36 million to 74 million. Fully 20 percent of the population remained poor during this prosperous time. But most families of ample as well as modest means exhibited a great deal of conformity in their consumer behavior, reflecting widely shared beliefs about the good life. They poured their money into homes, domestic appliances, televisions, automobiles, and family vacations. As prosperity spread throughout the 1950s, expenditures for food and clothing increased modestly, and spending on household appliances, recreation, automobiles, and televisions more than doubled. Homeowners moved into more than 1 million new suburban houses each year.

Nuclear families who settled in the suburbs provided the foundation for new types of community life and leisure pursuits, sometimes at the expense of older ones grounded in ethnic neighborhoods and kinship networks. Family-oriented amusement parks such as Disneyland in Anaheim, California, which opened in 1955, catered to middle-class tastes, in contrast to older venues such as Coney Island, known for their thrill rides, class and ethnic mixing, and erotic environments. Religious affiliation rose to an all-time high as Americans built and joined suburban churches and synagogues, complete with youth programs and summer camps. Families piled into the car for outings to local drive-in theaters and weekend excursions or shared leisure time gathered around television sets. In 1949, fewer than 1 million American homes had a television. Within the next four years, the number soared to 20 million.

The house and commodity boom had tremendous propaganda value during the Cold War, as Nixon demonstrated in the Kitchen Debate. Although they may have been unwitting soldiers, consumers who marched off to the nation's shopping centers to equip their new homes joined the ranks of Americans taking part in the Cold War. As early as 1947, newscaster and noted cold warrior George Putnam described shopping centers as "concrete expressions of the practical idealism that built America...plenty of free parking for all those cars that we capitalists seem to acquire. Who can help but contrast [them] with what you'd find under communism?"

The Cold War made a profound contribution to suburban sprawl. In 1951 the *Bulletin of Atomic Scientists* devoted an issue to "defense through decentralization" that argued in favor of depopulating the urban core to avoid a concentration of residences or industries in a potential target area for a nuclear attack. Joining this effort was the American Road Builders' Association, a lobbying group second only in power and wealth to the munitions industry. As a result of these pressures, Congress passed the Interstate Highway Act of 1956, which provided $100 billion to cover 90 percent of the cost for 41,000 miles of national highways. When President Dwight D. Eisenhower signed the bill into law, he stated one of the major

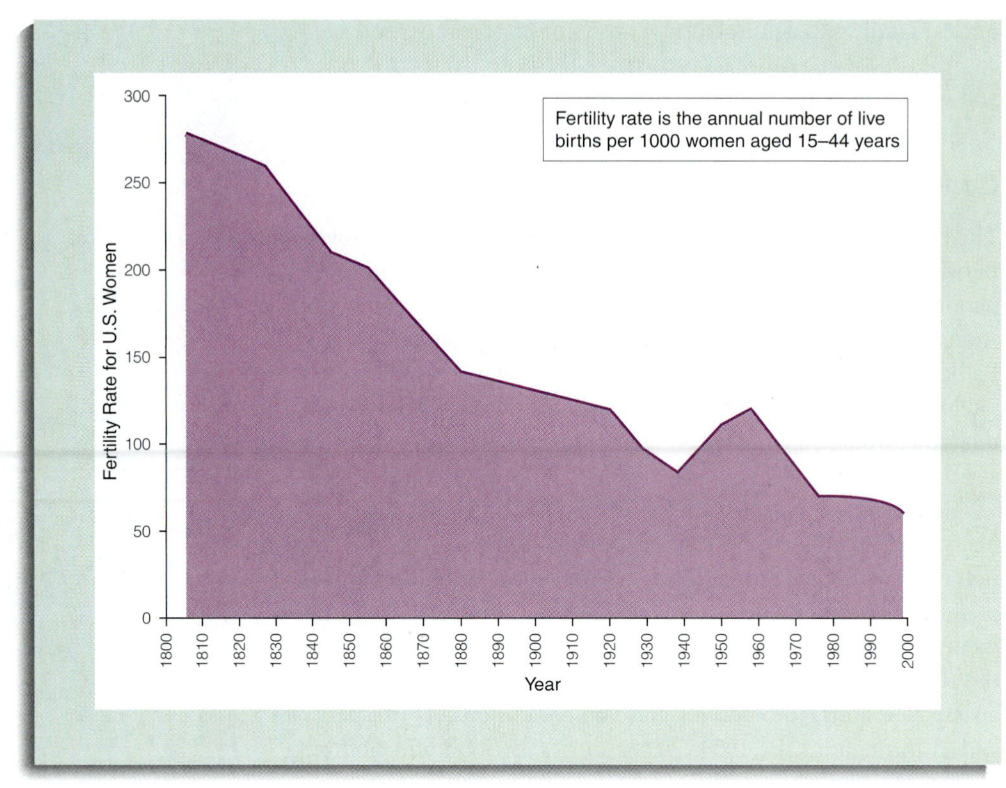

▶ FIGURE 25.2 THE BABY BOOM IN HISTORICAL CONTEXT After a decline of nearly a century and a half, the fertility rate of American women surged during and after World War II, producing the baby boom. The boom resulted from the high marriage rate, the lower marriage age, and the rise in the average number of children per couple.

reasons for the new highway system: "[In] case of atomic attack on our key cities, the road net must permit quick evacuation of target areas."

Many people believed that the suburbs also provided protection against labor unrest, which might lead to class warfare. According to the Cold War ethos of the time, class conflict within the United States would weaken the nation and harm its image abroad, bolstering the Soviet Union and making the United States vulnerable to communism. In the suburbs, working-class and middle-class Americans could pursue the American dream of individualism and upward mobility through private life, rather than collective action at work.

The worst-case scenario was communist takeover and the defeat of the United States in the Cold War. Pentagon strategists and foreign policy experts feared that the Soviet Union might gain the military might to allow its territorial expansion and, eventually, world domination. But observers also worried that the real dangers to America were internal: racial strife, emancipated women, class conflict, and familial disruption. To alleviate these fears, Americans turned to the family as a bastion of safety in an insecure world. Most postwar Americans longed for security after years of economic depression and war and saw family stability as the best bulwark against the new dangers of the Cold War.

Race, Class, and Domesticity

Many Americans think of the 1950s as a golden era of economic prosperity and happy families nestled in comfortable suburban homes. Large numbers of Americans achieved this lifestyle, but it was not available to everyone. The government subsidized suburban developments and restricted who could live in them. After World War II, the nation faced a severe housing shortage. The federal government gave developers financial subsidies to build affordable single-family homes and offered Federal Housing Authority (FHA) loans and income tax deductions to homebuyers. These benefits enabled white working-class and middle-class families to purchase houses. Second- and third-generation European immigrants moved out of their neighborhoods in the cities and into the suburbs.

In many suburbs, contracts for the sale of houses included restrictions that excluded Jews and prevented racial minorities from purchasing homes in white neighborhoods. Gradually, these restrictions began to lift. But it remained difficult for people of color to move to the suburbs. Despite the expansion of the black and Latino middle class and the increase in home ownership among racial minorities, most suburban developments excluded nonwhites. The FHA and lending banks maintained policies known as **red lining,** which designated certain neighborhoods off limits to racial minorities. They refused mortgage loans to people of color wishing to buy houses in redlined areas, even if the prospective buyers could afford the purchase price, because they feared that property values would decline in racially mixed neighborhoods. Although racial minorities remained concentrated in urban and rural areas, some did move to the suburbs, usually into segregated communities.

National Archives

▲ During the 1950s, churches and synagogues sprang up in suburban communities across the country, helping to strengthen community ties for newcomers to the suburbs. In the same decade, Congress inserted the phrase "under God" to the Pledge of Allegiance and added "In God We Trust" to U.S. currency.

For Americans of color, suburban home ownership offered inclusion in the postwar American dream. In her powerful 1959 play *A Raisin in the Sun,* African American playwright Lorraine Hansberry articulated with great eloquence the importance of a home in the suburbs, not to assimilate into white America but to live as a black family with dignity and pride. Asian Americans also had good reason to celebrate home and family life. With the end of the exclusion of Chinese immigrants during World War II, wives and war brides began to enter the country, helping build thriving family-oriented communities. After the disruptions and anguish of internment, Japanese Americans were eager to put their families and lives back together. Mexican Americans and Mexican immigrants, including ***braceros,*** established flourishing communities in the Southwest. Puerto Ricans migrated to New York and other eastern cities, where they could earn four times the average wage on the island.

Racial segregation did not prevail everywhere. For example, in Shaker Heights, Ohio, a suburb of Cleveland, white residents made a conscious decision, as a community, to integrate their neighborhood. Drawing on postwar liberal ideals of civil rights and racial integration, they welcomed black homeowners. They succeeded in this effort by emphasizing class similarity over racial difference. White residents encouraged other white families to move into Shaker Heights, pointing out that their prosperous black neighbors were "just like us." The City of Claremont, California, established an interracial housing cooperative of Mexican and African American residents along with white married college students at the edge of the Arbol Verde barrio, a Mexican American neighborhood. Desegregation experiments such as these established harmonious, racially integrated communities at a time when residential segregation was the norm across the country.

White attitudes toward racial integration began to shift, but only slightly. In the late 1950s, 60 percent of whites outside the South said they would stay in their homes if a black family moved next door, but only 45 percent said they would remain in the neighborhood if large numbers of people of color moved in. In 1964, demonstrating their belief in property rights over civil rights, 89 percent of those polled in the North and 96 percent in the South believed that "an owner of property should not have to sell to a Negro if he doesn't want to." Disapproval of racial integration was strongest in the most intimate realm of life: the family. During the 1950s, most white Americans—92 percent in the North and 99 percent in the

▲ **The Women's Council of St. Paul, Minnesota, was one of many service organizations in which black and white women joined in common projects. Volunteer activities enabled women to serve their communities as well as develop important political and leadership skills.**

South—approved of laws banning marriage between whites and nonwhites. As late as the mid-1960s, more than half of northern whites and more than three-fourths of southern whites still opposed interracial marriage.

As residents and businesses migrated to the suburbs, slum housing and vacant factories remained in the central cities. With declining tax bases, city governments had few resources to rebuild and revitalize urban neighborhoods. The Housing Acts of 1949 and 1954, promising a "decent home and suitable living environment for every American family," granted funds to municipalities for urban renewal. However, few of those federal dollars provided low-income housing. Mayors, bankers, and real estate interests used the money to bulldoze slums and build gleaming office towers, civic centers, and apartment complexes for affluent citizens, leaving the poor to fend for themselves in the remaining dilapidated corners of the cities.

Although intended to revitalize cities, urban renewal actually accelerated the decay of inner cities and worsened conditions for the urban poor. Federally funded projects often disrupted and destroyed ethnic communities. In St. Paul, Minnesota, the construction of U.S. Highway 94, while enabling suburbanites to commute to the city, obliterated the thriving urban African American neighborhood of Rondo. In Los Angeles, the Dodgers' stadium built in Chávez Ravine offered baseball fans and their families access to the national pastime, but it destroyed the historically rooted Mexican American neighborhood in its path. The $5 million project displaced 7,500 people and demolished 900 homes.

Along with the urban poor, rural Americans reaped few benefits of postwar affluence. Many rural residents had no electricity or running water during the 1950s and therefore had no TV sets or washing machines. Much of rural America, especially in the South, remained poor. The 1950s marked the greatest out-migration from the South as the mechanization of farms—particularly the mechanical cotton picker—reduced the number of workers on the land. More than one-fourth of the population left Kentucky and West Virginia, where unemployment in some areas reached 80 percent.

Women: Back to the Future

The **nuclear family** ideal of the 1950s included a full-time wife and mother and a breadwinner husband. This vision of domesticity contrasted with the expanded opportunities and experiences for women during World War II. It also masked a major postwar trend: the proportion of women who fit the mold of full-time homemaker was rapidly shrinking. Although most American women married, had children, and carried the lion's share of responsibility for housework and child-rearing, increasing numbers of married women also held jobs outside the home. The employment of married women began to rise during World War II and kept rising after the war, even though most of the well-paying and highly skilled jobs returned to men at the war's end.

For the majority of white working-class and middle-class women, the end of the war closed off a number of opportunities for occupational training, professional education, and careers. Often a woman's best chance to secure a decent standard of living was to marry a competent breadwinner. But the pressures on blue-collar as well as white-collar men to earn enough money for the trappings of middle-class affluence strained their ability to provide. Married women took jobs to help pay the bills. College-educated women often worked in clerical positions as secretaries or clerks; but these jobs did not make use of their knowledge and skills. Working-class women found work in the "pink collar" service sector of the economy—such jobs as waitress and hairdresser—with low pay and few chances for advancement. For most Mexican women, pink-collar work was an improvement over migrant labor or factory work. African American women also found these jobs preferable to domestic work in white middle-class homes.

Many women worked part-time while their children were at school, as they considered themselves homemakers, not wage-earners. With few other opportunities for creative work, women embraced their domestic roles and turned homemaking into a profession. Many fulfilled their role with pride and satisfaction and extended their energies and talents into their communities, where they made important contributions as volunteers in local parent-teacher associations (PTAs) and other **civic organizations.** Most postwar mothers finished childbearing by the time they were 30 and had many years ahead of them when their child-rearing responsibilities ended. Some expanded part-time employment into full-time occupations when their children left the nest. Others felt bored and frustrated and drowned their sorrow with alcohol or tranquilizers. In 1963 author Betty Friedan described the constraints facing women as the "problem that has no name" in her feminist manifesto *The Feminine Mystique.*

Park Forest, Illinois, 1953. Courtesy, Sandra Weiner. Photo by Dan Weiner

▲ **Commuters, mostly men, left their suburban homes each morning to go to jobs in the cities, returning home at night. Suburbs served as "bedroom communities," inhabited mostly by women and children during the day.**

Despite the powerful cultural expectation that women's primary responsibilities were to care for their homes and families, many single and married women followed alternative paths.

National Archives

▶ After World War II, women were forced out of most of the high-paying skilled jobs that they had occupied during wartime to make room for the returning men. The jobs available to women were mostly "pink-collar" jobs in the service industry. Here, women operate rolling food carts that enabled a New Jersey factory to feed its workers lunch in a mere 20 minutes.

Women pursued careers in a wide range of fields, including the arts, business, and politics. Harvard Medical School admitted its first female students in 1945, although the medical profession remained heavily male dominated. Some women managed to buck the prevailing gender role with ease; others found it difficult. Minnesota Democrat Coya Knudson, a member of the U.S. House of Representatives, paid a heavy price for her political ideals. While she was in Washington, D.C., working to pass legislation for such causes as college scholarships and school lunches, her husband told *Life* magazine that his wife had abandoned her domestic responsibilities to dally in the male world of politics. The article, titled "Coya Come Home," cast aspersions on Knudson's morals and featured a photo of the family having Thanksgiving dinner in a seedy Washington, D.C., cafeteria. Knudson lost her seat in Congress to a Republican challenger who used "Coya Come Home" as a campaign slogan.

Education was one avenue available to women, as students as well as teachers. But higher education did not open its doors fully to women. Because few women gained access to graduate and professional schools and most well-paying jobs were reserved for men, college degrees for white women did not necessarily open up career opportunities or greatly improve their job and earning prospects. By 1956, one-fourth of white female students married while still in college. Many of these women dropped out of school to take jobs in order to support their husbands through college. But the situation was quite different for black women. Like their mothers and grandmothers, most black women had to work to help support their families. Even in the prosperous postwar years, few black families could survive on the meager earnings of a single breadwinner. Job prospects for black women generally were limited to menial, low-paying occupations. Young black women knew that a college degree could mean the difference between working as a maid for a white family and working as a secretary, teacher, or nurse. Although few in number, more than 90 percent of black women who entered college completed their degrees.

Russell Lee/Library of Congress

◀ At a time when many corporations and professions excluded African Americans, many black entrepreneurs opened their own establishments to serve their own communities. This black-owned dress shop in Chicago catered to middle-class African American women.

Black women also aspired to the role of homemaker, but for very different reasons than white women. Although poverty still plagued large numbers of black citizens, the black middle class expanded during the 1950s. Postwar prosperity enabled some African Americans, for the first time, to strive for family life in which the earnings of men were adequate to allow women to stay home with their own children rather than tending to the houses and children of white families. Celebrating that possibility in 1947, *Ebony* magazine proclaimed: "Goodbye Mammy, Hello Mom." World War II "took Negro mothers out of white kitchens, put them in factories and shipyards. When it was all over, they went back to kitchens—but this time their own. . . . And so today in thousands of Negro homes, the Negro mother has come home, come home perhaps for the first time since 1619 when the first Negro families landed at Jamestown, Virginia." For a black woman, domesticity meant "freedom and independence in her own home." It is no wonder that in the early 1960s, women of color bristled when white feminists such as Betty Friedan called upon women to break free from the "chains" of domesticity.

The Civil Rights Movement

As the civil rights movement gained momentum in the South, African American activists faced fierce opposition from local white authorities and contempt from national leaders. Persistent racial discrimination proved to be the nation's worst embarrassment throughout the Cold War. Black leaders and federal officials understood that the national government needed to promote civil rights at home to save face abroad. The Soviet Union and other communist countries pointed to American race relations as an indication of the hypocrisy and failure of the American promise of freedom for all. Yet national leaders paid only lip service to racial justice and failed to provide the strong support necessary to defeat the system of racial segregation in the South known as the "Jim Crow" system. **Jim Crow** was a legal, or *de jure,* set of institutions that prevailed throughout the South. Although the nation's leaders acknowledged the need to address Southern segregation, they did nothing to address the unofficial, or *de facto,* segregation that prevailed throughout the rest of the country.

Nevertheless, at the grassroots level, racial minorities continued to work for equal rights. For example, Mexican Americans in the Southwest continued to press for desegregation of schools, residential neighborhoods, and public facilities through organizations such as the middle-class League of United Latin American Citizens (LULAC) and the Asociación Nacional México-Americana (ANMA), a civil rights organization that emerged out of the labor movement. It was not until 1963 that the power of the civil rights movement—and the violence of southern white opposition—finally compelled the federal government to take action.

Brown v. Board of Education

Brown v. Board of Education of Topeka, Kansas

The first major success in the struggle to dismantle the Jim Crow system in the South came in the 1954 Supreme Court decision *Brown v. Board of Education*. Civil rights strategists decided to pursue their cause in the courts rather than through Congress. They knew that Southern Democrats in Congress, who held disproportionate power through their seniority and control of major committees, would block any civil rights legislation that came before the House or Senate. They believed that they had a better chance of success through the courts.

Initially, civil rights attorneys worked within the system of segregation. The *Plessy v. Ferguson* decision in 1896 justified Jim Crow laws on the principle of providing "separate but equal" facilities. The attorneys argued that southern school systems violated the segregation laws because the separate, racially segregated schools were far from equal. In Clarendon County, South Carolina, for example, public funds provided $179 per white child but $43 per black child. Soon the lawyers shifted their strategy to claim that "separate" was inherently unequal and began the push to overturn *Plessy v. Ferguson*. Leading the charge was Thurgood Marshall, general counsel of the NAACP and a graduate of Howard University Law School.

Ed Clark/TimePix/Getty Images

▲ **Children in segregated schools studied in wretched physical conditions but benefited from dedicated African American teachers. The Supreme Court struck down school segregation in the landmark 1954 case *Brown v. Board of Education*, arguing in its unanimous decision that separate facilities were inherently unequal.**

The NAACP lawyers filed suit against the Topeka, Kansas, Board of Education, on behalf of Linda Brown, a black child in a segregated school. The case reached the U.S. Supreme Court, where NAACP general counsel Thurgood Marshall argued that separate facilities, by definition, denied African Americans their equal rights as citizens. A key argument in the case was the psychological effect of the stigma of segregation on black children. Psychologist Kenneth Clark, testifying as an expert

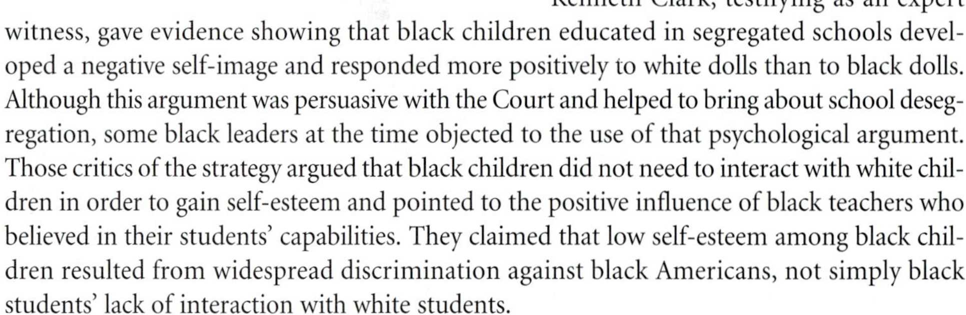

witness, gave evidence showing that black children educated in segregated schools developed a negative self-image and responded more positively to white dolls than to black dolls. Although this argument was persuasive with the Court and helped to bring about school desegregation, some black leaders at the time objected to the use of that psychological argument. Those critics of the strategy argued that black children did not need to interact with white children in order to gain self-esteem and pointed to the positive influence of black teachers who believed in their students' capabilities. They claimed that low self-esteem among black children resulted from widespread discrimination against black Americans, not simply black students' lack of interaction with white students.

In 1953, during the three-year period that the Supreme Court had the *Brown* case before it, President Eisenhower appointed Earl Warren as chief justice. Warren had been state attorney general and then governor of California during World War II and had approved the internment of Japanese Americans—a decision he later deeply regretted. He now used his political and legal skills to strike a blow for justice. He knew that such a critical case needed a unanimous decision to win broad political support. One by one, he persuaded his Supreme Court colleagues of the importance of striking down segregation. On May 17, 1954, Warren delivered the historic unanimous ruling: "To separate [black children] from others of similar age and qualifications solely because of their race generates a feeling of inferiority as to their status in the community that may affect their hearts and minds in a way unlikely ever to be undone. . . . We conclude that in the field of public education the doctrine of 'separate but equal' has no place. Separate educational facilities are inherently unequal."

White Resistance, Black Persistence

Winning the *Brown* case was a great triumph, but it was only the first step. Desegregation would be meaningful only when it was enforced, and that was another matter entirely. At first, there seemed to be some cause for optimism. In Hoxie, Arkansas, for example, the all-white-male school board agreed to integrate the schools, believing it was the right thing to do. Integration happened easily and without incident. Black and white children got along well and their families—long accustomed to living side by side in this small southern town—had almost no problems with their children attending integrated schools. But when the national media showcased Hoxie's successful integration, segregationists from Little Rock came to the town and mobilized some of the white residents to fight against integration. The resulting turmoil led to the resegregation of Hoxie's schools.

In the face of the kind of organized resistance that destroyed integration efforts in places like Hoxie, local officials were reluctant to implement the *Brown* decision. The national government did little to enforce integration. Even the Supreme Court delayed its decision on implementation for a full year and then simply called for the process to begin "with all deliberate speed" but specified no timetable. Political leaders did not come forward to work on the task, leaving sympathetic educators and eager black Americans with no support.

President Eisenhower expressed neither "approbation nor disapproval" of the *Brown* decision. Instead of calling for immediate desegregation, he said, "I don't think you can change the hearts of men with laws or decisions." Eisenhower remarked that "the Supreme Court decisions set back progress in the South at least fifteen years. . . . The fellow who tries to tell me that you can do these things by force is just plain nuts."

In 1955, the year after the *Brown* decision, several white Mississippians murdered 14-year-old Emmett Till for allegedly whistling at a white woman. The boy had come from Chicago to Mississippi, where he was visiting relatives. His mutilated body was found in the Tallahatchie River. Although Till's killers confessed to the murder, an all-white jury found them not guilty.

CORBIS

▲ **Teacher Marjorie Beach with an integrated kindergarten class in Washington, D.C., as the school year began in September 1954 following the Supreme Court's ruling in *Brown v. Board of Education* the previous spring.**

Eisenhower remained silent about Till's murder and the travesty of justice, even when E. Frederick Morrow, his one black adviser, beseeched him to condemn the lynching.

Eisenhower's hands-off policy emboldened southern segregationists to resist the Supreme Court's desegregation decision. When it became clear that the federal government would do nothing to enforce the ruling, white resistance spread across the South. State legislatures passed resolutions vowing to protect segregation, and most southern members of Congress signed the 1956 "Southern Manifesto" promising to oppose federal desegregation efforts.

A crisis at Central High School in Little Rock, Arkansas, finally forced Eisenhower to act. Under a federal district court's order to desegregate, school officials were prepared to comply and had carefully mobilized community support. But Arkansas Governor Orville Faubus, facing reelection, decided to play the race card. Using Central High's integration plan as his target, he created a crisis by instructing National Guard troops to maintain "order" by blocking the entry of black students into the school.

Eisenhower initially refused to intervene in the crisis. Hoping for a compromise, he met with Faubus, who agreed to allow the school to integrate peacefully. But Faubus broke his word, withdrew the National Guard troops, and left Little Rock, leaving the black students unprotected. On September 23, 1957, as nine black students attempted to enter Central High, a huge crowd of angry whites surrounded them. With international news cameras broadcasting pictures of the shrieking and menacing mob, Eisenhower took action to stop the embarrassing fracas. Furious at Faubus for his insubordination, Eisenhower denounced the "disgraceful occurrence," federalized the Arkansas National Guard, and sent 1,000 paratroopers to Little Rock. Unwilling to "acquiesce in anarchy and the dissolution of the union," Eisenhower acted to maintain federal authority. Although the Little Rock Nine, as the courageous students came to be called, finally gained entry to Central High, Governor Faubus closed the schools in Little Rock for the entire next year. Out of 712 school districts that had desegregated after the *Brown* decision, only 49 remained desegregated by the end of Eisenhower's term. Most of the others reverted to segregation.

Boycotts and Sit-Ins

Under Jim Crow laws in the South, black passengers were required to sit in the back section of buses, leaving the front of the bus for whites. If the "white" section at the front of the bus filled up, black passengers were required to give up their seats for white passengers. On December 1, 1955, Rosa Parks and the black community of Montgomery, Alabama, were ready to take on the system. Parks, who worked as a seamstress, was a widely respected leader in Montgomery's black community, active in her church, and secretary of the local NAACP. On her way home from work that day, sitting in the first row of the "colored" section of the bus when the front of the bus filled with passengers, she refused to move when a white man demanded her seat. Parks was arrested, and black Montgomery sprang into action.

Literally overnight, the Montgomery bus boycott was born. E. D. Nixon, president of the Alabama NAACP and the head of the local chapter of the Brotherhood of Sleeping Car Porters, and Jo Ann Robinson, the leader of the local Women's Political Council (a black alternative to the segregated League of Women Voters), mobilized the boycott. They gathered with 50 community representatives that night at the Dexter Avenue Baptist Church to plan strategy. They mobilized other black churches to spread the word to their congregations on Sunday, and black-owned taxi companies geared up to take the place of buses. By Monday, all of black Montgomery had heard the news of the boycott. The buses that day were empty of black riders. For 381 days, more than 90 percent of Montgomery's black citizens sacrificed their comfort and convenience for the sake of their rights and dignity. As one elderly black woman replied when a white reporter offered her a ride as she walked to work, "No, my feets is tired but my soul is rested."

Martin Luther King Jr., pastor of the Dexter Avenue Baptist Church, was a newcomer to Montgomery when the bus boycott began. He embraced the opportunity to become the leader

▲ **MAP 25.1 MAJOR EVENTS OF THE AFRICAN AMERICAN CIVIL RIGHTS MOVEMENT, 1953–1963**
Most of the major events of the early stages of the black freedom struggle took place in the South. Black southerners formed the backbone of the movement, but the grassroots protest movement drew participants from all regions of the country, all racial and ethnic groups, cities and rural areas, churches and universities, old and young, lawyers and sharecroppers.

of the boycott and, eventually, the most powerful spokesperson for the civil rights movement. His stirring and impassioned words inspired thousands of black citizens to join the cause. As he told the 5,000 listeners who gathered in his church on the first night of the boycott, "If you will protest courageously and yet with dignity and Christian love, in the history books that are written in future generations, historians will have to pause and say, 'there lived a great people—a black people—who injected a new meaning and dignity into the veins of civilization.' This is our challenge and our overwhelming responsibility."

The bus boycott ended a year later when the Supreme Court ruled that Montgomery's buses must integrate. The momentum generated by the boycott galvanized the civil rights movement. King and other leaders formed the Southern Christian Leadership Conference (SCLC), which united black ministers across the South in the cause of civil rights. The boycott tactic spread to other southern cities. As boycotts continued, a new strategy emerged: the **sit-in.**

On February 1, 1960, four African American students at North Carolina Agricultural and Technical College in Greensboro, inspired by the example of the bus boycott, entered the local Woolworth store and sat down at the lunch counter. When they were told, "We do not serve Negroes," they refused to leave, forcing the staff at Woolworth's to physically remove the nonviolent protesters. Undaunted, the students returned to the lunch counter the next day with 23 classmates. By the end of the week, more than a thousand students joined the protest. By this time, white gangs had gathered, waving Confederate flags and menacing the black undergraduates. But the students responded by waving American flags. An expression of their patriotism as well as their political shrewdness, the flag identified the protestors not as subversives acting against social order but as citizens claiming the values and identity of the nation.

In May 1961 members of the Congress of Racial Equality (CORE) organized the Freedom Rides, in which black and white civil rights workers attempted to ride two interstate buses from Washington, D.C., to New Orleans in an effort to challenge segregation at facilities used in interstate travel. Their journey began peacefully, but when they reached Rock Hill, South Carolina, a group of whites beat John Lewis, one of the young black riders, for entering a whites-only rest room. In Anniston, Alabama, a mob slashed the tires of one of the buses, threw a fire bomb through a window, and pummeled the riders with fists and pipes. After the brutal beatings, reinforcements from the Student Nonviolent Coordinating Committee (SNCC) arrived to continue the Freedom Rides. They persevered, facing beatings along the way until they reached Jackson, Mississippi, where they were immediately arrested and jailed for violating local Jim Crow laws. By August, 300 additional protesters had been locked in the jail, all refusing bail. The spirit and strength of the civil rights workers inspired many others to join them in the movement. They came from all over the South as well as the North, white as well as black, giving up comfort and safety, risking—and in some cases sacrificing—their lives.

The Eisenhower Years

Dwight D. Eisenhower, elected president in 1952, chose not to provide strong support for the civil rights movement. A respected and widely admired World War II general, Eisenhower could have used his leadership to bolster the cause. His reluctance to do so allowed southern segregationists to block implementation of the *Brown* decision and opened the way for violent resistance to the civil rights movement. His presidency was notable largely for moderation and maintaining the status quo, with very few major new initiatives and a style of leadership that rested more on his personal stature than his actions. Ike, as he was known, presided over the nation during a time of great prosperity, and his policies encouraged business expansion. However, the former general did try to stem the defense buildup. In his farewell address at the end of his second term as president, Eisenhower warned the nation against the growing power of the **military-industrial complex,** the term he coined to describe the armed forces and the politically powerful defense industries that supplied arms and equipment to them.

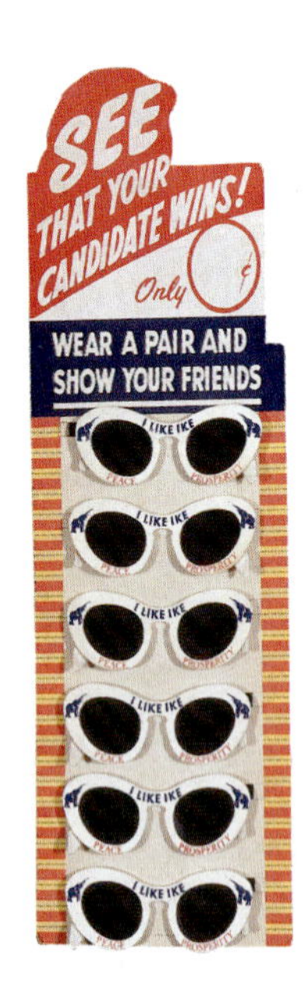

The Middle of the Road

Born in Texas, raised in Kansas, and educated at the U.S. Military Academy at West Point, Eisenhower became a career soldier who served as the supreme commander of the Allied forces in western Europe during World War II. Eisenhower planned and carried out the daring Allied invasion at Normandy on D-Day. As early as 1948, both the Democrats and the Republicans courted Eisenhower as a presidential candidate. But he resisted, believing that military leaders should not get involved in politics; indeed, he had never even registered to vote. In 1952, however, when he was president of Columbia University, he changed his mind and accepted the Republican nomination, choosing California Senator Richard M. Nixon—known as a dogged anticommunist crusader—as his running mate. The Democrats nominated Illinois Governor Adlai E. Stevenson. The cerebral Stevenson, dubbed an "egghead" by the press, was no match for the former general whose supporters donned campaign buttons boasting "I Like Ike." The popular Eisenhower won the election with the largest landslide up to that time and was reelected by an even wider margin in 1956.

As president, Eisenhower pursued a path down the middle of the road. His pro-business legislative agenda and appointments pleased conservatives, and he gratified liberals by extending many of the policies of the welfare state enacted during the New Deal. He agreed to the expansion of Social Security and unemployment compensation and an increase in the minimum wage. He also made concerted efforts to reduce defense spending, believing that continued massive military expenditures would hinder the nation's economic growth. In December 1953 Eisenhower announced the New Look, a streamlined military that relied less on expensive conventional ground forces and more on air power and advanced nuclear capabilities.

Eisenhower's plans to reduce defense spending derailed on October 4, 1957, when the Soviet Union launched *Sputnik,* the first artificial Earth satellite. Although *Sputnik* could not

The Texas-Louisiana Coast

The discovery of the Spindletop Oil Field near Beaumont, Texas, in 1901 helped transform the economies of coastal cities from lumbering, milling, and farming to centers of petroleum and petrochemical processing and shipping. Houston, the largest city in Texas, experienced explosive growth during the oil boom of the 1970s and 1980s. NASA's Manned Spacecraft Center was established in Clear Lake, 30 miles south of Houston, in 1961. Renamed in 1973 in honor of President Lyndon B. Johnson, the Center leads NASA's efforts in human space exploration.

In 1900, a deadly hurricane, described by the National Weather Service as "the deadliest natural disaster in American history," struck the city of Galveston, Texas, killing perhaps as many as 10,000 people. More recently, chemicals from nearby refineries and spills from oil rigs in the Gulf of Mexico have severely polluted some coastal regions.

In 2000, the Great Texas Coastal Birding Trail was completed, running along the coast for 500 miles from the Louisiana border to Mexico. More than 300 bird species can be observed from 310 wildlife viewing sites near major roads and highways. ■

AP/Wide World

▲ American popular culture reflected the playful part of the Cold War, poking fun at the competition between the superpowers, Here a customer in an Atlanta, Georgia, restaurant eagerly anticipates her first bite of a "Sputnikburger," complete with a large satellite olive pierced with three toothpicks for antennae, and topped with a miniature cocktail hotdog.

be seen with the naked eye—it was only 22 inches in diameter and weighed only 184 pounds—it emitted a beeping noise that was broadcast by commercial radio stations in the United States, making its presence very real and causing near hysteria among the public. The Soviet's launching of *Sputnik II* a month later seemed to confirm widespread fears that the United States was behind in the space race and, more significantly, in the arms race. Eisenhower's popularity in the polls suddenly dropped 22 points.

Acquiescing to his critics, the president allotted increased funds for military, scientific, and educational spending. The National Aeronautics and Space Administration (NASA), which developed the program of space exploration, was one result of this increase. But Eisenhower believed that "the most critical problem of all" was the lack of American scientists and engineers. He proposed that the federal government subsidize additional science and math training for both teachers and students. He also called for an improvement in overall education so that the next generation would be "equipped to live in the age of intercontinental ballistic missiles." On September 2, 1958, Eisenhower signed Public Law 85-864, also known as the National Defense Education Act (NDEA), which authorized more than $1 billion in education spending.

"What's Good for General Motors..."

Eisenhower's secretary of defense, former head of General Motors Charles Wilson, made the memorable comment that "what's good for General Motors business is good for America." But not everyone agreed. Eisenhower's pro-business policies had a devastating impact on the nation's environment. Eisenhower promoted the passage of the Submerged Land Act, which removed from federal jurisdiction more than $40 billion worth of oil-rich offshore lands. Under the control of state governments, oil companies could—and did—gain access to them. The *New York Times* called the act "one of the greatest and surely the most unjustified give-away program" in the nation's history. The administration's willingness to allow businesses to expand with little regulation, and with virtually no concern for the environment, contributed to increasing pollution of the air, water, and land during the 1950s and helped spark the environmental movement of the 1960s and 1970s.

DOCUMENT

National Defense Education Act

Eisenhower also supported the Federal-Aid Highway Act of 1956, inspired in part by Cold War concerns. An interstate highway system could allow the swift movement of military supplies and, presumably, the evacuation of urban centers in the event of a nuclear attack. The Highway Act had its greatest impact on business and transportation, however. As the largest public works project the nation had ever mounted, this centrally planned transportation system was a boon to the auto, trucking, oil, concrete, and tire industries. In addition, it contributed to the national pastime of family road vacations and tourism. Cheap gas also fueled America's car culture. Cars gave Americans increased mobility, and enabled suburban dwellers to drive to work in the cities. But reliance on the automobile doomed the nation's passenger train system and led to the decline of public transportation. Cars also contributed to suburban sprawl, air pollution, and traffic jams.

Eisenhower's Foreign Policy

The New Look, while containing military spending, also shifted American military priorities from reliance on conventional weapons to nuclear deterrence and covert operations. During Eisenhower's presidency, the United States and the Soviet Union both solidified their separate alliances. The North Atlantic Treaty Organization (NATO), formed in 1949, increased American influence in western Europe. The 12 NATO nations agreed that an attack on any one of them would be considered an attack on all, and they maintained a force to defend the West against a possible Soviet invasion. NATO expanded in 1952 to include Greece and Turkey, and West Germany joined in 1955. The Soviet Union formed a similar alliance, the Warsaw Pact, with the countries of eastern Europe. Confrontations between the United States and the Soviet Union over the fate of Europe gave way to more subtle maneuvers regarding the Third World—a term originally referring to **unaligned nations** in the Middle East, Africa, Asia, and Latin America.

When Joseph Stalin died in 1953, Nikita Khrushchev became the new leader of the Soviet Union and called for peaceful coexistence with the United States. To limit military expenditures and improve relations, the superpowers arranged high-level summit meetings. In 1955 delegates from the United States, the Soviet Union, Britain, and France met in Geneva. Although the meeting achieved little of substance, it set a tone of cooperation. In 1959 Khrushchev came to the United States, met with Eisenhower, and toured the country. Despite the Soviet downing of an American U-2 spy plane in 1960 and the capture of American pilot Gary Powers, the superpowers began to discuss arms limitation. Both countries agreed to limit aboveground testing of nuclear weapons in light of the health and environmental risks such tests posed.

In April 1955 in Bandung, Indonesia, representatives from 29 nations—primarily from Asia, Africa, and the Middle East—met in what President Sukarno of Indonesia called "the first international conference of colored peoples in the history of mankind."

As the United States and the Soviet Union worked toward greater cooperation, they faced challenges from within their separate "spheres of influence" and vied for the loyalty of newly independent states in the Third World. In 1956 the Soviet Union faced armed uprisings in Poland and Hungary, two "satellite" nations chafing under Soviet domination. In Poland, rebels resisting Moscow's control took to the streets, demanding that the Soviet Union recognize Wladyslaw Gomulka, who had been an opponent of Stalin, as the leader of Poland. After three days of fighting, the Soviet Union capitulated to the rebels' demand. In Hungary, maverick communist Imre Nagy took power and pledged to create a multiparty democracy. As revolution spread across Hungary, Soviet troops brutally crushed the rebellion, killing Nagy and thousands of other Hungarians.

While the United States and the Soviet Union competed with each other to gain influence in Third World countries, leaders from those countries came together to discuss ways to achieve self-determination. In April 1955 in Bandung, Indonesia, representatives from 29 nations—primarily from Asia, Africa, and the Middle East—met in what President Sukarno of Indonesia called "the first international conference of colored peoples in the history of mankind." Nearly all the participants came from countries that had previously been colonized by western European countries. Most were former colonies of Britain, France, Belgium, Holland, or Portugal. Although they shared no specific political ideology, the conference carried an implicit condemnation of Western powers and a commitment to eliminating the vestiges of colonialism and racial discrimination worldwide. Suspicious of the motives of the participants and worried about the outcome, Eisenhower sent no greeting to the gathering and tried to ignore or sabotage it. However, Adam Clayton Powell, one of three black members of the U.S. Congress, attended the conference as a "journalist," providing an unofficial U.S. presence.

The Eisenhower administration continued to distrust countries that maintained neutrality in the Cold War, fearing that those not aligned with the United States might turn to

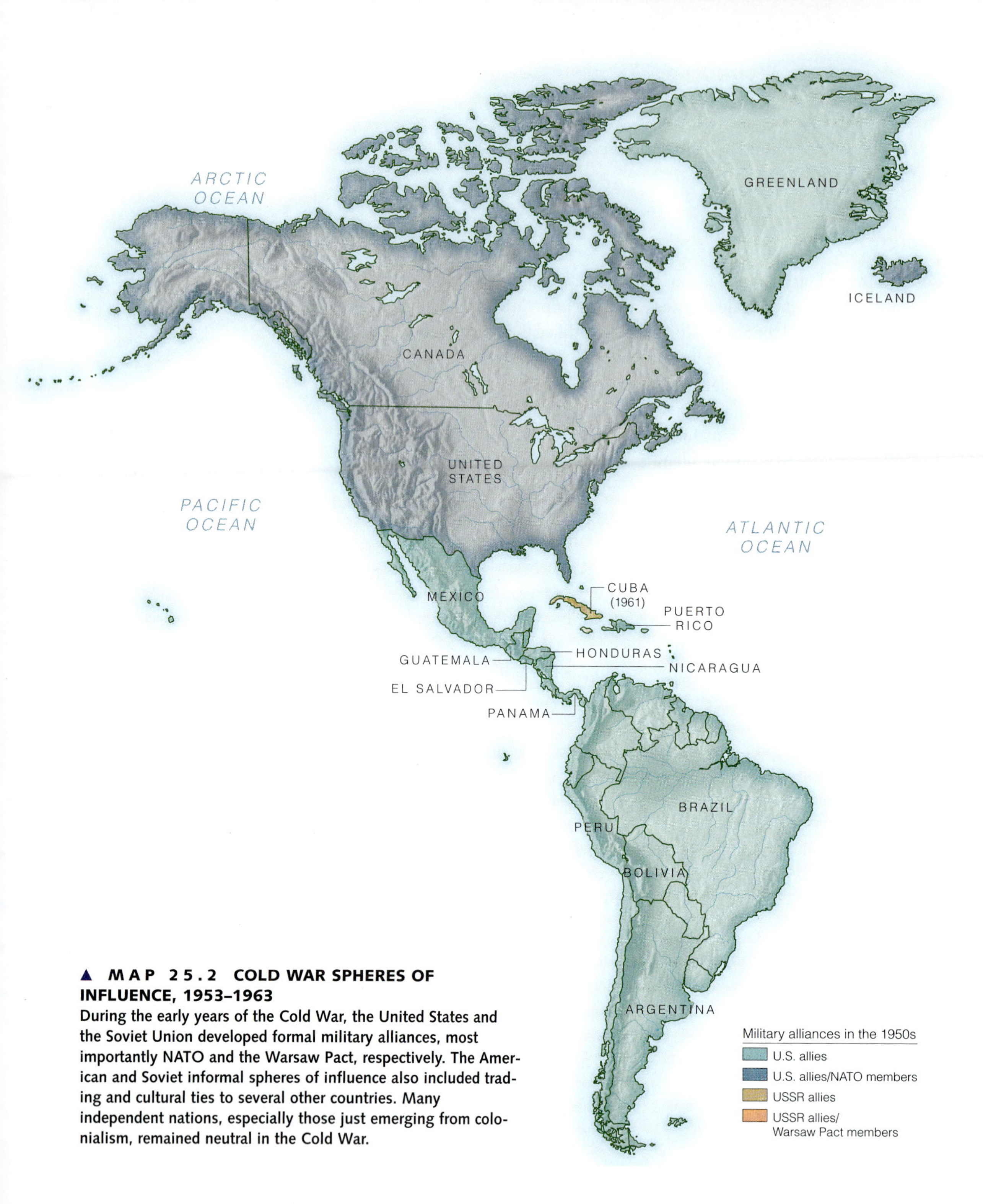

▲ MAP 25.2 COLD WAR SPHERES OF INFLUENCE, 1953–1963
During the early years of the Cold War, the United States and the Soviet Union developed formal military alliances, most importantly NATO and the Warsaw Pact, respectively. The American and Soviet informal spheres of influence also included trading and cultural ties to several other countries. Many independent nations, especially those just emerging from colonialism, remained neutral in the Cold War.

communism and become allies of the Soviet Union. In 1956 Secretary of State John Foster Dulles declared that neutrality "is an immoral and shortsighted conception." Anticommunism became the guiding principle behind nearly all U.S. foreign policy, taking precedence over other American ideals, such as support for democratically elected governments and national self-determination. Acting on its anticommunist priority, the United States helped overthrow democratically elected leaders and prop up corrupt and often brutal dictatorships.

The Central Intelligence Agency (CIA) was a major player in this drama, with 15,000 agents working around the world by the end of the 1950s. Congress established the CIA in 1947 to gather strategic intelligence from foreign countries and to engage in covert political activity. Through

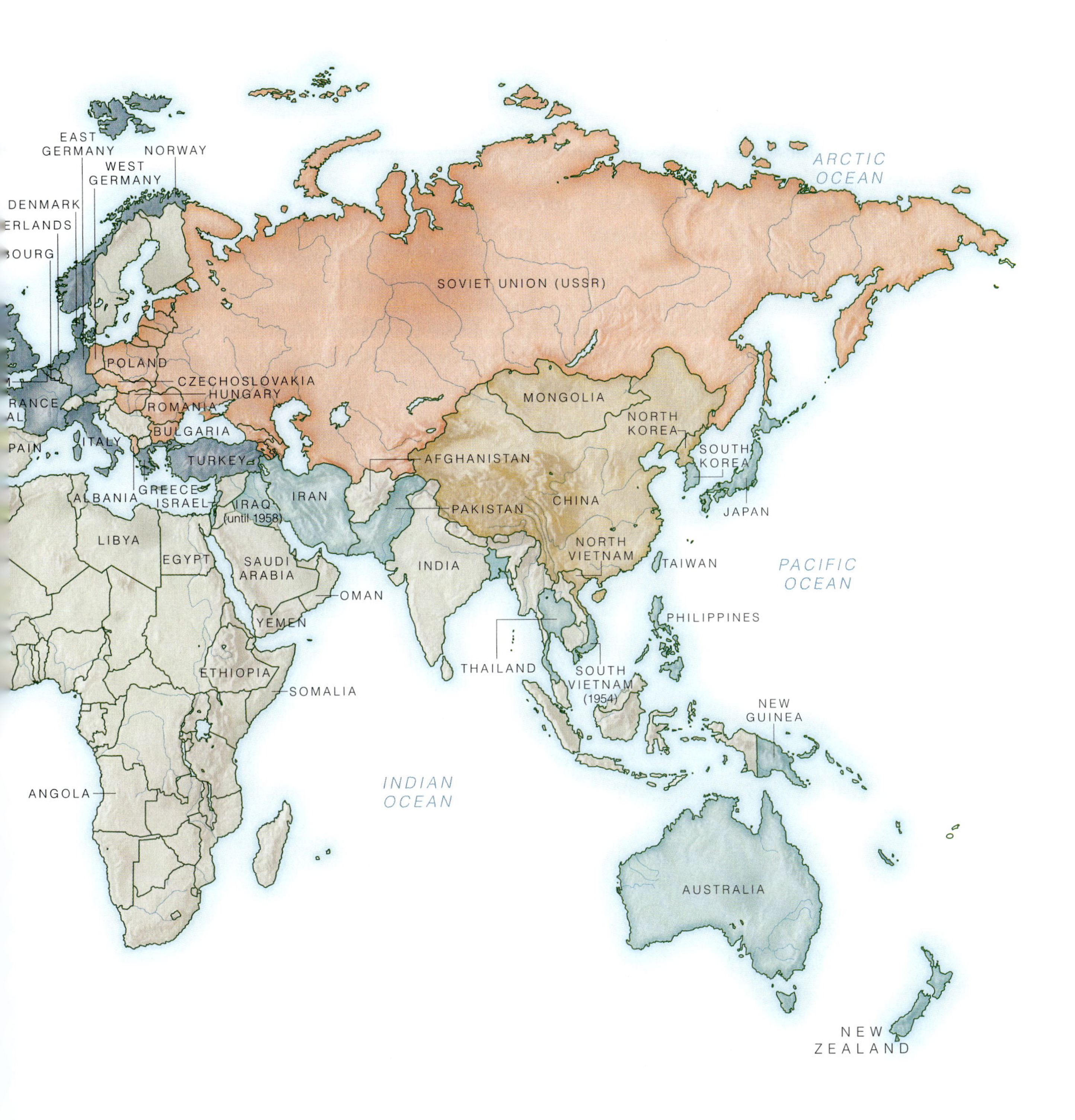

covert operations, the CIA helped overthrow the elected government in Iran—which had seized control of Western-owned oil fields in the country—and restore the dictatorship of Shah Reza Pahlavi, whose unpopular Western-leaning regime was finally overthrown by Muslim fundamentalists in 1979. In 1954 the CIA helped overthrow the elected government of Jacobo Arbenz in Guatemala. U.S. officials considered Arbenz a communist because he sought to nationalize and redistribute large tracts of land, much of it owned by the Boston-based United Fruit Company. Eisenhower also supported unpopular anticommunist dictators in Peru and Venezuela. In 1958 Latin Americans expressed their displeasure when Vice President Richard M. Nixon, on a good will tour of South America, faced angry protesters wherever he went. Nixon was nearly killed in Caracas, Venezuela, when demonstrators attacked his motorcade.

In 1959 revolutionary leader Fidel Castro overthrew Cuba's U.S.-friendly dictator Fulgencio Batista. Castro established a regime in Cuba based on principles of socialism. His government took control of foreign-owned companies, including many owned by Americans. Castro's socialist policies alarmed U.S. officials and investors in Cuba. Eisenhower's hostility encouraged Castro to forge an alliance with the Soviet Union. The CIA then launched a plot to overthrow Castro, which would culminate in an ill-fated invasion in 1961. In 1960–1961, the CIA also helped orchestrate the overthrow and assassination of charismatic left-leaning Patrice Lumumba, the first minister of the Republic of the Congo, soon after its independence from Belgium.

U.S. policymakers, with their anticommunist preoccupations, and people in Third World countries, with their campaigns against colonialism and racism, had little interest in each other's priorities. A case in point was Egypt, where in 1952 Gamal Abdul Nasser overthrew the corrupt monarchy of King Farouk and established a government neutral in the Cold War. In 1954 Nasser declared himself prime minister of the new government and accepted aid from both the United States and the Soviet Union. When Nasser engaged in trade with Soviet-bloc countries and extended diplomatic recognition to communist China, the United States canceled loans that were to support the building of the huge Aswan Dam, a major development project for the Egyptian economy. In response, Nasser nationalized the British-controlled Suez Canal in 1956, arguing that canal tolls would provide alternative funding for the dam. The British government, with the help of France and Israel, launched an attack against Egypt to regain control of the canal.

Although he distrusted Nasser, Eisenhower strongly criticized Britain for its effort to retain its imperial position in the Middle East. To avoid further antagonizing Nasser and other Third World leaders, Eisenhower denounced Britain's Suez attack and threatened economic sanctions, forcing the British to back down. Although leaders in Africa and Asia applauded Eisenhower's actions, the episode weakened U.S. relations with Nasser, who forged ties with the Soviet Union. Eisenhower now feared that "Nasserism" might spread throughout the Middle East.

In the spring of 1957, Congress approved the Eisenhower Doctrine, a pledge to defend Middle Eastern countries "against overt armed aggression from any nation controlled by international communism." However, U.S. policymakers rarely distinguished between nationalist movements and designs by "international communism," which they defined as Soviet aggression. Because American leaders believed that struggles for national self-determination in Third World countries were inspired and supported by the Soviet Union, they used the Eisenhower Doctrine to provide justification for U.S. military intervention to support pro-Western governments. When leaders in Lebanon and Jordan appeared friendly to Nasser, Eisenhower stepped in, sending 14,000 U.S. marines to Lebanon and setting up an anti-Nasser government there. Britain intervened in Jordan, restoring King Hussein to the throne.

CORBIS/Sygma

▲ Jackson Pollock shocked the art world when he began dripping paint on large canvasses. Abstract expressionist painters like Pollock celebrated their break from conventional forms and representations. National leaders embraced abstract expressionism as symbolic of American artistic freedom, and thousands of Americans hung reproductions of abstract art on the walls of their suburban homes.

Outsiders and Opposition

The 1950s often are remembered as a time of political and cultural complacency among white Americans, with most of the opposition to the nation's institutions emanating from people of color. There is a good deal of truth to this picture. But some young whites, in the South as well as North, joined in the struggle for civil rights; their numbers increased in the 1960s. Others were drawn to the music and dance of black America, especially the fusion of rhythm-and-blues with country-and-western, which took the form of early rock 'n' roll. Distinct forms of protest also emerged from within the white middle class: the rebellion of the Beats who rejected staid conformity, the stirrings of discontent among women, and the antinuclear and environmental movements. The arts also reflected a rejection of mainstream values, as Jackson Pollock and other abstract expressionist painters challenged the artistic conventions of the time and shifted the center of the art world from Paris to New York. Even the sexual revolution of the 1960s had its roots in the widespread defiance of the rigid sexual codes of the 1950s.

Youth, Sex, and Rock 'n' Roll

One clue that all was not tranquil in America was the widespread panic that the nation's young were out of control. Adult authorities worried about an epidemic of juvenile delinquency, blaming everything from parents to comic books. New celebrities such as movie stars Marlon Brando and James Dean portrayed misunderstood youth in rebellion against a corrupt and uncaring adult world. In the classic youth movie *Rebel Without A Cause,* Dean played a good-hearted but angry young man who suffers from a domineering mother and a wimpish apron-clad father who refuses to stand up to her. When asked, "What are you rebelling against, Johnny?" Brando's tough-guy character in *The Wild One* answers, "I dunno; what've you got?" In these films, and in J. D. Salinger's novel *Catcher in the Rye,* young women and men strain against the authority and expectations of their parents and the adult world, dreaming of freedom and personal fulfillment.

Sexual mores were rigid in the 1950s—and were widely violated. Single young women who became pregnant faced disgrace and ostracism unless they married quickly, which many did. Abortion, which had been illegal since the late nineteenth century but tacitly accepted until after World War II, became increasingly difficult to obtain, with hospitals placing new restrictions on legal therapeutic abortions. Illegal abortionists who had long practiced without interference faced increasing harassment, forcing the practice underground, where it became much more dangerous. A double standard encouraged men to pursue sexual conquest as a mark of manhood and virility but tarnished the reputation of women who engaged in sexual intercourse prior to marriage.

In many ways, the youth of the 1950s were already undermining the constraints that toppled in the next decade. Nowhere is this development more obvious than in the explosion of rock 'n' roll, with its roots in African American rhythm-and-blues, its raw sexuality, and its jubilant rebelliousness. Chuck Berry's hit "School Days" expressed youthful restlessness, and Little Richard's "Long Tall Sally" and "Rip It Up" exulted in sensual pleasure. Bill Haley and his Comets invited youngsters to "Rock Around the Clock."

Rock 'n' roll emerged out of the fusion of musical traditions. Artists from many ethnic backgrounds experimented with a variety of forms. Jewish songwriters Jerry Leiber and Mike Stoller wrote dozens of songs for black artists, including "Hound Dog" for black blues singer Willie Mae Thornton, later recorded by white Southerner Elvis Presley. The first Mexican American rock 'n' roll star, Ritchie Valens,

Social Welfare History Archives, University of Minnesota Libraries, American Social Health Association Records, box 179

▲ **Since sex was rarely discussed in most middle-class families, many parents relied on schools to provide elementary sex education, and a generation of suburban children learned the facts of life from nervous teachers and a variety of simplified texts.**

Photofest

▲ In *The Wild One* (1954), Marlon Brando portrayed a young man angry at the world. The young actor from Omaha, Nebraska, had already earned acclaim on Broadway. Two decades later he won an Oscar playing the title role in *The Godfather* (1972).

sang romantic ballads such as "Donna" along with jazzed-up versions of Mexican folk songs like "La Bamba." Rosie and the Originals—an all-girl band led by Mexican American Rosie Mendez—sang rock 'n' roll hits such as "Angel Baby."

Performances as well as lyrics carried erotic power. Chuck Berry pumped his electric guitar and shimmied across the stage, Little Richard danced on top of the piano and tore off his shirt, and James Brown begged "Please, please, please," while collapsing on the floor. Elvis Presley thrust his hips in his trademark style, sending young audiences into a frenzy. Criticism of his sexually charged gyrations persuaded producers to show him only above the waist during his appearance on Ed Sullivan's TV show. Rock 'n' roll music and dancing added powerful elements of sexuality and rebellion to the youth culture of the 1950s. Many of those impulses found political expression in the 1960s.

Rebellious Men

Men, too, were in revolt. According to widely read sociological tracts of the time, including William Whyte's *The Organization Man,* C. Wright Mills's *White Collar,* and David Riesman's *The Lonely Crowd,* middle-class men were forced into boring, routinized jobs, groomed to be "outer-directed" at the expense of their inner lives, and saddled with the overwhelming burden of providing for ever growing families with insatiable consumer desires.

A few highly visible American men provided alternative visions. Hugh Hefner built his Playboy empire by offering men the trappings of the "good life" without its burdensome responsibilities. The Playboy ethic encouraged men to enjoy the sexual pleasures of attractive women without the chains of marriage and to pursue the rewards of consumerism in well-appointed "bachelor flats" rather than appliance-laden homes. *Playboy* magazine celebrated this lifestyle, epitomized in the airbrushed photographs of nearly nude, young, female "bunnies" who seemed to promise sex without commitment.

Beat poets, writers, and artists offered a very different type of escape. In their literary works, such as Allen Ginsberg's poem *Howl* and Jack Kerouac's epic *On the Road,* and in their highly publicized lives, the Beats celebrated freedom from conformity, eccentric artistic expression, playful obscenity, experimentation with drugs, open homosexuality, and male bonding. While eschewing the sort of luxurious consumerism Hefner extolled, the Beats shared with the Playboy ethic a vision of male rebellion against conformity and responsibility. The mainstream men who indulged in these fantasies were more likely to enjoy them vicariously than to bolt from the breadwinner role. The dads who were honored on the new consumer holiday of Father's Day far outnumbered the freewheeling Beats and bachelors.

Mobilizing for Peace and the Environment

Some women did not wait for the new feminist movement to make their voices heard. Marine biologist Rachel Carson was one such woman. She wrote several books and articles, including her 1951 best-seller *The Sea Around Us.* Carson became increasingly concerned about the impact of manufactured chemicals on the environment, especially the insecticide DDT, which had been poisoning the earth since World War II. Her 1962 book, *Silent Spring,* brought attention to the worldwide problem of pesticide poisoning and helped launch the environmental movement that has flourished ever since.

Women also led the movement to stop the testing and proliferation of nuclear weapons. On November 1, 1961, 50,000 suburban women in more than 60 communities staged a protest,

Women Strike for Peace (WSP). Participants lobbied government officials to "End the Arms Race—Not the Human Race." The strikers were mostly educated, middle-class mothers; 61 percent did not work outside the home. WSP leaders were part of a small group of feminists who had worked on behalf of women's rights throughout the 1940s and 1950s. According to *Newsweek* magazine, the strikers "were perfectly ordinary looking women. . . . They looked like the women you would see driving ranch wagons, or shopping at the village market, or attending PTA meetings. . . . Many [were] wheeling baby buggies or strollers." Within a year their numbers grew to several hundred thousand. The FBI kept the group under surveillance, and in 1962 the leaders were called before the House Un-American Activities Committee (HUAC). Under questioning, these women spoke as mothers, claiming that saving American children from nuclear extinction was the essence of "Americanism." They brought their babies to the hearings and refused to be intimidated by their congressional inquisitors as supporters cheered and threw flowers from the gallery. These women carried the banner of motherhood into political activism, much as their nineteenth-century predecessors had done.

Decades later, the antinuclear protesters would be vindicated—unfortunately too late for many people exposed to radiation during the early years of the Cold War. At the time, the real dangers of nuclear testing had not yet come to light. But in the 1980s and 1990s, declassified top-secret documents confirmed that people living in the path of fallout from nuclear test sites, as well as military personnel working at or near the sites during the 1940s and 1950s, suffered disproportionately from cancer and other illnesses caused by radioactivity.

▲ **On November 1, 1961, 50,000 women in communities across the country took to the streets to protest nuclear testing. Under the sponsorship of Women Strike for Peace, these demonstrators used their authority as mothers, and brought along their children, to highlight their stake in the future.**

The Kennedy Era

John Fitzgerald Kennedy was the first American president born in the twentieth century and the first Catholic president. In his inaugural address, he claimed that "the torch has been passed to a new generation." It was a fitting metaphor for a young man who had been reared to compete and to win, whether the contest was athletic, intellectual, or political. But at the time of his election, it was not clear that a new generation had grabbed the torch. The young candidate was largely the creation of his father, Joseph, whose forebears had emigrated from Ireland during the 1840s. Joseph Kennedy rose to power and wealth as a financier, Hollywood executive, and ambassador to England. Ambitious and demanding, the elder Kennedy was known for his ruthlessness in business and politics and for his blatant philandering. He groomed his oldest son, Joseph P. Kennedy Jr., for greatness, specifically for the presidency. But when young Joe was killed in World War II, the father's ambitions settled on the next in line, John.

John (Jack) Kennedy became a hero during World War II, winning military honors for rescuing his crewmates on his patrol boat, PT-109, when it was rammed by a Japanese destroyer. The rescue left him with a painful back impairment and exacerbated the symptoms of Addison's disease, which plagued him all his life and necessitated daily cortisone injections. His father coached him to bear up under the pain, hide his infirmity, and project an image of health and vitality. "Vigor" was a word Kennedy used often and an aura he projected, inspiring a national craze for physical fitness that survives to this day. Young JFK also emulated his father's brash sexual promiscuity, even after his marriage to Jacqueline Bouvier in 1953.

In 1946 Kennedy won election to the House of Representatives, and in 1952 he defeated the incumbent Republican Henry Cabot Lodge to become the Democratic senator from Massachusetts. JFK's father financed all of his political campaigns, and in 1960 the elderly Kennedy bankrolled and masterminded JFK's narrowly successful run for the White House. Kennedy selected as his running mate the powerful Senate majority leader, Lyndon B. Johnson of Texas, whom he had battled for the nomination. Concerned that his Catholicism would be a liability

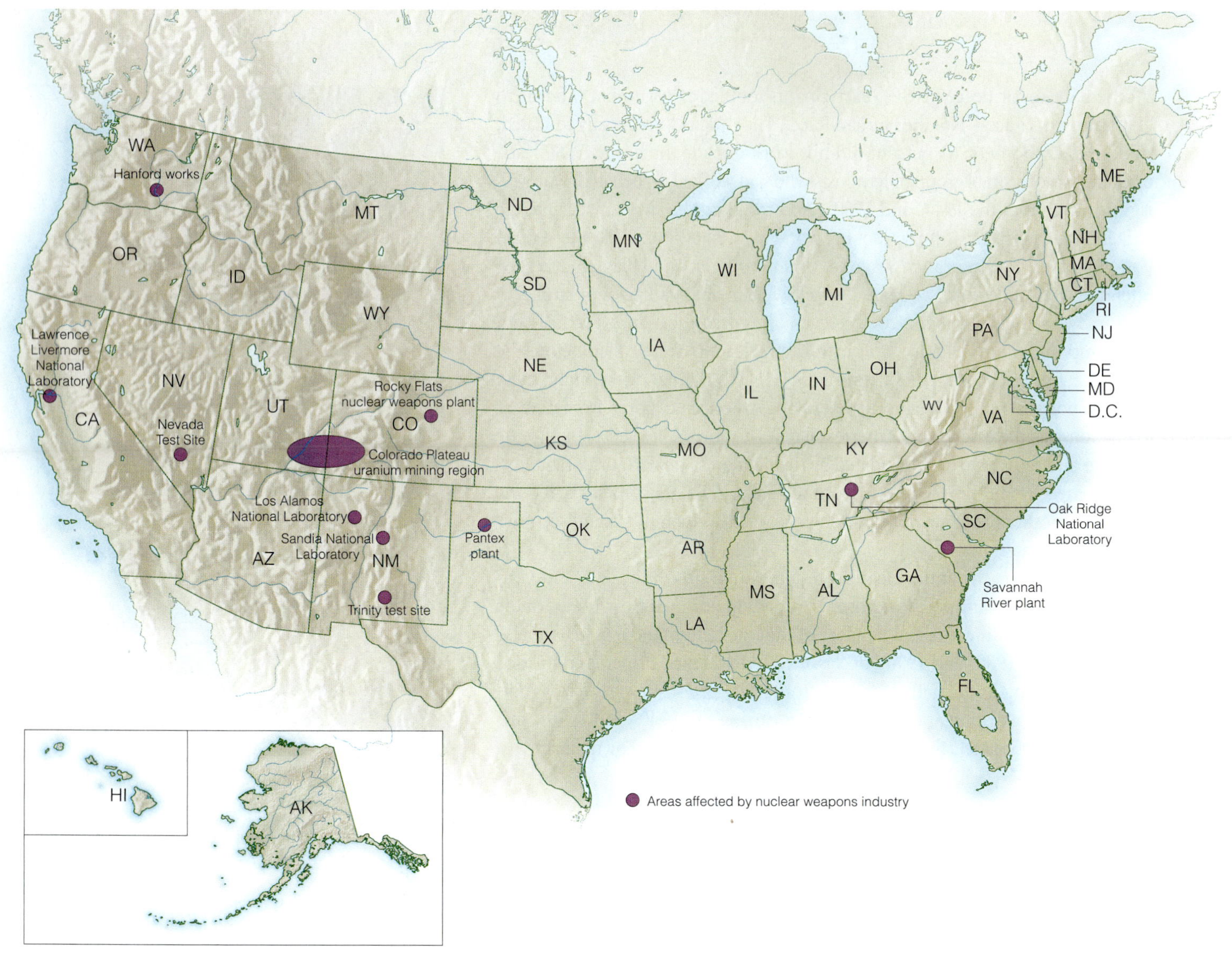

▲ **MAP 25.3 THE NUCLEAR LANDSCAPE**
The production and testing of nuclear weapons affected many regions across the country, especially in the West and South. Sites established during World War II remained active during the Cold War, as the nuclear arms race accelerated. The sites included testing grounds, uranium mining areas, laboratories, and plants where weapons were manufactured.

in the campaign, Kennedy spoke publicly about his faith, explaining that his religious beliefs would not interfere with his ability to do the job.

Just before the election, with the help of his brother Robert—whom he later appointed attorney general—Kennedy arranged to have Martin Luther King Jr. released from prison in Georgia, where hostile authorities had sentenced him to six months in jail for a minor traffic violation. This intervention secured the African American vote for Kennedy and the support of other minorities. Mexican Americans formed "Viva Kennedy" clubs throughout the Southwest. Voters of color helped Kennedy defeat his Republican foe, Eisenhower's vice president, Richard Nixon, by a slim margin.

Domestic Policy

With such a thin margin of victory, Kennedy lacked a popular mandate for change. But he quickly established himself as an eloquent leader. In his inaugural address, the new president inspired the nation with his memorable words, "And so, my fellow Americans, ask not what your country can do for you; ask what you can do for your country." Focusing his address on

Rachel Carson, *Silent Spring*

In 1962, Silent Spring, *Rachel Carson's eloquent exposé of the chemical industry's deadly impact on the health of the planet, landed on the best-seller list, where it stayed for months. The book, which eventually sold 1.5 million copies and remains in print today, galvanized the environmental movement of the 1960s and 1970s. Carson called the chemical industry "a child of the Second World War" and creator of "elixirs of death." She reported that annual pesticide production increased from 124 million pounds in 1947 to 637 million pounds by 1960. Twenty years later it had reached 2.4 billion pounds. "In the course of developing agents of chemical warfare," she noted, "some of the chemicals created in the laboratory were found to be lethal to insects. The discovery did not come by chance: insects were widely used to test chemicals as agents of death for man."*

Alfred Eisenstaedt/TimePix/Getty Images

Environmentalist Rachel Carson, author of *Silent Spring.*

It took hundreds of millions of years to produce the life that now inhabits the earth—eons of time in which that developing and evolving and diversifying life reached a state of adjustment and balance with its surroundings. The environment, rigorously shaping and directing the life it supported, contained elements that were hostile as well as supporting. Certain rocks gave out dangerous radiation; even within the light of the sun, from which all life draws its energy, there were short-wave radiations with power to injure. Given time—time not in years but in millennia—life adjusts, and a balance has been reached. For time is the essential ingredient; but in the modern world there is no time.

The rapidity of change and the speed with which new situations are created follow the impetuous and heedless pace of man rather than the deliberate pace of nature. Radiation is no longer merely the background radiation of rocks, the bombardment of cosmic rays, the ultraviolet of the sun that have existed before there was any life on earth; radiation is now the unnatural creation of man's tampering with the atom. The chemicals to which life is asked to make its adjustment are no longer merely the calcium and silica and copper and all the rest of the minerals washed out of the rocks and carried in rivers to the sea; they are the synthetic creations of man's inventive mind, brewed in his laboratories, and having no counterparts in nature.

To adjust to these chemicals would require time on the scale that is nature's; it would require not merely the years of a man's life but the life of generations. And even this, were it by some miracle possible, would be futile, for the new chemicals come from our laboratories in an endless stream; almost five hundred annually find their way into actual use in the United States alone. The figure is staggering and its implications are not easily grasped—500 new chemicals to which the bodies of men and animals are required somehow to adapt each year, chemicals totally outside the limits of biologic experience.

Among them are many that are used in man's war against nature. Since the mid-1940s over 200 basic chemicals have been created for use in killing insects, weeds, rodents, and other organisms described in the modern vernacular as "pests"; and they are sold under several thousand different brand names.

These sprays, dusts, and aerosols are now applied almost universally to farms, gardens, forests, and homes—nonselective chemicals that have the power to kill every insect, the "good" and the "bad," to still the song of the birds and the leaping of fish in the streams, to coat the leaves with a deadly film, and to linger on in the soil—all this though the intended target may be only a few weeds or insects. Can anyone believe it is possible to lay down such a barrage of poisons on the surface of the earth without making it unfit for all life? They should not be called "insecticides" but "biocides."

Questions

1. *What connection does Carson make between time and the environment?*
2. *Why does Carson believe insecticides should be called biocides?*

foreign policy, he declared: "Let every nation know...that we shall pay any price, bear any burden, meet any hardship, support any friend, oppose any foe to assure the survival and the success of liberty." In his first two years, he sought mainly to avoid division at home and to wage the Cold War forcefully abroad. He believed that prosperity was the best way to spread the fruits of affluence, rather than government programs that would promote a redistribution of wealth. Accordingly, he supported corporate tax cuts to stimulate the economy, which grew at a rate of 5 percent each year from 1961 to 1966.

Kennedy-Nixon Debate

Although Democrats held strong majorities in both houses, powerful southern conservatives often teamed up with Republicans to form a functional majority in Congress to defeat reform legislation. Kennedy knew that it would be futile to champion the cause of civil rights in the face of that alliance. But he did support issues important to his working-class constituents and proposed a number of legislative initiatives, including increasing the minimum wage, health care for the aged and increased Social Security benefits, and the creation of the Department of Housing and Urban Development (HUD).

When the steel industry challenged Kennedy's authority and threatened his economic policy by announcing a major price increase shortly after he had helped negotiate a new contract with the steel union that would have kept prices stable, he mobilized all the power of his administration to force the steel magnates to back down. Kennedy also demonstrated strong leadership in the space program, presiding over the first manned space flight and declaring that the United States would land a man on the moon by the end of the 1960s.

Foreign Policy

Kennedy was the first U.S. president to understand and recognize the legitimacy of movements for national self-determination in the Third World. In 1957, while still in the Senate, he gave a speech calling on the French to grant independence to Algeria, which was still under French rule. As president, he endeavored to support movements to end colonial rule while at the same time containing the spread of communism. His efforts earned him a great deal of goodwill among Africans and other non-Europeans. But if nationalist movements appeared friendly to the Soviet Union, Kennedy worked against them. He sharply increased military spending and nuclear arms buildup as a show of strength and preparedness against possible Soviet aggression.

John F. Kennedy, Space Program Speech

One of Kennedy's most popular initiatives was the creation of the Peace Corps, a program that sent Americans, especially young people, to nations around the world to work on development projects. In 1961 Kennedy signed the Charter of Punta del Este with several Latin American countries, establishing the Organization of American States (OAS) and the Alliance for Progress, a program designed to prevent the spread of anti-Americanism and communist insurgencies in Latin America. The alliance offered $20 billion in loans to OAS countries for democratic development initiatives.

Kennedy continued the strategies of Truman and Eisenhower to fight communism in South Vietnam by supporting the corrupt regime of Ngo Dinh Diem. But the National Liberation Front (NLF), founded in 1960 and supported by Ho Chi Minh's communist regime in North Vietnam, gained the upper hand in its struggle against Diem. In response, Kennedy increased the number of military advisers in South Vietnam from 800 to 17,000. By 1963 it was obvious that Diem's brutal regime was about to fall to the NLF, and Kennedy allowed U.S. military advisers and diplomats to encourage Diem's overthrow.

One of Kennedy's most popular initiatives was the creation of the Peace Corps, a program that sent Americans, especially young people, to nations around the world to work on development projects.

Kennedy also faced a crisis brewing in Cuba. Fidel Castro's revolution initially represented the sort of democratic insurgency that Kennedy wanted to support. But Castro's socialism turned the United States against him, and he established close ties with the Soviet Union. Kennedy now saw the strategically located island as a major threat where "communist influence...festers some 90 miles off the coast of Florida." During the Eisenhower administration, the CIA began planning an invasion of Cuba with the help of Cuban exiles in Florida. Kennedy's national security advisers persuaded Kennedy to allow the invasion to proceed.

On April 17, 1961, U.S.-backed and -trained anticommunist forces, most of them Cuban exiles, landed at the Bahia de Cochinas (Bay of Pigs) on the southern coast of Cuba. Castro expected the invasion—his agents in Florida had infiltrated the Cuban exiles—so his well-prepared troops quickly surrounded and captured the invaders. No domestic uprising against Castro occurred to support the invasion. Kennedy quickly realized that his only chance of success would be to call in the military with large-scale air support. Unwilling to take that step, Kennedy pulled back in humiliating defeat, telling his adviser Clark Clifford, "I have made a tragic mistake." Nevertheless, the president continued to support covert efforts that tried but failed to destabilize Cuba and assassinate Castro.

Another crisis soon erupted in Berlin. Located 200 miles deep in East Germany, with only two highways connecting it to West Germany, West Berlin was a showcase of Western material superiority and an espionage center for the Western powers. In June 1961, Khrushchev threatened to end the Western presence in Berlin and unite the city with the rest of East Germany. His plan was motivated in part to stop the steady stream of East Germans into West Berlin. Kennedy refused to relinquish West Berlin. On August 13, 1961, the East German government constructed a wall to separate East and West Berlin. Guards patrolled the wall with orders to shoot anyone who tried to cross, and many who tried lost their lives. Two years later, Kennedy stood in front of the wall and pledged to defend the West Berliners, making his memorable statement of solidarity, "*Ich bin ein Berliner*" ("I am a Berliner").

The most serious foreign policy crisis of Kennedy's presidency came in 1962, when the Soviet Union, at Castro's invitation, began to install intermediate-range nuclear missiles in Cuba. Kennedy's close advisers presented a series of options for actions that could be taken in response. The most dramatic and dangerous would be a full-scale military invasion of the island, which would topple Castro but would surely prompt military retaliation by the Soviet Union. Another option was a more limited military intervention, an air strike to destroy the missiles before they became operational. Others proposed a blockade of Cuban ports to prevent the missiles from entering. Another possibility was to negotiate secretly with Castro, Soviet leaders, or both. Kennedy decided against behind-the-scenes negotiations as well as the drastic move of military intervention and instead established a "quarantine" around the island to block Soviet ships from reaching Cuba, hoping that the Soviet Union would back down and withdraw the missiles. A quarantine, unlike a blockade, was not considered an act of war; nevertheless, Kennedy put the Strategic Air Command on full alert for possible nuclear war.

The Cuban Missile Crisis

"We will not prematurely or unnecessarily risk the costs of worldwide nuclear war in which even the fruits of victory would be ashes in our mouth, but neither will we shrink from that risk at any time it must be faced."

It was a risky move. On national television, Kennedy warned the Soviet Union to remove the missiles or face the military might of the United States: "We will not prematurely or unnecessarily risk the costs of worldwide nuclear war in which even the fruits of victory would be ashes in our mouth, but neither will we shrink from that risk at any time it must be faced." Khrushchev accused Kennedy of bringing the two nations to the brink of nuclear war. For the next five days, tensions mounted as Russian ships hovered in the water beyond the quarantine zone. Finally Khrushchev proposed an agreement, offering to remove the missiles if the United States would agree not to invade Cuba. Kennedy also privately promised to remove the Jupiter missiles in Turkey as soon as the crisis was over. The two leaders managed to diffuse the crisis, but they were both sobered by the experience of having come to the brink of nuclear war. They soon established a telephone "hotline" linking the White House and the Kremlin for quicker communication in any future crisis. In 1963 the two leaders signed a nuclear test ban treaty.

A Year of Turning Points

In 1963 the President's Commission on the Status of Women, which Kennedy had appointed under the leadership of Eleanor Roosevelt, published a report that documented widespread discrimination against women in jobs, pay, education, and the professions. In response to the findings, Kennedy issued a presidential order requiring the civil service to hire people "without regard to sex" and supported passage of the Equal Pay Act of 1963. The commission's report, along with the publication the same year of Betty Friedan's call to arms, *The Feminine Mystique,* provided fuel for the feminist movement that burst across the nation in the next few years.

Also in 1963, in Birmingham, Alabama, Martin Luther King Jr. led a silent and peaceful march through the city. Chief of Police Bull Connor unleashed the police, who blasted the demonstrators with fire hoses and attacked them with police dogs. Four black children were later killed when segregationists bombed an African American church. The Kennedy administration responded by bringing the full force of its authority to bear on the officials in Birmingham. But the crisis intensified. Alabama's segregationist governor, George Wallace, refused

Anticommunism

Throughout the twentieth century, American leaders have felt uneasy about revolutionary movements. On one hand, the United States was the great model of a successful anticolonial rebellion against a European colonial power. But on the other hand, the United States wanted to preserve order and stability in the world. The Russian Revolution of 1917 raised particular concerns because the victorious new communist regime denied Soviet citizens the essential democratic and economic principles that Americans cherished: free speech and elections, freedom of religious expression, private property, and capitalism. The United States officially refused to recognize the Soviet government from 1917 to 1933, as well as the People's Republic of China from 1949 until 1978 and Fidel Castro's Cuba from 1961 until today.

With these national principles and policies providing a foundation, anticommunism tapped widespread political and emotional passions within the United States. At times those passions, whipped up in moments of unsettling international or domestic events, led to extensive domestic repression of the very freedoms Americans have long cherished: free speech and political choice.

The first major wave of anticommunism in the United States came after World War I, in the wake of the founding of the American Communist party. The success of the Bolshevik revolution and the establishment of the Soviet Union energized a segment of socialists to form a Communist party in the United States in support of Soviet communism. The Red Scare of 1919–1920 was a wave of political repression that targeted not only communists but also left-leaning immigrants, radicals, and labor unions. Immigration officials rounded up thousands of foreign-born radicals and deported many, including the anarchist Emma Goldman. Many employers also used the rallying cry of anticommunism to break strikes and suppress unions. The Red Scare effectively silenced the Communist party and much of the left throughout the 1920s.

During the Great Depression of the 1930s, as fascism emerged in Europe, the Communist party attracted new members as well as thousands of liberal sympathizers. But enthusiasm for communism diminished in 1939 with the Nazi-Soviet pact and the communist opposition to Roosevelt's foreign policy. Anticommunist sentiment declined in 1941, when Hitler invaded Russia and the Soviet Union became an ally. The alliance was tense, however, as the United States vied with the Soviet Union over power in the postwar world.

The Cold War transformed anticommunism from a right-wing to a mainstream ideology and made it central to American politics and domestic culture. Because the United States vied with the Soviet Union for strategic power and territorial influence, the

to admit two black students to the University of Alabama, threatening to stand in the doorway to block their entrance.

Civil Rights March on Washington

Finally, on June 10, 1963, Kennedy federalized the Alabama National Guard and for the first time went before the American people to declare himself forcefully on the side of the civil rights protesters and to propose a civil rights bill. The violence in the South had raised "a moral issue," he declared, "as old as Scriptures and…as clear as the Constitution." A few months later, on August 28, more than 250,000 people gathered at the nation's capital in front of the Lincoln Memorial for the culmination of the March on Washington, a huge demonstration for jobs as well as freedom, where Martin Luther King Jr. delivered his inspiring "I Have a Dream" speech, which included these words:

> I say to you today, my friends, that in spite of the difficulties and frustrations of the moment, I still have a dream. It is a dream deeply rooted in the American dream.
>
> I have a dream that one day this nation will rise up and live out the true meaning of its creed: "We hold these truths to be self-evident: that all men are created equal."
>
> I have a dream that one day on the red hills of Georgia the sons of former slaves and the sons of former slave owners will be able to sit down together at a table of brotherhood. I have a dream that one day even the state of Mississippi, a desert state, sweltering with the heat of injustice and oppression, will be transformed into an oasis of freedom and justice. I have a dream that my four children will one day live in a nation where they will not be judged by the color of their skin but by the content of their character. . . . Let freedom ring from every hill and every molehill of Mississippi. From every mountainside, let freedom ring. When we let freedom ring, when we let it ring from every village and every hamlet, from every state and every city, we will

Communist party, with its links to the USSR, was considered a subversive organization. In 1947 the Truman administration barred from government jobs anyone associated with communists, and in 1949 the Justice Department prosecuted the 11 top leaders of the party for violation of the 1940 Smith Act, which made it illegal "to teach and advocate the overthrow and destruction of the United States government by force and violence." They were all convicted and sentenced to prison terms. Under the Smith Act, several hundred communists went to jail, while the House Un-American Activities Committee (HUAC) investigated suspected communist subversives. Hollywood became a primary target of anticommunism in the late 1940s and early 1950s, leading to the blacklisting of dozens of filmmakers and actors who refused to "name names" before HUAC.

Senator Joseph McCarthy and other zealots used anticommunism to further their own political ambitions at

Library of Congress

Anticommunist pamphlet published by the Catholic Library Service.

a time when Democrats were on the defensive for being allegedly "soft" on communism. Official anticommunism targeted not only members of left-wing political organizations but also gays, lesbians, and others who allegedly might be vulnerable to blackmail and therefore should not be allowed to work in government offices. The Federal Bureau of Investigation (FBI), under the leadership of J. Edgar Hoover, made anticommunism a high priority. The FBI targeted Martin Luther King Jr. and other civil rights activists who Hoover believed were communist agents seeking to destabilize American society. By the late 1950s the anticommunist hysteria had subsided, but it remained part of the political culture throughout the Cold War. During the 1980s, President Ronald Reagan revived anticommunist rhetoric when he called the Soviet Union the "evil empire." Today, anticommunist sentiments are still strong in south Florida, where many Cuban exiles and their children believe that the United States should continue to pursue a hard line against Fidel Castro's regime. This exile community, a potent voting bloc in a swing-state in presidential elections, has a large voice in local, state, and even national politics. ■

be able to speed up that day when all of God's children, black men and white men, Jews and Gentiles, Protestants and Catholics, will be able to join hands and sing in the words of the old Negro spiritual, "Free at last! Free at last! Thank God Almighty, we are free at last!"

In the fall of 1963, a confident Kennedy began planning his reelection campaign for the next year. To mobilize support he visited Texas. "Here we are in Dallas," he said on November 22, 1963, "and it looks like everything in Texas is going to be fine for us." Within an hour of uttering those optimistic words, the president lay dying of an assassin's bullet.

As shock and grief spread across the nation, a bizarre series of events confounded efforts to bring the assassin to justice. Police arrested Lee Harvey Oswald, who had previously lived in the Soviet Union and who had loose ties to organized crime. Oswald claimed that he was innocent. But before he could be brought to trial, Oswald himself was murdered. Jack Ruby, a nightclub owner who also had links to organized crime, shot Oswald while he was in the custody of the Dallas police—an event witnessed by millions on live television. Ruby later died in prison. The newly sworn-in president, Lyndon B. Johnson, appointed a commission to investigate the assassination under the leadership of Supreme Court Chief Justice Earl Warren. The Warren Commission eventually issued a report concluding that Oswald and Ruby had both acted alone. The commission findings created a heated controversy. Many people at the time and since believed that there was evidence of a conspiracy. In 1978 a panel of the House of Representatives suggested that Kennedy may have been the victim of a plot, possibly involving the Mafia. Conspiracy theories continue to circulate to this day, finding expression in dozens of books, articles, and motion pictures.

Conclusion

During the years between the election of Dwight D. Eisenhower and the assassination of John F. Kennedy, the nation experienced unprecedented prosperity as increasing numbers of Americans moved into middle-class suburbs and enjoyed the fruits of a rapidly expanding consumer economy. Men and women rushed into marriage and childbearing, creating the baby boom and a powerful domestic ideology resting on distinct gender roles for women and men. At the same time, the Cold War set the tone for foreign policy as well as domestic life, fostering fears of nuclear war, intense anticommunism, and pressures to conform to mainstream political and cultural values.

Beneath the apparently tranquil surface, anxiety and discontent simmered. Some Americans began to resist the limitations and exclusions of the widely touted "American way of life." African Americans in the South demanded their rightful place as full citizens, challenging the Jim Crow system and accelerating the civil rights movement through nonviolent protests, boycotts, and sit-ins. Young people created a vibrant youth culture to the pulsating rhythms of rock 'n' roll. Beatniks, peace activists, and environmentalists expressed incipient political and cultural dissent.

President Dwight D. Eisenhower personified the politically moderate side of the 1950s. He promoted business interests but worried about the growth of the "military-industrial complex," and reluctantly supported the civil rights movement. John F. Kennedy's election in 1960 ushered in a new era of Cold War militance, tempered by caution in the face of the Cuban missile crisis. He also actively supported the civil rights movement at home and anticolonialism abroad. Kennedy inspired many young Americans to become involved in politics. His assassination in 1963 traumatized the nation. But by that time the rumblings of vast social change had already begun and would explode in the years ahead.

Sites to Visit

We Shall Overcome: Historic Places of the Civil Rights Movement

www.cr.nps.gov/NR/travel/civilrights/index.htm

This site of the National Register of Historic Places provides maps and information about the historic locations of the civil rights movement.

Dwight David Eisenhower

www.ipl.org/ref/POTUS/ddeisenhower.html

This site contains basic information about Eisenhower's election and presidency, and an online biography.

The Literature and Culture of the American 1950s

dept.english.upenn.edu/~afilreis/50s/home.html

This site by University of Pennsylvania Professor Al Filreis contains a large array of 1950s documents, literature, and images.

Levittown: Documents of an Ideal American Suburb

tigger.uic.edu/~pbhales/Levittown/

Peter Bacon Hales of the Art History Department at the University of Illinois at Chicago developed this website, which includes images, articles, and information about the post–World War II Levittown suburb.

Hollywood and the Movies During the 1950s

lib.berkeley.edu/MRC/50sbib.html

This site from the University of California at Berkeley libraries includes information about Hollywood during the 1950s, and links to related sites, such as the Hollywood blacklist and film noir.

Rock and Roll

www.rockhall.com/home/default.asp

This website of the Rock and Roll Hall of Fame and Museum includes information about the history and major artists of rock and roll.

Little Rock 1959: Pages from History—The Central High Crisis

www.ardemgaz.com/prev/central/

This site documents the events surrounding the effort to desegregate Central High in Little Rock, Arkansas, in 1959.

From *Plessy v. Ferguson* to *Brown v. Board of Education*: The Supreme Court Rules on School Desegregation

www.yale.edu/ynhti/curriculum/units/1982/3/82.03.06.x.html

This site includes information about the landmark Supreme Court decision compiled by the Yale–New Haven Teachers Institute.

Civil Rights Era

lcweb2.loc.gov/ammem/aaohtml/exhibit/aopart9.html

This Library of Congress site includes information about the people, events, and developments of the civil rights movement.

John F. Kennedy

www.ipl.org/ref/POTUS/jfkennedy.html

This site contains basic information about Kennedy's election and presidency, and an online biography.

For Further Reading

General

Taylor Branch, *Parting the Waters: America in the King Years, 1954–1963* (1988).

William H. Chafe, *The Unfinished Journey: America Since World War II* (1986).

Pete Daniel, *Lost Revolutions: The South in the 1950s* (2000).

Eric Foner, *The Story of American Freedom* (1998).

Godfrey Hodgson, *America In Our Time* (1976).

Cold War, Warm Hearth

Stephanie Coontz, *The Way We Never Were: American Families and the Nostalgia Trap* (1992).

Barbara Ehrenreich, *The Hearts of Men: American Dreams and the Flight from Commitment* (1984).

Ruth Feldstein, *Motherhood in Black and White: Race and Sex in American Liberalism, 1930–1965* (2000).

Kenneth T. Jackson, *Crabgrass Frontier: The Suburbanization of the United States* (1985).

George Katona, *The Mass Consumption Society* (1964).

Christina Klein, *Cold War Orientalism: Asia in the Middlebrow Imagination, 1945–1961* (2003).

Elaine Tyler May, *Homeward Bound: American Families in the Cold War Era* (1999).

The Civil Rights Movement

Clayborne Carson, *In Struggle: SNCC and the Black Awakening of the 1960s* (1981).

Jennifer Delton, *Making Minnesota Liberal: Civil Rights and the Transformation of the Democratic Party* (2002).

Mary Dudziak, *Cold War Civil Rights: Equality as Cold War Policy, 1946–1968* (2000).

Hugh Davis Graham, *The Civil Rights Era: Origins and Development of National Policy* (1990).

Steven F. Lawson, *Running for Freedom: Civil Rights and Black Politics in America Since 1941* (1990).

Harvard Sitkoff, *The Struggle for Black Equality, 1954–1992* (1993).

The Eisenhower Years

Stephen E. Ambrose, *Eisenhower* (1983–84).

Thomas Borstelmann, *The Cold War and the Color Line: Race Relations and American Foreign Policy Since 1945* (2001).

Robert F. Burk, *The Eisenhower Administration and Black Civil Rights* (1984).

Robert A Divine, *The Sputnik Challenge* (1993).

Peter B. Dow, *Schoolhouse Politics: Lessons from the Sputnik Era* (1991).

Dwight D. Eisenhower, *The White House Years: Waging Peace, 1956–1961* (1965).

Fred I. Greenstein, *The Hidden-Hand Presidency: Eisenhower as Leader* (1994).

Outsiders and Opposition

Wini Breines, *Young, White, and Miserable: Growing Up Female in the Fifties* (1994).

Paul Brooks, *The House of Life: Rachel Carson at Work* (1972).

Rachel Carson, *Silent Spring* (1962).

Betty Friedan, *The Feminine Mystique* (1963).

James Gilbert, *A Cycle of Outrage: America's Reaction to the Juvenile Delinquent in the 1950s* (1986).

Charlie Gillett, *Sound of the City: The Rise of Rock and Roll* (1983).

Serge Guilbaut, *How New York Stole the Idea of Modern Art* (1985).

Joyce Johnson, *Minor Characters: A Young Woman's Coming-of-Age in the Beat Orbit of Jack Kerouac* (1999).

Joanne Meyerowitz, ed., *Not June Cleaver: Women and Gender in Postwar America, 1945–1960* (1994).

Leslie Reagan, *When Abortion Was a Crime: Women, Medicine, and the Law in the United States, 1867–1973* (1997).

Rickie Solinger, *Wake Up Little Susie: Single Pregnancy and Race Before* Roe v. Wade (1992).

The Kennedy Era

Elizabeth Cobbs Hoffman, *All You Need Is Love: The Peace Corps and the Spirit of the 1960s* (1998).

Roger Hilsman, *To Move a Nation: The Politics of Foreign Policy in the Administration of John F. Kennedy* (1967).

Herbert S. Parmet, *J.F.K.: The Presidency of John F. Kennedy* (1983).

Arthur M. Schlesinger Jr., *A Thousand Days: John F. Kennedy in the White House* (1965).

CHAPTER 26

The Nation Divides: The Vietnam War and Social Conflict, 1964–1971

CHAPTER OUTLINE

Lyndon Johnson and the Apex of Liberalism

Into War in Vietnam

The Movement

The Conservative Response

Conclusion

Sites to Visit

For Further Reading

Paul Schutzer/TimePix/Getty Images

▲ The deployment of hundreds of thousands of American soldiers in Vietnam intimately affected life there, sometimes in terrible ways and sometimes in helpful ways.

THE SOFT-SPOKEN BLACK MAN WITH THE STRANGE ACCENT FIRST SHOWED UP IN THE small town of McComb, Mississippi, in the summer of 1961. Robert Parris Moses had come on a mission of democracy: he was there to encourage impoverished African Americans to register to vote. He had grown up in Harlem, attended Hamilton College in upstate New York on a scholarship, and done graduate work in philosophy at Harvard. Moses was teaching math at an elite private school in Manhattan when the student sit-in movement against segregation spread across the upper South in the spring of 1960. Deeply impressed by the courage and leadership of those young black southerners, he went south that summer to work with Martin Luther King Jr.'s Southern Christian Leadership Conference. The following spring, Moses returned to the South as a full-time organizer for the new Student Nonviolent Coordinating Committee (SNCC).

Encouraging citizens to vote in the leading nation of the "free world" was a subversive act in 1961, at least when the citizens had dark skin and lived in the southeastern states of the former Confederacy. Over the next four years in the Deep South, Bob Moses paid a price for his commitments. Local police imprisoned him, white supremacists beat him severely, and they murdered dozens of his fellow activists in the black freedom movement. But Moses remained committed to nonviolence and racial integration. His quiet courage became legendary in the movement. One summer night in 1962, he returned to a deserted SNCC office in Greenwood, Mississippi, that had just been ransacked by a white mob; three other SNCC workers had barely escaped with their lives. Moses looked around, made up a bed in the corner of the devastated main room, and went to sleep. He refused to be intimidated.

For all his distinctiveness, Moses did not promote himself as a charismatic leader. Like his comrades in SNCC, he did not believe in traditional, top-down leadership. The women and men in SNCC worked instead to get local black communities to organize themselves and to find their leadership among their own members. When others became too dependent on his guidance, Moses even dropped his biblical surname and became simply "Bob Parris" to reduce his public profile. Such rejection of hierarchy put SNCC at odds with other civil rights organizations and with the national Democratic party, which sought black support. By 1964 Moses and other freedom workers grew disillusioned with white liberal leadership, especially after the Democratic convention that August, where President Lyndon Johnson crushed the integrated Mississippi Freedom Democratic party's bid to replace the all-white regular Mississippi delegation. Two trips to Africa expanded Moses' sense of connection to the Third World, and he became increasingly involved with the growing movement against the U.S. war in Vietnam. The federal government responded by drafting him. Moses moved to Canada to avoid being inducted to fight a war he opposed, and then went to east Africa, where he and his wife taught school and raised a family in Tanzania for almost a decade. He returned to the United States only after President Jimmy Carter's general amnesty for draft resisters in 1977.

A leading spokesperson for the Black Muslims, Malcolm X converted to orthodox Islam and softened his antiwhite rhetoric in the two years before his murder in 1965. Like SNCC's Bob Moses, Malcolm increasingly identified with the Third World. Here he is shown in Egypt on a 1964 pilgrimage to Mecca, Saudi Arabia.

The trajectory of Bob Moses' life across these years suggests much about the 1960s. An extraordinary number of idealistic young people became involved in public life in an effort to make real their nation's abstract promises of freedom and justice. The civil rights movement inspired the social movements that followed: for ending the war, for preserving the environment, and for liberating women, Latinos, Indians, and gay men and lesbians. But organizing for change inevitably brought activists up against fierce resistance from what they called "the establishment." Disillusionment and radicalization often followed. Whereas Moses went to Africa, other young African Americans moved toward **black nationalism** at home, a proud cultural identity at odds with the pursuit of integration. Public life became deeply contentious by 1968 as young radicals challenged more conservative citizens on issues of race, war, and gender.

The escalating American war in Southeast Asia loomed over all. Lyndon Johnson brought the nation to its apex of liberal reform with his extensive Great Society legislation. His purpose was to complete and surpass the New Deal promise of his hero, Franklin Roosevelt. However, the high-flying hopes of Democratic liberals crashed to earth with the destructive war that the Johnson administration waged against seasoned communist revolutionaries in far-off Vietnam. Out of the wreckage of 1968 emerged a Republican president, Richard Nixon, and a growing conservative backlash against the social changes advocated by people of color, the counterculture, the antiwar movement, and the rising tide of women's liberation. By the beginning of the 1970s, American politics turned to the right, even as American culture generally remained more tolerant of different lifestyles and values than it had been before the 1960s. This libertarian combination of distrusting government while accepting greater cultural diversity has predominated in American life ever since.

The escalating American war in Southeast Asia loomed over all.

Lyndon Johnson and the Apex of Liberalism

Wealth provided the foundation on which the Great Society was built. American economic expansion since World War II had created history's richest nation by 1960. From 1961 to 1966, the economy accelerated at an annual growth rate of more than 5 percent with very low inflation, stimulated by large tax cuts and extensive military spending. The 41 percent increase in per capita income during the 1960s was not evenly distributed, however. Economist Paul Samuelson explained in 1970, "If we made an income pyramid out of a child's blocks, with each layer portraying $1000 of income, the peak would be far higher than the Eiffel Tower, but almost all of us would be within a yard of the ground." And the distribution of wealth (stocks and real estate) was far more skewed than that of income. U.S. policymakers believed that economic expansion would continue indefinitely and the nation could therefore afford government policies to improve the welfare of less affluent Americans.

The New President

Lyndon Baines Johnson was one of the most remarkable American characters of the twentieth century. Journalist David Halberstam called him "a man of stunning force, drive and intelligence, and of equally stunning insecurity"—both a giant among political leaders and a bully with those who worked for him. Johnson grew up in a family struggling to stay out of poverty in the Texas hill country west of Austin. He entered Democratic politics early as an avid supporter of Franklin Roosevelt and the New Deal, aided by the business savvy and loyalty of his wife, Lady Bird Johnson, who grew wealthy through ownership of TV and radio stations. As First Lady, she became widely known for her leadership in highway beautification. Lyndon Johnson rose like a rocket through Congress to become perhaps the most powerful Senate majority leader ever (1954–1960) and then vice president (1961–1963). Kennedy's assassination catapulted him into the Oval Office as the nation's first Texan president.

Lyndon Baines Johnson Library & Museum. Photo by Cecil Stoughton

Lyndon Johnson took the presidential oath of office on board Air Force One, returning to Washington from Dallas, where John Kennedy had just been assassinated on November 22, 1963. His wife, Lady Bird, is on his right, and Jacqueline Kennedy, still in blood-stained clothes, stands on his left. Johnson adroitly channeled the public outpouring of grief for the murdered young president into support for their shared legislative goals.

Like his home state, Johnson was physically big and at times intimidating. His earthy humor and homely style contrasted sharply with Kennedy's telegenic sophistication. Eastern elites cringed at the idea of Johnson as Kennedy's successor in the White House; the fact that Kennedy was killed in Texas did not help. But Johnson retained Kennedy's cabinet and advisers and used the memory of the fallen young president to rally support for his administration. Johnson turned out to be the more liberal of the two men in part because his early years in Texas had given him a visceral understanding of poverty and discrimination that his predecessor lacked. Johnson's focus was different, too. He retained Kennedy's anticommunist commitments abroad, but his heart remained at home. "I don't want to be the President who built empires, or sought grandeur, or extended dominion," he told the nation. He wanted to perfect American society: to enhance American security by refashioning the central nation of the "free world" into a model for all others.

First he had to win reelection because less than a year remained until voters went to the polls in 1964. The Republicans nominated right-wing Senator Barry Goldwater of Arizona, a sign of the party's sharp swing away from its moderate northeastern elements toward its fiercely conservative western and southern constituencies. Conservative organizers such as the Young Americans for Freedom considered such Republican leaders as Dwight Eisenhower and Richard Nixon too much like Democrats. Goldwater instead believed in unrestricted markets and a minimal role for the federal government in every aspect of American life except the military. He spoke casually about using nuclear weapons against communists abroad. Goldwater declared that "extremism in the defense of liberty is no vice," but Johnson zeroed in on that extremism and swept to the largest electoral majority of any president (61 percent). Voters also chose the most liberal Congress since the Great Depression. Few realized then that Goldwater, not Johnson, was the better indicator of where American politics would soon be heading.

The Great Society: Fighting Poverty and Discrimination

Johnson, "The War on Poverty"

In pursuit of what he called the Great Society, Johnson first declared a "War on Poverty." No citizen in the richest nation on earth should live in squalor, he believed. The president's sensitivity to this issue, despite his personal rise to wealth, fit with a growing national concern, stimulated

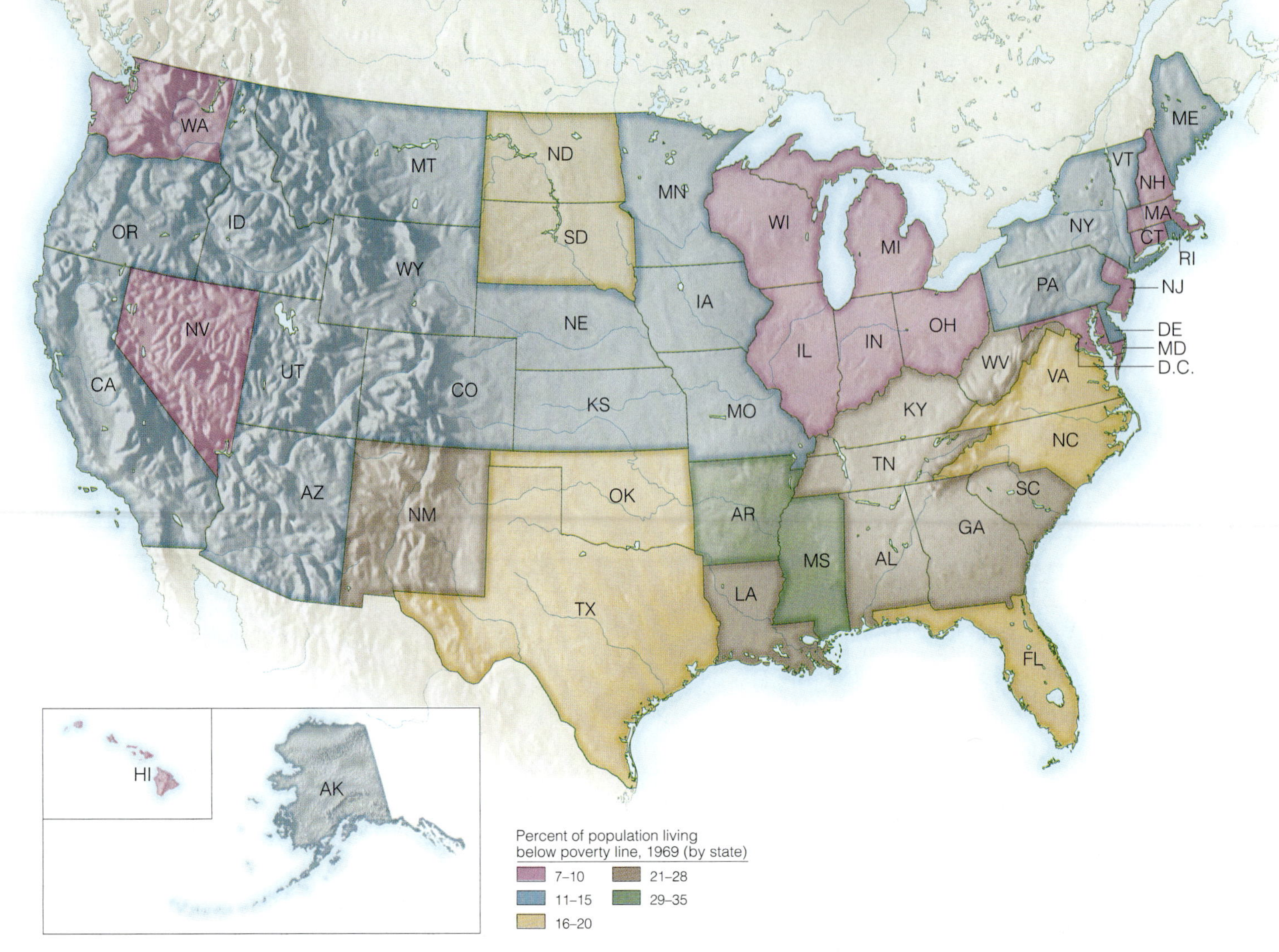

▲ **MAP 26.1 PERCENTAGE OF POPULATION LIVING BELOW THE POVERTY LINE, 1969 (BY STATE)**

The United States in the 1960s was a nation of unprecedented wealth and comfort. Yet millions of Americans still lived in poverty. Prodded by other reformers, President Johnson sought to reduce the number of impoverished citizens through the Great Society programs. The southeastern and south central states had the highest poverty rates, a legacy of slavery and limited industrialization.

in part by political activist Michael Harrington's widely read book *The Other Americans* (1962). The poor were everywhere, from decaying inner cities to rural areas such as Appalachia. More than one out of five Americans lived below the conservatively estimated official poverty line ($3,022 for a nonfarm family of four in 1960), and 70 percent of them were white.

The president and a large congressional majority passed several measures to alleviate poverty. They sharply increased the availability of money and food stamps through the Aid to Families with Dependent Children ("welfare") program, and they raised Social Security payments to older Americans. Several programs focused on improving educational opportunities as an avenue out of poverty: Head Start offered preschool education and meals for youngsters, the Elementary and Secondary Education Act sent federal funds to the least affluent school districts, and an expanded system of student loans facilitated access to college. The Job Corps provided employment training, and Volunteers in Service to America (VISTA) served as a domestic Peace Corps, funneling people with education and skills into poor communities to serve as teachers and providers of other social services.

How well did these programs work? Americans have debated this question ever since. Some defended the programs as reducing the number of people living in poverty and giving educational and employment opportunities to many previously deprived of such chances. Critics on the right believed that the programs instead encouraged dependence on government and thus actually worsened the problem. Critics on the left argued that the programs did not go far enough in attacking the root causes of poverty. Three conclusions seem clear about the War on Poverty. First, it did not eliminate poverty. Second, it did help reduce the number of poor people by one-third between 1960 and 1969 (22 percent to 14 percent). Third, the elderly benefited most from the higher payment schedules put into place by the War on Poverty, as the share of Americans over age 65 in the poor population dropped from 40 percent in 1959 to 16 percent by 1974.

No barrier to opportunity in the early 1960s was higher than the color bar. Both opportunist and idealist, Johnson as president shed his segregationist voting record (necessary for election in Texas before 1960) and became the most vocal proponent of racial equality ever to occupy the Oval Office. Two factors facilitated his change in position. Blatant inequalities for American citizens weakened the United States in its competition with the Soviets and Chinese for the loyalty of the nonwhite Third World majority. Moreover, the African American freedom struggle in the South had reached a boiling point. Black frustration was mounting over white brutality and the seeming indifference or even hostility of the national government. The persistence of local organizers across the South, such as Bob Moses, forced the U.S. government to move.

Impact of the Voting Rights Act of 1965

The Civil Rights Act of 1964 fulfilled the implicit promise of the *Brown v. Board of Education* decision a decade earlier. The 1964 act made desegregation the law of the land as it outlawed discrimination in employment and in public facilities such as restaurants, theaters, and hotels. When Alabama police beat peaceful marchers on the Edmund Pettis Bridge outside Selma on March 7, 1965, horrifying most national television viewers, Johnson seized the opportunity to push through Congress the Voting Rights Act. This legislation outlawed poll taxes and provided federal voting registrars in states that refused the ballot to African Americans. The single most important legislation of the twentieth century for bringing political democracy to the South, the Voting Rights Act increased the percentage of blacks voting in Mississippi from 7 percent to 60 percent in two years. Black electoral power began to bring unprecedented change to Dixie's political and racial landscape.

The Great Society: Improving the Quality of Life

Johnson's vision of the Great Society extended to the broader quality of life in the United States. Health care was perhaps the most fundamental issue for citizens' sense of personal security. After 1965, the new Medicare system paid for the medical needs of Americans over 65, and Medicaid underwrote health care services for the indigent. Rising concern about the quality of corporate products led to new federal efforts to protect citizens as consumers. In 1964, when more than half of adults smoked tobacco, the surgeon general issued the first government report linking smoking to cancer. A year later, consumer advocate Ralph Nader used research studies to show that Chevrolet's sporty new Corvair was "unsafe at any speed." Despite industry resistance, higher federal standards for automotive safety followed. Public pressures also led to the establishment of new requirements for publishing the nutritional values of packaged food. The federally funded Public Broadcasting System (PBS) was established to provide television programs that were more educational than the fare tied to advertising on the three corporate networks (NBC, CBS, and ABC). In fact, most Great Society measures targeted all Americans rather than just the disadvantaged.

Ansel Adams, *Moon over Half Dome*, 1960. Ansel Adams Publishing Rights Trust/CORBIS

▲ **The moon rises over Half Dome in Yosemite Valley, Yosemite National Park, California, 1960. With this and other spectacular shots, renowned photographer Ansel Adams contributed to a growing national appreciation for wilderness in the years after World War II.**

Nothing more directly threatened the quality of American life than the degradation of the natural environment. The costs of the

Coming to America

The United States is an immigrant nation. Even the ancestors of the oldest inhabitants of North America, who today are known as Native Americans or Indians, came to this continent across the frozen Bering Strait from Asia. Since the first European expeditions across the Atlantic Ocean, waves of newcomers from Europe, Africa, Asia, and the rest of the Americas have shaped and reshaped the history of the United States. They have come, above all, for economic opportunity and greater personal freedom.

This immigrant heritage has defined American identity. Different nations have different criteria for determining who is a citizen and how someone can become a citizen. Germany and Israel, for example, use ethnicity and religion as criteria: Jews from anywhere can become citizens of Israel, while people of German ethnicity whose families have lived elsewhere for generations can become citizens of Germany. In the United States, by contrast, people born on American soil are U.S. citizens, along with immigrants who—after meeting certain requirements, including a substantial period of residence—can become naturalized U.S. citizens. New citizens become Americans by accepting a set of constitutional rights and duties—by choice and commitment, not by prior ethnicity, race, or religion.

Who would be allowed to make that choice and commitment has changed dramatically since the nation's birth. The first Naturalization Act of 1790 used a racial definition to restrict naturalization to only "free white persons." People of African ancestry were added in 1870, after the Civil War and the end of slavery. Asians remained ineligible for citizenship, and in 1882 Congress specifically excluded any more Chinese from even entering the country. Thus began four decades of narrowing restrictions on who could come to the United States, a response primarily to the millions of new arrivals from southern and eastern Europe. These restrictions culminated in the immigration statutes of 1921 and 1924, heavily favoring northwestern Europeans. Immigration slowed to a trickle by the 1930s.

The imperatives of foreign policy—first in World War II and then in the Cold War—reversed this restrictive trend. Acknowledging the importance of China to the U.S. struggle against Japan, Congress in 1943 passed the first law allowing Asians—a small, symbolic number of Chinese—to become naturalized U.S. citizens. In 1952, in the midst of the Korean War that the United States was fighting with a South Korean ally, Congress created limited quotas for immigrants from each formerly excluded Asian nation.

unrestrained and much-heralded economic growth since World War II showed up in the nation's air, water, and land. The leaded gasoline that fueled products of the booming auto industry created smog, industrial effluents polluted lakes and rivers, and petrochemical wastes poisoned the ground. Biologist Garrett Hardin called these developments "the tragedy of the commons," wherein the pursuit of narrow individual self-interest leads to the despoiling of the common environment. For example, the very low price of gasoline in the United States compared with that of other industrialized nations did not (and still does not) recoup any of the vast environmental costs of its use. The products of science that had contributed so much to the production of wealth were turning out to have hidden costs, and a new wave of citizen action to protect the environment began to build.

Growing public awareness prompted the Clean Air Act (1963) and the Clean Waters Act (1966), which set federal guidelines for reducing smog and preserving public drinking sources from bacterial pollution. Even the long dam-building tradition in the American West faced new questions. A quarter century after Hoover Dam blocked the Colorado River, engineers completed the Glen Canyon Dam (1963) upstream at the Arizona-Utah border, drowning one of the nation's most spectacular canyons under the new Lake Powell. Demands for the dam's removal began immediately (they continue to this day) and helped spur passage of the Wild and Scenic Rivers Act in 1968. Meanwhile, Congress passed the Wilderness Act in 1964, setting aside 9 million acres of undeveloped public lands (almost all west of the Mississippi River) as a place "where man is a visitor who does not remain." In a nation growing more urban and more crowded, most Americans began to accept the idea that what little wilderness remained should be preserved. By the year 2000, the wilderness system incorporated 95 million acres of roadless areas.

Denis Poroy/AP/Wide World Photo

Denis Poroy/AP/Wide World Photos

U.S. soldiers and sailors take the oath of citizenship during a naturalization ceremony at Camp Pendleton, California, in January 2004. Afterward, they are greeted by another naturalized U.S. citizen, Austrian-born California governor Arnold Schwarzenegger.

The weakening system of restricting immigration by race and ethnicity finally fell in 1965. The landmark immigration statute of that year, passed soon after major civil rights legislation, eliminated the old system of national origins and quotas. Gone, suddenly, was the nearly 200-year effort to preserve an identity as a white nation. Who could be an American now? People from every corner of the earth. With racial discrimination at last illegal in the United States, so, too, was such discrimination banished from the nation's conception of who its citizens should be. The rising immigration of the final decades of the twentieth century included many Europeans, but the majority of newcomers came from Asia and Latin America. ■

The Liberal Warren Court

Just as the government's executive branch responded to pressures for reform, so did the judicial branch. Dwight Eisenhower did not expect liberal leadership from Earl Warren when he named him chief justice of the U.S. Supreme Court in 1953. As California's secretary of state, Warren had helped implement the internment of Japanese Americans during World War II, but he later came to regret that policy. The Warren Court produced the unanimous 1954 school desegregation case, *Brown v. Board of Education* (see Chapter 25), and steadily expanded the constitutional definition of individual rights. This shift in interpreting the law reached even those deemed to have lost many of their rights: prisoners. *Gideon v. Wainwright* (1963) established the right of indigent prisoners to legal counsel, and *Escobedo v. Illinois* (1964) confirmed the right to counsel during interrogation, a critical hindrance to the use of torture. After *Miranda v. Arizona* (1966), police were required to inform anyone they arrested of their rights to remain silent and to speak to a lawyer. Reading suspects their "Miranda rights" became a touchstone scene for a whole generation of television police shows.

The Warren Court bolstered other rights of individuals against potentially coercive community pressures. Decisions in 1962 and 1963 strictly limited the practice of requiring prayers in public schools. In 1963 the Court narrowed standards for the definition of "obscenity," allowing freer expression in the arts but also in pornography. *Griswold v. Connecticut* (1965) established the use of contraceptive devices as a matter of private choice protected by the Constitution. In 1967 the Court heard the case of Mildred Jeter, a black woman, and Richard Loving, a white man, Virginians who had evaded their state's ban on interracial marriage by traveling to Washington,

D.C., for their wedding and then returning to Caroline County to live. In the aptly titled *Loving v. Virginia,* the Court declared marriage one of the "basic civil rights of men" and overturned the laws of the last 16 states restricting interracial unions. Also in 1967 President Johnson appointed the esteemed chief NAACP legal counsel, Thurgood Marshall—who had mounted the successful argument in *Brown v. Board of Education* 13 years earlier—as the first black Supreme Court justice.

Johnson's accomplishments at home were forever overshadowed by the war he sent Americans to fight in the quiet rice paddies and beautiful highland forests of Southeast Asia.

The Supreme Court's interpreting of the Constitution to expand individual rights disturbed many conservative Americans. They saw the Court as another arm of an intrusive national government that was extending its control over matters previously left to local communities. For them, the goal of integration did not justify the busing of schoolchildren. Rising crime rates worried them more than police brutality. Many Roman Catholics were troubled by the legalization of contraceptives. Incensed by the ban on requiring school prayer, Protestant fundamentalists sought redress through political involvement, which they had previously shunned, initiating a grassroots religious conservative movement that helped bring Ronald Reagan to power in 1980. The Warren Court served as a lightning rod for traditionalists' distress at changes in Americans' private behavior. In the contest between local and national authorities ongoing since the Articles of Confederation of the 1780s, the 1960s represented a high-water mark of Washington's influence in the lives of individual citizens.

Into War in Vietnam

The 1960s also marked the culmination of the U.S. government's efforts to control revolutionary political and social change abroad. The Truman Doctrine's logic of containing communism spanned the entire globe, but few imagined that the United States would overreach itself, tragically, in Vietnam. Johnson's accomplishments at home were forever overshadowed by the war he sent Americans to fight in the quiet rice paddies and beautiful highland forests of Southeast Asia. The Vietnam War of 1965–1973 might be better named the "American War": it reflected the beliefs and commitments of Cold Warriors in Washington more than the realities of life on the ground in Southeast Asia. An aggressive U.S. anticommunist policy abroad collided with leftist revolutionaries throughout the Third World, and it was ill fortune for the Vietnamese that this collision struck them hardest of all. "They were just in the intersection when our convertible rolled up," former Stanford University student body president and draft resistance organizer David Harris recalled.

The Vietnamese Revolution and the United States

Americans viewed the conflict in Vietnam as part of a broader struggle between communist and noncommunist nations. It did not start out that way, however. It began as one of many efforts to end European colonialism. Vietnamese nationalists, varying in ideologies but led by Ho Chi Minh and the Indochinese Communist party, sought since the 1930s to liberate their country from French colonial rule. Japanese advances during World War II put the Vietminh (Vietnamese nationalists) on the same side as the Americans, and Ho worked closely with the U.S. Office of Strategic Services (OSS), precursor to the Central Intelligence Agency (CIA).

After the defeat of Germany and Japan, the French wanted to regain control of their colonies in Africa and Asia, including Vietnam. Their British friends provided troop transport ships for French soldiers, and the United States provided most of the funds to support France in its war against the Vietminh (1946–1954). Cold War priorities won out: a weakened France had to be bolstered as the linchpin of a reintegrated, anticommunist western Europe, while the Vietminh were led by Communist party members. But the Vietnamese defeated the much more heavily armed French, capped by the climactic victory at the battle of Dien Bien Phu in May 1954, which surprised most Western observers. Two months later, the Geneva Accords divided the country temporarily at the 17th parallel until national elections could be held within two years to reunify Vietnam. Like the 38th parallel in Korea, the 17th parallel was an arbitrary latitude on the map used to divide peoples who did not want to be separated. Ho's forces solidified their control of the north, the French pulled out entirely, and the Eisenhower administration made a fateful decision to intervene directly to preserve the southern part of Vietnam from communism. The United States created a new government led by the Roman Catholic, anticommunist Ngo Dinh Diem in a new country called "South Vietnam." "This is our offspring," Senator John Kennedy observed of the rulers in the capital city of Saigon, but most Americans still knew nothing about South Vietnam.

The Vietnamese revolution was only half over, however. The French colonialists withdrew, but the Saigon regime did not hold elections. In North Vietnam, the sometimes brutal internal revolution for the creation of a socialist society proceeded with an extensive program of land redistribution. In South Vietnam, Diem ruled for eight years with increasing repression of communists and other dissenters. U.S. funding kept him in power. Southern members of the old Vietminh began a sabotage campaign against the Saigon government and formed the National Liberation Front (NLF) in 1960, with the support of the government of North Vietnam in Hanoi. Diem and his American supporters called them Viet Cong or VC, roughly equivalent to the derogatory American term *Commies.* As the struggle to overthrow Diem intensified in the early 1960s, President Kennedy increased the number of U.S. military personnel from the 800 under Eisenhower to 16,000. They made little difference, however, as the unpopular Saigon government continued to lose ground to the NLF guerrillas. Just three weeks before Kennedy's murder, several of Diem's own generals assassinated him with the tacit support of U.S. officials in South Vietnam and Washington.

Faced with the choice of escalating U.S. involvement to prevent an NLF victory or withdrawing entirely from the country, Johnson escalated.

Johnson's War

Lyndon Johnson inherited his predecessors' commitment to preserving a noncommunist South Vietnam. Bolstered by Kennedy's hawkish advisers, especially Secretary of Defense Robert McNamara (1961–1968), he believed that American credibility was at stake. But Johnson faced a swiftly deteriorating military situation. The NLF, which the administration portrayed as merely a tool of North Vietnam, was winning the political war for the South, taking control of the countryside from the demoralized Army of the Republic of Vietnam (ARVN). Faced with the choice of escalating U.S. involvement to prevent an NLF victory or withdrawing entirely from the country, Johnson escalated.

How he did so was crucially important. There was neither a national debate nor a congressional vote to declare war. Johnson did not want to distract Congress from his Great Society agenda, nor did he want to provoke the Soviet Union or China. But he believed he had to preserve a noncommunist South Vietnam or else face a debilitating backlash from Republicans, who would skewer him as McCarthy had done to Truman over the "loss" of China 15 years earlier. So the president used deception, describing offensive American actions as defensive and opening up a credibility gap between a committed government and a skeptical public. This gap widened steadily until it finally drove Johnson not to run for reelection in 1968.

In August 1964, North Vietnamese ships in the Gulf of Tonkin fired on the U.S. destroyer *Maddox,* which was aiding South Vietnamese sabotage operations against the North. The president portrayed the incident as one of unprovoked communist aggression, and Congress expressed almost unanimous support through its Gulf of Tonkin Resolution. With this substitute for a declaration of war, Johnson ordered American planes to begin bombing North Vietnam, and the first American combat troops splashed ashore at Da Nang in South Vietnam on March 8, 1965. In July the administration made the key decision to add 100,000 more soldiers, with more to follow as necessary.

▲ **MAP 26.2 THE AMERICAN WAR IN VIETNAM**
Before U.S. combat troops entered Vietnam in 1965, few Americans knew where this Southeast Asian country was. Vietnam's geography and place names quickly became familiar in the United States as hundreds of thousands of young Americans served there and some 58,000 died there. Vietnam's elongated shape, its borders with Cambodia and Laos, and its proximity to China all affected the course of the fighting for Americans between 1965 and 1973.

The president also offered a piece of the Great Society to his opponents in Vietnam if they would halt their struggle. He promised a vast economic development program for the Mekong River delta "on a scale even to dwarf our" Tennessee Valley Authority. Like most of his compatriots, the president assumed that foreign peoples fundamentally wanted to be like Americans. Johnson and his advisers tended to believe that, in the words of a U.S. officer in the film *Full Metal Jacket* (1987), "Inside every Vietnamese there is an American trying to get out."

Johnson, The Tonkin Gulf Resolution Message

The carrot of American-style economic development was accompanied by the stick of U.S. military force. American strategy had two goals: to limit the war so as not to draw in neighboring China (to avoid a repeat of the Korean War) and to force the NLF and North Vietnam to give up their struggle to reunify the country under Hanoi's control. The problem was the political nature of the guerrilla war in the South: a contest for the loyalty of the population, in which NLF operatives mingled easily with the citizenry. This kind of war made the enemy difficult to find, as was often true for the British in fighting the American revolutionaries in the 1770s. Because guerrillas were like fish swimming in the sea of citizens who supported them, in Chinese leader

Mao Zedong's formulation, U.S. commanders decided to drain the sea. The "strategic hamlet" program uprooted rural peasants and concentrated them in fortified towns, creating "free fire zones" in their wake where anything that moved was a target. The U.S. Air Force pounded the South as well as the North, dropping more bombs on this ancient land (smaller than either Germany or Japan) than had been used in all theaters on all sides in World War II.

These tactics destabilized and traumatized society in South Vietnam as one-fourth of the population became refugees. The American war urbanized the South by force: from 85 percent rural in 1965, it became 65 percent urban by 1974. The strategy of attrition wielded by General William Westmoreland, the commander of U.S. forces in Vietnam, also alienated the citizenry of the South. Lacking a clear military front in a guerrilla conflict, U.S. commanders used body counts of enemy dead as a primary method of demonstrating progress in the war. This strategy created great pressure on officers to produce bodies. In a war where Americans had difficulty distinguishing the enemy from noncombatants, a new rule became increasingly standard: "If it's dead and Vietnamese, it's VC."

Americans in Southeast Asia

Given America's wealth, size, and superior weaponry, most U.S. soldiers who went to Vietnam in 1965–1966 had no doubt they would win the war. Their confidence reflected generations of American successes on battlefields across Europe and the Pacific Ocean. As emissaries from a culture that valued material wealth and technological sophistication, they tended to dismiss Vietnamese people as primitive and weak. They typically looked down on Asians. Very few knew anything about Vietnamese history or culture, and almost none spoke the Vietnamese language. This war, unlike World War II of their parents' generation, had no D-Day on the beaches of France as in 1944, with a staging across the narrow channel in familiar England. Although a small number of Americans worked closely with their South Vietnamese allies, most GIs encountered Vietnamese in subservient roles as laundry workers, prostitutes, waitresses, and bartenders. Blinkered by anticommunism and far removed from their own revolutionary roots, Americans from the top brass to the lowest "grunts" marched into a country they did not understand but assumed they could control.

President Johnson spoke of the conflict as a case of one sovereign nation—North Vietnam—invading another one—South Vietnam. However, few Vietnamese saw the war in those terms.

Universal Press Syndicate

▲ **Cartoonist Jules Feiffer suggested in 1966 some of the ongoing confusion of many Americans about Asia and its many nations and peoples, and why the United States was involved in a war in Vietnam. Anti-Asian prejudice had long contributed to problems in U.S.-Asian relations. President Johnson claimed that the United States was protecting the lives and interests of South Vietnamese against both North Vietnam and China.**

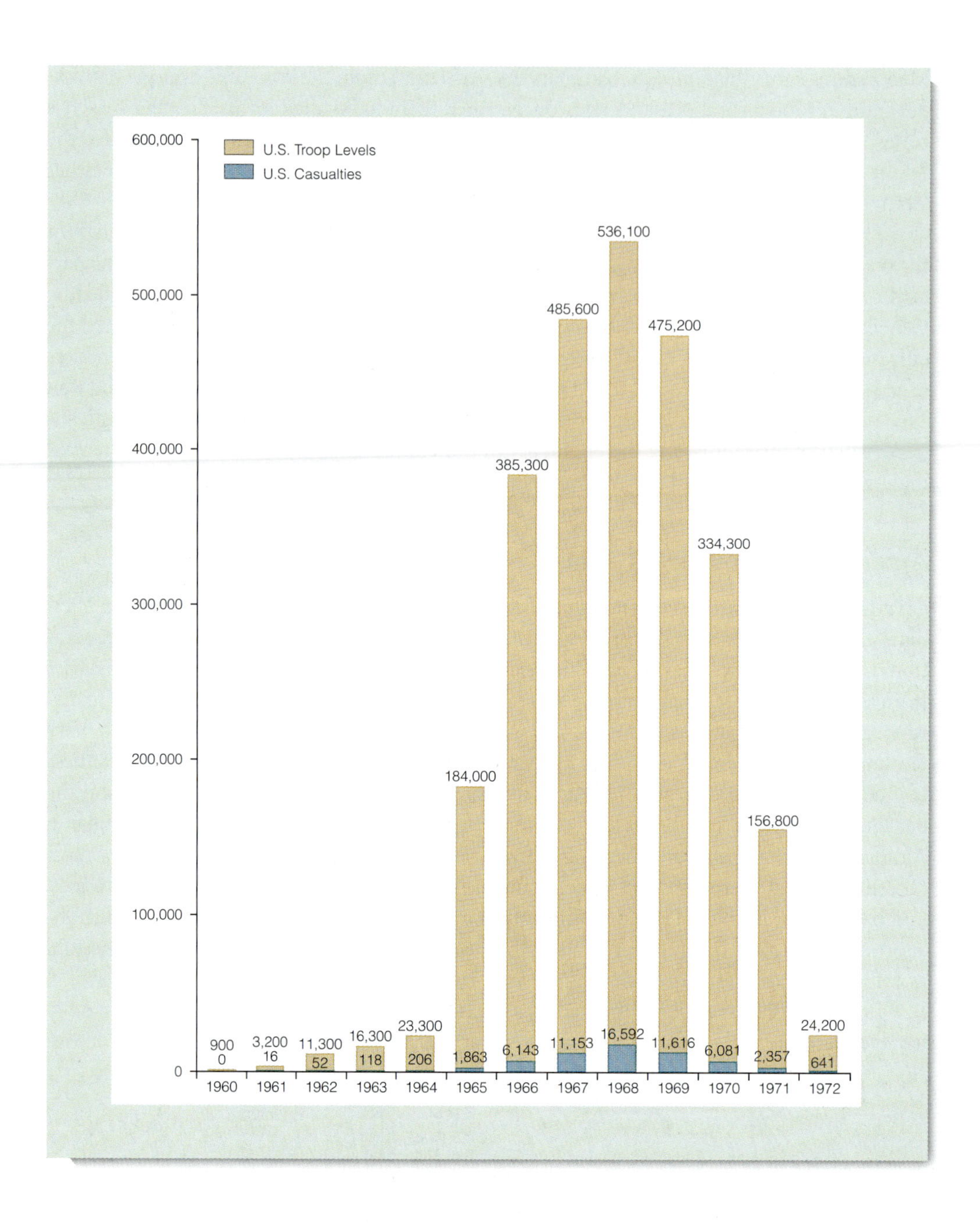

▶ **FIGURE 26.1**
U.S. TROOPS AND DEATHS IN VIETNAM (AS OF DECEMBER 31 OF EACH YEAR)

The United States, dismissing the failure of the French before them, had intervened not so much in an international war as in an ongoing revolution that aimed to reunify the country. Few Vietnamese, whatever their opinions of communism, viewed the corrupt Saigon regime as legitimate or democratic. After all, it was kept in place by foreigners, whereas the North was ruled by people who had expelled the French foreigners. Even the U.S. embassy admitted privately that "if any elected assembly sits in Saigon, it will be on the phone negotiating with Hanoi within one week." One U.S. sergeant concluded that "anticommunism is a lousy substitute for democracy."

Initial U.S. optimism reflected a grave underestimation of the NLF and the North Vietnamese. From President Johnson down to soldiers on patrol in the jungle, Americans assumed that communists did not have popular support and that the inferior weaponry of communist forces could not withstand the firepower of the world's strongest military, which dominated the air and the surrounding sea. These assumptions were fatal miscalculations. Ho Chi Minh was an extremely popular leader, and intervention from the other side of the world only strengthened his position. As the war expanded, NLF recruiting in the south snowballed, and the people of North Vietnam remained loyal to their authoritarian government. Communist forces proved willing to endure fantastic hardship and sacrifices to prevail, some even living underground in the labyrinthine tunnels of Cu Chi to avoid U.S. bombs. Their morale was much higher than that of the ARVN.

Who were the 3 million Americans who went to Vietnam? The initial forces contained experienced soldiers, but as the war escalated this professional army was diluted with hundreds of thousands of young draftees. Student deferments protected more comfortable Americans, so GIs were predominantly those who lacked money and education. Although 70 percent were white men, black, Hispanic, and Native American enlistees shipped out in disproportionate numbers. It became a teenage army, filled with 18-year-olds whose main aim, one ABC correspondent reported, "was to become 19." In sharp contrast to the motives of the NLF and the North Vietnamese army, these young men (along with 10,000 women who volunteered as nurses) were not in Vietnam to win the war regardless of the cost or duration. They had only to survive 12 months before returning home to the safety of a peacetime society.

North Vietnamese regular army units came south to match the growing number of U.S. forces, and they occasionally engaged the Americans in large set battles, as at Ia Drang valley in the fall of 1965. U.S. troops fought well in such firefights, making devastating use of their superior weapons and air power. However, the bulk of the fighting consisted of smaller engagements with deceptive enemies on their home turf who faded in and out of the civilian population with ease. Ambushes and unexpected death haunted Americans on patrol, and relentless heat and humidity wore them down.

American soldiers felt mounting frustration and rage over the nature of the war that they were ordered to fight. Lacking a clear battlefront and an understandable strategy for winning the war, they were commanded simply to kill the often mysterious enemy. Yet distinguishing civilians from combatants in a popular guerrilla war was not always easy, especially when so many civilians evidently supported the NLF and so few Americans spoke Vietnamese. "How can you tell the enemy?" one GI asked. "They all look the same." The U.S. ally, the ARVN, was riddled with NLF infiltrators and rarely fought effectively. Realizing that few of the people they were supposed to be defending actually wanted them there but under orders to produce enemy bodies,

◀ **Vietnamese villagers flee from an accidental U.S. napalm raid 26 miles southwest of Saigon in the Mekong River delta. U.S. Air Force planes dominated the skies above Vietnam, dropping conventional bombs and antipersonnel weapons such as napalm over both the North and the South. At least 2 million Vietnamese died, many of them civilians caught in the crossfire of a guerrilla war, but sheer destructiveness was unable to win the war for the United States.**

University of Maine, Ngo Vinh Long Collection

▲ A North Vietnamese militia fighter named Kim Lai escorts an American pilot whom she captured after his plane crashed over the North. American GIs often were struck by the diminutive size of the average Vietnamese in comparison to the average American. Bigger, better equipped, and much better armed than their opponents, most U.S. soldiers and officers before 1968 went into the field in Vietnam certain that they would be victorious.

U.S. troops on the ground began to slide toward a racial war against all Vietnamese. "You can't have a feeling of remorse for these people," said one marine. "I mean, like I say, they are an enemy until proven innocent."

Many GIs resisted this logic, sometimes showing real kindness to Vietnamese civilians. But atrocities on both sides inevitably followed from this kind of war. The worst came in the village of My Lai on March 16, 1968, where 105 soldiers from Charlie Company—enraged by the recent deaths of several comrades in ambushes—slaughtered, often after torturing or raping, more than 400 Vietnamese women, children, and old men. The U.S. Army covered up the massacre for a year and a half, and eventually found only Lieutenant William Calley, the leader of Charlie Company's First Platoon, guilty of murdering Vietnamese civilians.

1968: The Turning Point

In late 1967 the public face of the war effort remained upbeat, as General Westmoreland declared that he could now see "some light at the end of the tunnel." But other prominent members of the administration, including Secretary of Defense McNamara, were beginning to express doubts privately to the president. Any remaining hopes of an imminent victory were crushed by the startling Tet Offensive (named for the Vietnamese New Year) that began on January 30, 1968. NLF insurgents and North Vietnamese troops attacked U.S. strongholds throughout South Vietnam, even occupying the courtyard of the U.S. embassy for six hours. This risky tactic paid off for the communists with enormous political gains, despite military losses. U.S. troops killed thousands of their enemy as they ended and then reversed the advances of Tet. But the blow to American public confidence in Johnson and his military commanders proved irreversible. Far from being on the verge of defeat, as the administration had been claiming, the communists had shown that they could mount simultaneous attacks around the country. Revered television newscaster Walter Cronkite announced that "we are mired in stalemate" in Vietnam.

The Tet Offensive coincided with two other crises in early 1968 to convince American political and business elites that U.S. international commitments had become larger than the nation could afford. First, a week before Tet began, the North Korean navy seized the U.S. intelligence ship *Pueblo* in the Sea of Japan and temporarily imprisoned its crew. U.S. commanders were left scrambling to find enough forces to respond effectively without weakening American commitments in Europe and elsewhere. Second, a British financial collapse devalued the pound and caused the London government to announce its imminent withdrawal from its historic positions east of the Suez Canal, placing new military burdens on the United States in the Middle East. These events reduced international confidence in the U.S. economy, causing a currency crisis in March 1968 as holders of dollars traded them in for gold. The chair of the Federal Reserve Board warned Wall Street leaders of "either an uncontrollable recession or an uncontrollable inflation" as fears rose of another 1929. Financial leaders added their powerful voices to those of other dismayed Americans demanding a deescalation of the war.

The political career of Lyndon Johnson was a final casualty of these events. His support on the left withered as the antiwar and **black power** movements expanded. Meanwhile, his more centrist supporters were joining the backlash against civil rights, urban violence, and antiwar protesters, peeling off to the Republican party. On March 12 antiwar challenger Senator Eugene McCarthy of Minnesota nearly defeated the incumbent president in the New Hampshire Democratic primary. Johnson's vulnerability was obvious. Senator Robert Kennedy of

New York joined the race two weeks later. In a televised speech on March 31 that caught the divided nation by surprise, Johnson announced an end to U.S. escalations in the war, the start of negotiations in Paris with North Vietnam, and an end to his own career: "I shall not seek, and I will not accept, the nomination of my party for another term as your President."

The Movement

While national leaders were defending what they called the "frontiers of freedom" abroad, young Americans in the mid- and late 1960s organized to expand what they considered the frontiers of freedom at home. Television for the first time tied the country together in a common culture whose shared images were transmitted simultaneously around the nation. The expanding war in Vietnam radicalized people who had initially been optimistic about reforming American society. Black power, the New Left, the counterculture, women's liberation, and other liberation movements often had quite divergent goals. But participants overlapped extensively and activists spoke of "the Movement" as if it were a unified phenomenon. At the heart of the youth movements of the decade lay a common quest for authenticity—a rejection of hypocrisy and a distrust of traditional authorities—that fused cultural and political protest. Few American households remained untouched.

At the heart of the youth movements of the decade lay a common quest for authenticity—a rejection of hypocrisy and a distrust of traditional authorities.

From Civil Rights to Black Power

The black freedom struggle in the South that broke into the national consciousness so dramatically in the early 1960s inspired other activists. By 1966, however, the civil rights movement fractured as it confronted the limits of its success. It had achieved the goals of ending legal discrimination and putting southern African Americans in the voting booth, but it had not brought about a colorblind society. Racial prejudice among many white conservatives remained virulent, and white liberals, such as those in the Kennedy and Johnson administrations, revealed themselves as not always trustworthy allies. Expecting only hostility from conservatives, civil rights workers were more disillusioned with what they saw as liberal betrayals.

The Justice Department and the Federal Bureau of Investigation (FBI) did little to restrain the violence of the Ku Klux Klan until the murders of white organizers Michael Schwerner and Andrew Goodman along with black co-worker James Chaney in the summer of 1964. Two months later, at the national Democratic party convention in Atlantic City, New Jersey, Johnson crushed the effort of the biracial Mississippi Freedom Democratic party (MFDP) to replace the state's regular, all-white Democratic delegates. The president was determined to avoid further alienating white southern voters as he pursued a huge victory in the November elections. Former sharecropper and MFDP organizer Fannie Lou Hamer, who had suffered permanent damage when beaten by Mississippi police for her efforts to register black voters, expressed the anger of African Americans at this defense of segregation by the president and his party. To a national television audience, Hamer declared, "If the Freedom Democratic Party is not seated now, I question America. Is this America? The land of the free and the home of the brave?" Even the thousand white volunteers from northern and western colleges who courageously went to Mississippi for the 1964 "Freedom Summer" wound up unintentionally alienating many younger black organizers. The confident style and skills of volunteers from Yale, Stanford, and other elite universities highlighted anew the tendency of even well-intentioned whites to try to take over and manage African Americans' lives.

The black freedom struggle for centuries had woven together elements of racial separatism with elements of integration into the larger American culture. For many younger African Americans the pendulum swung toward a need for greater independence from the white majority.

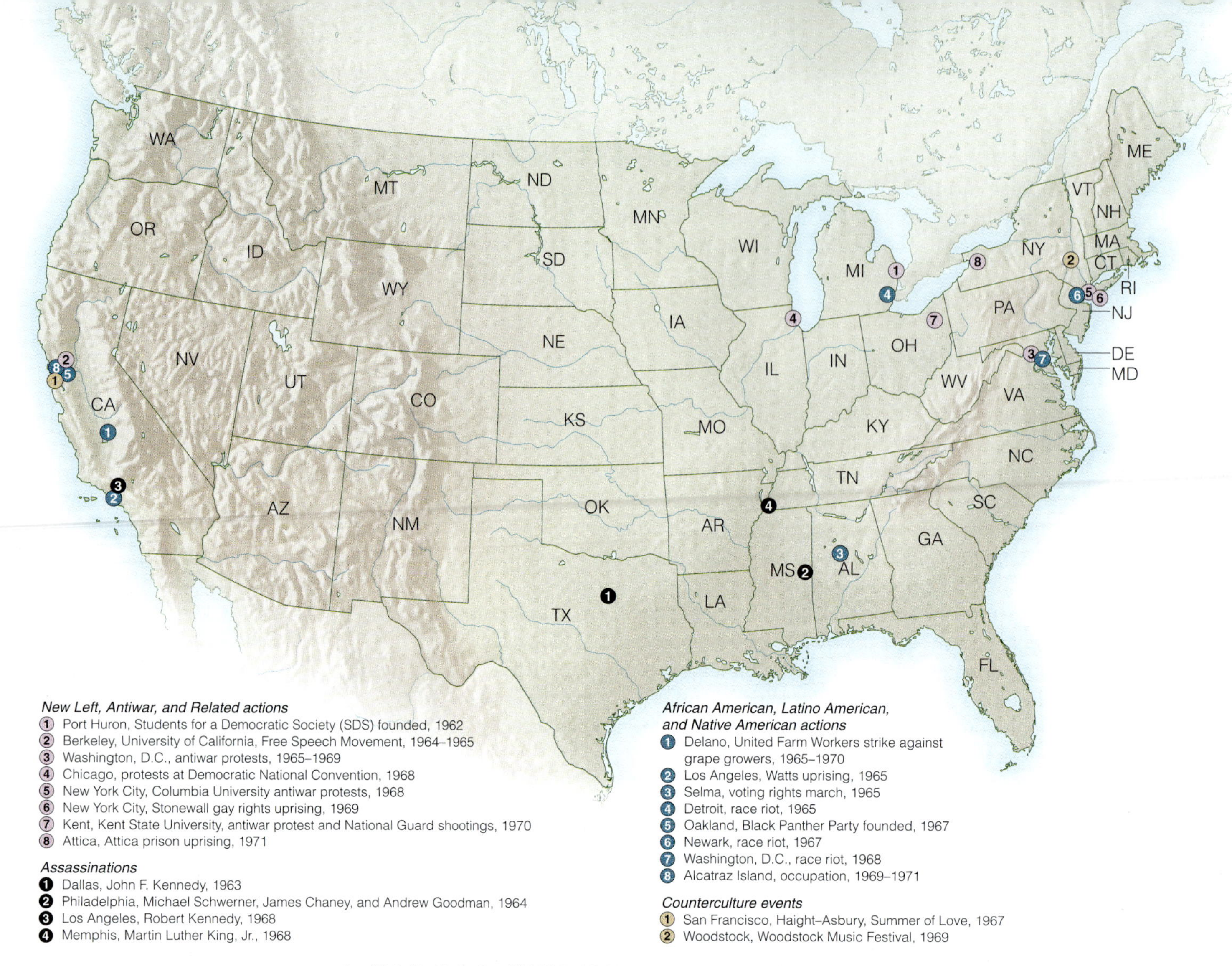

▲ **MAP 26.3 MAJOR SOCIAL AND POLITICAL PROTESTS, 1962–1971**
While not the first decade to witness dramatic public protests, the 1960s did become synonymous with large groups of citizens—especially young ones—demanding changes in public policies that they perceived as unjust. Foremost among these groups were civil rights workers, antiwar activists, women's rights supporters, and countercultural youth. Students emerged as important agents of change in the 1960s.

They took inspiration from Malcolm X, the fiery and eloquent minister of the Nation of Islam (Black Muslims), who until his murder in 1965 captivated listeners with denunciations of white perfidy and demands for black self-respect. After winning the heavyweight boxing title in 1964, Cassius Clay announced that he was a Black Muslim and was changing his name to Muhammad Ali. After fielding hostile questions from journalists at the news conference, Ali declared, "I don't have to be what you want me to be." In 1966 SNCC members began to speak of the need for "black power" rather than for the integrated "beloved community" they had initially sought in 1960.

The issue of violence loomed large in the shift from civil rights to black power. The Black Panther party formed in Oakland, California, in response to police brutality. The heavily armed Panthers engaged in several shootouts with police and were eventually decimated by an FBI campaign against them. White Americans were shocked by the uprisings and riots that swept through black urban communities during the summers of 1964 to 1968. Triggered by the actions of white police, the riots expressed the fierce frustrations of impoverished people whose lives remained largely untouched by the achievements of the civil rights struggle. The most destructive outbreaks occurred in the Watts district of Los Angeles in 1965 and in Detroit and Newark in 1967. The violence in Watts killed 34 people, wounded 1,000, and destroyed $45 million of property. Ninety people died and 4,000 were injured across the country in the 1967 riots, most of them African Americans killed by police as fires and looting spread through

Martin Luther King Jr. and the Vietnam War

Most Americans approved of the war in Vietnam until at least 1968. Appreciative of Lyndon Johnson's commitment to reduce poverty and end racial discrimination at home, African Americans generally supported the president's policies in Southeast Asia. However, younger, more radical civil rights workers were among those who opposed the first insertion of U.S. combat troops in 1965. Within two years, the nation's most prominent black leader, Martin Luther King Jr., decided that he could no longer keep quiet about his growing unease with the American war effort. A storm of criticism greeted his public denunciation of the war, most of it suggesting that he should limit himself to domestic civil rights work. But King no longer believed that events at home and abroad could be separated. The following excerpt is from his speech at Riverside Church, New York City, April 4, 1967.

A few years ago there was a shining moment in that struggle [against poverty and discrimination]. It seemed as if there was a real promise of hope for the poor—both black and white—through the Poverty Program. There were experiments, hopes, new beginnings. Then came the build-up in Vietnam and I watched the program broken and eviscerated as if it were some idle political plaything of a society gone mad on war. . . . I was increasingly compelled to see the war as an enemy of the poor and to attack it as such. . . .

We were taking the black young men who had been crippled by our society and sending them 8,000 miles away to guarantee liberties in Southeast Asia which they had not found in Southwest Georgia and East Harlem. So we have been repeatedly faced with the cruel irony of watching Negro and white boys on TV screens as they kill and die together for a nation that has been unable to seat them together in the same schools. . . .

As I have walked among the desperate, rejected and angry young men [in the ghettos of the North the last three summers] I have told them that Molotov cocktails and rifles would not solve their problems. I have tried to offer them my deepest compassion while maintaining my convictions that social change comes most meaningfully through non-violent action. But they asked—and rightly so—what about Vietnam? They asked if our own nation wasn't using massive doses of violence to solve its problems, to bring about the changes it wanted. Their questions hit home, and I knew that I would never again raise my voice against the violence of the oppressed in the ghettos without having first spoken clearly to the greatest purveyor of violence in the world today—my own government. . . .

[Our troops in Vietnam] must know after a short period there that none of the things we claim to be fighting for [such as freedom, justice, and peace] are really involved. Before long they must know that their government has sent them into a struggle among Vietnamese, and the more sophisticated surely realize that we are on the side of the wealthy and the secure while we create a hell for the poor.

TimePix/Getty Images

His birthday now a national holiday, Martin Luther King Jr. has become widely accepted as a heroic figure in the American past. But in the last few years of his life, King's increasingly sharp criticisms of injustice in American society disturbed many fellow citizens.

Questions

1. *How does King believe that the U.S. war in Vietnam is related to problems at home in American society?*
2. *What might have been the more negative and positive racial aspects of the Vietnam War?*
3. *What precisely does King believe to be wrong with the U.S. war in Vietnam?* ■

Source: Bruce J. Schulman, *Lyndon B. Johnson and American Liberalism* (Boston: Bedford, 1995), pp. 208–212.

African American neighborhoods. "Our nation is moving toward two societies, one black, one white—separate and unequal," the National Advisory Commission on Civil Disorders announced in its 1968 report.

Black power thrived primarily as a cultural movement that promoted pride in African American and African history and life. The slogan "black is beautiful" captured this spirit: long degraded by their white compatriots as inferior, black Americans in the late 1960s and 1970s reversed this equation to celebrate their cultural heritage. This could be as basic as a hairstyle, the natural Afro replacing hair straightened to look like European American hair. At universities, new departments of African American studies fostered the exploration of black history. Unlearning habits of public deference to whites, most African Americans began referring to themselves as "black" rather than "Negro."

Division of Rare & Manuscript Collections, Cornell University Library

▲ African American students march out of the student union at Cornell University in April 1969 after occupying the building during the annual Parents' Weekend on campus. With the support of radical white students such as those in SDS and some faculty, the black Ivy Leaguers were protesting racial discrimination, racial threats, and a recent cross-burning on campus, and they demanded the creation of a black studies program. The weapons in the picture went unused, but their presence on university grounds symbolized the extreme divisiveness and anger in American society between 1968 and 1970.

Cultural black power mixed with a different kind of political black power by the late 1960s: the election of black officials. Although militant black power advocates garnered the most media attention, most African Americans supported Lyndon Johnson and used the Voting Rights Act to pursue their goals in the realm of electoral politics. In 1966, Carl Stokes of Cleveland was elected the first black mayor of a major American city. African Americans won local offices across the South, and in 1972 Andrew Young of Georgia and Barbara Jordan of Texas became the first black U.S. representatives elected from the South since Reconstruction.

The New Left and the Struggle Against the War

In the summer of 1962 a group of young liberal college activists met at a labor union summer camp in Michigan. The Students for a Democratic Society (SDS) wrote a charter that became known as the Port Huron Statement, which called for a rejuvenation of American politics and society to replace the complacency that they saw pervading the country. Racial bigotry and poverty particularly troubled these optimistic young reformers, along with the overarching threat of nuclear destruction (highlighted anew by the missile crisis in Cuba a few months later). They hoped to become a kind of "white SNCC," promoting participatory democracy to redeem the promise of Cold War America.

SDS served as the central organization of the New Left. Communism was simply not important to these activists, nor was conservatism, which was then at its nadir. They focused instead on the behavior of the liberals who ran the U.S. government from 1961 to 1968. They developed a critique of "corporate **liberalism**" as promoting the interests of the wealthy and the business community far more than providing for the needs of the disadvantaged. From this perspective, communism was a false threat and anticommunism a distraction from the real problems of the nation, especially as the war in Vietnam expanded.

After 1965, SDS's initially broad reform agenda narrowed to stopping the Vietnam War. Protests about other issues also disrupted college campuses, such as the Free Speech Movement at Berkeley in 1964–1965; this successful effort to eliminate restrictions on students' lives set a precedent for campus activists elsewhere. But the escalation of the war moved draft-age opponents to focus on ending it. "Hell no, we won't go!" became their slogan. SDS members organized the first major antiwar protest outside the White House on April 17, 1965, bringing their organization into alliance with the small group of religious and secular pacifists already working against the war. Then mainstream Democrats began abandoning Johnson over the war as it grew. The president had alienated the powerful chair of the Senate Foreign Relations Committee, J. William Fulbright of Arkansas, with his misleading reports during the brief U.S. military intervention in the Dominican Republic in April 1965 to defeat a left-leaning but not communist coup attempt. Fulbright then held televised hearings on the American war in Southeast Asia in January 1966, raising grave doubts about its wisdom. Draft resistance increased as young men moved to Canada, as did SNCC's Bob Moses, or went to jail, as did boxing champion Muhammad Ali. "Man, I ain't got no quarrel with the Vietcong," the boxer explained.

Antiwar protesters followed the same trajectory of radicalization as black power advocates. Their dismay turned to rage as the Johnson administration continued to expand a

war that was destroying much of Vietnam while killing tens of thousands of American soldiers and many more Vietnamese for no reason its opponents considered legitimate. Having long admired Castro's revolution in Cuba, SDS began cheering for Ho Chi Minh and imagining itself as "the NLF behind Lyndon Johnson's lines." In combination with or in support of black militants, white radicals took over buildings on university campuses in 1968–1969: Columbia, Cornell, Harvard, San Francisco State, and many others. SDS ultimately broke apart in the confusion and exhilaration of its growing demand for revolution against the larger systemic enemies, imperialism and capitalism, not just corporate liberalism. Such fantasies of violence, as well as real bombings by a splinter group called the Weather Underground, alienated most Americans, including most peaceful antiwar protesters. But radical rage could not be understood apart from the ongoing destruction of Vietnam by a government acting in the name of all Americans.

"Protests Against the Vietnam War"

Cultural Rebellion and the Counterculture

While the New Left moved from wanting to reform American society to wanting to overthrow it, the counterculture sought to create an alternative society. Called "hippies" by those who disliked them, these young people were alienated by the materialism, competition, and conformity of American life in the Cold War. Like utopian idealists in previous centuries, they envisioned an America free from hypocrisy and artificiality. They tried to live out alternative values of gentleness, tolerance, and inclusivity. Sporting headbands, long hair, and beads, many identified with traditional Native Americans, who had repeatedly challenged the greed and deceptions of white culture from the time of Metacom and Popé in the seventeenth century. In place of junk foods, they promoted health foods; in place of profit-seeking businesses, they established co-ops. Referring to themselves as "freaks" for not fitting into "straight" society, they pursued what they saw as an authentic life. "Do your own thing" was the common slogan.

While the New Left moved from wanting to reform American society to wanting to overthrow it, the counterculture sought to create an alternative society.

In reaction against the conformity of mainstream society, members of the counterculture explored the limitations of consciousness to expand their self-knowledge. They went beyond the nicotine and alcohol that were the common stimulants of their parents' culture to experiment with such mind-altering drugs as marijuana, peyote, hashish, LSD, cocaine, and even heroin. Spirituality was an important path into consciousness for many in the counterculture. Religious traditions associated with Asia, particularly Buddhism, gained numerous adherents, as did spiritual customs and practices of traditional Native Americans. Others rediscovered the "authentic" Jesus obscured by the institutional structures of the formal Christian church (earning themselves the nickname "Jesus freaks"); Campus Crusade for Christ, InterVarsity, and other evangelical college groups spread across the country. Music served as the most common coin of the countercultural realm, from the political folk sound of Joan Baez and Bob Dylan to the broadly popular Beatles and the more distinctly countercultural rock 'n' roll of the Grateful Dead and Jefferson Airplane.

By its nature the counterculture had no clear membership. Millions of American youth dabbled in it to varying extents, smoking marijuana and listening to rock 'n' roll. A much smaller, more committed group pursued the building of communities—communes—that might coexist with the quest for unrestrained individual expression. These young people were centered in the Haight-Ashbury neighborhood of San Francisco until the 1967 Summer of Love. Counterculture youth gathered at the Woodstock music festival in upstate New York in August 1969, and they established 3,500 rural communes from Vermont to New Mexico by 1970. With the nation at war against communists in Southeast Asia, critics pointed to communes at home as subversive of the nuclear family and of American capitalist values.

Older Americans experienced the counterculture largely as spectacle. The mainstream media emphasized the alternative aspects of the hippie lifestyle in its coverage. Viewers were varyingly

The San Francisco Bay Area

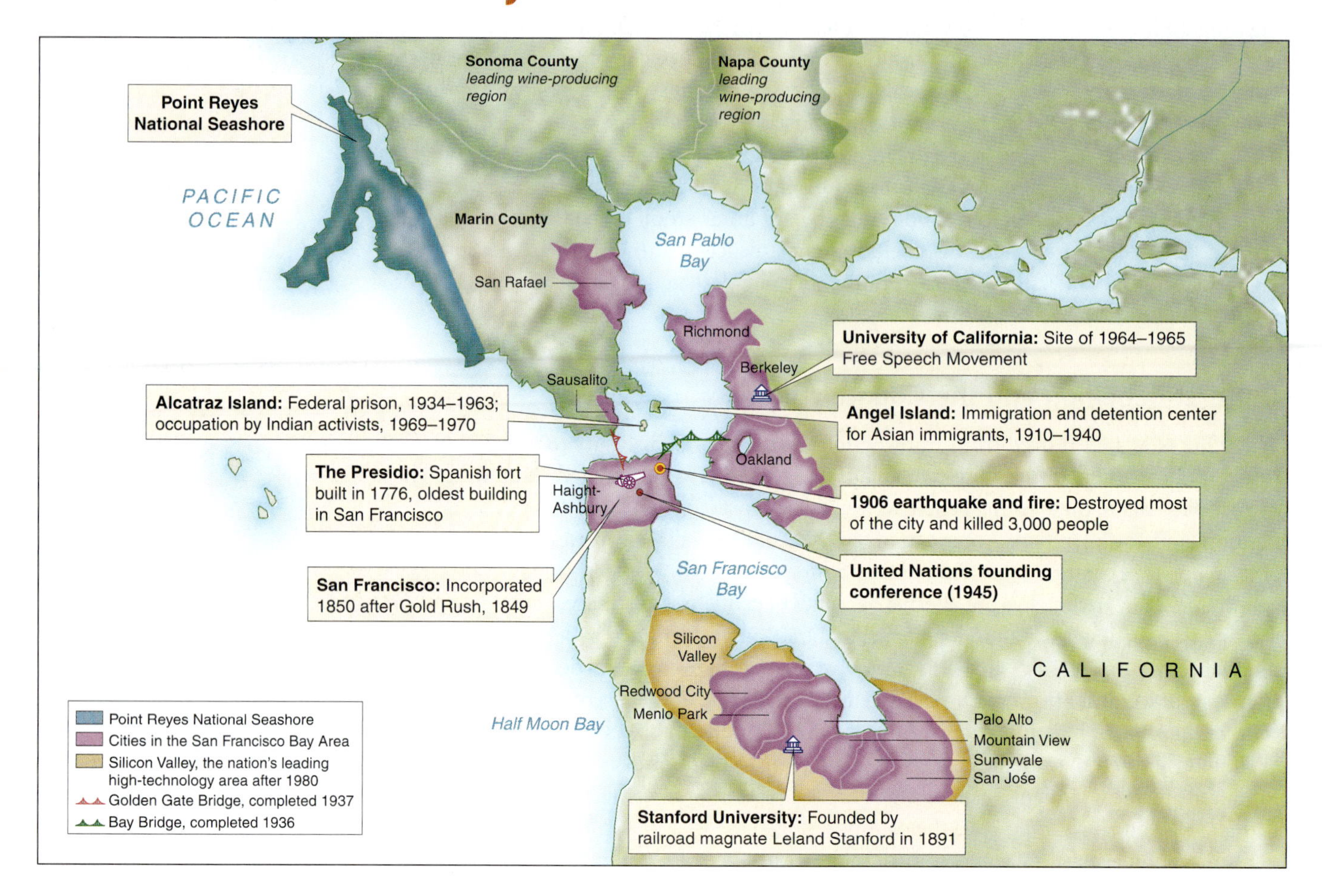

Known for its steep hills and breathtaking vistas, San Francisco was built by early Spanish settlers on a peninsula guarding the mouth of a kidney-shaped bay, the best natural harbor on the West Coast south of Puget Sound. The San Francisco Bay drains the Sierra Nevada mountains and California's fertile central valley, making it a hub of trade and commerce. The San Andreas Fault runs directly beneath the city, however, resulting in common small tremors and occasional large earthquakes, such as the devastating 1906 quake. In the 1960s California was still a bit exotic for most Americans from the East and the Midwest. But continuing migration to the Golden State and the emergence of air travel as a common means of transportation tied the nation more closely together. San Francisco, or "the City" to locals, became a hub of the counterculture and rock 'n' roll music as well as a place known for tolerance and diversity. Such innovative bands as the Grateful Dead and the Jefferson Airplane helped shape the "San Francisco sound" by the mid-1960s, and the city developed a large, vibrant gay and lesbian community. By the 1980s the "Silicon Valley" area around Stanford University became the epicenter of the computer and information technology boom in the United States. ■

Golden Gate Bridge, San Francisco

Campus Crusade for Christ, International

▲ **The search by many young people in the 1960s counterculture for greater consciousness led them to a spiritual path. These young evangelists held a Campus Crusade for Christ rally at the University of Texas at Austin in 1969. The emphasis of evangelical Christians on the person of Jesus rather than on a particular denominational tradition attracted many converts. The sandals, long hair, and gentleness associated with Jesus made a particularly good fit with the style and values of the "hippies," although most evangelicals appeared traditionally clean-cut and held conservative political views.**

disgusted by, attracted to, and titillated by the hair, clothing, nudity, and blurred gender distinctions. Celebrating the counterculture and its rock 'n' roll sound, the musical show *Hair* took Broadway by storm in 1968. Meanwhile, entrepreneurs realized that they could market the antimaterialist counterculture profitably. Young Americans eagerly bought up records, clothing, jewelry, and natural foods—a revealing demonstration of how consumer values pervaded American life.

One of the most visible changes of the 1960s was often called the sexual revolution. Changes in Americans' sexual behavior in the 1960s reflected in part the counterculture's goal of living an authentic, honest life in which words matched actions. The sexual revolution removed some of the penalties for the premarital and extramarital sex that had previously been fairly common but unacknowledged. The appearance of the birth control pill in 1960 underpinned the shift to more open sexual relationships by freeing women from the fear of pregnancy. Attitudes toward abortion also became more tolerant. New York passed the first state law legalizing some abortions in 1970, and three years later the Supreme Court established a woman's constitutional right to abortion in the landmark case of *Roe v. Wade*. For American women the sexual revolution proved a double-edged sword. It legitimated female sexuality and helped remove the old stereotyping of women as either "madonna" (virginal until married) or "whore" (lustful and degraded). But it also created pressures from men, especially within the counterculture, for women to have sex with many partners lest they be cast as "uptight" and unliberated.

Women's Liberation

The movement for women's liberation arose in the late 1960s as a way to resist these kinds of limitations and expectations. Women's liberation built on developments earlier in the decade.

National Organization of Women, Statement of Purpose

In 1963 writer Betty Friedan, a former labor journalist and then homemaker, published *The Feminine Mystique,* a widely read book that captured the frustrations of many women who had accepted the role of suburban homemaker after World War II. Friedan condemned the middle-class home as a "comfortable concentration camp" for women that limited their growth as individuals with the often monotonous routines of housework and child-rearing. Friedan and other liberal feminists founded the National Organization for Women (NOW) in 1966 to lobby against sexual discrimination in the public sphere in such areas as employment, wages, education, and jury duty. These challenges had radical implications for women's and men's earnings and thus for responsibilities within families, but NOW did not yet focus on issues inside the private sphere of the home.

The shift to the view that "the personal is political" came from younger, mostly white women who had been active in the civil rights and antiwar struggles. Inspired by the courage and successes of the protest movements in which they figured prominently, these female activists had also learned that traditional gender roles restricted them even in organizations dedicated to participatory democracy. Ironically, radical men could be as patronizing and disrespectful of women's abilities as mainstream men. Younger feminists in 1967 and 1968 began to organize themselves to promote their own liberation from the shackles of traditional gender roles. They agreed with NOW's challenge to discrimination in the public sphere, but they focused even more on the personal politics of women's daily lives, on critical issues such as parenting, child care, housework, and abortion. Feminism should liberate men as well as women, they believed, for men also had the contours of their lives unnecessarily constrained by gendered expectations.

Bettmann/CORBIS

▲ The new wave of organizing for women's rights that emerged in the late 1960s had many faces. Some protests against sex discrimination and disrespect for women were angry and others were gentle, as in this 1970 scene. "Raising consciousness" was a central strategy of the movement, as women and men became more aware of the gendered assumptions that had long governed—and channeled—their lives and their thoughts.

Many Americans discovered the women's liberation movement when a hundred activists picketed the 1968 Miss America Pageant in Atlantic City, New Jersey. The young feminists were protesting the promotion of physical appearance and charm as the primary measures of women's worth. They crowned a live sheep "Miss America" and paraded it along the boardwalk, making fun of the way contestants—like all women—"are appraised and judged like animals at a county fair." They objected to "the tyranny of beauty" and the extensive expectations of how women should present themselves for male approval. One protester sprayed Toni Home Permanent hair spray at the booth of a pageant sponsor, only to be charged with disorderly conduct and "emanating a noxious odor"—an irony that underlined the activists' point. Other feminists set up a "Freedom Trash Can" into which they threw items they considered unnatural sources of discomfort and exploitation: high-heeled shoes, girdles, hair curlers, bras, and copies of *Playboy* and *Cosmopolitan.* There was talk of burning the contents of the "Freedom Trash Can," an event that did not happen but that the media helped parlay into a myth of "bra-burning" militant feminists.

The new wave of feminism that washed through American culture at the end of the 1960s triggered fierce debates about the nature of gender. Was there a uniquely feminine way of knowing, seeing, and acting, or were women in essence the same as men, distinguishable ultimately by their individuality? Was womanhood biologically or only culturally constructed? Feminists disagreed sharply in their answers. Other differences inevitably divided a broad movement that addressed the lives of 51 percent of the entire American people. For example, NOW did not support gay rights until 1973, whereas many radical feminists believed lesbianism to be critical for women's full independence and autonomy. Women of color often found hierarchies of race and class more significant than those of sex; to them, as to many white working-class women, Friedan's statement that she wanted "something more than my husband and my children and my house" seemed the distant complaint of a woman of the leisure class. One's sex alone did not define one's entire identity.

However, diversity within the feminist movement did not hide a common commitment to expanding women's possibilities. One critical aspect was the need to unlearn niceness and passivity, just as black power advocates sought to unlearn deference. White men would no longer be the sole proprietors of assertiveness; grown women would no longer be "girls" nor grown black men "boys." The women's movement that emerged out of the 1960s permanently transformed women's lives and gender relations in American society, in areas ranging from job and educational opportunities, sexual harassment, and gender-neutral language to family roles, sexual relations, reproductive rights, and athletic facilities.

The Many Fronts of Liberation

Like the women's movement, the Chicano, pan-Indian, and gay liberation movements of the late 1960s were grounded in older organizing efforts within those communities. The struggles for "brown power," "red power," and "gay power" also reflected the newer influence of black

▲ **Cesar Chávez led a march during the United Farm Workers strike—*huelga*—against large grape growers in Delano, in California's central valley, in 1966. The UFW effort, in which women such as UFW Vice President Dolores Huerta (a mother of 11) figured prominently, included not only union organizing but also building a broader network of community institutions to improve the lives of Mexican American laborers. The Roman Catholic faith and pacifism of Chávez and others in the movement deeply impressed many non-Chicanos who supported the strike, such as Senator Robert F. Kennedy.**

power and its determination to take pride in what the dominant American society had denigrated for so long. Activists on college campuses successfully pressured administrations to establish interdisciplinary ethnic studies programs, such as the first Chicano studies program at California State University at Los Angeles in 1968. Ethnic cultural identity went hand in hand with the pursuit of political and economic integration into mainstream American life.

The Chicano, pan-Indian, and gay liberation movements of the late 1950s were grounded in older organizing efforts within those communities.

The most prominent push to organize Latinos was the effort led by Cesar Chávez to build a farm workers' union in California and the Southwest. These primarily Mexican American migrant workers harvested most of the hand-picked produce that Americans ate, but their hard work under severe conditions failed to lift them out of poverty. National consumer support for boycotts of table grapes and iceberg lettuce helped win recognition for the United Farm Workers (UFW) union and better pay by 1970, despite efforts by conservative leaders such as President Richard Nixon and California governor Ronald Reagan to encourage grape consumption in support of large growers. Younger Mexican Americans organized to oppose the discrimination against them that remained common across the Southwest, especially in schools. They looked with pride on their Mexican heritage, even appropriating the formerly pejorative term *Chicano*. In March 1968, 10,000 youngsters walked out of their East Los Angeles schools to demand curriculum revisions that would include Latino history, recruitment of more Mexican American teachers, and an end to tracking Chicanos into vocational education classes. Two years later 20,000 people attended the Chicano Moratorium in East Los Angeles to protest the U.S. war in Vietnam.

Puerto Ricans, the largest Spanish-speaking ethnic group located primarily on the East Coast, experienced a similar growth in militancy and nationalist sentiment during the late 1960s. By the 1960s more than a million natives of the Caribbean island had moved to the East Coast, most to the New York City area. The majority came after World War II, and 47,000 served in the Vietnam War. Despite being the only Latino immigrants already holding American citizenship when they arrived, Puerto Ricans experienced similar patterns of both discrimination and opportunity as Mexican Americans. Younger Puerto Ricans formed the Young Lords in 1969 as a more militant and nationalist alternative to established Puerto Rican community organizations, one that combined pride in Puerto Rican identity and the Spanish language with leftist politics and opposition to the Vietnam War.

The most destitute of Americans, Indians also sought to reinvigorate their communities. On the Northwest coast they staged "fish-ins" in the mid-1960s to assert treaty rights, and in 1968 urban activists in Minneapolis formed the American Indian Movement (AIM). On November 20, 1969, just days after the largest antiwar march in Washington, 78 Native Americans seized the island of Alcatraz in San Francisco Bay "in the name of all American Indians by right of discovery." For a year and a half they used their occupation of the former federal prison site to publicize grievances about anti-Indian prejudice and to promote a new pan-Indian identity that reached across traditional tribal divisions. In 1973 armed members of AIM occupied buildings for two months at Wounded Knee near Pine Ridge, South Dakota, site of the infamous 1890 U.S. Army massacre of unarmed Sioux. AIM sought to bring down the conservative tribal government of the Oglala reservation, but the failure of that effort led to internal dissent and FBI harassment that eventually dissolved the organization. Tribal governments sought "red power" in their own quieter way. They asserted greater tribal control of reservation schools across the country. They also regained sovereignty over some lands previously lost, such as Blue Lake in northern New Mexico, which the Taos Indians reacquired.

Although they lacked a unifying ethnic identity, gay men and lesbians also found opportunities to construct coalitions in the more open atmosphere of the late 1960s. Building on the earlier but quieter community organizing of older homosexuals in New York, San Francisco, and Los Angeles, more militant youth began to express openly their anger at the homophobic prejudice and violence prevalent in American society. The demand for tolerance and respect reached the headlines when gay patrons of the Stonewall Bar in New York fought back fiercely

Michael Evans/New York Times

▲ **The first gay pride parade was a daring and hasty political protest by some 200 men and women, who walked for an hour up the Avenue of the Americas in New York City in 1970. They were taking a public stand against widespread discrimination and violence against homosexuals. Such discrimination and violence did not disappear over the next three decades, but the movement for gay rights dramatically altered the visibility and mainstream acceptance of gays and lesbians in the United States. By 1999 the gay pride parade had become a six-hour party sponsored by the likes of Budweiser beer and United Airlines and attended by First Lady Hillary Rodham Clinton and the Republican mayor of New York, Rudolph Giuliani.**

against a typically forceful police raid on June 27, 1969. Activists of the new Gay Liberation Front emphasized the importance of "coming out of the closet": proudly acknowledging one's sexual orientation as legitimate and decent. Like "black is beautiful," this tactic represented an effort to recast the terms of one's identity apart from an ongoing tradition of prejudice. The American Psychiatric Association listed homosexuality as a mental disorder until 1973.

The Conservative Response

The majority of Americans had mixed feelings about the protests that roiled the nation. They were impressed by the courage of many who stood up against discrimination, and by 1968 they wanted to find a way out of the war in Southeast Asia. But they were alienated by the style and values of others who loudly demanded change in American society. Moderate and conservative citizens and generations of recent European immigrants resented what they saw as a lack of appreciation for the nation's virtues and successes. Powerful backlashes developed against the counterculture, antiwar radicals, and changes in race and gender relations. The political and social upheavals of 1968 opened the door to a Republican return to the White House, and Richard Nixon slipped through.

Backlashes

The backlash first developed in response to the increasing assertiveness of people of color. European Americans in every part of the United States had long been accustomed to deference from nonwhites and racial segregation, either by law in the South or by custom elsewhere. Like most white Americans, conservatives resented what they considered blacks' ingratitude at the civil rights measures enacted by the federal government, including black power's condemnation of whites as "crackers" and "honkies." Urban riots and escalating rates of violent crime, along with the Supreme Court's expansion of the rights of the accused, deepened their anger. They associated crime with urban African Americans, for although whites were still the majority of criminals, blacks (like any other population with less money) were disproportionately represented in prisons. Many in the white working class feared that desegregating schools and neighborhoods would lead to a decline in their property values. While keeping darker-skinned Americans economically and socially subordinated, most whites still expected them to want to emulate mainstream white American society. They were troubled by the militancy of Chicanos in the Southwest, Puerto Ricans in the Northeast, Indians on reservations and in cities, and African Americans almost everywhere.

Asian Americans seemed less volubly angry than other Americans of color. Conservatives appreciated this, dubbing them a "model minority"—that is, one that worked hard, succeeded academically and in other ways, and did not "complain." In fact, many young Americans of Japanese, Chinese, and Filipino ancestry were also involved in antiwar and antiracist organizing in the late 1960s. But it was true that the 1965 Immigration Act allowed the Chinese American and Filipino American populations to nearly double by the end of the decade, as new arrivals brought with them traditional immigrant ethics of hard work and a focus on achieving material success. These new immigrants joined an important group of earlier refugees from China's communist revolution, who were often very well educated and fairly affluent when they arrived. A prominent example was Shanghai-born An Wang, who was earning a Ph.D. in physics at Harvard University when the communist revolution at home prevented him from returning. Wang's innovative work on computer memory led him to found Wang Laboratories in 1961, and he became, for a time, one of America's richest people and a major philanthropist.

The broad backlash of the late 1960s was not only about race. It also represented a defense of traditional hierarchies against the cultural rebellions of the 1960s. Proud of their lives and values, conservatives rejected a whole array of challenges to American society. Raised to believe

Universal Press Syndicate

▲ **Cartoonist Jules Fieffer portrayed the generation gap that separated many younger Americans from many older ones by the early 1970s. Movements for black and Native American civil rights and against the U.S. war in Vietnam led to a profound shift in how many citizens, especially younger ones, understood their nation and its politics. A new generation of historians began to cast serious doubts on many long-accepted truisms about the American past.**

in respecting one's elders, they resented the disrespect of many youth, who warned, "Don't trust anyone over 30." A generation that had fought and sacrificed in the "good war" against the Nazis found the absence of patriotism among many protesters unfathomable. The United States remained one of the most religious of industrialized societies, and conservative churchgoers emphasized obedience to authorities. They feared the effects of illegal drugs on their children. They resented being told that their assumptions about the roles and behavior of men and women, on which they had built their daily lives, were wrong. They did not want to argue about the behavior of the U.S. government; "America: Love It or Leave It" became a favorite bumper sticker.

The backlash against the social changes of the 1960s contained elements of class antagonism as well. Working-class whites resented both the often affluent campus rebels and the black and Latino poor targeted by some Great Society programs. They believed that their values of hard work, restraint, and respectability were increasingly unappreciated and even mocked. Politicians seized on these feelings of working-class alienation for political gain. Republican leaders from Goldwater to Nixon to Reagan gave voice to these resentments and drew votes away from Democratic blue-collar strongholds. Democratic governor George Wallace of Alabama also became a spokesperson for the anger of many "forgotten" whites on both sides of the Mason-Dixon line. Even television gave voice to the backlash in the likable character of Archie Bunker on *All in the Family,* a wildly popular program from its first airing in January 1971.

The United States remained one of the most religious of industrialized societies, and conservative churchgoers emphasized obedience to authorities.

The Turmoil of 1968 at Home

The traumas of 1968 brought the conservative backlash to the critical stage. First came the Tet Offensive in Vietnam, creating fears that the war might become an interminable quagmire. Conservatives, like most other Americans, found it incredible that the mighty United States could not vanquish so small an enemy. Then, on April 4, just five days after President Johnson announced his retirement plans, a gunman named James Earl Ray assassinated Martin Luther King Jr. in Memphis, where he had gone to support a strike by sanitation workers. King had become more openly radical in his final years, opposing the war and working on class-based organizing of poor people. But he remained the nation's leading apostle of nonviolence, and his murder evoked despair among millions of citizens, especially African Americans. Police battled rioters and arsonists in black neighborhoods of 130 cities across the nation, with 46 people dying in the clashes. National Guard troops ringed the White House as smoke from hundreds of fires rose over Washington, D.C.; large parts of the nation's capital looked like a war zone.

Summer brought more shocking news. Charismatic Senator Robert Kennedy's entry into the presidential campaign inspired renewed hopes among Democratic liberals. On the night of his victory in the June 5 California primary, Kennedy was shot by a deranged gunman, Sirhan Sirhan, and died the next morning. Americans were stunned by this second murder of a Kennedy. Vice President Hubert Humphrey seemed assured of the nomination at the Democratic convention in Chicago in August, despite his association with Johnson's war policies. Some 10,000 antiwar activists, including hundreds of FBI *agents provocateurs* (spies seeking to provoke violence), showed up to engage in protests outside the convention. Chicago's Democratic mayor Richard Daley unleashed thousands of police on protesters, bystanders, and photographers in an orgy of beatings that subsequent investigations called a police riot. Ninety million Americans watched on television as a deeply divided Democratic party appeared helpless before the violence.

Into the vacuum of public anger and alienation that accompanied the liberals' self-destruction in Chicago stepped two men. The spread of the conservative backlash from 1964 to 1968 gave George Wallace a wider constituency for his right-wing populist message of hostility to liberals, blacks, and federal officials. With the national Democratic party committed to racial integration, the former Alabama governor ran for president as an independent candidate and won 13.5 percent of the popular vote in November. Republican candidate Richard Nixon, fresh from a unified convention in Miami, campaigned as the candidate of "law and order" and promised that he had a secret plan to end the war in Vietnam. His contacts with the South Vietnamese government helped ensure that no last-minute breakthrough in the Paris peace talks would boost Humphrey's popularity, and the former vice president squeezed past the current one by less than 1 percent of the popular vote.

The Nixon Administration

A lonely, aloof man of great tenacity and ambition, Richard Nixon had worked hard to remake his public image for 1968. Widely viewed as a somewhat unscrupulous partisan since his early career in Congress, he had refashioned himself as a statesman with a broad vision for reducing international tensions between the great powers. Foreign policy fascinated him, and unlike Johnson, he found domestic governance utterly dull—a matter of "building outhouses in Peoria." He won the Republican presidential nomination primarily because he bridged the gap between the party's conservative Sunbelt wing and its moderate eastern wing. He sounded like a conservative in the campaign against Humphrey, but once in the White House he governed as the most liberal Republican since Theodore Roosevelt, pressed by a Congress still controlled by Democrats.

Nowhere was this clearer than on issues related to natural resources. Much had happened to the environment since the Republican Roosevelt's conservation efforts, none of it for the better. A powerful movement was building to protect natural resources and human health from the effects of air and water pollution. Biologist Paul Ehrlich's best-selling *The Population Bomb* (1968) warned of the dire consequences of the globe's runaway growth in human population. In 1969, the government banned the carcinogenic pesticide DDT, its original usefulness against mosquito-born malaria in World War II now almost forgotten in light of its broadly toxic effects on wildlife and aquatic ecosystems. That same year a huge oil spill off Santa Barbara fouled 200 miles of pristine California beaches, and the Cuyahoga River in Cleveland, its surface coated with waste and oil, caught fire and burned for days. *Apollo 8* astronauts brought home unprecedented pictures of the earth that seemed to dramatize the vulnerability of the small blue-green planet as it hung alone in space. Environmentalists around the country proclaimed April 22, 1970, as "Earth Day."

Congress responded with legislation that mandated the careful management of the nation's natural resources. The Environmental Protection Agency was established in 1970. Amendments to the Clean Air (1970) and Clean Water (1972) acts tightened restrictions on harmful emissions from cars and factories. The Endangered Species Act (1973) created for the first time the legal right of nonhuman animals to survive, a major step toward viewing the quality of human life as inextricable from the earth's broader ecology. Nixon did not take the lead in promoting environmental laws, about which he personally cared little, telling business supporters that "in a flat choice between smoke and jobs, we're for jobs." But the president recognized the bipartisan popularity of actions to limit ecological damage, and he followed Congress's lead.

What Nixon did care deeply about at home was politics, not policy. Antiwar demonstrations reached their height during Nixon's first two years in the White House (1969–1970). He and Vice President Spiro Agnew loathed the protesters, whom they saw as weakening the nation. The two men pursued what Agnew called "positive polarization": campaigning to further divide the respectable "silent majority," as the president labeled his supporters, from voluble liberal Democrats in Congress and radical activists on the streets, whom they associated with permissiveness and lawlessness. In this broad cultural battle for political supremacy, the president appealed to conservative white southern and northern ethnic Democrats. His "Southern strategy" centered on opposing the use of court-ordered busing to desegregate public schools. He nominated two very conservative Southerners to the Supreme Court, only to see the Senate vote both of them down.

Early in his administration Nixon began wielding the power of the federal government to harass his political opponents. Johnson had used the FBI, the CIA, and military intelligence agencies to infiltrate and thin the ranks of antiwar demonstrators and nonwhite nationalists. Nixon continued those illegal operations, agreeing with his predecessor that radical activists constituted a threat to national security. Nixon went beyond other presidents in assembling an "enemies list" that included prominent elements of the political mainstream, especially liberals, the press, and his Democratic opponents. The president was particularly concerned about controlling secret information. The Pentagon Papers were a classified Defense Department history of U.S. actions in Vietnam revealing that the government had been deceiving the American public about the course of the war. When disillusioned former Pentagon official Daniel Ellsberg leaked the study to the *New York Times* for publication in 1971, Nixon was enraged. The White House created a team of covert operatives nicknamed the "plumbers" to "plug leaks" by whatever means necessary, including breaking into the office of Ellsberg's psychiatrist in search of information they might use to discredit him publicly.

Courtesy, National Aeronautics and Space Administration

▲ On July 20, 1969, astronauts Neil Armstrong and Edwin "Buzz" Aldrin put the first footprints on the moon. The U.S. flag they planted epitomized the sense of national accomplishment in space, even as divisions wracked American society at home. The actual flag here was made of rigid material because no lunar breeze existed to make the flag wave.

Escalating and Deescalating in Vietnam

Nixon recognized that in Vietnam the Truman Doctrine (see Chapter 24) had been stretched to the breaking point. The United States simply could not afford to send its troops everywhere abroad to contain the expansion of communism. The president and his national security adviser, Henry Kissinger, had ambitious plans for shifting the relationships of the great powers to America's advantage. To deal with China and the Soviet Union, they first had to reduce the vast U.S. engagement in the small country of Vietnam, which had grown wildly out of proportion to actual U.S. interests there. Under the Nixon Doctrine, the United States would provide military hardware rather than U.S. soldiers to allied governments, which would have to do their own fighting against leftist insurgencies. In South Vietnam this doctrine required "Vietnamization," or withdrawing American troops so ARVN could shoulder the bulk of the war.

The key to a successful withdrawal from Vietnam for Nixon was to preserve U.S. "credibility." The perception of power could be as important as its actual exercise, and the president wanted other nations, both friend and foe, to continue to respect and fear American military might. There was no immediate pullout but a gradual process that lasted for four years (1969–1973), during which almost half of the total U.S. casualties in Vietnam occurred. To avoid a humiliating collapse of the Saigon regime as soon as Americans left, Nixon did his utmost to weaken the communist forces during the slow withdrawal. The administration escalated in order to deescalate. The president ordered the secret bombing and invasion of neighboring Cambodia and Laos, an intensified aerial assault on North Vietnam, and the mining of Haiphong Harbor near Hanoi. Enormous protests rocked the country after the announcement of the Cambodian invasion on April 30, 1970, including a strike by hundreds of thousands of students that disrupted classes on more than 700 college campuses. National Guard troops killed four students at a demonstration at Kent State University in Ohio and two at Jackson State College in Mississippi, deepening the sense of national division.

Kent State Demonstrations

A majority of Americans now opposed the nation's war effort, a level of dissent unprecedented in U.S. history. Most telling of all was the criticism of some veterans returning from Vietnam. Although most stayed quiet about their traumatic experiences, some organized the Vietnam Veterans Against the War and even held public hearings into atrocities—war crimes—they and others had committed. These dissenters, including a young officer and future U.S. senator named John Kerry, were extremely hard for prowar Americans to discredit. The morale of American soldiers still in Vietnam plummeted as the steady withdrawal of their comrades made clear that they were no longer expected to win the war. Drug abuse and racial conflict increased sharply among GIs. Even "fragging" (killing one's own officers) escalated before the peace accords were signed in Paris and the United States evacuated its last combat troops in 1973.

Conclusion

Between 1964 and 1971, young, nonwhite, and female Americans laid claim to greater equality. The ratification of the Twenty-Sixth Amendment in 1971 reduced the voting age from 21 to 18, in acknowledgment of the sacrifices of young people sent to fight in Vietnam. In large numbers, women challenged and overcame traditional limits on their personal and work lives. Racial discrimination and segregation were outlawed. Immigration law for the first time welcomed new Americans equally, regardless of nation of origin or color of skin.

These years also witnessed striking disjunctures. The nation accomplished humanity's age-old dream of walking on the surface of the moon when Neil Armstrong stepped out of the *Apollo 11* spacecraft on July 20, 1969, while at home the country sometimes appeared to be coming apart at the seams. Poverty rates dropped to their lowest point ever, yet violence seemed to pervade the land. The slaughter of 43 people (mostly African Americans) by white state police retaking the Attica prison in upstate New York after an inmate insurrection in 1971 was one of the single most deadly confrontations between Americans since the Civil War.

The Vietnam War ended the Cold War consensus about the nation's duty to oppose communism abroad. The loss of this cornerstone of public purpose disoriented many citizens. The deceptive manner in which Johnson and Nixon waged the war eroded Americans' faith in their public officials. American life also grew more informal as the egalitarian style of the various social movements of the 1960s spread into the broader culture. But the removal of some of the most blatant distinctions of race and gender did not extend to differences of class. In the watershed cases of *San Antonio Independent School District v. Rodriguez* (1973) and *Milliken v. Bradley* (1974), the Supreme Court, led by Chief Justice Warren Burger, affirmed the autonomy of local school districts. Wealthier districts did not have to share financing with poorer ones, nor did they have to share students by means of busing. The Court ruled that there was no constitutional right to an education of equal quality. The ladder of social mobility remained slippery in a nation whose neighborhoods were still stratified between the affluent and the poor.

Sites to Visit

The Sixties Project

lists.village.virginia.edu/sixties/

This University of Virginia site has extensive exhibits, primary documents, and personal narratives from the 1960s.

Lyndon B. Johnson Library and Museum

www.lbjlib.utexas.edu/

This presidential library site has images and online exhibits.

The Wars for Vietnam: 1945 to 1975

http://vietnam.vassar.edu

Historian Robert Brigham's site offers an excellent overview of the U.S. war in Vietnam, along with critical documents and helpful links to other sites.

My Lai Court Martial (1970)

www.law.umkc.edu/faculty/projects/ftrials/mylai/mylai.htm

This site contains images, chronology, and court and official documents maintained by Doug Linder at the University of Missouri–Kansas City Law School.

Digger Archives

www.diggers.org

This site provides information about the San Francisco Diggers, a prominent countercultural group in the Haight-Ashbury scene of 1966–1968.

U.S. Latino History and Culture (Smithsonian Institution)

www.si.edu/resource/faq/nmah/latino.htm

This site offers exhibits, photos, resources, and links to other useful sites on the lives of Latino Americans.

Stonewall and Beyond: Lesbian and Gay Culture

www.columbia.edu/cu/lwweb/eresources/exhibitions/sw25/

This site includes articles from the New York City press as well as firsthand accounts of the 1969 Greenwich Village riots that are commemorated throughout the country during Gay Pride celebrations.

Malcolm X

http://www.brothermalcolm.net

This website includes a rich array of information about this key figure in the black freedom struggle.

For Further Reading

General

William H. Chafe, *The Unfinished Journey: America Since World War II,* 5th ed. (2003).

David Farber, *The Age of Great Dreams: America in the 1960s* (1994).

———, ed., *The Sixties: From Memory to History* (1994).

David Farber and Beth Bailey, *The Columbia Guide to America in the 1960s* (2001).

Maurice Isserman and Michael Kazin, *America Divided: The Civil War of the 1960s,* 2nd ed. (2004).

James T. Patterson, *Grand Expectations: The United States, 1945–1974* (1996).

Jeremi Suri, *Power and Protest: Global Revolution and the Rise of Détente* (2003).

Lyndon Johnson and the Apex of Liberalism

Robert Caro, *The Years of Lyndon Johnson,* 3 vols. (1982, 1990, 2002).

Robert Dallek, *Flawed Giant: Lyndon Johnson and His Times, 1961–1973* (1998).

Allen J. Matusow, *The Unravelling of America: A History of Liberalism in the 1960s* (1984).

Lucas A. Powe Jr., *The Warren Court and American Politics* (2000).

Bruce J. Schulman, *Lyndon B. Johnson and American Liberalism* (1995).

Into War in Vietnam

Lloyd C. Gardner, *Pay Any Price: Lyndon Johnson and the Wars for Vietnam* (1995).

Michael Herr, *Dispatches* (1977).

George C. Herring, *America's Longest War: The United States and Vietnam, 1950–1975,* 4th ed. (2001).

Fredrik Logevall, *Choosing War: The Lost Chance for Peace and the Escalation of War in Vietnam* (1999).

Robert D. Schulzinger, *A Time for War: The United States and Vietnam, 1941–1975* (1997).

Marilyn B. Young, *The Vietnam Wars, 1945–1990* (1991).

The Movement

Terry H. Anderson, *The Movement and the Sixties: Protest in America from Greensboro to Wounded Knee* (1995).

Alice Echols, *Daring to Be Bad: Radical Feminism in America, 1967–1975* (1989).

Sara Evans, *Personal Politics: The Roots of Women's Liberation in the Civil Rights Movement and the New Left* (1979).

Todd Gitlin, *The Sixties: Years of Hope, Days of Rage* (1987).

Malcolm X, *The Autobiography of Malcolm X* (1965).

Timothy Miller, *The '60s Communes: Hippies and Beyond* (1999).

William L. Van Deburg, *New Day in Babylon: The Black Power Movement and American Culture, 1965–1975* (1992).

Tom Wells, *The War Within: America's Battle over Vietnam* (1994).

The Conservative Response

Stephen Ambrose, *Nixon: The Triumph of a Politician, 1962–1972* (1989).

Dan T. Carter, *The Politics of Rage: George Wallace, the Origins of the New Conservatism, and the Transformation of American Politics,* 2nd ed. (2000).

Jeffrey Kimball, *Nixon's Vietnam War* (1998).

Lisa McGirr, *Suburban Warriors: The Origins of the New American Right* (2001).

Hal K. Rothman, *The Greening of a Nation? Environmentalism in the United States Since 1945* (1998).

Melvin Small, *The Presidency of Richard Nixon* (1999).

CHAPTER 27

Reconsidering National Priorities, 1972–1979

George Segal, "Walk, Don't Walk," 1976. © George and Helen Segal Foundation/Licensed by VAGA, New York. Purchase, with funds from the Louis and Bessie Adler Foundation, Inc., Seymour M. Klein, President, the Gilman Foundation, Inc., the Howard and Jean Lipman Foundation, Inc., and the National Endowment for the Arts. Photograph © 1996: Whitney Museum of American Art, New York (79.4)

▲ This 1976 sculpture by George Segal hinted at the uncertainties that pervaded American society in the mid-1970s.

CHAPTER OUTLINE

Twin Shocks: Détente and Watergate

Discovering the Limits of the U.S. Economy

Reshuffling Politics

Diffusing the Women's Movement

Conclusion

Sites to Visit

For Further Reading

The Susquehanna River flows southward through the pretty hills of Pennsylvania toward the Chesapeake Bay. Ten miles south of Harrisburg, the state capital, two nuclear power plants sit on Three Mile Island in the middle of the river. In the quiet early morning darkness of March 28, 1979, one of the two reactors began to malfunction. Pumps and valves that controlled the cooling water for the nuclear core shut down. Plant operators misunderstood what was happening and reacted with mistaken procedures that deepened the emergency. The core began to melt down.

Before plant operators managed to stop the meltdown, Three Mile Island's containment buildings filled with deadly levels of radioactivity. Some radioactive materials were released into the air, and throughout the five days of the crisis, the possibility of further releases of poisonous gases encouraged one-fifth of the population within a 20-mile radius to evacuate voluntarily.

Three Mile Island was the largest but not the only scare of the 1970s regarding nuclear energy. In 1972 Karen Silkwood, a divorced mother of three, began working as a laboratory analyst at Kerr-McGee's plutonium processing plant in Crescent, Oklahoma. There the highly poisonous radioactive material was made into fuel rods for nuclear power plants, such as those at Three Mile Island. In 1974 Silkwood was elected a local official of the union that represented many Kerr-McGee workers and began organizing for greater worker safety. She learned of numerous incidents of radioactive contamination at the plant. She also uncovered evidence of significant quantities of missing plutonium and of doctored quality assurance records for defective fuel rods. On November 5, she was mysteriously contaminated with potentially lethal levels of plutonium. On November 13 Silkwood set out for Oklahoma City to meet a national representative of her union and a *New York Times* reporter, intending to give them documents proving that Kerr-McGee was knowingly manufacturing defective nuclear products. She never made it. Her car was forced off the road and she died instantly when it crashed into a concrete culvert.

Karen Silkwood became a symbol of courage to many.

Karen Silkwood challenged the power of one of the nation's largest energy corporations and paid with her life. Her brief career as a whistleblower brought together major issues of the 1970s: labor organizing, environmental damage, the safety record of nuclear energy, and the power of corporations over individual citizens. Her dismissive treatment by some fellow workers, her employers, and the media also suggested the lack of respect that women had long endured, especially when they moved out of the traditional homemaker role. ABC television news anchor Howard K. Smith began his coverage of a women's rights march in New York City in 1970 by quoting with approval the words of Vice President Spiro Agnew: "Three things have been difficult to tame. The ocean, fools, and women. We may soon be able to tame the ocean, but fools and women will take a little longer."

Condescension toward women pervaded American society, and few men even noticed it. The political upheavals of the 1960s had barely touched the relationships between most women and men by the start of the new decade. But all this changed as the 1970s unfolded. The spread of ideas about women's liberation in the 1970s transformed the personal lives of almost every American, female and male alike. **Feminism** challenged the most basic and intimate assumptions about relationships, family, work, and power. It also sharply expanded women's opportunities. At the end of the decade, Dr. Martha Hurley of

Kansas City recalled, "In the middle of an operation today, I looked around the room—to the first assistant, my scrub nurse, and circulating nurse, the anesthesia doctor, nurse anesthetist, and the patient—and suddenly realized that we were performing major surgery and there was not a man in the room!"

Who were the feminists? They were mothers and wives, college students, professional women, and working-class women. Their growing awareness of gender discrimination had made them angry but also optimistic about change. And some feminists were men who realized that the movement could liberate them from their own narrowly defined masculine roles.

Many Americans resented challenges to their beliefs about men's and women's proper roles. J. Edgar Hoover, director of the Federal Bureau of Investigation (FBI), exemplified the resistance that could catalyze against demands for fair treatment of women. Well known for his dislike of leftists, African Americans, homosexuals, and anyone else who questioned the existing social order—including labor organizers such as Karen Silkwood—Hoover ordered his agents to infiltrate the women's liberation movement. (Ironically, Hoover was a cross-dresser in private and perhaps also gay, an apparent case of self-loathing.) Feminists, he warned FBI regional directors, "should be viewed as part of the enemy, a challenge to American values." At one point, the director instructed an FBI field office to "identify the officers and aims and objectives of this organization." But despite determined digging for information, a paid informant could report only that "this movement has no leaders, dues or organizations." Women's liberation was both nowhere and everywhere. No one could trace it to a specific group of conspirators.

In a certain sense, Hoover was right: the feminist wave did call traditional values and hierarchies into question as it washed over the United States in the 1970s. It joined with other developments of the decade to force Americans to reexamine much that they had taken for granted. Elected on the promise to end the war in Southeast Asia "with honor," President Nixon escalated the fighting before eventually withdrawing U.S. forces from Vietnam. At the same time, he repaired relations with both China and the Soviet Union as those two communist powers drew apart. Americans thus suffered their first clear defeat in war while also seeing the Cold War splinter. Scandal in the White House then forced the first resignation of a U.S. president and deepened public distrust of political authorities. American economic growth—the foundation of the country's power—stumbled because of spending on the Vietnam War and oil shortages. High-paying manufacturing jobs declined as factories began to move overseas in pursuit of cheaper labor, and skilled blue-collar workers saw their status as middle-class Americans start to slip. Unemployment grew sharply. And a growing environmental movement raised disturbing questions about whether an expanding economy and exploitation of natural resources should continue to top the country's list of priorities.

> ***The feminist wave called traditional values and hierarchies into question as it washed over the United States in the 1970s.***

The nation celebrated its two-hundredth birthday in 1976 amid these uncertainties. That year, one-term Georgia governor Jimmy Carter won election to the White House by promising to restore honesty and trust to the federal government. In his first two years in office, Carter shifted the nation's foreign-policy focus away from fighting communism toward building warmer relations with the Third World. He saw Americans' dependence on imported oil as a primary national security problem and implored citizens to scale back their lavish consumption of fossil fuels. But his presidency eventually foundered on persistent economic stagnation and inflation at home, upheavals abroad, and Carter's own limitations as chief executive.

Journalist Tom Wolfe dubbed the 1970s the "Me Decade," a phrase that proved even more appropriate for the 1980s. The label did have some merit: many Americans turned away from the public sphere after the exhilarating but divisive politics of the 1960s and pursued self-exploration and self-fulfillment instead. Crime, divorce, premarital and extramarital sex, and drug use all increased while the nation's economic health and international status declined. But the 1970s also witnessed a rethinking of long-standing assumptions: about how democracy should work at home, what role the nation should play in international affairs, how people ought to treat the environment, and how men and women should relate to each other. The decade offered a window of opportunity for Americans to reimagine their values and priorities for the future.

Twin Shocks: Détente and Watergate

Richard Nixon had long been the nation's leading anticommunist. No one had more fiercely opposed leftists at home and communists in China and the Soviet Union. However, the president was more a savvy political opportunist than an ideologue. He and his national security adviser, Henry Kissinger, saw a chance to use mounting Chinese-Soviet tensions to the advantage of the United States as they withdrew American armed forces from Vietnam.

At the same time that Nixon manipulated the Cold War abroad, the Republican president initiated a campaign of illegal actions at home to destroy his political opponents in the Democratic party. This strategy backfired in a scandal that drove him from office in 1974. Having undercut the logic of anticommunism abroad by warming relations with communist leaders in Beijing and Moscow, Nixon eroded the bipartisan consensus at home that had long supported the Cold War.

Triangular Diplomacy

Nixon and Kissinger prided themselves on their "realpolitik" approach to foreign policy: their pragmatic assessment of other powers' security needs, regardless of ideology, and their collaboration with those powers on issues of common concern. In 1969 China and the USSR gave Nixon and Kissinger an ideal opportunity to exercise their realpolitik skills. That year, tensions that had been building between the two communist states erupted in brief skirmishing between Chinese and Soviet troops on their shared border. For two decades, Americans had seen the communist bloc as impenetrable. But Nixon realized he could play China and the USSR against each other, and he seized the chance. That is, he saw a way to make not only Chinese leader Mao Zedong but also Soviet leader Leonid Brezhnev into another "Tito," an independent communist with ties to the West, like Premier Josef Tito of Yugoslavia. Nixon thus envisioned a "triangular diplomacy" that he hoped would divide the communist world.

Any fundamental revision of the nation's foreign policy, Nixon and Kissinger believed, could happen only if they concentrated all decision-making in the White House.

The president and Kissinger, a former Harvard professor with an intriguing German accent, also shared a commitment to secrecy. Any fundamental revision of the nation's foreign policy, they believed, could happen only if they concentrated all decision-making in the White House. They set out to keep Congress, the press, and even their own State Department in the dark. Diplomatic innovation thus went hand in hand with an unprecedented extension of the secretive national security state.

In February 1972, after a secret foray by Kissinger to Beijing, Nixon stunned Americans and the world by announcing that he would be the first U.S. president to visit China. The Soviets and the Vietnamese expressed dismay at the news, and liberal Democrats at home could

▶ MAP 27.1 NUCLEAR WEAPONS BEFORE DÉTENTE
The massive nuclear arsenals of the United States and the Soviet Union utterly surpassed those of the other nuclear powers. During the 1970s the Soviets achieved rough parity with the Americans in total nuclear warheads. The numbers for both sides were sufficient to destroy the entire populated world many times over.

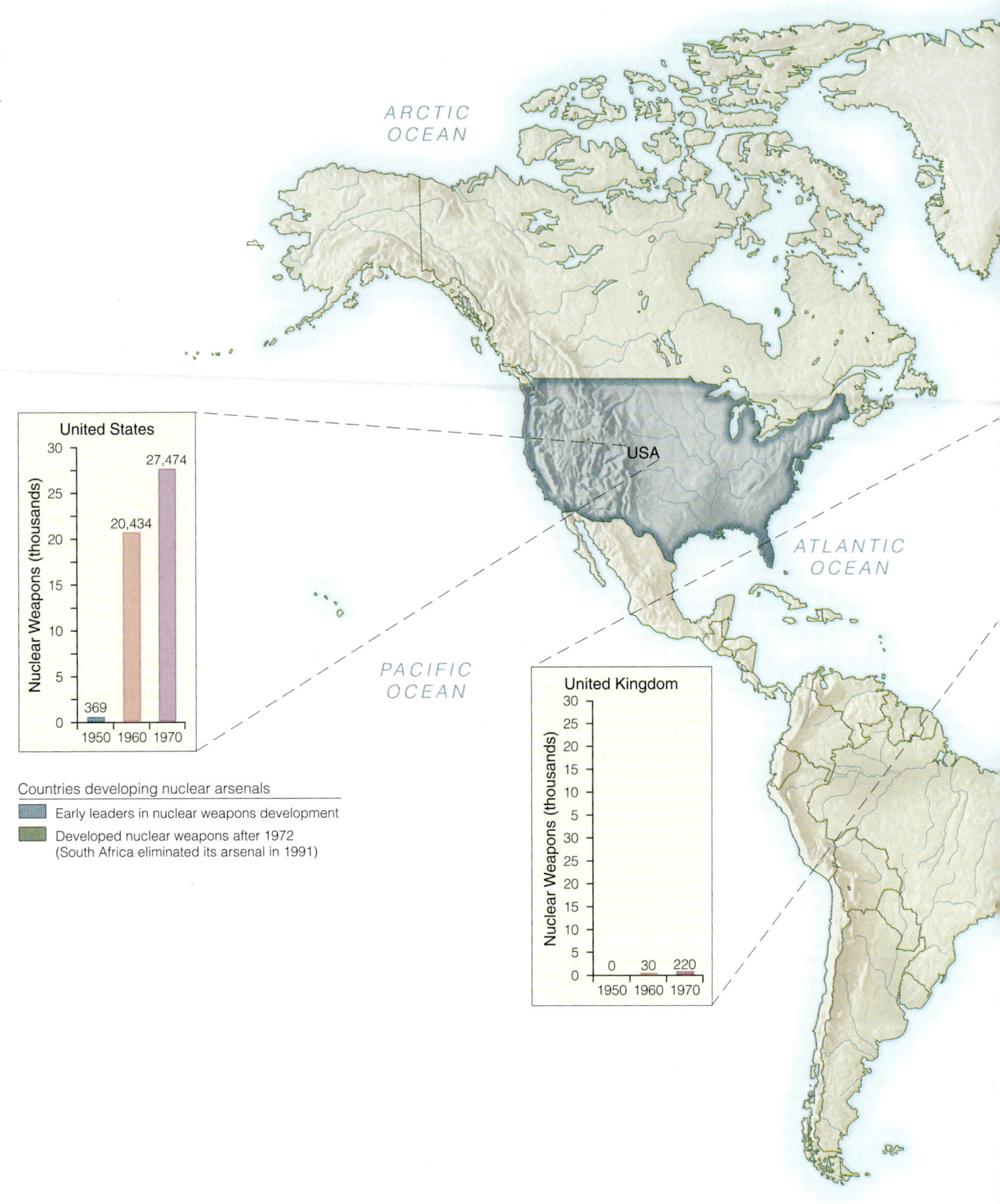

only gape, speechless, at their opponent's diplomatic coup: how could Nixon, a dyed-in-the-wool anticommunist, go to China? But that was precisely the point: as Democratic party insider Clark Clifford explained, Nixon was "the first president since the [Second World] War who didn't have to worry about Richard Nixon" attacking him for being "soft" on communism.

As it turned out, Nixon's visit brought a host of benefits. Live television coverage showed Nixon toasting Mao while a Chinese military band played "America the Beautiful" and "Home on the Range." Americans' impression of the People's Republic as a grim, forbidding land began to give way to a renewed interest in China as an exotic but intriguing place. Cultural exchanges

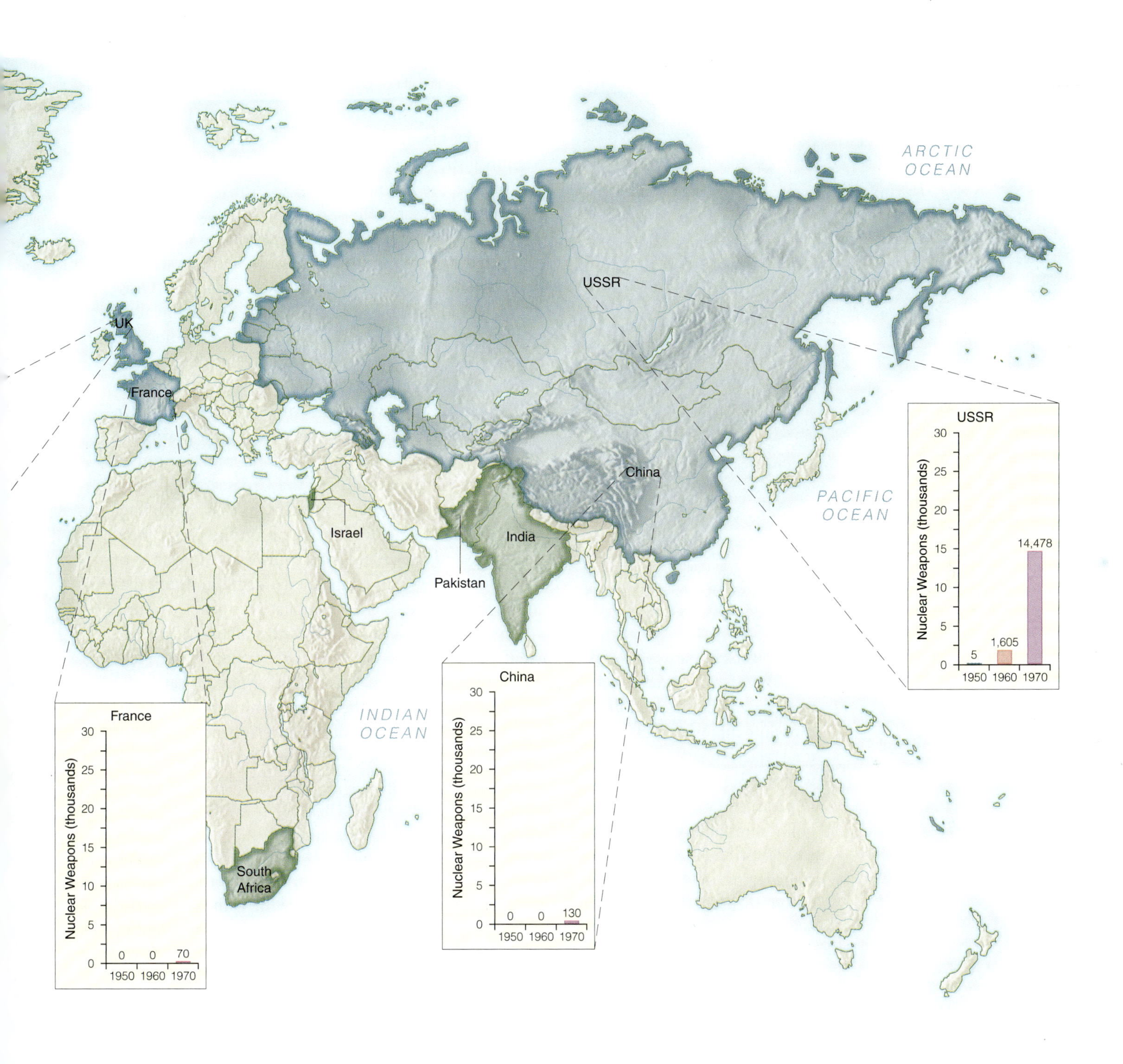

soon proliferated: first ping-pong teams, eventually legions of students. U.S. businesses also cast a covetous eye at the immense China market. Trade between the two nations rose dramatically over the next three decades.

Nixon and Kissinger now constructed the other leg of their diplomatic triangle. As they anticipated, the Soviets had taken alarm at the warming of relations between their two greatest rivals. They signaled their concern to Washington and suggested that the United States include them in the new arrangements. The Russians and the Americans both wanted to reduce the costliness of maintaining enormous nuclear arsenals, and each side saw lucrative trading possibilities with the other. Nixon flew to Moscow for a summit meeting with Brezhnev in May 1972

National Archives

▲ President Nixon met the premier of the People's Republic of China, Mao Zedong, in Beijing on February 29, 1972. The U.S. government had shunned China since its communist revolution in 1949. Richard Nixon's amiable visit there stunned observers and altered the dynamics of the Cold War.

that initiated a policy of **détente** (relaxation of tensions). A trade pact quickly followed. The two superpowers also agreed to limit offensive nuclear weapons (the Strategic Arms Limitations Treaty, or SALT I) and to ban antiballistic missile defense systems (the ABM treaty).

Like the Soviet leaders, Nixon and Kissinger sought to preserve the existing international balance of power. Deal making with China and the USSR constituted one step in this process. In another, the two men sought to stifle socialist revolutions in Third World nations by bolstering pro-American allies there. For instance, the duo feared that the democratic election of socialist Salvador Allende in Chile in 1970 would lead to "another Cuba." A socialist leader might nationalize the investments of U.S. corporations in Chile and perhaps challenge Washington's capitalist hegemony in the Western Hemisphere. Determined to block these possibilities, the CIA secretly funded a right-wing military coup in Chile in September 1973. Allende died in the assault on the presidential palace, and the rebel forces murdered thousands of his supporters and established a brutal military dictatorship under General Augusto Pinochet. "I don't see why we need to stand by and watch a country go Communist because of the irresponsibility of its own people," Kissinger explained privately.

There was little danger of such voter "irresponsibility" in South Africa, a nation that would not see democratic elections for another two decades. Still, the Nixon administration backed the white minority regime there, despite worldwide criticism of the government's policies of total racial segregation, or apartheid. Nixon's "southern strategy" of appealing to segregationist whites at home during the 1968 election campaign thus had an international parallel. He sought to preserve a pro-American order in South Africa, the southern tip of a continent rife with political instability.

Nixon and Kissinger reached beyond Latin America and Africa. They also bolstered the autocratic regime of Shah Reza Pahlavi of Iran. They sold him unlimited arms in return for Iranian oil shipments and political support in the strategic Middle East, where the United States had few allies. The president could not know it at the time, but preserving the shah's oppressive rule carried a high price—one that the United States would begin to pay before the 1970s were over.

Scandal in the White House

On June 17, 1972, Washington police caught agents of Nixon's reelection campaign breaking into the Democratic National Committee headquarters in the Watergate hotel and office complex. The burglars' goal was to put in place secretive listening devices, or "bugs." Later, the White House tried to cover up its connections to the break-in.

Ironically, the Republicans hardly needed to resort to illegal actions to hold onto the White House in 1972. The New Deal coalition that had kept the Democrats as the majority party since the 1930s was fast unraveling. White Southerners and many ethnic European Northerners were abandoning the party amid its increasing identification with black civil rights, feminism, and cultural liberalism. Middle- and upper-middle-class liberal activists had helped nominate Senator George McGovern of South Dakota, a former World War II pilot and college professor, as the Democratic presidential candidate, primarily on the basis of his principled and longstanding opposition to the war in Vietnam. Playing upon voter anxiety about cultural changes, the Republicans tarred McGovern's supporters with favoring "the 3 A's": acid (the drug LSD), abortion, and amnesty for draft evaders. McGovern's campaign never overcame that image of radicalism, and in November Nixon won 61 percent of the popular vote. He also swept the electoral votes of every state but one. Bumper stickers reading "Don't blame me, I'm from Massachusetts" proliferated as the Watergate scandal deepened.

But the Watergate break-in was only one step in Nixon's broader campaign of illegal warfare against his political opponents. The conflict still raging in Vietnam had polarized Americans more than at any time since the Civil War, and the president compiled a lengthy and secret "enemies list."

Nixon and Kissinger had taken things even further in May 1969, when they established the first in a long series of wiretaps without court warrants on their own staffs and on reporters. They were determined to discover the source of a newspaper story that had mentioned secret American bombing of neutral Cambodia. Several wartime presidents in the past had successfully silenced dissenters, but Nixon overreached still further. The president ultimately poisoned the very heart of American politics by his clandestine use of the government's powerful executive branch to undermine the mainstream opposition party and others who seemed to challenge his policies.

After the bungled Watergate break-in, the president directed the cover-up from the beginning, then lied about it to the public.

The president and his aides regularly discussed "how we can use the available federal machinery to screw our political enemies," in the words of White House counsel John Dean. They persuaded the FBI and the CIA to monitor and harass antiwar activists and pushed the Internal Revenue Service to investigate prominent Democrats. They extorted large contributions to the Republican party from corporate executives by making it clear that federal agencies would otherwise impede the pursuit of their business interests. The *New York Times*'s publication of the classified Pentagon Papers in 1971 stiffened the resolve of the Committee to Reelect the President (CREEP) to stop any further leaks. The committee assembled a group of undercover operatives (the "plumbers") to engineer "dirty tricks" against the Democrats. Their activities included smearing the reputation of one leading presidential candidate, Senator Edmund Muskie of Maine, and sowing dissent and distrust among Democratic voters.

After the bungled Watergate break-in, the president directed the cover-up from the beginning, then lied about it to the public. He also used the CIA to hinder the FBI's investigation into the matter. He approved payments of hush money to the burglars to keep them quiet about their ties to the White House. Nixon's abuse of power escalated as he pressured his subordinates to perjure themselves in court. For most of a year the cover-up held, and Nixon won reelection in 1972.

Richard Nixon, "I am not a crook"

But the persistent investigations by *Washington Post* journalists Bob Woodward and Carl Bernstein kept the heat on. In early 1973, the administration began to crack due to a grand jury probe in the federal court of Judge John Sirica. The president's men lost confidence that the cover-up would hold and began looking for ways to save their own skins. Convicted Watergate burglar James McCord wrote Judge Sirica that the White House had indeed been involved in the break-in. White House counsel Dean and former Attorney General John Mitchell refused Nixon's requests to absorb full blame and become scapegoats. Congress initiated its own televised investigations that mesmerized a national audience. The Senate Watergate committee, chaired by eloquent conservative North Carolina Democrat Sam Ervin, methodically exposed the criminal actions in the White House with growing bipartisan support. The key issue, as framed by Republican committee member Howard Baker of Tennessee, became "What did the president know, and when did he know it?"

On July 16, 1973, White House aide Alexander Butterfield told the Ervin committee that a built-in recorder taped all conversations in the Oval Office. Almost certainly, these tapes would provide answers to questions about the president's role. Both Congress and Justice Department special prosecutor Archibald Cox subpoenaed the White House tapes, but Nixon refused to hand them over. Instead, he fired Cox on October 20 in what became known as the Saturday

TimePix/Getty Images

Dennis Brack/Black Star/Stock Photo

▲ **On August 9, 1974, Richard Nixon became the only U.S. president to resign from office. As he left by helicopter one last time from the south lawn of the White House, he offered a defiant victory gesture rather than a presidential salute (inset). Vice President Gerald Ford, with his wife, Betty, then walked back to the White House to be sworn in as the nation's 38th president.**

Night Massacre. Outraged, Congress initiated impeachment proceedings against the president. In the spring of 1974, the House of Representatives passed bills of impeachment for his specific abuses of power. Before the Senate could vote on whether to find Nixon guilty of the House charges, the Supreme Court ruled that the White House had to turn over the subpoenaed tapes. The content of the tapes revealed the extent of the president's involvement in the cover-up and his personal crudeness, vindictiveness, and ethnic and racial prejudices. Facing a certain guilty verdict, Nixon resigned on August 9, 1974, less than halfway through his second term.

Committee's Conclusion on Impeachment

The Nation After Watergate

Never before had a U.S. president resigned from office. Many citizens celebrated the outcome of the Watergate investigations as evidence of democracy's resilience and power to uncover criminal activity in the White House and bring down a corrupt president. But the affair also discredited political institutions Americans had long respected. If you can't trust the president, U.S. citizens lamented, whom *can* you trust? Indeed, the Nixon administration proved quite corrupt. A whole raft of senior officials, including the president's closest aides, H. R. Haldeman and John Ehrlichman, went to prison. Even Vice President Spiro Agnew had been forced to resign amid the Watergate investigations when a Maryland jury found him guilty of tax evasion dating back to his years as governor there. The actions of Nixon and those who served him permanently tarnished the reputation of politicians, and some citizens responded by disengaging from the political process. The percentage of eligible voters actually casting ballots sank from 61 percent in 1968 to 53 percent in 1980, diminishing the practice of democracy: rule by the people.

Since 1945, the executive branch had grown increasingly powerful during the international crises of the Cold War, but Nixon's fall crippled the "imperial presidency." After Watergate,

Congress began to reclaim its constitutional responsibilities in international affairs. As the bicentennial of American independence approached, citizens' suspicion of corruption in high places recalled the Whiggish attitudes of the country's revolutionary leaders two centuries before. Most immediately, Congress swung strongly to the Democrats in the 1974 elections, slowing the Republicans' rise to the status of majority party.

The man who replaced Nixon in the White House faced a daunting situation. Gerald Ford, longtime Republican member of Congress from Grand Rapids, Michigan, and House minority leader, had been tapped by Nixon to replace Agnew as vice president. Well liked by members of both parties, Ford seemed to embody the antidote to the extreme styles of both Nixon and Agnew. To restore decency and trust in the government, Ford saw his role as healing what he called "the wounds of the past." Within a month, he granted a "full, free, and absolute pardon" to Nixon for any crimes he may have committed as president, precluding any trial and punishment within a court of law. However, most Americans believed that Nixon should have faced justice for his actions, as had the people who carried out his orders. Ford's approval ratings plummeted overnight from 72 percent to 49 percent and never fully recovered.

If Ford inherited the fallout from Watergate at home, abroad he inherited the pending defeat in Vietnam. Few Americans wanted to dwell on the meaning of the disastrous U.S. involvement in Southeast Asia. Military veterans returned to a nation determined to ignore or demean their sacrifices, and they quickly learned to keep their combat-induced traumas to themselves. When Saigon finally fell to the combined invasion of National Liberation Front and North Vietnamese fighters on April 30, 1975, Americans watched the televised images with both bitterness and relief. Two weeks later, Cambodian communist forces briefly seized the U.S. container ship *Mayaguez*, provoking Ford to demonstrate that the United States was still ready and willing to flex its military muscle. But 41 U.S. soldiers died in the rescue mission to save

▼ The last U.S. combat troops left Vietnam in 1973. Forces of the National Liberation Front and North Vietnam swept into the capital of South Vietnam, Saigon, on April 30, 1975. Here, one day earlier, a U.S. Marine helicopter on the roof of the U.S. embassy loads Americans and a few Vietnamese allies onto one of the last flights out.

Bettmann/CORBIS

Bettmann/CORBIS

▲ Many South Vietnamese fled the communist victory in their country in 1975, including this woman and her family crossing the Mekong River. Most of the refugees undertook extremely perilous journeys by boat to other Southeast Asian nations, and hundreds of thousands eventually made their way to the United States.

39 sailors whom, it turned out, Cambodia had already released. Ford and Kissinger, serving as the new president's secretary of state, continued to pursue détente with the Soviets at summit meetings in Vladivostock (1974) and Helsinki (1975). At the same time, they supported anticommunist forces in various Third World conflicts, such as the civil war that erupted in Angola after that country achieved its independence in 1975.

Discovering the Limits of the U.S. Economy

Generation after generation of Americans had watched their incomes rise, and most children expected to be wealthier than their parents had been. Since World War II had pulled the U.S. economy out of the Great Depression, median family income had doubled. Most Americans saw themselves as citizens of the world's richest country and prized the status that came with this privilege. But by 1973, the famous American standard of living began to decline. The three pillars of postwar prosperity—cheap energy, rising wages, and low inflation—simultaneously crumbled. The costs of the Vietnam War struck home at the same time that an oil embargo spawned by conflict in the Middle East gripped the country. Moreover, a widening environmental movement raised questions about the pursuit of endless economic growth on a planet that more and more people realized had limited natural resources. For the first time since the 1930s, Americans started to doubt what the economic future had in store for them.

The End of the Long Boom

Stagnation and inflation typically do not strike an economy at the same time. With stagnation, prices and wages stay level or even decline; with inflation, prices rise and jobs multiply. During the 1970s, however, a terrible new economic scourge dubbed "stagflation" hit the United States. For the first time, employment and wages stagnated while prices climbed. What explained this phenomenon? Spending on the Vietnam War had pulled prices upward. The government had never raised enough taxes to cover the expense of the war, so it paid the bills by simply printing more dollars—a sure-fire way to create inflation. In 1971, annual inflation stood at 4.5 percent, more than twice the pre-Vietnam rate; two years later it reached 10 percent, and by 1980 it topped out at 18 percent.

These figures devastated Americans' sense of economic security. Average real wages (income adjusted for inflation) dropped by 2 percent a year from 1973 to the 1990s. Unemployment rose to 9 percent in 1975, driven in part by continued automation of the workplace. Only the continued flow of women into the workforce, seen by most families as an economic necessity, kept the majority of U.S. families afloat financially. The portion of citizens living in poverty, which had dropped sharply through the 1960s to 11 percent in 1973, rose again, hitting 15 percent by 1982. The gap between rich and poor began widening, a process that persisted into the next millennium.

So ended the long boom of economic growth that had buoyed American life from 1945 to 1973. But perhaps the most telling evidence of the weakening economy came with the drop in the growth of productivity: output per worker-hour had risen at an annual average of more than 3 percent during the boom. From 1974 to 1992, it rose at less than half that rate.

This decline stemmed in part from competition from abroad, particularly West Germany and Japan. With U.S. assistance (and without the military expenditures that so burdened the United States), those countries had finally rebuilt their economies after World War II and boasted new, more efficient industrial facilities. Imported cars, for example, grew from just 8 percent of the U.S. market in 1970 to 22 percent in 1979 as Hondas, Toyotas, Volkswagens, and Mercedes streamed onto American highways. And the trade surplus that had long symbolized global U.S. economic superiority evaporated in 1971. That year, U.S. imports overtook exports for the first time in the twentieth century. Worried international investors traded in dollars for gold, forcing Nixon to end the 27-year-old Bretton Woods monetary system that had linked all other currencies to the dollar at fixed exchange rates. Freed from the fixed rate of $35 per ounce of gold, the dollar dropped like a stone; by the end of the decade, it took $800 to buy an ounce of gold.

Average real wages dropped by 2 percent a year from 1973 to the 1990s.

In this competitive environment, the *Wall Street Journal* reported, American companies "seek places where labor, land, electricity, and taxes are cheap." Corporations found those places in the American South and Southwest, regions characterized by scarce unions, low wage rates, minimal taxes, and negligible local government regulations. Many more such places were in neighboring Mexico, where U.S. companies established *maquiladoras* as early as 1965. These assembly plants, often just a few hundred yards across the Mexican-U.S. border, allowed corporations to hire primarily female workers at low wages and avoid strict U.S. environmental, labor, and safety laws. "The worst drawback of maquiladora work is all the damage we do to our health" by working with toxic chemicals and solvents, one employee reported. The wages, cheap by U.S. standards, were nonetheless higher than elsewhere in Mexico and drew laborers from central Mexico north to the border region. The long-term decline of the U.S. Rustbelt—the series of urban industrial centers strung across the American Northeast and Midwest—accelerated in the 1970s.

High unemployment and shrinking real wages contributed to rising anti-immigrant sentiment. Two white autoworkers in Detroit in 1982 got into an altercation in a bar with Vincent Chin, a Chinese American (and son of a World War II veteran) whom they called a "Jap." Angered that Japanese auto sales were undercutting jobs in Detroit, they made Chin a scapegoat for their rage, chasing him down the street and beating him to death with a baseball bat. At the same time, Vietnamese refugees who had fled the communist victory in their homeland in 1975 to make a life as shrimp fishers on the Gulf Coast of Texas found their equipment sabotaged by some white competitors.

From Texas to California, Latinos also suffered violence at the hands of both officials and private citizens. For example, three members of the Ku Klux Klan abducted a Latino hitchhiker outside San Diego and delivered him to the U.S. Immigration Service for deportation to Mexico, even though he was an American citizen. A wave of police brutality against Latinos alarmed even the White House by 1978, thanks to the lobbying of outraged Latino citizen organizations.

Black Americans also faced an increasing backlash against hard-won civil rights gains. While court-ordered busing to integrate schools in segregated neighborhoods proceeded slowly but peacefully in the South, northern urban whites dug in their heels. In Boston, violence erupted in the school hallways and the streets from 1975 to 1978 as economically vulnerable working-class whites harassed African Americans attending schools in white ethnic neighborhoods of South Boston, and blacks defended themselves.

Stanley J. Forman, *The Soiling of Old Glory*, Pulitzer Prize 1976

▲ **White resistance to school busing in Boston sometimes turned violent in the mid-1970s. On April 5, 1976, white high school students from South Boston and Charlestown met with a city council member who supported their boycott of classes. Outside City Hall, they chanced upon lawyer Theodore Landsmark and assaulted him. Photographer Stanley J. Forman won the Pulitzer Prize for this photo.**

The Oil Embargo

Nothing revealed Americans' newfound economic vulnerability more than the 1973–1974 boycott initiated by the Oil Producing and Exporting Countries (OPEC). The United States and the Soviet Union, along with Mexico and Venezuela, retained large oil reserves. But the largest producers were the Arab countries around the Persian Gulf, especially Saudi Arabia. These nations had resented the creation of Israel in 1948 and the resulting displacement of the Palestinians. Hostility intensified with the events of 1967. That year, Israel seized control of the West Bank of the Jordan River and the Gaza Strip. Six years later, Egypt and Syria struck back, attacking and threatening to overrun Israel.

At this point, the United States intervened. Nixon instructed the Pentagon to "send everything that will fly" to the Israelis—a massive resupply of weapons, combined with intelli-

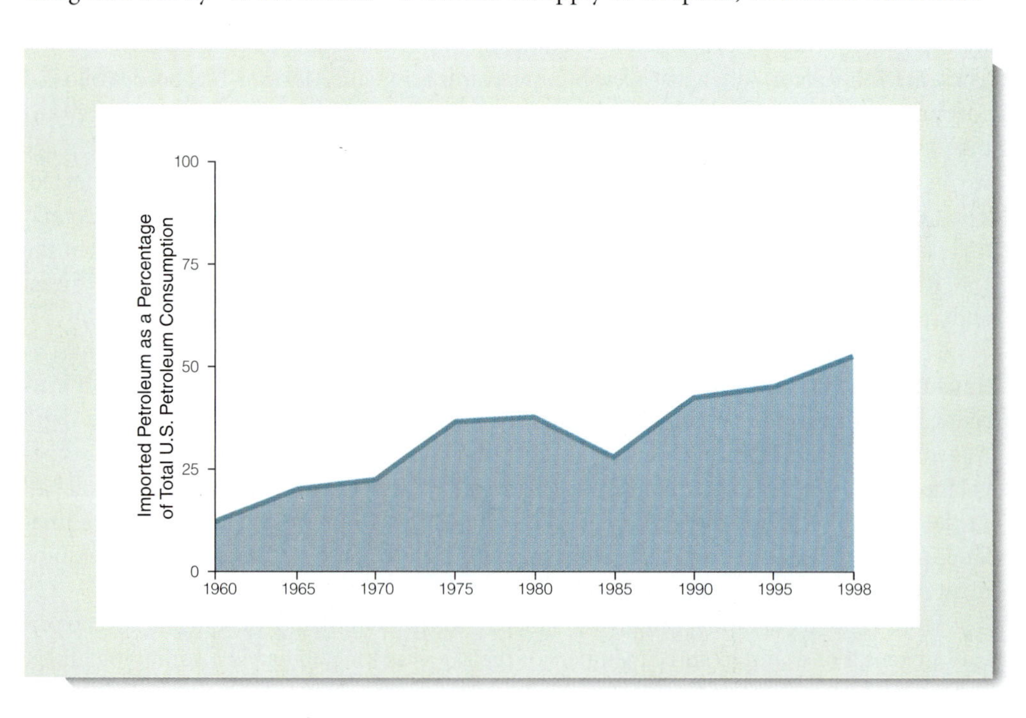

▶ **FIGURE 27.1** IMPORTED PETROLEUM AS SHARE OF U.S. CONSUMPTION
Abundant natural resources, especially coal and oil, encouraged Americans' long-standing feeling of national strength and autonomy. After World War II, however, the United States switched from exporting oil to importing oil. Conservation measures in the 1970s temporarily reversed America's growing dependence on oil from abroad.

gence on Arab troop movements. "We will not let Israel go down the tubes," the president declared. The tide of battle turned. Henry Kissinger then shuttled between Tel Aviv and Cairo to negotiate a ceasefire. His diplomatic skills won him the Nobel peace prize and laid the groundwork for a warming of U.S. relations with Egypt (the most populous Arab nation but not an oil producer).

However, the other Arab states expressed outrage at this demonstration of America's close links with the Israelis, and Kissinger's being Jewish only underlined the point. The U.S. commitment to Israel had never been clearer, and Arabs of all political persuasions were determined to voice their displeasure. In October 1973, the OPEC nations initiated an embargo on selling oil to the United States and to western European nations that had supported Israel in the war. Never before in peacetime had foreign policy affected Americans so directly. Oil supplies dwindled, and prices at gas pumps skyrocketed to four times their previous levels. Even when OPEC lifted the embargo after five months, it kept prices high by limiting production.

The U.S. commitment to Israel had never been clearer, and Arabs of all political persuasions were determined to voice their displeasure.

Steeper energy costs powerfully accelerated inflation. Decades of easy access to cheap gasoline came to a sudden halt. As American drivers formed long lines at the pump, President Ford urged them to drive at lower speeds to conserve gas. Americans confronted new and sobering limits on their mobility.

The Environmental Movement

The oil embargo encouraged many U.S. citizens to rethink the nation's cavalier use of natural resources. Environmental consciousness spread rapidly in the 1970s as evidence revealed the impact of industrial growth on the quality of life in the United States. Environmental organizations such as the Sierra Club, the National Wildlife Federation, and the Audubon Society saw their memberships soar. For the first time, the media began to examine the daunting range of environmental problems plaguing the United States and the rest of the world: acid rain, groundwater contamination, smog, rainforest destruction, oil spills, nuclear waste disposal, species extinction, ozone depletion, and global warming. A growing interest in ecology—human interaction with the wider web of life—expanded the efforts of older conservationists to preserve parklands. Residents of an urbanized mass society began to contemplate the wider consequences of small private acts such as watering the lawn, flushing the toilet, or leaving the lights on.

A new generation of Americans, unable to remember Depression scarcities and wartime rationing, was wasteful, sometimes extravagantly so. U.S. soldiers had expressed surprise when displaced Vietnamese civilians built shelters out of the aluminum cans the troops threw away so casually. Home to only 6 percent of the global population, the United States consumed as much as a third of the world's energy from nonrenewable fossil fuels such as oil and coal. Polluted air hung over the largest U.S. cities. The first evidence of global warming began to appear in the 1970s. Scientists also noticed the rapid thinning of the ozone layer in the earth's atmosphere in 1973. They attributed the problem in part to the widespread use of aerosol spray cans—especially by Americans, the world's wealthiest people. The production of inexpensive plastics from oil had also soared since World War II. Styrofoam cups and plastic containers littered the roadsides. Disposable diapers and other nonbiodegradable products accumulated in landfills in what became known as the throwaway culture.

Environmentalists argued that the idea of unlimited consumption of natural resources was fundamentally irresponsible, both to future human generations and to other species. They urged Congress and the Environmental Protection Agency (EPA) to require fuel-efficient engines from carmakers and to promote renewable energy sources such as water, solar, and wind power. Citizen groups such as the Clamshell Alliance in New England and the Abalone Alliance in California protested the construction of new nuclear power plants. These operations, they pointed out, had no reliable method in place for disposing of nuclear waste. What if the public were exposed to radiation? Their warnings had merit: cancer rates began to rise in populations that had close

Energy Use in the United States

Most Americans who lived through the 1970s remember gasoline shortages and price hikes as one of the decade's most distinctive features. No previous generation had experienced so steep a decline in the availability of a primary source of energy that was the key to its transportation system. In World War II the government had rationed gasoline to conserve it for military use. But never before had international market forces confronted Americans with their growing dependence on imported petroleum.

The Arab oil embargo of 1973–1974 and the decline in oil supplies after the Iranian revolution of 1979 battered a U.S. economy already weakened by spending on the Vietnam War. The oil shocks drove inflation sharply upward. They raised fundamental questions—not asked since the Great Depression of the 1930s—about whether the world's largest economy could continue to grow. And the oil price rise suggested that energy independence might be a crucial component of real national security.

Rich natural resources had long satisfied Americans' needs for energy sources. During the colonial period, wood from abundant forests and coal deposits provided heat. Whale oil powered lamps. Transportation came from the work of domesticated animals as well as sailing vessels that captured the force of the wind. In the era of the American Revolution, manufacturers built the first factories on riverbanks next to falls, where waterwheels produced the power to drive mechanical equipment.

In the 1800s, the spread of the Industrial Revolution increased the demand for energy, particularly coal. By the 1830s, coal fired the steam engines that pushed ships across the Atlantic Ocean and the railroads that would one day tie the growing nation together.

In 1859, on the eve of the Civil War, drillers near Titusville in northwestern Pennsylvania made a momentous discovery: oil. Refined into kerosene, oil lighted many American homes and city streets for more than a generation. Then Thomas Edison designed the first electricity-generating station in New York City in 1892, beginning the era of coal-fired electric utilities that spread rapidly over the next two decades.

Oil's real significance emerged in the twentieth century. Refined into gasoline, oil powered the new internal combustion engines that revolutionized transportation. Gasoline allowed the Wright brothers' airplane to leave the ground in 1903 and fueled the automobiles that began to pour off Henry Ford's assembly line with the first Model T in 1908. Inexpensive gasoline enabled cars to become Americans' foremost means of transportation. U.S. military forces depended on oil in all their wars of the twentieth century. Indeed, the United States fought in the Persian Gulf War of 1991 primarily to

contact with radioactive materials from the early Cold War years forward, such as communities near the Hanford nuclear facility in south central Washington state and towns downwind from the Atomic Test Site in Nevada. One Utah mother who lost a daughter to cancer felt "disappointed and hurt" by the "horrific neglect and indifference" of a government that would permit such contamination and then deny that there was any danger. "We were used. We were conned," another woman testified to Congress about government secrecy regarding the impact of radiation. "They knew and they didn't tell us."

A broad critique of the chemical industry's impact on public health also emerged in the 1970s. As it turned out, pesticides worked their way up the food chain into people's bodies. Some artificial sweeteners proved carcinogenic, and the lead that manufacturers had added to gasoline and house paint for generations caused brain damage. Long-standing industrial dumping of toxic chemicals made headlines. In 1975, investigations revealed that tons of cancer-causing polychlorinated biphenyls (PCBs) from General Electric plants lined the bottom of the Hudson River north of New York City. Four years later, the EPA announced that the nation had 32,000 to 50,000 major sites containing hazardous waste.

The crisis at Love Canal in New York helped bring the issue of toxic waste home to Americans. The Hooker Chemical Company had buried tons of poisonous waste in a dry canal in the town of Niagara Falls between 1947 and 1952 and then covered it over with dirt. The company gave the land to the town, which promptly built a school on it. A middle-class neighborhood soon grew up around the site. But the ground smelled odd and oozed mysterious substances.

preserve western access to oil from the Gulf region.

In the 1970s, the oil shocks and the growing environmental movement encouraged both energy conservation and the development of alternative, renewable sources. Many citizens paid increasing attention to solar, wind, water, and geothermal power. But corporations, encouraged by the federal government, paid far more attention to another alternative: nuclear energy. (The first American nuclear power plant had been built at Shippingport, Pennsylvania, in 1957.) Despite creating radioactive waste, nuclear power generated one-fifth of the nation's electricity by the twenty-first century.

In 2001, fossil fuels continued to provide 85 percent of the total energy used in the United States: oil, 40 percent; natural gas, 25 percent; and coal, 20 percent. Coal-burning plants created just over half the nation's electricity, and the United States had one-fourth of the world's coal supplies. However, unlike renewable energy sources, fossil fuels are a finite resource that eventually will be used up. Burning them also contributes to air pollution, atmospheric ozone depletion, and global warming. Nonetheless, at the turn of the twenty-first century, fossil fuels remain the cheapest source of power, a temptation too strong to resist. ■

Library of Congress

Oil derricks cover a hillside near Titusville, Pennsylvania, in the era of the Civil War. Unlike renewable energy sources such as falling water or the sun, fossil fuels such as oil and coal have to be burned and create serious air pollution in the process. The extraction of fossil fuels—so basic to the modern American economy—often involves damaging natural landscapes as well.

Sometimes it even caught on fire for no apparent reason. By the 1970s local rates of cancer and other severe illnesses had soared. The chemical and industrial plant workers who lived in the neighborhood began to suspect that their quiet loyalty to their employers was no longer worth the risk to the health of their families. Persistent activism by community members, led by housewife and mother Lois Gibbs and publicized by reporter Michael Brown, finally overcame local, state, and company officials' efforts to keep the contents of the buried canal secret. In August 1978, New York governor Hugh Carey at last agreed to buy out the entire neighborhood, seal it off, and move residents elsewhere. The Love Canal debacle accelerated American workers' loss of faith in the corporations and governments they had once trusted. "There are ticking time bombs all over," an EPA official concluded. "We just don't know how many potential Love Canals there are."

Discovering the limits of the U.S. economy so soon after the Vietnam War and the Watergate scandal spawned a crisis of confidence. Some Americans resented the idea of limits: on how much gas they could buy, how much the economy could grow, how much influence the United States could have abroad. At the same time, others began to embrace the idea of creating a healthier lifestyle that focused less on material consumption. Cigarette smoking started to decline. Organic food sales picked up. Exercise, especially running, began to become an increasingly common activity for middle-class adults. The wildly successful Nike athletic shoe company was founded in 1972; co-founder Bill Bowerman, the University of Oregon track coach, poured urethane rubber over a waffle iron to create the first waffle-sole running show. Entrants in the New York City Marathon ballooned from 126 in 1970 to 10,000 by 1978. Interest in outdoor recreation—

Peter Menzel/StockBoston

▶ Thousands of runners surge up the Hayes Street hill in San Francisco in the annual 7-mile Bay-to-Breakers race across the city. In the 1970s regular exercise began to become a common part of daily life for many Americans. At the same time, fast food and higher-fat diets contributed to a growing pattern of Americans being overweight and even obese.

hiking, camping, and bicycling—grew exponentially. Recycling also started its climb from a fringe activity to common practice in a few parts of the country. The government began to get the message, too. Federal agencies banned the use of hazardous products such as the pesticide DDT and the artificial sweetener sodium cyclamate in the original Gatorade formula. And in January 1974, Congress reduced the national speed limit to 55 miles per hour to conserve fuel.

Reshuffling Politics

The skepticism toward authority and tradition spawned by the counterculture, the Vietnam War, and the Watergate scandal spread through American culture in the 1970s. The use of illegal drugs, especially marijuana, was widespread. Casual sexual relationships proliferated in a decade when contraceptive pills had become widely available and the AIDS virus had not yet been identified. Popular and critically acclaimed films featured tales of malfeasance in high places. *All the President's Men* (1976) told the story of the Nixon administration's Watergate crimes. *Apocalypse Now* (1975) revealed the madness of the American war in Vietnam. *Three Days of the Condor* (1975) portrayed the CIA as a rogue agency beyond democratic control. *Chinatown* (1975) suggested the vast corruption marring the early twentieth-century growth of Los Angeles. *Blazing Saddles* (1974) hilariously spoofed the heroic Westerns that had long served as the staple of American moviegoers' diet. And *One Flew Over the Cuckoo's Nest* (1975) used novelist Ken Kesey's story of an insane asylum to imply that those in charge were more dangerous than the inmates. In this atmosphere Congress began to reassert its authority against the "imperial presidency," and in 1976 voters put an obscure, devout Georgia peanut farmer and former one-term governor in the White House.

Congressional Power Reasserted

The double shock of defeat in Vietnam and the Watergate scandal reawakened a Congress that had grown accustomed to deferring to the White House in foreign affairs. Tellingly, Congress had never formally declared war on North Korea or North Vietnam, although such declaration is its constitutional duty. Angered by the illegalities and deception in both the Johnson and Nixon administrations, Congress passed the War Powers Act in 1973 to limit the president's capacity to wage undeclared wars. The bill required the chief executive to obtain explicit congressional approval for keeping U.S. troops in an overseas conflict longer than 90 days.

Congress did not limit its muscle-flexing to keeping Americans out of conflicts with Third World leftists. It also promoted human rights within the communist bloc, cutting against the grain of Secretary of State Kissinger's realpolitik approach to Moscow. The Jackson-Vanik Amendment of 1974 sought to make the Soviet Union pay for its repression of Jewish dissidents by linking détente directly to human rights, much to Kissinger's dismay. To acquire most-favored-nation trading status with the United States, Moscow would have to let Jews emigrate.

With encouragement from voters and journalists, Congress also uncovered its eyes and began to investigate the covert side of American foreign policy that had gathered momentum since 1945. After Watergate popped the cork on the bottled-up secret abuses of the executive branch, other troubling news spilled out about the nation's intelligence agencies. Dissident former CIA agents such as Philip Agee began revealing "dirty tricks" that the agency had long used. And investigative reporter Seymour Hersh, author of the My Lai massacre exposé a few years earlier, uncovered the CIA's Operation Chaos. This program of illegal domestic espionage against antiwar dissidents paralleled FBI abuses such as the Cointelpro campaigns to defame Martin Luther King Jr. and destroy the Black Panthers and the American Indian Movement. Congressional committees led by Otis Pike of New York in the House and Frank Church of Idaho in the Senate initiated their own investigations of the national security state's tactics. Their documentation of CIA involvement in assassination attempts against foreign leaders such as Fidel Castro of Cuba and Patrice Lumumba of the Congo suggested that United States government agencies would secretly go to any lengths to prevail in the Cold War.

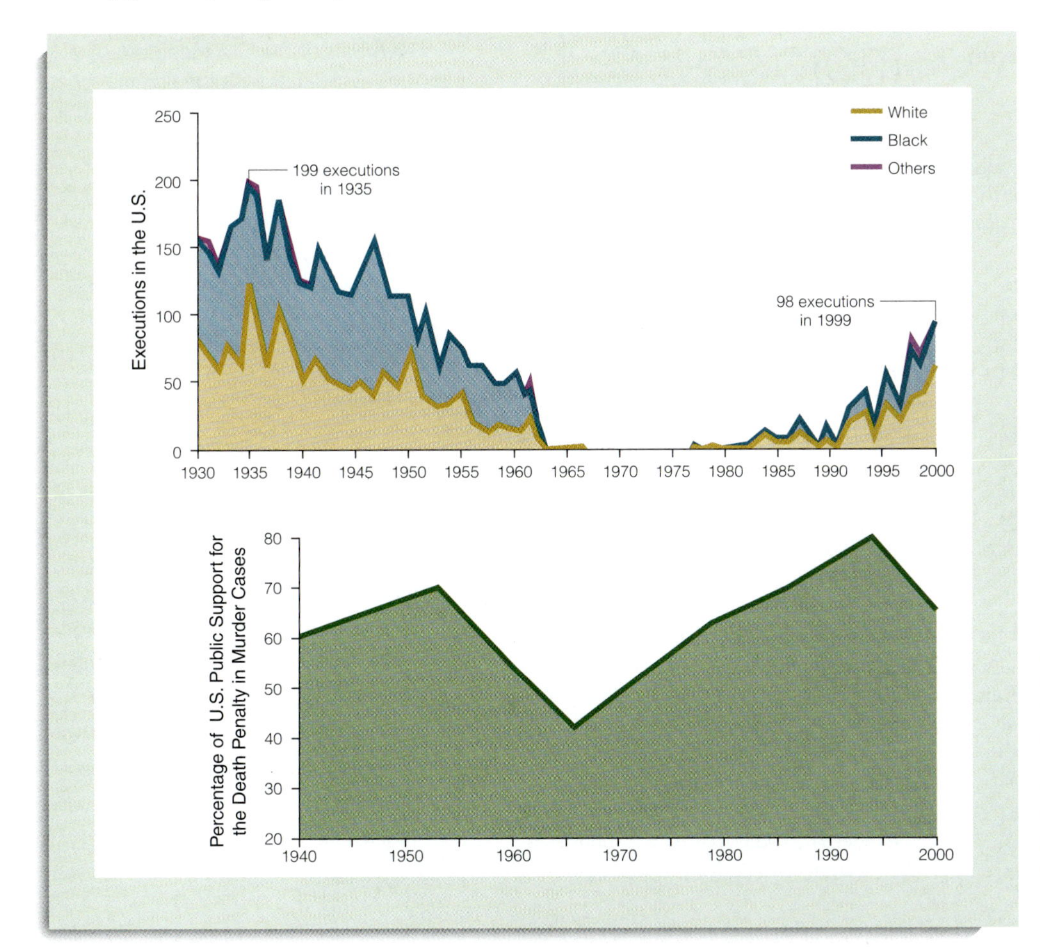

FIGURE 27.2
THE DEATH PENALTY: PRACTICES AND OPINIONS
The use of the death penalty distinguished the United States from most other industrialized nations, which had banned it. In 1972, the Supreme Court struck down existing capital punishment statutes as "arbitrary and capricious." Four years later, the Court upheld rewritten state and federal laws that provided clearer guidance for the imposition of the death penalty.

The Church Committee and CIA Covert Operations

In 1975–1976 the U.S. Senate Select Committee to Study Governmental Operations with Respect to Intelligence Activities engaged in the first comprehensive review by Congress of the actions of the Central Intelligence Agency. Under the leadership of Frank Church (D-Idaho), the committee investigated both intelligence gathering ("spying") and covert operations, the secret side of American foreign policy during the Cold War. One of the most controversial issues that the Church committee examined was evidence of the CIA's attempted use of assassination as a means of dealing with key figures in Cuba, the Congo, the Dominican Republic, South Vietnam, and Chile.

Bettmann/CORBIS

A star baseball pitcher who once turned down an offer to sign with the New York Giants, Fidel Castro led a leftist, anti-American revolution in Cuba in 1959. U.S. hostility and Castro's evolving politics led him to declare Cuba a communist state in 1961. The CIA tried unsuccessfully to arrange for Castro's assassination.

Alleged Assassination Plots Involving Foreign Leaders (Interim Report, November 20, 1975)

The Committee has received evidence that ranking Government officials discussed, and may have authorized, the establishment with the CIA of a generalized assassination capability. . . .

The evidence establishes that the United States was implicated in several assassination plots. . . . Our inquiry also reveals serious problems with respect to United States involvement in coups directed against foreign governments. . . .

Once methods of coercion and violence are chosen, the probability of loss of life is always present. There is, however, a significant difference between a coldblooded, targeted, intentional killing of an individual foreign leader and other forms of intervening in the affairs of foreign nations. . . .

Non-attribution to the United States for covert operations was the original and principal purpose of the so-called doctrine of "plausible denial."

Evidence before the Committee clearly demonstrates that this concept, designed to protect the United States and its operatives from the consequences of disclosures, has been expanded to mask decisions of the President and his senior staff members. . . .

"Plausible denial" can also lead to the use of euphemism and circumlocution, which are designed to allow the President and other senior officials to deny knowledge of an operation should it be disclosed. . . .

It is possible that there was a failure of communication between policymakers and the agency personnel who were experienced in secret, and often violent, action. Although policymakers testified that assassination was not intended by such words as "get rid of Castro," some of their subordinates in the Agency testified that they perceived that assassination was desired and that they should proceed without troubling their superiors. . . .

Running throughout the cases considered in this report was the expectation of American officials that they could control the actions of dissident groups which they were supporting in foreign countries. Events demonstrated that the United States had no such power. This point is graphically demonstrated by cables exchanged shortly before the coup in Vietnam. Ambassador Lodge cabled Washington on October 30, 1963, that he was unable to halt a coup; a cable from William Bundy in response stated that "we cannot accept conclusion that we have no power to delay or discourage a coup." The coup took place three days later. . . .

Officials of the CIA made use of persons associated with the criminal underworld in attempting to achieve the assassination of Fidel Castro. These underworld figures were relied upon because it was believed that they had expertise and contacts that were not available to law-abiding citizens. . . .

It may well be ourselves that we injure most if we adopt tactics "more ruthless than the enemy."

Questions

1. *What are the dangers to the United States of using assassination as a tool of U.S. foreign policy? Is the use of assassination compatible with the practice of democracy? How might it affect American society at home, as well as the way other nations perceive the United States?*
2. *Did the attacks of September 11, 2001, change the way Americans view the possible use by their government of assassination and other covert operations abroad? Should the attacks have altered Americans' attitudes about these issues?*

These revelations stirred fierce controversy among those who took an interest in national and international politics. Many citizens decried what their government had done in their names and without their knowledge. However, officials claimed that the extreme conditions of the Cold War and the duplicity of the Soviets necessitated secrecy. Convinced that information gathered by the Church and Pike committees threatened to undermine public trust in U.S. foreign policy officials, congressional leaders stopped official publication of the Pike report (although the *Village Voice* published a leaked copy). Nonetheless, in combination with the Freedom of Information Act of 1974—which forced the public release of most federal documents after 25 years—these congressional reports created a paper trail that altered Americans' perceptions of what their government did abroad.

At the core of this controversy were two burning questions. How transparent could a democratic society and its government afford to be when they also had global interests to protect? And when democratic openness and imperial self-interest conflicted, which should win out?

"I Will Never Lie to You"

In the backwash of Watergate, two presidential candidates—both outsiders to national politics—became advocates for opposing sides in the debate about power and openness in 1976. Former California governor Ronald Reagan made a strong run at the Republican nomination, falling just short at the Kansas City convention as incumbent Gerald Ford held on to head the GOP ticket. Reagan articulated conservative Americans' anger at seeing U.S. autonomy and power abroad hemmed in. He opposed détente with the Soviets, supported anticommunists everywhere, and warned against a treaty that would return control of the Panama Canal to the Panamanians. Ford found himself burdened by the faltering economy, weakened by Reagan's criticisms from the right, and hampered by widespread resentment of his pardon for Nixon. He struggled back from a 33-point deficit in opinion polls to fall just short with 49 percent of the votes in the general election. The hopes of moderate Republicans faded as the party moved to the right after 1976.

Ford Campaign Ad: Feeling Good About America

Jimmy Carter was the winner. The former Georgia governor had worked relentlessly to gain the Democratic nomination after starting out as the choice of just 4 percent of primary voters. He based his candidacy on moral uplift. Contrasting himself to the Nixon administration, he told audiences, "I will never lie to you." Instead, Carter promised openness, accountability, and a government "as good and decent as the American people." He pledged to heal a nation exhausted by conflict. The emphasis on morality came naturally to the born-again Christian who taught Sunday school, the first president to hail from the Deep South in more than a century. His open faith and cultural conservatism won him support from less liberal Democrats whom the McGovern campaign had alienated in 1972.

Carter was also a Naval Academy graduate, a former nuclear engineer, and a successful peanut farmer and businessperson. Yet the unusual green color of his campaign buttons and posters conveyed a subtle conservationist message, and liberals appreciated his attention to issues of poverty. Moreover, his support for civil rights during his governorship in Georgia had made him a symbol for a pragmatic new generation of white and black Southerners. Americans were not sure who their new president really was. Carter kept his diminutive first name: Jimmy, not James or even Jim. He wore denim, and he carried his own bags. At his inaugural parade, he and his wife Rosalynn chose to walk down Pennsylvania Avenue rather than ride in a limousine.

The new president entered the White House at a time of unusual resistance to executive authority. He encountered an assertive and suspicious Congress. He served an alienated and isolationist public that had given him a slim victory with no clear mandate. He had to grapple with an alert and skeptical media that had dropped most vestiges of its traditional deference to the Oval Office. And he faced an economy still mired in stagflation as unemployment and prices kept rising and interest rates reached 21 percent.

Politics and ideology also hamstrung the new president, limiting his ability to lead his own party in governing the nation. The New Deal coalition of the working class, people of color,

Jimmy Carter Library

▲ After his inauguration as president, Jimmy Carter got down to work in the Oval Office. Serious, conscientious, and extremely hard working, Carter immersed himself in many of the details of his administration's policies. The image of him sequestered and industrious at his desk came to symbolize, for many, both the strengths and weaknesses of his presidency.

and liberals had been unraveling for more than a decade. Carter had campaigned almost as an independent and developed few ties to the main Democratic constituencies. Thus he enjoyed little loyalty from his own party. The Georgian was also the first Democratic president since the 1930s who did not fully subscribe to the New Deal principle of government regulation of the economy. As a social moderate but an economic conservative, Carter had a strong desire to balance the federal budget. This vision placed him closer to the Republicans than to many in his own party. A businessperson, he also considered fiscal responsibility a primary virtue. Powerful liberal Democrats in Congress, by contrast, remained committed to government spending on programs such as Social Security and welfare, which Carter supported with less enthusiasm.

Carter's tendency to take moralistic stands did not mesh well with the horse-trading style of compromise that characterized Congress. The president and his aides tried to govern as outsiders to the federal government. They viewed insiders as selfish and narrow minded. They failed to cultivate relationships with Democratic leaders in Congress such as powerful House Speaker Thomas ("Tip") O'Neill of Massachusetts. Meanwhile, seasoned legislators of both parties looked down on the new administration as inexperienced and naive. With suspicion and condescension flowing in both directions between the White House and Capitol Hill, one senior Democratic member of Congress complained that Carter's popularity with the legislature was so low that he "couldn't get the Pledge of Allegiance through Congress" if he needed to.

Rise of a Peacemaker

Carter's idealism proved more effective, at least during his first two years, in refashioning U.S. foreign policy. The president started the national healing process with his first official act in office: he granted a "full, complete, and unconditional pardon" to those who had evaded the draft during the Vietnam War. He also tried to replace indiscriminate anticommunism with the promotion of human rights as the main theme in international affairs. "We are now free of that inordinate fear of Communism which once led us to embrace any dictator who joined us in that fear," he told an audience at Notre Dame University.

All presidents since 1945 had loudly supported human rights in the Soviet bloc. Carter defended dissidents in authoritarian countries friendly to the United States as well. His commitment to ending racial discrimination at home and his promotion of human rights abroad led to his administration's strong support for an end to white minority rule in southern Africa, including the establishment of Zimbabwe out of the old white-ruled Rhodesia in 1980. In a highly symbolic move, Carter appointed black civil rights leader and fellow Georgian Andrew Young as UN ambassador and point man on Africa policy.

Upon taking office, Carter fired the director of the CIA, George H. W. Bush. In the wake of the congressional investigations of the CIA, he reined in the agency's covert operations. Carter wanted to shift Americans' attention away from East-West Cold War tensions. Instead, he encouraged the public to acknowledge the burgeoning problems between industrialized nations of the Northern Hemisphere and mostly poor countries of the Southern Hemisphere. The president made control over the Panama Canal a test case for this reorientation. The canal symbolized U.S. dominance of the hemisphere and served as a focus of resentment among many Latin Americans. Since 1903, the United States had ruled the 10-mile-wide Canal Zone

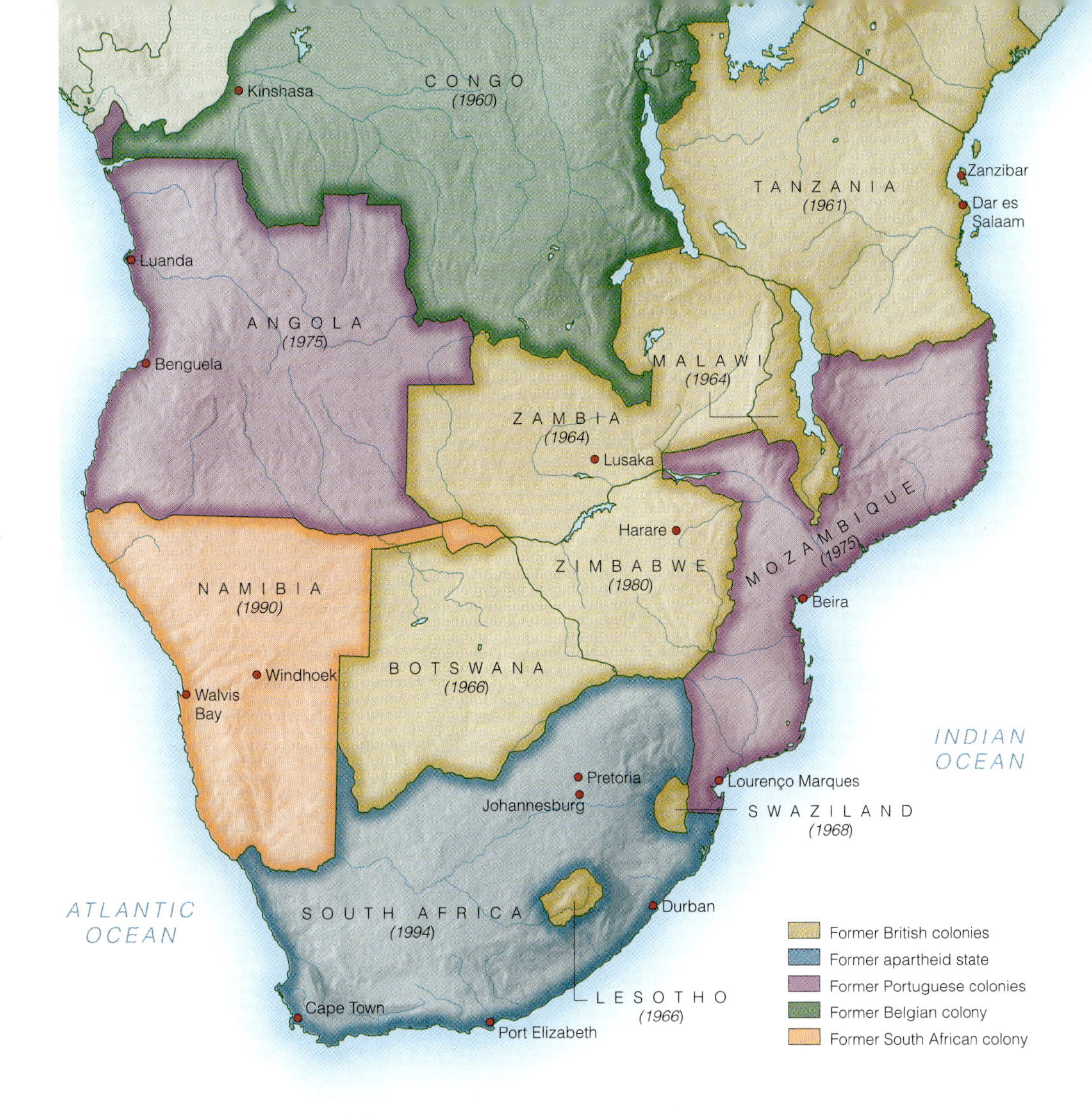

▲ **MAP 27.2 THE GRADUAL LIBERATION OF SOUTHERN AFRICA FROM WHITE MINORITY RULE**
The Carter administration supported the ending of white minority rule in southern Africa. The last redoubts of "white supremacy" included Rhodesia, which became Zimbabwe in 1980, and South Africa, which granted independence to Namibia in 1990 and ended apartheid in 1994.

as its own colony. Acknowledging this colonialist past, Carter signed treaties on September 7, 1977, to return sovereignty of the canal to Panama.

Defenders of U.S. control of the canal, led by prominent Republican Ronald Reagan, fought the treaties fiercely. They saw them as irresponsibly giving away an American asset. "We built it, we paid for it, and we're going to keep it," Reagan insisted. But other prominent conservatives, including Henry Kissinger and movie star John Wayne, acknowledged the symbolic importance of the canal for strengthening U.S. relations with Latin America. They supported the president. Carter threw all his political weight into the campaign, and the Senate approved the treaties by a thin margin in the spring of 1978.

The Carter administration's other great diplomatic achievement came with the Camp David accords, an agreement between Egypt's president Anwar Sadat and Israel's prime minister Menachem Begin. The Arab-Israeli conflict had remained one of the most intractable problems in modern diplomacy, yet Carter had unusual credibility in tackling the issue. His concern as a Christian for the "Holy Land" claimed by both Jewish Israelis and mostly Muslim Palestinians gave him sympathy for both sides. Sadat himself created an opening for diplomacy in 1977 by becoming the first Arab leader to visit Israel. Carter then took action. He invited Sadat and Begin to Camp David, the presidential retreat in rural western Maryland. There his persistence, plus promises of American aid to all parties, kept the marathon negotiations on track. In March 1979, the Egyptian and Israeli leaders signed two accords: Egypt became the first Arab state to grant official recognition to Israel. In turn, Israel agreed to withdraw its troops from the Sinai peninsula and apparently to stop building additional settlements on the Palestinian West Bank of the Jordan River. The framework for peace implied eventual autonomy for the Palestinians in the West Bank and the Gaza strip.

Though promising, the Camp David accords failed to bring peace to the Middle East. Israeli settlements in the West Bank continued to proliferate, and anti-Israeli terrorism by Palestinians persisted. But Carter had persuaded two major players in the region to take a big step back from open hostility. The world rightly proclaimed him a peacemaker.

The War on Waste

Within three months of taking office, Carter called for the "moral equivalent of war" to meet the deepening national energy crisis. The OPEC oil embargo of 1973 and his own thoughtfulness allowed the president to understand better than his immediate predecessors that the country's addiction to imported oil put Americans at the mercy of other oil-producing nations. He exhorted his fellow citizens to stop being "the most wasteful nation on Earth." Conserve energy, he implored them. Switch off lights and turn down thermostats.

The administration created the Department of Energy and granted tax incentives to promote development of alternative sources such as solar energy. The EPA required U.S. automakers to meet stricter fuel efficiency standards for their engines. High prices encouraged a renewed search for domestic sources of oil. In 1977 workers completed the 800-mile-long, 48-inch-wide

▼ Mt. McKinley in Alaska's Denali National Park rises to 20,320 feet above sea level, the tallest peak in North America. Its scale and beauty inspired many supporters of the Alaska National Interest Lands Conservation Act of 1980, which dramatically expanded the nation's parklands and wilderness areas. The Alaska Lands Act and the new Trans-Alaska Pipeline, completed three years earlier, helped many residents of the lower 48 learn more about the nation's largest and most remote state.

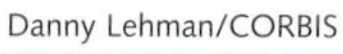

Danny Lehman/CORBIS

Alaska

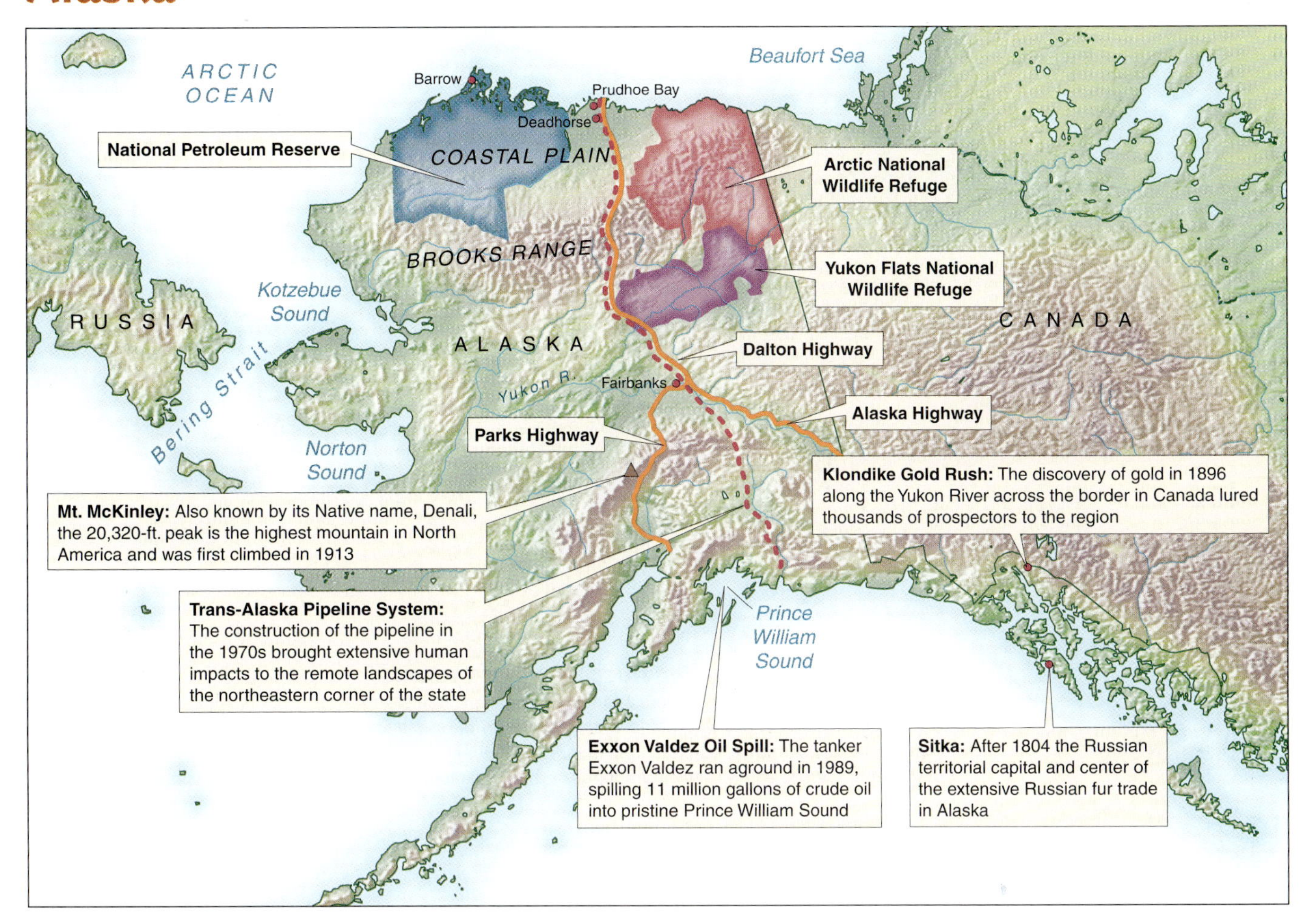

The discovery of oil at Prudhoe Bay in 1968 and its development in the 1970s brought extensive human impacts to beautiful, remote northern Alaska. Workers completed the Trans-Alaska Pipeline in 1977, allowing oil to flow 800 miles south, past the state capital of Fairbanks to the ice-free port of Valdez. Caribou and other wildlife had to accommodate themselves to the new human presence in their midst—trucks, cars, generators, oil rigs, buildings, and trash now littered the coastal area around Prudhoe Bay. The tundra turned out to be quite vulnerable to human incursions, depite the forbiddingly cold climate. Congress established the Arctic National Wildlife Refuge in 1960 and expanded it further in 1980 with the important Alaska Lands Act. In 2001, the George W. Bush administration began working to open the Arctic National Wildlife Refuge to oil drilling but was stymied by broad resistance in the U.S. Congress and among the American public. Alaskan residents tended to favor economic development in their vast state, including expanded oil production. But they also savored the wildness that made Alaska so distinctive. ■

The Image Bank/Getty Images

Northern Lights over Fairbanks, Alaska

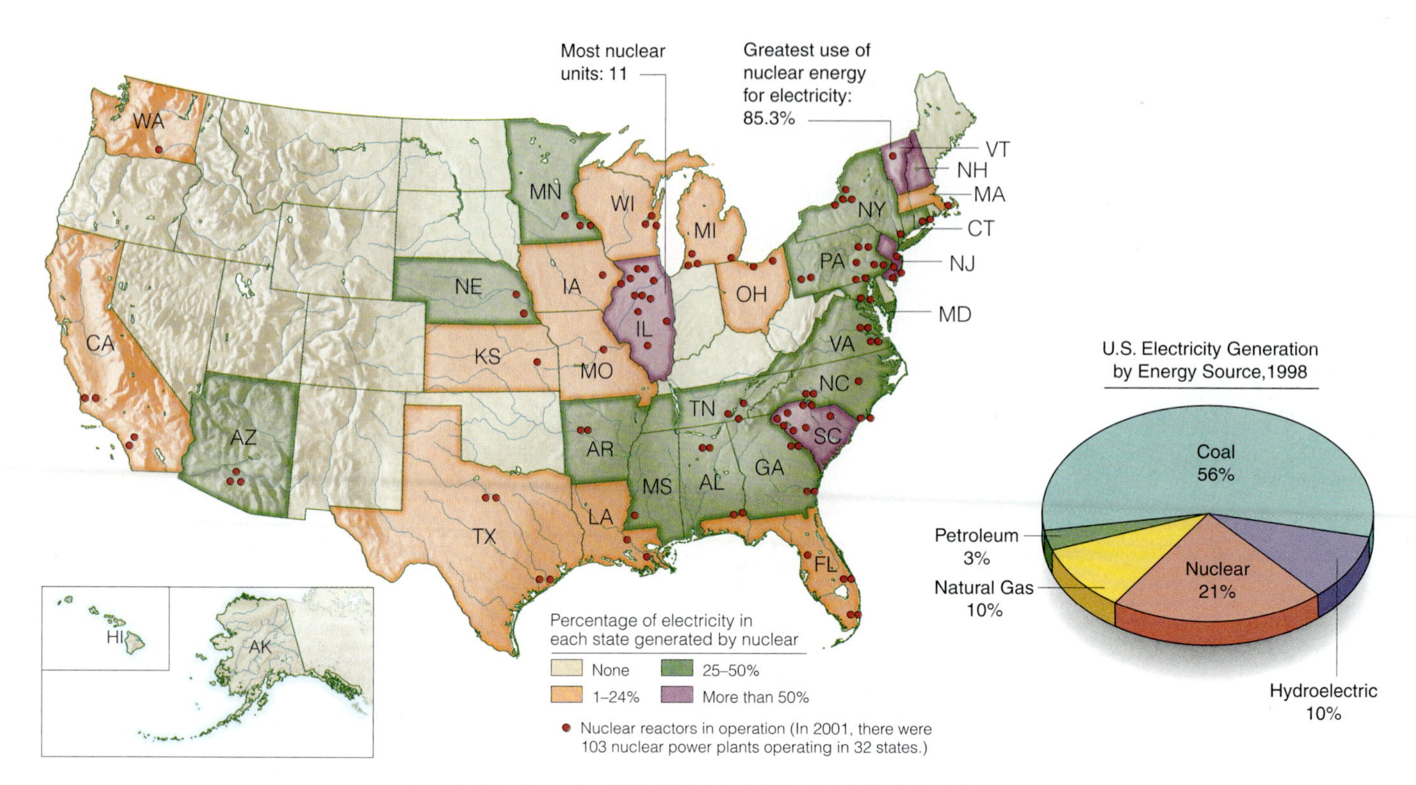

▲ MAP 27.3 BUILDING NUCLEAR POWER PLANTS
Between 1969 and 1980, all of the nation's 103 commercial nuclear power reactors either came on line (56) or were in the process of being planned or built (47). The United States has roughly one-quarter of the 434 commercial nuclear power reactors in the world. Despite nuclear energy's important role in U.S. electricity production, there is still no system in place for the permanent disposal of radioactive waste.

Trans-Alaska Pipeline System. The system linked the state's northern oil fields at Prudhoe Bay on the Arctic Ocean with a tanker terminal in Valdez, on Alaska's southern coast on the Pacific Ocean. With new oil now flowing freely, Carter worked with Congress to pass the 1980 Alaska National Interest Lands Conservation Act. This legislation created the single largest addition ever to the nation's wilderness system, 47 million acres, and the new Wrangell–St. Elias National Park.

The most controversial power alternative came in the form of nuclear energy. Obtained by harnessing the force of splitting atoms, nuclear energy seemed to promise unlimited pollution-free power. But it entailed the use of a deadly radioactive fuel, uranium. In March 1979, the partial meltdown of the nuclear core of the Three Mile Island reactor in Pennsylvania leaked radiation and forced a major evacuation. Nevertheless, existing nuclear power plants continued to generate 11 percent of the nation's electricity in 1979, a figure that climbed to 22 percent by 1992 as other plants under construction came on line. However, because of negative public opinion and the high cost per unit of nuclear power, no new plants ordered by utility companies after 1974 were ever completed.

In 1979, a revolution in Iran cut off the United States from the world's second-largest oil producer. The event initiated a new round of energy price increases, escalated inflation, and further intensified public anxieties. In an unusual display of frankness for a country's leader, President Carter acknowledged that the nation seemed adrift. He gathered an array of advisers at Camp David for extended reflection on how the nation might set a new direction for itself. He emerged to give a major speech on July 15, 1979. In it, he linked America's energy problems to a broader national "crisis of confidence." "In a nation that was proud of hard work, strong families, close-knit communities and our faith in God," he explained, "too many of us now tend to worship self-indulgence and consumption."

Carter and the "Crisis of Confidence"

But Carter proved more effective at identifying the problem of America's insatiable appetite for energy than he was at offering a remedy. His call for sacrifice and unity made for courageous but ultimately self-defeating politics in a society accustomed to unrestrained consumption. Other politicians, such as Ronald Reagan, moved swiftly to smooth Americans' ruffled feathers with a cheerful message: U.S. citizens were fine just as they were. As one supporter of the oil and gas industry claimed, "This country did not conserve its way to greatness. It produced its way to greatness."

John S. Zeedick/AP/Wide World

▲ The cooling towers of the Three Mile Island nuclear power plant loom over the Susquehanna River just south of Harrisburg, Pennsylvania. Nuclear energy epitomized the centralization of power: citizens benefited from the electricity produced but had little knowledge or control of a technology that could go astray more easily than authorities liked to admit.

Diffusing the Women's Movement

"Good morning, boys and girls!" This standard classroom greeting reveals the central place of gender in how Americans identify people from a young age. Few people consider the phrase offensive, even though they probably would protest if a teacher addressed class members as "blacks and whites" or "tall people and short people." Should one's sex (a biological characteristic) or gender (the social assumptions associated with sex) constitute the fundamental dividing line among human beings? The spread of feminism through U.S. society from the 1970s onward raised this question.

The Meanings of Women's Liberation

In a decade marked by hard rethinking of major issues, feminists provided one of the most profound challenges of all. Few American households avoided at least some reconsideration of the roles of men and women. Just as the nation reimagined its foreign policy in less assertive terms and with greater concern for human rights, feminists called for equality between the sexes while honoring their differences. This call resonated with a growing number of Americans. The women's movement cast a spotlight on the need for justice in both the private sphere of personal relationships and the public sphere of the workplace and the law.

Between 1968 and 1973 some 500 new feminist publications cropped up in the United States. Gloria Steinem's *Ms.* magazine became the most prominent, selling out the 250,000 copies of its first issue in January 1972 within eight days. Its then revolutionary name symbolized women's desire not to have their marital status revealed through the title of "Miss" or "Mrs." After all, the title "Mr." said nothing about a man's marital status, so why should not a woman's title be similarly neutral? Thousands of consciousness-raising meetings also made women aware that their own experiences with discrimination were part of a broader pattern of injustice toward women.

The millions of American women who found their lives changing in the 1970s did not agree on all issues. African American and Latino American women balanced identities as women with identities as people of color, which aligned them closely with men of their communities. Like Karen Silkwood, the Oklahoma nuclear plant worker, working-class women

Sophia Smith Collection, Smith College, Gloria Steinem Papers

▲ Gloria Steinem, with hands on her knees, speaks at a meeting of a women's consciousness-raising group in the early 1970s. Similar groups gathered informally in homes around the country and helped women articulate their common struggles against discrimination.

of all colors often focused on issues common to all workers, including wages, workplace conditions, and union representation. Community organizers such as Lois Gibbs of Love Canal zeroed in on neighborhoods and families. The educated white women who tended to form the most visible part of the movement for equality differed among themselves on such issues as pornography: some found it inherently exploitive of women, while others considered it primarily a matter of free expression.

However, all women shared certain concerns. Even as many female Americans remained wary of the label *feminist*—fearing associations with anger, militancy, and dislike of men—they nonetheless tended to side with feminist positions on issues from equal pay for equal work, to abortion rights, to more egalitarian distribution of household chores within families. Even women who still chose to wear makeup and dress in traditionally feminine fashion shared a desire for men to take women more seriously for their ideas and beliefs than for their appearance.

The women's movement also sought to unmask the violence constraining all women's lives: sexual harassment, domestic abuse, and rape. Many men were sympathetic, but not all. A "Take Back the Night" march of 300 undergraduates at the University of California at Davis in 1982 protested the threat of male violence against women. When the marchers reached "fraternity row," they encountered graphic hostility: young men hung out of windows shouting obscenities; a driver backed his car directly into the crowd; a young man urinated on several marchers while others "mooned" them; some men threatened to rape the female marchers later. University disciplinary action against the perpetrators could not mask the reality that a peaceful march for a rape-free society apparently still threatened some men. Even a woman's home was not safe at times. Until the mid-1970s, a husband could force himself sexually on his wife and not be considered a rapist by the law.

New Opportunities in Education, the Workplace, and Family Life

In the 1970s, educated women gained access to a host of new opportunities in the workplace. Young women in college, unlike their mothers, expected to choose and develop a career after graduation even more than they anticipated getting married. The number of women entering graduate and professional schools soared. The percentage of female students in law school shot up from 5 percent to 40 percent between 1970 and 1980. In addition, most single-sex private colleges and universities, such as Yale and Vassar, went coeducational. Many dormitories housed both men and women, allowing young people from the middle and upper classes to live in close physical proximity for the first time.

A similar process unfolded in the workplace. Employment in the United States, formerly divided into "men's" and "women's" work, saw a blurring of those lines. Help-wanted advertisements stopped categorizing jobs as male and female, and women joined the ranks of police officers and construction workers. The post-1950 pattern of women flocking into the paid workforce passed a milestone in 1980. That year, more than half of women with children under six years old had paying jobs outside the home. However, most of these jobs were lower-wage service positions that offered neither union support nor much upward mobility. Women fared better in the professions; the percentage of female lawyers and Ph.D.s tripled in the 1970s, and that of female physicians doubled.

Despite these gains, professional women still averaged only 73 percent of the pay of their male colleagues. They also encountered stubborn traditional gender expectations. Late in the decade, one New York City judge ordered a female attorney—dressed in a tailored designer pantsuit and silk blouse—to leave his courtroom and not return unless she showed up in a skirted suit that demonstrated "proper respect" for the court.

Not surprisingly, family life also changed shape in these years. In the 1950s more than 70 percent of American families with children had had a father who worked outside the home and a mother who stayed at home. By 1980, only 15 percent of families were configured that way. Yet society's growing acceptance of mothers in the workforce did not necessarily mean that these women enjoyed a lighter domestic load. Most working mothers still had primary responsibility for parenting. For example, President Nixon vetoed a 1970 bill to establish a federally funded daycare system. Such a program, he declared, "would lead to the Sovietization of American children." Although many fathers accommodated their wives' work lives, working mothers continued to bear the brunt of the "second shift": child-rearing and housework in addition to a full-time paid job.

Changing roles brought new marital stresses, and divorce rates climbed in this decade. In 1970, one-third as many divorces as marriages occurred annually; in 1980, the figure was one-half. No-fault divorce laws, beginning with California's in 1970, eased the process and the stigma attached to divorce, although its emotional impact on adults and children remained hard to measure. Men benefited financially when marriages split up. Their average living standard rose sharply, whereas that of women and their children plummeted. Children living with both parents had a 1-in-19 chance of growing up poor. The likelihood rose to 1 in 10 for children living with just a father; for those living with just a mother, the odds reached 1 in 3.

▲ The hit 1977 film *Saturday Night Fever* starred John Travolta, Karen Gorney, and the popular disco music of the late 1970s. Disco's many critics granted its success as dance music but condemned it as banal and uncreative. Punk was an angrier and edgier musical style that evolved in the same years out of the rock 'n' roll of the late 1960s and early 1970s.

Equality Under the Law

Paralleling the logic of the black civil rights movement, the modern women's movement pressured lawmakers to eliminate the legal underpinnings of sex-based discrimination. Title IX of the Educational Amendments of 1972 required schools to spend comparable amounts on women's and men's sports programs. This critical step symbolized women's shift away from spectatorship and cheerleading to the female athleticism that helped define American popular culture by the end of the twentieth century. Mia Hamm and her teammates on the wildly popular U.S. women's soccer team that won the 1999 world championship represented the first generation of women to grow up with strong institutional support for girls' sports.

Pat Summitt's extraordinary success as a college women's basketball coach demonstrates the impact of the change in federal law. Raised on a farm in rural Tennessee, Summitt starred as a player in college and on the U.S. Olympic team. With Title IX newly in place, the 22-year-old became the part-time head coach of an obscure University of Tennessee women's team in 1974. Thirty years later, she had become the most successful women's basketball coach in college history, with over 850 victories and 6 national titles. More than 12,000 fans now pour into Knoxville's Thompson-Boling Arena for home games. Summitt's annual salary approaches $1 million, and she has become one of the most recognizable faces in the state of Tennessee—and, indeed, in college sports. Summitt recognizes that her contribution to the rise of women's athleticism in the United States hinged on the support the university chose to give her: "I can't say enough about what U. of T. did when Title IX was passed."

Bettye Lane

▲ **Congress passed Title IX of the Educational Amendments of 1972, denying federal funds to schools that did not provide equal money to women's and men's sports programs. A New Jersey court ruled in 1973 that the nation's largest youth baseball program must admit girls, and these Hoboken youngsters became the first girls to play Little League.**

After languishing for decades among failed proposals in Congress, the proposed Equal Rights Amendment to the Constitution finally rode to an overwhelming victory among senators and representatives in 1972. The legislature then sent it to the states for possible ratification by 1980. Simple in its language, the ERA declared "Equality of rights under law shall not be denied or abridged by the United States or by any State on account of sex." On January 22, 1973, in the landmark case of *Roe v. Wade*, the Supreme Court ruled (by a 7–2 vote) that constitutional privacy rights were "broad enough to encompass a woman's decision whether or not to terminate her pregnancy" in its first six months. This decision established women's constitutional right to determine the course of their own pregnancies. Feminists had pointed out that the question was never *whether* women would have abortions but *how:* they would have them either in the offices of skilled physicians or at the hands of illegal and often dangerous practitioners.

Roe v. Wade

Backlash

Even as the majority of Americans accepted the fundamental tenets of feminism, some fiercely defended existing gender roles. The mainstream media often painted women's rights activists as angry man-haters. Indeed, the media seized the opportunity to associate feminism with "bra-burning," a titillating way to blend women's rights with the sexual revolution and thus avoid the serious issues that women were raising. One Chicana worker involved in a strike against the Farah slacks company in Texas responded, "I don't believe in burning your bra, but I do believe in having our rights."

The women's movement posed a daunting challenge to traditional ideas about masculinity. Men wondered what equality for women really meant and how it might change their intimate and professional relationships with them. Should men still open doors for women? Should they begin to do half (or more) of housework and parenting? Should they not comment on a female colleague's appearance?

Women's growing economic independence and educational opportunities often altered the dynamics of power in male-female relationships. Many men from all classes and ethnicities, feeling defensive about assumptions and behaviors that were increasingly labeled sexist, resisted these changes. One Latino graduate student at Stanford University resolved never to date "college girls." "When I want a real woman, I go to the barrio in East San Jose and pick up a high school girl." Many men also found the increasingly open acknowledgment of lesbianism threatening because it implied their potential irrelevance to women. The challenge to machismo took the form of public spectacle in 1973. That year, women's tennis champion Billie Jean King (age 29) agreed to play 55-year-old former Wimbledon champion Bobby Riggs in a nationally televised "Battle of the Sexes" in the Houston Astrodome. More than 45 million Americans watched King crush her self-proclaimed "male chauvinist pig" opponent in straight sets.

That men would have mixed feelings about women's liberation surprised no one. But some of the stiffest resistance came from women who had built their identities on motherhood and homemaking and now fiercely defended that tradition. Led by Illinois lawyer Phyllis

Schlafly, antifeminists sought to uphold an established family structure that they believed divorce, gay rights, abortion, and daycare would destroy. In their view, femininity meant service to one's family. "Feminists praise self-centeredness," Schlafly declared, "and call it liberation." In addition to defending their own choices, female antifeminists also worried about the impact of dual-career families on children.

Opponents of women's liberation made two major legislative gains in the late 1970s. First, Congress passed the Hyde Amendment in 1976, which forbade the use of Medicaid funds for abortions. In practice, the amendment limited access to abortion to those women who could afford to pay for it themselves. Second, Schlafly's Stop-ERA campaign helped defeat the Equal Rights Amendment by limiting its ratification to only 35 of the required 38 states. Schlafly claimed that the amendment would "destroy the family, foster homosexuality, and hurt women." ERA opponents condemned "unisex toilets" and the drafting of women into combat that they believed the amendment would bring. In these women's views, the ERA would also draw out the worst in men, letting husbands opt out of supporting their wives and freeing divorced men from paying alimony. Antifeminists resented the disrespect for motherhood that they felt from some feminists. Still, they agreed with feminists that tens of millions of American women were just one man removed from welfare. At the heart of the controversy, the two sides differed on the best way to protect women's interests. Should women's economic independence be enhanced, or should men be tied more tightly to their families?

Courtesy of Colorado Great Women

◀ Many American women had flown airplanes before the 1970s, most famously solo flier Amelia Earhart and the female pilots in World War II. But none piloted a major commercial airliner until 1973. That year, 34-year-old Emily Howell Warner of Denver, Colorado, became the first woman hired as a pilot by a scheduled U.S. carrier, Frontier Airlines. Within three years, she was promoted to the first female captain, and in 1986, Warner commanded the first all-female flight crew on a commercial route.

Though discouraging for some, the narrow defeat of the ERA could not mask feminism's growing influence throughout American culture. The "first woman" stories that began showing up in the media during the 1970s marked the entrance of women into previously all-male roles. Like physicians, lawyers, and other figures of cultural authority, religious leaders now increasingly consisted of women, including the first Lutheran pastor (1970), the first Jewish rabbi (1972), and the first Episcopal priest (1974). In 1981 Sandra Day O'Connor became the first female Supreme Court justice. And mainstream organizations such as churches and municipalities ran feminist-created community institutions, including rape crisis centers, women's health clinics, and battered women's shelters. In 1978 the National Weather Service began using male as well as female names for hurricanes. By the 1980s, the movement had made major inroads into gender discrimination, although subtle forms of it remained. Younger women, confident that their fair treatment under the law was secure, began shying away from the term *feminism* and its lingering associations with rejection of men.

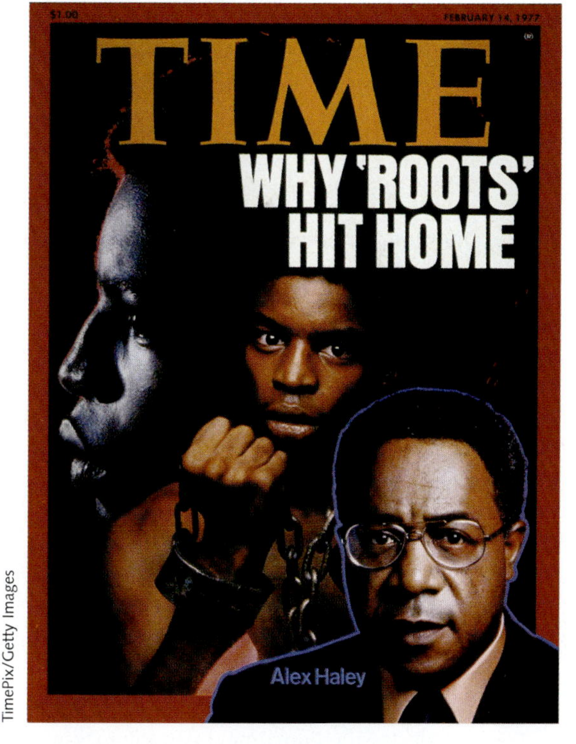

TimePix/Getty Images

▲ The 1977 miniseries version of Alex Haley's *Roots* captured the largest television audience ever to that time. The powerful drama about Haley's ancestors offered tens of millions of Americans an intimate and sympathetic understanding of the horrific story of black slavery and survival. *Roots* also represented the post-1960s emphasis on preserving and respecting group histories and identities rather than emphasizing only individual success and assimilation into the mainstream.

Conclusion

In 1978 a divided U.S. Supreme Court handed down a ruling on the contentious policy of affirmative action. The justices decided by a 5–4 vote in the *Bakke* case that strict racial quotas were unconstitutional but that universities could consider race as one of several factors in determining a candidate's qualifications for admission. The Court, like the American public, was wrestling with the broader 1970s problem of how to reform American society in ways that would preserve its historic strengths while removing the ills that the previous decade's political activism had laid bare.

A central problem was the tension between the ideal of colorblind integration and new expressions of pride in distinctive racial and ethnic identities. In 1973 armed American Indian Movement activists for two months occupied buildings in Wounded Knee, South Dakota—site of the infamous 1890 U.S. Army massacre of defenseless Sioux—to promote a pan-Indian nationalist consciousness. In 1977 ABC's enormously popular eight-part television miniseries *Roots* dramatized the human pathos contained in the long saga of African American slavery. Many white ethnic Americans in these years leavened their long-standing cultural assimilation with renewed attention to their own roots in particular European countries, especially Ireland and Italy.

Americans' self-confidence and pride as a nation had been deeply shaken by the combination of the Vietnam War, the Watergate scandal, and the economic downturn after 1973. Disillusioned by the corruptions of public life, many citizens turned inward and heeded the advice of Robert J. Ringer in his 1977 best-seller *Looking Out for Number One*. But others found motivation in the decade's events—especially the revelation that presidents, corporate executives, and other authorities had lied to them. They learned what earlier Americans had discovered in the 1760s about imperious British officials and the corrupting effects of managing a global empire. Like the revolutionaries of George Washington's generation, they sought to strengthen representative government. They pressed Congress to investigate the executive branch, and they elected an unusual outsider as president in 1976. Historians in this decade began to write more skeptically about those in power and more sympathetically about average Americans whom the history books had long ignored. The resurgence of conservatism in the 1980s recast many public policies, but it could not erase the vision of gender equality, environmental responsibility, and egalitarian governance that had taken hold among many citizens.

Sites to Visit

Divining America: Religion and the National Culture

www.nhc.rtp.nc.us/tserve/divam.htm

This site has essays by prominent historians on diverse aspects of the religious history of the United States.

Documents from the Women's Liberation Movement

http://scriptorium.lib.duke.edu/wlm/

Provocative and fascinating articles from feminists of the late 1960s and 1970s make this site worthy of a visit.

National Security Archive at George Washington University

www.gwu.edu/~nsarchiv/

This extraordinary site includes the most recent declassified documents on the making of U.S. foreign policy.

Natural Resources Defense Council

www.nrdc.org/

This site contains considerable information and links about environmental issues, particularly those that emerged into public consciousness in the 1970s.

Oyez Project of Northwestern University

http://www.oyez.org/oyez/frontpage

Arguments from important Supreme Court cases plus information about Supreme Court justices make this a most useful site for legal history.

Gerald R. Ford Library and Museum

www.ford.utexas.edu/

The Ford presidential library maintains this site, with documents and photographs from the mid-1970s.

Revisiting Watergate

www.washingtonpost.com/wp-srv/onpolitics/watergate/splash.html

The *Washington Post* created this informative site about the Watergate scandal 30 years after the events took place.

Accident at Three Mile Island

http://echo.gmu.edu/tmi/index.html#1medinfo

This site offers grassroots recollections of the nuclear accident near Harrisburg, Pennsylvania, in 1979, along with links to other useful sites regarding the event and its aftermath.

For Further Reading

General

William C. Berman, *America's Right Turn: From Nixon to Bush* (1994).

Peter N. Carroll, *It Seemed Like Nothing Happened: America in the 1970s* (1990).

William H. Chafe, *The Unfinished Journey: America Since World War II*, 5th ed. (2003).

E. J. Dionne Jr., *Why Americans Hate Politics* (1991).

Bruce J. Schulman, *The Seventies: The Great Shift in American Culture, Society, and Politics* (2001).

Twin Shocks: Détente and Watergate

Stephen E. Ambrose, *Nixon*, 3 vols. (1987, 1989, 1991).

Walter Isaacson, *Kissinger* (1992).

Jeffrey Kimball, *Nixon's Vietnam War* (1998).

Stanley I. Kutler, *The Wars of Watergate: The Last Crisis of Richard Nixon* (1992).

Melvin Small, *The Presidency of Richard M. Nixon* (1999).

Discovering the Limits of the U.S. Economy

Douglas Little, *American Orientalism: The United States and the Middle East Since 1945* (2002).

J. Anthony Lukas, *Common Ground: A Turbulent Decade in the Lives of Three American Families* (1985).

Allen J. Matusow, *Nixon's Economy: Booms, Busts, Dollars, and Votes* (1998).

Thomas J. McCormick, *America's Half-Century: United States Foreign Policy in the Cold War and After*, 2nd ed. (1995).

Hal K. Rothman, *The Greening of a Nation? Environmentalism in the United States Since 1945* (1998).

Daniel Yergin, *The Prize: The Epic Quest for Oil, Money, and Power* (1991).

Susan Zakin, *Coyotes and Town Dogs: Earth First! and the Environmental Movement* (1993).

Reshuffling Politics

Samuel P. Hays, *Beauty, Health, and Permanence: Environmental Politics in the United States, 1955–1985* (1987).

Burton I. Kaufman, *The Presidency of James Earl Carter, Jr.* (1993).

Melani McAlister, *Epic Encounters: Culture, Media, and U.S. Interests in the Middle East* (2001).

John Ranelagh, *The Agency: The Rise and Decline of the CIA* (1986).

Gaddis Smith, *Morality, Reason, and Power: American Diplomacy in the Carter Years* (1986).

U.S. Congress, Church Committee, *Alleged Assassination Plots Involving Foreign Leaders: Interim Report of the Select Committee to Study Governmental Operations with Respect to Intelligence Activities* (1976).

Diffusing the Women's Movement

Susan J. Douglas, *Where the Girls Are: Growing Up Female with the Mass Media* (1994).

Alice Echols, *Daring to Be Bad: Radical Feminism in America, 1967–75* (1989).

Sara M. Evans, *Tidal Wave: How Women Changed America at Century's End* (2003).

Arlie Russell Hochschild, *The Second Shift: Working Parents and the Revolution at Home* (1997).

Ruth Rosen, *The World Split Open: How the Modern Women's Movement Changed America* (2000).

Gloria Steinem, *Outrageous Acts and Everyday Rebellions* (1983).

1979 Iranian Revolution; militants take American hostages.
Soviet Union invades Afghanistan.
Sandinista rebels seize control of Nicaragua.

1980 Failed attempt to rescue American hostages in Iran.
Ronald Reagan elected president.

1981 President Anwar Sadat of Egypt assassinated.
Iran releases American hostages.
U.S. funds Contras to try to overthrow Nicaraguan government.

1982 Recession hits United States.
Nuclear freeze movement holds large protests in the United States and Western Europe.

1983 HIV identified as virus that causes AIDS.
First compact discs (CDs) marketed.
241 U.S. marines killed in bombing of Beirut barracks.
Strategic Defense Initiative proposed.
Martin Luther King Jr.'s birthday designated a national holiday.

1984 Russia boycotts summer Olympic games in Los Angeles.

1985 First Reagan-Gorbachev summit in Geneva.

1986 Chernobyl nuclear power plant disaster (Ukraine).
Iran-Contra scandal revealed.
Congress passes sanctions against South African apartheid government.

1987 Intermediate Nuclear Force Treaty.
Stock market crash.

1988 Indian Gaming Regulatory Act.
Libyan terrorist bomb downs Pan Am Flight 103 over Lockerbie, Scotland.

1989 Grounding of oil tanker *Exxon Valdez* off Alaska coast.
Last Soviet troops withdraw from Afghanistan.
Berlin Wall falls.
U.S. invades Panama to seize Manuel Noriega.

1990 Radiation Exposure Act.
Nelson Mandela freed from prison in South Africa.
Iraq invades and occupies Kuwait.

1991 Persian Gulf War against Iraq.
Los Angeles police beat and arrest Rodney King.
Soviet Union dissolves into Russia and other component states.

P A R T T E N

Global Connections, at Home and Abroad: New Threats and Possibilities, 1979–2004

Soon after the beginning of the twenty-first century, Americans confronted a frightening paradox: the defeat of old enemies gave rise to new ones. The Cold War had ended with the demise of the Soviet Union. And yet the post–Cold War world continued to be a violent and in certain respects even more terrifying place. As colonial and totalitarian political systems collapsed around the globe, local ethnic and religious conflicts rose to the surface. To some extent, those conflicts remained confined within regions: the Balkans, Indonesia, the former Soviet Union, and parts of Africa. However, the spread of worldwide terrorist networks threatened all parts of the globe. Instances of mass murder on American soil, especially the attacks on the World Trade Center and the Pentagon in 2001, proved that the United States was vulnerable to horrific acts of violence initiated from home and abroad.

In the 1980s, President Ronald Reagan left his imprint on both domestic and foreign affairs. Reagan gave voice to conservatives, including those who favored a federal retreat from social welfare programs. Bolstered by the Moral Majority and other fundamentalist Christian groups, conservatives engaged in the so-called culture wars with liberals. Conservatives disapproved of feminists, black power advocates, gay rights activists, and environmentalists. Reagan and Congress implemented policies that shrank the federal government's commitment to social welfare programs. Reagan also reinvigorated Cold War rhetoric—he denounced the Soviet Union as an "evil empire"—and pushed military spending to unprecedented levels. Yet Reagan welcomed the initiatives of Soviet leader Mikhail Gorbachev, who sought to ease tensions with the West.

Unable to meet the basic needs of its own people and bogged down in an unwinnable war in Afghanistan, the Soviet Union disintegrated in 1991. Simultaneously, the United States embarked on a remarkable period of economic growth and expansion. President Bill Clinton favored free trade policies, such as the North American Free Trade Agreement (NAFTA), which he and others hoped would knit the world's nations together in pursuit of political and economic progress.

Nevertheless, domestic and foreign conflicts thwarted much of this hopeful vision. At home, the AIDS epidemic and drug addiction claimed many lives. Clashes among African Americans, Latinos, and Koreans in Los Angeles in 1992; the bombing of an Oklahoma City federal building by domestic antigovernment terrorists in 1995; attacks on abortion clinics; and a series of shootings by high school students revealed persistent faultlines in American society. Backed by the Supreme Court, a number of state and local governments passed anti-immigrant and anti-affirmative action laws. The culture wars were hot and, in some cases, deadly.

Violent assaults on the United States came from forces outside as well as within it. The Middle East had become a tinderbox of fears and resentments. In Iran, Islamic militants overthrew the U.S.-backed shah in 1979. Throughout the region, many Islamic fundamentalists expressed their resentment over the military and political presence of the United States in Israel and Saudi Arabia. During the 1991 Gulf War, the United States successfully reversed Iraq's seizure of oil fields in Kuwait. Yet U.S. attempts to protect its economic and political interests in the Middle East continued to outrage Islamic militants.

By the end of the 1990s, some Americans were able to focus inward and enjoy prosperity. The stock market was booming. Cheap gas prices encouraged affluent Americans to purchase huge sport utility vehicles with little regard for their environmental impact. However, ten years of high employment masked the hidden effects of a transformed economy, one characterized by a decline in labor union membership and the rise of an ill-paid service sector. A substantial proportion of Americans lived from paycheck to paycheck.

On September 11, 2001, Americans were forced to confront their own vulnerabilities. Anti-U.S. terrorists hijacked four commercial airliners and flew two of them into the Twin Towers of the World Trade Center in New York City and one into the Pentagon outside Washington, D.C. The fourth plane crashed in a field near Shanksville, Pennsylvania. Some 3,000 people were killed. Within a month, anthrax-laced letters caused death and havoc in the offices where they were delivered and the postal centers that processed them, heightening pervasive fear and insecurity among Americans.

The events of September 11 highlighted grim realities: certain foreign groups despised such cherished American values as democracy, liberalism, and consumerism. Moreover, U.S. foreign policies in the Middle East fanned the fires of antiwestern extremism. Terrorists were becoming more successful in enlisting people who were willing to die in attacks on the United States and more resourceful in using modern technology in those attacks. These terrorists were stateless, freed from the political tasks of protecting their own citizens, monitoring national borders, or dealing with internal dissidents. In 2002 these realities prompted the United States to invade Afghanistan and displace the ruling Taliban, hosts to Al Qaeda's training network. The following year the United States attacked Iraq, a preemptive attack on what the Bush administration called a dangerous, destabilizing regime—the dictatorship of Saddam Hussein. At home, issues related to war, terrorism, and civil liberties became increasingly divisive and bitter among Americans.

1992 South central Los Angeles riots follow acquittal of police in Rodney King case.
FBI shootout at Ruby Ridge, Idaho.

1993 FBI storms compound of the Branch Davidian cult in Waco, Texas.
Congress approves North American Free Trade Agreement (NAFTA).
Arab-Israeli peace talks.
18 American soldiers die in Somalia; United States withdraws.

1994 House leadership announces "Contract with America."
O. J. Simpson murder trial.
Freedom of Access to Clinic Entrances Act.

1995 Truck bomb destroys federal building in Oklahoma City.
Congress revokes 55 mph speed limit.
U.S. intervenes against Serbs in war in Bosnia.
Dayton peace accords signed.

1996 Welfare Reform Act.

1997 Dow Jones average passes 8,000.

1998 Lewinsky-Clinton affair revealed.
Clinton impeached by House of Representatives.

1999 Senate acquits Clinton.
Dow Jones passes 10,000.
U.S. bombing campaign frees province of Kosovo from Serbian rule.
Elian Gonzales affair.

2000 Supreme Court decides contested election; George W. Bush becomes president.

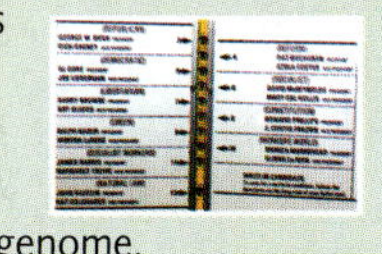

Scientists map human genome.

2001 Terrorists attack World Trade Center and Pentagon.
Anthrax in letters causes illness and death in Florida, Washington, D.C., and New York City.
U.S.-backed Afghan forces overthrow Taliban government in Afghanistan.

2002 Sexual abuse scandal in Roman Catholic church.

2003 United States invades and occupies Iraq, capturing Saddam Hussein.
Space shuttle *Columbia* disintegrates.
Supreme Court legalizes gay sexual conduct.

2004 Massachusetts court legalizes gay marriage.

CHAPTER 28

The Cold War Returns—and Ends, 1979–1991

▲ After the economic and international uncertainties of the 1970s, the 1980s brought a renewed sense of patriotism and a concentration on material acquisitions for many Americans.

CHAPTER OUTLINE

Anticommunism Revived

Republican Rule at Home

Cultural Conflict

The End of the Cold War

Conclusion

Sites to Visit

For Further Reading

On July 16, 1979, just west of Albuquerque, New Mexico, a dam holding wastewater and residue from a uranium mine broke. Some 94 million gallons of radioactive water flooded into the Rio Puerco, giving it what one resident called "a terrible odor and a dark chocolatey color" as it flowed toward the Rio Grande. One of the worst nuclear accidents in U.S. history, the flooding proved far graver than the well-publicized meltdown of the Three Mile Island reactor in Pennsylvania a few months earlier. Yet few Americans heard about it, for it affected mostly Navajo and Laguna Indians.

Nearby, the Anaconda Copper Company operated the nation's largest uranium mine, producing the fuel for nuclear power. The mine closed in the early 1980s. At public hearings in 1986 concerning the future of the mine and its small mountain of poisonous tailings, Anaconda's scientists argued that the mine did not threaten human health in the area. Thus, they said, the tailing piles and the polluted ponds did not need to be cleaned up. Herman Garcia, a Laguna Indian who lived in the adjoining village of Paguate, listened carefully but remained unconvinced. "We lost five people from cancer" the preceding year in tiny Paguate alone, he explained. "I'm no expert," he concluded, but "I'd like for some of these experts to go out there and swim in those ponds. Then when I see them swim, then maybe I feel more secure."

The Native American West and the nuclear West have overlapped to a remarkable extent ever since participants in the Manhattan Project began building the first atomic bomb in 1942. Repeatedly, the U.S. government constructed major nuclear sites in the West on lands surrounded by Indian settlements. These included the laboratories of Los Alamos, New Mexico; bomb factories and nuclear waste dumps in Hanford, Washington; the Nevada Test Site for atomic weapons north of Las Vegas; and uranium mines in the Black Hills of South Dakota and in the Four Corners region, where New Mexico, Arizona, Colorado, and Utah meet. Some of this overlap resulted from geological coincidence: almost 90 percent of the nation's uranium lay on or adjacent to Indian lands. Some of it stemmed from politics. The sparse populations of Pueblo, Western Shoshone, and Yakima lacked the political clout to prevent their lands from becoming what the National Academy of Science called "national sacrifice areas."

Ronald Reagan loved spending time at his ranch near Santa Barbara, California.

In the 1980s, nuclear weapons and waste once again sparked controversy in the United States. President Ronald Reagan expanded the nation's nuclear arsenal, and his administration publicly discussed fighting and winning a nuclear war against the Soviet Union. An accident in 1986 at the Chernobyl nuclear power plant outside the Soviet city of Kiev only heightened public concerns. The disaster killed more than 100 people and irradiated hundreds of thousands more. Frightened by rising U.S.-Soviet tensions, citizens in western Europe and the United States organized an international movement to freeze further development of nuclear weapons.

Native Americans responded to the renewed focus on nuclear weaponry with a combination of resistance and accommodation. Along with their non-Indian supporters, some protested at the Nevada Test Site. At the same time, former Navajo uranium miners—many of them now stricken with cancer—sued the government for failing to inform them of the risks in handling radioactive materials. Other Indians, such as the Mescalero Apache in New Mexico and the Goshute in Utah, allowed nuclear waste storage facilities on their land. In their view, this move would gain them both money and control over radioactive materials that were within their borders anyway. In 1990 the U.S. Congress finally passed the Radiation Exposure Act. The law designated funds to provide some compensation for those damaged by the nation's quest for nuclear supremacy during the Cold War.

The controversies over nuclear power, weapons, and radioactive waste revealed key themes of the 1980s, especially U.S. military standing, government deregulation, and renewed anticommunism. In 1979 two international incidents raised questions about U.S. military effectiveness. That year, a revolution in Iran led to the taking of American hostages and a dramatic rejection of American cultural values, and the Soviet Union sent troops into Afghanistan to prop up a Soviet-allied but weakening government. Angered, Americans put tough-talking Republicans in the White House for 12 years. These leaders' emphasis on military might challenged the Soviet leadership, while changes in eastern Europe and the USSR brought an end to the Cold War and the breakup of the Soviet Union.

Fed up with humiliating events overseas and with relentless inflation at home, American voters elected Ronald Reagan as president.

The Reagan administration also avidly promoted free markets. Its policies produced astounding wealth at the top of the socioeconomic ladder, increasing the distance between the daily experiences of the rich and the poor. These policies also catalyzed bitter struggles over natural resources, particularly those on western public lands.

Finally, the newly organized religious right clashed with liberal opponents over such issues as abortion and homosexuality. In these years, Christian fundamentalists and their allies sought to reverse cultural liberties that had emerged since the late 1960s.

Anticommunism Revived

"We're going down!" cried U.S. political officer Elizabeth Swift on the phone to the State Department. These were her last words as a crowd of young Iranians poured into the U.S. embassy in Teheran on the morning of November 4, 1979, and cut telephone lines. In a move that shocked Americans, Islamic militants seized 52 embassy personnel and held them for over a year.

In the late 1970s, revolutionaries of a different political bent—socialist and leftist—took the offensive against authoritarian regimes in Central America. Indeed, the Third World seemed to be turning away from U.S. leadership in the wake of the American defeat in Vietnam. To make matters worse, the Soviet Union stepped up its support for leftists abroad. In December 1979, the Red Army invaded Afghanistan. Fed up with these humiliating events overseas and with relentless inflation at home, American voters elected Ronald Reagan as president—the most conservative chief executive since Calvin Coolidge. Reagan promised to resurrect the Cold War, and he delivered.

Iran and Afghanistan

In January 1979, the Iranian people overthrew the longtime authoritarian government of Shah Reza Pahlavi. Under the shah's rule, the nation's enormous oil wealth had flowed into the hands of a small elite. Meanwhile, the impoverished majority of devout Shi'a Muslims grew increasingly resentful of the Shah's closeness with his American allies. His secret police had detained 50,000 political prisoners; in the shah's time, his critics said, "only the cemeteries prospered." The revolution found its leader in the austere religious figure Ruhollah Khomeini, who shouldered aside more moderate opposition groups. Returning from exile in Iraq and then Paris, Ayatollah Khomeini created a popular theocratic state grounded in a strict interpretation of Islamic law.

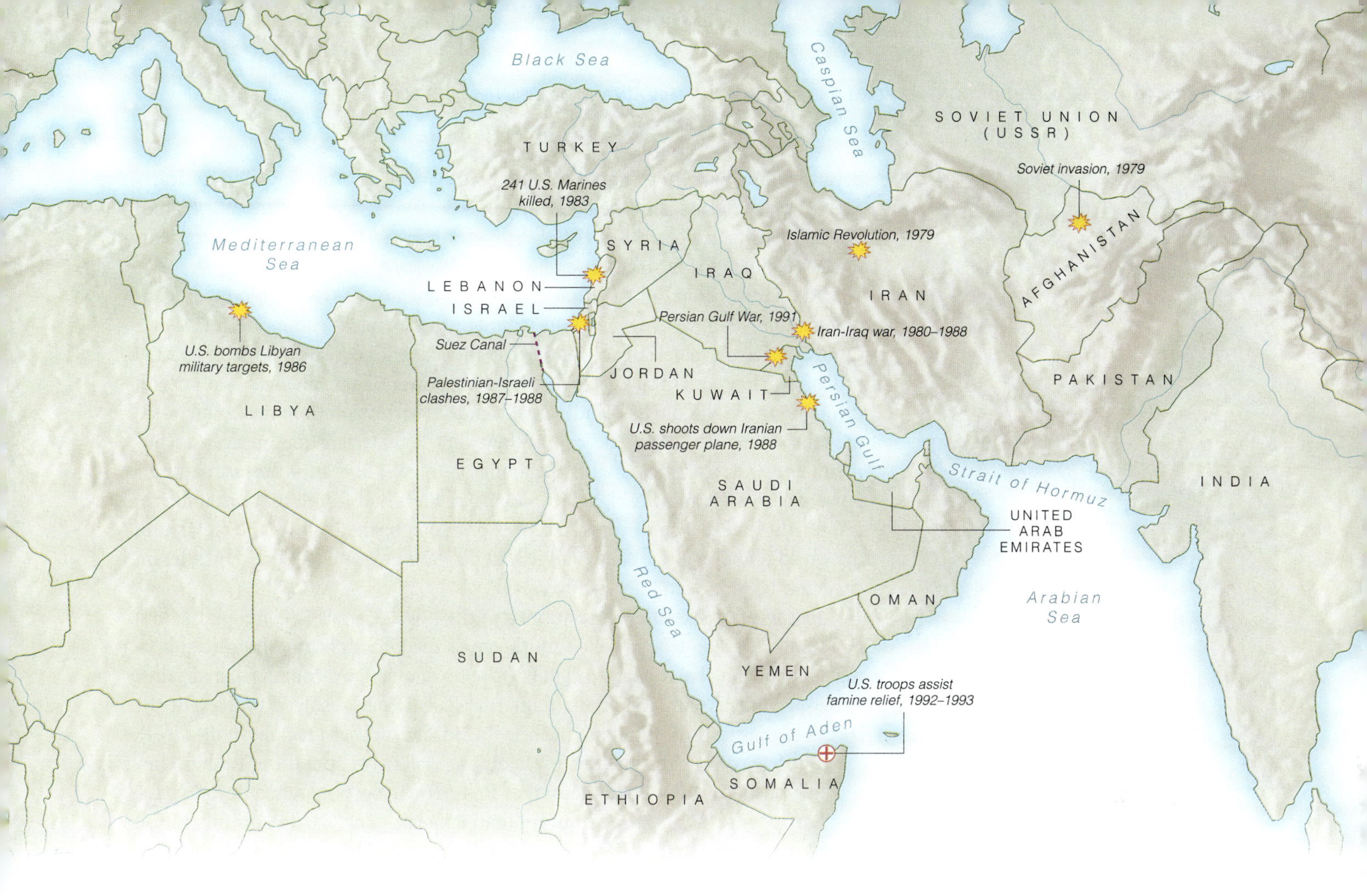

▲ MAP 28.1 TROUBLE SPOTS IN THE MIDDLE EAST, 1979–1993
Oil production around the Persian Gulf and the close American relationship with Israel made political instability in the Middle East a central concern of the U.S. government. American leaders particularly feared the spread of either Soviet influence or Islamic revolution, both of which opposed American cultural values and U.S. strategic interests.

For the United States, connections with both Iran and Saudi Arabia since the 1940s had formed the two pillars of American policy toward the oil-rich Persian Gulf. Indeed, the CIA had engineered the 1953 coup that overthrew the short-lived Iranian nationalist government of Muhammad Mussadiq and restored the young shah to power. American officials maintained close ties with the shah thereafter.

The drop in Iran's oil production that accompanied the 1979 revolution unleashed the United States' second oil shock of the 1970s. By that time, the nation depended on imports for as much as 42 percent of its oil. American gas prices soared by 60 percent amid shortages, sending another wave of inflation rolling through the U.S. economy.

Hunted by the rebels, the shah took his money and fled Iran. Several months later, the Carter administration let him fly to New York to seek treatment for cancer. Enraged that the United States harbored their nation's most wanted criminal, Iranians demanded the shah's extradition to Teheran to stand trial. Washington refused. Within a month, militants stormed the U.S. embassy—"that nest of spies," Khomeini called it, referring to the CIA's presence in Iran.

The hostages' captors paraded them before television cameras to force Washington to return the Shah. Carter refused to give in, but he focused the rest of his presidency on engineering the hostages' release. He thus had little energy and few resources to devote to his campaign for reelection. ABC television created the news show *Nightline* to provide daily reports on the crisis. In April 1980, Carter finally approved a military rescue effort. But mechanical failures forced the mission to abort, and the collision of two helicopters during the attempt killed several U.S. soldiers. Secretary of State Cyrus Vance resigned in protest against the attempted use of force. He was the first State Department head to quit over a matter of principle since William Jennings

Bettmann/CORBIS

▲ **Ruhollah Khomeini led the 1979 revolution in Iran that established the modern world's first Islamic theocratic state. The events in Iran encouraged Islamic revolutionaries across the Middle East, Asia, and North Africa. For Americans, the closest analogy was the Bolshevik revolution of 1917 in Russia, which provided a model for other communist revolutions abroad.**

Bryan resigned in 1915 to express his desire to stay out of World War I. Americans' frustration deepened, and their resentment of anti-American radicals in the Third World intensified. Not until after the shah's death in 1980 did the two governments finally negotiate the hostages' release.

At its root, what did the Iranian challenge mean for American power? Khomeini and his followers despised the values they associated with modern U.S. culture: secularism, materialism, gender equality, alcohol consumption, and sexual titillation. They sought to export the cleansing power of a puritanical Islamic faith throughout the Middle East and beyond. Indeed, the revolutionaries condemned the atheistic Soviets just as fiercely as they did the materialistic Americans. Khomeini applauded all movements that sought "to gain liberation from the superpowers of the left and the right." U.S. policymakers had feared that instability in Iran might lead to a communist takeover of that country. Instead, the creation of the world's first revolutionary Islamic state in 1979 presented an entirely different challenge to American interests overseas.

Just seven weeks after the outbreak of the hostage crisis in Teheran, the first of 110,000 Russian troops rolled south across the USSR's border into neighboring Afghanistan. Their goal: to stabilize the pro-Soviet government there against anticommunist Islamic guerrilla fighters. Moscow had resolved to prevent the spread of Islamic revolution into the heavily Muslim southern regions of the USSR.

But few Americans saw this invasion as a defensive operation. Rather, they feared a push toward vulnerable Iran as Red Army troops marched beyond eastern Europe for the first time in more than 30 years. The Carter administration halted most trade with the Soviets and withdrew the Strategic Arms Limitation Treaty (SALT II) nuclear arms control treaty from Senate consideration. In addition, the president organized a western boycott of the 1980 Olympics in Moscow and increased military spending. The "Carter Doctrine" proclaimed the U.S. commitment to preserve the status quo in the Persian Gulf region, even if it meant the use of military force. And the CIA began funding the Afghan guerrillas. Détente was dead; containment was back. Next came efforts to roll back the Soviets.

The Conservative Victory of 1980

By mid-1980, Carter's public approval rating had dropped to the lowest level of any modern president. Interest rates surpassed 20 percent, and inflation reached 17 percent. Even the president acknowledged a "crisis stage." With their dollars no longer buying what they used to, Americans wondered what the future would bring. For many voters, Carter's inability to free the hostages in Teheran or reverse the Soviet occupation of Afghanistan symbolized the limitations of his presidency. Even his own party threatened to abandon him, as the vigorous challenge in the Democratic primaries by liberal Senator Edward Kennedy of Massachusetts revealed.

Onto this stage strode Ronald Reagan. Long considered too conservative to win the presidency, the former California governor projected the confidence and strength that many Americans wanted, even if they did not share all of his views. The 69-year-old one-time actor sailed through the Republican primaries. For his main tactic, he appealed to nostalgia, particularly among white men, for a rosier past—a time of rising wages and U.S. military might. While Carter spoke of learning to live within limits, Reagan insisted that "we are too great a nation to limit ourselves to small dreams."

Reagan's electoral victory in 1989 symbolized the meshing of politics and entertainment. An actor on the ultimate stage, he understood the presidency as a matter of public performance more than substantive policies. With little interest in the actual process of governing, he gave his advisers minimal guidance. He focused his own efforts on selling an idealized version of America to the public. He deeply believed in this version, even when his stories about it derived from film plots. For example, he claimed to have filmed the liberation of Nazi death camps in Europe in World War II, when in fact he did not leave the United States during the war. Nevertheless, with his sunny disposition and ease before the camera, Reagan projected the image of an attractive, competent leader.

Reagan Presidential Ad: A Bear in the Woods

The media loved Reagan. Indeed, his presidency fit with the new emphasis on constant entertainment, as cable television, VCRs (1976), MTV (1981), and CDs (1983) swept the culture. Daily newspaper readership plummeted from 73 percent to 50 percent during the 1980s. Equally telling, the average length of an uninterrupted "sound bite" on the evening news dropped from 42 seconds in 1968 to fewer than 10 seconds in 1988. Anything longer, the networks believed, would bore viewers. And no one projected simplicity with greater warmth or sincerity than Reagan. Even his fiercest opponents admired his irrepressible good humor when, after being shot by would-be assassin John Hinkley in 1981, the president surveyed the surgeons standing around his operating table and quipped, "I hope you're all Republicans."

Yet the 1980 election was about more than just Reagan's likable personality. It revealed the nation's renewed interest in conservative ideas. Republicans won control of the Senate for the first time since 1952, managing to defeat several of the chamber's most respected liberal Democratic members. Several basic values united the party: an unhindered private sector and entrepreneurial initiative to create affluence, plus free markets and individual responsibility to solve the nation's social problems. Republicans, like most Democrats, also believed that the United States had a moral obligation to preserve world order and halt further expansion of communist influence. Reagan proclaimed that "government was the problem, not the solution." The United States' key European allies also moved to the right in the 1980s, especially Great Britain under the leadership of Margaret Thatcher.

Renewing the Cold War

"Sometimes in our administration," Reagan once joked, "the right hand doesn't know what the far-right hand is doing." But all hands in the White House agreed on the importance of restoring confidence in the nation's engagements abroad, particularly in the Third World. In the 1970s, leftist insurgencies in Asia, Africa, and Latin America—especially Vietnam, Cambodia, Angola, Ethiopia, El Salvador, and Nicaragua—had suggested the retreat of U.S. power. Equally troubling to many, when the U.S. government did assert its power, it often seemed to support antidemocratic or racist governments—as long as they were anticommunist and open to foreign investment. Never much concerned with foreign affairs in the best of times, most Americans now felt disillusioned.

Reagan set out to heal the public's bruised pride. Reagan blamed the Soviet Union for "all the unrest that is going on." He rejected the 1970s policy of détente that had emerged during the Nixon administration and had taken further shape under Ford and Carter. Often, Reagan spoke as though the Chinese-Soviet split had never happened. His was "a kind of 1952 world," one aide recalled. "He sees the world in black and white terms." Pointing to the Soviet occupation of Afghanistan and its 1983 shoot-down of a Korean Air Lines civilian jet that had strayed into Soviet airspace, the president denounced the USSR as "an evil empire." His pronouncement echoed the language of the wildly popular film *Star Wars* (1977) and its two sequels. The three movies cast the plucky heroes—like Americans and their allies—as righteous rebels against a malignant imperial power. Americans, Reagan vowed, must overcome their post-1973 "Vietnam syndrome" and stand ready once again to use force abroad.

Reagan, "Evil Empire" Speech

The Reagan administration backed up the president's words by launching the largest peacetime military buildup in American history. The Pentagon's budget ballooned 40 percent between

1980 and 1984. The new president also revived covert operations. He gave CIA director William Casey the green light to provide secret assistance to anticommunist governments and insurgencies throughout the Third World, despite their sometimes gruesome human rights records.

However, the administration's aggressive rhetoric about rolling back communism masked an unwillingness to put U.S. soldiers in harm's way abroad. The one exception came during the civil war in Lebanon in 1983. U.S. forces initially deployed as peacekeepers there began siding with the Israeli-backed Christian government troops against Syrian-supported Muslim rebels. Within weeks, a Muslim suicide bomber—one of the first of many to come in the Middle East—drove a truck full of explosives into the American barracks at the Beirut airport, killing 241 marines. The administration quietly backed off from mediating further Middle East conflicts. It covered its retreat with an invasion two days later of the tiny Caribbean island of Grenada. There, thousands of U.S. troops quickly overthrew a Marxist government and a small contingent of Cuban supporters.

▲ Critics of Reagan's policies toward Central America believed that he ignored the indigenous problems encouraging revolutions there, blaming instead the USSR and Cuba. The cartoon suggests that the Democratic party took a different view than the president. Many Democrats in the Congress did, and they were responsible for limiting Reagan's promotion of the Nicaraguan Contras. But many others went along with the popular president in defending the Contras and supporting right-wing regimes in the region.

In Central America, extreme inequalities between landowning elites and vast peasant majorities had fueled leftist insurgencies against the authoritarian governments of El Salvador, Guatemala, and Nicaragua. Moreover, some small assistance from Cuba and the Soviet Union had found its way to the rebels. Reagan passionately opposed these insurgents. He authorized the CIA to work hand in hand with the regimes, even though they used death squads to torture and murder dissidents and slaughtered whole villages and towns to wipe out possible resistance.

In Nicaragua, the Sandinista rebels had managed to overthrow the pro-American dictatorship of Antonio Somoza in 1979. The Sandinistas set about building a more egalitarian and socialistic state while still preserving 60 percent of the nation's wealth in private hands. Carter had adopted a wait-and-see attitude. But after Reagan took office in 1981, the CIA created the counterrevolutionary "Contras," recruited primarily from Somoza's brutal former National Guard. The Contras waged an undeclared war on the new government in the Nicaraguan capital of Managua. By 1987, 40,000 Nicaraguans had died in the fighting, most of them civilians. Reagan called the Contras "freedom fighters" and declared them "the moral equal of our Founding Fathers."

Nevertheless, several European and Latin American allies considered the Contras an illegitimate force of terrorists. A large coalition of church and university groups in the United States agreed. They organized fact-finding visits to Nicaragua and lobbying trips to Washington. Christian activists formed the "Sanctuary" movement to aid refugees from the right-wing dictatorships in Central America that sympathized with the Contras. The Pentagon, for its part, had no interest in sending troops to fight a popular government abroad. The opposition finally prevailed; Congress passed the Boland Amendments of 1982 and 1984 to restrict U.S. assistance to the Contras.

Reagan, Support for the Contras

The plight of refugees fleeing the civil wars in Central America exposed the politicized thinking that had influenced U.S. immigration policies for decades. Officials distinguished between "political" refugees and "economic" refugees. The former, they felt, had a well-founded fear of persecution. The latter were supposedly looking only for better economic opportunities. The Reagan administration used this distinction to justify supporting certain foreign governments while opposing others. For example, the U.S. government had warmly welcomed and financially assisted people fleeing communist regimes, such as Hungary in the 1950s and

Cuba since the 1960s. Likewise, Nicaraguan immigrants were treated well because their choice to leave Nicaragua provided ammunition in the propaganda war against the Sandinistas. However, Salvadorans and Guatemalans, deemed "economic" refugees, were turned away. In 1984, U.S. officials admitted only 328 Salvadorans into the country while refusing 13,045—a ratio opposite that for Nicaraguans.

These policies encouraged the emergence of militantly anticommunist expatriate communities in the United States. Such groups then lobbied to sustain U.S. hostility toward leftist regimes in their homelands. The anti-Castro Cuban community in Miami offered the most dramatic example. Immigrants who left Vietnam and Cambodia after the communist victories there in 1975 brought a similar perspective.

Republican Rule at Home

Lori was what the president called a "welfare cheat." Writer Barbara Ehrenreich told the story of a young neighbor in New York City representative of welfare recipients: a single white mother with one child. Lori had been married for two years to a man who beat her and once chased her around the house with a gun. Welfare had made it possible for her to leave him, a move she described as like being born again, "as a human being this time." Lori sometimes earned close to $100 a week from cleaning houses and waiting tables—not enough to support herself and her daughter, but a useful supplement to the small government payments. She chose not to report this to the welfare office, spending it instead on little things deemed inessential by welfare regulations: deodorant, hand lotion, and an occasional commercial haircut.

Lori's story helps illuminate some of the major trends of the 1980s. Inflation finally eased and the stock market perked up. Congress and the White House slashed taxes. However, annual budget deficits and the national debt (the accumulation of previous deficits) soon soared as tax revenues decreased and military spending increased. The administration shrank government programs for the poor and portrayed welfare recipients like Lori as lazy and irresponsible. Washington turned a cold shoulder to concerns over the environment and opened public lands in the West to new commercial uses. By the 1990s, the gap between rich and poor widened so much that the vaunted American middle class threatened to shrink dramatically.

> ***Annual budget deficits and the national debt soared as tax revenues decreased and military spending increased.***

"Reaganomics" and the Assault on Welfare

Taxes played a crucial role in the Reagan administration's efforts to reduce government involvement in the economy. Compared with America's closest allies in Europe, U.S. tax rates were already low because of the country's smaller welfare provisions. But a tax revolt had begun brewing in the 1970s, exemplified by California's Proposition 13 (1978), which cut property taxes by more than half. In 1981, Reagan proposed a new tax law to lower federal income tax rates by 25 percent over three years. Congress passed the legislation, and the top individual rate—paid only by the wealthiest Americans—dropped from 70 percent to 28 percent. Congress also slashed taxes on corporations, capital gains, and inheritances, further benefiting the most affluent Americans.

While taxes shrank, federal spending on the military soared. The Pentagon bolstered its conventional and nuclear arsenals and gave service personnel a morale-boosting salary increase. After 1983, billions of dollars poured from the U.S. Treasury into the president's proposed Strategic Defense Initiative (SDI) for a national missile defense system. The funds for the weapons buildup could come from only one source: social programs at home. However, most domestic spending went to popular programs, such as Social Security and Medicare, which primarily benefited the middle class. Leaving those in place, Reagan instead reduced funding for welfare programs, including food stamps, school lunches, job training, and low-income housing. His administration derided impoverished single mothers as "welfare queens." The welfare state, the administration contended, was only encouraging dependence and stifling individual responsibility.

The assault on welfare had links to racial issues as well. Reagan portrayed welfare recipients—most of whom were white and lived in rural areas—as primarily urban and African American. The president had made a blunt appeal to white southern voters in 1980. He had campaigned in Philadelphia, Mississippi, a tiny town but a national symbol of antiblack violence since three civil rights workers had been murdered nearby in 1964. There, Reagan spoke of his support for "states' rights"—the same language that those who supported the killers had used. The Reagan administration also opposed any form of affirmative action, calling instead for the "colorblind" application of law. The president and his supporters argued that prejudice no longer had any effect on the decisions that employers and others made. Ironically, Reagan's own Justice Department demonstrated the opposite: it sought unsuccessfully to win tax-free status for Bob Jones University in Greenville, South Carolina, and other schools and colleges that discriminated against people of color.

Despite some problems, "Reaganomics" helped the national economy recover somewhat from the traumas of the 1970s.

Reducing welfare spending did not close the budgetary gaps that lower taxes and higher military outlays had opened. "Supply-side" economists had promised that tax cuts would encourage investment and thereby generate wealth and eventually more tax revenues, even with lowered rates. But Reagan's own vice president and former challenger in the Republican primaries, George H. W. Bush, had dismissed these assumptions as "voodoo economics." Bush's perspective had merit. To close the budget gaps, the government resorted to borrowing money. Formerly the world's largest creditor nation, the United States became its largest debtor nation. Between 1981 and 1989, the national debt ballooned to almost $3 trillion. Moreover, during the 12 years of Republican rule ending in 1993, annual budget deficits jumped from $59 billion to $300 billion. Paying the interest on the new debt pushed interest rates higher and siphoned off funds that could have been used instead for productive purposes.

Despite these problems, "Reaganomics" helped the national economy recover somewhat from the traumas of the 1970s. The tight money policies of the Federal Reserve Board after 1979 eventually tamed inflation, which dropped from 14 percent in 1980 to less than 2 percent in 1983. The Fed's high interest rates also choked off the nation's cash flow and provoked a severe recession in 1981–1982, with unemployment reaching above 10 percent. However, the economy revived again in 1983 and was growing at a robust annual rate of 6.8 percent by 1984.

In that year, rising confidence in the economy helped Reagan crush his opponent, Carter's former vice president, Walter Mondale. Even the novelty of placing a woman, Geraldine Ferraro, on a major ticket as the vice presidential candidate could not bolster the Democratic challenge. Reagan, now 73 and limiting his campaign appearances to well-orchestrated photo opportunities, won reelection handily and continued his economic course. After several years of excellent returns on Wall Street, the stock market crash of October 1987 caught investors by surprise. Nevertheless, it did not provoke a broader economic downturn, as the 1929 crash had done.

An Embattled Environment

The 1980 election marked the sharpest turn ever in American environmental politics. The new administration reversed two decades of growing bipartisan consensus on the need for greater protection of the environment. Reagan instead supported corporations' demands for fewer environmental regulations and easier access to natural resources on public lands. The president ridiculed the idea of preserving wilderness for its own sake. Noting that plants emit carbon dioxide, he even claimed that "trees cause more pollution than automobiles do."

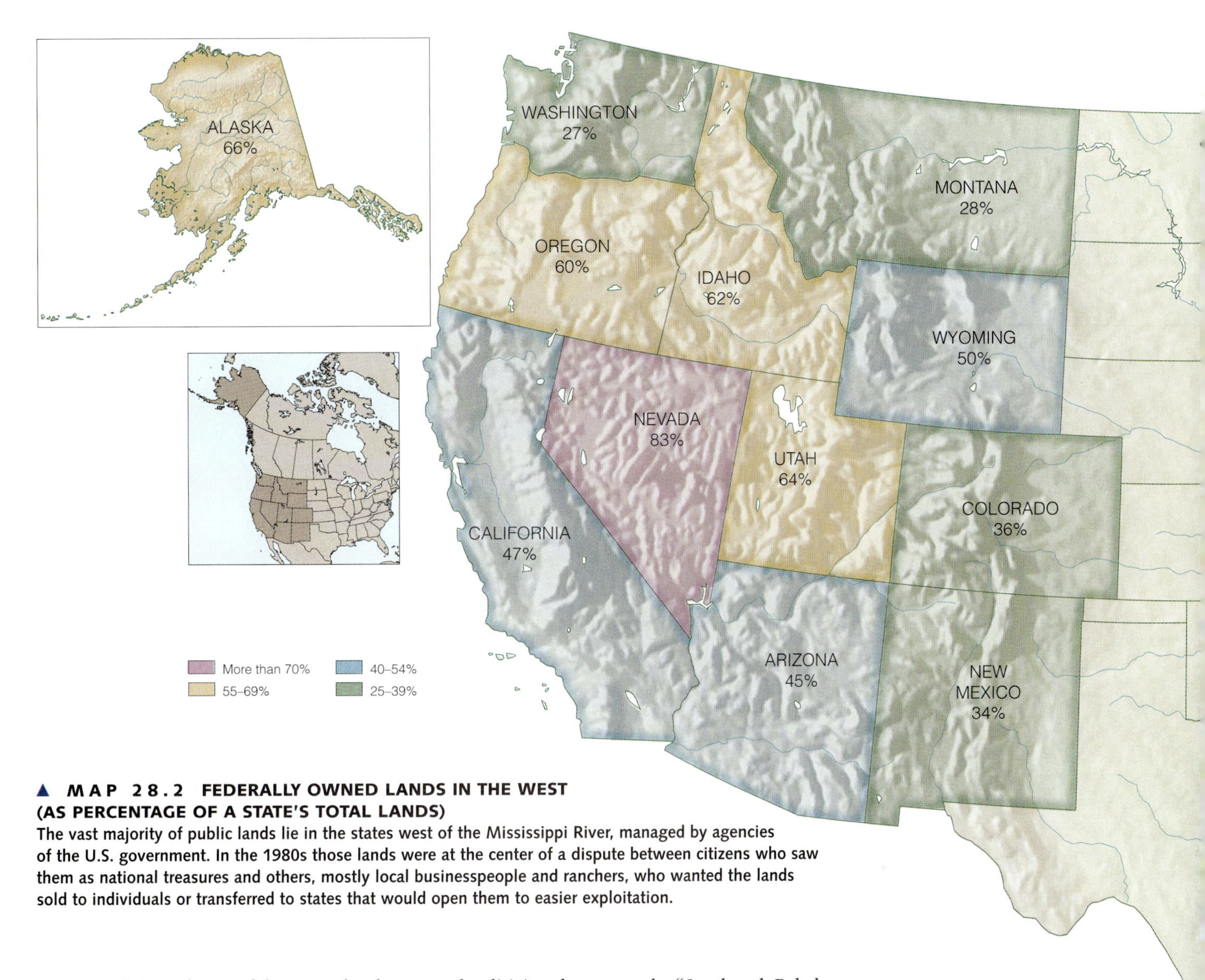

▲ **MAP 28.2 FEDERALLY OWNED LANDS IN THE WEST (AS PERCENTAGE OF A STATE'S TOTAL LANDS)**
The vast majority of public lands lie in the states west of the Mississippi River, managed by agencies of the U.S. government. In the 1980s those lands were at the center of a dispute between citizens who saw them as national treasures and others, mostly local businesspeople and ranchers, who wanted the lands sold to individuals or transferred to states that would open them to easier exploitation.

A coalition of powerful western land users and politicians known as the "Sagebrush Rebellion" had an ally in the White House. Emboldened, they launched a quest to turn federal lands over to the states and open them to commercial use. These lands, most of them in the West, were administered by the U.S. Forest Service and the Bureau of Land Management (BLM). They had ended up in federal hands primarily because successive waves of settlers had deemed them undesirable. They included snowy mountains in the Rockies and Sierras and vast deserts in the Great Basin of Nevada and Utah. By the 1980s, different groups desired them for two mutually exclusive purposes: corporations and ranchers wanted to harvest timber and minerals from them and use them for grazing, and environmentalists and outdoor enthusiasts sought to designate them for recreational and scenic use.

The officials Reagan appointed to oversee these lands and assume responsibility for protecting them had little respect for the agencies they ran. Critics described the situation as "foxes guarding the chicken house." The officials openly disdained environmentalists, including those in the moderate wing of the Republican party. Anne Gorsuch at the Environmental Protection Agency (EPA), Robert Burford at the BLM, and John Crowell in charge of the Forest Service explicitly rewrote regulations to favor private enterprise. They sold grazing, logging, and mining rights on public lands at prices far below market value, despite their stated commitment to market economics.

▶ James Watt, Reagan's first secretary of the interior, became one of the most polarizing figures in a polarized decade. He made clear that he considered environmentalists his opponents as he worked to promote the interests of mining and timbering companies as well as ranchers. The Department of the Interior manages the national parks, monuments, and wildlife refuges, as well as the Bureau of Land Management's extensive lands (national forests fall under the Department of Agriculture's jurisdiction).

Gorsuch, Burford, and Crowell were moderates in comparison to James Watt, the new secretary of the interior who controlled national parks and wildlife refuges. A native of Wheatland, Wyoming, Watt had worked as a lawyer in Denver for a private foundation dedicated to helping businesses gain access to public lands. An ideologue, he declared that only two kinds of people lived in the United States: "liberals and Americans." Watt was also a Christian fundamentalist who believed that the end of time was very near. In his Senate confirmation hearings, he suggested that the nation had little need for long-term public land management because Christ would soon be returning and the known world would pass away—an interpretation of stewardship that not even all fundamentalists shared, much less the broader American public. Watt's abrasive personal style eventually alienated even the White House, and he resigned in 1983.

The administration's reversal of federal environmental policies alarmed a wide range of citizens and stimulated a powerful backlash. Membership in environmental organizations soared, in such traditional groups as the Sierra Club and the Audubon Society, as well as in more radical ones, such as Greenpeace. Most Americans wanted to breathe cleaner air, drink safe water, and make recreational use of national forests, national parks, and BLM lands. In much of the rural West, jobs in the recreation industry now outnumbered those in the logging, mining, and ranching businesses. The public also took alarm at the 1986 Chernobyl nuclear accident in the USSR. Three years later, concerns intensified when the oil tanker *Exxon Valdez* ran aground in Prince William Sound in Alaska, coating 1,000 miles of pristine coastline with crude oil.

A Society Divided

As the Reagan administration eased corporate access to the nation's natural resources, the disparity between rich and poor expanded further. Whereas most Americans' real wages (wages after inflation is factored in) declined, the professional classes fared well, and the wealthiest citizens gained enormously. For example, the salary of an average corporate chief executive officer was 40 times greater than that of a typical factory worker in 1980; by 1989, it was 93 times greater. By 1989, the top 1 percent of American families possessed more assets than the bottom 90 percent—a ratio typical of Third World nations.

Roger Worth/Woodfin Camp

Elaine Thompson/AP/Wide World

▲ On May 18, 1980, a spectacular volcanic eruption blew the top off of Mount Saint Helens in Washington's Cascade Range. The hot ash and lava flows killed 57 people and created an ash-covered landscape out of a previously lush forest. The eruption reminded Americans of all political persuasions of the power and unpredictability of nature, just months before the Reagan administration initiated new environmental policies opening up natural resources to easier exploitation.

A series of corporate mergers and consolidations further enriched well-off Americans, as did financial speculation and manipulation on Wall Street. *Business Week* wrote of a "casino economy" in which insider trading and leveraged buyouts (business takeovers financed by debt) created paper wealth rather than actual products. Defenders of the aggressive new tactics on Wall Street argued that those taking great risks deserved great rewards and that new wealth trickled down to the broader American citizenry. "Greed is all right," fabulously wealthy financier and corporate takeover specialist Ivan Boesky assured the 1986 graduating class of the business school of the University of California at Berkeley. "I want you to know that. I think greed is healthy. You can be greedy and still feel good about yourself." Six months later, however, Boesky began a three-year prison term for illegal insider trading.

The explosion of wealth at the top fueled an emerging culture of extravagance, reminiscent of similar trends in the late nineteenth century and the 1920s. Newly identified "yuppies" (young urban professionals) embodied the drive for material acquisition, in contrast to the anticonsumerist inclinations of the late 1960s and early 1970s. Jerry Rubin, a member of the anarchist "yippies" in the 1960s, once dropped dollar bills onto the floor of the New York Stock Exchange—which traders scurried madly to grab—to dramatize the stock market's pursuit of profit. By the 1980s, however, Rubin was working as an investment banker. Ronald and Nancy Reagan were older but shared similar values. They relished lavish amenities like those made popular on the television shows *Dynasty*, *Dallas*, and *Lifestyles of the Rich and Famous.*

As the affluence gap widened, the broad middle class watched its job security slip. Early in the decade, the recession had prompted factory shutdowns and mass layoffs. More than a million industrial jobs disappeared in 1982 alone. Manufacturers' decisions to keep moving plants abroad for cheaper labor only worsened the situation. Although the 1980s saw the creation of 20 million new jobs, most of these were in the nonunionized service sector and offered low pay and few benefits. In his first year in office, Reagan broke a strike by the nation's 12,000

Is Material Success Corrupting?

Ted Thai/CORBIS/Sygma

Wealthy Americans have had varying attitudes about how to deal with their good fortune. The newly rich of the 1980s seemed eager to display their wealth publicly. Here New York real estate tycoon Donald Trump and his wife Ivana pose with part of the domestic staff that catered to their daily needs.

"Will you tell me," former president John Adams asked former president Thomas Jefferson in 1819, "how to prevent riches from becoming the effects of temperance and industry? Will you tell me how to prevent riches from producing luxury? Will you tell me how to prevent luxury from producing effeminacy, intoxication, extravagance, vice and folly?"

Adams had his finger on one of the enduring dilemmas in American life. Discipline and hard work—"temperance and industry"—tended to lead to material success. But acquiring riches tended to change people. It made them more self-indulgent and less virtuous as citizens of a republic, Adams feared.

Adams's concerns mirrored those of his Puritan ancestors who had arrived in Massachusetts almost two centuries earlier. So strongly had the Puritans rejected what they saw as the spiritual and material corruptions of life in England that they left to start anew across the Atlantic Ocean, a profoundly dangerous enterprise. Once they had survived the terrible first winters and established secure colonies in what they called New England, they began to face a new problem. Building a godly society meant "doing good": following the model of Jesus. But their disciplined lives led many Puritans also to "do well": make money. Were these two compatible? After all, Jesus himself had warned, "It is easier for a camel to go through the eye of a needle than for a rich man to enter into the kingdom of God" (*Matthew* 19:24). Puritans and their descendants wrestled with this problem for generations.

Waves of immigration since the 1600s replenished American society

DOCUMENT

Reagan, The Air Traffic Controllers Strike

air traffic controllers by firing the protesting public employees and hiring permanent replacements. By 1990, 8 million Americans had tried the unskilled work available at McDonald's fast-food restaurants. "To work at McDonald's you don't need a face, you don't need a brain," one of them recalled. "You need to have two hands and two legs and move 'em as fast as you can. That's the whole system. I wouldn't go back there for anything."

The poorest Americans fared badly in the 1980s. The bottom tenth saw their already meager incomes decline by another 10 percent. In 1986, a full-time worker at minimum wage earned $6,700 per year—almost $4,000 short of the poverty level for a family of four. Homelessness worsened in cities as the government cut funding for welfare and institutional care for the mentally ill while housing costs rose. More than 1 million people lived on the streets, one-fifth of them still employed. One out of eight children went hungry and 20 percent lived in poverty, including 50 percent of black children.

These Americans received minimal sympathy from the nation's political leaders. By contrast, Congress and the White House provided huge federal subsidies to "needy" businesses such as the Chrysler Corporation. The collapse of the savings and loan (S&L) industry pro-

Photo by George Cohen

Neither homelessness nor poverty in general was new in American society in the 1980s. But the numbers of Americans living on the streets increased sharply. They were especially visible in the centers of large cities, such as these sleeping in New York City's Pennsylvania Station in January 1990.

with people seeking opportunity. The hardships that attend moving to a new country ensured that new Americans tended to be strivers and risk-takers. Some came for religious and political freedom, but many others were drawn by the possibility of "doing well" economically. With effort, most fared much better than they had previously. The United States remained, in the old words of nineteenth-century Chinese immigrants, "the Golden Mountain."

Despite their enthusiasm for pursuing private material success, Americans in the twentieth century at times indicated public ambivalence about great wealth. During the trauma of the Great Depression and the national unity of World War II, displays of extravagance drew scorn, and government policies became somewhat more redistributive of the national wealth. The communes of the 1960s, like earlier utopian communities, sought to create a life free from what their members saw as the corruptions of materialism. In the Cold War competition for influence abroad, U.S. officials sent diplomats and aid workers to Africa but worried that Soviet and especially Chinese personnel, accustomed to fewer material comforts at home than Americans, were fitting much better into poor African societies and making more positive impressions on their hosts.

In other periods of modern American history, however, public life celebrated the success of the nation's richest citizens. During the Gilded Age of the late 1800s and the Jazz Age of the 1920s, political and cultural leaders admired and shared the affluence associated with names such as Rockefeller, Carnegie, and Ford. The 1980s became another era for ostentatious displays of wealth. "If you've got it, flaunt it," became a familiar expression. The proliferation of stretch limousines epitomized a decade marked by "conspicuous consumption." ■

vides the most striking example. Deregulation in the late 1970s had reduced oversight of the formerly sedate financial practices of S&Ls by federal regulators. But S&Ls remained insured by the U.S. government. As a result, some S&L executives, such as Charles Keating, engaged in rampant speculation and fraud. A decline in real estate prices bankrupted 600 shaky S&Ls by 1991, leaving taxpayers with a bill for nearly $500 billion. Federal Deposit Insurance Corporation chair William Seidman described the U.S. government as "a full partner in a nationwide casino."

Despite Reagan's record, 40 percent of union household members and 50 percent of all blue-collar workers cast their ballots for this staunch opponent of unions. Why? Part of the explanation lies in the decline of working-class voting during the 1970s. Disillusioned with a political process they saw as corrupt, numerous workers neglected to go to the polls on voting day. Many of those who did vote decided that the Democratic party had become increasingly co-opted by cultural liberalism and no longer spoke for the working class. Reagan's charisma and appeal to patriotism also attracted many citizens who might once have voted for their economic interests instead. Finally, white Americans increasingly defined their political loyalties on the

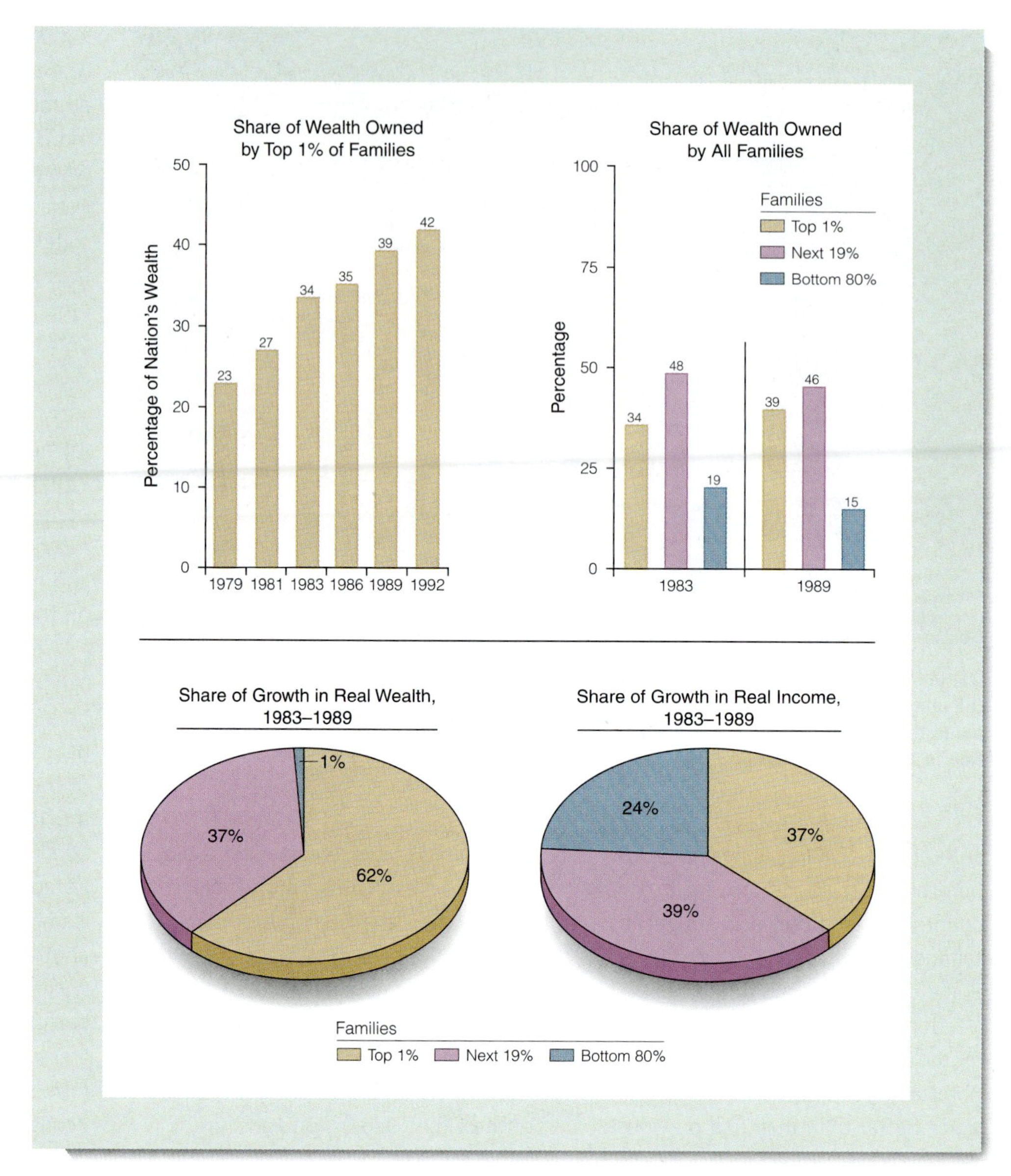

▶ **FIGURE 28.1**
DISTRIBUTION OF WEALTH AND INCOME
The 1980s were excellent years for wealthy Americans. The "trickle-down" effect touted by some Reagan administration officials—predicting that greater wealth accumulation among the rich would trickle down to the less affluent—had little impact.

basis of social and cultural issues—such as opposition to abortion, homosexuality, and affirmative action—rather than economic interests. Conservative Christians, in particular, strongly supported the Republican cause.

Cultural Conflict

One of the nation's foremost religious figures, Reverend Pat Robertson controlled the Christian Broadcasting Network and ran unsuccessfully for the 1988 Republican presidential nomination. Like other social conservatives of this era, he promoted "family values" and traditional gender roles. Robertson went so far as to declare that feminism "encourages women to leave their husbands, kill their children [and] practice witchcraft." In contrast, author Susan Faludi wrote the 1991 best-seller *Backlash* about opposition to the women's movement. She became an important critic of gender roles in American society and how they limit people's life experiences and possibilities. In contrast to Robertson, Faludi concluded, "All women are feminists. It's just a matter of time and encouragement."

Throughout the 1980s, Americans embroiled themselves in a contentious debate about values. Their society had changed in the previous generation in ways that some citizens disdained but others applauded. Americans argued primarily about issues that had come to the fore during the social movements of the 1960s and 1970s: sexuality, gender roles, the place of religion in public life, and multiculturalism. These often bitter "culture wars" dominated talk shows and newspaper editorial pages throughout much of the last two decades of the twentieth century.

The Rise of the Religious Right

Some of the Americans most troubled by the state of American society were conservative white Protestants. Disproportionately from the South, they had long avoided political involvement and sought to keep church and state separate. They had particularly distrusted Roman Catholicism and state aid for religious education that would include parochial schools. But anti-Catholicism declined sharply among these conservative Christians after the Supreme Court banned organized school prayer in 1962 and legalized abortion in 1973. Increasingly, conservative white Protestants saw secularism as their real enemy and conservative Catholics as allies.

Together these groups criticized the post-1960s shift in mainstream values away from respect for traditional authorities—the church, political leaders, and the military—and toward freer sexual expression and general self-indulgence. What the nation needed, they believed, was a return to reverence for God. The growth of this Christian fundamentalism paralleled rising religious fundamentalism around the globe, whether among Jews in Israel, Hindus in India, or Muslims in Iran and the Arab Middle East. For all their differences, religious people in these cultures shared a common quest: preserving spiritual purity and cultural traditions in an increasingly secular, integrated world.

Conservative Protestants were not a fringe group. As many as 45 million Americans—20 percent of the population—considered themselves fundamentalist Christians in 1980. In combination with a similar number of Catholics, they represented a vast potential force in American politics. And their ranks were growing, while membership in the more liberal mainline Protestant denominations, such as the Presbyterians and Episcopalians, declined steadily after the 1960s. Rather than emphasizing theological doctrine, these groups focused on individuals' emotional connection with a forgiving God. They built church schools, Bible colleges, and publishing houses to reinforce their message. Evangelism on secular college campuses expanded through such organizations as Intervarsity and Campus Crusade for Christ. Hal Lindsey's apocalyptic story about the second coming of Christ, *The Late Great Planet Earth*, sold more than 10 million copies in the 1970s.

> ***Increasingly, conservative white Protestants saw secularism as their real enemy and conservative Catholics as allies.***

Conservative Christians mobilized in the 1980 campaign to support Reagan's candidacy. Critics noted that Reagan himself attended church only occasionally and seemed an indifferent father. They contrasted the divorced candidate with his born-again, Sunday-school-teaching opponent, Jimmy Carter. But Reagan's conservative views on abortion and gay rights and his support for school prayer resonated with fundamentalists. They flocked to the Republican party and to new right-wing religious organizations, such as the Moral Majority, founded in 1979 in Lynchburg, Virginia, by Reverend Jerry Falwell. More than 60 million people each week watched—and many sent money to—"televangelists," including Falwell, Robertson, and Jim Bakker.

Suffusing the GOP with a distinctly southern, grassroots flavor, the religious right also highlighted a major faultline in the modern Republican party: the tension between social conservatives, who emphasized community and tradition, and free marketeers, who promoted entrepreneurial capitalism. In its quest for profits, unrestrained capitalism had no inherent respect for tradition. Indeed, it could bring unwelcome changes, as Rustbelt industrial workers had discovered when their employers moved south and overseas. Marrying Jesus to the market proved

Religion and Politics in the 1980s

In 1979, Baptist minister Jerry Falwell founded the Moral Majority in Lynchburg, Virginia. The organization represented the growing engagement of conservative evangelical Christians in American politics, and Falwell emerged as the most prominent figure of the new religious right. However, not all Christians were conservative. Robert McAfee Brown, a Presbyterian minister and theologian, represented more liberal elements of the church that understood both the Bible and the problems of American society differently than Falwell.

William E. Savro/New York Times, Nov. 11, 1980

Before he became involved in politics, Jerry Falwell had already made a name for himself as a prominent preacher in his hometown of Lynchburg, Virginia, as the senior minister of the large Thomas Road Baptist Church and the founder of Liberty University. His organization, the Moral Majority, became the most well-known conservative evangelical Christian organization of the 1980s.

The Goals of the Moral Majority (1980) by Jerry Falwell

We must reverse the trend America finds herself in today. Young people. . . have learned to disrespect the family as God established it. They have been educated in a public-school system that is permeated with secular humanism. They have been taught that the Bible is just another book of literature. They have been taught that there are no absolutes in our

difficult. Should the state play a minimal role in the economy and society, as free-market libertarians believed, or should it monitor personal behavior, as social conservatives implied?

Reagan managed to keep the two wings of the party together, often referring to his "11th commandment" to "speak no ill of another Republican." But tensions persisted. When Falwell called on "all good Christians" to oppose the 1981 Supreme Court nomination of Arizona's conservative Sandra Day O'Connor on the grounds that she was insufficiently hostile to abortion, Arizona senator and party elder Barry Goldwater—a staunch proponent of small government and personal privacy—retorted that "every good Christian ought to kick Jerry Falwell right in the ass."

Gender and sexuality issues particularly aroused the ire of religious conservatives. They blamed feminism for weakening male authority in the family and for increasing divorce rates. A growing anti-abortion movement gained national visibility by 1980. During the 1970s, 22 states repealed their sodomy laws, reflecting a slowly increasing acceptance of gays and lesbians. But the religious right, which viewed homosexuality as an abomination, fiercely resisted this trend. Dismayed by the prevalence of casual sexual relationships in the 1970s, church conservatives urged abstinence on young Americans.

The heyday of the sexual revolution ended in the early 1980s, when researchers identified the human immunodeficiency virus (HIV), which causes acquired immunodeficiency syndrome (AIDS). The deadly epidemic spread swiftly through the gay male communities of San Francisco and New York as a result of unprotected sex. Many fundamentalists viewed AIDS world today. . . . These same young people have been reared under the influence of a government that has taught them socialism and welfarism. . . .

I personally feel that the home and the family are still held in reverence by the vast majority of the American public. I believe there is still a vast number of Americans who love their country, are patriotic, and are willing to sacrifice for her. I remember that time when it was positive to be patriotic. . . . I remember as a boy. . . when the band struck up "The Stars and Stripes Forever," we stood and goose pimples would run all over me. . . .

It is now time to take a stand on certain moral issues. . . . We must stand against the Equal Rights Amendment, the feminist revolution, and the homosexual revolution. . . .

Americans have been silent much too long. We have stood by and watched as American power and influence have been systematically weakened in every sphere of the world. . . .

The hope of reversing the trends of decay in our republic now lies with the Christian public in America. We cannot expect help from the liberals. They certainly are not going to call our nation back to righteousness and neither are the pornographers, the smut peddlers, and those who are corrupting our youth.

The Politics of the Bible (1982) by Robert McAfee Brown

In Christian terms, and I think in terms with which all Jews could also agree, my real complaint about the Moral Majority's intrusion of the Bible into American politics, is that they are not biblical enough. . . .

The Moral Majority's biblically inspired political agenda involves a very selective, very partial, and therefore very distorted use of the Bible. They have isolated a set of concerns that they say get to the heart of what is wrong with America—homosexuality, abortion, and pornography. . . .

Take the issue of homosexuality. If one turns to the scriptures as a whole, to try to come up with their central concerns, homosexuality is going to be very low on such a list even if indeed it makes the list at all. There are perhaps seven very ambiguous verses in the whole biblical canon that even allude to it. . . . [But there are] hundreds and hundreds of places where the scriptures are dealing over and over again with question of social justice, the tendency of the rich to exploit the poor, the need for all of us to have a commitment to the hungry, . . . [and] the dangers of national idolatry, that is to say, making the nation into God, accepting uncritically whatever we have to do as a nation against other nations. . . .

When one looks over the agenda of the Moral Majority there is absolutely no mention of such things. . . . We seem to be living in two different worlds, reading two different books.

Questions

1. *Which specific issues in American society most trouble Jerry Falwell? What specifically about "liberals" does he seem most unhappy about?*
2. *What does Robert McAfee Brown find most unpersuasive about Jerry Falwell's use of the Bible to understand American society and its problems?*
3. *Which of these two interpretations do you find most persuasive, and why?* ■

Source: Irwin Unger and Robert R. Tomes, *American Issues*, 2nd ed. (Prentice-Hall, 1999), vol. 2, pp. 362–364, 375–377.

as a divine punishment for homosexual activity. "The poor homosexuals," Reagan aide Pat Buchanan wrote. "They have declared war on nature and now nature is exacting an awful retribution." The Reagan administration refused to help mobilize a campaign against the new plague. AIDS continued to spread during the 1990s and beyond, among gays and heterosexuals, both in the United States and abroad—especially in such places as China, southern Africa, and Russia. New drugs slowed the onset of actual AIDS in many HIV-infected Americans while scientists continued the frustrating quest for a cure for the disease.

Yet another epidemic swept through the United States during the 1980s, striking impoverished urban neighborhoods especially hard. The culprit was crack cocaine. Powerfully addictive, it contributed to gang violence and record homicide rates in several cities. Drug-related convictions skyrocketed, stimulating a boom in prison building, a doubling of the nation's inmate population, and new police special weapons and tactics (SWAT) teams to deal with heavily armed drug operators.

This effort tended to ignore the real forces behind drug dealing, which included persistent poverty and a consumer culture obsessed with immediate gratification. Dealing crack offered a rare avenue to wealth to the poorest communities. On the wall of one Detroit crack house, a dealer posted this notice for employees: "[With] hard work and dedication we will all be rich within 12 months." Yet for all the mayhem they caused, crack and other illicit drugs killed less than 1 percent as many Americans per year as the 500,000 felled by tobacco and alcohol. Clearly, addiction to legal as well as illegal substances remained a pervasive problem.

Dissenters Push Back

The liberal and radical reform energies that had percolated in the late 1960s and early 1970s did not evaporate entirely in the conservative 1980s. Nuclear threats engaged activists from both the peace and environmental movements. The accidents at Three Mile Island (1979) and Chernobyl (1986) intensified public anxieties about the dangers of nuclear energy. Nuclear weapons were even deadlier: after all, their very purpose was to wreak destruction on a scale that would create what scientists called "nuclear winter," a depopulated planet shrouded in radioactivity. The sharp increases in both Soviet and U.S. nuclear arsenals alarmed residents in those countries and across Europe, where many of the missiles were located. Americans and others who remembered Hiroshima expressed shock when Reagan administration officials spoke of winning a nuclear war and the president wrongly claimed that commanders could recall submarine-based missiles after firing them. The broad-based nuclear freeze movement that emerged in the United States and western Europe in the early 1980s instead encouraged arms control negotiations that would bear fruit a few years later.

Racial justice remained a primary concern for Americans of color and liberal and leftist activists, particularly in light of the Republican administration's opposition to affirmative action. Determined to honor the foremost leader of the civil rights movement, antiracists convinced Congress in 1983 to designate Martin Luther King Jr.'s birthday a national holiday. By 1985, a robust antiapartheid movement—inspired by South African church leader and Nobel peace prize winner Desmond Tutu—successfully campaigned to reduce U.S. investments in racially segregated South Africa. Perhaps the most prominent face of left-leaning politics in the decade was that of Reverend Jesse Jackson, a former aide to Martin Luther King Jr. Jackson sought the Democratic nomination for president in 1984 and 1988, winning a handful of primaries in 1988 with his multiracial Rainbow Coalition. Jackson's candidacy encouraged several million African Americans to register to vote for the first time.

Eric Draper/AP/Wide World

▲ **While immigrants brought their own distinctive cultures to the United States, American popular culture spread abroad. The broadcast of National Basketball Association (NBA) games in dozens of other countries helped basketball become the world's second most popular game (after soccer). Personable stars like Earvin "Magic" Johnson of the Los Angeles Lakers and particularly Michael Jordan of the Chicago Bulls became popular icons around the world.**

Gay rights advocates also raised their voices in the 1980s. Faced with the twin scourge of AIDS and homophobic violence, homosexuals and their heterosexual supporters lobbied for the inclusion of sexual orientation as a category of discrimination in civil rights laws. Others took to the streets, organized by the militant organization AIDS Coalition to Unleash Power (ACT-UP). In October 1987, nearly half a million Americans marched in Washington in support of gay rights. A few widely admired figures, such as tennis champion Martina Navratilova, publicly acknowledged their homosexuality, helping others to view this sexual orientation as acceptable rather than deviant. By the end of the 1980s, the record was mixed. Gays and lesbians remained the only Americans against whom tens of millions of their fellow citizens openly believed it acceptable to discriminate, but the rights of homosexuals, nonetheless, had much wider support than ever before.

Sexual harassment did not exist in the United States until the 1980s—at least not legally. "Boys will be boys," the saying went about adult men. But what some men called flirting, many women found offensive, and by the late 1970s feminists had begun challenging the legality for such behavior. Legal scholar Catherine MacKinnon identified two forms of sexual harassment: one when sexual submission to a supervisor becomes a condition of employment, and a second when behavior toward a woman in the workplace creates a hostile environment that interferes with her work. MacKinnon helped represent Mechelle Vinson of Washington, D.C., who sued Meritor Savings Bank and the vice president who had hired Vinson and promoted her for four years while maintaining a sexual relationship with her. When Vinson tried to end the relationship, the vice president raped her and the bank eventually fired her. In the landmark case of *Meritor Savings Bank v. Vinson* (1986), the U.S. Supreme Court unanimously found the bank and its vice president guilty of sexual harassment in both its forms. The Court agreed with an earlier appeals court that "sexual harassment which creates a hostile or offensive environment for members of one sex is every bit the arbitrary barrier to sexual equality at the workplace that racial harassment is to racial equality."

The New Immigration

For two decades after the restrictive immigration law of 1924, the flow of newcomers from abroad had slowed to a trickle. The trickle became a stream again after World War II, and then legislation in 1965 opened the gates even wider. As a result, a wave of new immigrants, 3.5 million in the 1960s and 4.5 million in the 1970s, hit the United States. The 1980s set the record as 6 million people entered the country legally, along with a similar number without documentation.

These newcomers brought an unprecedented cultural and ethnic diversity. Communist rule in eastern Europe and prosperity in western Europe had reduced the emigration from that continent; only 10 percent of the most recent arrivals in the United States were Europeans. Forty percent came instead from Asia—particularly China, the Philippines, and South Korea—and 50 percent from Latin America and the Caribbean, particularly Mexico. From 1965 to 1995, 7 million Latinos and 5 million Asians moved to the United States. Mexicans had been journeying north in smaller numbers since that country's 1910 revolution. But between 1970 and 1990, the Mexican American population of the southwestern states tripled, and the Asian American population of the western states increased sixfold.

Forty percent of immigrants now came from Asia and 50 percent from Latin America and the Caribbean.

The new immigrants came for the same reasons their predecessors had. Many were fleeing political and religious persecution in their home countries, but most sought new economic opportunity. A small number, primarily from South Korea and Hong Kong, arrived with some assets that helped them get started in business. However, most came with few resources and took what work they could find in garment sweatshops, on farms, as domestic servants and janitors, and as gardeners. They willingly endured profound hardship to build better lives for their families. They also rekindled the nation's long-standing cultural diversity, especially in Sunbelt cities from Miami, Florida, to San Diego, California. In 1981, citizens of San Antonio elected Henry Cisneros as the first Mexican American mayor of a major city. In Los Angeles, one-third of residents were foreign born by 1990.

Most Americans had foreign-born ancestors who had come to the United States with the same dreams that motivated the newest arrivals. Still, the non-European origins of the latest immigrants troubled some white citizens. Conservatives, in particular, worried about the growing diversity of American society and feared a decline of the Eurocentric culture they had grown up with. They were also anxious that poor immigrants might drain taxpayers' dollars by winding up on welfare. The Immigration and Naturalization Service (INS) stepped up patrols of the 2,000-mile U.S. border with Mexico to limit the rising number of undocumented Mexican workers heading north. By the early 1990s, the INS was apprehending and expelling 1.7 million undocumented workers every year. The desperate efforts of migrants to elude Border Patrol officers and cross into the United States led to deaths from thirst and

Southern Florida

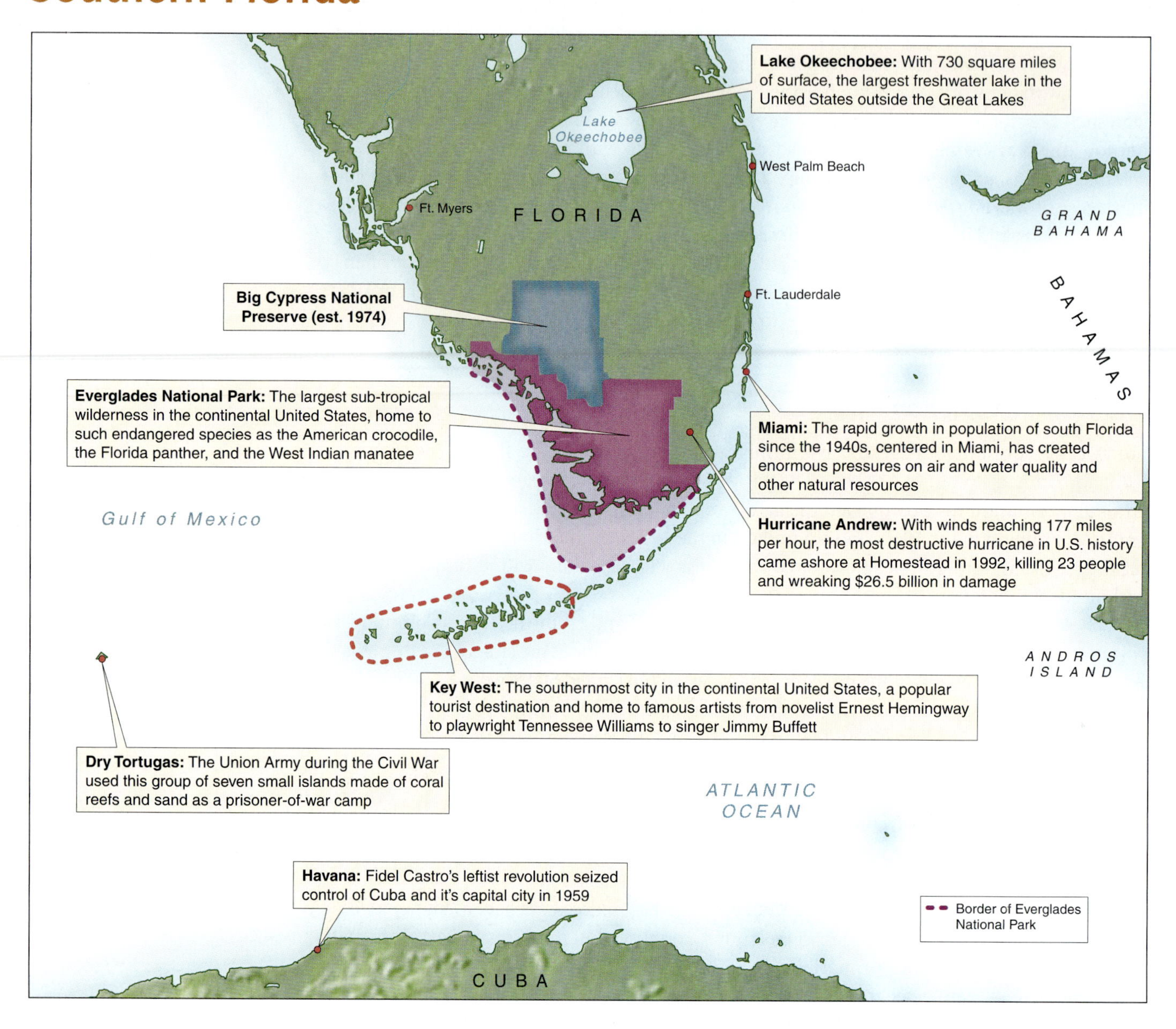

Dramatic population growth in southern Florida since the middle of the twentieth century has brought dramatic changes to a beautiful but fragile landscape. Three forces have driven the transformation of this formerly sleepy tropical region: winter tourism, retirees from the northern United States, and refugees and immigrants from the Caribbean islands and the rest of Latin America. Air conditioning has been crucial for taming the intense summer heat and humidity. Key West has long been a mecca for artists and writers, while Miami—far the biggest city in the region—has emerged as an economic, political, and cultural hub for much of the northern part of Latin America, including a large and influential population of Cuban refugees. However, the encroachment of a growing urban population has damaged air quality, water quality, and wildlife populations in the Everglades National Park, home to the largest designated wilderness area east of the Rocky Mountains. ■

exposure in the deserts that stretched across much of the region. A sign on one California freeway near the border showed the silhouette of a fleeing family as a warning to drivers to watch for pedestrians.

Despite the distaste that some Americans of European heritage felt for the new immigrants, the Latin American and especially Asian origins of the recent arrivals mirrored the rising economic significance of the Pacific Rim countries to the United States. In 1979 U.S. trade across the Pacific surpassed trade across the Atlantic for the first time. By 1996, the value of American trade with Asia was more than twice that with Europe. And Latin Americans, particularly Mexicans, provided a convenient supply of workers for the U.S. economy. They were available when companies needed them, and they could be shut out when that need evaporated.

In the early 1980s Americans worried that Japan's economy, the world's second largest, was growing much faster than that of the United States. Bitter bumper stickers reflected competitive anxieties and old racial antagonisms, such as "Toyota—By the Same People Who Brought You Pearl Harbor." But Americans in this decade also began to consume large quantities of sushi (to go with the new popularity of Thai restaurants, along with the nation's 35,000 Chinese restaurants), and millions of American children began to enjoy creative Japanese cartoons and electronic games such as Nintendo's Super Mario (1985). Other aspects of Asian cultures spread widely in American society, including martial arts traditions from across East Asia and Chinese traditional medicine such as herbal remedies and acupuncture. (The American Association of Acupuncture and Oriental Medicine was founded in 1981.) The warming of U.S. relations with the People's Republic of China allowed thousands of Chinese intellectuals to visit the United States, dovetailing with an existing tradition of Chinese American academic success. With its one-child family policies to prevent population growth, China became the largest source of international adoptions for American parents. The total number of Asian Americans doubled in the 1980s, reaching almost 7 million by the end of the decade.

Scott Teven, photohouston.com

▲ Young Mexican American women participate in a Cinco de Mayo celebration in Houston, Texas.

The End of the Cold War

"My fellow Americans, I'm pleased to tell you today that I've signed legislation that will outlaw Russia forever. We begin bombing in five minutes." Ronald Reagan, in 1984, thought he was telling a joke at a microphone that was not turned on. He was wrong. Indeed, after three years of the president's military buildup and confrontational rhetoric toward the Soviet Union ("the focus of evil in the world")—including talk of fighting and winning a nuclear war—many Americans found his attempted humor appalling. However, by the end of his presidency four years later, a stunning reversal had occurred. Reagan had traveled to Moscow, embraced Soviet leader Mikhail Gorbachev in front of Lenin's tomb, and announced that the Soviets had changed.

For Americans, the greatest surprise of the 1980s came with this warming of U.S.-Soviet relations after 1985. Few had imagined such a scenario during Reagan's first two years in office, when his administration became the first in four decades not to collaborate on nuclear arms control with the USSR. But in the Soviet Union, the rise to power of Communist party reformer Gorbachev permanently changed the face of international politics. The American president finally agreed to work toward the common goal of reducing tensions between the two superpowers.

East News/Sipa Press

▲ **Workers in Prague, Czechoslovakia, haul away a statue of Josef Stalin after the peaceful "Velvet Revolution" that overthrew communist rule there in 1989. Similar scenes unfolded across eastern Europe as Czechs, Poles, Hungarians, and others removed symbols of four and a half decades of Soviet domination. Accustomed to often extravagant accounts of the strength of the Soviet Union, Americans were stunned by the swiftness with which the Soviet empire and then the USSR itself unraveled.**

At the same time, the Reagan administration stumbled at home when a scandal involving Iran and the Nicaraguan counterrevolutionaries (Contras) came to light in 1986. The disaster revealed a secret foreign policy apparatus and a president out of touch with the daily governance process. Dramatic events in Europe then unfolded with little input from the administrations of either Reagan or George H. W. Bush, his successor in the White House. In 1989 eastern Europeans tore down the Berlin Wall and ended Soviet rule in their countries. Two years later, the Soviet Union unraveled into its separate components, Russia being the largest. The end of the Cold War enabled Bush to focus on the Middle East, where an international force drove Iraq out of occupied Kuwait and reestablished the status quo in that oil-rich region.

From Cold War to Détente

In the 1980s, internal Soviet politics finally ended the Cold War. Gorbachev and other reformers, like many Americans in the 1960s, boldly questioned orthodox thinking. They could see that the vast military expenditures of the 1960s and 1970s had devastated the Soviet economy. By the 1980s, the USSR's state-run economy was creaking to a halt. It simply could not provide the consumer products that Soviet citizens had learned about from the world outside their borders. Gorbachev warned of the danger of Russia becoming merely "an Upper Volta with missiles"—an impoverished nation that had squandered its wealth to build a nuclear arsenal.

As the 1980s unfolded, events further weakened the authority of the Soviet government. The USSR's occupation of Afghanistan became a quagmire resembling the United States' disastrous involvement in Vietnam, and the last Soviet troops finally withdrew in 1989. Initial government efforts to cover up the nuclear accident at Chernobyl only worsened matters, revealing the costs of corrupt communist rule. Nationalist movements for independence in the Baltic states, the Caucasus region, and central Asia gathered momentum. In his six years in power (1985–1991), Gorbachev tried to preserve the Soviet system by reforming it through *glasnost* (greater political liberty) and *perestroika* (economic restructuring allowing some private enterprise). However, his government proved unable to control the forces for change that it had helped unleash.

Reagan's primary role in ending the Cold War was to support Gorbachev's quest for change within the Soviet Union. To that end, Reagan moved from confrontational rhetoric to pursuing a policy of détente. Gorbachev became head of the Soviet Communist party in 1985, at the start of Reagan's second term. The American president had already built up the U.S. military and was now thinking about his place in history. He wanted to leave office having earned a reputation as a peacemaker.

Beneath Reagan's strident rhetoric about national military strength ran a streak of radical idealism, including a desire to eliminate the threat of nuclear warfare. This desire prompted him to launch the Strategic Defense Initiative. He expected the United States eventually to share the technology with the Soviets. Despite his Cold War posturing during his first term, the U.S. president had been troubled by the 1983 television drama *The Day After* and its sobering images of the aftermath of a nuclear war on American soil. The Soviet downing of a Korean Air Lines civilian jet that fall reminded him and others of the tragic costs of making mistakes with weapons.

Once he felt convinced of Gorbachev's seriousness about internal reform and rapprochement with the United States, Reagan took action. At a summit conference in Reykjavik, Iceland, in 1986, the two leaders came within a whisker of agreeing to eliminate nearly all of their nations' nuclear arsenals. The next year, they signed the more limited but still symbolically important Intermediate Nuclear Force (INF) treaty. The agreement removed short-range and intermediate-range missiles from Europe and enabled each side to conduct on-site verification of the other side's compliance. The INF treaty marked the first actual reduction in the total number of nuclear weapons stored in the two nations' arsenals.

Bettmann/CORBIS

▲ **U.S. Lieutenant Woody Lee guards the briefcase (known as "the football") containing the codes to be used by President Reagan if he were to decide to launch nuclear weapons. Lee's job was to remain close to the president at all times and to protect "the football" with his life. Ironically, Lee stands here in Moscow's Red Square in 1988, where Reagan was holding a summit meeting with Soviet leader Mikhail Gorbachev, so many of those U.S. nuclear missiles, presumably, were aimed at them.**

The Iran-Contra Scandal

Failures elsewhere offset Reagan's success with the Russians. His administration suffered its worst damage when it tried through illegal means to solve two foreign policy challenges with one stroke. Its main strategy consisted of linking a problem in the Middle East with one in Central America.

Revolutionary fervor intensified in the Middle East after the 1979 Iranian revolution, and hostage-taking and terrorism—the "poor man's nuclear bomb"—proliferated. In 1981 U.S. warplanes shot down two Libyan fighter jets when the jets tried to restrict American pilots' movements over the Mediterranean Sea. In 1986 Americans bombed the Libyan capital of Tripoli in retaliation for apparent Libyan involvement in the killing of two U.S. soldiers in Germany. In 1988 things took an even nastier turn when an American warship in the Persian

Gulf killed 290 civilians by shooting down an Iranian airliner, apparently by mistake. In revenge, pro-Iranian Libyan agents exploded a bomb on Pan Am Flight 109 over Lockerbie, Scotland, before the end of the year, killing 11 on the ground and 259 aboard the plane, including 35 students from Syracuse University.

Islamic revolutionaries also threatened moderate Arab leaders and assassinated Egyptian president Anwar Sadat in 1981. Lebanon became the center of a radical anti-Israeli campaign to seize Americans as hostages, especially after the United States' 1983 engagement against Muslim forces in the civil war there. Despite his 1980 campaign promise never to negotiate with terrorists, Reagan approved the illegal sale of U.S. arms to Iran in return for the freeing of a handful of hostages held by pro-Iranian radicals in Lebanon.

Events were heating up in Central America as well. The CIA-created Contras failed to overturn the new Sandinista government in Nicaragua. Even though the Contras lacked public support in Nicaragua and the United States, the president and his advisers were determined to keep them afloat. But they had a problem: how to fund the effort. Most Americans did not share Reagan's enthusiasm for the Contras and feared greater U.S. military involvement in Central America. Beginning in 1982, Congress passed the Boland Amendments, restricting aid to the Nicaraguan counterrevolutionaries. These restrictions culminated in a 1984 ban on helping them "directly or indirectly" beyond a token dose of humanitarian assistance. Faced with their chief's expressed desire to shore up the Contra cause, the president's men found an alternative solution.

Fred Ward/Black Star/Stock Photo

▲ Lieutenant Colonel Oliver North of the National Security Council became the public face of the Iran-Contra scandal. North displayed his medals from the Vietnam War in testimony before Congress, but his smug version of patriotism and his admitted deceitfulness alienated many senators and congressmen.

The National Security Council (NSC) established a secret operation run by staff member Lieutenant Colonel Oliver North. Free from public or congressional oversight, North worked closely with CIA director William Casey. North and his colleagues solicited funds for the Contras from wealthy, conservative Americans and from sympathetic foreign governments, including Saudi Arabia and Taiwan. Then North hit on what he called the "neat idea" of "using the Ayatollah Khomeini's money to support the Nicaraguan freedom fighters." Iran desperately needed weapons for its war against neighboring Iraq (1980–1988), so North and his colleagues started diverting profits to the Contras from new sales of U.S. Army property to Teheran. One operative joked about the "Contra-bution," although some of the funds wound up in the private accounts of North and others involved in the diversion.

The NSC's action was illegal: it sold U.S. government property without authorization from the Pentagon, and it broke U.S. laws banning aid to the Contras. When news of the operation finally leaked out in November 1986, it shocked the nation. Details emerged from separate investigations by a presidential commission, a Justice Department independent prosecutor, and a congressional committee.

North's televised testimony before Congress made him a hero to some. He indicted Congress for its failure to support the president's policies in Central America, and he painted his own actions as patriotic. Others thought him a scoundrel. After all, he had run a private foreign policy that subverted the legislature's constitutional responsibilities and then had shredded documents that detailed his role. He later admitted, "I tried to avoid telling outright lies [before Congress], but I certainly wasn't telling the truth." His celebrity status among conservatives almost won him a victory as the Republican candidate for the U.S. Senate from Virginia in 1992.

What did the president know, and when did he know it? The old Watergate question about Richard Nixon came to the fore again. Reagan called North a "national hero" but claimed ignorance of any illegal activities, including the diversion of funds from Iranian arms sales to the Nicaraguan rebels. When some of Reagan's aides testified that he had approved negotiating with terrorists for the release of hostages, the president denied it. Questioned by investigators, the president said he could not remember details about his decisions and policies. This possibility gained credence a few years later when the public learned of his affliction with Alzheimer's disease.

But in early 1987, 90 percent of Americans did not believe Reagan was telling all he knew. People could not decide which scenario was worse: that Reagan knew about the Iran-Contra deal and approved it or that he did not know what his own administration was doing in his name. Reagan's job approval ratings dropped from 67 percent to 46 percent. The first round of memoirs by former aides also appeared in the final years of his administration, revealing an isolated president out of touch with the government he nominally headed. For example, the former actor breezily admitted that he was happiest when "each morning I get a piece of paper that tells me what I do all day long." The leaking of news that an astrologer—hired by First Lady Nancy Reagan—had helped set the president's schedule for years did not help either. Nonetheless, Reagan held onto much of his personal popularity to the end of his term. In the phrase of Representative Pat Schroeder of Colorado, he was the "Teflon president" to whom no bad news could stick.

Some of the most dramatic events of the twentieth century unfolded during George H. W. Bush's presidency.

A Global Police?

Although George H. W. Bush had made his career in the Texas oil business and then in that state's Republican party, his roots lay in the party's moderate northeastern elite. His father, Prescott Bush, had been a U.S. senator from Connecticut, and he himself ran the CIA in 1975–1976. After losing in the 1980 party primaries, Bush agreed to run as Reagan's vice presidential candidate. He then moved to the political right throughout the 1980s.

When Bush's turn at the presidency finally came in 1988, he ran a bruising campaign that made a caricature of his Democratic opponent, Governor Michael Dukakis of Massachusetts. Bush skewered his opponent as a liberal and a "card-carrying member" of the American Civil Liberties Union, an organization dedicated to defending the Bill of Rights. Senator Joseph McCarthy had used precisely this phrase to describe members of the American Communist party four decades earlier. Thus, Bush implied that liberals were subversives.

Bush also accused Dukakis of coddling criminals. His campaign ads focused on Willie Horton, a black man convicted of murder. While on parole from a Massachusetts prison during Dukakis's governorship, Horton raped a white woman and killed her husband. Republicans appealed to whites' anxieties about race, sex, and safety. "If I can make Willie Horton a household name," Bush's campaign strategist Lee Atwater promised, "we'll win the election." He succeeded on both fronts.

As president, however, Bush proved cautious. Hemmed in by a Democratic-controlled Congress, he had what his chief of staff called a "limited agenda" at home. His most enduring domestic action came with his 1991 appointment of archconservative Clarence Thomas, an African American lawyer from Georgia, to fill the seat of retiring Supreme Court justice Thurgood Marshall. Only 43 years old and with little experience as a judge, Thomas was chosen because of his conservative views and his race. The Senate narrowly confirmed him, 52–48, after contentious hearings in which a former aide, Anita Hill, accused Thomas of sexual harassment.

"I much prefer foreign affairs," the president once confided in his diary. Yet he proceeded just as carefully in this realm as he did with domestic policy. Some of the most dramatic events of the twentieth century unfolded during his presidency. Poles, Czechs, and Hungarians—encouraged by Gorbachev's promise not to intervene militarily in other Warsaw Pact nations—peacefully overthrew their communist rulers in 1989. East Germans did the same. The Berlin Wall—the 28-year-old symbol of Cold War tensions—finally toppled on November 8. Three months later, Nelson Mandela walked out of the South African prison where he had been held for 27 years. The white supremacist government there agreed to hold the first elections in which all South Africans could vote. The Baltic states of Lithuania, Latvia, and Estonia also seceded from the USSR in 1990 and 1991. Rather than rejoicing at the shrinking of Soviet power, Bush urged Soviet citizens to move cautiously. The president feared that too much change too fast might create unrest across Russia and eastern Europe. But after a failed coup attempt by Communist hard-liners in August 1991, the Soviet Union broke into its 16 constituent states. Russian president Boris Yeltsin replaced Gorbachev as the major figure in Moscow.

The Bush administration acted more boldly in its own hemisphere. In Panama, under the brutal leadership of Manuel Noriega, tensions grew between the Panamanian Defense Forces (PDF) and U.S. soldiers based in the Canal Zone. Bush and Noriega had known each other since the mid-1970s, when each had headed his country's intelligence agency. They had worked together in the early 1980s when Noriega provided logistical support for the Contras' war in nearby Nicaragua. But the Panamanian dictator had since parted ways with the Americans and had deepened his lucrative role as an intermediary in smuggling Colombian cocaine into the United States. Meanwhile, the crack cocaine epidemic tightened its grip in poor

▼ MAP 28.3 THE SOVIET BLOC DISSOLVES

No change in world politics since World War II was greater than the collapse of the Soviet Union and its satellite states in eastern Europe. Eastern European countries soon sought membership in NATO, and post-communist Russia built closer relations with the United States and western Europe. The transition from socialist to capitalist economies was difficult, however, and many poorer citizens found daily life little easier than it had been before.

Robert Trippett/Sipa Press

▲ **In the 1970s antifeminists defeated the Equal Rights Amendment in part by opposing the idea of American women in combat. Attitudes about women had changed enough by 1991 that thousands of female service personnel participated in the Persian Gulf War with no public outcry. In Bethesda, Maryland, one soldier says goodbye to her family before shipping out to the Persian Gulf in September 1990.**

American neighborhoods. Rising popular concern about crack-related violence increased Americans' willingness to take action against Noriega. When the dictator overturned Panamanian election results that went against him and further confrontations erupted between American and Panamanian soldiers, Bush decided to step in.

In December 1989, 24,000 U.S. troops invaded the small Central American nation. They crushed the PDF, and thousands of civilians died in the crossfire. Noriega took refuge in the home of the Vatican emissary in Panama City. U.S. commanders applied psychological pressure. Knowing Noriega's distaste for rock 'n' roll music, they set up enormous speakers and floodlights outside the residence. At a deafening volume, they blared such songs as Linda Ronstadt's "You're No Good" and Sonny Curtis's "I Fought the Law (and the Law Won)." Noriega eventually surrendered and was brought to Miami, where he was convicted of drug trafficking and imprisoned.

Developments in the Middle East provoked the most important move of the George H. W. Bush administration: the initiation of the Persian Gulf War of 1991. After the Iranian revolution, Iraq and Iran had clashed over disputed border territories. The Reagan administration had provided weapons to both sides at different points. The president wanted neither combatant to win a decisive victory that would destabilize the area. With two-thirds of the world's known oil reserves in the states surrounding the Persian Gulf, the U.S. government especially dreaded seeing control of the region's oil prices and supplies shift from conservative Saudi Arabia to revolutionary Iran.

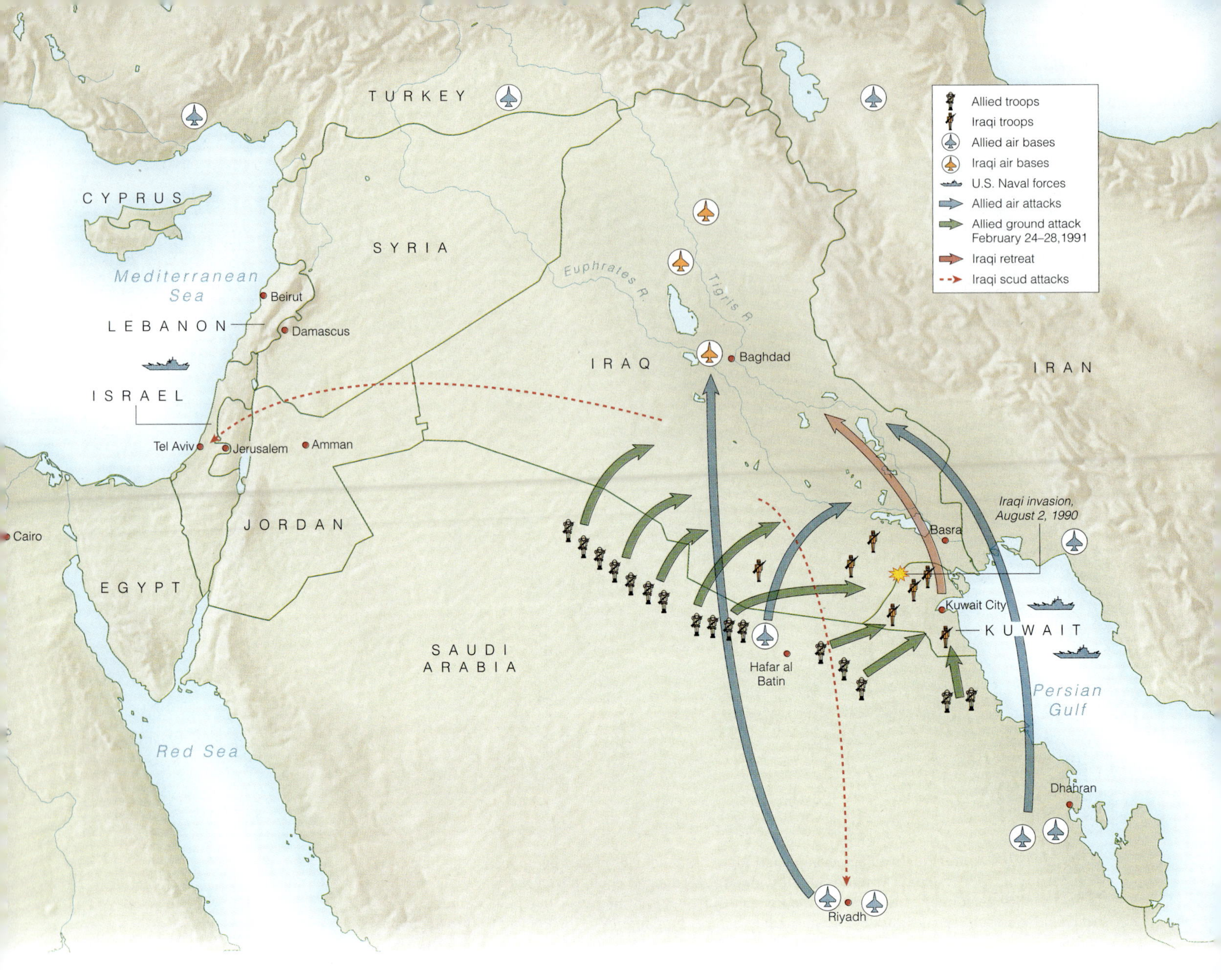

▲ **MAP 28.4 THE PERSIAN GULF WAR**

Rarely had U.S. strategic and economic interests been so openly the motivation for war. Oil brought American soldiers to defend Saudi Arabia and drive Iraqi troops out of Kuwait. But many Arab states supported the U.S.-led coalition because they opposed Iraqi President Saddam Hussein's occupation of Kuwait.

Iraq ended the war in a strong position in 1988, and two years later it invaded tiny, neighboring, oil-rich Kuwait, annexing it as Iraq's "19th province." With Americans and their Japanese and European allies dependent on Middle Eastern oil, Bush declared the invasion unacceptable. He rushed more than 200,000 troops to Saudi Arabia in "Operation Desert Shield" to discourage further aggression by Iraqi leader Saddam Hussein. At the same time, the United Nations slapped economic sanctions on Iraq.

Bush's Early Response in the Persian Gulf War

Within three months, Bush shifted his attention to liberating Kuwait. He doubled the number of U.S. troops in the region to 430,000. He also gained the support of the UN, which demanded Iraqi withdrawal by January 15, 1991. The U.S. Congress backed him as well, voting to support any actions necessary to drive Iraq out of Kuwait. Bush went on the offensive because he faced a shrinking window of opportunity. He had wide international support, including troops from several Arab nations, but growing clashes in Jerusalem between Israelis and Palestinians threatened to break up this alliance by rekindling Arab anger at Israel.

On January 16, 1991, U.S.-led coalition forces began five and a half weeks of bombing against Iraq. Then, on February 25, coalition forces poured across the border from Saudi

AP/Wide World Photo

▲ At five in the afternoon on October 17, 1989, the San Andreas fault system in northern California had its first major quake since 1906. The quake was responsible for 62 deaths, 3,757 injuries, and over $6 billion in damage, including this freeway in Oakland. The earthquake damaged 18,000 homes and 2,600 businesses and left about 3,000 people homeless.

Arabia in "Operation Desert Storm." The offensive freed Kuwait and sent Iraqi troops in headlong retreat toward Baghdad. The Iraqis burned oil wells as they fell back, blanketing the battlefield in smoke. Four days later, Bush halted the U.S. advance, having restored Kuwaiti sovereignty. Saddam Hussein remained in power and later crushed uprisings by Iraqi dissidents. The politics of coalition warfare helped prohibit further U.S. action, for no Arabs wanted Americans ruling Iraq.

What did the Gulf War reveal? It showed Bush at his most successful, managing an international coalition few would have thought possible a few years earlier. The war's outcome seemed to validate two strategic lessons that U.S. commanders had learned during the Vietnam War. The first was the importance of preserving absolute control of the media. During the Persian Gulf conflict, the Pentagon kept journalists away from most of the action to limit the images that Americans saw of the fighting. The public viewed endless videos of "smart" bombs hitting their targets in Baghdad but none of the tens of thousands of Iraqi soldiers being slaughtered during their retreat from Kuwait. Second, General Colin Powell, the African American chair of the Joint Chiefs of Staff who emerged from the war as a national hero, insisted on marshaling overwhelmingly superior forces before going into battle, thus ensuring the success of the operation.

Some 35,000 American women in the volunteer armed forces served in the war, mostly in rear support positions but also as pilots flying reconnaissance and search and rescue missions. Fifteen died, and enemy forces captured two others. Even though many of these female service personnel in the war had small children, their assignments close to the line of fire generated little public outcry. American women could now be warriors.

The 1991 Persian Gulf War raised the question of whether the U.S. military had become a mercenary force, with allies chipping in more than seven times what Washington spent to fund U.S. soldiers. "Why should I fight?" one wealthy Kuwaiti sitting out the war in comfort in Cairo asked. "We can pay other countries to fight for us." The conflict seemed to demonstrate a U.S. willingness to act as a global police force in the post–Cold War era. But the war

The Middle East in the 1980s and 1990s

also stimulated the further growth of anti-Americanism among Islamic revolutionaries, including Saudi-born Osama bin Laden; they considered it sacrilege for non-Muslim American soldiers to operate bases in Saudi Arabia, home to Mecca, Islam's holiest site. Finally, the war foreshadowed Bush's defiant claim at a 1992 international environmental conference that, when it came to oil, "the American lifestyle is not negotiable."

Conclusion

The Republican era of Ronald Reagan and George H. W. Bush reshaped American relations with the rest of the world, as well as politics and economics in the United States. Both sets of changes hinged on the elevation of individualism and market forces above communal values and government planning. At home, the Republican ascendancy successfully challenged five decades of New Deal assumptions about government's role in economic regulation and its responsibilities toward the poor. A booming stock market underwrote a culture increasingly focused on the individual acquisition of wealth. Popular television shows of the 1980s such as *Dynasty* reflected a widespread admiration for affluence and conspicuous consumption.

The collective dreams represented by the Soviet experiment evaporated into history in these years, leaving capitalism unchallenged as a system of economic organization across most of the globe. U.S. military power stepped into the vacuum left by the Soviet demise, most visibly in the 1991 Persian Gulf War. But that military revival came at the cost of vast deficit spending and a sharp recession in 1991–1992, which paved the way for Bill Clinton's victory over George H. W. Bush in the 1992 presidential campaign.

Sites to Visit

Digital Atlas of the United States, 1990

130.166.124.2/USpage1.html

This site offers an overview of the geography and demography of the U.S. population in 1990.

National Immigration Forum

http://www.immigrationforum.org/index.htm

This pro-immigration site offers a wealth of useful statistics, guides to key issues, and references to other useful sites.

Divining America: Religion and the National Culture

http://www.nhc.rtp.nc.us/tserve/divam.htm

This site has essays by prominent historians on diverse aspects of the religious history of the United States.

American Experience: The Presidents—Ronald Reagan

http://www.pbs.org/wgbh/amex/presidents/40_reagan/index.html

This Public Broadcasting System site has essential information about Reagan and his presidential administration as well as his most important speeches.

National Security Archive at George Washington University

http://www.gwu.edu/~nsarchiv/

This extraordinary site includes the most recent declassified documents on the making of U.S. foreign policy.

Cold War International History Project

http://wwics.si.edu/index.cfm?fuseaction=topics.home&topic_id=1409

The Woodrow Wilson International Center for Scholars maintains this excellent site, which offers newly released documents and up-to-date interpretive essays on the American-Soviet struggle.

Persian Gulf War

http://www.pbs.org/wgbh/pages/frontline/gulf/

The Public Broadcasting System's *Frontline* series created this site with information about the 1991 Persian Gulf War, including oral histories of U.S. commanders and of Americans taken as prisoners of war.

For Further Reading

General

E. J. Dionne Jr., *Why Americans Hate Politics* (1991).

Frances FitzGerald, *Way Out There in the Blue: Reagan, Star Wars, and the End of the Cold War* (2000).

Neil Postman, *Amusing Ourselves to Death: Public Discourse in the Age of Show Business* (1985).

Ronald Reagan, *Reagan, In His Own Hand: The Writings of Ronald Reagan That Reveal His Revolutionary Vision for America* (2001).

Michael Schaller, *Reckoning with Reagan: America and Its President in the 1980s* (1992).

Anticommunism Revived

James A. Bill, *The Eagle and the Lion: The Tragedy of American-Iranian Relations* (1988).

David Farber, *Taken Hostage: The Iran Hostage Crisis and America's First Encounter with Radical Islam* (2004).

Thomas Ferguson and Joel Rogers, eds., *The Hidden Election: Politics and Economics in the 1980 Presidential Campaign* (1981).

Michael T. Klare and Peter Kornbluh, *Low-Intensity Warfare: Counterinsurgency, Proinsurgency, and Antiterrorism in the Eighties* (1988).

Walter LaFeber, *Inevitable Revolutions: The United States in Central America*, 2nd ed. (1993).

William E. Pemberton, *Exit with Honor: The Life and Presidency of Ronald Reagan* (1998).

Republican Rule at Home

Thomas Byrne Edsall and Mary D. Edsall, *Chain Reaction: The Impact of Race, Rights and Taxes on American Politics* (1991).

Barbara Ehrenreich, *The Worst Years of Our Lives: Irreverent Notes from a Decade of Greed* (1990).

J. R. McNeill, *Something New Under the Sun: An Environmental History of the Twentieth-Century World* (2000).

Kevin Phillips, *The Politics of Rich and Poor: Wealth and the American Electorate in the Reagan Aftermath* (1990).

Mark Robert Rank, *Living on the Edge: The Realities of Welfare in America* (1994).

Cultural Conflict

Susan J. Douglas, *Where the Girls Are: Growing Up Female with the Mass Media* (1994).

Todd Gitlin, *The Twilight of Common Dreams: Why America Is Wracked by Culture Wars* (1995).

Martin E. Marty and R. Scott Appleby, *The Glory and the Power: The Fundamentalist Challenge to the Modern World* (1992).

Nicolaus Mills, ed., *Culture in an Age of Money: The Legacy of the 1980s in America* (1990).

David M. Reimers, *Still the Golden Door: The Third World Comes to America*, 2nd ed. (1992).

Randy Shilts, *And the Band Played On: Politics, People and the AIDS Epidemic* (1987).

The End of the Cold War

Theodore Draper, *A Very Thin Line: The Iran-Contra Affairs* (1991).

John Robert Greene, *The Presidency of George Bush* (2000).

Dilip Hiro, *Desert Shield to Desert Storm: The Second Gulf War* (1992).

Michael J. Hogan, ed., *The End of the Cold War: Its Meanings and Implications* (1992).

Jane Mayer and Doyle McManus, *Landslide: The Unmaking of the President, 1984–1988* (1989).

David Remnick, *Lenin's Tomb: The Last Days of the Soviet Empire* (1993).

CHAPTER 29

Post–Cold War America, 1991–2000

CHAPTER OUTLINE

The Economy: Global and Domestic

Tolerance and Its Limits

Violence and Danger

The Clinton Presidency

The Nation and the World

The Contested Election of 2000

Conclusion

Sites to Visit

For Further Reading

▲ Underwater explorers examine shells at the manufactured beach in Biosphere 2, an artificially created ecosystem in the Arizona desert inhabited by eight "biospherians" from 1991 to 1993. The attempt to create a self-sustaining "mini-earth" failed within two years.

On a cold December night in 1997, 23-year-old Julia Butterfly Hill climbed onto a small platform that had been constructed 180 feet above ground in a giant redwood tree in a forest in Humboldt County, California. She remained there for two years, trespassing in an act of civil disobedience on the property of the Pacific Lumber Company, which was threatening to cut down the 1,000-year-old tree as part of its logging operations. Hill had not planned to become an internationally famous environmental activist. She grew up in Arkansas, the daughter of an itinerant preacher. When friends invited the restless young woman to join them on a drive to California, she eagerly went along. "I had been on a journey, searching for my purpose in life," she recalled. "I ended up finding it in the redwoods." When she first saw the giant redwoods, "Gripped by the spirit of the forest, I dropped to my knees and began to sob. . . . I could feel my whole being bursting forth into new life in this majestic cathedral."

Hill's spiritual connection to the forest drew her to political activism, and she joined Earth First!, an environmental group that was working to save the redwoods from the logging industry. She discovered that 97 percent of the old-growth redwoods had already been destroyed and that the rest were threatened by clear-cutting, toxins, and diesel fuel. Tree sitting was a strategy the Earth First! activists developed to protest the destruction of the trees. They had named this particular tree Luna, after the goddess of the moon, because they had built the small platform in it by moonlight. Julia Hill took a forest name—Butterfly—and settled in for her turn at tree sitting. Although the strategy usually involved tree sitting for a week at a time, Hill decided that to have an impact the protest needed to be taken to "a different level." "I realized I had to give more. I needed to give my word that my feet would not touch the ground" until the tree was safe from destruction.

Julia "Butterfly" Hill in the giant redwood tree where she lived for two years.

Those two years were rough. The young woman survived rain and hail storms, 90-mile-per-hour winds that tossed the tiny platform into the air, and bone-chilling cold that turned her feet black. Friends and supporters provided her with food and other supplies using a rope pulley. She ate mostly raw fruits and vegetables, slept in a hammock, took sponge baths, and used a bucket for a toilet. She faced harassment from the logging company and derision from some skeptics. But she also had a powerful network of supporters and celebrities who raised money, brought her food, and publicized her protest.

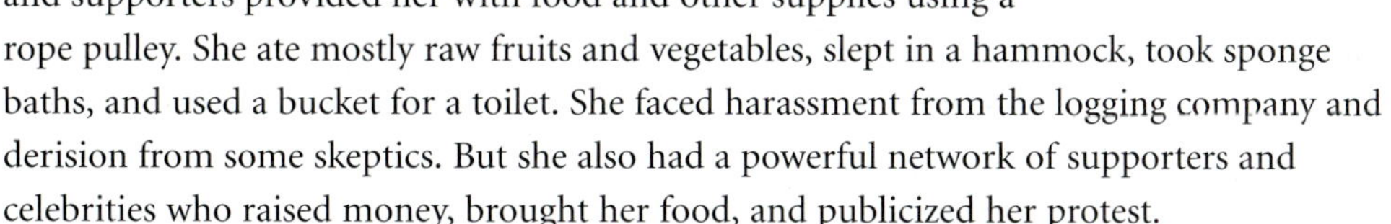

Hill's effort to save an ancient tree as old as the last millennium was conducted using the global technology of the new millennium. Critical to the success of her protest was her ability to communicate with the entire world from her treetop perch. She set up a Web site on the Internet visited by people from all across the globe. Schoolchildren in Germany sent her pictures of themselves in front of their favorite trees. People responded to her from as far away as Turkey and Australia. She used a solar-powered cell phone to speak with radio stations, schools, rallies, religious groups, reporters, and talk show hosts. The lumber company also used state-of-the-art technology in its efforts to stymie her protest, cutting down trees to make them fall in her direction, flying helicopters to hover noisily over her head, and using air horns to keep her awake at night.

The president of Pacific Lumber, John Campbell, eventually came to the tree to negotiate with Hill, and they made a deal. The company agreed never to cut down the tree or other trees in a 2.9-acre buffer zone. Hill agreed to come down. For her civil disobedience, she paid a $50,000 fine, contributed by supporters, which the court designated to Humboldt State University for forestry research. Although her success was modest in terms of saving endangered forests, her actions raised environmental awareness across the globe.

Activists such as Julia Butterfly Hill addressed political concerns through personal beliefs and direct action as part of social movements that evolved out of a century of such protests. The issues had reached a global scale. Internationally, Cold War power struggles gave way to other issues: regional and civil wars, ethnic strife, the environment and global warming, trade and labor relations, and terrorism. Domestically, concerns of environmentalists ranged from the protection of a single tree to climate change affecting the entire planet. The labor movement turned much of its attention to service workers and the global economy, addressing such issues as the export of jobs and the existence of sweatshops at home and abroad.

In the United States the economy expanded throughout the 1990s. Increasing numbers of Americans invested in the soaring stock market, many for the first time. The crime rate declined. Yet the strong economy also emboldened consumers to buy and use products and resources, such as huge gas-guzzling sport utility vehicles, with little concern for the environmental impact. Moreover, as the economy grew, so did the gap between the wealthy and the poor. As the new millennium dawned, the economy began to falter. The stock market fell, and there were signs of an impending recession.

The 2000 U.S. Census revealed a number of striking changes in the nation's population during the 1990s. Among the most dramatic was the 60 percent growth in the Latino population, from 22.4 million to 35.3 million, making the number of Latinos—most of them Mexican American—nearly equal to that of African Americans. Immigrants from Asia and Latin America also added increasing linguistic diversity, fueling controversies over bilingual education and "English-only" political initiatives.

Domestically, concerns of environmentalists ranged from the protection of a single tree to climate change affecting the entire planet.

In national politics the rifts between liberals and conservatives that had opened up in the 1960s persisted. Struggles over cultural issues such as abortion and gay rights polarized the political climate. Throughout most of the 1990s, one party controlled the White House while the other controlled the Congress. A Democratic Congress during the Republican administration of George H. W. Bush passed the 1990 Americans with Disabilities Act, requiring reasonable accommodation for disabled persons in employment and access to public places. The Clean Air Act, passed in the same year, reduced smokestack and auto emissions. New legislation also increased funding for Head Start and boosted the minimum wage. The Twenty-Seventh Amendment to the Constitution, ratified in 1992, prohibited midterm congressional pay raises.

In 1992 Democrats took back the White House, but in 1994 Republicans swept into control of Congress with a conservative agenda, hemming in President Bill Clinton, a Democrat of liberal social inclinations who, nonetheless, presided over the final destruction of the Aid to Families with Dependent Children (AFDC) program, which had been a central feature of the national welfare system since the New Deal of the 1930s.

Throughout the decade, racial hostilities flared, intensified by such events as the beating of motorist Rodney King and the murder trial of media celebrity O. J. Simpson. Anti-immigrant sentiments increased in response to recent immigration from Asia, Latin America, and especially Mexico. Nevertheless, studies showed that Americans had become more accepting of people whose racial or national backgrounds were different from their own. Americans' faith in political leadership, at low ebb since Watergate, sank even farther as Republicans doggedly pursued Clinton's unseemly sexual behavior, leading to his impeachment by the House of Representatives, although he was acquitted by the Senate and remained in office.

Money continued to pour into politics, even as voters called for campaign finance reform. Third-party candidates tapped widespread eagerness for a new type of politics. A Supreme Court dominated by conservatives nevertheless upheld liberal decisions, including abortion rights in *Planned Parenthood of Southeastern Pennsylvania v. Casey* (1992); gender equality in *U.S. v. Virginia* (1996), stating that the Virginia Military Institute could not exclude women; and the rights of gays and lesbians in *Romer v. Evans* (1996), which declared unconstitutional a Colorado amendment that nullified civil rights protections for homosexuals. In 2000, however, the Supreme Court decided one of the closest and most divisive elections in the nation's history, handing the White House to the Republican candidate, George W. Bush, son of the former president.

The post–Cold War era raised new questions about the role of the United States in the world. Americans no longer looked to Russia as a threat but to new international foes, especially terrorist networks operating outside the authority of particular countries. Within the nation, episodes of domestic terrorism, such as the bombing of a federal building in Oklahoma City and a series of school shootings by children made Americans feel that dangers lurked within their previously safe havens.

The post–Cold War era raised new questions about the role of the United States in the world.

The Economy: Global and Domestic

After the sharp recession of 1991–1992, by nearly all measures, the economy expanded in the 1990s. The stock market boomed, unemployment declined, and most Americans appeared to be better off financially at the end of the decade than at the beginning. But the overall growth of the economy did not benefit everyone, and many actually lost ground—especially those who lost jobs to mechanization, nonunionized workers who toiled for low wages under grim working conditions, and the nation's most vulnerable workers: poor single mothers, new immigrants, and unskilled people of color.

The Post–Cold War Economy

The end of the Cold War had a profound effect on the nation's economy. The demise of the Soviet Union put a final end to the arms race against a superpower foe and made cutting the defense budget politically acceptable. But the closing of defense-related plants in southern California, once the center of the nation's Cold War defense contracts that absorbed nearly a fifth of all federal defense dollars, devastated the regional economy. By the mid-1990s, half the workers in the southern California aerospace industry had been laid off, part of a national trend that resulted in the loss of more than half a million jobs. Many workers lost not only their jobs but also their homes, their economic security, and their sense of community. Louis Rodriguez, president of the International Federation of Professional and Technical Engineers Local 174, explained how he felt when his Long Beach, California, shipyard closed: "The shipyard has been a second family to me. When I get out of here...I will have lost my family."

While defense industries shrank, the technology sector of the economy expanded, opening up new opportunities for young computer experts and entrepreneurs and generating fortunes for corporate executives. At the same time, mergers of giant multinational companies concentrated wealth and power in an ever-smaller number of ever larger corporations. In the last three years of the decade, mergers totaled $5 trillion. Media giants America Online and

Front Range, Rocky Mountains

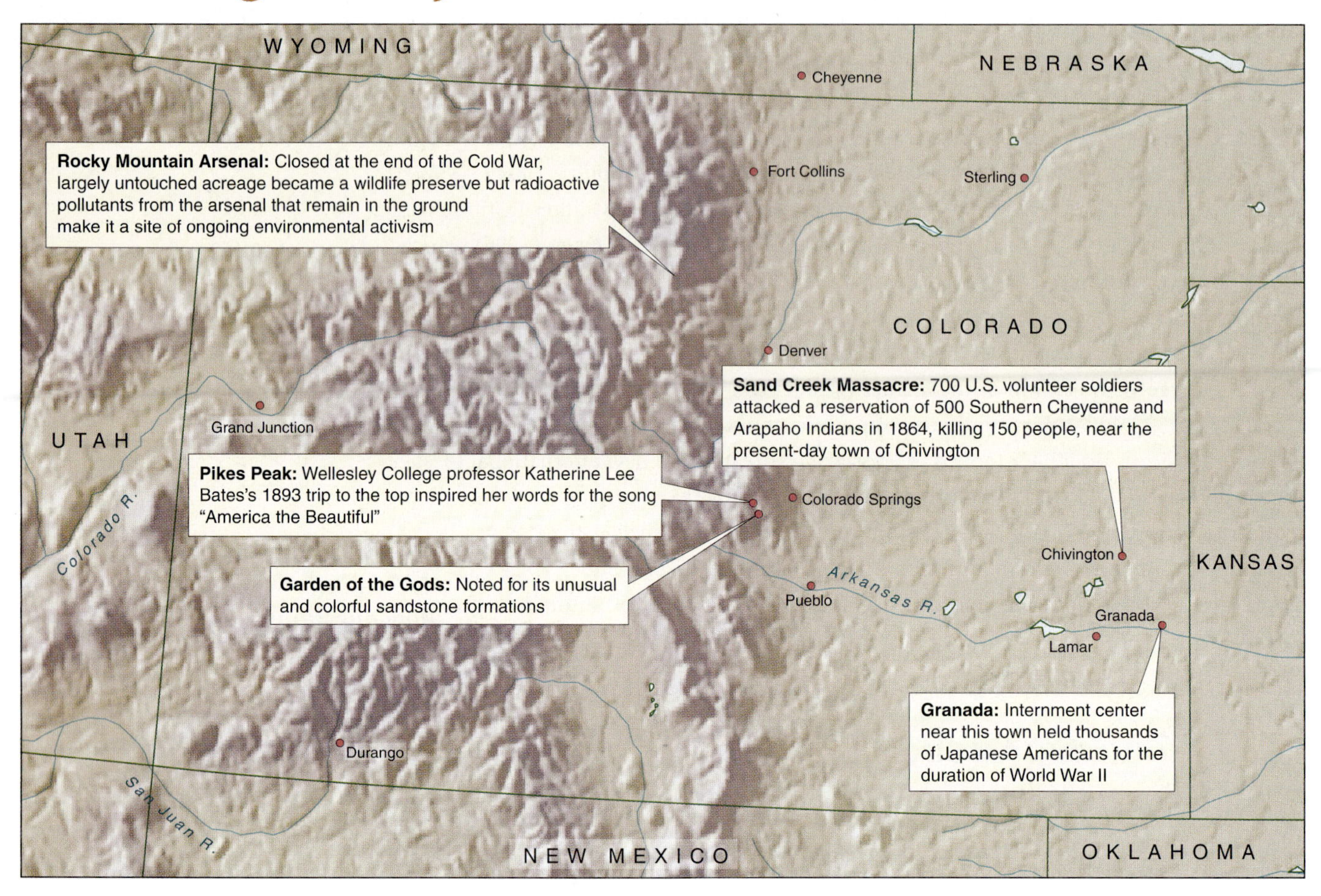

Prior to World War II, Colorado's Front Range cities—Denver, Boulder, Colorado Springs, and Pueblo—were still little more than frontier mining outposts. By the mid-1950s, however, these towns had developed into modern cities.

Mining helped make Denver the state's transportation and financial center and the biggest city in the inter-mountain West. During the national energy crises of the 1970s and 1980s, Denver, located in a region overflowing with coal, natural gas, oil, and uranium, experienced economic booms and busts. Boulder has maintained a more even keel due to the employment generated by the University of Colorado at Boulder. Recently Boulder has become one of the top computer and high-tech startup zones in the nation.

With its proximity to Pikes Peak and the Garden of the Gods, Colorado Springs was the Front Range's original tourist city. In the 1950s, Colorado Springs became home to the U.S. Air Force Academy and the North American Air Defense Command Center (NORAD), which is located at a site hidden deep within Cheyenne Mountain. Tourism, military expenditures, and defense contracts help diversify the economy of Colorado Springs. ■

Long's Peak, Rocky Mountain National Park, Colorado

Time-Warner merged in 2000. In 2001 Nestlé bought Ralston-Purina for $10 billion. Many of the largest mergers crossed national boundaries, such as German automobile maker Daimler-Benz and U.S. Chrysler. American companies were the largest target of global buyouts. In 1999 alone, foreigners paid $233 billion to buy American companies.

While corporations expanded, so did efforts to control their power. Microsoft initially lost an antitrust suit that ordered the computer software giant to be split into two companies. Microsoft appealed the ruling in 2001, and ultimately the Justice Department settled the suit with minor sanctions against the company. The controversial settlement generated opposition. Nine states that participated in the original suit refused to endorse the agreement, and calls for tougher penalties continued. In several states, civil suits against huge tobacco companies limited cigarette advertising and marketing and levied fines on tobacco companies totaling in the billions.

Miguel Gandert/CORBIS

▲ Casino Sandia on the Sandia Pueblo in New Mexico. Many Native American communities across the country built gambling facilities on tribal lands. Although casinos brought needed income, they remained controversial.

Across the country, innovative business ventures proliferated. The 1988 Indian Gaming Regulatory Act enabled Indian entrepreneurs to build lucrative Las Vegas–style casinos on tribal lands, bringing new jobs and an estimated $4 billion a year to formerly impoverished communities. The Mashantucket Pequot east of Hartford, Connecticut, opened Foxwoods in 1992, and it quickly became the largest casino in the Western Hemisphere. The Oneida followed suit a few years later with the Turning Stone casino near Utica, New York. In Arizona, casinos brought in $830 million a year. Some Indian casinos failed, however, and gambling always took a largely hidden toll in the losses of already poor local residents. Indian communities remained divided over the wisdom of trying to profit from America's growing inclination to take risks in hopes of winning big. Jose Lucero of New Mexico's Santa Clara tribe near Santa Fe feared that rebuilding Indian life around gambling was "like a leisure virus—we're trading our souls for money [when] we are supposed to be stewards of this land."

However, the advantages for the tribes were substantial. The Oneida tribe of Wisconsin, for example, used the profits from its 2,000-slot-machine complex outside Green Bay for an electronic components factory, an industrial park, a printing firm, a bank, a hotel, and four convenience stores. Tribal government outlays increased from $40 million to $250 million over the decade, providing subsidized housing, health care, student counseling, a new daycare center, and a new elementary school built in the shape of a turtle, a sacred creature in Oneida mythology. The money also helped revive the Oneida language, with a new written form and a CD of ancestral tales told by tribal elders. The tribe also spent $11 million in 1995 recovering property it once owned, bringing it into the tax-free zone of the reservation. In addition to this communal spending, the tribe paid out $225 a year to all its members. By comparison, the tiny band of Minnesota Shakopee, just south of Minneapolis and St. Paul, used much of the profits from its bustling casino to provide annual bonuses of $400,000 to each member.

The Widening Gap Between Rich and Poor

Some policy experts believed that promoting business and expanding the wealthiest class would stimulate the economy, create jobs, and boost consumer spending. Others disagreed. In the mid-1990s, two liberal economists noted, "The tide of economic growth no longer lifts all boats. We see the recent period as one in which the large yachts, moored in the safe harbors, rose with the tide, while the small boats ran aground. The notion that we can 'grow our way out' of the economic problems facing so many families is now obsolete." In the last decade of the

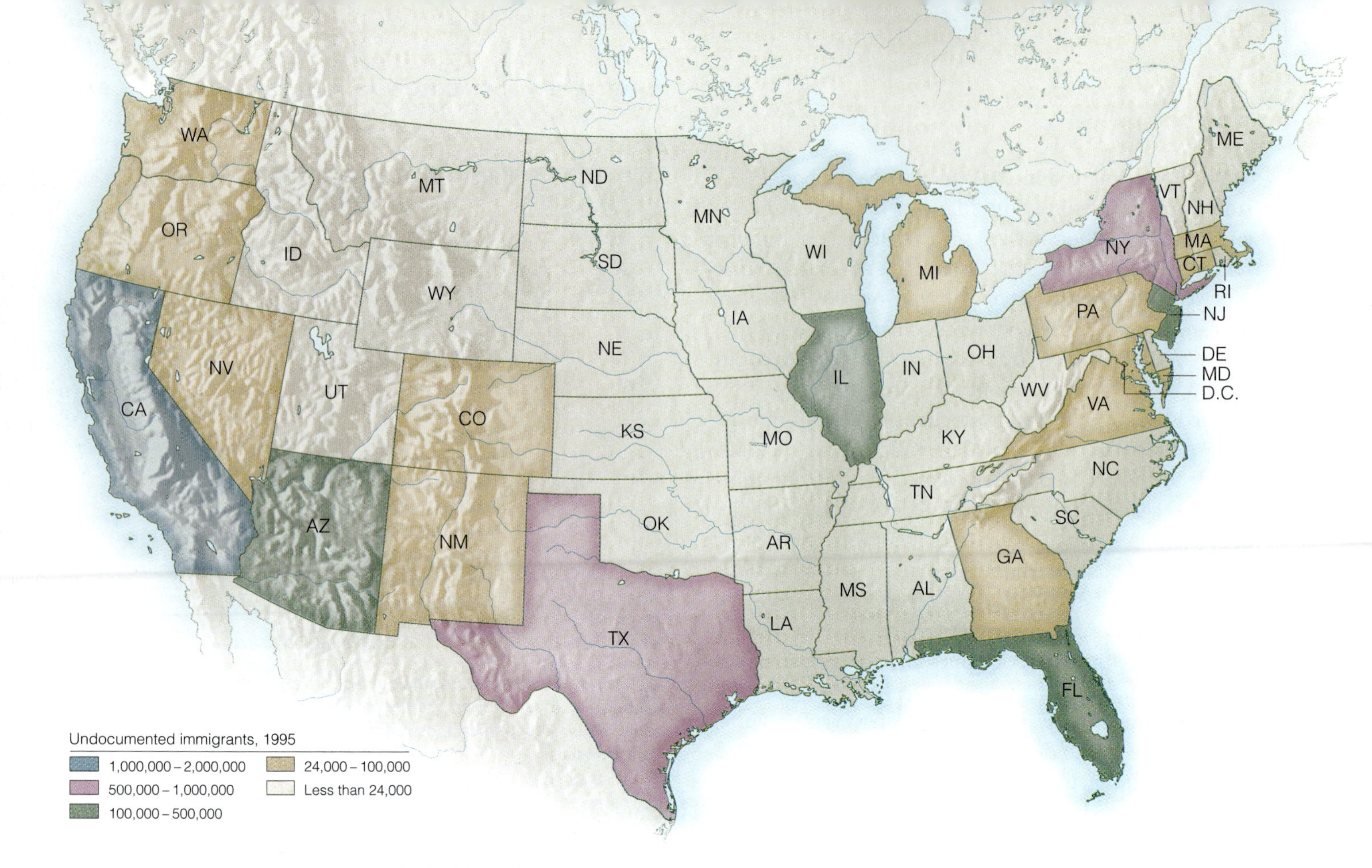

▲ MAP 29.1 STATES WITH LARGE NUMBERS OF UNDOCUMENTED IMMIGRANTS, 1995
In the 1990s fully 77 percent of all undocumented immigrants entered the country legally, with visas in hand. Although in 1900 the total proportion of the foreign born in the United States, including those with and without legal status, was 15 percent, by the 1990s it had dropped to 8 percent, almost half. Immigrants paid $133 billion dollars annually in local, state, and federal taxes, and generated an annual contribution to the American economy in the range of $25 to $30 billion.

century, the bottom 60 percent of the population saw their real income decline, even as the economy boomed. Accumulated wealth—property and investments—was an even better measure of security and influence, and the top 1 percent of Americans owned more wealth than the bottom 90 percent combined. Microsoft chair Bill Gates alone was wealthier than the bottom 45 percent of all U.S. households together. A century earlier, famed capitalist J. P. Morgan insisted that no corporate chieftain should earn more than 20 times what his workers were paid, but by 1980 a typical chief executive of a large U.S. company took home 40 times the earnings of an average factory worker; by 1990 the ratio had grown to 85 times, and by 1998 it reached 419 times.

Although one-third of the nation's African Americans were part of the middle class, black families had fewer assets and resources, making their hold on middle-class status more precarious than that of their white peers. The poorest African Americans were concentrated in low-paying jobs, lacking the quality health care and education that would make social and economic mobility possible. Full-time employment did not necessarily mean an escape from poverty. Among fully employed black heads of households without a high school education, 40 percent of the women and 25 percent of the men did not earn enough to achieve economic self-sufficiency. Almost 50 percent of all black children lived in households below the poverty line, compared to 16 percent of white children. The rate of unemployment was more than twice as high for blacks as for whites.

Recent immigrants from Asia, Africa, and Latin America joined African Americans in jobs at the bottom of the economy. Despite the controversy over illegal immigration, a quarter of a million undocumented workers toiled in the fields of agribusiness. At the same time, 2 percent of able-bodied citizens were in jail, nearly half of them black, because of the arrest and incarceration policies of the **war on drugs** that hit minority communities particularly hard. Prisoners were often required to work while incarcerated. Convicts provided data entry, packed golf balls, and filled a wide array of jobs for less than minimum wage, and most of their earnings went back to the government. These and other workers at the bottom of the labor force gained little or nothing from the economic boom of the 1990s.

M. Sofronski/Sipa Press

▲ Sweatshops like this one in the 1990s resemble those of a century earlier. Immigrant women labor in garment factories, working long hours in miserable conditions for meager wages.

Labor Unions

Low-wage workers in the service industries and certain sectors of the meat industry had one advantage over laborers working for multinational corporations: their jobs could not be exported. Many service workers organized successfully for better wages and working conditions. In 2000, for example, striking janitors of Service Employees International Union Local 1877 in Los Angeles marched eight miles past cheering crowds to the upscale business center of Century City. A few weeks later, the janitors had achieved a wage increase of 26 percent, raising their hourly pay from less than $8 to more than $10. This was a tremendous triumph for a union whose membership was 98 percent immigrant: 80 percent Central Americans, more than half women, and all of them poor.

Other service workers also won improved contracts. Unionized hotel workers in San Francisco negotiated a five-year contract that increased pay for the lowest-paid workers, room cleaners and dishwashers, by 25 percent, from $12 to $15 an hour. In Las Vegas, African American hotel worker Hattie Canty, who helped organize 40,000 employees of large casino hotels, said of her efforts, "It has not been a picnic for me, but I don't think I'd like to go on a picnic every day. I have enjoyed the struggle. I'm not the only Hattie. There's lots of Hatties out there." Yatta Staples went out on the picket line in front of the Minneapolis hotel where she worked as a waitress, telling reporters, "I'll stay here as long as it takes." In the summer of 1997, 185,000 Teamsters went on strike against United Parcel Service and won an improved contract with higher wages and benefits for part-time as well as full-time workers.

Jan Bauer/AP/Wide World Photos

▲ The lobby of the Daimler-Chrysler headquarters in Berlin on November 17, 1998, decorated to celebrate the merger of Daimler-Benz and Chrysler, on the day the new company began trading on the Frankfurt stock exchange. Daimler-Chrysler had its debut on Wall Street soon after.

Strikes did little to benefit nonunionized workers, especially undocumented immigrants, and sweatshop laborers both inside and outside the United States. There were some attempts to improve working conditions for those most exploited by the global economy. In April 1997 representatives from clothing manufacturers, human rights groups, and labor organizations drafted an agreement that tried to improve conditions for garment workers around the world. Companies that agreed to the voluntary pact would limit workweeks to 60 hours, with a maximum of 12 hours of overtime. The companies had to pay "at least the minimum wage required by local law or the prevailing industry wage, whichever is higher." The pact forbade employment of children under age 15 and contained policies protecting workers from harassment and unsafe working environments. Even full compliance with such minimal standards would leave workers in the global garment industry subject to much longer hours, lower wages, and worse working conditions than legally permitted in the United States. Critics also raised questions about how enforceable such voluntary standards would be. Nevertheless, the pact at least called attention to widespread exploitation in the global economy.

Tolerance and Its Limits

Racial discrimination had eased over the course of the twentieth century, but persistent inequalities of power and economic opportunity continued to disadvantage Americans of color, who remained disproportionately poor, in prison, and on welfare. The economic downturn of the early 1990s widened the chasm between affluent white and poor nonwhite Americans. Highly publicized incidents of police brutality directed against racial minorities generated protests and, occasionally, violence. Nevertheless, there were signs that Americans were becoming more tolerant of one another and more willing to accept and even appreciate their diversity.

"We Can All Get Along"

Shortly after midnight on March 3, 1991, police pulled over Rodney King, an African American motorist, after a high-speed chase on a Los Angeles freeway. The four officers dragged the unarmed black man from his car and kicked and beat him with their batons for 15 minutes. The beating left King with a fractured cheekbone, broken bones at the base of his skull, and a broken leg. A bystander recorded the beating on videotape, which was broadcast repeatedly on national television, sparking outrage among Americans of all races.

Lee Celano/Sipa Press

▲ In the aftermath of the violent uprising that followed the acquittal of police officers in the beating of motorist Rodney King, Koreans and African Americans in Los Angeles express their solidarity, hoping to heal the wounds and divisions that tore apart their city.

At the highly publicized trial in April 1992, defense lawyers for the police officers argued that King, who was clearly cowering on the videotape, was resisting arrest and that the police responded appropriately. The jury of ten whites, one Asian, and one Latino acquitted the officers. The acquittal ignited five days of rioting in the African American community of South Central Los Angeles, leaving 58 people dead and $1 billion in property destroyed. Community leaders called for calm; even Rodney King implored the public: "We can all get along. We've just got to." Months later, a federal court in Los Angeles convicted two of the officers involved in the beating of violating King's civil rights—too late to avert the violence that erupted after the initial verdict.

Of the 58 people who died in the violence, 18 were Latino, 26 were black, 10 were white, and 2 were Asian. Of the 4,000 businesses that were destroyed, most belonged to Latinos and Koreans. Perpetrators of the violence, as well as the victims, came from all racial groups. Antonia Hernandez, president of the Mexican American Legal Defense and Educational Fund, noted, "The hardest part is rebuilding the spirit of the city—what holds us together as Angelinos. It's the rebuilding of trust. . . . It's connecting communities that have never been connected." Several community groups came together in an effort to ease tensions, including the Japanese American Citizens League, Chinese for Affirmative Action, and the Asian Pacific Legal Center. "I think that much of the cause of the race relations problem comes down to economics—who has jobs, who has businesses, where is the money going," said Los Angeles City Council member Michael Woo. Jimmy Franco, director of the League of United Latin American Citizens, concurred: "These areas are the poorest areas of the city. If it weren't Rodney King, it would have been something else. It just took something like this to set off the anger."

Values in Conflict

In 1991 former University of Colorado football coach Bill McCartney formed the Promise Keepers, a conservative Christian group dedicated to restoring the traditional privileges and responsibilities of husbands and fathers in the home. The Promise Keepers held evangelical revivals that drew tens of thousands of mostly working-class white and some black men to rallies across the country. They believed that men should be good providers for their families, strong role models for their children, and committed spouses. Other groups and initiatives appeared that appealed to men across the political spectrum: the National Fatherhood Initiative, Father to Father (launched by Vice President Al Gore in 1995), the Fatherhood Project, the Institute for Responsible Fatherhood and Family Revitalization, and Fathers' Education Network.

Although white men continued to control nearly all the major economic and political institutions in the nation, a 1993 poll found that a majority of white men believed that their advantage in terms of jobs and income, along with their influence over American culture, was declining. African American men also felt the need to bolster manhood and fatherhood. Efforts geared specifically toward African American men included M.A.D. D.A.D.S. (Men Against Destruction—Defending Against Drugs and Social Disorder) and the 1995 Million Man March, organized by Nation of Islam Reverend Louis Farrakhan, which drew hundreds of thousands of black men to demonstrate their solidarity at a rally in Washington, D.C.

At the same time, gay men and lesbians mobilized to gain acceptance and legitimacy for the families that they formed. Although a 1994 poll showed that 52 percent of respondents "claimed to consider gay lifestyle acceptable," 64 percent were opposed to legalizing gay marriage or allowing gay couples to adopt children. Vermont became the first state to grant legal status to civil unions between same-sex couples.

Values also collided around the rights and traditions of American Indians as tribal communities came into conflict with non-Indian environmentalists, sports enthusiasts, and scientists. In the upper Midwest, treaties with the government in 1837 and 1842 granted the Chippewa hunting, fishing, and gathering rights in the territories ceded to the United States. Federal courts consistently upheld these treaties, which include rights to take up to half of the fish and game allowed by state conservation requirements and to use methods such as spear fishing that are illegal for non-Indians. In the 1980s and 1990s, non-Indians challenged these policies and accosted Native Americans in fishing boats with rocks and insults.

Native American cultural practices also clashed with environmentalist sensibilities over religious practices involving the gathering and sacrificing of golden eaglets. The Department of the Interior, weighing laws protecting Indian religious freedoms against those protecting national parks and wildlife, allowed the Hopi to gather up to 40 young eagles a year. The Hopi usually took about 15 birds for a ceremony that culminated in their sacrifice. The Interior Department's policy is consistent with long-standing treaties as well as recent law,

Vermont Civil Union Law

On April 26, 2000, Vermont became the first state to grant legal recognition to same-sex couples, affording them all the legal protections, privileges, and responsibilities of married couples. The law unleashed a storm of controversy and raised questions about the legal status in other states of civil unions contracted in Vermont. Nevertheless, in the first year after its enactment, 2,479 same-sex couples forged civil unions in Vermont, 478 of them among Vermonters, and the rest from other states. Two-thirds were lesbian unions. Several states began to consider similar bills, but others moved to prohibit such unions. Nebraska amended its state constitution to outlaw same-sex marriage and civil unions. On the national level, conservative lawmakers endeavored to introduce a constitutional amendment that would ban civil unions and restrict marriage to heterosexual couples. Among other provisions, the Vermont Civil Union Law stipulated the following:

Jim Bourg/TimePix/Getty Images

Kathleen Peterson and Carolyn Conrad exchange vows in front of Justice of the Peace T. Hunter Wilson. The ceremony in Brattleboro, Vermont, on July 1, 2000, marked the first legal union under Vermont's Civil Union Law. Vermont was the first state to provide recognition and legal status to gay and lesbian couples.

(1) Civil marriage under Vermont's marriage statutes consists of a union between a man and a woman. . . .

(2) Vermont's history as an independent republic and as a state is one of equal treatment and respect for all Vermonters. . . .

(3) The state's interest in civil marriage is to encourage close and caring families, and to protect all family members from the economic and social consequences of abandonment and divorce, focusing on those who have been especially at risk.

(4) Legal recognition of civil marriage by the state is the primary and, in a number of instances, the exclusive source of numerous benefits, responsibilities and protections under the laws of the state for married persons and their children.

(5) Based on the state's tradition of equality under the law and strong families, for at least 25 years, Vermont Probate Courts have qualified gay and lesbian individuals as adoptive parents.

(6) Vermont was one of the first states to adopt comprehensive legislation prohibiting discrimination on the basis of sexual orientation. . . .

(7) The state has a strong interest in promoting stable and lasting families, including families based upon a same-sex couple.

(8) Without the legal protections, benefits and responsibilities associated with civil marriage, same-sex couples suffer numerous obstacles and hardships.

(9) Despite longstanding social and economic discrimination, many gay and lesbian Vermonters have formed lasting, committed, caring and faithful relationships with persons of their same sex. These couples live together, participate in their communities together, and some raise children and care for family members together, just as do couples who are married under Vermont law.

(10) While a system of civil unions does not bestow the status of civil marriage, it does satisfy the requirements of the Common Benefits Clause. Changes in the way significant legal relationships are established under the constitution should be approached carefully, combining respect for the community and cultural institutions most affected with a commitment to the constitutional rights involved. Granting benefits and protections to same-sex couples through a system of civil unions will provide due respect for tradition and long-standing social institutions, and will permit adjustment as unanticipated consequences or unmet needs arise.

(11) The constitutional principle of equality embodied in the Common Benefits Clause is compatible with the freedom of religious belief and worship guaranteed in Chapter I, Article 3rd of the state constitution. Extending the benefits and protections of marriage to same-sex couples through a system of civil unions preserves the fundamental constitutional right of each of the multitude of religious faiths in Vermont to choose freely and without state interference to whom to grant the religious status, sacrament or blessing of marriage under the rules, practices or traditions of such faith.

Questions

1. *What political principles and values provided the foundation for Vermont's civil union law?*
2. *In what ways does the Vermont civil union law distinguish between civil marriages and civil unions?* ■

including the American Indian Religious Freedom Act of 1978. But many environmentalists agreed with the news columnist who wrote, "When native peoples, no matter how badly abused by us in the past, seek to perpetrate equally senseless barbarities on helpless creatures, we should stand on principle and use our awesome power to stop, not to enable them." Animal rights activists raised similar arguments against mainstream institutions, including scientific laboratories that used animals for research, and the meat industry, which engaged in inhumane practices.

Mary Ann Chastain/AP/Wide World Photos

▲ Two protesters dressed as monkeys imprisoned in cages take part in a demonstration against Procter and Gamble's use of animals in product testing. An animal-rights group, People for the Ethical Treatment of Animals (PETA), staged the protest on January 23, 1998, in front of Procter and Gamble's manufacturing facility in Greenville, South Carolina.

Courtroom Dramas

Two of the most controversial legal spectacles of the decade centered on accusations against successful black men and exposed deep chasms along lines of class and gender as well as race. The first of these episodes was the Senate hearing of October 1991 to confirm the appointment of conservative Judge Clarence Thomas to the U.S. Supreme Court. President George H. W. Bush nominated Thomas to replace the retiring liberal Justice Thurgood Marshall. Both jurists were black but otherwise had little in common; they occupied opposite ends of the political and judicial spectrum. Although Bush claimed that Thomas was the "best man for the job," the American Bar Association gave him the lowest rating of any justice confirmed in the previous three decades. Many people became skeptical during the confirmation hearings when Thomas claimed that he had not formed any opinion on the highly charged issue of abortion. Support for Thomas among the senators on the Senate Judiciary Committee fell largely along party lines. But when University of Oklahoma law professor Anita Hill accused Thomas of sexual harassment when she worked for him at the Equal Opportunity Employment Commission in the early 1980s, the question of Thomas's professional qualifications faded to the background and the hearings focused exclusively on Hill's accusations.

In live televised hearings, the African American law professor testified that Thomas had made crude and lurid remarks to her as well as unwanted sexual overtures. Several of the all-white-male panel of senators questioned Hill's credibility, wondering why she continued to work for Thomas after the alleged harassment. Thomas drew on the long history of black men being falsely accused of sexual aggression to counter the charge of sexual harassment, accusing his Democratic opponents of conducting a "high-tech lynching." In the end Thomas was confirmed. But Hill's testimony, and what appeared to her supporters as the insensitive behavior of the senators, brought the issue of sexual harassment to a high level of national consciousness. The hearings also highlighted the fact that Congress was overwhelmingly white and male, motivating female candidates and their supporters to alter that reality the following year. As a result of the 1992 elections, the number of female senators tripled from two to six, including the first black female senator, Carol Moseley Braun, Democrat from Illinois. The number of congresswomen rose from 28 to 47.

In 1994 television viewers were again riveted by a media spectacle, this time a sensational murder case in Los Angeles. The victims were the white ex-wife of black celebrity

O. J. Simpson, former football star and film actor, and her male companion. Simpson's blood was found at the scene, hair and other forensic and DNA evidence linked him to the crime, he had no reliable alibi, and a motive was evident in his pattern of jealous rage and brutality against the murdered woman. No other suspects in the case were ever identified. But Simpson's team of lawyers unearthed evidence that before the Simpson case, white police detective Mark Fuhrman had boasted of planting evidence and had made racist comments. The mostly black and female jury was sympathetic to the possibility that Fuhrman had framed Simpson. In Los Angeles, in the wake of the Rodney King beatings, African Americans had good reason to distrust the police.

Finally, in early October 1996, after a trial that lasted nearly a year, it took the jury only two hours to acquit Simpson of all charges. Pundits focused on the racial divide: blacks were more inclined to believe Simpson was innocent, and whites more likely to consider him guilty. Simpson was later convicted in a wrongful death civil suit (with lower standards for conviction than a criminal case), which found him responsible for the deaths and ordered him to pay damages.

The Changing Face of Diversity

These highly charged events illuminated racial tensions, but there was also evidence that Americans were accepting the nation's diversity and adopting a more inclusive vision. The number of immigrants represented 10 percent of the population, the highest proportion of foreign-born residents since the 1930s. The numbers of Asians and Pacific Islanders increased by 45.9 percent, with those of Chinese ancestry forming the largest group, followed by those with origins in the Philippines. The Latino population grew by 39.7 percent. Among the nation's Latinos, nearly two-thirds were of Mexican ancestry.

Not everyone celebrated these developments. In California, with one-third of the nation's Latino population, voters responded with Proposition 187 to deny public education and most other public social services to undocumented immigrants, and Proposition 227 to end bilingual education. Large numbers of Latino voters opposed these measures. In subsequent elections many young Latinos and new citizens marshaled their political power and voted for the first time. In Los Angeles during the 1990s, Latinos became the largest single ethnic group. By 2000 whites no longer constituted a majority of California's multiethnic population, dropping from 57 percent in 1990 to 47 percent in 2000.

Jack Smith/AP/Wide World

▲ **Golf superstar Tiger Woods celebrates his triumph at the U.S. Amateur Championships in North Plains, Oregon, August 25, 1996. Woods, the son of an African American father and a Thai mother, was one of several mixed-race celebrities in the 1990s.**

At the same time, politics and ideas based on distinct and rigid racial lines gave way to a growing recognition of intermixing. Artists actively explored this hybridity. In her widely acclaimed one-woman play *Twilight, Los Angeles,* mixed-race dramatist Anna Deveare Smith explored the uprising in South Central Los Angeles by interviewing and then performing the perspectives of a wide range of white, black, Asian, Latino, male, female, young, and old people who were involved in the conflict. By transforming herself on stage into each of those people, she suggested that we, as a society, were all of those people as well. In his 1996 film *Lone Star,* John Sayles examined a Texas border town where white, black, Latino, and Indian peoples were all interwoven and connected in their lives, communities, and families. From cross-racial love to debates over the local school's history curriculum, the film explored in microcosm the challenges and rewards of an inclusive American identity.

In the world of sports, young golfer Tiger Woods, son of a black Vietnam veteran father and a Thai mother, became the reigning superstar of the sport most closely identified with the world of the white elite. Pop star Prince was one of many artists who crafted a persona that highlighted both racial and gender ambiguity. On job and college application forms, a growing number of mixed-race Americans refused to be identified as belonging to one particular racial group. Reflecting this development, the U.S. Census of 2000 allowed people to check more than one box to indicate their identity group.

Violence and Danger

Violence was nothing new in American society, but new types of mayhem in the 1990s—including domestic terrorism and school shootings—sparked national soul-searching and wide-ranging debate over the causes of violence. Meanwhile, ordinary Americans inflicted various harms on themselves, often in class-distinct ways. Eating disorders and obesity reached epidemic proportions, and Americans continued to turn to drugs, most of them legal, to make themselves feel better.

Investigations throughout the decade uncovered networks of antigovernment militias, tax resisters, and white supremacist groups, many of them heavily armed and isolated in remote rural areas.

Domestic Terrorism

On the morning of April 19, 1995, a two-ton homemade bomb exploded at the Alfred P. Murrah Federal Building in Oklahoma City. The huge building crumbled, killing 168 people, including 19 children. The attack was the worst act of terrorism in the nation's history to that date. Initial news reports speculated that the terrorists were Arabs, but it turned out that the attack was carried out by American citizens with a hatred for the government. Timothy McVeigh, a veteran of the first U.S.-Iraq war, and his accomplice, Terry Nichols, were found guilty of the bombing.

Antigovernment individuals and groups had long operated within the United States, and during the 1990s their activities—as well as FBI efforts to curtail them—intensified. Investigations throughout the decade uncovered networks of antigovernment militias, tax resisters, and white supremacist groups, many of them heavily armed and isolated in remote rural areas. Some antigovernment extremists acted alone, like former mathematics professor Theodore Kaczynski, known as the "Unabomber," who for two decades sent bombs through the mail, killing 3 people and injuring 29. His demand to have his antigovernment manifesto published in major national newspapers led to his identification and arrest.

The FBI tried to prevent these extremists from causing harm, but some of their efforts went awry. In 1992 an FBI agent shot and killed the wife and son of Randall Weaver, a former Green Beret and antigovernment militia supporter who had failed to appear for trial on weapons charges, in a shootout at their Idaho home. The following year in Waco, Texas, the FBI stormed the heavily armed compound of an antigovernment religious sect known as the Branch Davidians. The leader of the group, David Koresh, had barricaded the compound. The FBI, acting on reports of abuse of members, particularly women and children, tried to force Koresh and his group out of the building. But a fire broke out, killing 80 men, women, and children inside. The FBI came under intense criticism for its aggressive tactics in these cases. For antigovernment extremists, these actions prompted revenge. The Oklahoma City bombing apparently was intended in part as retaliation for the FBI assault against the Branch Davidians precisely two years earlier. Timothy McVeigh was sentenced to death for the Oklahoma City bombing. The execution by lethal injection took place on June 11, 2001.

The McVeigh case revived a debate about the death penalty, particularly in light of recent evidence of many botched legal defenses in capital cases. Opponents pointed to the preponderance of convicts of color on death row, representation by incompetent attorneys, and the

▲ Abortion remained one of the most controversial political issues throughout the 1990s. Here abortion rights advocate Inga Coulter of Harrisburg, Pennsylvania, and antiabortion crusader Elizabeth McGee of Washington, D.C., take opposing sides in a demonstration outside the Supreme Court building on December 8, 1993.

execution of mentally retarded offenders, to argue that the death penalty should be abolished. The governor of Illinois declared a moratorium on executions when a study revealed that many death row inmates were cleared of charges as a result of new DNA evidence. Public opinion began to shift, but the majority—including the U.S. presidents from both parties throughout the decade—continued to support the death penalty.

The Oklahoma City bombing was the worst but not the only example of domestic terrorist attacks. After the Supreme Court's 1973 decision in *Roe* v. *Wade* legalized abortion, antiabortion activists worked to have the decision reversed. Most antiabortion protesters were peaceful and law-abiding. But a small militant fringe of antiabortion crusaders switched their targets of protest from elected officials to abortion providers and turned to violence. In 1993 half of all abortion clinics reported hostile actions, including death threats, fires, bombs, invasions, blockades, and shootings. In 1993 and 1994 vigilantes shot and killed one abortion provider, tried to kill another, and shot employees at two clinics in Brookline, Massachusetts.

The violence spurred Congress to pass the Freedom of Access to Clinic Entrances Act in 1994, making it a federal crime to block access to clinics. But ultimately, the intimidation and violence were effective. Although abortion remained legal, the procedure became increasing difficult to obtain. Few medical residency programs in obstetrics and gynecology routinely taught the procedure, and considering the dangers posed by antiabortion terrorists, few physicians were willing to perform abortions. By the end of the decade, there were no abortion providers in 86 percent of largely rural counties in the country. Abortions continued to be available in cities, mostly in specialized abortion clinics. Between 1990 and 1997, the number of abortions declined by 17.4 percent. But the political battles continued. After years of controversy and debate, the French abortion pill RU-486 received FDA approval for use in the United States, making it possible for individual doctors to prescribe the pill and for women to avoid surgery.

Kids Who Kill

Although violent crime declined throughout the decade, especially crimes committed by youths, a spate of school shootings in which children murdered other children sparked national soul searching and finger pointing as Americans wondered whom and what to blame. The murderers were mostly white middle-class boys who appeared to be "normal kids." The worst of these shootings occurred on April 20, 1999, at Columbine High School in a suburb of Denver, Colorado, where two boys opened fire and killed 12 of their schoolmates and a teacher before killing themselves.

The common factors in all of these killings were that the children used guns and that they got the weapons easily, often from their own homes. **Gun control** advocates noted that the easy access to firearms in the United States was unique among western industrial nations. In 1992, 367 people were killed by handguns in Great Britain, Sweden, Switzerland, Japan, Australia, and Canada combined. The total population of those countries equaled that of the United States, where in that same year, handguns killed 13,220 people. Public opinion polls showed that most Americans favored gun control, but the powerful gun lobby and the National Rifle Association argued that the Second Amendment to the Constitution guaranteed individuals the unlimited right to bear arms. Congress enacted the Brady Bill, a gun control measure named for James Brady, the White House press secretary who was gravely wounded in the 1981 assassination attempt on President Ronald W. Reagan. The bill required a waiting period for handgun purchases and banned assault rifles. Nevertheless, access to firearms remained easy. In the 2000 election, only two states, Oregon and Colorado, where two of the worst school shootings occurred, voted to establish some controls on the purchase of guns.

Adam Nadel/AP/Wide World Photos

▲ **The 1995–1996 government budget impasse resulted in shutdowns, including Statue of Liberty tourists being turned away.**

A Healthy Nation?

Despite the nation's near obsession with fitness, both the wealthy and the poor suffered from a number of afflictions. Eating disorders plagued millions of Americans. Among the affluent, anorexia nervosa (self-starvation) and bulimia (frequent binging and purging) affected an estimated 5 million Americans, especially young women, fed in part by a fashion fad that glamorized emaciated bodies. Men also strove for a fashionable body, sometimes with the aid of drugs to enhance athletic performance or muscle buildup. In 2000 the Mayo Clinic reported a 30 percent increase in eating disorders per year, mostly among young women, but in a growing number of men as well. The opposite problem plagued the lower end of the class ladder, where obesity increased dramatically, especially among children. With popular fast-food chains offering "supersized" high-fat meals, childhood obesity jumped from 5 percent in 1964 to 20 percent in 2000.

The sale and use of illegal drugs, including marijuana, cocaine, and heroin, remained widespread in spite of the harsh penalties and long prison terms that were the central feature of the government's "war on drugs." However, illegal drugs represented only one dimension of Americans' desire to solve their problems through the use of chemical substances. Some mind-altering drugs were legal and available by prescription, such as Prozac and other antidepressants. While these medications proved very effective in treating mental illness, some mental health experts worried that these drugs were being overprescribed, especially for children, as life's normal ups and downs were increasingly diagnosed as maladies such as depression and attention deficit disorder. Aging **baby boomers** also boosted the profits of pharmaceutical companies. Women turned to hormone replacement therapies to offset the effects of menopause. Skyrocketing sales of Viagra, a drug for treating male impotence, reflected middle-aged men's concerns about waning sexual potency.

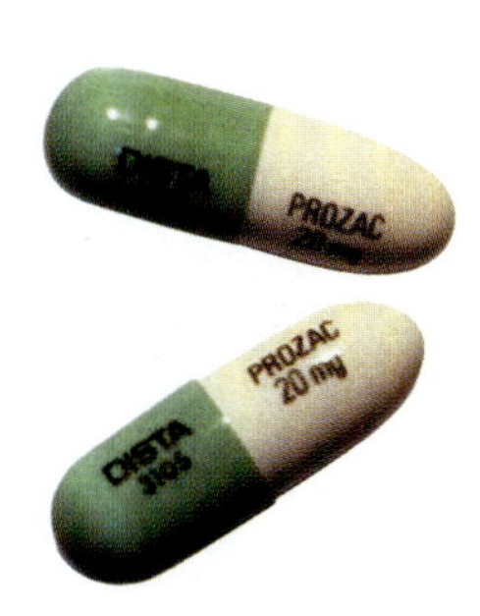

Medical developments brought new cures and new worries. Antibiotics were so widely prescribed that forms of drug-resistant bacteria began to proliferate. Tuberculosis appeared in new deadly forms that did not respond to treatment with available antibiotics. In 1997 researchers in Scotland cloned a sheep, raising hopes that cloning could lead to new medical breakthroughs and fears that human cloning might be next. In 2000 scientists charted the entire human genome, or genetic code, offering the hope of finding causes and cures for genetically linked diseases.

Advances in reproductive medicine provoked controversies over the benefits and dangers of such procedures as embryo selection, in vitro fertilization for postmenopausal women, and

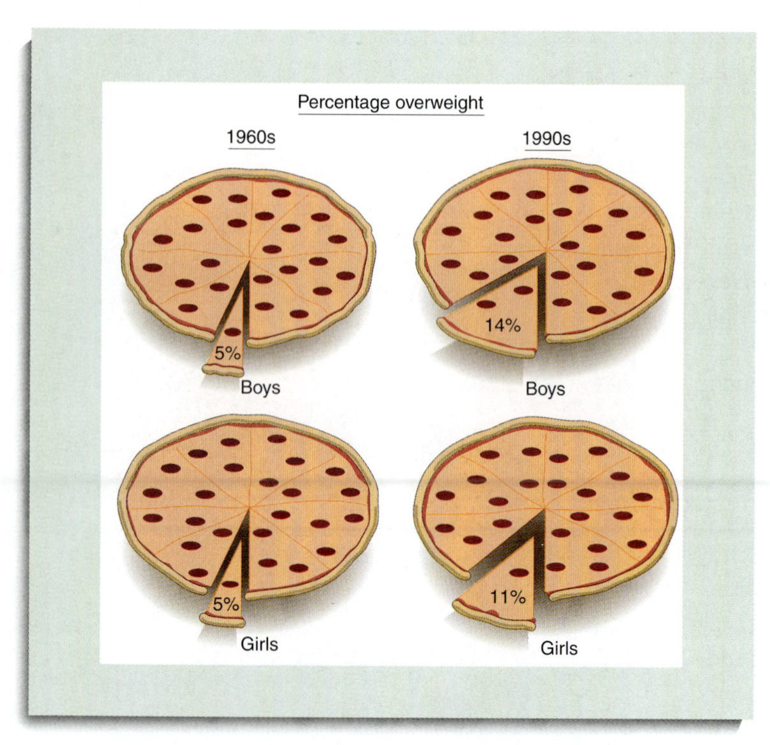

▲ **FIGURE 29.1 CHILDHOOD OBESITY RATES FOR BOYS AND GIRLS AGE 6–17, 1960s AND 1990s**
During the last half-century, obesity rates among children in the United States rose dramatically, especially in the 1990s. Childhood obesity is associated with a wide range of medical problems that can affect the health of overweight children throughout their lives. In the 1960s, boys and girls were equally likely to be overweight. But by the 1990s, obesity had become more prevalent among boys.

the long-term implications of egg and sperm donation. In one 1999 case that sparked a debate among medical ethicists, a couple advertised for an egg donor in the student newspapers of prestigious colleges, offering $50,000 to a donor who was athletic and tall, had no major family medical problems, and had scored at least 1400 on the Scholastic Achievement Test. Like the eugenic campaigns of earlier decades, these sorts of cases raised concerns about efforts to create "superior" children.

The Clinton Presidency

William Jefferson Clinton was the first American president born after World War II. Raised in Arkansas in a working-class family, Clinton attended Georgetown University and studied at Oxford University in England as a Rhodes Scholar. Like many college students of his generation, he opposed the Vietnam War and avoided the draft. He attended Yale Law School, where he met Hillary Rodham from Illinois, whom he married in 1975. In 1978, at the age of 33, he was elected governor of Arkansas. After one term he was defeated in his bid for reelection, but he reclaimed his job as governor four years later by defining himself as a centrist New Democrat. When he ran for president in 1992, Clinton received the support of the Democratic Leadership Council, a group of **New Democrats** who shifted the national party to the right of its previous New Deal liberal position.

VIDEO
Clinton Presidential Campaign Ad (1992)

Clinton was a brilliant campaigner and a charismatic leader with a disarming personal style that contributed to his victory over the incumbent George H. W. Bush. The sluggish economy also helped Clinton win the election. Throughout his presidency, despite political failures and scandals, Clinton achieved consistently high presidential job performance ratings in national polls. He also benefited from the recovery of the economy during his administration. But accusations of corruption and sexual impropriety plagued him throughout his two terms. Ultimately, during his second term as president, an affair with a young White House intern led to his impeachment by the House of Representatives. Although he was not removed from office, the incident cast a cloud over his presidency.

Clinton: The New Democrat

In 1992 the incumbent president, George H. W. Bush, faced an uphill battle. The recession of 1991–1992 hit white-collar as well as blue-collar workers as unemployment climbed above 8 percent. During 12 years of Republican presidents, the national debt had more than quadrupled to $4.4 trillion. The Republican party platform, reflecting pressures from the right wing of the party, attacked permissiveness in American society, opposed abortion and gay rights, and called for a smaller government. The Democrats nominated the 46-year-old Clinton, who selected as his running mate Al Gore, senator from Tennessee. A wildcard in the election was the Reform party candidacy of H. Ross Perot, a Texas billionaire who financed his own campaign and used the national media to tap into voter discontent with the two major parties.

Much of the campaign reflected the culture wars, pitting what many saw as the socially permissive legacy of the 1960s against conservative efforts to restore traditional "family values" to American public life. Many Americans worried that the prevalence of single-parent families, the high rate of divorce, and the pervasiveness of sex and violence in the popular culture all reflected a decline in moral standards and an erosion of American society. In May 1992 Vice President Dan Quayle delivered a speech criticizing the popular television show *Murphy Brown,* whose unmarried title character had given birth to a child. But Republicans were not the only critics of popular culture. Al Gore's wife, Tipper, for example, had long been an advocate of parental advisories and ratings of popular music.

Clinton won the election by a comfortable margin, but Perot garnered 19 percent of the popular vote, the largest showing for a third-party candidate since Theodore Roosevelt ran on the Progressive party ticket in 1912. Clinton began his term with a solidly Democratic House and Senate, which included a new infusion of women, along with the nation's first senator of American Indian descent, Ben Nighthorse Campbell of Colorado. Saying that he wanted his advisers to "look like America," Clinton appointed 2 Latinos, 3 blacks, and 3 women to the 14-member cabinet.

Many Americans worried that the prevalence of single-parent families, the high rate of divorce, and the pervasiveness of sex and violence in the popular culture all reflected a decline in moral standards and an erosion of American society.

Clinton's Domestic Agenda and the "Republican Revolution"

Clinton ran into trouble early in his administration when he tried to fulfill his campaign promise to allow gays and lesbians to serve openly in the military. Top military officials, already unhappy with having a new commander in chief who had avoided military service during the Vietnam War, vehemently opposed lifting the ban against gays. Ultimately, Clinton compromised and established a new policy of **"don't ask, don't tell,"** which allowed homosexuals to serve as long as they did not make their sexual orientation known.

Clinton's effort to reform the health care system was equally unsuccessful. With rising health care costs and millions of uninsured citizens, Clinton's campaign promises to provide national health insurance and reduce the cost of health care had wide public support but fierce opposition from the medical establishment and the pharmaceutical industry. Clinton appointed his wife, Hillary Rodham Clinton, an attorney and longtime advocate on behalf of children and families, to head a task force to develop a plan. But the task force, deliberating behind closed doors, failed to come up with a workable strategy acceptable to all sides. After a year of hearings and no action in Congress on the complicated task force proposal, the Clintons abandoned the effort.

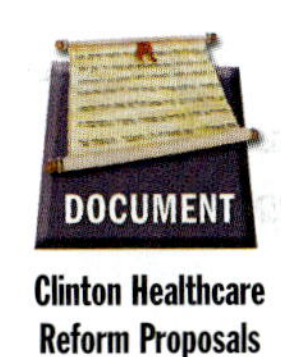

Clinton Healthcare Reform Proposals

Clinton achieved a major success when he pushed through Congress a budget that raised taxes on the wealthiest Americans, cut spending to reduce the deficit, and expanded tax credits for low-income families. In the next three years the economy markedly improved. Other legislative successes included passage of the "motor voter" act, which allowed eligible voters to register when applying for drivers' licenses, and the Family and Medical Leave Act, which required employers to grant unpaid medical leave for up to 12 weeks. Clinton appointed two relatively liberal Supreme Court Justices, Ruth Bader Ginsburg in 1993 and Stephen Breyer in 1994.

The 1994 congressional elections dealt a devastating blow to Clinton's legislative agenda. In the midst of the campaign, about 300 Republican congressional candidates, under the leadership of Speaker of the House Newt Gingrich, stood on the Capitol steps and endorsed a "Contract with America," calling for **welfare reform,** a balanced budget, more prisons and longer sentences, increased defense spending, an end to legal abortion, and other conservative measures. Only 39 percent of the electorate voted, and a whisker-thin majority of those voted Republican. Nevertheless, the Republicans declared a "Republican Revolution" as they took control of both the House and Senate for the first time in 40 years and pushed Congress to the right of center.

The new Congress passed a large tax cut and a tough anticrime bill, increased military spending, and reduced federal regulatory power over the environment. Clinton used his veto power to limit the Republican agenda, but he also undercut the conservative momentum by taking on some of their issues as his own, such as **free trade** and welfare reform. The "Republican Revolution" did not last long. In 1995 and again in 1996, Congress forced a shutdown of the federal government rather than agree to Clinton's proposed budget, leading to widespread frustration and anger as Democrats and Republicans blamed each other for the stalemate. Support for the "Contract with America" wore thin, and the public was quickly disenchanted with the gridlock in Washington. In his 1996 State of the Union address, Clinton announced that the "era of big government is over," and he signed the Welfare Reform Act, abolishing the 60-year-old program Aid to Families with Dependent Children (AFDC).

Public opinion polls showed a growing concern over the vast amounts of money poured into elections, but campaign finance reform remained a difficult issue for lawmakers, whose own success at the polls depended on large financial contributions.

Clinton won reelection easily in 1996, defeating the 73-year-old Senate Majority Leader, Republican Bob Dole of Kansas. Republicans lost some seats but stayed in control of both houses of Congress. The 1996 campaign was the most expensive in history, with Democrats spending $250 million and Republicans $400 million. Billionaire H. Ross Perot ran again, although his showing at the polls was much weaker than in 1992. Public opinion polls showed a growing concern over the vast amounts of money poured into elections, but campaign finance reform remained a difficult issue for lawmakers, whose own success at the polls depended on large financial contributions.

The Impeachment Crisis

Clinton's personal behavior left him vulnerable to political enemies, who took full advantage of every opportunity to discredit him. In 1993 the Clintons were investigated for possible complicity in a failed Arkansas investment scheme known as Whitewater. Although a few of the Clintons' close associates were found guilty of conspiracy, tax evasion, and mail fraud in the deal, four years of persistent investigation cleared the Clintons of any wrongdoing. Nevertheless, the Whitewater scandal activated the Office of the Independent Counsel, an independent investigative unit put into place during the Nixon administration to investigate the Watergate break-in. The independent counsel, former judge Kenneth Starr, with the help of the congressional Republicans, pursued Clinton throughout his two terms and nearly brought down his presidency. In the end, however, it was not Clinton's financial dealings but rather his sexual behavior that led to his impeachment.

Clinton's sexual behavior became an issue well before he entered the White House. During the 1992 campaign, Gennifer Flowers, a former nightclub singer, told a tabloid that she and Clinton had had an affair when he was governor. Early in his presidency, Paula Jones, a former Arkansas state employee, filed a sexual harassment suit against Clinton, claiming that he had propositioned her when he was governor of Arkansas. Eventually, the case was dismissed, but it came back to haunt him later.

In 1998, Kenneth Starr reported to the House Judiciary Committee that he had evidence that Clinton had an extramarital affair with a young White House intern, Monica Lewinsky. Starr claimed that Clinton had broken the law in an effort to cover up the affair. Lewinsky and Clinton had both been called to testify in the Paula Jones case, and both denied having had a sexual relationship. Starr claimed that Clinton had lied under oath and had instructed his close adviser and friend, Vernon Jordan, to find Lewinsky a job to keep her quiet. Starr charged Clinton with perjury, witness tampering, and obstruction of justice. As proof of the affair, Starr produced 20 hours of taped phone conversations recorded by Lewinsky's co-worker and confidante, Linda Tripp. Clinton vehemently denied the charges, but Lewinsky had saved a dress with a stain containing the president's DNA, providing the investigation with the "smoking gun" it needed.

As Starr and congressional Republicans pressed the investigation with relentless determination, the media saturated the nation and the world with sordid and graphic details of the president's sexual encounters with the young intern. Polls showed that Americans disapproved of Clinton's personal behavior, but they did not want him removed from office. With the economy booming, Clinton garnered high job performance ratings, rising to 79 percent at the height of the scandal. Negative sentiment against Kenneth Starr and congressional Republicans mounted as the investigation dragged on for four years at a cost to taxpayers of $40 million.

Public opinion notwithstanding, the House of Representatives impeached Clinton on December 19, 1998, charging him with perjury and obstruction of justice, based on Clinton's false testimony in the Paula Jones case. Removal from office requires two steps: the House of Representatives brings formal charges known as "articles of impeachment," and the Senate tries the impeached official on these articles. A two-thirds vote of the Senate is required for conviction. The vote in the House of Representatives fell strictly along party lines. The Bill of Impeachment was then sent to the Senate, where the majority of senators determined that Clinton's misdeeds did not meet the standard for "high crimes and misdemeanors" required to remove a president from office.

Articles of Impeachment Against Clinton (1999)

The Nation and the World

In foreign affairs, Clinton focused on peacekeeping and peacemaking while expanding trade and diplomatic relations, especially to countries that had been considered unfriendly during the Cold War. Clinton took on the role of peace broker by facilitating negotiations in long-standing conflicts in Northern Ireland and the Middle East. But hostilities in those areas proved too deep to be fully resolved. Military interventions in Somalia, Haiti, and Kosovo yielded mixed results, and trade agreements generated heated controversy. Episodes of international terrorism against U.S. embassies and military personnel killed hundreds of people and highlighted the strength of extremist groups whose members were deeply hostile to the United States and its interventions around the world.

Trade Agreements

In 1993, with the president's strong encouragement, Congress approved the North American Free Trade Agreement (NAFTA), eliminating tariffs and trade barriers among the United States, Mexico, and Canada and thus creating the largest free trade zone in the world. In 1994 Congress approved the General Agreement on Tariffs and Trade (GATT), which reduced tariffs on thousands of goods and phased out import quotas imposed by the United States and other industrialized nations. Supporters argued that these measures would increase global competition and improve the U.S. economy. Businesses would benefit from the easing of trade barriers, and consumers would have access to lower-priced goods.

▲ Activists protest at the opening of the meeting of the World Trade Organization (WTO) in Seattle, Washington, on November 1, 1999. During the four days of the meeting, hundreds of demonstrators took to the streets in opposition to the organization's environmental and labor policies.

▲ **Senator Hillary Rodham Clinton listens as Secretary of State Colin Powell testifies before the Senate Budget Committee on March 14, 2001. Elected to the Senate as a Democrat from New York in 2000, the former First Lady generated heated controversy. Her supporters hailed her as a pioneer, while her adversaries vilified her for her liberal positions and her violation of traditional roles and expectations.**

But NAFTA and GATT barely passed Congress. Clinton faced strong opposition from liberal Democrats in industrial areas and from labor unions, who feared that these measures would result in jobs going abroad, declining American wages, and a relaxation of environmental controls over companies moving outside U.S. borders. In the first few years of NAFTA and GATT, these fears seemed justified. Some jobs went abroad, and threats of moving gave employers a negotiating edge over workers. In Mexico the impact of NAFTA was even worse. The peso collapsed as money and goods flowed across the border, and the average wages for workers fell from $1.45 to $.78 per hour.

Equally controversial were Clinton's efforts to grant China **most-favored-nation status,** which would designate China as a full trading partner with the United States. Human rights activists argued that China's dismal record of violent suppression and imprisonment of political dissenters should preclude such favorable trading terms. But with an eye to China's huge potential market for American goods and favorable site for U.S.-owned factories, Congress approved Clinton's proposal.

Despite this new alliance with a former foe, Cold War politics did not entirely disappear from foreign policy. The tiny communist nation of Cuba, suffering severe economic hardship since the collapse of its benefactor, the Soviet Union, remained off limits to U.S. trade and tourism. Cuban Americans in southern Florida, who had fled Cuba after Fidel Castro's successful revolution, blocked any efforts to ease relations between the two countries. Democrats as well as Republicans were reluctant to alienate these voters; their numbers and political clout in the most populous part of the nation's fourth largest state gave them considerable power.

Relations between the United States and Cuba were strained anew in November 1999 when a small boat carrying a group of Cubans trying to escape to Florida capsized, drowning everyone aboard except a six-year-old boy, Elian Gonzales, who was found floating on an inner tube off the coast of Florida. Elian's relatives in Miami argued that the boy should stay in the United States, where he could grow up in a democratic society—a goal his mother died trying to achieve. However, his father wanted him back in Cuba, and a court decided that the boy should be returned to his remaining parent. After months of intense media coverage in both countries and futile efforts at negotiation, in April 2000 U.S. government agents

Richard Vogel/AP/Wide World Photos

▲ **Bill Clinton was the first American president to visit Vietnam since 1969. He is pictured here during his historic visit on November 17, 2000, walking with Vietnamese President Tran Duc Luong (left) as they passed Vietnamese soldiers during official welcoming ceremonies.**

stormed the small house where Elian was staying and seized the boy, who eventually returned to Cuba with his father.

Efforts at Peacemaking

Clinton endeavored to ease hostilities in some of the world's most conflict-ridden areas. Northern Ireland had been fraught with violence for 30 years. Irish Catholic nationalists wanted to break ties with England and join the Republic of Ireland; Protestants loyal to Great Britain wanted to remain part of the United Kingdom. The United States, with political and diplomatic connections to London as well as strong ties to the Irish, wanted to help resolve the crisis. Clinton made several trips to Ireland to promote peace. He appointed former Senator George Mitchell of Maine as negotiator, who spent months working on a settlement. Despite dissent and violence by extremists on both sides, by the time Clinton left office, an agreement had been reached that established a shared coalition government.

In the Middle East, Clinton brought Yasser Arafat, leader of the Palestine Liberation Organization (PLO), and Yitzak Rabin, Israeli Prime Minister, to Washington for talks that led to a historic 1993 handshake and pledges to pursue a peace agreement. As in Northern Ireland, those efforts were hampered by violent extremists on both sides. Rabin was assassinated by a fanatical right-wing Israeli, leading to the election of a hawkish new prime minister, Benjamin Netanyahu. The peace process fell apart for several years until negotiations finally resumed in the late 1990s. But just when an agreement seemed to be within reach, large-scale violence between Palestinians and Israelis erupted again in the summer of 2000. Clinton left office with no agreement in sight.

In the final weeks of Clinton's presidency in 2000, he made a historic visit to Vietnam—the first by an American president since the war. Because Clinton had protested against the war decades earlier, his visit held great symbolic power and his was the first administration to reopen formal relations with the Vietnamese government. Although the United States lost the war, westernization had taken hold in Vietnam, with investment beginning to flow in from Europe, the United States, and Japan, as well as American popular culture and technology. Cheering crowds welcomed the president of the superpower that Vietnam had vanquished 25 years earlier.

Military Interventions and International Terrorism

The end of the Cold War raised new questions about how and when to use American military force. Most of the overseas crises stemmed from problems of national disintegration, ethnic conflict, and humanitarian disasters resulting from political chaos and civil wars.

On the Caribbean island of Haiti, a military coup in 1991 had ousted the democratically elected President Jean Bertrand Aristide. In a striking departure from former Cold War policies, Clinton backed the black populist Aristide against the coup leaders, who had strong ties to the CIA. In 1994, the United States received UN support for an invasion to restore Aristide to power. To avert a large-scale military conflict, Clinton sent former President Jimmy Carter to Haiti to negotiate a settlement. The resulting agreement allowed the coup members to leave the country, and Aristide returned. Six years later, however, the United States criticized Aristide for corruption and fraud in his 2000 reelection.

In 1992 President Bush had sent U.S. marines to Somalia in east Africa as part of a UN effort to provide famine relief and to restore peace in the war-torn nation. After Clinton took office, Somali warlord Mohammed Farah Aidid killed 50 Pakistani UN peacekeepers. The U.S. forces then mobilized against Aidid, shifting the peacekeeping mission to military engagement. As part of the effort to hunt down Aidid, U.S. soldiers killed hundreds of Somali citizens, creating intense anti-American sentiment among the population. Amid that hostile atmosphere, in September 1993, Aidid's forces killed 18 American soldiers in a firefight and

▲ **MAP 29.2 THE BREAKUP OF THE FORMER YUGOSLAVIA**
Created in 1919 as a multiethnic nation, Yugoslavia split apart in 1991–1992. After Slovenia and Croatia gained their independence swiftly, Bosnia deteriorated into fierce ethnic fighting dominated by Serb atrocities and encouraged by the Serbian government of Slobodan Milosevic. A brief U.S. bombing campaign in 1995 finally brought the Serbs to peace negotiations. Similar ethnic fighting in the province of Kosovo in 1999 led to another U.S. bombing campaign and Kosovo's quasi-independence under NATO guidance.

dragged the body of one victim through the streets. The outraged American public viewed the grim spectacle on TV, and the experience left Clinton with no clear guidelines on **humanitarian intervention** abroad. Largely as a result of the disaster in Somalia, when ethnic conflict led to genocide in Rwanda in central Africa in 1994, the United States and other western nations refused to intervene.

Ethnic conflict was also the cause of trouble in the Balkans. From 1945 to 1980 Marshal Josip Broz Tito ruled over a unified communist Yugoslavia, maintaining stability by suppressing ethnic rivalries. But after Tito's death in 1980 and the end of the Cold War in 1989, ethnic nationalism pulled Yugoslavia apart, with Slovenia and Croatia breaking away in 1991–1992. The region erupted in bloody conflicts. After sustained Serbian attacks on Muslims in Bosnia between 1992 and 1995, Clinton reluctantly agreed to air strikes against the Serbs, leading to the 1995 Dayton Accords, which brought an end to the war. When Serbian president Slobodan Milosevic embarked on a murderous campaign to drive the majority Muslim ethnic Albanians out of Serbia's southern province of Kosovo, Clinton finally ordered air strikes that forced the Serbs to retreat. Milosevic was voted out of office in 2000. The following year, Serbian authorities arrested Milosevic and turned him over to the War Crimes Tribunal in The Hague, which had indicted Milosevic for crimes against humanity.

The Balkan Proximity Peace Talks Agreement

In some regions of the world, resentment against the United States found expression in violence and terrorism. In June 1996 a truck bomb killed 19 U.S. airmen in Dhahran, Saudi Arabia. Two years later, bombs exploded at two U.S. embassies in east Africa, killing 224 people in Nairobi, Kenya, and Dar es Salaam, Tanzania. Four men were convicted of conspiracy in the terrorist attacks. They were identified as followers of Islamic militant Osama bin Laden, who was also indicted in connection with the embassy bombings. Bin Laden, originally from Saudi Arabia, was living in Afghanistan under the protection of the fundamentalist Taliban regime and remained a fugitive. He was known to be the leader of the Al Qaeda terrorist network operating in several countries throughout the Middle East. On October 12, 2000, a small boat pulled up next to the destroyer USS *Cole* in Yemen's port of Aden. A bomb exploded and ripped a hole in the destroyer, killing 17 Americans and wounding 39 others. Two suicide bombers carried out the attack. U.S. officials believed that they, too, were associated with Osama bin Laden.

Islamic fundamentalists also struck at home. On February 26, 1993, a bomb exploded in the parking garage underneath the World Trade Center, the skyscrapers dominating the New York skyline in Lower Manhattan. Five people were killed and more than a thousand were injured. Eight years later the same twin towers were attacked again, with far more devastating consequences.

The Contested Election of 2000

The first presidential election of the new millennium was the most bitterly contested in more than a century. The Democratic candidate won the national popular vote, but with ballot counts incomplete in the key state of Florida, the Supreme Court ultimately declared the Republican candidate the victor. The election exposed defects in the election process, from faulty ballots and voting machines to the role of the media, and raised serious questions about the value of the electoral college. The election also revealed that flaws in the system disfranchised large numbers of poor and minority voters. But in the end, the transfer of power took place smoothly, and the nation accepted the outcome.

The election exposed defects in the election process, from faulty ballots and voting machines to the role of the media, and raised serious questions about the value of the electoral college.

The Campaign, the Vote, and the Courts

The Democrats nominated Vice President Al Gore, who hoped to benefit from Clinton's high approval rating and the healthy economy. The Republicans nominated George

Voting

One of the most troubling revelations to surface in the wake of the 2000 election was the news that millions of citizens, in Florida and elsewhere, were thwarted in their effort to vote or to have their votes count. Studies conducted after the election showed that 4 to 6 million Americans were disfranchised as a result of faulty equipment, confusing ballots, erroneous voter registration lists, long lines at polling places, and problems with absentee ballots. Voters in low-income precincts with a large percentage of citizens of color were much more likely to have their votes discarded, or to be turned away at the polls, than voters in more affluent and whiter districts. These revelations sparked outrage among Americans who believe that voting is one of the fundamental rights of democratic citizenship. But the disfranchisement of potential voters has a long history in the United States, beginning with the founding of the nation.

The Constitution does not guarantee anyone the right to vote. After the American Revolution, the majority of Americans—including women, slaves, most free black men, propertyless white men, apprentices, indentured laborers, felons, and those considered mentally incompetent—were denied the right to vote. New Jersey was the only state to allow women the vote.

Debates over who should vote, and efforts both to expand and to restrict suffrage, continued for most of the nation's history. During the first half of the nineteenth century, Democrats viewed the vote as a right of all white men, whereas Whigs argued that voting was a privilege to be reserved for the elite. Although the United States was the first western nation to expand the electorate by lowering economic barriers to voting, for a long time after that, the laws governing the right to vote actually limited rather than broadened access to the polls.

Hightower Lowdown 2(12), December 2000, p. 1.

The 2000 election exposed many problems in the voting process. This political cartoon suggests that the controversial Florida ballots and methods of counting them were only the final symptoms of an electoral system that was flawed at many levels.

Between the Revolution and the Civil War, race and gender replaced property as the primary criteria for voting. Nearly every state disfranchised free blacks while dropping the property requirements for white men. States in the West tended toward more inclusive voting rolls. Several gave the vote to aliens who had established permanent residence and to Native Americans who had relinquished tribal citizenship. Some politicians were eager to expand suffrage to portray themselves as champions of the common people and win the votes of the newly enfranchised.

But several states restricted voting well into the twentieth century. Rhode Island required foreign-born citizens to meet a property requirement to vote, and California prevented Asians from voting. In 1921 New York adopted English literacy tests to prevent immigrants from voting, disfranchising hundreds of thousands of citizens as late as the 1960s. As a result of these restrictions, voter turnout began to decline in the late nineteenth century. This shrinking of the electorate was not accidental. In 1907 the voter registration board of Pittsburgh boasted that in only two years the Pennsylvania registration law had cut the number of registered voters in half. Women achieved the right to vote in 1920, but most women of color and many immigrant women remained disfranchised for decades.

African Americans officially gained the right to vote in 1870 with the ratification of the Fifteenth Amendment. But by 1900, almost all blacks as well as poor whites in the South had been disfranchised through poll taxes and literacy and property requirements. Not until passage of the 1965 Voting Rights Act were African Americans in the South able to vote. Suffrage expanded again in 1971 when the Twenty-Sixth Amendment lowered the voting age from 21 to 18. The Vietnam War revived claims made since the Revolution that citizens old enough to fight and die for their country were old enough to vote.

By the time of the 2000 election, universal suffrage was the law of the land. Although only half of all eligible voters went to the polls that year, the number of voters had increased tenfold since 1888. Still, questions remained about the fairness of the process, whether intentional or not. When the winner of the popular vote lost the election to a candidate without a clear victory in the electoral college, critics of the system called for direct election of the president. In the end, however, it was neither the voters nor the electoral college but the justices of the U.S. Supreme Court who elected the president by a vote of 5–4. ■

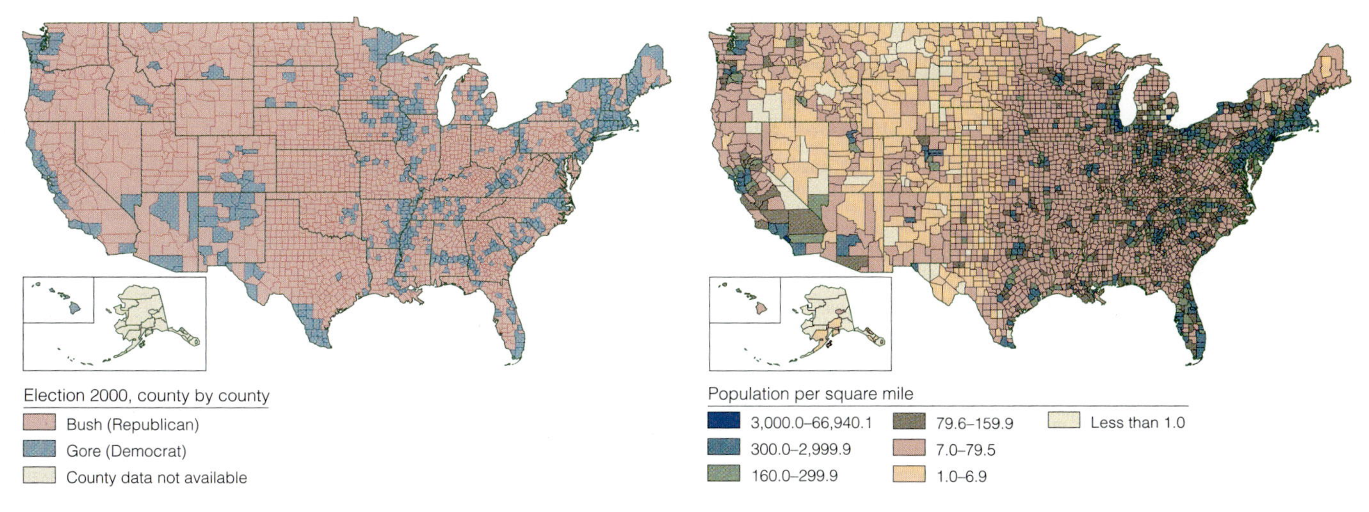

▲ MAP 29.3 THE CONTESTED ELECTION OF 2000
The 2000 election was so close and so fraught with problems that it was ultimately decided by a 5–4 vote of the Supreme Court. As these maps show, Democratic votes were concentrated in the densely populated urban areas and Republican votes in the sparsely populated rural areas.

W. Bush, governor of Texas and son of the former president. Bush chose as his running mate Dick Cheney, who had been the elder Bush's Secretary of State. Gore chose Senator Joe Lieberman from Connecticut as his running mate, the first Jew to run on a presidential ticket.

Only half of the nation's eligible voters turned out to vote. Even before all the polls had closed, the national media began to report the results. Early in the evening, they declared that Florida, a key state with 25 electoral votes, had gone to Gore. But soon after that announcement, they changed their projection and put Florida back into the "undecided" group of states. It became clear that whoever took Florida, where Bush's brother Jeb Bush was governor, would win the election. By the next day, Gore had won the national popular vote by half a million votes, but Bush was ahead in Florida. Bush's lead was so narrow that it triggered an automatic recount.

With all eyes on Florida, a number of serious irregularities surfaced. Voters in Palm Beach County had been given a confusing "butterfly" ballot, resulting in more than 20,000 mismarked ballots. In other counties, registered voters had been turned away at the polls because of inaccurate and incomplete voter registration lists. Some voter lists inaccurately listed eligible voters as felons. Most of these disfranchised voters were African American, who usually voted Democratic. In several largely minority counties, old voting machines that used a punched-ballot system had failed to count thousands of ballots.

For weeks after the election, the outcome was still unknown. Democrats insisted that because Bush's lead had narrowed to a few hundred votes, tallied by inaccurate voting machines, ballots in four Florida counties should be recounted by hand. Republicans pointed out that it would be unfair to recount votes in only four heavily Democratic counties, especially with no standard way of determining voter intent on punch-card ballots with ambiguous marks on them. Florida's secretary of state, Katherine Harris, a Republican who headed Florida's campaign for George W. Bush, refused to extend the deadline to allow the recounts to take place and declared Bush the winner by 537 votes out of 6 million cast statewide.

Gore contested the results, and the Florida Supreme Court ordered that the recount proceed. Bush then appealed to the U.S. Supreme Court to reverse the decision of the Florida Supreme Court. After 36 days of partial vote counting and court battles, a U.S. Supreme Court ruling stopped further vote counting in Florida, effectively giving the presidency to Bush in a sharply divided 5–4 decision, with the most conservative judges voting in favor of Bush. The four dissenting judges issued a stinging rebuke of their five colleagues responsible for the decision. In his dissenting opinion, Justice Stephen Breyer wrote that the majority ruling "can only lend confidence to the most cynical appraisal of the work of judges throughout the land."

The Aftermath

What became clear in the months after the election were the widespread flaws in the election system in Florida and elsewhere. Across the country, outdated voting machines yielded inaccurate vote counts, and long lines at polling places prevented voters from casting ballots. Low-income and minority voters were more likely to be disfranchised because they lived in precincts with faulty voting machines or overcrowded polling places. The U.S. Civil Rights Commission estimated that, in Florida, black voters were nine times more likely than white voters to have had their votes rejected.

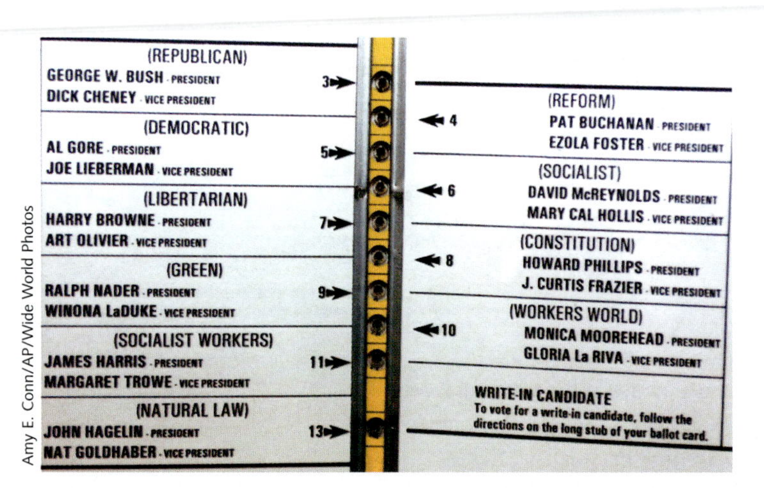

Amy E. Conn/AP/Wide World Photos

▲ **In Palm Beach, Florida, voters received this confusing "butterfly ballot." Thousands of voters in the predominantly Democratic county accidentally voted for Reform candidate Pat Buchanan instead of Democrat Al Gore. With only a few hundred votes separating Bush and Gore in Florida, it is quite possible that the butterfly ballot may have cost Gore the election.**

In addition to those whose votes did not count, many others were prevented from voting altogether. In Florida, "suspected felons" were removed from voter registration lists without being informed and without the opportunity to demonstrate that they were law-abiding citizens eligible to vote. An estimated 15 percent of the list was inaccurate, and more than half of those voters were African American. According to the U.S. Civil Rights Commission, "Perhaps the most dramatic undercount in Florida's election was the non-existent ballots of countless unknown eligible voters, who were turned away, or wrongfully purged from the voter registration rolls...and were prevented from exercising the franchise." As a result, hundreds of African American citizens with no criminal record arrived at the polls, only to discover that they had been disfranchised. An investigation by scholars of constitutional law concluded that the disfranchisement of African American voters in Florida constituted a violation of the 1965 Voting Rights Act. They determined that if those African American voters had been able to cast ballots, they would have provided more than the 537 votes Gore needed to win.

The election also renewed a national debate over the value of the electoral college. Opponents argued that Gore was the rightful winner because he won a majority of the popular vote. Advocates claimed that the electoral college protected the interests of less populous states and that Bush was fairly elected because he won the majority of states. Congress and state legislatures began discussions of various forms of electoral reform, but abolishing the electoral college was not among them. Representatives of small states would likely block any such measures.

Policymakers and media moguls also debated the role of the media in reporting election returns. Some argued for a blackout on early returns until all polls across the country were closed, to avoid the possibility that early results might influence voters who had not yet voted. Others proposed that only official results be announced, to avoid the problem of erroneous reporting that occurred on election night 2000. But media representatives countered that a free press should be able to report the news as it happens, although they agreed on the need to ensure accuracy.

Legacies of Election 2000

In addition to the unprecedented Supreme Court decision, the 2000 election was remarkable in other ways. For the first time, a First Lady was elected to public office: Hillary Rodham Clinton became a Democratic senator from New York. In another Senate race, a deceased candidate was elected. Mel Carnahan, Democratic governor of Missouri, had run against Republican incumbent senator John Ashcroft. But Carnahan died in a plane crash a few weeks before the election, too late to have his name removed from the ballot. The acting governor pledged to appoint Carnahan's widow if he won the election, and she picked up the campaign. Carnahan was elected and his widow went to the Senate. (The defeated candidate, John Ashcroft, became George W. Bush's attorney general.)

For the first time, a First Lady was elected to public office: Hillary Rodham Clinton became a Democratic senator from New York.

Third-party politics also critically influenced the outcome of the presidential election. Several third-party candidates had achieved national visibility during the 1990s and won elections at the state and local levels, including professional wrestler Jesse Ventura, elected governor of Minnesota in 1998 on the Reform party ticket. In 2000 Ralph Nader wreaked havoc for the Democrats with his Green party candidacy for president. Although Nader gained fewer than 3 percent of the votes, his candidacy drew off some of the left-leaning elements of the Democratic party—enough votes to cost Al Gore the election.

The election results left the Congress almost evenly divided, with a thin Republican majority in the House and a 50–50 split in the Senate. Within a year, Senator James M. Jeffords from Vermont bolted the Republican party and became an Independent, giving the Democrats a majority in the Senate. The closely divided Congress began to take up issues raised by the contested election, including various measures to improve the voting process, and campaign finance reform.

President George W. Bush immediately began to reverse several Clinton-era policies, including a number of environmental protections. His first major legislative success was the passage of a major tax cut. During his first year in office, the economy went from boom to bust and headed into a recession. The robust stock market of the 1990s wilted in early 2001. Nevertheless, as the new millennium dawned, the United States remained the wealthiest and most powerful nation in the world. Bush retreated from international treaties on issues ranging from global warming to nuclear test ban agreements, and he revived the Reagan-era proposal for a nuclear missile shield. But the place of the nation in the global community was yet to be defined. Soon, monumental events shattered the nation's sense of security and prompted Bush to engage in the world in unprecedented ways.

Conclusion

In the 1990s the role of the nation in the world shifted and a half-century of political certainties evaporated. The end of the Cold War meant that the United States had to develop a new international mission. The struggle against the Soviet Union and the communist foe had come to an end. Russia was our friend; China was our trading partner. With the Cold War now over, conflicts around the globe, many of them grounded in ancient ethnic and religious hostilities, posed challenges for the world's most powerful nation. The United States focused on markets and trade, the nation's supply of oil, the need for political order to maintain international stability, and the danger of **rogue nations** developing nuclear arms. President Clinton promoted peace initiatives in Northern Ireland and the Middle East, although conflicts in those regions persisted.

At home, Americans demonstrated increasing tolerance for people who looked and acted differently from themselves. Polls showed declining levels of racial, ethnic, and religious hostility and greater acceptance of homosexuality, single parenthood, and family arrangements that deviated from the nuclear family model. But episodes of racial discrimination—by police, courts, and voting officials—continued. Politics remained an arena in which culture wars flared over abortion, gun control, and welfare reform. A Democratic president faced impeachment by his Republican foes in Congress while maintaining high approval ratings from the public.

At the dawn of the new century, several crises challenged Americans' sense of security. A deeply flawed presidential election revealed profound problems in the nation's voting system. A sharp and sudden downturn in the economy shattered the optimism many middle-class people felt during the booming Clinton years and forced many of the working poor into desperate circumstances. Already reeling from these disturbing developments, the nation was soon shaken to its core by a terrorist attack that forced a new reckoning at home and abroad.

Sites to Visit

William Jefferson Clinton

www.ipl.org/ref/POTUS/wjclinton.html

This site contains basic information about Clinton's election and presidency and an online biography.

Distribution of Wealth and Income

www.inequality.org/factsfr.html

This site provides facts and figures about the distribution of wealth and income in the 1990s.

American Identities

xroads.virginia.edu/~YP/ethnic.html

This site of the American Studies program at the University of Virginia includes information and resources for studying America's multiple ethnic identities.

The O. J. Simpson Trial

www.cnn.com/US/OJ/index.html

This CNN site provides basic facts and interpretive essays, plus additional links about the O. J. Simpson trial.

Investigating the President: The Trial

www.cnn.com/ALLPOLITICS/resources/1998/lewinsky/

This CNN site provides information and documents about the scandals surrounding President Clinton's impeachment.

Focus on Kosovo

www.cnn.com/SPECIALS/1998/10/kosovo/

This in-depth CNN interactive site looks at the development and resolution of the turmoil in Kosovo.

Oklahoma City Bombing

www.cnn.com/US/9703/okc.trial/

This CNN interactive site has information about the domestic terrorist bombing in Oklahoma City and the trial that followed.

Why Do Campaign Polls Zigzag So Much?

www.psych.purdue.edu/%7Ecodelab/Invalid.Polls.html

This site, created by Gerald S. Wasserman of the Psychological Sciences Department at Purdue University, examines polling data from the 1996 presidential campaign.

For Further Reading

General

Stephanie Coontz, *The Way We Really Are: Coming to Terms with America's Changing Families* (1997).

Thomas L. Friedman, *The Lexus and the Olive Tree: Understanding Globalization* (2000).

Clara E. Rodriguez, *Changing Race: Latinos, the Census and the History of Ethnicity in the United States* (2000).

Leland T. Saito and Roger Daniels, *Race and Politics: Asian Americans, Latinos, and Whites in a Los Angeles Suburb* (1998).

The Economy: Global and Domestic

Sheldon Danziger and Peter Gottschalk, *America Unequal* (1995).

Julia Butterfly Hill, *The Legacy of Luna: The Story of a Tree, a Woman, and the Struggle to Save the Redwoods* (2000).

Jacqueline Jones, *American Work: Four Centuries of Black and White Labor* (1998).

William A. Orme, *Understanding NAFTA: Mexico, Free Trade, and the New North America* (1996).

Tolerance and Its Limits

Jeffrey Abramson, ed., *Postmortem: The O.J. Simpson Case: Justice Confronts Race, Domestic Violence, Lawyers, Money, and the Media* (1996).

Robin D. G. Kelley, *Yo' Mama's Disfunktional!: Fighting the Culture Wars in Urban America* (1998).

Jane Mayer and Jill Abramson, *Strange Justice: The Selling of Clarence Thomas* (1994).

Michael Omi and Howard Winant, *Racial Formation in the United States: From the 1960s to the 1990s* (1994).

Alan Wolfe, *One Nation, After All: What Americans Really Think About God, Country, Family, Racism, Welfare, Immigration, Homosexuality, Work, the Right, the Left and Each Other* (1998).

Violence and Danger

Joan Jacobs Brumberg, *Fasting Girls: The History of Anorexia Nervosa* (2000).

Joan Jacobs Brumberg, *The Body Project: An Intimate History of American Girls* (2000).

Susan Faludi, *Stiffed: The Betrayal of the American Man* (1999).

Peter D. Kramer, *Listening to Prozac* (1997).

Rickie Solinger, ed., *Abortion Wars: A Half Century of Struggle, 1950–2000* (1998).

Judith Stacey, *In the Name of the Family: Rethinking Family Values in the Postmodern Age* (1996).

Steven Wisotsky and Thomas Szasz, *Beyond the War on Drugs: Overcoming a Failed Public Policy* (1999).

The Clinton Presidency

William C. Berman, *From the Center to the Edge: The Politics and Policies of the Clinton Presidency* (2001).

James MacGregor Burns and Georgia J. Sorenson, *Dead Center: Clinton-Gore Leadership and the Perils of Moderation* (1999).

Bill Clinton, *My Life* (2004).

Steven E. Schier, ed., *The Postmodern Presidency: Bill Clinton's Legacy in U.S. Politics* (2000).

The Nation and the World

John Dumbrell and David M. Barrett, *The Making of U.S. Foreign Policy* (1998).

Thomas H. Henriksen, *Clinton's Foreign Policy in Somalia, Bosnia, Haiti, and North Korea* (1996).

Richard A. Melanson, *American Foreign Policy Since the Vietnam War: The Search for Consensus from Nixon to Clinton* (2001).

The Contested Election of 2000

Alan M. Dershowitz, *Supreme Injustice: How the High Court Hijacked Election 2000* (2001).

E. J. Dionne and William Kristol, eds., *Bush v. Gore: The Court Cases and the Commentary* (2001).

Alexander Keyssar, *The Right to Vote: The Contested History of Democracy in the United States* (2000).

Charles Lewis, *The Buying of the President 2000* (2001).

Richard A. Posner, *Breaking the Deadlock: The 2000 Election, the Constitution, and the Courts* (2001).

Bill Sammon, *At Any Cost: How Al Gore Tried to Steal the Election* (2001).

CHAPTER 30

A Global Nation for the New Millennium

CHAPTER OUTLINE

The George W. Bush Administration

America's Place in a Global Economy

The Stewardship of Natural Resources

The Expansion of American Popular Culture Abroad

Identity in Contemporary America

Conclusion

Sites to Visit

For Further Reading

Nam June Paik, *Global Encoder*, 1994. Courtesy of Nam June Paik and Carl Solway Gallery, Cincinnati, Ohio. Photo by Tom Allison and Chris Gomien

▲ At the beginning of the new millennium, computer technology and the Internet linked Americans closely to each other and to events around the globe. Electronic circuitry enabled information to flow at a pace unimaginable to previous generations.

WHAT HELD AMERICANS TOGETHER AS THEY SET OFF INTO THE TWENTY-FIRST CENTURY was a common loyalty to a set of ideas about economic opportunities and individual liberties. Unlike such nations as Germany and Israel, where citizenship was extended automatically to people of a certain ethnicity, the United States awarded citizenship to those who were born within its borders, regardless of ethnicity or race. Those born elsewhere became citizens on the basis not of their past lineage but of their future commitments—of their newly sworn loyalty to the U.S. Constitution, with its guarantees of freedom and its responsibilities of citizenship. In a vast society of multiple political and cultural beliefs, the scope of specific freedoms and the nature of individual responsibilities inevitably remained matters of ongoing tension and conflict. Nonetheless, the United States continued to address most of its problems through an orderly legal system, in contrast to the ethnic and religious strife marking so many of the world's nations.

That strife from abroad impinged on Americans in a shocking new way on September 11, 2001. On a sunny Tuesday morning, 19 hijackers—four of them trained as pilots—seized control simultaneously of four large commercial jets and turned them into suicidal missiles. At 8:48 a.m., one flew into the 110-story north tower of New York City's World Trade Center, igniting an enormous fireball. Fifteen minutes later, the second plane flew into the south tower. In less than two hours, both towers collapsed, killing the thousands of people still inside. Among the dead were hundreds of firefighters, police officers, and other rescue workers who had raced into the towers to evacuate the occupants. The third plane flew into the Pentagon. The fourth was also being directed toward Washington, apparently to destroy the White House or the Capitol Building, but when the passengers rushed the hijackers in the cockpit, the plane crashed in a field 75 miles southeast of Pittsburgh.

Val McClatchey

Smoke rises from the crash of United Airlines Flight 93 near Shanksville, Pennsylvania. For almost all Americans, the hijackings and destruction of September 11, 2001, came indeed out of a clear blue sky. Anti-American actions of the previous decade by Islamic terrorists had created little anxiety in a powerful nation that had imagined itself safe from major attack.

The carefully coordinated assaults killed some 3,000 people, destroyed the two tallest buildings in the country's largest city, and left a gaping hole in the headquarters of the nation's military command. Not since the Japanese assault on Pearl Harbor 60 years earlier had the United States experienced such a devastating attack on its soil. During the intervening half-century of the Cold War, the Soviet Union and other communist forces had never attempted direct aggression against the American homeland. Who was responsible for the most horrific act of terrorism against civilians in U.S. history?

The 19 perpetrators were self-styled holy warriors of a secretive, extremist Islamic organization known as Al Qaeda, organized by wealthy, charismatic Saudi Arabian expatriate Osama bin Laden. Al Qaeda worked out of Afghanistan, hosted by the most repressive Islamic government on Earth, the Taliban, which rose to power in 1996 out of the chaos that followed the withdrawal of the Soviet army in 1989. The rage of bin Laden and other Islamic terrorists against the United States had been building throughout the 1990s, fueled by the presence of "infidel" American troops in Saudi Arabia since the 1991 Persian Gulf War, by American support for Israel, and by the rapid spread of secular American popular culture around the globe. At odds with moderate Islamic mainstream thought throughout the world, bin Laden announced in 1998: "To kill Americans and their allies is an individual duty of every Muslim who is able."

At the heart of American society remained a common assumption, that the United States is a democratic country. The events on United Airlines Flight 93, one of the four doomed planes on September 11, 2001, revealed the tenacity of the belief in majority rule. After the hijackers seized control and herded the passengers into the rear of the cabin, a dozen passengers and crew members were able to communicate by phone with people on the ground. They learned that two other planes had already crashed into the World Trade Center towers in New York City, and they realized that these hijackers—unlike previous ones who sought concrete gains and an escape—planned only destruction for them all. Face to face with imminent death and the certainty that many others would perish if they failed to act, the passengers discussed what to do. They made a plan to rush the hijackers, led by several large, athletic passengers, including Mark Bingham, a prominent gay businessperson and rugby player from San Francisco. Should they proceed? Quintessential Americans, they took a vote. GTE Airfone operator Lisa Jefferson heard the rest: "Are you guys ready?" asked Todd Beamer, a tall father of two from Cranbury, New Jersey. Screams and a sustained scuffle followed before the line went dead. The plane, headed for the heart of Washington, crashed in an unpopulated part of western Pennsylvania with no casualties on the ground.

The events on United Airlines Flight 93, one of the four doomed planes on September 11, 2001, revealed the tenacity of the belief in majority rule.

The George W. Bush Administration

The attacks of September 11, 2001, constituted perhaps the most significant event in American life since Japan's surrender in 1945. People remember where they were when they first learned what had happened, and they recall vividly the terrible televised images of destruction. As citizens of the sole remaining superpower after the collapse of the Soviet Union in 1991, Americans had grown accustomed to unprecedented global power and influence. They had no great power rival. For most of those ten years, they had experienced rapid economic growth as well. The nation, it seemed, was wealthy and secure.

The events on September 11 changed all that. The economy, already sliding into recession, accelerated its downward course. Just seven months in office, the administration of President George W. Bush responded by leading the nation into a "war on terrorism" abroad and at home. Within two years, U.S.-led efforts succeeded in overthrowing the governments of Afghanistan and Iraq. Complicated, long-term military occupations ensued, with U.S. forces continuing to engage in bloody battles against insurgents in both countries. In an effort to prevent further terrorist attacks at home, Congress passed the "USA Patriot Act," granting greater powers to the executive branch of the federal government. Authorities detained hundreds of immigrants, primarily young men of Middle Eastern descent. These policies then faced the test of public approval in the elections of November 2004.

The President and the War on Terrorism

George W. Bush did not have an auspicious record of achievement before his election as governor of Texas in 1994 and as president of the United States six years later. He certainly had opportunities. He grew up primarily in Midland, Texas, the grandson of a U.S. senator from Connecticut and the eldest son of a wealthy oilman, diplomat, and eventual U.S. president, George H. W. Bush. "W.," as he was sometimes called to distinguish him from his father, attended the elite Phillips Academy in Andover, Massachusetts, and he earned degrees from

Yale and Harvard Business School, though his modest academic achievements hinted at the benefits of unofficial forms of affirmative action for the scions of wealthy and powerful families. His sociability and charisma earned him many friends. He avoided going to Vietnam when he was of draft age by serving in the Air National Guard, though he apparently failed to show up for much of a year of that service in 1972.

After a mixed career in business and a strong taste for the partying life, Bush gave up drinking at age 40 and became a devout, conservative Christian. This ambitious and now more serious man made his way up in Republican political circles, benefiting from family connections as well as a warm, "regular guy" personality that appealed to many working-class Americans. His awkward public syntax caused him to be, in his words, "misunderestimated" by many. Despite his father's strongly international orientation, Bush himself before his presidency had left the United States only three times to go anywhere besides Mexico. "I'm not going to play like a person who has spent hours involved with foreign policy," he admitted during the 2000 campaign. Once president, he took a unilateralist and almost isolationist stance, to the dismay of close U.S. allies abroad. The United States rejected or withdrew from international agreements limiting global warming, weapons testing, and war crime prosecutions.

George W. Bush, Address to Congress (September 20, 2001)

The events of September 11 stunned all Americans and gave the president a new focus. Finding and destroying Al Qaeda and its allies was now "the purpose of this administration," Bush told his cabinet. He became more openly religious in his public addresses, urging Americans to remember that "our calling as a blessed country is to make this world better." Four weeks after the attacks on New York and Washington, U.S. planes initiated the "war on terrorism" by bombing Taliban and Al Qaeda positions in Afghanistan. By October 19, U.S. special operations forces were working on the ground with anti-Taliban Afghan insurgents. Several European nations provided troops and other military assistance. By December, the Taliban had been driven from power throughout the country, and U.S. and allied forces had killed and captured hundreds of Taliban and Al Qaeda fighters. Many of the prisoners were transferred to the U.S. naval base at Guantanamo Bay, Cuba, to be held indefinitely and interrogated as "enemy combatants." Despite continued pursuit and a reward offer of $25 million, the United States was not able to find Osama bin Laden, who was assumed to be hiding in the remote, snowy mountains of the Pakistan-Afghanistan border region.

Security and Politics at Home

The war on terrorism was not only a foreign affair. Just as the onset of the Cold War in the late 1940s had incorporated a hunt for domestic traitors, the war on terrorism in the early 2000s included a search for potential Al Qaeda sympathizers at home. Like the Cold War, the war on terrorism was framed as a long-term struggle against a maniacal, evil enemy who would not be easily defeated. Indeed, also as in the Cold War, American leaders announced that some civil liberties would have to be curtailed in order to protect the nation. The USA Patriot Act of October 2001 increased the U.S. Justice Department's range of options for spying on and detaining citizens and noncitizens suspected of pro-terrorist activities. Determined to prevent another major terrorist attack, Attorney General John Ashcroft oversaw the arrest of hundreds of illegal immigrants and their imprisonment in what the Justice Department later admitted were often unduly harsh conditions—not unlike Guantanamo, observers noted. Congress created the Department of Homeland Security (DHS) in an effort to better coordinate intelligence, police, and military authorities for defending the nation from future attacks.

Like the Cold War, the war on terrorism was framed as a long-term struggle against a maniacal, evil enemy who would not be easily defeated.

Beyond terrorism, George W. Bush sought to move the nation in the direction of what he called "compassionate conservatism." Unlike his father, George H. W. Bush, who served as Ronald Reagan's vice president for eight years but turned out to be more moderate once in the Oval Office himself, the younger Bush's administration—in the approving words of a conservative activist—turned out to be "more Reaganite

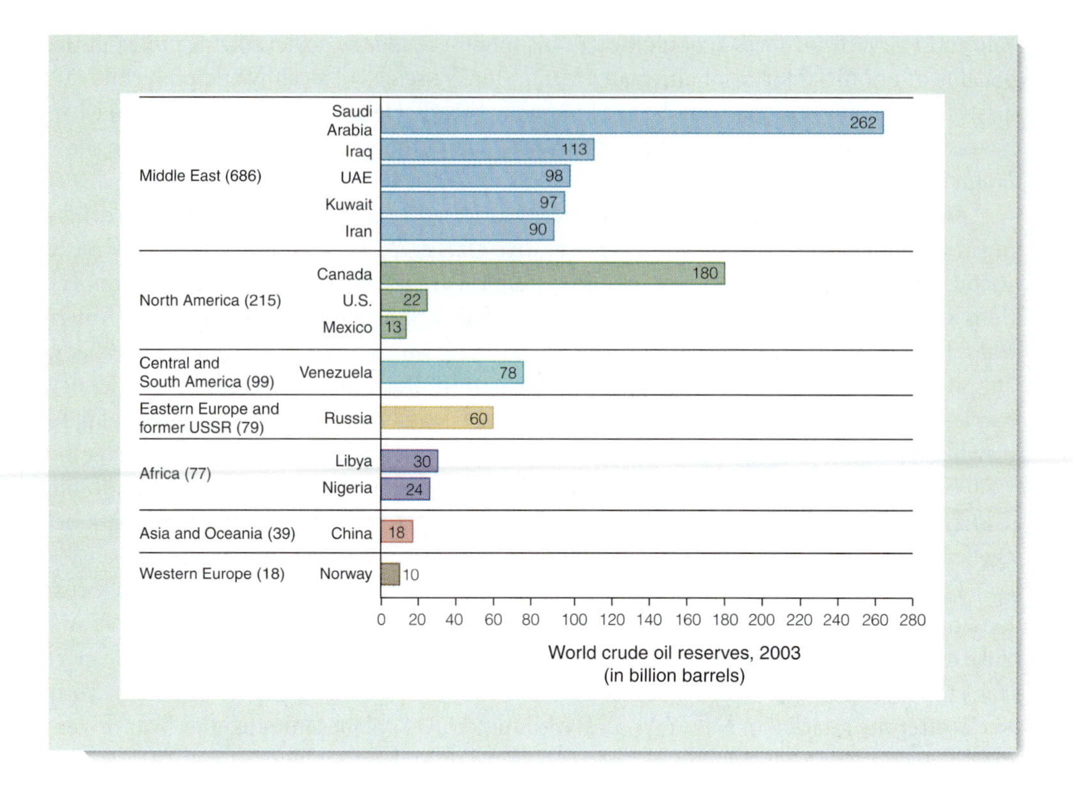

▶ **FIGURE 30.1** WORLD CRUDE OIL RESERVES, 2003 (IN BILLION BARRELS)

than the Reagan administration." In the economic realm, this meant promoting the private sector and reducing federal spending on social programs for the poor. It meant reducing the government's role in regulating health and safety issues in the workplace. And it meant pushing large tax cuts through Congress in 2001 and 2003 to the disproportionate benefit of the wealthiest 1 percent of Americans. The budget surpluses of Bill Clinton's last years disappeared, as the Bush administration ran enormous annual deficits by retaining the tax cuts while sharply increasing military spending. The nation's debt grew rapidly under Bush, restricting options for solving current social problems and burdening future generations. Multimillionaire Vice President Dick Cheney claimed that "Reagan proved deficits don't matter"—at least not to affluent Americans.

Bush's conservatism did not include conserving natural resources. Former oil executives Bush and Cheney were closely allied with corporate interests, particularly in the energy business, that sought easier access to public resources. The administration promoted oil drilling offshore and in the Arctic National Wildlife Refuge, encouraged mining and timber clear-cutting across western federal lands, and refused to regulate carbon dioxide emissions despite overwhelming evidence of global warming. The administration also loosened federal regulations on industrial air pollution, on water pollution by the coal industry, and on arsenic levels in drinking water. It eased off Clinton-era efforts to enforce an array of environmental standards. Northeastern moderate Republicans, such as Representative Sherwood Boehlert of New York and Senator Lincoln Chafee of Rhode Island, found themselves increasingly isolated in a party now far distant from its conservationist heritage in Theodore Roosevelt's presidency.

Sexual issues remained flashpoints of political controversy. Explicit and suggestive sexuality pervaded popular culture, including two-thirds of television shows, causing particular concern among parents of young children. At the same time, Americans were increasingly accepting of homosexual couples. In *Lawrence v. Texas* (2003), the U.S. Supreme Court overturned state laws banning private homosexual behavior between consenting adults. A year later, Massachusetts legalized gay marriage. Wal-Mart, the nation's largest private employer, expanded its antidiscrimination policy to include gay and lesbian workers. One-third of the nation's largest companies now offered employees in same-sex marriages or committed relationships the same benefits and supports, such as health care insurance, that they offered employees with traditional families. President Bush opposed gay marriage on the grounds that marriage between a man and a woman was "one of the most fundamental, enduring institutions of our civilization." But marriage and family remained social institutions in transition, for better or worse: only 56 percent of adults were now married, compared with 75 percent 30 years earlier. And only 26 percent of American households consisted of a married couple with children.

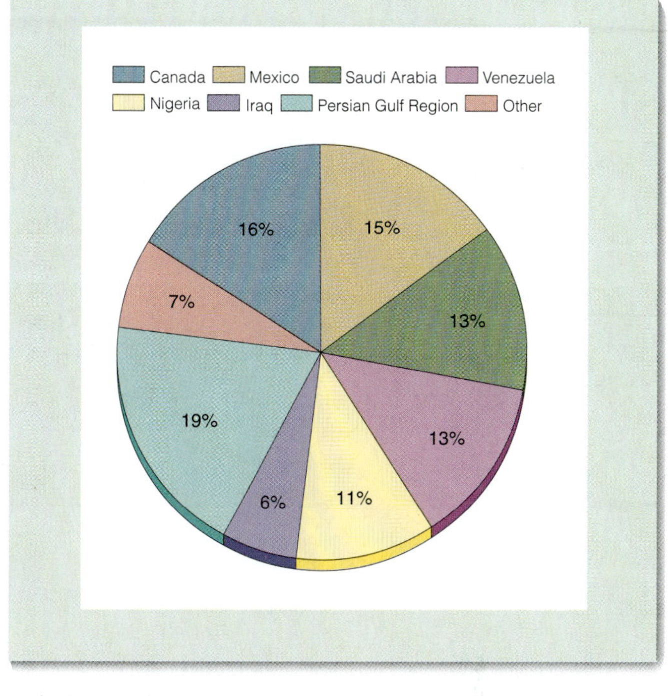

▲ **FIGURE 30.2** U.S. PETROLEUM IMPORTS BY LEADING COUNTRIES OF ORIGIN, APRIL 2004

Source: U.S. Department of Enerergy, Energy Information Administration (www.eia.doe.gov).

The War in Iraq

President Bush's most momentous decision was to invade and occupy Iraq in the spring of 2003. This was a very different proposition than the attack on Afghanistan. The effort to destroy Al Qaeda and its Taliban hosts in Afghanistan had widespread support in the United States and across much of the world. By contrast, invading a sovereign nation that had not attacked or even threatened the United States divided Americans and alienated most of the rest of the world. The United Nations refused to support the invasion. America's western European allies were dismayed. Among America's major allies, only the British government of Prime Minister Tony Blair provided enthusiastic political support and a significant number of troops. Given this lack of support, why did the Bush administration invade Iraq?

Some observers pointed to personal reasons. Bush would be "finishing" the Persian Gulf War of 1991, when his father oversaw the liberation of Kuwait from Saddam Hussein's invading Iraqi forces but did not send troops to Baghdad to overthrow Saddam. Bush would also be avenging Saddam's effort to assassinate the elder Bush on a visit to Kuwait. Other observers emphasized the centrality of Iraq's oil reserves, the largest in the world after those of Saudi Arabia and Canada. The president himself claimed two primary reasons for the invasion: that Saddam possessed "weapons of mass destruction"—chemical, biological, or nuclear—and could attack the United States or its allies "on any given day," and that Iraq had ties to Al Qaeda "and was equally as bad, equally as evil and equally as destructive." But after U.S. forces occupied Iraq, these two official reasons for the war were placed in doubt. U.S. troops found no weapons of mass destruction (though Saddam had indeed used chemical weapons on dissident Iraqi civilians 15 years earlier), and Secretary of State Colin Powell admitted there was no "smoking gun" proof of a link between Al Qaeda's religious zealots and Saddam's fiercely secular dictatorship. The bipartisan reports of both the 9/11 Commission and the Senate Intelligence Committee in 2004 found that the primary reasons the president gave for invading Iraq were not true.

A deeper reason for the U.S. invasion of Iraq appeared to be the administration's view of September 11 as an opportunity to preemptively reshape the Middle East into a region less hostile to the United States and Israel. A liberated Iraq, right in the center of the Middle East, might have a "demonstration effect" of pro-American capitalist democracy that would turn the rest of the region away from authoritarianism and Islamic revolution. Bush spoke of the overthrow of Saddam as "a watershed event in the global democratic revolution." This statement represented a highly optimistic view of how Americans might bring change to the Middle East, part of a new U.S. strategic doctrine emphasizing preemptive action against the nation's enemies. "We must

▲ **MAP 30.1 IRAQ AND THE MIDDLE EAST**

The U.S. invasion and occupation of Iraq in the spring of 2003 put more than 100,000 American soldiers in the center of the volatile Middle East. The Bush administration hoped their presence would influence other nations in the region to reduce their support for anti-American and anti-Israeli terrorism and to move toward greater political and economic liberty. Whether this would happen, or whether the U.S. troops would instead become a magnet for anti-American insurgents from around the region, remained unclear at the end of 2004. Most Middle Easterners continued to see Israeli policies in the Palestinian-Israeli conflict as the key problem in the region.

take the battle to the enemy" in the war on terrorism, Bush declared in 2002, "and confront the worst threats before they emerge." Terrorism was now "a permanent condition," and indeed Islamic terrorists continued to unleash attacks in nations as varied as Indonesia, Kenya, Turkey, Saudi Arabia, Spain, and Israel. The most powerful nation in the world therefore had to go on the offensive, the president announced, a prospect that startled most other countries and contributed to a building wave of anti-American sentiment. This feeling grew particularly strong in Muslim nations, where Bush was believed to be targeting all Muslims rather than just terrorists.

The U.S.-led offensive in Iraq that began on March 19, 2003, was a successful military action. Some 200,000 U.S. and British troops, with a few other allied forces, overran Saddam's defenses and occupied the entire nation of 25 million people within four weeks. The rapid military victory and the presence of so many U.S. troops initially stunned neighboring Iran and Syria into reducing aid to anti-Israeli terrorist groups. Most Iraqis celebrated their liberation from Saddam's brutal regime, and many seemed to welcome the American soldiers. Seven months later, U.S. soldiers captured Saddam himself.

Behrouz Mehri, Agence France-Presse/Getty Images

▲ **Nothing undercut the U.S. effort to extend its influence in the Middle East more than the photographs that emerged in the spring of 2004 of U.S. troops abusing Iraqi detainees at Abu Ghraib prison outside Baghdad. Here, two of these photographs are displayed on a street in neighboring Iran. The Abu Ghraib scandal dismayed America's allies, enraged Muslims everywhere, and almost certainly enhanced Al Qaeda recruiting. An Iraqi-American observed that the Bush administration had "done a good job of occupying the land of Iraq, but a horrible job of occupying the hearts of the Iraqi people."**

But military occupations rarely age well, especially without sufficient troops for the task. Widespread looting ravaged Baghdad, and essential services and personal security deteriorated in the aftermath of the old government's defeat. "Baghdad," one gasoline station owner observed, "is like the Wild West now." Saddam loyalists, Iraqi nationalists of various stripes, and arriving foreign Islamic revolutionaries initiated a multi-sided insurgency against the American occupiers. The number of U.S. and Iraqi deaths shot upward, as did the number of American troops sent to Iraq. The U.S. invasion of Iraq seemed to be increasing rather than reducing the threat of terrorism to Americans and others. Indeed, some observers suggested that Osama bin Laden might be pleased to have so many U.S. troops trying to control an unhappy Muslim population for the stimulus it provided to recruiting anti-American jihadists. One CIA officer noted that, for bin Laden, the invasion and occupation of Iraq was like "a Christmas present you long for but never expected to receive." Critics of U.S. postwar planning now included some prominent Republicans, and the commander of allied forces in Iraq, General Ricardo Sanchez, told Americans flatly "we're still at war."

The Bush administration turned over official sovereignty to a new Iraqi government on June 28, 2004, with 130,000 U.S. troops remaining in the country in an effort to provide security against insurgents. "We don't do empire," insisted Secretary of Defense Donald Rumsfeld. But two months earlier, photographs and eyewitness reports were made public of U.S. troops abusing, torturing, and sexually humiliating Iraqi detainees at the Abu Ghraib prison outside Baghdad. After a week's delay, the president finally apologized. For most Middle Easterners and for Muslims around the world, however, this was compelling evidence that Bush's rhetoric about liberating Iraq was merely a cover for what they saw as fundamental American disrespect and disdain for Muslims.

The Election of 2004

President Bush entered his campaign for reelection with solid support in his own party but mixed reviews from others. Many other nations considered the U.S. attack on Iraq to be unjustified and unwise. Western Europeans resented Bush's lack of interest in their concerns, making him perhaps the least-popular American president in Europe in 80 years. Less than three years after the attacks of September 11, 2001, Americans still tended to support him on foreign policy matters. But many voters were troubled by the growing insurgency in Iraq and by a still-weak economy, and the president's approval ratings remained below 50 percent.

The Democratic Party hoped to exploit Bush's vulnerability. Former Vermont governor Howard Dean railed against the president and the war and created an early wave of enthusiasm in the Democratic primaries. The upbeat charm and poverty-to-riches personal story of first-term U.S. Senator John Edwards of North Carolina earned him the vice-presidential nomination. But for the top of their ticket, Democrats rallied to the candidacy of Senator John Kerry of Massachusetts, a decorated Vietnam War hero with a moderately liberal legislative record. Bush and Kerry had graduated from Yale within two years of each other, and both had very wealthy families. Democratic party activists hoped to blunt the appeal of the president's "war on terrorism" and emphasis on patriotism by nominating a man whose courage under fire in Vietnam contrasted with Bush's safe spot in the Texas National Guard during that war.

It did not quite work. The president prevailed in a narrow popular-vote victory of 51 percent to Kerry's 48 percent, a contrast to Bush's defeat in the popular vote in the 2000 election. The Electoral College outcome of 2004 hinged on Ohio, where a difference of 136,000 votes put Bush over the top. Two issues predominated in the minds of the majority of voters. One was the war on terrorism, which they tended to see as the same as the war in Iraq (despite evidence to the contrary) and on which they trusted Bush's leadership more than Kerry's. The second was what voters described as "moral values," a sense that Bush—even if they sometimes did not agree with his specific policy choices—had personal integrity, a quality they were less sure

AP/Wide World Photos

▲ Citizens stand in line for their chance to vote on November 2, 2004. A hard-fought campaign and anxieties about the war in Iraq contributed to a relatively strong turnout of 59 percent of registered voters.

of with Kerry's nuanced views of complicated policy issues. Christian conservatives were particularly important in getting Republican voters to the polls, passing initiatives in 11 states to ban gay marriage and winning four new seats in the Senate and four in the House to give the president a larger majority in Congress.

▲ The U.S.-Mexico border divides a great deal of wealth from stark poverty. Here a shack in Ciudad Juarez contrasts with El Paso in the background. But the border region from Texas to California is also a vibrant economy where the languages and cultures of the two countries mix in fascinating ways.

America's Place in a Global Economy

Mollie Brown grew up in the small Virginia town of Cartersville, 45 miles west of Richmond. In 1950, at age 19, she moved to Paterson, New Jersey, joining the broad river of black Southerners who sought better economic opportunities and greater personal freedom in the North. There she married Sam James, another migrant from Virginia, who worked at a foundry in Paterson, and together they raised four children. A working mother, like most African American women, Mollie James took a job in 1955 with the Universal Manufacturing Company in Paterson, where the wages and decent treatment were unlike what had been available to her in Virginia. She stayed with Universal for 34 years, becoming its first female union steward and one of its first black union stewards. With union-negotiated wages, overtime work, and company-paid health insurance, she helped pull her family into the middle-class world of owning their own home and car and saving for retirement. But the peace of mind that came from a secure job vanished in 1989 when Universal closed the Paterson plant and moved its manufacturing operations to Matamoros, Mexico, just across the Rio Grande River from Brownsville, Texas.

"On the Internet, nobody knows you're a dog."

◄ The Internet provides both immediate connections with other people around the world and the safety of personal anonymity. Internet users cannot be judged by their appearance or material possessions, only by the words they type. Many Americans debate whether the popularity of the Internet represents a new kind of virtual community that will strengthen their connections to each other, or merely another way for citizens to remain isolated in their own homes rather than engaged with each other in civic organizations.

The Internet and the World Wide Web

For students entering college after the mid-1990s, the Internet and the World Wide Web were an integral part of daily life. Electronic mail (e-mail) made communicating with friends and relatives easy and nearly instantaneous, whether they were on the same college campus or on the other side of the world. The Web transformed the availability of information about nearly all subjects. The foremost symbol of the process of globalization, it linked people everywhere who had access to computers, reducing the importance of a person's geographic location.

The Web had limitations: Internet access remained disproportionately available to people with higher incomes, and there were no controls on the accuracy or usefulness of the information it carried. Risks accompanied the Web as well, including the dissemination of pornography to children, the emergence of sexual predators via e-mail, and the rise in the theft of personal information. But the Web did connect students and other researchers to vast resources for knowledge that seemed destined to grow indefinitely. For a society and an economy increasingly centered on the management of information, the establishment of the Internet and the Web appeared to mark the beginning of a new era.

Yet the Internet and the Web were only the most recent in a long line of developments in telecommunications linking distant parts of the globe more closely together. In the 1830s, the telegraph first enabled instantaneous communication on the same continent. The first undersea cable laid across the floor of the Atlantic Ocean in 1866 allowed Americans to get news directly from Europe. Ten years later, Alexander Graham Bell added the human voice to the technology of the telegraph by creating the telephone. In 1895, Italian inventor Guglielmo Marconi freed long-distance communications from the earthly constraints of copper wires by sending the first radio ("wireless") transmission; in 1901, he established the first radio link from North America to Europe. By 1940 the ability to transmit images enabled television broadcasts in the United States and England, and in the 1950s TV became widely popular and available.

The ENIAC computer, built at the University of Pennsylvania in 1945, and its successors were vast machines that filled entire rooms. Altair offered the first microcomputer, or personal computer (PC), as a kit in 1975. Apple followed with the fully assembled Apple I in 1977 and the Macintosh in 1984, the latter initiating the use of a mouse to point and click at items on a screen. The entry of powerful International Business Machines (IBM) into the PC market in 1981 marked the movement of computers into the mainstream of American society.

James's job did not disappear. It moved and was inherited by 20-year-old Balbina Duque Granados. She, too, had grown up in a small town located in an agricultural area, in the Mexican province of San Luis Potosí, and she, too, had moved 400 miles north to find better-paying work in a booming manufacturing city. She was thrilled to land the difficult, repetitive job—her "answered prayer"—at a *maquiladora,* one of the foreign-owned assembly plants along Mexico's border with the United States that wed First World engineering with Third World working conditions. Her employer was also satisfied, paying her 65 cents an hour to do what James had been paid $7.91 an hour for. But Granados's job was no more secure than James's had been. The beginnings of successful worker organizing in Matamoros encouraged the company to shift many of its operations 60 miles upriver to Reynosa, where the union movement was weaker. A journalist asked Granados whether she would move there if her job did. "And what if they were to move again?" she replied. "Maybe to Juarez or Tijuana? What then? Do I have to chase my job all over the world?"

The Logic and Technology of Globalization

Like many other workers in the United States and abroad, Mollie James and Balbina Duque Granados learned firsthand the relentlessly international logic of the economic system known as **capitalism.** Those who had capital—extra money—invested it in corporations, whose purpose was to produce a profit for their shareholders. A corporation's profitability depended on keeping costs—labor and materials—down and expanding into new markets. Those markets were not limited by nationality; a manufacturer tried to sell not just to Americans but to

Photofest

Photofest

The popular 1998 film *You've Got Mail!* starred Tom Hanks and Meg Ryan as bitter New York business rivals by day who unknowingly fall in love through an anonymous computer chat room. Since the mid-1990s, e-mail has provided a quick and convenient form of communication that falls somewhere between a telephone call and a traditional letter. Many American workers find the efficiency of e-mail somewhat offset by the need to spend more time reading and sending it.

The search by the U.S. Department of Defense for a communication network invulnerable to nuclear attack led to the creation of ARPANET in 1969, a forerunner of the Internet, which began to function in 1983. These systems transmitted only text—words—between computers that were connected to each other by telephone links. In 1990, software researchers created the World Wide Web, which used the Internet to send graphic and multimedia information as well as text. Audio and visual capacity now joined words on the growing web of connected networks. In 1993, the White House joined the rush of users establishing sites on the Web, and by 1995, public access to the World Wide Web was widely available in the United States. ■

customers wherever they might be found. The technological innovations facilitating the integration of the U.S. economy into the world economy in the late 1900s were not so much a new force as an acceleration of an older trend. Just as the telegraph and telephone had helped create a nation unified by rapid communication, the spread of personal computers and the Internet linked Americans even more closely to other nations. In the 1920s, the head of General Electric, Owen Young, spoke of his ambition to "obliterate the eastern, western, northern and southern boundaries of the United States," for "the sphere of our activities is the world." Capitalists were rarely nationalists but rather internationalists.

At the close of the twentieth century, engineering breakthroughs sped up the process of **globalization.** Bill Gates of Seattle became the world's wealthiest person in the 1990s, with assets at one point worth $100 billion as the company he headed, Microsoft, provided the software for operating most personal computers. At just 34 years old, Michael Dell of Austin leapt to fifth place on the list of wealthiest Americans in 1999 by selling computers through a mail-order business, Dell Computers. The integration of computers into every aspect of commerce and private life increased the efficiency with which businesses could operate. Retailers, for example, could monitor their inventory much more closely and eliminate unnecessary expenses. Computers boosted American productivity (the amount of work performed by a person in a given time period), which had declined between 1973 and 1996, and the U.S. economy enjoyed its longest-ever expansion during the presidency of Bill Clinton. Americans were plugged in: Since the 1980s the spread of cable television and videocassette recorders (VCRs) provided constant entertainment, and Cable News Network (CNN) offered a standardized package of world news available 24 hours a day around the globe. Atlanta-based CNN was

▶ MAP 30.2 TOP TEN U.S. TRADING PARTNERS (RANKED, WITH TOTAL VALUE OF IMPORTS AND EXPORTS COMBINED FOR APRIL 2004)
Americans do the most business with Canada and Mexico, followed by east Asia and then western Europe. U.S. economic vitality has always depended to some extent on foreign trade, but that dependence grew steadily in the past generation.

so international in its aims that its founder, Ted Turner, banned the word *foreign* from its broadcasts.

Americans were also speeding up their daily routines as the new millennium approached. The desire for immediate gratification and efficiency that had nurtured fast food and microwave ovens encouraged the spread of cell phones, beepers, fax machines, overnight package delivery, and constant news headlines scrolling across TV screens. Computers processed more information faster on ever-smaller silicon chips. Cell phones proliferated among businesspeople, students, and drivers. As prices dropped, they even reached into poorer areas. International air travel for business and pleasure quadrupled between 1980 and 1998, and international tourism vied with oil as the world's largest industry. The spread of the Internet and the use of electronic mail (e-mail) after the early 1990s best represented the shift toward instant global communication. Just as the Berlin Wall had long symbolized the divided world of the Cold War, the Internet became the emblem of the post–Cold War era of an increasingly unified global economy.

Free Trade and the Global Assembly Line

The ideology of free trade underpinned the tighter meshing of Americans' lives with the world economy. Free trade meant the reduction of tariffs, or taxes on imported and exported goods. Nations that supported free trade had industries that were eager to expand and were strong enough to compete successfully in a global market; nations with less competitive industries used tariffs to protect those industries from less expensive and higher-quality imports. As a new nation in the late 1700s and 1800s, the United States had enacted high tariffs to protect its domestic producers, while England, the world's leading economic power at the time, had sought to reduce tariffs and increase trade with America. When the United States emerged after World War II as the new leading economic nation and U.S. manufacturers and farmers looked increasingly to foreign markets, U.S. tariff rates plummeted. From averages of 30–50 percent before 1945, they dropped to 5 percent by 1990. In 1965, the sum of all exports and

imports amounted to 10 percent of the U.S. gross national product (GNP); by 1990, it had surpassed 25 percent and continued to climb.

Advocates of free trade argued that global markets unhindered by national tariffs benefited consumers everywhere by giving them access to the best goods at the lowest prices. America's NAFTA treaty with Canada and Mexico reflected this belief (see Chapter 29), as did the European Union with its newly unified currency, the euro. In the United States, by the start of the new millennium, most leaders of both major political parties, corporate executives, bankers, and most other elites supported free trade. But others objected to this internationalist economic ideology. Environmentalists and labor unions led the forces opposing unregulated globalization of the U.S. economy. Environmentalists warned of the pollution costs to the world's environment of U.S. factories relocating to poorer and less regulated nations, such as Mexico and China. Labor organizers decried the flight of American jobs as manufacturers sought less expensive and more compliant—often desperate—workers abroad. Human rights activists spotlighted the grim working conditions in many overseas plants, including the prevalence of child labor. In 1999, in Seattle, and in 2001, in Genoa, Italy, thousands of antiglobalization protesters disrupted meetings of the World Trade Organization and of the leaders of the largest industrialized nations.

A "race to the bottom" for labor and environmental standards resulted from the development of a global assembly line. With capital able to move swiftly around the world and take its factories with it, nations and localities felt that they had little choice but to compete in offering multinational corporations the most advantageous terms possible. Such terms meant minimal government regulation, little protection for workers, nonexistent pollution standards, and even local subsidies in place of corporate taxes. Just as industries in the 1890s had formed national trusts to evade state regulations on commerce, the multinational corporations of a century later escaped the reach of national governments. This trend also represented an extension of the same logic that created the American Sunbelt over the previous half-century, when businesses from the Northeast and Midwest relocated to states (that happened to be warmer) with lower wage rates, fewer unions, weaker environmental standards, and minimal taxes. Corporate income taxes, which had been dropping since the 1950s, shrank by another third between 1986 and 2000. The *maquiladoras* on the Mexican border were part of a broader pattern of the corporate search for efficiency and profit, as companies, like Mollie James's Universal Manufacturing Company and RCA, took their production lines first to the American South and then abroad.

Was the new Boeing 777, manufactured piece by piece in 12 different countries, an "American" airplane?

As a result, corporations and their products became less identifiable by nationality. Boeing Aircraft had long been the largest employer in the Seattle area, but was its new Boeing 777, manufactured piece by piece in 12 different countries, an "American" airplane? Japanese companies also moved many manufacturing plants overseas, including to the United States, to be closer to important markets. Was a Toyota made by American workers in Georgetown, Kentucky, a "foreign" car? A worker sewing the "American" company label on a trendy piece of clothing might be in Malaysia or Taiwan. Or she might be a Mexican American working in a southern California garment factory—and have a sister across the border in Mexico sewing for the same company at still lower wages. In an age of globalization and international commerce, insistence on purity of product lineage—"Buy American" campaigns—seemed to make little more sense than discredited notions of "racial purity."

Who Benefits from Globalization?

The increasing globalization of the U.S. economy at the end of the twentieth century created enormous wealth while sharpening class inequalities. The stock market skyrocketed. The Dow Jones average of the value of 30 top companies' stocks rose steadily from 500 in 1956, to 1,000 in 1972, and to 3,000 in 1991. Then it more than tripled in value in just eight years, surpassing 10,000 in 1999. Wealthy Americans who owned the bulk of corporate stock reaped the most gain, but middle- and even working-class Americans with retirement funds invested in the market also benefited handsomely. The process of globalization and the steady expansion of the U.S. economy after 1992 also encouraged a growing belief among Americans, especially affluent ones, that markets alone offered the best solution to social problems. But markets and their strict dependence on the profit motive proved unable to preserve the quality of the environment, to pull the 36 million officially poor Americans above the poverty line ($17,000 for a family of four in 1999), or to preserve the security of the vast middle class that had stabilized American politics since World War II. Inequalities within the United States reflected growing global inequality as 20 percent of the world's people (mostly in Europe and North America) consumed 86 percent of its goods and services.

American consumers enjoyed many of the fruits of the more integrated world economy. At least in industries not dominated by monopolies, the corporate quest for lower production costs, along with fierce international competition and technological innovation, reduced prices of many goods and services. Computers, airline travel, and gasoline were all significantly less expensive in real dollars (adjusted for inflation) than they had been a generation earlier. Competition abounded in the robust retail sector of the U.S. economy, including catalog and Internet shopping. Wal-Mart represented the epitome of how the globalized economy could benefit consumers. By 2000, the discount store that Sam Walton had opened in Arkansas in 1962 surpassed General Motors as the largest American company, responsible for 6 percent of all U.S. retail sales. It sold 20,000 pairs of shoes an hour. Wal-Mart's success resulted from relentlessly cutting costs through sharp management, using cheaper imported goods and employing a nonunion workforce, and passing its savings along to customers in the form of lower prices. In towns across the United States, Wal-Mart put smaller local competitors out of business, and its efficiency became the standard to which other large retailers aspired.

The benefits that the working-class majority of Americans experienced as consumers in the global economy were offset by their declining status as workers. As manufacturers moved to the Sunbelt and then overseas, high-wage, unionized jobs providing health insurance and pension benefits disappeared. Average real wages declined steadily after 1973, and union membership slid from one-third of the workforce in the early 1950s to one-tenth in 2000. Family incomes were maintained only by the addition of second and third wage earners, especially women. Americans spent more than they earned. The average household had 11 credit cards and carried $7,000 in debt on them, in addition to owing car and home mortgage payments.

"Meritocracy worked for my grandfather, it worked for my father, and it's working for me."

▲ An important tension in American history was the conflict between the ideal of equal opportunity for all and the reality of inherited wealth and privilege. The efforts of the George W. Bush administration to eliminate the federal estate tax, which affected the inheritances of less than 1 percent of U.S. citizens, represented the latest round in the debate about the relationship between political democracy and inherited economic inequality. In a pure meritocracy, all citizens would be rewarded for their personal achievements rather than those of their parents or ancestors.

Already wider in the United States than in any other industrialized nation, the distance between rich and poor continued to grow, whittling away at Americans' self-image as a middle-class society. The share of the national income going to the richest 1 percent nearly doubled in the last quarter of the twentieth century, while the share going to the bottom 80 percent shrank. Three million Americans lived in gated communities in extremely affluent suburbs, but one of five American children grew up in poverty and 21 million citizens sought emergency food assistance each year. One of the nation's leading newspapers unknowingly captured this disparity with two articles a few pages apart, headlined "As Closets Bulge, Americans' Taste in Gifts Often Turns Toward the Taste Buds" and "Food Drives Find Cupboard Is Nearly Bare."

The political system, which helps determine how wealth and opportunity are distributed in a society, seemed to offer little respite from the widening gap between haves and have-nots. The fraction of eligible citizens who make the effort to vote in presidential elections declined to just half in 2000 and in off-year congressional elections to a mere third, with the likelihood of voting closely correlated to a person's affluence. The fierce partisanship, personal attacks, and culture of scandal that dominated American politics alienated others.

Many citizens were also disillusioned by the blatant manner in which money came to dominate the political process. With the average cost of a successful Senate campaign at $5 million and a House campaign approaching $1 million, few but the wealthy could campaign for Congress, and elected members spent inordinate amounts of time raising money from wealthy donors. Democratic Senator Richard Durbin of Illinois admitted that the system of fund-raising is corrupting: "It forces you into compromising yourself." Republican Senator John McCain of Arizona called campaign financing "an elaborate influence-peddling scheme in which both parties conspire to stay in office by selling the country to the highest bidder." For average Americans, exclusive fund-raising dinners that sometimes reaped more than $30 million signaled a kind of political access they could not hope to match. The ability of business to outspend labor 15 to 1 in contributing to campaigns helped ensure minimal publicity to any discussions of the gulf between rich and poor.

The Stewardship of Natural Resources

No issue at the beginning of the twenty-first century was more global than the environment. Winds and waters do not respect political boundaries, nor do the materials borne on them. The condition of the natural environment affects all living creatures, yet the prevailing calculus of the market and private ownership does not apportion responsibility for its care. The free market system has no mechanism for offsetting, or even measuring, the costs of depleted natural resources. A generation ago, biologist Garrett Hardin warned of the tragedy of the commons: that individuals' incentives to preserve the quality of their own property do not carry over to resources held in common. Litter is an obvious example, and air, water, and ground pollution are the more serious cases. American culture had long celebrated human domination of the natural world and the benefits it brought, especially the growth in productivity that permitted living standards to rise dramatically across decades and centuries. At the same time, the rise of environmentalism and ecological understanding since 1960 offered a different way of imagining people's place on the earth.

Ecological Transformations

Ecosystems are always dynamic, and changes in weather and Native American land use had reshaped the North American environment long before the followers of Christopher Columbus arrived on the continent. But European settlement and industrialization altered the face of the land in ways that would dumbfound a time traveler from the 1500s. Even a visitor from 1900 would be astonished by the intensity of human development of the land: vast cities with

Stuart Westmorland/CORBIS

▲ **Clear-cutting scars mountainsides on both private and public lands, especially in the Pacific Northwest and here on Kupreanof Island in the Tongass National Forest of southeastern Alaska. Clear-cutting is a more efficient method of timber harvesting than selective tree thinning, but it encourages soil erosion, mudslides, and flooding.**

Puget Sound and Western Washington

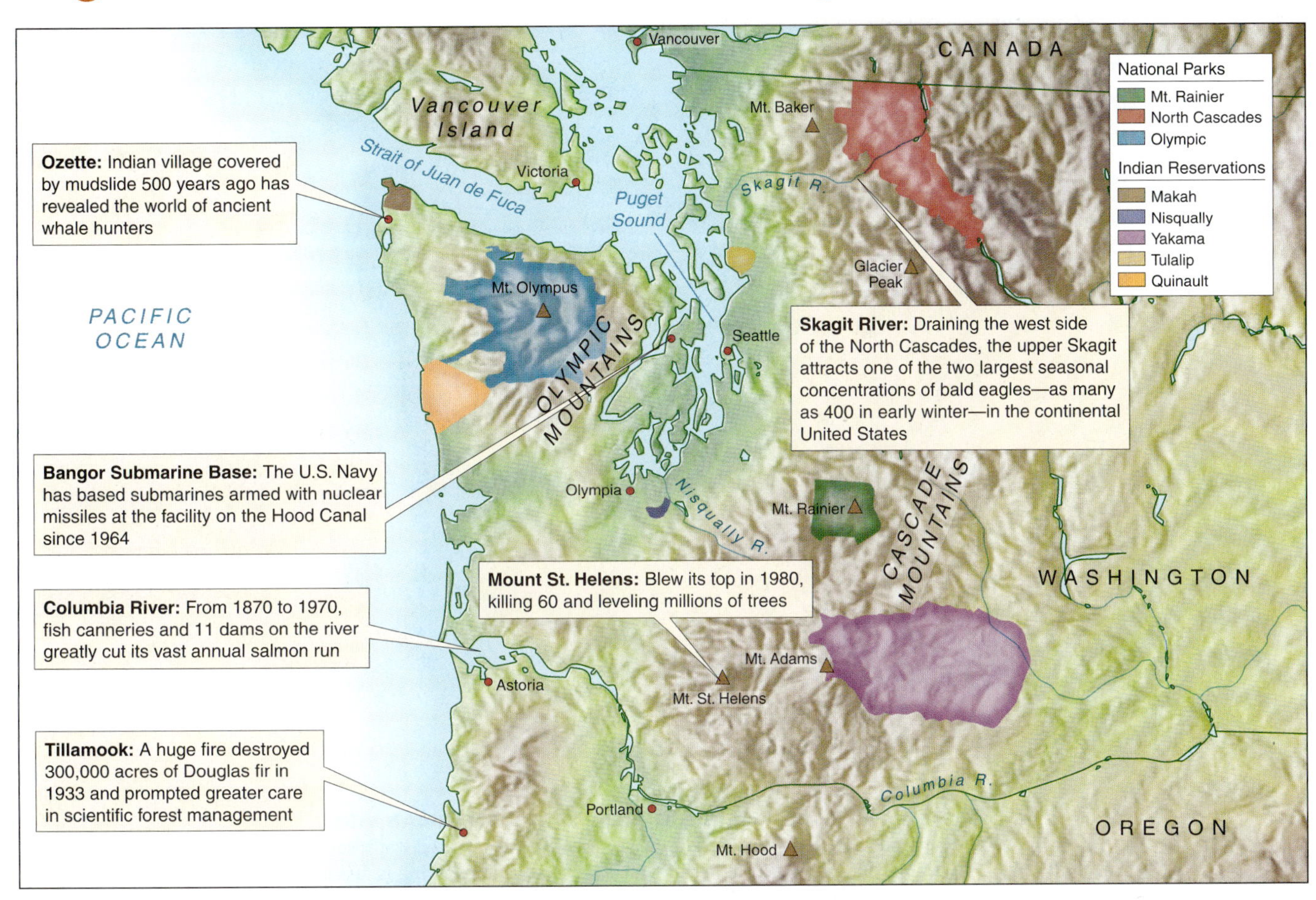

Nestled between two dramatic mountain ranges, the Olympics and the Cascades, the lush and mild Puget Sound region provided abundant natural resources for fishing, timbering, and farming for Native Americans for thousands of years before the arrival of British Captain George Vancouver and Lieutenant Peter Puget in 1792. Seattle grew in the twentieth century as a trading port, particularly with east Asian markets, and as the original aircraft manufacturing site of Boeing Corporation. With the permanently snow-capped volcanic peaks of the Cascade range visible on clear days, Seattle continued to attract new residents and tourists alike. The population of the former frontier state of Washington nearly doubled from 1970 to 2003, topping 6 million.

Seattle was also the departure point for most Americans traveling north to Alaska. Passenger ferries crisscrossed Puget Sound, providing an alternative method of commuting to work in Seattle for residents of other area communities. In the 1980s the city became associated with the extraordinary business success of computer software giant Microsoft and coffee retailer Starbucks. Recreation Equipment Incorporated (REI) began in Seattle as a consumer cooperative for buying products for outdoor activities such as rock-climbing and backpacking. By 2000 REI had built stores across the United States. ■

Getty Images

Mt. Rainier, Mount Rainier National Park, Washington

▲ **MAP 30.3 WATER SOURCES IN THE AMERICAN WEST**
Rapid population growth has put great pressure on the limited water sources of the arid interior West. The water in the region's major rivers is fully allocated, and pumping is fast depleting underground reserves, such as the Ogallala Aquifer below the Plains states. Access to water will help determine the course of future growth in the western half of the country.

their sprawling suburbs and roads and highways everywhere. The key factor was population growth. Just as the number of people in the world quadrupled from 1.5 billion to 6 billion during the twentieth century, the population of the United States almost quadrupled from 75 million to 281 million, with the largest increase for a single decade (33 million) coming in the 1990s. Immigration and natural reproduction accounted for much of this, as did the much longer average lifespan ushered in by antibiotics and antiviral vaccines.

The most dramatic changes in the land in the twentieth century resulted from the exploitation of wood, minerals, and water, particularly in the majority of the country lying west of the Mississippi River. Commercial logging destroyed all but 3 percent of the old-growth forests of the 50 states. The clear-cuts scarring the mountainsides and hillsides of the Pacific Northwest and Alaska told the tale, as did the erosion caused by the overgrazing by cattle of public lands managed by the Interior Department's Bureau of Land Management in Utah, New Mexico, and other western states. The Mining Act of 1872 still granted to private corporations the rights to such valuable minerals as gold and copper on public land for the remarkable nineteenth-century price of $2.50 per acre. Mining companies took full advantage of the opportunity, resulting in rock and chemical wastes piled in vast slagheaps and dumped in toxic holding ponds from Arizona to Montana. In the arid but increasingly populated western states, water was the most critical resource for population growth. The U.S. Army Corps of Engineers and the Bureau of Reclamation built huge dams from the 1930s to the 1980s, providing irrigation, flood control, and hydropower but also destroying wild rivers and causing silt to begin filling up the reservoirs. Increasing diversions of the Rio Grande left that now misnamed river so dry that, by 2001, it failed to reach the Gulf of Mexico, trickling to a halt 50 feet short. Groundwater pumping for agricultural irrigation in the plains states and on the eastern slope of the Rocky Mountains was draining the vast underground Ogallala Aquifer at a rate that will empty it within a few more decades.

American prosperity came at a price. The prodigious growth of the U.S. economy in the twentieth century depended on the consumption of ever-increasing amounts of energy, most of it from coal, oil, and natural gas. Though making up less than 5 percent of the world's population, Americans accounted for a quarter of the globe's energy consumption. They depended on other countries to provide much of it for them: the United States imported 22 percent of its total energy needs and 69 percent of its oil, primarily from Saudi Arabia, Venezuela, Canada, and Mexico. Fossil fuels, such as coal and oil, could not be renewed; once burned, they were gone, and the world had a finite supply of such fuels. Americans were constructing a lifestyle that was unsustainable in the long run.

Courtesy, National Aeronautics and Space Administration

▲ A nighttime photograph taken from a satellite above the south Pacific Ocean reveals the use of electricity in North America. Only Alaska and some parts of the inland western states (Nevada, Idaho, eastern Oregon) appear mostly unlit. The growth of the Sunbelt states of the South and West after 1970 was dramatic, but the bulk of the U.S. population remained east of the Mississippi River, especially in the Northeast and Midwest. The demand for electrical power even with most citizens in bed was enormous.

Pollution

The world's growing population was consuming five times as much fossil fuel in 2000 as in 1950, helping stimulate a steady rise in the earth's average temperatures. Americans caused 36 percent of carbon-based emissions, the largest contribution to the foremost environmental problem, global warming. The release of large amounts of carbon dioxide from burning coal, oil, and other fossil fuels helps trap extra heat within the earth's atmosphere—the greenhouse effect—and melt ice in high-altitude and polar regions. In the summer of 2000, startled scientists found open water at the North Pole, a sight humans had never before seen. Greenhouse gases also contribute to a thinning of the ozone layer of the atmosphere, which enables more of the sun's ultraviolet rays to reach the earth's surface and causes skin cancer rates to soar.

At the end of the twentieth century, industrial manufacturing still figured importantly in the human assault on the air and the atmosphere, but the internal combustion engine had long since surpassed coal burning as the leading cause of pollution. The United States produced and used more cars and trucks than any other nation. The automobile and its symbolism of convenience and personal freedom defined much of American culture. With minimal public transportation outside a handful of major cities, Americans were deeply committed to a car-dependent lifestyle. As a price, they quietly accepted an annual death toll of more than 40,000 people from accidents on the road, two-thirds the number each year of all U.S. deaths in the Vietnam War. The highway infrastructure strained under the pressure of a 60 percent rise in the number of licensed drivers from 1970 to 2000 but only a 6 percent growth in total miles of roads. Negotiating traffic jams was a standard part of the daily lives of the majority of Americans who lived in the suburbs created by urban sprawl, especially around such cities as Los Angeles and Atlanta. Citizens spent three times as many hours stalled in traffic in 1999 as they did in 1982. Smog increasingly obscured the once sublime spectacular vistas of Arizona's Grand Canyon. Thousands of cars daily jammed Yosemite National Park in the Sierra Nevada mountains of California, making it an almost urban setting with air quality on the verge of

Justin Sullivan/AP/Wide World

▲ **The oil crises of the 1970s led automobile manufacturers to improve the efficiency of gas mileage in their cars. By the 1990s, however, gasoline was once again inexpensive and growing numbers of Americans were buying large new sport utility vehicles (SUVs) such as the Chevrolet Suburban, despite their low gas mileage. A few environmentalists placed bumper stickers on other people's SUVs to highlight the key role of auto emissions in the accelerating process of global warming.**

violating federal standards. Yet park managers' efforts to limit automobile access to the valley were repeatedly defeated by popular opposition.

Daily life in the United States came to depend in countless ways on the use of synthetic chemicals, production of which was 350 times greater in 1982 than in 1940. Many chemicals were crucial components of Americans' comfortable modern lives. But more than 50,000 known toxic waste dumps in the United States leached poisonous chemicals and heavy metals into the soil and water, such as the polychlorinated biphenyls that lined the bottom of the Hudson River north of Albany and the arsenic and cadmium that clogged the Milltown Dam on Montana's scenic Clark Fork River six miles upstream from Missoula. Cancer rates among Americans grew sharply in the twentieth century, partly because people lived significantly longer lives (giving more time for cancers to appear) and partly because they were exposed to a much larger array of carcinogenic materials in the environment.

No synthetic product was more pervasive in the United States than plastic, a post-1945 product made from petroleum. Its prevalence and extraordinary durability helped it become a major factor in loading up the nation's landfills. The most deadly and durable pollutants remained the radioactive wastes created by five decades of nuclear development. No one knew yet how to dispose safely of millions of tons of materials impregnated with plutonium and other human-made radioactive elements, 30 percent of it casually poured into dirt or stored in flimsy containers prone to leakage. The chain of nuclear poison arched across the American West—from the bomb factory at Hanford in south-central Washington through the weapons testing site in southwestern Nevada—then eastward to the uranium-processing plants in Paducah, Kentucky, and Barnwell, South Carolina. The U.S. nuclear weapon complex of some 3,000 sites put its often fatal touch on the lives of millions of Americans: uranium miners, military workers, soldiers used to observe test explosions at close range, and citizens living downwind from the Nevada Test Site in Nevada and Utah. The National Academy of Sciences concluded in 2000 that many of these sites would be permanent national sacrifice zones, toxic to humans for at least tens of thousands of years.

Environmentalism and Its Limitations

The ideas of most Americans about how to manage natural resources changed in the twentieth century. Environmental consciousness blossomed since the 1960s, rediscovering a tradition that linked eighteenth-century naturalist William Bartram with nineteenth-century transcendentalist Henry David Thoreau and twentieth-century conservationists of both major political parties. Awareness of humans' connections with their broader ecological context led to significant reforms, such as the banning of carcinogenic pesticides and leaded gasoline, the cleaning up of polluted water in the Great Lakes, and the introduction of catalytic converters to reduce harmful emissions from automobile exhaust pipes and factory smokestacks. Recycling became common, and some dams were destroyed, freeing long-constricted rivers, such as the Penobscot in Maine.

Yet issues of public land management and pollution control remained among the most controversial problems in American public life. Since 1980, the Republican party has supported the exploitation of natural resources to produce wealth and raise standards of living, departing at least in tone from the party's earlier conservationist bent. Meanwhile, the Democratic party became associated with environmental protection. This contrast was dramatically displayed in January 2001 when President Clinton rushed to provide new protections to a swath of federal lands in the West before his term ended, while president-elect George W. Bush was appointing as secretary of the interior Colorado attorney Gale Norton, who strongly opposed such protections. Both Bush and his vice president, Dick Cheney, had extensive experience in the energy industry, and their administration promoted new oil and gas drilling in wilderness locations that included Alaska's Arctic National Wildlife Refuge.

Beyond partisan differences and the broad tendency of even the most well-known corporate polluters to pose as friendly to the environment, the relationship of Americans to their natural environment continued to be paradoxical. By large majorities in public opinion polls, they supported strong antipollution laws and the preservation of public lands from economic development. They flocked to such films as *Erin Brockovich* (2000) and *A Civil Action* (1998), in which average citizens and lawyers won court cases against large corporate polluters.

Americans consumed natural resources—particularly gasoline, electricity, and water—in quantities unmatched by other societies.

But in their daily lives, Americans consumed natural resources, particularly gasoline, electricity, and water, at a rate unmatched by other societies. Measures that had reduced some of the nation's energy consumption since the 1970s were reversed by 2000: Congress revoked the national 55 mph speed limit in 1995, and ever larger cars, trucks, and especially sport utility vehicles steadily reduced the average gas mileage of passenger vehicles. While scientists and some utilities urged a reduction in the nation's expanding use of fossil fuels, Vice President Cheney dismissed conservation as merely "a sign of personal virtue" rather than a basis for a sound energy policy. Many residents across the arid Southwest, most of them newcomers, remained determined to recreate the green lawns they had left behind in the East and Midwest. When an investigator for the Las Vegas city water district confronted one resident about his wasteful sprinkler, the man responded, "Man, with all these new rules, you people are trying to turn this place into a desert."

The Expansion of American Popular Culture Abroad

Just as the U.S. economy and American environmental problems could not be separated from the outside world, the nation's cultural life grew more closely tied to that of other nations at the dawn of the new millennium. During the Cold War, from the 1940s through the 1980s, American foreign relations hinged on problems of national security and the projection of military might abroad. The dissolution of the Soviet Union in 1991 and the retreat of communism ended the bipolar division of the world and left the United States the sole remaining superpower. By 2000, American popular culture rather than armed strength had emerged as the leading edge of U.S. influence around the world.

Over the first half of the twentieth century, the United States slowly replaced Great Britain as the dominant force in international affairs. The economic and military aspects of this shift of influence were clear by the end of World War II, and its cultural elements soon followed. American power extended the preeminence of English as the global language of commerce and diplomacy, and ambitious and privileged youth from beyond Europe aimed no longer for an education at England's Oxford and Cambridge but rather at prestigious U.S. universities. American culture had become less regionally distinctive and more nationally homogeneous in the twentieth century because of improvements in transportation and communication. By the end of the century, this same process of homogenization of popular consumer culture was at work on a worldwide scale. American themes and products stood out in an increasingly global popular culture, although they were resisted by some abroad who preferred more local identities and traditions, often rooted in ethnicity or religious conviction.

A Culture of Diversity and Entertainment

Known for its informality and diversity, American culture proved powerfully attractive to peoples all over the world, partly because racial and ethnic diversity was more pronounced in the United States than in any other major power. African Americans, Latino Americans, and Asian Americans all figured prominently in the popular realms of sports, music, and films. Television was the leading medium for this culture of entertainment, beaming CNN, MTV, and "reality" shows, such as *Survivor,* around the world. From jazz to rock 'n' roll to rap, American popular music spread across the globe, as did such clothing of American youth as jeans and sneakers, symbols of informality and comfort. Hollywood's movies dominated cinemas and VCRs everywhere, providing 85 percent of films screened in Europe.

The idea of individual choice pervaded American culture, backed by constitutional guarantees of freedom of expression. Freedom to choose included matters of religion, politics, and other weighty areas, which had long made the United States a beacon of liberty to people oppressed for their beliefs. But freedom of choice came increasingly by the end of the twentieth century to refer to options for consumption in the marketplace. The United States was the largest market in the world, and its affluent citizens had unparalleled choices of what to buy. In 1960, Americans already had 3,000 shopping centers and 4 square feet of retail space per person. By 2000, those numbers had soared to 40,000 and 19, respectively, for their children and grandchildren. The premium placed on acquiring material goods seemed to many foreign observers the primary American value.

Advertising grew in prominence as the central link between popular culture and the selling of products. Sports became steadily more commercialized. Postseason college football games began in 1985 to include the names of their corporate sponsors, creating such events as the Chick-Fil-A Peach Bowl and the Weed Eater Independence Bowl. By 2000, newspapers ranked bowl games—once hallowed for their own traditions—by the simple criterion of how much money sponsors paid to participating teams. In the 1990s "hoops" joined baseball as a popular U.S.

AP/Wide World Photos

▲ **Perhaps no other element of American popular culture spread abroad as quickly as rock 'n' roll music. Like jazz after the 1920s, rock 'n' roll after the 1950s captured a vast listening audience overseas. Most Russian leaders during the Soviet era before 1991 appeared publicly as stiff, serious figures, but by 1996, Russian president Boris Yeltsin joined Russian rock 'n' rollers onstage in an event during his successful campaign for reelection.**

export. National Basketball Association (NBA) games were telecast to more than 190 countries in 41 languages. Sports also brought foreigners to the United States as professional baseball and basketball teams began recruiting Latin American, European, African, and Asian athletes.

U.S. Influence Abroad Since the Cold War

Cultural influences flowed both ways for Americans, with immigrants in particular bringing with them traditions and perspectives that refreshed the cultural mix of life in the United States. Japanese Pokémon trading cards, Thai cuisine, and Cuban salsa music pervaded daily routines for many Americans. But increased trade and communication since the end of the Cold War above all enabled the further spread of American popular culture. American-accented English straddled the globe, the language of international commerce and of 80 percent of listings on the World Wide Web. The informality and individualism of the Internet made it seem quintessentially American in style. The U.S. dollar remained the world's primary trading currency and became the de facto and even the de jure currency of many other nations. Mickey Mouse's empire expanded to EuroDisney outside Paris and to Tokyo Disneyland. American studies became a major field of scholarship at universities around the world.

▲ **By 2000, the process of globalization tied the world more closely together than ever before. Increasing trade, tourism, and communication encouraged the mixing of different cultures. American popular culture was a powerful influence around the globe, including American music, fast food, television, clothing, and movies. Mickey Mouse's ears famously symbolized the Disney Company, American television and films, and their worldwide prominence in popular entertainment.**

America's most popular eatery served 20 million customers a day at its 23,000 franchises across the globe. McDonald's Golden Arches appeared everywhere, from Japan and France to Russia and China. Even Mecca in Saudi Arabia, Islam's holiest site and the destination of millions of Muslim pilgrims, had a McDonald's. The company generated half of its revenues from non-U.S. operations.

Nor did only U.S. material interests spread abroad swiftly in recent years. American religious missionaries worked in poor countries around the world, combining their spiritual mission with a commitment to improving daily life in concrete ways involving health care, education, and agriculture. Pentecostalists gained millions of converts in Latin America since the 1970s, and mainstream denominations, such as the Lutherans, Episcopalians, and Roman Catholics, saw their numbers rise sharply in Africa. The most fully homegrown American religion was especially active in proselytizing abroad. As a result, the Church of Jesus Christ of Latter Day Saints (Mormons), headquartered in Salt Lake City, had 5 million members in the United States and another 5 million worldwide.

The United States retained its military superiority, with a defense budget larger than that of the next ten biggest military powers combined. But the difficulties of unconventional warfare, from Vietnam in the 1960s to Somalia in 1993, combined with the apparent disappearance of a major threat to the nation's security after the demise of the Soviet Union, made U.S. policymakers and citizens reluctant to put American troops in harm's way abroad, at least until after the terrorist attacks of September 11, 2001. Instead, the expansion of American culture abroad seemed a safer and more effective way to influence other nations.

Resistance to American Popular Culture

Like Christian, Jewish, and Hindu fundamentalists, all of whom grew prominent in the final decades of the twentieth century, Muslim fundamentalists rejected the radical egalitarianism

The Slow Food Movement

For many people in countries other than the United States, as for many Americans, McDonald's and other U.S.-based fast food restaurants offered an attractive dining experience. Customers everywhere appreciated the efficient and friendly service, clean surroundings, and the consistent quality of the food. Their enthusiasm explained the extraordinary international growth and profitability of such chains as Burger King and Kentucky Fried Chicken at the end of the twentieth century.

For other people, the rapid spread of fast food franchises around the globe threatened cherished values and lifestyles. The Slow Food Movement emerged in western Europe in the late 1980s as a loose-knit organization, headquartered in the northern Italian town of Bra. The movement sought to preserve and celebrate traditional cuisines and methods of food production in Europe and around the world. Slow Food's 60,000 members objected not only to the specific taste of fast food, but also to broader cultural changes symbolized by McDonald's and its competitors: the speeding up of daily life, including the loss of sociability around more leisurely meals; the gradual replacement of family farming and food production by corporate agriculture; and the erosion of distinctive local cooking and dining traditions.

Hasan Hamali/AP/Wide World

The spread of American fast food chains around the globe suggested that American culture may be a more powerful influence abroad than U.S. military might. The end of the Cold War led to McDonald's restaurants proliferating in downtown Moscow and Beijing, the capital cities of America's greatest opponents since World War II. The Golden Arches even invaded Mecca, Saudi Arabia, the holiest city of Islam.

The Slow Food Manifesto (November 9, 1989)

Our century, which began and has developed under the insignia of industrial civilization, first invented the machine and then took it as its life model.

We are enslaved by speed and have all succumbed to the same insidious virus: *Fast Life,* which disrupts our habits, pervades the privacy of our homes and forces us to eat *Fast Foods.*

To be worthy of the name, *Homo sapiens* should rid himself of speed before it reduces him to a species in danger of extinction.

A firm defense of quiet material pleasure is the only way to oppose the universal folly of *Fast Life.*

May suitable doses of guaranteed sensual pleasure and slow, long-lasting enjoyment preserve us from the contagion of the multitude who mistake frenzy for efficiency.

Our defense should begin at the table with *Slow Food.* Let us rediscover the flavors and savors of regional cooking and banish the degrading effects of *Fast Food.*

In the name of productivity, *Fast Life* has changed our way of being and threatens our environment and our landscapes. So *Slow Food* is now the only truly progressive answer.

That is what real culture is all about: developing taste rather than demeaning it. And what better way to set about this than an international exchange of experiences, knowledge, projects?

Slow Food guarantees a better future.

Slow Food is an idea that needs plenty of qualified supporters who can help turn this (slow) motion into an international movement, with the little snail as its symbol.

Slow Food operates to protect the right to pleasure, the respect of the rhythms of life and a harmonious relationship with nature. It also seeks to explore, describe and improve the culture of food, to develop a proper education of taste and smell from childhood and to safeguard and defend the agroindustrial heritage while respecting the cuisines of each single country.

The Slow Food Manifesto was ratified in Paris at the Founding Congress of the International Slow Food Movement on December 9, 1989.

Source: http://www.slowfood.com

Questions

1. *What, precisely, do slow food advocates object to about fast food?*
2. *How important is fast food in the lives of people you know, and how does it affect their lives?* ■

and the unbridled pursuit of pleasure—especially the sexual titillation—so prevalent in American popular culture. The relative equality of women and the lack of respect for traditional social and religious hierarchies seemed to them emblems of American decadence, as the Islamic rulers of Afghanistan (known as the Taliban) demonstrated in the 1990s in their brutal repression of women's rights. Osama bin Laden and his followers resented U.S. policies of supporting Israel and certain oil-producing Arab nations, but they also fiercely condemned the secular, egalitarian character of American society, which they considered anti-Islamic. During the 1991 Persian Gulf War, Saudi Arabian officials tried to isolate U.S. troops from Saudi citizens, fearing the effects of contact with such diverse forces as female soldiers, bawdiness, Christianity, and American music and television.

▲ By the start of the new century, the hopes of nine U.S. presidents that the communist leader of Cuba would be swept out of power had been dashed. Four decades after leading the leftist revolution of 1959, and ten years after the collapse of communism in Russia and eastern Europe, Castro remained defiant toward the United States. He continued to denounce free market capitalism, whose price, he claimed, was paid in human misery, child labor, prostitution, and vast social inequalities.

The demise of communist regimes in Russia and eastern Europe opened the gates to a flood of western influences and brought the opportunities and inequalities of a suddenly privatized economy. State-provided safety nets disappeared, class differences widened, women's economic status declined, and the old Communist parties regained some popularity among voters scared by the instabilities of American-style capitalism. Western Europeans also remained ambivalent about the spread of American values and lifestyles. Although many of them, especially among the young, found American culture attractive and learned English in record numbers, traditionalists who were proud of their own national culture took a dim view of such innovations as fast food.

Other nations sometimes found the U.S. government overbearing and resented its unparalleled military power. Rapidly modernizing China, the world's most populous country, seemed a growing rival to the United States in Asia, even as the two nations became major trading partners. In April 2001, a U.S. surveillance plane collided over the South China Sea with a Chinese fighter jet that had been following it. The Chinese pilot died, but the American plane managed to crash-land safely at a Chinese military airport on Hainan Island. China detained the crew of 24 men and women for ten days. Public and congressional anger in the United States paralleled the outrage in China, but the two governments, mindful of their growing economic interdependence, resolved the crisis after a brief standoff. Americans were surprised by the intensity of anti-American nationalism within Chinese society.

Two opposing trends characterized world affairs. One consisted of the unifying forces of economic internationalism and globalization, carrying with them a tide of American-dominated cultural styles. The other was made up of the resisting forces of political and ethnic nationalism. A world more tightly integrated in economic ways was at the same time divided by ethnic conflicts, revealed in wars in the Balkans in southeastern Europe, the Caucasus region on Russia's southern border, and central Africa. As people around the world felt themselves increasingly sucked into the vortex of a powerful global economy that they could not control, many of them responded by renewing their allegiances to older, more local traditions. Ethnic, religious, and national identities often offered more meaningful alternatives to a purely economic identity as consumers. "I don't find foreign countries foreign," Gillette Corporation chair Alfred M. Zeien said, and many people in other nations felt the same way about the United States. But for others, as the terrorist attacks of 2001 made all too clear, American life seemed fundamentally alien and increasingly threatening.

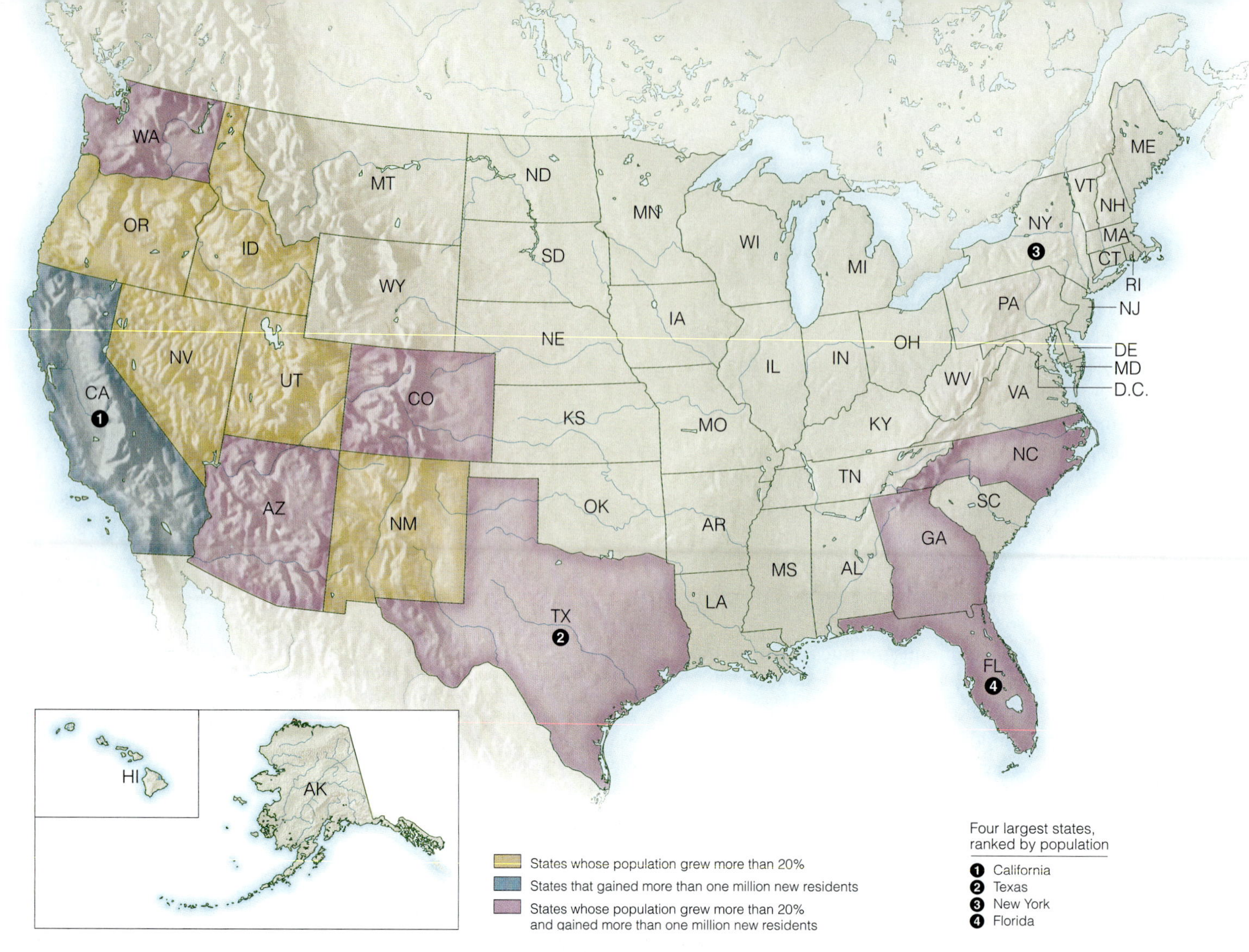

▲ **MAP 30.4 STATE POPULATION GROWTH, 1990–2000**
The population of the United States continued to shift slowly out of the long-urbanized Northeast to the Sunbelt of the South and West. Los Angeles replaced Chicago as the nation's second largest city, after New York. Retirees and workers alike seemed to prefer sunnier, warmer climates.

Identity in Contemporary America

The 2000 U.S. Census revealed a society in the midst of change. Americans have long been known as a particularly restless and mobile people, and one out of five changed residences every year. The post-1965 wave of immigrants continued to rise (and foreign adoptions rose dramatically), bringing in millions of new Americans of Asian heritage. Latino Americans surpassed African Americans as the nation's largest minority. This latest surge in immigration boosted the number of Roman Catholics and Buddhists as American society remained by far the most openly religious—still primarily Protestant—of the industrialized nations. Geographically, Americans lived farther south and west than earlier generations.

Americans were older than they used to be: life expectancy rose to 77 from 45 years in 1900. More than half lived in suburbs. Average household size dropped by 50 percent over the twentieth century, as only one in four consisted of a married couple with children. Whereas in 1900 just 6 percent of married women worked outside the home, 61 percent did so by 2000, including 64 percent of those with children under age six. The "family wage" that so many men earned in the mid-twentieth century was disappearing, helping bring in its wake changes in gender roles as women became crucial breadwinners as well as homemakers and child-raisers.

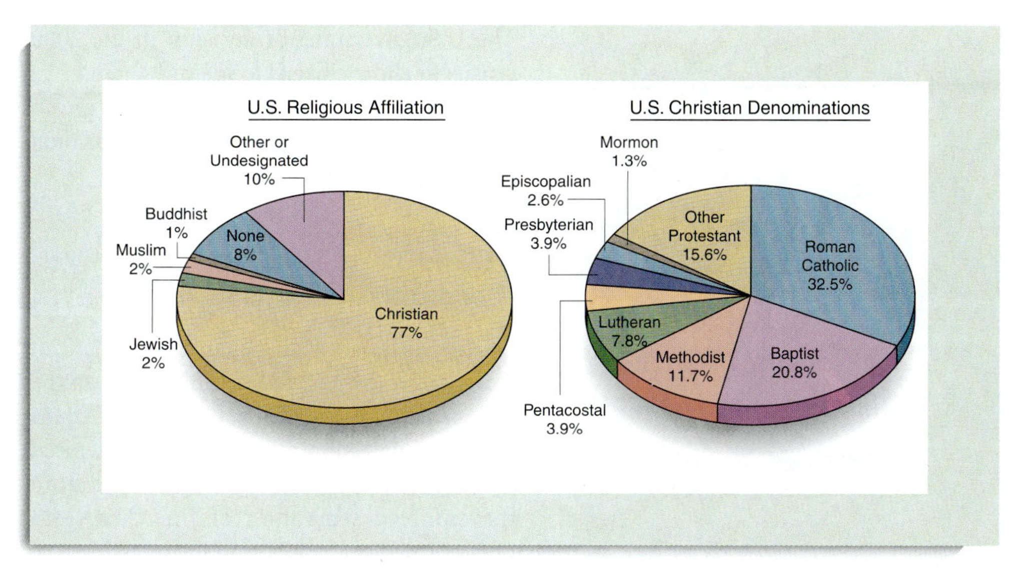

◀ FIGURE 30.3 SELF-DESCRIBED RELIGIOUS AFFILIATION IN THE UNITED STATES, 2000
The most noticeable change during the last 30 years in American religious life has been the growth of evangelical and fundamentalist Protestant congregations (shown here as Pentecostal and "Other Protestant") and the shrinking of mainline Protestant denominations.

Negotiating Multiple Identities

Americans derived their sense of identity from myriad sources, including nationality, work, socioeconomic status, religion, race, ethnicity, family, gender, region, and sexual orientation. Since the struggles for equality that emerged dramatically in the 1960s, individual identities and group identities have often been in tension. The achievement of legal equality and the outlawing of explicit discrimination did not immediately change deeply embedded patterns of exclusionary behavior. The policy of affirmative action had developed as a preference in hiring or admission for members of an underrepresented group who were roughly comparable to others in qualifications. It aimed to balance some of the effects of existing but little-noticed habits of "affirmative action" for white Americans and men, as when colleges used lower admission standards for children of alumni or when powerful white men tended to hire other white men. Opponents of affirmative action called it "reverse discrimination" and argued that race and sex should no longer be criteria for success in a colorblind society that promoted individual achievement. By 2000, these opponents had succeeded in eliminating affirmative action from the admission process of the large state university systems of Texas and California. Supporters of the policy observed that employers and others were certainly not colorblind yet, so that a group remedy, such as affirmative action, remained essential for the advancement of more than a token few from groups that had faced discrimination in the past.

Ideas about racial identity remained at the heart of the controversy over affirmative action. Those who used the term *race* to group people according to skin color and other visible features, such as eye shape, commonly assumed that race had an important biological meaning as a way of distinguishing one human population from another. However, biologists noted that the genetic differences between races are miniscule compared with differences between individuals of the same race. They suggested that categorizing people by skin color made as much sense as organizing library books by the size and color of their covers rather than their internal contents. The mapping of the entire human genome by 2001 further clarified the biological insignificance of race. Indeed, the racial category "white" had changed over time to encompass such formerly excluded groups as Irish Americans and Jewish Americans. Despite its lack of scientific basis, the use of race as a primary marker of identity long served to preserve a higher status for Americans of European heritage. One could be mostly white yet still be "black," thanks to the one-drop tradition regarding African heritage (that any observable percentage of African "blood" defined a person as black). Thus, a white woman could have a black child in the United States, for example, but a black woman could not have a white child.

Photograph by Michael O'Brien

▲ One aspect of American identity that continued to distinguish the United States from the industrialized countries of western Europe was enthusiastic support for the death penalty. Most surviving victims and relatives of victims of the 1995 Oklahoma City federal building bombing were eager for the execution of the confessed and unrepentant perpetrator, Timothy McVeigh, in 2001. However, a few overcame their grief and rage to oppose having the government kill the killer, including (left to right) Bud Welch, Kathy Wilburn, Patrick Reeder, and Rosemary Koelsch, each of whom lost loved ones in the mass murder.

The U.S. government's decision in the 2000 census to allow citizens to identify themselves as belonging to more than one racial group reflected the complications and occasional absurdities of racial categorization.

Social Change and Abiding Discrimination

One of the most striking changes in American society over the past five decades has been the desegregation of public life. Latinos and Asians became much more numerous in the United States, and African Americans emerged from the enforced separation of Jim Crow into greater prominence. Roughly one-third of blacks were middle-class, and thousands won election to local, state, and national political offices. Black Americans became central in the nation's cultural life in music, literature, theater, and sports. By 2001, even a new president from the Republican party—known since 1964 for its lack of support from black voters—appointed two African Americans to run the nation's foreign relations: Secretary of State Colin Powell and National Security Advisor Condoleezza Rice. Workplaces were racially integrated to an extent that would have been hard to imagine in 1950, and interracial marriages rose steeply in the final decades of the twentieth century.

The lives of women in the United States also changed dramatically during the last half of the twentieth century. Most worked outside the home, from jobs in the service and manufacturing sectors to careers in the professions and politics. In 2000, women made up one-third of the students in the nation's medical schools and one-half in law schools. Their presence in leading political positions ranged from local officials to more than a dozen U.S. senators, two U.S. Supreme Court justices, a U.S. attorney general, and a U.S. secretary of state. The passage of Title IX in 1972, prohibiting gender discrimination in school programs that received federal money, created a tidal wave of social change for American girls. In 1971, one in 27 girls played high school sports; by 1998, the ratio was one in three. Sports programs and teams for girls comparable to those for boys nourished a new generation of American women for whom athletic competition and achievement were the norm rather than the exception.

Anti-homosexual attitudes persisted as one of the nation's fiercest prejudices but nonetheless declined in mainstream American society during the 1980s and 1990s. Gay men and lesbians became more open and prominent in such public venues as television and politics, helping millions of other Americans shed some of the homophobia they had unknowingly learned during childhood.

These improvements for the majority of Americans who were not heterosexual white men jostled against abiding forms of discrimination and inequality. Violence and the threat of violence against homosexuals, people of color, and particularly women (primarily domestic violence at the hands of husbands and lovers) remained very real, but most prejudices found more subtle avenues of expression. Working women continued to average less than three-quarters the wages of working men. Many employers, police officers, store owners, bank loan officers, and others in positions of authority treated African Americans and Latino Americans with greater suspicion than they did other citizens, a practice that became known as racial profiling. Poverty and unemployment disproportionately affected black communities and families. Given the powerful legacy of the past, white individuals on average possessed ten times more real wealth (much of it inherited) than their African American counterparts. Residential neighborhoods and public schools remained largely segregated by race, and the deeply symbolic Confederate flag still occupied a place of public honor in several southern states. Popular black comedian Chris Rock reminded mostly white audiences of the enduring but unstated advantage of being white in the United States: "Ain't no white man here willing to trade places with me—and I'm rich!"

AFP/CORBIS

▲ Defender Brandi Chastain celebrates after her decisive penalty kick against China gave the U.S. women's soccer team the 1999 World Cup title. Ripping off her shirt just as male soccer players often did, Chastain shocked some viewers but impressed others who saw muscular athleticism rather than the sexual suggestiveness of bikini swimsuits. Teammate and high scorer Mia Hamm became a household name.

Native Americans shared this combination of improving status and continuing discrimination. Their numbers were reviving, from a mere 250,000 in 1900 to 2 million in 2000. A series of federal court decisions in the 1970s and 1980s strengthened Indians' "unique and limited" sovereignty over the tribal reservations, which constituted 2 percent of U.S. land. Starting with the Iroquois of upstate New York in 1970, several eastern Indian nations sued state and federal governments for the return of parts of lands that had been illegally seized from them in the past, or for compensation. From Florida to Maine, these nations won a combination of small portions of public land and millions of dollars in compensation in cases from the 1970s through the 1990s. Casino revenues in the 1990s brought much-needed resources to a number of Indian nations. At the same time, the process of assimilation continued as a majority of Indians lived in urban areas and were married to non-Indians. Reservations suffered from severe unemployment rates and remained some of the poorest communities in the country, dependent on federal assistance for food and other basic necessities. Anti-Indian sentiments continued to surface in states as diverse as Montana, Wisconsin, Arizona, and New York.

Still an Immigrant Society

Economic opportunity and individual liberty still lured millions of people from other nations to the United States at the start of the new millennium. Some 800,000 now came legally each year, and another 300,000 entered without official papers. For the first time since the 1930s, one in ten Americans had been born abroad; in New York City the ratio was one in four. Fifteen percent came from Europe, 26 percent arrived from Asia, and 51 percent moved north from Latin America and the Caribbean. Like Italy in 1900, Mexico in 2000 became the most important single source of new Americans. The demographic transition of California in 2000 from a white majority to a more diverse ethnic and racial mix like that of Hawaii symbolized the nation's turn to the South and West, even as the aspirations and work habits of the newcomers remained very much the same as those of their European predecessors.

Only the hardiest and most motivated people made the difficult, emotionally wrenching, and often dangerous move to the United States. Many fled political persecution in countries such as Guatemala, Haiti, Vietnam, and Cuba. In contrast to the left-leaning and often socialist attitudes of immigrants in 1900, political refugees in 2000 were sometimes fierce anticommunists who helped pressure the U.S. government to take an even harder line toward regimes in Havana and Hanoi. Most immigrants came to stay, but some worked to save money and return home to their families, carrying with them not only money, but also bits of American culture. Other people flowed outward too, as American students and tourists traveled all over the globe. Some Americans worked abroad, usually for U.S.-based multinationals such as oil companies, to earn better wages and then return home. Others served in the military, worked for aid agencies and church groups, or joined in the resurgence of the Peace Corps.

Despite increasing contacts overseas, Americans responded to the wave of newcomers with an ambivalence common in previous periods of high immigration. Many in the working class feared competition from highly motivated laborers accustomed to much lower wages. Many elites worried whether cultural diversity might weaken national unity. Conservative political leaders promoted new restrictions and stronger border patrols. Some members of Congress ridiculed the idea of there being value in traveling abroad by boasting that they did not even have passports. In 1998, the Republican House majority leader, Dick Armey of Texas, announced: "I've been to Europe once; I don't have to go again." Such disdain for other cultures among some American political leaders dismayed U.S. allies overseas.

Most Americans got used to having more immigrants around. Americans cheered for the one in four major league baseball players who were born in Latin America or had parents from there, and they became accustomed to the high number of Asian Americans in college classrooms. They also cheered for baseball players from Japan and heard more Spanish on college walkways. Many churches worked to help new arrivals adjust to life in the United States. Nearly all-white Iowa even began an immigrant recruitment drive to sustain a vibrant state economy that lacked sufficient workers. Above all, American employers depended on immigrant workers to keep the nation's powerful economy afloat—to pick its fruits and vegetables, tend its young children, and work in its factories.

Conclusion

The story of the American past draws together four primary themes: the distribution of wealth and power, the identities Americans construct for themselves in a multicultural society, the international ties that help shape American life, and the natural environment in which the United States builds its future. These four themes come together in the story of southern Nevada.

In Las Vegas and across the country, immigrant labor was prized. Undocumented immigrants worked hard for low wages and caused few problems for those who hired them. But Latino or Hispanic Americans did not form a single, coherent community, despite the prominence of people of Mexican extraction. Their roots ranged from the southern tip of Chile in South America to the Rio Grande, from the Caribbean islands to the Pacific coast. They were not all in the working class: the first Spanish-speaking people drawn to modern Las Vegas for its economic opportunities were middle-class Cuban refugees from Fidel Castro's 1959 revolution, which eliminated Havana's gambling palaces and put skilled casino operators out of work. Nor were they all immigrants. The area that is now southern Nevada was part of Mexico for more than two centuries after the Pilgrims sailed into Massachusetts Bay in 1620, and many of its current Latino residents were born in the United States. Latinos represented a large part of the future of Las Vegas, where their numbers more than doubled in the 1990s to constitute 18 percent of the population, and they made up the fastest-growing ethnic group in the United States.

For most of the twentieth century, Nevada seemed to outsiders a distant desert state where the rules that governed most American lives could be bent. Prostitution was legal, as was gambling—"gaming," as industry spokespeople called it—and divorce could be easily obtained.

A reputation as a mecca for pleasure tourism drew visitors to Las Vegas, especially with the advent of jet airline service in the 1960s. With its population more than quadrupling since 1970, the fastest-growing metropolitan area in the nation had 1.5 million residents in 2000. Even as the city drew migrants to it, its values seemed to spread outward: a nation that had long condemned gambling as a vice now embraced the gaming business as a partial replacement for declining industrial employment. By 2000, most states had lotteries or some other form of legalized betting, and casinos spread from Atlantic City, New Jersey, to riverboats on the Mississippi River and Indian reservations across the country. The early nickname for Las Vegas—"Sin City"—no longer fit a place that had become a model of the new service economy and the American demographic shift to the Sunbelt of the West and South.

Las Vegas offered unskilled but industrious workers an opportunity for real upward mobility. Inexpensive housing and a low cost of living were important, and a mostly unionized work force provided the linchpin, just as it had in Detroit's auto plants. The organized housekeepers and other service employees in the city's vast hotels and casinos, whose large and diverse Culinary Workers Union was led in 2002 by an African American woman, Hattie Canty, earned decent wages and crucial benefits, such as health insurance and pension plans, that could pull them into the middle class. The traditional American dream of improving one's socioeconomic status through sheer hard work was a more viable option here than in most places in the United States, after three decades of declining real wages for those without a college education and two generations of shrinking union membership.

These economic dreams and successes were built on a slim and imperiled natural resource base, however. Unplanned and largely unregulated urban sprawl spread like an environmental cancer across Las Vegas and surrounding Clark County as roads, housing developments, and shopping malls swallowed thousands of acres of fragile desert landscape, bringing congestion, smog, and other pollutants to a harsh but once pristine climate. Like its spectacular casinos built to resemble New York City or the Egyptian pyramids, Las Vegas was in many ways an artificial city. Everything was imported from elsewhere: people, food, capital, grass, and especially water. Annual rainfall was less than five inches, yet vast fountains and swimming pools graced the grounds of the large casinos. Limited in the share of water it could divert from the nearby Colorado River, the city pumped groundwater to quench its growing thirst—the same process that was drying up underground aquifers across much of the arid West. "There is no lack of water here," essayist Edward Abbey warned about the parched Great Basin country of Nevada and Utah, "unless you try to establish a city where no city should be."

Sites to Visit

Smithsonian Center for Latino Initiatives

http://latino.si.edu/

This site offers an array of links to information on Latino culture and history.

How Race Is Lived in America

www.nytimes.com/library/national/race/most-recent.html

This is a collection of revealing articles from the *New York Times* in 2000 on race relations and racial identities in contemporary America.

Muslim Life in America

http://usinfo.state.gov/products/pubs/muslimlife/

Here, researchers can find information on Muslims in modern America and links to other sources for research.

Online Encyclopedia of Washington State History

www.historylink.org

This site provides an array of historical information about one of the fastest growing areas in the country.

September 11 Digital Archive

http://911digitalarchive.org

Created by the Center for History and New Media and George Mason University and the American Social History Project at City University of New York Graduate Center, this site offers a large collection of stories and images from September 11, 2001, when terrorists attacked New York City and Washington, D.C.

Native Americans

www.americanwest.com/pages/indians.htm

This site contains information about American Indian history and culture, along with links to the home pages of many Indian nations.

National Security Archive at George Washington University

www.gwu.edu/~nsarchiv/

This extraordinary site includes the most recent declassified documents on the making of U.S. foreign policy.

Natural Resources Defense Council

www.nrdc.org/

This site contains information and links about an array of current environmental issues.

For Further Reading

General

Thomas Bender, ed., *Rethinking American History in a Global Age* (2002).

Godfrey Hodgson, *More Equal Than Others: America from Nixon to the New Century* (2004).

Harvard Sitkoff, ed., *Perspectives on Modern America: Making Sense of the Twentieth Century* (2001).

National Commission on Terrorist Attacks, *The 9/11 Commission Report* (2004).

The George W. Bush Administration

Ivo H. Daalder and James M. Lindsay, *America Unbound: The Bush Revolution in Foreign Policy* (2003).

John Keegan, *The Iraq War* (2004).

Phebe Marr, *The Modern History of Iraq*, 2nd ed. (2004).

John Newhouse, *Imperial America: The Bush Assault on the World Order* (2003).

America's Place in a Global Economy

William M. Adler, *Mollie's Job: A Story of Life and Work on the Global Assembly Line* (2000).

Jefferson Cowie, *Capital Moves: RCA's Seventy-Year Quest for Cheap Labor* (1999).

Barbara Ehrenreich, *Nickel and Dimed: On (Not) Getting By in America* (2001).

Thomas L. Friedman, *The Lexus and the Olive Tree: Understanding Globalization* (1999).

William Greider, *One World, Ready or Not: The Manic Logic of Global Capitalism* (1997).

Robert Kuttner, *Everything for Sale: The Virtues and Limits of Markets* (1996).

The Stewardship of Natural Resources

David Goodstein, *Out of Gas: The End of the Age of Oil* (2004).

J. R. McNeill, *Something New Under the Sun: An Environmental History of the Twentieth-Century World* (2000).

David Quammen, *The Song of the Dodo: Island Biogeography in an Age of Extinction* (1996).

Hal K. Rothman, *Saving the Planet: The American Response to the Environment in the Twentieth Century* (2000).

James Gustave Speth, *Red Sky at Morning: America and the Crisis of the Global Environment* (2004).

The Expansion of American Popular Culture Abroad

Benjamin R. Barber, *Jihad vs. McWorld: How the Planet Is Both Falling Apart and Coming Together and What This Means for Democracy* (1995).

Chalmers Johnson, *Blowback: The Costs and Consequences of American Empire* (2000).

Richard F. Kuisel, *Seducing the French: The Dilemma of Americanization* (1993).

Richard Pells, *Not Like Us: How Europeans Have Loved, Hated, and Transformed American Culture Since World War II* (1997).

Reinhold Wagnleitner and Elaine Tyler May, eds., *"Here, There and Everywhere": The Foreign Politics of American Popular Culture* (2000).

Identity in Contemporary America

Charles Hirshman and Philip Kasinitz, eds., *The Handbook of International Migration: The American Experience* (1999).

David A. Hollinger, *Postethnic America: Beyond Multiculturalism*, rev. ed. (2000).

Gary Y. Okihiro, *Common Ground: Reimagining American History* (2001).

Robert D. Putnam, *Bowling Alone: The Collapse and Revival of American Community* (2000).

Ruth Rosen, *The World Split Open: How the Modern Women's Movement Changed America* (2000).

Alan Wolfe, *One Nation After All: What Americans Really Think About God, Country, Family, Racism, Welfare, Immigration, Homosexuality, Work, the Right, the Left and Each Other* (1998).

Appendix

The Declaration of Independence

The Articles of Confederation

The Constitution of the United States of America

Amendments to the Constitution

Presidential Elections

Mapping History in the United States

Present Day World

For additional reference material, go to
www.ablongman.com/jonescreatedequal/appendix
The online appendix includes the following:

The Declaration of Independence
The Articles of Confederation
The Constitution of the United States of America
Amendments to the Constitution
Presidential Elections
Vice Presidents and Cabinet Members by Administration
Supreme Court Justices
Presidents, Congresses, and Chief Justices, 1789–2001
Territorial Expansion of the United States (map)
Admission of States of the Union
U.S. Population, 1790–2000
Ten Largest Cities by Population, 1700–1900
Birthrate, 1820–2000 (chart)
Death Rate, 1900–2000 (chart)
Life Expectancy, 1900–2000 (chart)
Urban/Rural Population, 1750–1900 (chart)
Women in the Labor Force, 1890–1990 (chart)
United States Physical Features (map)
United States Native Vegetation (map)
Ancient Native American Communities (map)
Native American Peoples, c. 1500 (map)
Present Day United States (map)

The Declaration of Independence

In Congress, July 4, 1776

The Unanimous Declaration of the Thirteen United States of America

When, in the course of human events, it becomes necessary for one people to dissolve the political bonds which have connected them with another, and to assume, among the powers of the earth, the separate and equal station to which the laws of nature and of nature's God entitle them, a decent respect to the opinions of mankind requires that they should declare the causes which impel them to the separation.

We hold these truths to be self-evident: That all men are created equal; that they are endowed by their Creator with certain unalienable rights; that among these are life, liberty, and the pursuit of happiness; that, to secure these rights, governments are instituted among men, deriving their just powers from the consent of the governed; that whenever any form of government becomes destructive of these ends, it is the right of the people to alter or to abolish it, and to institute new government, laying its foundation on such principles, and organizing its powers in such form, as to them shall seem most likely to effect their safety and happiness. Prudence, indeed, will dictate that governments long established should not be changed for light and transient causes; and accordingly all experience hath shown that mankind are more disposed to suffer, while evils are sufferable, than to right themselves by abolishing the forms to which they are accustomed. But when a long train of abuses and usurpations, pursuing invariably the same object, evinces a design to reduce them under absolute despotism, it is their right, it is their duty, to throw off such government, and to provide new guards for their future security. Such has been the patient sufferance of these colonies; and such is now the necessity which constrains them to alter their former systems of government. The history of the present King of Great Britain is a history of repeated injuries and usurpations, all having in direct object the establishment of an absolute tyranny over these states. To prove this, let facts be submitted to a candid world.

He has refused his assent to laws, the most wholesome and necessary for the public good.

He has forbidden his governors to pass laws of immediate and pressing importance, unless suspended in their operation till his assent should be obtained; and, when so suspended, he has utterly neglected to attend to them.

He has refused to pass other laws for the accommodation of large districts of people, unless those people would relinquish the right of representation in the legislature, a right inestimable to them, and formidable to tyrants only.

He has called together legislative bodies at places unusual, uncomfortable, and distant from the depository of their public records, for the sole purpose of fatiguing them into compliance with his measures.

He has dissolved representative houses repeatedly, for opposing, with manly firmness, his invasions on the rights of the people.

He has refused for a long time, after such dissolutions, to cause others to be elected; whereby the legislative powers, incapable of annihilation, have returned to the people at large for their exercise; the state remaining, in the mean time, exposed to all the dangers of invasions from without and convulsions within.

He has endeavored to prevent the population of these states; for that purpose obstructing the laws for naturalization of foreigners; refusing to pass others to encourage their migration hither, and raising the conditions of new appropriations of lands.

He has obstructed the administration of justice, by refusing his assent to laws for establishing judiciary powers.

He has made judges dependent on his will alone, for the tenure of their offices, and the amount and payment of their salaries.

He has erected a multitude of new offices, and sent hither swarms of officers to harass our people and eat out their substance.

He has kept among us, in times of peace, standing armies, without the consent of our legislatures.

He has affected to render the military independent of, and superior to, the civil power.

He has combined with others to subject us to a jurisdiction foreign to our constitution, and unacknowledged by our laws, giving his assent to their acts of pretended legislation:

For quartering large bodies of armed troops among us;

For protecting them, by a mock trial, from punishment for any murder which they should commit on the inhabitants of these states;

For cutting off our trade with all parts of the world;

For imposing taxes on us without our consent;

For depriving us, in many cases, of the benefits of trial by jury;

For transporting us beyond seas, to be tried for pretended offenses;

For abolishing the free system of English laws in a neighboring province, establishing therein an arbitrary government, and enlarging its boundaries, so as to render it at once an example and fit instrument for introducing the same absolute rule into these colonies;

For taking away our charters, abolishing our most valuable laws, and altering fundamentally the forms of our governments;

For suspending our own legislatures, and declaring themselves invested with power to legislate for us in all cases whatsoever.

He has abdicated government here, by declaring us out of his protection and waging war against us.

He has plundered our seas, ravaged our coasts, burned our towns, and destroyed the lives of our people.

He is at this time transporting large armies of foreign mercenaries to complete the works of death, desolation, and tyranny already begun with circumstances of cruelty and perfidy scarcely paralleled in the most barbarous ages, and totally unworthy the head of a civilized nation.

He has constrained our fellow-citizens, taken captive on the high seas, to bear arms against their country, to become the executioners of their friends and brethren, or to fall themselves by their hands.

He has excited domestic insurrection among us, and has endeavored to bring on the inhabitants of our frontiers the merciless Indian savages, whose known rule of warfare is an undistinguished destruction of all ages, sexes, and conditions.

In every stage of these oppressions we have petitioned for redress in the most humble terms; our repeated petitions have been answered only by repeated injury. A prince, whose character is thus marked by every act which may define a tyrant, is unfit to be the ruler of a free people.

Nor have we been wanting in our attentions to our British brethren. We have warned them, from time to time, of attempts by their legislature to extend an unwarrantable jurisdiction over us. We have reminded them of the circumstances of our emigration and settlement here. We have appealed to their native justice and magnanimity; and we have conjured them, by the ties of our common kindred, to disavow these usurpations, which would inevitably interrupt our connections and correspondence. They, too, have been deaf to the voice of justice and of consanguinity. We must, therefore, acquiesce in the necessity which denounces our separation, and hold them, as we hold the rest of mankind, enemies in war, in peace friends.

We, therefore, the representatives of the United States of America, in General Congress assembled, appealing to the Supreme Judge of the world for the rectitude of our intentions, do, in the name and by the authority of the good people of these colonies, solemnly publish and declare, that these United Colonies are, and of right ought to be, FREE AND INDEPENDENT STATES; that they are absolved from all allegiance to the British crown, and that all political connection between them and the state of Great Britain is, and ought to be, totally dissolved; and that, as free and independent states, they have full power to levy war, conclude peace, contract alliances, establish commerce, and do all other acts and things which independent states may of right do. And for the support of this declaration, with a firm reliance on the protection of Divine Providence, we mutually pledge to each other our lives, our fortunes, and our sacred honor.

JOHN HANCOCK

New Hampshire
Josiah Bartlett
William Whipple
Matthew Thornton

Massachusetts
John Adams
Samuel Adams
Robert Treat Paine
Elbridge Gerry

New York
William Floyd
Philip Livingston
Francis Lewis
Lewis Morris

Rhode Island
Stephen Hopkins
William Ellery

New Jersey
Richard Stockton
John Witherspoon
Francis Hopkinson
John Hart
Abraham Clark

Pennsylvania
Robert Morris
Benjamin Rush
Benjamin Franklin
John Morton
George Clymer
James Smith
George Taylor
James Wilson
George Ross

Delaware
Caeser Rodney
George Read
Thomas McKean

Maryland
Samuel Chase
William Paca
Thomas Stone
Charles Carroll of Carrollton

North Carolina
William Hooper
Joseph Hewes
John Penn

Virginia
George Wythe
Richard Henry Lee
Thomas Jefferson
Benjamin Harrison
Thomas Nelson, Jr.
Francis Lightfoot Lee
Carter Braxton

South Carolina
Edward Rutledge
Thomas Heyward, Jr.
Thomas Lynch, Jr.
Arthur Middleton

Connecticut
Roger Sherman
Samuel Huntington
William Williams
Oliver Wolcott

Georgia
Button Gwinnett
Lyman Hall
George Walton

The Articles of Confederation

Between the States of New Hampshire, Massachusetts Bay, Rhode Island and Providence Plantations, Connecticut, New York, New Jersey, Pennsylvania, Delaware, Maryland, Virginia, North Carolina, South Carolina, Georgia

Article 1

The stile of this confederacy shall be "The United States of America."

Article 2

Each State retains its sovereignty, freedom and independence, and every power, jurisdiction, and right, which is not by this confederation expressly delegated to the United States, in Congress assembled.

Article 3

The said states hereby severally enter into a firm league of friendship with each other for their common defence, the security of their liberties and their mutual and general welfare; binding themselves to assist each other against all force offered to, or attacks made upon them, or any of them, on account of religion, sovereignty, trade, or any other pretence whatever.

Article 4

The better to secure and perpetuate mutual friendship and intercourse among the people of the different states in this union, the free inhabitants of each of these states, paupers, vagabonds, and fugitives from justice excepted, shall be entitled to all privileges and immunities of free citizens in the several states; and the people of each State shall have free ingress and regress to and from any other State, and shall enjoy therein all the privileges of trade and commerce, subject to the same duties, impositions, and restrictions, as the inhabitants thereof respectively; provided, that such restrictions shall not extend so far as to prevent the removal of property, imported into any State, to any other State of which the owner is an inhabitant; provided also, that no imposition, duties, or restriction, shall be laid by any State on the property of the United States, or either of them.

If any person guilty of, or charged with treason, felony, or other high misdemeanor in any State, shall flee from justice and be found in any of the United States, he shall, upon demand of the governor or executive power of the State from which he fled, be delivered up and removed to the State having jurisdiction of his offence.

Full faith and credit shall be given in each of these states to the records, acts, and judicial proceedings of the courts and magistrates of every other State.

Article 5

For the more convenient management of the general interests of the United States, delegates shall be annually appointed, in such manner as the legislature of each State shall direct, to meet in Congress, on the 1st Monday in November in every year, with a power reserved to each State to recall its delegates, or any of them, at any time within the year, and to send others in their stead for the remainder of the year.

No State shall be represented in Congress by less than two, nor by more than seven members; and no person shall be capable of being a delegate for more than three years in any term of six years; nor shall any person, being a delegate, be capable of holding any office under the United States, for which he, or any other for his benefit, receives any salary, fees, or emolument of any kind.

Each State shall maintain its own delegates in a meeting of the states, and while they act as members of the committee of the states.

In determining questions in the United States, in Congress assembled, each State shall have one vote.

Freedom of speech and debate in Congress shall not be impeached or questioned in any court or place out of Congress: and the members of Congress shall be protected in their persons from arrests and imprisonments, during the time of their going to and from, and attendance on Congress, except for treason, felony, or breach of the peace.

Article 6

No State, without the consent of the United States, in Congress assembled, shall send any embassy to, or receive any embassy from, or enter into any conference, agreement, alliance, or treaty with any king, prince, or state; nor shall any person, holding any office of profit or trust under the United States, or any of them, accept of any present, emolument, office or title, of any kind whatever, from any king, prince, or foreign state; nor shall the United States, in Congress assembled, or any of them, grant any title of nobility.

No two or more states shall enter into any treaty, confederation, or alliance, whatever, between them, without the consent of the United States, in Congress assembled, specifying accurately the purposes for which the same is to be entered into, and how long it shall continue.

No State shall lay any imposts or duties which may interfere with any stipulations in treaties entered into by the United States, in Congress assembled, with any king, prince, or state, in pursuance of any treaties already proposed by Congress to the courts of France and Spain.

No vessels of war shall be kept up in time of peace by any State, except such number only as shall be deemed necessary by the United States, in Congress assembled, for the defence of such State or its trade; nor shall any body of forces be kept up by any State, in time of peace, except such number only as, in the judgment of the United States, in Congress assembled, shall be deemed requisite to garrison the forts necessary for the defence of such State; but every State shall always keep up a well regulated and disciplined militia, sufficiently armed and accoutred, and shall provide, and constantly have ready for use, in public stores, a due number of field pieces and tents, and a proper quantity of arms, ammunition and camp equipage.

No State shall engage in any war without the consent of the United States, in Congress assembled, unless such State be actually invaded by enemies, or shall have received certain advice of a resolution being formed by some nation of Indians to invade such State, and the danger is so imminent as not to admit of a delay till the United States, in Congress assembled, can be consulted; nor shall any State grant commissions to any ships or vessels of war, nor letters of marque or reprisal, except it be after a declaration of war by the United States, in Congress assembled, and then only against the kingdom or state, and the subjects thereof, against which war has been so declared, and under such regulations as shall be established by the United States, in Congress assembled, unless such States be infested by pirates, in which case vessels of war may be fitted out for that occasion, and kept so long as the danger shall continue, or until the United States, in Congress assembled, shall determine otherwise.

Article 7

When land forces are raised by any State for the common defence, all officers of or under the rank of colonel, shall be appointed by the legislature of each State respectively, by whom such forces shall be raised, or in such manner as such State shall direct; and all vacancies shall be filled up by the State which first made the appointment.

Article 8

All charges of war and all other expences, that shall be incurred for the common defence or general welfare, and allowed by the United States, in Congress assembled, shall be defrayed out of a common treasury, which shall be supplied by the several states, in proportion to the value of all land within each State, granted to or surveyed for any person, as such land and the buildings and improvements thereon shall be estimated according to such mode as the United States, in Congress assembled, shall, from time to time, direct and appoint.

The taxes for paying that proportion shall be laid and levied by the authority and direction of the legislatures of the several states, within the time agreed upon by the United States, in Congress assembled.

Article 9

The United States, in Congress assembled, shall have the sole and exclusive right and power of determining on peace and war, except in the cases mentioned in the 6th article; of sending and receiving ambassadors; entering into treaties and alliances, provided that no treaty of commerce shall be made, whereby the legislative power of the respective states shall be restrained from imposing such imposts and duties on foreigners as their own people are subjected to, or from prohibiting the exportation or importation of any species of goods or commodities whatsoever; of establishing rules for deciding, in all cases, what captures on land or water shall be legal, and in what manner prizes, taken by land or naval forces in the service of the United States, shall be divided or appropriated; of granting letters of marque and reprisal in times of peace; appointing courts for the trial of piracies and felonies committed on the high seas, and establishing courts for receiving and determining, finally, appeals in all cases of captures; provided, that no member of Congress shall be appointed a judge of any of the said courts.

The United States, in Congress assembled, shall also be the last resort on appeal in all disputes and differences now subsisting, or that hereafter may arise between two or more states concerning boundary, jurisdiction or any other cause whatever; which authority shall always be exercised in the manner following: whenever the legislative or executive authority, or lawful agent of any State, in controversy with another, shall present a petition to Congress, stating the matter in question, and praying for a hearing, notice thereof shall be given, by order of Congress, to the legislative or executive authority of the other State in controversy, and a day assigned for the appearance of the parties by their lawful agents, who shall then be directed to appoint, by joint consent, commissioners or judges to constitute a court for hearing and determining the matter in question; but, if they cannot agree, Congress shall name three persons out of each of the United States, and from the list of such persons each party shall alternately strike out one, in the petitioners beginning, until the number shall be reduced to thirteen; and from that number not less than seven, nor more than nine names, as Congress shall direct, shall, in the presence of Congress, be drawn out by lot; and the persons whose names shall be drawn, or any five of them, shall be commissioners or judges to hear and finally determine the controversy, so always as a major part of the judges who shall hear the cause shall agree in the determination; and if either party shall neglect to attend at the day appointed, without shewing reasons which Congress shall judge sufficient, or, being present, shall refuse to strike, the Congress shall proceed to nominate three persons out of each State, and the secretary of Congress shall strike in behalf of such party absent or refusing; and the judgment and sentence of the court to be appointed, in the manner before prescribed, shall be final and conclusive; and if any of the parties shall refuse to submit to the authority of such court, or to appear or defend their claim or cause, the court shall nevertheless proceed to pronounce sentence or judgment, which shall, in like manner, be final and decisive, the judgment or sentence and other proceedings being, in either case, transmitted to Congress, and lodged among the acts of Congress for the security of the parties concerned: provided, that every commissioner, before he sits in judgment, shall take an oath, to be administered by one of the judges of the supreme or superior court of the State where the cause shall be tried, "well and truly to hear and determine the matter in question, according to the best of his judgment, without favour, affection, or hope of reward": provided, also, that no State shall be deprived of territory for the benefit of the United States.

All controversies concerning the private right of soil, claimed under different grants of two or more states, whose jurisdictions, as they may respect such lands and the states which passed such grants, are adjusted, the said grants, or either of them, being at the same time claimed to have originated antecedent to such settlement of jurisdiction, shall, on the petition of either party to the Congress of the United States, be finally determined, as near as may be, in the same manner as is before prescribed for deciding disputes respecting territorial jurisdiction between different states.

The United States, in Congress assembled, shall also have the sole and exclusive right and power of regulating the alloy and value of coin struck by their own authority, or by that of the respective states; fixing the standard of weights and measures throughout the United States; regulating the trade and managing all affairs with the Indians not members of any of the states; provided that the legislative right of any State within its own limits be not infringed or violated; establishing and regulating post offices from one State to another throughout all the United States, and exacting such postage on the papers passing through the same as may be requisite to defray the expences of the said office; appointing all officers of the land forces in the service of the United States, excepting regimental officers; appointing all the officers of the naval forces, and commissioning all officers whatever in the service of the United States; making rules for the government and regulation of the said land and naval forces, and directing their operations.

The United States, in Congress assembled, shall have authority to appoint a committee to sit in the recess of Congress, to be denominated "a Committee of the States," and to consist of one delegate from each State, and to appoint such other committees and civil officers as may be necessary for managing the general affairs of the United States, under their direction; to appoint one of their number to preside; provided that no person be allowed to serve in the office of president more than one year in any term of three years; to ascertain the necessary sums of money to be raised for the service of the United States, and to appropriate and apply the same for defraying the public expences; to borrow money or emit bills on the credit of the United States, transmitting, every half year, to the respective states, an account of the sums of money so borrowed or emitted; to build and equip a navy; to agree upon the number of land forces, and to make requisitions from each State for its quota, in proportion to the number of white inhabitants in such State; which requisitions shall be binding; and, thereupon, the legislature of each State shall appoint the regimental officers, raise the men, and cloathe, arm, and equip them in a soldier-like manner, at the expence of the United States; and the officers and men so cloathed, armed, and equipped, shall march to the place appointed and within the time agreed on by the United States, in Congress assembled; but if the United States, in Congress assembled, shall, on consideration of circumstances, judge proper that any State should not raise men, or should raise a smaller number than its quota, and that any other State should raise a greater number of men than the quota thereof, such extra number shall be raised, officered, cloathed, armed, and equipped in the same manner as the quota of such State, unless the legislature of such State shall judge that such extra number cannot be safely spared out of the same, in which case they shall raise, officer, cloathe, arm, and equip as many of such extra number as they judge can be safely spared. And the officers and men so cloathed, armed, and equipped, shall march to the place appointed and within the time agreed on by the United States, in Congress assembled.

The United States, in Congress assembled, shall never engage in a war, nor grant letters of marque and reprisal in time of peace, nor enter into any treaties or alliances, nor coin money, nor regulate the value thereof, nor ascertain the sums and expences necessary for the defence and welfare of the United States, or any of them: nor emit bills, nor borrow money on the credit of the United States, nor appropriate money, nor agree upon the number of vessels of war to be built or purchased, or the number of land or sea forces to be raised, nor appoint a commander in chief of the army or navy, unless nine states assent to the same; nor shall a question on any other point, except for adjourning from day to day, be determined, unless by the votes of a majority of the United States, in Congress assembled.

The Congress of the United States shall have power to adjourn to any time within the year, and to any place within the United States, so that no period of adjournment be for a longer duration than the space of six months, and shall publish the journal of their proceedings monthly, except such parts thereof, relating to treaties, alliances or military operations, as, in their judgment, require secrecy; and the yeas and nays of the delegates of each State on any question shall be entered on the journal, when it is desired by any delegate; and the delegates of a State, or any of them, at his, or their request, shall be furnished with a transcript of the said journal, except such parts as are above excepted, to lay before the legislatures of the several states.

Article 10

The committee of the states, or any nine of them, shall be authorized to execute, in the recess of Congress, such of the powers of Congress as the United States, in Congress assembled, by the consent of nine states, shall, from time to time, think expedient to vest them with; provided, that no power be delegated to the said committee for the exercise of which, by the articles of confederation, the voice of nine states, in the Congress of the United States assembled, is requisite.

Article 11

Canada acceding to this confederation, and joining in the measures of the United States, shall be admitted into and entitled to all the advantages of this union; but no other colony shall be admitted into the same, unless such admission be agreed to by nine states.

Article 12

All bills of credit emitted, monies borrowed and debts contracted by, or under the authority of Congress before the assembling of the United States, in pursuance of the present confederation, shall be deemed and considered as a charge against the United States, for payment and satisfaction whereof the said United States and the public faith are hereby solemnly pledged.

Article 13

Every State shall abide by the determinations of the United States, in Congress assembled, on all questions which, by this confederation, are submitted to them. And the articles of this confederation shall be inviolably observed by every State, and the union shall be perpetual; nor shall any alteration at any time hereafter be made in any of them, unless such alteration be agreed to in a Congress of the United States, and be afterwards confirmed by the legislatures of every State.

These articles shall be proposed to the legislatures of all the United States, to be considered, and if approved of by them, they are advised to authorize their delegates to ratify the same in the Congress of the United States; which being done, the same shall become conclusive.

The Constitution of the United States of America

Preamble

We the People of the United States, in Order to form a more perfect Union, establish Justice, insure domestic Tranquility, provide for the common defence, promote the general Welfare, and secure the Blessings of Liberty to ourselves and our Posterity, do ordain and establish this Constitution for the United States of America.

Article I

Section 1

All legislative Powers herein granted shall be vested in a Congress of the United States, which shall consist of a Senate and House of Representatives.

Section 2

The House of Representatives shall be composed of Members chosen every second Year by the People of the several States, and the Electors in each State shall have the Qualifications requisite for Electors of the most numerous Branch of the State Legislature.

No Person shall be a Representative who shall not have attained to the Age of twenty five Years, and been seven Years a Citizen of the United States, and who shall not, when elected, be an inhabitant of that State in which he shall be chosen.

Representatives and direct Taxes shall be apportioned among the several States which may be included within this Union, according to their respective Numbers, *which shall be determined by adding to the whole Number of free Persons, including those bound to Service for a Term of Years, and excluding Indians not taxed, three fifths of all other Persons.** The actual Enumeration shall be made within three Years after the first Meeting of the Congress of the United States, and within every subsequent Term of ten Years, in such Manner as they shall by Law direct. The Number of Representatives shall not exceed one for every thirty Thousand, but each State shall have at Least one Representative; *and until such enumeration shall be made, the State of New Hampshire shall be entitled to chuse three, Massachusetts eight, Rhode-Island and Providence Plantations one, Connecticut five, New York six, New Jersey four, Pennsylvania eight, Delaware one, Maryland six, Virginia ten, North Carolina five, South Carolina five, and Georgia three.*

When vacancies happen in the Representation from any State, the Executive Authority thereof shall issue Writs of Election to fill such Vacancies.

The House of Representatives shall chuse their Speaker and other Officers; and shall have the sole Power of Impeachment.

Section 3

The Senate of the United States shall be composed of two Senators from each State, *chosen by the Legislature thereof,* for six Years; and each Senator shall have one Vote.

Immediately after they shall be assembled in Consequence of the first Election, they shall be divided as equally as may be into three Classes. The Seats of the Senators of the first Class shall be vacated at the Expiration of the second Year, of the second Class at the Expiration of the fourth Year, and of the third Class at the Expiration of the sixth Year so that one third may be chosen every second Year; and if Vacancies happen by Resignation, or otherwise, during the Recess of the Legislature of any state, the Executive thereof may make temporary Appointments until the next Meeting of the Legislature, which shall then fill such Vacancies.

No Person shall be a Senator who shall not have attained to the Age of thirty Years, and been nine Years a Citizen of the United States, and who shall not, when elected, be an Inhabitant of that State for which he shall be chosen.

The Vice President of the United States shall be President of the Senate, but shall have no Vote, unless they be equally divided.

The Senate shall chuse their other Officers, and also a President *pro tempore,* in the Absence of the Vice President, or when he shall exercise the Office of President of the United States.

The Senate shall have the sole Power to try all Impeachments. When sitting for that Purpose, they shall be on Oath or Affirmation. When the President of the United States is tried the Chief Justice shall preside: And no Person shall be convicted without the Concurrence of two thirds of the Members present.

Judgment in Cases of Impeachment shall not extend further than to removal from Office, and disqualification to hold and enjoy any Office of honor, Trust or Profit under the United States: but the Party convicted shall nevertheless be liable and subject to Indictment, Trial, Judgment and Punishment, according to Law.

Section 4

The Times, Places and Manner of holding Elections for Senators and Representatives, shall be prescribed in each State by the Legislature thereof; but the Congress may at any time by Law make or alter such Regulations, except as to the Places of chusing Senators.

The Congress shall assemble at least once in every Year, *and such Meeting shall be on the first Monday in December, unless they shall by Law appoint a different Day.*

Section 5

Each House shall be the Judge of the Elections, Returns and Qualifications of its own Members, and a Majority of each shall constitute a Quorum to do Business; but a smaller Number may adjourn from day to day, and may be authorized to compel the Attendance of absent Members, in such Manner, and under such Penalties as each House may provide.

*Passages no longer in effect are printed in italic type.

Each House may determine the Rules of its Proceedings, punish its Members for disorderly Behaviour, and, with the Concurrence of two thirds, expel a Member.

Each House shall keep a Journal of its Proceedings, and from time to time publish the same, excepting such Parts as may in their Judgment require Secrecy; and the Yeas and Nays of the Members of either House on any question shall, at the Desire of one fifth of those Present, be entered on the Journal.

Neither House, during the Session of Congress, shall, without the Consent of the other, adjourn for more than three days, nor to any other Place than that in which the two Houses shall be sitting.

Section 6

The Senators and Representatives shall receive a Compensation for their Services, to be ascertained by Law, and paid out of the Treasury of the United States. They shall in all Cases, except Treason, Felony and Breach of the Peace, be privileged from Arrest during their Attendance at the Session of their respective Houses, and in going to and returning from the same; and for any Speech or Debate in either House, they shall not be questioned in any other Place.

No Senator or Representative shall, during the Time for which he was elected, be appointed to any civil Office under the Authority of the United States, which shall have been created, or the Emoluments whereof shall have been encreased during such time, and no Person holding any Office under the United States, shall be a Member of either House during his Continuance in Office.

Section 7

All Bills for raising Revenue shall originate in the House of Representatives; but the Senate may propose or concur with Amendments as on other Bills.

Every Bill which shall have passed the House of Representatives and the Senate, shall, before it become a Law, be presented to the President of the United States; If he approve he shall sign it, but if not he shall return it, with his Objections to the House in which it shall have originated, who shall enter the Objections at large on their Journal, and proceed to reconsider it. If after such Reconsideration two thirds of that House shall agree to pass the Bill, it shall be sent, together with the Objections, to the other House, by which it shall likewise be reconsidered, and if approved by two thirds of that House, it shall become a Law. But in all such Cases the Votes of both Houses shall be determined by yeas and Nays, and the Names of the Persons voting for and against the Bill shall be entered on the Journal of each House respectively. If any Bill shall not be returned by the President within ten Days (Sundays excepted) after it shall have been presented to him, the Same shall be a Law, in like Manner as if he had signed it, unless the Congress by their Adjournment prevent its Return, in which Case it shall not be a Law.

Every Order, Resolution, or Vote to which the Concurrence of the Senate and House of Representatives may be necessary (except on a question of Adjournment) shall be presented to the President of the United States; and before the Same shall take Effect, shall be approved by him, or being disapproved by him, shall be repassed by two thirds of the Senate and House of Representatives, according to the Rules and Limitations prescribed in the Case of a Bill.

Section 8

The Congress shall have Power To lay and collect Taxes, Duties, Imposts and Excises, to pay the Debts and provide for the common Defence and general Welfare of the United States; but all Duties, Imposts and Excises shall be uniform throughout the United States;

To borrow Money on the credit of the United States;

To regulate Commerce with foreign Nations, and among the several States, and with the Indian Tribes;

To establish an uniform Rule of Naturalization, and uniform Laws on the subject of Bankruptcies throughout the United States;

To coin Money, regulate the Value thereof, and of foreign Coin, and fix the Standard of Weights and Measures;

To provide for the Punishment of counterfeiting the Securities and current Coin of the United States;

To establish Post Offices and post Roads;

To promote the Progress of Science and useful Arts, by securing for limited Times to Authors and Inventors the exclusive Right to their respective Writings and Discoveries;

To constitute Tribunals inferior to the supreme Court;

To define and punish Piracies and Felonies committed on the high Seas, and Offences against the Law of Nations;

To declare War, grant Letters of Marque and Reprisal, and make Rules concerning Captures on Land and Water;

To raise and support Armies, but no Appropriation of Money to that Use shall be for a longer Term than two Years;

To provide and maintain a Navy;

To make Rules for the Government and Regulation of the land and naval Forces;

To provide for calling forth the Militia to execute the Laws of the Union, suppress Insurrections and repel Invasions;

To provide for organizing, arming, and disciplining, the Militia, and for governing such Part of them as may be employed in the Service of the United States, reserving to the States respectively, the Appointment of the Officers, and the Authority of training the Militia according to the discipline prescribed by Congress;

To exercise exclusive Legislation in all Cases whatsoever, over such District (not exceeding ten Miles square) as may, by Cession of particular States, and the Acceptance of Congress, become the Seat of the Government of the United States, and to exercise like Authority over all Places purchased by the Consent of the Legislature of the State in which the Same shall be, for the Erection of Forts, Magazines, Arsenals, dock-Yards, and other needful Buildings;—And

To make all Laws which shall be necessary and proper for carrying into Execution the foregoing Powers, and all other Powers vested by this Constitution in the Government of the United States, or in any Department of Officer thereof.

Section 9

The Migration or Importation of such Persons as any of the States now existing shall think proper to admit, shall not be prohibited by the Congress prior to the Year one thousand eight hundred and

eight, but a Tax or duty may be imposed on such Importation, not exceeding ten dollars for each Person.

The Privilege of the Writ of Habeas Corpus shall not be suspended, unless when in Cases of Rebellion or Invasion the public Safety may require it.

No Bill of Attainder or ex post facto Law shall be passed.

No Capitation, or other direct, Tax shall be laid, unless in Proportion to the Census or Enumeration herein before directed to be taken.

No Tax or Duty shall be laid on Articles exported from any State.

No Preference shall be given by any Regulation of Commerce or Revenue to the Ports of one State over those of another: nor shall Vessels bound to, or from, one State, be obliged to enter, clear, or pay Duties in another.

No Money shall be drawn from the Treasury, but in Consequence of Appropriations made by Law; and a regular Statement and Account of the Receipts and Expenditures of all public Money shall be published from time to time.

No Title of Nobility shall be granted by the United States: And no Person holding any Office of Profit or Trust under them, shall, without the Consent of the Congress, accept of any present, Emolument, Office, or Title, of any kind whatever, from any King, Prince, or foreign State.

Section 10

No State shall enter into any Treaty, Alliance, or Confederation; grant Letters of Marque and Reprisal; coin Money; emit Bills of Credit; make any Thing but gold and silver Coin a Tender in Payment of Debts; pass any Bill of Attainder, ex post facto Law, or Law impairing the obligation of Contracts, or grant any Title of Nobility.

No State shall, without the Consent of the Congress, lay any Imposts or Duties on Imports or Exports, except what may be absolutely necessary for executing its inspection Laws: and the net Produce of all Duties and Imposts, laid by any State on Imports or Exports, shall be for the Use of the Treasury of the United States; and all such Laws shall be subject to the Revision and Controul of the Congress.

No State shall, without the Consent of Congress, lay any Duty of Tonnage, keep Troops, or Ships of War in time of Peace, enter into any Agreement or Compact with another State, or with a foreign Power, or engage in War, unless actually invaded, or in such imminent Danger as will not admit of delay.

Article II

Section 1

The executive Power shall be vested in a President of the United States of America. He shall hold his Office during the Term of four Years, and, together with the Vice President, chosen for the same Term, be elected, as follows:

Each State shall appoint, in such Manner as the Legislature thereof may direct, a Number of Electors, equal to the whole Number of Senators and Representatives to which the State may be entitled in the Congress: but no Senator or Representative, or Person holding an Office of Trust or Profit under the United States, shall be appointed an Elector.

The Electors shall meet in their respective States, and vote by Ballot for two Persons, of whom one at least shall not be an Inhabitant of the same State with themselves. And they shall make a List of all the Persons voted for, and of the Number of Votes for each; which List they shall sign and certify, and transmit sealed to the Seat of the Government of the United States, directed to the President of the Senate. The President of the Senate shall, in the Presence of the Senate and House of Representatives, open all the Certificates, and the Votes shall then be counted. The Person having the greatest Number of Votes shall be the President, if such Number be a Majority of the whole number of Electors appointed; and if there be more than one who have such Majority, and have an equal Number of Votes, then the House of Representatives shall immediately chuse by Ballot one of them for President; and if no Person have a Majority, then from the five highest on the List the said House shall in like Manner chuse the President. But in chusing the President, the Votes shall be taken by States, the Representation from each State having one Vote; A quorum for this Purpose shall consist of a Member or Members from two thirds of the States, and a Majority of all the States shall be necessary to a Choice. In every Case, after the Choice of the President, the Person having the greatest Number of Votes of the Electors shall be the Vice President. But if there should remain two or more who have equal Votes, the Senate shall chuse from them by Ballot the Vice President.

The Congress may determine the time of chusing the Electors, and the Day on which they shall give their Votes; which Day shall be the same throughout the United States.

No person except a natural born Citizen, *or a Citizen of the United States, at the time of the Adoption of this Constitution,* shall be eligible to the Office of President; neither shall any Person be eligible to that Office who shall not have attained to the Age of thirty five Years, and been fourteen Years a Resident within the United States.

In Case of the Removal of the President from Office, or of his Death, Resignation, or Inability to discharge the Powers and Duties of the said Office, the Same shall devolve on the Vice President, and the Congress may by Law provide for the Case of Removal, Death, Resignation or Inability, both of the President and Vice President, declaring what Officer shall then act as President, and such Officer shall act accordingly, until the Disability be removed, or a President shall be elected.

The President shall, at stated Times, receive for his Services, a Compensation, which shall neither be encreased nor diminished during the Period for which he shall have been elected, and he shall not receive within that period any other Emolument from the United States, or any of them.

Before he enter on the Execution of his Office, he shall take the following Oath or Affirmation:—"I do solemnly swear (or affirm) that I will faithfully execute the Office of President of the United States, and will to the best of my Ability, preserve, protect and defend the Constitution of the United States."

Section 2

The President shall be Commander in Chief of the Army and Navy of the United States, and of the Militia of the several States, when called into the actual Service of the United States; he may require the Opinion, in writing, of the principal Officer in each of the executive Departments, upon any Subject relating to the Duties of their respective Offices, and he shall have

Power to grant Reprieves and Pardons for Offences against the United States, except in Cases of Impeachment.

He shall have Power, by and with the Advice and Consent of the Senate, to make Treaties, provided two thirds of the Senators present concur; and he shall nominate, and by and with the Advice and Consent of the Senate, shall appoint Ambassadors, other public Ministers and Consuls, Judges of the supreme Court, and all other Officers of the United States, whose Appointments are not herein otherwise provided for, and which shall be established by Law: but the Congress may by Law vest the Appointment of such inferior Officers, as they think proper in the President alone, in the Courts of Law, or in the Heads of Departments.

The President shall have Power to fill up all Vacancies that may happen during the Recess of the Senate, by granting Commissions which shall expire at the End of their next Session.

Section 3

He shall from time to time give to the Congress Information of the State of the Union, and recommend to their Consideration such Measures as he shall judge necessary and expedient; he may, on extraordinary Occasions, convene both Houses, or either of them, and in Case of disagreement between them, with Respect to the Time of Adjournment, he may adjourn them to such Time as he shall think proper; he shall receive Ambassadors and other public Ministers; he shall take Care that the Laws be faithfully executed, and shall Commission all the officers of the United States.

Section 4

The President, Vice President and all civil Officers of the United States, shall be removed from Office on Impeachment for, and Conviction of, Treason, Bribery or other high Crimes and Misdemeanors.

Article III

Section 1

The judicial Power of the United States, shall be vested in one supreme Court, and in such inferior Courts as the Congress may from time to time ordain and establish. The Judges, both of the supreme and inferior Courts, shall hold their offices during good Behaviour, and shall, at stated Times, receive for their Services, a Compensation, which shall not be diminished during their Continuance in Office.

Section 2

The judicial Power shall extend to all Cases, in Law and Equity, arising under this Constitution, the Laws of the United States, and Treaties made, or which shall be made, under their Authority;—to all Cases affecting Ambassadors, other public Ministers and Consuls;—to all Cases of admiralty and maritime Jurisdiction;—to Controversies to which the United States shall be a Party;—to Controversies between two or more States;—*between a State and Citizens of another State;*—between Citizens of different States;—between Citizens of the same State claiming Lands under Grants of different States, and between a State, or the Citizens thereof, and foreign States, Citizens or Subjects.

In all Cases affecting Ambassadors, other public Ministers and Consuls, and those in which a State shall be Party, the supreme Court shall have original Jurisdiction. In all the other Cases before mentioned, the supreme Court shall have appellate Jurisdiction, both as to Law and Fact, with such Exceptions, and under such Regulations as the Congress shall make.

The Trial of all Crimes, except in Cases of Impeachment, shall be by Jury; and such Trial shall be held in the State where the said Crimes shall have been committed, but when not committed within any State, the Trial shall be at such Place or Places as the Congress may by Law have directed.

Section 3

Treason against the United States, shall consist only in levying War against them, or in adhering to their Enemies, giving them Aid and Comfort. No person shall be convicted of Treason unless on the Testimony of two Witnesses to the same overt Act, or on Confession in open Court.

The Congress shall have Power to declare the Punishment of Treason, but no Attainder of Treason shall work Corruption of Blood, or Forfeiture except during the Life of the Person attainted.

Article IV

Section 1

Full Faith and Credit shall be given in each State to the public Acts, Records, and judicial Proceedings of every other State. And the Congress may by general Laws prescribe the Manner in which such Acts, Records and Proceedings shall be proved, and the Effect thereof.

Section 2

The Citizens of each State shall be entitled to all Privileges and Immunities of Citizens in the several States.

A Person charged in any State with Treason, Felony, or other Crime, who shall flee from Justice, and be found in another State, shall on Demand of the executive Authority of the State from which he fled, be delivered up, to be removed to the State having Jurisdiction of the Crime.

No Person held to Service or Labour in one State, under the Laws thereof, escaping into another, shall, in Consequence of any Law or Regulation therein, be discharged from such Service or Labour, but shall be delivered up on Claim of the Party to whom such Service or Labour may be due.

Section 3

New States may be admitted by the Congress into this Union; but no new State shall be formed or erected within the Jurisdiction of any other State; nor any State be formed by the Junction of two or more States, or Parts of States, without the Consent of the Legislatures of the States concerned as well as of the Congress.

The Congress shall have Power to dispose of and make all needful Rules and Regulations respecting the Territory or other Property belonging to the United States; and nothing in this Constitution shall be so construed as to Prejudice any Claims of the United States, or of any particular States.

Section 4

The United States shall guarantee to every State in this Union a Republican Form of Government, and shall protect each of them against Invasion; and on Application of the Legislature, or of the Executive (when the Legislature cannot be convened) against domestic violence.

Article V

The Congress, whenever two thirds of both Houses shall deem it necessary, shall propose Amendments to this Constitution, or, on the Application of the Legislatures of two thirds of the several States, shall call a Convention for proposing Amendments, which, in either Case, shall be valid to all Intents and Purposes, as Part of this Constitution, when ratified by the Legislatures of three fourths of the several States, or by Conventions in three fourths thereof, as the one or the other Mode of Ratification may be proposed by the Congress; Provided *that no Amendment which may be made prior to the Year One thousand eight hundred and eight shall in any Manner affect the first and fourth Clauses in the Ninth Section of the first Article;* and that no State, without its Consent, shall be deprived of its equal Suffrage in the Senate.

Article VI

All Debts contracted and Engagements entered into, before the Adoption of this Constitution, shall be as valid against the United States under this Constitution, as under the Confederation.

This Constitution, and Laws of the United States which shall be made in Pursuance thereof; and all Treaties made, or which shall be made, under the Authority of the United States, shall be the supreme Law of the Land; and the Judges in every State shall be bound thereby, any Thing in the Constitution or Laws of any State to the Contrary notwithstanding.

The Senators and Representatives before mentioned, and the Members of the several State Legislatures, and all executive and Judicial Officers, both of the United States and of the several States, shall be bound by Oath or Affirmation, to support this Constitution; but no religious Test shall ever be required as a Qualification to any Office of public Trust under the United States.

Article VII

The Ratification of the Conventions of nine States, shall be sufficient for the Establishment of this Constitution between the States so ratifying the Same.

Done in Convention by the Unanimous Consent of the States present the Seventeenth Day of September in the Year of our Lord one thousand seven hundred and Eighty seven and of the Independence of the United States of America the Twelfth† IN WITNESS whereof We have hereunto subscribed our Names,

George Washington
President and Deputy from Virginia

Delaware
George Read
Gunning Bedford, Jr.
John Dickinson
Richard Bassett
Jacob Broom

Maryland
James McHenry
Daniel of St. Thomas Jenifer
Daniel Carroll

Virginia
John Blair
James Madison, Jr.

North Carolina
William Blount
Richard Dobbs Spraight
Hugh Williamson

South Carolina
John Rutledge
Charles Cotesworth Pinckney
Charles Pinckney
Pierce Butler

Georgia
William Few
Abraham Baldwin

New Hampshire
John Langdon
Nicholas Gilman

Massachusetts
Nathaniel Gorham
Rufus King

Connecticut
William Samuel Johnson
Roger Sherman

New York
Alexander Hamilton

New Jersey
William Livingston
David Brearley
William Paterson
Jonathan Dayton

Pennsylvania
Benjamin Franklin
Thomas Mifflin
Robert Morris
George Clymer
Thomas FitzSimons
Jared Ingersoll
James Wilson
Gouverneur Morris

†The Constitution was submitted on September 17, 1787, by the Constitutional Convention, was ratified by conventions of the several states at various dates up to May 29, 1790, and became effective on March 4, 1789.

Amendments to the Constitution

Amendment I

Congress shall make no law respecting an establishment of religion, or prohibiting the free exercise thereof; or abridging the freedom of speech, or of the press; or the right of the people peaceably to assemble, and to petition the Government for a redress of grievances.

Amendment II

A well regulated Militia being necessary to the security of a free State, the right of the people to keep and bear Arms, shall not be infringed.

Amendment III

No Soldier shall, in time of peace be quartered in any house, without the consent of the Owner, nor in time of war, but in a manner to be prescribed by law.

Amendment IV

The right of the people to be secure in their persons, houses, papers, and effects, against unreasonable searches and seizures, shall not be violated, and no Warrants shall issue, but upon probable cause, supported by Oath or affirmation, and particularly describing the place to be searched, and the persons or things to be seized.

Amendment V

No person shall be held to answer for a capital, or otherwise infamous crime, unless on a presentment or indictment of a Grand Jury, except in cases arising in the land or naval forces, or in the Militia, when in actual service in time of War or public danger; nor shall any person be subject for the same offense to be twice put in jeopardy of life or limb; nor shall be compelled in any criminal case to be a witness against himself, nor be deprived of life, liberty, or property, without due process of law; nor shall private property be taken for public use, without just compensation.

Amendment VI

In all criminal prosecutions, the accused shall enjoy the right to a speedy and public trial, by an impartial jury of the State and district wherein the crime shall have been committed, which district shall have been previously ascertained by law, and to be informed of the nature and cause of the accusation; to be confronted with the witnesses against him; to have compulsory process for obtaining witnesses in his favor, and to have the Assistance of Counsel for his defence.

Amendment VII

In Suits at common law, where the value in controversy shall exceed twenty dollars, the right of trial by jury shall be preserved, and no fact tried by a jury, shall be otherwise re-examined in any Court of the United States, than according to the rules of the common law.

Amendment VIII

Excessive bail shall not be required, nor excessive fines imposed, nor cruel and unusual punishments inflicted.

Amendment IX

The enumeration in the Constitution, of certain rights, shall not be construed to deny or disparage others retained by the people.

Amendment X*

The powers not delegated to the United States by the Constitution, nor prohibited by it to the States, are reserved to the States respectively, or to the people.

Amendment XI
[Adopted 1798]

The Judicial power of the United States shall not be construed to extend to any suit in law or equity, commenced or prosecuted against one of the United States by Citizens of another State, or by Citizens or Subjects of any Foreign State.

Amendment XII
[Adopted 1804]

The Electors shall meet in their respective states, and vote by ballot for President and Vice President, one of whom, at least, shall not be an inhabitant of the same state with themselves; they shall name in their ballots the person voted for as President, and in distinct ballots the person voted for as Vice President, and they shall make distinct lists of all persons voted for as President, and of all persons voted for as Vice President, and of the number of votes for each, which lists they shall sign and certify, and transmit sealed to the seat of the government of the United States, directed to the President of the Senate;—The President of the Senate shall, in the presence of the Senate and House of Representatives, open all the certificates and the votes shall then be counted;—The person having the greatest number of votes for President, shall be the President, if such number be a majority of the whole number of Electors appointed; and if no person have such majority, then from the persons having the highest numbers not exceeding three on the list of those voted for as President, the House of Representatives shall choose immediately, by ballot, the President. But in choosing the President, the votes shall be taken by states, the representation from each state having one vote; a quorum for this purpose shall consist of a

*The first ten amendments (the Bill of Rights) were ratified and their adoption was certified on December 15, 1791.

member or members from two-thirds of the states, and a majority of all the states shall be necessary to a choice. And if the House of Representatives shall not choose a President whenever the right of choice shall devolve upon them, before *the fourth day of March* next following, then the Vice President shall act as President, as in the case of the death or other constitutional disability of the President.—The person having the greatest number of votes as Vice President, shall be the Vice President, if such number be a majority of the whole number of Electors appointed, and if no person have a majority, then from the two highest numbers on the list, the Senate shall choose the Vice President; a quorum for the purpose shall consist of two-thirds of the whole number of Senators, and a majority of the whole number shall be necessary to a choice. But no person constitutionally ineligible to the office of President shall be eligible to that of Vice President of the United States.

Amendment XIII
[Adopted 1865]

Section 1

Neither slavery nor involuntary servitude, except as a punishment for crime whereof the party shall have been duly convicted, shall exist within the United States, or any place subject to their jurisdiction.

Section 2

Congress shall have power to enforce this article by appropriate legislation.

Amendment XIV
[Adopted 1868]

Section 1

All persons born or naturalized in the United States, and subject to the jurisdiction thereof, are citizens of the United States and of the State wherein they reside. No State shall make or enforce any law which shall abridge the privileges or immunities of citizens of the United States; nor shall any State deprive any person of life, liberty, or property, without due process of law; nor deny to any person within its jurisdiction the equal protection of the laws.

Section 2

Representatives shall be apportioned among the several States according to their respective numbers, counting the whole number of persons in each State, excluding Indians not taxed. But when the right to vote at any election for the choice of electors for President and Vice President of the United States, Representatives in Congress, the Executive and Judicial officers of a State, or the members of the Legislature thereof, is denied to any of the male inhabitants of such State, being twenty-one years of age, and citizens of the United States, or in any way abridged, except for participation in rebellion, or other crime, the basis of representation therein shall be reduced in the proportion which the number of such male citizens shall bear to the whole number of male citizens twenty-one years of age in such State.

Section 3

No person shall be a Senator or Representative in Congress, or elector of President and Vice President, or hold any office, civil or military, under the United States, or under any State, who, having previously taken an oath, as a member of Congress, or as an officer of the United States, or as a member of any State legislature, or as an executive or judicial officer of any State, to support the Constitution of the United States, shall have engaged in insurrection or rebellion against the same, or given aid or comfort to the enemies thereof. But Congress may by a vote of two-thirds of each House, remove such disability.

Section 4

The validity of the public debt of the United States, authorized by law, including debts incurred for payment of pensions and bounties for services in suppressing insurrection or rebellion, shall not be questioned. But neither the United States nor any State shall assume or pay any debt or obligation incurred in aid of insurrection or rebellion against the United States, or any claim for the loss or emancipation of any slave; but all such debts, obligations and claims shall be held illegal and void.

Section 5

The Congress shall have power to enforce, by appropriate legislation, the provisions of this article.

Amendment XV
[Adopted 1870]

Section 1

The right of citizens of the United States to vote shall not be denied or abridged by the United States or by any State on account of race, color, or previous condition of servitude.

Section 2

The Congress shall have power to enforce this article by appropriate legislation.

Amendment XVI
[Adopted 1913]

The Congress shall have power to lay and collect taxes on incomes, from whatever source derived, without apportionment among the several States, and without regard to any census or enumeration.

Amendment XVII
[Adopted 1913]

The Senate of the United States shall be composed of two Senators from each State, elected by the people thereof, for six years; and each Senator shall have one vote. The electors in each State shall have the qualifications requisite for electors of the most numerous branch of the State legislatures.

When vacancies happen in the representation of any State in the Senate, the executive authority of such State shall issue writs of election to fill such vacancies: *Provided,* That the legislature of any State may empower the executive thereof to make temporary appointments until the people fill the vacancies by election as the legislature may direct.

This amendment shall not be so construed as to affect the election or term of any Senator chosen before it becomes valid as part of the Constitution.

Amendment XVIII
[Adopted 1919, repealed 1933]

Section 1

After one year from the ratification of this article the manufacture, sale, or transportation of intoxicating liquors within, the importation thereof into, or the exportation thereof from the United States and all territory subject to the jurisdiction thereof for beverage purposes is hereby prohibited.

Section 2

The Congress and the several States shall have concurrent power to enforce this article by appropriate legislation.

Section 3

This article shall be inoperative unless it shall have been ratified as an amendment to the Constitution by the legislatures of the several States, as provided in the Constitution, within seven years from the date of the submission hereof to the States by the Congress.

Amendment XIX
[Adopted 1920]

The right of citizens of the United States to vote shall not be denied or abridged by the United States or by any State on account of sex.

Congress shall have power to enforce this article by appropriate legislation.

Amendment XX
[Adopted 1933]

Section 1

The terms of the President and Vice President shall end at noon on the 20th day of January, and the terms of Senators and Representatives at noon on the 3d day of January, of the years in which such terms would have ended if this article had not been ratified and the terms of their successors shall then begin.

Section 2

The Congress shall assemble at least once in every year, and such meeting shall begin at noon on the 3d day of January, unless they shall by law appoint a different day.

Section 3

If, at the time fixed for the beginning of the term of the President, the President elect shall have died, the Vice President elect shall become President. If a President shall not have been chosen before the time fixed for the beginning of his term, or if the President elect shall have failed to qualify, then the Vice President elect shall act as President until a President shall have qualified; and the Congress may by law provide for the case wherein neither a President elect nor a Vice President elect shall have qualified, declaring who shall then act as President, or the manner in which one who is to act shall be selected, and such person shall act accordingly until a President or Vice President shall have qualified.

Section 4

The Congress may by law provide for the case of the death of any of the persons from whom the House of Representatives may choose a President whenever the right of choice shall have devolved upon them, and for the case of the death of any of the persons from whom the Senate may choose a Vice President whenever the right of choice shall have devolved upon them.

Section 5

Sections 1 and 2 shall take effect on the 15th day of October following the ratification of this article.

Section 6

This article shall be inoperative unless it shall have been ratified as an amendment to the Constitution by the legislatures of three fourths of the several States within seven years from the date of its submission.

Amendment XXI
[Adopted 1933]

Section 1

The eighteenth article of amendment to the Constitution of the United States is hereby repealed.

Section 2

The transportation or importation into any State, Territory, or possession of the United States for delivery or use therein of intoxicating liquors in violation of the laws thereof, is hereby prohibited.

Section 3

This article shall be inoperative unless it shall have been ratified as an amendment to the Constitution by conventions in the several States, as provided in the Constitution, within seven years from the date of the submission hereof to the States by the Congress.

Amendment XXII
[Adopted 1951]

Section 1

No person shall be elected to the office of the President more than twice, and no person who has held the office of President, or acted as President, for more than two years of a term to which some other person was elected President shall be elected to the office of the President more than once. But this Article shall not apply to any person holding the office of President when this Article was proposed by the Congress, and shall not prevent any person who may be holding the office of President, or acting as President, during the term within which this Article becomes operative from holding the office of President or acting as President during the remainder of such term.

Section 2

This article shall be inoperative unless it shall have been ratified as an amendment to the Constitution by the legislatures of three-fourths of the several States within seven years from the date of its submission to the States by the Congress.

Amendment XXIII
[Adopted 1961]

Section 1

The District constituting the seat of Government of the United States shall appoint in such manner as the Congress shall direct:

A number of electors of President and Vice President equal to the whole number of Senators and Representatives in Congress to which the District would be entitled if it were a State, but in no event more than the least populous State; they shall be in addition to those appointed by the States, but they shall be considered, for the purposes of the election of President and Vice President, to be electors appointed by a State; and they shall meet in the District and perform such duties as provided by the twelfth article of amendment.

Section 2

The Congress shall have power to enforce this article by appropriate legislation.

Amendment XXIV
[Adopted 1964]

Section 1

The right of citizens of the United States to vote in any primary or other election for President or Vice President, for electors for President or Vice President, or for Senator or Representative in Congress, shall not be denied or abridged by the United States or any state by reason of failure to pay any poll tax or other tax.

Section 2

The Congress shall have the power to enforce this article by appropriate legislation.

Amendment XXV
[Adopted 1967]

Section 1

In case of the removal of the President from office or his death or resignation, the Vice President shall become President.

Section 2

Whenever there is a vacancy in the office of the Vice President, the President shall nominate a Vice President who shall take the office upon confirmation by a majority vote of both houses of Congress.

Section 3

Whenever the President transmits to the President pro tempore of the Senate and the Speaker of the House of Representatives his written declaration that he is unable to discharge the powers and duties of his office, and until he transmits to them a written declaration to the contrary, such powers and duties shall be discharged by the Vice President as Acting President.

Section 4

Whenever the Vice President and a majority of either the principal officers of the executive departments or of such other body as Congress may by law provide, transmit to the President pro tempore of the Senate and the Speaker of the House of Representatives their written declaration that the President is unable to discharge the powers and duties of his office, the Vice President shall immediately assume the powers and duties of the office as Acting President.

Thereafter, when the President transmits to the President pro tempore of the Senate and the Speaker of the House of Representatives his written declaration that no inability exists, he shall resume the powers and duties of his office unless the Vice President and a majority of either the principal officers of the executive department or of such other body as Congress may by law provide, transmit within four days to the President pro tempore of the Senate and the Speaker of the House of Representatives their written declaration that the President is unable to discharge the powers and duties of his office. Thereupon Congress shall decide the issue, assembling within 48 hours for that purpose if not in session. If the Congress, within 21 days after receipt of the latter written declaration, or, if Congress is not in session, within 21 days after Congress is required to assemble, determines by two-thirds vote of both houses that the President is unable to discharge the powers and duties of his office, the Vice President shall continue to discharge the same as Acting President; otherwise, the President shall resume the powers and duties of his office.

Amendment XXVI
[Adopted 1971]

Section 1

The right of citizens of the United States, who are 18 years of age or older, to vote shall not be denied or abridged by the United States or any state on account of age.

Section 2

The Congress shall have the power to enforce this article by appropriate legislation.

Amendment XXVII
[Adopted 1992]

No law, varying the compensation for the services of the Senators and Representatives shall take effect, until an election of Representatives shall have intervened.

Presidential Elections

Year	Candidates	Parties	Popular Vote	Electoral Vote	Voter Participation
1789	**George Washington**		*	69	
	John Adams			34	
	Others			35	
1792	**George Washington**		*	132	
	John Adams			77	
	George Clinton			50	
	Others			5	
1796	**John Adams**	Federalist	*	71	
	Thomas Jefferson	Democratic-Republican		68	
	Thomas Pinckney	Federalist		59	
	Aaron Burr	Dem.-Rep.		30	
	Others			48	
1800	**Thomas Jefferson**	Dem.-Rep.	*	73	
	Aaron Burr	Dem.-Rep.		73	
	John Adams	Federalist		65	
	C. C. Pinckney	Federalist		64	
	John Jay	Federalist		1	
1804	**Thomas Jefferson**	Dem.-Rep.	*	162	
	C. C. Pinckney	Federalist		14	
1808	**James Madison**	Dem.-Rep.	*	122	
	C. C. Pinckney	Federalist		47	
	George Clinton	Dem.-Rep.		6	
1812	**James Madison**	Dem.-Rep.	*	128	
	De Witt Clinton	Federalist		89	
1816	**James Monroe**	Dem.-Rep.	*	183	
	Rufus King	Federalist		34	
1820	**James Monroe**	Dem.-Rep.	*	231	
	John Quincy Adams	Dem.-Rep.		1	
1824	**John Quincy Adams**	Dem.-Rep.	108,740 (30.5%)	84	26.9%
	Andrew Jackson	Dem.-Rep.	153,544 (43.1%)	99	
	William H. Crawford	Dem.-Rep.	46,618 (13.1%)	41	
	Henry Clay	Dem.-Rep.	47,136 (13.2%)	37	
1828	**Andrew Jackson**	Democratic	647,286 (56.0%)	178	57.6%
	John Quincy Adams	National Republican	508,064 (44.0%)	83	
1832	**Andrew Jackson**	Democratic	687,502 (55.0%)	219	55.4%
	Henry Clay	National Republican	530,189 (42.4%)	49	
	John Floyd	Independent		11	
	William Wirt	Anti-Mason	33,108 (2.6%)	7	
1836	**Martin Van Buren**	Democratic	765,483 (50.9%)	170	57.8%
	William Henry Harrison	Whig		73	
	Hugh L. White	Whig	739,795 (49.1%)	26	
	Daniel Webster	Whig		14	
	W. P. Magnum	Independent		11	
1840	**William Henry Harrison**	Whig	1,274,624 (53.1%)	234	80.2%
	Martin Van Buren	Democratic	1,127,781 (46.9%)	60	
	J. G. Birney	Liberty	7069	—	

*Electors selected by state legislatures.

Year	Candidates	Parties	Popular Vote	Electoral Vote	Voter Participation
1844	**James K. Polk**	Democratic	1,338,464 (49.6%)	170	78.9%
	Henry Clay	Whig	1,300,097 (48.1%)	105	
	J. G. Birney	Liberty	62,300 (2.3%)	—	
1848	**Zachary Taylor**	Whig	1,360,967 (47.4%)	163	72.7%
	Lewis Cass	Democratic	1,222,342 (42.5%)	127	
	Martin Van Buren	Free-Soil	291,263 (10.1%)	—	
1852	**Franklin Pierce**	Democratic	1,601,117 (50.9%)	254	69.6%
	Winfield Scott	Whig	1,385,453 (44.1%)	42	
	John P. Hale	Free-Soil	155,825 (5.0%)	—	
1856	**James Buchanan**	Democratic	1,832,955 (45.3%)	174	78.9%
	John C. Frémont	Republican	1,339,932 (33.1%)	114	
	Millard Fillmore	American	871,731 (21.6%)	8	
1860	**Abraham Lincoln**	Republican	1,865,593 (39.8%)	180	81.2%
	Stephen A. Douglas	Democratic	1,382,713 (29.5%)	12	
	John C. Breckinridge	Democratic	848,356 (18.1%)	72	
	John Bell	Union	592,906 (12.6%)	39	
1864	**Abraham Lincoln**	Republican	2,213,655 (55.0%)	212[*]	73.8%
	George B. McClellan	Democratic	1,805,237 (45.0%)	21	
1868	**Ulysses S. Grant**	Republican	3,012,833 (52.7%)	214	78.1%
	Horatio Seymour	Democratic	2,703,249 (47.3%)	80	
1872	**Ulysses S. Grant**	Republican	3,597,132 (55.6%)	286	71.3%
	Horace Greeley	Dem.; Liberal Republican	2,834,125 (43.9%)	66[†]	
1876	**Rutherford B. Hayes ‡**	Republican	4,036,298 (48.0%)	185	81.8%
	Samuel J. Tilden	Democratic	4,300,590 (51.0%)	184	
1880	**James A. Garfield**	Republican	4,454,416 (48.5%)	214	79.4%
	Winfield S. Hancock	Democratic	4,444,952 (48.1%)	155	
1884	**Grover Cleveland**	Democratic	4,874,986 (48.5%)	219	77.5%
	James G. Blaine	Republican	4,851,981 (48.2%)	182	
1888	**Benjamin Harrison**	Republican	5,439,853 (47.9%)	233	79.3%
	Grover Cleveland	Democratic	5,540,309 (48.6%)	168	
1892	**Grover Cleveland**	Democratic	5,556,918 (46.1%)	277	74.7%
	Benjamin Harrison	Republican	5,176,108 (43.0%)	145	
	James B. Weaver	People's	1,041,028 (8.5%)	22	
1896	**William McKinley**	Republican	7,104,779 (51.1%)	271	79.3%
	William Jennings Bryan	Democratic People's	6,502,925 (47.7%)	176	
1900	**William McKinley**	Republican	7,207,923 (51.7%)	292	73.2%
	William Jennings Bryan	Dem.-Populist	6,358,133 (45.5%)	155	
1904	**Theodore Roosevelt**	Republican	7,623,486 (57.9%)	336	65.2%
	Alton B. Parker	Democratic	5,077,911 (37.6%)	140	
	Eugene V. Debs	Socialist	402,283 (3.0%)	—	
1908	**William H. Taft**	Republican	7,678,908 (51.6%)	321	65.4%
	William Jennings Bryan	Democratic	6,409,104 (43.1%)	162	
	Eugene V. Debs	Socialist	420,793 (2.8%)	—	
1912	**Woodrow Wilson**	Democratic	6,293,454 (41.9%)	435	58.8%
	Theodore Roosevelt	Progressive	4,119,538 (27.4%)	88	
	William H. Taft	Republican	3,484,980 (23.2%)	8	
	Eugene V. Debs	Socialist	900,672 (6.0%)	—	
1916	**Woodrow Wilson**	Democratic	9,129,606 (49.4%)	277	61.6%
	Charles E. Hughes	Republican	8,538,221 (46.2%)	254	
	A. L. Benson	Socialist	585,113 (3.2%)	—	
1920	**Warren G. Harding**	Republican	16,152,200 (60.4%)	404	49.2%
	James M. Cox	Democratic	9,147,353 (34.2%)	127	
	Eugene V. Debs	Socialist	919,799 (3.4%)	—	
1924	**Calvin Coolidge**	Republican	15,725,016 (54.0%)	382	48.9%
	John W. Davis	Democratic	8,386,503 (28.8%)	136	
	Robert M. La Follette	Progressive	4,822,856 (16.6%)	13	

[*]Eleven secessionist states did not participate.
[†]Greeley died before the electoral college met. His electoral votes were divided among the four minor candidates.
[‡]Contested result settled by special election.

Year	Candidates	Parties	Popular Vote	Electoral Vote	Voter Participation
1928	**Herbert Hoover**	Republican	21,391,381 (58.2%)	444	56.9%
	Alfred E. Smith	Democratic	15,016,443 (40.9%)	87	
	Norman Thomas	Socialist	267,835 (0.7%)	—	
1932	**Franklin D. Roosevelt**	Democratic	22,821,857 (57.4%)	472	56.9%
	Herbert Hoover	Republican	15,761,841 (39.7%)	59	
	Norman Thomas	Socialist	881,951 (2.2%)	—	
1936	**Franklin D. Roosevelt**	Democratic	27,751,597 (60.8%)	523	61.0%
	Alfred M. Landon	Republican	16,679,583 (36.5%)	8	
	William Lemke	Union	882,479 (1.9%)	—	
1940	**Franklin D. Roosevelt**	Democratic	27,244,160 (54.8%)	449	62.5%
	Wendell L. Willkie	Republican	22,305,198 (44.8%)	82	
1944	**Franklin D. Roosevelt**	Democratic	25,602,504 (53.5%)	432	55.9%
	Thomas E. Dewey	Republican	22,006,285 (46.0%)	99	
1948	**Harry S Truman**	Democratic	24,105,695 (49.5%)	304	53.0%
	Thomas E. Dewey	Republican	21,969,170 (45.1%)	189	
	J. Strom Thurmond	State-Rights Democratic	1,169,021 (2.4%)	38	
	Henry A. Wallace	Progressive	1,156,103 (2.4%)	—	
1952	**Dwight D. Eisenhower**	Republican	33,936,252 (55.1%)	442	63.3%
	Adlai E. Stevenson	Democratic	27,314,992 (44.4%)	89	
1956	**Dwight D. Eisenhower**	Republican	35,575,420 (57.6%)	457	60.6%
	Adlai E. Stevenson	Democratic	26,033,066 (42.1%)	73	
	Other	—	—	1	
1960	**John F. Kennedy**	Democratic	34,227,096 (49.9%)	303	62.8%
	Richard M. Nixon	Republican	34,108,546 (49.6%)	219	
	Other	—	—	15	
1964	**Lyndon B. Johnson**	Democratic	43,126,506 (61.1%)	486	61.7%
	Barry M. Goldwater	Republican	27,176,799 (38.5%)	52	
1968	**Richard M. Nixon**	Republican	31,770,237 (43.4%)	301	60.6%
	Hubert H. Humphrey	Democratic	31,270,533 (42.7%)	191	
	George Wallace	American Indep.	9,906,141 (13.5%)	46	
1972	**Richard M. Nixon**	Republican	47,169,911 (60.7%)	520	55.2%
	George S. McGovern	Democratic	29,170,383 (37.5%)	17	
	Other	—	—	1	
1976	**Jimmy Carter**	Democratic	40,828,587 (50.0%)	297	53.5%
	Gerald R. Ford	Republican	39,147,613 (47.9%)	241	
	Other	—	1,575,459 (2.1%)	—	
1980	**Ronald Reagan**	Republican	43,901,812 (50.7%)	489	52.6%
	Jimmy Carter	Democratic	35,483,820 (41.0%)	49	
	John B. Anderson	Independent	5,719,722 (6.6%)	—	
	Ed Clark	Libertarian	921,188 (1.1%)	—	
1984	**Ronald Reagan**	Republican	54,455,075 (59.0%)	525	53.3%
	Walter Mondale	Democratic	37,577,185 (41.0%)	13	
1988	**George H. W. Bush**	Republican	48,886,000 (53.4%)	426	57.4%
	Michael S. Dukakis	Democratic	41,809,000 (45.6%)	111	
1992	**William J. Clinton**	Democratic	43,728,375 (43%)	370	55.0%
	George H. W. Bush	Republican	38,167,416 (38%)	168	
	H. Ross Perot	Independent	19,237,247 (19%)	—	
1996	**William J. Clinton**	Democratic	45,590,703 (50%)	379	48.8%
	Robert Dole	Republican	37,816,307 (41%)	159	
	H. Ross Perot	Reform	7,866,284		
2000	**George W. Bush**	Republican	50,456,167 (47.88%)	271	51.2%
	Al Gore	Democratic	50,996,064 (48.39%)	266*	
	Ralph Nader	Green	2,864,810 (2.72%)	—	
	Other		834,774 (< 1%)	—	
2004	**George W. Bush**	Republican	60,934,251 (51%)	286	50.0%
	John F. Kerry	Democratic	57,765,291 (48%)	252	
	Other		699,309 (2.72%)	0	
	Ralph Nader	Independent	405,933 (0%)	0	

*One District of Columbia Gore elector abstained.

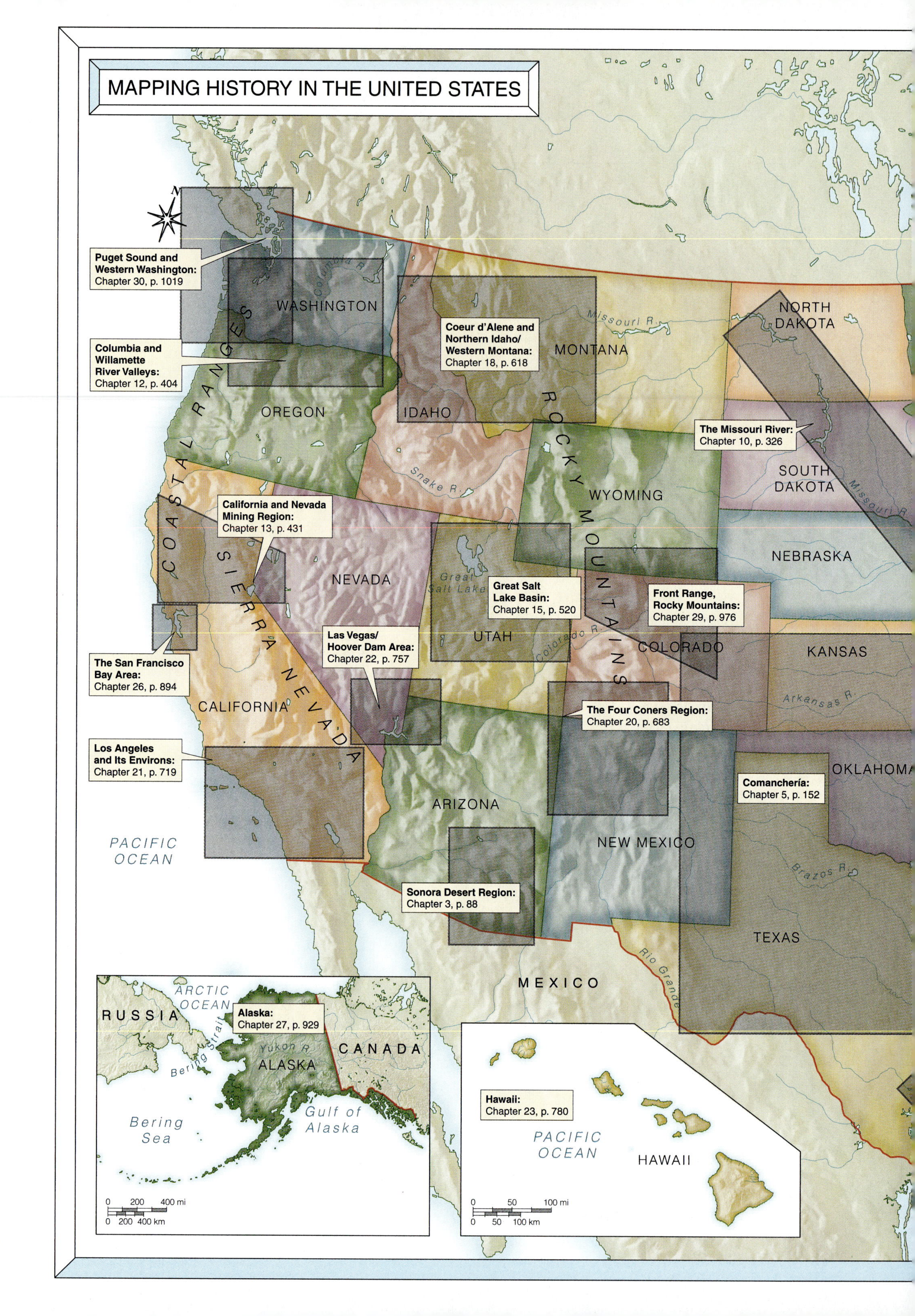

MAPPING HISTORY IN THE UNITED STATES
Puget Sound and Western Washington: Chapter 30, p. 1019
Columbia and Willamette River Valleys: Chapter 12, p. 404
Coeur d'Alene and Northern Idaho/ Western Montana: Chapter 18, p. 618
The Missouri River: Chapter 10, p. 326
California and Nevada Mining Region: Chapter 13, p. 431
Great Salt Lake Basin: Chapter 15, p. 520
Front Range, Rocky Mountains: Chapter 29, p. 976
Las Vegas/ Hoover Dam Area: Chapter 22, p. 757
The San Francisco Bay Area: Chapter 26, p. 894
The Four Coners Region: Chapter 20, p. 683
Los Angeles and Its Environs: Chapter 21, p. 719
Comanchería: Chapter 5, p. 152
Sonora Desert Region: Chapter 3, p. 88
Alaska: Chapter 27, p. 929
Hawaii: Chapter 23, p. 780
WASHINGTON
OREGON
IDAHO
MONTANA
NORTH DAKOTA
SOUTH DAKOTA
WYOMING
NEBRASKA
NEVADA
UTAH
COLORADO
KANSAS
CALIFORNIA
ARIZONA
NEW MEXICO
OKLAHOMA
TEXAS
MEXICO
COASTAL RANGES
SIERRA NEVADA
ROCKY MOUNTAINS
PACIFIC OCEAN
Missouri R.
Columbia R.
Snake R.
Great Salt Lake
Colorado R.
Arkansas R.
Brazos R.
Rio Grande
RUSSIA
ARCTIC OCEAN
CANADA
ALASKA
Yukon R.
Bering Strait
Bering Sea
Gulf of Alaska
0 200 400 mi
0 200 400 km
PACIFIC OCEAN
HAWAII
0 50 100 mi
0 50 100 km

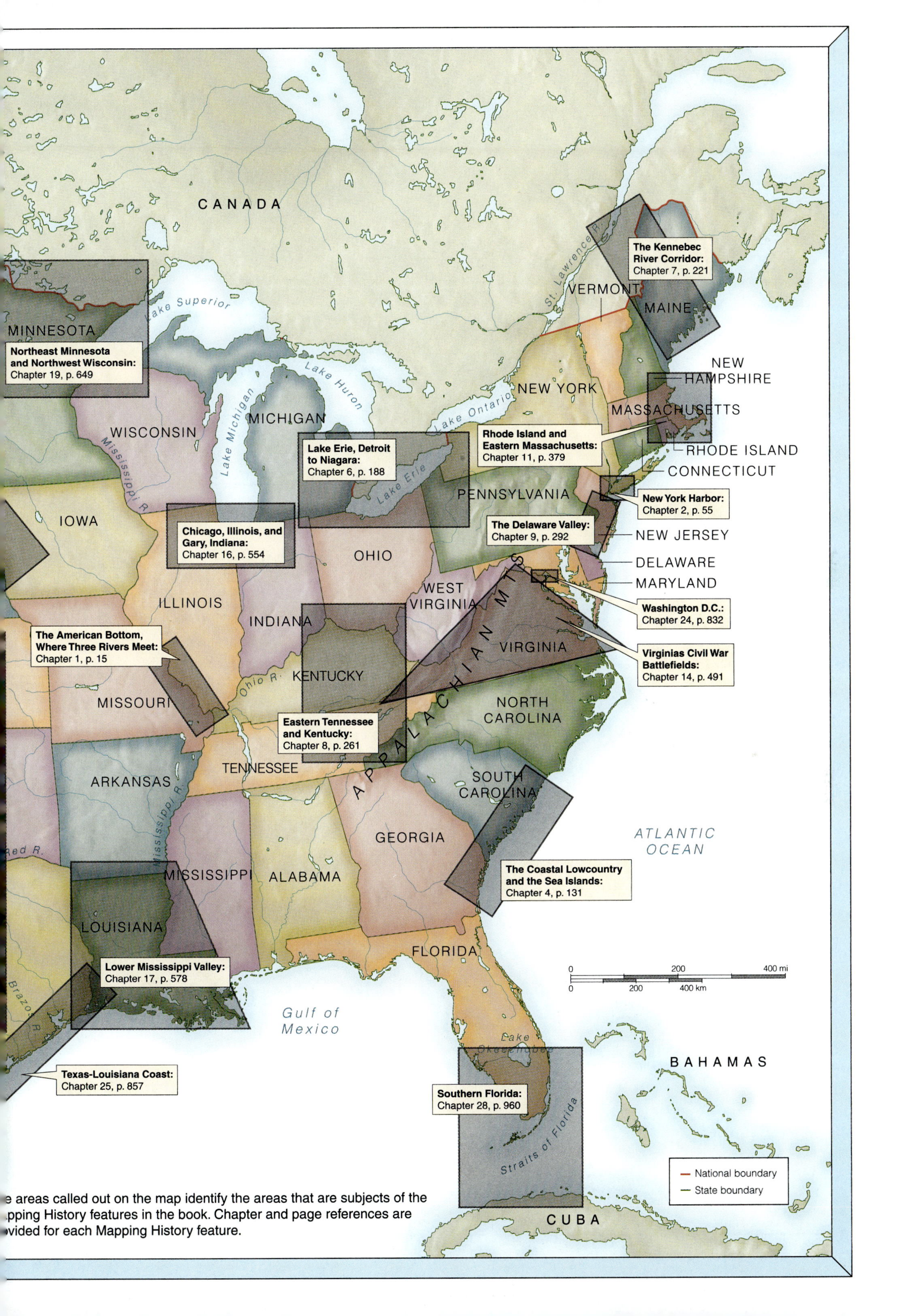

CANADA
Lake Superior
Lake Michigan
Lake Huron
Lake Ontario
Lake Erie
St. Lawrence R.
Mississippi R.
Ohio R.
Red R.
Brazos R.
MINNESOTA
Northeast Minnesota and Northwest Wisconsin: Chapter 19, p. 649
WISCONSIN
MICHIGAN
IOWA
ILLINOIS
INDIANA
OHIO
MISSOURI
KENTUCKY
TENNESSEE
ARKANSAS
MISSISSIPPI
ALABAMA
LOUISIANA
GEORGIA
FLORIDA
SOUTH CAROLINA
NORTH CAROLINA
VIRGINIA
WEST VIRGINIA
PENNSYLVANIA
NEW YORK
VERMONT
MAINE
NEW HAMPSHIRE
MASSACHUSETTS
RHODE ISLAND
CONNECTICUT
NEW JERSEY
DELAWARE
MARYLAND
APPALACHIAN MTS.
The Kennebec River Corridor: Chapter 7, p. 221
Rhode Island and Eastern Massachusetts: Chapter 11, p. 379
Lake Erie, Detroit to Niagara: Chapter 6, p. 188
New York Harbor: Chapter 2, p. 55
The Delaware Valley: Chapter 9, p. 292
Chicago, Illinois, and Gary, Indiana: Chapter 16, p. 554
Washington D.C.: Chapter 24, p. 832
Virginias Civil War Battlefields: Chapter 14, p. 491
The American Bottom, Where Three Rivers Meet: Chapter 1, p. 15
Eastern Tennessee and Kentucky: Chapter 8, p. 261
The Coastal Lowcountry and the Sea Islands: Chapter 4, p. 131
Lower Mississippi Valley: Chapter 17, p. 578
Texas-Louisiana Coast: Chapter 25, p. 857
Southern Florida: Chapter 28, p. 960
ATLANTIC OCEAN
Gulf of Mexico
Lake Okeechobee
Straits of Florida
BAHAMAS
CUBA
0 200 400 mi
0 200 400 km
National boundary
State boundary
e areas called out on the map identify the areas that are subjects of the
pping History features in the book. Chapter and page references are
vided for each Mapping History feature.

PRESENT DAY WORLD
ARCTIC OCEAN
Beaufort Sea
ALASKA (U.S.)
Bering Sea
Gulf of Alaska
CANADA
Hudson Bay
Baffin Bay
GREENLAND
ICELAND
Labrador Sea
Great Lakes
UNITED STATES
ATLANTIC OCEAN
MEXICO
Gulf of Mexico
PACIFIC OCEAN
Hawaiian Is. (U.S.)
BELIZE
GUATEMALA
SURINAME
FRENCH GUIANA (FR.)
EL SALVADOR
Galapagos Is. (EQ.)
ECUADOR
Kiribati
Tokelau
Samoa
Am. Samoa
Cook Is.
French Polynesia
Tonga
PERU
BRAZIL
BOLIVIA
PARAGUAY
CHILE
URUGUAY
ARGENTINA
Falkland Is. (U.K.)
South Georgia (U.K.)
Weddell Sea
ANTARCTICA
MOROCCO
WESTERN SAHARA
MAURITANIA
CAPE VERDE
SENEGAL
THE GAMBIA
GUINEA
GUINEA BISSAU
SIERRA LEONE
LIBERIA
CÔTE D'IVOIRE
GHANA
SÃO TOMÉ and PRÍNCIPE
UNITED STATES
0 200 400 600 mi
0 200 400 600 km
BAHAMAS
ATLANTIC OCEAN
Turks and Caicos Is. (U.K.)
CUBA
DOMINICAN REPUBLIC
Cayman Is. (U.K.)
U.S. Virgin Is.
Antigua and Barbuda
JAMAICA
HAITI
PUERTO RICO
Guadaloupe
Dominica
Martinique
St. Lucia
Barbados
HONDURAS
Caribbean Sea
NICARAGUA
St. Vincent and the Grenadines
Curaco
Grenada
Trinidad and Tobago
COSTA RICA
VENEZUELA
GUYANA
PANAMA
COLOMBIA

0
1000
2000
3000 mi
0
1000
2000
3000 km
Svalbard Is. (NOR.)
Novaya
Zemlya
Barents
Sea
Kara
Sea
Laptev
Sea
New Siberian Is.
ARCTIC
OCEAN
East
Siberian
Sea
RUSSIA
Sea
of
Okhotsk
Lake
Baikal
Sakhalin
KAZAKHSTAN
Aral
Sea
Lake
Balkhash
MONGOLIA
N. KOREA
S. KOREA
JAPAN
PEOPLE'S
REPUBLIC
OF CHINA
AFGHAN.
PAKISTAN
IRAN
IRAQ
ISRAEL
JORDAN
TUNISIA
LIBYA
EGYPT
BAHRAIN
QATAR
SAUDI
ARABIA
U.A.E.
OMAN
NEPAL
BHUTAN
BANG.
INDIA
BURMA
(MYANMAR)
East
China
Sea
TAIWAN
PACIFIC
OCEAN
MACAO
LAOS
VIETNAM
Philippine
Sea
PHILIPPINES
Northern
Mariana
Is.
Arabian
Sea
Bay of
Bengal
South
China
Sea
THAILAND
CAMBODIA
SRI
LANKA
BRUNEI
MALAYSIA
SINGAPORE
INDONESIA
PAPUA
NEW GUINEA
Nauru
Marshall
Is.
Solomon Is.
Tuvalu
NIGER
CHAD
SUDAN
ERITREA
YEMEN
DJIBOUTI
SOMALIA
ETHIOPIA
CENT.
AFRICAN REP.
CAMEROON
EQUA.
GUINEA
UGANDA
KENYA
GABON
DEM. REP.
OF
CONGO
RWANDA
BURUNDI
TANZANIA
REP.
OF
CONGO
ANGOLA
MALAWI
ZAMBIA
ZIMB.
NAMIBIA
BOTSWANA
MADAGASCAR
MAURITIUS
MOZAMBIQUE
SOUTH
AFRICA
SWAZILAND
LESOTHO
INDIAN
OCEAN
Coral
Sea
Vanuatu
Fiji
New Caledonia (FR.)
AUSTRALIA
Tasman
Sea
NEW
ZEALAND
N
NORWAY
FINLAND
SWEDEN
0
200
400
600
800 mi
0
200
400
600
800 km
North
Sea
ESTONIA
IRELAND
DENMARK
LATVIA
Baltic
Sea
LITHUANIA
RUSSIA
UNITED
KINGDOM
NETHERLANDS
POLAND
BELARUS
ATLANTIC
OCEAN
BELGIUM
GERMANY
LUX.
CZECH
REPUBLIC
UKRAINE
FRANCE
LIECHT.
SLOVAKIA
SWITZ.
AUSTRIA
HUNGARY
MOLDOVA
Caspian Sea
SLOVENIA
CROATIA
ROMANIA
BOSNIA
HERZ.
SERBIA
BULGARIA
Black Sea
GEORGIA
ARMENIA
AZERBAIJAN
PORTUGAL
SPAIN
Adriatic Sea
ITALY
MACEDONIA
ALBANIA
TURKEY
GREECE
Aegean
Sea
Mediterranean
Sea
CYPRUS
SYRIA
IRAQ
LEBANON

Glossary

Abdicate To give up a throne or high position, to renounce sovereign power. 99

Accommodationist A person who adapts or modifies a position to ease conflict rather than holding fast to convictions in the face of opposition. 614

Acculturate To change the behavior of a group to conform to the behavior of the larger society. 625

Adage A familiar saying that embodies a common observation or a wise idea. 216

Aliens Foreign-born residents of the United States who have not been naturalized as U.S. citizens. 612

Allies Members of an alliance, such as the military coalition led by the United States, the Soviet Union, and Great Britain during World War II. 778

Almshouse A privately financed home for the poor; a poorhouse. 166

Amphibious landing A military assault that begins on the water and ends on land. 420

Anarchists Persons who reject all forms of government as inherently oppressive and undesirable. 593

Annexation Addition of territory that had belonged to one nation into another nation. 418

Annulment An official pronouncement nullifying a marriage, or declaring it invalid. 35

Antebellum The extended period before a war; usually refers to the several decades immediately before the American Civil War. 348

Anthropology The study of the origin and development of humankind. 610

Anti-Semitism Prejudice against Jews. 545

Aqueduct An elevated conduit or channel built to transfer water flowing from a distant source, using gravity. 360

Archipelago A group of islands, such as the Hawaiian archipelago. 17

Ardent Passionate, devoted, zealous, fiery. 271

Armistice A truce in a military conflict; a temporary halt in hostilities by agreement between the opposing sides. 633

Asiento A contract negotiated by the Spanish crown (between 1595 and 1789) with other European powers such as Portugal, France, England, and the Netherlands to provide a fixed number of slaves annually to Spain's American colonies for a set payment. 114

Assembly line A form of industrial production popularized by the Ford Motor Company in which workers perform one task repeatedly as the products they are jointly assembling move along a conveyor. 657

Atlatl A weighted, handheld device that enabled early Native Americans to throw spears with added power and velocity. 8

Avid Eager, greedy, enthusiastic. 222

Axis A political alignment or alliance, such as the military coalition between Germany, Italy, and Japan during World War II. 775

Babel A city described in the Old Testament where constructing a tower was made impossible by the confusion of varied languages. This term from the Book of Genesis is used to describe any scene of clamor and confusion. 148

Baby boom The period of increased U.S. childbirths from roughly the early 1940s to the early 1960s. 842

Baby boomers The generation of Americans born during the era from the early 1940s to the early 1960s. 987

Barracoon An enclosure or barrack used for the confinement of slaves before their forced deportation from the African coast. 124

Blacklist A (figurative or real) list of persons to be denied jobs because of their alleged loyalty to a particular cause or institution. 588

Black nationalism A shared identification among peoples of African descent, with a goal of cultural or economic separatism within the United States. 875

Black power The slogan used by young black nationalists in the mid- and late 1960s. 888

"Bloody shirt" A partisan rallying cry used to stir up or revive sectional or party animosity after the American Civil War; for example, post–Civil War Republicans "waved the bloody shirt," associating some Democrats with a treasonous acceptance of secession during the war, while opponents had spilled their blood for the Union. 562

Bolsheviks The Communist revolutionaries who overthrew the Russian czar in 1917 and established the Union of Soviet Socialist Republics (USSR). 695

Boston marriages Unions of two women based on long-term emotional bonds in which the women live together as if married to each other. 661

Braceros Mexican nationals working in the United States in low-wage jobs as part of a temporary work program between 1942 and 1964. (The *Bracero* program was established by an executive agreement between the presidents of Mexico and the United States, providing Mexican agricultural labor in the Southwest and the Pacific Northwest.) 847

Brunt The principal force, shock, or stress, especially of an attack. 266

Bull Moosers Supporters of Theodore Roosevelt in the 1912 presidential election when he broke from the Republican party and ran as a third-party candidate on the ticket of the Progressive (or Bull Moose) party. 671

Burgess A representative elected to the popular branch of the colonial legislature in either Virginia or Maryland. 62

Cajuns The Louisiana word for French-speaking people from Acadia (Nova Scotia) who were forced to move south in 1755 during the French and Indian War. Many of these refugees eventually moved to French Louisiana, where they have had a lasting impact on the culture. 160

Canal locks An enclosure on a canal or other waterway equipped with gates that can be closed so that boats can be raised or lowered by adjusting the water, in order to pass from one level to another. 359

Capitalism The now almost worldwide economic system of private ownership of property and profit-seeking corporations. 1012

Capitulation The act of formal surrender, upon specified terms. 243

Carpetbaggers A negative term applied by Southerners to Northerners who moved to the South after the Civil War to pursue political or economic opportunities. 505

Causeway A raised roadway crossing above open water or wet ground. 12

Cede To surrender possession of. 433

Civic organizations Membership organizations that exist to further the public life and welfare of a community. 849

Coalition An alliance of parties, factions, or nations. 426

Coffle A procession or train of enslaved prisoners, bound together for travel (from the Arabic word for "caravan"). 124

Cold War The conflict and competition between the United States and the Soviet Union (and their respective allies) that emerged after 1945 and lasted until 1989. 807

Colonialism The centuries-old system of mostly European nations controlling and governing peoples and lands outside of Europe. 820

Comfort women Women, mostly Chinese and Korean, forced into sexual slavery by Japanese troops during World War II. 798

Commercial farming Agricultural system producing for markets and intended to yield a profit after crops are sold. 434

Common school system Tax-supported public education to provide elementary schooling free to young children. 413

Communism A totalitarian form of government, grounded in the theories of German philosopher Karl Marx and the practices of V. I. Lenin in Russia, that eliminated private ownership of property in supposed pursuit of complete human equality; the system of government also featured a centrally directed economy and the absolute rule of a small group of leaders. 807

Complicit Assisting in an activity, serving as an accomplice. 454

Conclave A private meeting, secret assembly, gathering, or convention. 277

Conservationists Advocates of conserving and protecting the natural world through the use of renewable natural resources. 609

Conspicuous consumption A term coined by the American social theorist Thorstein Veblen to describe the behavior of wealthy persons who flaunt their status through their purchase of fine clothes, large houses, fancy cars, and other highly visible material goods. 616

Containment The U.S. policy during the Cold War of trying to halt the expansion of Soviet and communist influences. 818

Contraband Goods (or, during the Civil War, slaves) seized from the enemy during war. 475

Cooperatives Organizations that produce or market goods and that are owned collectively by people who share in their profits or benefits. 527

Cotton press A mill that produces cottonseed oil, a material used in the manufacture of paints, soaps, and other products. 592

Coverture French term for the dependent and legal status of a woman during marriage. Under English law, the male family head received legal rights, and his wife lost independent status, becoming, in legal terms, a *femme covert.* 92

Creoles People born in the United States but retaining a strong cultural identification with their forebears; especially persons of mixed Spanish or French and African descent speaking a dialect of Spanish or French. 350

Czar The monarch (king) of Russia before the 1917 revolution. 678

De facto government A government that is exercising power as if legally constituted. 207

Demobilize To discharge from military service, to disband. 254

Détente The lessening of military or diplomatic tensions, as between the United States and the Soviet Union. 812

Diaspora The dispersion of a population abroad, whether forced or voluntary. The term is often applied to Jewish settlement outside the eastern Mediterranean region, and to the spread of Africans across the Americas, due to the Atlantic slave trade. 143

Dispossession Act of taking land or other property from a group of people. 430

Don't ask, don't tell A policy established by the Clinton administration allowing gays and lesbians to serve in the military so long as they do not disclose their sexual orientation. 989

Double V The campaign by African Americans during the Second World War to fight simultaneously for victory against fascism abroad and racial discrimination at home. 773

Dust Bowl The plains regions of Oklahoma, Texas, Colorado, and New Mexico affected by severe drought in the 1930s. 745

Ecology The web of interconnections between organisms (particularly humans) and the natural environment. 362

Educated franchise The notion that literacy should be a qualification for voting. 623

Emancipation National or state-sponsored program to free slaves. 427

Embargo A government order prohibiting the entry or departure of commercial ships from a port. 329

Emigrants People who leave one place and move to another. 340

Encomienda The Spanish encomienda system, imposed in Spain's American empire, requiring Indian communities to supply labor or pay tribute to a local colonial overlord (identified as an encomendero). 85

Enemy race A concept applied by Americans during the Second World War to their Japanese—but not their white German and Italian—adversaries. 781

Enfranchised citizens Persons who are entitled to vote in government elections. 337

Entente The alliance of Britain, France, and Russia, later joined by the United States, during World War I. 677

Entrepreneur A person who organizes, manages, or assumes the risks in a business venture. 344

Established churches Religious denominations that receive special favors, financial or otherwise, from state governments. 308

Ethnic niches Businesses or sectors of the economy dominated by a particular ethnic group. 548

Evangelicals Christians, especially Protestants, who emphasize the importance of personal faith, as well as seeking new converts. 407

Exposé A piece of investigative journalism that exposes corruption in government, business, or other institutions. 530

Extractive enterprises Businesses that harvest or extract natural products from the land or sea (fish, timber, minerals, crops). 543

Fall line The geographical division between the Piedmont and the Atlantic coastal plain where the land slopes sharply to the sea. 289

Family wage A level of income sufficient for an individual worker, usually a man, to support a spouse and family through a single salary. 762

Fatigue work Unskilled manual labor. 483

Feminism The belief that women and men are of equal value and that gender roles are, to a considerable degree, created by society rather than being simply natural. 907

Fireside chats The broadcasts by President Franklin Delano Roosevelt during which he spoke directly to American families, often gathered around a radio in their living room. 740

Flappers Young women in the 1910s and 1920s who rebelled against the gender conventions of the era with respect to fashion and behavior. 707

Flotilla Any sizeable fleet of ships, or, more specifically, a naval term for a unit consisting of two or more squadrons of small warships. 176

Foreclosure A legal process of seizing private property, such as a home or farm, in order to pay off a debtor's creditors. 266

Foundling home A residence for orphaned children. 648

Free trade International economic relations characterized by multinational investment and a reduction or elimination of tariffs. 990

Free labor ideology The ideas, represented most forcefully by the antebellum Republican party, that workers should profit from their own labor and that slavery is wrong. 437

Freighter Person, vehicle, or vessel that transports goods. 441

Fusion A combination, alliance. 621

Geographic mobility The phenomenon of people moving frequently from one place to another. 622

Glacier A large body of ice that endures for centuries, advancing or receding slowly as climactic conditions change. 6

Globalization The process of integration—economic, but also cultural—of different parts of the world into a more unified system of trade and communication. 1013

Grain elevator Warehouse or tall storage bin, usually beside a railroad track, where, for a price, farmers can store their corn, wheat, or oats before these crops are shipped to market. 584

Grassroots democracy A political system that relies on the active participation of people at the local level. 606

Great Migration The movement of African Americans out of the South to northern cities, particularly during World War I. 688

Guerrilla war A conflict fought not on the basis of conventional warfare, but rather by mobilizing small groups of fighters who attack and harass superior forces. 397

Gun control The legal regulation of firearms. 986

Hard currency Coins made of precious metals such as silver, gold, or nickel, as opposed to paper bills; also called hard money or specie. 290

Harry To torment an enemy by destructive raids or repeated small attacks. 217

Hayseeds A derogatory term applied to rural people deemed uneducated and naive (in contrast to self-proclaimed sophisticated city dwellers). 616

Headright Under the headright system, English colonial governments granted a fixed amount of land, usually 50 acres, to any head of household for every family member or hired hand that person brought into the colony. Sometimes fewer acres were granted for women and children on the grounds that they would clear and plant less land. 62

Hinterland A rural area that is linked to a nearby city through trade networks. 341

Hobo Migrant worker or poor and homeless vagrant who traveled on trains from location to location, usually in search of employment. 743

Hoovervilles Shantytowns, named for president Hoover and occupied largely by people who lost their homes and farms during the Great Depression. 732

Horticultural Pertaining to the art and science of growing fruits and vegetables. 9

Humanitarian intervention Warfare undertaken ostensibly in furtherance of humanitarian objectives. 995

Hyperbole An extravagant statement or figure of speech ("I'm so hungry I could eat a horse"). 559

Impressment A policy that authorizes the seizure of persons or private property in the service of a government. 288

Indenture A document binding one person to work for another for a given period of time. Indentured servants received food, shelter, and clothing, plus "freedom dues" when their terms of service ended to help them get started independently. 116

Injunction A court order prohibiting a party from certain kinds of behavior—for example, barring a labor union from striking. 619

Internal improvements Turnpikes, canals, bridges, seaports, and other projects intended to facilitate trade and transportation within the country. 337

Iroquois League A Native American confederacy, located in central New York, originally composed of the Cayuga, Mohawk, Oneida, Onondaga, and Seneca Indians, and later including the Tuscarora as well. 52

Isthmus A narrow strip of land connecting two larger land areas (such as the isthmus of Panama). 28

Itinerant minister A preacher who travels from place to place without invitation, or who visits a circuit of churches on a regular basis. 172

Jim Crow The name given to the set of legal institutions that ensured the segregation of nonwhite people in the South. 851

Juke joint A small, inexpensive establishment where patrons could eat and drink or dance to music from a jukebox. *Juke* is a word of West African origin popularized by African Americans in the Sea Islands of South Carolina.707

Kachina An Indian religious system, inspired by Mexican traditions, and present in the American Southwest for more than 800 years. The kachina cult used masks for group performances associated with rain, curing, fertility, warfare, and the ancestors. Among many Pueblo and Hopi Indians, this tradition was epitomized by kachina (or katsina) dolls. 87

Kayak A highly maneuverable, decked-in canoe used by Native Alaskans for travel and hunting. The light frame is covered with skins, and the paddle has a blade at each end. Popular modern versions of this traditional boat are made with canvas or fiberglass. 184

Kickbacks Money paid illegally in return for favors (for example, to a politician by a person or business that has received government contracts). 512

Land speculation The act of buying land in the hope of making a profit by selling it in the future. 305

Levellers Radicals during the English Civil War who advocated equality before the law and religious toleration. Americans who have advocated reducing or eliminating social differences have sometimes received the same label. 199

Liberalism Originally a nineteenth-century belief in free-market capitalism; in the twentieth century, a belief in using the power of the federal government to increase opportunity and provisions for the least affluent citizens; by the twenty-first century, increasingly a belief in multicultural tolerance and inclusion. 892

Litigation A lawsuit or legal contest. 262

Longevity Length of life, a long duration of life. 281

Longshoremen Dockworkers who load and unload ships. 361

Lost Generation A group of writers critical of American social and cultural life who moved to France after World War I and were known for their heavy drinking and partying as well as their art. 730

Manumission A formal emancipation from slavery; the act (by an individual owner or government authority) of granting freedom to an enslaved person or persons. 136

Market revolution The combined effects of transportation innovation, technological change, and economic growth, especially during the first half of the nineteenth century. 343

McCarthyism The political campaign led by Senator Joseph McCarthy (R-Wisconsin) to blame liberals at home for setbacks to U.S. interests abroad, due to what he considered liberals' sympathies with communism. 826

Meager Thin, sparse, scanty; lacking fullness, richness, or strength. 218

Merchant-capitalist An entrepreneur who hires workers to perform piecework in the worker's home. 344

Mesoamerica The transitional region between North and South America, composed of Mexico and Central America. 9

Mestizo A person of mixed European and American Indian ancestry. 86

Middle ground The geographical region occupied by diverse cultural groups engaged in trade. 285

Middle passage For European slave ships, the middle passage was the second of three legs in the triangular round-trip voyage from Europe to Africa to America and back to Europe. For enslaved Africans, the middle passage came to mean not only the transatlantic journey itself, but the entire process of removal from an African homeland and ultimate sale to an American master. 123

Military-industrial complex The term given by President Dwight D. Eisenhower to the military arms industry nexus. 856

Monetary policy Government policies designed to affect the national economy through bank lending policies, interest rates, and control of the amount of money in circulation. 288

Monogamy Custom of being married to only one person at a time. 414

Mortise-and-tenon A traditional method of securing frames (without using costly nails) by inserting a narrow end (tenon) on one piece of wood into a matching cavity or slot (mortise) in another piece of wood. Often a wooden pin or peg through both pieces holds the joint in place. 72

Most-favored-nation status A designation allowing countries to export their products to the United States with tariffs no greater than those levied against most other nations. 992

Muckrakers The name given to a group of investigative journalists in the early twentieth century whose exposés often challenged corporate and government power. 662

Mulatto A person of mixed European and African ancestry; the first-generation offspring of a Caucasian and a Negroid parent. 86

Muse In Greek mythology, one of the nine sister goddesses who preside over music, poetry, and the arts. 65

Mutual aid society An organization of people who voluntarily pool their resources in order to help members in times of illness or other personal crises. 343

NAACP National Association for the Advancement of Colored People, founded in 1909. 677

National security state The reorientation of the U.S. government and its budget after 1945 toward a primary focus on military and intelligence capabilities. 830

Nativists American citizens born in the United States who oppose further immigration, especially from anywhere outside northwestern Europe. 323

Nemesis A formidable and usually victorious rival. 231

New Democrats Members of the Democratic party, many of them organized in the Democratic Leadership Council, who espouse center to center-right policies. 988

Nisei Japanese Americans born in the United States of Japanese immigrant parents. 781

NSC-68 The 1950 directive of the National Security Council that called for rolling back, rather than merely containing, Soviet and communist influences. 830

Nuclear family A basic family structure that has parents and their children at its center, or nucleus, but does not include grandparents, cousins, or other relatives. 849

Nullification The doctrine that a state has the right to ignore or nullify certain federal laws with which it disagrees. 372

Okies Migrants from Oklahoma who left the state during the Dust Bowl period in search of work. 746

Operative A machine tender. 338

Ordnance Cannons, artillery, and by extension general military supplies including weapons, ammunition, combat vehicles, and tools. 220

Overspeculation Buying stocks and land that turn out to be not as valuable as the investors had originally believed. 408

Pachucos Young Mexican American members of neighborhood gangs. 792

Parochial schools Schools sponsored by the Catholic Church or some other religious denomination (in contrast to public schools). 614

Patronage System that rewards political supporters with jobs and other favors. 464

Pest house In colonial times, a shelter to quarantine those possibly infected with contagious diseases (such as newcomers arriving in American ports from Africa or Europe) to prevent the spread of shipborne pestilence. 130

Placate To soothe or pacify, usually by granting concessions. 12

Planned obsolescence A concept whereby producers intend for their products to eventually become obsolete or outdated and require replacement, thus perpetuating a cycle of production and consumption. 722

Pocket veto An indirect veto of a legislative bill made when an executive (such as a president or governor) simply leaves the bill unsigned, so that it dies after the adjournment of the legislature. 502

Political machine A group that effectively exercises control over a political party, usually at the local level and organized around precincts and patronage. 712

Popular sovereignty The idea that residents of a state should be able to make decisions on crucial issues, such as whether or not to legalize slavery. 448

Postbellum Period after a war, especially after the Civil War, 1865–1877. 507

Precedent An earlier occurrence of something similar; something done or said setting an example or pattern that can justify later actions. 114

Preemptive attack A form of military aggression on the part of one country designed to thwart a perceived imminent attack from another. 632

Preservationists Advocates of the idea that nature must remain in an unaltered state. 609

Presidio A military garrison or fortified settlement in an area under Spanish control. 185

Privateers Ships (and their crew members) licensed to harass enemy shipping in wartime. 103

Producer economy An economic system dominated by individuals who are self-producers of manufactured goods and foodstuffs rather than employees working for wages. 707

Progressivism A notion of political reform central to the "Progressive Era" (the first two decades of the twentieth century), when urban reformers with a faith in progress sought to address local and national social problems through political and civic means. 661

Public domain Lands owned by the federal government. 609

Putting out System in which workers labor in their homes to produce goods for a merchant, who usually provides raw materials and pays them not by the hour but by each piece they finish. 344

Quitrent A fixed rent paid annually by a tenant to a proprietor or landowner. 93

Race suicide A fear articulated by Theodore Roosevelt and others that the low birthrate of Anglo-Saxon Americans, along with the high birthrate of immigrants from southern and eastern Europe, would result in a population in which "inferior" peoples would outnumber the "American racial stock". 656

Radiocarbon analysis The process, crucial to modern archaeology, of measuring the radioactive substance known as carbon 14 that occurs in bits of charcoal. Scientists measure the decay of this substance to obtain increasingly accurate dates for ancient campfires and objects found near them. 8

Realignment Change in a coalition or alliance between political parties. 426

Redemption system An eighteenth-century arrangement in which potential migrants in Europe signed up with an agent who agreed to pay for their Atlantic passage. Reaching America, the newcomer signed a pact to work for several years for an employer. In exchange for much-needed labor, the employer agreed to pay back the shipper, "redeeming" the original loan that had been made to the immigrant "redemptioner." 157

Red lining A business practice in which lending institutions deny credit to racial or ethnic minorities who live in poor neighborhoods. 847

Redress A remedy for a wrong; a correction or reparation. As a verb, to redress means to correct, to set right, or to remove the cause of a grievance. 199

Red Scare Post–World War I repression of socialists, communists, and other left-wing radicals ("Reds"). 702

Regressive tax A tax that decreases in rate as the base increases, so that someone with a large holding pays a relatively small amount. A fixed tax of $100 is regressive, since persons with $1,000 or $1 million shoulder very different relative burdens. This is the opposite of a progressive tax, where those with less pay at a lower rate. 201

Rejuvenation To restore the youthful vigor or appearance of a thing or a person. 627

Republican Mother A wife and mother whose primary role is caring for and socializing future citizens (her children); an ideal favored by some elites after the American Revolution. 312

Requisition To request, demand, or formally require something of someone. 234

Rescate In the colonial Southwest, the organized process of tribute in which Spaniards paid a ransom to Indians for the release of captives that one tribe had taken from another. The ransomed Indians often became Christians working as servants in Spanish households. Some were sold into slavery in Mexico. 151

Restitution Giving back to the rightful owner something that has been lost or taken away. 422

Rogue nations A label used by the U.S. government to refer to nations it considers hostile, unpredictable, and potentially dangerous. 999

Rosie the Riveter A heroic symbol of women workers on the homefront during World War II. 787

Sachem Algonquin Indian term for a Native American leader or chief. 95

Safety valve The West as a destination for eastern farmers and city-dwellers, a place where people can begin life anew by taking advantage of economic opportunities. 607

Scalawag A negative term applied by southern Democrats after the Civil War to any white Southerner who allied with the Republican party. 505

Scuttle To scuttle a ship is to sink it or attempt to destroy it, usually by creating holes in the vessel's hull. 204

Secession Withdrawal of a state from the authority of the federal government. 337

Second New Deal The agenda of policies and programs initiated by President Franklin Delano Roosevelt beginning in 1935 that was intended to strengthen the lot of American workers while simultaneously preserving the capitalist system. 752

Sedentary farming Activity that requires cultivators to live in one place for extended periods of time. 304

Sedition Acts that stir up rebellion against a government. 294

Separation of powers The constitutional doctrine upholding the independence of each of the three branches of the federal government: executive (president), legislative (Congress), and judicial (Supreme Court). 511

Sit-down strike A strategy employed by workers agitating for better wages and working conditions in which they stop working and simply sit down, thus ceasing production and preventing strikebreakers from entering a facility to assume their jobs. 765

Sit-in A form of civil disobedience in which activists sit down somewhere in violation of law or policy in order to challenge discriminatory practices or laws. The tactic originated during labor struggles in the 1930s and was used effectively in the civil rights movement in 1960. 855

Social Darwinism A late-nineteenth-century variation on the theories of British naturalist Charles Darwin, promoting the idea that only the "fittest" individuals will, or deserve to, survive (i.e., the idea that society operates on principles of evolutionary biology). 566

Speakeasies Establishments where alcohol was illegally sold during the Prohibition era. 712

Squatters People who live on land that they do not own, without the landowner's permission. 362

Staples Important trade items or foodstuffs. 486

Steerage Section of a ship providing the cheapest accommodations for passengers. 599

Subsidies Government assistance in the form of tax breaks or cash bonuses given to a person or business. 427

Subsistence homesteading Farming to provide only for the necessities of one's family. 434

Substitute During war, a man paid to serve in combat in another man's place. 469

Suffrage The right to vote. 681

Sunbelt The band of states from the Southeast to the Southwest that experienced rapid economic and population growth during and after World War II. 825

Sweatshop A small factory where employees work long hours for low wages under poor conditions (especially in the garment industry). 625

Swords into plowshares Turning weapons of war into productive implements, such as plows, based on the biblical passage in Isaiah 2:4. 253

Tariff A government tax on imported goods. 288

Tejanos Spanish-speaking residents of the Mexican state of Texas. 362

Temperance A social movement embracing either total opposition to alcohol consumption or support for its moderate use. 410

Tenements Densely inhabited apartment buildings generally found in crowded and poor areas of cities where immigrants and ethnic minorities lived in unhealthy conditions. 429

Texians The name used by U.S.-born citizens who lived in the Mexican state of Texas. 362

Tithe A levy or donation (generally a tenth part) given to provide support, usually for a church. 35

Total war The attacking of both military and civilian targets. 795

Townsend Plan A proposal by Dr. Francis Townsend in 1934 for a 2 percent national sales tax that would fund a guaranteed pension of $200 per month for Americans older than age 60. 759

Travois A French Canadian term for the A-frame device used by many traditional Native Americans to draw heavy loads over long distances. It consisted of two trailing poles attached to a dog or horse and supporting a platform to carry belongings. 150

Treaties Legally binding documents ratified by nations pledging them to engage or refrain from engaging in certain actions or policies. 709

Trickle-down economics An economic concept whereby the government aids the wealthiest strata as well as large corporations in the belief that the benefits of this aid will "trickle down" to the middle and lower classes. 709

Truman Doctrine President Truman's March 1947 speech articulating the new policy of containment. 819

Trusts A combination of firms or corporations created for the purpose of reducing competition and controlling prices throughout an industry. 545

Tundra A cold and treeless plain typical of arctic and subarctic regions. 6

Two-party system A system of government characterized by two major political parties that compete against each other in "winner take all" elections. 287

Unaligned nations Countries that remained neutral during the Cold War, refusing to align themselves with either the United States or the Soviet Union. 859

Unicameral legislature A legislative body that has only one chamber, or house. 94

Vagrancy The state of being unemployed and wandering from place to place. 430

Vestiges Traces, remnants. 505

Victorians Middle-class (chiefly Protestant) people living during the reign of Queen Victoria of England (1837–1901) who identified with British culture and who professed social values such as self-control, sexual restraint, and personal ambition. 612

Vigilantes People who seek to take the law into their own hands and punish or intimidate alleged criminals or persons who resist a certain social order (for example, white supremacy). 505

Vocational instruction Schooling intended to prepare the student for a specific trade (in contrast to a broader liberal-arts education). 612

Wage slavery The idea that wage earners are exploited by employers as harshly as slaves are exploited by their owners. 438

War chest A fund accumulated to finance a war or earmarked to conduct some specific action or campaign. 256

War hawks Politicians who favor specific forms of military action as a tool of U.S. foreign policy. 330

War on drugs The global campaign spearheaded by the federal government to eliminate the production of illegal drugs and their importation into the United States, and its domestic counterpart in which drug violations are treated harshly by the legal and criminal justice system. 979

Welfare reform The legislative campaign in the 1960s through the 1990s to abolish Aid to Families with Dependent Children in favor of a program that sets limits on the amount of time a poor family can receive government aid (culminating in the Temporary Aid to Needy Families Act of 1996). 989

Welfare state A nation in which the government provides a "safety net" of entitlements and benefits for citizens unable to economically provide for themselves. 742

Wildcat banks Small banks that make loans unsupervised by the state or other financial institutions. 364

Wobblies Members of the Industrial Workers of the World (IWW), a radical labor union formed in 1905. 665

Yellow journalism Newspaper articles, images, and editorials that exploit, distort, or exaggerate the news in order to inflame public opinion. 631

Yeoman A farmer who owns a modest amount of land (but no slaves). 436

Yiddish A language derived largely from German spoken mainly by Jews from eastern Europe. 643

Zionism The movement to create a modern Jewish state in Palestine, where ancient Israel had been. 680

Zoot suits Distinctive clothing in the 1940s worn largely by Mexican American and African American men, characterized by flared pants, long coats, and wide-brimmed hats. 792

Credits

Chapter 15

Page 524 (table): From *Americans and Their Forests: A Historical Review* by Michael Williams. Copyright © 1989 by Cambridge University Press. Reprinted by permission of Cambridge University Press.

Part 6 Opener

Page 534 (Top): The Library of Congress

Page 534 (Middle): Library of Congress

Page 534 (Bottom): Collection of The New-York Historical Society, Liman Collection, 2000.715.

Page 535 (Top): Courtesy, Janice L. and David Frent

Page 535 (Middle): Chicago Historical Society, ICHi-02437

Page 535 (Bottom): The Granger Collection, NY

Chapter 16

Page 539: Collection of The New-York Historical Society, Liman Collection, 2000.715.

Page 542 (figure): Adapted from *Americans and Their Forests: A Historical Review* by Michael Williams. Copyright © 1989 by Cambridge University Press. Reprinted by permission of Cambridge University Press.

Page 544 (figure): Adapted from "How Indians Used the Buffalo" from *The Native American Almanac* by Arlene B. Hirschfelder and Martha Kreipe de Montano. Copyright © 1998. Reprinted by permission of Hungry Minds.

Page 560 (Top): Rio Grande Historical Collections/Hobson-Hunstinger University Archives, New Mexico State University Library

Page 560 (Bottom): Century Magazine, May 1890

Chapter 17

Page 571: Ben Wittick, Museum of New Mexico, Palace of the Governors (Neg. #15821 & #58591)

Page 600: Courtesy, Janice L. and David Frent

Chapter 18

Page 605 (Top): Reproduced by permission of The Huntington Library, San Marino, California, photCL11(52)

Page 605 (Bottom): Reproduced by permission of The Huntington Library, San Marino, California, photCL11(53)

Page 606: Chicago Historical Society, ICHi-02437

Page 629 (Top): Fair Street Pictures

Part 7 Opener

Page 640 (Top): From the Collections of The Henry Ford

Page 640 (Middle): Courtesy, The Lilly Library, Indiana University, Bloomington, Indiana

Page 640 (Bottom): Hulton|Archive/Getty Images

Page 641 (Top): Fair Street Pictures

Page 641 (Middle): Library of Congress

Page 641 (Bottom): Rare Book, Manuscript and Special Collections Library, Duke University

Chapter 19

Page 643: Brown Brothers

Page 657 (Bottom): From the Collections of The Henry Ford

Chapter 20

Page 690: Fair Street Pictures

Chapter 21

Page 707: AP/Wide World Photos

Page 723 (figure): "Changes in Farm and Nonfarm Populations: 1880–1980" from *America's Northern Heartland: An Economic and Historical Geography of the Upper Midwest* by John R. Borchert. Copyright © 1987, published by the University of Minnesota Press. Used by permission.

Part 8 Opener

Page 736 (Top): Courtesy, Janice L. and David Frent

Page 736 (Middle): Kobal Collection/United Artists

Page 736 (Bottom): Gift of Mr. and Mrs. Jim Kawaminami, Japanese American National Museum. Photo by Norman Sugimoto

Page 737 (Top): Harry S. Truman Library

Page 737 (Middle): Cathy Crawford/CORBIS

Page 737 (Bottom): Joseph Sohm; ChromoSohm Inc./CORBIS

Chapter 22

Page 739: Bettmann/CORBIS

Page 766: Kobal Collection/United Artists

Chapter 23

Page 773: U.S. Marine Corps/The National Archives

Page 781: Gift of Mr. and Mrs. Jim Kawaminami, Japanese American National Museum. Photo by Norman Sugimoto

Page 794: Interview with Zelda Anderson in R. T. King, ed., from *War Stories: Veterans Remember World War II.* Published by the University of Nevada Oral History Program, 1995. Used by permission of Zelda Anderson and the University of Nevada Oral History Program.

Part Opener 9

Page 838 (Top, Middle): Library of Congress

Page 838 (Bottom): Courtesy, Janice L. and David Frent

Page 0839 (Top): Courtesy, National Aeronautics and Space Administration

Page 839 (Middle): Courtesy, Janice L and David Frent

Page 839 (Bottom): TimePix/Getty Images

Chapter 25

Page 856: Courtesy, Janice L and David Frent

Pages 870–871: Martin Luther King, Jr., "I Have a Dream" (speech delivered August 28, 1963, Washington, D.C.) Reprinted by arrangement with The Heirs to the Estate of Martin Luther King Jr., c/o Writers House, Inc. as agent for the proprietor. Copyright 1963 by Martin Luther King Jr., copyright renewed 1991 by Coretta Scott King.

Chapter 26

Page 875: Black Star/Stock Photo

Page 880: Courtesy, Janice L. and David Frent

Page 891: "A Time to Break Silence" by Martin Luther King, Jr. Reprinted by arrangement with the Estate of Martin Luther King Jr., c/o Writers House as agent for the proprietor. Copyright 1963 by Martin Luther King Jr., copyright renewed 1991 by Coretta Scott King.

Page 892: Library of Congress

Chapter 27

Page 907: Sean Sweeney
Page 925: Courtesy, Janice L. and David Frent

Part 10 Opener

Page 938 (Top): Bettmann/CORBIS
Page 938 (Bottom): Photofest
Page 939 (Top): Justin Sullivan/AP/Wide World Photos
Page 939 (Bottom): Amy E. Conn/AP/Wide World Photos

Chapter 28

Page 941: Ronald Reagan Presidential Library
Page 945: Photofest
Page 950 (Bottom): Sipa Press
Pages 956–957: From *Listen America* by Jerry Falwell, copyright © 1980 by Jerry Falwell. Used by permission of Doubleday, a division of Random House.
Page 957: "The Need for a Moral Minority" by Robert McAfee Brown. Reprinted by permission of the estate of Robert McAfee Brown.

Chapter 29

Page 973: SIPA Press
Page 977 (Bottom): W. Cody/CORBIS

Index

Entries followed by *f, t, m,* and *i* refer to figures, tables, maps, and illustrations, respectively.

A

AAA. *See* Agricultural Adjustment Act
Abalone Alliance, 919
Abbey, Edward, 1033
ABC. *See* American Broadcasting Company
Aberdeen Saturday Pioneer, 560
ABM treaty, 912
Abolitionist movement
  mid-19th century
    factions in, 526
    Native American rights movement and, 597
    women's rights movement and, 526, 626
Abortion
  Bolsheviks and, 700
  in 1940s, 825
  in 1950s, 825, 864
  in 1960s, 864, 895, 897
  in 1970s, 934–935
  in 1980s, debate over, 942, 954, 956
  in 1990s
    anti-abortion violence, 939, 986
    Clinton policies on, 986
    debate over, 974, 983, 986, 986*i*, 988
    decline in numbers of, 986
  early 20th century, 681–682
Abraham Lincoln Brigade, 775, 804
Abstinence movement, 956
Abstract expressionism, 862–863, 863*i*
Abu Ghraib prisoner abuse scandal, 1009, 1009*i*
Acadia National Park, 688
Acheson, Dean, 816, 819
Acid rain, 919
Acquired immunodeficiency syndrome. *See* AIDS
ACT-UP. *See* AIDS Coalition to Unleash Power
Adams, Ansel, 879*i*
Adams, Henry, 580
Adamson Act (1916), 688
Addams, Jane, 599, 661, 663, 665, 690
Adoption of foreign orphans, 961
The Adventures of Huckleberry Finn (Twain), 534*t*
Advertising
  early development of, 561
  in 1920s, 561, 716, 728–729, 728*i*
  psychology and, 561
  late 19th century
    agencies, 561
    mass merchandising, 534, 538–540, 539*i*, 543*i*, 556, 559–562, 560*i*, 567
    minorities and, 534–535, 561
  late 20th century, 561, 836, 1024
AEF. *See* American Expeditionary Force
Aerospace industry, 975
Affirmative action
  debate over, 1028
  Reagan administration and, 954
  Supreme Court on, 839*t*, 935–936
Afghanistan
  Soviet invasion of, 938, 938*t*, 942, 943*m*, 944, 945
  Taliban regime in, 995, 1003–1005, 1007, 1027
  U.S. intervention in (2001), 939, 939*t*, 1004–1005, 1007
AFL. *See* American Federation of Labor
Africa
  African-American return to, early 20th century, 715, 715*i*
  AIDS in, 957
  Carter policy in, 927*m*
  Europeans and
    imperialism in, 774, 811, 815, 820
African-American women
  Feminism and, 851, 896, 931
  in World War I, 696, 696*i*
  in World War II, 783–784, 787, 793, 794, 794*i*
  in 1920s, 719*i*
  in 1930s
    employment, 763
    New Deal and, 764, 767
  in 1990s, first in Senate, 983
  suffrage movement and, 526, 664
  19th century, 561
    authors, 603
    reform movements and, 526
  volunteerism and, 848*i*
  post–World War II
    employment, 812, 814, 850–851
    role and status of, 850–851
African Americans. *See also* Race; Slaves
  late 19th century
    businesses of, 561, 564*i*
    lynchings of, 579, 593, 594*i*, 601, 606, 611
    settlement houses and, 625
    Social Darwinism and, 566
    in Spanish-American War, 632
    as strikebreakers, 622
    temperance movement and, 600, 624–626
    unions and, 528–529, 592
    voting rights, 526, 621, 996
  and 2000 election, 996, 998
  in 1920s
    Harlem Renaissance, 719, 719*i*, 721–722
    music of, 707–708, 712, 715–723
    nationalist movements of, 715, 715*i*
    and race riots, 676, 704
    in South, 724
  in 1930s
    Communist Party and, 758–759
    employment, 736*t*, 743–744, 758, 763–764
    party affiliation, 766
    Roosevelt policies and, 758–759, 766–767
    Scottsboro Boys, 736*t*, 743–744, 744*i*
    welfare state and, 763–764, 766–767
  in 1950s
    aspirations of, 840*i*
    first major league baseball player, 814, 814*i*
    home ownership, 812, 847–848, 851
    Red Scare and, 827
  in 1960s
    as Democrats, 867, 892
    Islam among, 875*i*, 890
    riots, 890–891
    Vietnam War and, 887
    voting rights, 879, 889, 996
  in 1980s
    in armed forces, 969
    Rainbow Coalition and voting by, 958
  in 1990s
    crime and, 978–979
    population of, 974
  in World War I
    migration to cities in, 694
    as soldiers, 694, 697*i*
    as strikebreakers in, 694
  in World War II
    in armed forces, 773, 774, 792–794, 793*i*, 794*i*
    employment, 783–784
    Northward migration and, 783–784, 792
    racial tension and, 791–793
  post–Civil War (*See also* Reconstruction)
    aspirations of, 506, 579
    as buffalo soldiers, 579–580, 580*i*, 581*m*

African Americans, *cont.*
churches of, 508, 510, 579
citizenship of, 504–505
class divisions among, 508, 579
as cowboys, 523
education and, 498*i*, 508, 579
employment and, 506–508
marriage and family, 505–507, 511*t*, 610*i*
mutual aid among, 508–509, 579
office holding among, 511–512, 513*i*, 515
political organization, 508, 511–512
rights of, 504–508
sharecropping system, 508, 576*m*, 585*t*
unions and, 592
voting rights, 504, 508, 513, 526, 996
white efforts to control, 504–507
20th century
as cowboys, 523
early 20th century
Great Migration of, 674*i*, 688–689, 688*i*
lynchings of, 640, 664, 665, 676, 680
migrations north, 674*i*
mid-20th century
violence against, 812
late 20th century
crime and, 978–979
cultural impact of, 1030
employment, 1031
men's movements in, 981
poverty and, 952, 978–979
racial profiling and, 1031
role and status of, 1030
violence against, 980–981, 980*i*, 1030
back-to-Africa movement, 715, 715*i*, 734
intermarriage with Native Americans, 610, 610*i*
post–World War II
in armed forces, 807, 812, 814
party affiliation, 826, 892
African National Congress, 677
Agee, Philip, 923
Agnew, Spiro, 902, 907, 914
Agribusiness, late 19th century, 519, 521, 540*i*, 588*i*
Agricultural Adjustment Act (AAA) (1933), 737*t*, 753, 763*t*, 764
Agriculture
in 2000s, water and, 1020–1021, 1020*m*
19th century (*See also* Sharecropping system)
agribusiness, 519, 521, 540*i*, 588*i*
drought, 585–586, 586*i*
economics of, 538, 584–587
government aid to, 541
in Midwest, 527, 541*m*, 588*i*
percentage engaged in, 623*t*
railroads and, 538, 584
regions, 541*m*
technological advances in, 541
20th century
drought, 745*i*, 747*m*
economics of, 978
in Southwest, 745–746, 747*m* (*See also* Dust Bowl)
technological advances in, 823*i*
Aguinaldo, Emilio, 535*t*, 632, 637*i*
Ah Quin, 575*i*
Ah Sue, 575*i*
Aid to Families with Dependent Children
ending of, 974, 990
under Johnson, 878
Aidid, Mohammed Farah, 994
AIDS, 922, 938, 938*t*, 956–958
AIDS Coalition to Unleash Power (ACT-UP), 958
AIM. *See* American Indian Movement
Air conditioning, impact of, 825, 960
Air traffic controllers strike, 951–952
Aircraft
development of, 701, 920
industry, 825
Airline industry
development of, 640, 1016, 1033
traffic in, 1014
women pilots in, 935*i*
Al Qaeda, 939, 995, 1003–1005, 1009*i*
internment in Cuba, 1005
ties to Iraq, 1007
Alabama, 587
civil rights struggle in, 869–870
readmission to Union, 513
Alabama, University of, 869–870
Alaska, 677, 929*i*
and Alcan highway, 825
Native Americans of, 814
natural resources in, 525, 670, 928*i*, 929*m*, 1018*i*
oil industry in, 839*t*, 928–930, 928*i*, 929*m*, 950, 1006, 1022
Russia in, 524–525
statehood, 825, 842
U.S. purchase of, 524–525
Alaska National Interest Lands Conservation Act (1980), 928*i*, 930
Alaska Native Brotherhood, 814
Albania, 966*m*
Alcan (Alaska-Canada) Highway, 825
Alcatraz Island
Indian seizure of (1969), 839*t*, 894*m*, 898
prison, 894*m*
Alcohol, 944. *See also* Temperance movement
mortality from, 957
Native Americans and, 597
Aldrin, Edwin "Buzz," 839*t*, 903*i*
Aleutian Islanders, 525
Alfred P. Murrah Federal Building. *See* Oklahoma City Federal Building bombing
Ali, Muhammad, 890, 892
Alien Land Act (California, 1913), 678
"All America" team (football), 557
All in the Family (TV show), 901
All the President's Men (film), 922
Allende, Salvador, 912, 924
Alliance for Progress, 868
Allied powers (World War I), 684, 689–690, 694–695, 695*m*, 697
Allied powers (World War II), 774–778, 795–802, 795*m*
Alperovitz, Gar, 818
Alsace-Lorraine, 677, 699*m*
Altair Co., 1012
Altgeld, John P., 594*i*
Alvord, John W., 500*i*
Amador, Refugio, and family, 560*i*
Amalgamated Association of Steel and Iron Workers, 537
Amalgamated Clothing Workers of America, 765
The Ambassadors (James), 615
America First Committee, 777
America Online, 975, 977
American and European Labor Association, 573
American Association of Acupuncture and Oriental Medicine, 961
American Bar Association, 983
American Broadcasting Company (ABC), 879, 887, 936, 943
American Civil Liberties Union (ACLU), 726, 965
American Communist party. *See* Communist party
American Dilemma (Myrdal), 789
American exceptionalism, 697
American Expeditionary Force (AEF), 694–695, 695*m*, 696, 697
American Federation of Labor (AFL)
in 1930s
membership of, 765
early 20th century, 665, 687
activism of, 684, 702
anticapitalism of, 682
and election of 1912, 684
membership restrictions, 528–529, 592
late 19th century
rise of, 593–594, 623
in World War II, blacks and, 792
American GI Forum, 814, 827
American identity
21st century, 1028–1032
20th century
and immigrants, 647–648
inclusiveness and, 984
in 1930s, 739
19th century character of, 538, 607–608
American Indian Movement (AIM), 839*t*, 897–898, 923, 936
American Indian Religious Freedom Act (1978), 983
American League, 557
American Legion, 702
American Medical Association, 826
American Museum of Natural History, 628

American National Exhibition (1959), 842–844, 843*i*
American Psychiatric Association, 899
American Railway Union (ARU), 594, 619
American Relief Administration, 747
American Revolution
    economic consequences of, 590
    events leading to
        rural unrest, 590
American Road Builders' Association, 845
American System, 540–541
American Telephone and Telegraph (AT&T), 722
American Tobacco Co., 687
American Tract Society, 500*i*
American Victorianism, home decoration and, 526, 625*i*
American Woman Suffrage Association (AWSA), 527, 623
Americans with Disabilities Act (1990), 974
Americas. *See also* North America
Amusement parks
    late 19th century, 539
An Wang, 900
Anaconda Copper Co., 618*m*, 941
Anarchists
    post–World War I, 678, 702, 713, 714*i*
    late 19th century, 593–594, 594*i*, 599, 602
Anderson, Marian, 761, 761*i*
Anderson, Zelda Webb, 794, 794*i*
Angel Island, 647*m*, 651, 894*m*
Angelou, Maya, 787
Angola, 927*m*
    civil war in, 916, 945
Animal rights, 983, 983*i*
ANMA. *See* Associación Nacional México-Americana
Anorexia nervosa, 987
Antarctica, 677
Anthony, Susan B., 526–527, 526*i*, 529
Anthrax, 939, 939*t*
Anti-Imperialist League, 634
Anti-Saloon League, 712
Antibiotics
    development of, 821
    late 20th century, 987, 1020
Anticommunism
    backlash against, 892, 926
    Cold War and, 860–862
    history of, 826–827, 870–871
    Nixon and, 827*i*, 909
    Reagan and, 871
    of refugee immigrants, 1031–1032
    in 1940s, 814–816, 822, 826–828, 871*i*
    in 1970s, 909
Antidepressants, 987
Antisemitism
    Father Coughlin and, 760
    German, 775
    Holocaust and, 775, 789–791, 790*m*
    in Russia and Eastern Europe, 545, 653–654
    early 20th century, 653–654, 658
    U.S., in World War II era, 658, 777
Antislavery movement. *See* Abolitionist movement
Antiwar protests
    Vietnam War, 839*t*, 892–893
    World War II, 777, 781
Apache
    alliances with whites, 516
    assimilation of, 605*i*
    and nuclear waste storage, 941
    reservations for, 517, 583*m*, 609*m*, 613*m*, 683*m*
    resistance to whites, 534*t*
    in Southwest, 683
    white wars against, 517, 572, 580
Apartheid in South Africa
    activism against, 677, 958
    ending of, 926, 927*m*, 938*t*, 958, 966
    U.S. support for, 912
Apex Mining Act (1872), 524
Apocalypse Now (film), 922
Apollo 8, 902
Apollo 11, 903*i*, 904
Appeasement, in World War II, 776
Arab-Americans
    civil liberties of, post-9/11 attacks, 1004
    and Israel, 821
Arabian peninsula
    immigration from, 651*m*
Arabic pledge, 691
Arabs
    hostility to Israel, 821
    oil embargo (1973-1974), 918–920
    peace talks with Israel, 939*t*
Arafat, Yasser, 993
Arapahos
    alliance with whites, 516
    Ghost Dance and, 581
    land loss by, 583*m*, 609*m*
    white wars against, 517*m*, 976*m*
Arbenz, Jacobo, 861
Arches National Park, 520, 520*m*, 687*m*
Architecture
    early 20th century, 638
    late 19th century, 549
Arctic, exploration of, 627–628, 627*i*, 640*t*, 675, 675*i*
Arctic National Wildlife Refuge, 929, 929*m*, 1006, 1023
Area 51, 757*m*
Arikara
    trade, 518
Aristide, Jean Bertrand, 994
Arizona
    Indian reservations in, 613*m*
    Native Americans rights in, 773, 814
    Native Americans' suffrage in, 737*t*, 814
    racial prejudice in, 648
    statehood, 677
    Sunbelt prosperity of, 825
Arizona Copper Co., 648
Arkansas
    Clinton as governor of, 988
    Creationism in, 726
    Phillips County massacre, 702
    readmission to Union, 513
    sharecroppers in, 759
Armed forces
    desegregation of, 807, 826
    homosexuals in, 989
    19th century, segregation in, 579
    women in, 967*i*, 969
    World War II, segregation in, 792–794, 807
Armenia, immigration from, 19th century, 545
Armey, Dick, 1032
Armijo, Antonio, 757
Armour Meatpacking, 538
Arms race
    in Cold War, 838, 859
    nuclear arms stockpiles, 910*m*–911*m*, 947, 958
    nuclear deterrence and, 801, 838, 859, 869
Arms reduction treaties
    ABM treaty, 912
    Intermediate Nuclear Force (INF) treaty, 938*t*, 963
    nuclear test ban treaty of 1963, 869
    Strategic Arms Limitations Treaties (SALT I and II), 1005
    early 20th century, 709
Armstrong, Neil, 839*t*, 903*i*
Army Corps of Engineers, 723–724, 724*i*, 1020
Army-McCarthy hearings, 827
Army of the Republic of Vietnam (ARVN), 883, 903
Arnett, Benjamin W., 568
ARPANET, 1013
Arthur, Chester A., 563
Arts and Crafts Movement, 638
ARU. *See* American Railway Union
ARVN. *See* Army of the Republic of Vietnam
Ashcan School, 660*i*, 661
Ashcroft, John, 999, 1005
Asia
    20th century, 650–651, 651*m*, 731, 841
        anticolonialism in, 811, 820–821, 820*m*
        political change in, 815, 820–821, 820*m*
        trade with, 961
        The Ugly American and, 641, 885
Asian-Americans, 20th century
    citizenship and, 575–576, 828, 961
    population of, 984
    in U.S. culture, 641
Asian Pacific Legal Center, 981
Associación Nacional México-Americana (ANMA), 852
Associated Press (AP), 594
Astaire, Fred, 717
Aswan Dam, 862
Atchison, Topeka and Santa Fe Railroad, 571

Athabascan (languages, people), 525
Atlanta
  Sherman's march to, 500–501
  late 19th century, 588, 611*i*
Atlanta Compromise, 613
Atlanta University, 614
Atlantic Charter, 777–778
Atomic bomb. *See also* Nuclear arms
  bombing of Japan, 737, 798*m*, 800–801, 801*i*, 803, 803*i*, 818
  development of, 683*m*, 737*t*, 799, 800, 803
Atomic Energy Commission, 821–822
AT&T. *See* American Telephone and Telegraph
The Attack of the Crab Monsters (film), 822
Attention deficit disorder, 987
Attlee, Clement, 799
Atwater, Lee, 965
Audubon Society, 919, 950
Auschwitz-Birkenau camp, 790*m*
Australia
  in World War II, 797, 798*m*
Austria, in World War II and after
  Allied occupation of, 810*m*, 817*m*, 833
  German annexation of, 776
Austria-Hungary
  immigration from, 714*f*
  and World War I, 694–695, 697
    casualties in, 685*f*
    causes of, 677, 678
    impact of, 698
The Autobiography of Alice B. Toklas (Stein), 730
Automobiles
  development of, 541, 640
  federal safety standards for, 879
  fuel efficiency standards for, 919, 928, 1022*i*, 1023
  importation of, 917
  industry
    racial discrimination in, 792
    worker unrest in, 766
    World War II conversion of, 784
  number of, 722, 825, 845, 858
    in 2000, 1021
  pollution and, 824*i*, 825, 842, 859, 880, 1021
  in 1920s, 707–708, 716, 722, 728*i*, 733–734
  safety of, 879, 1021
  sport utility vehicles, 939, 974, 1022*i*
  and Western growth, 683, 722–723, 825
The Awakening (Chopin), 616
Axis Pact, 775–777, 795*m*, 808
Ayatollah Khomeini. *See* Khomeini, Ruhollah

B

Babbitt (Lewis), 729
Baby and Child Care (Spock), 825, 842
Baby boom, 737, 802, 824–825, 839, 845, 845*i*, 872
  drug use and, 987
  as expression of optimism, 842
  in historical context, 846*f*
Backlash (Faludi), 954
Bacon's Rebellion, 590
Baez, Joan, 893
Baker, Howard, 913
Baker, Josephine, 561, 721
Bakke case (1978), 839*t*, 935–936
Bakker, Jim, 955
Baldwin-Felts, 702
Balkans
  early 20th century
    immigration from, 646
    nationalism in, 677–678
  late 20th century, ethnic violence in, 938, 994*m*, 995
Ballinger, Richard A., 670
Bandung Conference (1956), 859
Bank(s)
  Federal Reserve, 686, 888
  Great Depression and, 641, 708, 732, 736*t*, 752
  New Deal and, 753, 763*t*
  in Progressive Era, 669
  savings and loan crisis of 1980s and, 952–953
  19th-century role of, 544, 550, 591
  and World War I, 684, 689–690
Banks, Nathaniel, 502
Bannock Indians, 517*m*, 524
Baptists, 612, 1029*f*
Barry, Leonora, 588
Barton, Bruce, 728
Bartram, William, 1022
Baseball
  Negro leagues in, 568, 814
  20th century
    Black Sox scandal and, 703
    foreigners in, 1025, 1032
    integration of, 814, 814*i*
    sports heroes in, 767
  late 19th century, 536*i*, 556–557, 568, 615
Baseball cards, 557*i*
Basketball
  as American popular culture, 958*i*, 1024–1025
  foreigners in, 1025
  invention of, 615
  women's, 933
Bass, Morris, 654
Bataan Death March, 797
Bates, Katherine Lee, 976*m*
Bathtub gin, 713
Batista, Fulgencio, 862
Battle of Britain, 776–777, 795*m*
Battleship, development of, 628
Bauer, Sybil, 708
Baum, L. Frank, 560
Baumfree, Isabella. *See* Truth, Sojourner
Baum's Bazaar, 560
Bay of Pigs invasion (1961), 838*t*
Bayan Mongol, 717*i*
Beamer, Todd, 1004
Beatles, 716, 893
Beats, 864
The Beautiful and the Damned (Fitzgerald), 729
Beecher, Eunice, 526
Beecher, Henry Ward, 526, 566
Begin, Menachem, 927
Beijing summit (1972), 909–911, 912*i*
Beirut, bombing of marine barracks in, 938*t*, 943*m*
Belgium
  Communist Party rise in, 810
  and World War II, 774, 776, 795*m*
Bell, Alexander Graham, 540, 568
Bell Telephone, establishment of, 544
Bellamy, Edward, 534*t*, 591–592
Belleau Wood, Battle of, 694
Benedict, Ruth, 789
Berger, Victor, 693
Bergman, Ingmar, 716
Berlin
  siege of (World War II), 796–797, 808–809
  post–World War II
    Allied occupation of, 810*m*, 819
    Soviet blockade of, 751, 817*m*, 819, 868–869
Berlin Wall
  construction of, 810*m*, 838*t*, 869
  fall of, 818, 938*t*, 962, 965
Bernstein, Carl, 913
Berry, Chuck, 717*i*, 814, 863
Bessemer process, 541
Bicentennial celebrations (1976), 839*t*, 908
Bicycle, 540–541, 548, 606, 922
Biddle, Francis, 781
Big Cypress National Preserve, 960*m*
Bikini Islands, 821, 822*i*
Bilingual education, 974, 984
Bill Haley and the Comets, 814, 863
Billboard, 814
Billboards, 561, 876
Biloxi, Mississippi, 578*m*
Bin Laden, Osama, 970, 995, 1003–1005, 1009, 1027
Bingham, Mark, 1004
Biological weapons, 1007
Biosphere 2, 972*i*
Birmingham, Alabama
  civil rights march (1963), 869
  Great Depression in, 758–759
  iron industry in, 577, 622
Birth control. *See* Contraception
The Birth of a Nation (film), 641*t*, 680
Birthrate, 846*f*
  and Baby Boom, 824–825, 844, 845, 845*i*, 846*f*
  early 20th-century white native-born, 656
  in World War II, 788
Black Americans. *See* African Americans
Black Codes, 504
Black Elk, 543
Black Hills, 518, 522
Black Kettle, 516
Black Muslims, 875*i*, 890, 981

Black nationalism, 876
Black Panther party, 890, 923
Black Power movement, 889–892
Black Scare, post-World War I, 702
Black Sox, 703
Black Star Line, 715
Black Tuesday, 732
Blackfeet, 618*m*
  white encroachment on, 524
Blackwell, Henry, 527
Blaine, James G., 564, 629
Blair, Tony, 1007
Blair Mountain, Battle of, 702
Blazing Saddles (film), 922
Blind, education of, 663
BLM. *See* Bureau of Land Management
The Blob (film), 822
Bloomingdale's Department Store, 560*i*
The Blues, 721
Boas, Franz, 680
Boat people, 916*i*
Bob Jones University, 948
Body and Soul (film), 721
Boehlert, Sherwood, 1006
Boeing Aircraft, 1016, 1019
Boesky, Ivan, 951
Boland Amendments (1982, 1984), 946, 964
Bolden, Charles "Buddy," 661
Bolshevik revolution in Russia, 641, 641*t*, 676, 678
  U.S. fear of, 698, 700, 944*i*
  World War I and, 677, 685*f*, 691, 694–695, 695*m*, 698
Bonanza farms, 540*i*, 544
Bondelid, Almira, 788
Bonneville Power Administration, 756
Bonnin, Gertrude, 612
Bonsack, James, 577
Bontemps, Arna, 719
Bonus March, 736*t*, 749
Borglum, Gutzon, 758
Bosnia, 939*t*, 966*m*, 994*m*, 995
Boston
  19th century
    budget of, 555
  20th century
    police strike in, 702
    1970s racial violence in, 918, 918*i*
Boston Fruit Co., 544
Boston Indian Citizenship Committee, 597
Boston marriages, 661
Botswana, 927*m*
Boulder, Colorado, 976
Boundary Waters Canoe Area, 649, 649*m*
Bourke-White, Margaret, 741*i*, 756*i*
Bourne, Randolph, 690
Bow, Clara, 717
Bowerman, Bill, 921
Boxer Rebellion, 535*t*, 633, 633*i*, 668
Boxing
  professionalization of, 557
  1930s celebrities in, 767–768
Boycotts
  20th century
    civil rights and, 854–856
    of grapes and lettuce, 897
    Taft-Hartley Act and, 815
Bozeman Trail, 517*m*, 618*m*
Bracero program, 784, 825, 847
Bradley, Aaron, 499
Bradley, Omar, 835
Brady, James, 987
Brady Bill, 987
Braille, 663
Brain Trust, 753
Branch Davidian compound, FBI assault on, 939*t*, 985
Brandeis, Louis, 680, 680*i*, 765
Brando, Marlon, 863, 864*i*
Brandywine Springs Amusement Park, 556
Braun, Carol Moseley, 983
Brazil, 653
Brest-Litovsk Treaty (1918), 697
Bretton Woods monetary system, 917
Breyer, Stephen, 989, 998
Brezhnev, Leonid, 909
Briand, Aristide, 710
Bright Eyes, 597
Brooklyn, New York, 550*i*
Brooklyn Bridge, 550*i*
Brotherhood of Sleeping Car Porters, 791, 854
Brown, Ed, 730
Brown, James, 717*i*, 863
Brown, Jere A., 592
Brown, Linda, 852
Brown, Michael, 921
Brown, Robert McAfee, 956–957
Brown, William, 702
Brown, Willie Mae, 730
Brown v. *Board of Education* (1954), 838*t*, 852–853, 852*i*, 855*m*, 881–882
  implementation of, 853–854, 854*i*, 879
Bruce, Blanche K., 515
Bryan, William Jennings
  and election of 1896, 620
  and election of 1900, 635
  Scopes trial and, 726–727, 727*i*
  on Social Darwinism, 726
  World War I and, 691, 943–944
Bryan-Chamorro Treaty (1916), 679
Bryant, Louise, 703
Buchanan, Pat, 957, 998*i*
Buchenwald camp, 790*m*
Buck, Carrie, 726
Buck, Doris, 726
Buck v. *Bell* (1927), 640*t*, 723, 724–726
Buddhism, 893, 1028, 1029*f*
Buffalo
  extermination of, 523*i*, 543, 543*i*, 544*i*, 557, 597
  Indians and, 544*i*, 581, 597
Buffalo soldiers, 579–580, 580*i*, 581*m*
Buford (ship), 702
Bulgaria, 699*m*, 966*m*
Bulge, Battle of, 795*m*, 796
Bulimia, 987
Bull Moose party, 671
Bulletin of Atomic Scientists, 845
Bully pulpit, 750
Bundy, William, 924
Bunker, Archie, 901
Burdick, Eugene, 841
Bureau of Indian Affairs, 828
Bureau of Land Management (BLM), 687*m*, 949–950, 950*i*, 1020
Bureau of Reclamation, 757, 1020
Bureau of Refugees, Freedmen, and Abandoned Lands. *See* Freedmen's Bureau
Burford, Robert, 949–950
Burger, Warren, 904
Burger King, 1026
Burlingame, Anson, 519
Burlingame Treaty (1868), 519
Burma
  independence of, 820*m*
Burton, Maria Amparo Ruiz de, 521
Bush, George H. W.
  background of, 965
  as CIA director, 926, 965
  and election of 1988, 965, 974
  and election of 1992, 988–989
  foreign policy, 965–970
  Panama intervention and, 966–967
  Persian Gulf War and, 962, 967–970, 968*m*
  and Soviet Union collapse, 962, 965–966
  on supply-side economics, 948
  Supreme Court appointments, 965, 983
  as vice president, 965, 1005
  in World War II, 785*i*
Bush, George W.
  background of, 1004–1005
  budget deficits and, 1006
  campaign financing and, 1017
  domestic policies of, 999, 1005–1007, 1022
  and election of 2000, 939*t*, 975, 995–999, 997*m*, 998*i*
  and election of 2004, 1010–1011
  environmental policy of, 929, 999, 1023
  foreign policy of, 1005, 1007, 1010, 1025
  and Iraq War, 1007–1010, 1008*m*
  on same-sex marriage, 1007
  on taxes, 1006, 1017*i*
Bush, Jeb, 997
Business. *See also* Corporations; Industry
  in 1930s, 739, 767
  in 1950s, Eisenhower and, 858
  20th century
    African American, 851*i*
    and China, 910–911
    flight overseas, 908, 977
    World War I earnings, 693
  late 19th century
    development of national markets, 537–549, 559–562

Business, *cont.*
nnovations in, 539–543
mass merchandising, 534, 538–540
mergers and integrations, 544, 565
Business Week, 951
Busing, court-ordered, 876, 882, 900, 918i
Butler Act (Tennessee, 1925), 726
Butterfield, Alexander, 913
Butterfly ballot, 997, 998*i*
Buttonmakers, 588

C

Cabarets, 659–660, 660*i*
Cabinet, first woman in, 753
Cable News Network (CNN), 1013–1014, 1024
Cady, Elizabeth. *See* Stanton, Elizabeth Cady
Cahuila Indians, 522*i*
Cajuns
20th century, 857, 857*m*
California, 837. *See also* Los Angeles; San Francisco
Indian reservations in, 613*m*
21st century
recall of governor in (2003), 662
19th century
Chinese Exclusion Act and, 573–576
Chinese in, 515, 518–519, 521*i*, 547*m*, 573–576, 621*i*
economy of, 519, 521
Native Americans in, 519, 522*i*, 613*m*
property rights in, 521
women in, 521
20th century
anti-Asian legislation, 650, 880
compulsory sterilization in, 656, 726
defense spending and, 825, 831*i*, 975
Depression-era poverty in, 746*i*, 760–761
and Dust Bowl, 745–746, 747*m*
environmentalism in, 973–974
ethnicity in, 974, 984
federal lands in, 949*m*
immigration to, 825
Japanese in, 652–653
Latino population, 897
military spending and, 825
motion picture industry in, 659
politics in, 760–761
Proposition 13, 839*t*, 947
Proposition 187, 984
Proposition 227, 984
voting rights, 664
California, University of (Berkeley), 892–893, 894*m*, 951
California, University of (Davis), 932
California Sanitary Canning company, 787
Calley, William, 888
Cambodia
Communist revolution in, 945
independence of, 820*i*
USS Mayaguez incident, 839*t*, 915–916
refugees from, 947
Vietnam War and, 839*t*, 884*m*, 903, 913
Cameron, Lucille, 664
Camp, Walter, 557
Camp Cedar Grove, 625
Camp David Accords, 839*t*, 927–928
Campaign financing
in 2000s, 975, 990, 1017
late 19th century, 620
Campbell, Ben Nighthorse, 989
Campbell, John, 973
Campus Crusade for Christ, 893, 895*i*, 955
Canada
21st century
oil reserves and exports, 1006*f*, 1007*f*, 1021
trade with U.S., 1014*m*–1015*m*
20th century
immigration from, 689, 714
Vietnam War draft resisters and, 875
Cancer
chemical carcinogens and, 920–922, 1022
nuclear technology and, 821, 822*i*, 865, 919–920
ozone depletion and, 1021
Canned food, introduction of, 541
Canty, Hattie, 979, 1033
Capital gains taxes, in 1980s, 947
Capitalism
cyclical nature of, 1012
19th century
opposition to, 562, 595
20th century
characteristics of, 741, 1012
in Cold War, 807
foreign investment and, 678*m*–679*m*, 679–680
opposition to, 758–760, 1027*i*
public opinion of, 758
U.S. commitment to, 641, 769
Capitol Reef National Park, 520*m*, 687*m*
Capone, Al, 713
Carbon-based emissions. *See* Global warming
Carcinogens. *See* Cancer
Carey, Hugh, 921
Caribbean
immigration from, 959, 960
Spanish-American War in, 630–636, 632*i*, 634*m*, 635*m*, 638
U.S. interests in, 525, 678–680, 678*m*–679*m*, 704
Carlisle Indian boarding school, 605, 605*i*, 612
Carnahan, Mel, 999
Carnegie, Andrew, 537–538, 537*i*, 544–545, 566–567, 567*i*, 577, 617, 634
Carnegie Endowment for International Peace, 538
Carnegie family, 537–538
Carnegie Steel Co., 537, 537*i*, 617
Carolina colonies. *See also* North Carolina; South Carolina
Carpetbaggers, 505, 512
Carrington, Morris, 621
Carson, Rachel, 838*t*, 864, 866*i*
Cartels. *See* Trusts
Carter, Jimmy, 839*t*, 926*i*
and election of 1976, 908, 922, 925
and election of 1980, 944–945
as emissary, 994
foreign policy, 926–928, 927*m*, 946
and fundamentalist Christians, 955
political style of, 925, 925*i*
Vietnam War draft resistance amnesty and, 875, 926
in World War II, 785*i*
Carter Doctrine, 944
Casey, William, 946, 964
Casino Sandia, 977*i*
Casinos
in Las Vegas, 757, 977, 1032
Native Americans and, 977, 977*i*, 1033
Cassettari, Rosa, 546
Cassettari, Santino, 546
Castle Garden, 546
Castro, Fidel, 870–871, 893, 992, 1027*i*
and Bay of Pigs invasion, 868
Cold War and, 862
U.S. assassination attempts, 868, 923, 924*i*
Catcher in the Rye (Salinger), 863
Catholic Library Service, 871*i*
Catholicism
19th century
adherents, 535
education and, 614
religious instruction in, 614
20th century
anticommunism of, 827, 841
and Chicano movement, 898*i*
eugenics and, 656, 726
first presidential candidate, 711, 867
fundamentalism and, 955
missions, 841, 1025
orphanages of, 648
population and, 1028, 1029*f*
Protestant fear of, 648, 711, 955
sexual abuse scandal in, 939*t*
and Spanish Civil War, 775
Catt, Carrie Chapman, 681
Cattle drives, 523, 586, 590
Cattle ranching, 586, 609
in California, 522*i*
Federal land management and, 667, 949–950, 1020
railroads and, 517*m*, 523
social conflict and, 523–524, 590, 600
Cayuga Indians. *See also* Iroquois Confederacy
CBS. *See* Columbia Broadcasting System

CCC. *See* Civilian Conservation Corps
CDs (compact discs), 945
Celebrities, in 1920s/1930s, 707*i*, 708, 767–768
Cell phones, impact of, 973, 1014
Censorship, in World War II, 785
Census
of 2000
demographic data, 974, 1028
ethnic identity in, 974, 985, 1028–1029
of 1890 and American frontier, 607
of 1920 and urbanization, 689
Central America, 20th century
U.S. foreign policy in, 945–947, 946*i*, 963–964
U.S. intervention in, 678–680, 678*m*–679*m*, 704
Central Europe, post–World War II, Soviet domination of, 816–819, 818*m*
Central Intelligence Agency (CIA), 832*m*, 841
abuses of power by, 902–903, 913, 922–923, 924, 924*i*
in Afghanistan, 944
under Carter, 943–944
in Chile, 912
Cold War operations, 833, 838, 859–862, 923
creation of, 833
in Cuba, 862, 868, 923–924, 924*i*
in Haiti, 994
in Iran, 838*t*, 861, 943
Iran-Contra scandal and, 839*t*, 938*t*, 964
on Iraq War, 1009
and Korean War, 835
in Nicaragua, 946, 964
under Nixon, 902–903, 912–913, 923
under Reagan, 946
and Vietnam War, 841, 882, 913
and Watergate break-in, 913
Central Pacific Railroad, 516, 516*i*, 518, 521*i*, 614
Central Powers (World War I), 678, 684, 689–690, 695*m*, 701
Century Magazine, 560*i*
A Century of Dishonor (Jackson), 565
Chaco Canyon site, New Mexico, 683*m*
Chafee, Lincoln, 1006
Chan Young, 574
Chaney, James, 889
Channel Islands National Park, 720*m*
Channel One (closed-circuit TV), 561
Chaplin, Charlie, 716, 766, 766*i*
Character, American
origins of, 538, 607–608
in 2000s, 1009*i*, 1017, 1021, 1023–1025, 1027
Charity, in Great Depression, 748
Charity girls, 660
Charleston (dance), 707
Charter of Punta del Este (1961), 868
Chastain, Brandi, 1031*i*
Château-Thierry, Battle of, 694
Chávez, Cesar, 792, 897, 898*i*
Chemical industry, late 20th century, environmental impact of, 866, 880, 920, 1022
Chemical weapons, 684, 701, 1007
Cheney, Dick, 997, 1006, 1023
Chernobyl nuclear accident, 938*t*, 941, 950, 958, 963
Cherokee. *See also* Five Civilized Tribes
19th century
land sales by, 583*m*
Cherokee Female Seminary, 612
Cherokee Outlet, 608, 609*m*
Chesapeake and Ohio Canal, 832*m*
Chesapeake Bay region. *See also* Virginia
economy of
19th century, 542
Chew, William, 830
Cheyenne
alliance with whites, 516
assimilation of, 584
Ghost Dance and, 581
land loss by, 583*m*, 584, 609*m*
removal of, 584
reservations for, 518, 583*m*, 584, 613*m*
and Sand Creek massacre, 516
white war against, 516, 517*m*, 518, 580, 584*i*
in World War II, 793
Chiang Kai-shek (Jiang Jieshi), 797–798, 829
Chicago
Hull House in, 599, 625
19th century
immigration to, 546
20th century
and Jazz Age, 721
migration to, 688–689, 688*i*, 784
organized crime, 713
race riots in, 676, 702
World War II and, 788–789
late 19th century
design and architecture of, 549
economy of, 549–551, 554*m*
immigration to, 546–547, 551, 554, 592
pollution in, 543, 555
World's Fair (Columbian Exposition; 1893), 535*t*, 606, 607, 628
Chicago, University of, 615, 616
Chicago Defender, 688
Chicago Sanitary and Ship Canal, 554*m*, 555
Chicano Moratorium, 897
Chicanos
pacifism among, 898*i*
as term, 792, 897
Chickasaw. *See also* Five Civilized Tribes
Child labor
laws on, 663, 663*i*, 688
20th century, 662–663, 663*i*, 688, 709, 979–980
Childhood
in 1990s
obesity and, 987, 988*f*
violence and, 986–987
mid-20th century, 825, 842
Children's Bureau, 681
Chile, in 1970s, U.S. intervention in, 912, 924
Chin, Vincent, 917
China
crude oil reserves of, 1006*f*
in 2000s
anti-Americanism in, 1027
trade with U.S., 992, 1014*m*–1015*m*
U.S. spy plane and, 1027
19th century
Boxer Rebellion, 633, 668
Christian missions in, 829
immigration from, 518, 545–546, 547*m*, 564, 592
Open Door policy and, 633, 678
trade, 633, 829
20th century
AIDS in, 957
Cold War and, 829–830, 830*i*
communist revolution in, 797–798, 829–830
cultural exchanges with, 961
establishment of People's Republic (PRC), 737*t*, 829
immigration from, 650, 678, 714, 900, 959
Japanese imperialism and, 678, 700, 797–798, 829
Korean War and, 834*m*, 835–836
loss of China debate, 830
Nationalist revolution in, 676, 678
nuclear arms stockpiles, 910*m*–911*m*
population control programs in, 961
social evils in, 650
Soviet Union and, 816, 829–830, 830*i*, 836, 909
trade, 829, 911, 992
U.S. relations with, 829–830, 834*m*, 835–836, 839*t*, 908–912, 912*i*, 961
Vietnam War and, 884*m*, 909
war with Japan, 736*t*, 774, 797–798, 800
World War II and, 774, 797–798, 800
Chinatown (film), 922
Chinatowns
decline of, 830
San Francisco, 549
Chinese-Americans
assimilation of, 847
citizenship of, 575–576
discrimination against, 515, 518–519, 534*t*, 549, 564, 573–576, 650, 678, 830
education and, 575–576
FBI and, 830

Chinese-Americans, *cont.*
food and, 678
mission homes and, 575*i,* 599, 624
population of, 984
prostitution and, 599–600, 624, 650–651
and railroads, 516*i,* 518–519, 521*i,* 532
return to China, 650
as strikebreakers, 529
Chinese Communist Party (CCP), 829–830
Chinese Exclusion Act (1882), 534*t,* 563–564, 573–576, 650, 784
Chinese Exclusion Act (1902), 650, 880
Chinese for Affirmative Action, 981
Chinese Mission Home (San Francisco), 575*i,* 624
Chinese Nationalists, 676, 678, 829, 835–836
Chippewa, 649*m,* 981
Chisholm Trail, 523
Choctaw. *See also* Five Civilized Tribes
Cholera, late 19th century, 555
Chopin, Kate, 616
Chrichlow, Ernest, 840*i*
Christian Broadcasting Network, 954
Christian Science, 616, 638
Christianity. *See also* Catholicism; Fundamentalist Christians; Protestantism
"African" churches, 508, 510
in civil rights movement, 854, 855, 855*m*
21st century
denominations of, 1028*f*
20th century
and Central America, 946
missions, 841, 1025
in 1960s, 893, 895*i*
in 19th century
domestic missions and, 599–600, 624
foreign missions and, 535, 551, 633
Native Americans and, 597, 605
Chrysler Corp., 952, 977, 979*i*
Church, Frank, 923–925
Church, Frederic Edwin, 628
Church of Christ, Scientist, 616
Church of Jesus Christ of Latter-Day Saints. *See* Mormons
Churchill, Winston
Atlantic Charter and, 777–778
on iron curtain, 737*t,* 819
loss of office, 799, 810–811
World War II and
peace settlement, 736, 799
strategy, 777, 796
CIA. *See* Central Intelligence Agency
Cigar Makers' International Union, 593
Cincinnati, Ohio, 19th century, 554
Cinco de Mayo, 961*i*
CIO. *See* Congress of Industrial Organizations
Circuses, 558
Cisneros, Henry, 959
Cities
19th century
culture of, 549, 551–552
design and architecture in, 549
growth of, 546, 551, 625
rural migration to, 551
20th century
black migration to, 688–689, 688*i*
first black mayor, 892
ghettos in, 708
growth of, 723, 723*f,* 733
immigration and, 674*i*
migration to, 688–689
suburban growth and, 823
Citizenship
criteria for, 880, 1003
naturalization and, 880–881, 881*i*
19th century
freed slaves and, 501, 508
Native Americans and, 597–598, 601
requirements for, 610, 612
20th century
Asians and, 828
race and, 658–659, 880–881
World War II and, 783
City government, late 19th century, 530, 530*i,* 555
A Civil Action (film), 1023
Civil liberties
in Cold War, 826–828
under Warren Court, 852–853, 881–882
in World Wars I and II, 693, 784–785, 789, 804, 826
Civil Rights Act (1866), 504
Civil Rights Act (1875), 530, 531, 564, 574
Civil Rights Acts (1964, 1965), 838*t,* 839, 879
Civil Rights Bill (1866), 504
Civil rights movement
foreign relations and, 851
Johnson and, 879
Kennedy and, 867, 870
Roosevelt (F.D.) and, 740, 766
in 1940s, World War II and, 826
in 1950s, 851–856, 855*m,* 872
in 1960s, 855*m,* 869–871, 872, 879, 889
backlash against, 839, 876, 900
strains in, 889–892
19th century, 525–526
early 20th century
and New Deal, 766–767
Truman and, 826
voting rights and, 879, 996
Civil Service
desegregation of, 826
reform, late 19th century, 564
Civil Service Commission, 564
Civil unions. *see* Marriage, same-sex
Civil War
as agrarian revolt, 591
impact on South, 501
veterans' pensions, 616
Civil Works Administration (CWA), 753–754, 763*t*
Civilian Conservation Corps (CCC), 736*t,* 754, 763*t,* 784
Clamshell Alliance, 919
Claremont housing cooperative, 847
Clark, Harvey E., 812
Clark, Kenneth, 852
Clark, Tom, 826
Clark Field, 779
Class. *See* Middle class
Class struggle
20th century
Cold War and, 824, 846
protest movements and, 901
late 19th century, 616–627
Clay, Cassius. *See* Ali, Muhammad
Clayton Anti-trust Act (1914), 687
Clean Air Act (1963), 880, 902
Clean Air Act Amendments (1970), 902
Clean Air Act (1990s), 974
Clean Water Act (1966), 838*t,* 880
Clean Water Act Amendments (1972), 902
Clear and present danger standard, 693
Clearcutting, 1018, 1020
Clemenceau, Georges, 698, 776
Clemens, Samuel. *See* Twain, Mark
Cleveland, Grover
and election of 1884, 564
and election of 1888, 565
and election of 1892, 617
and election of 1896, 620
and Hawaii, 629–630
Monroe Doctrine and, 629
unions and, 619, 620*i*
Clifford, Clark, 868, 910
Clinton, Bill. *See* Clinton, William Jefferson "Bill"
Clinton, Hillary Rodham, 514, 751*i,* 899*i,* 988–989, 992*i,* 999
Clinton, William Jefferson "Bill," 514*i,* 1000
affirmative action and, 989
background and early career, 514, 988
cabinet of, 989
campaign financing and, 990
and deficit, 989
domestic policies, 988–990
and election of 1992, 974, 988–989
and election of 1996, 974
environmental policy, 999, 1023
foreign policy, 991–995
impeachment of, 514, 939*t,* 975, 988, 990–991, 1000
media and, 751, 751*i*
and Republican Revolution, 974, 989–990
scandals, 751, 939*t,* 974–975, 988, 990–991
Supreme Court appointments, 989
trade policy, 938, 990, 991–992
in Vietnam, 993, 993*i*
Cloning, 987

CNN. *See* Cable News Network
Coal
company towns and, 552
energy from, 920–921, 930*m,* 1021
mining of, 520, 521, 672
Coca-Cola, 815*i*
Cocaine, 957, 966–967, 987
Code talkers, 773, 773*i,* 779, 793, 797
Cody, William "Buffalo Bill," 535, 557, 557*i*
Wild West shows of, 535, 557–558, 582, 605
Coeur d'Alene, gold rush in, 535*t,* 539, 617, 618, 618*m*
COINTELPRO, 923
Coit Tower (San Francisco), 762*i*
Cold War, 807–808, 818, 836, 838–839, 859–862, 868–869, 872, 970
arms race in, 800–801, 843, 846
civil liberties in, 822
class conflict in, 818, 824
covert operations in, 833, 839, 859 (*See also* Central Intelligence Agency)
cultural struggle in, 818, 843–844, 843*i*
culture in, 806*i,* 822–828, 1023
Eisenhower and, 845–846
end of, 961–963, 965, 975
Europe divided by, 817*m*
and highway construction, 838*t,* 845–846, 858
Kennedy and, 751
McCarthyism in, 808, 822
and national security state, establishment of, 830–831, 833, 870
Nixon and, 843, 843*i,* 909
origins of, 697, 818
Reagan and, 938, 945–947, 961–963
roots of, in World War I, 697
in 1980s, 942
space exploration and, 842
spheres of influence in, 817*m,* 820*i,* 859, 860*m*–861*m*
suburban sprawl and, 845–846
in Third World, 859, 882–889
United Nations and, 701
U.S. covert operations in, 833, 839, 859 (*See also* Central Intelligence Agency)
USS Cole, 995
Colfax, Schuyler, 530
Collective bargaining rights
in 1930s, 755, 758, 761–762, 763*t*
early 20th century, 684
late 19th century, 588–589
post–World War II, 815
Collier, John, 755, 755*i,* 773
Collier's, 643, 662
Colonialism
19th century American, 606
early 20th century European, 677–680, 774
post–World War II
collapse of, 774, 811, 820–821, 820*m,* 828, 838, 927*m,* 938
discrediting of, 811, 828–829, 868
Colonies, British
revolt of (*See* American Revolution)
Colorado, 683*m*
cattle ranching in, 523
Dust Bowl in, 745–746, 747*m*
front range area of, 976
gun control in, 987
and homosexual civil rights, 975
Indian population, 570*i*
mining in, 522, 546, 570*i,* 682, 683*i,* 684
women's voting rights and, 601
Colorado, University of, 976
Colorado Cottage Home, 600
Colorado Fuel and Iron Co., 682
Colorado River Relocation Center (Poston, Arizona), 781*m,* 782*i*
Colorado Springs, Colorado, 976
Colored Farmers' Alliance, 586
Colored Masons, 579
Colored National Labor Union, 528
Colored Odd Fellows, 579
Columbia Broadcasting System (CBS), 879
Columbia River, 756
Columbia (space shuttle), 857*m,* 939*t*
Columbia University, 680, 750, 893
Columbian Exposition (1893), 535*t,* 606, 607, 628
Columbine High School shootings, 939, 986
Colville Confederated Tribes, 756
Comanche
alliance with whites, 516
removal of, 609*m*
white wars against, 572, 580
Comfort women, 798
Comic books, 863
Comintern, 700
Command of the Army Act (1867), 510
Commission for Relief in Belgium, 747
Commissioners from Edisto Island, 507
Committee of Fifteen, 531
Committee on Public Information (CPI), 693
Committee to Reelect the President (CREEP), 913
Common man. *See also* Workers
post–Civil War, debt and, 527
19th century
and competition for jobs, 545, 584, 588
economic plight of, 527
Communes, in 1960s, 893
Communication(s)
history of, 1012–1013
19th century, 516, 540
early 20th century, 767
late 20th century
and cultural homogenization, 945, 1023
Communism. *See also* Containment policy; Red scare
in Cold War, 807, 838
McCarthyism and, 808
U.S. fear of, 737, 814–815, 846
as economic system, 741–742
post–World War I, spread of, 698, 870
in 1930s
increased interest in, 758–759, 870
New Deal and, 758–761, 767
in 1940s
increased interest in, 814–816
in 1950s, Cuban revolution, 838*t,* 862, 868, 924, 924*i*
Communist bloc
in Asia, 820*m*
in Europe, 817*m*
Communist Party
before World War II, 704, 751, 758, 767, 870
in Birmingham, Alabama, 758–759
increased interest in, 758
Scottsboro Boys and, 744
strategy of, 758, 777
post–World War II, 814–815, 826, 827, 870
Communists, civil liberties of, in Cold War, 815, 826–828
Commuters, 849*i*
Company towns, 552
Compassionate Conservatism, 1005
Compromise of 1877, 531, 531*m*
Computers. *See also* ENIAC; personal computers
impact of, 1013–1014, 1016
industry, 687, 977, 978, 1013
Comstock, Anthony, 527
Comstock, Sarah, 643
Concentration camps, Nazi, 789–791, 790*m,* 799
Conestoga Indians, 590
Coney Island, New York, 556, 845
Confederate flag, in late 20th century, 1031
Congo, 927*m*
CIA in, 862, 923, 924
Congregationalists
missions in South, 499
Congress
and election of 2000, 999
and election of 2004, 1011
post–Civil War
Black members of, 512–515, 513*i,* 515
Confederates in, 504
Reconstruction policies, 510, 512*m,* 513
20th century
first black senator, 983
first female member of, 681
first Indian senator, 989
power of, 914–915
shutdown of government, 987*i,* 990
Congress of Industrial Organizations (CIO)
in 1930s
activism of, 765–766, 787
establishment of, 736*t,* 765

(CIO), *cont.*
post–World War II
communist influence in, 814–815
Operation Dixie, 815
Congress on Racial Equality (CORE), 736*t*
freedom rides and, 855–856, 855*m*
Connecticut
voting rights
of African Americans, 504
Conner, Howard, 773
Connor, Bull, 869
Conscription
in 1960s, resistance to, 892–893
in World War I, 692
late 20th century
amnesty, 839*t*, 875, 926
women and, 935
Conservationism. *See also* Environmentalism
21st century
Cheney on, 1023
20th century
and Ecology, 919
Roosevelt (F.D.) and, 667, 754
vs. preservationism, 609, 667
late 19th century, 524, 568, 609
Conservatives, late 20th century
and election of 1980, 944–945
on immigration, 1031–1032
policy goals of, 882, 938
Constitution, U.S.
and voting rights, 513, 526, 996
Constitution (Atlanta newspaper), 576
Consumer culture
and fall of Soviet Union, 962–963
in 1920s, 641, 707, 716, 722–723, 728–729, 733–734, 742
in 1950s, 822–823, 836, 838, 842–844, 843*i*, 872
in 1980s, 940*i*, 951
in 1990s, 974
in 2000s, 1017
in 1960s/1970s, 842–844, 895
late 20th century, global spread of, 1024
late 19th century, rise of, 534, 538–539, 541, 556–562, 568, 584, 616
Consumer protection movement
in 1960s, 879
early 20th century, 662
Containment policy, 818
China and, 829–830
Korean War and, 836
Nixon and, 903
Truman and, 815, 819, 830–831, 833, 882
Vietnam War and, 882, 903
Contraception
post–World War II, 825, 922
the Pill, 838*t*, 842, 895, 922
Supreme Court on, 881–882
early 20th century, activism for, 640, 681–682
Contract with America, 939*t*, 989–990
Contras, Nicaraguan, 938*t*, 946, 946*i*, 962–964, 966
Convict labor
19th century, 577
Cook, James, 780, 780*m*
Cooke, Jay, 524
Coolidge, Calvin, 734
on business, 708
and election of 1924, 709
and election of 1928, 710–711
as President, 641, 708, 709–710
Cooperatives, farmers', 527
Coral Sea, Battle of, 797, 798*m*
CORE. *See* Congress on Racial Equality
Corn
production areas of, 541*m*, 554*m*
Cornell University, 540, 893
Corporations. *See also* Business
20th century
antitrust suits, 666, 670, 671, 687, 750
culture and, 838, 892
environment and, 948–950
executive compensation, 950, 978
flight overseas, 908, 951, 977, 1011–1012, 1016
mergers, 951, 975, 977
multinational expansion, 838, 977, 1016
power of, 907
taxation of, 686, 947
World War I earnings, 693
late 19th century, rise of, 534, 548*t*
Corregidor, 797
Corruption
Clinton administration and, 988
in Reconstruction, 512–513
and Prohibition, 713
late 19th century, in local government, 530–531, 530*i*, 555–556
Cosmopolitan (magazine), 896
Cotton economy
in Great Depression, 753, 759*i*
post–Civil War, 506–507, 509, 509*i*, 511*t*, 576*m*
production and export, 577*i*
sharecropping and, 576*m*, 585*t*
slavery and, 508
Cotton plantations
black life and labor on, 508, 509, 509*i*, 511*t*
post–Civil War, sharecropping system, 508, 509*i*, 511*t*, 576*m*, 585*t*
19th century
labor supply for, 509
sharecropping system, 508, 576*m*, 585*t*
Cotton States Exposition (1895), 613
Coughlin, Charles E., 759–760
Coulter, Inga, 986*i*
Country Club Plaza, 728–729
Court of Private Land Claims, 572, 608
Cowboys, 523, 683
African Americans as, 523
in Cody's Wild West show, 558
labor unrest by, 590
Cox, Archibald, 913–914
Coxey, Jacob S., 619, 620, 620*i*
Coxey's Army, 535*t*, 619, 620, 620*i*
CPI. *See* Committee on Public Information
Crack cocaine, 957, 966–967
Crane, Stephen, 615–616
Crazy Horse, 518, 519*i*
Crazy Mule, John, 584*i*
Creationists, 727
Credit cards, first, 823
Crédit Mobilier, 530
Creek Indians. *See also* Five Civilized Tribes
and Seminoles, 580*i*
Creel, George, 693
CREEP. *See* Committee to Reelect the President
Creeping socialism, 755
Crews, Henry, 730
The Crisis, 666
Croatia, 966*m*, 994*m*, 995
Cronkite, Walter, 888
Crook, George, 517, 597
Cross of Gold speech, 620
Crow Indians, 518, 524
Crowell, John, 949–950
Crummel, Alexander, 568
Cu Chi, tunnels of, 887
Cuba
in 1980s
and leftist revolutions, 946, 946*i*
in 1990s
Elian Gonzalez case and, 992
U.S. relations with, 992, 1027*i*
in 1950s and 1960s
Bay of Pigs invasion (1961), 838*t*, 862, 868
communist revolution in, 838*t*, 862, 868, 870, 893, 924, 924*i*
Cuban Missile Crisis (1962), 751, 801, 838, 838*t*, 869, 892
refugees from, 871, 947, 960, 992
19th century
immigration from, 547
revolution of 1895, 630–631
and Spanish-American War, 629–633, 635*m*, 638
U.S. designs on, 606
early 20th century
constitution of 1901, 633
U.S. intervention in, 641*t*, 669, 678–680, 678*m*–679*m*
Cubism, 661
Culinary Workers Union, 1033
Culpeper's Rebellion, 590
Cultural imperialism, U.S.
post–World War II, 815*i*, 818
Culture
in 1980s
conflicts in, 938, 954–959

sexuality, 944
viewer attention span, 945
in 1990s, conflict in, 989
in 1960s and 1970s
backlash against, 876, 899–902
Cold War and, 910
counterculture, 839, 845, 889–899, 893, 895
sexuality, 909
television and, 889
uncertainties of, 906*i*
post–World War II
global spread of, 833
in Cold War
as battleground, 839, 845, 889–899
McCarthyism, 808
19th century, 538, 556–562
Europe and, 599, 604*i*
literature and art, 560, 604*i*
psychology as discipline, 615, 616
sexuality and women, 527
shows and entertainments, 556–558, 558*i*, 559*i*
Victorianism, 526, 552*f*, 566, 612, 625*i*, 627
westward migration and, 557–558
20th century (*See also* Music; Sexuality)
African Americans and, 707–708, 712, 715–723, 719, 719*i*
characteristics of, 1023–1025
conservative backlash in, 899–902
and counterculture, 893, 895
global resistance to, 1025–1027
homogenization of, 1023
literature and art, 763*t*
overseas spread of American, 815*i*, 1023–1025, 1027
sexual mores, 909
Slow Food movement challenge to, 1026
youth, 839, 845, 889–899, 893, 895, 900–901
Cunard shipping lines, 599
Currency, U.S., 529, 677
crisis of 1968, 888
Federal Reserve and, 686, 888
and gold, 620, 917
"In God We Trust" on, 847*i*
as international currency, 686, 1025
silver coinage and, 587
Custer, George, 500, 516–517, 517*m*, 518*i*, 519*i*, 558, 558*i*, 579, 582
CWA. *See* Civil Works Administration
Czechoslovakia, 698, 699*m*, 776, 962*i*, 965, 966*m*

D

D-Day, 737*t*, 795*m*, 796, 796*i*
Da Nang, 883, 884*m*
Dachau camp, 790*m*, 799
The Daily Graphic, 526*i*
Daimler-Benz, 977, 979*i*
Dairy industry, 541*m*
Daisy Miller (James), 615
Dakota Indians. *See* Sioux
Daley, Richard, 901
Dallas (TV series), 951
Dalton, Henry, 522*i*
Dalton, Mrs. L. L., 600
Dalton Highway, 929*m*
Dams, 20th century, 667, 919, 1020
DAR. *See* Daughters of the American Revolution
Darrow, Clarence, 726–727
Darwin, Charles, 566, 726
Daughters of the American Revolution (DAR), 761, 761*i*
Davis, Bette, 767
Davis, Gray, 662
Davis, John W., 709
Dawes General Allotment (Severalty) Act (1881), 534*t*, 565, 565*i*, 598, 613*m*, 647, 755
The Day After (TV drama), 963
Day care
in World War II, 787–788
in 1970s, 933
Dayton Accords (1995), 939*t*, 995
DDT, 864, 902, 922
de Burton, Maria Amparo Ruiz, 521
Deaf
education of, 663
workers in World War II, 787
Dean, James, 863
Dean, John, 913
Death penalty
debate on, 923*f*, 985–986
executions (1930-2000), 923*f*
moratorium on (Illinois), 986
public opinion on (1940-2000), 923*f*
Death Valley National Park, 687*m*, 720*m*
Debs, Eugene V., 619, 665, 690, 693
December 7 (film), 785
Declaration of Independence, 811
Declaration of war, War Powers Act (1973) and, 923
Deerfield Village, 658
Del Rio, Dolores, 718
DeLarge, Robert G., 513*i*
Deliver Us from Evil (Dooley), 841
Dell, Michael, 1013
Dell Computers, 1013
DeMille, Cecil B., 717
Democracy
direct, 662
grassroots, 606
Democratic Leadership Council, 988
Democratic National Committee, 912–913
Democratic National Convention (Chicago, 1968), 901
Democratic party
convention of 1964, 889
convention of 1968, 901
and election of 1868, 513
and election of 1872, 530
and election of 1876, 531, 531*m*
and election of 1880, 563
and election of 1884, 564
and election of 1888, 565
and election of 1892, 617
and election of 1896, 620
and election of 1900, 635
and election of 1904, 667
and election of 1912, 671
and election of 1916, 690
and election of 1920, 704, 750
and election of 1924, 709
and election of 1928, 710–711
and election of 1932, 751
and election of 1936, 764, 766
and election of 1940, 778
and election of 1944, 796
and election of 1948, 826
and election of 1952, 836, 856
and election of 1960, 867
and election of 1964, 877
and election of 1968, 888–889, 901
and election of 1972, 912–913
and election of 1974, 915
and election of 1976, 925–926
and election of 1980, 944–945
and election of 1984, 948, 958
and election of 1996, 974
and election of 2000, 995–999, 997*m*
and election of 2004, 1010–1011
19th century
and farmers, 587
Populists and, 620
post–Civil War policies, 500, 505, 512*m*
and race, 579
tariff and, 562
20th century
alliance with labor, 684
blacks and, 766, 875
constituency, 766–767
environmental policies, 1022
loss of blue-collar vote, 901
New Democrats, 988
Student Non-Violent Coordinating Committee (SNCC) and, 875
Dempsey, Jack, 708
Denali National Park, 928*i*. *See also* Mount McKinley
Denmark
and World War II
German invasion of, 776
Jews in, 791
Denver, Colorado, 976
Department of Agriculture
discrimination by, 591
establishment of, 541
19th century, policies of, 591, 608
Department of Commerce, 711, 722, 724
Department of Defense, 832*m*, 833, 835, 918–919, 969, 1013
under Reagan, 945–946
Department of Homeland Security, 832, 832*m*, 1005
Department of Housing and Urban Development (HUD), 867

Department of Labor, 684
Department of the Interior, 687*m*, 709, 950, 950*i*, 981, 1020
Department stores, rise of, 544, 554, 557*i*, 559
Depressions, cycle of, 740, 809. *See also* Economy
Desegregation
in late 20th century, 1030
in 1940s
of armed forces, 737*t*, 807, 826
of interstate transportation, 737*t*
in 1950s and 1960s, 838*t*, 847, 879
backlash against, 876, 900
black debate over, 890
Brown v. *Board of Education* and, 852*i*
of buses, 869–871
Civil Rights Act (1964), 839, 879
and court-ordered busing, 876, 882, 900, 918*i*
implementation of, 853–854
in Northern communities, 847
Desert Land Act (1877), 523
Détente, 911–912, 916, 923, 925, 944–945
Detroit
20th century
black riots in, 737*t*, 838*t*, 890, 900
migration to, 545, 640, 688–689
Rustbelt decline of, 825
Detroit Publishing Co., 568, 672
Dewey, George, 632, 634*m*
Dewey, Thomas E.
and election of 1944, 796
and election of 1948, 826
DeWitt, John L., 781
Dexter Avenue Baptist Church, 854
Diaz, José, 792
Didrikson, Babe, 768
Dien Bien Phu, Battle of, 882–883
Dies, Martin, 767
Diggers, 904
diMaggio, Joe, 767
Diné. *See* Navajo
Diner's Club, 823
Dinosaur National Monument, 520*m*
Diptheria, late 19th century, 555
Disabled persons, 839
Disarmament agreements. *See also* Arms reduction treaties
1920s, 709
Disco music, 933*i*
Discrimination. *See also* Prejudice; Racism
in 1930s, 744
WPA and, 766–767
in 1950s and 1960s
in housing, 812, 823, 830, 918
in workplace, 839
post–World War II
discrediting of, 808
opposition to, 826
in World War II
in defense industries, 791–792
21st century
against homosexuals, 1006
19th century
against African Americans, 584
against Chinese, 518–519, 573–576, 584
employment and, 584
20th century, 641, 980
in USDA loan program, 591
Disease
19th century
industry and, 588
in Spanish-American War, 633
urban water and, 555
20th century
AIDS epidemic, 922, 938, 938*t*, 956–958
drug-resistant bacteria, 987, 1020
flu epidemic (1918), 700, 705
polio, 750–751, 842
radioactive fallout and, 821–822, 822*i*, 942
in World War I, 700, 705
Disney Corporation
global spread of, 838*t*, 1025, 1025*i*
Disneyland, 838*t*, 845
District of Columbia, 572, 832, 832*m*. *See also* Washington, D.C.
Diversity. *See also* Ethnicity
in 20th century, 974, 984–985
Division of Forestry, 609
Divorce
in 1920s, 707, 712
in 1970s, 844*f*, 909, 933, 935
20th century, 640, 661, 700, 844*f*, 1032
late 19th century, 527, 626, 956
Dixiecrats (State-Rights Democratic party), 826
DNA analysis, 984, 986, 990
Dodge, Grenville, 500
Dodge, Mabel, 703
Doheny, Edward L., 709
Dole, Robert, 990
Dollar. *See* Currency
Dollar Diplomacy, 670
Dollinger, Genora Johnson, 766
Dominican Republic
and Jewish refugees, 791
U.S. designs on, 19th century, 525
U.S. intervention in, 20th century, 641*t*, 669, 678–680, 678*m*–679*m*, 892, 924
"Don't ask, don't tell" policy, 989
Dooley, Tom, 841, 841*i*
"Double V," 773, 792–793, 802
Douglass, Frederick, 568
unions and, 529
on women's rights, 526
Dr. Seuss, 791*i*
Draft. *See* Conscription
Dreiser, Theodore, 661
Drought
in 1930s, 745–747, 745*i*, 747*m*
late 19th century, 585–586, 586*i*
Drug use
in 1970s, 909, 922
in 1980s, 957
in 1990s, 938, 978, 985
in 1950s-1960s, 864, 893, 895
Dry Tortugas, Florida, 960*m*
Du Bois, W. E. B., 535*t*, 614, 634, 665–666, 672, 694, 789, 827
Du Pont Chemical Co., 687
Dukakis, Michael, 965
Duke, James Buchanan, 577
Dulles, John Foster, 860
Duluth, Daniel Greysolon Sieur, 649
Duluth, Minnesota, 649, 649*m*
Duniway, Abigail Scott, 600
Durbin, Richard, 1017
Dust Bowl, 745–746, 745*i*, 747*m*, 748, 769, 770
Dylan, Bob, 649*m*, 893
Dynasty (TV series), 951, 970
Dysentery
in Spanish-American War, 633

E

E-mail, 1012–1014, 1013*i*. *See also* Internet
Earhart, Amelia, 768, 768*i*, 935*i*
Earth Day, establishment of, 902
Earth First!, 973
Easter Rising (1916), 685, 700
Eastern Europe
post–World War I, political order in, 698–699, 699*m*
19th century, immigration from, 592
post–World War II
Soviet domination of, 816–819, 818*m*
Warsaw Pact and, 818*m*
late 20th century
culture in, 1026
Soviet Union collapse and, 938, 938*t*, 962–963, 962*i*, 965–966, 966*m*
Eating disorders, in 1990s, 985, 987
Ebony (magazine), 844, 851
Ecology, 919, 972*i*, 1018, 1020
Economy
in 1920s, 708–709
in 1930s (*See* Great Depression)
in 1950s, 809, 822–823
in 1960s, 842, 876
in 1970s, 908, 916–917, 925–926
in 1980s, 947–948
in 1990s, 974, 975, 977–978, 988–989, 1013
in 2000s, 999
21st century
recession of 2001-2003, 999, 1010
U.S. trading partners in, 1014*m*–1015*m*
world integration and, 1016
19th century
depression of 1873, 528–529

post–Civil War, 527
regional characteristics, 527
20th century
currency crisis of 1968, 888
early (*See* Great Depression)
energy and, 1006
immigration and, 978*m*
oil and, 918–921 918*f*
panic of 1907, 669
recession of 1913-1914, 684, 692*i*
recession of 1981-1982, 938*t*, 948
recession of 1991-1992, 975, 988
stock market crash of 1929, 641
Vietnam War and, 916–917
World War I and, 692–693
World War II and, 778, 787–789, 802, 809
late 19th century, 606
and city growth, 550–551
depression of 1873, 528–529
depression of 1893, 535*t*, 606, 619, 620*i*
labor supply and, 550–551
Eddy, Mary Baker Eddy, 616, 638
Edens, Bessie, 731
Ederle, Gertrude, 641*t*, 707*i*, 708
Edgar Thomson Steelworks, 537, 545
Edison, Thomas A., 534*t*, 540, 920
Edmunds Act (1882), 563
Education
bilingual, 974, 984
compulsory attendance laws, 614*m*
higher
20th century, 824, 948, 1023
in 1970s
racial quotas and, 935–936
women and, 897, 932–933
in 1950s and 1960s
for minorities, 852–853, 852*i*, 854*i*
prayer in public schools, 881–882
sex education, 864*i*
in 1980s and 1990s
prayer in schools, 881–882
racial discrimination in, 948
violence in, 939, 975, 986–987
19th century
African Americans and, 498*i*, 508
Chinese Americans and, 575–576
common school system and, 508
engineering and, 539–540
of immigrants, 575–576, 612
of Indians, 598, 605, 605*i*, 612
Native Americans and, 598, 605, 605*i*, 612
parochial schools, 614
segregated, 508, 579
Victorianism and, 612
and voting rights, 623, 996
women and, 527, 623
20th century
Cold War and, 858
desegregation of, 851–856, 852*i*, 918
GI Bill and, 811–812, 813*f*
segregated, 851–856, 852*i*
standardization in, 655
of women, 681*i*, 813*f*, 824, 850, 897
Educational Amendments of 1972, Title IX, 933, 934*i*
Edwards, John, 1010
Efficiency, industrial labor and, 549
Efficiency experts, 549, 657
Egypt, 875*i*, 938*t*
Camp David Accords, 927–928
and Israel, 918–919
under Nasser, 862
U.S. relations with, 919
Ehrenreich, Barbara, 947
Ehrlich, Paul, 902
Ehrlichman, John, 914
Eight hour day. *See* Work day
Eighteenth Amendment, 641, 641*t*, 693, 712–713
Einstein, Albert, 800
Eisenhower, Dwight D., 872
background of, 796–797, 856
civil rights movement and, 853–854
and defense budget, 856
and desegregation of schools, 853–854
domestic policies, 856, 858–859
on Dooley, Tom, 841
and election of 1952, 827, 836, 856
and election of 1956, 856
foreign policy, 859–862
Interstate Highway Act and, 845–846
Sputnik and, 856, 858
Supreme Court appointments, 852, 881
on Tennessee Valley Authority, 755
Vietnam War and, 841, 868, 883
in World War II, 785*i*, 796–797, 856
Eisenhower Doctrine, 838*t*, 862
El Alamein, Battle of, 795*m*
El Congreso de Pueblos de Habla Española, 736*t*, 767
El Paso, Texas, 679, 689, 1011*i*
El Salvador, 945–947
Election(s)
of 1866, 505
of 1868, 513
of 1872, 527, 530
of 1876, 531, 531*m*
of 1880, 563
of 1884, 564
of 1888, 565
of 1892, 617
of 1896, 620
of 1900, 635
of 1904, 667
of 1908, 669–670
of 1912, 671
of 1916, 690
of 1920, 709, 750
of 1924, 709
of 1928, 710–711
of 1932, 740, 751
of 1936, 764
of 1940, 778
of 1944, 796
of 1948, 826
of 1952, 827, 836, 856
of 1956, 856
of 1964, 877
of 1968, 888–889, 901–902
of 1972, 912–913
of 1974, 915
of 1976, 922, 925
of 1980, 944–945
of 1984, 948, 958
of 1988, 954, 958, 965
of 1992, 964, 988–989
of 1994, 989
of 1996, 974
of 2000, 995–999, 997*m*
of 2004, 1010–1011, 1010*i*
Electoral College
debate over, 709, 996, 998
and election
of 2000, 997–998
of 2004, 1010
Electric chair, 713
Electric light
invention of, 540, 920
use as indicator of population, 1021*i*
Electric utilities, 668, 754*m*, 920, 1021*i*
and nuclear power, 919, 921, 930*m*
and power marketing, 668
Electrification, rural, 754–755, 754*m*, 1021*i*
Elementary and Secondary Education Act, 878
Elephant Rock, Nevada, 757*i*
Elevators, introduction of, 552–553
Elliott, Robert B., 513*i*
Ellis Island, 535*t*, 647*m*, 651
Ellsberg, Daniel, 903
Emergency Banking Act (1933), 752, 763*t*
Emergency Relief Appropriation (1935), 764
Emmons, Delos, 782
Empire State Building, 758
Empire Zinc Mining Co., 828*i*
Employment
19th century
categories of, 548*t*, 623*t*
and competition for jobs, 588
and firm size, 548*t*
20th century
and Great Depression, 732, 736*t*, 742, 778
1970s crisis in, 917
and World War II, 778, 787–789, 802, 814
Encyclopedia Britannica, 610
End Poverty in California (EPIC) plan, 760–761
Endangered Species Act (1973), 839*t*, 902
Energy. *See also* Nuclear power; Oil
conservation of, 921, 928, 1023
industry, and politics, 1006
renewable, 919, 921, 921*i*, 928
Energy use, U.S.
history of, 920–921
20th century, 677, 919, 921, 928, 930–931, 1021

Engineering
electrical, 540
rise of, 539–540, 567
and space exploration, 858
England/Great Britain
21st century
and Iraq War, 1007–1008
trade with U.S., 1014*m*–1015*m*
19th century
in Americas, 629
immigration from, 545, 714*f*
U.S. rivalry with, 628–629
20th century
Communist Party rise in, 810–811
cultural impact of, 716
Empire of, 778, 820–821, 888
Five-Power Treaty, 709
and Great Depression, 742
immigration from, 783
in Middle East, 695, 862, 888
nuclear arms stockpiles, 910*m*–911*m*
politics in, 945
Socialist Party rise in, 810–811
in Vietnam, 882
weakening of, 819, 820*m*, 821, 888, 1023
World War I and, 677, 685*f*, 689, 694–695, 695*m*, 697
World War II and
Battle of Britain, 776–777, 795*m*
diplomacy of, 774, 776, 796, 799
Empire of, 778
English Channel, first woman to swim, 707*i*, 708
English language
and English-only initiatives, 974
20th century, global reach of, 1023, 1025
ENIAC computer, 1012
Enola Gay, 801
Environmental damage. *See also* Pollution
in 1930s, Dust Bowl, 745–746, 745*i*, 747*m*
in 1960s, 880
in 1970s, 902
in 1980s, 949–950
in 1990s, 973–974
in 2000s, 1018
19th century, 539, 542–543, 542*f*, 609, 638
20th century, 638, 683, 864, 880
nuclear industry and, 821, 907
oil drilling and, 858, 902
pesticides/insecticides and, 864, 866, 880, 902, 920, 1022
and quality of life, 919
uranium mining and, 941–942
Environmental Protection Agency (EPA)
environmentalists and, 919
establishment of, 902
and hazardous waste sites, 920–921, 1022
under Reagan, 949–950
Environmentalism. *See also* Conservationism
in 1960s, 839, 858, 876, 879–880, 879*i*
in 1970s, 858, 902, 908, 919–922
in 1980s, 947, 948–950
in 1990s, 973–974, 973*i*
in 2000s
global support for, 1018
in 21st century, 1006, 1022–1023
early 20th century
New Deal and, 754–755
late 19th century, 524, 568, 609
late 20th century, 936
EPA. *See* Environmental Protection Agency
Episcopalians, 677, 935, 955, 1025, 1029*f*
Epps, Charles H., 624*i*
Equal Opportunity, ideal of, 1017*i*
Equal Opportunity Employment Commission, 983
Equal Pay Act (1963), 838*t*, 869
Equal Rights Amendment (ERA), 641*t*, 711–712, 934, 967*i*
Equal Rights Association, 526
ERA. *See* Equal Rights Amendment
Erin Brockovich (film), 1023
Ervin, Sam, 913
Escobar, Carmen Bernal, 745
Escobedo v. *Illinois* (1964), 881
Eskimo, 525, 610, 627–628, 627*i*, 675
Espionage Act (1917), 693
Estate tax
in 1980s, 947
in 2000s, 1017*i*
early 20th century, 670, 686, 709, 747
Estonia, 699*m*, 966, 966*m*
Ethiopia
and Italian imperialism (1896), 677, 775
1980s revolution in, 945
Ethnic studies programs, 897
Ethnicity. *See also* Diversity
as criterion for citizenship, 880, 1003
19th century
class struggle and, 548
employment and, 548
by region, 551*m*
late 20th century
diversity of, 959, 974, 984–985, 1000
and resistance to American culture, 1023–1025, 1027
Eugenics movement
in 1920s, 640, 656–657, 724–726
in 1990s, 988
Euro (European currency), 1015
Europe. *See also* Eastern Europe
21st century
Bush (G.W.) and, 1007, 1010
19th century
Americans in, 599, 604*i*
imperialism of, 627–637, 638
20th century
Bush (G.H.W.) and, 962
Communism in, 698–703, 810*m*
immigration from, 714*f*, 959
loans to, after World War I, 709, 742
Reagan and, 962
European Recovery Program. *See* Marshall Plan
Everglades National Park, 960, 960*m*
Everglades wetlands, 729, 960
Everybody's, 662
Evian conference on Jewish refugees, 790
Evolution of human species, 726–727, 727*i*, 728
Exceptionalism, 607–608
Executive Order 7046, 766–767
Executive Order 8802, 792
Executive Order 9066, 736*t*, 781
Exercise, popularity of, 921–922, 922*i*
Exodusters, 580
Exoticism, 627–628
Extractive industry, 521–524, 534, 539, 542–543, 623*t*, 683, 731, 949–950. *See also* Mining; Naval stores; Timber
Exxon Valdez oil spill, 938*t*, 950

F

Fair Employment Practices Commission (FEPC), 792
Fair Labor Standards Act (1938), 736*t*, 763*t*
Fairbanks, Alaska, 929, 929*m*
Fairbanks, Douglas, 606, 716
Fall, Albert, 709
Faludi, Susan, 954
Falwell, Jerry, 955–957, 956*i*
Family
in Cold War, 823–825
in Great Depression, 743–746, 762–763
in 1970s, 932–933
19th century
Cotton Belt, 511*t*
Victorianism and, 526, 625*i*, 627
mid-20th century
nuclear, 838, 844–846, 849
women's role in, 808, 838, 849–851
Victorianism and, 526, 566, 625*i*, 627
in World War II, 788–789
Family and Medical Leave Act, 989
Farah slacks company, 934
Fargo, North Dakota, 718*i*
Farm Mortgage Act (1933), 753, 763*t*
Farm Relief Act (1933), 753
Farm Security Administration (FSA), 746*i*, 804
Farm subsidies, 709, 753, 763*t*
Farmers
19th century
plight of, 585–587, 616
unrest, 585–587, 590–591
20th century
decline in numbers of, 723*f*
in World War II, 787
Farmers' Alliance, 617
Farmers' Holiday Association, 590*i*, 591

Farming, mechanization of, 541–542, 621*i*
Farouk, King of Egypt, 862
Farrakhan, Louis, 981
Fascism
  beginnings of, 716, 742, 760, 767
  discrediting of, 808–809
  programs of, 774–776, 789–791, 790*m*, 802
"Fat Boy," 801*i*
Father to Father, 981
Fatherhood Project, 981
Father's Day, establishment of, 824, 864
Fathers' Education Network, 981
Faubus, Orville, 853–854
FBI. *See* Federal Bureau of Investigation
FDIC. *See* Federal Deposit Insurance Corporation
Fear, Freedom from, 774, 777*i*
Federal Aid Highway Act (1956), 858
Federal Aid Highways Act (1916), 722
Federal Bureau of Investigation (FBI)
  American Indian Movement and, 898
  antisubversive activities of, 826, 902–903
  Black Panthers and, 890
  and Democratic Convention of 1968, 901
  and domestic terrorism, 985
  excesses of, 871, 901, 902–903
  Ku Klux Klan and, 889
  Nixon and, 902–903
  1990s assaults by, 939*t*
  and Vietnam War opponents, 913
  and Watergate break-in, 913
  and women's liberation, 908
Federal Deposit Insurance Corporation (FDIC), 763*t*, 768
  creation of, 753
  and Savings and Loan crisis, 1980s, 952–953
Federal Emergency Relief Act (1933), 753, 763*t*
Federal Emergency Relief Administration (FERA), 736*t*
Federal government
  in 1980s and 1990s
    Republican view of, 945
    shutdown of, 987*i*, 990
  20th century
    employee loyalty program, 826
    growth of, 666, 777
  late 19th century, strike breaking by, 562–563, 619–620
Federal Highways Act (1916), 772
Federal Housing Administration (FHA), 763*t*, 823
Federal Housing Authority (FHA), 736*t*, 846
Federal lands
  21st century, exploitation of, 1006
  19th century, 608–609
  20th century, 667, 670, 949–950, 949*m*, 951*i*
Federal One program, 763*t*, 764
Federal Radio Commission, 722
Federal Reserve
  Great Depression and, 732
  and inflation, 948
Federal Reserve Act (1913), 640*t*, 686
Federal Theater Project, 764
Federal Trade Commission, 687
Federal Writers Project, 770
Feebleminded persons, sterilization of, 656, 726
Feis, Herbert, 818
Fellini, Federico, 716
The Feminine Mystique (Friedan), 838*t*, 849, 869, 896
Feminism, 936. *See also* Women's rights movement
  20th century
    and African Americans, 851, 896, 931
    backlash against, 934–935, 954, 956
    and Gay rights, 896
    and Latinos, 931
    opposition to nuclear weapons and, 864–865
    rise of, 839, 849, 869, 895
    in 1960s, 876, 889, 896–897, 897*i*
    in 1970s, 907–908, 931–935, 932*i*, 934*i*, 935*i*
    and sexual harassment, 958–959
  19th century precursors of, 626
FEPC. *See* Fair Employment Practices Commission
FERA. *See* Federal Emergency Relief Administration
Ferraro, Geraldine, 948
Fertility rate, 1800-2000, 788
FHA. *See* Federal Housing Administration; Federal Housing Authority
Fieffer, Jules, 885*i*, 900*i*
Fifteenth Amendment, 513, 526–527, 610, 996
Fillmore, Millard, 552
Film. *See* Motion picture industry
Final Solution, 789–791, 790*m*, 795, 799
Finland
  20th century
    immigration from, 658–659, 659*i*
    independence of, 698, 699*m*
    Soviet Union and, 776
Fireside chats, 750–751, 750*i*, 752, 767
First Amendment
  advertising and, 561
  in Cold War, 822
  Supreme Court on, 693
Fiscal policy, late 19th century, 529
Fishing industry, 539, 542, 588
Fitzgerald, F. Scott, 641*t*, 725, 729–730, 733, 733*i*
Fitzgerald, Zelda, 729–730, 733, 733*i*
Five Civilized Tribes
  removal of, 609*m*
Five Nations. *See* Iroquois Confederacy
Five-Power Treaty, 641*t*, 709
Flanagan, Hallie, 764
Flappers, 706*i*, 707, 717, 734
Flathead Indians, 755*i*
Flight 93, 1003–1004, 1003*i*
Flight 109 (Pan Am), 938*t*, 964
Florida
  2000 election and, 995–999, 997*m*
  19th century
    readmission to Union, 513
  20th century
    Cuban refugees in, 947, 960
    hurricanes in, 641, 729
    1920s land boom in, 729
    Southern, growth of, 960, 960*m*
Florida Keys, 960*m*
Flowers, Gennifer, 990
Flynn, Elizabeth Gurley, 665*i*
Follies Bergeres, 659
Fong Dai Sing, 650
Food
  exotic, 1025
  labeling of, 879
  Slow Food movement, 1026
Food rationing, World War II, 784, 811
Football
  as college sport, 557, 615, 1024
  history of, 534*t*, 557
Forbes, Charles R., 709
Ford, Betty, 914*i*
Ford, Gerald R., 936
  Arab oil embargo and, 919
  assumption of presidency, 839*t*, 914–915, 914*i*
  and election of 1976, 925
  Nixon pardon, 915, 925
  Vietnam and, 915
  in World War II, 785*i*
Ford, Henry, 657–658, 722, 920
Ford, John, 785
Ford Motor Co., 640*t*, 657–658
Foreign aid, 839
Foreign policy, 704. *See also* Containment policy
  1920s, 708
  early 20th century, 668–669, 677–680
  late 19th century, 606
  late 20th century, 837, 991–995
Forest Reserve Act (1891), 609
Forests, 542–543, 542*f*. *See also* Logging; Timber
  19th century
    management of, 618
    railroad construction and, 524*t*
    Timber Culture Act (1873), 523
  20th century
    destruction of, 647
    management of, 667
Forman, Jim, 807
Forman, Stanley J., 918*i*
Forsyth, James, 583
Fort Concho, 580
Fort Dearborn, 554*m*
Fort Jackson, 578*m*
Fort Laramie Treaty (1851), 517
Fort Lauderdale, Florida, 960*m*

Fort Myers, Florida, 960
Fort Peck Dam, 756*i*
"40 acres and a mule," 507
Fossil fuels
  and pollution, 902, 920–921
  supply of, 918–921
  20th century, consumption, 918*f*, 919–922
Foster, William Z., 751
Four Corners area, 683*m*, 821, 941
Four Freedoms, 736*t*, 774, 777, 777*i*
The Four Horsemen of the Apocalypse (film), 718*i*
14 Points, 641*t*, 697–698
Fourteenth Amendment, 504–505, 510
Fox Indians
  land loss by, 609*m*
Fox Studios, 659
Foxwoods (casino), 977
Fragging, 903
France
  21st century
    trade with U.S., 1014*m*–1015*m*
  20th century
    in Africa and Middle East, 862, 868
    and Great Depression, 742
    and NATO, 817*m*
    nuclear arms stockpiles of, 910*m*–911*m*
    in Vietnam, 811, 828, 835, 838*t*, 882–883
    World War I and, 677, 685*f*, 694–695, 695*m*, 697
    World War II and, 774, 776, 795*m*, 796, 799, 810
Franco, Francisco, 775–776
Franco, Jimmy, 981
Franklin, Benjamin
  newspaper ventures, 561
Free labor ideology, 501–502
Free speech
  advertising and, 561
  in Cold War, 822
  Supreme Court on, 693
Free Speech, 611
Free Speech Movement, in 1960s, 892
Free trade. *See also* Tariffs
  21st century
    support for, 1015
    U.S. trading partners and, 1014*m*–1015*m*
  late 20th century
    as conservative principle, 990, 1014
    debate over, 1015
    history of, 1014–1015
  post–World War II, U.S. commitment to, 815
Freed, Alan, 814
Freedman, Rose Rosenfeld, 645, 645*i*
The Freedman's Third Reader, 500*i*
Freedmen's Bureau
  activities of, 499, 502, 504, 505, 506*i*
  Black family life and, 506, 506*i*
  budget of, 506
  establishment of, 499, 502
  impact of, 507–510
  land redistribution and, 503*i*, 507
  Southern opinion of, 510
Freedom of Access to Clinic Entrances Act (1994), 939*t*, 986
Freedom of Information Act (1974), 925
Freedom rides, 838*t*, 855–856, 855*m*
Freedom Summer, 889
Freedom to choose, late 20th century, 974, 983, 986, 986*i*, 988
Fremont Indians, 520
Freud, Sigmund, 615
Frick, Henry Clay, 537, 617
Friedan, Betty, 838*t*, 849, 851, 869, 896
Front Page (film), 767
Frontier. *See also* West
  as America's defining concept, 607–608
  disappearance of, 607, 607*m*
Frontier Airlines, 935*i*
FSA. *See* Farm Security Administration
Fuchs, Klaus, 826
Fuhrman, Mark, 984
Fulbright, J. William, 892
Full Metal Jacket (film), 884
Fundamentalism, worldwide religious, 955. *See also* Fundamentalist Christians, 20th/21st century; Islamic fundamentalism
Fundamentalist Christians, 20th/21st century
  agenda of, 882, 954, 981
  cultural impact of, 938
  and election of 2004, 1011
  and environment, 950
  rise of, 942, 955–956
  sexuality and, 956–957

G

Galarza, Ernesto, 722
Galveston, Texas, 857, 857*m*
Gangsters, in 1920s, 713
Garbo, Greta, 716, 718
Garcia, Herman, 941
Garcia, John, 779
Garden of the Gods, 976, 976*m*
Garfield, James A., 563
Garland, Hamilton, 587
Garment industry, 588, 592, 640*t*, 643. 665, 979–980
Garvey, Marcus, 715, 715*i*, 734
Gary, Indiana, 554
Gasoline
  conservation and speed limit, 922, 939*t*
  leaded, 880, 920, 1022
  price of, 919, 920, 943, 1016
  rationing, World War II, 784, 811, 920
Gasoline engines
  fuel-efficiency of, 919, 928, 1022*i*, 1023
  and pollution, 824*i*, 825, 880, 1021
  and transportation, 824*i*, 825, 858, 920
Gates, Bill, 978, 1013
Gates, Merrill, 606
Gatorade, 922
GATT. *See* General Agreement on Tariffs and Trade
Gay Liberation Front, 899
Gay Liberation movement, 876, 897–899
  and Feminist movement, 896
Gay Pride parade (New York City), 899*i*, 905
Gays. *See* Homosexuality
Gaza Strip, 918–919, 928
Gender roles
  1960s Feminist movement and, 896–897, 897*i*
  1970s Feminist movement and, 931–935, 932*i*, 934*i*
  in 1920s-1930s, 707, 734, 763, 768*i*, 769
  in World War II, 788–789
  post–World War II, 824
  late 19th century, challenges to, 626
General Agreement on Tariffs and Trade (GATT), 991
General Electric, 920, 1013
General Federation of Women's Clubs (GFWC), 624
General Motors, 722, 766, 823, 858, 879, 1016–1017, 1022*i*
Geneva Accords (1954), 883
Geneva summit meeting (1955), 859
Gentlemen's Agreement (1907), 640*t*, 653
George, Henry, 550, 591
George, Presley, Sr., 508
Georgia
  19th century
    readmission to Union, 513
Geothermal power, 921
German American Bund, 777
German Americans
  20th century
    and World War I, 693
    and World War II, 783
Germany
  post–World War I
    fascism in, 742, 774–776
    immigration from, 714*f*
    imperialism of, 775
    U.S. loans to, 689–690, 732, 742
    Weimar Republic, 704, 775
  in 2000s, trade with U.S., 1014*m*–1015*m*
  19th century
    immigration from, 545, 714*f*
    unification of, 701
    universities of, 599
    U.S. rivalry with, 628
  World War I and, 677, 689, 694–695, 695*m*, 697
    casualties in, 685*f*
    causes of, 677, 701
    impact of, 694, 698
    peace settlement, 698–699, 699*m*, 704
  World War II, 736*t*, 795–797, 795*m*
    atomic research in, 800

firebombing of, 799, 800
immigration from, 783
Jews in, 774–776, 789–791, 790*m*
nonaggression pact with Soviet Union, 776–777, 796
post–World War II
East German refugees and, 869
and NATO, 817*m*, 835
occupation of, 799, 807, 810*m*, 816, 833
reconstruction of, 819
reunification of, 965
war crimes trials in, 819
Geronimo, 517, 534*t*
GFWC. *See* General Federation of Women's Clubs
Ghost dance, 573, 580–584, 582*i*
GI Bill. *See* Servicemen's Readjustment Act of 1944
Gibbs, Lois, 921, 932
Gideon v. *Wainwright* (1963), 881
Gilded Age, 563
The Gilded Age (Twain and Warner), 563
Gillette Corp., 1027
Gilman, Charlotte Perkins, 626
Gingrich, Newt, 989
Ginsberg, Allen, 864
Ginsburg, Ruth Bader, 989
Giuliani, Rudolph, 899*i*
Glacier National Park, 609, 687*m*, 688
Glackens, William, 661
Glasnost, 963
Glen Canyon Dam, 683*m*, 880
Global warming, 919, 921, 1005–1006, 1021–1022, 1022*i*
Globalization
beginnings of, 716–717, 815*i*, 833
21st century
debate over, 1016–1017, 1025*i*, 1026–1027
and U.S. world trade, 1014*m*–1015*m*
late 20th century, 974, 977, 1013
impact of, 818, 979–980
opponents of, 1015
GNP
1930s fall in, 743
1920s growth in, 708
The Godfather (film), 864*i*
Gold
discovery of
in Black Hills, 518, 522
in Coeur d'Alene, Idaho, 539, 617, 618, 618*m*
mine pollution
in California, 542–543
in Colorado, 683*m*
price of, 917
reserves of, 619, 620
standard, 619
Gold rush
Coeur d'Alene, 539, 617, 618, 618*m*
The Golden Bowl (James), 615
Golden Gate bridge, 758, 894*i*, 894*m*
Goldman, Emma, 593, 626, 665, 672, 702, 704
Goldstein, Mildred, 752
Goldwater, Barry M., 877, 901, 956
Golf, 985
Gompers, Samuel, 593, 602, 634, 684
Gomulka, Wladyslaw, 859
Gonzales, Elian, 939*t*, 992
Gonzales, Lucia, 593
Goodman, Andrew, 889
Goodyear Tire & Rubber Co., 559
Gorbachev, Mikhail, 938, 938*t*, 961–963, 965–966
Gore, Al, 988
and election of 2000, 995–999, 997*m*, 998*i*
Gore, Tipper, 989
Gorney, Karen, 933*i*
Las Gorras Blancas, 571–572, 585, 590, 601
Gorsuch, Anne, 949–950
Goshute Indians, 941
Gospel of Wealth, 567
Grady, Henry, 576, 579
Graham, Billy, 737*t*, 827
Grain elevators, 584, 588*i*
Granada, Colorado, 976*m*
Granados, Balbina Duque, 1012
Grand Army of the Republic, 562
Grand Coulee Dam, 756
The Grange, 527, 559, 565
Grange, Red, 708
Grant, Cary, 767, 767*i*
Grant, Madison, 680
Grant, Ulysses S.
and election of 1868, 513
and election of 1872, 530
as President, 530
Reconstruction and, 510–511, 514–515
The Grapes of Wrath (film), 785
The Grapes of Wrath (Steinbeck), 746
Grateful Dead, 893
Great Britain. *See* England/Great Britain
Great Depression, 641, 704, 736, 739–769, 770. *See also* New Deal
anti-capitalism in, 758–760
causes of, 732, 734, 739, 741–743
celebrities during, 767–768
consumer debt and, 742
culture in, 740
employment in, 732, 742
end of, 778, 787, 809
and family life, 743–746
farmers and, 590*i*, 743
Fascism and, 775
foreign loans and, 742
Hoover policies and, 747–750
minorities in, 758–759, 764, 766–767
political impact of, 740
poverty in, 742–746, 745*i*, 746*i*
private charity in, 748
tariffs and, 742–743
Weimar Republic and, 704, 775
Great Flood of 1927, 723–724, 724*i*, 725*m*
The Great Gatsby (Fitzgerald), 641*t*, 725, 729, 733
Great Labor Uprising of 1877, 534*t*, 562–563, 563*i*, 588, 596
Great Migration, 545, 640, 688–689, 688*i*, 705
Great Northern Railroad, 517*m*
Great Plains, 532, 585–586, 586*i*, 607*m*, 823*i*, 1020*m*, 1021
Great Salt Basin, 520, 520*m*, 549
Great Salt Lake, 520, 520*m*
Great Sand Dunes National Monument, 683*m*
Great Society, 839, 876–879, 880*i*, 901
Great Texas Coastal Birding Trail, 857
Great War. *See* World War I
Greece
19th century, immigration from, 545
20th century
immigration from, 714
and NATO, 817*m*
Truman Doctrine and, 815, 817–818, 817*m*, 819
Greeley, Horace, 530
Green Mountain Boys, 590
Green party, late 20th century, 999
Greenback Labor Party, 529, 617
Greenhouse gases. *See* Global warming
Greenland
Peary expedition to, 627–628, 627*i*
Greenpeace, 950
Greenwood riots, 675–676, 702
Grenada, U.S. invasion of (1983), 946
Grey, Edward, 684
Griffith, D. W., 680
Griswold v. *Connecticut* (1965), 838*t*, 881
Gross National Product. *See* GNP
Guadalcanal, Battle of, 786*i*, 797, 798*m*
Guam, 535*t*, 633
Guantanamo, U.S. base at, 633, 635*m*, 1005
Guatemala
in 1950s, U.S. in, 861
in 1980s
refugees from, 947
U.S. in, 946–947
Guggenheim, David, 670
Guiana, British, 629
Guinan, Mary Louise, 712*i*
Guiteau, Charles J., 534*t*, 563
Gulf of Tonkin Resolution, 838*t*, 883, 884*m*
Gulf War. *See* Persian Gulf War (1991)
Guns
gun control debate, 986–987
Guthrie, Woody, 746, 748–749, 748*i*, 756
Gypsies (Romani), 774, 790, 790*m*

H

Haidas, 525
Haight-Asbury, in 1960s, 893, 904
Haiphong Harbor, mining of, 903
Hair (musical), 895
Haiti
20th century, U.S. intervention in, 640*t*, 669, 678–680, 678*m*–679*m*, 991, 994

Halberstam, David, 876
Haldeman, H. R., 914
Haleakala National Park, 780*m*
Haley, Alex, 839*t*, 935*i*
Haley, Bill, 814, 863
Half Dome, 879*i*
Hamer, Fanny Lou, 889
Hamm, Mia, 933, 1031*i*
Hampton Institute, 598, 598*i*
Hampton Normal and Agricultural Institute, 613
Hancock, Winfield S., 563
Handguns, deaths from, 986–987
Hanford Works (nuclear weapons plant), 821, 865*m*, 919, 941, 1022
Hanna, Marcus "Mark," 620–621, 634
Hansberry, Lorraine, 847
Hardin, Garrett, 880, 1018
Harding, Warren G., 641, 704, 708–709, 710*i*, 734
Harlan, John Marshall, 610–611
Harlem Renaissance, 715, 719, 719*i*, 721–722, 734
Harper, Frances Ellen Watkins, 579, 600
Harper's Weekly, 530*i*, 559*i*, 560
Harrington, Michael, 878
Harris, David, 862
Harris, Joel Chandler, 638
Harris, Katherine, 997
Harrison, Benjamin
  and election of 1888, 565
  and election of 1892, 617
  Indian Territory and, 609
  policies, 617
Hart, William S., 605
Harvard (College, University), 615, 750, 850, 893
Harvard Medical School, first female students, 850
Hashish, 893
Hawai'i Volcanoes National Park, 780*m*
Hawaiian Islands
  European contact, 629, 780, 780*m*
  19th century
    annexation of, 535*t*, 545, 629–630, 632, 780
    immigration to, 545, 547, 629
    planter revolt in (1893), 535*t*, 629, 629*i*, 638
    population of, 629
    Protestant missions in, 629, 780, 780*m*
    sugar economy in, 629
    U.S. in, 629
  20th century
    Japanese in, 652, 689*i*, 782
    statehood for, 780, 825, 842
    tourism and, 780
    World War II and, 780, 780*m*, 782
Hawley-Smoot Tariff (1930), 732, 736*t*
Hay, John, 633
Hayes, Rutherford B., 531, 531*m*, 532, 563
Haymarket bombing, 534*t*, 593–594, 594*i*, 596, 603
Head Start, 878, 974
Health
  environmental pollution and, 821, 822*i*, 865, 919–922, 1022
  in 1970s, 921
  in 1990s, 987–988, 988*f*
Health care
  Clinton reform efforts, 989
  in Johnson administration, 879
  in 1940s, 826
  in 21st century, 1006–1007
  early 20th century, 640, 655, 655*i*
Health foods, 893, 921
Healy, Dorothy Ray, 787
Hearst, William R., 630–631
Hefner, Hugh, 864
Helsinki summit (1975), 916
Henri, Robert, 661
Henry, Edward L., 498*i*
Henry Street Settlement, 625
Henson, Matthew, 640*t*, 675, 675*i*
Hepburn, Katharine, 767
Hernandez, Antonia, 981
Hernandez v. *Texas* (1954), 575
Herndon, Angelo, 758
Heroin, 987
Herrera, Juan Jose, 571
Herrera, Nicanor, 571
Herrera, Pablo, 571
Hersh, Seymour, 923
Herzl, Theodor, 677
Hetch Hetchy Valley, 667–668, 668*i*, 669*i*
The Hidden Persuaders (Packard), 561
High schools, spread of, 614
Highway construction
  in 1920s, 722
  2000s need for, 1021
  post–World War II, 823, 824*i*, 825, 842, 845–846, 848, 858
Hill, Anita, 938*t*, 965, 983
Hill, Julia Butterfly, 973–974, 973*i*
Hillman, Sidney, 765
Hindman Settlement School, 625
Hine, Lewis, 661, 663*i*
Hine, Thomas J., 525*i*
Hinkley, John, 945
Hippies, 893, 895, 895*i*
Hirano family, 782*i*
Hiroshima, atomic bombing of, 737, 798*m*, 800–801
His Girl Friday (film), 767, 767*i*
Hispanics. *See also* Latinos; Mexican Americans
  19th century, 638
    culture of, 535, 571
    land rights of, 571
  20th century
    civil rights activism, 876, 897, 918
    liberation movement, 897
    New Deal coalition and, 767
Hiss, Alger, 827*i*
Hitler, Adolf, 658, 704, 736*t*
  aggression of, 775–776
  death of, 797
  domestic policies, 775–776
  Final Solution of, 789–791, 790*m*, 795, 799
  and Olympic Games, 630
HIV (human immunodefficiency virus), 938*t*, 956–957
Ho Chi Minh, 698, 811, 828, 868, 882–883, 893
Hobos, in 1930s, 743–744, 748
Holland
  Indonesian independence and, 811, 820*m*
  World War II and, 774, 776, 795*m*, 798*m*
Hollywood
  early 20th century, 659, 707, 715–718, 720, 734, 739
  mid-20th century, Red Scare, 827, 872
  late 20th century, 922
Holmes, Oliver Wendell, 726
Holocaust, 774–776, 789–791, 790*m*, 799, 804
Home decoration, Victorian, 526, 625*i*
Home Insurance Building (Chicago), 549
Home Owners' Loan Corporation, 755, 763*t*
Home ownership, 842–848
Homeland Security. *See* Department of Homeland Security
Homelessness, in 1980s, 953*i*
Homestead, Florida, 960*m*
Homestead Steelworks, 537, 617
Homosexuality
  early 20th century, 661, 663, 730
  mid-20th century
    Beats and, 864
    Nazis and, 774, 775, 790, 790*m*
    World War II and, 774, 784, 789
    post–World War II, 825, 827
    1960s rights activism, 839, 898–899, 899*i*
  late 20th century
    acceptance of, 981
    activism, 876, 958
    AIDS and, 956–958
    discrimination against, 841–842, 871, 958, 1030
    gay families and, 981
    gay marriage and, 939*t*, 981
    military service and, 989
    religious right and, 942, 954, 956–957
    repeal of laws against, 956, 958
    women's liberation and, 896, 935
  21st century, 1006–1007, 1011
    and decline of homophobia, 1030
Honduras, 678–680, 678*m*–679*m*
The Honeymooners (TV show), 844
Hong Kong, 959
Hooker Chemical Co., 920
Hoover, Herbert, 734
  background of, 711, 747
  as Commerce secretary, 711, 722, 724, 747
  economic policies, 711, 746

and election of 1928, 710–711
and election of 1932, 746, 749, 751
and food relief, 747–749
as president, 641, 711, 747–750
and stock market crash of 1929, 732, 734, 747
Hoover, J. Edgar, 781, 871, 908
Hoover Dam, 736*t,* 756–757, 757*m,* 880
Hoovervilles, 732
Hope, Bob, 786
Hope, John, 614
Hope, Lugenia Burns, 626
Hope (ship), 627
Hopis, 981, 983
Hopkins, Harry, 753, 764
Horizontal integration, 545
Hormone replacement therapy, 987
Horses
late 18th century urban use of, 553
Seabiscuit, 768, 769*i*
Horton, Willie, 965
Hotline, 869
House Un-American Activities Committee (HUAC), 736*t,* 767, 826–828, 827*i,* 871
Women Strike for Peace movement and, 865, 867*i*
Household appliances, 641, 842–845
Household structure
late 19th century, 511*t*
late 20th century, 1028
Housing
20th century, 811, 812, 823, 843–848
discrimination in, 812, 823, 847
GI Bill and, 812, 846
homelessness and, 952
Housing Acts (1949, 1954), 848
How the Other Half Lives (Riis), 594–596, 596*i*
Howard, Merriman, 512
Howard, Oliver O., 500, 503*i*
Howells, William Dean, 638
Howl (Ginsberg), 864
HUAC. *See* House Un-American Activities Committee
HUD. *See* Department of Housing and Urban Development
Huerta, Dolores, 898*i*
Hughes, Charles E., 690, 709
Hughes, Langston, 719, 721, 721*i*
Hughes, Robert P., 636–637
Hull House, 599, 625
Human Genome mapping, 939*t,* 987, 1029
Human immunodefficiency virus. *See* HIV
Human rights, 20th century
in U.S. foreign policy, 923, 926, 992
Humboldt State University, 974
Humphrey, Hubert, 901
Hungary
in 1950s
refugees from, 946
uprising in, 817*m,* 859
19th century, immigration from, 545
20th century
and collapse of Soviet Union, 962*i,* 965, 966*m*
creation of, 699*m*
worker unrest in, 698
Hunton, Addie W., 696
Hurley, Martha, 907–908
Hurricanes
Andrew (1992), 960*m*
Galveston, Texas (1900), 857
naming of, 935
Hussein, Saddam
Iraq War and, 939, 939*t,* 1007–1008
Persian Gulf War and, 968–969, 968*m*
Huston, John, 786
Hyde Amendment (1976), 839*t,* 935
Hydrogen bomb, development of, 800, 822, 838

I

"I Have a Dream" speech, 870–871
Ia Drang valley, Battle of, 887
IBM. *See* International Business Machines
Ickes, Harold L., 753, 755*i*
Idaho, 618, 618*m*
Chinese immigrants in, 576
indian reservations in, 613*m*
statehood, 539
women's voting rights and, 601
Identity, American
21st century, 1028–1032
20th century
and immigrants, 647–648
inclusivness and, 984
in 1930s, 739
19th century character of, 538, 607–608
ILD. *See* International Labor Defense
Illinois
death penalty moratorium in, 986
Imamura, Ichiro, 799
Immigration
settlement houses and, 599, 624–625
21st century, 1031–1032
origins of, 1031
political refugees in, 1031–1032
19th century
from China, 518–519, 880
city growth and, 550–551, 592
and competition for jobs, 545, 584, 588, 621
cultural impact of, 539, 584
discrimination and, 611
ethnic diversity and, 538–539
impact of, by region, 551*i*
imperialism and, 635
labor supply and, 545, 584
opponents of, 610–612
reasons for, 538–539, 545
by region, 551*m,* 647*m*
and return home, 545
to South, 546, 551*m,* 610–611
stereotypes and, 610–611
volume of, 534, 545, 646*f*
20th century, 641, 646–655, 647*m,* 880–881, 959, 961, 970
areas of settlement, 647*m,* 978*m*
Cold War refugees and, 946–947
cultural impact of, 716–718, 959
debate over, 713–714
discrimination against, 641, 646, 711, 880, 917, 974
diversity and, 880, 959, 974
economic impact of, 978*m*
employment and, 917
illegal, 978*m,* 984, 1005
to Midwest, 647*m*
and neutrality in World War I, 685
origins of, 714*f,* 959
poverty and, 648*i*
quotas for, 713–714, 790, 880
restrictions on, 641, 652–653, 652*m,* 709, 713–714, 734, 790–791, 880, 959
and return home, 646, 1032
to Southwest, 647*m,* 1028, 1028*m*
undocumented, 978*m,* 984, 1005
U.S. policy on, 713–714, 880–881, 959, 961, 1005
volume of, 646, 646*f,* 714*f,* 783, 959, 978*m,* 984
to West Coast, 647*m*
by women, 783
World War II and, 790–791, 959
Immigration and Naturalization Service (INS), 652*i,* 959
Immigration Restriction League, 611
Impeachment
of Clinton, 514, 939*t,* 975, 988, 990–991
of Johnson, 513, 514, 532
process of, 991
Imperialism
cultural, of U.S., 1016–1017, 1025*i,* 1026–1027
20th century
Taft and, 633, 669
Third World backlash against, 828–829
late 19th century, 627–637, 638
critics of, 634–635
lure of, 627
in Pacific, 628–629
Spanish-American War, 630–636, 632*i,* 634*m,* 635*m,* 638
Inchon landing, 835
Income tax
deductions, and housing, 846
introduction of, 686
in 1980s, 947
Supreme Court on, 620
early 20th century, 686, 709, 747
India
20th century
anticolonialism in, 698, 700, 811
immigration from, 651*m*
independence, 811, 820*m,* 821
nuclear arms and, 911*m*

Indian boarding school movement, 598, 612, 755
Indian Claims Commission, 828
Indian Gaming Regulatory Act (1988), 938*t*, 977
Indian Office, 597
Indian Reorganization Act (1934), 736*t*, 755, 763*t*
Indian Rights Association, 597
Indian Territory
  Native American removal to, 580*i*, 609*m*, 675
  opening to settlers, 609, 609*m*, 675
  white incursions in, 523, 597
Indiana
  compulsory sterilization in, 640*t*, 656
Individualism, in 19th century, 566–567
Indonesia, 21st century
  Islamic terrorism in, 1008
Indonesia, 20th century
  anticolonialism in, 811
  conflict in, 938
  immigration from, 651*m*
  independence of, 820*m*
  and World War II, 774, 797, 798*m*, 828
Industrial Christian Home Association, 600
Industrial education. *See* Vocational instruction
Industrial Workers of the World (IWW), 593, 640*t*, 665, 665*i*
  anticapitalism of, 682
  World War I and, 693–694, 694*i*
Industry
  19th century
    and American system of manufacturing, 540–541
    centers of, 622*m*
    company towns, 552
    disease and, 588
    distribution of, 622*m*
    factory system, 538, 540, 568
    growth of, 548*t*, 622*m*, 623*t*
    mechanization and, 539–541, 559, 622
    in Northeast, 622*m*
    technological innovation and, 539–549, 567
    worker unrest, 535, 584–585, 588–594
  20th century
    defense and, 737, 825, 831*i*, 975
    evils of, 662
    flight overseas, 908
    Great Depression and, 732, 762*i*
    mass production and, 657–658
    post–World War II peacetime reconversion, 811–812, 822–823
    in World War II, 784
INF Treaty. *See* Intermediate Nuclear Force (INF) treaty
Infant mortality, 681, 712
The Influence of Sea-Power in History, 1660-1763 (Mahan), 628
Influenza
  early 20th century, 641*t*, 700, 705
Inheritance tax. *See* Estate tax
Initiative (petition for popular vote), 662
INS. *See* Immigration and Naturalization Service
Insider trading, 951
Installment buying, in 1920s, 728
Institute for Responsible Fatherhood and Family Revitalization, 981
Integration. *See also* Desegregation
  Cold War efforts towards, 847
  White attitudes on, 847
Intelligence agencies, 832, 832*m*
Intermediate Nuclear Force (INF) treaty, 938*t*, 963
Internal Security Act (1950), 737*t*, 826
International Business Machines (IBM), 1012
International Federation of Professional and Technical Engineers, 975
International Labor Defense (ILD), 744
International Typographical Union, 593
Internet, 561, 973–974, 973*i*, 1002*i*, 1011*i*, 1012–1014, 1016, 1025
Internment
  of Japanese, 736, 773, 781–783, 781*m*, 791*i*
  of Muslims, 1005
The Interpretation of Dreams (Freud), 615
Interstate Commerce Act (1887), 534*t*, 565
Interstate Commerce Commission, establishment of, 565
Interstate Highway Act (1956), 838*t*, 845–846, 858
Interstate roads, development of, 824*i*, 845–846, 858
InterVarsity, 893, 955
Inuit, 675
Iowa Indians, 609*m*
Iran, 21st century
  and U.S. in Iraq, 1008
Iran, 20th century
  hostage crisis in, 938*t*, 942–944
  Islamic revolution in, 839*t*, 930, 938*t*, 939, 942–944, 943*m*, 963
  oil exports of, 943, 967
  Soviet Union and, 816–817
  U.S. arms for hostages and, 964
  U.S. involvement in, 838*t*, 861, 912, 938*t*, 942–944, 943*m*, 963–964
  war with Iraq (1980-1988), 964, 967–968
Iran-Contra scandal, 938*t*, 962–964
Iraq
  oil exports to U.S., 1007*f*
  war with Iran (1980-1988), 964, 967–968
Iraq War (2003-), 939, 939*t*, 1004, 1007–1009, 1008*m*. *See also* Persian Gulf War (1991)
  civil disorder in, 1009
  insurgency after, 1009–1010
  other nations' view of, 1007, 1010
  prisoner abuse in, 1009, 1009*i*
Ireland
  Northern, peace efforts in, 991, 993
  21st century
    trade with U.S., 1014*m*–1015*m*
  19th century
    immigration from, 545
  20th century
    independence of, 685, 700
Irish-Americans
  and Democratic party, 548
  and railroads, 518
  return to Ireland, 646
  World War I and, 685, 700
Iron Curtain, 818
Iron Molder's International Union, 528
Iron range, 647–648, 649
Iroquois Confederacy
  20th century
    land reclaimed by, 1031
Iroquois League. *See* Iroquois Confederacy
Islam
  among African Americans, 875*i*
Islamic fundamentalism
  mid-20th century
    Iranian revolution and, 942–944, 944*i*
    rise of, 839
  late 20th century
    anti-Americanism, 939, 1003, 1025, 1027
    Arab leaders and, 964
    Gulf War and, 970
    September 11th terrorist attacks and, 1003–1004, 1003*i*
    terrorism by, 938–939, 995, 1003–1004, 1003*i*
    women and, 1027
Isolationism, 641, 775, 777, 925
Israel
  Arab conflicts, 821, 862, 918
    1987–1988 clashes, 943*m*
    1967 War, 918
    1973 War, 918–919
    1990s clashes, 968, 993
    2000s terrorism, 1008
  Camp David Accords, 927–928
  creation of, 737*t*, 821, 918
  Gulf War and, 968
  peace negotiations, 939*t*, 993
  settlement policy of, 928
  U.S. support for, 821, 1003
Italian Americans, in World War II, 783
Italy
  19th century, immigration from, 545–547, 592–593, 610, 714*f*
    to South, 611
    unification of, 654
  20th century
    Communist Party rise in, 810
    fascism in, 742, 775
    Five-Power Treaty, 709
    immigration from, 654–655, 654*m*, 714, 714*f*, 783
    imperialism of, 677

World War I and, 677, 685*f*, 689, 694–695, 695*m*, 697
World War II and, 775, 795*m*, 796
Ivory Soap, 561
Iwo Jima, 773, 797, 797*i*, 798*m*
IWW. *See* Industrial Workers of the World

J

Jackson, Graham, 809*i*
Jackson, Helen Hunt, 565
Jackson, Jesse, 958
Jackson-Vanik Amendment (1974), 923
James, Henry, 599, 615
James, Mollie Brown, 1011–1012, 1016
James, William, 615
Japan
19th century
rise to power of, 633
and Sino-Japanese War, 633
pre–World War II, 698, 742, 776
fascism in, 775, 776
Five-Power Treaty, 709
German alliance, 775
immigration from, 547, 651*m*, 652–653, 678, 689*i*, 714, 731
imperialism of, 678, 700, 774, 776, 779
and Russo-Japanese War, 640*t*, 677, 678
World War II and
brutality of, 776, 798
in China, 776–777, 779
Kamikaze pilots, 811*i*
in Pacific, 773, 778–781, 797–799, 798*m*, 811*i*
Pearl Harbor attack, 736, 736*t*, 773, 778–781, 778*i*, 780*m*
propaganda, 786
in Southeast Asia, 774, 776, 882
surrender, 802, 802*i*, 811*i*
U.S. atomic bombing of, 737, 798*m*, 800–801, 801*i*, 803, 803*i*, 809, 818
U.S. firebombing of cities, 799–801, 809
post–World War II
economy, 819, 836, 917, 961
reconstruction, 819
U.S. occupation, 819, 833
war crimes trials in, 819
in 2000s, trade with U.S., 1014*m*–1015*m*
Japanese American Citizens League, 827, 981
Japanese-Americans
discrimination against, 653, 678, 791*i*
post-war reintegration of, 812*i*, 847
World War II and
internment of, 736, 773, 781–783, 781*m*, 791*i*, 802–803, 828
prejudice against, 781–783, 785, 791*i*
reparations for, 783
in U.S. Army, 773, 782–783
Jazz, origins of, 659, 661, 707, 804
Jazz Age, 707–708, 708*i*, 712, 715–723, 719, 719*i*, 721–722, 729, 734
The Jazz Singer (film), 641*t*
Jefferson, Lisa, 1004
Jefferson Airplane, 893
Jeffords, James M., 939*t*, 999
Jenney, William LeBaron, 549
Jeter, Mildred, 881
Jews. *See also* Israel
19th century
immigration by, 545, 547, 592, 610
in South, 611, 611*i*
early 20th century
assimilation by, 654, 680*i*
Grand Migration from Europe, 654*m*
immigration by, 642*i*, 645, 653–655, 714
motion picture industry and, 659, 707–708, 716–717
racial classification of, 659, 775
return to Europe, 646
Zionist movement and, 677, 680*i*
in World War II
casualties in, 774, 790
Holocaust and, 774–776, 789–791, 790*m*, 799, 827
immigration by, 790–791
in Nazi Germany, 774, 775–776
U.S. antisemitism and, 777, 790–791
post–World War II
growing tolerance of, 827
in Palestine, 821
Protestant fear of, 658, 777
Soviet repression of, 923
women as rabbis, 935
in 1990s, first on presidential ticket, 997
in 2000s, 1029*f*
Jiang Jieshi, 797–798, 829
Jim Crow system. *See also* Segregation
decline of, 839, 851–856
height of, 610–611, 675, 694, 708, 719, 794
origins of, 579–580
Job Corps, 878
John Robinson Circus, 558
John Stands-in-Timber, 584
Johnson, Andrew, 514*i*
background of, 502, 514
on black voting rights, 504, 512*m*
impeachment of, 513, 514, 532
and pardons, 502–504
political career of, 502
Reconstruction policy, 500, 502–505, 512*m*, 514
Johnson, Earvin "Magic," 958*i*
Johnson, Eastman, 564*i*
Johnson, Hiram W., 671
Johnson, Jack, 664
Johnson, Kathryn M., 696
Johnson, Lady Bird, 876, 877*i*
Johnson, Lyndon B., 904, 922
assumption of presidency, 838*t*, 839, 876–877, 877*i*
background of, 876–877
civil rights and, 879
and Democratic convention of 1964, 875, 889
discrimination and, 814, 879
and election of 1960, 867
and election of 1964, 877
and election of 1968, 888–889
environmentalism, 880
foreign policy of, 877
Great Society and, 839, 876–879
health care and, 879
and New Deal, 876
Supreme Court appointments, 882
as vice president, 867, 876
Vietnam War and, 690, 883–889, 885*i*
voting rights and, 879
and War on Poverty, 877–879, 878*m*
and Warren Commission, 871
in World War II, 785*i*
Johnson-Reid Act (1924), 641*t*, 713–714
Johnston, Eric, 785
Jolson, Al, 641*t*
Jones, Joe, 738*i*
Jones, Paula, 990–991
Jordan
and Israel, 918, 928
mid-20th century, British intervention in, 862
Jordan, Barbara, 892
Jordan, Michael, 958*i*
Jordan, Vernon, 990
Joseph, Chief, 500, 517*m*, 584*i*
Jung, David, 678
The Jungle (Sinclair), 640*t*, 662, 760
Justice Department
Ku Klux Klan and, 889
and national security, 693

K

Kaczynski, Theodore, 985
Kaiser, Henry, 783
Kalakaua, David (King of Hawaii), 629
Kamekeha, Lydia. *See* Liliuokalani, Queen
Kamikaze pilots, 811*i*
Kampuchea. *See* Cambodia
Kansas
Creationism in, 726
and drought of 1886, 585–586
Dust Bowl in, 745–746, 747*m*
settlement of, 515, 580
voting rights in, 526
Kansas Pacific Railroad, 523*i*
Kearney, Belle, 664
Kearney, Denis, 573
Keating, Charles, 953
Keefe, Tim, 557*i*
Keller, Helen, 663
Kelley, Florence, 625, 663
Kellie, Luna, 617
Kellogg, Frank, 710
Kellogg, Noah S., 539

Kellogg-Briand Pact (1928), 710
Kelly, Gene, 717
Kelly, Oliver H., 527
Kennan, George, 818, 831
Kennedy, Edward, 944
Kennedy, Jacqueline Bouvier, 867, 877*i*
Kennedy, John F.
assassination of, 838*t*, 839, 871, 877*i*
background and early career, 866–867
and Berlin Wall, 868–869
Catholicism of, 867
civil rights movement and, 869–871
and Cuba, 868–869
and Cuban Missile Crisis, 751, 838, 869
on discrimination against women, 869
domestic policy, 867
and election of 1960, 711, 750–751, 867
foreign policy, 867, 868–869
inaugural address, 866, 867
media and, 750–751
Monroe Doctrine and, 869
and Peace Corps, 841
Vietnam War and, 868, 883
in World War II, 785*i*, 867
Kennedy, Joseph, 866–867
Kennedy, Joseph P., Jr., 867
Kennedy, Robert, 839*t*, 867, 888–889, 898*i*
assassination of, 901
and election of 1968, 888–889, 901
Kenney, Abbott, 720*m*
Kent State shootings, 839*t*, 903
Kentucky
late 20th century rural decline of, 848
Kentucky Federation of Women's Clubs, 625
Kentucky Fried Chicken, 1026
Kenya
Islamic terrorism in, 995, 1008
Kerouac, Jack, 864
Kerr-McGee, 907
Kerry, John Forbes
and election of 2004, 1010–1011
and Vietnam War, 903, 1010
Kesey, Ken, 922
Key West, Florida, 960
Khmer Rouge, 884*m*
Khomeini, Ruhollah, 942–943, 944*i*, 964
Khrushchev, Nikita, 838*t*, 842–844, 843*i*, 859, 869
Kickapoo Indians, 609*m*
Kicking Bear, 518*i*
Kim Il-Sung, 834
Kim Lai, 888*i*
King, Billie Jean, 934
King, Martin Luther, Jr.
assassination of, 839*t*, 901
Birmingham civil rights march (1963), 869
birthday holiday for, 891, 938*t*, 958
FBI and, 923
"I Have a Dream" speech of, 870–871
and March on Washington, 870
and Montgomery bus boycott, 854–855, 876
release from prison, 867
Vietnam War and, 891
King, Rodney, 938*t*, 939*t*, 974, 980–981, 980*i*, 984
Kinji Ushijima, 548
Kinsey, Alfred, 825
Kinsey Reports (1948, 1953), 825
Kiowa
alliance with whites, 516
removal of, 609*m*
white wars against, 580
Kisatchie National Forest, 578*m*
Kissinger, Henry
and Arab-Israeli War (1973), 919
and China, 909
and Panama Canal, 927
and Soviet Union, 911–912, 916, 923
and Vietnam War, 903
Kitchen Debate, 842–844, 843*i*, 845
Knickerbocker Base Ball Club, 556
Knights of Labor, 529, 534, 590–594, 684
demise of, 593–594
farmers and, 572, 587
and Haymarket bombing, 593–594
labor unrest and, 571–572, 590–594
local issues and, 572, 590
minorities and, 573, 592
Populists and, 619
women and, 588, 592*i*
Knights of St. Crispin, 529, 529*t*
Knudson, Coya, 850
Kolko, Gabriel, 818
Korea. *See also* Korean War; North Korea; South Korea
and airliner downed by Soviet Union, 945, 963
immigration from, 651*m*, 880, 981
Japanese annexation of, 678, 833
in World War II, 798, 833–834, 834*m*
Korean War, 737*t*, 803, 807, 831, 833–836, 833*i*, 834*m*, 837, 838
brain-washing and propaganda in, 842
casualties in, 833*i*, 835–836
China and, 834*m*, 835–836
as Cold War outbreak, 829
cultural impact of, 822, 842
McCarthy and, 827
political impact of, 836
refugees in, 835*i*, 836
Koresh, David, 985
Kosovo, 939*t*, 966*m*, 991, 994*m*, 995, 1000
Krajczar, Norma, 787
Kristallnacht, 775–776
Kroger, establishment of, 544
Ku Klux Klan
19th century
founding of, 505, 510
violence by, 513–514, 611
in 20th century, 680, 702, 711, 714–715, 734, 889, 917–918
Ku Klux Klan Act (1871), 514
Kuramoto, Kazuko, 776
Kurihara, Joseph Y., 782
Kurosawa, Akiro, 716
Kuwait
Persian Gulf War and, 938*t*, 939, 968–969, 968*m*, 1007

L

La Follette, Phil, 760
La Follette, Robert "Bob" , 760
La Follette, Robert M., 671, 709, 760
Labor contracts, 505–507, 509, 509*i*
Labor supply, late 19th century, 505–508
LaFlesche, Joseph, 597
LaFlesche, Susan, 598, 598*i*
LaFlesche, Susette, 597
Laguna Indians, 941
Laissez-faire
in economics
19th century, 562, 565
early 20th century, 686
late 20th century, 947–948
on social questions
19th century, 562, 565
Lake Mead, 757*m*
Lake Mohonk conferences, 597
Lake Powell, 683*m*, 880
Lake Superior area, 649, 649*m*
Lakota Indians. *See* Sioux
Land management
19th century, 608–609
20th century, 667, 670, 949–950, 949*m*, 950*i*
Land ownership
19th century, as conflict source, 503*i*, 507, 608–609
Land redistribution, post-Civil War, 503*i*
Landsmark, Theodore, 918*i*
Lange, Dorothea, 746, 746*i*
Lansing, Robert, 691, 698
Laos
Dooley missions in, 841
independence of, 820*m*
Vietnam War and, 883, 884*m*, 903
Las Vegas, Nevada
infrastructure of, 757, 757*m*, 1033
Latinos in, 757, 1032
nuclear tests and, 821, 822*i*
water and, 667, 756–757, 1020–1021, 1020*m*, 1023, 1033
Lasky, Jesse, 659
Lassen Volcanic National Park, 687*m*, 688
The Late Great Planet Earth (Lindsey), 955
Latin America, 20th century
immigration from, 959, 960
U.S. in, 678–680, 678*m*–679*m*
U.S. relations, 927
Latinos. *See also* Hispanics; Mexican Americans
20th century
discrimination against, 792, 917–918
Feminism and, 931, 934

liberation of, 876, 897
political power of, 918
population of, 974, 984
prejudice against, 792, 917–918
in U.S. culture, 1032, 1033
veterans organizations, 814, 827
Latvia, 699*m*, 966, 966*m*
Lau Dai Moy, 650
Laughlin, Harry, 726
Lawrence, Benjamin, 730
Lawrence, Jacob, 674*i*
Lawrence, Myrtle Terry, 730
Lawrence Livermore National Laboratory, 865*m*
Lawrence v. *Texas* (2003), 1006
Lazarus, Emma, 545–546
Lea, Tom, 772*i*
League of Nations, 641*t*, 697–699, 701
League of United Latin American Citizens (LULAC), 814, 852, 981
League of Women Voters, 711–712
Leave It to Beaver (TV show), 844
Lebanon
20th century
U.S. arms for hostages in, 964
U.S. intervention in, 862, 938*t*, 943*m*, 946, 964
Lederer, William, 841
Lee, Erika, 652, 652*i*
Lee Chi Yet, 651–652, 652*i*
Lee Yow Chun, 624
Legal counsel, right to, 881
Leiber, Jerry, 863
LeMay, Curtis, 799, 835
Lemlich, Clara, 643, 646, 650, 665
Lend-Lease program, 777, 809
Lenin, Vladimir, 695, 700*i*
Leningrad, Battle of, 795*m*
Lesbians, 661, 730, 784, 789, 841, 871, 956, 982
Lesotho, 927*m*
Let There Be Light (film), 786
Leung, Tom, 678
Levees, Mississippi River, 723–724, 724*i*
Leveraged buyouts, 951
Levi-Strauss, 538
Levitt, Alfred, 823
Levitt, William, 823, 827
Levittown, 823, 872
Lewinsky, Monica, 514, 939*t*, 990
Lewis, John, 856
Lewis, John L., 765–766
Lewis, Sinclair, 729
Lewis and Clark Expedition, 541
Liberation movements. *See* Feminism; Gay Liberation movement
Liberty University, 956*i*
Libraries, Carnegie, 567
Libya
crude oil reserves of, 1006*f*
and terrorism, 938*t*, 964
U.S. conflict with (1981, 1986), 943*m*, 963
Lieberman, Joe, 995
Life expectancy, 20th century, 1028
of Native Americans, 793
Life (magazine), 756*i*, 844, 850
Lifestyles of the Rich and Famous (TV show), 951
Light bulb, invention of, 540
Liliuokalani, Queen, 535*t*
Lincoln, Abraham
on free blacks, fate of, 501–502
Gettysburg Address of, 750
oratory skill of, 750
Reconstruction policy, 499, 501–502, 512*m*
on reentry of Confederate states, 501–503
second inaugural address, 750
Lincoln Brigade. *See* Abraham Lincoln Brigade
Lindbergh, Charles, 641*t*, 708, 777
Lindsey, Hal, 955
Ling Sing v. *Washburn* (California, 1862), 574
Linganfield, Lorimer and Marsha, 707
Literacy tests, 610, 612, 996
Lithuania, 699*m*, 966, 966*m*
Little, Keith, 773, 779, 793
Little, Kenneth Marion, 657*i*
Little, Lora C., 657, 657*i*
Little Big Horn, Battle of, 517*m*, 518, 518*i*, 519*i*, 532, 582
Little League, girls, 934*i*
Little Richard, 814, 863
Little Rock, Arkansas, school desegregation in, 838*t*, 853–854, 855*m*, 872
Little Rock Nine, 854
Lloyd George, David, 698
Local government, late 19th century corruption in, 530–531, 530*i*, 555–556
Lockwood, Belva, 601
Lodge, Henry Cabot, 636–637, 699, 867, 924
Logging
21st century, 1006, 1018*i*
19th century, 501, 521, 539, 542, 542*f*, 577, 578, 608*i*, 609
company towns and, 552
20th century, 647, 731, 949–950, 950*i*, 973–974, 973*i*, 1020
Lomax, Alan, 748
Lomax, John and Ruby, 770
Lôme, Dupuy de, 631
London, Jack, 644
Lone Star (film), 984
The Lonely Crowd (Riesman), 864
Long, Huey P., 759–760
Long, Jefferson, 513*i*
Longoria, Felix, 814
Looking Backward (Bellamy), 534*t*, 591
Looking Out for Number One (Ringer), 936
Lord & Taylor stores, 559
Los Alamos, New Mexico, 683*m*, 800, 865*m*, 941
Los Angeles, California
area of, 720
founding of, 720
growth of, 922
Mexican immigration and, 689, 720
water and, 667–668, 720, 1020–1021, 1020*m*
in World War II, racial unrest in, 792
late 20th century
air pollution in, 825
foreign immigration to, 959, 1028
population of, 1028*i*
race rioting in, 737*t*, 890, 900, 938*t*, 939, 939*t*, 980–981, 980*i*
urban renewal in, 848
Los Angeles American Indian Protective Association, 606
Los Angeles Aqueduct, 667–669
Lost Generation, 730, 734
Louis, Joe, 736*t*, 767–768
Louisiana. *See also* New Orleans
Cajuns, 857, 857*m*
19th century
immigration to, 546
political violence in, 513–515
readmission to Union, 513
20th century
coast of, 857, 857*m*
immigration to, 654*m*
Love, Emanuel, 568
Love Canal, 920–921, 932
Loving, Richard, 812, 881–882
Loving v. *Virginia* (1967), 812, 881–882
Loyalty, American, 827
LSD, 893
Lucero, Jose, 977
Ludendorff, Erich, 694
Ludlow massacre, 682, 682*i*, 683*m*, 684, 704
Luks, George, 660*i*
LULAC. *See* League of United Latin American Citizens
Lumber. *See* Logging
Lumumba, Patrice, 862, 923
Luna, Grace, 680
Lunas, 629
Lusitania (ship), 641*t*, 691
Lutherans, 935, 1025, 1029*f*
Lynchings
in Great Depression, 743–744, 761
"high-tech (in 1990s), 983
Mexicans and, 665
early 20th century, 640, 664, 665, 676, 680, 702, 721
late 19th century, 579, 593, 594*i*, 601, 606, 611
mid-20th century, 812

M

MacArthur, Douglas
Bonus March and, 749
in Korea, 835
in occupied Japan, 819
in Philippines, 797, 798*m*
Macedonia, 966*m*, 994*m*
MacKinnon, Catherine, 959

Macy's stores, 559
M.A.D. D.A.D.S (Men Against Destruction-Defending Against Drugs and Social Disorder), 981
USS Maddox, 883
Mahan, Alfred Thayer, 628
Mail order catalogs, 538, 559, 561
Maine
    19th century tourism in, 609
Maine (ship), 535*t,* 631, 632*i*
Malaria
    in Spanish-American War, 633
Malawi, 927*m*
Malaya, Japanese attack on, 779, 828
Malaysia
    independence of, 820*m*
Malcolm X, 875*i,* 890
Mallon, Mary, 655–656
The Man That Nobody Knows (Barton), 728
Manchuria, 776
Mandate system, 698
Mandela, Nelson, 938*t,* 966
Manhattan Project, 800–801, 941
Manifest destiny, 634
Manila Bay, Battle of, 632, 634*m*
Manly, Alex, 611
Mann Act (1910), 663–664
Manufacturing. *See* Industry
Mao Anying, 829*i*
Mao Zedong (Mao Tse-tung), 797–798, 829–830, 829*i,* 830*i,* 884–885
    and Nixon, 909–912, 912*i*
Maquiladoras, 917, 1011–1012, 1016
March on Washington (1963), 855*m,* 870
Marconi, Guglielmo, 1012
Marcos, Ferdinand, 938*t*
Marcus, David, 821
Marijuana, 893, 922, 987
Marketing. See Advertising
Marriage
    same-sex, 939*t,* 981–982, 1006–1007, 1011
    21st century, 1007
    20th century, 824, 844, 844*f,* 846*f,* 872, 939*t,* 981–982
        immigrant picture brides, 653
        interracial, 812, 847–848, 881–882, 1030
        same-sex, 939*t,* 981–982
        in World War II, 788
    late 19th century, 626
Marshall, George C., 801, 819, 821
Marshall, Thurgood, 838*t,* 852, 882, 965, 983
Marshall Field
    establishment of, 544, 554
    as "palace of consumption," 559
Marshall Plan, 817*m,* 819
Marti, José Julian, 630
Marx, Karl, 595
Masons
    colored, 579
Mass merchandising, rise of, 534, 538–540, 559–560
Mass production, development of, 539–541, 559, 657–658
Massachusetts
    21st century, same-sex marriage in, 939*t,* 1006
Massachusetts Institute of Technology (MIT), 540
May Day (May 1, international labor day), 594
USS Mayaguez, 839*t,* 915–916
Mayflower (ship), 751
Mayo Clinic, 987
McAdoo, William G., 709
McCain, John, 1017
McCarran-Walter Act (1952), 737*t,* 828
McCarthy, Eugene, 888
McCarthy, Joseph, 737*t,* 808, 827, 836, 871, 965
McCarthyism, 808, 826–828
McCartney, Bill, 981
McClure's, 662
McCord, James, 913
McCormick reapers, 538, 593
McDonald's, 952, 1025–1026, 1026*i*
McGee, Elizabeth, 986*i*
McGovern, George S., 912–913, 925
McKinley, William
    assassination of, 640*t*
    and election of 1896, 620–621
    and election of 1900, 635–636
    and Hawaiian Islands, 629, 631
    policies, 629–636, 638
    Spanish-American War and, 630–636, 632*i,* 634*m,* 635*m,* 638
McKinley Tariff (1890), 616, 629
McLaurin v. *Oklahoma* (1950), 812
McNamara, Robert, 883, 888
McNary-Haugen bills (1926,1928), 709
McParlan, James, 589
McVeigh, Timothy, 985
Me Decade, 909
Meat Inspection Act (1906), 662
Meatpacking industry, 538, 554, 562, 588, 622*m,* 662
Media. *See also* Television
    Carter and, 925
    Clinton and, 750, 750*i*
    and election of 2000, 751, 997–998
    Gulf War and, 969
    Kennedy and, 750–751
    Reagan and, 750–751
    Roosevelt (F.D.) and, 750–751, 750*i,* 759–760
    Roosevelt (T.) and, 750
    late 20th century, 975, 977
Medicaid
    abortion and, 839*t,* 935
    introduction of, 879
Medicare
    introduction of, 879
    Reagan and, 947–948
Medicine
    19th century
        Christian Science and, 616
    20th century
        advances, 655, 821, 842, 957, 987
        ethics in, 988
        oriental, popularity of, 961
        politics of, 712, 841–842
        population growth and, 1020
        reproductive, 987–988
Memminger, Christopher, 504
Mendez Rosie, 863
Mendez v. *Westminster* (1946), 814
Men's movements, 981
Mental illness, treatment of, 922
Mercer, Erminia Pablita Ruiz, 743
Mercer, Lucy, 761
Meredith, James, 855*m*
Meritor Savings Bank, 959
Meritor Savings Bank v. *Vinson* (1986), 959
Methodists, 1029*f*
Metro Goldwyn Mayer, 659, 716
Metropolitan Life Insurance Co., 645
Mexican American Legal Defense and Educational Fund, 981
Mexican Americans
    20th century
        assimilation of, 847
        as Democrats, 867
        deportation of in 1930s, 745, 759
        employment, 648, 745, 897
        as farm labor, 680, 714, 759, 759*i,* 825, 897
        in Great depression, 745, 759, 759*i*
        hostility toward, 648, 792, 814, 897
        immigration of, 641, 647*m,* 648–649, 679, 689, 714, 825
        lynching of, 665
        population of, 974, 984
        unions and, 648, 759, 759*i,* 828*i,* 897
        women of, 648, 680, 828*i,* 961*i*
    mid-19th century
        as cowboys, 523
Mexico
    oil reserves and exports, 1006*f,* 1007*f,* 1021
    in 2000s
        trade with U.S., 992, 1014*m*–1015*m*
        U.S. border region, 1011–1012, 1011*i*
    19th century
        immigration from, 546
        and U.S.-Mexican War, 516
    20th century
        immigration from, 641, 647*m,* 648–649, 679, 689, 714, 714*f,* 784, 825, 959
        industry flight to, 917
        NAFTA and, 992
        oil industry in, 918
        Revolution of 1911, 640, 640*t,* 648, 676, 678–680, 700, 703–704
        U.S. border with, 714, 959
        U.S. intervention in, 640*t,* 669, 678–680, 678*m*–679*m*
        World War I and, 691
        World War II and, 784

Miami, Florida, 729, 959, 960
Micheaux, Oscar, 721–722
Michigan Carlson Works, 543*i*
Microsoft Corp., 687, 977, 978, 1013, 1019
Mid-Atlantic, forest clearing in, 542*f*
Middle class
  19th century
    alliance with workers, 584, 589
    culture of, 535, 539, 559
    fear of poor, 596
    growth of, 538, 547
    reformers in, 535, 596
    Social Darwinism and, 566
    values of, 526–527, 539, 559
  20th century, 842–848
    blacks and, 850–851, 851*i*
    1980s shrinkage of, 947, 951
Middle East
  21st century
    U.S. policy in, 1007–1009, 1008*i*
  20th century
    British withdrawal from, 815, 820–821, 862
    crude oil reserves of, 1006*f*
    instability in, 942–944, 943*m*, 963
    U.S. policy in, 862, 939, 946, 963–964, 967–970, 991, 1007–1008
Midvale steelworks, 657
Midway Island, Battle of, 797, 798*m*
Midwest
  19th century
    economy, 527
    ethnic groups in, 546
    forest clearing in, 542*f*, 647
    population of, 607*m*, 723*f*
    rural unrest in, 585–587, 590–591
    settlement of, 546
  20th century
    Great Depression in, 590*i*
    mining in, 647–648
    population of, 723*f*
Migrant labor
  in 19th century, 585, 621
  in 20th century, 678, 680, 714, 743, 746, 748, 768, 978
Migration(s). *See also* Immigration
  20th century, 646–655, 674*i*
    to Midwest, 647
Military districts, post–Civil War, 510, 512*m*
Military-industrial complex, 856
Militias, state
  as strikebreakers, 682, 684, 702
Miller, Glenn, 717*i*
Milliken v. *Bradley* (1974), 904
Million Man March, 981
Mills, C. Wright, 864
Milosevic, Slobodan, 994*m*, 995
Mineral Act (1866), 523
Minik, 627–628, 627*i*
Minimum wage, 663, 763*t*, 856, 867, 974
Mining
  Chinese and, 519, 574*i*
  environmental impact of, 950, 1020
  hazards of, 588, 589*i*, 731
  methods of, 524
  21st century, 1006
  technology of
    engineers and, 540
    hydraulic extraction in, 539, 542
  19th century, 519, 521–524, 529, 539, 546
    company towns and, 552
    disease and, 588
    environmental impact of, 524, 618*m*
    labor unrest in, 588–589, 617
    and Native Americans, 570*i*
    in Northeast, 622*m*
    in West, 522, 587, 976
  20th century
    environmental damage and, 950, 950*i*
    Federal land management and, 667, 949–950
    labor unrest in, 665, 682, 682*i*, 683*m*, 684, 787
    in Midwest, 649
    in West, 682–684, 682*i*, 792, 949–950
  worker unrest in, 588–589, 665, 682, 682*i*, 683*m*, 684, 787
Mining Act (1872), 524, 1020
Minnesota
  Black voting rights in, 504
  indian reservations in, 613*m*, 647
  migration to
    20th century, 647, 647*m*, 649
Minnesota Farmer-Labor party, 760
Minorities
  in 1930s
    motion picture industry and, 721–722
    role and status of, 739
    as sports celebrities, 814, 814*i*
  19th century
    advertising and, 534–535, 561
    rights of, 508
    unions and, 528–529, 592
  early 20th century, women's suffrage movement and, 664
  World War II and, 773
    GI Bill, 811–812, 813*f*
Miranda rights, 881
Miranda v. *Arizona* (1964), 881
Miss America Pageant (1968), 896
Mission homes, late 19th century, 638
Mississippi
  19th century
    Black Codes, 504
    readmission to Union, 513
  20th century
    civil rights struggle in, 855–858, 855*m*, 875
    economy of, 578
    and Reagan on states rights, 948
  post–Civil War
    African American suffrage in, 610
    Black Codes, 504
    readmission to Union, 513
Mississippi Basin. *See* Mississippi Valley
Mississippi Delta, 515, 578
Mississippi Freedom Democratic Party, 875, 889
Mississippi River
  20th century
    Great Flood of 1927, 641, 723–724, 724*i*, 725*m*
    levee construction on, 515, 723–724, 724*i*
    navigation of, 515
Mississippi River Commission, 724
Mississippi Valley
  19th century, economy of, 578, 578*m*
Mississippian cultures. *See* Mississippi Valley, Native American cultures in
Mitchell, George, 993
Mitchell, John (Attorney General), 913
Mitchell, John (UMW president), 666
Moapa River Indian Reservation, 757*m*
Mobility, American experience and, 622, 722, 730, 731*m*
Model T Ford, 657, 920
Modern Times (film), 766
Mohawk. *See also* Iroquois Confederacy
Molano, Elvira, 828*i*
Molly Maguires, 589
Moloka'i Leper Colony, 780*m*
Mondale, Walter, 948
Monetary policy
  in 1970s, 917
  in 1980s, 948
  early 20th century, 686
  late 19th century, 529
Money Trust, 687
Monopolies. *See* Trusts
Monroe, Marilyn, 787
Monroe Doctrine
  Roosevelt Corollary to, 640*t*, 669
  in 20th century, 678–679, 684
  in late 19th century, 629
Montana, 618, 618*m*
  Indian reservations in, 613*m*
  mining in, 589*i*, 617, 792
  statehood, 539
Montenegro, 966*m*
Montgomery bus boycott, 838*t*, 854–855, 855*m*
Montgomery Ward, 559, 561
Moon, U.S. landing on, 839*t*, 903*i*
Moral Majority, 938, 955–957, 956*i*
Moral values and 2004 election, 1010–1011
Morehouse College, 614
Moreno, Luisa, 787, 828
Morgan, John Pierpont, 537*i*, 567, 619–620, 670, 687, 978
Morgan v. *Virginia* (1946), 737*t*, 812
Mormon Corridor, 550
Mormon Tabernacle, 549
Mormon Trail, 520*m*
Mormons, 549, 563
  plural marriage and, 563, 600
  late 20th century, 1025
Morrow, E. Frederick, 853
Morton, Ferdinand "Jelly Roll," 661

Moscow summit (1972), 911–912
Moses, Robert Parris, 875–876, 875*i*, 879, 892
Moses, Simon, 611
Motherhood
  in 1920s, rejection of, 707
Mothers
  in 1920s, education for, 681, 712
  1980s single, as welfare queens, 948
Mother's Day, establishment of, 681
Motion picture camera, invention of, 659
Motion picture industry. *See also* Hollywood
  diversity in, 1024
  in 1950s, 863, 864*i*, 872, 922
  early 20th century, 640–641, 659, 707, 716–718, 767, 767*i*
    African-American, 721–722
  in World War II, 785
Motion Picture Producers' Association, 785
Motor Voter Act, 989
Mount, Julia Luna, 745
Mount McKinley, 677, 687*m*, 928*i*
Mount Rainier National Park, 609, 687*m*, 1019*m*
Mount Rushmore, 758
Mount St. Helens, 951*i*
The Movement, 889–899
Mozambique
  independence of, 927*m*
Ms. Magazine, 839*t*, 931
MTV (MTV-Music Television)
  Rock'n'Roll Inaugural Ball (1993), 751, 751*i*
  and spread of American culture, 1024
  start of, 945
Muckraking, 662
Mugwumps, 564
Muir, John, 524, 609, 667–668
Mullan road, 517*m*
Muller v. *Oregon* (1908), 640*t*, 663
Munich agreement (1938), 776
Murphy, Frank, 766
Murphy Brown (TV show), 989
Music
  African American, 564*i*, 659, 661, 707, 814, 862
    The Blues as, 721
    Jazz as, 707, 721–722
  on compact discs (CDs), 938*t*, 945
  country and western, 862
  of Depression Era, 748–749, 748*i*
  Disco, 933*i*
  diversity in, 1024
  Punk, 933*i*
  ragtime, 606, 659
  record industry and, 722, 814
  rhythm and blues, 814, 862–863
  Rock 'n' roll, 716, 719*i*, 751, 814, 833, 839, 862–864, 872, 893, 1024*i*
  1960s counterculture and, 893, 894
  and spread of American culture, 1024
Muskie, Edmund, 913
Muslims. *See also* Islam; Islamic fundamentalism
  in U.S., post-9/11, 1029*f*, 1033
  worldwide, post-9/11, 1008–1009
Mussadiq, Muhammad, 943
Mussolini, Benito, 775
My Lai massacre, 800, 839*t*, 888, 904, 923
Myer, Dillon S., 828
Myers, Isaac, 528
Myrdal, Gunnar, 789

N

NAACP. *See* National Association for the Advancement of Colored People
NACW. *See* National Association of Colored Women
Nader, Ralph, 879, 999
NAFTA. *See* North American Free Trade Agreement
Nagasaki, atomic bombing of, 737, 798*m*, 800–801, 801*i*, 803*i*
Nagy, Imre, 859
Namibia, 927*m*
Namouna (ship), 604*i*
Nanticoke, 609
Napalm, 800, 887*i*
NASA. *See* National Aeronautics and Space Administration
Nasser, Gamal Abdul, 862
Nast, Thomas, 513*i*, 530*i*
The Nation, 599, 615, 746
Nation of Islam. *See* Black Muslims
National Academy of Sciences, 941, 1022
National Advisory Commission on Civil Disorders, 891
National Aeronautics and Space Administration (NASA), 903*i*
  Cold War and, 858
  Manned Spacecraft Center (Houston), 857
National-American Woman Suffrage Association (NAWSA), 535*t*, 623, 681
National Association for the Advancement of Colored People (NAACP), 784
  anti-lynching campaign, 666, 680
  anti-segregation activism, 812, 814, 852–856
  establishment of, 640*t*, 666, 677
  first presidential address to, 826
  Red Scare and, 827
  Scottsboro Boys and, 744
National Association of Colored Women (NACW), 624
National Association of Window Trimmers, 560
National Baseball League, 556–557
National Basketball Association (NBA), 958*i*, 1025
National Broadcasting Company (NBC), 722, 879
National Child Labor Committee, 663*i*
National Congress of Mothers, 624
National Consumer League (NCL), 625, 663
National debt
  in 1980s, 947–948, 988
National Defense Education Act (NDEA) [1958], 838*t*, 858
National Equal Rights Party, 601
National Farmers' Alliance, 534*t*, 586–587, 587*m*
National Farmers' Alliance and Industrial Union, 586
National Fatherhood Initiative, 981
National Grange of the Patrons of Husbandry. *See* The Grange
National Guard
  Bush (G.W.) in, 1005, 1010
  and flood relief, 724
  in school integration, 853–854, 870
  as strikebreakers, 622, 731, 766
  and student protests, 839*t*, 903
National Industrial Recovery Act (NIRA) (1933), 755, 758, 763*t*, 764
National Labor Relations (Wagner) Act (1935), 736*t*, 761–762, 763*t*
National Labor Union (NLU), 501, 527–529
  and African Americans, 528
  member unions of, 529*t*
National Liberation Front (Viet Cong; NLF), 839, 868, 883–889, 884*m*, 915
National Organization for Women (NOW), 838*t*, 896
National Park Service, 524, 667, 687*m*, 688
National park system
  development of, 524, 667
  early 20th century, 667, 687*m*, 688
  in West, 520, 520*m*, 524, 687*m*
National Petroleum Reserve (Alaska), 929*m*
National Recovery Administration (NRA), 755, 763*t*
National Rifle Association, 987
National security, post–World War II
  declassified documents on, 830–831, 833, 836, 936, 970, 1034
  redefinition of, 816, 830–831, 832*m*, 833
National Security Act (1947, 1949), 833
National Security Agency (NSA), 832*m*
National Security Council (NSC), 832*m*
  creation of, 833
  document 68 (NSC-68), 830–831, 833
  Iran-Contra scandal and, 964, 964*i*
National Security League, 693
National security state
  establishment of, 830–831, 833
  tactics of, 909, 923
National Socialist (Nazi) party (Germany)
  eugenics program, 726
  rise to power, 775
National Union for Social Justice, 759
National Weather Service, 935
National Wildlife Federation, 919
National Woman Suffrage Association (NWSA), 526–527, 623
National Women's Party (NWP), 664, 681, 711–712
National Youth Administration, 763*t*, 764, 784

Nationalism
 20th century
  American, 677–680, 698
  in Asia, 828
Nationalist movement, 592
Native American Grave and Burial
 Protection Act, 628
Native-American women
 crafts, 518
 first physician, 598, 598*i*
Native Americans, 1034
 intermarriage of
  with African Americans,
   610, 610*i*
  with non-indians, 1031
 19th century
  alcohol and, 597
  assimilation of, 584, 596–598,
   605–606, 605*i*
  in California, 519, 583*m*
  and citizenship, 597–598, 601
  education, 605*i*
  land losses, 583*m*, 584
  land rights of, 565, 583*m*
  railroad and, 516, 535
  reformers and, 596
  religion, 580–584
  removals, 580, 583*m*, 647
  reservations for, 516–518, 583*m*,
   584, 596–598, 613*m*, 647
  resistance by, 535, 580–584, 610
  rights of, 565, 583*m*, 996
  Social Darwinism and, 535, 566
  subduing of, 535, 583–584
  white views on, 582–584
  white wars against, 516–518,
   517*m*
 20th century
  activism, 814, 839, 897–898
  assimilation of, 723*i*, 755, 828,
   1031
  autonomy of, 755
  casinos and, 977, 977*i*, 1031
  citizenship for, 996
  compensation debate, 828
  counterculture and, 893
  discrimination against, 793, 814,
   1031
  education of, 755
  environmental movement and,
   981, 983
  federal policy on, 755–756, 755*i*,
   763*t*, 773, 828, 1031
  first U.S. senator and, 989
  life expectancy, 793
  militancy of, 876, 897–898
  and New Deal, 755–756, 755*i*,
   763*t*, 773
  nuclear contamination and, 821,
   941–942
  population of, 1031
  rights of, 773, 814, 828, 839
  role and status of, 739*i*, 1031
  science and, 981
  in Southwest, 773, 814
  sports and, 981
  voting rights, 814, 996
  white awareness of, 723*i*
  in World War II, 773, 773*i*, 793
Nativists
 in 20th century, 648, 652
Natural resources
 21st century
  exploitation of, 1006, 1018,
   1020–1021, 1023
 19th century, exploitation of, 534,
  539, 542–543, 542*f*, 554, 609
 20th century
  energy needs and, 918–922, 918*f*
  exploitation of, 942
Natural Resources Defense Council, 936,
 1034
Naturalists, 1022
Naturalization Act (1790), 880
Navajos
 changing homeland of, 683*m*
 environment and, 756
 Indian Reorganization Act and, 756
 nuclear contamination and, 821
 reservations for, 583*m*, 613*m*, 683*m*
 in Southwest, 683, 756
 voting rights of, 814
 World War II and, 717, 773, 773*i*,
  793, 797
Naval stores, 521
Navarro, Ramon, 718
Navratilova, Martina, 958
Navy, British
 in World War I, 690–691
Navy, U.S.
 and Five-Power agreement (1922), 709
 in Spanish-American War, 632–633,
  632*i*, 634*m*, 635*m*, 638
 Teapot Dome scandal and, 709, 710*i*
 19th century, growth of, 628
 in World War I, 692
NAWSA. *See* National-American Woman
 Suffrage Association
Nazis. *See* National Socialist (Nazi) party
NBA. *See* National Basketball Association
NBC. *See* National Broadcasting
 Company
NCL. *See* National Consumer League
 (NCL)
NDEA. *See* National Defense Education
 Act
Nebraska
 and drought of 1886, 585–586, 586*i*
 Populist party in, 617
 and same-sex marriage, 982
 settlement of, 515
The Negro World, *715*
Neighborhood Guild of New York City,
 599
Neighborhood Union, 625–626
Neighborhoods, destruction of, 848
Nestlé, 977
Net worth. See Wealth
Netanyahu, Benjamin, 993
Netherlands. See Holland
Neutrality, U.S. in World War I, 684–685,
 689–690
Neutrality Acts (1935, 1936, 1937),
 776–777
Nevada
 economy of, 20th century, 757
 federal lands in, 949*m*
 indian reservations in, 613*m*
 mining in, 522
 nuclear testing in, 821, 822*i*, 865*m*,
  920, 941, 1022
 prostitution in, 1032
 southern area of, 757, 757*m*,
  1032–1033
New Americanism, 767–768
"The New Colossus" (Lazarus), 545–546
New Deal, 619, 736, 740, 752–765, 763*t*,
 768–769, 770
 construction projects in, 754–755,
  756–758
 critics of, 758–761, 769, 777
 effects of, 736, 740, 752–765, 768–769
 Eisenhower and, 755, 856
 and election of 1932, 751
 goals of, 752–758
 Indian policies, 755–756, 755*i*
 legislation, 736*t*, 753–758, 763*t*
 media and, 750–751, 750*i*, 759–760
 minorities and, 758–759, 764,
  766–767
 second, 752, 761–764
New Deal coalition, 766–767
 and election of 1972, 912
 in 1970s, 912, 925
New Democrats, 988
New England Society of New York, 576
New Freedom (Wilson), 671, 680
New Jersey
 19th century
  labor unrest in, 589
 20th century
  agricultural economy of, 812*i*
  race riots in, 890
New Lands Act (1902), 640*t*
New Left, in 1960s, 889, 892–893
New Look, 856, 859
New Mexico
 Santa Fe, 522
 19th century
  Hispanic culture of, 560*i*, 571
  Hispanic land rights in, 571–572
  Knights of Labor in, 572, 590
  Santa Fe Ring in, 522
 20th century
  Dust Bowl in, 735–736, 747*m*
  federal lands in, 949*m*
  Indian population, 613*m*, 814
  Native Americans' suffrage in,
   737*t*, 814
  statehood, 677
  women's suffrage in, 664, 712
New Nationalism, 670–671
New Northwest, 600
New Orleans, Battle of, 578*m*
New Orleans, Louisiana
 19th century
  in Civil War, 502
  lynchings in, 535*t*, 611

New Orleans, Louisiana, *cont.*
 20th century
  and development of Jazz, 661, 721
 post–Civil War, 505, 508, 578*m*, 610, 616
New Orleans Times-Picayune, *598*
New Republic, 599
"New South," 576–577, 587
New York
 19th century
  African American voting rights in, 996
New York Charity Organization Society, 655
New York City
 19th century
  corruption in, 530–531, 530*i*, 555–556
  immigration to, 546, 551, 625
  union unrest, 591
 early 20th century
  entertainment in, 659
  migration to, 688–689
  prohibition in, 712
  Triangle Shirtwaist Company fire, 643–644, 643*i*, 645, 672
 late 19th century
  architecture of, 549, 550, 550*i*
  culture of, 549
  immigration, 546
  poverty in, 594–596, 596*i*, 625
  reform in, 594–596, 625
 late 20th century
  Gay Pride parade, 899*i*, 905
  Marathon in, 921
  Puerto Rican migration to, 897
New York Freeman, 592
New York Journal, 630–631
New York Nine (baseball team), 556
New York Sun, 530, 561
New York Times
 on Indian policy, 566
 on offshore oil, 858
 Pentagon Papers and, 903
 Rogers (Will) and, 739
 Silkwood case and, 907
 on Tammany Hall, 530
New York Tribune, 530, 594
New York World, 630
Newark, New Jersey, in 1960s, black riots in, 838*t*, 890
Newfoundland, 777
Newland Act (1902), 679
Newspapers
 in 1980s, readership, 945
 19th century, 530, 630–631
Newsweek, 865
Nez Perce Indians
 culture, 518
 removal of, 500, 584*i*, 618
Ngo Dingh Diem, 841, 868, 883
Niagara Movement, 666
Nicaragua
 20th century
  refugees from, 947
  Sandinista revolution in, 938*t*, 945–946, 964
  U.S. foreign policy in, 938*t*, 946–947, 964
  U.S. intervention in, 669, 678–680, 678*m*–679*m*
Nichols, Jesse Clyde, 728–729
Nichols, Terry, 985
Nigeria, oil reserves and exports, 1006*f*, 1007*f*
Nightline (news program), 943
Nike Shoe Co., 921
Nimitz, Chester, 797
9/11 Commission, 1007
Nineteenth Amendment, 640, 641*t*, 664, 681, 704
Nintendo, 961
NIRA. *See* National Industrial Recovery Act
Nisquallys, 1019*m*
Nixon, E.D., 854
Nixon, Richard M.
 abuses of power by, 839*t*, 908, 912–914, 922–923
 and Arab-Israeli War (1973), 918–919
 child care and, 933
 in China, 839*t*, 908–912, 912*i*
 Cold War and, 843, 843*i*, 909
 constituency of, 899–902
 domestic policies, 902–903
 economic policy, 916–919
 and election of 1960, 750–751, 867
 and election of 1968, 876, 899, 901–902
 and election of 1972, 912–913
 enemies list of, 902–903, 913
 and environment, 902
 foreign policy, 838*t*, 903
 impeachment of, 908, 914
 Latin Americans and, 861
 pardon of, 915, 925
 political style of, 902
 resignation of, 839, 839*t*, 908, 914, 914*i*
 Southern strategy of, 902, 912
 in Soviet Union, 842–844, 843*i*, 908
 and Supreme Court, 902
 unions and, 897
 as vice president, 842–844, 843*i*, 856, 867
 Vietnam War and, 839, 876, 903–904, 908
  suppression of dissent, 902, 913
 Watergate scandal, 839*t*, 908, 909, 912–914
  historians' view of Cold War and, 818
  impact of, 922
 in World War II, 785*i*
Nixon Doctrine, 903
NLF. *See* National Liberation Front
NLU. *See* National Labor Union
Nonimportation movement. *See* Boycotts, in American Revolution
NORAD. *See* North American Air Defense Command
Noriega, Manuel, 938*t*, 966–967
Norris, Clarence, 744
North
 19th century
  agriculture in, 541*m*
  in Civil War (*See* Union)
  population of, 607*m*
North, Oliver, 964, 964*i*
North America
 crude oil reserves of, 1006*f*
North American Air Defense Command (NORAD), 976
North American Free Trade Agreement (NAFTA), 938, 939*t*, 991, 1015
North American Review (periodical), 562
North Atlantic Treaty Organization (NATO), 737, 807, 817*m*, 819
 in Balkans, 994*m*, 995
 ex–Warsaw Pact states and, 966*m*
 France and, 817*m*, 820
 Greece and, 817*m*, 859
 in 1950s, 859, 860*m*–861*m*
 Spain and, 817*m*
 Turkey and, 817*m*, 859
 West Germany and, 817*m*, 835, 859
North Carolina
 19th century
  African American women organizations in, 624
  free blacks in, 501–502
  readmission to Union, 513
North Carolina Agricultural and Mechanical College, 612
North Dakota
 indian reservations in, 613*m*, 647
 statehood for, 539
North Korea. *See also* Korean War
 Pueblo incident, 888
 Soviet Union in, 816, 820*m*, 833–834
North Pole, 677
 global warming and, 1021
 Peary expedition to, 640*t*, 675, 675*i*
North Vietnam, 884*m*. *See also* Vietnam War
 establishment of, 838*t*, 883
 morale of, 886–887
 refugees from, 841
 U.S. bombing of, 883, 884*m*, 887*i*
 and U.S.-China detente, 909
Northeast
 19th century
  forest clearing in, 542*f*
  population of, 607*m*
Northern Alliance, 586
Northern Ireland, 993
Northern Pacific Railroad, 517, 517*m*, 524, 539, 609
Northern Securities Co., 666
Norton, Gale, 1023
Norway
 crude oil reserves of, 1006*f*
 20th century
  German invasion of, 776, 795*m*
Notre Dame University, 926
Novel, 19th century American, 615–616

NOW. *See* National Organization for Women
NRA. *See* National Recovery Administration
NSC. *See* National Security Council
Nuclear arms. *See also* Arms race
atomic bomb
bombing of Japan, 737, 798*m*, 800–801, 801*i*, 803, 803*i*, 821
development of, 683*m*, 737*t*, 799–800
cultural impact of, 845, 858
debate over, 800–801, 821–822, 842, 877, 961
environmental damage from, 821–822, 822*i*, 865*m*, 942, 950, 1022
hydrogen bomb, development of, 800, 822
in Iraq, 1007
production and test sites, 800, 821, 822*i*, 865*m*, 1022
proliferation of, 701, 801, 838, 864–865, 868, 910*m*–911*m*, 1007
protests against, 864–865, 867*i*, 941
Soviet acquisition of, 800, 809, 830
stockpiles of
in 1970s, 910*m*–911*m*
in 1980s, 947, 958
testing of, environmental damage from, 821–822, 822*i*, 865*m*, 920, 1022
Nuclear deterrence, 801, 838, 859, 869
Nuclear freeze movement, 938*t*, 941, 958
Nuclear power, 842, 921
accidents involving, 907, 931*i*, 938*t*, 941–942, 958
controversy over, 907, 919, 930, 931*i*, 941
as percent of total, 930, 930*m*
plant locations, 921, 930*m*, 931*i*
protests against, 919, 958
Nuclear test ban treaty of 1963, 869
Nuclear waste, 821–822, 919, 921, 930*m*, 941, 1022
Nuclear winter, 801, 958
Nuremberg trials, 819
Nurses
20th century
in public health, 655, 681, 712
in World War I, 694
NWP. *See* National Women's Party
NWSA. *See* National Woman Suffrage Association
Nylon, 836

O

Oak Ridge National Laboratory, 865*m*
Oakley, Annie, 557–558
OAS. *See* Organization of American States
Oberlin College, 515
Obesity, prevalence of, 922*i*, 985, 987, 988*f*
Obscenity. *See* Pornography
Occupational hazards. *See* Safety, industrial
O'Connor, Sandra Day, 935, 956
O'Donnell, Edward, 588
Office of Independent Counsel, 990
Office of Strategic Services (OSS), 882
Office of War Information (OWI), 784–785, 789, 804
Ogallala aquifer, 1020*m*, 1021
Ohio
21st century
and election of 2004, 1010
Oil
Arab oil embargo (1973-1974), 839*t*, 918–920, 928, 930–931
energy from, 930*m*, 1021
Iranian revolution and, 816–817, 861, 912, 930, 942–944
Mexican revolution and, 679
Persian Gulf War (1991) and, 939, 967, 969–970
spills and pollution, 902, 919, 929, 938*t*, 950
supply of, 857, 857*m*, 908, 928, 943, 1006*f*, 1007*f*
U.S. dependence on, 825, 918*f*, 919, 1021
U.S. economy and, 825, 918*f*
U.S. importation of, 908, 918*f*, 1007*f*, 1021
U.S. industry
and Arctic National Wildlife Refuge, 929, 1006, 1023
development of, 560, 686, 720, 857, 857*m*, 920, 921*i*, 1014
and offshore drilling, 858, 902, 1006
and Standard Oil Trust, 534*t*, 541*m*, 545
Teapot Dome scandal and, 709, 710*i*
Oil Producing and Exporting Countries (OPEC), 839, 839*t*, 918–919, 928
Ojibwa, 649
O'Keefe, Georgia, 683*m*
Okies, 745–746, 748, 759, 784
Okinawa, 797, 798*m*, 807
Oklahoma
19th century
land rush in, 608, 609*m*
Native American removal to, 580*i*, 609*m*
20th century
Dust Bowl in, 745–746, 745*i*, 747*m*
indian reservations in, 613*m*
oil boom in, 675–676
racial violence in, 675, 702
statehood for, 609*m*, 640*t*
Oklahoma City Federal Building bombing (1995), 939, 939*t*, 985, 986, 1000
Oklahoma Territory, establishment of, 608, 609*m*
Old Faithful, 525*i*
Olney, Richard, 619
Olson, Floyd, 760
Olympia National Park, 687*m*, 1019
Olympic Games
of 1912, 680
of 1936, 630
of 1972, 630
of 1980, 630, 944
of 1984, 938*t*
of 2004, 631
history of, 630–631, 631*i*
Winter games, 520, 630
Omahas, 597
On the Road (Kerouac), 864
One Flew over the Cuckoo's Nest (film), 922
One Flew over the Cuckoo's Nest (Kesey), 922
Oneida. *See also* Iroquois Confederacy
casinos and, 977
O'Neill, Thomas "Tip," 926
Onondaga. *See also* Iroquois Confederacy
OPEC. *See* Oil Producing and Exporting Countries
Open Door policy, 633, 678
Operation Chaos, 923
Operation Desert Shield, 968–969, 968*m*
Operation Desert Storm, 969
Operation Dixie, 815
Operation Vittles, 819
Order of the Eastern Star, 579
Oregon Equal Suffrage Association, 600
Oregon (territory, state)
agriculture in, 540*i*
direct democracy in, 662
gun control in, 987
Indian reservations in, 613*m*
The Organization Man (Whyte), 864
Organization of American States (OAS), establishment of, 737*t*, 868
Organized crime
in film, 767
in 1920s, 713
Oriental foods, popularity of, 961
Orientalism, 628
OSS. *See* Office of Strategic Services
Oswald, Lee Harvey, 871
The Other Americans (Harrington), 878
Ottoman Empire, World War I and, 677, 685*f*, 694–695, 695*m*, 697–698, 700
Our Country (Strong), 566
Owens, Jesse, 630
OWI. *See* Office of War Information
Oyster fishing, 542
Ozone depletion, 919, 921, 1021

P

Pachucos, 792
Pacific Gas & Electric Co. (PG&E), 667–668
Pacific Islanders, population of, 984
Pacific Lumber, 973–974
Pacific Ocean
20th century
trade, 961

Pacific Ocean, *cont.*
in World War II, 773, 773*i*, 779, 797–799, 797*i*, 798*m*, 811*i* (*See also* Pearl Harbor)
Pacifism, and Chicano movement, 898*i*
Packard, Vance, 561
Padre Island National Seashore, 857*m*
Pahlavi, Reza (Shah of Iran), 861, 912, 942–943
Paiute Indians, 581, 757
Pakistan
independence of, 820*m*
nuclear arms and, 911*m*
Palestine
Jewish hopes for homeland in, 677, 680*i*, 821
post–World War II
British withdrawal from, 821
refugees of, 821
Palestinian Liberation Organization (PLO), 993
Palmer, A. Mitchell, 702
Palmer raids, 702
Pan Am Flight 109, 938*t*, 964
Pan-American Conference (1890), 629
Panama, 678–680, 678*m*–679*m*, 926–927
in 1980s, U.S. intervention in, 938*t*
U.S. intervention in (1989), 966–967
Panama Canal
construction of, 668, 677, 678*m*–679*m*
return of, 925–927
U.S. management of, 926
Panic of 1907, 669
Pantex plant (nuclear weapons), 865*m*
Pape, Eric, 628
Paper industry, 588
Paramount pictures, 659
Parent-teacher associations (PTAs), 849
Paris conference (1919), 698
Park, David, 806*i*
Parker, Alton B., 667
Parks, Rosa, 854
Parochial schools, late 19th century, 614
Parrish, Mary E. Jones, 676
Parsons, Albert, 593, 595, 595*i*
Parsons, Lucia Gonzalez, 593
Parties
19th century, 623
The Passing of the Great Race (Grant), 680
Pathet Lao, 884*m*
Patriot Act (2001). *See* U.S.A. Patriot Act (2001)
Patriotism, 20th century, 818*i*, 826, 901, 940*i*, 953
Patronage system
reform of, 564
late 19th century, 530
Paul, Alice, 664, 681
Pawnee
reservations for, 608, 613*m*
Paxton Boys, 590
Payne-Aldrich Tariff (1909), 670
PBS. *See* Public Broadcasting System
PCBs (polychlorinated biphenyls), 920, 1022
Peace Corps, 841, 868, 1032
Peace movements
in 1930s, 777
Pearl Harbor
Japanese attack on, 736, 736*t*, 773, 778–781, 778*i*, 779*i*, 780*m*, 802, 1003
U.S. base at, 534*t*, 628, 778*i*, 779, 780
Peary, Robert, 627–628, 627*i*, 640*t*, 675, 675*i*
Pendleton Act (1883), 534*t*, 564
Penicillin, 821
Pennsylvania
19th century
African American voting rights, 504, 996
labor unrest in, 617
oil industry in, 920, 921*i*
Pennsylvania Railroad, 537–538, 562
Pension Act (1890), 616
Pentagon, terrorist attack on. *See* September 11th terrorist attacks
Pentagon Papers, 839*t*, 903, 913
Pentecostalists, 1025, 1029*f*
Peonage, 640
People for Ethical Treatment of Animals (PETA), 983*i*
People's Cooperative Grocery Store, 611
People's party. *See* Populist Party
People's Republic of China (PRC). *See also* China
establishment of, 737*t*, 829
U.S. relations with, 829–830, 870, 909–912, 912*i*, 961
Pequot, 977
Perestroika, 963
Perkins, Charles Elliott, 976
Perkins, Frances, 753
Perot, H. Ross, 988–989, 990
Pershing, John J., 680, 694
Persian Gulf War (1991), 938*t*, 939, 943*m*, 967–970, 968*m*, 1007
Carter Doctrine and, 944
Islam and, 970, 1026
oil and, 920–921, 967, 969, 1007
United Nations and, 701, 968
women in, 967*i*, 969, 1026
Personal computers, impact of, 1002*i*, 1012–1013
Peru, 861
PETA. *See* People for Ethical Treatment of Animals
Petroleum. *See also* Oil
plastics and, 842, 919
Philadelphia
19th century
immigration to, 546
early 20th century, migration to, 688–689
Philadelphia Gazette, 561
Philanthropy, 537, 567, 612
Philippines
19th century
Spanish-American War and, 535*t*, 630–636, 632*i*, 634*m*, 635*m*, 638
U.S. purchase of, 633, 634*m*
U.S. subjugation of, 535*t*, 606, 633, 634*m*, 636–637, 637*i*
20th century
immigration from, 900, 959, 984
independence of, 669, 677, 820–821, 820*m*
Marcos regime in, 938*t*
U.S. in, 669, 670, 835
World War II and, 736*t*, 779, 797, 828
Phonograph, invention of, 534*t*, 540, 722
photography, 525*i*, 568, 786
Phyllis Wheatley Settlement, 625
Picture brides, 653
Pike, Otis, 923, 925
Pikes Peak, 976, 976*m*
Pillsbury Flour, 538
Pinchot, Gifford, 609, 670
Pine Ridge Reservation, 517*m*, 582, 582*i*, 605, 613*m*, 898
Pink collar work, 849, 850*i*
Pinkerton, Allan, 589
Pinkerton National Detective Agency, 537, 588–589, 617, 622, 702
Pinochet, Augusto, 912
Pinups, in World War II, 786, 786*i*
Pittsburgh, Pennsylvania
late 19th century, 537
Plains Indians
culture, 518
Dawes Severalty Act and, 565, 565*i*, 598, 613*m*, 647, 755
Ghost Dance and, 573, 580–584, 582*i*
independence movement, 517–518
removal of, 517–518, 647
resistance by, 516–518, 535
treaties, 516
white war against, 500, 501, 516–518, 517*m*, 581*m*
Planned obsolescence, invention of, 722
Planned Parenthood of Southeastern Pennsylvania v. *Casey* (1992), 975
Plantation agriculture. *See also* Cotton plantations; Rice plantations
Chinese and, 546, 547*m*
failure of immigration to aid, 546, 547*m*
on Hawaiian Islands, 629
early 20th century, 724
Plastics, 836, 919, 1022
Platt Amendment (1901), 633
Plausible denial doctrine, 924
Playboy ethic, 864
Playboy (magazine), 864, 896
Pledge of Allegiance, 612, 827, 847*i*
Plessy, Homer, 610
Plessy v. *Ferguson* (1896), 535*t*, 610, 852, 873
PLO. *See* Palestinian Liberation Organization
Plumbers, 839*t*, 903, 912–913
Pogroms, 654, 677
Point Reyes National Seashore, 894*m*
Pokémon, 1025
Poland
immigration from, 545, 547, 592, 610, 714, 783

World War I and, 698, 699*m*
World War II and, 774, 776, 810*m*, 816
in 1950s, uprising, 859
and collapse of Soviet Union, 962*i*, 965, 966*m*
Police power, international
Roosevelt Corollary and, 640*t*, 669
late 20th century, 969
Polio
FDR and, 750–751
early 20th century, 645
vaccine development, 838*t*
Politics, late 19th century
characteristics of, 555–556
corruption in, 530–531, 530*i*, 555–556
Poll taxes, 610, 879
Pollard, Red, 769*i*
Pollock, Jackson, 862–863, 863*i*
Pollock v. *Farmers' Loan and Trust Company* (1895), 620
Pollution. *See also* Environmental damage
21st century, 1018, 1021–1022
air pollution, 1006, 1021
public opinion on, 1023
water and, 1006, 1020–1021
19th century, urban
industrial, 538
water supplies, 542–543, 555
20th century
air pollution, 667, 824*i*, 825, 839, 858, 880, 902
fossil fuels and, 824*i*, 825, 880
new materials and, 836, 880
pesticides/insecticides and, 836, 864, 866, 902, 920, 1022
radioactive, 821–822, 907, 941–942
water and, 821, 839, 858, 880, 902, 919
Polowsky, Joseph, 807
Polychlorinated biphenyls. *See* PCBs
Polyester, 836
Polygamy
among Mormons, 600
outlawing of, 563, 600
Polynesians, 629, 780, 780*m*
Ponca Indians, 597
Pony Express, 557
Popular Front, 758
Population
in 2000s, 1018, 1020, 1028*m*
19th century
density of, 607*m*
immigrant, 539
increase in, 539, 636
20th century, 970
The Population Bomb (Ehrlich), 902
Populism, in New Deal, 760–761
Populist party
constituency of, 535, 587, 588*i*, 616, 618–619
demise of, 621
and election of 1892, 617, 619
and election of 1896, 620
and election of 1900, 635
platform of, 584, 587, 591, 617, 619
predecessors of, 587
rise of, 529, 535, 535*t*, 587, 617
Pornography
feminism and, 527, 932
Supreme Court on, 881
Port Arthur, Texas, 857*m*
Port Huron Statement, 892
Portrait of a Lady (James), 599
Portugal
19th century, immigration from, 545
Post Dispatch (St. Louis), 630
Potawatomi Indians
land loss, 609*m*
Potsdam Conference (1945), 799
Poverty
in 1920s, 708, 730–731, 733, 742
in 1930s, 740, 741*i*, 742, 753
in 1960s, 845, 877–879, 878*m*
in 1970s, 904, 917, 933
in 1980s, 952, 970
drug dealing and, 957
in 1990s, 978–979
in 2000s, 1016–1017, 1031
19th century
reform movements and, 535, 594–596, 599
urban, 594–596, 596*i*, 599
20th century, 655
and divorce, 933
freedom from, 774, 777*i*
Powderly, Terence V., 590, 592, 592*i*
Powell, Adam Clayton, 859
Powell, Colin, 969, 1007, 1030
Powers, Gary, 859
Powhatan Indians, 19th century, 610*i*
Pratt, Richard Henry, 605, 612
Prayer in schools, religious right and, 881–882
PRC. *See* People's Republic of China
Pre-marital sex, 661, 825, 863, 909
Prejudice. *See also* Discrimination
19th century, 573
20th century
interracial sex and, 847–848, 895, 1030
in suffrage movement, 664
Presbyterian College of the Southwest, 612
Presbyterians, 612
decline of, 955
mission homes, 600, 624
missions in South, 499
Preservationism, *vs.* conservationism, early 20th century, 609, 667
Presidency
and media, 750–751, 750*i*, 751*i*
late 20th century
Nixon resignation and, 914
President's Commission on the Status of Women, 761, 869
President's Committee on Civil Rights, 826
Presley, Elvis, 719*i*, 814, 863–864
Prince (pop star), 985
Principles of Psychology (James), 615
The Principles of Scientific Management (Taylor), 657
Printing and publishing. *See also* Newspapers
18th century
in Early Republic, 561
19th century
investigative journalism, 530, 530*i*
newspapers and, 530, 630–631
Prisons
and abuse in Iraq, 1009, 1009*i*
prisoners' rights and, 881
20th century boom in, 957, 979
Proctor & Gamble Co., 561, 983*i*
Productivity
20th century
slowing growth in, 917
Professionals
organizations of, 654
Progress and Poverty (George), 591
Progressive Era, 606, 619, 642–671
African Americans and, 665–666, 688–689
close of, 703, 733
conservationism and, 662
evaluation of, 640, 704, 741
New Deal and, 752
Progressive party
and election of 1912, 671, 989
and election of 1924, 709
and election of 1948, 826
formation of, 640*t*
in Wisconsin, 760
Progressivism, 619, 661–666
decline of, 641, 703
environmentalism and, 662
New Deal and, 752
Protestants and, 661–662
reformers and, 662–664, 680*i*, 703
Roosevelt and, 703
World War I and, 690
Prohibition, 640, 664, 693, 704, 709, 712*i*, 734
and election of 1928, 711
repeal of, 712–713, 753
Promise Keepers, 981
Property ownership
and extractive industries, 521
and voting rights, 996
Proposition 13 (California), 839*t*, 947
Proposition 187 (California), 984
Proposition 227 (California), 984
Prostitution
automobile and, 723
Chinese-Americans and, 599–600, 624, 650–651
in Nevada, 1032
vice crusaders and, 663–664
Protect the Emperor Society, 650
Protest movements. *See also* Reform movements
antiwar protests
Vietnam War, 875–876, 888–889, 892–893, 901–903, 913
World War II, 777, 781
in 1960s
backlash against, 876, 899–902

Protestantism. *See also* Fundamentalist Christians
  19th century, 538
    education and, 508, 612
    Indian assimilation and, 596–598
    reform movements and, 596
    religious instruction in, 612
  20th century
    dislike of Catholics, 648, 955
    missionary activities of, 1025
    population and, 1028, 1029*f*
    rise of fundamentalism in, 641, 955
Prozac, 987
Prudhoe Bay, Alaska, 929–930, 929*m*
Psychology
  and impact of segregation, 852
  introduction as discipline, 615, 616
PT-109, 867
PTAs. *See* Parent-teacher associations
Public Broadcasting System (PBS), 879
Public Law 85-846. *See* National Defense Education Act (NDEA) [1958]
Public schools, 512
Public Works Administration (PWA), 763*t*
USS Pueblo incident, 888
Pueblo Indians
  nuclear contamination and, 941
Puerto Ricans
  citizenship for, 677
  in 1960s, militancy of, 897
  in Vietnam War, 897
Puerto Rico, 635*m*
  annexation of, 535*t*
  commonwealth status for, 737*t*
  early 20th century, U.S. in, 641*t*, 678*m*–679*m*, 679
Puget, Peter, 1019
Puget Sound area, 1019, 1019*m*
Pujo, Arsene, 687
Pulitzer, Joseph, 630
Pullman, George M., 552
Pullman cars, 524, 552
Pullman Palace Car Co., 552, 619, 620
Pure Food and Drug Act (1906), 640*t*, 662
Pusan perimeter (Korea), 834*m*, 835, 835*i*
Putnam, George, 845
PWA. *See* Public Works Administration
Pyle, Ernie, 798–799

Q

Qisuk, 627–628, 627*i*
Quayle, Dan, 988
Quinaults, 1019*m*

R

Rabin, Yitzak, 993
Race
  in 2000s
    decreasing usefulness as category, 1029
  19th century
    as classification, 610, 610*i*
    as justification for exploitation, 610–611
    and social class, 610
  20th century
    and birthrate, 656
    as classification, 658, 680, 985, 1033
    definition of whiteness, 658–659, 1029
    interracial sex, 663–664, 847–848, 881–882, 1030
    mixing of, 985
    Nazis and, 774, 775–776
    stereotypes of, 767, 1028
    in Vietnam War, 887–888
The Races of Mankind (Benedict), 789
Racial profiling, 1031
Racial quotas, Supreme Court on, 935–936
Racism. *See also* Discrimination; Lynchings; Prejudice
  19th century
    growth of, 564, 593
    imperialism and, 535
    Social Darwinism and, 535, 566, 635
  20th century
    challenges to, 808, 892
    eugenics and, 656, 724–726
    Fascism and, 775–776
    race riots, 675–676, 688, 702, 890–891, 900
    Tulsa race riot (1921), 641*t*, 675–676
Radcliffe College, 663
Radiation Exposure Act (1990), 938*t*, 942
Radical politics. *See also* Protest movements; Reform movements
  early 20th century, 664–665
Radio
  advertising and, 561, 722
  disc jockeys and, 814
  Father Coughlin and, 759–760
  invention of, 722, 1012
  Roosevelt (F.D.) and, 750–751, 750*i*, 752, 767
  in 1920s, 641, 641*t*, 708, 716, 722, 734
  World War II morale and, 785–786
Radioactive fallout, 821–822, 822*i*, 865*m*, 920, 1022
Radioactive waste, 821–822, 919, 921, 930*m*, 941–942, 1022
Railroad(s)
  19th century
    big business and, 538, 541*m*
    and buffalo, 543
    and Civil War, 501, 563
    consolidation of, 544, 565, 686
    early development of, 920
    farmers and, 541*m*, 565, 584, 591
    impact of, 512, 515–516, 517*m*, 524*t*, 538, 543
    Indians and, 516–518, 516*i*, 517*m*
    intercontinental project, 629
    and national integration, 515–516, 538
    refrigerated cars, 538
    regulation of, 565
    resource exploitation and, 524*t*, 542–543
    segregation on, 610, 613
    strikes, 562–563, 563*i*, 588–589, 593, 665
    technology and, 540, 567
    tourism and, 523*i*, 524, 609
    transcontinental lines, 500, 515–516, 516*i*, 521*i*, 568
    trees used in building, 543
    westward migration and, 515–516
    worker unrest, 562–563, 563*i*
    workers for, 516*i*, 521*i*, 532, 538, 577
  20th century, 644, 791
    regulation of, 686, 688, 692–693
    strikes and, 815
    Trans-Siberian line, 677
Railroad Administration, U.S., establishment of, 692–693
Rain-in-the-Face, 519*i*
Rainbow Coalition, 958
Rainey, Joseph H., 513*i*
Rainey, Ma, 721
Rainforests, concern for, 919
A Raisin in the Sun (Hansberry), 847
Raker Act (1913), 668
Ralston-Purina, 977
Ramabai, Pandita, 624
Ramabai Circles, 624
Randolph, A. Philip, 690, 736*t*, 791
Range Creek ruins, 520, 520*m*
Rankin, Jeannette, 641*t*, 681, 781
Rape, Feminist activism against, 932, 935
Ray, Dorothy, 759
Ray, James Earl, 901
Rayburn, Sam, 808
RCA, 1016
Reagan, Nancy, 965
Reagan, Ronald W., 941*i*, 970
  on abortion, 955
  and AIDS, 956–957
  Alzheimer's disease and, 965
  anticommunism of, 925
  assassination attempt against, 945, 987
  budget deficits and, 947–948, 989
  business and, 947
  Cold War and, 801, 925, 941, 945–947, 961
  constituency of, 901
  domestic policies, 938, 947–948
  economic policies, 942, 947–948
  and election of 1976, 925
  and election of 1980, 938*t*, 944–945, 965
  and election of 1984, 948
  11th Commandment of, 956
  environmental policies, 948–950
  foreign policy, 938, 938*t*, 945–947, 961–965

fundamentalist Christians and, 955–956
on gay rights, 955
as "Great Communicator," 751, 945
impact of, 965
Iran-Contra scandal and, 938*t*, 963–965
media and, 750–751
nuclear arsenal and, 941, 947
optimism of, 931, 963
Panama Canal and, 927
personality of, 751, 944–945, 961, 963, 965
on school prayer, 955
social programs and, 947–948
Soviet Union and, 925, 945, 961–963
Strategic Defense Initiative and, 801
support for, 931, 965
unions and, 897
vision of, 944–945, 963
World War II and, 785*i*, 789
Reaganomics, 947–948
Realism, in art, 660*i*, 661
Realpolitik, 909, 923
Rebel Without a Cause (film), 863
Recall (of elected officials), 662
Reconstruction, 499–515
close of, 530
corruption in, 512–513
debate over, 500, 512–515
under Johnson, 500, 502–505, 512*m*, 514
land redistribution and, 503*i*, 507
Reconstruction Act (1867), 510
Reconstruction Finance Corporation, 748
Recycling, 1022
Red Army. *See* Soviet Union
The Red Badge of Courage (Crane), 615–616
Red-baiting, 826–827, 871
Red Cloud, 517–518
Red Cross, 694, 696, 724, 776
Red lining policies, 847
Red Power (Native American rights), 898
Red Scare
civil liberties and, 702, 870
and Korean War, 836
post–World War I, 702, 713, 731
post–World War II, 808, 814–815, 826–828, 870
Reed, John, 703–704
Referendum (direct popular vote), 662
Reform Darwinism, 599
Reform movements. *See also* Protest movements
19th century, 535, 612
trans-Atlantic networks, 599
women and, 599–600
20th century, 655–657, 661–666, 711–715
World War I and, 690
Reform party, 988, 999
Religion, 705, 936, 970
as criterion for citizenship, 880
19th century
"African" churches, 508, 510
Christian Science, 616, 638
instruction in, 612, 614
Psychology and, 615
summer colonies and, 609
20th century (*See also* Fundamentalist Christians)
affiliations, 1028, 1029*f*
anticommunism and, 827
black churches and civil rights, 854, 855, 855*m*
in census of 2000, 1028
characteristics of, 893, 901
counterculture spirituality and, 893
eastern influences on, 893
evangelical, 893, 895*i*, 955–957, 981, 1029*f*
freedom of, 774
fundamentalism in, 955
global evangelism, 827
prayer in public schools, 881–882
and resistance to American culture, 1023–1025, 1027
in 1960s, 845, 847*i*, 867, 893, 901
science and, 726–727, 734
Scopes trial and, 726–727, 727*i*
in suburbs, 845, 847*i*
Religious right. *See* Fundamentalist Christians
Remington, Frederic, 582*i*
Reparations
after World War I, 698
to Japanese Americans, 783
Republican party
and election of 1868, 513
and election of 1872, 530
and election of 1876, 531, 531*m*
and election of 1880, 563
and election of 1884, 564
and election of 1888, 565
and election of 1892, 617
and election of 1896, 620
and election of 1900, 635
and election of 1904, 667
and election of 1910, 671
and election of 1912, 671
and election of 1916, 690
and election of 1920, 704, 708
and election of 1924, 709
and election of 1928, 710–711
and election of 1932, 751
and election of 1936, 764
and election of 1940, 778
and election of 1944, 796
and election of 1946, 815
and election of 1948, 826
and election of 1952, 827, 836, 856
and election of 1960, 867
and election of 1964, 877
and election of 1968, 898–899, 901–902
and election of 1972, 912–913
and election of 1976, 925
and election of 1980, 944–945
and election of 1984, 948
and election of 1992, 988–989
and election of 1994, 939*t*, 989
and election of 1996, 974
and election of 2000, 995–999, 997*m*
and election of 2004, 1010–1011
post–Civil War
land policies, 524–525
office holders in South, 512, 515
policies, 505
Reconstruction policy, 500, 501
20th century
affirmative action and, 954
blacks and, 766
environmental policies, 1022
factions in, 670–671
platform of, 988
Red Scare and, 826–828
Republican Revolution (1994), 989
Versailles Treaty and, 698–699
late 19th century, 620
Populists and, 621
tariff and, 562
Reservations, Native American
creation of, 517–518, 582, 582*i*, 583*m*, 605, 608, 613*m*, 647, 649*m*
in 20th century, 898
Resumption Act (1875), 529
Revels, Hiram, 513*i*
Revenue Act (1916), 686
Revenue Act (1926), 709
Reykjavik summit (1986), 963
Reynolds, E. B., 581–582
Rhee, Syngman, 834–835
Rhodesia, 926, 927*m*
Rice, Condoleezza, 1030
Rice plantations
black life and labor on, 507–508
Rich and Brothers Dry Goods, 611*i*
Richmond, California, 783–784
Richmond, Virginia
19th century, labor unrest in, 572, 592
Rickey, Branch, 814*i*
Riegner, Gerhard, 790
Riesman, David, 864
Riggs, Bobbie, 934
Rights. *See also* Civil liberties; Civil rights; Human rights; Voting rights; Women's rights movement
Riis, Jacob, 594–596, 596*i*
Riley, Charles S., 636–637
Ringer, Robert J., 936
Rio Grande River, 941–942, 1021
Rio Puerco Valley, New Mexico, nuclear contamination, 941
The Rising Tide of Color Against White World Supremacy (Stoddard), 724
Road construction. *See also* Highway construction
Roaring twenties, 707–708, 715–723
Robertson, Pat, 954–955
Robeson, Paul, 827–828
Robinson, Jackie, 737*t*, 814, 814*i*
Robinson, Jo Ann, 854
Robinson, John, circus, 558

Rock, Chris, 1031
Rock 'n' roll, 716, 719*i*, 751, 814, 839, 862–864, 872, 893, 1024*i*
Rock Springs (Wyoming) massacre, 574
Rockefeller, John D., 544–545, 566–567, 568, 615, 662, 682, 684
Rockefeller Center, 758
Rockford (Illinois) Female Seminary, 599
Rockwell, Norman, 777*i*
Rocky Flats, Colorado (nuclear weapons plant), 821, 865*m*
Rocky Mountain Arsenal, 976*m*
Rocky Mountain National Park, 687*m*, 688
Rodriguez, Louis, 975
Roe v. *Wade* (1973), 839*t*, 895, 934, 986
Roger Williams University, 614
Rogers, Ginger, 786
Rogers, Will, 720*m*, 722, 742, 752, 767, 769
  and Roosevelt (F.D.), 739–740, 739*i*, 760
Roller coasters, 556
Rolling Stones, 716
Romani. *See* Gypsies
Romania
  collapse of Soviet Union and, 966*m*
  World War I and, 685*f*, 695*m*, 699*m*
Romer v. *Evans* (1996), 975
Roosevelt, Eleanor
  activism of, 761, 761*i*, 762, 767, 769
  background of, 750, 761
  flying lessons for, 768*i*
  letters to, 753
  marriage of, 750, 761, 808
  and President's Commission on the Status of Women, 761, 869
Roosevelt, Franklin D., 750*i*, 768–769, 770
  background of, 750–751
  blacks and, 740, 766
  cabinet of, 753
  and Chinese revolution, 797–798
  conservationism and, 754–755
  death of, 797, 808, 809*i*
  early career of, 750–751
  and election of 1932, 739*i*, 746, 751
  and election of 1936, 764–765
  and election of 1940, 778
  and election of 1944, 736, 796
  fireside chats, 740, 750–751, 750*i*, 752, 767
  first hundred days, 753–756
  Four Freedoms speech, 736*t*, 774, 777
  inaugural address, first, 752
  Japanese internment and, 781–783, 781*m*
  Manhattan Project and, 800
  marriage of, 750, 761, 808
  media and, 750–751, 750*i*, 752, 767
  and New Deal, 736
    legislation, 752–765, 763*t*
    opposition to, 758–761
    second, 761–764
  Pearl Harbor attack and, 778–781, 778*i*, 780*m*
  policies of
    on banks, 752
    on immigrants, 752
    on strikes, 766
  polio, 750–751
  Rogers (Will) and, 739–740, 739*i*, 760
  second term, 764–768
  supporters of, 740, 764–767
  Supreme Court packing scheme, 736*t*, 764–765
  World War II and
    Atlantic Charter and, 777–778
    discrimination in defense industry, 791–792
    domestic opposition to, 777, 781
    Four Freedoms, 774, 777, 777*i*
    Holocaust and, 790–791
    Japanese aggression and, 777
    Japanese internment and, 736, 773, 781–783, 781*m*, 791*i*
    peace settlement, 799, 803
    racial unrest and, 791–792
    strategy for, 774, 795–796
Roosevelt, Theodore, 666–667, 672
  on Americanization (assimilation), 666–667
  background, 591, 666
  death of, 703
  domestic policies of, 641
  early career of, 666
  and election of 1900, 635, 666
  and election of 1904, 667
  and election of 1908, 669
  and election of 1912, 671
  environmentalism and, 627, 662, 667, 670, 688
  eugenics movement and, 656
  foreign policy, 631, 653
  on frontier, 627
  ideology of, 627, 662, 670
  on immigrants, 666–667
  media and, 750
  and muckrakers, 662
  Progressive party and, 640*t*, 662
  Roosevelt Corollary, 640*t*, 669
  Rough Riders and, 632, 635
  on segregation, 667
  and Spanish-American War, 631, 633
  World War I and, 690
Roosevelt Corollary, 640*t*, 669
Root, Elihu, 690
Roots (Haley), 839*t*, 935*i*, 936
Rosebud Reservation, 517*m*, 605, 613*m*
Rosenberg, Ethel and Julius, 737*t*, 826
Rosenthal, Joe, 797*i*
Rosenwald, Julius, 612
Rosewood, Florida, riots in (1923), 702
Rosie the Riveter, 787–789, 787*i*
Rough Riders, 632
Royal Air Force (British), 776
RU-486, 986
Rubin, Jerry, 951
Ruby, Jack, 871
Ruby Ridge, Idaho, 939*t*
Rumrunners, 713
Rumsfeld, Donald, 1009
Rural areas
  20th century
    life in, 848
  late 19th century
    population, 551
    unrest in, 585–587
    Women's rights movement, 587
Rural Free Delivery, 561
Russell, Rosalind, 767, 767*i*
Russia. *See also* Soviet Union
  crude oil reserves of, 1006*f*
  19th century
    immigration from, 545, 587, 610
  early 20th century
    Allied intervention in, 700, 704
    anti-Americanism in, 700
    antisemitism in, 654
    Bolshevik revolution in, 641, 641*t*, 676, 678, 691, 694–695, 695*i*, 700, 870
    immigration from, 654, 654*m*, 678, 714*f*
    World War I and, 677, 685*f*, 694–695, 695*m*, 697–698
  late 20th century
    AIDS in, 957
    and dissolution of Soviet Union, 938*t*, 966*m*
Russo-Japanese War (1905), 640*t*, 677, 678, 799
Rustbelt, decline of, 20th century, 825, 917, 955
Rusticating, 609, 627
Ruth, Babe, 708
Rwanda, genocide in, 995

S

Sacco, Nicola, 641*t*, 713, 714*i*
Sadat, Anwar, 927, 938*t*, 964
Safety, consumer
  and automobiles, 879
  and tobacco, 879
Safety, industrial
  21st century, 1006
  19th century, 588–589, 589*i*
  20th century, 640, 643–644, 643*i*, 645, 663
    and nuclear industry, 907
    and women, 663
Sagebrush Rebellion, 591, 949–950, 949*m*, 950*i*
Said, Edward, 821
St. Louis, Missouri, 676, 721
St. Mihiel, Battle of, 694
Saipan, 797, 798*m*
Salinger, J. D., 863
Salk, Dr. Jonas, 842
SALT. *See* Strategic Arms Limitations Treaties
Salt Lake City
  late 19th century, 549–550, 600
  modern, 520, 520*m*
Salt of the Earth (film), 828*i*
Samoa
  late 19th century, 628

Samuelson, Paul, 876
San Antonio, Texas, 857*m*
 20th century growth of
  Mexican immigration and, 689, 959
San Antonio Independent School District v. Rodriguez (1973), 904
San Diego, California, 521, 720*m*, 779*i*, 959
San Francisco, California
 founding of, 894, 894*m*
 19th century
  Chinese in, 519, 572, 573–576
  labor unrest in, 572
  regional economy of, 519, 521, 550
 20th century
  Bay-to-Breakers race, 922*i*
  Chinatown, 644, 644*i*
  earthquake (1906), 640*t*, 641, 644, 644*i*, 894, 894*m*
  Golden Gate Bridge, 758
  Haight-Asbury, 893, 904
  immigration to, 825
  Japanese in, 653
  water and, 667–668, 668*i*, 669*i*
San Francisco Bay area, 894, 894*m*
San Francisco Boot and Shoemakers' White Labor League, 611
San Francisco Chronicle, 650
San Francisco Examiner, 630
San Francisco Presbyterian Chinese Mission Home, 575*i*, 599, 624
San Francisco State University, 893
San Francisco Workingmen's Party, 534*t*, 563–564
San Gabriel mission, 720
San Joaquin Valley Cotton Strike, 759*i*
San Juan Hill, Battle of, 632, 635*m*
Sanchez, Ricardo, 1009
Sanctuary movement, 946
Sand Creek massacre, 516, 683*m*, 684, 976*m*
Sandia National Laboratory, 865*m*
Sandia Pueblo, 977*i*
Sandinistas, 938*t*, 946
Sanger, Margaret, 682
Sanitary porcelain, 560*i*
Sanitation, early 20th century, 655
Santa Clara Pueblo, 977
Santa Fe
 19th century, 571*i*
 20th century, 683, 683*m*
Santa Fe Railroad. *See* Atchison, Topeka and Santa Fe Railroad
Santa Fe Ring, 522
Santiago Bay, Battle of, 632, 635*m*
Sargent, John Singer, 628
Saturday Evening Post, 777*i*, 793
Saturday Night Fever (film), 933*i*
Saturday Night Massacre, 913–914
Saudi Arabia
 and Iran-Contra scandal, 964
 Islam in, 875*i*, 970
 McDonalds in, 1025, 1026*i*
 oil industry in, 918, 967, 1007*f*, 1021
 terrorism in, 1008
 U.S. bases in, 970, 995, 1003
Sauk
 land loss, 609*m*
Savannah, Georgia
 post–Civil War
  education in, 499, 500*i*
 and Sherman's March to Sea, 499, 500–501
 19th century
  slave market of, 499
Savannah Education Association (SEA), 499, 499*i*, 500*i*, 508
Savannah River plant (nuclear weapons), 865*m*
Savings and loan crisis (1980s), 952–953
Sayles, John, 984
Scalawags, 505, 512
Scales, Jesse Sleet, 655
Scandinavia
 19th century, immigration from, 545–546, 585
 20th century, Communist Party rise in, 810
Scanlon, Emily, 556
Schenck v. *United States* (1919), 693
Schlafly, Phyllis, 934–935
Schlesinger, Arthur, Jr., 818
Schmeling, Max, 736*t*, 768
Schofield, John, 510
School shootings, 986–987
Schroeder, Pat, 965
Schwarzenegger, Arnold, 662, 881*i*
Schwerner, Michael, 889
Science. *See also* Medicine
 early 20th century
  eugenics and, 724–726
  public health and, 655, 681, 712
  religion and, 726–727, 734
 mid-20th century
  pollution and, 842
  space exploration and, 842, 858
Science Digest, 799
Science fiction, 822, 842
Scientific management, 657–658
SCLC. *See* Southern Christian Leadership Conference
Scopes, John Thomas, 726
Scopes trial, 641*t*, 723, 726–727, 727*i*, 734
Scott, Emmett, 621
Scott, Garrett, 621
Scott, Thomas A., 537, 562
Scottsboro Boys, 736*t*, 743–744, 744*i*, 769
Scribner's, 650
SDI. *See* Strategic Defense Initiative
SDS. *See* Students for a Democratic Society
The Sea Around Us (Carson), 864
Sea Islands
 in Civil War, 501–502, 503*i*
 cotton and, 501–502, 507
 land redistribution on, 503*i*, 507
Seabiscuit (horse), 768, 769*i*
Sears, Richard, 559
Sears Roebuck, 559, 561
SEATO. *See* Southeast Asia Treaty Organization
Seattle, Washington, 1019, 1019*m*
Seattle General Strike Committee, 702*i*
SEC. *See* Securities and Exchange Commission
Secession
 Confederate, 501
Secularism, 641, 944, 955, 1003
Securities and Exchange Act (1934), 763*t*
Securities and Exchange Commission (SEC), creation of, 736*t*, 753, 768
Sedition Act (1918), 641*t*, 693, 826
Segal, George, 906*i*
Segregation
 Supreme Court on, 535*t*, 610, 812, 823, 830, 881–882
 19th century
  among blacks by class, 508
  black resistance to, 577–579, 592
  temperance movement and, 600, 624–626
  textile industry and, 549
  unions and, 528–529, 592
  in West, 579–580
 20th century
  Asians and, 653
  black protests against, 812, 839, 869–871, 879
  continuation after World War II, 812, 814
  de facto, 851
  in education, 851–856, 852*i*
  in federal government, 680
  in Great Flood refugee camps, 724
  in housing, 812, 823, 830, 844
  opposition to, 879
  psychological effects of, 852
  resistance to, 812, 839, 879
  in World War I, 694, 697*i*
  in World War II, 793, 807
Seidman, William, 953
Selective Service Act (1915), 692
Self-determination
 in Atlantic Charter, 777–778
 post–World War I, 698
 in UN Human Rights Declaration, 811
Selma, Alabama, civil rights march, 879
Seminole. *See also* Five Civilized Tribes
 as buffalo soldiers, 580*i*
 U.S. war on, 580*i*
Seneca. *See also* Iroquois Confederacy
Seneca Falls Convention, 526–527
Separation of powers
 in U.S. constitution, 512, 670
September 11th terrorist attacks, 938–939, 939*t*, 995, 1003–1004, 1003*i*, 1034
 and Iraq War, 1007
 and racial profiling, 1031
Serbia, 939*t*, 966*m*, 994*m*, 995
Service Employees International Union, 979
Servicemen's Readjustment Act of 1944 (GI Bill), 737*t*, 811–812, 813*f*, 844

Settlement houses, 599, 624–625
Sevara, 570*i*
Seventeenth Amendment, 686
Sewall, Arthur, 620
Seward, William H., 524
Sexual harassment, 958–959, 965, 983
Sexuality
in World War II, 784, 788–789
late 20th century, Islamic fundamentalism and, 944
in 1920s, 707, 711, 723, 734
in 1950s, 825, 863–864, 864*i*
in 1960s, 839, 842, 863–864, 864*i*, 895
in 1970s, 909, 922
in 1980s, 956–957
in 1990s, 983
in 2000s
and Catholic Church, 939*t*
and television, 1006
early 20th century, 641, 660–661
interracial intimacy, 663–664
mid-19th century, 527
Shakopee, 977
Share-Our-Wealth Plan, 760
Sharecroppers' Union, 591
Sharecropping system
rise of, 508
19th century, 508, 511*t*, 521, 527, 535, 576*m*, 578, 585*t*, 629
20th century, 724, 730–731, 736, 753, 759, 768
Shawnee Indians
land loss, 583*m*, 609*m*
Shays' Rebellion, 591
Shelley v. *Kraemer* (1948), 812
Sheppard-Towner Act (1921), 641*t*, 681, 712
Sheridan, Philip H., 500
Sherman, William T., 499, 500, 507
Sherman Anti-Trust Act (1890), 535*t*, 565, 620
Supreme Court on, 620
in early 20th century, 667, 687
Sherman Silver Purchase Act (1890), 616
Shi'ite Muslims, 942
Shima, George, 548
Shinn, Everett, 661
Shipbuilding
in California, 975
in World War II, 783
Shipping
centers for agricultural products, 541*m*
Shopping centers
and consumer culture, 1024
mid-20th century, 842, 845
Short Line Railroad, 517*m*
Shoshones
19th century
culture, 518
white encroachment on, 517*m*, 524
20th century, nuclear contamination and, 941
The Show Window, *560*
Shtetls, *653–654*
Siegel, Ben "Bugsy," 757
Sieh King King, 650, 665
Sierra Club, 609, 667–668, 919, 950
"The Significance of the Frontier in American History" (Turner), 607–608
Silent Spring (Carson), 838*t*, 864–865, 865*i*
Silicon Valley, 894*m*
Silkwood, Karen, 907, 907*i*, 931–932
Silver, currency and, 587, 616–617
Simpson, Nicole Brown, 984
Simpson, O.J., 939*t*, 974, 983–984, 1000
Sinclair, Harry F., 709
Sinclair, Upton, 640*t*, 662, 760–761
Singapore, 820*m*, 828
Sioux, 649
Black Hills and, 518
19th century
assimilation of, 605–606, 612
Black Hills and, 518
culture, 567, 605
education among, 605, 612
Ghost Dance and, 573, 580–584, 582*i*
reservations for, 517*m*, 518, 565*i*, 613*m*, 647
resistance, 517, 517*m*
white wars against, 500, 517–518, 517*m*, 580
in Wild West show, 535, 582
20th century
AIM occupation at Wounded Knee, (1973), 839*t*, 898
Sirhan Sirhan, 901
Sirica, John, 913
Sister Carrie (Dreiser), 661
Sit-down strikes, in 1930s, 736*t*, 765–766, 765*i*
Sit-ins
in 1960s, 838*t*, 839, 854–856, 855*m*
Site of Ancient Memphis (Pape), 628
Sitting Bull, 518, 518*i*, 535, 557–558, 558*i*, 582–583, 739
Sixteenth Amendment, 640*t*, 686
Skyscrapers
introduction of, 549, 552–553
20th century, 644, 655, 758
Slavery
19th century
emancipation, 501
as political issue, 501
Slaves
Middle Passage and, 935*i*
on plantations, life and labor of, 935*i*
resistance by, 935*i*
runaway
advertisements for, 561
18th century, 561
Slavs, immigration by
19th century, 592
20th century, 714
Sloan, Alfred P., Jr., 722
Sloan, John, 661
Slovenia, 966*m*, 994*m*, 995
Slow Food movement, 1026
Smallpox
vaccination against, 656–657, 657*i*
Smith, Alfred E., 709–711
Smith, Anna Deveare, 984
Smith, Bessie, 721
Smith, Howard K., 907
Smith, Mary Rozet, 661
Smith Act (1940), 736*t*, 783, 871
Smith-Connally Act (1943), 737*t*, 787
Smith v. *Albright* (1944), 812
Smithsonian Institute, *Enola Gay* exhibit, 801
Smog, 824*i*, 825, 919, 1021
SNCC. *See* Student Nonviolent Coordinating Committee
Snuff. *See* Tobacco
"So Long, It's Been Good to Know Yuh" (song), 748–749
Soapine, 561*i*
Soccer, women's, 933, 1031*i*
Social Darwinism, 535, 566, 568, 635, 726
Social Gospel, 599
Social Security
Carter and, 926
Eisenhower and, 856
Johnson and, 878
Kennedy and, 867
Reagan and, 947–948
Social Security Act (1935), 736, 736*t*, 759, 762–764, 763*t*, 768
Social Security Administration, establishment of, 762
Social settlement houses, 599, 624–625
Socialism
as economic system, 741–742, 966*m*
in 1930s
increased interest in, 742
New Deal and, 758, 767
early 20th century
advocates of, 662, 665, 682
late 19th century, 591, 595
international links in, 594, 621
unions and, 591, 593–594
World War I, suppression of, 693–694
post–World War II, increased interest in, 810–811, 816
Socialist party
and election of 1932, 751
early 20th century, 665, 682, 690, 767
and World War I, 693
Society of American Indians, 640*t*
Sod houses, 585
Solar energy, 919, 921, 928, 973
Somalia, U.S. intervention in, 939*t*, 943*m*, 991, 994
Somoza, Antonio, 946
Sony Corp., 716
Sooners, 608
South. *See also* Civil War; Slavery
pre–Civil War
and Civil War
impact of, 501
education in, 612
voting rights in, 610
19th century
rural unrest in, 586–587, 590–591
20th century (*See also* Segregation)
Black migration from, 688–689, 688*i*, 731*m*, 784, 792, 848

economy, 825
New Deal and, 736
poverty in, 878*m*
rural life in, 730
sharecropping system in, 730–731
sunbelt prosperity in, 825
voting rights in, 879
post–Civil War
African Americans in, 511–512, 511*t*
black flight from, 577, 579
Chinese in, 546, 547*m*
Democratic party in, 512–513, 512*m*, 513–515
economy, 576–577
education in, 498*i*, 508, 510
immigrants in, 546
impact of War, 501
labor issues in, 505–508, 577
"New South" concept and, 576–577, 577*i*
occupation of, 531, 531*m*, 534*t*
population of, 607*m*
Republican party in, 511–515, 512*m*
sharecropping system in, 508, 511*t*, 576*m*, 585*t*
white reassertion of control, 512–513
white supremacy doctrine in, 610–611
South Africa, apartheid in
activism against, 677, 958
ending of, 926, 927*m*, 938*t*, 958, 966
nuclear arms stockpiles of, 910*m*–911*m*
U.S. support for, 912
South Carolina
19th century
readmission to Union, 513
South Dakota
Indian reservations in, 613*m*
statehood, 539
South Korea. *See also* Korean War
immigration from, 959
independence of, 820*m*
in 2000s, trade with U.S., 1014*m*–1015*m*
World War II and, 833–834, 834*m*
South Pole, exploration of, 677
South Vietnam, 884*m*. *See also* Vietnam War
Army of, 883
bombing in, 884*m*, 885, 887*i*
establishment of, 838*t*, 883
fall of, 915, 915*i*, 916*i*
Johnson and, 883–889
Kennedy and, 868
morale of, 883, 886–887
refugees in or from, 885, 916*i*, 947
Southeast
19th century
forest clearing in, 542*f*
Southeast Asia Treaty Organization (SEATO), 838*t*
Southern Alliance, 586
Southern Christian Leadership Conference (SCLC), 855, 875
Southern Homestead Act (1866), 523
Southern Manifesto, 853
Southern Tenant Farmers Union (STFU), 591, 730, 759
Southwest
19th century
forest clearing in, 542*f*
labor unrest in, 572, 590
land conflict in, 583*m*
property rights in, 521
20th century
immigration to, 648, 731*m*
water in, 1020–1021, 1020*m*, 1023
Soviet Union
in Cold War, 818*i*
American sympathizers with, 827
atomic arms acquisition, 830
Berlin Blockade and, 751, 817*m*, 819, 868–869
Berlin Wall construction, 810*m*, 838*t*, 869
and China, 909–910
Cuban Missile Crisis, 838, 869
foreign policy, 816, 846
Korean Airliner downed by, 945, 963
mutual defense treaty with China, 829, 830*i*
nuclear arms stockpiles, 910*m*–911*m*, 962
and revolutionary movements, 816
space program of, 842, 856, 858
sphere of influence, 859, 860*m*–861*m*
spies, 826, 827*i*
U.S. relations, 816–819, 868–869, 908, 911–912
in 1930s
economy of, 742, 758
and Spanish Civil War, 775
post–World War II
economy of, 816
expansionism of, 809–811, 810*m*, 815, 816–818
and occupation of Germany, 807
policy goals, 809, 816
repression of Jews, 923
U.S. relations, 807, 814, 816–819, 870
World War II and, 774, 795*m*
casualties in, 774, 796
immigration from, 783
nonaggression pact with Germany, 776–777, 796, 870
U.S. relations, 777, 795–796, 807*i*, 870
war with Japan, 798*m*, 799
late 20th century
in Afghanistan, 938, 938*t*, 944, 962–963
Carter and, 944
in Caucasus, 938, 963
Chernobyl nuclear accident, 938*t*, 941, 950, 958, 963
collapse of, 818, 938, 938*t*, 962–963, 962*i*, 965–966, 966*m*
economy of, 962–963
nationalist movements in, 963
oil industry in, 918
Reagan and, 945, 961–963
support of revolutionary movements, 942, 946*i*
Sozodont dentrifice, 559–560
Space exploration
Apollo 8, 838*t*, 902
Cold War and, 838, 856, 858, 868
moon landing, 868, 903*i*
Spain
21st century
Islamic terrorism in, 1008
19th century
Spanish-American War, 535, 535*t*, 630–636, 632*i*, 634*m*, 635*m*, 638
20th century
civil war in, 736*t*, 775, 776
fascism in, 775
Spanish-American War, 630–636, 632*i*, 634*m*, 635*m*
Spanish influenza, early 20th century, 641*t*, 700, 705
Speakeasies, 712–713, 712*i*
Special Commission on Wartime Relocation and Internment of Civilians, 783
Speech, freedom of, 774, 777*i*
speed limit, 55 mph, 922, 939*t*, 1023
Speert, Edith, 788
Spindletop Oil Field, 857, 857*m*
Spirit of St. Louis, 708
Spock, Benjamin, 824–825, 842
Spoils system
reform of, 564
late 19th century, 530, 564
The Spokesman, 715
Sports
in 1920s and 1930s
celebrities, 707*i*, 708
women and, 707*i*, 708
late 19th century, 536*i*, 539, 556–557, 557*i*, 615
late 20th century
commercialization of, 1024
diversity and, 1024
women and, 897, 1030, 1031*i*
Spotted Tail, 518
Sprague, Julian, 553
Sprague Electric Railway and Motor Co., 553
Spring Valley Water Co., 667–668
Sputnik, 838*t*, 842, 856, 858
Sputnik II, 858
Stackpole, Ralph, 762*i*
Stagflation, 916, 925
Stalin, Joseph
Cold War and, 809, 816–819, 818*m*
and collapse of Soviet Union, 962*i*
communist bloc and, 817*m*, 859
death of, 737*t*, 859
World War II and, 736, 776–777, 795–796, 799
Stalingrad, Battle of, 795*m*, 796
Stamp Act (1765), 561

Standard Oil Trust, 534*t*, 541*m*, 545, 568, 662
Standardization
  in education, 655
  late 19th century
    industry and, 540–541, 568, 629
    railroads and, 538–539
Standing armies
  World War I and, 690
Standing Bear, Luther, 605–606
Standing Bear (Ponca leader), 597
Standing Bear (Sioux leader), 605
Standing Bear v. *Crook* (1879), 597
Standing Rock Reservation, 565*i*, 583, 613*m*
Stanford, Leland, 615
Stanford University, 615, 894*m*, 934
Stanton, Edwin, 510, 513
Stanton, Elizabeth Cady, 526–527, 623
Staples, Yatta, 979
Star Wars. *See* Strategic Defense Initiative
Star Wars (film), 945
Starbucks, 1019
Starks, Margaret, 784
Starr, Ellen Gates, 599
Starr, Kenneth, 990–991
State-Rights Democratic party (Dixiecrats), and election of 1948, 826
States' rights
  post-Reconstruction, 504
Statue of Liberty, 546, 549, 646, 987*i*
Steamboats
  introduction of, 920
Steel industry
  20th century, 665, 693, 758, 766, 868
  late 19th century, 537–538, 547, 554, 588, 592, 622*m*
Steel Workers Organizing Committee, 766
Steffens, Lincoln, 662
Steichen, Edward, 661
Stein, Gertrude, 729–730, 729*i*
Steinbeck, John, 746
Steinem, Gloria, 931, 932*i*
Stephens, Alexander H., 504
Stephens, Uriah, 529
Sterilization, compulsory, 640, 640*t*, 641*t*, 656–657, 726, 734
Stettheimer, Florine, 706*i*
Stevens, Thaddeus, 510
Stevenson, Adlai E., 836, 856
STFU. *See* Southern Tenant Farmers Union
Stieglitz, Alfred, 661
Stock market
  1929 collapse of, 641, 641*t*, 708, 732, 734, 770
  1987 crash of, 938*t*, 948
  in Progressive Era, 669
  in 1980s, 947, 970, 1016
    abuses in, 951
  in 1990s, 939, 939*t*, 974, 1016
  in 2000s, 1016
  1930s regulation of, 753
Stoddard, Lothrop, 724
Stokes, Carl, 892
Stoller, Mike, 863
Stone, Lucy, 526–527
Stonewall riots, 839*t*, 898–899, 899*i*, 905
Stop-ERA campaign, 935
Strategic Arms Limitations Treaties (SALT I and II), 912, 944
Strategic Defense Initiative (Star Wars; SDI), 801, 938*t*, 947, 963
Strategic hamlet program, 885
Streetcars, electric, 553, 555, 644
Strikes
  21st century
    of hotel workers, 979
    of janitors, 979
  19th century, 622
    Great Labor Uprising of 1877 and, 562, 563*i*, 588, 596
    of miners, 535*t*, 562, 588–589
    of Pullman workers, 535*t*, 619, 620
    of railroad workers, 562, 619, 665
    of shoemakers, 529
    of steelworkers, 535*t*, 617
    suppression of, 534, 562–563, 580, 588–589, 617, 622
  20th century, 682
    1945-1960, 815–816
    of agricultural workers, 759, 759*i*, 897, 898*i*
    of air traffic controllers, 951–952
    of automobile workers, 766
    and civil rights movement, 901
    of garment workers, 640*t*, 643–644, 665
    during Great Depression, 758–759
    Ludlow massacre and, 682, 682*i*, 683*m*, 684, 704
    of miners, 648, 666, 693, 702, 787, 828*i*
    of railroad workers, 815
    Seattle General Strike and, 702, 702*i*
    sit-down tactics in, 765–766, 765*i*
    of steelworkers, 702
    of Teamsters, 979
    of textile mill workers, 682, 731
    during World War I, 693
    during World War II, 787
Strong, Josiah, 551, 566
Stuck, Hudson, 677
Student Nonviolent Coordinating Committee (SNCC), 855*m*, 856, 875, 890
Students for a Democratic Society (SDS), 838*t*, 892
Styrofoam, 836, 919
Submarine warfare, in World War I, 690, 701
Submerged Land Act, 858
Suburbs
  20th century
    arms race and, 845–846
    as bedroom communities, 849*i*
    blacks and, 847
    growth of, 737, 822–823, 842, 845
    and labor unrest, 846
    religion and, 845, 847*i*
    sex education in, 864*i*
    and urban sprawl, 825, 845, 848
  late 19th century, 538, 555
Subways, 644
Sudetenland, 776
Suez Canal, 677, 862, 888, 943*m*
Suffrage. *See* Voting rights
Sugar plantations
  in Cuba, 631
  in Hawaii, 547, 629, 689*i*, 780
Sugar Trust, 545, 620
Sukarno, 859
Sullivan, Anne, 663
Sullivan, Ed, 864
Sullivan, John L., 557
Summer of Love, 893
Summitt, Pat, 933
Sumner, Charles, 510, 525
Sumner, William Graham, 566, 635
Sun Yat-sen, 678
Sunbelt, 20th century
  foreign immigrants in, 959
  growth of, 825, 1017, 1033
  immigration to, 825, 1016, 1028*m*
Sundance Film Festival, 520
Supply-side economics, 948
Supreme Court, 936
  on abortion, 895, 934, 955, 975
  on advertising, 561
  on affirmative action, 839*t*, 935–936, 939
  on African American rights, 812, 853, 855, 900
  on Civil Rights Act of 1875, 530
  on compulsory sterilization, 656, 726, 734
  on contraception, 881
  on death penalty, 923*f*
  on desegregation of schools, 812, 814, 852–853, 881
    implementation of, 853–854, 854*i*
  and election of 2000, 939*t*, 975, 996–999, 997*m*
  on First Amendment, 693
  first black Justice, 838*t*, 882
  first female Justice, 935, 956
  first Jewish Justice, 680, 765
  on free speech, 881
    clear and present danger standard, 693
  on gay rights, 939*t*, 975, 1006
  on income tax, 620
  on integration of public transportation, 855
  on interracial marriage, 812, 881–882
  on interstate commerce, 565, 620
  on Japanese internment, 783
  on local school autonomy, 904
  on minority rights, 575
  on New Deal legislation, 764–765
  on Nixon White House tapes, 914
  on pornography, 881
  on prayer in public schools, 881
  on racial discrimination, 575, 648, 830

on racial quotas, 935–936
on right to legal counsel, 881, 900
Roosevelt court-packing scheme, 764–765
on school prayer, 881, 955
Scottsboro Boys and, 744
on segregation, 535*t*, 610, 812, 823, 830, 881–882
on sexual harassment, 959
Warren Court, 881–882
on women's rights, 601, 895, 934, 975
on worker protection legislation, 663
Survivor (TV show), 1024
Sussez pledge, 691
Svan, John, 658–659
Sweatshops
19th century, 546
activism against, 625
20th century, 643–645, 646, 663, 663*i*, 974, 979–980, 979*i*
Sweatt v. *Painter* (1950), 812
Sweden
19th century, immigration from, 546
Swift, Elizabeth, 942
Sylvis, William, 528
Syria, 918, 1008

T

Taft, William Howard, 672
and election of 1908, 669–670
and election of 1912, 671
on Filipinos, 633
as governor-general of Philippines, 669
Taft-Hartley Act (1947), 737*t*, 815
Taiwan
Chinese Nationalists on, 829
and Iran-contra scandal, 964
trade with U.S., 1014*m*–1015*m*
U.S. defense of, 835, 836
Taliban
internment in Cuba, 1005
regime in Afghanistan, 939, 1003–1005, 1007, 1027
Tamiami Trail, 641*t*, 729
Tammany Hall, 530, 530*i*, 555
Tanzania, 927*m*
Tanzania, embassy bombing in, 995
Taos, New Mexico, 683, 683*m*
Taos Indians, 898
Tape, Joseph, 575
Tape, Mamie, 575
Tape, Mary, 575–576
Tape v. *Hurley* (1885), 575–576
Tarawa, Battle of, 798*m*
Tarbell, Ida, 662
Tariff Act of 1930, 732
Tariffs
and Great Depression, 742–743
history and purpose of, 562, 1014
early 20th century, 670, 686, 709, 732
late 19th century, 562, 565, 616–617
late 20th century, 991
Taxation. *See also* Tariffs
in 1960s, 867, 876
in 1970s, and renewable energy, 928
in 1980s, 947
in 1990s, 989
in 2000s, 999
early 20th century, 686, 709, 747
late 19th century
of Chinese workers, 574
city growth and, 555
Taylor, Frederick Winslow, 549, 657
Teapot Dome scandal, 709, 710*i*
Technology
19th century
in agriculture, 527, 541, 585–587
export of, 541
in industry, 539–541
in transportation, 567
late 19th century
in agriculture, 585–587
education and training in, 539–540, 567
and growth of cities, 553, 555, 644
innovations, 534, 540–541, 567
mining, 539–540, 542
urban design and architecture, 549
communications
history of, 1012–1013
19th century, 516, 540
early 20th century, 767
late 20th century, 945
of mining
hydraulic extraction in, 539, 542
early 20th century
household appliances and, 641
World War I and, 690–691, 691*i*
mid-20th century
and new materials, 836
Soviet advances in, 838, 842
late 20th century
computer industry and, 975, 977, 1002*i*, 1012–1013
employment and, 975
entertainment and, 945
globalization and, 977
transportation
20th century, 541, 640, 701, 920
Teheran Conference (1943), 799
Telegraph
invention of, 1012–1013
and railroads, 516
service to Europe, 1012
Telemarketing, 561
Telephone
invention of, 534*t*, 540, 1012
service to Europe, 677
spread of, 767, 1013
Televangelism, 955, 956
Television
advertising and, 561
and family life, 844–845
introduction of, 1012
politicians' use of, 751
in 1950s and 1960s, 827, 842, 845
and slavery, 935*i*, 936
and spread of U.S. culture, 1024–1025, 1025*i*
21st century programming, 1006
Teller Amendment (1898), 631
Temperance movement
19th century, 573
women's rights movement, 600, 624–626
20th century, Prohibition, 640, 664, 693, 704, 709, 711–713, 734
late 19th century, 600, 624–626
African American women and, 600, 624–626
Ten Days That Shook the World (Reed), 704
Ten Percent Plan, 502, 512*m*
Tenancy system, late 19th century, in South, 576*m*
Tenement House Commission, 594
Tenements, 594, 646, 648*i*
Tennessee
19th century
readmission to Union, 513
20th century
Creationism in, 726
Tennessee, University of, and women's sports, 933
Tennessee Coal, Iron, and Railway Company, 577
Tennessee Valley Authority (TVA), 736*t*, 754–755, 754*m*, 763*t*
Tennis, 934
Tenure of Office Act (1867), 510, 513, 514
Terrell, Mary Church, 624
Territories. *See also* Frontier
Terrorism, 20th/21st century
anti-U.S., 975, 991, 995
Bush doctrine on, 1007–1008
domestic, 975, 985–986
by Islamic fundamentalists, 939, 991, 1003, 1008
September 11th attacks, 938–939, 995, 1003–1004, 1003*i*
Terrorism, white
post–Civil War, 505
Tet Offensive, 839*t*, 884*m*, 888, 901
Texas
19th century
labor unrest in, 590
readmission to Union, 513
20th century
coast of, 857, 857*m*
Dust Bowl in, 745–746, 747*m*
immigration to, 917
Mexican Americans in, 961*i*
Texas, University of (Austin), 895*i*
Texas Rangers, 580, 590
Textile industry
19th century, 548
company towns in, 552
distribution of, 622*m*
segregation of, 549
in South, 549, 577, 622*m*
workers in, 537, 549, 588
20th century
unions and, 665, 682, 731
Thanksgiving, 552*f*, 739
Thatcher, Margaret, 945

Them! (film), 822
Third Reich. *See* Germany, World War II
Third World
  Carter and, 908, 942–944
  civil rights movement and, 875, 875*i*
  Cold War in, 838, 859, 923
  Eisenhower and, 859–860
  Kennedy and, 868
  U.S. anticommunism and, 838, 859, 861–862, 868, 882
Thirteenth Amendment, 503, 504
38th Parallel (Korea), 834–835, 834*m*
This is the Army (film), 789
This Side of Paradise (Fitzgerald), 729
Thomas, Clarence, 938*t*, 965, 983
Thomas, Norman, 751
Thoreau, Henry David, 1022
Thornton, Willie Mae, 863
Thorpe, Jim, 680
Three Days of the Condor (film), 922
Three Mile Island nuclear accident, 839*t*, 907, 930, 931*i*, 936, 958
Throwaway culture, 919
Thurmond, J. Strom, 826
Tibet, 820*m*
Tiffany and Co., 628
Tijuana (Mexico), 720*m*
Tilden, Samuel J., 531, 531*m*
Till, Emmett, 853, 855*m*
Timber, 521, 539, 542, 542*f*, 608*i*, 920, 1018*i*
  Federal management of, 609, 667, 949–950, 950*i*
  trade in, 501, 973–974
Timber Culture Act (1873), 523
Time (magazine), 815*i*
Time-Warner, 977
Title IX, Educational Amendments of 1972, 933, 934*i*, 1030
Tito, Josip Broz, 817*m*, 909, 995
Titusville, Pennsylvania, oil fields, 920, 921*i*
Tlingits, 524
Tobacco
  19th century
    cigarette-rolling machine, 577
    marketing of, 557*i*, 628
  20th century
    advertising, 728, 977
    civil suits against, 977
    decline in use of, 921
    exports to China, 829
    mortality from, 957
    surgeon-general's warnings on, 879
Tobacco Road *(film)*, 785
Tojo, Hideki, 779
Toklas, Alice B., 729–730, 729*i*
Tokyo, World War II firebombing of, 799, 801
Toland, Greg, 785
Tongass National Forest, 1018*i*
Tonkawa, reservations for, 608
Totalitarian governments
  American embrace of, 816, 860–862, 912, 945
  late 20th century collapse of, 938, 942
Tourism
  20th century
    automobile and, 722
    Hawaii and, 780
    international, 1014
    South Florida and, 960
    in West, 683, 722, 723*i*, 757–758, 950, 976
  late 19th century, 523*i*, 524, 599, 604*i*, 609
    railroads and, 523*i*, 524, 609
Townsend, Francis, 759
Townsend Plan, 759
Toxic waste, 919, 1022
Toynbee Hall, 599
Toyota, 961, 1016
Trade. *See also* Free trade
  most favored nation status in, 923, 992
  in Pacific region, 961
  in 2000s, U.S. trading partners, 1014*m*–1015*m*
  20th century
    with China, 829, 911, 961
    most-favored nation status, 923, 992
    in 1930s, 743
Tragedy of the commons, 880, 1018
Trans-Alaska Pipeline System, 839*t*, 928–930, 928*i*, 929*m*
Trans-Siberian railroad, 677
Transcontinental railroad, 500, 515–516, 515*i*
Transportation. *See also* Automobiles
  19th century, 623*t*
    Chicago and, 554
    infrastructure growth, 549
  20th century
    and cultural homogenization, 1023
    desegregration of, 854–856
    and impact of automobile, 858–859
    innovations in, 640, 677, 722
Travolta, John, 933*i*
Treaty(ies)
  with Native American peoples
    renunciation of (1871), 516
    as white manipulation, 583*m*
  U.S. bilateral defense, 820*m*
Treaty of Fort Laramie (1868), 517
Treaty of Medicine Lodge Creek, 516
Triangle Shirtwaist Company fire, 640*t*, 643–644, 643*i*, 645, 672
Triangular diplomacy, 909
Trickle-down economics, 948, 954*f*
trinity Site, 683*m*
Triple Alliance, 677
Triple Entente, 677, 678, 695, 701
Tripp, Linda, 990
Truman, Bess Wallace, 694
Truman, Harry, 836
  assumption of presidency, 737, 737*t*, 797
  atomic bomb and, 737, 798*m*, 799, 800–801, 830–832
  China and, 829
  on civil rights, 826
  containment and, 815, 819
  and election of 1944, 796
  and election of 1946, 815
  and election of 1948, 826
  Israel and, 821
  on Japanese-Americans in World War II, 783
  Korean War and, 833–836
  McCarthyism and, 826–828
  policies of
    New Deal and, 825–826
    trade and, 815–816
    War and, 800–801
  post-War vision of, 815
  and Soviet atomic bomb, 830–832
  unions and, 815
  in World War I, 694
  World War II peace and, 799
Truman Doctrine, 737*t*, 815, 817–818, 817*m*, 819, 829, 833, 882, 903
Trust busting, 666, 670, 671, 687, 750
Trusts
  regulation of, 535*t*, 565, 620, 667, 687, 741 (*See also* Clayton Anti-Trust Act (1914); Sherman Anti-Trust Act)
  late 19th century, rise of, 544–545, 565, 1016
Truth, Sojourner, 526
Tsimshian, 525
Tuberculosis
  in 1990s, 987
  early 20th century, 655
Tulsa race riots (1921), 641*t*, 675–676, 702
Tumulty, Joseph, 702
Turkey, post–World War II, 815, 817, 817*m*, 819, 869, 1008
Turner, Benjamin S., 513*i*
Turner, Frederick Jackson, 607–608
Turner, Ted, 1014
Turning Stone (casino), 977
Turpentine. *See* Naval stores
Tuskegee Airmen, 793*i*, 804
Tuskegee Institute, 613
Tutu, Desmond, 958
TVA. *See* Tennessee Valley Authority
Twain, Mark, 534*t*, 563, 634, 638
Tweed, William M. "Boss," 530, 530*i*, 555
20th Century Fox Television, 645
Twenty-First Amendment, 736*t*, 753
21 Demands, 678
Twenty-Seventh Amendment, 974
Twenty-Sixth Amendment, 904, 996
Twilight, Los Angeles (Smith), 984
Typhoid
  in Spanish-American War, 633
  early 20th century, 655
Typhoid Mary, 655, 655*i*

U

U-2 spy plane incident, 838*t*, 859
U-boats, in World War I, 690
UAW. *See* United Auto Workers
UFW. *See* United Farm Workers

The Ugly American (Lederer & Burdick), 841
UMW. *See* United Mine Workers
Unabomber, 985
Underwood-Simmons Tariff (1913), 686
Unemployment
after World War II, 814
in Great Depression, 742–746, 758–759
in 1970s, 908
in 1990s, 988
Unemployment Councils, 736
UNIA. *See* Universal Negro Improvement Association
Union. *See also* Civil War
Union Army
pensions for, 616
"Union Maid" (song), 748–749
Union of Soviet Socialist Republics (USSR). *See* Russia; Soviet Union
Union Pacific (film), 606
Union Pacific Railroad, 500, 516, 516*i*, 574
Unions. *See also* Collective bargaining rights
late 19th century
African Americans and, 528–529, 592
corruption and, 531, 562
efforts to suppress, 562–563, 588–589
minorities and, 528–529, 592
rise of, 528, 529*t*, 584–585, 588–594
segregation in, 528–529, 592
Social Darwinism and, 566
strikes, 529, 537, 562, 584–585, 592
women and, 529
in 1920s and 1930s, 768
legitimization of, 731, 755, 761–762, 763*t*
militancy of, 731, 738*i*, 765–767
opposition to, 709, 758
strikes, 731, 758
women and, 731
in 1950s and 1960s, minorities and, 852, 897
in 1970s and 1980s
and environmental concerns, 907
early 20th century
alliance with Democratic party, 684
fear of, 641, 702
legitimization of, 687, 693, 702
resistance to, 702
strikes, 643–644, 693, 702, 702*i*
women and, 665
post–World War II
communist influence in, 808
strikes, 814
World War II and, 787, 814
late 20th century
decline of, 939, 951, 953, 1016–1017
free trade and, 992
globalization and, 951, 992, 1015
strikes, 951–952
United Auto Workers (UAW), 766
United Daughters of Ham, 579
United Farm Workers (UFW), 792, 897, 898*i*
United Fruit Co., 861
United Labor party, 591
United Mine Workers (UMW), 594, 622, 666, 684, 702, 765, 787
United Nations, 926
Declaration of Human Rights (1948), 761, 811
establishment of, 701, 737*t*, 811, 894*m*
General Assembly, 701, 811
and Iraq War, 1007
and Korean War, 835
and Persian Gulf War, 701, 968
Security Council, 701, 811
and Somalia, 994
United Provinces. *See* Holland
United States v. *E. C. Knight* (1895), 620
Unity, national, in 2000s, 1010
Universal Manufacturing Co., 1011–1012, 1016
Universal Negro Improvement Association (UNIA), 715, 715*i*
Universities
Red scare and, 827
spread of, 614
and women, 850
Uprising of twenty thousand, 640*t*, 643–644
Uranium
mining of, 821, 865*m*, 941, 1022
radioactive waste and, 821–822, 930, 941–942, 1022
Urban renewal, mid-20th century, 848
Urban sprawl, 848
U.S. Air Force Academy, 976
U.S. Army. *See also* Union Army
19th century
segregation in, 579–580
20th century
segregation in, 793, 807
U.S. Border Patrol, 959
U.S. Civil Rights Commission, 998
U.S. Forest Service, 687*m*, 949–950
U.S. Geological Survey (USGS), establishment of, 541
U.S.-Mexican War
territory acquired in, 516
U.S. Military Academy (West Point), 579
U.S. Postal Service, 561
U.S. Steel, 554*m*, 687, 702, 766
U.S. v. *Virginia* (1996), 975
U.S.A. Patriot Act (2001), 1004–1005
USDA. *See* Department of Agriculture
Utah
Indian reservations in, 613*m*
settlement of, 520*m*, 549
19th century, women's voting rights and, 600–601
20th century, nuclear testing in, 821
Ute, 683, 683*m*
removal of, 570*i*
white war against, late 19th century, 570*i*, 580

V

V-E (Victory in Europe) Day, 737*t*, 797
V-J (Victory in Japan) Day, 737*t*, 801–802, 802*i*
Vaccination, compulsory, 656–657, 657*i*
Valdez, Alaska, 929–930
Valens, Ritchie, 863
Valentino, Rudolph, 716, 718, 718*i*
Valera, Eamon de, 700
Valley of Fire State Park, Nevada, 757*i*, 757*m*
Vance, Cyrus, 943
Vancouver, George, 1019
Vanzetti, Bartolomeo, 641*t*, 713, 714*i*
Vassar College, 932
VCRs (videocassette recorders), 945, 1013, 1024
Veblen, Thorstein, 616
Velez, Lupe, 718
Velvet Revolution, 962*i*
Venereal disease, in World War II, 789
Venezuela, 629, 861, 918
oil reserves and exports, 1006*f*, 1007*f*, 1021
Venice Beach (California), 720*m*
Ventura, Jesse, 999
Vera Cruz
U.S. occupation of (1914), 678*m*–679*m*, 680
Vermont
in 1990s, same-sex marriage in, 981–982
Versailles, 698
Versailles Treaty (1919), 641*t*, 676, 698–699, 699*m*, 704, 775, 811
Vertical integration, 544
Veterans Administration, 811, 823
Veterans Bureau, 709
Viagra, 987
Vice crusaders, early 20th century, 663
Victorianism
core values of, 526, 566, 612
education and, 612
food of, 552*f*
home decoration and, 526, 625*i*
men and, 627, 660
popular culture and, 558, 625*i*
Victory gardens, 787
Victory girls, 789
Viet Cong. *See* National Liberation Front
Vietminh, 882
Vietnam, 698, 776
Clinton visit to, 993, 993*i*
post–World War II
French in, 811, 828, 835, 838*t*, 882–883
independence of, 811, 820*m*, 821
in 1970s
flight from, 916*i*, 917, 947
reunification of, 839*t*, 915
Vietnam Veterans Against the War, 903

Vietnam War, 800, 803, 807, 838, 874*i*, 882–889, 884*m*, 904
- African Americans and, 887
- antiwar movement and, 875–876, 888–889, 892–893, 901–903, 913
- atrocities in, 874*i*, 887–888, 887*i*, 903
- bombing in, 883, 884*m*, 885, 887*i*, 903
- casualties in, 839, 874*i*, 886*f*, 887–888, 887*i*, 903
- civil disorder in, 903
- civil liberties in, 913
- civil unrest in, 903, 913
- and Cold War consensus, 818
- combat in, 874*i*, 884*m*, 887–888, 887*i*, 888*i*
- containment and, 882
- credibility gap in, 883, 888, 903
- draft resistance in, 875, 892–893
- under Eisenhower, 841, 868, 883
- escalation of, 883, 884*m*, 886*f*, 889
- events leading to, 868, 882–883, 885*i*
- fall of South Vietnam, 839*t*, 915, 915*i*, 916*i*
- financial cost of, 916–917
- Ford and, 915
- guerilla warfare in, 633, 886–888
- historians' view of Cold War and, 818
- impact of, 874*i*, 888–889, 922
- Johnson and, 839, 883–889, 884*m*
- Kennedy (John F.) and, 868, 883
- Kennedy (Robert) and, 888–889
- Laos and Cambodia in, 841, 884*m*, 915–916
- Nixon and, 839, 876, 903–904, 908
- parallels to
  - American Revolution, 884
  - in Philippines, 633, 636–637
- peace negotiations, 884, 903
- strategic hamlet program in, 885
- Tet Offensive, 884*m*, 888, 901
- as tragedy, 874*i*, 922
- U.S. economy and, 904
- U.S. reasons for fighting, 885
- U.S. strategy in, 884–885, 884*m*
- U.S. troops in, 874*i*, 884*m*, 886*f*, 915
  - characteristics of, 887, 903
  - morale of, 885–888, 903
  - as POWs, 888*i*
- U.S. view of, 885, 885*i*, 887–888, 887*i*, 891, 892–893, 902–904
- Vietnamese view of, 885–886, 887*i*
- Vietnamization of, 903

Vietnamese, U.S. view of, 885, 885*i*, 917

Vigilantes
- post–Civil War, 505
- late 19th century, in South, 579, 611

Villa, Francisco "Pancho," 680, 694, 704

Village Voice, 925

Vinson, Mechelle, 959

Vinyl, 836

Virgin Islands, early 20th century, U.S. intervention in, 678*m*–679*m*, 679

Virginia. *See also* Richmond, Virginia
- 19th century
  - readmission to Union, 513
- 20th century, eugenics laws, 726

Virginia Colony for Epileptics and Feebleminded, 726

Virginia Military Institute, gender integration of, 975

Virginia State Board of Pharmacy v. *Virginia Citizens Council, Inc.* (1976), 561

VISTA. *See* Volunteers in Service to America

Vladivostock summit (1974), 916

Vocational instruction, 605, 612

Volstead Act (1919), 641, 712–713

Volunteers in Service to America (VISTA), 878

Voter participation
- after Nixon resignation, 914
- and Motor Voter Act, 989
- in 2000s, 1010

Voting age, Twenty-Sixth Amendment and, 904, 996

Voting rights. *See also* Women's suffrage movement
- post–Civil War
  - of African Americans, 504, 508, 513, 996
  - of Confederates, 510
- 18th century
  - in Constitution, 996
  - property requirements for, 996
  - of women, 996
- 19th century
  - of African Americans, 504, 508, 512*m*, 610
  - state efforts to limit, 504, 512*m*, 610
  - of women, 526–527, 600, 996
- late 19th century
  - of African Americans, 508, 610
  - literacy and, 610, 612
  - of women, 526–527, 623
- history of, 532, 996
- 20th century
  - of African Americans, 812, 838, 879
  - and election of 2000, 996, 998
  - of women, 664, 996

Voting Rights Act (1965), 879, 892, 996, 998

W

Wabash *v.* Illinois *(1886)*, 565

WACs. See Women's Army Corps

Wade-Davis Bill (1864), 502

Wagner Act (1935), 761–762

Wagner-Rogers Bill, 790

Wal-Mart, 1006, 1016–1017

Wald, Lillian, 625

Walden, Dana, 645

Walker, Madame C. J., 561

Walkowitz, Abraham, 642*i*

Wall Street Journal, 739, 917

Wallace, George, 744, 869, 901

Wallace, Henry A., 753, 796, 826

Walls, Josiah T., 513*i*

Walsh, Frank, 684

Walton, Sam, 1016

Wanamakers stores, 559, 605

Wang Laboratories, 900

War
- atrocities during, 684–685, 790–791, 795, 798–799
- industrialized, 684–685
- total, 795

War Bonds, World War II, 777*i*, 785

War Crimes Tribunal (The Hague), 995

War Industries Board, 693

War Labor Board, 693

War on Drugs
- in 1980s, 957
- in 1990s, 979, 987

War on Poverty, 877–879, 879*m*

War on Terrorism, 1004–1005, 1010

War Powers Act (1973), 923

Warner, Charles Dudley, 563

Warner, Emily Howell, 935*i*

Warner Brothers, 789

Warren, Adelina Otero, 664, 712

Warren, Earl
- Japanese internment and, 781, 881
- and segregation, 853
- Supreme Court under, 852, 881–882
- Warren Commission and, 871

Warren Commission, 871

Warsaw Pact, 817*m*, 859, 860*m*–861*m*, 965

Washington, Booker T., 568, 612–614, 667

Washington, D.C.
- and death of Martin Luther King, Jr., 901
- late 19th century labor unrest in, 572
- national security agencies in, 832, 832*m*
- race riots in (1919), 702
- SDS protests in (1965), 892

Washington, George
- on entangling alliances, 684, 701

Washington (territory, state), 1033
- Indian reservations in, 613*m*, 1019*m*
- Native Americans in, 500
- New Deal in, 756
- nuclear weapons plants in, 821
- settlement of, 608*i*
- statehood, 539
- Western area of, 1019, 1019*m*
- women's suffrage in, 600, 664

Washington Post, 913

Water
- 19th century, and disease, 542–543, 555
- 20th century
  - agriculture and, 1020*m*, 1021
  - and disease, 655
  - Federal land management and, 667
  - and pollution, 821, 839, 858, 880, 919, 1022
  - in West, 1020–1021, 1020*m*

Water cure, 633

Water power, 920, 921

Watergate scandal, 839, 839*t*, 908–909,

912–914, 936
historians' view of Cold War and, 818
impact of, 922–923, 974
Waters, Ethel, 721
Watson, Thomas E., 620
Watt, James, 950, 950*i*
Watts (Los Angeles), 719, 720*m*, 740
in 1960s, black riots in, 838*t*, 890, 900
WAVES (Women Accepted for Voluntary Emergency Service), 788
Wayne, John, 927
WCTU. *See* Women's Christian Temperance Union
Wealth
after World War II, 809
attitudes towards, 537, 567
distribution of
in Great Depression, 732, 742
in 1960s, 876
in 1970s, 917
in 1980s, 942, 947, 950, 954*f*
in 1990s, 977–978, 1000
in 2000s, 1016–1017
early 20th century, 682, 708
late 20th century, 842–848, 916, 942, 950
"*Wealth*" (Carnegie), 567
Weapons, 20th century, 795
access to, and violence, 986–987
atomic bombs, 683*m*, 737, 737*t*, 798*m*, 799, 800–801, 803
ballistic missiles, 800–801, 831*i*, 858, 869, 912
submarine-based, 958
firebombing and, 799–801
machine guns, 684, 701
of mass destruction, 1007
missile defense systems (Star Wars), 801, 938*t*, 947
napalm, 800, 887*i*
poison gas, 684, 701
Weapons of mass destruction, 1007
Weather Bureau, establishment of, 935
Weather Underground, 893
Weaver, James B.
and election of 1880, 563
and election of 1892, 617
Weaver, Randall, 985
The Web. *See* Internet
The Weekly Toiler, 587
Weimar Republic, 704, 775
Welfare capitalism, 742
Welfare Reform Act (1996), 939*t*, 990
Welfare state
backlash against, 839, 938, 1005–1006
definition of, 742
in 1930s, 762–763
women and, 762
in 1940s, 811–812
in 1960s, 878–879
in 1980s, 947–948, 970
in 1990s, reform of, 974, 989–990
Wells, Ida B., 568, 601, 611, 664–666
Wells-Barnett, Ida B. *See* Wells, Ida B.
West
19th century
African Americans in, 579–580
culture of, 600–601
economy of, 500, 519, 521–524, 587
forest clearing in, 542*f*
Indian land losses in, 518*m*, 583*m*
migration to, 518–524
mining in, 522, 587, 976
mission homes in, 638
Native Americans in, 613*m*
population of, 607*m*
property rights in, 521
railroads and, 515–516, 522–523, 587
segregation in, 579
women's rights and, 600–601
20th century
growth of, 731*m*, 825
labor activism in, 693
land management in, 667, 670, 949–950, 949*m*, 950*i*
nuclear sites in, 821, 822*i*
public lands in, 947, 949*m*
radioactive waste and, 821–822, 919, 930*m*, 941–942, 1022
sunbelt prosperity in, 825
water and, 683, 1020–1021, 1020*m*
West, Mae, 767
West Germany, economy, in 1970s, 917
West Point. *See* U.S. Military Academy
West Virginia
late 20th century rural decline of, 848
Western Federation of Miners, 617
Westinghouse Corporation, 568, 672, 692*i*
Westmoreland, William, 885, 888
Whaling, 920
What the Social Classes Owe to Each Other (Sumner), 566
Wheat, production of
19th century, 541*m*, 588
20th century
and Dust Bowl, 746
and irrigation, 823*i*
Wheat, work hours per bushel
late 19th century, 541
late 20th century, 823*i*
Wheatley, Phyllis, 625
Wheeler, Harry, 693–694
Wherry, Kenneth, 829
"Which Side Are You On?" (song), 748–749
Whig party
19th century
decline of, 505
Whiskey Rebellion, 591
White Collar (Mills), 864
White League, 611
White Man's Union (WMU), 621
White race, definition of, 658–659, 1029
White supremacy doctrine. *See also* Apartheid
late 19th century, impact of, 579, 611
Whitewater scandal, 990
Whitfield, Louise, 538
Whitman, Walt, 515
Why Change Your Wife (film), 717
Whyte, William, 823, 864
Wichita, 609*m*
Wilcox, Waldo, 520
Wild and Scenic Rivers Act (1968), 839*t*, 880
The Wild One (film), 863, 864*i*
Wild West shows, 535, 557–558, 557*i*, 582, 605, 739
Wilderness Act (1964), 838*t*, 880
Wildlife
Native American rights over, 981
refuges for, 667
Wilhelm II, Kaiser of Germany, 689, 694*i*, 701
Wilkie, Wendell L., 778
The Will to Believe (James), 615
Willard, Frances, 600–601, 601*i*
Williams, John D., 509
Williams, William Appleman, 818
Willoughby, Charles, 782
Wills, Helen, 708, 768
Wilson, Charles, 858
Wilson, Edith, 702
Wilson, Jack, 581
Wilson, William B., 684
Wilson, Woodrow
antitrust activities, 687
background of, 671, 677, 686*i*
conservationism and, 688
domestic policies, 641, 680
and election of 1912, 640*t*, 671
and election of 1916, 690
on imperialism, 698
on Latin America, 678–679
and League of Nations, 698–699, 701
on Mexico, 680
minorities and, 694
monetary policy, 686
and Russia, 698–700
on segregation, 702–703
stroke suffered by, 699, 702
Supreme Court appointments, 680
unions and, 684
and women's suffrage, 680–681, 681*i*
World War I and
14 Points, 641*t*, 697–698
peace settlement and, 697–699, 699*m*
purpose of fighting, 676
sympathy for allies, 689
U.S. entry into, 690
U.S. neutrality and, 684–685, 689–690
Wind energy, 919, 921
Windmills, 586*i*
Windtalkers (film), 717
The Wings of the Dove (James), 615
Winner-take-all electoral system, implications of, 623
The Winning of the West (Roosevelt), 627
Winslow, Paul and Rose, 681

Winter Quartels disaster, 520, 520*m*
Wisconsin
  Black voting rights in, 504
  Indian reservations in, 613*m*, 647, 649*m*
  migration to
    19th century, 527
    20th century, 647, 647*i*, 649
Wisconsin Progressive party, 760
Wise, Stephen S., 791
Within Our Gates (film), 721
The Wizard of Oz (Baum), 560
WMU. *See* White Man's Union
Wobblies. *See* Industrial Workers of the World
Wolfe, Tom, 909
Woman's Medical College of Philadelphia, 598
Women, 704. *See also* Mothers
  19th century
    education and, 498*i*
    employment, 588, 599
    industrialization and, 588
    unions and, 586–588
    voting rights, 526–527, 996
  late 19th century
    clubs and organizations, 599–600, 624, 665
    politics and, 616
    reform movements and, 596, 599–600, 624–625
    unions and, 586–588
    voting rights, 526–527, 996
    working conditions of, 587–588
  first Cabinet official, 753
  first in Senate, 983
  first trans-Atlantic solo flight, 768, 768*i*, 935*i*
  in World War II
    in armed forces, 788, 794, 802
    child care and, 787–788
    employment, 787–789, 787*i*, 802, 808, 849
    immigration to U.S. by, 783
    unions and, 787
  Native American
    crafts, 518
    first physician, 598, 598*i*
  in 1920s
    role and status of, 680–681, 706*i*, 707, 711–712
    sports and, 707*i*
  in 1930s
    employment of, 743
    as heroes, 707*i*, 708
    sports and, 707, 708
    welfare state and, 762
  in 1970s
    employment, 907, 917, 932–933
    labor activism of, 907
    role and status of, 896–897, 897*i*, 931–935, 932*i*, 934*i*, 935*i*
  in 1950s and 1960s
    activism of, 848*i*, 849, 896–897
    discrimination against, 849–850, 850*i*, 869
    employment of, 849–850, 869
    role and status of, 824, 844, 849, 869
  late 20th century
    in Afghanistan, 1027
    eating disorders and, 987
    education of, 1030
    employment, 1028, 1030–1031
    and military combat, 967*i*
    in political office, 1030
    role and status of, 931–935, 932*i*, 934*i*, 935*i*, 1028
    sports and, 934*i*, 958, 1030
    violence against, 1030
  early 20th century
    employment, 640, 663, 692*i*
    reform movements and, 640, 711
    social roles of, 680–681
    voting rights, 640, 680–681, 681*i*, 996
    in World War I, 692*i*
  post–World War II
    child care and, 808, 824–825
    education, 932–933
    employment, 787, 802, 808, 812, 812*i*, 849
    gender roles and, 808, 812, 849
Women and Economics (Gilman), 626
Women Strike for Peace (WSP), 864–865, 867*i*
Women's Army Corps (WACs), 788
  African Americans in, 793, 794, 794*i*
Women's Bureau, 788
Women's Christian Temperance Union (WCTU), 600–601, 601*i*, 712
  African Americans and, 600, 624–626
Women's clubs, 599–600, 624, 665
Women's Council, 848*i*
Women's Emergency Brigade, 766
Women's Foreign Missionary Society, 599–600
Women's liberation movement. *See* Feminism
Women's National Indian Association, 597–598
Women's Political Council, 854
Women's rights movement
  in 1960s, 839, 895–897, 897*i*
  in 1970s, 907, 931–935, 932*i*, 934*i*, 935*i*
    backlash against, 876, 907, 934–935
  19th century, 501, 526–527
    abolitionist movement and, 501, 626
    temperance movement and, 600, 624–626
  20th century, 680–682, 711–712, 733
    work restrictions and, 663, 711
Women's suffrage movement
  19th century, 526–527, 600, 623, 638
  early 20th century, 664, 680–681, 681*i*, 734
Women's Trade Union League (WTUL), 665
Women's U.S. World Cup soccer team (1999), 933, 1031*i*
Wong Lan Fong, 652, 652*i*
Woo, John, 717
Woo, Michael, 981
Wooden Leg, 582
Woodhull, Victoria, 527, 626
Woods, Tiger, 984*i*, 985
Woodstock, 893
Woodward, Bob, 913
Woolworth lunch counter sit-ins, 855
Work day, 588, 646, 711, 763*t*
  eight-hour, 592–593, 619, 663, 666, 688, 693
  ten-hour limit on, 663
Workers. *See also* Common man
  19th century
    skilled, 622
  early 20th century
    conditions of, 646, 682, 684
    discrimination among, 792
    protective legislation for, 768
    in 1920s, 730–731
    in 1930s, 758–760, 764, 765–767
    unrest, 682–684, 693, 814
  late 19th century
    anarchist movement and, 593–594, 594*i*, 599, 602
    dangers faced by, 588–589, 589*i*
    immigrants as, 545, 592
    industrial unrest, 584–585, 588–594, 602
    mechanization and, 539, 541–542, 584, 621*i*, 622
    mobility of, 622
    numbers per firm, 548*t*
    plight of, 601, 616
    and rise of corporations, 534, 545
    Social Darwinism and, 566
    unrest, 534–535
  late 20th century
    and exportation of jobs, 1011–1012, 1015
    in 1970s, 901
    in 1980s, 952–954
    in 1990s, 975
    service, 974, 979
Workers' compensation, introduction of, 688
Workers' Council of Colored People, 764
Workingmen's Party of California, 573
Workplace
  end of discrimination in, 839
Works Progress Administration (WPA), 762*i*, 763*t*, 764, 770, 784
  discrimination and, 766–767
World Jewish Congress, 790–791
World Trade Center
  2001 attacks on (*See* September 11th terrorist attacks)
  bombing of (1993), 995
World Trade Organization (WTO), protests against, 991*i*, 1015
World War I, 640, 640*t*, 674*i*, 676, 704, 777, 802–803
  African Americans in, 676, 694–695, 697*i*
  banks and, 684, 689–690

casualties in, 684–685, 685*f,* 691*i*, 693
causes of, 677, 701
civil liberties in, 693–694
context of, 676–677
disease in, 700, 705
employment and, 692*i,* 693
Europe and Western front, 694–695, 695*m,* 697
horrors of, 684–685, 691*i*
impact of, 641, 692–693, 698–699, 699*m,* 712
peace settlement for, 697–699, 698–699, 699*m*
reparations after, 698
repression of dissent in, 693–694
U.S. entry into, 641*t,* 690
U.S. neutrality in, 684–685, 689–690
U.S. preparation for, 690
women in, 692*i*

World War II, 736, 770, 772*i*
African Americans in, 773–774, 783–784, 787, 789, 802
casualties in, 774, 779*i,* 798–799, 802, 809
civil liberties in, 785
cultural impact of, 737, 774, 783–789
destructiveness of, 774, 786, 799, 802, 808–809
domestic opposition to, 777, 781
in Europe, 736*t,* 774, 795–797, 795*m*
events leading to, 701, 736*t*
horrors of, 786, 798–799
Japanese-Americans in
internment of, 736, 773, 781–783, 781*m,* 791*i,* 828
prejudice against, 781–783, 785
reparations for, 783
in U.S. Army, 773
Jews in
casualties, 774
Holocaust, 774–776, 789–791, 790*m,* 799
immigration by, 790–791
in Nazi Germany, 774–776, 789–791, 790*m*
minorities and, 773–774, 774, 787, 802
mobilization for, 779*i,* 783–784, 795–796
Native Americans in, 773–774, 773*i,* 793, 802
in North Africa, 795*m,* 796
in Pacific, 773, 778–781, 797–799, 798*m,* 811*i*
peace settlement, 799, 803
Pearl Harbor attack, 736, 736*t,* 773, 778–781, 778*i,* 780*m*
post-War occupations, 793
presidential service in, 785*i*
propaganda during, 786
segregation in, 791–794, 807
U.S. armed forces
African Americans in, 792–794, 793*i,* 794*i*
morale of, 786
women in, 788, 794
U.S. censorship in, 785–786
U.S. domestic impact, 774, 783–789
U.S. entry into, resistance to, 774, 777, 781
U.S. home front, 784–789, 804
morale in, 784–786, 803
racial tension in, 791–792
women workers, 787–789, 787*i*
U.S. migrations in, 783–784, 793
U.S. power following, 802–803
U.S. racial hostility in Pacific, 798–799
U.S.-Soviet relations in, 795–796
U.S. strategy in, 795–796, 799
war crimes trials, 819
women in
in armed forces, 788, 794, 802
as workers, 787–789, 787*i,* 808

World War II veterans, 809
African Americans as, 812, 814
GI Bill and, 811–812, 813*f,* 844
Latino veterans organizations, 814, 827

World Wide Web, 561, 1012–1013. *See also* Internet

Wounded Knee, AIM occupation at (1973), 839*t,* 898, 936

Wounded Knee massacre, 517*m,* 535*t,* 582–584, 582*i,* 605

Wovoka, 580–581

WPA. *See* Works Progress Administration

Wrangell-St. Elias National Park, 930

Wright, Frances, 626

Wright, Orville and Wilbur, 640*t*

WSP. *See* Women Strike for Peace

WTUL. *See* Women's Trade Union League

Wyoming
Indian reservations in, 613*m*
Rock Springs massacre, 574
statehood, 535*t,* 539
women's voting rights and, 600–601

Wyoming Stock Growers Association, 587

Y

Yakima Indians, 941, 1019

Yale (College, University), 932
late 19th century, 615

Yalta Conference (1945), 799

Yank, 787

Yellow fever, 633

Yellow Hand, 557

Yellow journalism, 631

Yellowstone National Park, 524, 525*i,* 687*m*

Yeltsin, Boris, 966, 1024*i*

Yemen, attack on *USS Cole* in, 995

Yeoman farmers, 514, 551

Yick Wo, 574–575

Yick Wo v. *Hopkins* (1886), 575

Y2K problem, 939*t*

YMCA. *See* Young Men's Christian Association

Yosemite National Park, 524, 609, 667–668, 687*m,* 879*i,* 1021–1022

Young, Andrew, 892, 926

Young, Owen, 1013

Young Americans for Freedom, 877

Young Lords, 897

Young Men's Christian Association (YMCA)
World War I and, 696

Young Women's Christian Association (YWCA)
African Americans and, 624, 696
World War I and, 696

Youth culture (1960s-1970s), 839, 845, 889–899, 893, 895, 900*i*

You've Got Mail (film), 1013*i*

Yucca Flat, 822*i*

Yugoslavia
collapse of, 698, 994*m,* 995
creation of, 698, 699*m*

Yukon Flats National Wildlife Refuge, 929*m*

Yuppies, 951

YWCA. *See* Young Women's Christian Association

Z

Zambia, 927*m*

Zeien, Alfred M., 1027

Zgodat, 614

Zimbabwe, establishment of, 926, 927*m*

Zimmerman, Arthur, 691

Zimmerman telegram, 691

Zionist movement, 677, 680*i,* 821

Zitkala-Sa, 612

Zoning
early 20th century, 663
late 19th century, 555

Zoos, Scopes trial and, 728

Zoot suits, 737*t,* 792, 804

Zybach, Frank, 823*i*